T

~~(810) 560-1216 (h)~~

~~(310) 331-7408 (o)~~

personal copy

(310) 720-7408

(310) 812-9029

INTRODUCTION TO STATISTICAL DECISION THEORY

INTRODUCTION TO STATISTICAL DECISION THEORY

John W. Pratt, Howard Raiffa, and Robert Schlaifer

The MIT Press
Cambridge, Massachusetts
London, England

Third printing, 2001

This book was set in Times Roman by Asco Trade Typesetting Ltd., Hong Kong, and was printed and bound in the United States of America.

Library of Congress Cataloging-in-Publication Data

Pratt, John W. (John Winsor), 1931–
Introduction to statistical decision theory / John Pratt, Howard Raiffa, and Robert Schlaifer.
p. cm.
Includes bibliographical references and index.
ISBN 0-262-16144-3
1. Statistical decision. I. Raiffa, Howard, 1924– . II. Schlaifer, Robert. III. Title.
QA279.4.P73 1994
519.5′42—dc20 94-7958
CIP

Dedicated to

Robert O. Schlaifer (1915–1994): An original, deep, creative, indefatigable, persistent, versatile, demanding, sometimes irascible scholar, who always was an inspiration to us both.

John Pratt and Howard Raiffa

Contents

Preface

This book is an introduction to Bayesian statistics, that is, to the mathematical analysis of the problems that arise when the consequence of action depends on the uncertain "state of the world," about which the decision maker either has obtained or can obtain additional information by sampling or experimentation. Our approach is based on the fact that if the decision maker is willing to scale both his preferences for the possible consequences and his judgments concerning the uncertain states and to accept two simple principles of consistent behavior, then he can by straightforward calculations determine which strategy for experimentation and action he *should* adopt in order to be consistent, in the sense of these principles, with his own preferences and judgments. Thus for us probability assessments reflect a state of mind, and the task is how to think coherently about such uncertainties and decisions as when to act on the basis of what we already know, when to accumulate further information that can inform us about the uncertain states of the world, and how to balance the costs and benefits of accumulating evidence before action.

As its title indicates, this book is intended as an *introduction* to the subject. The only specialized background we assume is familiarity with the basic concepts of calculus; we do not assume any previous training in probability or statistical inference, but readers who have it will find that it enriches study of this book besides contributing a little more of that nebulous quality sometimes called "mathematical sophistication." The language of sets is described in a very brief appendix; a slightly longer appendix supplies the rudimentary matrix theory that is needed in the chapters on multivariate distributions (chapters 21 and following). Earlier versions of the present book have been used as the basis for a course taken by some mathematically advanced undergraduates and by graduate students with undergraduate degrees mainly in engineering, the physical sciences, and mathematics, but also in the social sciences and the humanities.

This book has as direct ancestors Schlaifer's *Probability and Statistics for Business Decisions* (McGraw-Hill, 1959) and Raiffa and Schlaifer's *Applied Statistical Decision Theory* (Harvard Business School, 1961) but it differs radically from them. On the one hand, *PSBD* was completely nonmathematical and therefore very restricted in both scope and rigor, while on the other, *ASDT*, was written very specifically for people who were already fully trained in classical mathematical statistics. In general approach and notation, however, the present book agrees almost exactly with *ASDT*, and anyone who has gone through it should have no trouble in understanding what *ASDT* has to say on topics that are not treated herein.

In 1965 we distributed in mimeographed form a preliminary edition of this book under the auspices of McGraw-Hill. It had too many rough edges and incomplete and missing chapters to be published as a finished book at the time, but it was complete enough to constitute the text of a serious course, and our very cooperative publishers filled orders for copies from outside individuals and institutions. Unfortunately the decision to distribute a preliminary edition took the heat off of us to complete the enormous amount of work we had already invested in developing the manuscript. Also, more fundamentally, in the mid-1960s we gradually realized the importance of the application of the Bayesian approach much more generally to a much wider class of problems of decision making under uncertainty, and we collectively helped develop a body of techniques and approaches now known as *decision analysis*. Roughly speaking, *statistical* decision theory deals with decision problems in which data gathered by sampling or other structured observation can be processed to update our knowledge about a state parameter (such as a population mean). But there are hosts of decision problems in economics and management, in public policy and life, where such data play little or no role although uncertainties abound, and where decision theory illuminates analysis although the paradigm of *statistical* decision theory is too narrow. It remains our view, however, that statistical decision theory is an important branch of decision theory and deserves special attention. Thus we regret our delay in finishing our manuscript.

In the intervening years from 1965 to 1992, two of us (Pratt and Raiffa, but mostly Pratt) continued periodically to teach a course in statistical decision theory at Harvard using our manuscript and we (again, mostly Pratt) developed supplements to the preliminary edition. Revisions of those supplements as well as missing chapters have been added to the manuscript. We are indeed indebted to the MIT Press for publishing this book that is over a quarter of a century in the making.

Description of This Book for the Knowledgeable Reader

In the first part of the book, chapters 1 through 6, we examine both informally and formally (i.e., axiomatically) the logical and philosophical justification of the Bayesian approach—or more accurately, the subjectivistic approach—and show how this methodology can be implemented in simple discrete problems.

In the preliminary edition we used and hoped to establish more widely the term *preference* in lieu of the more popular term *utility*. We felt at the time that much confusion was arising because the literature was using *utility* in both ordinal (Marshallian) and cardinal (von Neumann) senses. To dispel this confusion and avoid questionable connotations, we introduced the more descriptive term *preference* for the latter. We have long since given up this crusade to change terminology; in this book, utility is always cardinal, and if you find the term *preference* lingering on it is meant to be synonymous with *utility*.

Although our treatment of the foundations fully develops the conceptual theory of utility, not much is done with it throughout the book. After brief discussion in chapter 4, we specialize rapidly to the case of linear utility or expected value, which greatly facilitates statistical decision theory. Nevertheless, we feel utility is critical to the foundations of the subject of decision making under uncertainty and include as appendix 3 to the entire book a considerable amount of new material on utility theory. We decided not to make this an appendix to chapter 4 because it is more sophisticated and more compactly written than the earlier part of the book and it exploits probability theory presented later on.

In the second part of the book, chapter 7 extends the foundations to the continuous case, and chapter 8 introduces the terminology and manipulation of random variables and expectation operators. Chapter 9 is not to be read as a unit; it is a catalogue where many useful formulas about specific distributions are collected for easy reference as need arises later in the book. Chapter 10 is a rather intricate discussion of Bayes' theorem for the continuous case that can easily be skipped.

The third part of the book, chapters 11 through 14, first introduces the Bernoulli process and develops distribution theory for inference and forecasting. We then use these results to analyze three "standard" statistical decision problems: (1) the problem of choosing between two acts when the value of each is linear in the unknown mean of a process or population, (2) the problem of estimation with quadratic loss, and (3) the problem of estimation with symmetric or asymmetric linear losses, which has additional interest because it is isomorphic with certain order-quantity and other decision problems. These problems serve to illustrate such economic concepts as opportunity loss, expected value of perfect information, expected value of sample information, and expected net gain of sampling. For each of the problems, we show, first, how to carry out *terminal analysis*, that is, how to select an optimal terminal act after a sample has already been taken, and second, how to carry out *preposterior analysis*, that is, how to select the optimal sample size if one and only one (more) sample can be taken before choosing a terminal act. In a new closing section of chapter 14 we discuss optimal sequential Bernoulli sampling for the two-act problem.

The fourth part of the book describes other univariate sampling models and illustrates their use in terminal and preposterior analysis of various decision problems, always including the three "standard" problems described above. Chapters 15 through 18 deal successively with the Poisson process, the Normal process with known variance, the Normal process with unknown variance, and large-sample theory. Of these four chapters, the preliminary edition included only the two most essential ones for the rest of the book, chapter 16 on the Normal process with known variance and chapter 18 on large-sample theory.

The fifth part of the book comprises chapters 19 and 20. Chapter 19 looks at the problem of optimal experimentation and action from a different point of view, using the so-called *normal form* of analysis instead of the *extensive form* used in previous chapters. In the extensive form, the analysis proceeds by working backward down a decision tree, and judgmental probabilities for the possible states of the world enter the analysis from the beginning. In the normal form, the analysis starts with a listing of all possible strategies for experimentation and action and evaluates each one conditionally on each possible state of the world; judgmental probabilities for the states are brought in at the last stage of the analysis. Since classical statistical procedures do not employ judgmental distributions for state parameters, classical and Bayesian procedures can be compared most instructively by looking at analyses in normal form.

A new appendix to chapter 19 develops the objectivistic theory of statistical decision theory, à la Abraham Wald. The focus is on complete class theory and shows how certain Bayes Decision Rules—not with subjectively assessed priors but with purely formal weighting functions—can be used to generate admissible (i.e., non-dominated) decision rules that (almost) form a complete class. This material is not central to the (subjective) Bayesian view we adopt, but is included for completeness' sake and to highlight the relations and distinctions between subjectivist and objectivist approaches.

In chapter 20, standard classical procedures such as unbiased and maximum likelihood estimation, confidence intervals, and one- and two-tailed tests of hypotheses are described and interpreted from the Bayesian point of view. Sufficient statistics are sketched in a new appendix, deferred to this point to highlight the differences and similarities between the classical (objectivistic) and Bayesian (subjectivistic) concepts.

The sixth and last part of the book, chapters 21 to 24, takes up what might be called multivariate problems. After introducing multivariate distributions in chapter 21 and the multivariate Normal distribution in chapter 22, we devote chapter 23 to a study of four representative applications of the multivariate Normal distribution: (1) selection of the best of several processes or treatments, (2) analysis when the sampling process is biassed to an unknown extent, (3) stratified sampling, (4) selection of an optimal portfolio of securities. For the first three of these we discuss terminal analysis and the optimal choice of a single experiment of fixed size. The book closes with an introduction to the Normal linear regression model in chapter 24, amplified by new material on the choice of statistical models (section 24.6) and an extensive discussion of causation (section 24.7).

The exercises and case material are an integral part of the text, and they often supply additional motivation for the theory and suggestions for additional applications. In this sense the book is written more for classroom use than for individual study. There is plenty of room for the instructor occasionally to reconstruct the big picture, or even to draw medium-size landscapes when the going gets rough. A good many of the mathematical details are left as formal exercises for the reader, but the more difficult of these, and some omitted topics, are developed in coordinated sequences of exercises where each step to be supplied by the student crosses a small gap rather than a wide chasm.

Acknowledgments

Ronald Rubel was of great assistance in the physical preparation of the preliminary manuscript, and in addition he prepared solutions for most of the exercises and cases in the text. Irving LaValle and José Faus made numerous useful corrections and comments on an early draft of the manuscript. Gordon Kaufman, Arthur Schleifer, and Richard Meyer also contributed helpfully. Chris Avery did a splendid detailed editing of the final book and helped correct several errors, some substantial. Our very special thanks to Shi Leyuan, who used results in *ASDT* to write a fine first draft of the present chapter 17 on the Normal process with unknown mean and variance. And finally, our thanks go to all our students at Harvard who have used the preliminary manuscript and uncovered all too many typos as well as more serious errors.

Finally, we would like to express our deep gratitude to the administration of the Harvard Graduate School of Business Administration for their encouragement and support of our research in the use of mathematical models for the prescriptive analysis of the decision problems under uncertainty, and we would like to thank the National Science Foundation for financial support for a three-year period in the early 1960s.

John W. Pratt
Howard Raiffa
Robert Schlaifer

Boston, Massachusetts
April 1993

1 Introduction

1.1 The Problem of Decision under Uncertainty

When all of the facts bearing on a decision are accurately known beforehand—when the decision is made "under certainty"—careless thinking or excessive computational difficulty are the only reasons why the decision should turn out, after the fact, to have been wrong. But when the relevant facts are not all known—when the decision is made "under uncertainty"—it is impossible to make sure that every decision will turn out to have been right. Under uncertainty, the decision maker is forced, in effect, to gamble. His previous actions have put him in a position where he must place bets, hoping that he will win but knowing that he may lose. Under such circumstances, a right decision consists in the choice of the best possible bet, whether it is won or lost after the fact. A woman who buys fire insurance does not censure herself for wasting money if her house has not burned down by the time the insurance expires, and the following examples are typical of other decisions which must be made and judged in this way.

1.1.1 Some Typical Examples

An Inventory Problem

A retailer is about to place an order for a number of units of a perishable commodity which spoils if it is not sold by the end of the day on which it is stocked. The retailer does not know what the demand for the item will be, but must nevertheless decide on a definite number of units to stock.

A Scrap-Allowance Problem

A manufacturer has contracted to deliver at least 100 good pieces of a nonstandard product at a fixed price for the lot. He feels virtually sure that there will be some defectives among the first 100 pieces produced. Since setting up for a second production run to fill out a shortage would cost a substantial amount of money, he wishes to schedule some additional pieces on the original run as a scrap allowance. On the other hand, once 100 good pieces have been produced, the direct manufacturing cost of any additional production will be a total loss, and therefore he does not wish to make the scrap allowance excessively large. If the manufacturer knew exactly how many pieces would have to be produced in order to get exactly 100 good pieces, it would be easy to set the right size for the production order; but he must decide on some definite size for the order even without that information.

A Problem in Manufacturing Methods

A manufacturer is about to tool up for production of a newly developed product. This product can be manufactured by either of two processes, one of which requires a relatively small capital investment but high labor cost per unit produced, while the other will have much lower labor costs but requires a much greater investment. The former process will thus be the better one if sales of the product are low, while the latter will be better if sales are high; however, the manufacturer must choose between the two processes without knowing what sales will actually be.

A Marketing Problem

The brand manager for a certain grocery product is considering a change of package design in the hope that the new package will attract more attention on the shelf and thereby increase sales. She has done a certain amount of store testing and has found that during the past week sales of the new package were greater than sales of the old in some stores, but that the contrary was true in other stores. She still feels uncertain whether adoption of the new package will increase or decrease her total national sales, but she must nevertheless either decide on one package or the other or else decide to spend more money on additional testing. In the latter case she must decide whether she should simply continue the test for a few more weeks in the same stores she has already used or spend still more money to draw new stores into her sample.

An Investment Problem

An oil wildcatter who holds an option on a plot of land in an oil-producing region must decide whether to drill on the site before the option expires or to abandon his rights. The profitability of drilling will depend on a large number of unknowns—the cost of drilling, the amount of oil or gas discovered, the price at which the oil or gas can be sold, and so forth—none of which can be predicted with certainty. His problem is further complicated by the fact that it is possible to perform various tests or experiments that will yield a certain amount of information on the geophysical structure below the land on which he has an option. Since some structures are more favorable to the existence of oil than others, this information would be of considerable help in deciding whether or not to drill; but the various tests available cost a substantial amount of money, and hence it is not at all obvious that any of them should be performed. The wildcatter must nevertheless decide which if any of the tests to perform and ultimately, if not now, he must decide whether or not to drill.

1.2 Decision Trees

The examples described above, like all the problems we shall study in this book, have two essential characteristics:

1. A *choice*, or in some cases a sequence of choices, must be made among various possible courses of action.

2. This choice or sequence of choices will ultimately lead to some *consequence*, but the decision maker cannot be sure in advance what this consequence will be, because it depends not only on his or her choice or choices but on an unpredictable *event or* sequence of events.

The essence of any such problem can be brought out very clearly by a type of diagram known as a *decision tree*, which can best be explained by examples.

1.2.1 A Simple Decision Tree

As an example that will illustrate all the essential points involved in the construction of a decision tree without useless complexities, we shall take a somewhat simplified version of the oil-drilling problem described just above. For our present purpose we shall assume that:

1. If the well is drilled at all, it will be drilled on a fixed-price contract for \$100,000;

2. If oil is struck, the wildcatter will immediately sell out to a major producer for \$450,000;

3. Only one type of test or experiment, namely a seismic sounding, can be performed before deciding whether or not to drill. This experiment costs \$10,000; if it is performed, it will reveal with certainty whether the structure is of type A (very favorable to the existence of oil), type B (less favorable), or type C (very unfavorable).

On these assumptions the wildcatter's decision problem can be represented by the tree shown as figure 1.1. We imagine the decision maker as standing at the base of the tree (the left side of the diagram) and as being obliged to choose first between having the seismic sounding made and not having it made. If the wildcatter chooses to take the sounding, then one of three events will occur: the subsurface structure will be revealed to be of type A, B, or C. If the wildcatter chooses not to take the sounding, then only one event can occur at this stage: no information.

Nodes under the decision maker's control will be called *choice nodes* and designated by squares; nodes not under the decision maker's control will be called *event nodes* and designated by circles.

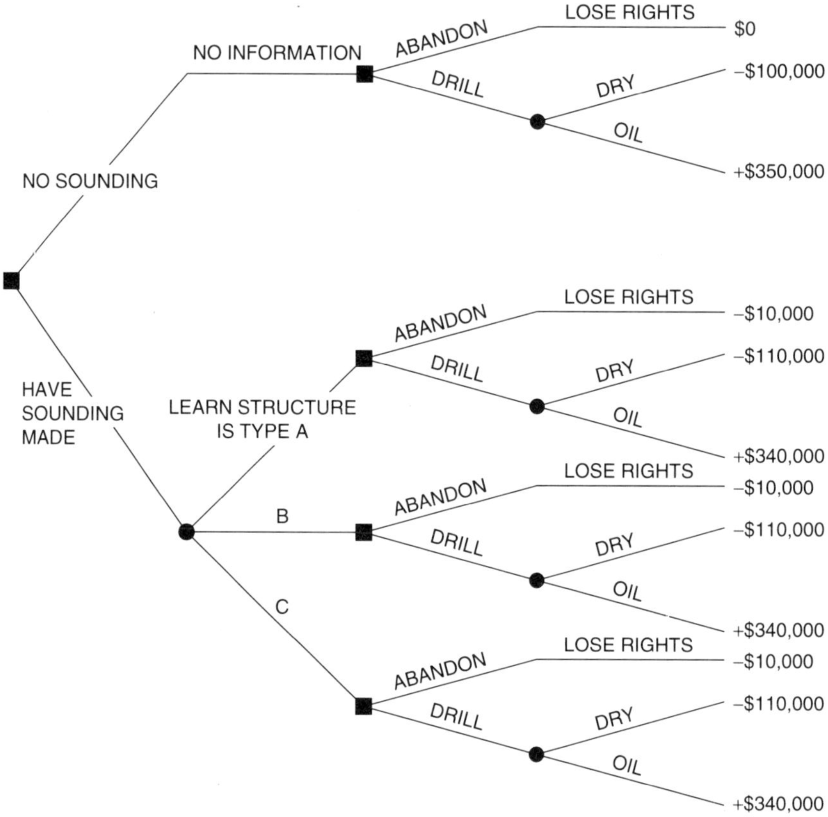

Figure 1.1
The oil wildcatter's decision tree

Whatever the wildcatter's first-stage choice may be and whatever the first-stage event, the wildcatter must now enter a second stage by making a choice between drilling and abandoning the option. If he drills, then one or the other of two events will occur: oil or dry hole; if he chooses to abandon the option, then the only possible event is "option rights lost."

Finally at the end (right) of the tree we write down a description of the consequence of each possible sequence of choices and events. If the wildcatter chooses not to have the sounding made and to abandon his option, the consequence is simply $0—we neglect whatever he may originally have paid for the option because this is a sunk cost that cannot be affected by any present decision and therefore is irrelevant to the decision problem. Suppose on the contrary he decides to drill even though he has learned nothing about the subsurface structure; if he strikes a dry hole, he loses the $100,000 drilling cost, whereas if he strikes oil, his profit is the $450,000 for which he sells the rights less the $100,000 cost of drilling. If in the first stage he decides to have the sounding made, then the consequences of abandoning the option, drilling a dry hole, or striking oil are all reduced by the $10,000 cost of the sounding.

The wildcatter may feel quite sure that, for example, he would decide to drill if he knew that the structure was of type A or B and would decide not to drill if he knew that the structure was of type C; however, his immediate problem is to decide whether or not to spend $10,000 in order to learn what the structure is. While it is obvious that this information has value, it is not at all clear whether the value is greater or less than the $10,000 the information will cost.

1.2.2 More Complex Decision Trees

The problem faced by any real wildcatter is of course far more complicated than the simplified problem represented by figure 1.1. Since there is more than one possible experiment that will tell him something about the chances of striking oil, the first fork in the real tree would have not just two branches corresponding to "sounding made" and "no sounding," but a branch for each possible experiment and one for no experiment at all. Each branch corresponding to a particular experiment would be followed by a whole set of branches corresponding to the possible outcomes of that experiment. Then, since there is nothing to prevent the wildcatter from performing a second experiment if he feels that the first one is not decisive, each of these "outcome" branches would be followed by a fork corresponding to the various possible second-stage experiments, each of which has to be followed by a fork corresponding to *its* possible outcomes. Thus even if there are just two possible experiments, I and II, each of which has just two possible outcomes, F(avorable) and U(nfavorable), the simple two-branch fork at the extreme left of figure 1.1 would have to be replaced by the whole diagram shown as figure 1.2. Notice that this diagram has been simplified as much as possible by omitting such sequences as "no experiment in the first stage followed by experiment I in the second stage," since this is equivalent to "experiment I in first stage followed by no experiment in the second stage."

In the same way, the possible "terminal" choices in the real problem are far more numerous than the two choices "drill" and "abandon" that are represented in figure 1.1. After all experimentation is over (or after a decision not to experiment at all), the wildcatter is not faced with just these two alternatives; in actual fact, he can make all kinds of risk-sharing deals with other wildcatters and investors. If the experimental possibilities were correctly represented by figure 1.2, then every one of the 12 different path-ends at the right of that figure would yield a branch for each of the possible drilling deals plus one for "abandon."

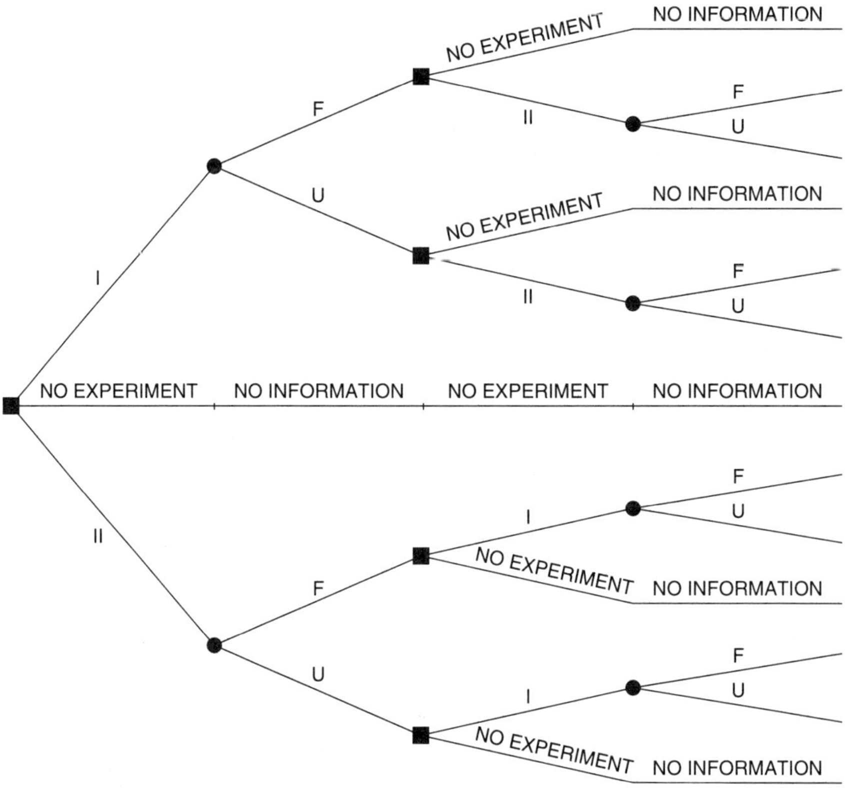

Figure 1.2
Decision tree with choice of experiment in two stages

Finally, the possible outcomes of drilling (at sole or shared risk) would not in reality be the single possibility "sell out for $450,000" which was assumed in constructing figure 1.1. The value of the oil would depend on its estimated amount, the depth at which it was found, and so forth; therefore, we must think of each "oil" branch in figure 1.1 as replaced by a whole bundle of branches, each corresponding to a different value attached to the well.

1.3 The Problem of Analysis

1.3.1 Analysis of the Simplest Problems

Before we even try to say what we mean by a "reasoned solution" of a complex decision problem of the kind we have just described, let us start by seeing how a sensible decision maker might solve a much simpler problem.

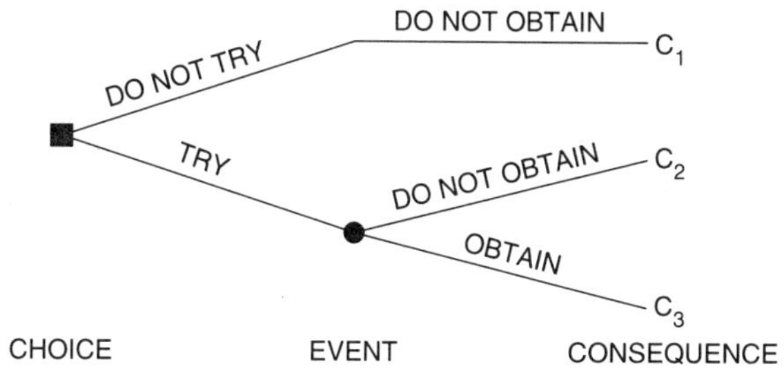

Figure 1.3
The simplest nontrivial decision tree

We consider an example. A manufacturer, Mr. L. K. Jones, has recently experienced a serious decline in demand for his product and as a result will be forced to lay off a substantial portion of his work force, spend money for protective treatment of idle machinery, and so forth, unless he can obtain a large order which the XYZ Company is about to place with some supplier. To have a chance at obtaining this order, Jones will have to incur considerable expense both for making samples and for sending a team of sales engineers to visit the XYZ Company. He must now decide whether or not to incur this expense. Formally, his problem can be described by the tree shown in figure 1.3, where the three possible consequences of the two possible acts are represented by symbols:

C_1 = layoff of substantial part of work force, cost of protecting machinery;

C_2 = same as C_1, and in addition the cost of unsuccessful attempt to obtain order;

C_3 = substantial monetary profit on order, less cost of obtaining it, and layoff averted.

The structure of this problem is simple enough to make quite clear to anyone the issues that are involved in its solution. Jones (or any other sensible decision maker faced with a problem of this sort) will feel that his decision will depend on two separate considerations: (1) his judgment concerning his chances of getting the order if he tries, and (2) a comparison of the cost of trying with the advantages which will accrue to him if he succeeds. If the cost is quite small relative to the advantages which would accompany success, he will make the attempt even if he thinks the chances of success are quite small; if, on the other hand, the cost of trying to get the order is so large that it would eat up most of the profits, he will not make the attempt unless he feels virtually sure that the attempt will succeed.

Sometimes a decision maker who is thinking about a problem of this kind will go even further and *quantify* some, if not all, of his reasoning. He may say, for example, that there is so much to be gained by obtaining the order that he would try to obtain it even if there were only 1 chance in 3 of success; he may then conclude either (a) that he will make the effort because in his opinion the chances are at least as good as 1 in 3, or else (b) that he will not make the effort because in his opinion the chances of success are less than 1 in 3. Alternatively, the decision maker may start from the other side of the problem, say that in his opinion he has about 1 chance in 3 of getting the order if he tries, and then conclude either (a) that he will make the attempt because the gains which would accrue from success are so great that a 1/3 chance of obtaining them is well worth the cost or trying, or else (b) that he will not make the attempt because the gains are too small to warrant the cost when there is only 1 chance in 3 of success.

1.3.2 The Bases of Decision: Preference and Judgment

The problem we have just discussed suffices to make it clear that there is in general no "objectively correct" solution to any realistic decision problem. Since Jones is personally responsible for the decision to try or not to try to get the order, his decision must necessarily rest on:

1. How good *he feels* the chances of obtaining the order would have to be to make it worth his while to try;
2. How good *in his opinion* the chances of obtaining the order actually are.

What the decision maker actually does when he answers questions of type 1 is quantify his *personal preference* for C_1 relative to C_2 and C_3; what he does when he answers questions of type 2 is quantify his *personal judgment* concerning the relative strengths of the factors that favor and oppose certain events. If he behaves reasonably, he then chooses the solution of the problem which is *consistent* with this personal preference and this personal judgment.

1.3.3 Analysis of Complex Problems: The Role of Formal Analysis

Since reasonable decisions in even the simplest problems must rest necessarily on the responsible decision maker's personal judgments and personal preferences, clearly these same elements must be involved in the solution of complex problems represented by decision trees with many levels and many branches at each level. It would be folly, in other words, to look for a method of analysis that will lead to an "objectively correct" solution of the oil-drilling problem we have used as an example in sections 1.2.1 and 1.2.2. A reasonable decision maker wants his decision to agree with his preferences and his best judgments, and he will have (and should have) no use for any proposal that purports to solve his problem by some "formula" that does *not* incorporate his preferences and judgments. This assertion does not of course imply that the decision maker should ignore objective evidence that is relevant and available; on the contrary, we shall be concerned throughout this book with methods that ensure that all available objective evidence is duly taken into account in arriving at considered judgments.

We shall show informally in the second chapter and more formally in the third chapter that any decision problem, no matter how complex, can in principle be reduced to a number of problems, each of which individually has the same simple structure as the problem described by the tree of figure 1.3. If in each of these simple problems the decision maker will (1) quantify his *preference*[1] by telling us how good the chances of obtaining C_3 *would have to be* to make him willing to gamble on C_2 or C_3 rather than to take C_1 for certain, and (2) quantify his *judgment* by telling us how good in his opinion the chances of obtaining C_3 *actually are*, and if in addition he accepts certain simple principles of "reasonable," "consistent," or "coherent" behavior, then we shall see that it is possible by purely logical deduction to find that solution of the complex problem which is *logically consistent with the decision maker's own preferences and judgments.*

Naturally we shall be concerned with decision problems where this kind of analysis by decomposition and evaluation produces fruitful results. There are, of course, many problems—some would say "most problems"—where although in principle such an analysis could be made, it would not be profitable to do so. In many situations, the incremental advantage to be gained from formal analysis cannot be expected to repay the effort, time, and cost of the analysis; in others, the decision maker may not be able, especially without training, to quantify his or her preferences and judgments in the way required for a formal analysis; in still others, the decision problem may be faithfully abstracted into the proper form only to prove to be too complicated for the analytical tools we have available. Even after granting all these exceptions, however, there remain many problems in which formal analysis can be of considerable help to a decision maker who wishes to take advantage of it. These are the types of problems that we shall study in this book.

1. See the preface for a discussion of "preference" versus "utility."

2 An Informal Treatment of Foundations

2.1 Introduction

In section 1.3.3 we said that if a decision maker will (1) quantify his or her preferences and judgments in a number of decision problems each of which individually has a very simple structure, and (2) accept certain principles of "reasonable," "consistent," or "coherent" behavior, then we can by pure deductive logic find that solution of any decision problem, however complex, which is logically consistent with the decision maker's own preferences and judgments. In the present chapter we shall give a very informal presentation of the logical foundation for this assertion; the same basic ideas will then be presented formally and rigorously in chapter 3.

2.1.1 Lotteries and Prizes

Since some, if not all, of the possible courses of action open to a decision maker in any real decision problem may result in any of a number of different possible consequences depending on an unpredictable event, choosing among the available alternatives is logically the same kind of problem as choosing among a number of different *lotteries*; and we shall find it convenient in what follows to keep attention focussed on this logical character of the problem by using the word *lottery* in place of the lengthier and less clear expression *possible course of action.*

In the simplest lotteries, the prizes are consequences in the sense in which we have been using that word. Thus the participant may be entitled to receive \$10,000 if a certain coin falls heads, otherwise nothing; or the participant may be assured of a \$10,000 profit if a certain order is obtained, and a \$0 profit if it is not. We shall, however, also have to consider more complicated lotteries in which the prizes are themselves lotteries. Thus in a lottery conducted by tossing a coin, tails may entitle the participant to spin a roulette wheel and then receive \$10,000 for red and \$5,000 for black, whereas heads obliges the participant to roll a die and pay \$7,000 for an ace and \$2,000 for any other face. Or in the business lottery "try to obtain the order," failure may result in a loss of a known amount but success may simply award the decision maker another lottery in the sense that profit depends on various unknown factors that will determine the cost of filling the order.

2.1.2 Mutually Exclusive and Collectively Exhaustive Events

Suppose that we have an urn containing serially numbered balls and that each ball bears in addition to its serial number some other distinguishing mark—as an example, suppose that some of the balls are marked A, the remainder B. If then a ball marked A is drawn from the urn, we shall say that the event A has occurred.

The idea of an event of this sort does not of course depend on the fact that the name of the event is actually marked on certain balls in the urn. We can equally well define the event A by saying that A occurs if and only if the serial number of the ball drawn from the urn is, say, greater than 7 but not greater than 25, in which case we shall say that the event A consists of outcomes 8 through 25. The only thing essential to the definition of an event is that we have some way of telling whether the event has or has not occurred.

A single outcome may of course correspond to any number of "overlapping" events. Thus, in our previous example, if the ball numbered 10 is drawn from the urn, we may obviously say that the event A and the event 10 have both occurred. The reader can easily generalize further. We shall however be particularly interested in certain *lists of events* that are drawn up in such a way that:

1. All the events on the list are *mutually exclusive* in the sense that *no more than one* of them *can* occur;

2. The events taken together are *collectively exhaustive* in the sense that *some one* of them *must* occur.

Thus, if the balls in an urn are serially numbered, a list of these numbers is a list of mutually exclusive and collectively exhaustive events. If, in addition, every ball in the urn bears one and only one of the labels A, B, or C, then $\{A, B, C\}$ is another list of mutually exclusive and collectively exhaustive events; and so forth.

2.2 Canonical Probability

In section 1.3.1 we suggested that a decision maker can and often does quantify his preferences and/or judgments in terms of "chances"—for instance, by saying that he would be willing to try for a particular order if the chances of success were 1 in 3 or better, or by saying that he thinks the chances of obtaining the order actually are 1 in 3. We shall now give a definite, operational meaning to such statements by introducing the concept of *canonical* chance or *canonical* probability.

2.2.1 Equally Likely Outcomes

Suppose that a person is offered a free chance at some prize under the following conditions. Balls numbered 1 to 100 have been placed in an urn and one of these balls has then been drawn and put in a closed box. The person in question is presented with 100 tickets numbered from 1 to 100 and is allowed to choose one of them. If the number he chooses matches the number on the ball which has been drawn from the urn, he will receive the prize; if not, he will receive nothing. Suppose further that even though the prize is one which he would very much like to win, he does not feel that it is worth the slightest effort to look for a ticket with any particular number on it and simply takes the first one which comes to hand.

In such a situation we shall say that *in this particular person's opinion* the 100 possible outcomes are *equally likely*. Notice very carefully that we do not and cannot assert that the outcomes are "in fact" equally likely; the fact is that the ball which has been drawn has some one particular number and no other. But even though someone who knew which ball has been drawn would not be indifferent among the 100 tickets, a person's decisions must be based on what he knows or believes about the facts of the world—they cannot be based on the unknown truth about these facts. Therefore, if he is indifferent in the way described, then for him the 100 outcomes are equally likely *by definition.*

2.2.2 Canonical Experiments

In what follows we shall continually have occasion to deal with experiments whose outcomes are all equally likely for some particular decision maker, and to be brief we shall say that any such experiment is *canonical* for the particular decision maker in question. A canonical experiment may consist of drawing one ball from an urn containing some known number of serially numbered balls, but it may equally well consist of rolling a die or tossing a coin, and so forth—in all cases the "canonicity" of the experiment arises solely from the fact that all possible outcomes are regarded as equally likely by the particular decision maker with whom we are dealing. For brevity we shall sometimes talk of a drawing from a "canonical urn," a toss of a "canonical coin," and so forth, or we shall say that a ball is drawn from an urn "canonically," that a coin is tossed "canonically," and so forth. All of these expressions mean simply that the decision maker is assumed to consider the outcomes equally likely.

2.2.3 Canonical Chances

Consider a canonical experiment with N possible outcomes and assume that the event A corresponds to n of these outcomes—we may have placed the label A on n of the N balls in an urn, or we may simply have listed n outcomes as defining the event A. Then we shall say that the *canonical chance* of the event A is n/N by *definition.*

2.2.4 Canonical Lotteries

Assuming that the reader understands the everyday meaning of the word "lottery," we shall use the term *canonical lottery* to designate a lottery in which the prize will be determined by a canonical experiment.

A complete description of such a lottery would consist of a list of all possible outcomes of the canonical experiment and a statement of the prize associated with every one of these outcomes. Since, however, the outcomes are all equally likely, the only thing that really matters is the *number* of outcomes associated with each prize, or equivalently, the *canonical chance* at each prize. Therefore, a canonical lottery can be adequately described by simply listing the prizes and the canonical chance at each.

2.3 Basic Assumptions

In a systematic though informal fashion, we next set forth the various assumptions that we need to make if we are to reduce complex decision problems to a number of very simple problems.

2.3.1 Existence of a Canonical Basis

In order to get a meaningful basis for *quantification* of preferences and judgments, we assume that given any positive integer N, the decision maker can imagine an experiment with N possible outcomes that is canonical as defined in section 2.2.2; and in order to get a basis for *comparison* of lotteries, we further assume that if two canonical lotteries involve only the same two prizes, the decision maker will prefer the one that offers the greater chance at the better prize. These assumptions can be given a self-contained expression as follows:

Basic Assumption 1 (Canonicity and Monotonicity) Suppose the decision maker prefers prize W to L. Given any positive integer N, the decision maker can imagine there exists an experiment[1] with N possible outcomes such that, if one lottery entitles him to a prize W contingent on the occurrence of one of n_1 possible outcomes, and L otherwise, whereas another lottery entitles him to prize W contingent on the occurrence of one of n_2 possible outcomes, and L otherwise, then he will prefer the former lottery to the latter if and only if $n_1 > n_2$.

The reader should observe that this assumption *implies* that the outcomes are equally likely in the sense of section 2.2.1.

1. For example, "one can imagine" shuffling a deck of N identical playing cards and drawing one card "at random."

2.3.2 Quantification of Preferences

Consider a decision maker who is comparing the attractiveness of (1) \$50,000 profit for certain with (2) a canonical lottery that gives a chance p at \$100,000 and a complementary chance $(1 - p)$ at nothing at all. His preference will obviously depend on the value of p. We may start with the trivial observations that (1) if $p = 0$, the lottery is equivalent to \$0 certain and hence is obviously less attractive than \$50,000 certain, while (2) if $p = 1$, the lottery is equivalent to \$100,000 certain and hence is obviously more attractive than \$50,000 certain. It also seems eminently sensible to argue that, loosely speaking, the attractiveness of the lottery to any reasonable person will increase "smoothly" as p increases from 0 to 1, and hence that there must exist some value of p—call it π—which makes the lottery *neither more nor less attractive* than \$50,000 certain.

The value of this "indifference probability," π, will of course depend on the individual decision maker. A man with large assets might very reasonably decide that he would be indifferent between the alternatives if the chance of winning the \$100,000 were exactly 1/2, whereas a man in serious need of \$50,000 might just as reasonably decide that he would prefer the \$50,000 certain unless the chance of winning in the lottery were at least 3/4 or even 9/10 or some larger number. All that we assume is that for any particular decision maker there exists *some* number π such that he would be indifferent between the certainty and the lottery if the chance of winning in the lottery were π.

Observe that although all the "prizes" in our example were sums of money, nothing in our argument turned on this fact. All that was really required for the argument was that one of the prizes in the lottery be *more* attractive and the other be *less* attractive than the consequence being compared with the lottery. Consider for example the problem facing Mr. L. K. Jones, which we described in section 1.3.1 and figure 1.3. We assume that Mr. Jones can *imagine* a situation wherein, if he tries to obtain the order, the XYZ Company will actually award the order by drawing a ball from a canonical urn in which a fraction p of the balls are labelled "L. K. Jones" while the others bear the names of other potential suppliers. If $p = 0$, Jones will obviously be unwilling to make the effort; if $p = 1$, he will obviously be willing; and we assume that as p increases from 0 toward 1 it will pass through some value π which is *just* large enough to make Jones feel that it is worth the trouble of trying to get the order in the imagined situation.

We sum up this discussion by making the following

Basic Assumption 2a (Quantification of Preferences) Given any decision problem with any set of possible consequences, the decision maker can select a consequence c^* which he finds at least as attractive, and another consequence c_* which he finds at least as unattractive, as any of the possible consequences; and he can then quantify his preference for any possible consequence c by specifying a number $\pi(c)$ between 0 and 1 inclusive such that he would be indifferent between (1) c for certain, and (2) a lottery giving a canonical chance $\pi(c)$ at c^* and a complementary chance at c_*.

Henceforth the number $\pi(c)$ will be called the *utility* of the consequence c (relative to the norming of c^* and c_*). The utility, $\pi(c)$, is that number for which the decision maker is indifferent between receiving c for certain or the lottery that yields prize c^* with canonical probability $\pi(c)$ and prize c_* with the complementary canonical probability.

The utility number $\pi(c)$ quantifies the decision maker's preferences for consequences c, c^*, c_*. Note that $\pi(c^*) = 1$ and $\pi(c_*) = 0$.

2.3.3 Quantification of Judgments

To see how judgments about real-world events can be quantified in much the same way that preferences for real-world consequences are quantified, consider first a gambler who is offered a choice between (1) winning \$1,000 if Wisconsin defeats Michigan in their next football game, and (2) winning \$1,000 if a red ball is drawn from a canonical urn. The gambler will obviously prefer option (1) if the fraction p of red balls in the urn is 0; she will obviously prefer option (2) if the fraction p is 1; furthermore we assume that as p increases from 0 toward 1 it will pass through some value P at which the gambler is indifferent between the two options.[2] We shall say that this value P is *by definition* the *judgmental probability* that *this particular gambler* assigns to the real-world event "Wisconsin defeats Michigan."

Observe that we do *not* say or imply that P as thus defined is the "true probability" that Wisconsin will defeat Michigan, nor do we say that it is this gambler's "best estimate" of the "true probability." If something is to be "estimated," we must know what that something is, and we frankly have no idea whatever of what is or can conceivably be meant by the "true probability" that Wisconsin will defeat Michigan. We might of course say that this "true probability" is 1 if in fact Wisconsin will defeat Michigan and 0 otherwise; but there is nothing to be gained except confusion by dragging the words "probability 0" and "probability 1" into the discussion when what we are talking about is ascertained facts. What we are interested in in this book is the making of decisions when the facts have *not* been ascertained, and for this purpose what we need is a quantification of

2. Assume the gambler has no preference for the outcome of the game other than the monetary rewards involved.

the judgment of the *responsible decision maker* concerning what the facts may be.

Observe also that it would be completely nonsensical for our purpose to distinguish between the probability that Wisconsin wins as defined *before* the game is played and the probability of the same event as defined *after* the game is played. If the game has in fact been played, but the gambler has learned nothing bearing on its outcome, she will make exactly the same choice between options (1) and (2) that she would have made before the game was played. The probabilities that are relevant in problems of decision under uncertainty *depend on what the decision maker knows*; they are not determined either by the "true facts" or by what some other person knows.

Now returning to a business context, consider once again Mr. L. K. Jones's problem of deciding whether to try to obtain the order from the XYZ Company, recalling that he has already evaluated his *preferences* regarding the *consequences* involved by saying that he would be just as willing to try to get the order if there were a certain canonical chance π of getting the order. We now assume that he can evaluate his *judgment* concerning his *real* chances of getting the order by imagining that he has actually made the required effort and the XYZ Company has already decided who is to get the order, but at this moment the president of XYZ, just for fun, gives him a choice between the following two options: (1) accept the decision as made, and (2) let the decision be remade by drawing a ball from a canonical urn. If the fraction of winning balls in the urn is 0, Jones will clearly prefer option 1; if it is 1, he will clearly prefer option 2. We assume furthermore that as the fraction increases from 0 toward 1 there will be *some* value where *Jones* is indifferent between the two options. This value we shall call the *judgmental probability* which *Jones* assigns to the real-world event "the attempt to get XYZ's order succeeds." And if we denote this event by Θ_0, we can denote the probability of the event by $P(\Theta_0)$.

We can sum up this discussion by making the following

Basic Assumption 2b (Quantification of Judgments) Let Θ_0 be any real-world event, and let c^* and c_* be the consequences defined in Basic Assumption 2a. The decision maker can quantify his judgment concerning Θ_0 by specifying a number $P(\Theta_0)$ between 0 and 1 such that *he* would be *indifferent* between (1) the right to receive c^* if Θ_0 occurs, otherwise c_*, and (2) a lottery giving a canonical chance $P(\Theta_0)$ at c^* and a complementary chance at c_*.

The decision maker's *preferences* for consequence c (relative to c^* and c_*) is quantified by the *utility* number $\pi(c)$. The decision maker's *judgments* about the uncertain event θ_0 is quantified by the *probability* number $P(\theta_0)$. For the purpose of this book probabilities are always judgmental, and gradually we shall dispense with modifier "judgmental" as in judgmental probability.

2.3.4 Transitivity

In a purely logical argument, a statement of premises does not by itself enable one to draw any conclusions whatever; there must also exist a set of agreed "rules" or "principles" of logical inference. In just the same way, the decision maker's preferences for consequences and judgments concerning events do not by themselves determine which is the best solution of a problem of decision under uncertainty. We must also use certain rules or principles of "reasonable," "consistent," or "coherent" behavior. The first of the two principles we propose to use is stated in the following

Basic Assumption 3 (Transitivity) Let l', l'', and l''' denote any three lotteries. If the decision maker has any preferences among these lotteries, then these preferences should be transitive in the sense that:

a. If he is indifferent between l' and l'' and between l'' and l''', then he is indifferent between l' and l'''.

b. If he is indifferent between l' and l'' but prefers l'' to l''', then he prefers l' to l''', and so forth.[3]

We do not mean by this assumption to imply that a reasonable person's *intuitive* preferences are necessarily transitive, and it has in fact been well established that they sometimes are not. What we are assuming is that the decision maker would *like* his preferences to be transitive, and the reasonableness of this assumption seems scarcely open to question. For suppose that we could find an "intransitive" *decision maker* (not a mere conversationalist) who prefers l' to l'', prefers l'' to l''' or is indifferent, and prefers l''' to l' or is indifferent. If these preferences mean anything at all, they mean that if the decision maker owns l', he would be willing to exchange it for l''', would then be willing to exchange l''' for l'', and would then pay a premium to exchange l'' for l'. In the vernacular he would be said to be a "money pump," especially if he could be pumped repeatedly or sucked dry—but one pump suffices for the argument.

2.3.5 Substitution of Prizes

To illustrate the second (and last) principle of reasonable or consistent behavior that we shall adopt, suppose that a coin is to be tossed and that

---

3. Notice that the Transitivity Assumption does not assume that the decision maker has a preference ordering for any two lotteries. It says that insofar as preferences exist, they should be transitive.

a decision maker is given a free choice of one of two lotteries whose outcomes are based on this toss. Both lotteries award the *same* prize if the coin comes up heads, but they differ as regards the prize associated to tails: lottery A offers a certain new automobile; lottery B offers a power boat plus $1,125 cash. Our principle asserts in effect that if the decision maker would be indifferent between the new automobile *for certain* and the power boat plus $1,125 cash *for certain*, then he will be indifferent between the *lottery* in which the automobile is the prize and the *lottery* in which the boat plus cash is the prize.

The principle itself can now be stated in the form of the following

Basic Assumption 4 (Substitutability) Let a lottery be modified by replacing just one of its prizes by another. If the decision maker is indifferent between the original and new prizes, he should be indifferent between the original and modified lotteries.

2.4 Comparison of Simple Canonical Lotteries

2.4.1 Introduction

We now have available all the material needed to compare any set of lotteries, where, as usual, the term "lotteries" includes possible courses of action in ordinary decision problems. Ultimately we shall show how the analysis is actually carried out by solving successively problems of three increasing degrees of complexity:

1. Comparison of *simple canonical* lotteries, where by "simple" we mean that after the decision maker has made a single choice, a single canonical event determines the ultimate consequence.
2. Comparison of *simple "real"* lotteries, where the logical structure is the same as in a simple canonical lottery but the events are in the real world and not in an imaginary canonical experiment.
3. Comparison of *compound "real"* lotteries, where there may be a whole sequence of choices by the decision maker alternating with chance events before the consequence is finally determined.

The first of these three classes of problems will be the subject of the present section; the second will occupy sections 2.5 through 2.8; the third and last will be the subject of chapter 6.

2.4.2 A Typical Problem

As a typical example of choice between simple canonical lotteries we shall suppose that a decision maker is offered the opportunity to participate if

Table 2.1
Description of lotteries l' and l''

Description of lottery l'			Description of lottery l''		
Label on ball	Number of balls	Prize	Label on ball	Number of balls	Prize
1	100	$-$ \$9,000	1	100	0
2	300	0	2	900	+ \$3,000
3	600	+ \$9,000		1,000	
	1,000				

Table 2.2
Utilities for consequences

c	π(c)
$-$ \$9,000	.20
0	.85
+3,000	.90
+9,000	.98

he likes in either, but not both, of two lotteries l' and l'' defined as follows: Lottery l' will be conducted by drawing one ball from an urn containing the mix of bals described by the first two columns of table 2.1 and then awarding the prize indicated in the third column of that table. A plus sign means that the participant will receive the amount of money in question, whereas a minus sign means that he will have to pay out that amount of money to the bank. Lottery l'' is of the same general nature, but is based on an urn with a different mix of balls and with different prizes, as shown in the last three columns of table 2.1.

2.4.3 Quantification of Preferences

In accordance with our Basic Assumption 2a (section 2.3.2) we assume that our decision maker can now select a pair of *reference consequences* c^* and c_* and quantify his preference for every consequence in table 2.1 by comparing it with a canonical *reference lottery between* c^* and c_*. Specifically, we shall assume that our decision maker selects

$$c^* = +\$10{,}000, \qquad c_* = -\$10{,}000,$$

and then makes the utility evaluations shown in table 2.2. Convenient methods for actually making such evaluations will be discussed in chapter 4.

Table 2.3
Description of lottery l'_Δ

Primary lottery		Chances in secondary lottery	
Label on ball	Number of balls	of winning \$10,000	of losing \$10,000
1	100	.20	.80
2	300	.85	.15
3	600	.98	.02
	1,000		

2.4.4 Substitution of Prizes

Recalling from section 2.3.2 that the first entry in table 2.2 means that this particular decision maker is *indifferent* between (1) a loss of \$9,000 certain, and (2) a lottery giving a .20 chance of winning \$10,000 and a .80 chance of losing \$10,000, we now argue in accordance with our fourth fundamental assumption (section 2.3.5) that the attractiveness of lottery l' *to this particular decision maker* will be left exactly the same if we replace the −\$9,000 prize for a ball numbered 1 by a "secondary" lottery giving a .20 chance at +\$10,000 and a .80 chance at −\$10,000. We then argue that the attractiveness of lottery l' will still be left exactly the same if this modified version is further modified by replacing the 0 prize for a ball numbered 2 by a "secondary" lottery giving a .85 chance at +\$10,000 and a .15 chance at −\$10,000; and similarly for the last prize in the lottery. The end result of these three modifications is to convert the original lottery l' into the lottery l'_Δ described by table 2.3.

2.4.5 Reduction of Compound Canonical Lotteries

The objective of our strategy of analysis should now be clear. We have reduced the original lottery l', which could result in any of three different prizes, to the modified lottery l'_Δ, which will ultimately result in one of just two prizes, +\$10,000 or −\$10,000. The reader can see at once that lottery l'' can be similarly reduced by use of table 2.2 to a lottery l''_Δ involving *these same two prizes.* As between l'_Δ and l''_Δ, the better choice is obviously the one with the better chance of winning, and hence necessarily the smaller chance of losing, \$10,000. Therefore all that remains is to compute the chance of winning \$10,000 in each of the two modified lotteries.

Rather than reasoning about these chances abstractly, we can make them concrete by simply building each secondary lottery into the mechanism of the primary lottery. Starting with the first line in table 2.3, we observe that if a ball labelled 1 is drawn, the participant is to be given a .20 chance at winning and a .80 chance at losing \$10,000; and we argue that

Table 2.4
Description of lottery $l'_{\Delta\Delta}$

Primary label	Number of balls	Number with secondary label W
1	100	$.20 \times 100 = 20$
2	300	$.85 \times 300 = 255$
3	600	$.98 \times 600 = 588$
	1,000	863

since there are 100 equally likely balls labelled 1, we can accomplish this by simply placing a secondary label W (win) on $.20 \times 100 = 20$ of these balls and placing a secondary label L (lose) on the remainder. Proceeding to row 2 of the table we similarly build in the secondary lottery by placing a secondary label W on $.85 \times 300 = 255$ of the 300 equally likely balls labelled 2 and placing a secondary label L on the remainder. Proceeding similarly for the last row of the table, we end up with the "single-stage" lottery $l'_{\Delta\Delta}$ described in table 2.4, and we see at once that the chances of winning $10,000 in this lottery are $863/1000 = .863$. In exactly the same manner the reader can show that lottery l'' can be reduced to a lottery $l''_{\Delta\Delta}$ in which the chances of winning are .895 and thus greater than the corresponding chances in lottery $l'_{\Delta\Delta}$ (exercise 4).

2.4.6 Solution of the Example

Since lottery $l''_{\Delta\Delta}$ involves the same two prizes as lottery $l'_{\Delta\Delta}$ and gives a greater chance at the better prize (.895 against .863), we conclude by our first basic assumption (section 2.3.1) that in accordance with common sense the decision maker should prefer $l''_{\Delta\Delta}$ to $l'_{\Delta\Delta}$. Then since $l'_{\Delta\Delta}$ and $l''_{\Delta\Delta}$ were derived from l' and l'' respectively by a series of modifications, each of which left the attractiveness of the lottery in question unchanged, and since $l''_{\Delta\Delta}$ is preferable to $l'_{\Delta\Delta}$ as just shown, we conclude by our third basic assumption (Transitivity, in section 2.3.4) that the decision maker should prefer l'' to l'. We remind the reader that when we say "should," we mean should if he wishes to behave in a way that agrees with his own preferences as revealed in table 2.2 and with the principles of consistent behavior expressed in our third and fourth basic assumptions.

We leave it to the reader (exercise 5) to show that, given the basic preferences revealed in table 2.2, this particular decision maker should prefer participating in *either* lottery to a refusal to participate at all.

2.4.7 Generalization

Let us now reexamine what was really involved in the process by which we reduced lotteries l' and l'' to two lotteries both of which involved the *same*

Table 2.5
Reduction of lottery l'

Primary label	Fraction so labelled	Fraction relabelled W	Product
1	.1	.20	.020
2	.3	.85	.255
3	.6	.98	.588
	1.0		.863

two prizes and could therefore be compared by simply comparing the *chances* of winning the better prize. The reduction of l' was carried out in table 2.4, and examination of that table will convince the reader that the number of balls in the urn on which the lottery was based played no real role whatever in the argument. What we wanted was the *fraction* of winning balls in the urn, not the *number*; and that fraction can be calculated directly, as shown in table 2.5.

From this way of presenting the calculation, the reader can easily infer the following generalization of our result concerning reduction of canonical lotteries to reference lotteries:

Let $c_1, \ldots, c_i, \ldots, c_n$ be the prizes in a canonical lottery l, let m_i be the chance which the lottery gives at c_i, and let $\pi(c_i)$ be the decision maker's quantified preference for c_i relative to reference consequences c^* and c_*. Then the decision maker should be indifferent between l and a canonical lottery in which the consequence will be either c^* or c_*, and in which the chance at c^* is

$$\Pi = \sum_{i=1}^{n} m_i \pi(c_i).$$

From this result we have immediately the following result for choice between any two canonical lotteries:

Let l' be a canonical lottery which gives chances m_i' at prizes c_i' which $i = 1, \ldots, n'$; let l'' be a canonical lottery which gives chances m_i'' at prizes c_i'' where $i = 1, \ldots, n''$; and compute the indices

$$\Pi' = \sum_{i=1}^{n'} m_i' \pi(c_i'), \qquad \Pi'' = \sum_{i=1}^{n''} m_i'' \pi(c_i'').$$

Then l' should be preferred to l'' if and only if Π' is greater than Π''.

The preference indices $\pi(c_i')$ and $\pi(c_i'')$ must of course be evaluated relative to the *same* reference consequences c^* and c_*.

2.4.8 Reduction of Compound Canonical Lotteries: A Generalization

It will be helpful for the discussion to follow if at this point we formalize a generalization of the ideas introduced in section 2.4.5. Let l' be a lottery

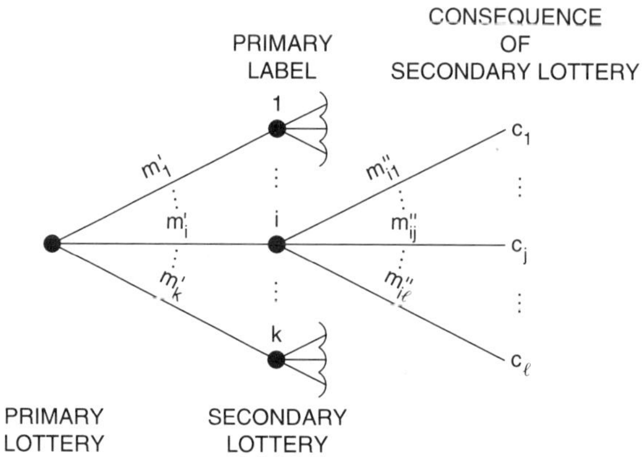

Figure 2.1
Compound lottery

which can result in one of the labels $1, \ldots, i, \ldots, k$ with canonical probabilities $m'_1, \ldots, m'_i, \ldots, m'_k$ respectively. If l' results in label i, then as shown in figure 2.1 let a secondary lottery l'' be performed that will result in one of the consequences $c_1, \ldots, c_j, \ldots, c_l$ with canonical probabilities $m''_{i1}, \ldots, m''_{ij}, \ldots, m''_{il}$ respectively. *The canonical chance that the compound lottery will result in consequence* c_j *is* $\sum_{i=1}^{k} m'_i m''_{ij}$, *for* $j = 1, \ldots, l$. This assertion can be proved by using balls in an urn with double labellings (as done in section 2.4.5), and the details are left to the reader as an exercise (exercise 7).

2.5 Comparison of Simple "Real" Lotteries: An Introduction

2.5.1 A Simplified Example

Our next task is to show how the method of comparing *canonical* lotteries, which we developed in the previous section, can be extended to comparison of *real* lotteries, in other words of available courses of action in real decision problems. To exhibit the basic logic without distracting complexities, we shall base our exposition on the following extremely simple example. A painting contractor must choose between two available contracts. Contract l' will yield a profit of about \$9,000 if it can be completed by the deadline specified in the contract, but the contract provides late-completion penalties which will reduce the profit to zero if the completion is up to a month late, and will lead to an actual loss of about \$9,000 if the completion is over a month late. Contract l'' will yield a profit of about \$3,000 if it is completed on time; however, the profit will be reduced to zero if the deadline is not met regardless of the extent of the delay. The

Table 2.6

Contract l'		Contract l''	
Event	Consequence	Event	Consequence
Θ'_1: on time	+$9,000	Θ''_1: on time	+$3,000
Θ'_2: up to one month late	0	Θ''_2: late	0
Θ'_3: over one month late	−$9,000		

data of the problem can be represented in tabular form as shown in table 2.6, where the reader should understand the event Θ'_1 to mean that contract l' will be completed on time *if* it is signed, and similarly for all the other events in the table.

2.5.2 A Proposed Method of Analysis

Comparing table 2.6 with table 2.1, we see at once that in most respects the contractor's decision problem that we are now discussing is identical to the problem of choosing between two canonical lotteries that we solved in section 2.4 by showing that both lotteries could be "reduced" to canonical lotteries having the same two prizes and differing only as regards the canonical chance of winning the better prize. The only real difference between that problem and the present problem is the fact that there we knew the canonical chance associated with each possible outcome of lotteries l' and l'', whereas here the outcomes of contracts l' and l'' depend on events that do *not* have definite chances associated with them.

We have pointed out repeatedly, however, that even though no definite numerical chances come already attached to the consequences in table 2.6, the contractor should nevertheless think quantitatively about chances before choosing between contracts l' and l''. If he believes, for example, that there is a very good chance that he will be able to complete l' on time, then he will certainly try for $9,000 with l' rather than settle for a maximum of $3,000 with l''; whereas if he thinks that there is a substantial chance that he might be over a month late in completing l', then he may very well take l'' instead. What is more, we have remarked that decision makers frequently assign definite numerical values to such chances, saying, for example, "I think that there is about one chance in ten that I cannot complete l' on time." In section 2.3.3 we took it as Basic Assumption 2b that a decision maker *can* scale his judgments about events in this way if he believes it useful to do so.

This way of looking at the problem suggests that if the contractor assigns a numerical chance to every event in table 2.6 as well as a numerical

Table 2.7

	Act	
Event	Property I	Property II
Θ_1	\$10,000	\$0
Θ_2	0	10,000

preference π to every consequence in the table, then he may be able to solve his problem by exactly the same method of analysis that we used to solve the problem of choosing between the two canonical lotteries of table 2.1. Specifically, if the decision maker says that the chance that Θ'_1 will occur is some number $P(\Theta'_1)$, and so forth, then it seems plausible that he should be indifferent (1) between contract l' and a canonical reference lottery between c^* and c_* in which the chance of c^* is

$$\Pi' = P(\Theta'_1)\pi(+9{,}000) + P(\Theta'_2)\pi(0) + P(\Theta'_3)\pi(-9{,}000),$$

and (2) between l'' and a reference lottery in which the chance of c^* is

$$\Pi'' = P(\Theta''_1)\pi(+3{,}000) + P(\Theta''_2)\pi(0),$$

and *if* these indifferences should hold, then clearly he should prefer l' to l'' if and only if Π' is greater than Π''.

Ultimately we shall show that these plausible conjectures are in fact consequences of our basic assumptions and that the problem can in fact be solved in this way. However, before we can show this we must first digress to examine some logical inconsistencies that can arise in the decision maker's evaluations of the chances of the various possible events.

2.6 Consistency Requirements for Evaluations of Events

2.6.1 An Example of Inconsistent Evaluations

To see how inconsistencies can arise in the assignment of numerical values to the chances of real-world events, let us leave our contractor's problem for a moment and consider an example chosen to bring out the problem of consistency as clearly as possible. A real estate investor, Dianne Myers, knows for certain that a new highway will be built along one of just two possible routes, I and II. The investor owns a plot of land on route I which she is sure will be worth \$10,000 as a site for a filling station *if* the highway follows route I, but will be worthless if the highway follows route II. She has an opportunity to make an even trade of this property for a similar one located on route II; furthermore, she feels sure that this alternate

Table 2.8

Urn		Prizes	
Label	Fraction of all balls	Lottery I	Lottery II
I	$P(\Theta_1)$	$10,000	$0
II	$P(\Theta_2)$	0	10,000

property will be worth $10,000 if the highway follows route II, and otherwise nothing. The investor's problem is thus simply to decide whether she prefers a plot on route I to one on route II or the contrary. The problem can be laid out in the way shown in table 2.7, where Property I means that the investor chooses the property on route I, whereas event Θ_2 means that the highway actually follows route II, and so forth. In this particular problem, the relevant events happen to be the same for both acts.

Without implying that any investor would really want to make a formal analysis of so simple a problem, for the sake of the argument over principles, we shall nevertheless inquire into what might happen if she did. To apply the method of analysis that we recommended to the contractor of the previous section, the investor must evaluate the events Θ_1 and Θ_2 in such a way that she can reduce her real decision problem to the canonical problem of table 2.8. And it is quite conceivable that in assigning these two probabilities she might reason as follows: Looking first at the real-world event Θ_1, she might decide that she would just be indifferent between (1) the right to receive $10,000 if Θ_1 occurs, and (2) a .40 canonical chance at that same prize. Then looking at the real-world event Θ_2, she might decide that even though this event is more likely in her judgment than event Θ_1, she is nevertheless so uncertain about the factors that determine which route the highway will follow that she would definitely *prefer* a *known* 50-50 chance at $10,000 to the right to receive $10,000 if Θ_2 occurs; and she might thus finally conclude that she would be *indifferent* between (1) the right to receive $10,000 if Θ_2 occurs, and (2) a .45 canonical chance at the same prize.

If we point out to this investor that $P(\Theta_1) = .40$ and $P(\Theta_2) = .45$ do not add to 1, it is very possible that she will answer that she nonetheless does in fact prefer a known .50 chance at $10,000 to *either* a chance based on the occurrence of Θ_1 *or* a chance based on the occurrence of Θ_2. Since she thinks the chances of Θ_2 are better than those of Θ_1, she will of course choose Property II if she decides *without* the use of formal analysis. If our method of analysis cannot arrive at this conclusion without forcing her to change her feeling that *neither* Property I nor Property II is as good as a known .50 chance at $10,000, then it is the method of analysis that will have to be changed, not her considered opinions.

2.6.2 Implications of the Inconsistencies

Rather than argue about whether this investor "should" hold these opinions, let us test whether she really does hold them. To do so, we have only to point out to the investor that if, instead of choosing either Property I or Property II outright, she chooses to toss a coin and to take I if the coin falls heads, II if it falls tails, then she will have a known objective .50 chance of making $10,000 whichever route the highway actually follows. If therefore she really meant it when she said that a known .50 chance at $10,000 was better than a chance at $10,000 depending on the occurrence of either Θ_1 or Θ_2, then she presumably *will* (not "should") immediately revise her decision to choose Θ_2 and adopt the coin-tossing strategy instead. If, on the other hand, she says that it would be absurd for her to take property Θ_1 just because a coin falls heads, when in her judgment Θ_2 is the better bet, then she *must* (not "should") admit that she did not really mean it when she said that she preferred a known .50 chance at $10,000 to a chance at $10,000 depending on the occurrence of either Θ_1 or Θ_2. Which of these two alternatives the investor will choose is up to her, but this book is for those decision makers who wish to act in accordance with their best judgment, uncertain as it may be, and not in accordance with the toss of a coin.[4]

2.6.3 Consistency Requirement for the Example

Assuming that our investor has decided not to determine her action by tossing a coin, but to follow the dictates of her own best judgment and revise her assertions about $P(\Theta_1)$ and $P(\Theta_2)$ accordingly, we can now give a simple argument to show that she *should* assign values to these two numbers that *add to 1*. To do so we shall examine some further implications of the fact that by "randomizing" her choice she *could* obtain a definite .50 chance at $10,000; more specifically, we shall argue that even though the investor would not actually want to randomize her choice, she will nevertheless want to avoid making any statements which falsely imply that the randomized choice would not give her a .50 chance at $10,000.

In order to make the argument a little easier to follow, let us now imagine the randomized choice as being based not on the toss of a coin but on drawing a ball from an urn in which one half of the balls are marked "take Property I" and the other half "take Property II." If the investor chooses a number $P(\Theta_1)$ such that she would really be indifferent between Property I and a $P(\Theta_1)$ canonical chance at $10,000, then the

4. Exercises 2.17 and 2.18 further examine this behavioral inconsistency.

value to her of this lottery will be left unchanged if we modify the lottery by taking the balls labelled "take I" and relabel a fraction $P(\Theta_1)$ of them "win \$10,000" and the remainder "win \$0." If the investor similarly chooses $P(\Theta_2)$ so that she would really be indifferent between Property II and a $P(\Theta_2)$ canonical chance at \$10,000, then the value of the lottery to her will again be left unchanged if we take the balls originally labelled "take II" and relabel a fraction $P(\Theta_2)$ of them "win \$10,000," and the remainder "win \$0."

Recalling that half the balls in the urn were originally labelled "take I" and half were labelled "take II," we see that the fraction of *all* balls that now bear the label "win \$10,000" is

$$\tfrac{1}{2}P(\Theta_1) + \tfrac{1}{2}P(\Theta_2) = \tfrac{1}{2}[P(\Theta_1) + P(\Theta_2)].$$

We already know, however, that *before* the balls were relabelled the lottery gave a .50 canonical chance at \$10,000, and it follows at once that the direct and the indirect evaluations of the lottery will agree if and only if

$$\tfrac{1}{2}[P(\Theta_1) + P(\Theta_2)] = \tfrac{1}{2},$$

i.e., if and only if $P(\Theta_1) + P(\Theta_2) = 1$.

The reader can easily verify that the argument leading to this conclusion involved just two basic assumptions: the principle of substitutability of equivalent prizes discussed in section 2.3.5 and the principle of transitivity discussed in section 2.3.4.

2.6.4 General Consistency Requirements

Having shown by this example why consistency requirements are not really obvious but need proof, we shall now proceed a little more formally to develop a set of three consistency requirements that govern the evaluation of events in all decision problems, no matter how many events may be involved.

1. If Θ_0 is any event whatever, then

$$P(\Theta_0) \geq 0.$$

This non-negativity requirement follows directly from Assumption 2b in section 2.3.3 and requires no proof.

2. If Θ is an event that is *certain* to occur, then

$$P(\Theta) = 1.$$

The decision maker should obviously be indifferent between (1) the right to receive a valuable prize if an event occurs that he believes is certain to occur, and (2) the right to receive that same prize if a ball marked "win" is drawn from a canonical urn in which all the balls are marked "win."

Table 2.9

	Lottery l_1			Lottery l_2	
	Red	Black		Red	Black
Θ_1	win	lose	Θ_1	win	lose
Θ_2	lose	win	Θ_2	win	lose
Θ_3	lose	lose	Θ_3	lose	lose

3. If Θ_1 and Θ_2 are *mutually exclusive* events and (Θ_1 *or* Θ_2) is the event that one *or* the other of these two events occurs,

$$P(\Theta_1 \text{ or } \Theta_2) = P(\Theta_1) + P(\Theta_2).$$

Let event Θ_3 be defined in such a manner that events Θ_1, Θ_2, and Θ_3 are mutually exclusive and collectively exhaustive. In other words, let $\Theta_3 \equiv$ not (Θ_1 *or* Θ_2).

The consistency requirement that we developed for the two-route example in the previous section was simply a special case of this rule—special because in that example Θ_1 and Θ_2 were not only mutually exclusive but also collectively exhaustive, so that $P(\Theta_1) + P(\Theta_2) = 1$. We now proceed to prove the general rule.

Consider first the two "compound" lotteries described in table 2.9, both of which will pay out either \$10,000 or nothing, and in both of which the payout depends *both* on the color of a ball drawn from an urn *and* on which one of a set of mutually exclusive and collectively exhaustive real-world events occurs. More specifically:

1. In lottery l_1, the urn contains 100 red and 100 black balls and the \$10,000 will be paid if either (a) the ball is red and event Θ_1 occurs, or (b) the ball is black and even Θ_2 occurs.

2. In lottery l_2, the urn contains 100 red and 100 black balls and the \$10,000 will be paid if the ball is red and the event (Θ_1 *or* Θ_2) occurs—that is, if *either* Θ_1 or Θ_2 occurs.

In figure 2.2 we exhibit two different decision tree representations of the lotteries l_1 and l_2. In terms of these representations we shall prove successively that the decision maker should be indifferent between:

1. l_1 and l_2 (proof uses the first representations of l_1 and l_2);

2. l_1 and a canonical chance of $\frac{1}{2}[P(\Theta_1) + P(\Theta_2)]$ at W (proof uses the second representation of l_1); and

3. l_2 and a canonical chance of $\frac{1}{2}[P(\Theta_1 \text{ or } \Theta_2)]$ at W (proof uses the second representation of l_2).

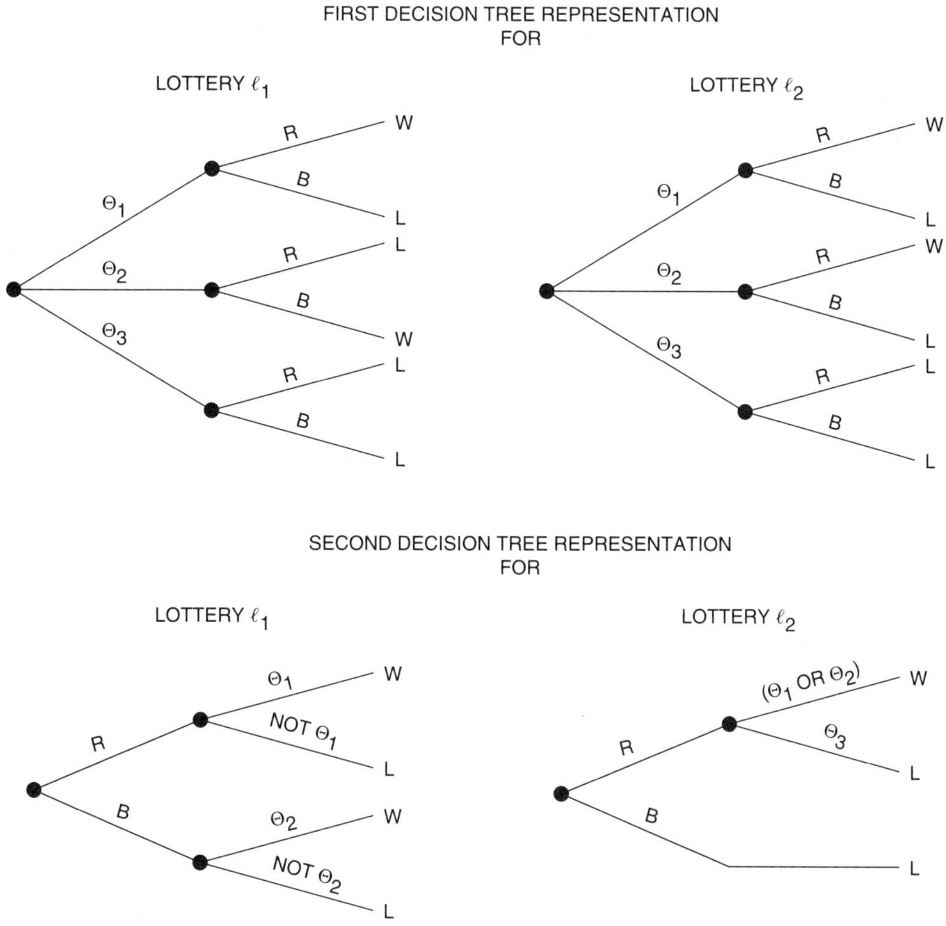

Figure 2.2
Additivity of probability

From these indifferences it is clear by transitivity that $[P(\Theta_1) + P(\Theta_2)]$ must equal $P(\Theta_1 \text{ or } \Theta_2)$.

Regarding 1

From the first representations of l_1 and l_2, we observe that l_2 is a modification of l_1 which arises from changing the prize if Θ_2 occurs; however, since the decision maker is indifferent between the old and the new prizes—both give a canonical chance of $\frac{1}{2}$ at W—then by Basic Assumption 4 he must be indifferent between the original and the modified lotteries.

Table 2.10

Original lottery l	
Event	Consequence
Θ_1	c_1
Θ_2	c_2
Θ_3	c_3

Regarding 2

From the second representation of l_1, the prize associated with event R is indifferent to a secondary lottery which gives a canonical chance of $P(\Theta_1)$ at W, and the prize associated with event B is indifferent to a secondary lottery which gives a canonical chance of $P(\Theta_2)$ at W. Making these substitutions successively, which by Basic Assumptions 4 and 3 do not change the desirability of l_1, we replace l_1 by a compound *canonical* lottery which is easily shown to be reducible to a lottery which gives a canonical chance of $\frac{1}{2}[P(\Theta_1) + P(\Theta_2)]$ at W.

Regarding 3

From the second representation of l_2, the prize associated with event R is indifferent to a secondary lottery which gives a canonical chance of $P(\Theta_1$ *or* $\Theta_2)$ at W. Arguing in a similar fashion as above, l_2 is shown to be indifferent to a lottery which gives a canonical chance of $\frac{1}{2}P(\Theta_1$ *or* $\Theta_2)$ at W. Arguing in a similar fashion as above, l_2 is shown to be indifferent to a lottery which gives a canonical chance of $\frac{1}{2}P(\Theta_1$ *or* $\Theta_2)$ at W.

2.7 Reduction of Acts to Reference Lotteries

Now that we have shown that the decision maker should observe certain consistency requirements in assigning probabilities to events, we are ready to show how probabilities that meet these requirements can be used to simplify the problem of selecting the best of a set of available "real lotteries," that is, available acts in a real decision problem. What we shall prove is that, given *any* act, the decision maker can find a canonical reference lottery between the two reference consequence c^* and c_* that is neither more nor less attractive *to him* than the given act; the best act will then be the one corresponding to the reference lottery that gives the greatest chance at c^*.

Table 2.11

	Modified lottery l_Δ	
	Prize: secondary lottery with	
Event	Chance at c^*	Chance at c_*
Θ_1	π_1	$(1-\pi_1)$
Θ_2	π_2	$(1-\pi_2)$
Θ_3	π_3	$(1-\pi_3)$

Table 2.12
Scheme for conducting l_Δ

Urn		Prize chart			
Label	Number	Θ_1	Θ_2	Θ_3	Number relabelled c^*
Γ_1	$\pi_1 N$	c^*	c^*	c^*	$(P_1+P_2+P_3)\pi_3 N$
Γ_2	$(\pi_2-\pi_3)N$	c^*	c^*	c^*	$(P_1+P_2)(\pi_2-\pi_3)N$
Γ_3	$(\pi_1-\pi_2)N$	c^*	c^*	c^*	$P_1(\pi_1-\pi_2)N$
Γ_4	$(1-\pi_1)N$	c^*	c^*	c^*	0
Total	N				$(P_1\pi_1+P_1\pi_1+P_1\pi_1)N$

2.7.1 Reduction When There Are Only Three Consequences

To simplify the exposition, we shall prove the reducibility asserted above only for the special case where the original act has just three possible consequences, but it will be obvious to the reader how the proof could be generalized to the case where the act has any finite number of possible consequences.

Let $\{\Theta_1, \Theta_2$, and $\Theta_3\}$ be a set of mutually exclusive and collectively exhaustive events, and consider the act or lottery l defined by table 2.10; suppose, furthermore, that the decision maker assigns probability $P(\Theta_i)$ to Θ_i and utility $\pi(c_i)$ to c_i, and abbreviate the notation by defining

$$P_i \equiv P(\Theta_i), \qquad \pi_i \equiv \pi(c_i).$$

As the first step in the reduction of the act l described by table 2.10, we observe that the decision maker should be indifferent between l and the "compound" lottery described in table 2.11, where, for each i, prize c_i of l has been replaced by a canonical lottery giving a π_i chance at c^* and a complementary chance at c_*. Formally, the equivalence of the two lotteries follows by Basic Assumption 4 from the fact that the prize associated with each Θ_i in l_Δ is equivalent to the corresponding prize in the original l.

For reasons which will become clear in a moment, we next point out that the compound lottery l_Δ can be conducted in the following manner. Assuming without loss of generality that the Θ_i have been numbered in such a way that $\pi_1 \geq \pi_2 \geq \pi_3$, we first construct an urn containing N balls all of which bear one or another of the labels, $\Gamma_1, \Gamma_2, \Gamma_3$, or Γ_4, the number bearing each label being as shown in the second column of table 2.12. Before it is known which of the three Θ_i has occurred, one ball is drawn canonically from this urn and its label is read; as soon as it is learned which Θ_i has occurred, the prize is determined by consulting the Prize Chart in table 2.12. Thus if the ball is labelled Γ_2 and Θ_3 has occurred, the prize is c_*; if the ball is labelled Γ_3 and Θ_1 has occurred, the prize is c^*; and so forth. It is easily verified that for any Θ_i, this scheme gives the chances at c^* and c_* called for by table 2.11. If, for example, Θ_2 occurs, the prize will be c^* if the ball drawn from the urn was labelled Γ_1 or Γ_2; and since the number of balls bearing one or the other of these two labels is

$$N\pi_3 + N(\pi_2 - \pi_3) = N\pi_2,$$

the chance at c^* given Θ_2 is $N\pi_2/N = \pi_2$ in agreement with table 2.11.

Now consider the decision maker's position after the ball has been drawn but before it is known which of the three possible Θ_i has occurred. Take the case where a ball labelled Γ_2 is drawn: What the decision maker has at this point, as shown by table 2.12, is essentially a secondary lottery which will pay c^* if (Θ_1 *or* Θ_2) occurs, and c_* otherwise. By Assumption 2b, he is indifferent between this secondary lottery depending on the occurrence or nonoccurrence of the event (Θ_1 *or* Θ_2) and a canonical secondary lottery which gives a canonical chance $P(\Theta_1 \text{ or } \Theta_2)$ at c^* and a complementary chance at c_*. Hence it follows by Assumption 4 that the attractiveness of l_Δ as a whole will remain unchanged for this decision maker if, *before* any ball is drawn from the urn, we put a supplementary label c^* on a fraction

$$P(\Theta_1 \text{ or } \Theta_2) = P(\Theta_1) + P(\Theta_2) \equiv P_1 + P_2$$

of the Γ_2-balls, put a label c_* on the remaining Γ_2-balls, and then let the prize associated with drawing a Γ_2-ball be determined immediately by this supplementary label, *without* waiting to see which Θ_i occurs and then using the Prize Chart in table 2.12.

Applying this logic and this procedure to all four kinds of balls in the urn, we end up by putting the supplementary label c^* on the numbers of balls shown in the last column of table 2.12; and adding the entries in this column we find that out of the N balls in the urn, a fraction $(P_1\pi_1 + P_2\pi_2 + P_3\pi_3)$ bear the label c^* while the remainder bear the label c_*.

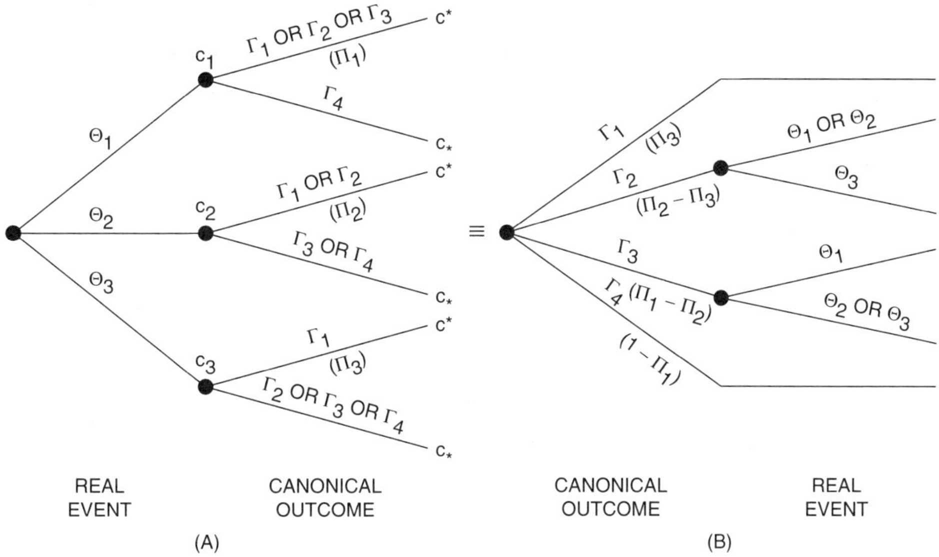

Figure 2.3
Reduction of a real lottery to a canonical lottery

Since each successive relabelling (or substitution of prizes) left the attractiveness of l_Δ as a whole unchanged, we conclude by transitivity that *the decision maker should be indifferent between* l_Δ *and a reference lottery giving a canonical chance* $(P_1\pi_1 + P_2\pi_2 + P_3\pi_3)$ *at* c^* *and a complementary chance at* c_*. Finally, since we have already seen that the decision maker should be indifferent between the original act l and the lottery l_Δ, it follows again by transitivity that he should be indifferent between the act l and the reference lottery we have just described. The proof of reducibility is thus complete.

The basic strategy of this proof can also be explained in terms of equivalent decision tree representations of a compound lottery whose outcome depends jointly on which real-world event Θ_1, Θ_2, or Θ_3 is true and which outcome $\Gamma_1, \Gamma_2, \Gamma_3$, or Γ_4 of a canonical experiment is true. These two representations are given in figure 2.3. In figure 2.3A the prize of the primary lottery is determined by the real-world event and the consequence of the secondary lottery is determined by a canonical experiment. The secondary canonical experiment is so arranged that if Θ_i occurs at the first stage, then the canonical chance of getting c^* at the second stage is π_i, so that the secondary lottery is indifferent to c_i. In figure 2.3B the prize of the primary lottery is determined by the outcome of the canonical experiment and the consequence of the secondary lottery is determined by the real-world event. The representation in figure 2.3B is straightforward to analyze: Each secondary lottery is of a form which can be replaced by an equivalent canonical lottery which does not change the attractiveness of the compound lottery (this uses Assumptions 2b, 4, and 3). The combination of these substitutions produces a compound *canonical* lottery which we already know how to analyze.

2.7.2 Generalization

We leave it to the reader to verify the truth of the following generalization of the result just obtained.

Let $\{\Theta_1, \ldots, \Theta_i, \ldots, \Theta_n\}$ be a set of mutually exclusive and collectively exhaustive events; let l be an act that will have consequence c_i if Θ_i occurs; let $P(\Theta_i)$ be the decision maker's scaled probability judgment of Θ_i; and let $\pi(c_i)$ be his scaled utility preference for c_i relative to c^* and c_*. Then the decision maker should be indifferent between l and a canonical lottery in which the consequence will be either c^* or c_* and the chance at c^* is

$$\Pi = \sum_{i=1}^{n} P(\Theta_i)\pi(c_i).$$

It follows trivially that if the decision maker is to choose one act from any number of available acts, then he or she should prefer the one whose index Π is greatest.

2.8 Conditional Utility and Conditional Probability

2.8.1 Conditional Assessments: An Example

In some situations the decision maker will wish to pay particular attention to some one particular piece of information for his assessments of probabilities and hence for his choice of an act. Thus consider an oil wildcatter who must decide whether or not to drill on a certain plot of land and who consults his geologist concerning the chances of striking oil. The geologist may well answer that he finds this question very difficult to answer directly, since the chance that there is oil beneath the surface depends on whether or not there is a closed geophysical structure beneath the surface, but he can say that in his opinion:

1. There is about 1 chance in 3 that there *is* a closed structure beneath this plot;

2. *If* such a structure does exist, then the chance of striking oil is quite good, say 4 in 5;

3. But *if* such a structure does *not* exist, then the chance of striking oil is very poor, say 1 in 10.

If our wildcatter feels that his opinions on matters such as these are of negligible value in comparison with the geologist's, he may well be ready to place his bets in accordance with what his geologist quotes as the "fair odds"; but because he must decide whether or not to drill without knowing whether or not a closed subsurface structure exists, none of the odds quoted by the geologist are directly relevant to his problem. What the wildcatter needs to know is "the" probability that he will strike oil, not a probability that is *conditional* on the existence or nonexistence of a closed subsurface structure. It seems plausible, however, that "the" (unconditional) probability of oil is in some way determined by and hence computable from the three probabilities that *have* been assessed. We shall now show that this conjecture is correct provided that the decision maker behaves in accordance with our four basic assumptions.

2.8.2 Notation

In order to discuss this problem clearly and concisely, we first define the symbols:

Θ_0: there is oil,

$\overline{\Theta}_0$: there is no oil,

$\Theta^\dagger$: there is closed structure,

$\overline{\Theta}^\dagger$: there is no closed structure.

From these basic symbols we can derive symbols for events with more complex descriptions, for example:

(Θ_0 *and* $\Theta^\dagger$): there is oil *and* there is closed structure,

[(Θ_0 *and* $\Theta^\dagger$) *or* (Θ_0 *and* $\overline{\Theta}^\dagger$)]: there is either (a) oil and closed structure, *or* (b) oil and no closed structue.

Observe incidentally that this last event is identical to the event Θ_0, since $\Theta^\dagger$ and $\overline{\Theta}^\dagger$ are collectively exhaustive, and therefore one or the other of them must accompany Θ_0 if Θ_0 occurs.

Regarding the notations for probabilities, we have already defined the symbol P in a way which implies that, for example:

$P(\Theta_0)$ = the *un*conditional probability that Θ_0 occurs (there is oil),

$P(\Theta^\dagger)$ = the *un*conditional probability that $\Theta^\dagger$ occurs (there is closed structure),

$P(\Theta_0$ *and* $\Theta^\dagger)$ = the *un*conditional probability that both Θ_0 and $\Theta^\dagger$ occur.

To express *conditional* probabilities, we shall write, for example:

$P(\Theta_0|\Theta^\dagger)$ = the conditional probability that there is oil *if* there is closed structure.

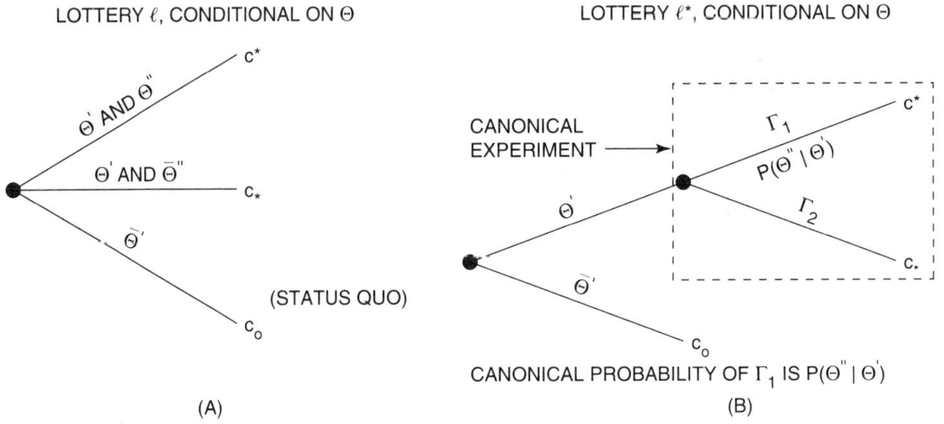

Figure 2.4
Interpretation of conditional probability

In this notation, the geologist in our example assessed $P(\Theta^{\dagger})$, $P(\Theta_0|\Theta^{\dagger})$, and $P(\Theta_0|\overline{\Theta}^{\dagger})$; what he wants to *compute* is $P(\Theta_0)$.

2.8.3 Definition of Conditional Probability

Although it is reasonably clear in common sense what is meant by a conditional probability such as the probability that there is oil *if* there is closed structure, we must be more precise about the meaning before we can derive logical rules for using such probabilities. Therefore, we shall adopt the following behavioral definition of conditional probability:

Let l and l^* be two lotteries, neither of which pays anything at all unless a specified event Θ' occurs. *Provided* that Θ' does occur, l will pay c^* if some other event Θ'' occurs, and otherwise will pay c_*, while l^* will give a canonical chance p at c^* and a complementary chance at c_*. The value of p which leaves the decision maker *indifferent* between l and l^* will be called the *conditional probability* of Θ'' *given* Θ' and will be denoted by $P(\Theta''|\Theta')$.

The reader should observe that this definition of conditional probability is identical to the definition of *un*conditional probability in Basic Assumption 2b (section 2.3.3), except for the proviso that the defining lotteries will actually pay off only on *condition* that Θ' occurs.

The value $P(\Theta''|\Theta')$ can be readily interpreted in terms of the tree representation in figure 2.4, where c_0 represents the consequence which pays nothing (i.e., the status quo). A decision maker should be indifferent between the two lotteries depicted in figure 2.4 provided that the canonical probability of outcome Γ_1 is $P(\Theta''|\Theta')$.

As an example of the application of the definition, we shall interpret the wildcatter's assignment of conditional probability 4/5 to the existence of oil *if* there is closed structure as having the following implication: The wildcatter would be *indifferent* between (1) a lottery l paying c^* if there is oil, otherwise c_*, and (2) a lottery l^* giving a 4/5 canonical chance at c^* and a complementary chance at c_*, *provided that it is understood that both lotteries are to be called off unless closed structure exists.*

2.8.4 Consistency among Conditional and Unconditional Probabilities

Our next step is to show that *conditional* probabilities like $P(\Theta''|\Theta')$ are related to *unconditional* probabilities like $P(\Theta')$ and $P(\Theta' \textit{ and } \Theta'')$ by a *consistency requirement* that is a consequence of the four basic assumptions of section 2.3. We will then be able to show that this new consistency requirement together with the three consistency requirements for unconditional probabilities already proved in section 2.6.4 enables us to compute $P(\Theta_0)$ from the given quantities $P(\Theta_0|\overline{\Theta}^\dagger)$, $P(\Theta_0|\Theta^\dagger)$, and $P(\Theta^\dagger)$.

The new consistency requirement relating conditional to unconditional probabilities is as follows:

LetΘ'* and Θ'' be any events. The decision maker *should* assess $P(\Theta')$, $P(\Theta' \textit{ and } \Theta'')$, and $P(\Theta''|\Theta')$ in such a way that

$$P(\Theta' \textit{ and } \Theta'') = P(\Theta')P(\Theta''|\Theta'),$$

implying that

$$P(\Theta''|\Theta') = \frac{P(\Theta' \textit{ and } \Theta'')}{P(\Theta')} \quad \text{if} \quad P(\Theta') > 0.$$

The remainder of this section will be devoted to the proof of this proposition.

When $P(\Theta') = 0$ the proof is trivial. We may write

$$\Theta' \equiv [(\Theta' \textit{ and } \Theta'') \textit{ or } (\Theta' \textit{ and } \overline{\Theta}'')]$$

because the *event* on the right is identical to the *event* on the left. We then have by the additivity rule in section 2.6.4 that

$$P(\Theta') = P(\Theta' \textit{ and } \Theta'') + P(\overline{\Theta}' \textit{ and } \overline{\Theta}''),$$

and since the probability on the left is 0 by hypothesis, both probabilities on the right must be 0 by the non-negativity rule in section 2.6.4.

When $P(\Theta') > 0$ the proof follows readily from figure 2.4. In figure 2.4A, lottery l, conditional on Θ', is indifferent (by section 2.7) to a canonical lottery for which the consequence will be either c^* or c_* and the chance at c^* is

$$\Pi = P(\Theta' \textit{ and } \Theta'') + P(\overline{\Theta}')\pi(c_0).$$

We will show below that in figure 2.4B lottery l^*, conditional on Θ', is indifferent to a canonical lottery for which thc consequence will be either c^* or c_*, and the chance at c^* is

$$\Pi^* = P(\Theta')P(\Theta''|\Theta') + P(\overline{\Theta}')\pi(c_0).$$

Since by the definition of $P(\Theta''|\Theta')$ the decision maker is indifferent between these two conditional lotteries, it follows that $\Pi = \Pi^*$, or

$$P(\Theta' \textit{ and } \Theta'') - P(\Theta')P(\Theta''|\Theta'),$$

as we want to show.

Now let us establish the formula for Π^*. If Θ' occurs in the lottery depicted in figure 2.4B, one can think of the resulting outcome as a consequence c, say, *which is the canonical experiment* blocked off in that figure. Using this interpretation, we immediately have

$$\pi(c) = P(\Theta''|\Theta'),$$

and from this vantage point the formula for Π^* is immediate. (There are some purists, however, who object to this kind of proof because they argue that we do not have the liberty to invent new consequences—especially like the kind we just did. For these purists we offer a slightly more complicated proof in the next chapter where we give a more formal treatment of the foundations.)

2.8.5 Indirect Assessment of Probabilities

We are now ready to complete the task of assessing the *un*conditional probability of oil from the various probabilities that were given in section 2.8.1, namely

$$P(\Theta^\dagger) = \tfrac{1}{3}, \qquad P(\Theta_0|\Theta^\dagger) = \tfrac{4}{5}, \qquad P(\Theta_0|\overline{\Theta}^\dagger) = \tfrac{1}{10}.$$

To do so, we observe first that we can compute

$$P(\overline{\Theta}^\dagger) = 1 - \tfrac{1}{3} = \tfrac{2}{3},$$

since

$$P(\Theta^\dagger) + P(\overline{\Theta}^\dagger) = P(\Theta^\dagger \textit{ or } \overline{\Theta}^\dagger)$$

(by the third consistency requirement in section 2.6.4), and since

$$P(\Theta^\dagger \textit{ or } \overline{\Theta}^\dagger) = 1$$

(by the second requirement in that section). Then using the new consistency requirement in section 2.8.4, we have

$$P(\Theta_0 \textit{ and } \Theta^\dagger) = P(\Theta^\dagger)P(\Theta_0|\Theta^\dagger) = \left(\frac{1}{3}\right)\left(\frac{4}{5}\right) = \left(\frac{4}{15}\right),$$

$$P(\Theta_0 \textit{ and } \overline{\Theta}^\dagger) = P(\overline{\Theta}^\dagger)P(\Theta_0|\overline{\Theta}^\dagger) = \left(\frac{2}{3}\right)\left(\frac{1}{10}\right) = \left(\frac{1}{15}\right),$$

and finally again using the third requirement in section 2.6.4, we have

$$P(\Theta_0) \equiv P[(\Theta_0 \textit{ and } \Theta^\dagger) \textit{ or } (\Theta_0 \textit{ and } \overline{\Theta}^\dagger)]$$

$$= P(\Theta_0 \textit{ and } \Theta^\dagger) + P(\Theta_0 \textit{ and } \Theta^\dagger)\left(\frac{4}{15}\right) + \left(\frac{1}{15}\right) = \left(\frac{1}{3}\right).$$

Generalizing this example, the reader can readily convince himself of the correctness of the following rule for getting a desired set of unconditional probabilities from (1) a set of conditional probabilities, and (2) the probabilities of the conditions.

Let $\{\Theta_1^\dagger, \ldots, \Theta_j^\dagger, \ldots, \Theta_m^\dagger\}$ be a mutually exclusive and collectively exhaustive set of events. Then, for any event Θ_0,

$$P(\Theta_0) = \textstyle\sum_j P(\Theta_j^\dagger)P(\Theta_0|\Theta_j^\dagger).$$

2.8.6 Posterior Probability

Suppose now that after making the calculations described in the previous section, our wildcatter learns that a seismic sounding made on a neighboring plot of land has shown that there *is* closed structure beneath both that plot and his own. Assuming that this is the *only* relevant new information, what probability should he now assign to Θ_0, the existence of oil?

It seems obvious that if the wildcatter previously assigned probability $P(\Theta_0|\Theta^\dagger) = \frac{4}{5}$ to the existence of oil *if* there was closed structure, then he should assign this same probability to the existence of oil *after actually learning* that there is closed structure, and this is in fact the point of view that we shall take. From a purely logical point of view, however, this proposition cannot be shown to follow from the four basic assumptions of section 2.3, all of which deal with preferences among lotteries in a situation where the relevant information remains *fixed*; therefore the proposition constitutes a *new basic assumption.*

To fit this new assumption into our overall system, we state it, not as a proposition about probabilities, but as a proposition about preferences among lotteries.

Basic Assumption 5 The decision maker *should* prefer l' to l'' after learning that $\Theta^\dagger$ has occurred if and only if he *would* have preferred l' to l'' without this information but with the understanding that both lotteries would be called off unless $\Theta^\dagger$ occurred.

From this new assumption together with our four original assumptions it can easily be proved that the assertions contained in the four original assumptions remain true when they are reworded to apply to preferences held *after* learning that $\Theta^\dagger$ has occurred; and it can also be proved that (1) the decision maker's *utility for any consequence c* as scaled by $\pi(c)$ should be the same *after* learning that $\Theta^\dagger$ has occurred as it was *before* learning that $\Theta^\dagger$ has occurred, whereas (2) the decision maker's *probability concerning* any event Θ_0 should be revised from $P(\Theta_0)$ *before* learning that $\Theta^\dagger$ has occurred to $P(\Theta_0|\Theta^\dagger)$ after learning that $\Theta^\dagger$ has occurred. These propositions are in fact so close to self-evident that we shall give no proof here.

Exercises

1. Describe an outcome of a simple experiment that you can perform to which you would assign a canonical probability of 3/4. Repeat for .76285.

2. On the basis of your current information assign a judgmental probability to the following events:

   a. From the opening of the stock market on Monday of next week until the closing of the stock market on Friday of next week the Dow-Jones Average will rise and (at the same time) IBM stock will fall.

   b. The winner of the first game of the next World Series will also win the second game.

   c. The Democratic nominee for president will obtain between 50 and .55 of the popular vote in the next election.

3. Suppose two dice are rolled in such a manner that you believe that all 36 pairs of numbers from (1, 1) to (6, 6) are equally likely. What is the canonical probability of getting a 7 or an 11? What is the conditional canonical probability of getting a 7 given that a 7 or an 11 has occurred?

4. Show that the lottery l'' in table 2.1 (section 2.4.2) can be reduced to a lottery $l''_{\Delta\Delta}$ in which the chances of winning are .895.

5. Given the preferences displayed in table 2.2 (section 2.4.3), should the decision maker participate in either l' or l'' in preference to the status quo?

6. You do not know which one of four possible events $\theta_1, \theta_2, \theta_3, \theta_4$ is true, but you do know that the event has been selected by a canonical experiment giving chances .4, .2, .3, and .1 to $\theta_1, \theta_2, \theta_3$, and θ_4 respectively. You as decision maker have to choose between acts a_1 and a_2. With either act there are two ultimate consequences, "Win" or "Lose." The consequence of either act for any θ event will also be determined by a canonical experiment: With act a_1, there is a .2 chance of Win if θ_1 is true, .3 if θ_2 is true, .6 if θ_3 is true, and .9 if θ_4 is true; with act a_2 there is a .7 chance of Win if θ_1 is true, .5 if θ_2 is true, .1 if θ_3 is true, and 0 if θ_4 is true. Which act would you choose and why?

7. Assume that we have the compound lottery shown in figure 2.1 (section 2.4.8). Show that the canonical chance the compound lottery will result in consequence c_j is given by

   $$m'_1 m''_{1j} + m'_2 m''_{2j} + \cdots + m'_k m''_{kj}.$$

In the following exercises we denote the canonical lottery which gives an m_i chance at c_i, where $m_i \geq 0$, for $i = 1, \ldots, n$, and where $\sum_{i=1}^{n} m_i = 1$, by the symbol $\{(m_1 : c_1), (m_2 : c_2), \ldots, (m_n : c_n)\}$ Also we define the following relationships:

$l_1 \sim l_2$: l_1 is indifferent to l_2;

$l_1 \precsim l_2$: l_1 is not preferred to l_2; i.e., l_2 is either preferred to or indifferent to l_1;

$l_1 \gtrsim l_2$: l_1 is not preferred to l_1;
$l_1 < l_2$: l_2 is preferred to l_1;
$l_1 > l_2$: l_2 is preferred to l_2.

8. Mr. Jones must choose between the following two canonical lotteries:

$$l_1 = \{(.3 : c_1), (.2 : c_2), (.1 : c_3), (.4 : c_5)\},$$
$$l_2 = \{(.2 : c_1), (.5 : c_3), (.2 : c_4), (.1 : c_6)\}.$$

Consequences c_1 to c_6 are themselves complex entities with both monetary and psychological implications; after due consideration he has expressed his relative preferences among them by the following assertion:

$$c_1 \lesssim c_2 \lesssim c_3 \lesssim c_4 \lesssim c_5 \lesssim c_6,$$
$$c_2 \sim \{(.9 : c_1), (.1 : c_6)\},$$
$$c_3 \sim \{(.6 : c_1), (.4 : c_6)\},$$
$$c_4 \sim \{(.3 : c_1), (.7 : c_6)\},$$
$$c_5 \sim \{(.2 : c_1), (.2 : c_6)\}.$$

Should Mr. Jones choose l_1 or l_2?

9. Mr. Black must choose between the following two canonical lotteries:

$$l_1 = \{(.3 : c_1), (.2 : c_2), (.4 : c_3), (.1 : c_4)\},$$
$$l_2 = \{(.1 : c_1), (.6 : c_2), (.1 : c_3), (.2 : c_4)\},$$

Consequences c_1, c_2, and c_3 are rather definite and Black feels that

$$c_1 > c_2 > c_4 \quad \text{and} \quad c_2 \sim \{(.6 : c_1), (.4 : c_4)\}.$$

Consequence c_3 on the contrary involves many intangibles, and although Black feels sure that $c_1 > c_3 > c_4$ he is still struggling to find a π such that

$$c_3 \sim \{(\pi : c_1), (1 - \pi : c_4)\}.$$

For what range of π values should Black prefer l_1 to l_2?

10. Mr. Smith must choose between the following two canonical lotteries:

$$l_1 = \{(.2 : c_1), (.3 : c_2), (.4 : c_3), (.1 : c_5)\},$$
$$l_2 = \{(.25 : c_1), (.45 : c_3), (.3 : c_4)\}.$$

After due consideration Smith has expressed his preferences for consequences by the following assertion:

$$c_1 > c_2 > c^3 > c_4 > c_5,$$
$$c_3 \sim \{(.6 : c_1), (.4 : c_5)\},$$
$$c_2 \sim \{(.75 : c_1), (.25 : c_3)\},$$
$$c_4 \sim \{(.5 : c_3), (.5 : c_5)\};$$

the subscript 3 in the last two of these statements is *not* a misprint. Which of the two lotteries should Smith choose?

11. Consider a decision problem involving two lotteries and four mutually exclusive and collectively exhaustive events $\theta_1, \theta_2, \theta_3$, and θ_4. Assume that each of the consequences has already been calibrated in terms of a canonical lottery involving reference consequences c^* and c_*; let the symbol $\langle\pi\rangle$ denote a basic reference lottery that gives c^* with canonical chance π and c_* with canonical chance $(1 - \pi)$; let

$$l_1 = \{(\theta_1 : \langle .8\rangle), (\theta_2 : \langle .4\rangle), (\theta_3 : \langle .6\rangle), (\theta_4 : \langle .2\rangle)\},$$

and

$$l_2 = \{(\theta_1 : \langle .3\rangle), (\theta_2 : \langle .2\rangle), (\theta_3 : \langle .4\rangle), (\theta_4 : \langle .9\rangle)\},$$

where, as an example, choice of l_2 means that if event θ_3 occurs the resulting consequence is indifferent to a .4 chance at c^* and a complementary chance at c_*. As regards judgments concerning events, the decision maker feels as follows:

a. He is indifferent between a prize conditional on event $\{\theta_1 \text{ or } \theta_2\}$ and the same prize with canonical probability 3/5.

b. If he were to learn that the true event is $\{\theta_1 \text{ or } \theta_2\}$, he would then be indifferent between a prize conditional on θ_2 and the same prize with canonical probability 2/3.

c. If he were to learn that the true event is $\{\theta_3 \text{ or } \theta_4\}$, he would then be indifferent between a prize conditional on θ_3 and the same prize conditional on θ_4.

Which lottery offers a better chance at c^*?

12. Five particular consequences are defined as follows:

c_1: The status quo.

c_2: You own the rights to select absolutely free any 25 compact discs of your choice with the understanding that they are for your own personal use.

c_3: You will be given a *very slightly* used set of the latest Encyclopedia Britannica, to do with as you choose.

c_4: You have the nontransferable rights to attend all concerts, plays, and sporting events in the city of your choice during the next calendar year and to choose any seat you desire; for a payment of \$200 you can obtain similar rights for someone to accompany you.

c_5: For any dozen evenings in the next calendar year you and a designated guest of yours have the nontransferable privilege of dining and drinking absolutely free in any restaurants of your choice.

Let c^* and c_* denote respectively the most favorable and least favorable of these 5 consequences; let $\pi(c_i)$ be such that *you* are indifferent between c_i and the lottery which gives a canonical chance of $\pi(c_i)$ at c^* and a complementary chance at c_*. What are your breakeven probabilities $\pi(c_i)$ for $i = 1, \ldots, 5$?

13. Consider the following two lotteries l_1 and l_2 which involve consequences $c_1, \ldots, c_5$ of the previous exercise:

Lottery l_1

Event	Consequence
In the next World Series the American League will	
lose	c_2
win in 4 games	c_5
win in 5 games	c_1
win in 6 games	c_3
win in 7 games	c_4

Lottery l_2

Event	Consequence
The number of enrolled students who will drop the course will be	
at most 2	c_5
3 or 4	c_1
at least 5	c_2

Which lottery would you choose and why?

14. Consider the following four canonical lotteries, where M stands for "million":

$l_1 = \{(1 : \$1\text{M})\}$, i.e., \$1 million certain,
$l_2 = \{(.10 : \$5\text{M}), (.89 : \$1\text{M}), (.01 : \$0\text{M})\}$,
$l_3 = \{(.10 : \$5\text{M}), (.90 : \$0\text{M})\}$,
$l_4 = \{(.11 : \$1\text{M}), (.89 : \$0\text{M})\}$

Show that if you let $c^* = \$5\text{M}$, $c_* = \$0\text{M}$ and $\$1\text{M} \sim \langle\pi\rangle$, then *no matter what value*

π *has*, logical consistency (according to our Basic Assumptions) requires you to prefer either (1) l_1 to l_2 and l_4 to l_3, or else (2) l_2 to l_1 and l_3 to l_4.

(M. Allais, a French mathematical economist, has shown that many subjects choose l_1 over l_2, and l_3 over l_4, and therefore implicitly violate some of our Basic Assumptions. (see Allais, 1953). The next exercise attempts to examine related types of behavior in detail.)

15. Mr. X is invited to participate in a lottery under the following conditions. An urn contains balls all of which are white or orange. One ball is drawn from the urn in Mr. X's presence and placed in a closed box; the drawing is made in such a way that Mr. X considers all balls equally likely. Mr. X is then told that if he participates in the lottery, the box will be opened and he will receive a certain prize Q if the ball is orange or will have his choice of prize R or prize S if the ball is white; in this latter case he must however announce his choice immediately upon seeing that the ball is white.

Mr. X inspects the three prizes carefully, announces that he is delighted to participate in the lottery, and decides that if the ball turns out to be white he will choose R rather than S.

a. Mr. X is now told that there is a slight change in the conditions of the lottery: If he wishes to participate, he must announce *before* the box is opened whether he wants to receive R or S as a prize if the ball is white. Mr. X replies that he would still like to participate but that under the new conditions he cannot tell whether he prefers R or S unless he knows how many white and orange balls there were in the urn before the drawing was made. Upon being told there were 11 white and 89 orange balls, Mr. X decides that the new conditions really change the picture substantially and therefore announces that if the ball is white he wants to receive prize S rather than R.

Comment on Mr. X's behavior.

b. Mr. X is next told that there has been a mistake concerning the prize to be awarded if the ball is orange. Prize Q actually belongs to someone who won it in a lottery conducted yesterday, and therefore it has been replaced by prize Q^*. Mr. X inspects prize Q^* carefully and then announces that while he still wants to participate in the lottery, this change in the prize to be awarded if the ball is orange has altered his preferences concerning the prize to be awarded if the ball is white; he now wants this prize to be R rather than S.

Comment on Mr. X's behavior.

c. Reconsider your answers to (a) and (b) for the special case where prize R is \$1 million certain while prize S is a ticket in a lottery offering a 10/11 chance at \$5 million and a 1/11 chance at \$0.

d. Specialize further to the case where prize Q is \$0 and prize Q^* is \$1 million.

(Allais showed that many people considered it reasonable to switch from S in part (a) to R in part (b). This denies the principle that if two lotteries are alike except as regards one prize, the better lottery is necessarily the one with the better prize, and thus implies that it is also reasonable to switch from R under the original conditions of the lottery to S in part (a).)

16. On each ball in a given urn there is a label consisting of an ordered pair of numbers, such as (84, −37). The decision maker is asked to carefully examine the balls and then to select either alternatives *left* or *right* with the understanding that after he makes his selection, a ball will be canonically drawn from the urn and he will receive the amount on the left or on the right of the label according to his previously announced selection. As an example, if he chooses "left" and then draws the ball with label (84, −37), he receives \$84; if he chooses "right" and then draws this same ball, he receives −\$37. Let us suppose that you are the decision maker and that after examining the urn very carefully you have decided to select "left."

Now suppose that before a ball is drawn an additional ball is added to the urn with a label having identical left and right components. Would knowledge of the common value on this ball have any effect on your choice to play this game or not? If you were compelled or have decided voluntarily to play the game with the new ball added to the urn, would you perhaps decide to change from "left" to "right"? How would you feel if an undisclosed number of new balls were added to the urn where each new ball had *identical left and right components*?

17. In a discussion about basic principles of decision theory a Mr. E was asked which of the following three options he would prefer:

i. Receive a Cadillac convertible if the University of Michigan beats or ties Wisconsin in their next annual football match.

ii. Receive the same Cadillac convertible if Wisconsin beats or ties Michigan in this same game.

iii. Receive the same Cadillac convertible conditional on whether heads appears in a toss of a fair coin, the toss to be made at the end of this game.

Mr. E stated that he would prefer option (iii) because this option gave him a known 50-50 chance at the prize whereas he knew almost nothing about the relative strengths of the Michigan and Wisconsin teams. "In fact," he continued, "I would still prefer option (iii) if \$300 were added to the prizes in the other two options."
Comment.

18. *The Ellsberg Paradox.* (Ellsberg 1961).
Imagine an urn known to contain 30 red balls and a total of 60 other balls which are either black or yellow in some unknown proportion. Consider the following lotteries whose outcome depends on a canonical drawing from this urn.

Lotteries

	l_1	l_2	l_3	l_4
30 {Red	\$100	\$0	\$0	\$100
60 {Black	0	100	100	0
60 {Yellow	0	0	100	100

a. If you were given a choice between l_1 and l_2, which would you choose?

b. If you were given a choice between l_3 and l_4, which would you choose?
(Most people when presented with these two choices prefer l_1 to l_2 and prefer l_3 to l_4 because l_1 and l_3 give known canonical chances at the \$100 prize where l_2 and l_4 do not.

c. Show that there is no possible assignment of judgmental probabilities to the events in the table which would lead a decision maker to prefer *both* l_1 to l_2 and l_3 to l_4.

d. If you think that it is unreasonable for someone to choose l_1 over l_2 and l_3 over l_4, how would you try to convince him that he was making a mistake?

19. Let $\{\theta_1, \theta_2, \theta_3\}$ be three mutually exclusive and collectively exhaustive events; let the consequences of lotteries l_1 and l_2 depend on which of these events occur according to the following table:

Lotteries

Events	l_1	l_2
θ_1	c_{11}	c_{12}
θ_2	c_{21}	c_{22}
θ_3	c_{31}	c_{32}

As a consequence of our general reduction result (cf. section 2.7), show that if $\pi(c_{31}) = \pi(c_{32})$, then the choice between l_1 and l_2 does not depend on the common value of $\pi(c_{31})$ and $\pi(c_{32})$. Comment on the behavioral plausibility of this result, and relate this exercise to exercises 15, 16, and 18.

3 A Formal Treatment of Foundations

3.1 Introduction

This chapter will contain a formal treatment of the material discussed in the previous chapter. Some concepts introduced in chapter 2 are repeated here in order to make this chapter relatively self-contained. We shall concentrate on the formal structure of the assumptions and their consequences rather than on motivation and interpretation, which were covered in the previous chapter.

3.1.1 Informal Statement of the Problem

We consider the problem faced by a person who on most occasions makes decisions intuitively and more or less inconsistently, like all mortals, but who on some one particular occasion wishes to make a particular decision in a reasoned, deliberate manner. To do so he must, of course, start by defining his problem, and we therefore assume that he has already specified the set of acts that he believes it worth his while to consider. As in the previous chapter we identify each act with a lottery and assume that the consequence of the lottery depends on some uncertain event. What we shall show is that if this decision maker is willing (1) to scale his *preferences* for the possible consequences and his *judgments* concerning the possible events in a manner to be described in a moment, and (2) to accept two simple principles of *consistent* behavior, then it is possible by straightforward calculation to determine which of the lotteries he *should* choose in order to be consistent, in the sense of these principles, with his own preferences and judgments.

3.1.2 Notation for Events, Consequences, and Lotteries

Our discussion will be considerably simplified if at the outset we introduce the idea of an "elementary event," an event which is described so finely that we shall never need to subdivide it further. We shall use the symbol θ to represent the generic elementary event and the symbol Θ to represent the set of all possible elementary events. Subsets of Θ will be denoted by subscripts or superscripts such as Θ_0, $\Theta_1, \ldots$, Θ', $\Theta^\dagger$, and so forth. We shall not need to make any assumption about the number of elements in Θ and we specifically leave open the possibility that Θ may have an infinite number of elementary events. There is no loss of generality if we assume that there is some true elementary state which has already been determined, but which is as yet unknown to the decision maker at the time he has to make his choice. We shall use the symbol $\tilde{\theta}$ (read: "θ tilde") to denote the as-yet-unknown, true, elementary event and the expression

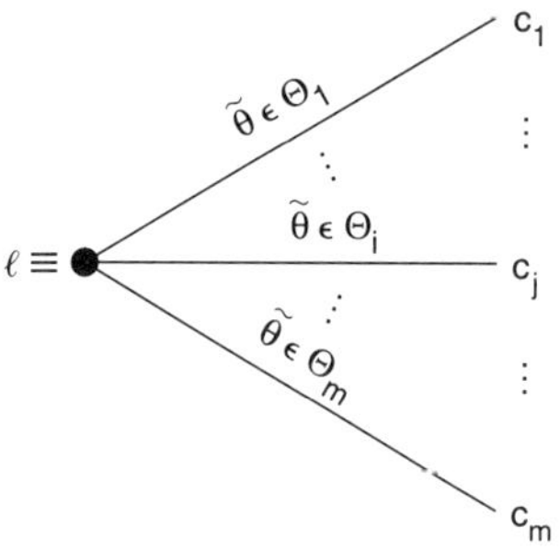

Figure 3.1
A typical lottery

"$\tilde{\theta} \in \Theta_0$" will be used to denote the event "the true elementary event belongs to the subset Θ_0."

It will be assumed that a lottery l can have at most a finite number of consequences. The generic consequence will be labelled by c, specific consequences will be labelled by $c_1, c_2, \ldots$, and the set of all consequences will be denoted by C.

Consider a lottery l that, for each possible θ, can result in one, and only one, of the consequences $c_1, c_2, \ldots, c_m$. Let c_i obtain if and only if the as-yet-unknown elementary event $\tilde{\theta}$ belongs to the subset Θ_i; that is, if $\tilde{\theta} \in \Theta_i$, then the resulting consequence is c_i. We assume that the subsets $\Theta_1, \Theta_2, \ldots, \Theta_m$ are mutually exclusive (i.e., $\tilde{\theta}$ can belong to at most one of these subsets) and collectively exhaustive (i.e., $\tilde{\theta}$ must belong to one of these subsets). In more formal terminology, we assume that the collection of subsets $\{\Theta_1, \Theta_2, \ldots, \Theta_m\}$ forms a *partition* of Θ. The lottery l which results in consequence c_i if and only if $\tilde{\theta} \in \Theta_i$ will be denoted by

$$l \equiv \{(c_1 : \Theta_1), \ldots, (c_i : \Theta_i), \ldots (c_m : \Theta_m)\}$$

and is exhibited in figure 3.1.

3.1.3 Formal Statement of the Problem

Our basic problem can now be posed in terms of a choice between two lotteries l' and l''. Given two lotteries

$$l' = \{(c'_1 : \Theta'_1), \ldots, (c'_m : \Theta'_m)\}$$

and

$$l'' = \{(c''_1 : \Theta''_1), \ldots, (c''_n : \Theta''_n)\}$$

how should the decision maker express his preferences for the consequences and his judgments concerning the events, and from these determine which,

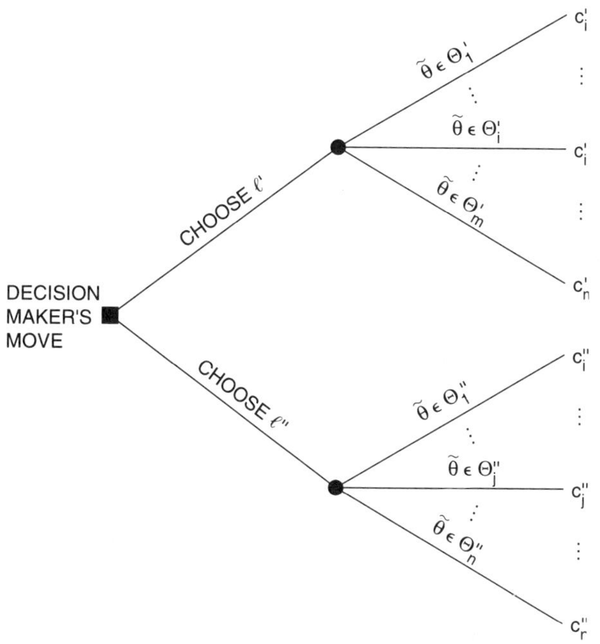

Figure 3.2
Decision tree for choice between lotteries

for him, is the better of the two lotteries? This choice problem is depicted graphically in figure 3.2.

3.2 The Canonical Basis

As a basis for the scaling of preferences and judgments and as a standard for comparison of lotteries, we shall now ask the decision maker to imagine an auxiliary experiment which is completely unrelated to the determination of the as-yet-unknown elementary event $\tilde{\theta}$. In particular, we ask him to imagine an experiment which will result in a pair of numbers γ and δ, each of which is in the interval 0 to 1. We can also think of the experiment as one which selects a point (γ, δ) in a unit square (see figure 3.3). As an approximation to what we have in mind, imagine that the outcome (γ, δ) of the auxiliary experiment is "equally likely" to fall anywhere in the unit square—a notion to be clarified shortly. Such an experiment will be called a *canonical* experiment and it will be used later to help calibrate the decision maker's preferences and judgments.

Using the expression "generalized interval" to denote any rectangle or finite union of rectangles with sides parallel to the γ and δ axes, we shall

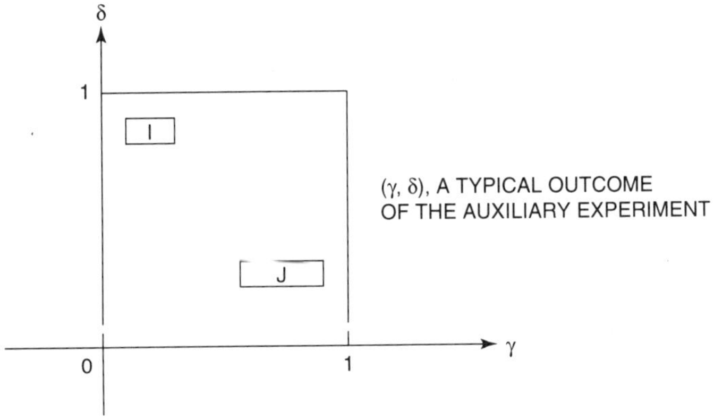

Figure 3.3
Canonical auxiliary experiment

consider lotteries which will yield a valuable prize if the point (γ, δ) falls within some specified generalized interval such as I or J in figure 3.3; and as a second approximation we shall say that the experiment is canonical if the decision maker prefers the lottery l_1 which gives the prize when (γ, δ) falls in I to the lottery l_2 which gives the prize when (γ, δ) falls in J provided that the area of I is larger than the area of J, regardless of where I and J are located.

There is no loss of generality if as before we assume that the canonical experiment has already been conducted but its outcome is as yet unknown to the decision maker. We shall denote this as-yet-unknown true outcome of the canonical experiment by $(\tilde{\gamma}, \tilde{\delta})$.

The definition of a canonical experiment given above neglects one point of considerable importance. If the canonical experiment is to serve as a standard for scaling of preferences and judgments and for comparison of acts, then clearly it must be of such a nature that its outcome in no way depends on the real-world events involved in the decision maker's real decision problem. In our original, informal discussion we took this independence for granted, but in the formal system we shall make the following assumption which requires it specifically:

Assumption Let Θ_0 denote any real-world event, and let I and J denote any two generalized intervals whose areas are equal. The decision maker can imagine that (γ, δ) will be determined in such a way that he will be indifferent between any two lotteries, one of which yields a valuable prize, if *both* $\tilde{\theta} \in \Theta_0$ *and* $(\tilde{\gamma}, \tilde{\delta}) \in I$, while the other yields that same prize if *both* $\tilde{\theta} \in \Theta_0$ *and* $(\tilde{\gamma}, \tilde{\delta}) \in J$.

That this assumption does in fact require the decision maker to think of $\tilde{\gamma}$ and $\tilde{\delta}$ as independent of $\tilde{\theta}$ is easily seen. For suppose, for example, that the decision maker feels that if $\tilde{\theta}$ belongs to some particular Θ_0, then high values of $\tilde{y}$ and $\tilde{\delta}$ are "more likely" than low values. He would then prefer a prize contingent on Θ_0 and an interval I in the upper right-hand corner of the unit square to the same prize contingent on Θ_0 and an interval J of the same area as I but located in the lower left-hand corner of the unit square, in contradiction to the assumption just stated. Notice, on the other hand, that we do not say in the assumption that he will *prefer* the prize contingent on Θ_0 and I to the prize contingent on Θ_0 and J if I is *larger* than J; the event Θ_0 may be so implausible that the decision maker would attach no value to the lottery whatever the areas of I and J might be.

3.3 Lotteries and Prizes

We are now going to generalize the notion of a lottery by allowing the consequence of a lottery to depend not only on the as-yet-unknown true elementary event $\tilde{\theta}$ but also possibly on the unknown true outcome $(\tilde{y}, \tilde{\delta})$ of the auxiliary canonical experiment. At first sight this seems as if we are progressing in the wrong direction: Not being able to resolve a choice between lotteries whose consequences depend only on $\tilde{\theta}$, we seemingly complicate matters by considering lotteries which depend also on $(\tilde{y}, \tilde{\delta})$. The strategy, however, is not unlike asking someone to choose between alternative A and B and, after meeting considerable hesitancy, introducing a hypothetical third alternative which is so constructed that the decision maker clearly sees that he prefers A to C and C to B; the introduction of C thus helps resolve the choice problem between A and B. It is in such a spirit that we introduce lotteries whose consequences depend on $(\tilde{\theta}, \tilde{y}, \tilde{\delta})$ in order to help the decision maker resolve his preferences between lotteries whose consequences depend merely on $\tilde{\theta}$.

3.3.1 Diagrammatic Representation of Lotteries

Most of the real and hypothetical lotteries that we shall have to consider can be represented by diagrams of the kind shown in figure 3.4. Figure 3.4A is to be interpreted as defining a lottery that pays, for example

$$c_{11} \quad \text{if} \quad 0 \le \tilde{y} \le a \quad \text{and} \quad \tilde{\theta} \in \Theta_1,$$

$$c_{23} \quad \text{if} \quad a < \tilde{y} \le b \quad \text{and} \quad \tilde{\theta} \in \Theta_3,$$

and so forth. Figure 3.4B is to be interpreted as defining a lottery that pays

$$c_1 \quad \text{if} \quad 0 \le \tilde{y} \le a \quad \text{and} \quad 0 \le \tilde{\delta} \le \alpha,$$

$$c_3 \quad \text{if} \quad a < \tilde{y} \le b \quad \text{regardless of } \tilde{\delta},$$

and so forth.

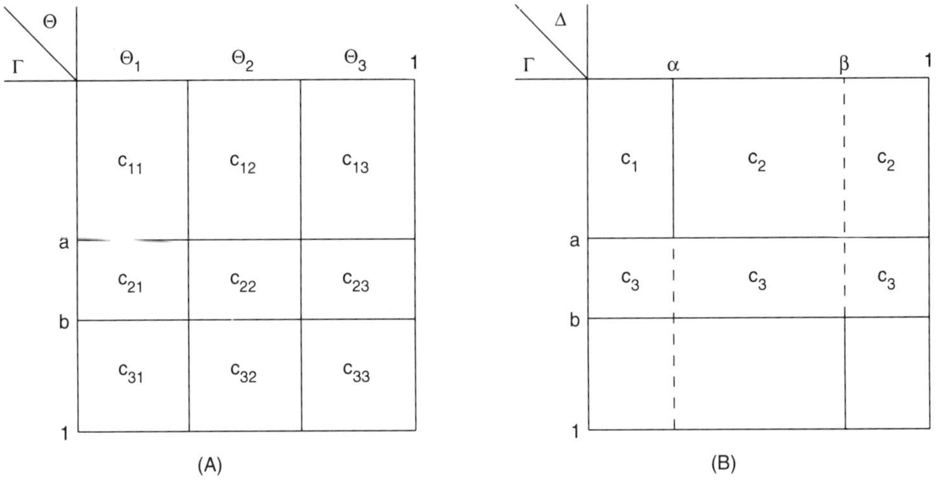

Figure 3.4
Lotteries on $\Theta \times \Gamma$ and $\Delta \times \Gamma$

3.3.2 Lotteries with Lotteries as Prizes

In evaluating *hypothetical* lotteries whose payoffs depend in whole or in part on $\tilde{\gamma}$ and/or $\tilde{\delta}$ we shall ask the decision maker to imagine that he will *never actually learn* the true values of these quantities—what he will learn is simply the consequence that the lottery pays out; nevertheless, we shall sometimes ask him to look at and compare such lotteries *conditionally* upon some given θ, γ, or δ.

Suppose then, for example, that we consider the lottery defined by figure 3.4A given that $\tilde{\theta} \in \Theta_2$; what we have is a lottery in which the payoff depends only on $\tilde{\gamma}$, yielding

$$c_{12} \text{ if } 0 \le \tilde{\gamma} \le a, \qquad c_{22} \text{ if } a < \tilde{\gamma} \le b, \qquad c_{32} \text{ if } b < \tilde{\gamma} \le 1.$$

If we consider the lottery defined by figure 3.4B *given* that $0 \le \tilde{\gamma} \le a$, we have a lottery that pays

$$c_1 \text{ if } 0 \le \tilde{\delta} \le \alpha, \qquad c_2 \text{ if } \alpha < \tilde{\delta} \le 1;$$

if we consider the lottery defined by figure 3.4B *given* that $a < \tilde{\gamma} \le b$, we have a *constant* lottery that pays c_3 regardless of the value of $\tilde{\delta}$; and so forth. In short, every row in a diagram like those in figure 3.4 defines a *row lottery*, and every column defines a *column lottery*.

This way of looking at the rows and columns of diagrams like those in figure 3.4 means that there are three possible ways of looking at the figures as a whole; we illustrate with figure 3.4A as an example.

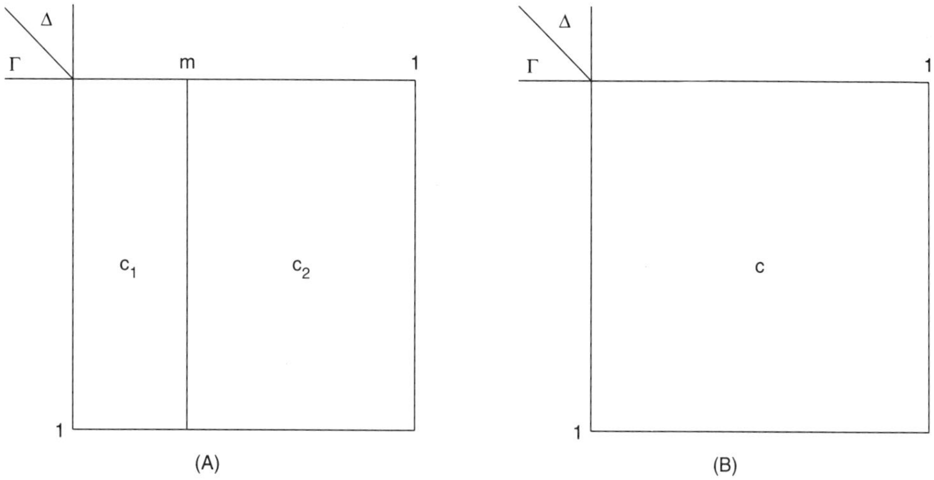

Figure 3.5
Lotteries depending on at most one argument

1. Figure 3.4A may be regarded as a lottery in which $\tilde{\theta}$ and $\tilde{\gamma}$ jointly determine a particular cell in the table and thus a particular consequence. When we regard it in this way, we shall call figure 3.4A a *lottery on* $\Theta \times \Gamma$ with *consequences as prizes.*

2. Figure 3.4A may be regarded as a lottery in which $\tilde{\theta}$ determines a column and $\tilde{\gamma}$ determines a cell within the column. When we regard it in this way, we shall call figure 3.4A a *lottery on* Θ with *lotteries on* Γ *as prizes.*

3. Figure 3.4A may be regarded as a lottery in which $\tilde{\gamma}$ determines a row and $\tilde{\theta}$ determines a cell within the row. When we regard it in this way, we shall call figure 3.4A a *lottery on* Γ with *lotteries on* Θ *as prizes.*

The reader must remember, however, that the second and third "aspects" which we have just defined do not imply that the value of one of the two "variables" is revealed to the decision maker *after* the other.

3.3.3 Notation for Lotteries

The diagrams in figure 3.5 represent notational devices which are virtually self-explanatory. As shown in figure 3.5A, we shall sometimes find it convenient to regard a lottery as a lottery $\Gamma \times \Delta$, say, even though the prize actually depends only on $\tilde{\delta}$, and similarly for lotteries depending only on $\tilde{\gamma}$ or $\tilde{\theta}$. As shown in figure 3.5B, we shall sometimes even find it convenient to describe a particular consequence as a "lottery" which is sure to yield that particular consequence with certainty; for example, we have already referred to the second row of figure 3.4B as defining a row lottery even though that row lottery is sure to pay c_3.

The formal notation for lotteries which we shall introduce in section 3.4 will be based on a complete systematization of this point of view. In order to avoid having to deal with preference relations between different *kinds* of entities, *all* lotteries (including row lotteries and column lotteries) will be formally treated as *functions* with all three of $\tilde{\theta}$, $\tilde{\gamma}$, and $\tilde{\delta}$ as arguments, even though the value of such a function will almost never actually depend on more than two of its three arguments, and may depend only on one or even none. Thus a consequence c will sometimes be treated as a "function" of $\tilde{\theta}$, $\tilde{\gamma}$, and $\tilde{\delta}$ *whose value is c for all values of $\tilde{\theta}$, $\tilde{\gamma}$, $\tilde{\delta}$*; a lottery on Θ with consequences as prizes will be treated as a function of $\tilde{\theta}$, $\tilde{\gamma}$, and $\tilde{\delta}$ *whose value depends only on $\tilde{\theta}$*; and so forth. We shall use the symbol $l(\theta, \gamma, \delta)$ to denote the consequence of l for the case $\tilde{\theta} = \theta$, $\tilde{\gamma} = \gamma$, $\tilde{\delta} = \delta$.

3.4 Formal Notation and Definitions

3.4.1 Basic Notation

In the remainder of this chapter, the basic notation of our formal system will be the following:

C: a finite set of "consequences," with generic element c.

Θ: a set of "real-world events," with generic element θ.

$\Gamma \times \Delta$, $\Gamma = \{\gamma: 0 \leq \gamma \leq 1\}$ and $\Delta = \{\delta: 0 \leq \delta \leq 1\}$: the set of possible "outcomes" of a hypothetical "canonical experiment."

L: the set of all functions ("lotteries") from $\Theta \times \Gamma \times \Delta$ to C, with the generic element l.

$\precsim$: a binary relation ("is not preferred to") defined for some members of $L \times L$; we do *not* assume that $L \times L$ is completely ordered by $\precsim$. We treat $\precsim$ as the primitive relation in the formal system.

3.4.2 Definitions

Starting from the primitive relation $\precsim$, we shall shortly define relations of preference and indifference between lotteries. In the interpretation, the statements $l_1 \precsim l_2$ and $l_2 \succsim l_1$ will both be used to mean that l_1 *is not preferred* to l_2; the statements $l_1 \succ l_2$ and $l_2 \prec l_1$ to mean that l_1 *is preferred* to l_2; and the statements $l_1 \sim l_2$ and $l_2 \sim l_1$ to mean l_1 is *equivalent* to l_2—that is, that the decision maker is indifferent between l_1 and l_2. Formally, we write:

Definition 1 (Preference and Indifference)

$l_1 \sim l_2 \quad \Leftrightarrow \quad l_1 \lesssim l_2$ and $l_2 \lesssim l_1$;

$l_1 \prec l_2 \quad \Leftrightarrow \quad l_1 \lesssim l_2$ and not $l_2 \lesssim l_1$;

$l_1 \gtrsim l_2 \quad \Leftrightarrow \quad l_2 \lesssim l_1$;

$l_1 \succ l_2 \quad \Leftrightarrow \quad l_2 \prec l_1$.

Since $\lesssim$ was taken as a primitive relation on $L \times L$ (i.e., among lotteries), and since $\succ$, $\sim$, etc., have all been defined in terms of $\lesssim$, we have as yet no way of expressing preference relations among consequences; and although such relations are not really necessary for the construction of the formal system, it will be very convenient to have them available. Since there is no difference in the interpretation between a consequence and a lottery which is sure to result in that consequence, we can introduce preference relations among consequences into the formal system by simply asserting that the statement "consequence c_1 is not preferred to consequence c_2" is identical in meaning to the statement "a lottery certain to result in c_1 is not preferred to a lottery certain to result in c_2."

Definition 2 (Preference between Consequences)

$c_1 \lesssim c_2 \quad \Leftrightarrow \quad l_1 \lesssim l_2$,

where l_1 and l_2 are defined by

$l_i(\theta, \gamma, \delta) \equiv c_i \quad$ for all θ, γ, δ; $\qquad i = 1, 2$.

Finally, we define a convenient special notation for lotteries in which the consequence depends on only one of the three arguments θ, γ, and δ.

Definition 3 Let Q be any one of Θ, Γ, Δ; let q be the corresponding one of θ, γ, δ; and let $\{Q_1, \ldots, Q_n\}$ form a partition of Q. The function l defined by

$l(\theta, \gamma, \delta) \equiv c_i \quad$ if $\quad q \in Q_i$

may be denoted by

$\{(Q_1 : c_1), \ldots, (Q_i : c_i), \ldots, (Q_n : c_n)\} \quad$ or $\quad \{(Q_i : c_i)\}$.

3.5 Axioms or Basic Assumptions

3.5.1 Canonical Basis

The idea of a canonical basis was introduced in section 3.2; the following axiom (or basic assumption) formalizes that discussion:

Axiom 1 Let c' and c'' be any consequences such that $c' \succ c''$; let $\Theta_0 \subset \Theta$; for $i = 1, 2$, let Z_i be a generalized interval in $\Gamma \times \Delta$ whose area is m_i; and let l_i be defined by

$$l_i(\theta, \gamma, \delta) = \begin{cases} c' & \text{if } \theta \in \Theta_0 \text{ and } (\gamma, \delta) \in Z_i, \\ c'' & \text{otherwise.} \end{cases}$$

a. (*Canonicity*)

For any $\Theta_0 \subset \Theta$: $\quad m_1 = m_2 \quad \Rightarrow \quad l_1 \sim l_2.$

b. (*Monotonicity*)

For $\Theta_0 = \Theta$: $\quad m_1 > m_2 \quad \Rightarrow \quad l_1 \succ l_2.$

Lemma 1 In the notation of Axiom 1,

for $\Theta_0 = \Theta$: $\quad l_1 \sim l_2 \quad \Rightarrow \quad m_1 = m_2.$

The proof of the lemma is immediate from Axiom 1b and Definition 1.

If a lottery l does not depend on $\tilde{\theta}$ and if l has a consequence c' if and only if $(\tilde{\gamma}, \tilde{\delta})$ belongs to a generalized interval Z' whose area is m', then we shall say that lottery l has consequence c' with *canonical probability* m'.

3.5.2 Scaling

The next axiom (or basic assumption) formalizes the assumption about scaling of preferences and judgments. It asserts that there are two basic reference consequences: c^*, a most preferred consequence of C, and c_*, a least preferred consequence of C; and that

a. for each consequence c there is a number $\pi(c)$ such that the decision maker is indifferent between obtaining c outright and obtaining a reference lottery which gives c^* with canonical probability $\pi(c)$ and c_* with canonical probability $1 - \pi(c)$;

b. for each subset Θ_0 there is a number $P(\Theta_0)$ such that the decision maker is indifferent between the following two lotteries: one which gives c^* if $\tilde{\theta}$ belongs to Θ_0 and c_* otherwise, the other which gives c^* with canonical probability $P(\Theta_0)$ and c_* otherwise.

This is formalized in terms of the following:

Axiom 2 The set C contains c^* and c_*, where $c^* > c_*$, with the following properties:

a. (*Evaluation of Consequences*) There exists a function π from C to $[0,1]$ such that[1] for any $c \in C$

$$c \sim \{(\Gamma_0 : c^*), (\bar{\Gamma}_0 : c_*)\} \quad \text{where} \quad \Gamma_0 \equiv [0, \pi(c)].$$

b. (*Evaluation of Events*) There exists a function P from subsets of Θ to $[0,1]$ such that for any $\Theta_0 \subset \Theta$

$$\{(\Theta_0 : c^*), (\bar{\Theta}_0 : c_*)\} \sim \{(\Delta_0 : c^*), (\bar{\Delta}_0 : c_*)\} \quad \text{where} \quad \Delta_0 \equiv [0, P(\Theta_0)].$$

The functions π and P will be shown to be unique in Lemma 3.

3.5.3 Consistency

The next axiom formalizes the first of the two principles of consistent behavior we shall invoke. We do not assert at the outset that the decision maker can compare any two lotteries and say which he or she prefers. We do insist, however, that if he or she asserts that l_2 is at least as desirable l_1 and that l_3 is at least as desirable as l_2, then l_3 should be at least as desirable as l_1. This assertion is formalized as our next axiom.

Axiom 3 (Transitivity)

$$l_1 \precsim l_2 \text{ and } l_2 \precsim l_3 \quad \Rightarrow \quad l_1 \precsim l_3.$$

Lemma 2

$$l_1 \sim l_2 \text{ and } l_2 \sim l_3 \quad \Rightarrow \quad l_1 \sim l_3;$$

$$l_1 \prec l_2 \text{ and } l_2 \sim l_3 \quad \Rightarrow \quad l_1 \prec l_3;$$

$$l_1 \sim l_2 \text{ and } l_2 < l_3 \quad \Rightarrow \quad l_1 \prec l_3.$$

The lemma follows immediately from Definition 1 and Axiom 3.

The second of the two consistency principles is formalized in our next and last axiom, which says in effect that if every row (column) lottery in a " compound" lottery like those in figure 3.4 is replaced by another row (column) lottery such that the decision maker is indifferent between each new row (column) lottery and the corresponding original row (column) lottery, then the decision maker should be indifferent between the original and modified compound lottery. The original and modified compound lotteries are respectively called l' and l'' in the axiom; their component row or column lotteries are respectively $\{l'_1, \ldots, l'_n\}$ and $\{l''_1, \ldots, l''_n\}$.

---

1. The complement of any set A is designated by $\bar{A}$. Note also that Axiom 2A implies the existence of c_* and c^* such that for any $c \in C$, $c_* \precsim c \precsim c^*$.

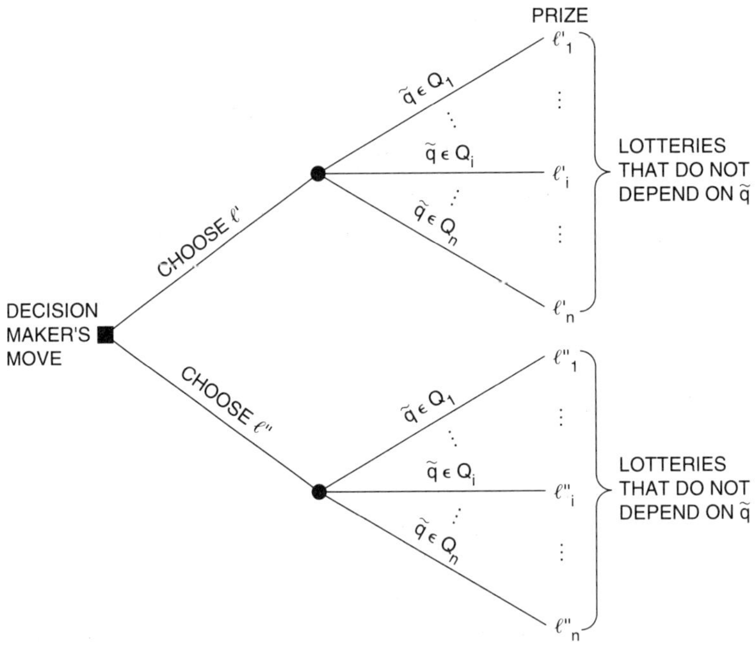

Figure 3.6
Decision tree representing substitutability

Another way of understanding the meaning of the next axiom is to structure it in terms of the decision tree in figure 3.6. Let $\tilde{q}$ represent one of the three unknowns $\tilde{\theta}$, $\tilde{\gamma}$, $\tilde{\delta}$; let lottery l' result in prize l_i' if $\tilde{q} \in Q_i$; let lottery l'' result in prize l_i'' if $\tilde{q} \in Q_i$; let l_i' and l_i'' be lotteries that do not depend on $\tilde{q}$. The axiom says that if l' and l'' are structured as in figure 3.6 and if the decision maker is indifferent between l_i' and l_i'' for all i, then he should also be indifferent between l' and l''.

Axiom 4 (Substitutability) Let Q be any one of Θ, Γ, Δ; let q be the corresponding one of θ, γ, δ; let $\{Q_1, \ldots, Q_n\}$ be a partition of Q; for $i = 1, \ldots, n$, let l_i' and l_i'' be functions from $\Theta \times \Gamma \times \Delta$ to C whose values depend only on arguments *other* than q; and let l' and l'' be defined by

$$\left.\begin{aligned} l'(\theta,\gamma,\delta) &= l_i'(\theta,\gamma,\delta) \\ l''(\theta,\gamma,\delta) &= l_i''(\theta,\gamma,\delta) \end{aligned}\right\} \quad \text{if } q \in Q_i.$$

Then

$$l_i' \sim l_i'' \quad \text{for all } i \quad \Rightarrow \quad l' \sim l''.$$

3.6 Results

3.6.1 Uniqueness of π and P

In Axiom 2, we assumed merely that, given any consequence c, there exists *some* number $\pi(c)$ such that the decision maker would be indifferent between (1) c for certain and (2) a canonical lottery giving a chance $\pi(c)$ at the better reference consequence c^* and a complementary chance at the worse reference consequence c_*; similarly, we assumed merely that for any Θ_0 there exists *some* number $P(\Theta_0)$ such that the decision maker would be indifferent between (1) a lottery giving him c^* if Θ_0 occurs, and otherwise c_*, and (2) a canonical lottery giving him a $P(\Theta_0)$ chance at c^* with a complementary chance at c_*. We shall now show that the monotonicity principle of Axiom 1b together with the transitivity principle of Axiom 3 require that these numbers should be unique—that is, that there exist only one $\pi(c)$ for any c and only one $P(\Theta_0)$ for any Θ_0.

Lemma 3 (Uniqueness of π and P) The functions π and P defined by Axiom 2 are unique.

Proof To show that π is unique, consider any $c \in C$ and for $i = 1, 2$ assume that there exists a number π_i in $[0, 1]$ such that $c \sim l_i \equiv \{(\Gamma_i : c^*), (\bar{\Gamma}_i : c_*)\}$ where $\Gamma_i = [0, \pi_i]$. From the transitivity of $\sim$ (Lemma 2), $l_1 \sim l_2$; and by Lemma 1, $\pi_1 = \pi_2$. This proves the uniqueness of π, and an analogous proof establishes the uniqueness of P. ∎

3.6.2 P as Probability Measure

We next show that the function P defined by Axiom 2b has the essential properties of a probability measure.

Theorem 1 (Axioms of Probability) For any $\Theta_0, \Theta_1, \Theta_2 \subset \Theta$,

$$P(\Theta_0) \geq 0,$$

$$P(\Theta) = 1,$$

$$P(\Theta_1 \cup \Theta_2) = P(\Theta_1) + P(\Theta_2) \quad \text{if} \quad \Theta_1 \cap \Theta_2 = \varnothing.$$

Proof That $P(\Theta_0) \geq 0$ is asserted directly by Axiom 2b (Evaluation of Events). To prove that $P(\Theta) = 1$, observe that

$$\{(\Theta : c^*), (\varnothing : c_*)\} \equiv \{(\Delta_0 : c^*), (\bar{\Delta}_0 : c_*)\}, \quad \text{where} \quad \Delta_0 = [0, 1] = \Delta,$$

and use Lemma 3 (Uniqueness of P). To prove that $P(\Theta_1 \cup \Theta_2) = P(\Theta_1) + P(\Theta_2)$ if Θ_1 and Θ_2 are disjoint, consider the four lotteries defined diagrammatically in figure 3.7, where a dot denotes c_*. We have

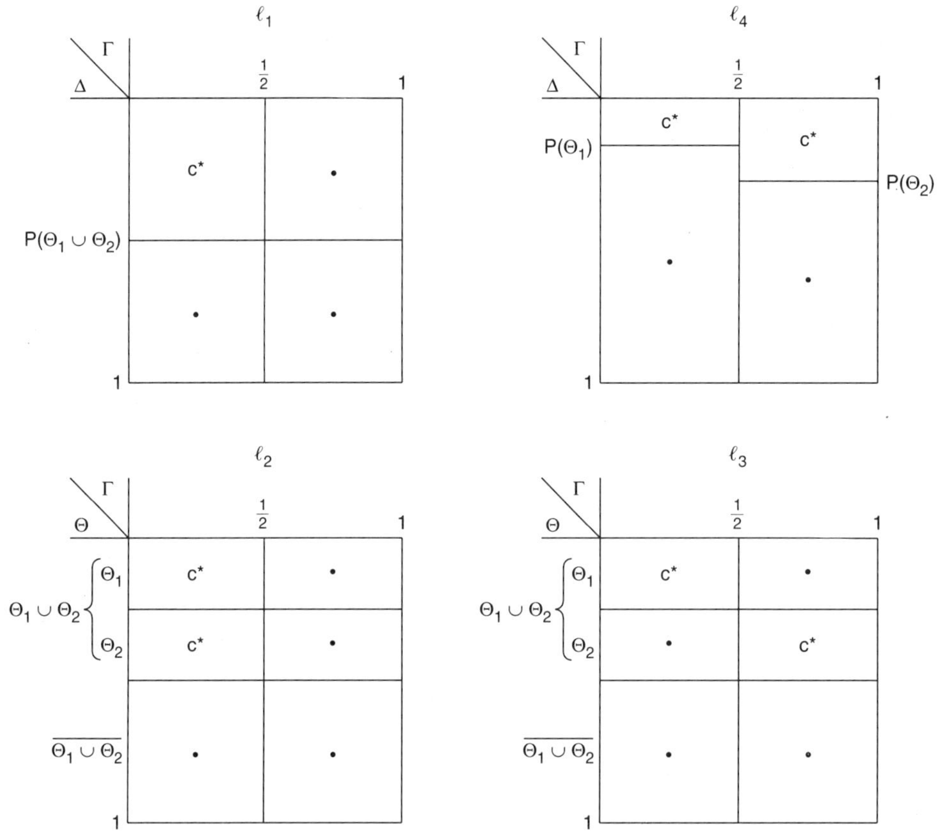

Figure 3.7
Proof of additivity of probability

$l_1 \sim l_2$ by Axiom 4 (Substitutability) because corresponding columns are equivalent by Axiom 2b (Evaluation of Events); $l_2 \sim l_3$ by Axiom 4 because corresponding rows are equivalent by Axiom 1a (Canonicity); $l_3 \sim l_4$ by Axiom 4 because corresponding columns are equivalent by Axiom 2b; and hence $l_1 \sim l_4$ by Lemma 2 (Transitivity). Since the areas associated to c^* in l_1 and l_4 are respectively $\frac{1}{2}P(\Theta_1 \cup \Theta_2)$ and $\frac{1}{2}P(\Theta_1) + \frac{1}{2}P(\Theta_2)$, the lemma follows by Lemma 1. ■

3.6.3 Comparison of Lotteries

The essence of the logic by which we shall arrive at a method of comparison of acts is contained in the following theorem, which says that, given any act (or lottery on Θ with consequences as prizes), we can find an equivalent *canonical reference lottery* involving only the two *reference consequences* c^* and c_*.

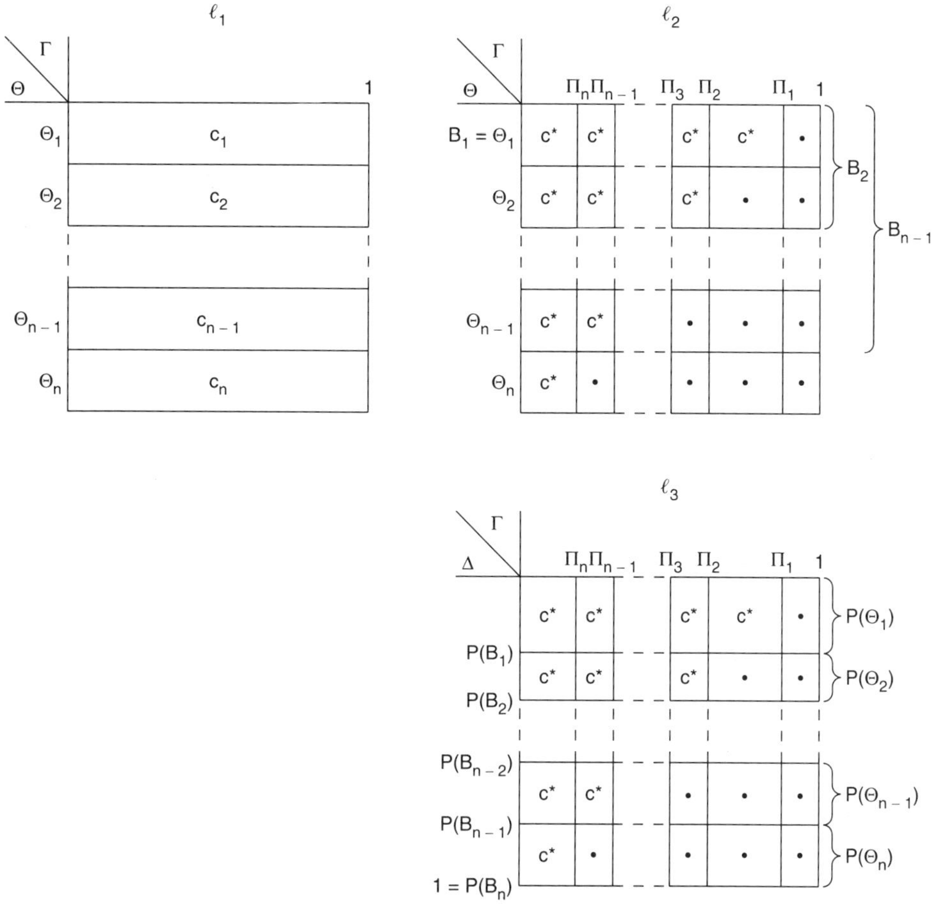

Figure 3.8
Reduction of real to canonical reference lottery

Theorem 2 (Reduction of Real to Canonical Reference Lotteries) Let $\{\Theta_1, \ldots, \Theta_n\}$ be a partition of Θ. Then

$$\{(\Theta_i : c_i)\} \sim \{(\Gamma_0 : c^*), (\bar{\Gamma}_0 : c_*)\},$$

where

$$\Gamma_0 \equiv [0, \Pi] \quad \text{and} \quad \Pi \equiv \textstyle\sum_i P(\Theta_i)\pi(c_i).$$

Proof Assume without loss of generality that $\pi(c_{i+1}) \leq \pi(c_i)$ for $i < n$ and consider the three lotteries defined diagrammatically in figure 3.8, where $\pi_i \equiv \pi(c_i)$, a dot denotes c_*, and

$$B_i \equiv \Theta_1 \cup \Theta_2 \cup \cdots \cup \Theta_i.$$

We have $\{(\Theta_i : c_i)\} \equiv l_1 \sim l_2$ by Axiom 4 (Substitutability) because corresponding rows are equivalent by Axiom 2a (Evaluation of Consequences); and $l_2 \sim l_3$ by Axiom 4 because corresponding columns are equivalent by Axiom 2b (Evaluation of Events). Since $B_i = B_{i-1} \cup \Theta_i$, we have

$$P(B_i) - P(B_{i-1}) \equiv P(\Theta_i)$$

by Theorem 1 (Additivity Axiom of Probability); the area associated with c^* in l_3 is therefore

$$P(\Theta_1)\pi_1 + P(\Theta_2)\pi_2 + \cdots + P(\Theta_n)\pi_n;$$

and the theorem now follows by Axiom 1a (Canonicity) and Lemma 2 (Transitivity). ■

We now come to our principal result concerning comparison of lotteries.

Theorem 3 (Comparison of Lotteries) Let $\{\Theta'_1, \ldots, \Theta'_i, \ldots, \Theta'_m\}$ and $\{\Theta''_1, \ldots, \Theta''_j, \ldots, \Theta''_n\}$ be two partitions of Θ; let

$$l' \equiv \{(\Theta'_1 : c'_1), \ldots, (\Theta'_i : c'_i), \ldots, (\Theta'_m : c'_m)\}; \qquad \Pi' \equiv \textstyle\sum_{i=1}^{m} P(\Theta'_i)\pi(c'_i);$$

$$l'' \equiv \{(\Theta''_1 : c''_1), \ldots, (\Theta''_j : c''_j), \ldots, (\Theta''_n : c''_n)\}; \qquad \Pi'' \equiv \textstyle\sum_{j=1}^{n} P(\Theta''_j)\pi(c''_j).$$

Then

$$\Pi' \left\{ \begin{matrix} > \\ = \\ < \end{matrix} \right\} \Pi'' \quad \Leftrightarrow \quad l' \left\{ \begin{matrix} > \\ \sim \\ < \end{matrix} \right\} l''.$$

The proof is immediate from Theorem 2 (Reduction of Acts), Axioms 1a and 1b (Canonicity and Monotonicity), and Lemma 2 (Transitivity).

3.6.4 Supplementary Results

One way of internalizing the logic by which probabilities P and preferences π combine to reduce a real-world act to an equivalent reference lottery is to think of the reduction as proceeding in two stages. Using only the P assessments, not the π assessments, we can replace any real-world act by a neither more nor less attractive canonical lottery having the *same consequences as the original real-world act*; then, as a separate operation, we can use the π assessments to replace each individual consequence in this canonical lottery by a secondary lottery between c^* and c_*, thus reducing the entire original lottery to a compound lottery between c^* and c_*. The following two theorems establish the validity of these two steps in inverse order:

Theorem 4 (Reduction From Canonical to Reference Lotteries) Let $\{\Delta_1, \ldots, \Delta_m\}$ be a partition of Δ, and let m_i be the length of Δ_i. Then

$$\{(\Delta_i : c_i)\} \sim \{(\Delta_0 : c^*), (\bar{\Delta}_0 : c_*)\} \quad \text{where} \quad \Delta_0 = [0, \textstyle\sum_i m_i \pi(c_i)].$$

The proof is similar to the proof of Theorem 2 but is even simpler and therefore omitted.

Theorem 5 (Reduction of Real to Canonical Lotteries) Let $\{\Theta_1, \ldots, \Theta_m\}$ be a partition of Θ and let

$$R_i \equiv \textstyle\sum_{j=1}^{i} P(\Theta_j),$$

$$\Delta_1 \equiv [0, R_1],$$

$$\Delta_i \equiv (R_{i-1}, R_i], \qquad i = 2, \ldots, m.$$

Then

$$\{(\Theta_i : c_i)\} \sim \{(\Delta_i : c_i)\}.$$

The theorem follows immediately from Theorems 2 and 4 and Lemma 2 (Transitivity).

From this last result it is easy to show that although the probability measure P is defined by reference to two particular consequences c^* and c_*, it would be unaffected if these two consequences were replaced by any other two consequences one of which is preferred to the other.

Theorem 6 (Nondependence of *P* on the Prizes) There exists one and only one function P from subsets of Θ to $[0, 1]$ such that for any c', $c'' \in C$

$$\{(\Theta_0 : c'), (\bar{\Theta}_0 : c'')\} \sim \{(\Delta_0 : c'), (\bar{\Delta}_0 : c'')\} \quad \text{where} \quad \Delta_0 = [0, P(\Theta_0)].$$

The theorem follows immediately from Theorem 5 (Reduction of Real to Canonical Lotteries), Lemma 1 (Monotonicity), and Lemma 2 (Transitivity).

We call the reader's attention to the fact that although the preference function π is not involved in the formal statement of Theorems 5 and 6, it is involved in the proof of both theorems because Theorem 6 depends on Theorem 5 and Theorem 5 depends on Theorems 2 and 4 both of which *do* involve π. In other words, the conceptual existence of the π function is necessary for Theorems 5 and 6 even though its actual values are irrelevant. In order to prove Theorem 5 *without* reference to the π function, we would have to strengthen Axiom 2b (Evaluation of Events) in such a way as to axiomatize rather than to prove the content of Theorem 6.

3.7 Conditional Probability

In the abstract theory of probability, the conditional probability of Θ_0 given $\Theta^\dagger$ is defined to be

$$P(\Theta_0|\Theta^\dagger) \equiv \frac{P(\Theta_0 \cap \Theta^\dagger)}{P(\Theta^\dagger)} \quad \text{if} \quad P(\Theta^\dagger) > 0.$$

We now inquire whether and in what sense this definition is meaningful when applied to the scaled judgments P that we have been discussing.

3.7.1 Evaluation of Conditional Lotteries

Let l_Θ be a lottery which gives consequence c^* of $\theta \in \Theta_0$, and gives c_* otherwise; let l_Γ be a lottery which gives c^* with canonical probability p and c_* with complementary probability $1 - p$. By Axiom 2b we know that $l_\Theta \sim l_\Gamma$ if and only if $p = P(\Theta_0)$. Now suppose we agree to "call off" both lotteries l_Θ and l_Γ unless $\tilde{\theta}$ belongs to some subset $\Theta^\dagger$ of Θ where $P(\Theta^\dagger) > 0$. Under these circumstances the value of p that makes these two conditional lotteries indifferent will generally shift. We will denote the new equilibrating value of p by $P(\Theta_0|\Theta^\dagger)$ and show in Theorem 7 that it agrees with the usual formula (stated above) for the conditional probability of Θ_0 given $\Theta^\dagger$. But first we must formalize the notion of a *conditional lottery*. We shall let the symbol c_0 denote the consequence "maintenance of the status quo" and adopt the following definition:

Definition 4 (Conditional Lotteries) Let $l \in L$, $c_0 \in C$, and $\Theta^\dagger \subset \Theta$. Then

$$l^\dagger(\theta, \gamma, \delta) \equiv \begin{cases} l(\theta, \gamma, \delta) & \text{if } \theta \in \Theta^\dagger, \\ c_0 & \text{if } \theta \notin \Theta^\dagger. \end{cases}$$

The way in which conditional probability can be used in evaluating such lotteries is then shown by the following theorem:

Theorem 7 (Evaluation of Conditional Lotteries) Let $\Theta^\dagger \subset \Theta$ be such that $P(\Theta^\dagger) > 0$, and let

$$l_\Theta \equiv \{(\Theta_0 : c^*), (\bar{\Theta}_0 : c_*)\},$$

$$l_\Delta \equiv \{(\Delta_0 : c^*), (\bar{\Delta}_0 : c_*)\}, \quad \text{where} \quad \Delta_0 \equiv [0, P(\Theta_0|\Theta^\dagger)],$$

where $P(\Theta_0|\Theta^\dagger) \equiv P(\Theta_0 \cap \Theta^\dagger)/P(\Theta^\dagger)$. Then

$$l_\Theta^\dagger \sim l_\Delta^\dagger.$$

Proof Consider the lotteries shown diagrammatically in figure 3.9, where a dot denotes c_*. Recalling that $\pi(c^*) = 1$ and $\pi(c_*) = 0$, we have $l_\Theta^\dagger \sim l^*$

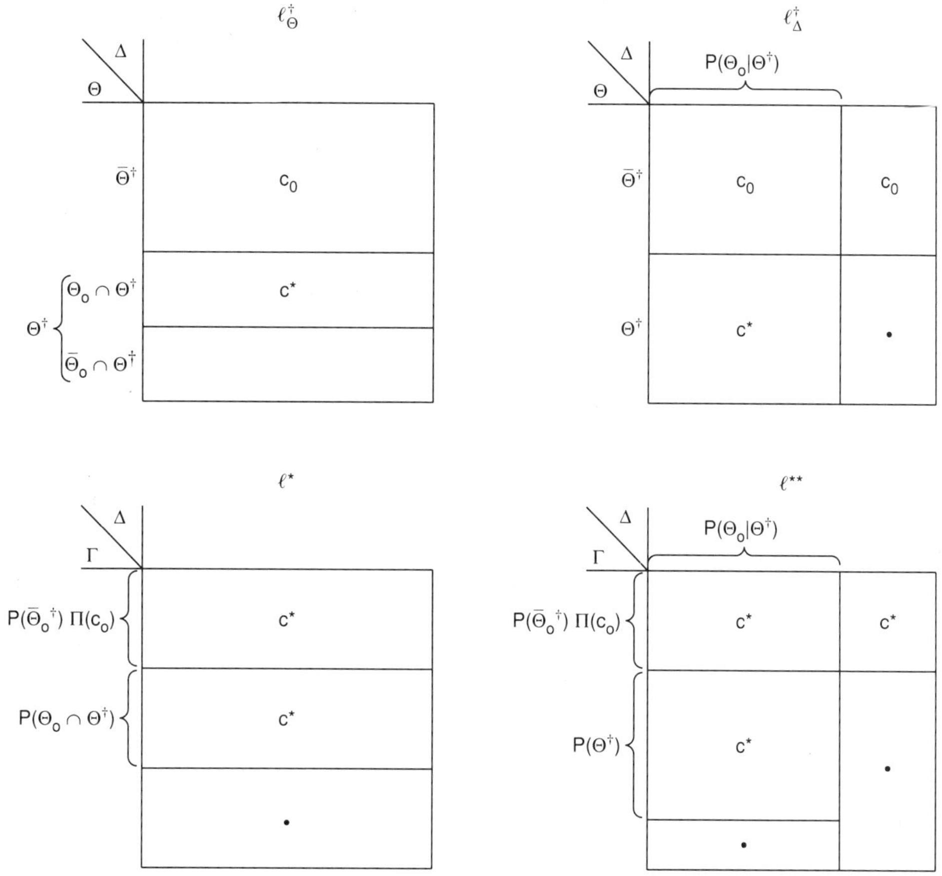

Figure 3.9
Evaluation of conditional lotteries

by Theorem 2 (Reduction of Acts to Reference Lotteries); $l^* \sim l^{**}$ by Axiom 1a (Canonicity) because the areas associated to c^* are equal by the definition of $P(\Theta_0|\Theta^\dagger)$; $l^{**} \sim l_\Delta^\dagger$ by Axiom 4 (Substitutability) because corresponding columns are equivalent by Theorem 2; and hence $l_\Theta^\dagger \sim l_\Delta^\dagger$ by Lemma 2 (Transitivity). ■

The following theorem illustrates the role of conditional probability in the evaluation of conditional lotteries.

Theorem 8 Let $\{\Theta_1', \ldots, \Theta_i', \ldots, \Theta_m'\}$ and $\{\Theta_1'', \ldots, \Theta_j'', \ldots, \Theta_n''\}$ be two partitions; let $\Theta^\dagger \in \Theta$ be such that $P(\Theta^\dagger) > 0$; let

$$l_1 = \{(\Theta_1' : c_1'), \ldots, (\Theta_m' : c_m')\}, \qquad \Pi_1^\dagger = \textstyle\sum_{i=1}^m P(\Theta_i'|\Theta^\dagger)\pi(c_i'),$$

$$l_2 = \{(\Theta_1'' : c_1''), \ldots, (\Theta_m'' : c_n'')\}, \qquad \Pi_2^\dagger = \textstyle\sum_{j=1}^n P(\Theta_j''|\Theta^\dagger)\pi(c_j'').$$

Then

$$l_1^\dagger \begin{Bmatrix} \succ \\ \sim \\ \prec \end{Bmatrix} l_2^\dagger \quad \Leftrightarrow \quad \Pi_1^\dagger \begin{Bmatrix} > \\ = \\ < \end{Bmatrix} \Pi_2^\dagger.$$

Proof Left as an exercise.

3.7.2 Posterior Preference and Probability

We now wish to formalize a basic assumption which states that the decision maker *should* prefer l_1 to l_2 after learning that $\Theta^\dagger$ has occurred if and only if he *would* have preferred l_1 to l_2 without this information, but with the understanding that both lotteries would be called off unless $\Theta^\dagger$ occurred.

Since we have as yet no language capable of distinguishing between preferences held before and after learning that $\tilde{\theta} \in \Theta^\dagger$, we now introduce a new primitive relation $\precsim''$ on $L \times L$:

$\precsim''$, which means: *is not preferred to when it is known that* $\tilde{\theta} \in \Theta^\dagger$ and rewrite the original relation $\precsim$ as $\precsim'$ to express preferences that obtain when it is not known whether or not $\theta \in \Theta^\dagger$. By adopting Definition 1 with $\precsim'$ or $\precsim''$ in place of $\precsim$, we can then define relations such as $\prec'$, $\prec''$, $\sim'$, and $\sim''$ and by a similar modification of Definition 2 we define preferences between consequences given $\Theta^\dagger$.

To relate $\precsim''$ to $\precsim'$ we adopt one additional axiom, an informal statement of which was given above:

Axiom 5 (Conditional and Posterior Preference)

$$l_1^\dagger \begin{Bmatrix} \succ \\ \sim \\ \prec \end{Bmatrix}' l_2^\dagger \quad \Leftrightarrow \quad l_1 \begin{Bmatrix} \succ \\ \sim \\ \prec \end{Bmatrix}'' l_2.$$

From this new axiom and our four original axioms it is easy to prove as a theorem that the statements of the four original axioms all hold when $\precsim$ is replaced by $\precsim''$, and also to show that the function π of the revised Axiom 2a is identical to the π of the original Axiom 2a; using Theorem 7 it is equally easy to show that the function P of the revised Axiom 2b is identical to the conditional-probability function $P(\cdot|\Theta^\dagger)$. In other words, after learning that $\theta \in \Theta^\dagger$ the decision maker "should" reassess all probabilities in accordance with the usual formula for conditional probability and then solve his decision problem by exactly the same *method* of analysis that he would have used if he had not learned whether or not $\tilde{\theta} \in \Theta^\dagger$. This result is of course equivalent to Theorem 8 with the additional assumption that the decision maker should actually follow his optimal rule when he learns that in fact $\tilde{\theta} \in \Theta^{\dagger}$.

It is perhaps worth remarking that Axiom 5 could be proved as a theorem from what may be regarded as three simpler assumptions which do not make use of the notion of called-off lotteries.

1. If the consequence of l_1 is equal to the consequence of l_2 for each $\theta \notin \Theta^{\dagger}$, then

$$l_1 \left\{ \begin{matrix} \succ \\ \sim \\ \prec \end{matrix} \right\}' l_2 \Leftrightarrow l_1 \left\{ \begin{matrix} \succ \\ \sim \\ \prec \end{matrix} \right\}'' l_2.$$

2. If the consequence of l_1 is equal to the consequence of l_2 for each $\theta \in \Theta^{\dagger}$, then $l_1 \sim'' l_2$.

3. If $l_1 \gtrsim'' l_2$ and $l_2 \gtrsim'' l_3$, then $l_1 \gtrsim'' l_3$.

From these assumptions about $\gtrsim''$ we wish to prove Axiom 5. From the first assumption we have

$$l_1^{\dagger} \left\{ \begin{matrix} \succ \\ \sim \\ \prec \end{matrix} \right\}' l_2^{\dagger} \Rightarrow l_1^{\dagger} \left\{ \begin{matrix} \succ \\ \sim \\ \prec \end{matrix} \right\}'' l_2^{\dagger};$$

from the second we have

$$l_1 \sim'' l_1^{\dagger}, \qquad l_2 \sim'' l_2^{\dagger};$$

combining these results, we have from the third assumption,

$$l_1^{\dagger} \left\{ \begin{matrix} \succ \\ \sim \\ \prec \end{matrix} \right\}' l_2^{\dagger} \Leftrightarrow l_1 \left\{ \begin{matrix} \succ \\ \sim \\ \prec \end{matrix} \right\}'' l_2,$$

■

4 Assessment of Utilities for Consequences

4.1 Indifference Probabilities and Utility Indices

4.1.1 Review

Consider a decision maker who wishes to choose among several acts when the consequence of one or more of these acts depends on which one of a set of possible events occurs. If the decision maker wishes to solve his problem by formal analysis, then as we saw in chapters 2 and 3, there are two sets of preliminary evaluations which he must make. He must on one hand quantify his *judgments* about the possible *events* by assigning a judgmental probability $P(\Theta_i)$ to each event Θ_i in a mutually exclusive and collectively exhaustive list, $\{\Theta_1, \ldots, \Theta_i, \ldots, \Theta_n\}$. He must on the other hand quantify his *preferences* among *consequences* by choosing appropriate reference consequences c^* and c_* and then assigning a number $\pi(c_i)$ to every consequence c_i, such that he would be indifferent between c_i for certain and a lottery giving a *canonical* chance $\pi(c_i)$ at c^* and a complementary chance at c_*. Given the assessments $P(\Theta_i)$ and $\pi(c_i)$, we have seen that the lottery $\{(\Theta_i : c_i)\}$ can be shown to be equivalent to a simple canonical *reference lottery* which gives a canonical chance

$$\Pi = \textstyle\sum_i \pi(c_i)P(\Theta_i) \tag{4.1}$$

at c^* and a complementary chance at c_*. Once all the acts have thus been reduced to two-valued lotteries, each with the same two prizes, c^* and c_*, the decision maker chooses the act corresponding to the lottery which gives the greatest chance at c^*.

4.1.2 Utility Functions

Let us take a closer look at the expression (4.1). We could think of the number $\pi(c_i)$ as a utility index or utility value of c_i. If, for example, the decision maker prefers c_3 to c_5, say, then the number $\pi(c_3)$ will exceed the number $\pi(c_5)$. We can also think of the number Π as a utility index or value of the lottery l in the sense that, given several lotteries, we would prefer the one with the highest associated utility index. Observe that the number Π is a *weighted average* of the numbers $\pi(c_1)$, $\pi(c_2), \ldots, \pi(c_n)$, where the weights are given by $P(\Theta_1)$, $P(\Theta_2), \ldots, P(\Theta_n)$ respectively. We have shown that if we scale each consequence c_i in terms of a utility index $\pi(c_i)$, then the weighted average of these indices is an appropriate utility index for the lottery. Is this utility scale unique? Obviously not. If, for example we doubled each number $\pi(c_i)$, then the index of the lottery would be doubled. If this doubling procedure were to be carried out for all lotteries, however, the relative rankings of the lotteries according to their associated indices *would not be altered.* If we arbitrarily added 5 units to each $\pi(c_i)$ value, then 5 units would be added to their weighted average, or 5 units to the utility index of the lottery. If this were done to all lotteries, then once again the rankings of lotteries according to their associated indices would not be altered. Adding 5 units to each $\pi(c_i)$ can be thought of as a change of origin of measurement; doubling each $\pi(c_i)$ value can be thought of as a change of the unit or scale of measurement. The discussion so far is not unlike a discussion of the relation between the Fahrenheit and Celsius temperature scales. We will discuss at a later point why it is desirable to have more than one utility scale, even though they all lead to identical rankings of lotteries.

We will now show in a more formal manner that a change in the origin and/or the scale of utility measurement does not alter the relative rankings of lotteries. Suppose now that after the decision maker has assigned an indifference probability $\pi(c_i)$ to every c_i, we select an arbitrary constant a and an arbitrary positive constant b, and define for every consequence c_i the quantity

$$u(c_i) \equiv a + b\pi(c_i) \qquad \text{for all } i; \tag{4.2}$$

and then compute for the lottery $\{(\Theta_i : c_i)\}$ the index

$$\begin{aligned} U &= \textstyle\sum_i u(c_i)P(\Theta_i) = \sum_i [a + b\pi(c_i)]P(\Theta_i) \\ &a \textstyle\sum_i P(\Theta_i) + b \sum_i \pi(c_i)P(\Theta_i) \\ &= a + b\Pi, \end{aligned} \tag{4.3}$$

rather than the quantity Π defined by (4.1). Since b is positive, U and Π will rank order lotteries identically.[1]

Definition Let C be a set of consequences with generic element c; let u be a function which assigns to each $c \in C$ a real number $u(c)$; let l' be a canonical lottery which gives chances m_i' at prizes c_i', where $i = 1, 2, \ldots, n'$; let l'' be a canonical lottery which gives chances m_i'' at prizes c_i'' for $i = 1, 2, \ldots, n''$; and let

$$U' \equiv \textstyle\sum_{i=1}^{n'} m_i' u(c_i'), \qquad U'' \equiv \sum_{i=1}^{n''} m_i'' u(c_i'').$$

If for all canonical lotteries l' and l''

1. Two points should be noted, however. First, *utility* has a precise meaning here in terms of lotteries, which need not coincide with any other concept of usefulness or desirability, though it may be related. Second, in economics it is often called *cardinal utility* or *von Neumann-Morgenstern utility* to distinguish it from *ordinal utility* which ranks certainties but cannot be used like cardinal utility in ranking lotteries.

$$l' \left\{ \begin{matrix} \succ \\ \sim \\ \prec \end{matrix} \right\} l'' \Leftrightarrow U' \left\{ \begin{matrix} > \\ = \\ < \end{matrix} \right\} U'',$$

then u is a *utility function.*

If u is a utility function, then the number $u(c)$ associated with a given consequence c will be called the *utility index* of c.

In terms of this new terminology, what we showed in the previous two chapters was that π, as defined in Basic Assumption 2a (section 2.3.2), is a utility function—provided, of course, that the other basic assumptions of chapters 2 and 3 are also accepted. We also see from (4.3) that provided that b is positive, $u \equiv a + b\pi$ is a utility function. We leave (as exercises 10 and 11) the verification of the following simple propositions to the reader:

1. If u_1 is a utility function, then for any constant a and any positive constant b, the function $u_2 = a + bu_1$ is also a utility function.

2. If u is a utility function, then there exist a constant a and a positive constant b such that

$$u(c) = a + b\pi(c) \qquad \text{for all } c \in C.$$

It follows from the above discussion that formal analysis of a decision problem does not require us to compare acts by computing Π for each act directly from the original indifference probabilities $\pi(c)$. We can just as well proceed indirectly, replacing all the original $\pi(c)$ values by the corresponding values of $u(c)$ of some utility function u, computing U for each act and then selecting the act with the greatest U. The next section will illustrate one reason why this indirect procedure is sometimes actually simpler than the direct procedure.

4.2 Utility Functions for Monetary Consequences

4.2.1 Introduction

We can avoid a great deal of needless confusion if, at the outset, we agree to measure monetary values from some fixed asset position. It is important that this asset position remain constant during a given discussion. For some purposes it is convenient to use one's present asset position as the reference standard from which incremental monetary amounts are measured. For other purposes it is more convenient to single out some other asset position, such as ruin or a particular target value, as the fixed reference point.

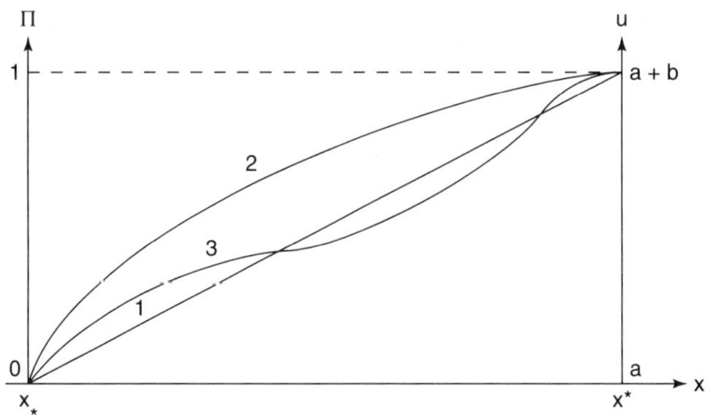

Figure 4.1
Qualitatively different Π-utility functions

Let us assume that we are concerned with a choice among lotteries, where a typical lottery l pays off monetary value x_i with canonical chance m_i, where $i = 1, 2, \dots, n$, and $\sum_{i=1}^{n} m_i = 1$. If y_0 is our fixed asset position for this discussion, this means that with canonical chance m_i the lottery l will result in asset position $y_0 + x_i$. Since y_0 is *not* to be changed during this discussion, we will suppress any further notational reference to y_0 in the sequel. We shall assume that the x_i's all lie in some interval x_* to x^*, and at this point we do not need to impose any restriction on the signs of x_* and x^*. Our notation is chosen so that x_* and x^* will play respectively the roles of c_* and c^*.

For any amount x, where $x_* \leq x \leq x^*$, let $\pi(x)$ be such that the decision maker is indifferent between obtaining x for certain and obtaining the reference lottery which gives him a $\pi(x)$ chance at x^* and a $1 - \pi(x)$ chance of x_*. If $x_1 < x_2$, then it is clear that for all but the most mystical people, $\pi(x_1) < \pi(x_2)$. We therefore shall assume henceforth that $\pi(x)$ is a strictly monotonic increasing function of x. We also know that $\pi(x_*) = 0$ and $\pi(x^*) = 1$. In figure 4.1 we exhibit three qualitatively different π functions which we shall eventually discuss. We shall also discuss at a later stage how a decision maker could obtain his π-utility function.

4.2.2 Change of Utility Scales

Suppose a decision maker has constructed a π-utility function and for some reason wants to change her π-utility function to a u-utility function, where

$$u(x) = a + b\pi(x), \qquad b > 0. \tag{4.4}$$

It is easy to see that her u-utility function and her π-utility function have the same shape, except that the vertical scale must be changed as shown in figure 4.1; $\pi = 0$ corresponds to $u = a$ and $\pi = 1$ corresponds to $u = a + b$.

Suppose we now choose three monetary amounts x_1, x, x_2 where $x_* \le x_1 \le x \le x_2 \le x^*$ and $x_2 > x_1$, and pose the following problem: Find the number α such that the decision maker is indifferent between obtaining x for certain, and obtaining the lottery which gives x_2 with canonical chance α and x_1 with canonical chance $(1 - \alpha)$. Introducing the notation $\{(\alpha : x_2), (1 - \alpha : x_1)\}$ to represent this lottery, α is such that

$$x \sim \{(\alpha : x_2), (1 - \alpha : x_1)\}. \tag{4.5}$$

If u is a utility function, then from (4.5) we must have

$$u(x) = \alpha u(x_2) + (1 - \alpha) u(x_1),$$

or

$$\alpha = \frac{u(x) - u(x_1)}{u(x_2) - u(x_1)}. \tag{4.6}$$

If the u-scale is so chosen that $u(x_1) = 0$ and $u(x_2) = 1$, then we obtain $\alpha = u(x)$. Symbolically, we have shown

$$x \sim \{(u(x) : x_2), (1 - u(x) : x_1)\} \quad \text{if} \begin{cases} u(x_2) = 1, \\ u(x_1) = 0. \end{cases} \tag{4.7}$$

Thus, if a utility function for money is given, then by suitably changing its scale, one can get a meaningful and direct probabilistic interpretation for $u(x)$ for all $x_1 \le x \le x_2$. The suitable change of scale is such that $u(x_1) = 0$ and $u(x_2) = 1$. This is a reason, but definitely not the main reason, as we shall soon see, for the introduction of u-utility functions.

4.2.3 Cash Equivalents

Let l be a lottery which pays off x_i with canonical chance m_i, $i = 1, 2, \ldots, n$. The *cash equivalent*[2] of l, denoted by CE(l), is the amount such that the decision maker is indifferent between obtaining the lottery l and obtaining the amount CE(l) for certain. Stated in a slightly different form, she would be just willing to sell the lottery l, if she had it, for the amount CE(l). It is in this sense that the cash equivalent of a lottery can be thought of as the *selling price* of a lottery.

More formally, the cash equivalent of l is that amount q such that

$$u(q) = \textstyle\sum_{i=1}^{n} m_i u(x_i), \qquad q = \mathrm{CE}(l). \tag{4.8}$$

2. In the literature, the "*cash* equivalent" of l is also referred to as the "*certainty* equivalent" of l; both are abbreviated as CE(l).

If the reference point for assets is the decision maker's present asset position, and if the decision maker would rather have the lottery than not, then $\mathrm{CE}(l) > 0$. If, however, the lottery is unfavorable, so that the decision maker would prefer not to have it, then $\mathrm{CE}(l) < 0$; it is natural in this case to think of l as an obligation and $-\mathrm{CE}(l)$ is the amount the decision maker would be just willing to pay to relieve herself of this obligation. We therefore say that the amount $-\mathrm{CE}(l)$ is the *insurance premium* for l.

It is important to recognize that the amount a decision maker would just be willing to pay for a certain lottery—assuming she does not have it—is in general different from the amount she would just be willing to sell this same lottery for—assuming she does have it. If this is not clear, imagine a lottery which would give you a .5 chance at $100,000 and a .5 chance at $0. Would you pay as much for this lottery if you did not have it as the price you would sell it for if you were lucky enough to have it in the first place?

We repeat once again: In this book, the *cash equivalent* of a lottery is the trading or selling price of the lottery assuming that *you already own the rights and obligations of this lottery.*

4.2.4 Expected Monetary Value

Now consider the special case where the π- or u-utility function is *linear* for x values from x_* and x^*. In this case we obtain

$$\pi(x) = \frac{x - x_*}{x^* - x_*}, \tag{4.9}$$

or

$$x = x_* + (x^* - x_*)\pi(x). \tag{4.10}$$

If we now compare (4.10) and (4.2) by letting $a = x_*$ and $b = x^* - x_*$, we see that the function $u(x) = x$ is a valid utility function. Alternatively this important conclusion may be phrased: *If π is linear, then the number x itself is a valid utility index for the monetary amount x.*

If a lottery l pays off the monetary value x_i with canonical chance m_i, $i = 1, 2, \ldots, n$, then the quantity

$$X = \textstyle\sum_{i=1}^{n} m_i x_i \tag{4.11}$$

is defined as the *expected monetary value* (EMV) of the lottery l. We shall also use the notation $\mathrm{EMV}(l)$ for X.

In terms of this definition of EMV, we now can assert that if a decision maker's utility function is linear, then

a. EMV is a valid index for choice among lotteries, and

b. the cash equivalent of a lottery is its EMV; i.e., $\mathrm{CE}(l) = \mathrm{EMV}(l)$.

This last proposition follows by comparing (4.8) and (4.11) and taking $u(x) = x$, which can be done because of proposition (a).

Our results so far have taken the form: "If π is linear, then...." We now propose to develop a simple rule to test whether a decision maker's π-function is linear. We first observe that if π is linear, then a lottery which gives a 50-50 chance at x_1 and x_2 has a cash equivalent of (x_1 and x_2)/2. The converse proposition is also true: If for *every* x_1 and x_2 between x_* and x^* the lottery $\{(.5 : x_1), (.5 : x_2)\}$ has a cash equivalent of (x_1 and x_2)/2, then the π-function must be linear between x_* and x^*. In symbolic form this can be restated as:

$$\begin{bmatrix} \pi \text{ is linear} \\ \text{from } x_* \text{ to } x^* \end{bmatrix} \Leftrightarrow \begin{bmatrix} \text{CE}\{(.5 : x_1), (.5 : x_2)\} = \dfrac{x_1 + x_2}{2} \\ \text{for all } x_* \leq x_1 < x_2 \leq x^* \end{bmatrix}. \qquad (4.12)$$

We now summarize this discussion by the following *Rule for the Use of EMV as a Criterion of Choice:*

If (1) all the consequences in a decision problem are adequately described by monetary values lying between an upper limit x^* and a lower limit x_*, and if (2) the decision maker would use EMV as a criterion in evaluating a 50-50 gamble involving any two sums of money lying between x_* and x^*, then he should use EMV as a criterion for choice among acts in his decision problem.

A large corporation would presumably want to make decisions involving small amounts of money so nearly in accordance with expected monetary value that its indifference probability function π is for all purposes linear in money. Even a large corporation, however, will be faced with some decisions where the consequences are so large that maximizing expected monetary value is not satisfactory. Furthermore, most individual investors do not use simple expected monetary value, and this brings into the picture utility indices which are not linear in money. For example, the whole investment portfolio selection problem hinges on this, whether it is looked at from the point of view of the individual investor or that of a mutual fund. Notice also that an individual will not have the same π function for money when acting for a corporation as when acting for himself, even if his actions for the corporation are in his own rather than the corporation's best interest. In section 4.3 we shall investigate the assessment of π functions for money.

4.2.5 Risk Aversion and Concave Utility Functions

We now digress to remind the reader what concave and strictly concave functions are, after which we shall relate the concept of concavity with a concept of risk aversion to be defined shortly.

A real-valued function w of a real argument x is called *concave* if for all x_1, x_2, and α, where $0 < \alpha < 1$,

$$w[\alpha x_1 + (1 - \alpha)x_2] \geq \alpha w(x_1) + (1 - \alpha)w(x_2). \tag{4.13}$$

A function w is called *strictly concave* if (4.13) holds with $>$ in place of $\geq$. These properties mean that the line segment or chord connecting any two points of the graph of w is:

a. nowhere above the graph for a concave w;

b. everywhere below the graph (except at the end points of the chord) for a strictly concave w.

In figure 4.1 utility function 2 is strictly concave, function 1 is concave (in a degenerate sort of sense), and function 3 is not concave (but it is strictly concave in portions of the range).

By definition a decision maker will be said to be *averse to risk* if he considers *no* lottery *more* desirable than its EMV, that is, if

$$\text{CE}(l) \leq \text{EMV}(l) \qquad \text{for all } l, \tag{4.14}$$

and he will be said to be *strictly risk averse* if (4.14) holds with $<$ in place of $\leq$ for all l with at least two possible payoffs. By saying that a payoff is "possible," we mean that it occurs with positive probability.

In the case that EMV(l) is negative, it is instructive to reinterpret (4.14) in terms of insurance. Multiplying both sides of (4.14) by -1 we obtain

$$-\text{CE}(l) \geq -\text{EMV}(l) \qquad \text{for all } l. \tag{4.15}$$

Now recalling our discussion in section 4.2.3 where we defined *insurance premium*, we can say that a person averse to risk is willing to pay an insurance premium *at least* equal to $-$EMV(l) to relieve himself of the obligation of an unfavorable lottery l. The words "at least equal to" can be replaced by "greater than" for *strict* risk aversion.

The reader may prove (exercise 13) the following propositions:

a. risk aversion $\Leftrightarrow$ concavity of the utility function,

b. strict risk aversion $\Leftrightarrow$ strict concavity of the utility function.

We now give a simple test for concavity of a utility function analogous to the one given for linearity in (4.12). It is not difficult to prove (exercise 14):

$$\begin{bmatrix} \pi \text{ is concave} \\ \text{from } x_* \text{ to } x^* \end{bmatrix} \Leftrightarrow \begin{bmatrix} \text{CE}\{(.5 : x_1), (.5 : x_2)\} \leq \dfrac{x_1 + x_2}{2} \\ \text{for all } x_* \leq x_1 < x_2 \leq x^* \end{bmatrix} \tag{4.16}$$

It has been shown in the literature that some decision makers sometimes behave as if their utility functions were not risk averse. For example, Grayson (1960) has shown that some oil wildcatters are not willing to sell their rights to a lottery for its EMV, especially when some of the possible, but not very probable, monetary prizes hold out the promise of a "new way of life." Some of their utility functions are of type 3 in figure 4.1. Nevertheless we suspect that decision makers in most business contexts are strictly risk averse.[3]

4.3 Construction of a Utility Function for Money

4.3.1 Fitting a Utility Function by Direct Responses

Since the action implications of a utility function are left unchanged when the function is multiplied by a positive constant or augmented by any constant, there is no loss of generality in arbitrarily choosing two monetary amounts x_0 and x_1, where $x_0 < x_1$, and assigning to them two arbitrarily chosen utility indices $u(x_0)$ and $u(x_1)$, provided, of course, that $u(x_1) > u(x_0)$. Starting from the pairs $[x_0, u(x_0)]$, $[x_1, u(x_1)]$, we propose to show how you (the decision maker) can generate a sequence of pairs $\{[x_i, u(x_i)]\}$. To this end, suppose you have already generated the sequence of pairs for $i = 0, 1, \ldots, n-1$. To generate $[x_n, u(x_n)]$, we allow you to choose any x_i and x_j where $x_i < x_j$ and where i and j are indices from 0 to $n-1$, and then ask you to respond to any one of the following three types of questions:

1. State the value x_n (between x_i and x_j) such that you would be indifferent between getting x_n outright and a lottery which gives a .5 chance at x_i and a .5 chance at x_j; that is, x_n is your cash equivalent for a 50-50 gamble between x_i and x_j. In this case the pair $[x_n, u(x_n)]$ satisfies the requirement

$$u(x_n) = \tfrac{1}{2}u(x_i) + \tfrac{1}{2}u(x_j).$$

2. State the value x_n (below x_i) such that you would be indifferent between getting x_i outright and a lottery which gives a .5 chance at x_n and a .5 chance at x_j. In this case thc pair $[x_n, u(x_n)]$ satisfies the requirement

$$u(x_i) = \tfrac{1}{2}u(x_n) + \tfrac{1}{2}u(x_j).$$

3. One notable exception is that some decision makers often prefer lotteries with incremental negative EMV to the EMV of that lottery. For example, some decision makers might prefer to take a 50-50 chance at $-\$100$ or \$0 to a vertainty of $-\$45$, say. See exercise 4.

3. State the value x_n (above x_j) such that you would be indifferent between getting x_j outright and a lottery which gives a .5 chance at x_i and a .5 chance at x_n. In this case the pair $[x_n, u(x_n)]$ satisfies the requirement

$$u(x_j) = \tfrac{1}{2}u(x_i) + \tfrac{1}{2}u(x_n).$$

We suggest that as you generate pairs $[x_i, u(x_i)]$ you plot these on a piece of graph paper and after obtaining a "moderate" number of points, you fair in (or fit) a smooth curve connecting these points. It may be helpful to police your responses as you go along so that your curve does not have to go through excessive local gyrations.

This is not the *only* way to obtain a utility curve; rather it is *a* way, which has the merit of using only lotteries with two equally likely payoffs.

4.3.2 Some Cautionary Remarks about Direct Assessments

We shall now briefly indicate some of the serious shortcomings of the approach used in the previous subsection for assessing a utility function.

If a utility function u is determined by fairing a curve through empirically determined points, then $u(x)$ can only be read from the curve or a table made from the curve. In complicated problems, like the sampling problems we shall encounter in this book, the analysis becomes almost hopeless unless we can work with utility functions expressed in analytical form. For example, we shall see later that we will often be concerned with an expression of the form $\int_b^a u(x)f(x)\,dx$ where f is a function related to probability assessments. While it is true that approximations to an integral of this kind can be found by numerical means, our task of analysis will become increasingly difficult unless we can systematically join together different analytical expressions and use the full power of the calculus.

If a utility function u is determined by fairing a curve through empirically determined points, it is often the case that some of the implications that can be drawn from this curve will contradict other strongly held feelings. Suppose, for example, that l is a lottery which with equal chance pays nothing or \$10,000 and that the decision maker is indifferent between receiving l and receiving an outright payment of \$3,000; and let us assume that his utility curve appropriately reflects this response. Now suppose we add \$5,000 to each of the prizes in l and let l' be the lottery which with equal chance pays \$5,000 or \$15,000. According to the decision maker's utility function u it might possibly turn out that he is indifferent between l' and a certainty of \$7,500. Now l' is equivalent to l plus \$5,000 cash, and the decision maker might very well argue that if he were \$5,000 richer he would *not* be content to trade l for \$3,000. In other words, this type of reflection might lead him to the conclusion that l' should be indifferent to some amount greater than \$5,000 + \$3,000, contrary to the conclusion

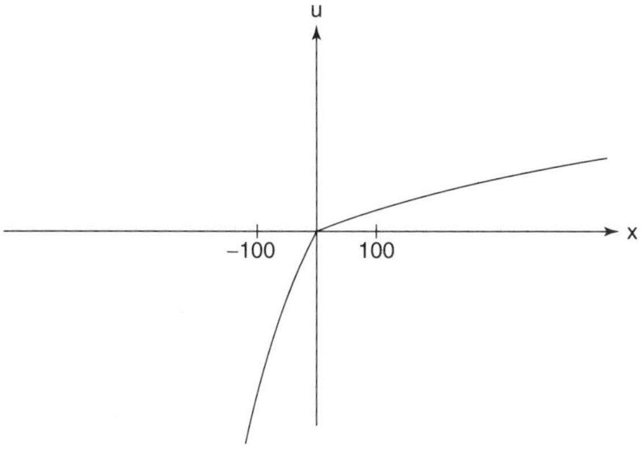

Figure 4.2
A utility function exhibiting a break in slope at current asset position

drawn from direct computations with his assessed utility function for incremental amounts of money.

As a second example, an investor may feel strongly that as his assets grow he should spend a proportionately larger share of his investment funds on growth stocks rather than less risky investments, whereas his empirically determined utility function may argue the reverse. While there is no way of proving *which* set of feelings should be altered, one set *must* be altered if the investor's utility function is to agree with his preferences.

As a third example, in many empirically derived utility functions for money, there is an actual break in the slope of u at $x = 0$, the point representing the decision maker's current assets. (See figure 4.2.) If we let l represent the lottery which gives equal chances at $-\$100$ and $+\$100$, then according to a utility function u of the type shown in figure 4.2, the insurance premium the decision maker would pay to avoid accepting a small gamble with EMV equal to zero would be greatly decreased if the decision maker's present assets were *either* increased or decreased by a fairly small amount—enough to carry him either to the right or to the left of the extremely concave portion of his utility curve. Such behavior would of course be perfectly self-consistent and in that sense "rational," but it seems doubtful that a person ordinarily judged "reasonable" would adhere to such a utility curve—or to the indifference statements underlying it—once its implications are pointed out. The phenomenon arises, we would guess, from very unconsidered first reactions to the possibility of out-of-pocket losses versus pure windfall gains. We imagine further that it is usually in conflict with the same person's real attitudes as revealed by his decision regarding serious investments.

To sum up, we have seen that *one* procedure for determining a decision maker's utility function is to ask him to state his cash equivalent for a number of very simple hypothetical gambles; we presume his responses express his *basic* attitudes toward risk. We then argued that the specific responses elicited by this direct approach might conflict with attitudes revealed by other more general types of questions, such as questions concerning the qualitative effect of changes in assets on the decision maker's reactions to a given lottery; and the general attitudes and preferences thus revealed may be more truly basic than those reflected in reactions to specific hypothetical gambles in the sense that when informed of the logical contradiction the decision maker will prefer to alter his original reactions to specific hypothetical gambles rather than to modify his attitudes toward the more general qualitative questions. In the construction of a utility function for money it is often preferable to use an analytical curve having certain specified qualitative features but with some adjustable parameters, whose values can be adjusted from questions about particular gambles. There must be as many questions as parameters to be determined. If extra questions are asked, then the parameters may be determined from some answers with the rest used to check the consequences, or the parameters may be chosen according to some criterion of "best fit" to all.

4.3.3 Boundedness of Utility Functions

We believe almost any decision maker could, if called upon, announce some large monetary value x_1 that he would prefer outright to a lottery which gives him a .5 chance at some small amount x_0 and a .5 chance at some amount x_2 *no matter how large that value may be.* This means that there exists some x_1 value such that

$$u(x_1) > \tfrac{1}{2}u(x_0) + \tfrac{1}{2}u(x_2)$$

for *all* x_2 however large! As a consequence of this proposition we observe that $u(x_2)$ must be bounded as x_2 increases, or more briefly stated: *u must be bounded from above.*

Now let us turn our attention to the behavior of $u(x)$ as x decreases. If $u(x)$ were to decrease without bound then for any monetary consequence x_1, however desirable, and any probability p, however small, there would be some monetary consequence x_2 so undesirable that the decision maker would prefer the status quo to a lottery giving the miniscule chance p at x_2 and the complementary almost certain chance $(1 - p)$ at x_1. What *monetary* consequence x_2 could be so terrible to counterbalance a p value of say 10^{-10} and an x_1 value of \$$10^7$? Because of the above considerations we conclude that u should also be bounded from below.

If a utility function u is risk averse (i.e., concave), it cannot be bounded from below *if* the domain of x is unlimited to the left. But the domain will always be limited strictly speaking by a ruin or bankruptcy condition.

The arguments about the boundedness of any reasonable utility function u should not, however, unduly limit our choice of suitable u functions. Although in all practical applications the range of possible monetary values is limited, there will be times when for analytical purposes it will be convenient to consider lotteries whose possible monetary outcomes are unlimited. Strictly speaking, we have argued that in cases of this kind we should use bounded utility functions. But since any utility index $u(x)$ is always multiplied by some probability $P(x)$ that the lottery will result in x, it may be mathematically expedient in some circumstances to let $u(x)$ increase without bound as x increases, as long as we neutralize this distortion by insisting that $P(x)$ goes to zero "fast enough" so that the product $u(x)\ P(x)$ also goes to zero "fast enough" as x increases. We can use unbounded utility functions, such as x itself, $\log x$, or $\sqrt{x}$, but we have to tread with care whenever we introduce at the same time idealized approximating lotteries whose possible monetary outcomes are unlimited. A similar comment applies to functions such as $\log x$ or $-1/x$ and outcomes near 0.

4.4 Monetary and Other Numeraires

4.4.1 Scaling of Complex Consequences by Equivalent Monetary Value

Even when some or all of the consequences in a decision problem are not fully described by the amount of money which the decision maker will receive or pay out, he may choose to *scale* these consequences in terms of equivalent monetary values. Thus if a particular consequence c consists of a combination of a certain monetary cost plus substantial administrative complications for a decision maker, he may be able to decide that he would be indifferent between c and a somewhat larger monetary cost x without the administrative complications. In this sense x can be thought of as the pure monetary equivalent for the complex consequence c. If it is reasonable in a given problem to substitute a pure monetary equivalent for each complex consequence then the subsequent analysis of the problem will in general be simplified, essentially because indifference probabilities or utility indices can be assigned to purely monetary consequences via a curve or simple mathematical function, whereas each complex consequence must usually be evaluated directly in terms of reference consequences. If, furthermore, all consequences can be scaled in terms of monetary equivalents which lie in the interval from x_* to x^* and if the utility function for money is linear in this range, then the problem can be evaluated in terms of expected monetary value without formally introducing any indifference probabilities or utility indices at all.

4.4.2 Other Numeraires

Even when consequences cannot be scaled in terms of monetary value, it may be possible to scale them (to reduce the description of each consequence to a single numerical value) in terms of some other quantity—hours worked, number of patients cured, and so forth. Thus, for example, the director of a clinic who must ultimately decide whether or not to adopt a new drug in place of an old one may well feel that the consequence of either act is measured almost entirely by the number of patients cured as a result. The new drug may differ from the old one not only as regards the *numeraire* "patients cured" but also as regards certain unpleasant or dangerous side effects. The most effective way of handling this complication, however, may well be to start by scaling these side effects in terms of a pure cure-rate equivalent.

If each of the consequences of a lottery can be scaled in terms of an equivalent value of some numeraire, then the subsequent analysis can proceed by means of a utility function over the domain of this numeraire. If the utility function is linear in the relevant range of this numeraire, then it is appropriate to analyze the problem in terms of the expected *numeraire* value just as we did in terms of the expected *monetary* value.

In some situations it is very difficult to describe a complex consequence in terms of a numeraire which is a single number. It may be reasonable, however, to define a pair of numeraires—or perhaps more—and then associate each consequence c with a pair of numbers (x_1, x_2) which adequately describes that consequence. In these circumstances we would then be confronted with the problem of constructing a utility function involving two variables. In this book, however, we shall not get involved in this type of intricate measurement problem. For further analysis of utility functions defined over several variables see Keeney and Raiffa (1976).

Appendix 3 more fully develops the theory of utility for monetary consequences. It assumes some background in probability theory and is written in a compact style. It can be omitted without interfering with understanding the rest of the book. Those interested in the material, unless they are well prepared, should wait at least until chapter 13 before reading it.

Exercises

1. Let u be a utility function for (incremental) amounts of money x and suppose that u is chosen such that $u(100) = 0$ and $u(300) = 1$. Show that

   i. if $100 \sim \{(.5 : -25), (.5 : 300)\}$, then $u(-25) = -1$;

   ii. if $300 \sim \{(.5 : 600), (.5 : 100)\}$, then $u(600) = 2$;

   iii. if $100 \sim \{(.5 : -100), (.5 : 600)\}$, then $u(-100) = -2$;

   iv. if $-100 \sim \{(.5 : -200), (.5 : 300)\}$, then $u(-200) = -5$;

   Plot these six points on a graph where the horizontal axis is labelled x and the vertical axis u. Fair a smooth curve through these points, and assume for the remainder of this exercise that this utility function is your own. From the graph, you will be able to answer the following questions:

   a. What is the CE of a lottery that gives a .5 chance at \$300 and a .5 chance at \$600?

   b. What is the CE for a lottery that gives a .75 chance at \$400 and a .25 chance at −\$200?

   c. You are offered a compound lottery with a canonical chance at the lottery l of part (b) as one prize and a complementary chance at no net gain. What would your chance of winning lottery l have to be before you would accept the offer?

   d. What is the insurance premium of a lottery that gives a .5 chance at \$0 and a .5 chance at −\$200?

   e. Given that the CE of a lottery is \$325, and the lottery gives a π chance at \$500 and a $(1 - \pi)$ chance at \$300, find π.

   f. What is the CE of a lottery that offers a .375 chance at \$500, a .125 chance at \$600, and a .5 chance at \$0?

   g. You are offered the lottery of part (f) for \$200; would you buy it? If you were an EMV'er would your choice change?

   h. Consider the lottery

   $$l = \{(.2 : \$0), (.5 : \$150), (.3 : \$600)\}.$$

   For how much would you just be willing to *sell* this lottery if you owned it?

   i. For how much would you just be willing to *buy* the lottery of part (h) if you did not own it?

2. Use the method of section 4.3.1 to obtain your utility function for incremental amounts of money from −\$10,000 to +\$10,000. Start off by letting $x_0 = \$0$ and $x_1 = \$10{,}000$. Use graph paper.

3. In section 4.4.1 we talked about the scaling of complex consequences by equivalent monetary values and in section 4.4.2 we very briefly indicated that this same procedure may be used with scales or numeraires other than money. Take for example a medical problem where such things as side effects of drugs, hours spent in research, etc., are all scaled in terms of the numeraire "number of patients cured," w. Obviously, if act a_1 leads for certain to a higher w than act a_2 does, then $a_1 > a_2$. Suppose, however, that act a_1 leads for certain to w_1 and act a_2 leads to a .5 chance at w_2 and a .5 chance at w_3 where $w_2 < w_1 < w_3$. Then one must compare w_1 and $\{(.5 : w_2), (.5 : w_3)\}$. In this situation do you think that the utility function $u(w)$ should be linear so that "expected patients cured" would be valid guide for action? Or would it be more natural for the u function to be concave?

4. An oil wildcatter with an option on a certain site must decide whether to abandon the option, to drill at his own risk, or to sell off some part of the risk and then drill. The first table following shows the possible acts and events and gives (in \$000) the discounted present value (DPV) of the cash flows which will result from each act-event pair:

Event	Judgmental probability	Do not drill	Keep all	Sell $\frac{1}{4}$	Drill, and sell $\frac{1}{2}$	Sell $\frac{3}{4}$
Dry hole	.60	0	−50	−37.5	−25	−12.5
100,000 bbls	.20	0	100	75	50	25
200,000 bbls	.10	0	200	150	100	50
500,000 bbls	.07	0	500	375	250	125
1,000,000 bbls	.03	0	1,000	750	500	250

The next table shows for each consequence the π of an equivalent canonical lottery between +\$1,000,000 and −\$50,000.

DPV (\$000)	π	DPV (\$000)	π	DPV (\$000)	π
−50.0	.000	+25.0	.202	+200.0	.520
−37.5	.040	50.0	.255	250.0	.600
−25.0	.075	75.0	.305	375.0	.740
−12.5	.110	100.0	.350	500.0	.835
0	.140	125.0	.395	750.0	.950
		150.0	.435	1,000.0	1.000

Which act should the wildcatter choose?

5. *St. Petersburg Paradox.* If a coin is tossed canonically until heads occurs, the probability that i tosses will be required is $(1/2)^i$. Now let l be the lottery which pays off $\$2^i$ if i tosses are required.

a. Show that a decision maker for whom EMV is a valid criterion of choice would be happy to pay out his entire assets for the rights to this lottery.

b. How much would *you* be willing to pay for this lottery?

c. Since there is not enough money in the whole world to make a payment of $\$2^{50}$, let us modify the lottery by assuming that if heads does not occur in the first 25 tosses, no prize will be awarded. The lottery will then be of the form

$$l = \left\{\left(\frac{1}{2} : \$2\right), \left(\frac{1}{4} : \$4\right), \left(\frac{1}{8} : \$8\right), \ldots, \left(\frac{1}{2^{25}} : \$2^{25}\right), (p : \$0)\right\}$$

where

$$p = 1 - \left\{\frac{1}{2} + \frac{1}{4} + \cdots + \frac{1}{2^{25}}\right\}.$$

Show that the EMV for this lottery is \$25.

d. How much would you be willing to pay for the modified lottery?

6. The following exercise should preferably be answered immediately after a cocktail party:

State an amount z so that *you* would be indifferent between the following two options:

Option A: In addition to your regular income you will receive a tax-free gift of z dollars per year for the rest of your life.

Option B: A single toss of a fair coin will determine whether you get *nothing* or the fabulous privilege of an *unlimited* ability to write checks in any amount you wish for the rest of your natural life.

In both options you cannot decide to set up your very own Foreign Aid program. The rules of the game—too bad it is only a game—specify that you must spend the money for consumption by you and your family. Yes, you can buy that yacht! It's also fun (?) to guess how others would respond to this gamble to end all gambles. Incidentally, one point of this exercise is to convince you that u should be bounded from above.

7. Let l_x denote the lottery

$$\{(\tfrac{1}{2}: -100 + x), (\tfrac{1}{2}: 100 + x)\}.$$

Let $g(x) \equiv \mathrm{CE}(l_x) - x$. Describe the behavior of your g function for $-500 \leq x \leq 500$ and compare your qualitative conclusions about g with that of a person whose utility function is given in figure 4.2.

8. Let u denote your utility function. Let b be the maximum amount you would be willing to spend to *buy* the lottery

$$l = \{(m_1 : x_1), \ldots, (m_n : x_n)\}.$$

Show that

$$u(0) = \textstyle\sum_{i=1}^{n} m_i u(x_i - b).$$

9. For any amount x, let $s(x)$ be such that

$$s(x) \sim \{(\tfrac{1}{2} : x), (\tfrac{1}{2} : 0)\},$$

as far as *your* preferences are concerned. Plot $s(x)$ against x for a range $-\$1{,}000 \leq x \leq +\$1{,}000$. Can your s function be determined from your u or π function? Can your u or π function be determined from your s function?

The following exercises include assertions made in the text that were not proved:

10. (End of section 4.1.2): If u_1 is a utility function, then for any constant a and any positive constant b, the function $u_2 = a + bu_1$ is also a utility function.

11. (End of section 4.1.2): If u is a utility function, then there exist a constant a and a positive constant b such that

$$u(c) = a + b\pi(c) \qquad \text{for all } c \in C.$$

Hint Use c^* and c_* to find a and b. Now consider two-valued lotteries.

12. Verify the proposition (4.12).

13. Verify the propositions (a) and (b) given in section 4.2.5. (This is essentially Jensen's inequality, usually stated as $\varphi(E\tilde{x}) \leq E\varphi(\tilde{x})$ if φ is a convex function and the expectations are defined.)

14. Verify the proposition (4.16).

CASE: WATERMAN ENGINEERING CORPORATION[4]

On August 14, 1969, Mr. L. E. Waterman had only a few more days in which to make up his mind whether or not to sign a proposed contract with a syndicate of businessmen in the city of Norwood. The contract provided that the Waterman Engineering Corporation, of which Waterman was president, should build a community television antenna according to certain specifications on a site some distance from the city

4. Adapted from Schlaifer (1969), pp. 81–83, 196–98. Adaptation copyright © 1976 by the President and Fellows of Harvard College. Used with permission and minor editing.

and link it to a distributing point near the center of the city; the local syndicate would then pay Waterman in cash for the complete system and take over its operation.

The Waterman Engineering Corporation's sole business was the design and construction of community antenna systems to service towns and small cities beyond the reach of existing television broadcast facilities. The company had been founded by Waterman in 1965, after he had received a master's degree in civil and electrical engineering from Georgia Tech in June 1963, and then spent two years working in the Broadcasting Facilities Department of a major television network. Its initial capital had consisted of $15,000 paid in by Waterman's father, a successful construction contractor. Since the founding of the company, all of its stock has been held by members of the Waterman family. The company's assets on August 14, 1969, amounted to $90,000, of which $57,000 represented cash while the remainder represented the net book value of the construction and office equipment. The firm's after-tax profit to date for the 1969–1970 fiscal year (Waterman's fiscal year was May 1–April 30) was $89,000, of which $40,000 had been used to repay the Waterman family for loans made in the 1968–1969 fiscal year.

In order to conserve working capital,[5] Waterman had a firm policy of avoiding involvement in the ownership and operation of any antenna system once it had been completed and tested. In developing a new location, the company obtained a franchise from the city government and then, before committing any resources to actual construction, tried to interest local businessmen and investors in forming a local company to purchase and operate the system as soon as it was completed and proved out. When Waterman failed to organize a local group which would contract for purchase of the system on satisfactory terms, he invariably preferred to forfeit the franchise rather than tie up his capital for an indefinite period of time. On August 14, 1969, Waterman held only one franchise, the one in the city of Norwood, and saw no prospect of getting another one within the next several months. The Norwood franchise would become invalid unless construction "begins not later than September 1 and continues thereafter with no unnecessary or undue delays."

The only suitable location for the antenna at Norwood was at a substantial distance from the city, and therefore it would be more economical to transmit the television signals from the antenna to the distributing point in the center of Norwood by microwave relay than by coaxial cable.

5. Working capital, also called net current assets, is equal to net liquid assets plus inventories at the lower of cost or market.

Such microwave transmission required a license from the Federal Communications Commission, however, and because there was a local television station in Norwood, it was not at all certain what action the FCC would take concerning Waterman's application for a license. The license might be granted without restrictions, but in similar circumstances in the recent past the FCC had sometimes restricted the license to prohibit transmission of programs that the local station wished to rebroadcast by use of kinescope recordings and sometimes refused to grant any license at all. The examiner's report on the Waterman case was not to be rendered until December 15, and Waterman knew of no way of getting any advance indication of the examiner's conclusion; he felt sure, however, that the commission would accept the examiner's recommendation in this case whichever way he ruled.

The granting of a restricted license would be disadvantageous to Waterman because the proposed contract with the Norwood syndicate specified a price of only \$120,000 for a system with a microwave connection and a restricted license, whereas it specified a price of \$150,000 for a system with a microwave connection and unrestricted license. The syndicate would also pay \$150,000 for a system with connection by coaxial cable, over which the FCC would have no control, but whereas construction of the system would cost only about \$110,000 if a microwave link was used, it would cost about \$180,000 if a cable connection was necessary. Although no money would have to be spent on equipment for either type of connection until after the examiner's report was received on December 15, the terms of the franchise meant that the antenna itself, which accounted for about \$80,000 of the total cost, would have to be nearly if not entirely completed before that date.

On August 15, 1969, before he had made up his mind whether or not to sign the contract with the local group in Norwood, Waterman learned quite unexpectedly that a competitor, the Electronics Service Corporation, was willing to sell him a franchise and contract held by Electronics in the city of Prescott; the price would be \$10,000 cash. Waterman had offered to buy the franchise and contract at that price some months before, but at that time Electronics had flatly refused to sell. Electronics now indicated that they had another offer for the franchise and contract, in the amount of \$9,000, which they would accept if Waterman did not close the deal within one week. Although the Prescott franchise had come along unexpectedly, Waterman felt quite sure that the chance of his being offered still another franchise within the next several months was virtually nil.

The contract with the local operating group at Prescott called for an antenna to be erected on a hill just outside the city and to be connected by cable with a distributing point in the city. The price to be paid by the group for the completed system was $140,000, and from the investigation he had conducted before making his original offer, Waterman had concluded that he could build the complete system for about $90,000 provided that he could get by with an antenna 100 feet high, as he hoped he could. There was some risk, however, that an antenna only 100 feet high would not receive a signal of the strength and clarity required by the contract, since a mountain range partially obstructed the antenna's reception. If the 100-foot antenna did prove insufficient, Waterman was certain he could increase its height to a point where the signal was not obstructed for an additional cost of $70,000; virtually none of this extra cost could be saved by building the higher antenna to begin with.

The local group and the city government had agreed to allow Electronics to sell the franchise and contract to Waterman. The franchise was valid provided that the system was in operation on April 1, 1970, and Waterman felt absolutely sure that construction would take less than three months even if he had to work on the Norwood job at the same time and even if the height of the antenna at Prescott had to be increased. Waterman would, however, have to deposit $5,000 with the operating group within one week of taking over the contract, and he would have to agree that if he should fail to complete the system, the deposit would be forfeited in lieu of any suit the operating group might have brought.

On August 16, 1969, Waterman decided to make a systematic analysis of the decision problem he faced regarding a proposed contract with a syndicate of local businessmen in the city of Norwood and an offer he had received from the Electronics Service Corporation. To do so, he first assessed the following probabilities:

License for microwave connection at Norwood:	
Granted without restrictions	.5
Granted with restrictions	.2
Refused	.3
	1.0
Increase in height of antenna at Prescott:	
Necessary	.4
Unnecessary	.6
	1.0

After thinking more carefully about the possible consequences of his courses of action, Waterman decided that his certainty equivalents for some of the gambles he might face would not be at all close to his corresponding mathematical expectations. After some further thought he decided to base his analysis on his preferences for net liquid assets on April 1, 1970, and selecting \$110,000 and \$25,000 as his reference terminal values, he assessed a utility curve which is shown in Exhibit 2. In doing so, he took his current nonmonetary assets as his base, assuming that none of the acts or events in the decision problem he was facing would in any way alter this base.

Waterman expected that in the current fiscal year, as in the previous one, the company would be taxed at 48%. Quarterly taxes had already been paid at that rate on the firm's profits prior to August 14, 1969.

Exhibit 1 *L. E. Waterman's preference assessments*
(certainty equivalents for 50-50 gambles for net liquid assets)

Gamble consequences		Certainty equivalent
1. \$110,000	\$25,000	\$40,000
2. \$110,000	\$40,000	\$60,000
3. \$ 40,000	\$25,000	\$30,000

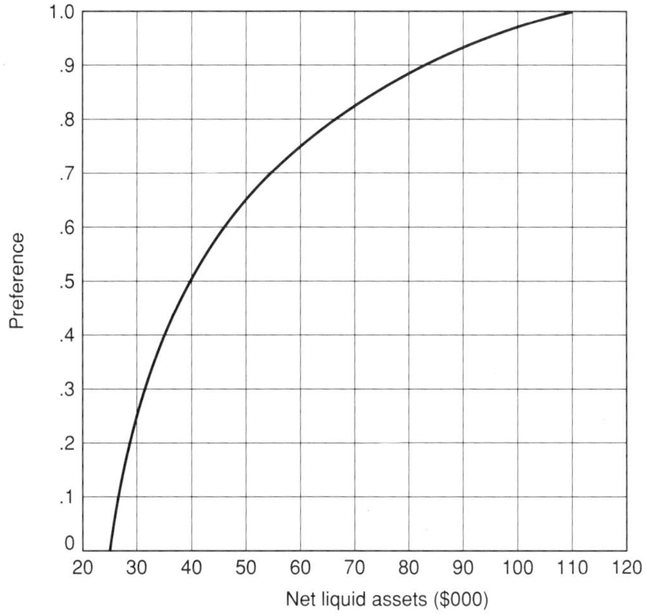

Exhibit 2
L. E. Waterman's preferences for net liquid assets relative to \$110,000 and \$25,000 in the presence of his base nonmonetary assets

Questions on "Waterman Engineering Corporation"

1. Draw a decision diagram of Waterman's decision problems and evaluate the *after tax* net liquid assets of the company at each possible end position. If you don't know how taxes work (lucky you!), please consult someone who does.
2. If Waterman's utility function were linear, what would be the value to him of the Norwood deal alone? The Prescott deal alone? Both together?
3. According to the utility curve in Exhibit 2 and the addendum, what are the values to him (certainty equivalents) of the deals individually and together?
4. What are the risk premiums in 2 and 3?
5. Why is or is not the value of the deals together equal to the sum of their individual values in 2 and 3?
6. Same question for the risk premiums.
7. If only Norwood or Prescott could be chosen, not both, which should Waterman prefer?

   (Some of the following questions are difficult and/or use appendix 3.)
8. Would the answer in 7 be the same for all risk averse utility functions?
9. Is Waterman decreasingly risk averse?
10. If Waterman had already accepted the Norwood deal, what utility function could he use to evaluate further opportunities concluding by April 1, 1970, under what assumptions? (Describe how to find values and find a few.)
11. Does the Prescott deal satisfy these assumptions?
12. What would be the certainty equivalent for the Prescott deal according to the utility function in 10? Can you evaluate it without evaluating this utility function?
13. Is it possible that, according to some utility function, Waterman would want to accept the Prescott deal and later, in some circumstances, forfeit the $5,000 deposit?

    Justify your answers.

Addendum

Waterman's utility function for net liquid assets in thousands of dollars is an increasing linear function of $u(x) = -e^{-Ax} - Ce^{-Bx}$ where $A = .1946761597$, $B = .0265123474$, and $C = .05581238$. It is tabulated below.

Table 4E

Value	Preference	Value	Preference	Value	Preference
25.000	.0000	44.000	.5649	78.000	.8793
25.500	.0327	45.000	.5795	79.000	.8848
26.000	.0632	46.000	.5935	80.000	.8902
26.500	.0918	47.000	.6071	81.000	.8954
27.000	.1187	48.000	.6202	82.000	.9005
27.500	.1439	49.000	.6329	83.000	.9055
28.000	.1676	50.000	.6452	84.000	.9103
28.500	.1899	51.000	.6571	85.000	.9151
29.000	.2111	52.000	.6687	86.000	.9196
29.500	.2311	53.000	.6799	87.000	.9241
30.000	.2500	54.000	.6908	88.000	.9285
30.500	.2680	55.000	.7014	89.000	.9327
31.000	.2851	56.000	.7117	90.000	.9368
31.500	.3014	57.000	.7216	91.000	.9408
32.000	.3170	58.000	.7314	92.000	.9447
32.500	.3318	59.000	.7408	93.000	.9486
33.000	.3461	60.000	.7500	94.000	.9523
33.500	.3597	61.000	.7589	95.000	.9559
34.000	.3728	62.000	.7676	96.000	.9594
34.500	.3855	63.000	.7761	97.000	.9628
35.000	.3976	64.000	.7844	98.000	.9662
35.500	.4094	65.000	.7924	99.000	.9694
36.000	.4207	66.000	.8002	100.000	.9726
36.500	.4317	67.000	.8078	101.000	.9757
37.000	.4423	68.000	.8152	102.000	.9787
37.500	.4526	69.000	.8224	103.000	.9816
38.000	.4626	70.000	.8294	104.000	.9844
38.500	.4723	71.000	.8363	105.000	.9872
39.000	.4818	72.000	.8429	106.000	.9899
39.500	.4910	73.000	.8494	107.000	.9925
40.000	.5000	74.000	.8557	108.000	.9951
41.000	.5173	75.000	.8618	109.000	.9976
42.000	.5338	76.000	.8678	110.000	1.0000
43.000	.5497	77.000	.8736		

Preference	Value	Preference	Value	Preference	Value
.0000	25,000	.1600	27.837	.3200	32.101
.0100	25.149	.1700	28.053	.3300	32.437
.0200	25.302	.1800	28.274	.3400	32.784
.0300	25.458	.1900	28.501	.3500	33.142
.0400	25.617	.2000	28.734	.3600	33.510
.0500	25.779	.2100	28.974	.3700	33.890
.0600	25.946	.2200	29.220	.3800	34.281
.0700	26.116	.2300	29.473	.3900	34.684
.0800	26.289	.2400	29.733	.4000	35.099
.0900	26.467	.2500	30.000	.4100	35.527
.1000	26.649	.2600	30.275	.4200	35.968
.1100	26.835	.2700	30.558	.4300	36.422
.1200	27.026	.2800	30.849	.4400	36.890
.1300	27.221	.2900	31.148	.4500	37.372
.1400	27.421	.3000	31.456	.4600	37.868
.1500	27.627	.3100	31.774	.4700	38.378

Table 4E (cont.)

Preference	Value	Preference	Value	Preference	Value
.4800	38.904	.6600	51.244	.8400	71.560
.4900	39.444	.6700	52.114	.8500	73.097
.5000	40.000	.6800	53.008	.8600	74.699
.5100	40.572	.6900	53.925	.8700	76.373
.5200	41.159	.7000	54.868	.8800	78.124
.5300	41.763	.7100	55.837	.8900	79.961
.5400	42.384	.7200	56.833	.9000	81.892
.5500	43.021	.7300	57.858	.9100	83.927
.5600	43.675	.7400	58.913	.9200	86.079
.5700	44.347	.7500	60.000	.9300	88.360
.5800	45.037	.7600	61.120	.9400	90.789
.5900	45.745	.7700	62.275	.9500	93.386
.6000	46.471	.7800	63.468	.9600	96.174
.6100	47.216	.7900	64.701	.9700	99.184
.6200	47.981	.8000	65.975	.9800	102.457
.6300	48.765	.8100	67.295	.9900	106.040
.6400	49.570	.8200	68.664	1.0000	110.000
.6500	50.396	.8300	70.084		

5 Quantification of Judgments

5.1 Introduction

In chapters 2 and 3 we saw how judgments about real-world events could be quantified in much the same way that preferences for real-world consequences could be quantified: When a decision maker assigns the number $P(\Theta_0)$ to the event Θ_0, he is saying that *he or she* would be indifferent between (1) the right to receive a desirable prize if Θ_0 occurs and nothing otherwise, and (2) a lottery giving a canonical chance $P(\Theta_0)$ at the same desirable prize and nothing otherwise. We can say in a more elliptical manner that the decision maker feels that if a real number x is drawn canonically from the interval $[0, 1]$, then the event Θ_0 and the event $\{0 \leq \tilde{x} \leq P(\Theta_0)\}$ are "equally likely" for him.

In this chapter we will be concerned with developing some preliminary attitudes and techniques to help the decision maker assign *reasonable* probabilities to events. We say "preliminary" because in a sense not only this chapter but the entire book will in large part be devoted to this same task. We shall also attempt to dispel the naive notion that because P-assessments are, in the last analysis, personal, they are arbitrary and capricious.

5.2 Consistency of a Set of Probability Assessments

We shall employ the concept, first introduced in chapter 3, of a so-called "elementary event," an event so finely described that we shall never need to subdivide it further. Let the possible elementary events be denoted by $\theta_1, \theta_2, \ldots, \theta_m$, where the notation implies that there is only a finite number of possibilities, and let Θ denote the set of all possible elementary events. It will be easier and entail no loss of generality in this discussion to assume that the true elementary event has already been physically determined, but that this information is not known by the decision maker; we shall designate the as-yet-unknown true elementary event by $\tilde{\theta}$ (read: "θ tilde") and write $(\tilde{\theta} \in \Theta_0)$ to designate the event that the as-yet-unknown true elementary event, $\tilde{\theta}$, belongs to some particular subset, Θ_0, of the set of all elementary events.

In chapters 2 and 3 we assumed that the decision maker could assign a number $P(\tilde{\theta} \in \Theta_0)$ to the event that $\tilde{\theta} \in \Theta_0$, or equivalently, a number $P(\Theta_0)$ to the subset $\Theta_0 \subset \Theta$; and we proved that if the decision maker wanted to be consistent with our first four basic assumptions, then the totality of all P assessments had to satisfy the following *internal consistency* requirements:

1. If Θ_0 is any subset of Θ, then $P(\Theta_0) \geq 0$;
2. $P(\Theta) = 1$;
3. If Θ_1 *and* Θ_2 are mutually disjoint (or equivalently if the events $\tilde{\theta} \in \Theta_1$ and $\tilde{\theta} \in \Theta_2$ are mutually exclusive), then

$P(\Theta_1 \cup \Theta_2) = P(\Theta_1) + P(\Theta_2)$.

We did not say (and never will say!) that the decision maker should by introspection assign a probability to each and every subset of Θ. This would clearly be an impossible task if the number of elementary events were even moderately large; if there are m elementary events in Θ, there are 2^m subsets of Θ (including Θ itself and the empty set). Our advice rather will be that, by introspection or by other means to be described in this book, the decision maker should assign probabilities directly to *some* subsets and by means of these assignments calculate the probabilities that must be given to other subsets in accordance with consistency requirements. The question of which subsets should be selected for direct assessment and which for indirect assessment will be left, in the final analysis, to the discretion of the decision maker, and the informal advice that we can give will best be communicated throughout the book in terms of illustrations rather than by a cookbook of recipes. We would maintain, however, that the decision maker *should assign probabilities to those events on which his experience bears most directly* and then use the internal consistency requirements of probability to assign probabilities to the events with which he has had less extensive experience.

5.2.1 Assignments to Elementary and Composite Events

If by some means or other the decision maker has assigned to each elementary event $(\tilde{\theta} = \theta)$ a probability $P(\tilde{\theta} = \theta)$ then internal consistency requires that:

1. $P(\tilde{\theta} = \theta) \geq 0$,
2. $\sum_{\Theta} P(\tilde{\theta} = \theta) = 1$, where the summation is taken over all $\theta \in \Theta$,
3. to any composite event $(\tilde{\theta} \in \Theta_0)$, he or she assign the probability

$P(\Theta_0) \equiv P(\tilde{\theta} \in \Theta_0) = \sum_{\Theta_0} P(\tilde{\theta} = \theta)$,

where the last summation is taken over all $\theta \in \Theta_0$.

If by some means or other the decision maker has assigned to the composite event $(\tilde{\theta} \in \Theta_0)$ a probability $P(\Theta_0)$, then internal consistency requires that

4. $P(\bar{\Theta}_0) = 1 - P(\Theta_0)$

where $\bar{\Theta}_0$ is the complement of Θ_0—or, equivalently, where $(\tilde{\theta} \in \bar{\Theta}_0)$ is the event that $(\tilde{\theta} \notin \Theta_0)$. Furthermore, the set of assignments $P(\tilde{\theta} = \theta)$ for all θ, must be such that (1), (2), and (3) are all satisfied, and in addition,

5. $P(\bar{\Theta}_0) = \sum_{\bar{\Theta}_0} P(\tilde{\theta} = \theta)$.

If, for example, we wish to know which of 87 different specific possibilities has caused the malfunction of an engine, it might be most natural to say that there is a 2-to-1 chance that the trouble lies in the carburetor; and if there are 13 specific possibilities all subsumed under the category of "carburetor," then, to be consistent with this assertion, the $P(\tilde{\theta} = \theta)$'s for these 13 possibilities should add up to $\frac{2}{3}$, and the $P(\tilde{\theta} = \theta)$'s for the remaining 74 categories should add up to $\frac{1}{3}$.

5.2.2 Consistency with Conditional Judgments

If the decision maker has assigned probabilities to all the subsets of Θ either directly or indirectly, then he could calculate a conditional probability statement such as $P(\Theta_0|\Theta_1)$, the conditional probability that $\tilde{\theta} \in \Theta_0$ given that $\tilde{\theta} \in \Theta_1$, from the formula

$$P(\Theta_0|\Theta_1) = \frac{P(\Theta_0 \text{ and } \Theta_1)}{P(\Theta_1)}. \tag{5.1}$$

Since, in sections 2.8 and 3.7, we have given a behavioral interpretation to conditional probabilities in terms of posterior preferences or of conditional lotteries, the decision maker could then check whether this derived assignment is reasonable or not. If he strongly feels that it is not reasonable, he might wish to make a direct assignment to $P(\Theta_0|\Theta_1)$ and to modify his original P assessments so that (5.1) is satisfied. In case of conflicting judgmental assessments, our attitude is that something "must give"—which statement it should be depends on the basic knowledge and feelings of the decision maker.

To continue with the example of the previous subsection, suppose we agree to give values $P(\tilde{\theta} = \theta)$ to the 13 elementary events that comprise the composite event Θ_0, "carburetor trouble," so that the total adds up to $\frac{2}{3}$. It may now be possible to decompose Θ_0 into two mutually exclusive and collectively exhaustive subsets Θ_{01} and Θ_{02}, say, so that given the knowledge $\tilde{\theta} \in \Theta_0$—that is, given that the cause of the difficulty lies in the carburetor—the decision maker might decide to assign conditional probability .4 to Θ_{01} and .6 to Θ_{02}. From the above assessments we can then obtain the *un*conditional probability assessments of Θ_{01} and Θ_{02} by the calculations

$$P(\Theta_{01}) = P(\Theta_{01}|\Theta_0) \times P(\Theta_0) = \frac{4}{10} \times \frac{2}{3} = \frac{4}{15},$$

$$P(\Theta_{02}) = P(\Theta_{02}|\Theta_0) \times P(\Theta_0) = \frac{6}{10} \times \frac{2}{3} = \frac{6}{15}.$$

By further decomposing the composite events Θ_{01} and Θ_{02}, we gradually can narrow down our assignments to smaller and smaller composite events until we finally reach the level of elementary events at which point we see no reason to subdivide still further.

As another somewhat more complicated example which illustrates how conditional judgments might be used for assessment purposes, suppose, for purely academic interest, we arbitrarily select a student from the 1,600 or so M.B.A. students at the Harvard Business School and wish to assess the probability that this student knows how to evaluate correctly $\int_0^{2\pi} \sin x\, dx$. Suppose we know that roughly 40% of the students have engineering backgrounds and that the remaining 60% are predominantly from liberal arts backgrounds. In assessing the probability of a correct answer (event S), it is helpful to assess first the conditional probabilities of S given that the student is an engineer (E) and then given that he is not an engineer ($\bar{E}$). If, for example, we assign the probabilities

$$P(S|E) = .70 \quad \text{and} \quad P(S|\bar{E}) = .20,$$

then we should assign $P(S) = .70(.40) + .20(.60) = .40$. In making the assessment for $P(S|\bar{E})$ we may wish to assess first the probabilities that a nonengineer has taken calculus (C) or has not ($\bar{C}$), and then to assess the conditional probabilities of S conditional on $\bar{E} \cap C$ and on $\bar{E} \cap \bar{C}$.

The point of this subsection is to draw the reader's attention at an early stage in this book to the idea that if we want to assess a probability distribution for some basic unknown quantity, it often is appropriate to introduce related factors, especially when our experience bears more directly on these related factors than on the basic quantity and when the probabilistic connections between the basic quantity and these related factors are also reasonably clear.

5.3 Relative Frequency and the Rational Assessment of Probabilities

Although we have indicated that the theory of probability can be used to show that certain probabilities are mutually inconsistent, and although we have said that such inconsistencies must be reconciled before final assignments of probabilities are made, we have as yet said nothing about the way in which a reasonable person will reconcile any inconsistencies that are discovered.

To cite a very simple but famous example, the eighteenth-century mathematician D'Alembert assigned weight $\frac{1}{3}$ to one occurrence of heads in two tosses of a coin, arguing that the pair of tosses must produce 0, 1, or 2 heads and that in his opinion these three events were equally likely. To see whether we would share this attitude we may reason as follows: An *elementary* event of a pair of tosses of a coin is described by stating the results of each of the two tosses in the order in which they occurred. If we use HT to denote the elementary event "heads on first toss, tails on second toss" and similar notation for all the other possibilities, then the four possible elementary events of the double toss are HH, HT, TH, and TT. If we feel that *these* four events are equally likely and therefore assign weight $\frac{1}{4}$ to each of them, we can add the weights assigned to HT and TH and find that we have implicitly assigned weight $\frac{1}{2}$ rather than $\frac{1}{3}$ to the compound event "one heads." To state the conclusion the other way around, D'Alembert implicitly assigned the same total weight to the *two* events HT and TH that he assigned to each of the single events HH and TT.

We have seen that it is inconsistent to assign probability $\frac{1}{3}$ to the event "one heads" and at the same time to assign probability $\frac{1}{4}$ to each of the events HT and TH, but we have given no reason for preferring either one of these assignments to the other. It is to this problem that we now turn our attention.

In our original discussion of the meaning of probabilities, we emphasized that any probability is necessarily an expression of a personal judgment and is therefore necessarily *subjective* in the sense that two reasonable people may assign different probabilities to the same event. This by no means implies, however, that reasonable people will assign probabilities *arbitrarily*. They should base the probabilities which they assign to events in the real world on their experience with such events, and when two reasonable people are subjected to the same overwhelming experience with a certain kind of event, they then tend to assign to it roughly the same probability.

5.3.1 Overwhelming Experience

As an extreme example of this principle, consider the situation where a decision maker has seen a certain coin tossed in a particular manner many times—say on the order of 100,000 tosses—and at each toss suppose that the coin spins an extremely large number of times before it falls. Suppose that a proportion p_0 of these tosses resulted in heads and that a careful scrutiny of the record shows no discernible pattern whatsoever: Heads occurred about as frequently on tosses which followed heads as on tosses which followed tails; more generally, heads seemed to have occurred just about as frequently on tosses which followed any particular pattern of heads and tails on previous tosses as it did overall; finally, the proportion of heads in any large segment of tosses (such as in the first 10,000 tosses, or in the middle 20,000 tosses, etc.) was practically p_0. On the basis of this overwhelming experience, how should the decision maker assess the probability $P(H)$ of heads on the next toss of the coin?

On the basis of the experience with this coin let us suppose the decision maker agrees with the two propositions stated below. For the time being we will leave aside the pertinent question of whether or not it is *reasonable* for him to agree with these propositions.

1. If in the next 10,000 tosses or so I were told the exact number of heads (*Hs*) and tails (*Ts*), but were not told anything about the particular sequence of *Hs* and *Ts*, then among the resulting possible sequences I would consider any particular sequence of *Hs* and *Ts* just as likely as any other particular sequence of *Hs* and *Ts*. (This is called the *exchangeability* principle.)

2. I would be very surprised indeed if the proportion p_1 of heads in the next 10,000 tosses did not come very close to p_0.

We shall now give a consistency argument that shows that *if a decision maker agrees with the above two propositions, then he or she should assign a probability near* p_0 *to the event "heads in the next toss."* We argue as follows:

a. If a list were made of *all* possible sequences of 10,000 tosses with a proportion p_1 of *Hs*, then a proportion p_1 of these sequences would start with an *H* on the first toss. (Why?)

b. If the decision maker were told that a proportion p_1 of the next 10,000 tosses were *Hs*, then by the exchangeability principle he would think all the sequences listed in (a) were equally likely; furthermore, since a proportion p_1 of these sequences start with an *H*, by consistency he must assign $P(H) = p_1$. (So far the argument has used only the exchangeability principle.)

c. By the second of the above propositions he is practically certain that p_1 will be very close to p_0, and therefore he is practically certain, without being told the value of p_1, that the appropriate value of $P(H)$ should be close to p_0.

Now let us return to the question of whether a reasonable decision maker should agree with propositions 1 and 2. All that we have proved so far is that *if* he does agree with them, *then* he *should* assign $P(H) = p_0$, approximately.

If the decision maker cannot discern any pattern whatsoever on the past 100,000 trials and if he believes the future will, in a loose sense, be like the past, then we feel that it is reasonable to believe that future trials will exhibit the same patternless stream. The exchangeability principle is merely a formal expression of this feeling. We also believe that "almost everyone" who has seriously scrutinized the outcomes of tosses of coins or rolls of dice would be of the same opinion. We cannot say "everyone" because there are those mystics who believe that by thinking hard enough they can influence the pattern of outcomes. Furthermore, we feel that most reasonable people would accept the exchangeability principle even if the particular coin had been tossed only a few times in the past, or even not at all! The justification of this feeling comes from overwhelming experience with other tossed or rolled objects.

Now let us consider the reasonableness of the second proposition. We purposely chose to describe a case where the tosses in the past were so numerous that by analyzing the past we could get some consensus on what to expect in the future. To be specific let us suppose that $p_0 = .45217$ and that the proportions of heads in the first 10,000 tosses, in the second 10,000 tosses, and so forth up to the last 10,000 tosses ranged from .4436 to .4625. Now we would imagine that some persons might balk at Proposition 2 because of its vagueness; for example, what is meant by "very close?" But with these figures at hand we would imagine that "almost everyone" would agree that the proportion p_1 in the next 10,000 tosses would almost surely lie between .43 and .47, say—they would be "surprised" otherwise. We would insist, therefore, that it would be entirely unreasonable for a decision maker to assign a probability $P(H)$ of heads at the next toss that differed from p_0 by as much as .03, say. An assignment such as $P(H) = .55$ would be completely unreasonable in light of the evidence at hand.

There is something a bit awkward about the above discussion. For us, at least, it is harder to think about what we might expect in the next 10,000 trials than about what we might expect in the long run, even though, as Keynes once remarked, "We will all be dead in the long run." In the next section we make the jump into the world of the mathematician and suggest a model of idealized long-run behavior. It is important to realize, however, that the previous argument leading to the plausibility of the assessment $P(H) = p_0$ does *not* depend on such an idealization. After we discuss this model, then we will go on to indicate that it is legitimate to think in this manner *provided* the exchangeability principle is adopted.

5.3.2 The Bernoulli Model

On the basis of an overwhelming amount of experience with tosses of coins we proceed to construct a nondeterministic model for the behavior of a tossed coin. According to the model there is a process that generates an unending sequence of *Hs* and *Ts* in such a manner that the ratio of heads to trials tends to limit p as the number of trials increases indefinitely. The model asserts further that in a very long run, the proportion of times heads will follow any predetermined pattern of previous tosses will be approximately p and approach p in the limit as the number of trials increases indefinitely. Such a model of an idealized data generating process will be called a *Bernoulli process* or *model with parameter p*, and this process will be further formalized and extensively analyzed in chapter 11. When we adopt the Bernoulli process with given parameter p as a model for the behavior of a tossed coin, we can think of p as being not unlike any other physical property of the coin, such as its weight, and talk about the "true" p of the coin, even though we cannot possibly determine its precise value.

When is it appropriate to use the Bernoulli process as a model for the behavior of a tossed coin? According to a result of Bruno de Finetti (1937) the question can be answered in terms of the *exchangeability principle*. He proves a theorem which says roughly:

> If the decision maker accepts the exchangeability principle for a given process that generates *Hs* and *Ts* (or 0s and 1s), then for the purposes of determining his best action, he can treat the process as a Bernoulli process with parameter p, where the possibly uncertain parameter $\tilde{p}$ is given a probability distribution.[1]

If we adopt a Bernoulli process as a model for the behavior of a coin, then we have essentially agreed to adopt the exchangeability principle. If we also know—or act as if we know—the parameter p_0 of the process, then we are saying that we would be very surprised if in a long series of trials the proportion of heads to trials did not come very close to p_0. Therefore, if we adopt the Bernoulli process with a *known parameter* p_0, then by the argument given in section 5.2.1 we *should assign* $P(H) = p_0$ *to the event "heads" at any particular toss.*

We are now able to say something definite about the probability which it is reasonable to assign to "one head" in D'Alembert's problem. If we have adopted a model of coin behavior in which heads occur in the long run on one-half of all tosses and in which half the heads are followed by

1. We discuss how the decision maker can assign a probability distribution to the unknown population parameter $\tilde{p}$ in chapter 11.

heads, and so forth (i.e., a Bernoulli process with parameter $p = \frac{1}{2}$), it is easy to see that in a long run of *pairs* of tosses the events HH, HT, TH, and TT will each occur $\frac{1}{4}$ of the time. Let us now consider a derived process which generates Ss and Fs, where S stands for HT or TH, where F stands for HH or TT, and where the sequence HH TH HT TT ... gives F S S F...; then this process is in turn a Bernoulli process with long-run relative frequency of S equal to $\frac{1}{2}$. Any one who has adopted this model of the behavior of a given coin should therefore assign probability $P(S) = \frac{1}{2}$ to the event S in *the next pair of tosses*—or equivalently, probability $\frac{1}{2}$ to the event "exactly one head in two tosses."

5.3.3 Limited Experience

Let us now consider the case where the decision maker has limited experience with a particular coin. Suppose, to be more specific, that after carefully examining this coin and finding it to be slightly asymmetric, he tossed this coin 10 times and observed the pattern $(H, T, T, T, T, H, T, H, T, T)$. Suppose that he now wishes to assess the probability $P(H)$ of heads on the next toss. In this situation, general experience with *other* coins and other objects such as dice may lead a reasonable person to accept the exchangeability principle for this particular coin, and according to de Finetti's result it is therefore legitimate to adopt a model of behavior of the coin based on the Bernoulli process with an *unknown* idealized limiting relative frequency p. Let us suppose that our hypothetical decision maker holds this opinion. If he has enough experience with this coin to feel sure that the long-run relative frequency of heads would be .3, then he should assign $P(H) = .3$ on the next toss. But with the limited experience he has had with this coin he probably would not want simply to equate p with the proportion of Hs in the record of just 10 tosses. Certainly, if he had tossed the coin just once and it had come up H, he would not assign $P(H) = 1$; if he had tossed the coin twice and had observed (H, H), he still would not assign $P(H) = 1$ to the next toss. The decision maker might feel on the basis of the examination of the coin and the record of 10 tosses that it is more likely that p is between .4 and .6, say, than between .2 and .4, say.

In chapter 11 we shall develop techniques that can help the decision maker analyze this problem in a systematic fashion. We shall show that his assessment of the probability of heads on the next toss should be substantially influenced by his observation of the shape of the coin and his knowledge (if any) about the limiting relative frequencies of other slightly asymmetric coins. In particular, we shall show that if the decision maker, *after* examining the coin but *prior* to observing this limited record of Hs and Ts, assesses a probability distribution of the unknown physical parameter $\tilde{p}$, then there is a definite rule that he should follow for revising this distribution on the basis of observed outcomes of tosses, and there is another definite rule that he should follow for revising his assessment $P(H)$ of heads on the next trial. We can think of this whole process as a model of how one *should* learn from experience starting from given judgmental inputs—or alternatively, as a model of a *rational adaptive process.*

5.3.4 Application to Business Problems

In exceptional circumstances the probabilities involved in a business problem can be simply equated to "known" relative frequencies in the same way that probability can be assigned to heads in the next toss of a coin that has already been tossed an overwhelming number of times. If 15% of the last 100,000 parts produced by some machine have been defective, if we have no reason either in theory or in observation to believe that defectives occur in streaks, and if a new production run is to be made under the same conditions as all these past runs, we will be strongly tempted to adopt a model of the behavior of the machine which is exactly like the model of coin behavior discussed above. We will be willing to predict that 15% of all future parts will be defective, that 15% of the defectives will be followed by defectives, and so on, and we will not change these predictions no matter what the pattern of quality happens to be in the next few pieces produced.

In the majority of cases, however, the problem will not be so simple. If the machine is new or has just been repaired, or if a new operator is employed, or if a slightly off-standard batch of raw material is received, we will be in the same position that we were when we assessed the probability of heads on a slightly deformed coin. The probability assigned to defective on the first piece will depend on judgment in the sense that two reasonable people may well assign different values. This probability will be revised as more experience is gained, and again judgment, as well as formal analysis to be described later in this book, will determine the relative weights given to the observed frequencies on the one hand and to other kinds of evidence on the other.

5.3.5 Mental Processes and Relative Frequency

We have discussed examples of the way in which models involving the relative frequencies of physical phenomena can be of use in assessing probabilities, but not how the same kind of argument can be of use in connection with mental phenomena. Frequency models of mental processes usually involve uncertainty about the actual value of the long-run frequency in exactly the same way that most frequency models of physical processes do. In both cases the frequency model is useful even though it is not completely decisive. For example, the value of a large tract of timber is often assessed by having it visually inspected by an experienced timber cruiser whose judgment has previously been calibrated by a comparison of his estimates of the amount of timber in a number of tracts with accurate measurements made on the same tracts. The probability that his present estimate will be low by 10% say, is then assessed largely on the basis of the relative frequency of errors of this magnitude on previous occasions.

In the same way, the accuracy of the predictions of a sales manager, who bases sales forecasts on his "feel of the market," can very usefully be treated as a "process." If we have extensive records of the errors he has made in his past forecasts, we will assess the probability that his current forecast will be low by 10% almost entirely on the basis of the relative frequency with which this event occurred in past forecasts. If, on the other hand, we have very little previous experience with his forecasts, or if the nature of the product or the market has been radically changed, we will have to make much larger use of other kinds of experience in assessing this probability, just as we have to depart from exclusive reliance on observed frequencies when we assess probabilities concerning the performance of a new machine or of an old machine under new conditions.

5.4 Abstract Probability

In this section we shall develop the basic axioms, definitions and theorems of the *abstract* or mathematical *theory of probability*. Although we took great pains to be clear just what we meant by "probability" when we were talking about probability in the real world, we proceed quite differently in developing the abstract or mathematical theory. Just as the mathematical theory of geometry does not define a point (e.g., as that which has no breadth, width, or extent—whatever that may mean) or a straight line, but instead takes these terms as primitive or undefined concepts and stipulates precise relationships among them (e.g., two distinct points determine one and only one line), the mathematical theory of probability does not *define* "probability" but rather *characterizes* it as anything that obeys some simple rules or axioms. When the mathematical theory of probability is used in applications, one must then *interpret* or give operational meaning to the word "probability" and verify that the axioms make sense with this interpretation in mind; if they do, then one is entitled to make use of all the results of the mathematical theory.

As soon as we have stated the axioms of the abstract system, we shall see that they are satisfied in a number of quite different applications, one being to the *judgmental probabilities* we have been discussing hitherto, another being to *proportions* among various kinds of physical units in a finite collection of physical units, and still another being to *relative frequencies* or idealized long-run relative frequencies.

5.4.1 Axioms and Basic Definitions

Axioms Let U denote the universal set; let V denote any subset of U; and let P be a function which associates numbers $P(V)$ to some Vs (not necessarily to all Vs). Any set V to which P associates a number will be called a *measurable* set. We assume

1. the universal set U is measurable;
2. if V is measurable, then so is $\bar{V}$;
3. if $V_1, \ldots, V_m$ are measurable, then so are

$$V_1 \cup \cdots \cup V_m \quad \text{and} \quad V_1 \cap \cdots \cap V_m.$$

The function P is defined to be a *probability measure* if and only if it obeys the following *axioms* for all measurable sets:

1. $P(V) \geq 0,$ (5.2a)

2. $P(U) = 1,$ (5.2b)

3. $P(V_1 \cup V_2) = P(V_1) + P(V_2) \quad \text{if} \quad V_1 \cap V_2 = \varnothing.$ (5.2c)

From (5.2c) we can prove by induction the property of

Finite Additivity If $V_1, V_2, \ldots, V_m$ are disjoint measurable sets, then

$$P(V_1 \cup V_2 \cup \cdots \cup V_m) = P(V_1) + P(V_2) + \cdots + P(V_m).$$

Interpretation as Judgmental Probability

If we interpret the universal set U as the set of all possible *elementary events*, then it is easy to see that the role of U was played in chapters 2 and 3 by the universal or certain event Θ, while the roles of subsets of U such as V_1 and V_2 were played by subsets of Θ, such as Θ_1, Θ_2, and so forth. Given these identifications, it is obvious that the three *axioms* of abstract probability correspond exactly to the three "consistency requirements" on judgmental probabilities which were proved as theorems in section 2.6.3 and again in chapter 3. We leave it to the reader to review at this point the "meaning" of those three consistency requirements.

Interpretation as Physical Proportion

Consider a population containing a set U of elements that are marked with various distinguishing labels. For any subset V of elements in the population, let $N(V)$ denote the number of elements in this subset. Define the *proportion* of all elements in subset V in the usual way,

$$P(V) \equiv \frac{N(V)}{N(U)}.$$

Then obviously

$$P(V) \geq 0;$$

$$P(U) = \frac{N(U)}{N(U)} = 1;$$

and for any two disjoint subsets V_1 and V_2,

$$P(V_1 \cup V_2) = \frac{N(V_1 \cup V_2)}{N(U)} = \frac{N(V_1) + N(V_2)}{N(U)} = P(V_1) + P(V_2).$$

Interpretation as Relative Frequency

Consider a process that generates one of the outcomes $\{a, b, c, d\}$ at each successive trial. As an example, let the process generate the sequence: a, d, c, c, b, b, a, b, c, ... Let V be any subset of the set $U = \{a, b, c, d\}$; let $N_n(V)$ denote the number of those outcomes in the first n trials which belong to V (e.g., in the sequence above if $V = \{a, c\}$, then $N_5(V) = 3$). For any n, the relative frequency of an outcome belonging to V in the first n trials is

$$P_n(V) \equiv \frac{N_n(V)}{n}.$$

Clearly, P_n satisfies the axioms of (5.2). If we also define long-run relative frequency by

$$P(V) \equiv \lim_{n \to \infty} \frac{N_n(V)}{n} = \lim_{n \to \infty} P_n(V),$$

and assume that the process goes on forever and that the limit exists, then P also satisfies axioms (5.2).

5.4.2 Definition of Conditional Probability: The "Multiplication Rule"

If P is a probability measure, the *conditional probability* is defined in the abstract system by

$$P(V|W) = \frac{P(V \cap W)}{P(W)} \quad \text{if} \quad P(W) > 0; \tag{5.3}$$

if $P(W) = 0$, then $P(V|W)$ is not defined.

From (5.3) we obtain the so-called "multiplication rule" by elementary algebra:

$$P(V \cap W) = P(W)P(V|W). \tag{5.4}$$

Interpretation as Judgmental Probability

In section 2.8 and again in chapter 3 we showed as a result of our behavioral Basic Assumptions that the conditional probability of an event Θ_0 given $\Theta^\dagger$,

$$P(\Theta_0|\Theta^\dagger) = \frac{P(\Theta_0 \cap \Theta^\dagger)}{P(\Theta^\dagger)},$$

in agreement with the *definition* of conditional probability in the abstract theory of probability.

Interpretation as Physical Proportion

Consider a population containing n elements, each of which has (1) either attribute x or not x, and (2) either attribute y or not y; and define

X: set of all elements that have attribute x,

X: set of all elements that have attribute y,

$X \cap Y$: set of all elements that have *both* attribute x and attribute y.

We can compute the (conditional) proportion of elements that have attribute y among those that have attribute x, by the formula

$$P(Y|X) = \frac{N(X \cap Y)}{N(X)} = \frac{N(X \cap Y)/n}{N(X)/n} = \frac{P(X \cap Y)}{P(X)}.$$

Interpretation as Relative Frequency

Consider, as before, the process that generates one of the outcomes for the set $U = \{a, b, c, d\}$ at each successive trial. Let V and W be subsets of U; let $N_n(V)$ be defined as before. In the first n trials, the conditional relative frequency of an outcome contained in V among those which resulted in W is

$$P_n(V|W) = \frac{N_n(V \cap W)}{N_n(W)} = \frac{N_n(V \cap W)/n}{N_n(W)/n}$$

$$= \frac{P_n(V \cap W)}{P_n(W)}.$$

Taking the limit, which is assumed to exist, gives

$$P(V|W) = \lim_{n\to\infty} P_n(V|W) = \frac{\lim_{n\to\infty} P_n(V \cap W)}{\lim_{n\to\infty} P_n(W)},$$

$$= \frac{P(V \cap W)}{P(W)},$$

which also agrees with the abstract definition of conditional probability.

5.4.3 Independence

In the abstract system two sets V and W, where $0 < P(V) < 1$ and $0 < P(W) < 1$, are defined to be *independent* if the following equivalent conditions are satisfied:

$$P(V \cap W) = P(V)P(W); \tag{5.5a}$$

$$P(V|W) = P(V|\bar{W}) = P(V); \tag{5.5b}$$

$$P(W|V) = P(W|\bar{V}) = P(W). \tag{5.5c}$$

The equivalence of these three conditions follows directly from (5.3). Notice that (5.5a) is a special form of the multiplication rule (5.4) which is valid *only* when V and W are independent.

We leave as an exercise the meaning of "independence" for each of the interpretations of P measure we have considered.

5.5 Results on Partitions, Double Partitions, and Two-Way Tables

From the axioms (5.2) on abstract P measures, we shall now derive some simple results that we shall need in the next chapter.

Let $Z \subset U$ and let $\{V_1, \ldots, V_m\}$ be a partition of Z. Since the V_i are disjoint by the definition of a partition, we have by the additivity axiom (5.2c)

$$P(Z) = \textstyle\sum_{i=1}^{m} P(V_i). \tag{5.6}$$

Next, let $\{V_1, \ldots, V_m\}$ be a partition of U itself, and let $Z \subset U$ as before. Then $\{V_1 \cap Z, \ldots, V_m \cap Z\}$ is a partition of Z and hence by our previous result

$$P(Z) = \textstyle\sum_{i=1}^{m} P(V_i \cap Z). \tag{5.7}$$

5.5.1 Joint Probabilities

Let $\{V_1, V_2, \ldots, V_m\}$ and $\{W_1, W_2, \ldots, W_n\}$ be two different partitions of a universal set U, and let P be a probability measure which assigns a

Table 5.4

	W_1		W_j		W_n	Total
V_1	$P(V_1 \cap W_1)$	$\dots$	$P(V_1 \cap W_j)$	$\dots$	$P(V_1 \cap W_n)$	$P(V_1)$
$\vdots$	$\vdots$		$\vdots$		$\vdots$	$\vdots$
V_i	$P(V_i \cap W_1)$	$\dots$	$P(V_i \cap W_j)$	$\dots$	$P(V_i \cap W_n)$	$P(V_i)$
$\vdots$	$\vdots$		$\vdots$		$\vdots$	$\vdots$
V_m	$P(V_m \cap W_1)$	$\dots$	$P(V_m \cap W_j)$	$\dots$	$P(V_m \cap W_n)$	$P(V_m)$
Total	$P(W_1)$	$\dots$	$P(W_j)$	$\dots$	$P(W_n)$	1

number $P(V_i \cap W_j)$ to sets of the form $V_i \cap W_j$ for all i, j. These *joint probabilities* can be conveniently displayed by means of a *two-way table* as shown in table 5.4.

5.5.2 Marginal Probabilities

Since $\{V_1, \dots, V_m\}$ is a partition of U, we have for any j that $\{V_1 \cap W_j, \dots, V_m \cap W_j\}$ is a partition of W_j, and hence by (5.7) that

$$P(W_j) = \textstyle\sum_{i=1}^{m} P(V_i \cap W_j), \qquad j = 1, \dots n. \tag{5.8}$$

The probability of W_j is thus the *sum* of all the joint probabilities in the *column* of table 5.4 which pertains to W_j, and this sum can be conveniently displayed at the bottom of the column in question. Similarly, the probability of V_i is the sum of all the joint probabilities in the *row* pertaining to V_i, and this sum can be conveniently displayed to the right of the row in question.

Because probabilities like $P(V_i)$ and $P(W_j)$ appear in the *margins* of tables showing joint probabilities like $P(V_i \cap W_j)$, they are often called *marginal probabilities.* The reader should observe that the adjective "marginal" conveys absolutely nothing about the *meaning* of a probability; it describes only the way in which the probability is or might be *computed.*

5.5.3 Conditional Probabilities

Given a table like 5.4, which shows both joint and marginal probabilities, it is easy to compute *conditional* probabilities from the definition (5.3):

$$\begin{aligned} P(V_i \mid W_j) &= \frac{P(V_i \cap W_j)}{P(W_j)}, \quad \text{if} \quad P(W_j) > 0, \\ P(W_j \mid V_i) &= \frac{P(V_i \cap W_j)}{P(V_i)}, \quad \text{if} \quad P(V_i) > 0. \end{aligned} \tag{5.9}$$

5.5.4 Operations on Two-Way Tables

If the original data do *not* give the joint probabilities directly but instead give

1. the marginal probabilities $P(W_j)$ for all j, and
2. the conditional probabilities $P(V_i | W_j)$ for all i, j,

then it is possible to compute the joint probabilities for formula (5.4):

$$P(V_i \cap W_j) = P(W_j)P(V_i | W_j). \tag{5.10}$$

From these joint probabilities it is then easy to compute

3. the marginal probabilities $P(V_i)$ for all i, and
4. the conditional probabilities $P(W_j | V_i)$ for all i, j.

To do so, we first use (5.8) and (5.10) to derive the formula

$$P(V_i) = \textstyle\sum_{k=1}^{n} P(W_k)P(V_i | W_k), \tag{5.11}$$

known as the *formula for marginal probabilities*; and we then use (5.9), (5.10), and (5.11) to derive the formula

$$P(W_j | V_i) = \frac{P(W_j)P(V_i | W_j)}{\sum_{k=1}^{n} P(W_k)P(V_i | W_k)}, \tag{5.12}$$

known as *Bayes' theorem for conditional probabilities.*

Conversely, if we are given the probabilities in (3) and (4), we can reverse the procedure and compute the probabilities (1) and (2).

Exercises

1. On the basis of what you already know assess your own probability for the proportion of students in the Harvard (or some other) Law School who could correctly evaluate $\int_0^{2\pi} \sin x \, dx$.

2. There are two jobs for which Ms. Jones can apply. She assigns probability .6 that she will be accepted for the first job and .5 that she will be accepted for the second job. She feels that if she were told that she was accepted for the first job, she would then revise her probability assignment for the second job from .5 to .7.

   a. What do these probabilities mean?

   b. What probability would she assign to landing *at least one* job? What does this mean?

   There is a third job for which Ms. Jones can apply provided that she does not apply for either of the first two, and she assesses the probability of getting this job as .8.

   c. If all three jobs are equally desirable as far as Ms. Jones is concerned, should she apply for the first two jobs and not the third or for the third and neither of the first two?

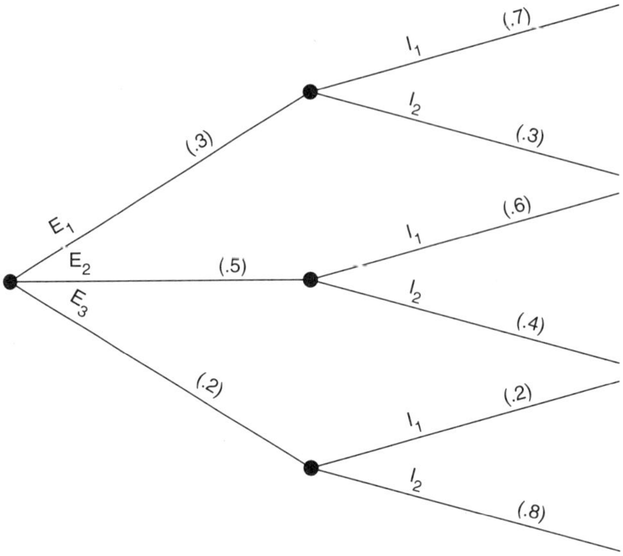

Figure 5E.1

3. In a certain diagnostic procedure a subject is first classified into one of two categories, 0 or 1, on measurement 1. If the subject is classified as a 1 on measurement 1, then measurement 2 is taken and he is classified on this second assignment as a 0, a 1, or a 2; if on the contrary the subject is classified as a 0 on measurement 1, then no second measurement is taken. The chances of the various possible outcomes depend on whether the subject is "normal" or "abnormal" and are shown in the trees in fig. 5E.1, where x_i stands for "i'th measurement."

   a. If the diagnosis is made according to the rule "Diagnose the subject as an 'abnormal' if and only if $x_1 = 1$ and $x_2 = 2$ or 1," what is the probability of *mis*classifying a normal? an abnormal?

   b. What are these probabilities if the rule is "Diagnose the subject as abnormal if and only if $x_1 = 1$ and $x_2 = 2$"?

   c. What information would you want to obtain before choosing between the above two rules?

The remaining exercises are based on the material in appendix 1 and sections 5.3 and 5.4.

4. From the axioms of probability given in (5.2), without interpreting what P means, prove the following results:

   a. $P(\varnothing) = 0$
   Hint For any set V, $V \cup \varnothing = V$ and $V \cap \varnothing = \varnothing$.

   b. $P(V_1 \cup V_2) = P(V_1) + P(V_2) - P(V_1 \cap V_2)$.

5. Using the definition of conditional probability, prove the equivalence of (5.5a), (5.5b), and (5.5c). Interpret independence according to judgmental probabilities and physical proportions.

6. For any V and W such that $0 < P(W) < 1$, prove that $P(V)$ lies between $P(V|W)$ and $P(V|\bar{W})$. Do not use any particular interpretation of P to prove this result. Now interpret this result.

7. In a given population of male adults above 30, individuals are classified by two factors. Factor 1 is an education factor with three levels: E_1 means not a high school graduate; E_2, high school but not a college graduate; E_3, a college graduate. Factor 2 is an income factor with two levels: I_1, less than \$15,000 per year; I_2, at least \$15,000 per year. The tree diagram below gives the proportions of individuals in different categories; for example, the high-school-but-not-college graduates constitute .5 of the population and of this group .6 earn less than \$15,000.

a. Exhibit a two-way table illustrating the proportions in different joint categories.

b. Exhibit a tree diagram depicting this data starting with Factor 2 (income) instead of Factor 1 (education).

8. Given that P is a probability measure (i.e., it satisfies (5.2a), (5.2b), and (5.2c)), show that the following two additional assumptions are equivalent:

a. (*Complete Additivity*). If $V_1, V_2, \ldots$ are disjoint measurable sets and if $(V_1 \cup V_2 \cup \ldots)$ is also measurable, then

$$P(V_1 \cup V_2 \cup \ldots) = P(V_1) + P(V_2) + \cdots.$$

b. (*Continuity or Nullity*). If the nested sequence of measurable sets

$$W_1 \supset W_2 \supset W_3 \supset \ldots$$

vanishes in the limit—in the sense that *no* element of U belongs to all the W_n sets (or, more formally, where $\bigcap_{n=1}^{\infty} W = \varnothing$)—then

$$\lim_{n\to\infty} P(W_n) = 0.$$

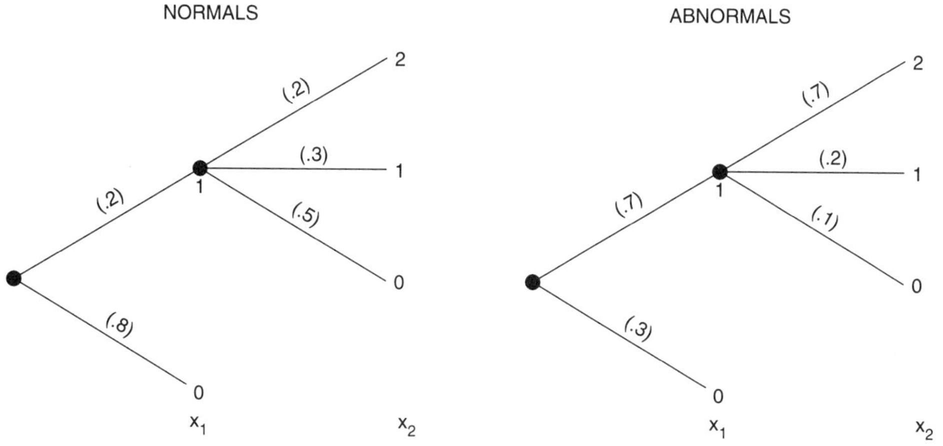

Figure 5E.2

6 Analysis of Decision Trees

6.1 Description of a Class of Decision Problems

In what follows we shall be concerned with the logical analysis of choice among courses of action when (a) the consequence c of any course of action a will depend upon the "state of the world" s, (b) the true state is as yet unknown, but (c) it is possible at a cost, by observing the outcome z of an experiment e, to obtain information about the true state. We assume that the person responsible for the decision has already eliminated a great many possible courses of action as being unworthy of further consideration and thus has reduced his problem to a choice from a well-defined set of contenders; we assume further that he wishes to choose among these contenders and among several possible experiments in a way which will be logically consistent with (a) his basic preferences concerning consequences, and (b) his basis judgments concerning the true state s and the as-yet-unobserved outcome z of each potential experiment e; and we assume that these basic preferences and judgments are respectively scaled in terms of a utility function u and a probability measure P.

6.1.1 The Basic Data and Notational Conventions

Formally, we assume that the decision maker can specify the following basic data defining his decision problem:

1. *Set of possible terminal acts:* $A = \{a_1, a_2, \ldots, a_n\}$. When we wish to refer to a typical or generic act from the set A, we shall use the symbol a without a subscript; this notation will not only make the typography clearer, but will also help when we generalize to cases in which A has an infinite number of elements.

2. *Set of possible "states of the world":* $S = \{s_1, s_2, \ldots, s_m\}$. The generic element of S will simply be written as s. The symbol $\tilde{s}$ will be read "the unknown true state" and, for example, the expression $(\tilde{s} = s_5)$ will denote the event that the unknown true state is s_5.

3. *Set of possible experiments:* $E = \{e_0, e_1, \ldots, e_q\}$. The generic element of E will simply be written as e. We reserve the symbol e_0 to designate the possibility that the decision maker may choose *not to experiment.*

4. *Set of potential outcomes of all experiments in E:* $Z = \{z_0, z_1, \ldots, z_p\}$. As in the cases above, the symbol z will represent the generic outcome of the experiment. The symbol $\tilde{z}$ will denote the as-yet-unobserved outcome and, for example, the expression $(\tilde{z} = z_7)$ will denote the event that the as-yet-unobserved outcome is z_7.

The fact that we are assuming that A has n elements, S has m elements, E has $(q + 1)$ elements and Z has $(p + 1)$ elements is completely unimportant, and we shall feel free to use the letters n, m, q, and p for other purposes as well.

5. *Utility function:* u. Associated with a choice of an experiment e and its outcome z, with the subsequent choice of a particular act a, and with a particular state s, there is a consequence to which the decision maker assigns a utility value $u(e, z, a, s)$.

6. *Probability measure:* P. We shall assume that the decision maker can, by one means or another, give an internally consistent set of probability assessments to events involving $\tilde{s}$ and $\tilde{z}$ for each given e.

6.2 The General Decision Problem as a Game

The general decision problem can usefully be represented as a game between the decision maker and a fictitious character we shall call "chance." The game has four moves: (1) The decision maker chooses e, (2) chance chooses z, (3) the decision maker then chooses a, and finally (4) chance chooses s. The play is then completed and the decision maker gets a consequence to which he assigns the utility value $u(e, z, a, s)$.

Although the decision maker has full control over his choice of e and a, he has neither control over, nor perfect foreknowledge of, the choices of z and s which will be made by chance. We have assumed, however, that he is able in one way or another to assign probability measures over these choices. We also assume that the probabilities assigned to $\tilde{s}$ do not depend on the choice of e.

6.2.1 The Decision Tree

The flow of the game can in principle be represented by a tree diagram; and although a complete diagram can actually be drawn only if the number of elements involved in E, Z, A, and S is very small, even an incomplete representation of the tree can aid our intuition considerably.

A partial tree of this sort is shown in figure 6.1, where D denotes decision and C denotes chance. In two examples to follow shortly we shall depict a complete tree and present an analysis of the problem in terms of this representation.

6.3 Illustrative Examples

6.3.1 Analysis of a Drilling Decision

In chapter 1 (section 1.2.1) we formulated, but did not analyze, a somewhat simplified version of an oil drilling problem and showed how that

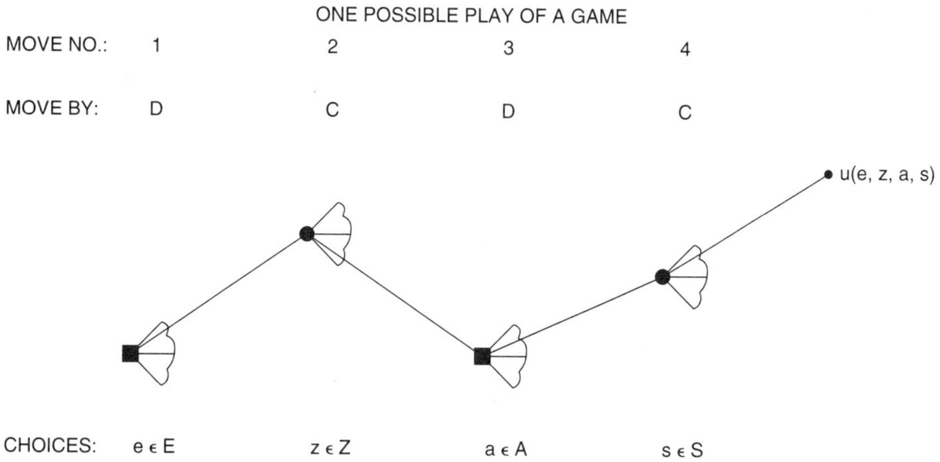

Figure 6.1
Decision tree for choice of experiment and terminal act

problem could be described in terms of a decision tree (see figure 1.1). In this section we shall complete the analysis of that simplified problem as an illustration of the theory discussed in this chapter.

For the convenience of the reader we shall first summarize the description of the problem and at the same time introduce the general notation we shall employ in this chapter. An oil wildcatter must choose between drilling a well at a given site (act a_1) and abandoning his option to drill at this site (act a_2); therefore the set of acts is $A = \{a_1, a_2\}$. In this simplified problem the desirability of drilling depends on whether there is "no oil" (state s_1) or "oil" (state s_2); therefore the set of states is $S = \{s_1, s_2\}$. If he wishes, the decision maker can act on the basis of his present information (i.e., choose the nonexperiment e_0), or he can obtain more geological and geophysical evidence by means of an expensive seismic sounding (experiment e_1); therefore the set of experiments is $E = \{e_0, e_1\}$. If the seismic sounding is made, we assume that it will reliably determine which one of the following three conditions prevails: (1) There is no subsurface structure (outcome z_1), (2) there is an open subsurface structure (outcome z_2), or (3) there is a closed subsurface structure (outcome z_3); we shall label the dummy outcome of the nonexperiment by z_0; therefore the set of all possible outcomes is $Z = \{z_0, z_1, z_2, z_3\}$. The possible sequences of choices by the decision maker and chance are shown on the decision tree (figure 6.2).

Assignment of Utilities

The psychological stimulus associated in the problem with an (e, z, a, s) sequence is highly complicated. Different wells entail different drilling

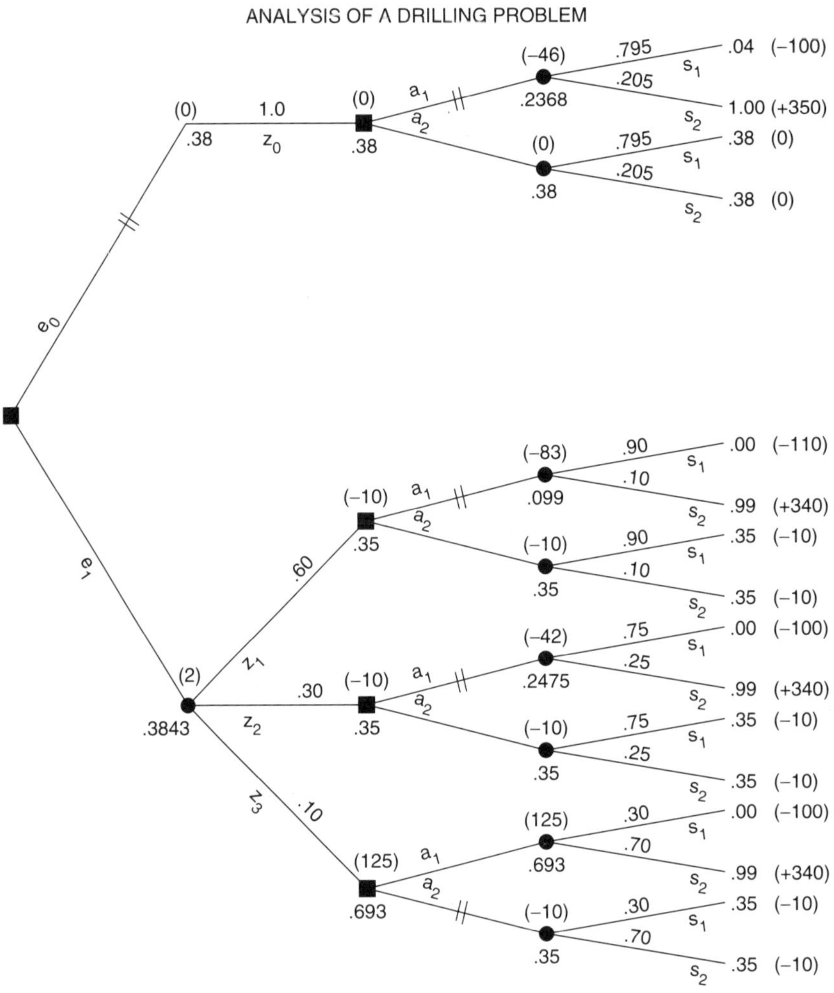

Figure 6.2
Analysis of a drilling problem

costs, and different strikes produce quantities and qualities of oil which can be recovered over different periods of time and sold at different prices. Furthermore, each potential consequence of the present drilling venture affects future potential drilling ventures. For example, geological information gained in one deal may be crucial for the next, and capital expenditures made in one deal may prohibit the acceptance of the next one, no matter how favorable it may then appear to be.

We shall assume that the decision maker can associate a monetary value with each (e, z, a, s) sequence, such that he would be indifferent between obtaining the full consequence arising from this (e, z, a, s) sequence and obtaining that amount of money outright. We shall assume further that no monetary payments are actually made during the course of the play so that the consequence includes in its description any monetary obligations that are incurred during the course of the (e, z, a, s) sequence. At the tip of the branch (e_1, z_1, a_1, s_2), for example, is the entry $(+340)$, where the branch and entry are interpreted as follows: The wildcatter imagines at the beginning of the play of the game what his position would be like if, after taking the seismic sounding, he drilled and struck oil; he knows that at that instance in time he would have to pay the costs of the seismic sounding and drilling expenses, which are in themselves uncertain, but he would then also be in the happy position of knowing that this particular site had oil deposits. The full monetary consequence associated with this (e_1, z_1, a_1, s_2) sequence, however, would remain uncertain even *after* learning that oil has been struck; the $+340$ figure indicates that before the game starts the wildcatter's *selling price* for the *consequence* (or better yet, *lottery*) associated with this (e_1, z_1, a_1, s_2) sequence is \$340,000. We assume that the wildcatter, in arriving at such a figure, will informally take into account all he knows about similar (and not so similar) deals in the past, and that perhaps he will make some calculations which he thinks may help him with this assessment. Actually the decision tree for this problem which extends only to the indication of "oil" or "no oil" is not complete; and in a general sense no decision tree is *ever* really complete. Life goes on after (e_1, z_1, a_1, s_2) and, in order to assign a selling price to the sequence, one could always look ahead still further by adding additional uncertain elements and additional moves in the game of "life itself." In practice, however, it will not always be worth the effort of *formally* looking very far ahead and, in order not to get bogged down in a never ending regress, the decision maker will be asked to make some judgmental assessments out at the tips of this curtailed decision tree.

The monetary amounts involved in this decision problem range from $-\$110{,}000$ to $+\$350{,}000$, and we shall suppose that the wildcatter's utility function u for money is far from linear over this range, so that EMV is

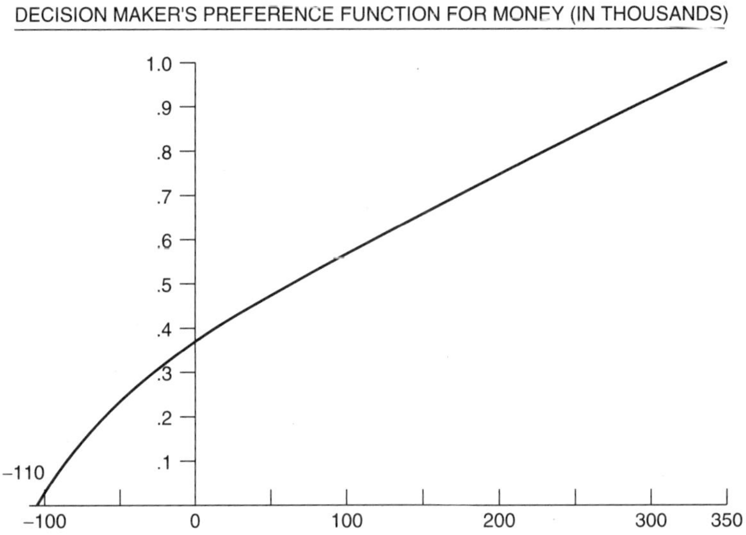

Figure 6.3
Decision maker's utility function for money (in thousands)

not an appropriate index for action purposes. We suppose that the decision maker, for example, is indifferent between receiving an outright payment of \$125,000 and a lottery which gives him an equal chance at \$0 and \$350,000; and we suppose that he is also indifferent between \$0 and a lottery which gives him an equal chance at a loss of \$100,000 and a gain of \$140,000. The utility function for (incremental) monetary values that we postulate for this decision maker is shown in figure 6.3. Some of the values we shall use subsequently are more precise than can be read off this graph, but figure 6.3 is included to help the reader check that these values are roughly correct. In our analysis we used a curve drawn on fine graph paper. We chose the origin and scale of measurement on the vertical axis so that

$$u(+\$350{,}000) = 1, \qquad \text{and} \qquad u(-\$110{,}000) = 0;$$

with this choice of scale it is possible to interpret utility values as indifference probabilities relative to the two basic consequences which are the most and least desirable of all the consequences at the tips of the tree in figure 6.2.

Assignment of Probabilities

It is not unreasonable to suppose in this example that previous experience with the existence of oil in the three possible types of geologic structures may make it possible to assign a nearly, if not completely, objective measure to the existence of oil given any particular outcome of the seismic sounding, whereas it would be much less clear what probability should be assigned to the existence of oil in the absence of knowledge of the structure. The following hypothetical probability assignments are given directly to the event ($\tilde{s} = s_2$)—that is, to the existence of oil—given respectively no structure (z_1), open structure (z_2) and closed structure (z_3):

$$P(\tilde{s} = s_2 | \tilde{z} = z_1) = .10, \quad P(\tilde{s} = s_2 | \tilde{z} = z_2) = .25, \quad P(\tilde{s} = s_2 | \tilde{z} = z_3) = .70.$$

At the same time, it will in general be meaningful to a geologist to assign probabilities to the various structures, which in this case means to assign probabilities to three simplified outcomes z_1, z_2, and z_3 of experiment e_1. The following hypothetical probability assignments are also given directly for experiment e_1:

$$P(\tilde{z} = z_1) = .60, \qquad P(\tilde{z} = z_2) = .30, \qquad P(\tilde{z} = z_3) = .10.$$

These probabilities, of course, do (and must) add to 1.0.

These probability assignments can be found on the branches of the decision tree (figure 6.2) which emanate from e_1.

It remains to assign probabilities to s_1 and s_2 *unconditionally*, in other words without being given the result of a seismic sounding. These probability assignments are needed on the fourth moves of the decision tree which emanate from e_0, and are obtained indirectly by use of the formula:

$$\begin{aligned} P(\tilde{s} = s_i) &= \textstyle\sum_{j=1}^{3} P(\tilde{s} = s_i \text{ and } \tilde{z} = z_j) \\ &= \textstyle\sum_{j=1}^{3} P(\tilde{s} = s_i | \tilde{z} = z_j) P(\tilde{z} = z_j); \end{aligned}$$

for example,

$$P(\tilde{s} = s_2) = (.10 \times .60) + (.25 \times .30) + (.70 \times .10) = .205.$$

We have now fully d scribed this particular drilling decision problem. We shall return to analyze this problem in section 6.4.2 after we first develop results for the analysis of the more general class of such problems.

6.3.2 The Imperfect Tester

Consider another example of a decision maker who must decide whether a certain component should be hand-adjusted at extra expense before it is installed in a complicated electronic system. Should the only available test, which is expensive and not infallible, be made on the component before a final decision is reached? The possible choices by the decision maker and chance are listed in table 6.1.

Table 6.1
Possible choices

Set	Elements	Interpretation
A	a_1	do not adjust
	a_2	adjust
S	s_1	component does not need adjustment
	s_2	component needs adjustment
E	e_0	do not experiment
	e_1	experiment
Z	z_0	outcome of e_0, i.e., no additional information
	z_1	outcome of e_1 that is more favorable to s_1
	z_2	outcome of e_1 that is more available to s_2

Assignment of Costs

We shall assume that (1) the cost of the necessary repairs when a defective component is installed in the system is \$100, (2) the cost of hand-adjustment to guarantee that there will be no need of repair is \$30, (3) the cost of the test to get a partial indication whether the component needs adjustment is \$10 if a critical condenser does not blow (indicating a favorable response), and is \$15 if this condenser does blow (indicating an unfavorable response). Figure 6.4 exhibits the decision tree for this problem giving the monetary costs for (e, z, a, s) plays at the tips of the tree. For example, the play (e_1, z_2, a_2, s_1) involves a cost of \$15 for experimentation (since z_2 means that the condenser blew), and an additional \$30 was required for hand-adjustment, for a total of \$45. We shall assume also that the decision maker has indicated that for the range of monetary costs involved in this problem, expected monetary cost is a valid "disutility" index.

Probability Assessments

We shall assume that on the basis of previous experience with this imperfect tester the decision maker has decided to make the following direct probability assessments of the two possible error responses for the test equipment:

$$P(\tilde{z} = z_2 | \tilde{s} = s_1; e_1) = .3,$$

and

$$P(\tilde{z} = z_1 | \tilde{s} = s_2; e_1) = .2.$$

Furthermore, on the basis of past performance of similar components from this particular supplier as well as from other suppliers, and on the

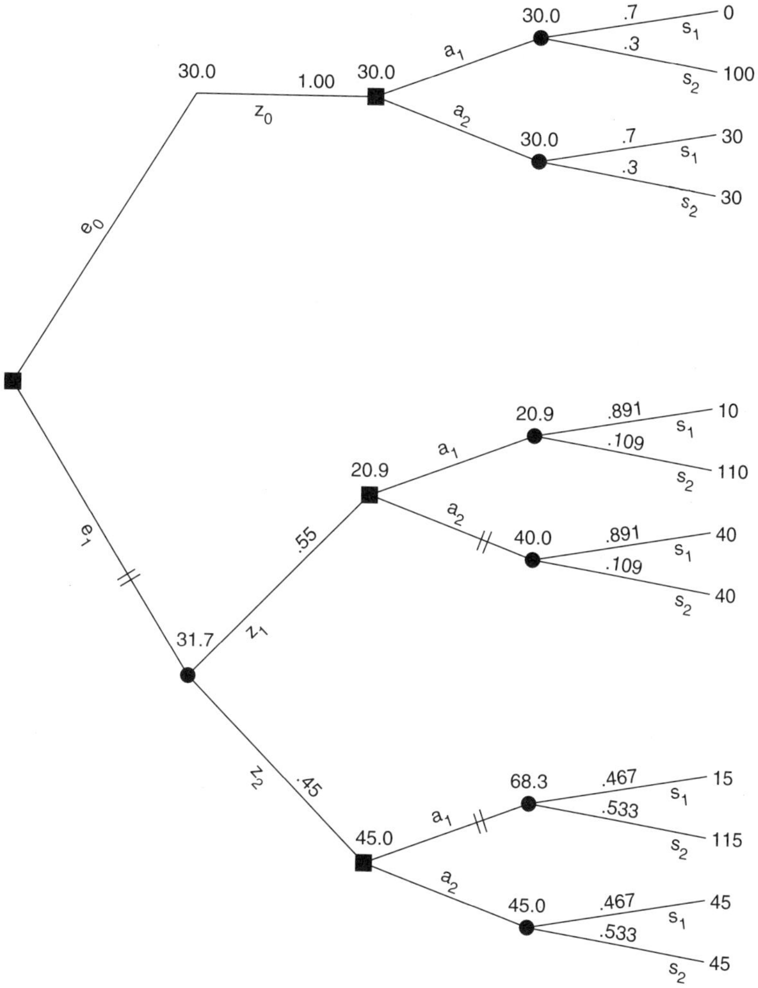

Figure 6.4
Analysis of an "imperfect tester"

Table 6.2
Marginal and joint probability measures associated with e_1

	s_1	s_2	$P(\tilde{z}=z)$
z_1	$.70 \times .70 = .49$	$.20 \times .30 = .06$	.55
z_2	$.30 \times .70 = .21$	$.80 \times .30 = .24$	.45
$P(\tilde{s}=s)$	.70	.30	1.00

Table 6.3
Conditional probabilities of states given outcomes

	s_1	s_2	Totals
z_1	$\frac{.49}{.55} = .891$	$\frac{.06}{.55} = .109$	1.00
z_2	$\frac{.21}{.45} = .467$	$\frac{.24}{.45} = .533$	1.00

basis of preliminary performance data submitted by the supplier on this particular component, the decision maker has also decided that he believes

$$P(\tilde{s} = s_1) = .7.$$

The above probability assignments suffice to fully determine the probability measure for all events involving $\tilde{s}$ and $\tilde{z}$. On the branches of the tree emanating from e_0, the probability assignments on move 4 are given directly in terms of the above data. On the branches of the tree emanating from e_1, however, the probability assignments on moves 2 and 4 require some calculations; these calculations will be discussed in terms of tables 6.2 and 6.3. In table 6.2 we start with the entries $P(\tilde{s} = s_1) = .70$ and $P(\tilde{s} = s_2) = .30$. The entry in row z_i and columns s_j is the assessment for $P(\tilde{z} = z_i \text{ and } \tilde{s} = s_j)$ and to compute these quantities we use the formula

$$P(\tilde{z} = z_i \text{ and } \tilde{s} = s_j) = P(\tilde{z} = z_i | \tilde{s} = s_j)P(\tilde{s} = s_j).$$

The entry in row z_i under the column label $P(\tilde{z} = z)$ is the assessment for $P(\tilde{z} = z_i)$ and to compute these quantities we use the formula

$$P(\tilde{z} = z_i) = P(\tilde{z} = z_i \text{ and } \tilde{s} = s_1) + P(\tilde{z} = z_i \text{ and } \tilde{s} = s_2).$$

Thus each entry in the last column is the sum of the entries in the corresponding row of the body of the table. The two probabilities $P(\tilde{z} = z_1) = .55$ and $P(\tilde{z} = z_2) = .45$ are shown on the branches of move 2 following experiment e_1.

It remains to compute probabilities of the form $P(\tilde{s} = s_j | \tilde{z} = z_i)$, which are needed on the branches of the fourth moves. These probabilities are computed from table 6.2 and exhibited in table 6.3. The entry corresponding to z_i and s_j in table 6.3 is the assessment for $P(\tilde{s} = s_j | \tilde{z} = z_i)$, and is computed from the formula

$$P(\tilde{s} = s_j | \tilde{z} = z_i) = \frac{P(\tilde{s} = s_j \text{ and } \tilde{z} = z_i)}{P(\tilde{z} = z_i)}.$$

This completes the full description of this particular problem. Its analysis will be deferred to section 6.4.3 and at that time the remaining entries to be found at the nodes of the decision tree figure 6.4 will be described.

6.3.3 Probability Assessments

In this subsection we wish to discuss further the assessment of probabilities for events involving $\tilde{s}$ and $\tilde{z}$ and to contrast how such assessments were made in the two preceding illustrative examples. We shall adopt the following notational and terminological conventions in describing the five different probability measures involved in such problems.

Let S_0 and Z_0 respectively denote subsets of S and Z.

a. The *joint* probability that $\tilde{s} \in S_0$ *and* $\tilde{z} \in Z_0$ when the experiment e is performed will be alternatively designated by

$$P(\tilde{s} \in S_0 \text{ and } \tilde{z} \in Z_0; e) \quad \text{or} \quad P_{s,z;e}(S_0, Z_0).$$

The probability measure $P_{s,z;e}$ defined on pairs of subsets, such as (S_0, Z_0), will be called the *joint* probability measure for the experiment e.

b. The *unconditional* probability that $\tilde{s} \in S_0$ will be alternatively designated by

$$P(\tilde{s} \in S_0) \quad \text{or} \quad P_s(S_0).$$

The probability measure P_s defined on subsets of S will also be called the prior probability measure on S. We shall continue to assume that P_s does not in any way depend on the choice or contemplated choice of an e.

c. The *conditional* probability that $\tilde{z} \in Z_0$ given that $\tilde{s} = s$ when the experiment e is performed will be alternatively designated by

$$P(\tilde{z} \in Z_0 | \tilde{s} = s; e) \quad \text{or} \quad P_{z|s;e}(Z_0).$$

d. The *conditional* probability that $\tilde{s} \in S_0$ given that $\tilde{z} = z$ has been observed will be alternatively designated by

$$P(\tilde{s} \in S_0 | \tilde{z} = z) \quad \text{or} \quad P_{s|z}(S_0).$$

The probability measure $P_{s|z}$ defined on subsets of S will also be called the *posterior* probability measure on S given z. The symbol e is suppressed, because, by assumption, all the relevant information for probability purposes is included in the description of z.

e. The *unconditional* probability that $\tilde{z} \in Z_0$ when the experiment e is performed will be alternatively designated by

$$P(\tilde{z} \in Z_0; e) \quad \text{or} \quad P_{z;e}(Z_0).$$

In the analysis of the drilling decision problem we assumed that the decision maker assessed directly the measures $P_{z,e}$ (the unconditional probability measure of subsurface structures) and $P_{s|z}$ (the conditional or posterior probability measure for $\tilde{s}$ given knowledge about the outcome of $\tilde{z}$). These assessments were used directly on the tree at all chance moves following e_1. From these measures we *calculated*

$$P_s(s_j) = \textstyle\sum_i P_{s|z_i}(s_j) P_{z;e_1}(z_i),$$

and we used these derived probabilities on the chance moves after the choice of e_0. In that illustration we did not even mention measures $P_{z|s;e}$ and $P_{s,z;e}$.

In the analysis of the problem of the imperfect tester, we indicated that the decision maker was able to make the most effective use of his experience by making direct probability assessments of the measures P_s (the unconditional or prior probability measure for $\tilde{s}$) and $P_{z|s;e}$ (the conditional probability measure for $\tilde{z}$ given knowledge of the state $\tilde{s}$). These probabilities could be directly applied only to chance moves following e_0. On the basis of these probabilities we computed, in sequential order, the joint probability measure $P_{s,z;e}$, the unconditional probability measure $P_{z;e}$ (table 6.2), and the conditional or posterior measure $P_{s|z}$ (table 6.3). The probability measures $P_{z;e}$ and $P_{s|z}$ were then used to make assignments on the branches of chance moves following e_1. This procedure represents the more typical case: Both experience and theory make it more meaningful in most cases to assign probability measures P_s and $P_{z|s;e}$ directly and then to *derive* the probability measures $P_{z;e}$ and $P_{s|z}$ that are necessary for the analysis of the problem.

6.4 Analysis of a Decision Tree

In this section we shall analyze the general problem formulated in sections 6.1 and 6.2. Although at first we shall describe the analysis in general terms, we suggest that the reader keep in mind the illustration of the oil drilling experiment and occasionally refer to the associated decision tree (figure 6.2). After describing the analysis of the general case, we shall complete the analyses of the oil drilling and imperfect tester problems.

The analysis will proceed by first assuming that the utility function u is represented in such a way that we can interpret the number $u(c)$ as a breakeven probability. In particular, we shall assume that any consequence c associated with an (e, z, a, s) sequence is at least as preferable as a basic reference consequence c_*, and at most as preferable as a basic reference consequence c^*; furthermore, we shall assume that the decision maker is indifferent between obtaining c outright and obtaining the reference lottery which gives a canonical chance $u(c)$ at c^* and a complementary canonical chance at c_*. With this interpretation for u we can associate with each (e, z, a, s) sequence a *payoff* which consists of a $u(e, z, a, s)$ chance at c^* and a complementary chance at c_*. Keeping this interpretation of u in mind, we shall develop a procedure for analyzing the tree which will amount to manipulating the us in a certain manner. We will then argue that if u is any equivalent utility function whatsoever, then these same manipulations will lead to the same suggested strategy for experimentation and action. In the previous chapters we reserved the symbol $\pi(c)$ to denote the breakeven probability associated with c; we prefer not to do the same thing here because it would require writing all formulas first in terms of πs and then in terms of us.

6.4.1 Backwards Induction

The analysis of the decision problem proceeds by working backwards from the end of the decision tree (the right side of figure 6.1) to the initial starting point: Instead of asking which experiment e the decision maker should choose at move 1 when she knows neither of the moves which will subsequently be made by chance, we start by asking which terminal act she should choose at move 3 *if* she has already performed a particular experiment e and has observed a particular outcome z. Even at this point, with a known history (e, z), the consequences of the various possible terminal acts are uncertain because the state s which will be chosen by chance at move 4 is still unknown; however, this difficulty is easily resolved by observing that for each choice a, there is an associated lottery with basic reference lotteries as prizes, and by recalling that a composite lottery of this sort can in turn be "reduced" to a basic reference lottery. The lottery associated with an (e, z, a) history is exhibited in table 6.4. Given the (e, z) information, the decision maker assigns a probability $P_{s|z}(s_i)$ to the event $\{\tilde{s} = s_i\}$, and if this event occurs, she gets a chance of $u(e, z, a, s_i)$ at c^* and a complementary chance at c_*. Therefore, if the decision maker chooses act a after observing (e, z), the resulting composite lottery is, in her regard, indifferent to a basic reference lottery where the chance at c^* is

$$\bar{u}''(e, z, a) = \textstyle\sum_i u(e, z, a, s_i) P_{s|z}(s_i), \tag{6.1}$$

Table 6.4
Reference lottery associated with an (e, z, a) history

State	Probability of state	Chance at c^* for given state
s_1	$P_{s\|z}(s_1)$	$u(e, z, a, s_1)$
s_2	$P_{s\|z}(s_2)$	$u(e, z, a, s_2)$
.	.	.
.	.	.
	.	.
s_m	$P_{s\|z}(s_m)$	$u(e, z, a, s_m)$

and the chance at c_* is $1 - \bar{u}''(e, z, a)$. We use the double prime superscript on u to denote "posterior to experimentation," and the bar on top of u to denote an *averaging* process.

Now since the decision maker wants to maximize her assessed chance of obtaining c^*, for a given history (e, z), she will wish to choose a to maximize $\bar{u}''(e, z, a)$. If we let a_z^o denote a maximizer of $\bar{u}''(e, z, a)$, where the superscript ^{o} is mnemonic for *optimum* and the subscript z serves as a reminder that the optimal a depends on the outcome z, we then have

$$\bar{u}''(e, z, a_z^o) = \max_a \bar{u}''(e, z, a), \tag{6.2}$$

where the operator $\max_a$ when applied to $\bar{u}''(e, z, a)$ denotes the *maximum* value of the set of numbers $\bar{u}''(e, z, a)$ as the argument a runs through all of its possible values. If the decision maker has already observed (e, z), then at move 3 she should choose act a_z^o and this choice will lead to a situation which she feels is indifferent to a chance $\bar{u}''(e, z, a_z^o)$ at c^* and a complementary chance at c_*.

After we have computed $\bar{u}''(e, z, a_z^o)$ in this way for all possible histories (e, z), we are ready to attack the problem of the initial choice of an experiment. For any choice e at move 1, the outcome z to be chosen by chance at move 2 is still unknown; but we resolve this difficulty in the same way as we did for choosing an appropriate act a, given (e, z). For each choice e, there is an associated lottery, as exhibited in table 6.5, which can be "reduced" to a basic reference lottery. If e is chosen, the decision maker assigns a probability $P_{z;e}(z_j)$ to the event $\{\tilde{z} = z_j\}$ and, if this event occurs, she is indifferent between the resulting situation and a basic reference lottery with a canonical chance of $\bar{u}''(e, z_j, a_z^o)$ at c^*. Therefore, if at move 1 she chooses experiment e, then before chance chooses z, she is faced with a situation which is equivalent in her regard to a basic reference lottery that gives c^* with canonical chance

$$\bar{\bar{u}}'(e) = \sum_j \bar{u}''(e, z_j, a_{z_j}^o) P_{z;e}(z_j); \tag{6.3}$$

Table 6.5
Lottery associated with choice of e

Experimental outcome	Probability	Assessed chance at c^* for given outcome
z_1	$P_{z;e}(z_1)$	$\bar{u}''(e, z_1, a^{\circ}_{z1})$
z_2	$P_{z;e}(z_2)$	$\bar{u}''(e, z_2, a^{\circ}_{z2})$
.	.	.
.	.	.
.	.	.
z_p	$P_{z;e}(z_p)$	$\bar{u}''(e, z_p, a^{\circ}_{zp})$

the double bar on u represents an averaging of $\bar{u}''$ values, and the single prime superscript denotes an evaluation made *prior* to experimentation.

Now again, the decision maker will wish to choose the e for which $\bar{\bar{u}}'(e)$ is maximum; if we let e^o denote a *maximizer* of $\bar{\bar{u}}'(e)$ we then have

$$\bar{\bar{u}}'(e^o) = \max_e \bar{\bar{u}}'(e). \tag{6.4}$$

This procedure of working back from the outermost branches of the decision tree to the base of the trunk is often called "backwards induction." More descriptively it could be called a process of "averaging out and folding back."

It will be convenient to label each node of the decision tree by the particular sequence of moves leading to that node. Thus, for example, the node at move 3 that results from e_3 being chosen on move 1 and z_5 on move 2 will be simply designated by (e_3, z_5). We can now summarize the analysis of the tree by backward induction in terms of an algorithm for assigning a preference index to each node of the decision tree.

1. At the end of move 4 assign to each node (e, z, a, s) the index $u(e, z, a, s)$.

2. At move 4 assign to each node (e, z, a) the index $\bar{u}''(e, z, a)$ which is computed from (6.1).

3. At move 3 assign to each node (e, z) the index $\bar{u}''(e, z, a^o_z)$, which is computed from (6.2); block off with double slash marks all branches emanating from (e, z) other than a^o_z.

4. At move 2 assign to each node (e) the index $\bar{\bar{u}}'(e)$, which is computed from (6.3).

5. At move 1 assign to the starting node the index $\bar{\bar{u}}'(e^o)$, which is computed from (6.4); block off with double slash marks all es other than e^o.

The optimal strategy for experimentation and action is to choose e^o at move 1, and for any outcome z at move 2 to choose a^o_z at move 3.

Throughout this discussion we interpreted the utility function u as the breakeven probability function π and used this interpretation to justify the process of backwards induction. We now wish to remove this restriction. The reader can easily verify that if at the end of move 4 each of the breakeven probability assignments $u(e, z, a, s)$ were multiplied by a positive constant β, and another constant α added to the product—so that $u(e, z, a, s)$ would become $\alpha + \beta\, u(e, z, a, s)$—then all the assignments at the nodes of the tree which are computed by the backwards induction process using formulas (6.1) to (6.4) will also be multiplied by β and α will be added to each; furthermore, the algorithm will result in the same optimal act a_z^o for each z, and the same optimal experiment e^o.

6.4.2 Analysis of the Drilling Problem

All the data required for the analysis appears on the decision tree in figure 6.2. Two numbers are recorded at each node of the tree: The number *not* in parentheses is the preference index (in this case the indifference probability) for the node, and the number in parentheses is the equivalent selling price at the node. Thus, for example, at the node (e_1, z_1, a_1), we obtain

$$\bar{u}''(e_1, z_1, a_1) = u(e_1, z_1, a_1, s_1)P_{s|z_1}(s_1) + u(e_1, z_1, a_1, s_2)P_{s|z_1}(s_2)$$

$$= (.00)(.90) + (.99)(.10) = .099,$$

and from the decision maker's utility curve (see figure 6.3) we obtain the equivalent selling price of $-\$83{,}000$; that is, $.099 = u(-\$83{,}000)$. At the node (e_1, e_2), for example, we observe that $a_{z_2}^o = a_2$, since

$$\bar{u}''(e_1, z_2, a_2) > \bar{u}''(e_1, z_2, a_1);$$

therefore the branch a_1 emanating from this node is blocked off and at this node the utility value $\bar{u}''(e_1, z_2, a_{z_2}^o) = .35$ is recorded; once again from figure 6.3 we observe that $.35 = u(-\$10{,}000)$, so that $-\$10{,}000$ is the equivalent selling price at (e_1, z_2). To obtain the entries at node (e_1), for example, we observe that

$$(.60 \times .35) + (.30 \times .35) + (.10 \times .693) = .3843$$

and from figure 6.3 that $.3843 = u(\$2{,}000)$. Since $\bar{u}'(e_1) = .3843$ and $\bar{u}'(e_0) = .38$, the optimal experiment is $e^o = e_1$.

The analysis shows that it is almost a standoff between e_0 and e_1 but it is slightly better to buy the seismic sounding (e_1). The optimal terminal act is then to drill (act a_1) if and only if a closed structure z_3 is revealed.

6.4.3 Analysis of the Problem of the Imperfect Tester

At the tips of the decision tree in figure 6.4 we have recorded the costs for all (e, z, a, s) sequences for the problem of the Imperfect Tester. We have already remarked that the decision maker has decided to use expected monetary costs as a valid "disutility" index. This shift in orientation from monetary value to monetary cost, or from utility to "disutility," means that at the decision maker's moves 1 and 3 it will be necessary to choose minimum rather than maximum values.

We are now ready to begin our analysis of the decision tree and our first step is to start from the end (extreme right), using the costs we find there to evaluate the expected costs for all (e, z, a) nodes. As a single example of the computation, the expected cost at node (e_1, z_1, a_1) is given by

$$(10)(.891) + 110(.109) = 20.9,$$

which is exhibited on the tree. Having computed expected costs at all (e, z, a) nodes, we are ready to move back one level and compute expected costs for all (e, z) nodes. As an example, at node (e_1, z_1), the decision maker has a free choice of a_1, which results in an expected cost of 20.9, or of a_2, which results in an expected cost of 45.0; naturally, he would rather choose a_1, and therefore at node (e_1, z_1), the number 20.9 is recorded and the a_2 branch at node (e_1, z_1) is blocked off with double slashes. Next we compute the entries at nodes e_0 and e_1. At node (e_1), for example, the entry is computed to be

$$(20.0)(.55) + 45(.45) = 31.7.$$

Since the entry at e_1 is larger than that at e_0 the optimal choice is to use e_0 and then it is a standoff between a_1 and a_2. Therefore it is better *not* to use the imperfect tester even though if it were used it would be powerful enough to clearly determine the decision maker's preferred action.

Exercises

1. Mr. Brown must choose between canonical lotteries l_1 and l_2 described by the decision tree in figure 6E.1. Observe that, as shown by the tree, the consequence c_0 of l_1 consists in giving Brown a free choice between c_3 for certain and a canonical lottery l_4 among c_1, c_4, and c_5. The numbers in parentheses on the branches of the tree are canonical probabilities. Brown's preferences among the possible *ultimate* consequences have been expressed by the following statements:

$$c_1 > c_2 > c_3 > c_4 > c_5;$$
$$c_2 \sim \{(.8 : c_1), (.2 : c_5)\},$$
$$c_3 \sim \{(.5 : c_1), (.5 : c_5)\},$$
$$c_4 \sim \{(.2 : c_1), (.8 : c_5)\}.$$

a. *If* Mr. Brown chooses l_1 and wins c_0, should he then choose l_3 (i.e., c_3) or l_4?

b. Should Mr. Brown choose l_1 or l_2?

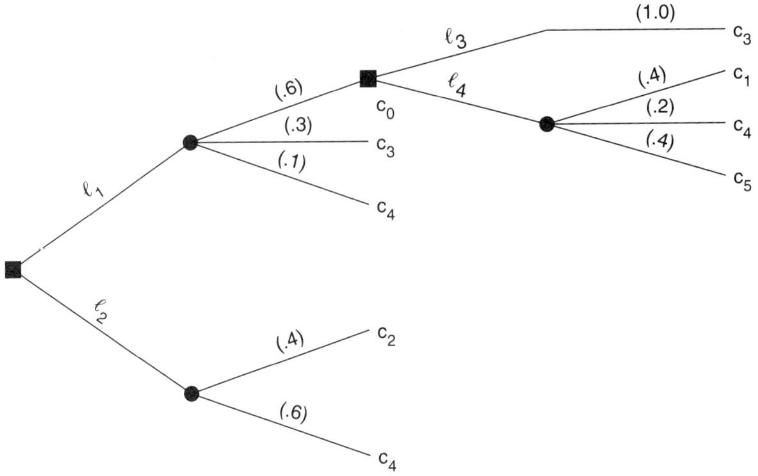

Figure 6E.1

2. A property owner has three properties which she wishes to sell at the prices shown in the second column of the table below. She goes to Mr. L. K. Jones, a real estate broker, and addresses him as follows: "Jones, I'm offering you only property A as of now, and if you don't sell it within a month I'll take all my business, including A, elsewhere. However, if you do sell A within a month, you can have your choice of B or C; if you sell that property within a month of the time it's put in your hands, you can have a month to sell the last one."

Property	Price	Advertising cost	Probability of sale
A	$25,000	$800	.7
B	50,000	200	.6
C	100,000	400	.5

Jones inspects the properties, decides on the amount he would spend advertising each one if it were put in his hands (figures in the third column of the table), and assesses his chances of selling each if he tries (figures in the last column of the table); he believes that success in selling any one property would not affect his chances of selling any other. His commission is 4% of the gross.

Jones next informs his consultant on decision theory that his financial position is such that:

1. He would be indifferent between getting $1,500 outright and taking a 50-50 chance at +$6,000 or −$1,000;

2. He would be indifferent between not betting and betting on a 50-50 chance at +$1,500 and −$1,000;

3. He would be indifferent between getting $3,200 for certain or taking a 50-50 chance at +$6,000 or −$1,500.

Given these data:

a. If you were Jones's consultant, how would you advise him?

b. What is the client's proposition worth to Jones (approximately)?

3. In the oil-drilling example discussed in this chapter, what is the optimal course of experimentation and action if the decision maker's utility function for money is linear (i.e., if he is an EMV'er for the monetary ranges involved in this problem)?

4. A lottery is to be conducted using 10 urns, 8 of which are of type I and 2 of which are of type II. Urns of type I contain 4 red and 6 black balls; urns of type II contain 9 red and 1 black balls. One of these 10 urns is selected canonically and you are asked to guess whether the selected urn is of type I or II. You will receive a reward or penalty according to whether your guess is correct or not as given in the accompanying table:

True state	Guess (Act)	
	Type I (a_1)	Type II (a_2)
Type I	+\$400	−\$50
Type II	−\$200	+\$1,000

Before making your guess you have the privilege of the following two options:

a. At a cost of \$50 you can make a single canonical drawing from the selected urn before guessing.

b. At a cost of \$80 you can take one canonical drawing, replace the ball, and take a second canonical drawing before guessing.

If your money were at stake would you play? If you wanted to play, or had to play, what strategy would you follow? If the privilege of playing this game were to be sold in an open auction to the highest bidder, up to what amount would you bid? Be sure to use your very own utility function for money as given in exercise 2 of chapter 4.

5. (Optional) The notion of a decision tree can be generalized in many ways. One possible way proceeds in terms of the primitive notions of *nodes* and a *successor* operation. Given any two nodes α and β it is possible to say whether or not β is a successor of α. If β is a successor of α, we shall write $\alpha \rightarrow \beta$. If $\alpha \rightarrow \beta$, we shall also say that α is a *predecessor* of β. We assume

i. There are a finite set of nodes.

ii. There is a unique *initial* node (i.e., one which has no predecessor).

iii. Each node, other than the initial node, has a unique predecessor. A node which has no successor is called a *terminating* node.

iv. To each terminating node γ there is assigned a utility value $u(\gamma)$.

The set of nonterminating nodes is partitioned into two classes: chance nodes and decision maker's nodes.

v. If α is a chance node and if $\{\alpha_1^+, \alpha_2^+, \ldots, \alpha_m^+\}$ is the complete set of successor nodes to α, there is a probability function which assigns to α_i^+ a nonnegative number $P(\alpha_i^+ | \alpha)$ such that $\sum_{i=1}^{n} P(\alpha_i^+ | \alpha) = 1$.

In terms of this generalized abstract tree representation of a decision problem, describe the averaging out and folding back process.

A *decision rule*, σ, assigns to each of the decision maker's nodes α a unique successor to α, labelled $\sigma(\alpha)$. Give a definition of an *optimal* decision rule and indicate how you would find it.

7 Random Variables

7.1 Introduction: Definition of a Random Variable

7.1.1 Quantities and Values

Hitherto we have talked about "events" in general; in most of the remainder of this book we shall be concerned with a special but very important class of events, namely those described by stating the *value* of some *quantity*. Thus we may be interested in the number of heads that have occurred in the last 100 tosses of a certain coin, in which case a possible event is described by saying that the number of heads was 47; or we may be interested in the ratio of heads to total tosses that would be approached if this coin were to be tossed indefinitely, in which case a possible event would be described by saying that the ratio is some particular real number, say .23607. As examples of quantities whose values may be of interest in business decision problems consider:

1. The number of loaves of bread sold by the ABC Supermarket on a certain day.
2. The number of barrels of reserves found by drilling an oil well on a certain site.
3. The number of defectives produced by a certain automatic screw machine in a certain production run of 1,000 pieces.
4. The fraction defective that this same machine "tends" to produce in its present condition; that is, the ratio of defectives to all pieces that would be approached if the present condition of the machine were to remain unchanged while production went on indefinitely.

7.1.2 Unknown Quantities

We are of course primarily interested in *unknown events,* and correspondingly in quantities whose values are unknown, or more briefly, in *unknown quantities.* Thus a decision problem may involve the number of units that will be sold tomorrow, or the number of barrels of reserves that can be found by drilling on a certain site, or the number of defectives that will be produced by a certain machine.

Remember, however, that by "unknown" we mean *unknown to some particular decision maker*, and that a quantity may well be unknown to a decision maker even though it is fully *determined* in fact or even actually *known* to some other person. Thus the number of defectives in a particular lot of purchased components may be an unknown quantity to the purchaser even though it is a perfectly well-determined quantity (the lot having been already produced) and may even be actually known to the vendor. Observe, on the other hand, that unknown quantities may be of very real importance in practical decision problems even though their values may not or even cannot ever be learned. Thus the decision maker may never learn the number of barrels of reserves under a certain site if he decides not to drill on this site; and the decision maker cannot ever learn exactly what fraction defective a machine would produce if its present condition could remain unaltered during an infinitely long production run.

7.1.3 Notation

As we have explained previously, any *unknown quantity* will be denoted by a letter with a tilde over it, $\tilde{x}$ for example, while the *generic value* of the unknown quantity will be denoted by the same letter without the tilde, x for example. The *event* that the unknown quantity $\tilde{x}$ has some particular value x will be written $\tilde{x} = x$; the event that $\tilde{x}$ has a value belonging to some particular *set* X_0 of values will be written $\tilde{x} \in X_0$; the event that $\tilde{x}$ has a value greater than some particular value x will be written $\tilde{x} > x$; and so forth.

7.1.4 Probability Assignments

Now consider a decision problem in which the consequence of one or more of the available acts depends on an unpredictable event of the form $(\tilde{x} = x)$—depends, that is, on the value of some unknown quantity.

If the number of possible values and hence the number of possible events is *finite*, then we have a problem of exactly the kind with which we have dealt in earlier chapters. The decision maker can conceptually write down the probability that he assigns to every possible event of the form $(\tilde{x} = x)$; the probability of every event of the form $(\tilde{x} \in X_0)$ that appears in the decision problem can then be computed (by use of the addition axiom) from the probabilities assigned to the events of the form $(\tilde{x} = x)$; and the problem can then be solved by the methods described already in chapter 2.

If, however, the number of possible values of the unknown quantity is *infinite*, then clearly it will not be possible to proceed in this simple way. Instead of actually writing down the probability assigned to each event, the decision maker will have to adopt some *formula* or rule with which he can work algebraically or algorithmically rather than numerically; and even more than this, he may have to make his basic assignment to events of some sort other than $(\tilde{x} = x)$. For suppose that the unknown quantity of interest in a particular problem is the fraction defective which some machine would generate in the long run if it remained in its present state of adjustment. If the decision maker believes that this fraction can have any value in the interval $[0, 1]$ or even in some small subinterval of $[0, 1]$, then he may be unwilling to assign a positive probability however small to *any* event of the form $(\tilde{x} = x)$—there may be *no* odds at which he is willing to bet for the proposition that the fraction is *exactly* equal to .1 and not, say, a decimal in which 1 is followed by a billion zeros and then another 1. Thus he may feel that $P(\tilde{x} = x) = 0$ for every x; such a view, however, does not prevent the decision maker from assigning probabilities to events of the form $(\tilde{x} \leq x)$—he may feel, for example, that there is one chance in three that the long-run fraction defective is *no greater than* .1, two chances in three that it is no greater than .15, and so forth—and we shall see later that our method of analysis can be extended to handle any decision problem turning on an unknown $\tilde{x}$ if the decision maker will give us a formula specifying $P(\tilde{x} \leq x)$ for all real numbers x. Thus a probability assignment for an unknown long-run fraction defective might take the form

$$P(\tilde{x} \leq x) = \begin{cases} 0 & \text{if} \quad -\infty < x < 0, \\ 1 - (1 - x)^2 & \text{if} \quad 0 \leq x \leq 1, \\ 1 & \text{if} \quad 1 < x < \infty. \end{cases}$$

Any probability measure P which assigns a value $P(\tilde{x} \leq x)$ for all real x may be called a (probability) *distribution* of $\tilde{x}$.

In general, the assessment of $P(\tilde{x} \leq x)$ is a matter of judgment, just as any probability assignment is a matter of judgment; however, again like any other probabilities, the values assigned to $P(\tilde{x} \leq x)$ for various x must obey the axioms of probability. In particular, the first axiom requires that

$$P(\tilde{x} \leq x) \geq 0 \qquad \text{for all real } x;$$

the second axiom requires that

$$P(\tilde{x} < \infty) = 1;$$

and the first and third axioms together require that

$$P(\tilde{x} \leq x_1) \leq P(\tilde{x} \leq x_2) \qquad \text{if} \quad x_1 \leq x_2,$$

because additivity implies that

$$P(x_1 < \tilde{x} \leq x_2) = P(\tilde{x} \leq x_2) - P(x \leq x_1)$$

and the left-hand side of this expression must be nonnegative by the first axiom.

Observe now that although this new method of stating basic probability assignments is not actually *needed* in problems where the unknown $\tilde{x}$ has only a finite number of possible values and the decision maker assigns a probability to each of these values directly, the decision maker's assignments can be *expressed* in terms of $P(\tilde{x} \leq x)$ just as well as in terms of $P(\tilde{x} = x)$ even in the finite case. Suppose, for example, that $\tilde{x}$ is the number turned up on the roll of a die, and suppose that the decision maker assigns probability 1/6 to each of the 6 possible values of $\tilde{x}$. This assignment can equally well be expressed by saying that the decision maker has specified

$$P(x \le x) = \begin{cases} 0 & \text{if} \quad -\infty < x < 1, \\ 1/6 & \text{if} \quad 1 \le x \le 2, \\ 1/6 & \text{if} \quad 2 < x < 3, \end{cases}$$

and so forth. What we shall see in the end is that in many decision problems where the consequence of one or more of the available acts depends on the value of an unknown quantity $\tilde{x}$, the decision maker might find it convenient to assign a probability to every event of the form $(\tilde{x} \le x)$; once these assignments have been made, he is ready to solve his decision problem using the theory of probability as required.

7.1.5 A Nullity Assumption

We are about to impose another assumption concerning probability assignments for a variable quantity $\tilde{x}$, but before we do so let us first illustrate what this assumption is designed to avoid.

Pathology 1

It is possible under our present assumptions to assign probabilities such that $P(\tilde{x} < \infty) = 1$ but $\lim_{x \to \infty} P(\tilde{x} \le x) < 1$. For example, let $\tilde{x}$ be an unknown positive integer. For any *finite* subset X^* let $P(\tilde{x} \in X^*) = 0$. In this case it is still possible to assign positive probabilities to events which contain an infinite number of integers. For example, if X_E and X_0 represent respectively the set of even and odd integers, we could let

$$P(\tilde{x} \in X_E) = P(\tilde{x} \in X_0) = \tfrac{1}{2}.$$

More generally, if X_1 is any infinite subset of positive integers and x_n is the nth integer in the set X_1 in order of increasing size, then we could let

$$P(\tilde{x} \in X_1) = \lim_{n \to \infty} \frac{n}{x_n},$$

provided this limit exists. In this case P assigns values to various subsets of integers in a consistent manner and $P(\tilde{x} < \infty) = 1$ but $\lim_{n \to \infty} P(\tilde{x} \le n) = 0$. This is all right for some purposes but in this book we do not want to deal with such pathological $\tilde{x}$'s.

Pathology 2

It is possible under our present assumptions to assign probabilities such that $\lim_{x \to -\infty} P(\tilde{x} \le x) > 0$. For example, all we have to do is use the unknown quantity $\tilde{x}$ where $(-\tilde{x})$ is as defined in Pathology 1.

Pathology 3

Similar considerations show that we could not rule out the following set of probability assignments: Let x_0 be some predetermined number and let

$$P(\tilde{x} < x) = 0 \qquad \text{for all } x < x_0,$$

$$P(\tilde{x} < x_0) = .50,$$

$$P(\tilde{x} \leq x_0) = .75,$$

$$P(\tilde{x} < x) = 1.00 \qquad \text{for all } x > x_0.$$

This is bothersome since it is not clear where all the probability mass is situated. In this case

$$P(\tilde{x} = x_0) = P(\tilde{x} \leq x_0) - P(\tilde{x} < x_0) = .25.$$

Where is the remaining .75 mass? Once again we do not want to deal with such pathological $\tilde{x}$'s.

These illustrations help motivate the following:

Nullity Assumption

a. Let $\{a_n\}$ be a monotone increasing sequence of (real) numbers which approach b (possibly infinite). Then

$$\lim_{n \to \infty} P(a_n < \tilde{x} < b) = 0.$$

b. Let $\{b_n\}$ be a monotone decreasing sequence of (real) numbers which approach a (possibly $-\infty$). Then

$$\lim_{n \to \infty} P(a < x < b_n) = 0.$$

It is left (exercise 12) for the reader to show that the nullity assumption rules out the three pathological examples given above.

7.1.6 Definition of a Random Variable

Any unknown real quantity $\tilde{x}$ for which probability assignments can be made for *all* intervals—that is, intervals of the form $(-\infty, b)$, $(-\infty, b]$, (a, b), $(a, b]$, $[a, b)$, $[a, b)$, $[a, b]$, (a, ∞), $[a, \infty)$—and for which the nullity assumption holds will be called a *random variable* (rv). The use of the words "random" and "variable" in the technical term "random variable" is purely a historical residue, and nothing but confusion will result if the reader tries to find any meaning in either word taken by itself.

The reader should observe that if $\tilde{x}$ is a rv, then

$$\lim_{x \to x_0, x < x_0} P(\tilde{x} \leq x) = P(\tilde{x} < x_0), \tag{7.1a}$$

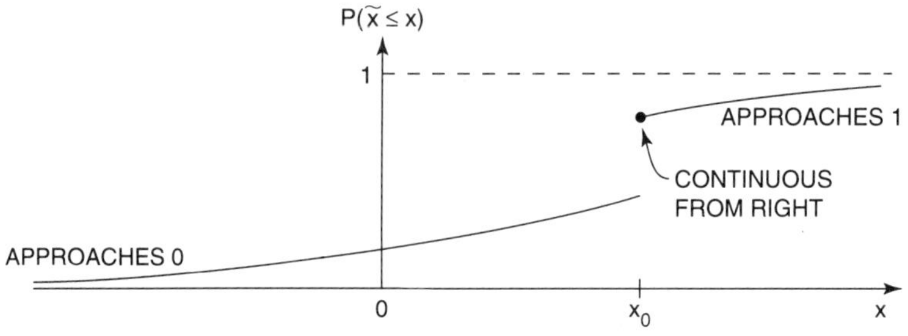

Figure 7.1
Probability of x or less

$$\lim_{x \to x_0, x > x_0} P(\tilde{x} \leq x) = P(\tilde{x} \leq x_0), \tag{7.1b}$$

and, in particular if $x_0 = +\infty$ and $-\infty$ respectively, we get

$$\lim_{x \to \infty} P(\tilde{x} \leq x) = 1, \tag{7.1c}$$

$$\lim_{x \to -\infty} P(\tilde{x} \leq x) = 0. \tag{7.1d}$$

This says, among other things, that the expression $P(\tilde{x} \leq x)$, treated as a function of x, approaches 0 as $x \to -\infty$ [by (7.1d)], approaches 1 as $x \to +\infty$ [by (7.1c)], is continuous from the right [by (7.1b)], but is perhaps discontinuous from the left (see figure 7.1).

It is not difficult to show that the function $P(\tilde{x} < x)$ approaches 0 at $-\infty$, approaches 1 at $+\infty$, and is continuous from the *left*.

Finally, observe that both expressions $P(\tilde{x} \leq x)$ and $P(\tilde{x} < x)$, treated as functions of x, are obviously nondecreasing because of the standard properties of any P-measure.

7.2 Discrete Random Variables: Mass Functions

7.2.1 Definition of a Discrete RV

Having defined random variables in principle, we are now ready to enter into the technical details of manipulating the probability assignments called for by the definition. Letting $\tilde{x}$ stand for the rv of interest, we start by considering the case where the *possible* values of $\tilde{x}$ constitute a discrete set X and probabilities like $P(\tilde{x} \leq x)$ are related to probabilities like $P(\tilde{x} = x)$ by

$$P(\tilde{x} \leq x) = \textstyle\sum_{t \leq x} P(\tilde{x} = t), \qquad t \in X, \tag{7.2}$$

where the summation on the right is over all members of X that are less than or equal to the real number x specified on the left.[1] Random variables having these properties will be called *discrete* rv's.

7.2.2 Definition of a Mass Function

If $\tilde{x}$ is a discrete rv with a set X of possible values, then the function f defined on the real line by

$$f(x) = \begin{cases} P(\tilde{x} = x) & \text{if} \quad x \in X, \\ 0 & \text{if} \quad x \notin X, \end{cases} \tag{7.3}$$

is called the *mass function* (mf) of the rv $\tilde{x}$.

In some situations the decision maker will start by assessing $P(\tilde{x} = x)$ for all possible events $(\tilde{x} = x)$ and these assessments will define the function f. More frequently, as we shall see in due course, the decision maker will start by selecting a function f on theoretical grounds and will then assess $P(\tilde{x} = x)$ by equating it to $f(x)$.

7.2.3 Properties of Mass Functions

A function f which to every real number x associates a real number $f(x)$—or alternatively, a real-valued function f defined on the real line—is capable of serving as the mass function of a discrete rv and will therefore be called a mass function if for some discrete set X

$$1.\ f(x) \begin{cases} \geq 0 & \text{for all } x \in X, \\ = 0 & \text{for all } x \notin X, \end{cases} \tag{7.4}$$

2. $\sum_X f(X) = 1,$

where $\sum_X$ denotes a summation over all $x \in X$; for if such a function is used to assign a measure P via (7.3) and (7.2), then clearly P will satisfy (7.1).

Example 1 Let $X = \{1, 2, 5\}$ and let f be defined by

$$f(x) \equiv \begin{cases} .2 & \text{if } x = 1, \\ .5 & \text{if } x = 2, \\ .3 & \text{if } x = 5, \\ 0 & \text{if } x \notin X. \end{cases} \tag{7.5}$$

---

1. In summations of this sort, t is a "dummy" or "running" variable in the same sense that these expressions are used in the calculus.

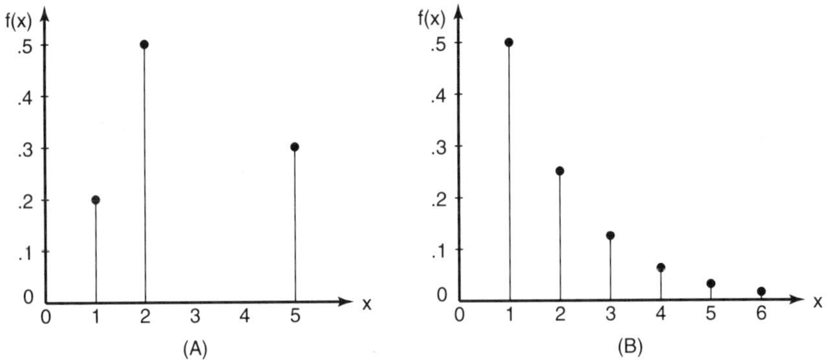

Figure 7.2
Two mass functions

Then

$\sum_X f(x) = .2 + .5 + .3 = 1$

and f is a mass function.

Example 2 Let $X = \{0, 1, 2, \ldots, 9\}$ and let f be defined by

$$f(x) \equiv \begin{cases} .1, & x \in X, \\ 0, & x \notin X, \end{cases} \tag{7.6}$$

Then

$\sum_X f(x) = .1 + .1 + \cdots + .1 = 1$

and f is a mass function.

Example 3 Let $X = \{1, 2, \ldots\}$ and let f be defined by

$$f(x) \equiv \begin{cases} (\frac{1}{2})^x, & x \in X, \\ 0, & x \notin X. \end{cases} \tag{7.7}$$

Then

$\sum_X f(x) = \frac{1}{2} + \frac{1}{4} + \frac{1}{8} + \cdots = 1$

and f is a mass function.

7.2.4 Graphic Representation of Mass Functions

Mass functions may be represented graphically in the way typified by figure 7.2, where the graph on the left depicts the mf defined by (7.5) while the graph on the right depicts the mf defined by (7.7). The only aspect of the graphs which has any real meaning is the points represented by heavy dots; the thin vertical lines are simply guides to the eye.

7.2.5 Cumulative Functions

If f is a mass function and X is a discrete set containing all x for which $f(x) > 0$, then the function F defined for *all real* x by

$$F(x) \equiv \textstyle\sum_{t \leq x} f(t), \qquad t \in X, \tag{7.8a}$$

will be called the *left-tail cumulative function* associated to f, and the function G defined by

$$G(x) \equiv \textstyle\sum_{t \geq x} f(t), \qquad t \in X, \tag{7.8b}$$

will be called the *right-tail cumulative function* associated to f. If f is in fact the mf of a random variable $\tilde{x}$, then by the additivity axiom of probability

$$F(x) = P(\tilde{x} \leq x), \qquad G(x) = P(\tilde{x} \geq x). \tag{7.9}$$

Example For the mf defined by (7.5),

$$F(0) = 0, \qquad F(1) = .2, \qquad F(3.5) = .2 + .5 = .7,$$

$$G(0) = 1, \qquad G(1) = 1, \qquad G(3.5) = .3.$$

We repeat that $F(x)$ and $G(x)$ are defined for *all* real x, not just for $x \in X$: if $\tilde{x}$ is a random variable, it is meaningful to talk about the probability that $\tilde{x} \leq 3.5$ or $\tilde{x} \geq 3.5$ even though $\tilde{x}$ cannot actually have the value 3.5. Observe also that

$$F(x) + G(x) = 1 + f(x) \tag{7.10}$$

where $f(x)$ may or may not be 0. In our example, $F(3.5) + G(3.5) = 1$ but $F(1) + G(1) = 1.2$ because $f(1)$ is counted in both $F(1)$ and $G(1)$.

7.2.6 Graphic Representation of Cumulative Functions

Cumulative functions may be represented graphically in the way typified in figure 7.3, where the graph on the left depicts the function F for the mf defined by (7.5) while the graph on the right depicts F for the mf defined by (7.7). The heavy horizontal lines are meaningful and the dots show which horizontal line applies at points where there is a jump in the function; the light vertical lines serve only as guides to the eye. The jumps occur, of course, at points where $f(x)$ is greater than 0; if $\tilde{x}$ is a rv, these points correspond to the values of $\tilde{x}$ to which nonzero probability is attached.

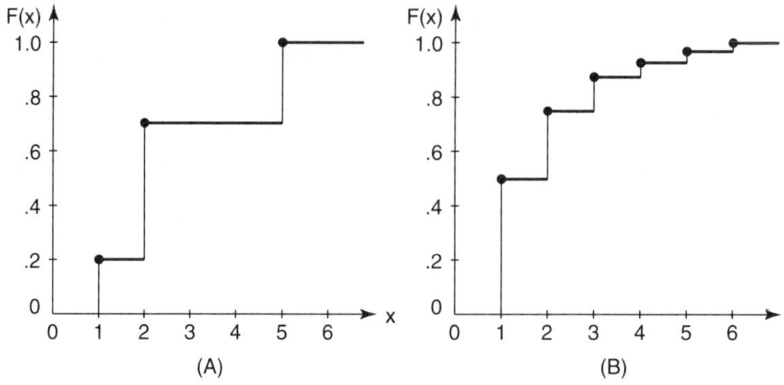

Figure 7.3
Two cumulative functions

7.2.7 Fractiles

Let $\tilde{x}$ be a discrete rv with left-tail cumulative function F, and let k be a real number in $[0, 1]$. Any real number x_k that satisfies the two conditions

$$F(x)\begin{cases} \leq k & \text{if} \quad x < x_k, \\ \geq k & \text{if} \quad x \geq x_k, \end{cases} \tag{7.11}$$

will be called a *k'th fractile* (or quantile) of the distribution of $\tilde{x}$.

The meaning of this definition can be brought out better by examples than by words; in both the following examples we shall let F be the function graphed in figure 7.3A.

Example 1 To locate $x_{.4}$ (i.e., the .4 fractile) in figure 7.3A, locate .4 on the vertical axis, read across horizontally to the graph, and read down to find 2 on the horizontal axis. It is easily verified (1) that $x_{.4} = 2$ satisfies the two conditions in (7.11), and (2) that if we tried to take any number other than 2 as $x_{.4}$, one or the other of the two conditions would be violated. Thus, for example, $x_{.4}$ is *not* equal to 1.8 because $F(1.8) < .4$; and $x_{.4}$ is *not* equal to 2.2 because $F(2.1) > .4$.

Example 2 To locate the $x_{.7}$ (i.e., the .7 fractile) in figure 7.3A, locate .7 on the vertical axis, read across horizontally, and encounter the "flat" in the graph extending horizontally from $x = 2$ to $x = 5$. *Any* real number from 2 to 5 inclusive is a .7 fractile of the distribution, as can readily be verified by checking against the conditions (7.11). Observe that, as shown by this example, *a fractile of the distribution of $\tilde{x}$ is not necessarily a possible value of $\tilde{x}$.*

A .5 fractile is also called a *median*; a .25 fractile is a first *quartile*; a .1 fractile is a first *decile*; a .01 fractile is a first *percentile*.

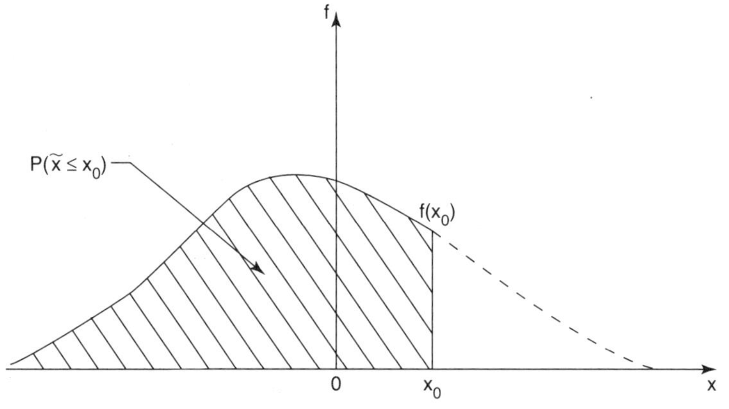

Figure 7.4
Density function and cumulative area

7.3 Continuous Random Variables: Density Functions

7.3.1 Definition of a Continuous RV and Its Density Function

We now take up the second special class of rv's that will be of concern to us in this course, namely rv's whose measure P is such that there exists a function f with the property

$$\int_{-\infty}^{x} f(t)\,dt = P(\tilde{x} \le x); \tag{7.12}$$

geometrically, $P(\tilde{x} \le x)$ is the area under the graph of f to the left of x, as shown in figure 7.4.

The property (7.12) implies that, regarded as a function of x, $P(\tilde{x} \le x)$ is *continuous*; and any rv having a measure P with the property (7.12) will itself be called continuous. The function f will be called the *density function* (df) of the rv $\tilde{x}$.

In the great majority of practical situations the decision maker will assign the measure P of a continuous rv indirectly, by first selecting a density function f and then using (7.12) to assess P.

7.3.2 Properties of Density Functions

A real-valued function f defined on the real line is capable of serving as the density function of a continuous rv and will therefore be called a density function if

$$(1)\quad f(x) \geq 0 \qquad \text{for all real } x, \tag{7.13}$$

$$(2)\quad \textstyle\int_R f(x)\,dx = 1,$$

where $\int_R$ denotes integration over the entire real line; if such a function is used to assign a measure P via (7.12), then clearly P will satisfy (7.1). Interpreted geometrically, the requirement that the complete integral of a density function be equal to 1 says simply that the *entire* area under the curve in figure 7.4 must be equal to 1.

Example 1 Let f be defined by

$$f(x) = \begin{cases} \dfrac{1}{b-a} & \textit{if} \qquad a \leq x \leq b, \\ 0 & \text{elsewhere.} \end{cases} \tag{7.14}$$

Then

$$\int_{-\infty}^{\infty} f(x)\,dx = \int_a^b f(x)\,dx = \int_a^b \frac{1}{b-a}\,dx = 1$$

and f is a density function. This particular df is called a *rectangular* or *uniform* df.

Example 2 Let f be defined by

$$f(x) = \begin{cases} 2x & \text{if} \qquad 0 \leq x \leq 1, \\ 0 & \text{elsewhere.} \end{cases} \tag{7.15}$$

Then

$$\int_{-\infty}^{\infty} f(x)\,dx = \int_0^1 2x\,dx = x^2 \Big|_0^1 = 1$$

and f is a density function. This particular df is called a *triangular* df.

Example 3 Let λ be a positive real number and let f be defined by

$$f(x) = \begin{cases} \lambda e^{-\lambda x} & \text{if} \qquad 0 \leq x < \infty, \\ 0 & \text{elsewhere.} \end{cases} \tag{7.16}$$

Then

$$\int_{-\infty}^{\infty} f(x)\,dx = \int_0^{\infty} \lambda e^{-\lambda x}\,dx = -e^{-\lambda x} \Big|_0^{\infty} = 1$$

and f is a density function. This particular density is called the *exponential* df with parameter λ.

Abridged Description of Density Functions

Henceforth we shall shorten our description of specific density functions by omitting any explicit reference to their values on intervals on which the value is everywhere 0. Thus the rectangular density defined in (7.14) will in the future be defined by writing simply

$$f(x) = \frac{1}{b-a}, \qquad a \le x \le b,$$

leaving it to the reader to infer that $f(x) = 0$ for all x *not* in $[a, b]$.

7.3.3 Probabilities of Intervals

It follows directly from the additivity axiom of probability that for any x and any positive ε

$$P(\tilde{x} \le x - \varepsilon) \le P(\tilde{x} < x) \le P(\tilde{x} \le x), \tag{7.17}$$

and when P is continuous in x, as it is in the case we are now considering, (7.17) implies immediately that

$$P(\tilde{x} < x) = P(\tilde{x} \le x). \tag{7.18}$$

By the additivity axiom of probability we have also that, for any rv $\tilde{x}$ and any real numbers x_1 and x_2 such that $x_1 \le x_2$,

$$P(x_1 < \tilde{x} \le x_2) = P(\tilde{x} \le x_2) - P(\tilde{x} \le x_1).$$

Hence we have by (7.12) that for any continuous $\tilde{x}$ with density f

$$\begin{aligned} P(x_1 < \tilde{x} \le x_2) &= \int_{-\infty}^{x_2} f(x)\,dx - \int_{-\infty}^{x_1} f(x)\,dx \\ &= \int_{x_1}^{x_2} f(x)\,dx; \end{aligned} \tag{7.19}$$

and by (7.18) this result is still valid when $<$ is replaced by $\le$ or $\le$ by $<$ in its left-hand member. Interpreted geometrically as in figure 7.5, the probability that a *continuous* rv lies between x_1 and x_2 *inclusive or exclusive* is equal to the *area under the graph of f between x_1* and x_2.

Observe that if $x_1 = x_2$, the area is zero, corresponding to the fact that *probability 0 is assigned to any particular exact value of $\tilde{x}$.*

Example 1 Let f be the rectangular df defined by (7.14) and let x_1 and x_2 be such that $a \le x_1 \le x_2 \le b$. Then

$$P(x_1 \le \tilde{x} \le x_2) = \int_{x_1}^{x_2} \frac{dx}{b-a} = \frac{x_2 - x_1}{b-a}.$$

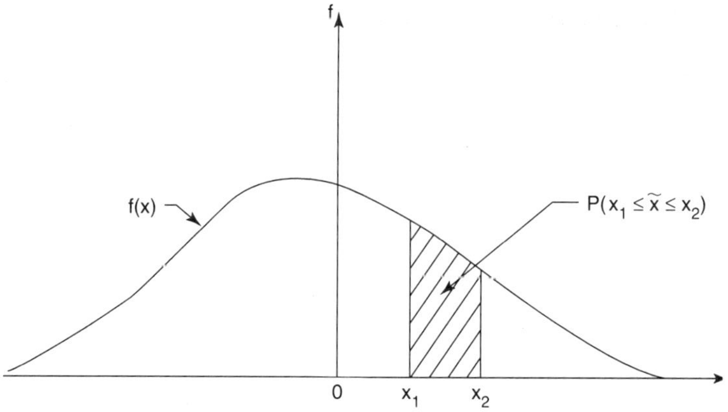

Figure 7.5
Density function and probability in an interval

The probability that x lies in $[x_1, x_2]$ when it must lie in $[a, b]$ is the ratio of the length of the former interval to the length of the latter.

Example 2 Let f be the triangular df defined by (7.15) and let x_1 and x_2 be such that $0 \le x_1 \le x_2 \le 1$. Then

$$P(x_1 \le \tilde{x} \le x_2) = \int_{x_1}^{x_2} 2x\,dx = x^2 \Big|_{x_1}^{x_2} = x_2^2 - x_1^2.$$

Example 3 Let f be the exponential df defined by (7.16) and let $0 \le x_1 \le x_2 < \infty$. Then

$$P(x_1 \le \tilde{x} \le x_2) = \int_{x_1}^{x_2} \lambda e^{-\lambda x}\,dx = -e^{-\lambda x}\Big|_{x_1}^{x_2} = e^{-\lambda x_1} - e^{-\lambda x_2}.$$

7.3.4 Cumulative Functions

If f is a density function, then the function F defined for all real x by

$$F(x) \equiv \int_{-\infty}^{x} f(t)\,dt \tag{7.20a}$$

will be called the *left-tail cumulative function* associated to f; and the function G defined for all real x by

$$G(x) \equiv \int_{x}^{\infty} f(t)\,dt \tag{7.20b}$$

will be called the *right-tail cumulative function* associated to f. Observe that

$$F(x) + G(x) = 1 \tag{7.21}$$

and contrast the corresponding relation (7.10) for the discrete case.

If f is the density of a rv $\tilde{x}$, then by (7.20), (7.12), and (7.18)

$$\begin{aligned} F(x) &= P(\tilde{x} \leq x) = P(\tilde{x} < x), \\ G(x) &= P(\tilde{x} \geq x) = P(\tilde{x} > x). \end{aligned} \tag{7.22}$$

Examples By the results of the examples in section 7.3.3 just above, we have the following relations among the rectangular, triangular, and exponential densities and their associated cumulative functions:

Domain	$f(x)$	$F(x)$	$G(x)$	Type
$[a, b]$	$\dfrac{1}{b-a}$	$\dfrac{x-a}{b-a}$	$\dfrac{b-x}{b-a}$	rectangular
$[0, 1]$	$2x$	x^2	$1-x^2$	triangular
$[0, \infty)$	$\lambda e^{-\lambda x}$	$1 - e^{-\lambda x}$	$e^{-\lambda x}$	exponential

7.3.5 Relation between Cumulative and Density Functions

By the definition (7.20a) of the left-tail cumulative function F, this function is the *integral* of the density function f. Differentiating both sides of the definition wrt (with respect to) x, we of course find that

$$f(x) = \frac{d}{dx} F(x);$$

the density function is the derivative of the left-tail cumulative function. Correspondingly,

$$P(x \leq \tilde{x} \leq x + \delta x) = F(x + \delta x) - F(x) = f(x)\delta x \quad (+\text{higher order terms}).$$

Interpreted geometrically, this means that

$$\text{large } f(x) \quad \Leftrightarrow \quad \text{steep } F(x),$$

$$\text{zero } f(x) \quad \Leftrightarrow \quad \text{flat } F(x).$$

It is especially important to keep these relations in mind when trying to understand a graph of F, since we think much more easily in terms of f than in terms of F.

7.3.6 Fractiles

Let $\tilde{x}$ be a continuous rv with left-tail cumulative function F, and let k be a real number in $[0, 1]$. A *k'th fractile* of the distribution of $\tilde{x}$ is any real number x_k that satisfies

$$F(x_k) = k. \tag{7.23}$$

If F is strictly monotone increasing, then x_k is unique for k in $[0, 1]$. Contrast the definition (7.11) for the discrete case, where the fact that F is a step function means that although most fractiles are unique, some are determined only within the interval between two successive possible values of the rv. Another contrast is that fractiles x_k may be equal for different values of k in the discrete case but not in the continuous case.

7.4 Mixed Random Variables

The most general type of random variable that we shall encounter in this course is one which has *both* a density *and* a mass function; a part $(1 - \lambda)$ of the total probability is spread out "continuously" over some interval or intervals on the real line, while the remaining part λ is assigned in "lumps" to a (finite or infinite) discrete set of values. The way of handling such mixed rv's is so obvious that we shall not go into details; it suffices to say that if f_1 is the mass function and f_2 is the density function then

$$P(\tilde{x} \le x) = \lambda \textstyle\sum_{t \le x} f_1(t) + (1 - \lambda) \displaystyle\int_{-\infty}^{x} f_2(t)\, dt, \tag{7.24}$$

and so forth.

7.5 Functions of Random Variables

7.5.1 Induced Probability Measures

Let $\tilde{x}$ be a rv and let φ be a function which assigns a single real value y to every real x; let

$$\tilde{y} \equiv \varphi(\tilde{x}). \tag{7.25a}$$

Since $P(\tilde{y} \le y)$ is defined for all real y by

$$P(\tilde{y} \le y) \equiv P(\tilde{x} \in X_y) \tag{7.25b}$$

where X_y is the set of all x such that $\varphi(x) \le y$, the unknown quantity $\tilde{y}$ is a rv provided that the set X_y has a P_x measure for all y. This will be the case if the function φ is reasonably well-behaved.

Example 1 Let

$$\tilde{y} = a\tilde{x} + b, \qquad a > 0.$$

Then

$$P(\tilde{y} \le y) = P\left(\tilde{x} \le \frac{y-b}{a}\right).$$

Example 2 Let

$$\tilde{y} = a\tilde{x} + b, \qquad a < 0.$$

Then

$$P(\tilde{y} \le y) = P\left(\tilde{x} \ge \frac{y-b}{a}\right).$$

Example 3 Let

$$\tilde{y} = \tilde{x}^2.$$

Then

$$P(\tilde{y} \le y) = P(-y^{1/2} \le \tilde{x} \le y^{1/2}).$$

7.5.2 Induced Mass and Density Functions

If the possible values of $\tilde{x}$ are *discrete*, then clearly the set of possible values of $\tilde{y}$ is finite or denumerable and the measure of $\tilde{y}$ will be wholly determined by a mass function.

It is not true, however, that if $\tilde{x}$ is continuous, then $\tilde{y}$ is necessarily continuous. Thus if φ is defined by

$$\varphi(x) \equiv \begin{cases} 0 & \text{if} \quad x \le 0, \\ 1 & \text{if} \quad x > 0, \end{cases}$$

then $\tilde{y} = \varphi(\tilde{x})$ is discrete regardless of the nature of the measure of $\tilde{x}$. If $\tilde{x}$ is continuous and φ is defined by

$$\varphi(x) \equiv \begin{cases} 0 & \text{if} \quad x \le 0, \\ x & \text{if} \quad x > 0, \end{cases}$$

then the measure of $\tilde{y} = \varphi(\tilde{x})$ will attach a mass equal to $P(\tilde{x} \le 0)$ to $(\tilde{y} = 0)$ and distribute the remaining probability continuously over values of $\tilde{y}$ greater than 0.

Provided that $\tilde{y}$ is continuous, its density can usually be found by writing down the formula for $P(\tilde{y} \le y)$ and differentiating wrt y. Thus let $\tilde{x}$ have density

$$f(x) = e^{-x}, \qquad 0 \le x < \infty, \tag{7.26a}$$

and let

$$\tilde{y} = \tilde{x}^{1/2}. \tag{7.26b}$$

Then

$$P(\tilde{y} \le y) = P(\tilde{x} \le y^2) = \int_0^{y^2} e^{-x}\, dx,$$

and since this is continuous and differentiable wrt y, $\tilde{y}$ has a density

$$g(y) = \frac{d}{dy} P(x \le y^2) = \frac{d}{dy}\left[\int_0^{y^2} e^{-x}\, dx\right] \qquad (7.26c)$$
$$= 2ye^{-y^2}.$$

7.6 Probability Assessments for a RV

7.6.1 Use of Judgmental Fractiles

In this section we shall consider one of many possible methods for assessing a probability distribution for some as yet unknown quantity $\tilde{\theta}$ of interest. We shall assume the true value of $\tilde{\theta}$ is some real number and set as our task the assessment of a left-tail cumulative function for $\tilde{\theta}$. We shall assume that $\tilde{\theta}$ is a continuous rv in the sense that for any value of θ, $P(\tilde{\theta} = \theta) = 0$ and $P(\tilde{\theta} \le \theta)$ can be represented as the area to the left of θ under some df.

We shall first introduce two preliminary definitions. Let $I_1, I_2, \ldots, I_m$ be m intervals. We shall say that these intervals are "equally likely" (with respect to $\tilde{\theta}$) if the decision maker is indifferent among the m lotteries $l_1, \ldots, l_i, \ldots, l_m$, where l_i gives a desirable consequence c^* if $\tilde{\theta} \in I_i$, and nothing otherwise. Given an interval I with left end point θ_l (possibly $-\infty$) and right end point θ_r (possibly $+\infty$), we shall say that the points θ_1, $\theta_2, \ldots, \theta_{n-1}$ where $\theta_1 < \theta_2 < \ldots < \theta_{n-1}$ *divide I into n* equally likely parts if the n intervals $[\theta_l, \theta_1]$, $[\theta_1, \theta_2], \ldots$, $[\theta_{n-2}, \theta_{n-1}]$, $[\theta_{n-1}, \theta_r]$ are equally likely.

The Method of Equally Likely Subintervals

Suppose we have already assessed a left-tail cumulative function F for $\tilde{\theta}$. The kth fractile of $\tilde{\theta}$, where $0 < k < 1$, will be designated by θ_k and is such that

$$P(\tilde{\theta} \le \theta_k) = F(\theta_k) = k.$$

Hence the generic point on the graph of F can be labelled by coordinates (θ_k, k). We now propos toereverse the procedure: Not being given F, we shall ask the decision maker to respond to a series of questions which will lead to a determination of θ_k values for such k as .5, .25, .75, .125, .375,

We then can plot these (θ_k, k) points and at some stage in the process we will obtain F by "fairing" a curve through (or possibly close to) these assessed points. Here is one way to generate (θ_k, k) points that we have found easy to apply.

Step 1 Find $\theta_{.5}$ by asking such a question as the following: "Thinking of the interval of all possible values that the unknown $\tilde{\theta}$ can assume, how would you divide this interval by a single cutting point into two equally likely subintervals? We are using the words 'equally likely' in the sense that you would just as soon receive a prize conditional on $\tilde{\theta}$ being in the left subinterval as on $\tilde{\theta}$ being in the right subinterval. In other words we are asking you for your judgmental 50-50 cutting point."

Step 2 Find $\theta_{.25}$ and $\theta_{.75}$ using either one of the two following procedures:

a. "How would you divide the interval to the left of $\theta_{.50}$ into two equally likely parts?" (This gives $\theta_{.25}$.) "How would you divide the interval to the right of $\theta_{.50}$ into two equally likely parts?" (This gives $\theta_{.75}$.)

b. "By means of 3 cutting points divide the possible values that $\tilde{\theta}$ can assume into 4 equally likely subintervals." (This gives $\theta_{.25}$, $\theta_{.50}$, and $\theta_{.75}$. Presumably $\theta_{.50}$ should agree with the answer obtained from step 1. If not, then this contradiction should be resolved by the modification of one of the answers.)

It should now be apparent how to proceed. The central idea is to ask the decision maker at any stage to subdivide a given interval (generated at a previous stage) into two judgmentally equally likely subintervals. How far should this procedure go? We have no pat answer for this. We advise plotting the (θ_k, k) points as they are generated until the shape of the F function becomes reasonably clear. If the problem requires careful assessment of probabilities in the tails of those distributions, then it might be wise to probe sequentially for such values as $\theta_{.25}, \theta_{.125}, \theta_{.0625}, \theta_{.03125}, \ldots$ and $\theta_{.75}, \theta_{.875}, \theta_{.9375}, \theta_{.96875}, \ldots$.

There is a point that needs to be emphasized here. We have suggested a procedure for generating a probability distribution for $\tilde{\theta}$ based on judgmental responses. At no point did we say how these responses are to be made. We definitely have in mind, however, that *the decision maker should attempt to utilize all the relevant information he has at hand which bears on* $\tilde{\theta}$. Some formal procedures for implementing this task in special cases will be developed later in the book.

7.6.2 Use of Historical Distributions of Relative Frequencies

There is one case where objective data bearing on $\tilde{\theta}$ is available and of such a form that it can be partially dealt with at this point by a mixture of

Table 7.1

Demand d	Number of occurrences	Relative frequency	Cumulative relative frequency
2	1	.063	.063
3	3	.187	.250
4	2	.125	.375
5	4	.250	.625
6	3	.187	.812
7	2	.125	.937
8	0	.000	.937
9	1	.063	1.000
10+	0	.000	1.000
	16	1.000	

formal and informal techniques. We shall illustrate this case by a simple example.

Suppose we are interested in the as yet unknown demand $\tilde{\theta}$ for a given product in the next time period. Suppose we have available a historical frequency distribution for demand in "similar periods" in the past as exhibited in table 7.1. There is a "dip" in the relative frequencies between demand for 3 units and demand for 5 units and another between 7 and 9 units. Before adopting a probability distribution for next period's demand which is a mere copy of this historical frequency distribution, we should ask ourselves whether such a distribution is reasonable in the light of whatever general knowledge we have of the factors affecting demand. This means that we must ask ourselves whether we would expect demand on a large number of periods "like" the next period to have a frequency distribution like that of table 7.1.

Under most circumstances almost any sensible person would answer immediately that it is not reasonable to expect demands for 7 and 9 units to occur with relative frequencies .125 and .063 while demands for 8 units never occur at all. Unless some definite, *assignable* cause can be found which *prevents* demands for 8 units, it is reasonable to believe that a long run of similar periods would produce demands for 8 units with a relative frequency somewhere *between* the frequencies of 7 and 9 units.

Similarly for the dip in relative frequency between 3 and 5 units: Unless a specific cause can be found to explain the dip, a reasonable person would be willing to bet that in a hypothetical long run the relative frequency of demands for 4 units would be between the frequencies for 3 and 5 units and would assign probabilities to next period's demand accordingly.

Finally, the fact that no demand for less than 2 or more than 9 units has occurred in the 16 days in the record is not in itself a proof that such

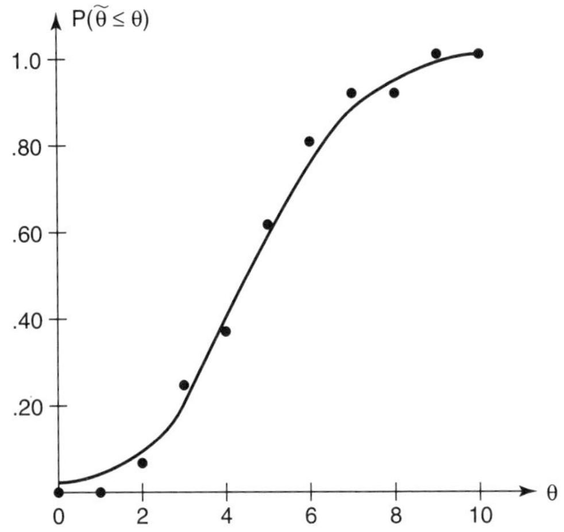

Figure 7.6
Smoothed cumulative distribution

demands are impossible, and a reasonable person might well want to assign them some small probability.

The above considerations lead to a need for smoothing out the irregularities in historical distributions of relative frequencies. We suggest the following in the way of partial advice for smoothing the historical cumulative distribution function. On ordinary graph paper for each value of θ on the horizontal axis plot the relative frequency $\hat{p}_\theta$ that past demands are less than or equal to θ. Based on these plotted points $(\theta, \hat{p}_\theta)$ draw in a smooth curve (for non-integral values of θ as well) keeping in mind the following points:

1. For $\hat{p}$ values close to 0 and to 1 there is very little information contained in the data, and no objective advice can take the place of your judgment in the particular situation, no matter how shaky that judgment may seem to you.
2. If $(\theta, \hat{p}_\theta)$ is a plotted point based on historical data where $\hat{p}_\theta$ is not close to 0 or 1, then the smoothed curve should pass "reasonably close" to the point $(\theta, \hat{p}_\theta)$.
3. If you take seriously the proposition that the long-run frequency distribution and therefore the probability distribution of demand should fall away smoothly on either side of a single most probable value, then the smoothed cumulative curve should be S-shaped and have its steepest ascent at the most probable value.

In figure 7.6 we plot points on the empirical cumulative distribution and then "fair" in a curve that seems to us to represent a reasonable

Table 7.2
Comparison of historical with smoothed relative frequencies

Demand d	Historical relative frequency	Historical cumulative	Smoothed cumulative: $P(\tilde{\theta} \leq \theta)$	Smoothed relative: $P(\tilde{\theta} = \theta)$
0	.000	.000	.005	.005
1	.000	.000	.020	.015
2	.063	.063	.090	.070
3	.187	.250	.230	.140
4	.125	.375	.400	.170
5	.250	.625	.610	.210
6	.187	.812	.800	.190
7	.125	.937	.900	.100
8	.000	.937	.960	.060
9	.063	1.000	.990	.030
10	.000	1.000	1.000	.010
10+	.000	1.000	1.000	.000
	1.000			1.000

compromise. In table 7.2 we compare the historical distribution of relative frequencies for events $(\tilde{\theta} = \theta)$ with P assessments for these events based on the *smoothed* cumulative function. For noninteger values of θ between 0 and 10, the smoothed value does not apply.

7.6.3 A Need for Analytical Procedures and Models

So far in this section we have discussed essentially two different types of procedures for the assessment of probability distributions. In section 7.6.1 the decision maker was asked, on the basis of all his current information about an unknown quantity $\tilde{\theta}$, say, to respond to a series of hypothetical questions such as "For what number θ^* do you think it is equally likely that $(\tilde{\theta} \leq \theta^*)$ and $(\tilde{\theta} > \theta^*)$?" On the basis of these responses we obtained numbers θ_k where $P(\tilde{\theta} \leq \theta_k) = k$, for a few values of k such as .50, .25, .75, and .125; next, we plotted those points with coördinates (θ_k, k) and faired in a smooth curve for the assessed cumulative probability distribution, $P(\tilde{\theta} \leq \theta)$. In section 7.6.2 we depended more on historical data and less on introspection. We argued that if the decision maker expected that the immediate future would be "like the past" then he might reasonably assess a cumulative distribution by possibly smoothing the cumulative historical relative frequency distribution. We now wish to point out some severe limitations of both these procedures.

In the decision problems we shall be concerned with in this book, the assessment of a probability distribution for some unknown quantity is not the end point of the analysis but typically a starting point. We shall be concerned with how the decision maker should combine such probability assessments with economic data in order to answer questions about whether it is desirable to sample or not before committing himself to an irrevocable action. In order for these problems to be fairly amenable to formal analysis without extensive computer programming or software, it is necessary to be able to express cumulative probability distributions in such a form that the full power of the calculus can be employed. If a cumulative probability distribution is given solely in terms of a graph, we will be hobbled by not being able to use some very powerful techniques of mathematical analysis. Many ideas and concepts are easier to understand and illustrate with formulas than with computers.

In many of the applications that we shall encounter it is often possible to argue cogently that for theoretical reasons the decision maker could choose with impunity a probability distribution from a well-specified family of probability distributions expressed in analytical form. The theory, however, might not be able to select a *particular* single probability distribution from this family, but usually the selection can be made in rational manner by asking the decision maker to respond to a few relatively simple hypothetical questions. It is tempting to try to give an illustration of what we have in mind, but with the limited tools and vocabulary we now have available it might be more confusing than helpful; we will give ample illustrations of this type of procedure starting in chapter 11.

Rather than smoothing the historical cumulative relative frequency distribution we shall show in chapter 11 and following that it often is convenient and appropriate to hypothesize a model which in principle is capable of generating data which is "qualitatively similar" to the observed historical data. Once again theory might be powerful enough to designate a model to help rationalize the data but it might not be able to specify values for critical parameters of the model. The Bernoulli process with parameter p, discussed briefly in chapter 5, is an example of the kind of model we have in mind. We shall show starting in chapter 11 how it is often possible with the aid of an accepted model to make effective use of the historical data, however sparse this data might be, in arriving at rational probability assessments of unknown quantities of interest.

Exercises

1. On the basis of what you already know, assess your own probability distribution for any two of the following quantities, which we presume are unknown to you:
   a. The Dow Jones Index one week hence
   b. The weight of your instructor in this course

c. The population of the city or town in which the course is given

d. The number of reported automobile fatalities in this state last year

e. The average length of time per day adults listen to TV on weekdays during this time of year

(Use the procedure discussed in sections 5.1.1 and 5.1.2.)

2. A certain product is stocked daily and a retailer knows at least approximately the effect which a variety of factors such as season, weather, and advertising exert on demand for this product; however, because no one combination of "values" of these factors is ever repeated exactly, he believes that it is impossible to build up a historical frequency distribution of demand on a number of "identical" days. Therefore, instead of looking at such a distribution before deciding how many units to order, he has based each order on a forecast of the next day's demand. The table below shows the record for the past 19 days of his forecast of demand and the demand which actually occurred; his forecast of tomorrow's demand is 100 units.

Day	Forecast	Demand	Day	Forecast	Demand
1	75	92	11	110	101
2	100	107	12	95	100
3	120	98	13	100	107
4	85	78	14	125	118
5	110	104	15	70	61
6	130	140	16	100	105
7	90	90	17	105	91
8	80	85	18	80	86
9	75	93	19	120	108
10	120	127			

On the basis of this record assess a probability distribution for tomorrow's demand.

3. There appears to be no pattern whatsoever in the daily demand for a given product. At the end of one day the manager notices that there are only 5 units left in stock and he puts in an order for 100 additional items. Demand for the item over the past 1,000 days has been as follows:

Number demanded	Number of occurrences	Number demanded	Number of occurrences
5	3	12	148
6	21	13	59
7	45	14	34
8	75	15	22
9	130	16	12
10	186	17	2
11	263		

a. Assuming that it takes one day to fill an order, assess a probability distribution for the number of unfilled orders tomorrow.

b. If there is a .4 chance that the order will take one day to fill and a .6 chance that it will take two days to fill, assess a probability distribution for the number of unfilled orders in the next two days. [Do this part as best you can. You will learn some techniques later that will help you in this assessment.]

4. For any two numbers x_1 and x_2 let $\max\{x_1, x_2\}$ denote the maximum of the two numbers and $\min\{x_1, x_2\}$ the minimum of the two numbers. Thus for example, $\max\{3, 7\} = 7$ and $\min\{3, 7\} = 3$, $\max\{3, -7\} = 3$ and $\min\{3, -7\} = -7$.

Let $\tilde{d}$ be the random variable designating the unknown demand for a product, let $\tilde{d}$ have the range and mass function given in the table below, and suppose the decision maker stocks 4 units.

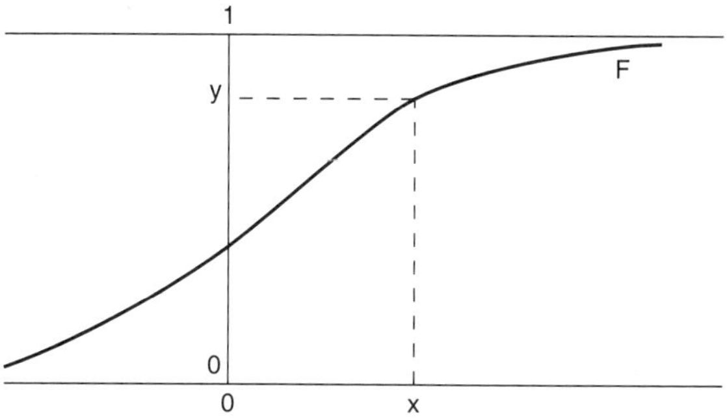

Figure 7E.1

Possible values of demand

d:	0	1	2	3	4	5	6	7
$P(\tilde{d} = d)$:	.05	.10	.15	.25	.20	.10	.10	.05

a. Interpret the rv $\tilde{y} = \max\{\tilde{d} - 4, 0\}$; give its mf.

b. Interpret the rv $\tilde{z} = \max\{4 - \tilde{d}, 0\}$; give its mf.

5. Let $\tilde{d}$ be the rv defined in problem 4 and define the random variable

$$\tilde{w} \equiv \max\{-4 + 2\tilde{d}, \tilde{d}\}.$$

Give the mf of $\tilde{w}$.

6. Let $\tilde{d}$ be the rv defined in problem 4. Assume that if $\tilde{d} = d$, monetary profit (in dollars) will be

$$v = \begin{cases} -4 + 3d & \text{if} \quad d \leq 4 \\ 8 & \text{if} \quad d > 4. \end{cases}$$

Since $\tilde{d}$ is a rv, so is $\tilde{v}$. Find the mf of $\tilde{v}$.

We recall some terminology used in chapter 3. A number y will be said to be drawn *canonically* from $[0, 1]$ if it is just as likely that y will fall in one interval as another of the same length. If $\tilde{y}$ denotes the as yet unknown canonically drawn number, then for any numbers a and b where $0 \leq a \leq b \leq 1$,

$$P(a \leq \tilde{y} \leq b) = b - a.$$

7. Consider a canonical experiment that can result in any real number y in the interval $[0, 1]$. What is the probability that y is *not* one of the numbers in $0, .1, .2, \ldots, .9, 1.0$?

8. Let f be a density function, let F be its associated left-tail cumulative function, and recall that the function F is a monotone increasing function of its argument and can assume all values in the interval $[0, 1]$. Now let a real number y be selected canonically from $[0, 1]$, and let x then be chosen such that $y = F(x)$. (See figure 7E.1.) Show that, if x is chosen in this manner, then (1) $P(a \leq \tilde{x} \leq b) = F(b) - F(a)$, for any a and b, and therefore (2) $\tilde{x}$ has the density f.

9. Let $\tilde{x}$ have a density function $f(x) = \lambda e^{-\lambda x}$, $x \geq 0$, $\lambda > 0$.

a. Show that if t and h are positive

$$P(\tilde{x} > t + h | \tilde{x} > h) = P(\tilde{x} > t).$$

b. If the rv $\tilde{x}$ denotes the as yet unknown waiting time for some particular event to happen (e.g., for a telephone call to terminate, for a light bulb to burn out, for a machine to break down), interpret the result in part (a).

Note If a continuous rv $\tilde{x}$ satisfies the property in part (a) for all t and h, then it can be shown that $\tilde{x}$ *must* have a density function of the form $f(x) = e^{-\lambda x}\lambda$ for some λ.

10. Find a formula for the kth fractile for each of the following density functions:

a. $f(x) = \dfrac{1}{b-a}$ for $a \le x \le b$;

b. $f(x) = 2x$ for $0 \le x \le 1$;

c. $f(x) = \lambda e^{-\lambda x}$ for $x \ge 0$.

11. Review the argument given in section 7.5.2, especially the result leading to (7.26c). In this exercise this result will be generalized.

Let $\tilde{x}$ have the df f; let $y = \varphi(x)$ or $x = \psi(y)$; let g be the df of $\tilde{y}$ (provided it exists); denote $\frac{d}{dy}\psi(y)$ by $\psi'(y)$ and assume the derivative exists. Show that

a. If $\psi'(y) > 0$ for all y, then

$$g(y) = \frac{d}{dy}P(\tilde{y} \le y) = f[\psi(y)]\psi'(y);$$

b. If $\psi'(y) < 0$ for all y, then

$$g(y) = \frac{d}{dy}P(\tilde{y} \le y) = -f[\psi(y)]\psi'(y);$$

c. If ψ or φ is monotone increasing or decreasing (i.e., case a or b holds) then

$$g(y) = f[\psi(y)]\,|\psi'(y)|.$$

d. Suppose φ is not monotonic but that the x-axis can be partitioned into a finite number of intervals $X_1, X_2, \ldots, X_m$ in such a manner that φ is monotone in each of these intervals. For $x \in X_i$ let

$$y = \varphi_i(x) \quad \text{and} \quad x = \psi_i(y).$$

Now, using the result

$$P(\tilde{y} \le y) = \sum_{i=1}^{m} P(\tilde{y} \le y \text{ and } \tilde{x} \in X_i),$$

show that

$$g(y) = \sum_{i=1}^{m} f[\psi_i(y)]\,|\psi_i'(y)|.$$

12. Show that the nullity assumption of section 7.1.5 rules out the three pathological examples given there.

13. a. In the analysis of the oil drilling problem described and analyzed in figure 6.2, the optimal strategy for experimentation and action will result in an uncertain monetary amount, which can be considered a rv $\tilde{x}$. Describe $\tilde{x}$ and draw its mf.

b. Let $\tilde{\pi}$ denote the uncertain preference index which will result in this situation. Describe the rv $\tilde{\pi}$ and draw its mf.

8 Continuous Lotteries and Expectations

8.1 Reduction of Lotteries with an Infinity of Consequences

8.1.1 Review

In an informal presentation in chapter 2 and a more formal presentation in chapter 3 we proved the following result:

Let $\Theta = \{\theta_1, \ldots, \theta_m\}$ be a set of mutually exclusive and collectively exhaustive real-world elementary events; let $P(\tilde{\theta} = \theta_i)$ be the decision maker's probability assignment for the event $(\tilde{\theta} = \theta_i)$ according to Basic Assumption 2b;[1] let l be a lottery which results in consequence $l(\theta_i)$ if event $(\tilde{\theta} = \theta_i)$ obtains; let $\pi[l(\theta_i)]$ be the decision maker's indifference probability assignment for the consequence $l(\theta_i)$ according to Basic Assumption 2a; let

$$\Pi = \textstyle\sum_{i=1}^{m} \pi[l(\theta_i)]P(\tilde{\theta} = \theta_i). \tag{8.1}$$

Then according to Basic Assumptions 1–4 the decision maker should be indifferent between l and the basic reference lottery which gives a canonical chance Π at c^* and a complementary chance at c_*.

The lottery l described in the above paragraph will result in some consequence which has an associated π-utility. Before the lottery is conducted, this π value is unknown and can be treated as a discrete rv $\tilde{\pi}$. It can take on the value $\pi[l(\theta_i)]$ with probability $P(\tilde{\theta} = \theta_i)$. The value Π defined in (8.1) will be called later the *expectation* of $\tilde{\pi}$ and the latter part of this chapter will be devoted to a development of the concept of expectation.

In many of the applications to follow in later chapters it will be convenient to assume that an unknown quantity $\tilde{\theta}$ can take on any one of an unlimited number of possible values and that the lottery l has an infinity of possible consequences. In this section we shall analyze such lotteries and show that some additional, very reasonable, basic assumptions allow us to reduce such a lottery to an equivalent basic reference lottery where the formula (8.1) for Π is replaced by an infinite sum or an integral; furthermore, we state wherever possible sufficient conditions for the validity of the reduction in terms of the existence (or convergence) of these infinite sums or integrals. We will not strive for complete generality but we will attempt to justify fully the reduction for each case that arises in the sequel.

As an example of such a lottery, consider a problem where it is natural to describe the elementary uncertain event by the (idealized) long-run relative frequency θ with which a given production process generates defective items. It is reasonable to imagine that the unknown $\tilde{\theta}$ can assume *any* real value from 0 to 1 inclusive. To be sure, the monetary consequences of the

1. Throughout this book we use the terms "basic assumption" and "axiom" interchangeably.

available acts may depend only on the number of defective items among the next 1,000 produced, say, and it would theoretically be possible to exclude the continuous variable θ from the discussion entirely. However, this would greatly increase the psychological difficulty of the probability assessment problem and greatly complicate the mathematics as well.

As another example, consider the result of an accurate measurement: the number of possible outcomes is finite but extremely large. Here too we may find it convenient to introduce a continuous variable, this time as an approximation to a physical variable already in the problem. (In the previous paragraph we introduced an idealized variable which was unobservable and could have been excluded.) The point is that it is much easier conceptually and mathematically to deal with quantities that are assumed to vary continuously over the continuum of real numbers than with some astronomically large but finite number of alternatives. The motivation for going to the infinite idealization is compelling, but if we adopt this idealization, then we should investigate carefully the rules we use to manipulate these idealized quantities.

For the convenience of the reader we summarize here in rather loose terms the Basic Assumptions made in chapter 3.

Basic Assumption 1 Let $\tilde{\gamma}$ and $\tilde{\delta}$ denote two as yet undisclosed numbers that have been canonically drawn from $[0, 1]$; let $\tilde{\theta}$ be the unknown, true, real-world, elementary event. The unknown $\tilde{\gamma}$, $\tilde{\delta}$, $\tilde{\theta}$ are completely unrelated to each other in the sense that knowledge about the true values of one or two of these does not give any information about the remainder. By "canonical" we mean that we would rather obtain a desirable prize conditional on the pair $(\tilde{\gamma}, \tilde{\delta})$ lying in one subset than in another subset of the unit square if and only if the first subset has greater area than the second—regardless of where these two subsets are located.

Basic Assumption 2 Let c^* and c_* represent two basic reference consequences and let the symbol $\langle\alpha\rangle$, where $0 \leq \alpha \leq 1$, be the lottery which gives c^* with canonical chance α and c_* with canonical chance $1 - \alpha$.

a. There is a real-valued function π defined on the set of consequences such that the decision maker is indifferent between any consequence c and $\langle\pi(c)\rangle$.

b. There is a real-valued function P defined on subsets of Θ such that the decision maker is indifferent between the lottery which gives c^* if Θ_0 occurs, c_* otherwise, and the lottery $\langle P(\Theta_0)\rangle$, for all subsets $\Theta_0 \subset \Theta$.

Basic Assumption 3 Preferences for lotteries, insofar as they exist, are transitive.

Basic Assumption 4 Let $\tilde{q}$ be any one of three arguments $\tilde{\theta}$, $\tilde{\gamma}$, $\tilde{\delta}$; let lotteries $l'_1, \ldots, l'_i, \ldots, l'_n$ and $l''_1, \ldots, l''_i, \ldots, l''_n$ not depend on $\tilde{q}$—that is, $\tilde{q}$ is an inactive argument in these lotteries; let the events $(\tilde{q} \in Q_1), \ldots, (\tilde{q} \in Q_n)$ be mutually exclusive and collectively exhaustive; let l' be the lottery which gives prize l'_i if $(\tilde{q} \in Q_i)$; let l'' be the lottery which gives prize l''_i if $(\tilde{q} \in Q_i)$. Then

$$[l'_i \sim l''_i \text{ for all } i] \quad \Rightarrow \quad l' \sim l''.$$

8.1.2 Additional Basic Assumptions

One of the bases of our reduction of lotteries with an infinity of possible consequences will be the following extension of our original Basic Assumption 4:

Basic Assumption 4*

a. (*Dominance*). If l' and l'' are two lotteries such that for *every* triplet of values (θ, γ, δ) the consequence of l'' is at least as desirable as the consequence of l', then l'' is at least as desirable as l'. Symbolically:

$$\left.\begin{matrix} l'(\theta,\gamma,\delta) \precsim l''(\theta,\gamma,\delta) \\ \text{for all } (\theta,\gamma,\delta) \end{matrix}\right\} \quad \Rightarrow \quad l' \precsim l''.$$

b. (*Continuous Substitution*). Let l be a lottery whose consequence depends on θ alone (i.e., γ and δ are inactive); let l' be a lottery whose consequence depends only on θ and γ (i.e., δ is inactive) which is defined by

$$l'(\theta,\gamma) = \begin{cases} c^* & \text{if} \quad \gamma \leq \pi[l(\theta)] \\ c_* & \text{if} \quad \gamma > \pi[l(\theta)] \end{cases};$$

then

$$l \sim l'.$$

Remarks on Part b If the event $(\tilde{\theta} = \theta)$ occurs, lottery l gives the *certain* consequence $l(\theta)$, and in the opinion of the decision maker this consequence is indifferent to a canonical chance of $\pi[l(\theta)]$ at c^* and a complementary chance at c_*. If the event $(\tilde{\theta} = \theta)$ occurs, the consequence of lottery l', on the other hand, is still *uncertain* since it depends on the canonically drawn value of $\tilde{\gamma}$; the consequence will be c^* if $\tilde{\gamma} \leq \pi[l(\theta)]$—that is, with canonical chance $\pi[l(\theta)]$—and it will be c_* otherwise. Hence no matter what event $(\tilde{\theta} = \theta)$ occurs, lotteries l and l' appear to be indifferent. The very reasonable assumption of continuous substitution says that the decision maker is indifferent between the lottery l and l' without knowing what event $(\tilde{\theta} = \theta)$ will indeed occur.

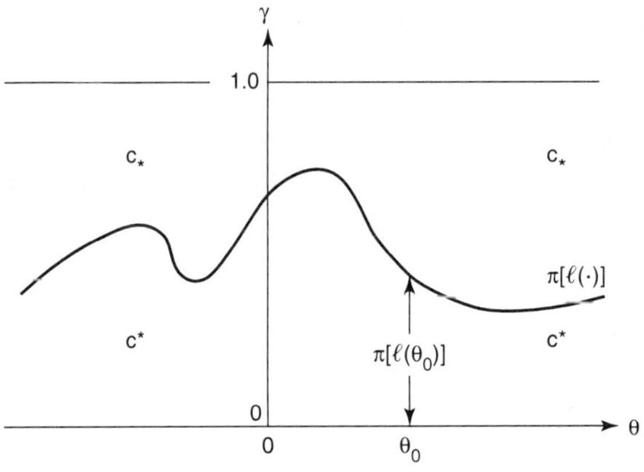

Figure 8.1
Reduction of continuous lottery to reference consequences

The lottery l' can be given a very suggestive pictorial representation for the case where θ can assume any value on the real line. In figure 8.1 we plot on θ, γ axes the curve $\pi[l(\theta)]$ as a function of θ. If $(\tilde{\theta} = \theta)$ and $(\tilde{\gamma} = \gamma)$, lottery l' gives payoff c^* if the point (θ, γ) is below or on the curve and gives c_* if the point is above the curve. In order to reduce l' to a basic reference lottery involving c^* and c_* we somehow have to evaluate the probability that the unknown pair $(\tilde{\theta}, \tilde{\gamma})$ will fall on or below the curve. A methodological difficulty arises since $\tilde{\theta}$ can assume a continuum of values and all the results we have proved so far involved *finite* partitions of Θ.

If the $\pi[l(\cdot)]$ function were a step function like the kind exhibited in figure 8.2, then we would know how to reduce l' to an equivalent basic reference lottery. In particular suppose that $\{\Theta_0, \ldots, \Theta_n\}$ is a finite partition of Θ and that

$$l'(\theta, \gamma) = \begin{cases} c^* & \text{if} \quad \theta \in \Theta_i \text{ and } \gamma \leq \gamma_i, \\ c_* & \text{if} \quad \theta \in \Theta_i \text{ and } \gamma > \gamma_i. \end{cases}$$

Then by the application of the results of chapters 2 and 3, l' is indifferent to the basic reference lottery $\langle \Pi' \rangle$ where

$$\Pi' = \textstyle\sum_i \gamma_i P(\tilde{\theta} \in \Theta_i).$$

The procedure we shall follow in order to reduce or evaluate a lottery of the type given in figure 8.1 is to approximate the function $\pi[l(\cdot)]$ more and more closely by step functions of the type shown in figure 8.2. More specifically we shall show how to "squeeze in" on the function $\pi[l(\cdot)]$ by a sequence of pairs of step functions which undercut and overcut $\pi[l(\cdot)]$ (see figure 8.3). Let l' be related to l as stated in part (b) of Basic Assumption 4.

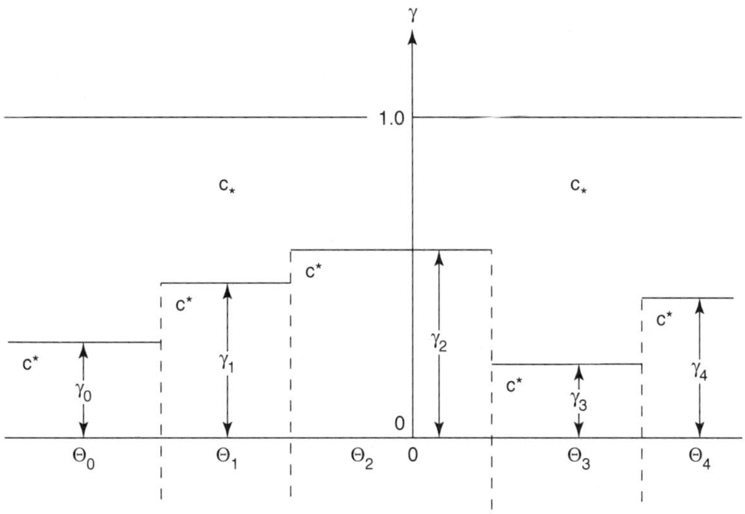

Figure 8.2
Step-function lottery

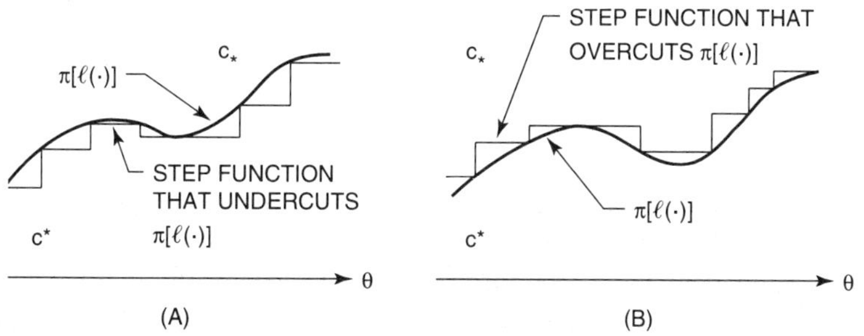

Figure 8.3
Undercutting and overcutting step functions

Let l_n^- be the nth lottery in a sequence of undercuts. The fact that it is an undercut means (see figure 8.3A)

$$l_n^-(\theta,\gamma) = c_* \quad \text{whenever} \quad l'(\theta,\gamma) = c_*.$$

Therefore $l_n^-(\theta,\gamma) \precsim l'(\theta,\gamma)$ for all (θ,γ), whence $l_n^- \precsim l'$ by the dominance part of Basic Assumption 4*. Letting Π_n^- be the number such that $l_n^- \sim \langle \Pi_n^- \rangle$ we have

$$\langle \Pi_n^- \rangle \sim l_n^- \precsim l' \sim l.$$

In a similar manner, let l_n^+ be the nth lottery in a sequence of overcuts, so that (see figure 8.3B)

$$l_n^+(\theta,\gamma) = c^* \qquad \text{whenever} \qquad l'(\theta,\gamma) = c^*.$$

Then $l_n^+(\theta,\gamma) \gtrsim l'(\theta,\gamma)$ for all (θ,γ), whence $l_n^+ \gtrsim l'$ by the dominance part of Basic Assumption 4*. Letting Π_n^+ be the number such that $l_n^+ \sim \langle \Pi_n^+ \rangle$, we have

$$\langle \Pi_n^+ \rangle \sim l_n^+ \gtrsim l' \sim l.$$

By transitivity we thus obtain the "squeeze"

$$\langle \Pi_n^- \rangle \lesssim l \lesssim \langle \Pi_n^+ \rangle.$$

This indicates what use we will be able to make of the next behavioral assumption.

Basic Assumption 6 (Continuity) If

$$\langle \Pi_n^- \rangle \lesssim l \lesssim \langle \Pi_n^+ \rangle, \qquad n = 1, 2 \ldots$$

and

$$\lim \Pi_n^- = \lim \Pi_n^+ = \Pi$$

then

$$l \sim \langle \Pi \rangle.$$

8.1.3 Special Reduction Formulas

On the basis of all of our basic assumptions we can *prove* that any lottery l, with possibly an infinity of different consequences, can be reduced to an equivalent basic reference lottery $\langle \Pi \rangle$, where the number Π, of course, depends on l. This assertion seems so very plausible that we were tempted at one point to use this assertion as a basic assumption in lieu of Basic Assumption 6 (continuity) and to prove that assumption as an immediate result. But Basic Assumption 6 seems to demand a bit less from the behavioral point of view. As a result of our assumptions, we shall show in the next subsection not only that to every l there *exists* an equivalent $\langle \Pi \rangle$ but also how to derive a formula for Π. In this subsection we shall give a statement of results for the determination of Π for the important cases we shall consider in later chapters. Throughout this section we assume that l is a lottery that gives consequence $l(\theta)$ if $(\tilde{\theta} = \theta)$.

We shall assume that $\tilde{\theta}$ is a random variable (rv) and consider three special cases for $\tilde{\theta}$: discrete, continuous, and mixed. For each of these cases we shall state a formula for Π but we shall defer all proofs to the next subsection where we shall show that all these results are special cases of a much more general reduction formula.

Case 1 (Discrete) Let $\tilde{\theta}$ be a discrete rv with mf f; in other words, let

a. $P(\tilde{\theta} = \theta) = f(\theta)$,

b. $f(\theta) \geq 0$, and $=$ holds except at valucs $\theta_1, \theta_2, \ldots$,

c. $\sum_i f(\theta_i) = 1$.

Let

$$\Pi \equiv \sum_i \pi[l(\theta_i)] f(\theta_i). \tag{8.2}$$

Then

$l \sim \langle \Pi \rangle$.

Case 2 (Continuous) Let $\tilde{\theta}$ be a continuous rv with df f; in other words,

a. $P(\tilde{\theta} \leq \theta) = \int_{-\infty}^{\theta} f(t)\, dt$

(where the integral is assumed to exist in the Riemann sense),

b. $f(t) \geq 0$ for all t,

c. $\int_{-\infty}^{\infty} f(t)\, dt = 1$.

Let

$$\Pi \equiv \int_{-\infty}^{\infty} \pi[l(\theta)] f(\theta)\, d\theta, \tag{8.3}$$

where the integral is assumed to exist (again in the Riemann sense). Then

$l \sim \langle \Pi \rangle$.

Case 3 (Mixed) Let f_1 be a mf and f_2 a df and assume $\tilde{\theta}$ is such that for any θ,

$$P(\tilde{\theta} \leq \theta) \equiv \lambda \sum_{-\infty}^{\theta} f_1(t) + (1 - \lambda) \int_{-\infty}^{\theta} f_2(t)\, dt, \tag{8.4}$$

where the sum is understood to be taken over all θ_i such that $\theta_i \leq \theta$ and $f_1(\theta_i) > 0$, and where $0 < \lambda < 1$. Let

$$\Pi \equiv \lambda \sum_{-\infty}^{\infty} \pi[l(\theta)] f_1(\theta) + (1 - \lambda) \int_{-\infty}^{\infty} \pi[l(\theta)] f_2(\theta)\, d\theta, \tag{8.5}$$

where the sum is taken over all θ_i such that $f_1(\theta_i) > 0$. Then

$l \sim \langle \Pi \rangle$.

In case 3, if $\lambda = 1$, we get case 1; if $\lambda = 0$, we get case 2.

8.1.4 General Reduction Formulas and Proofs[2]

All the results in this section are consequences of the following principal theorem:

Theorem 1 (General Reduction Formula) Let Θ be an arbitrary set of elements (possibly infinite); let h be a function from Θ to $[0,1]$; let l' be defined by

$$l'(\theta,\gamma) \equiv \begin{cases} c^* & \text{if} \quad \gamma \le h(\theta), \\ c_* & \text{if} \quad \gamma > h(\theta), \end{cases}$$

and let

$$\Theta_{i,n} \equiv \left\{\theta : \frac{i}{2^n} \le h(\theta) < \frac{i+1}{2^n}\right\} \quad \text{for} \quad \begin{cases} i = 0, 1, \ldots, 2^n, \\ n = 1, 2, \ldots. \end{cases} \tag{8.6}$$

Then

$$l' \sim \langle \Pi \rangle \quad \text{where} \quad \Pi = \lim \textstyle\sum_{i=0}^{2^n} \frac{i}{2^n} P(\Theta_{i,n}) \tag{8.7}$$

and the limit always exists.

The limit in (8.7) is usually written as

$$\Pi = \int_{\Theta} h(\theta)\, dP(\theta)$$

and is known as the *Lebesgue integral* of h with respect to P measure.

Proof For any i and n as in (8.6) define

$$l_n^-(\theta,\gamma) \equiv \begin{cases} c^* & \text{if} \quad \gamma \le \frac{i}{2^n} & \text{and} \quad \theta \in \Theta_{i,n}, \\ c_* & \text{if} \quad \gamma > \frac{i}{2^n} & \text{and} \quad \theta \in \Theta_{i,n}, \end{cases}$$

$$l_n^+(\theta,\gamma) \equiv \begin{cases} c^* & \text{if} \quad \gamma \le \frac{i+1}{2^n} & \text{and} \quad \theta \in \Theta_{i,n}, \\ c_* & \text{if} \quad \gamma > \frac{i+1}{2^n} & \text{and} \quad \theta \in \Theta_{i,n}. \end{cases}$$

Then by Basic Assumption 4* (Dominance)

2. The material in this section requires more mathematical preparation than is needed in the remainder of the book.

$l_n^-(\theta, \gamma) \precsim l'(\theta, \gamma) \precsim l_n^+(\theta, \gamma).$

Since

a. $l_n^- \sim \langle \Pi_n^- \rangle$ where $\Pi_n^- = \sum_{i=0}^{2^n} \frac{i}{2^n} P(\Theta_{i,n}),$

b. $l_n^+ \sim \langle \Pi_n^+ \rangle$ where $\Pi_n^+ = \sum_{i=0}^{2^n} \frac{i+1}{2^n} P(\Theta_{i,n}),$

c. $\{\Pi_n^-\}$ is an *increasing* sequence,

d. $\{\Pi_n^+\}$ is *decreasing* sequence,

e. $\Pi_n^+ - \Pi_n^- = \frac{1}{2^n}$ and therefore $\lim (\Pi_n^+ - \Pi_n^-) = 0,$

it follows that the limit in (8.7) exists and the theorem follows by Basic Assumption 6 (Continuity). ■

If one does not wish to assert that all subsets of Θ have P-measure, then some restrictions have to be placed on the function h to obtain the above result. If we assume that each of the sets $\Theta_{i,n}$ has P-measure, that all finite unions and intersections of sets that have P-measure also have P-measure, and that the complement of any set that has P-measure also has P-measure, then the result stated above is valid without restrictions.

Corollary If the lottery l is defined on Θ with consequence $l(\theta)$ for $\theta \in \Theta$ (i.e., l depends only on θ), then

$$l \sim \langle \Pi \rangle \quad \text{where} \quad \Pi = \int_{\Theta} \pi[l(\theta)]\, dP(\theta). \tag{8.8}$$

Proof By Basic Assumption 4*b (Continuous Substitution), $l \sim l'$ where l' is the lottery defined in the above theorem with $h(\theta) = \pi[l(\theta)]$. The result follows now from the general formula of Theorem 1.

The reduction formula (8.8) reduces respectively to (8.2), (8.3), and (8.5) in cases 1, 2 and 3 of section 8.1.3. This is a standard mathematical result which will not be proved here. ■

8.2 Expectations

8.2.1 Unified Notation for Sums and Integrals

For reasons which will become apparent immediately we can avoid a great deal of repetition by the following definitions. Let φ be any function defined on the real line and let P_x be the measure of a rv $\tilde{x}$. (1) If $\tilde{x}$ is *discrete* with mf f, then

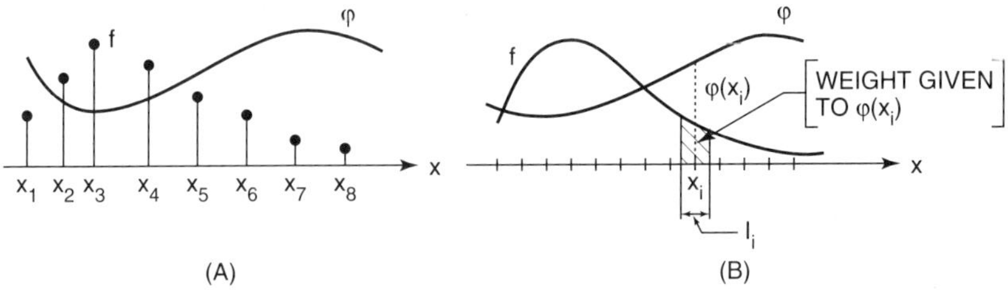

Figure 8.4
Discrete and continuous weighted averages

$$\int \varphi(x)\, dP_x \equiv \sum \varphi(x) f(x), \tag{8.9a}$$

where the sum is over all x for which f is positive. (2) If $\tilde{x}$ is *continuous* with df f, then

$$\int \varphi(x)\, dP_x \equiv \int \varphi(x) f(x)\, dx, \tag{8.9b}$$

where the integral on the right is over the entire real line. (3) If $\tilde{x}$ is *mixed*, where the mf f_1 is given a weight λ and the df f_2 is given a weight $(1 - \lambda)$, then

$$\int \varphi(x)\, dP_x \equiv \lambda \sum \varphi(x) f_1(x) + (1 - \lambda) \int \varphi(x) f_2(x)\, dx, \tag{8.9c}$$

where the sum and integral are over the same sets as before.

An interpretation of (8.9) for the cases where $\tilde{x}$ has a mf and a df respectively can be seen graphically from figure 8.4. In case $\tilde{x}$ has a mf as in figure 8.4A, $\int \varphi(x)\, dP_x$ is obtained by taking the values of φ where $\tilde{x}$ has a positive mass—in this case $\varphi(x_1)$, $\varphi(x_2), \ldots, \varphi(x_8)$—and taking a weighted average of these values by weighting them respectively by $f(x_1)$, $f(x_2), \ldots$, $f(x_8)$. These weights are, of course, all positive and add to one. In case $\tilde{x}$ has a df as in figure 8.4B, $\int \varphi(x)\, dP_x$ can once again be thought of as a continuous weighted average of the φ function where the weights are supplied by the f function. More precisely, the expression $\int \varphi(x)\, dP_x$ can be approximated by (1) dividing the x-axis into subintervals of I_1, $I_2, \ldots$, $I_i, \ldots, I_n$ of fine mesh, (2) for all i, choosing an x_i-value in subinterval I_i and computing $\varphi(x_i)$, and (3) taking a weighted average of these $\varphi(x_i)$ values where the weight given to $\varphi(x_i)$ is the area under f in the range of I_i. By the definition of f, these weights are nonnegative and add to one. The true value of $\int \varphi(x)\, dP_x$ is a limit of these approximations as the subdividing mesh becomes finer and finer assuming of course that this limit exists.

8.2.2 Expectation of a Random Variable

Let $\tilde{x}$ be a discrete, continuous, or mixed rv with measure P_x. The *expectation* or *mean* of $\tilde{x}$ is defined to be

$$\bar{x} \equiv E(\tilde{x}) \equiv \int x\,dP_x \tag{8.10}$$

provided that the expression on the right as defined by (8.9) converges absolutely; if it does not, we shall say that the expectation of $\tilde{x}$ does not exist.

The term "expected value" is sometimes used instead of "expectation" but will be avoided in this book as being excessively misleading. Notice that in both the first two examples below the expectation of the rv is *not* equal to a possible value of the rv.

Example 1 Let $\tilde{x}$ be a rv with mf f defined by (7.5). Then

$$\bar{x} \equiv E(\tilde{x}) = 1(.2) + 2(.5) + 5(.3) = 2.7.$$

Example 2 Let $\tilde{x}$ be a rv with f defined by (7.6). Then

$$\bar{x} \equiv E(\tilde{x}) = \textstyle\sum_{i=0}^{9} i(.1) = 4.5.$$

Example 3 Let $\tilde{x}$ be a rv with mf f defined by (7.7). Then

$$\begin{aligned}\bar{x} \equiv E(\tilde{x}) &= \textstyle\sum_X x(\frac{1}{2})^x = \sum_{i=1} i(\frac{1}{2})^i \\ &= 1(\tfrac{1}{2}) + 2(\tfrac{1}{4}) + 3(\tfrac{1}{8}) + \ldots = 2,\end{aligned}$$

where the last equality can be found (exercise 1) at the end of this chapter.

Example 4 Let X be the set of positive integers and let the rv $\tilde{x}$ have a mf f defined by

$$f(x) = \begin{cases} \dfrac{1}{x(x+1)} & \text{if} \quad x \in X, \\ 0 & \text{if} \quad x \notin X. \end{cases}$$

Then it can be shown that $\sum_X f(x) = 1$, so that f is a valid mass function; but also $\sum_X xf(x)$ diverges, so that the expectation of $\tilde{x}$ does not exist.

Example 5 Let the rv $\tilde{x}$ have the rectangular density defined by (7.14). Then

$$\bar{x} \equiv E(\tilde{x}) = \int_a^b \frac{x}{b-a}\,dx = \frac{a+b}{2}.$$

Example 6 Let the rv $\tilde{x}$ have the exponential density defined by (7.16). Then

$$\bar{x} \equiv E(\tilde{x}) = \int_0^\infty x\lambda e^{-\lambda x}\,dx = -\left(x + \frac{1}{\lambda}\right)e^{-\lambda x}\Big|_0^\infty = 1/\lambda.$$

8.2.3 Expectation of a Function of a Random Variable

Let $\tilde{x}$ be a rv with measure P_x and let φ be a real-valued function on the real line. Assume $\tilde{y} \equiv \varphi(\tilde{x})$ is a rv with induced measure P_y as discussed in section 7.5.1; by (8.10)

$$E\varphi(\tilde{x}) \equiv E(\tilde{y}) \equiv \int y\,dP_y. \tag{8.11}$$

If, however, all that we want to know about $\tilde{y} \equiv \varphi(\tilde{x})$ is its mean, we can avoid the trouble of computing P_y by using the alternative formula

$$E\varphi(\tilde{x}) = \int \varphi(x)\,dP_x. \tag{8.12}$$

We shall give examples of the two methods of computation before discussing the proof of their equivalence in some important special cases.

Example 1 Let $\tilde{x}$ be a rv with mf f defined by (7.5) and let

$\tilde{y} = \varphi(\tilde{x}) = x^2.$

Then formula (8.12) gives

$$E\varphi(\tilde{x}) = \int \varphi(x)\,dP_x = 1^2(.2) + 2^2(.5) + 5^2(.3) = 9.7$$

directly, whereas to use formula (8.11) we must first evaluate the mf of $\tilde{y}$,

$$g(y) = \begin{cases} .2 & \text{if} \quad y = 1^2 = 1, \\ .5 & \text{if} \quad y = 2^2 = 4, \\ .3 & \text{if} \quad y = 5^2 = 25, \end{cases}$$

and then compute

$$E\varphi(\tilde{x}) = \int y\,dP_y = 1(.2) + 4(.5) + 25(.3) = 9.7.$$

Example 2 Let $\tilde{x}$ be a rv with density f defined by (7.15) and let

$\tilde{y} = \varphi(\tilde{x}) = \tilde{x}^2.$

From formula (8.12) we can obtain directly

$$E\varphi(\tilde{x}) = \int_0^1 x^2 2x\,dx = \tfrac{1}{2}.$$

To use formula (8.11) we must first proceed as in section 7.5.2 to find the probability measure of $\tilde{y}$. We have

$$P(\tilde{y} \le y) = P(\tilde{x} \le y^{1/2}) = \int_0^{y^{1/2}} 2x\,dx.$$

Since this is continuous and differentiable, y has a density

$$g(y) = \frac{d}{dy}\int_0^{y^{1/2}} 2x\,dx = (\tfrac{1}{2}y^{-1/2})(2y^{1/2}) = 1, \qquad 0 \le y \le 1;$$

from this we have by (8.11)

$$E\varphi(\tilde{x}) = E(\tilde{y}) = \int_0^1 yg(y)\,dy = \tfrac{1}{2}.$$

Proof of the Equivalence When $\tilde{x}$ is Discrete It is very easy to prove that the right-hand sides of (8.11) and (8.12) are equal when $\tilde{x}$ is discrete. If $\tilde{x}$ is discrete, then $\tilde{y}$ can assume at most a denumerable number of values; denote its possible values by $y_1, \ldots, y_i, \ldots$, and let X_i be the set of all x such that $\varphi(x) = y_i$. Then

$$P(\tilde{y} = y_i) = P(\tilde{x} \in X_i) = \textstyle\sum_{X_i} f(x),$$

so that the right-hand side of (8.11) can be written

$$\textstyle\sum_i y_i \sum_{X_i} f(x) = \sum_i \sum_{X_i} y_i f(x),$$

and the right-hand side of this expression is obviously equivalent to

$$\textstyle\sum_X \varphi(x) f(x),$$

which is the right-hand side of (8.12).

Proof of the Equivalence When $\tilde{y}$ is Discrete We have seen in section 7.5.2 that $\tilde{y}$ may be discrete even though $\tilde{x}$ is not. We leave it to the reader (exercise 11) to show that only minor modifications are required to extend the proof given above to this more general case.

Proof of the Equivalence When $\tilde{y}$ is Not Discrete A proof of the equivalence of (8.11) and (8.12) is sketched in exercise 10 for the important special case where (a) $\tilde{x}$ has a df, and (b) the domain of $\tilde{x}$ can be partitioned into a finite number of intervals such that in each of these intervals the function φ is monotone; this special case will be general enough to satisfy all our needs in the remainder of the book.

8.2.4 Expectations of Special Functions

From (8.12) it is easy to show (exercise 2) that if a and b are constants, then

$$E(a) = a, \tag{8.13a}$$

$$E(b\tilde{x}) = bE(\tilde{x}). \tag{8.13b}$$

It is also easy to show, again from (8.12), that, if φ_1 and φ_2 are any two functions each of which assigns a single real value to every real x, then

$$E[\varphi_1(\tilde{x}) + \varphi_2(\tilde{x})] = E\varphi_1(\tilde{x}) + E\varphi_2(\tilde{x}), \tag{8.14}$$

provided that both the expectations on the right exist. From (8.13) and (8.14) we obtain the very frequently used result for *linear* functions

$$E(a + b\tilde{x}) = a + bE(\tilde{x}). \tag{8.15}$$

8.3 Variance of a Random Variable

8.3.1 Definition of Variance and Standard Deviation

Let $\tilde{x}$ be a rv. Then the quantity denoted

$$\breve{x} \equiv V(\tilde{x}) \equiv E(\tilde{x} - \bar{x})^2 \tag{8.16}$$

will be called the *variance* of $\tilde{x}$. The quantity denoted

$$\ddot{x} \equiv S(\tilde{x}) \equiv [V(\tilde{x})]^{1/2} = [E(\tilde{x} - \bar{x})^2]^{1/2} \tag{8.17}$$

will be called the *standard deviation* of $\tilde{x}$.

8.3.2 Direct Computation of Variance

The quantity $(\tilde{x} - \bar{x})^2$ which appears in (8.16) is a function of the random variable $\tilde{x}$, and therefore it follows from (8.12) that if P_x is the measure of $\tilde{x}$, then

$$\breve{x} \equiv V(\tilde{x}) = \int (x - \bar{x})^2 \, dP_x. \tag{8.18}$$

Observe that the variance is the *mean* of the *squares* of the *differences* between (1) each individual x and (2) the mean $\bar{x}$ of all the x's.

Example 1 Let $\tilde{x}$ be a rv with mf f defined by (7.5). Then since $\bar{x} = 2.7$, as shown in section 8.2.2, the variance of $\tilde{x}$ is

$$\breve{x} \equiv V(x) = (1 - 2.7)^2\,(.2) + (2 - 2.7)^2\,(.5) + (5 - 2.7)^2\,(.3) = 2.41$$

and the standard deviation of $\tilde{x}$ is

$$\ddot{x} = \sqrt{2.41} = 1.55.$$

Example 2 Let $\tilde{x}$ be a rv with mf f defined by (7.6). Then since $\bar{x} = 4.5$, as shown in section 8.2.2,

$$\check{x} \equiv V(\tilde{x}) = \textstyle\sum_{i=0}^{9} (i - 4.5)^2 (.1) = 8.25,$$

$$\ddot{x} \equiv S(\tilde{x}) = \sqrt{8.25} = 2.87.$$

Example 3 Let $\tilde{x}$ be a rv with mf f defined by (7.7). Then since $\bar{x} = 2$, as shown in section 8.2.2,

$$\check{x} \equiv V(\tilde{x}) = \textstyle\sum_{i=1}^{\infty} (i - 2)^2 (\frac{1}{2})^i = 2$$

as may be proved by extending exercise 1 or by taking $p = \frac{1}{2}$ in (9.134), and

$$\ddot{x} \equiv S(\tilde{x}) = \sqrt{2} = 1.41.$$

Example 4 Let $\tilde{x}$ be a rv with rectangular density f defined by (7.14). Then since $\bar{x} = \frac{1}{2}(a + b)$, as shown in section 8.2.2,

$$\check{x} \equiv V(\tilde{x}) = \int_a^b \left[x - \frac{1}{2}(a + b)\right]^2 \frac{1}{b - a}\,dx = \frac{1}{12}(b - a)^2,$$

and

$$\ddot{x} \equiv S(\tilde{x}) = \sqrt{1/12}(b - a) = .289(b - a).$$

Example 5 Let $\tilde{x}$ be a rv with exponential density f defined by (7.16). Then, since $\bar{x} = 1/\lambda$, as shown in section 8.2.2,

$$\begin{aligned}\check{x} \equiv V(\tilde{x}) &= \int_0^{\infty} (x - 1/\lambda)^2 \lambda e^{-\lambda x}\,dx \\ &= -(x - 1/\lambda)^2 \lambda e^{-\lambda x}\Big|_0^{\infty} + \int_0^{\infty} 2(x - 1/\lambda)\lambda e^{-\lambda x}\,dx \\ &= 1/\lambda^2,\end{aligned}$$

and

$$\ddot{x} \equiv S(\tilde{x}) = 1/\lambda.$$

8.3.3 Indirect Computation of Variance

Let $\tilde{x}$ be a rv with measure P_x. Then by (8.16)

$$\begin{aligned}\check{x} \equiv V(\tilde{x}) &\equiv E(\tilde{x} - \bar{x})^2 = E(\tilde{x}^2 - 2\tilde{x}\bar{x} + \bar{x}^2) \\ &= E(\tilde{x}^2) - E(2\tilde{x}\bar{x}) + E(\bar{x}^2)\end{aligned}$$

$$= E(\tilde{x}^2) - 2\bar{x}E(\tilde{x}) + \bar{x}^2$$

$$= E(\tilde{x}^2) - E^2(\tilde{x}), \qquad \text{where } E^2(\tilde{x}) \equiv [E(\tilde{x})]^2. \tag{8.19}$$

In many applications it is easier to compute $E(\tilde{x}^2)$ and then use (8.19) to compute the variance than it is to compute the variance directly from (8.18).

Example 1 Let $\tilde{x}$ be a rv with mf f defined by (7.5). Then by (8.12)

$$E(\tilde{x}^2) = \sum_x x^2 f(x) = 1^2(.2) + 2^2(.5) + 5^2(.3) = 9.7;$$

since $E(\tilde{x}) = 2.7$, as shown in section 8.2.2, by (8.19)

$$V(\tilde{x}) = E(\tilde{x}^2) - E^2(\tilde{x}) = 9.7 - 2.7^2 = 2.41$$

in agreement with the result obtained by direct computation in section 8.3.2.

8.3.4 Variance of a Linear Function

Let $\tilde{x}$ be a rv and let

$$\tilde{y} = a + b\tilde{x}.$$

Then it follows from (8.16), (8.15) and (8.13) that

$$V(\tilde{y}) = b^2 V(\tilde{x}).$$

8.4 Functions Defined as Expectations

In the analysis of decision problems we frequently encounter certain functions that are defined as expectations of other functions.

8.4.1 Partial Expectations

In contrast to the (complete) expectation of a rv $\tilde{x}$, given by (8.10), *the left-hand partial expectation* (up to ξ) and the *right-hand partial expectation* (from ξ on) of a rv $\tilde{x}$ are defined by

$$E^{(l)}(\xi) \equiv \int_{-\infty}^{\xi} x\, dP_x, \tag{8.20a}$$

$$E^{(r)}(\xi) \equiv \int_{\xi}^{\infty} x\, dP_x. \tag{8.20b}$$

In (8.20) we use the convention that if $\tilde{x}$ has a mf, then the end point ξ is *included* in the summation.

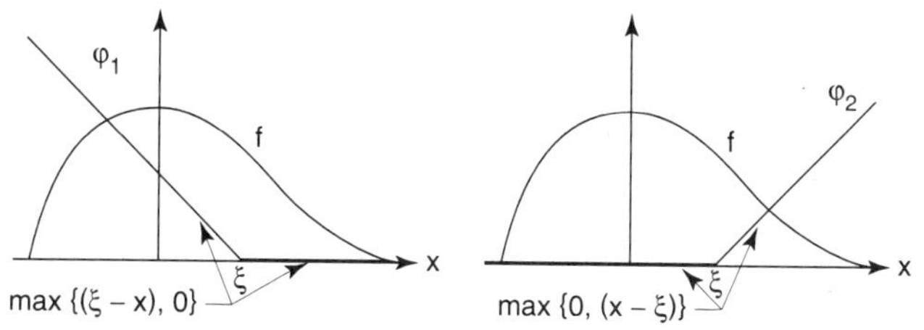

Figure 8.5
Linear loss functions

The reader is asked to show (exercise 9) that

$$E^{(l)}(\xi) + E^{(r)}(\xi) = \begin{cases} E(\tilde{x}), & \text{if } \tilde{x} \text{ has a df,} \\ E(\tilde{x}) + \xi f(\xi), & \text{if } \tilde{x} \text{ has a mf.} \end{cases} \tag{8.21}$$

8.4.2 Linear Loss Functions

Let $\tilde{x}$ have a mf or a df f, let ξ be any number (to be held fixed in this subsection). Define the functions, graphed in figure 8.5,

$$\varphi_1(x) \equiv \begin{cases} \xi - x, & \text{if } x \le \xi, \\ 0, & \text{otherwise,} \end{cases} \qquad \varphi_2(x) \equiv \begin{matrix} x - \xi, & \text{if } x \ge \xi, \\ 0, & \text{otherwise.} \end{matrix} \tag{8.22a}$$

In terms of the max operator these functions can be expressed as follows:

$$\varphi_1(x) = \max\{\xi - x, 0\}, \qquad \varphi_2(x) = \max\{x - \xi, 0\}. \tag{8.22b}$$

In terms of these functions we define the left- and right-hand *linear loss* functions by

$$L^{(l)}(\xi) \equiv E\max\{\xi - \tilde{x}, 0\} = \int_{-\infty}^{\xi} (\xi - x)\,dP_x, \tag{8.23a}$$

$$L^{(r)}(\xi) \equiv E\max\{\tilde{x} - \xi, 0\} = \int_{\xi}^{\infty} (x - \xi)\,dP_x. \tag{8.23b}$$

The reader can easily verify that

$$\varphi_1(x) - \varphi_2(x) = \xi - x$$

and taking expectations of both sides, we get

$$L^{(l)}(\xi) - L^{(r)}(\xi) = \xi - E(\tilde{x}), \tag{8.24a}$$

or

$$L^{(l)}(\xi) = L^{(r)}(\xi) + (\xi - \bar{x}). \tag{8.24b}$$

In chapter 9 we develop formulas for $L^{(r)}(\xi)$ for the principal types of distributions we shall encounter in this book. In chapter 12 we indicate the central role that the L functions play in the analysis of an important class of decision problems.

The reader is asked to show (exercise 9) that the $L^{(r)}$ and $L^{(l)}$ functions can be expressed in terms of the $E^{(r)}$ and $E^{(l)}$ functions as follows:

$$L^{(l)}(\xi) = \xi F(\xi) - E^{(l)}(\xi), \tag{8.25a}$$

$$L^{(r)}(\xi) = E^{(r)}(\xi) - \xi G(\xi). \tag{8.25b}$$

In chapter 9 we develop formulas for $E^{(r)}(\xi)$ for the principal types of distributions we shall encounter in this book.

8.5 Reduction of Lotteries Using the Expectation Operator

In section 8.1 we showed that if l is a lottery whose consequence depends on $\tilde{\theta}$ alone, then by (8.8),

$$l \sim \langle \Pi \rangle, \quad \text{where} \quad \Pi = \int_{\Theta} \pi[l(\theta)]\, dP(\theta)$$

where the integral on the right reduces to (8.2) if $\tilde{\theta}$ is a discrete rv, to (8.3) if $\tilde{\theta}$ is a continuous rv, and to (8.4) if $\tilde{\theta}$ is a mixed rv. From the results of section 8.2 we can also think of Π as the expectation of the composite function $\pi l(\cdot)$ of the rv $\tilde{\theta}$, viz.:

$$\Pi = E\{\pi[l(\tilde{\theta})]\}. \tag{8.26}$$

The expectation operator is taken with respect to the measure P_θ.

If $l(\tilde{\theta})$ is an as-yet-unknown monetary amount $\tilde{x}$, then we can say that l has monetary payoff $\tilde{x}$ with probability measure P_x, where P_x is induced from P_θ (cf. section 7.5.1). We then could write

$$\Pi = E[\pi(\tilde{x})], \tag{8.27}$$

where the expectation operator is taken with respect to the measure P_x.

Finally, we can think of the as yet unknown $\tilde{\pi}$ value of the lottery. We can say that l has a utility value $\tilde{\pi}$ with probability measure P_π where P_π is induced from P_θ or P_x. We could then write

$$\Pi = E(\tilde{\pi}), \tag{8.28}$$

where the expectation operator is taken with respect to P_π.

Exercises

1. (Result needed for example 3 of section 8.2.2).
   From the identity

$$\frac{1}{1-y} = 1 + y + y^2 + \dots, \qquad (|y| < 1)$$

show that

$$\frac{1}{(1-y)^2} = 1 + 2y + 3y^2 + \dots,$$

and therefore

$\sum_{i=1}^{\infty} i(\frac{1}{2})^i = 2.$

2. Prove (8.13), (8.14), and (8.15).

3. For any rv x which has a mf or a df and for which $E(x)$ exists, show that

$E(\tilde{x} - \bar{x}) = 0.$

4. Show that

$E(\tilde{x} - a)^2 = V(\tilde{x}) + (\bar{x} - a)^2$

provided that $V(\tilde{x})$ exists. From this argue that the function

$h(a) \equiv E(\tilde{x} - a)^2$

is minimized by setting $a = \bar{x}$.
Hint $E(\tilde{x} - a)^2 = E[(\tilde{x} - \bar{x}) + (\bar{x} - a)]^2$.

5. Prove the result in section 8.3.4; i.e.,

$V(a + b\tilde{x}) = b^2 V(\tilde{x})$.

6. Let $\tilde{x}$ be a rv with mf f where

x	-3	-2	0	1	2	3
$f(x)$	.05	.15	.30	.25	.10	.15

Let $\tilde{y} = |\tilde{x}|$.

$$\left(\text{Note.} \quad |x| = \begin{cases} x & \text{if} \quad x \geq 0 \\ -x & \text{if} \quad x < 0 \end{cases}.\right)$$

Find $E(\tilde{y})$ using (8.11) and (8.12) and check that they give the same result.

7. Let $\tilde{x}$ have the rectangular density function over the interval $[a, b]$. Find $E^{(r)}(\xi)$, $E^{(l)}(\xi)$, $L^{(r)}(\xi)$, $L^{(l)}(\xi)$ and verify (8.21), (8.24), and (8.25) for this special case.

8. Let $\tilde{x}$ have the exponential density defined by

$f(x) \equiv e^{-\lambda x}\lambda, \qquad 0 \leq x < \infty.$

a. Plot f against x.
b. Find $\bar{x}$, $\check{x}$, $E^{(r)}(\xi)$, and $L^{(r)}(\xi)$; find $E^{(l)}(\xi)$ and $L^{(l)}(\xi)$ from (8.21) and (8.24).

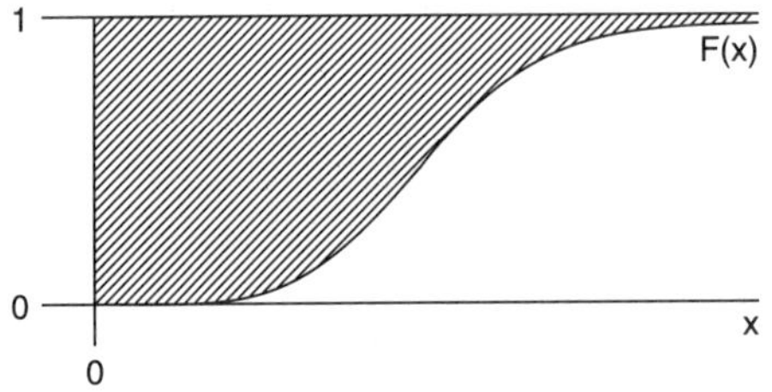

Figure 8E.1

Remark The following formulas can be found in tables of integrals:

$$\int e^{ax}\,dx = \frac{1}{a}e^{ax}$$

$$\int xe^{ax}\,dx = e^{ax}\left(\frac{x}{a} - \frac{1}{a^2}\right)$$

$$\int x^2e^{ax}\,dx = e^{ax}\left(\frac{x^2}{a} - \frac{2x}{a^2} + \frac{2}{a^3}\right)$$

9. Prove (8.21) and (8.25).

10. In this exercise we will outline the proof showing the equivalence of (8.11) and (8.12) for the important special case where $\tilde{y} = \varphi(\tilde{x})$, y has a df g, $\tilde{x}$ has a df f. In this case we must prove

$$\int_{-\infty}^{\infty} yg(y)\,dy = \int_{-\infty}^{\infty} \varphi(x)f(x)\,dx. \tag{A}$$

a. Let φ be a monotonic function and define ψ such that $x = \psi(y)$. In the integral on the right-hand side of (A) make a change of variable $x = \psi(y)$. We then get

$$\int_{-\infty}^{\infty} \varphi(x)f(x)\,dx = \int_{-\infty}^{\infty} yf[\psi(y)]\,|\psi'(y)|\,dy$$

and using the result of part (c) of exercise 11 of chapter 7 we get the left-hand side of (A).

b. Suppose φ is not monotonic but that the x-axis can be partitioned into a finite number of intervals $x_1, x_2, \ldots, x_m$ in such a manner that φ is monotone in each of these intervals. For $x \in X_i$, let

$$y = \varphi_i(x) \quad \text{and} \quad x = \psi_i(y).$$

Prove (A) for this case using part (d) of exercise 11 of chapter 7.

11. Modify the proof given in section 8.2.3 to the case where $\tilde{y}$ is discrete, even though $\tilde{x}$ is not.

12. Let $\tilde{x}$ have left-tail cumulative function F.

a. Show that $L^{(l)}(x) = \int_{-\infty}^{x} F(y)\,dy$ and $L^{(r)}(x) = \int_{x}^{\infty} [1 - F(y)]\,dy$.

b. Use one of these formulas to show that, if $F(0) = 0$, then $E(\tilde{x})$ is the shaded area in figure 8E.1

13. Show that, for any random variable $\tilde{x}$ and nonnegative function g

a. $Eg(\tilde{x}) = \int_0^\infty P(g(\tilde{x}) > t)\,dt$;

b. $\int_{-\infty}^{\infty} g(x)\,dx = \int_0^\infty G(t)\,dt$ where $G(t)$ is the total length or Lebesgue measure of the set $\{x : g(x) > t\}$, that is, $G(t) = \int_{-\infty}^{\infty} I(x, t)\,dx$ where $I(x, t) = 1$ if $g(x) > t$, $I(x, t) = 0$ otherwise.

c. What happens if g may have negative values?

9 Special Univariate Distributions

9.1 Introduction

In this chapter we will present in a formal style with a minimum of motivation the basic univariate mass and density functions that we shall encounter in this book. The chapter is written somewhat in the form of a catalogue where many of the useful formulas about specific distributions needed at later stages in the book are collected in one place for easy reference. This will simplify the presentation of material given in later chapters because it will not be necessary then to cut into the mainstream of the development with digressions about relevant distribution theory. The material of this chapter utilizes only the concepts and notations of the previous two chapters and thus it gives the reader many concrete examples in analytical form of mass and density functions and their related expectations, variances, and linear loss functions. We give some information about tables that were historical landmarks, but do not attempt to describe the abundant, constantly developing supply of computer programs, algorithms, and approximations available. Convenient, accurate calculator approximations are given by Peizer and Pratt (1968) and Ling and Pratt (1984); see also Alramowitz and Stegun (1964), Blyth (1986), Ling (1978), Maindonald (1984), Molenaar (1970), and, for exact calculation, current statistical computer packages and their documentation.

The order of presentation of distributions in this chapter follows very closely the order in which they appear in the remainder of the book. As a footnote to each section of this chapter we indicate where the reference material developed in that section is first used in later chapters.

9.2 Mathematical Preliminaries: Complete Beta and Gamma Functions

We define the following functions:

Complete Beta Function

$$B(\rho, \sigma) \equiv \int_0^1 t^{\rho-1}(1-t)^{\sigma-1}\,dt, \qquad \rho > 0,\ \sigma > 0. \tag{9.1}$$

Complete Gamma Function

$$\Gamma(\rho) \equiv \int_0^\infty t^{\rho-1}e^{-t}\,dt, \qquad \rho > 0. \tag{9.2}$$

The following standard results on beta and gamma functions can be found in books on calculus. For the reader who wishes to prove these results for herself we suggest that she follow the order given.

$$\Gamma(1) = 1, \tag{9.3}$$

$$\Gamma(\rho) = (\rho - 1)\Gamma(\rho - 1), \qquad \rho > 1, \tag{9.4}$$

$$\Gamma(n) = (n - 1)!, \qquad n \text{ integral}, \tag{9.5}$$

$$\frac{\Gamma(\rho)}{a^\rho} = \int_0^\infty v^{\rho-1} e^{-av}\, dv, \tag{9.6}$$

$$B(\rho, \sigma) = B(\sigma, \rho), \tag{9.7}$$

$$B(\rho, \sigma) = \frac{\Gamma(\rho)\Gamma(\sigma)}{\Gamma(\rho + \sigma)}, \tag{9.8}$$

$$B(\tfrac{1}{2}, \tfrac{1}{2}) = \pi, \tag{9.9}$$

$$\Gamma(\tfrac{1}{2}) = \sqrt{\pi}, \tag{9.10}$$

$$\int_{-\infty}^{\infty} e^{-(1/2)u^2}\, du = \sqrt{2\pi}. \tag{9.11}$$

9.3 The Beta Distribution[1]

9.3.1 Introduction

In an important class of decision problems we shall be concerned with situations where the unknown quantity of interest $\tilde{p}$ is some number between 0 and 1. For example, $\tilde{p}$ might represent the unknown proportion of members of a given population who have a given attribute; or $\tilde{p}$ might represent the unknown long-run proportion of defective items in a production process. In problems of this kind it is often appropriate and convenient to assess a df for $\tilde{p}$ from the so-called *beta* family. This family of distributions has two adjustable parameters ρ and ν and by appropriately choosing these parameters a wide variety of different shapes can be attained.

The function f_β of three arguments defined by

$$f_\beta(p|\rho, \nu) \equiv \frac{1}{B(\rho, \sigma)} p^{\rho-1}(1 - p)^{\sigma-1}, \qquad \begin{array}{l} 0 \le p \le 1, \\ \sigma \equiv \nu - \rho, \\ \rho, \sigma > 0, \end{array} \tag{9.12}$$

1. The material of this section will be needed for chapters 11–14.

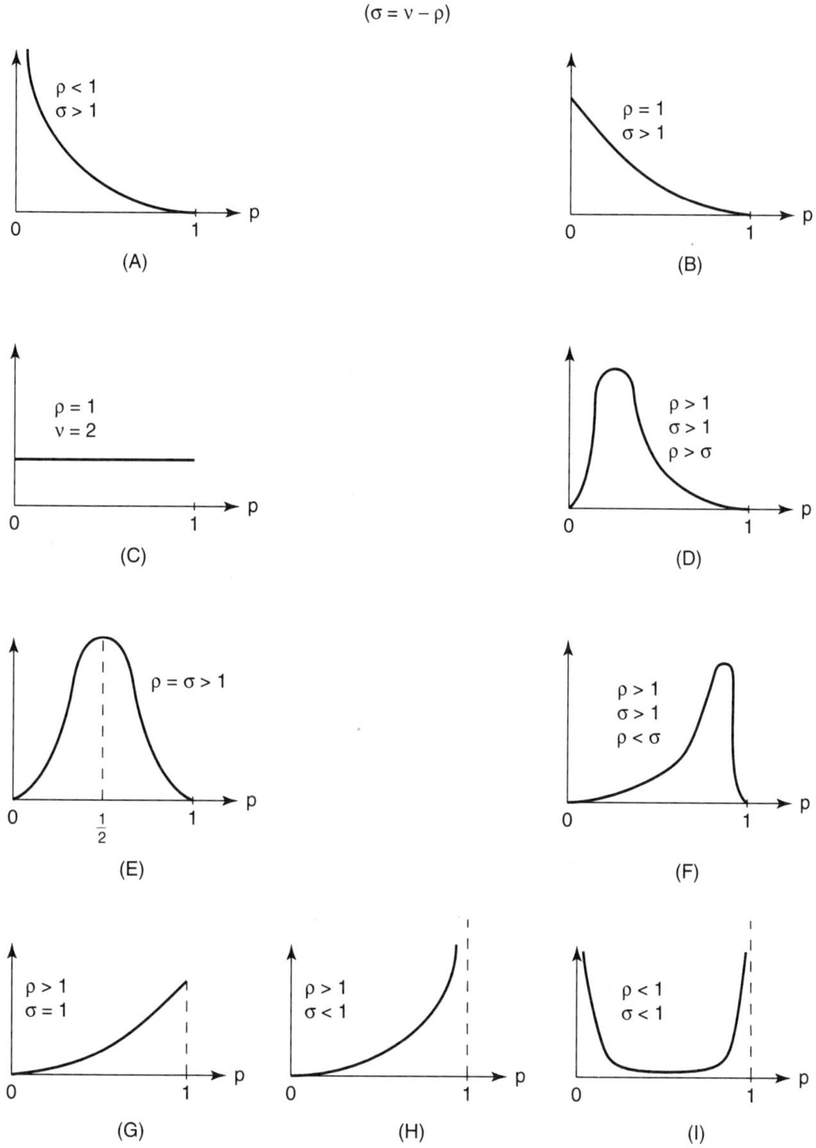

Figure 9.1
Beta density shapes

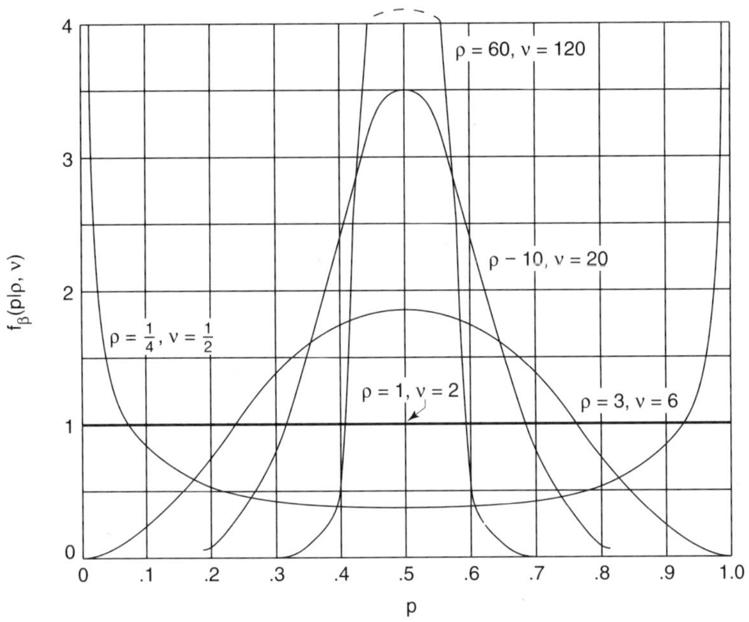

Figure 9.2
Symmetric beta densities

where $B(\rho, \sigma)$ is the complete beta function given in (9.1), is called a *beta* df with parameter (ρ, ν); any rv with a df of the form (9.12) will be called a *beta* rv with parameter (ρ, ν).

9.3.2 Graphs and Tables

Graphs of various beta density functions are shown in figures 9.1, 9.2, and 9.3.

The left- and right-tail cumulative functions defined by

$$\left.\begin{aligned} F_\beta(p|\rho, \nu) &\equiv \int_0^p f_\beta(t|\rho, \nu)\,dt, \\ G_\beta(p|\rho, \nu) &\equiv \int_p^1 f_\beta(t|\rho, \nu)\,dt \end{aligned}\right\} \quad 0 \le p \le 1, \tag{9.13}$$

cannot be evaluated in terms of elementary functions (except in special cases) but their values can be found from tables. The classical and most extensive tables appear in K. Pearson (1934), which gives

$$I_x(p, q) \equiv F_\beta(x|p, p + q),$$

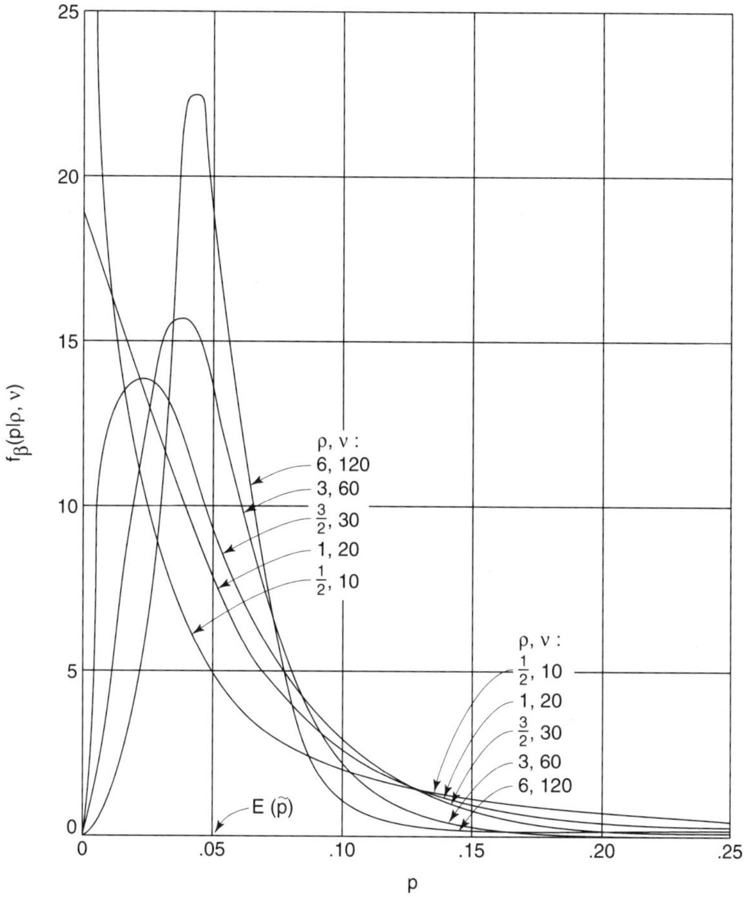

Figure 9.3
Beta densities with mean .05

to 7 decimal places for

$$p, q = .5(.5)10(1)50, \qquad p \geq q, \qquad x = .01(.01)1.$$

To use these tables we look up

$$\begin{aligned} F_\beta(p|\rho, \nu) &= I_p(\rho, \nu - \rho) \qquad \text{if} \quad \rho \geq \tfrac{1}{2}\nu, \quad \rho \leq 50, \\ G_\beta(p|\rho, \nu) &= I_{1-p}(\nu - \rho, \rho) \qquad \text{if} \quad \rho \leq \tfrac{1}{2}\nu, \quad \nu - \rho \leq 50. \end{aligned} \tag{9.14}$$

Values of F_β and G_β can also be found from tables of the binomial[2]

2. The binomial function will be discussed in section 9.4.

right-tail cumulative function G_b via the following relations which hold for any integral ρ and v, as proved in exercise 9,

$$F_\beta(p|\rho, v) = G_b(\rho|v - 1, p),$$
$$G_\beta(p|\rho, v) = G_b(v - \rho|v - 1, 1 - p). \tag{9.15}$$

An "inverse" table showing p for selected values of $F_\beta(p|\rho, v)$—that is, a table of selected *fractiles* of the distribution of $\tilde{p}$—is given at the end of this book.

9.3.3 Expectations

The reader is asked to prove as exercises the following propositions for a rv $\tilde{p}$ that has a beta df with parameter (ρ, v):

$$E_\beta(\tilde{p}|\rho, v) \equiv \bar{p} = \frac{\rho}{v},$$
$$V_\beta(\tilde{p}|\rho, v) \equiv \breve{p} = \frac{\rho(v - \rho)}{v^2(v + 1)} = \frac{\bar{p}(1 - \bar{p})}{v + 1}, \tag{9.16}$$

$$E_\beta^{(l)}(p|\rho, v) = \bar{p}F_\beta(p|\rho + 1, v + 1),$$
$$E_\beta^{(r)}(p|\rho, v) = \bar{p}G_\beta(p|\rho + 1, v + 1), \tag{9.17}$$

$$L_\beta^{(l)}(p|\rho, v) = pF_\beta(p|\rho, v) - \bar{p}F_\beta(p|\rho + 1, v + 1),$$
$$L_\beta^{(r)}(p|\rho, v) = \bar{p}G_\beta(p|\rho + 1, v + 1) - pG_\beta(p|\rho, v). \tag{9.18}$$

9.4 The Binomial Distribution[3]

9.4.1 Introduction

The function f_b of three arguments, defined by

$$f_b(r|n, p) \equiv C_r^n p^r (1 - p)^{n-r}, \qquad 0 \le p \le 1, \quad r, n = 0, 1, 2, \ldots, \quad r \le n, \tag{9.19}$$

where

$$C_r^n \equiv \frac{n!}{r!(n - r)!}, \tag{9.20}$$

3. The material of this section will be needed for chapter 14.

will be said to be a *binomial* mf with parameter (n, p); any rv with mf (9.19) will be called a *binomial* rv with parameter (n, p).

The reader is asked to show as an exercise that

$$\sum_{r=0}^{n} f_b(r|n, p) = 1, \tag{9.21}$$

so that f_b is a proper mf.

9.4.2 Tables

The binomial cumulative functions F_b and G_b, defined by

$$\begin{aligned} F_b(r|n, p) &\equiv \sum_{i=0}^{r} f_b(i|n, p), \\ G_b(r|n, p) &\equiv \sum_{i=r}^{n} f_b(i|n, p), \end{aligned} \tag{9.22}$$

are cumbersome to evaluate directly but many tables of their values exist. The most convenient complete table, unfortunately out of print, is U.S. Army (1952), which gives G_b to 7 decimal places for

$$n = 1\ (1)\ 150; \qquad p = .01\ (.01)\ .50; \qquad r = 0\ (1)\ n.$$

Another table, less complete for $n < 150$ but more accessible, is Harvard University (1955), which gives G_b to 5 decimal places for

$$n = 1\ (1)\ 50\ (2)\ 100\ (10)\ 200\ (20)\ 500\ (50)\ 1000; \qquad r = 0\ (1)\ n;$$

$$p = .01\ (.01)\ .50, \tfrac{1}{12}\ (\tfrac{1}{12})\ \tfrac{5}{12}, \tfrac{1}{16}\ (\tfrac{1}{16})\ \tfrac{7}{16}.$$

In using these tables it is often necessary to employ the following very simple results:

$$\begin{aligned} F_b(r|n, p) &= 1 - G_b(r + 1|n, p), \\ f_b(r|n, p) &= G_b(r|n, p) - G_b(r + 1|n, p) \\ &= F_b(r|n, p) - F_b(r - 1|n, p), \\ F_b(r|n, p) &= G_b(n - r|n, 1 - p); \end{aligned} \tag{9.23}$$

this last result is important because it makes it sufficient to tabulate G_b only for $p \leq .50$.

Tables of the binomial mass function (table MT-12R) are included in the back of this book. They show f_b to four decimal places for

$$n = 1\ (1)\ 20, 50, 100; \qquad r = 0\ (1)\ n; \qquad p = .01\ (.01)\ 1.0.$$

9.4.3 Expectations

The reader is asked to prove as exercises the following propositions for a rv $\tilde{r}$ that has a binomial mf with parameter (n, p):

$$E_b(\tilde{r}|n,p) \equiv \bar{r} = np,$$
$$V_b(\tilde{r}|n,p) \equiv \check{r} = np(1-p), \tag{9.24}$$

$$E_b^{(l)}(r|n,p) = \bar{r}F_b(r-1|n-1,p),$$
$$E_b^{(r)}(r|n,p) = \bar{r}G_b(r-1|n-1,p), \tag{9.25}$$

$$L_b^{(l)}(r|n,p) = rF_b(r|n,p) - \bar{r}F_b(r-1|n-1,p),$$
$$L_b^{(r)}(r|n,p) = \bar{r}G_b(r-1|n-1,p) - rG_b(r|n,p). \tag{9.26}$$

9.5 The Pascal Distribution[4]

9.5.1 Introduction

The function f_{Pa} of three arguments, defined by

$$f_{Pa}(n|r,p) \equiv C_{r-1}^{n-1} p^r (1-p)^{n-r}, \qquad 0 < p \leq 1, \quad r, n = 1, 2, \ldots, \quad n \geq r, \tag{9.27}$$

will be said to be a *Pascal* mf with parameter (r, p); any rv with a mf of the form (9.27) will be called a *Pascal* rv with parameter (r, p).

The reader is asked to show as an exercise that

$$\textstyle\sum_{n=r}^{\infty} f_{Pa}(n|r,p) = 1, \tag{9.28}$$

so that f_{Pa} is a proper mf.

9.5.2 Tables

The Pascal cumulative functions F_{Pa} and G_{Pa}, defined by

$$F_{Pa}(n|r,p) \equiv \textstyle\sum_{i=r}^{n} f_{Pa}(i|r,p),$$
$$G_{Pa}(n|r,p) \equiv \textstyle\sum_{i=n}^{\infty} f_{Pa}(i|r,p), \tag{9.29}$$

are cumbersome to evaluate directly and tables of their values do not exist, but we *can* express them in terms of the binomial cumulative function G_b and thus evaluate them by use of tables of G_b. In an exercise to chapter 14 an outline of a simple argument will be given leading to the result

$$F_{Pa}(n|r,p) = G_b(r|n,p). \tag{9.30}$$

---

4. The material of this section will be used in isolated sections of chapter 14.

9.5.3 Expectations

The reader is asked to prove as exercises the following propositions for a rv $\tilde{n}$ that has a Pascal mf with parameter (r, p):

$$E_{Pa}(\tilde{n}|r,p) \equiv \bar{n} = \frac{r}{p},$$
$$V_{Pa}(\tilde{n}|r,p) \equiv \breve{n} = \frac{r(1-p)}{p^2}, \tag{9.31}$$

$$E_{Pa}^{(l)}(n|r,p) = \frac{r}{p} F_{Pa}(n+1|r+1,p),$$
$$E_{Pa}^{(r)}(n|r,p) = \frac{r}{p} G_{Pa}(n+1|r+1,p), \tag{9.32}$$

$$L_{Pa}^{(l)}(n|r,p) = nF_{Pa}(n|r,p) - \bar{n}F_{Pa}(n+1|r+1,p),$$
$$L_{Pa}^{(r)}(n|r,p) = \bar{n}G_{Pa}(n+1|r+1,p) - nG_{Pa}(n|r,p). \tag{9.33}$$

9.6 The Hyperbinomial, Hyperpascal, and Hypergeometric Distributions[5]

9.6.1 The Hyperbinomial Distribution

The function f_{hb} of four arguments, defined by

$$f_{hb}(r|r',n',n) \equiv \frac{(r+r'-1)!(n+n'-r-r'-1)!n!(n'-1)!}{r!(r'-1)!(n-r)!(n'-r'-1)!(n+n'-1)!}, \quad \begin{array}{l} r = 0, 1, \ldots, \\ n = 1, 2, \ldots, \\ n \geq r, \\ n' > r' > 0, \end{array} \tag{9.34}$$

will be said to be a *hyperbinomial* mf with parameter (r', n', n); any rv with a mf of the form (9.34) will be called a *hyperbinomial* rv with parameter (r', n', n).

The reader is asked to show as an exercise that

$$f_{hb}(r|r',n',n) = \int_0^1 f_b(r|n,p) f_\beta(p|r',n')\,dp, \tag{9.35}$$

5. The material of this section will be needed in chapter 14.

and by this means to prove that

$$\textstyle\sum_{r=0}^{n} f_{hb}(r|r',n',n) = 1. \tag{9.36}$$

9.6.2 The Hyperpascal Distribution

The function f_{hp} of four arguments defined by

$$f_{hp}(n|r',n',r) \equiv \frac{(r+r'-1)!(n+n'-r-r'-1)!(n-1)!(n'-1)!}{(r-1)!(r'-1)!(n-r)!(n'-r'-1)!(n+n'-1)!}, \quad \begin{array}{l} n, r = 1, 2, \ldots, \\ n \geq r, \\ n' > r' > 0, \end{array} \tag{9.37}$$

will be said to be a *hyperpascal* mf with parameter (r',n',r); any rv with a mf of the form (9.37) will be called a hyperpascal rv with parameter (r',n',r).

The reader is asked to show as an exercise that

$$f_{hp}(n|r',n',r) = \int_0^1 f_{Pa}(n|r,p) f_\beta(p|r',n')\,dp, \tag{9.38}$$

and by this means to prove that

$$\textstyle\sum_{n=r}^{\infty} f_{hp}(n|r',n',r) = 1. \tag{9.39}$$

9.6.3 The Hypergeometric Distribution

The function f_{hg} of four arguments, defined by

$$f_{hg}(s|S,F,v) \equiv \frac{v!(S+F-v)!S!F!}{s!(v-s)!(S-s)!(F-v+s)!(S+F)!}, \quad \begin{array}{l} s, S, F, v = 0, 1, \ldots, \\ S, v \geq s, \\ F \geq v - s. \end{array} \tag{9.40}$$

will be said to be a *hypergeometric* mf with parameter (S,F,v); any rv with a mf of the form (9.40) will be called a *hypergeometric* rv with parameter (S,F,v).

As an exercise (with hints) the reader is asked to give a probabilistic interpretation to f_{hg} by observing that

$$f_{hg}(s|S,F,v) = \frac{C_s^S C_{v-s}^F}{C_v^{S+F}} \tag{9.41}$$

and from this to conclude (as part of the exercise) that

$$\textstyle\sum_{s=0}^{\min(v,S)} f_{hg}(s|S,F,v) = 1. \tag{9.42}$$

9.6.4 Tables

We define F_{hb}, F_{hp}, F_{hg}, G_{hb}, G_{hp}, G_{hg} in the obvious manner. From (9.30), (9.34), (9.37), we observe that

$$F_{hp}(n|r', n', r) = G_{hb}(r|r', n', n). \tag{9.43}$$

An argument is given in *ASDT*, pages 238–239, showing that

$$G_{hb}(r|r', n', n) = G_{hg}(r|n, n' - 1, r + r' - 1). \tag{9.44}$$

Exact Evaluation by Use of Hypergeometric Tables

When r' and n' are integral and $n' + n - 1$ has a value in the range 1 (1) 50 (10) 100, the evaluation can be made by use of tables of the function P defined and tabulated by Lieberman and Owen (1961), which directly or indirectly gives $P(N, n, k, x)$ to 6 decimal places for

$$N = 1\ (1)\ 50\ (10)\ 100;\ n = 1\ (1)\ N;\ k = 1\ (1)\ N;\ x = 0\ (1)\ n.$$

The basic relation between our functions and the function P is

$$F_{hb}(r|r', n', n) = P(N, n, r'', r) \tag{9.45a}$$

where

$$N \equiv n' + n - 1, \qquad r'' \equiv r' + r. \tag{9.45b}$$

This relation leads directly to tabled entries provided that

$$r'' \leq n \leq \tfrac{1}{2}N;$$

in other cases it is necessary to make use of the "symmetry relations" given on pages 4–5 of the introduction to the Lieberman-Owen tables and from which we can derive the formula

$$G_{hb}(r|r', n', n) = P(N, n' - 1, r'' - 1, r' - 1) \tag{9.46a}$$

which leads directly to tabled entries

$$r'' \leq n' \leq \tfrac{1}{2}(N + 1). \tag{9.46b}$$

From (9.43) and (9.44) it is now an easy matter to exhibit formulas for the cumulative hyperpascal and hypergeometric functions in terms of the tabulated $P(N, n, k, x)$ values. We choose only to give the formulas F_{hb} and G_{hb} because these will be used most directly in chapter 14.

Approximation by Use of Binomial Tables

It is shown in *ASDT*, page 241, that if

$$r' \ll n' \quad \textit{and} \quad r \ll n \quad \textit{and} \quad r' + r \ll \max\{n', n\}, \tag{9.47a}$$

then very good approximations to hyperbinomial cumulative functions can be obtained from binomial tables by use of the relation

$$G_{hb}(r|r', n', n) = G_b(r|n^*, p^*) \tag{9.47b}$$

where

$$n^* \equiv r' + r - 1, \qquad p^* \equiv \frac{n}{n' + n - 1}. \tag{9.47c}$$

9.7 The Normal Distribution[6]

9.7.1 The Normal Density Function

The function f_N of three arguments defined by

$$f_N(x|M, V) \equiv \frac{1}{\sqrt{2\pi V}} e^{-(1/2)[(x-M)^2/V]}, \qquad \begin{array}{c} -\infty < x < \infty, \\ -\infty < M < \infty, \\ 0 < V < \infty, \end{array} \tag{9.48}$$

will be said to be a *Normal* df with parameter (M, V); any rv with a df of the form (9.48) will be called a *Normal* rv with parameter (M, V).

The function f_{N*} defined by

$$f_{N*}(u) \equiv \frac{1}{\sqrt{2\pi}} e^{-(1/2)u^2} \qquad -\infty < u < \infty, \tag{9.49}$$

will be said to be a *standardized (or unit) Normal* density function; any rv with a df of the form (9.49) will be called a *unit Normal* rv.

From (9.48) and (9.49), we observe that

$$f_{N*}(u) = f_N(u|0, 1). \tag{9.50}$$

The reader is asked to prove as an exercise that if $\tilde{x}$ is a Normal rv with parameter (M, V), then

$$\tilde{u} = \frac{\tilde{x} - M}{\sqrt{V}} \tag{9.51}$$

is a unit Normal rv, and conversely.

6. The material of this section will be needed from chapter 16 on.

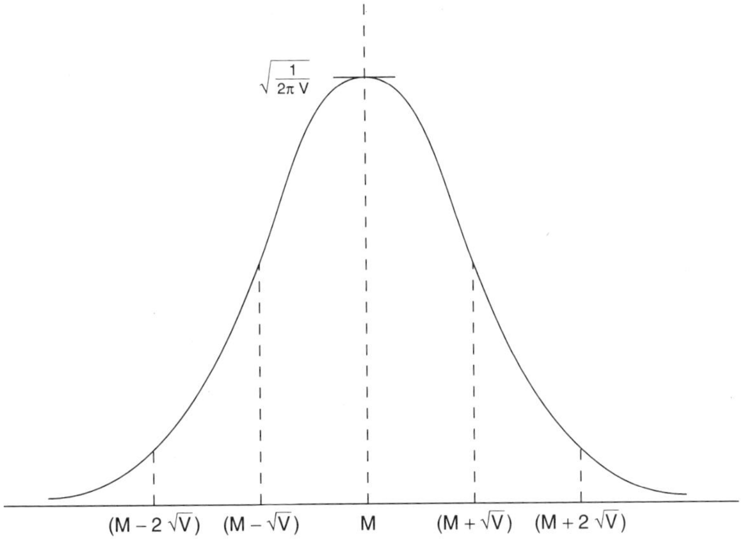

Figure 9.4
Normal density

In (9.11) we indicated that

$$\int_{-\infty}^{\infty} f_{N*}(u)\,du = 1, \tag{9.52a}$$

and by a simple change of variable we also conclude that

$$\int_{-\infty}^{\infty} f_N(x|M,V)\,dx = 1, \qquad \begin{array}{l} -\infty < M < \infty, \\ 0 < V < \infty. \end{array} \tag{9.52b}$$

9.7.2 Tables and Graphs

The Normal df with parameter (M, V) is a bell-shaped curve, which is symmetrical about the value $x = M$, as depicted in figure 9.4. It is concave in the interval $M - \sqrt{V} \le x \le m + \sqrt{V}$ and convex outside this interval. The parameter M is the center of symmetry of the df and the parameter V determines the spread.

The left- and right-tail cumulative functions defined by

$$\begin{array}{ll} F_N(x|M,V) \equiv \int_{-\infty}^{x} f_N(t|M,V)\,dt, & F_{N*}(u) \equiv \int_{-\infty}^{u} f_{N*}(t)\,dt, \\ G_N(x|M,V) \equiv \int_{x}^{\infty} f_N(t|M,V)\,dt, & G_{N*}(u) \equiv \int_{u}^{\infty} f_{N*}(t)\,dt \end{array} \tag{9.53}$$

cannot be evaluated in terms of elementary functions but their values can be found from tables.

At the end of this book, the functions $f_{N*}(u)$ and $G_{N*}(u)$ are tabulated to four significant figures for $u = 0(.01)\,4.00$. Values of f_{N*} and G_{N*} for negative values of u can be obtained from the easily proved relations:

$$f_{N*}(-u) = f_{N*}(u), \tag{9.54}$$

$$G_{N*}(-u) = 1 - G_{N*}(u). \tag{9.55}$$

Finally, values of f_N and G_N can be obtained from the easily proved relations:

$$f_N(x|M, V) = \frac{1}{\sqrt{V}} f_{N*}(u), \tag{9.56}$$

$$G_N(x|M, V) = G_{N*}(u), \tag{9.57}$$

where

$$u = \frac{x - M}{\sqrt{V}}. \tag{9.58}$$

9.7.3 Expectations

The reader is asked to prove as exercises the following propositions for a rv $\tilde{x}$ that has a Normal df with parameter (M, V):

$$E_N(\tilde{x}|M, V) \equiv \bar{x} = M, \tag{9.59}$$

$$V_N(\tilde{x}|M, V) \equiv \check{x} = V; \tag{9.60}$$

from (9.59) and (9.60) we observe that if $\tilde{x}$ is a Normal rv with parameter (M, V), then its mean and variance are respectively M and V.

From the easily proved result

$$\int_{-\infty}^{u} t f_{N*}(t)\,dt = -f_{N*}(u), \tag{9.61}$$

we get by a simple change of variables

$$E_n^{(l)}(x|M, V) \equiv \int_{-\infty}^{x} t f_N(t|M, V)\,dt$$

$$= M F_{N*}(u) - \sqrt{V} f_{N*}(u), \qquad u = V^{-1/2}(x - M), \tag{9.62}$$

and

$$E_N^{(r)}(x|M, V) \equiv \int_x^\infty t f_N(t|M, V)\, dt$$

$$= M G_{N*}(u) - \sqrt{V} f_{N*}(u), \qquad u = V^{-1/2}(x - M), \qquad (9.63)$$

From (9.61), we obtain

$$L_{N*}(u) \equiv \int_u^\infty (t - u) f_{N*}(t)\, dt = f_{N*}(u) - u G_{N*}(u). \qquad (9.64)$$

By a simple change of variables we get

$$L_N^{(l)}(x|M, V) \equiv \int_{-\infty}^x (x - t) f_N(t|M, V)\, dt$$

$$= \sqrt{V} L_{N*}(-u), \qquad u = V^{-1/2}(x - M), \qquad (9.65)$$

and

$$L_N^{(r)}(x|M, V) \equiv \int_x^\infty (t - x) f_N(t|M, V)\, dt$$

$$= \sqrt{V} L_{N*}(u), \qquad u = V^{-1/2}(x - M), \qquad (9.66)$$

At the end of this book, the function $L_{N*}(u)$ is tabulated to four significant figures for $u = 0(.01)\ 4.00$. Values of L_{N*} for negative values of u can be found by means of the easily verified relation

$$L_{N*}(-u) = u + L_{N*}(u). \qquad (9.67)$$

9.8 The Gamma-2 Distribution[7]

9.8.1 The Gamma-2 Density Function

The function $f_{\gamma 2}$ of three arguments defined by

$$f_{\gamma 2}(h|\mathrm{v}, \upsilon) \equiv \frac{e^{-(1/2)\upsilon \mathrm{v} h}(\frac{1}{2}\upsilon \mathrm{v} h)^{(1/2)\upsilon - 1}}{\Gamma(\frac{1}{2}\upsilon)} \tfrac{1}{2}\upsilon \mathrm{v}, \qquad h \geq 0,$$

$$\upsilon, \mathrm{v} > 0, \qquad (9.68)$$

will be said to be a *gamma-2* df with parameter (v, υ); any rv with a df of the form (9.68) will be called a *gamma-2* rv with parameter (v, υ).

The reader is asked to prove as an exercise that if $\tilde{x}$ is a (standardized) gamma rv with parameter $\upsilon/2$ then $\tilde{h} = 2\tilde{x}/\upsilon \mathrm{v}$ is a gamma-2 rv with parameter (v, υ).

7. The material of this section will be needed for chapter 17.

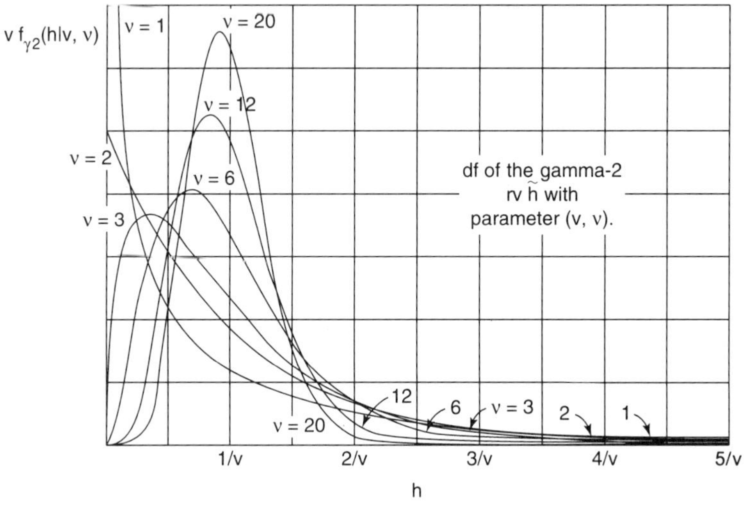

Figure 9.5
Gamma-2 densities

9.8.2 Graphs

In figure 9.5 several gamma-2 df's are shown for various values of (v, υ).

Let $\tilde{h}$ be a gamma-2 rv with parameter (s^2, υ), and let $\tilde{\sigma} \equiv \tilde{h}^{-1/2}$; density functions for $\tilde{\sigma}$ are shown in figure 9.6 for various values of (s^2, υ).

9.8.3 Expectations

The reader will be asked to prove as exercises the following propositions for a rv $\tilde{h}$ that has a gamma-2 df with parameter (v, υ).

$$E_{\gamma 2}(\tilde{h}|\mathrm{v}, \upsilon) \equiv \bar{h} = 1/\mathrm{v}, \tag{9.69}$$

$$V_{\gamma 2}(\tilde{h}|\mathrm{v}, \upsilon) \equiv \breve{h} = \frac{1}{\frac{1}{2}\upsilon\mathrm{v}^2}, \tag{9.70a}$$

$$(\breve{h})^{1/2} \equiv \ddot{h} = \sqrt{\frac{2}{\upsilon}}\bar{h}. \tag{9.70b}$$

Letting $\tilde{\sigma} = \tilde{h}^{-1/2}$ and $\mathrm{v} = s^2$, we obtain

$$E(\tilde{\sigma}) \equiv \bar{\sigma} = E_{\gamma 2}(\tilde{h}^{-1/2}|s^2, \upsilon) = s\sqrt{\tfrac{1}{2}\upsilon}\frac{(\frac{1}{2}\upsilon - \frac{3}{2})!}{(\frac{1}{2}\upsilon - 1)!}, \qquad \upsilon > 1, \tag{9.71}$$

$$V(\tilde{\sigma}) \equiv \breve{\sigma} = V_{\gamma 2}(\tilde{h}^{-1/2}|s^2, \upsilon) = s^2\frac{\upsilon}{\upsilon - 2} - \bar{\sigma}^2, \qquad \upsilon > 2. \tag{9.72}$$

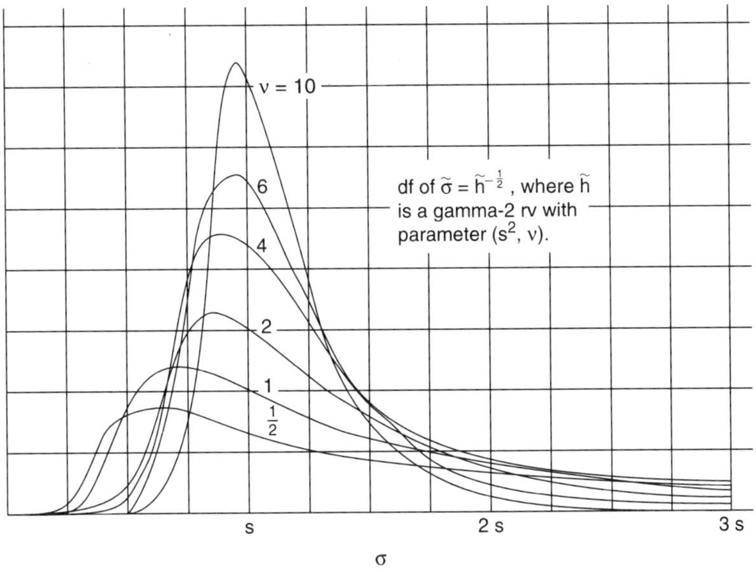

Figure 9.6
Density of $-\frac{1}{2}$ power of gamma-2 *rv*

9.9 The Student Distribution[8]

9.9.1 The Student Density Function

The function f_S of four arguments defined by

$$f_S(x|M,H,\upsilon) \equiv \begin{cases} \dfrac{\upsilon^{(1/2)\upsilon}}{B(\frac{1}{2},\frac{1}{2}\upsilon)}[\upsilon + H(x-M)^2]^{-(1/2)(\upsilon+1)}H^{1/2}, & \begin{cases} 0<\upsilon, H<\infty, \\ -\infty<M, x<\infty \end{cases} \\ (2\pi)^{-1/2}e^{-(1/2)H(x-M)^2}H^{1/2} & \begin{cases} 0<H<\infty \\ \upsilon=\infty, \\ -\infty<M, x<\infty, \end{cases} \end{cases} \tag{9.73}$$

will be said to be a *Student* df with parameter (M, H, υ); any rv with a df of the form (9.73) will be called a *Student* rv with parameter (M, H, υ).

The function f_{S*} of two arguments defined by

$$f_{S*}(t|\upsilon) \equiv f_S(t|0,1,\upsilon) \tag{9.74}$$

will be said to be a *standardized Student* df with parameter υ, any rv with

8. The material of this section will be needed for chapter 17.

a df of the form (9.74) will be called a *standardized Student* rv with parameter υ.

The reader is asked to prove as an exercise that if $\tilde{x}$ is a Student rv with parameter (M, H, υ) then

$$\tilde{t} = H^{1/2}(\tilde{x} - M) \tag{9.75}$$

is a standardized Student rv with parameter υ, and conversely.

Observe that by (9.48) and (9.73)

$$f_S(x|M, H, \infty) = f_N(x|M, H^{-1}). \tag{9.76}$$

The reader is asked to show as an exercise that

$$\int_0^\infty f_N(x|M, (hn)^{-1}) f_{\gamma 2}(h|\mathrm{v}, \upsilon)\, dh = f_S(x|M, n/\mathrm{v}, \upsilon), \tag{9.77}$$

which plays a central role in chapter 17.

9.9.2 Tables and Graphs

The Student df with parameter (M, H, υ) is a bell-shaped curve, which is symmetrically shaped about the value $x = M$. If a Student df is compared with a Normal df with the same .25, .50, and .75 fractiles, then the Student df falls off less slowly in the tails than does the Normal; as υ increases, the qualitative difference becomes less and less pronounced and the Student approaches the Normal in the limit.

The left- and right-tail cumulative functions defined by

$$\begin{aligned} F_S(x|M, H, \upsilon) &\equiv \int_{-\infty}^{x} f_S(w|M, H, \upsilon)\, dw, \quad F_{S*}(t|\upsilon) \equiv \int_{-\infty}^{t} f_{S*}(w|\upsilon)\, dw \\ G_S(x|M, H, \upsilon) &\equiv \int_{x}^{\infty} f_S(w|M, H, \upsilon)\, dw, \quad G_{S*}(t|\upsilon) \equiv \int_{t}^{\infty} f_{S*}(w|\upsilon)\, dw, \end{aligned} \tag{9.78}$$

cannot be evaluated in terms of elementary functions but their values can be found in tables.

The standardized functions f_{S*} and G_{S*} are tabulated in Bracken and Schleifer (1964). These tables are accurate to at least three and usually four significant figures, and the tabulations are for

$$\upsilon = 1, 1\tfrac{1}{2}, 2\ (1)\ 10, 12, 15, 20, 24, 30, 40, 60, 120, \infty,$$

and for nonnegative values of t in steps of .01 to some variable place beyond $t = 4.00$.

Values of f_{S*} and G_{S*} for negative values of t can be obtained from the easily proved relations

$$f_{S*}(-t|\upsilon) = f_{S*}(t|\upsilon), \tag{9.79}$$

$$G_{S*}(-t|\upsilon) = 1 - G_{S*}(t|\upsilon). \tag{9.80}$$

Finally, values of f_S and G_S can be obtained from the easily proved relations:

$$f_S(x|M, H, \upsilon) = H^{1/2} f_{S*}(t|\upsilon), \tag{9.81}$$

$$G_S(x|M, H, \upsilon) = G_{S*}(t|\upsilon), \tag{9.82}$$

where

$$t = H^{1/2}(x - M). \tag{9.83}$$

9.9.3 Expectations

The reader is asked to prove as exercises the following propositions for the rv $\tilde{x}$ which has a Student df with parameter (M, H, υ):

$$E_S(\tilde{x}|M, H, \upsilon) \equiv \bar{x} = M, \qquad \upsilon > 1, \tag{9.84}$$

$$V_S(\tilde{x}|M, H, \upsilon) \equiv \check{x} = \frac{1}{H}\frac{\upsilon}{\upsilon - 2}, \qquad \upsilon > 2. \tag{9.85}$$

From the easily proved result

$$\int_{-\infty}^{t} w f_{S*}(w|\upsilon)\, dw = -\frac{\upsilon + t^2}{\upsilon - 1} f_{S*}(t|\upsilon), \qquad \upsilon > 1, \tag{9.86}$$

we get by a simple change of variables

$$\begin{aligned} E_S^{(l)}(x|M, H, \upsilon) &\equiv \int_{-\infty}^{x} w f_S(w|M, H, \upsilon)\, dw \\ &= M F_{S*}(t|\upsilon) - \frac{1}{\sqrt{H}}\frac{\upsilon + t^2}{\upsilon - 1} f_{S*}(t|v), \qquad t = H^{1/2}(x - M), \end{aligned} \tag{9.87}$$

and

$$\begin{aligned} E_S^{(r)}(x|M, H, \upsilon) &\equiv \int_{x}^{\infty} w f_S(w|M, H, \upsilon)\, dw \\ &= M G_{S*}(t|\upsilon) - \frac{1}{\sqrt{H}}\frac{\upsilon + t^2}{\upsilon - 1} f_{S*}(t|\upsilon), \qquad t = H^{1/2}(x - M). \end{aligned} \tag{9.88}$$

From (9.86) we also obtain

$$L_{S*}(t|\upsilon) \equiv \int_t^\infty (w - t) f_{S*}(w|\upsilon)\, dw = \frac{\upsilon + t^2}{\upsilon - 1} f_{S*}(t|\upsilon) - t G_{S*}(t|\upsilon), \tag{9.89}$$

and by a simple change of variables we get

$$\begin{aligned} L_S^{(l)}(x|M, H, \upsilon) &\equiv \int_{-\infty}^{x} (x - w) f_S(w|M, H, \upsilon)\, dw \\ &= H^{-1/2} L_{S*}(-t|\upsilon), \qquad t = H^{1/2}(x - M), \end{aligned} \tag{9.90}$$

and

$$\begin{aligned} L_S^{(r)}(x|M, H, \upsilon) &\equiv \int_{x}^{\infty} (w - x) f_S(w|M, H, \upsilon)\, d\upsilon \\ &= H^{-1/2} L_{S*}(t|\upsilon), \qquad t = H^{1/2}(x - M). \end{aligned} \tag{9.91}$$

Bracken and Schleifer, in the tables cited above, tabulate L_{S*} for the same range of arguments of υ and t that f_{S*} and G_{S*} are tabulated, except that $\upsilon = 1$ is excluded from the L_{S*} table because the integral defining L_{S*} converges only for $\upsilon > 1$. Values of L_{S*} for negative values of t can be found by means of the easily verified relation

$$L_{S*}(-t|\upsilon) = t + L_{S*}(t|\upsilon). \tag{9.92}$$

9.10 The Exponential Distribution[9]

9.10.1 The Exponential Density Function

The function f_e of two arguments defined by

$$f_e(x|\lambda) \equiv \lambda e^{-\lambda x}, \qquad \lambda > 0,\ x > 0, \tag{9.93}$$

will be said to be an *exponential* df with parameter λ; any rv with a df of the form (9.93) will be called an *exponential* rv with parameter λ.

9.10.2 Cumulatives and Graphs

The right-tail cumulative function is given by

$$G_e(x|\lambda) \equiv \int_x^\infty f_e(\upsilon|\lambda)\, d\upsilon = e^{-\lambda x} \tag{9.94}$$

9. The material of this section will be needed for chapter 15.

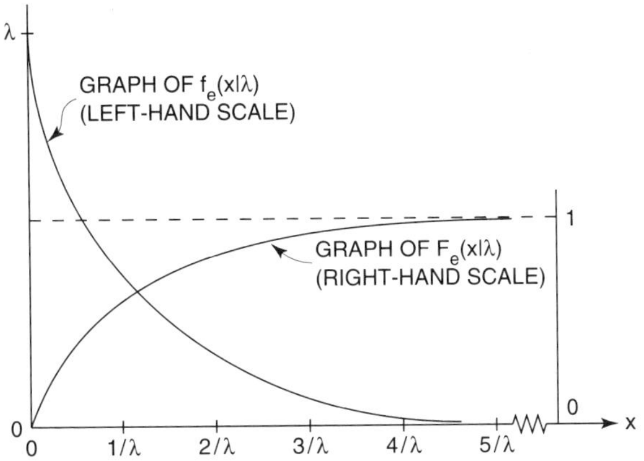

Figure 9.7
Exponential density and cumulative function

and the left-tail cumulative function is given by

$$F_e(x|\lambda) = 1 - G_e(x|\lambda) = 1 - e^{-\lambda x}. \tag{9.95}$$

The functions f_e and F_e are plotted in figure 9.7.

9.10.3 Expectations

The reader is asked to prove as exercises the following propositions for the rv $\tilde{x}$ which has an exponential df with parameter λ:

$$E_e(\tilde{x}|\lambda) \equiv \bar{x} = 1/\lambda, \tag{9.96}$$

$$V_e(\tilde{x}|\lambda) \equiv \breve{x} = 1/\lambda^2, \tag{9.97}$$

$$E_e^{(l)}(x|\lambda) \equiv \int_0^\infty \mathrm{v} f_e(\mathrm{v}|\lambda)\,d\mathrm{v} = -e^{\lambda \mathrm{v}}\left(\mathrm{v} + \frac{1}{\lambda}\right)\Bigg|_0^x$$

$$= -e^{-\lambda x}\left(x + \frac{1}{\lambda}\right) + \frac{1}{\lambda}, \tag{9.98}$$

$$E_e^{(r)}(x|\lambda) \equiv \int_x^\infty \mathrm{v} f_e(\mathrm{v}|\lambda)\,dv = -e^{-\lambda \mathrm{v}}\left(\mathrm{v} + \frac{1}{\lambda}\right)\Bigg|_x^\infty$$

$$= -e^{-\lambda x}\left(x + \frac{1}{\lambda}\right), \tag{9.99}$$

$$L_e^{(l)}(x|\lambda) \equiv \int_0^x (x - \mathrm{v}) f_e(\mathrm{v}|\lambda)\,d\mathrm{v} = x + \frac{1}{\lambda}e^{-\lambda x} - \frac{1}{\lambda}, \tag{9.100}$$

$$L_e^{(r)}(x|\lambda) \equiv \int_x^\infty (\mathrm{v} - x) f_e(\mathrm{v}|\lambda)\,d\mathrm{v} = \frac{1}{\lambda}e^{-\lambda x}. \tag{9.101}$$

9.11 The Gamma-1 Distribution[10]

9.11.1 The Gamma-1 Density Function

The function $f_{\gamma 1}$ of three arguments defined by

$$f_{\gamma 1}(y|\rho,\tau) \equiv \frac{e^{-y\tau}(y\tau)^{\rho-1}}{(\rho-1)!}\tau, \qquad \begin{array}{l} y \geq 0, \\ \rho, \tau > 0, \end{array} \tag{9.102}$$

where

$$(\rho-1)! \equiv \Gamma(\rho),$$

will be said to be a *gamma-1* df with parameter (ρ, τ); any rv with a df of the form (9.102) will be called a *gamma-1* rv with parameter (ρ, τ).

The function f_γ of two arguments defined by

$$f_\gamma(x|\rho) = \frac{e^{-x}x^{\rho-1}}{(\rho-1)!}, \qquad \begin{array}{l} x \geq 0, \\ \rho > 0, \end{array} \tag{9.103}$$

will be said to be a *standardized gamma* df with parameter ρ; any rv with a df of the form (9.103) will be called a *standardized gamma* rv with parameter ρ. From (9.102) and (9.103) we observe that

$$f_\gamma(x|\rho) = f_{\gamma 1}(x|\rho, 1). \tag{9.104}$$

The reader is asked to prove as an exercise that if $\tilde{y}$ is a gamma-1 rv with parameter (ρ, τ) then

$$\tilde{x} = \tau\tilde{y} \tag{9.105}$$

is a standardized gamma rv with parameter ρ and conversely.

From (9.2) we conclude that

$$\int_0^\infty f_\gamma(x|\rho)\,dx = 1 \tag{9.106a}$$

and by a simple change of variables we also conclude that

$$\int_0^\infty f_{\gamma 1}(y|\rho,\tau)\,dy = 1. \tag{9.106b}$$

10. The material of this section will be needed for chapter 15.

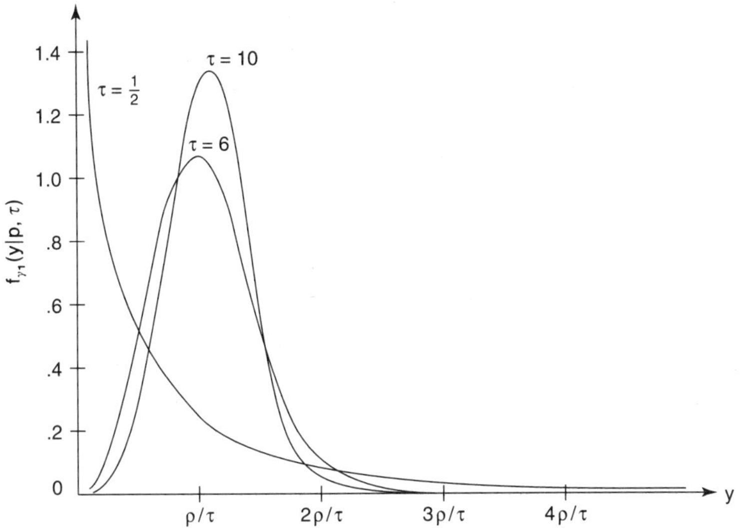

Figure 9.8
Gamma-1 densities

9.11.2 Graphs, Cumulatives, and Tables

In figure 9.8 several gamma-1 df's are shown for various values of (ρ, τ).

The left- and right-tail cumulative functions defined by

$$\begin{aligned} F_{\gamma 1}(y|\rho,\tau) &\equiv \int_0^y f_{\gamma 1}(w|\rho,\tau)\,dw, \\ G_{\gamma 1}(y|\rho,\tau) &\equiv \int_y^\infty f_{\gamma 1}(w|\rho,\tau)\,dw, \end{aligned} \tag{9.107}$$

cannot be evaluated in terms of elementary functions (except in special cases) but their values can be found from tables. Extensive tables can be found in K. Pearson (1922), which gives

$$I(u,p) \equiv F_\gamma(u\sqrt{p+1}|p+1)$$

to seven places for

$$p = -.95(.05)0 \text{ (table II); } 0(.1)5\ (.2)50 \text{ (table I)},$$

$$u = 0(.1)\infty.$$

To use these tables for gamma-1 cumulative probabilities we need

$$F_{\gamma 1}(y|\rho,\tau) = F_\gamma(\tau y|\rho) = I\left(\frac{\tau y}{\sqrt{\rho}}\middle|\rho - 1\right). \tag{9.108}$$

Values of the cumulative gamma function may also be obtained from tables of the cumulative Poisson function (see section 9.12.2).

Beyond the range of available tables, values of the cumulative function may be obtained from tables of the standardized Normal function by use of one of the three approximations which we list in order of increasing accuracy:

$$F_\gamma(x|\rho) \doteq F_{N*}(u) \text{ where } u = \begin{cases} \dfrac{x-\rho}{\sqrt{\rho}} & \text{direct,} \\ \sqrt{4x} - \sqrt{4\rho - 1} & \text{Fisher,} \\ 3\sqrt{\rho}\left[\sqrt[3]{\dfrac{x}{\rho}} - \dfrac{9\rho - 1}{9\rho}\right] & \text{Wilson-Hilferty.} \end{cases}$$

For a discussion of the accuracy of these and still more accurate approximations, see the references given in section 9.1.

9.11.3 Expectations

The reader is asked to prove as exercises the following propositions for a rv $\tilde{y}$ that has a gamma-1 df with parameter (ρ, τ):

$$E_{\gamma 1}(\tilde{y}|\rho,\tau) \equiv \bar{y} = \frac{\rho}{\tau}, \tag{9.109}$$

$$V_{\gamma 1}(\tilde{y}|\rho,\tau) \equiv \breve{y} = \frac{\rho}{\tau^2}, \tag{9.110}$$

$$E_{\gamma 1}^{(l)}(y|\rho,\tau) \equiv \int_0^y w f_{\gamma 1}(w|\rho,\tau)\,dw$$

$$= \bar{y}F_\gamma(\tau y|\rho + 1), \tag{9.111}$$

$$E_{\gamma 1}^{(r)}(y|\rho,\tau) \equiv \int_y^\infty w f_{\gamma 1}(w|\rho,\tau)\,dw$$

$$= \bar{y}G_\gamma(\tau y|\rho + 1), \tag{9.112}$$

$$L_{\gamma 1}^{(l)}(y|\rho,\tau) \equiv \int_0^y (y - w) f_{\gamma 1}(w|\rho,\tau)\,dw$$

$$= yF_\gamma(y\tau|\rho) - \bar{y}F_\gamma(y\tau|\rho + 1), \tag{9.113}$$

$$L_{\gamma 1}^{(r)}(y|\rho,\tau) \equiv \int_y^\infty (w - y) f_{\gamma 1}(w|\rho,\tau)\,dw$$

$$= \bar{y}G_\gamma(y\tau|\rho + 1) - yG_\gamma(y\tau|\rho). \tag{9.114}$$

9.12 The Poisson Distribution

9.12.1 The Poisson Mass Function

The function f_P of two arguments defined by

$$f_P(r|m) \equiv \frac{e^{-m}m^r}{r!}, \qquad \begin{array}{l} r = 0, 1, 2, \ldots, \\ m > 0, \end{array} \tag{9.115}$$

will be said to be a *Poisson* mf with parameter m; any rv with a mf of the form (9.115) will be called a *Poisson* rv with parameter m.

Since

$$e^m = \textstyle\sum_{r=0}^{\infty} \frac{m^r}{r!}, \tag{9.116}$$

it is clear that

$$\textstyle\sum_{r=0}^{\infty} f_P(r|m) = 1. \tag{9.117}$$

9.12.2 Cumulatives and Tables

The Poisson cumulative functions F_P and G_P defined by

$$\begin{aligned} F_P(r|m) &\equiv \textstyle\sum_{i=0}^{r} f_P(i|m), \\ G_P(r|m) &\equiv \textstyle\sum_{i=r}^{\infty} f_P(i|m), \end{aligned} \tag{9.118}$$

are cumbersome to evaluate directly but many tables of their values exist.

Molina (1942) gives 6-place tables of both $f_P(x|a)$ (table I) and $P(c, a) = G_P(c|a)$ (table II) for

$a = .001\ (.001)\ .01\ (.01)\ .3\ (.1)\ 15\ (1)\ 100$

$x, c = 0\ (1)\infty.$

Pearson and Hartley (1966, table 39) gives $f_P(i|m)$ to 6 places for

$m = .1\ (.1)\ 15.0$

$i = 0\ (1)\infty.$

table 7 (pp. 122–29) gives $F_P(c - 1|m)$ to 5 places for

$m = .0005\ (.0005)\ .005\ (.005)\ .05\ (.05)\ 1\ (.1)\ 5\ (.25)\ 10\ (.5)\ 20\ (1)\ 60,$

$c = 1\ (1)\ 35.$

We prove in (15.5) that for integral r,

$$F_P(r - 1|m) = G_{\gamma 1}(m|r, 1), \tag{9.119a}$$

and using (9.104) we get

$$F_P(r-1|m) = G_\gamma(m|r), \tag{9.119b}$$

so that cumulative gamma tables can be used to obtain cumulative Poisson probabilities (see section 9.11.2 for information about gamma tables).

9.12.3 Expectations

The reader is asked to prove as exercises the following propositions for a rv $\tilde{r}$ that has a Poisson mf with parameter m:

$$E_P(\tilde{r}|m) \equiv \bar{r} = m, \tag{9.120}$$

$$V_P(\tilde{r}|m) \equiv \breve{r} = m, \tag{9.121}$$

$$E_P^{(l)}(r|m) \equiv \textstyle\sum_{i=0}^{r} i f_P(i|m) = mF_P(r-1|m), \tag{9.122}$$

$$E_P^{(r)}(r|m) \equiv \textstyle\sum_{i=0}^{\infty} i f_P(i|m) = mG_P(r-1|m), \tag{9.123}$$

$$\begin{aligned} L_P^{(l)}(r|m) &\equiv \textstyle\sum_{i=0}^{r} (r-i) f_P(i|m) \\ &= rF_P(r|m) - mF_P(r-1|m), \end{aligned} \tag{9.124}$$

$$\begin{aligned} L_P^{(r)}(r|m) &\equiv \textstyle\sum_{i=r}^{\infty} (i-r) f_P(i|m) \\ &= mG_P(r-1|m) - rG_P(r|m). \end{aligned} \tag{9.125}$$

9.13 The Negative-Binomial Distribution[11]

9.13.1 The Negative-Binomial Mass Function

The function f_{nb} of three arguments defined by

$$f_{nb}(r|r',p) \equiv \frac{(r+r'-1)!}{r!(r'-1)!} p^r (1-p)^{r'}, \qquad \begin{aligned} &r = 0, 1, \ldots, \\ &r' > 0, \\ &0 < p < 1, \end{aligned} \tag{9.126}$$

will be said to be a *negative-binomial* mf with parameter (r', p); any rv with a mf of the form (9.126) will be called a *negative-binomial* rv with parameter (r', p).

11. The material of this section will be needed in chapter 15. The negative-binomial distribution would more appropriately be named according to our conventions as the "hyperpoisson" distribution. We defer, however, to common usage.

The reader is asked to show as an exercise a result that will be used later

$$\int_0^\infty f_P(r|\lambda t) f_{\gamma 1}(\lambda|r',t')\,d\lambda = f_{nb}\left(r|r', \frac{t}{t+t'}\right); \tag{9.127}$$

from this we obtain a characterization of the negative-binomial mf:

$$f_{nb}(r|r',p) = \int_0^\infty f_P(r|\lambda p) f_{\gamma 1}(\lambda|r', 1-p)\,d\lambda. \tag{9.128}$$

From the characterization of f_{nb} in (9.128) the reader can easily show that

$$\textstyle\sum_{r=0}^{\infty} f_{nb}(r|r',p) = 1. \tag{9.129}$$

9.13.2 Cumulatives and Tables

From (9.19) and (9.126), we have for r integral,

$$f_{nb}(r|r',p) = p f_b(r|r+r'-1, p), \tag{9.130}$$

and tables of the binomial mf can be used to evaluate terms of the negative-binomial mass function.

Let F_{nb} and G_{nb} be defined in the obvious manner.

In an exercise in chapter 14 we interpret a negative-binomial rv in terms of a Bernoulli process and from this interpretation the reader is asked to show that for r' integral

$$G_{nb}(r|r',p) = G_b(r|r+r'-1, p). \tag{9.131}$$

From (9.131) and from (9.15), which relates the binomial and the beta cumulatives, we get

$$G_{nb}(r|r',p) = F_\beta(p|r, r+r'). \tag{9.132}$$

In *ASDT*, page 237, a proof is given of (9.132), which holds for all values of r', integral or not.

Cumulative probabilities for a negative-binomial mf can be obtained by use of (9.131) and (9.132).

9.13.3 Expectations

The reader is asked to prove as an exercise the following propositions for a rv $\tilde{r}$ that has a negative-binomial mf with parameter (r', p):

$$E_{nb}(\tilde{r}|r',p) \equiv \bar{r} = r' \frac{p}{1-p}, \tag{9.133}$$

$$V_{nb}(\tilde{r}|r',p) \equiv \breve{r} = r' \frac{p}{(1-p)^2} = \frac{1}{1-p}\bar{r}', \tag{9.134}$$

$$E_{nb}^{(l)}(r|r',p) \equiv \sum_{j=0}^{r} jf_{nb}(j|r',p)$$
$$= r'\frac{p}{1-p}F_{nb}(r-1|r'+1,p), \tag{9.135}$$
$$E_{nb}^{(r)}(r|r',p) \equiv \sum_{j=r}^{\infty} jf_{nb}(j|r',p)$$
$$= r'\frac{p}{1-p}G_{nb}(r-1|r'+1,p), \tag{9.136}$$
$$L_{nb}^{(l)}(r|r',p) \equiv \sum_{j=0}^{r}(r-j)f_{nb}(j|r',p)$$
$$= rF_{nb}(r|r',p) - \bar{r}F_{nb}(r-1|r'+1,p), \tag{9.137}$$
$$L_{nb}^{(r)}(r|r',p) \equiv \sum_{j=r}^{\infty}(j-r)f_{nb}(j|r',p)$$
$$= \bar{r}G_{nb}(r-1|r'+1,p) - rG_{nb}(r|r',p). \tag{9.138}$$

Exercises

1. Using the binomial tables, find

   $F_\beta(.4|6,10)$, $F_\beta(.7|6,10)$, $G_\beta(.4|7,13)$.

2. Consider the beta density

$$f_\beta(p|\rho,\upsilon) = \text{constant} \times p^{\rho-1}(1-p)^{\upsilon-\rho-1}, \quad 0 \le p \le 1, \quad 0 < \rho < \upsilon.$$

   a. Show that $f_\beta(p|1,2)$ is rectangular in $[0,1]$.

   b. Show that $f_\beta(p|1,\upsilon)$ for $\upsilon > 2$ has the shape indicated in figure 9.1B. What happens as υ increases?

   c. Show that $f_\beta(p|\rho,\upsilon)$ for $\rho < 1$, $\upsilon > \rho + 1$ has the shape indicated in figure 9.1A.

3. Let p_k be such that $F_\beta(p_k|\rho,\upsilon) = k$. Use the beta fractile tables to construct a table of entries $(p_{.75} - p_{.25})$ for ρ values going from 1 to 14 in steps of 1 when $\upsilon = 2\rho$.

4. a. Use (9.19) to find $f_b(r|4,.3)$ for $r = 0, 1, 2, 3, 4$.

   b. Use (9.22) to find $G_b(r|4,.3)$ for $r = 0, 1, 2, 3, 4$. Verify (9.21) for this case.

   c. Check your answer to (b) by referring to the binomial probability tables.

5. Use the binomial tables to find

   $F_b(40|50,.7)$, $G_b(12|20,.6)$, $f_b(14|20,.6)$.

6. Use tables to evaluate the following:

   a.

$F_{N^*}(-3)$	$F_{N^*}(0)$
$F_{N^*}(-2)$	$F_{N^*}(.6745)$
$F_{N^*}(-1)$	$F_{N^*}(1)$
$F_{N^*}(-.6745)$	$F_{N^*}(2)$

b.

$G_N(3\mid 2, 1)$	$F_N(7\mid 5, \frac{9}{16})$
$G_N(3\mid 2, 4)$	$F_N(-1\mid 0, \frac{1}{4})$

7. Give the following fractiles of the standardized Normal df $f_{N^*}(\cdot)$:

   .01, .05 (.05) .95, .99.

8. Repeat for the Normal df with mean 5 and variance 100; i.e., for $f_N(\cdot\mid 5, 100)$.

9. *Proof of (9.15)* Keeping ρ and υ fixed, define the function $H(p)$ by

   $H(p) \equiv G_b(\rho\mid\upsilon - 1, p) = \sum_{j=\rho}^{\upsilon} C_j^{\upsilon-1}\, p^j(1-p)^{\upsilon-1-j}$.

   Show that

   $$\frac{d}{dp}H(p) \equiv H'(p) = f_\beta(p\mid\rho, \upsilon).$$

   Since $H(0) = 0$, obtain (9.15) by integrating $H'(t)$ for t from 0 to p.

10. Prove the formulas for beta expectations in section 9.3.3.

11. Prove (9.21) (binomial mass function has sum 1).

12. Prove the formulas for binomial expectations in section 9.4.3.

13. Prove (9.28) (Pascal mass function has sum 1).

14. Prove the formulas for Pascal expectations in section 9.5.3.

15. Prove formulas (9.35) and (9.36) for the hyperbinomial mass function.

16. Prove formulas (9.38) and (9.39) for the hyperpascal mass function.

17. Show that the hypergeometric mf is the probability of obtaining exactly s balls labelled S if a sample of v balls is drawn at random *without* replacement from an urn containing S balls labeled S and F balls labelled F. Derive (9.41) and (9.42).

18. Prove that unit and arbitrary Normal rv's are related by (9.51).

19. Prove formulas (9.59) and (9.60) for Normal expectations.

20. Prove the relation between gamma and gamma-2 rv's stated in section 9.8.1.

21. Prove the formulas for gamma-2 expectations in section 9.8.3.

22. Prove the relations (9.75) and (9.77) for Student rv's.

23. Prove formulas (9.84) and (9.85) for Student expectations.

24. Prove the formulas for exponential expectations in section 9.10.3.

25. Prove the relation (9.105) between gamma and gamma-1 rv's.

26. Prove the formulas for gamma-1 expectations in section 9.11.3.

27. Prove the formulas for Poisson expectations in section 9.12.3.

28. Prove formula (9.128) for the negative binomial mass function.

29. Prove the formulas for negative binomial expectations in section 9.13.3.

10 Conditional Probability and Bayes' Theorem

10.1 Introduction

In chapter 6 we discussed a class of decision problems represented by a decision tree with four moves: On move 1, the decision maker was required to choose an experiment e; on move 2, chance "responded" with an outcome z; on move 3, the decision maker was required to choose an act a; on move 4, chance responded with state s. After e was chosen on move 1, both z and s were treated as unknowns and, according to our notational conventions, were labelled $\tilde{z}$, $\tilde{s}$. In chapter 6 we assumed that both $\tilde{z}$ and $\tilde{s}$ could take on only a finite number of possible values. It is our purpose in this chapter to generalize the discussion of probabilities in that chapter to the case where $\tilde{s}$ is a continuous rv with a specified df; we continue to assume, however, that $\tilde{z}$ can be one of only a finite number of possible values. The generalization to the case where $\tilde{z}$ also is a continuous rv presents comparatively little additional conceptual difficulty, and discussion of it is deferred to chapter 13.

Here is the essence of the problem that confronts us: If S_0 is a subset of possible states and $P(\tilde{s} \in S_0) > 0$, our discussion in chapters 2 and 3 on conditional preferences and conditional probabilities allows us to deal meaningfully with the expression $P(\tilde{z} = z_0 | \tilde{s} \in S_0)$. However, if for any given state s_0, $P(\tilde{s} = s_0) = 0$ (this is the case if $\tilde{s}$ has a df), we have no mechanism so far for handling and interpreting the expression $P(\tilde{z} = z_0 | \tilde{s} = s_0)$; that is, we must extend our foundations in order to be able to handle conditional preferences and conditional probabilities when the conditioning event, such as $(\tilde{s} = s_0)$, has probability zero but is nevertheless possible.

We wish to have the flexibility in the sequel to interchange the roles of s and z, that is, to consider also expressions of the form $P(\tilde{s} \in S_0 | \tilde{z} = z_0)$ when $\tilde{z}$ is a continuous rv, and therefore we adopt a more neutral notation and develop results in terms of a pair (α, β) instead of (z, s).

10.2 Conditional Preferences for Lotteries[1]

10.2.1 Notation

In what follows we assume that the generic element θ is expressed as a pair (α, β), where α belongs to a set A and β belongs to a set B, and we adopt

1. Since the material in section 10.2 is rather abstract, we append at the end of this chapter a statement that gives the salient conclusions of this section that are necessary for an understanding of the rest of the book. The reader who wishes to can read the summary and skip section 10.2.

the following notation for events. The event that the unknown α lies in a subset A_0 will be designated $(\tilde{\alpha} \in A_0)$; the event that the unknown β lies in a subset B_0 will be designated $(\tilde{\beta} \in B_0)$; the event that consists of the simultaneous occurrence of both $(\tilde{\alpha} \in A_0)$ and $(\tilde{\beta} \in B_0)$ will be designated $(\tilde{\alpha} \in A_0, \tilde{\beta} \in B_0)$. If A_0 consists of a single element, α_i say, we write $(\tilde{\alpha} = \alpha_i)$, and so on.

We now propose to relate preference statements for lotteries held *prior* to obtaining information about $\tilde{\beta}$ with statements held *posterior* to obtaining this information, and we adopt the following notation:

$l' \gtrsim l''$: l' is preferred or indifferent to l'' prior to obtaining any information about $\tilde{\beta}$.

$l' \overline{\gtrsim | B_0}\, l''$: l' is preferred or indifferent to l'' posterior to learning the event $(\tilde{\beta} \in B_0)$.

$l' \overline{\gtrsim | \beta_0}\, l''$: l' is preferred or indifferent to l'' posterior to learning the event $(\tilde{\beta} = \beta_0)$.

$$l_{B_0} = \begin{cases} l & \text{if } \tilde{\beta} \in B_0, \\ c_0 \text{ (the status quo)} & \text{if } \beta \notin B_0. \end{cases}$$

10.2.2 Motivation from the Finite Case

In order to relate preferences held *before* learning $(\tilde{\beta} \in B_0)$ to preferences held *after* learning this fact, we assumed in Basic Assumption 5 of chapters 2 and 3 that

$$l' \overline{\lesssim | B_0}\, l'' \quad \Leftrightarrow \quad l'_{B_0} \lesssim l''_{B_0} \quad \text{if} \quad P(\tilde{\beta} \in B_0) > 0; \tag{10.1a}$$

that is, we related posterior preferences to prior preferences by means of an assumption involving "called-off" lotteries. This assumption then led to the conclusion that, posterior to learning $(\tilde{\beta} \in B_0)$, the lottery that gives c^* if $\tilde{\alpha} \in A_0$ and c_* otherwise is indifferent to a canonical lottery that gives a chance at c^* equal to

$$P(\tilde{\alpha} \in A_0 | \tilde{\beta} \in B_0) = \frac{P(\tilde{\alpha} \in A_0, \tilde{\beta} \in B_0)}{P(\tilde{\beta} \in B_0)} \tag{10.1b}$$

and gives a complementary chance at c_*.

When $P(\tilde{\beta} \in B_0) = 0$, the assumption (10.1a) does not enable us to relate prior and posterior preferences, because in this case $l'_{B_0} \sim l''_{B_0}$ for all l' and l''; however, we cannot simply ignore the problem of preferences conditional on an event of 0 probability, because it is often meaningful and useful to assign a probability to an event $(\tilde{\alpha} \in A_0)$ on the *hypothesis* that $\tilde{\beta}$ is known to have some *specific* value β even though $P(\tilde{\beta} = \beta) = 0$ for all

$\tilde{\beta}$, and even though it is not possible to *observe* that $\tilde{\beta}$ is equal to any exact infinite decimal.

In order to help motivate the additional behavioral assumption that we need in order to cope with the problem of conditional preferences when the conditioning event has zero probability, we first examine certain results that can be proved from our previous assumptions when the conditioning event has positive probability. In stating these results we use the following notation:

$l \sim \langle \Pi(l) \rangle$: the decision maker is indifferent between l and a reference lottery giving a canonical chance $\Pi(l)$ at c^* (and a complementary chance at c_*).

$l \overline{\sim | B_0} \langle \Pi(l|B_0) \rangle$: *given that* $\tilde{\beta} \in B_0$, the decision maker is indifferent between l and a reference lottery with chance $\Pi(l|B_0)$ at c^*.[2]

$l \overline{\sim | \beta_0} \langle \Pi(l|\beta_0) \rangle$: as before, but given that $\tilde{\beta} = \beta_0$.

Now consider the finite case where $B = (\beta_1, \ldots, \beta_r)$ and $P(\tilde{\beta} = \beta_i) > 0$ for all i, and let l be a lottery whose consequence depends on the unknown $\tilde{\alpha}$ and possibly but not necessarily on $\tilde{\beta}$. (Even if the consequence of l does not depend on $\tilde{\beta}$, information about $\tilde{\beta}$ may be relevant because knowledge about $\tilde{\beta}$ would affect the decision maker's judgments about $\tilde{\alpha}$ and therefore affect his evaluation of l.) It can easily be proved that if for all i

$$l \overline{\sim | \beta_i} \langle \Pi(l|\beta_i) \rangle, \tag{10.2}$$

then for any set $B_0 \subset B$

$$l \overline{\sim | B_0} \langle \Pi(l|B_0) \rangle \tag{10.3}$$

where

$$\Pi(l|B_0) = \textstyle\sum_{B_0} \Pi(l|\beta_i) P(\tilde{\beta} = \beta_i | \tilde{\beta} \in B_0), \tag{10.4}$$

the summation being over all $\beta_i \in B_0$; and since

$$P(\tilde{\beta} = \beta_i | \tilde{\beta} \in B_0) = \frac{P(\tilde{\beta} = \beta_i)}{P(\tilde{\beta} \in B_0)},$$

we have

$$\Pi(l|B_0) = \frac{1}{P(\tilde{\beta} \in B_0)} \textstyle\sum_{B_0} \Pi(l|\beta_i) P(\tilde{\beta} = \beta_i). \tag{10.5}$$

2. In the formal system the symbol $\overline{\succsim | B_0}$ is an undefined relation on $L \times L$ which satisfies Basic Assumptions 1 to 4, and also 5 whenever $P(B_0) > 0$.

If l is the special lottery which pays off c^* if $\tilde{\alpha} \in A_0$ and c_* otherwise, then by definition $\Pi(l)$ is $P(\tilde{\alpha} \in A_0)$ or simply $P(A_0)$, $\Pi(l|B_0)$ is $P(\tilde{\alpha} \in A_0 | \tilde{\beta} \in B_0)$ or simply $P(A_0|B_0)$, etc. Formulas (10.4) and (10.5) then specialize to the formulas

$$P(A_0|B_0) = \textstyle\sum_{B_0} P(A_0|\beta_i)P(\beta_i|B_0) \tag{10.4$'$}$$

$$P(\tilde{\alpha} \in A_0, \tilde{\beta} \in B_0) = P(A_0|B_0)P(B_0) = \textstyle\sum_{B_0} P(A_0|\beta_i)P(\beta_i). \tag{10.5$'$}$$

Our aim in the next section will be to introduce another assumption about conditional preferences for lotteries that will enable us to generalize formulas (10.5) and (10.5′) to the cases where $P(\tilde{\beta} = \beta) = 0$ for all β.

10.2.3 A Basic Assumption

We now turn to the case where B is infinite. We would like to extend formulas (10.5) and (10.5′) to infinite sums when B is denumerable and to integrals when B is the real line; and to do so we need another basic behavioral assumption. Rather than stating this assumption and commenting on it afterward, we prefer to introduce it informally before giving the more precise and concise formal version.

Suppose l is a lottery which results in consequence $l(\alpha, \beta)$ if the event $(\tilde{\alpha} = \alpha, \tilde{\beta} = \beta)$ occurs. Now if the decision maker were somehow to learn that $(\tilde{\beta} = \beta)$ but to learn nothing directly about $\tilde{\alpha}$, then the consequence of lottery l would still be uncertain since $\tilde{\alpha}$ is still unknown. Let us assume that given the knowledge that $(\tilde{\beta} = \beta)$, the decision maker is indifferent between l and $\langle \Pi(l|\beta) \rangle$. Now let us compare lottery l with a lottery l' whose consequence depends on the outcome of $\tilde{\gamma}$ and $\tilde{\beta}$, where as usual $\tilde{\gamma}$ represents the unknown result of a canonical drawing from the interval $[0, 1]$ and where $\tilde{\gamma}$ is completely unrelated to $\tilde{\beta}$; suppose that l' results in consequence c^* if the pair (β, γ) is such that $\gamma < \Pi(l|\beta)$, and results in c_* otherwise.

If the decision maker were somehow to learn that $(\tilde{\beta} = \beta)$, then the consequence of lottery l' would still be uncertain and would involve a canonical chance $\Pi(l|\beta)$ at c^* and a complementary chance at c_*. Thus, posterior to learning that $(\tilde{\beta} = \beta)$, the decision maker feels that both l and l' are indifferent to $\langle \Pi(l|\beta) \rangle$, and by transitivity l is indifferent to l' (still given β). Our next behavioral assumption says that since l and l' are indifferent given that $(\tilde{\beta} = \beta)$ no matter what $\tilde{\beta}$ is, lotteries l and l' should be *indifferent no matter what the decision maker learns about* $\tilde{\beta}$, such as $\tilde{\beta} \in B_0$.

This discussion is now formalized in terms of the following

Basic Assumption 7 (Conditional Substitutability) Let l be a lottery defined on pairs (α, β); let $\Pi(l|\beta)$ be defined for all β by

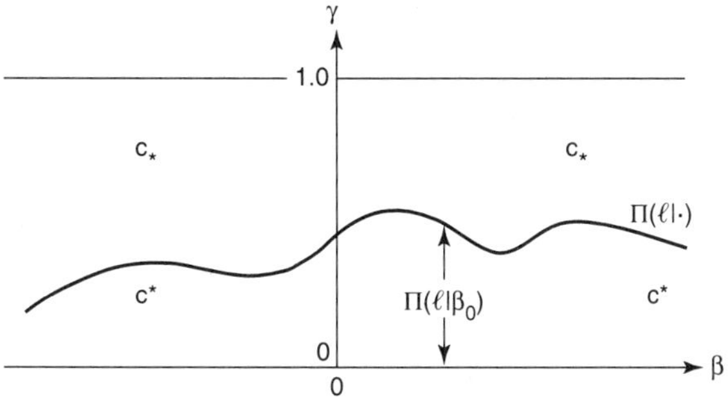

Figure 10.1
Reduction of conditional lottery to reference consequences

$l \;\overline{\sim|\beta}\; \langle\Pi(l|\beta)\rangle;$

let l' be defined on pairs (β, γ) by

$$l'(\beta,\gamma) = \begin{cases} c^* & \text{if} \quad \gamma \le \Pi(l|\beta), \\ c_* & \text{if} \quad \gamma > \Pi(l|\beta). \end{cases}$$

Then for any set B_0,

$l \;\overline{\sim|B_0}\; l'.$

Lottery l' can be given a very suggestive pictorial representation when β is a real number (see figure 10.1).

10.2.4 Statement of Results for Special Infinite Cases

We assume that $\tilde{\beta}$ is some unknown *real* number and consider three special cases for P. For each of these cases we state formulas which generalize the result of (10.5) and (10.5′) but defer all proofs to a later subsection.

Case 1 (Discrete) Let $\tilde{\beta}$ be a discrete rv with mf f; that is, let

a. $P(\tilde{\beta} = \beta) = f(\beta)$,
b. $f(\beta) \ge 0$, and $=$ holds except at values $\beta_1, \beta_2, \ldots$,
c. $\sum_i f(\beta_i) = 1$.

Then for any set B_0,

$$\Pi(l|B_0) = \frac{1}{P(\tilde{\beta} \in B_0)} \sum_{B_0} \Pi(l|\beta_i) f(\beta_i), \tag{10.6a}$$

and

$$P(\tilde{\alpha} \in A_0, \tilde{\beta} \in B_0) = \sum_{B_0} P(\tilde{\alpha} \in A_0 | \tilde{\beta} = \beta_i) f(\beta_i) \tag{10.6b}$$

where the sums are taken over all $\beta_i \in B_0$.

Case 2 (Continuous) Let $\tilde{\beta}$ be continuous rv with df f; that is, let

a. $P(\tilde{\beta} \leq \beta) = \int_{-\infty}^{\beta} f(t)\,dt$,

b. $f(t) \geq 0$, all t,

c. $\int_{-\infty}^{\infty} f(t)\,dt = 1$.

Then for any set B_0 such that $P(\tilde{\beta} \in B_0) > 0$,

$$\Pi(l|B_0) = \frac{1}{P(\tilde{\beta} \in B_0)} \int_{B_0} \Pi(l|\beta) f(\beta)\,d\beta, \tag{10.7a}$$

and

$$P(\tilde{\alpha} \in A_0, \tilde{\beta} \in B_0) = \int_{B_0} P(\tilde{\alpha} \in A_0 | \tilde{\beta} = \beta) f(\beta)\,d\beta, \tag{10.7b}$$

provided the integrals exist (Riemann sense).

Case 3 (Mixed) Let f_1 be a mf and f_2 be a df and assume that $\tilde{\beta}$ is such that for any β,

$$P(\tilde{\beta} \leq \beta) \equiv \lambda \textstyle\sum_{-\infty}^{\beta} f_1(t) + (1 - \lambda) \displaystyle\int_{-\infty}^{\beta} f_2(t)\,dt.$$

(See chapter 8, section 8.1.3.) Then for any set B_0 such that $P(\tilde{\beta} \in B_0) > 0$

$$\Pi(l|B_0) = \frac{1}{P(\tilde{\beta} \in B_0)} \left[\lambda \textstyle\sum_{B_0} \Pi(l|\beta) f_1(\beta) + (1 - \lambda) \displaystyle\int_{B_0} \Pi(l|\beta) f_2(\beta)\,d\beta \right] \tag{10.8a}$$

and

$$\begin{aligned} P(\tilde{\alpha} \in A_0, \tilde{\beta} \in B_0) &= \lambda \textstyle\sum_{B_0} P(\tilde{\alpha} \in A_0 | \tilde{\beta} = \beta) f_1(\beta) \\ &\quad + (1 - \lambda) \displaystyle\int_{B_0} P(\tilde{\alpha} \in A_0 | \tilde{\beta} = \beta) f_2(\beta)\,d\beta, \end{aligned} \tag{10.8b}$$

provided the integrals exist.

10.2.5 More General Results and Proofs[3]

In this section we generalize the results of section 10.2.4 and provide all proofs.

---

3. The material in this section requires more mathematical preparation than is needed in the remainder of the book.

Results for General B

Let the set B be completely general and suppose for a given lottery l that $\Pi(l|\beta)$ has been assessed for each β; let l' be as defined in Basic Assumption 7 (Conditional Substitutability); let $B_0 = B$ in that assumption. We then have $l \sim l'$ and therefore $\Pi(l) = \Pi(l')$. But by Theorem 1 of chapter 8, section 8.1.4, we have

$$\Pi(l) = \Pi(l') = \int_B \Pi(l|\beta)\, dP(\beta), \tag{10.9a}$$

where the integral is taken in the Lebsegue sense; the variable β plays the role of θ and $\Pi(l|\beta)$ plays the role of $h(\theta)$.

Since $[l \overline{\sim | B_0} \, l']$ by Basic Assumption 7, we have $\Pi(l|B_0) = \Pi(l'|B_0)$; and if $P(B_0) > 0$, it is only necessary to replace the P-measure on subsets of B by the conditional P-measure on subsets of B given B_0. We then get

$$\Pi(l|B_0) = \Pi(l'|B_0) = \int_{B_0} \Pi(l|\beta)\, dP(\beta|B_0) \tag{10.10a}$$

where for any $B_1 \subset B_0$

$$P(B_1|B_0) = \frac{P(B_1)}{P(B_0)}. \tag{10.11}$$

From (10.10a) and (10.11) we obtain the consistency requirement

$$\Pi(l|B_0) = \frac{1}{P(B_0)} \int_{B_0} \Pi(l|\beta)\, dP(\beta) \tag{10.12a}$$

for all B_0 such that $P(B_0) > 0$.

If l is the special lottery that gives c^* whenever $\tilde{\alpha} \in A_0$ and c_* otherwise, then by definition

$$\Pi(l) = P(A_0), \qquad \Pi(l|B_0) = P(A_0|B_0), \qquad \text{and} \qquad \Pi(l|\beta) = P(A_0|\beta).$$

In this case formulas (10.9a), (10.10a), and (10.12a) specialize to the cases:

$$P(A_0) = \int_B P(A_0|\beta)\, dP(\beta), \tag{10.9b}$$

$$P(A_0|B_0) = \int_{B_0} P(A_0|\beta)\, dP(\beta|B_0), \tag{10.10b}$$

and

$$P(A_0 \cap B_0) = P(A_0|B_0)P(B_0) = \int_{B_0} P(A_0|\beta)\,dP(\beta). \tag{10.12b}$$

The results (10.12a, 12b) reduce respectively to (10.6a, 6b) for the discrete case, to (10.9a, 9b) for the continuous case, and to (10.8a, 8b) for the mixed case. It is possible to prove the result in (10.6) for the discrete case with far less machinery than we brought to bear. Indeed, for the discrete case we could have obtained (10.6b) without use of Basic Assumption 7 (Conditional Substitutability).

10.3 Bayes' Theorem

10.3.1 The Posterior Mass Function Based on an Event of Positive Measure

Let us once again return to the situation where $\tilde{s}$ is the unknown state and $\tilde{z}$ is the unknown outcome of experimentation. In what follows $\tilde{s}$ will play the role of $\tilde{\beta}$ and $\tilde{z}$ the role of $\tilde{\alpha}$. We assume that before $\tilde{z}$ is observed, the initial probability assessments are given in terms of

a. a prior mf, f', for $\tilde{s}$, and
b. a family of conditional distributions, $P(\tilde{z} = z|\tilde{s} = s)$.

We assume that $\tilde{s}$ can either take on a finite or a denumerable number of values with positive probabilities. The results to be stated immediately below have already been proven for the *finite* case.

From these assessed probability inputs we now show that the *marginal* (or unconditional) probability that $\tilde{z}$ will assume some specific value z^* is given by

$$P(\tilde{z} = z^*) = \sum P(\tilde{z} = z^*)|\tilde{s} = t)f'(t) \tag{10.13}$$

(where t is a dummy variable of summation, and the summation is understood to be over all t values for which $f'(t) > 0$), and that, posterior to observing $\tilde{z} = z^*$, the rv $\tilde{s}$ will have a revised mf which is given by

$$f''(s|z^*) = \frac{P(\tilde{z} = z|\tilde{s} = s)f'(s)}{P(\tilde{z} = z^*)}, \tag{10.14}$$

provided that $P(\tilde{z} = z^*) > 0$.

Proof of (10.13) This follows immediately from (10.6b) and the observation that

$$P(\tilde{z} = z^*) = P(\tilde{z} = z^* \text{ and } \tilde{s} < \infty).$$

Proof of (10.14) We have by (10.6b)

$$P(\tilde{s} = s|\tilde{z} = z^*) = \frac{P(\tilde{s} = s \text{ and } \tilde{z} = z^*)}{P(\tilde{z} = z^*)}$$

$$= \frac{P(\tilde{z} = z^*|\tilde{s} = s)f'(s)}{P(\tilde{z} = z^*)}.$$

When (10.13) and (10.14) are combined, the resulting expression is given the name of *Bayes' Theorem* (for mf's):

$$f''(s|z^*) = \frac{P(\tilde{z} = z^*|\tilde{s} = s)f'(s)}{\sum_t P(\tilde{z} = z^*|\tilde{s} = t)f'(t)}. \tag{10.15}$$

10.3.2 The Posterior Density Function Based on an Event of Positive Measure

Once again, in what follows $\tilde{s}$ will play the role of $\tilde{\beta}$ and $\tilde{z}$ the role of $\tilde{\alpha}$. We assume that before $\tilde{z}$ is observed, the initial probability assessments are given in terms of

a. a prior df, f', for $\tilde{s}$, and

b. a family of conditional distributions, $P(\tilde{z} = z|\tilde{s} = s)$.

From these assessed probability inputs we will now show that the *marginal* (or unconditional) probability that $\tilde{z}$ will assume some specific value z^* is given by

$$P(\tilde{z} = z^*) = \int_{-\infty}^{\infty} P(\tilde{z} = z^*|\tilde{s} = t)f'(t)\,dt, \tag{10.16}$$

and that, posterior to observing $\tilde{z} = z^*$, the rv $\tilde{s}$ will have a revised df which is given by

$$f''(s|z^*) = \frac{P(\tilde{z} = z^*|\tilde{s} = s)f'(s)}{P(\tilde{z} = z^*)}, \tag{10.17}$$

provided that $P(\tilde{z} = z^*) > 0$.

Proof of (10.16) This follows immediately from (10.7b) and the observation that

$$P(\tilde{z} = z^*) = P(\tilde{z} = z^* \text{ and } \tilde{s} < \infty).$$

Proof of (10.17) We have by (10.7b)

$$P(\tilde{s} \leq s|\tilde{z} = z^*) = \frac{P(\tilde{s} \leq s \text{ and } \tilde{z} = z^*)}{P(\tilde{z} = z^*)}$$

$$= \frac{\int_{-\infty}^{s} P(\tilde{z} = z^*|\tilde{s} = t)f'(t)\,dt}{P(\tilde{z} = z^*)}$$

where the variable t in the last equality is merely the dummy variable of integration. Differentiating with respect to s, we get

$$f''(s|z^*) \equiv \frac{d}{ds} P(\tilde{s} \leq s|\tilde{z} = z^*)$$

$$= \frac{P(\tilde{z} = z^*|\tilde{s} = s)f'(s)}{P(\tilde{z} = z^*)}.$$ ■

When (10.16) and (10.17) are combined, the resulting expression is given the name of *Bayes' Theorem* (for df's):

$$f''(s|z^*) = \frac{P(\tilde{z} = z^*|\tilde{s} = s)f'(s)}{\int_{-\infty}^{\infty} P(\tilde{z} = z^*|\tilde{s} = t)f'(t)\,dt}. \tag{10.18}$$

10.3.3 The Likelihood Function

The expression $P(\tilde{z} = z|\tilde{s} = s)$ associates a number to every choice of z and s, and as such can be thought of as a function of two variables. If we hold s fixed, call its value s^*, then the expression $P(\tilde{z} = z|\tilde{s} = s^*)$ can be thought of as a function of the one variable z, and as such it is called the *conditional probability function* for $\tilde{z}$ given $\tilde{s} = s^*$. If we hold z fixed, call its value z^*, then the expression $P(\tilde{z} = z^*|\tilde{s} = s)$ can be thought of as a function of the one variable s, and as such it is called the *likelihood function* of $\tilde{s}$ given $\tilde{z} = z^*$. In a purely formal manner we define the symbol

$$L(s|z^*) \equiv P(\tilde{z} = z^*|\tilde{s} = s) \tag{10.19}$$

to emphasize the fact that in the likelihood function we think of z^* as a fixed value and s as a variable.

In terms of the likelihood notation we can express Bayes' Theorem as follows

$$f''(s|z^*) = C(z^*)L(s|z^*)f'(s), \tag{10.20}$$

where $C(z^*)$ does not depend on s and is given by

$$C(z^*) \equiv \frac{1}{P(\tilde{z} = z^*)}.$$

From (10.20) we draw the important observation: *The shape of the posterior density function of $\tilde{s}$ given z^* is given by the product of the likelihood function of $\tilde{s}$ given z^* and the prior df of $\tilde{s}$*—the factor $C(z^*)$ should be thought of merely as a "normalizing factor" which makes the area under the resulting product of $L(\cdot|z^*)$ and $f'(\cdot)$ equal to one. This observation is often given expression in terms of a formula where $C(z^*)$ is suppressed:

$$f''(s|z^*) \propto L(s|z^*)f'(s), \tag{10.21}$$

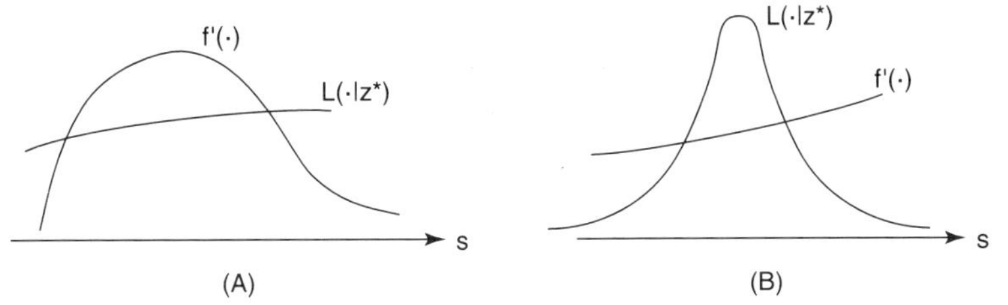

Figure 10.2
"Gentle" likelihood (A) or prior (B)

where the symbol $\propto$ is read "is proportional to." The product of $L(s|z^*)$ and an arbitrary function of z^* is also called a likelihood function because (10.20) and (10.21) remain true when $L(s|z^*)$ is replaced by such a product and $C(z^*)$ is redefined appropriately.

10.3.4 "Gentle" Priors

From formula (10.21) it is quite apparent how to draw qualitative conclusions about the shape of the posterior density function $f''(\cdot|z^*)$ in two extreme cases. If, as in figure 10.2A, L is *gentle* or slowly changing where f' is rapidly changing, and if L is not so large where f' is small as to make the product large, then the shape of their product will largely be determined by the prior df f'. In this case f'' will look like f' and we can say roughly that the observation z^* did not contain very much information. If as in figure 10.2B, f' is gentle or slowly changing where L is rapidly changing, and if f' is not so large where L is small as to make the product large, then the shape of their product will largely be determined by the likelihood function L. In this case f'' will look like L and we can say roughly that the likelihood function "swamped" the prior. When it is clear in a given situation that L swamps the prior f', it is often convenient as an approximation to treat f' as if it were strictly flat and to let $f''(s|z^*) \propto L(s|z^*)$.

10.4 Summary of Main Results of Section 10.2

Let the event that the unknown $\tilde{\alpha}$ lies in a subset A_0 be designated $(\tilde{\alpha} \in A_0)$; let the event that the unknown $\tilde{\beta}$ lies in a subset B_0 be designated $(\tilde{\beta} \in B_0)$; let the simultaneous occurrence of $(\tilde{\alpha} \in A_0)$ and $(\tilde{\beta} \in B_0)$ be designated $(\tilde{\alpha} \in A_0, \tilde{\beta} \in B_0)$. We adopt the abbreviated notation:

$P(A_0)$	for	$P(\tilde{\alpha} \in A_0)$,
$P(B_0)$	for	$P(\tilde{\beta} \in B_0)$,

$P(A_0|B_0)$ for $P(\tilde{\alpha} \in A_0|\tilde{\beta} \in B_0)$,

$P(A_0|\beta)$ for $P(\tilde{\alpha} \in A_0|\tilde{\beta} = \beta)$,

$P(A_0, B_0)$ for $P(\tilde{\alpha} \in A_0, \tilde{\beta} \in B_0)$.

Suppose $\tilde{\beta}$ is a discrete rv which can assume only a finite number of values $\{\beta_1, \ldots, \beta_i, \ldots, \beta_r\}$. Let f be the mf of $\tilde{\beta}$, that is,

$$P(\tilde{\beta} = \beta) = f'(\beta)$$

and $f'(\beta)$ is zero for all β other than $\beta_1, \ldots, \beta_r$. We have already proved the following results:

(1) $P(A_0, B_0) = \sum_{B_0} P(A_0|\beta) f'(\beta)$

where the summation is taken over all the β_i's that belong to B_0;

(2) $P(A_0) = \sum_B P(A_0|\beta) f'(\beta)$

where the summation is taken over all β_i's—the set B is understood to be the universal set for the β's.

If event $(\tilde{\alpha} \in A_0)$ is observed, then the conditional probability assessments for $\tilde{\beta}$ will in general be revised. Let $f''(\beta|A_0)$ denote $P(\tilde{\beta} = \beta|\tilde{\alpha} \in A_0)$. Hence the function $f''(\cdot|A_0)$—treated as a function of β—is the revised or posterior mf of the rv $\tilde{\beta}$ given $(\tilde{\alpha} \in A_0)$. We have already proved (cf. (5.11) and (5.12)) that

(3) $$f''(\beta|A_0) = \frac{P(A_0|\beta) f'(\beta)}{P(A_0)},$$

which is Bayes' formula for conditional probabilities.

We now wish to generalize formulas 1, 2, and 3 when $\tilde{\beta}$ is a continuous rv. It is often meaningful and useful to assign a probability to an event $(\tilde{\alpha} \in A_0)$ on the *hypothesis* that $\tilde{\beta}$ is known to have some specific value β even though $P(\tilde{\beta} = \beta) = 0$ for all β, and even though it is not possible to observe that $\tilde{\beta}$ is equal to any exact infinite decimal.

In chapters 2 and 3 (cf. Axiom 5) we related judgmental probabilities held prior and posterior to a given event $\Theta^\dagger$ by means of the notion of "called-off" bets. This required, however, that $P(\Theta^\dagger) > 0$. We run into difficulty if $\Theta^\dagger$ is the event $(\tilde{\beta} = \beta)$ and $P(\tilde{\beta} = \beta) = 0$. To circumvent this difficulty we need to adopt an additional basic assumption, which we call Conditional Substitutability. As a consequence of this additional assumption we prove that the set of assignments $P(A_0|\beta)$ for different values of β must be consistent with the assignments $P(A_0, B_0)$ for different subsets B_0. In particular for every B_0 we require a simple generalization of (1):

$$(1)^* \quad P(A_0, B_0) = \int_{B_0} P(A_0|\beta) f'(\beta)\, d\beta$$

where f' is the df of $\tilde{\beta}$ and the integral is taken over all β in the set B_0. From (1)* we immediately get

$$(2)^* \quad P(A_0) = \int_{-\infty}^{\infty} P(A_0|\beta) f'(\beta)\, d\beta.$$

If we let $f''(\cdot|A_0)$ denote the posterior density of $\tilde{\beta}$ given that $(\tilde{\alpha} \in A_0)$ has been observed, it is a simple matter to prove from (1)* that (3) *holds for df's as well as for mf's.*

As a by-product of the proof of the result leading to (1)* we also obtain the result that (1), (2), and (3) also hold when $\tilde{\beta}$ is a discrete rv with a denumerable number of possibilities.

This summary also touches on the material in sections 10.3.1 and 10.3.2 so that in returning to section 10.3 the reader should expect some redundancy.

11 Bernoulli Process

11.1 The Bernoulli Model

Many real-world processes of great practical importance can be described in terms of a number of distinct trials each of which has one or the other of two possible outcomes. Thus a worker or an automatic machine may produce pieces which are either "defective" or "good," a sample survey may draw households which are either "users" or "nonusers" of a certain product, and so forth. In order to have a standard terminology to use in discussing all processes of this kind, we shall call one of the two possible results of each trial a *success* (S) and the other a *failure* (F).

A simple class of processes of this kind are those in which there is absolutely no pattern to the occurrences of Ss and Fs: Ss tend to occur with exactly the same frequency in the first as in the last part of a long run; Ss tend to be followed by Fs exactly as frequently as Fs are followed by Fs, and so forth.

Although we will soon formalize this statement, roughly speaking, a process which meets these conditions will be called a *Bernoulli process*,[1] and the long-run fraction of successes (which is assumed to approach a limit) will be called the parameter p of the process. We can think of this parameter p as a property of the physical process which generates the sequence of Ss and Fs.

To keep a concrete situation in mind consider the case where an urn contains a proportion p of balls labelled S and the complementary proportion $1 - p$ labelled F and repeated canonical drawings are made from this urn with replacements; if the balls are thoroughly mixed up at each trial, the sequence of Ss and Fs will appear nearly patternless and experience has shown that the ratio of Ss to total trials will tend to a limit p. In the first part of this chapter we assume that p is known with certainty; later in the chapter we consider the case when p is uncertain and the decision maker, on the basis of his current information about $\tilde{p}$ assigns a probability distribution to $\tilde{p}$.

11.2 Probability Assignments for a Bernoulli Process with Known p

Consider a process which generates a sequence of trials $T_1, T_2, \ldots, T_i, \ldots$ such that every trial results in an S or an F. Let the *event* that trial T_i results in the outcome S be denoted by S_i, and similarly for F_i. Let H^n denote the "history" of the events of the first n trials; one possible history

1. The Bernoulli process was briefly mentioned in section 5.2.2 in connection with the assessment of judgmental probabilities when a great deal of empirical evidence is available.

would be

$$H^5 = S_1 S_2 F_3 S_4 F_5,$$

meaning that the outcome S occurred on trials 1, 2, and 4 while the outcome F occurred on trials 3 and 5.

Definition A process which generates Ss and Fs is said to be a *Bernoulli process with known parameter p* if after observing any particular history H^n of Ss and Fs in n trials, the probability that is assigned to the event S_{n+1} is p; in symbols,

$$P(S_{n+1}|H^n) = P(S_{n+1}) = p, \text{ for } n = 0, 1, \ldots, \text{ and all } H^n. \tag{11.1}$$

The fact that $P(S_{n+1}|H^n) = P(S_{n+1})$ means that events S_{n+1} and H^n are *independent*; similarly events F_{n+1} and H^n are independent; sometimes we express this independence by saying that the *trials are independent*. The fact that $P(S_{n+1}) = p$ for all n is sometimes expressed by saying that the process is *stable*. We shall also say that expression (11.1) is the fundamental set of probability assignments which describe a Bernoulli process with known p.

We now examine the probability that n trials will yield some one, particular history H^n. From (11.1) and the multiplication rule (5.4) it follows immediately that if $H^n = H^3 = S_1 S_2 F_3$, then the probability of this history is

$$\begin{aligned} P(S_1 S_2)P(F_3|S_1 S_2) &= P(S_1)P(S_2|S_1)P(F_3|S_1 S_2) \\ &= pp(1-p) = p^2(1-p); \end{aligned}$$

if $H^n = H^3 = S_1 F_2 S_3$, then the probability of this history is

$$p(1-p)p = p^2(1-p)$$

exactly as before; and similarly for $F_1 S_2 S_3$. Generalizing, we see (1) that the probability of any history H^n depends only on the number of trials n and the number of successes r, and (2) that if we let H_r^n denote any *one particular* history (sequence) with n trials and r successes, and hence $n - r$ failures, then, for a Bernoulli process with known p,

$$P(H_r^n) = p^r(1-p)^{n-r}. \tag{11.2}$$

11.3 Probability Assignments for a Bernoulli Process with Unknown p

11.3.1 Introduction

In many situations our general knowledge of the way a process works convinces us that it is (at least approximately) a Bernoulli process with *some* parameter p but we do not know the value p. In such situations we shall treat the unknown parameter as a random variable $\tilde{p}$ and assign it a probability distribution. Ordinarily, when p is unknown we will feel that no values in the interval $[0, 1]$ are absolutely impossible and in such circumstances we may wish to assign a density function to $\tilde{p}$. There are also many practical examples where the parameter p can assume only a finite number of possible values—for instance, where p is the proportion of individuals in a finite population that have some given attribute—and in these circumstances we may wish to assign a mass function to $\tilde{p}$. In addition, there will be times when no value of p in the interval $[0, 1]$ can be logically excluded, but it is nevertheless convenient as an approximation to use a mass function for $\tilde{p}$; there will be other times when p is limited to a finite number of possible values but it is convenient as an approximation to use a density function for $\tilde{p}$.

Assume that *before* observing any actual trials of the process in question, we assign some distributing[2] function f' to the rv $\tilde{p}$; assume further that we then observe some particular history H_r^n consisting of r successes and $(n - r)$ failures in some particular order; and assume finally that the conditional probability of event H_r^n given $(\tilde{p} = p)$ is

$$P(H_r^n | \tilde{p} = p) = p^r(1 - p)^{n-r}. \tag{11.3}$$

We now pose the fundamental problem: to find from these data the *revised* distributing function for $\tilde{p}$, which *takes into account the information contained in the observations* H_r^n.

We now make strong use of the results developed in chapter 10. Indeed, chapter 10 was partially developed so that at this very point in the argument we would not have to digress to develop the necessary techniques for handling conditional probabilities.

11.3.2 Posterior Distribution of $\tilde{p}$

Discrete Case Prior to observing the process, let $\tilde{p}$ have a mf f' where for some discrete set A of points

$$f'(p) \geq 0 \quad \text{for } p \in A,$$
$$= 0 \quad \text{for } p \notin A.$$

Posterior to observing some particular history H_r^n consisting of r successes and $(n - r)$ failures in some particular order, $\tilde{p}$ has a mf $f''(\cdot | H_r^n)$ where

2. We use the term *distributing* function to refer to either a mf or a df.

$$f''(p|H_r^n) = Cp^r(1-p)^{n-r}f'(p), \tag{11.4a}$$

and where

$$C = 1/\textstyle\sum_{p \in A} p^r(1-p)^{n-r}f'(p). \tag{11.4b}$$

Continuous Case Prior to observing the process, let $\tilde{p}$ have a df f'. Posterior to observing some particular history H_r^n consisting of r successes and $(n-r)$ failures in some particular order, $\tilde{p}$ has a df $f''(\cdot|H_r^n)$ where

$$f''(p|H_n^r) = Cp^r(1-p)^{n-r}f'(p), \tag{11.5a}$$

and where

$$C = 1\Big/\int_0^1 p^r(1-p)^{n-r}f'(p)\,dp. \tag{11.5b}$$

We can summarize both cases by stating: If $\tilde{p}$ has a prior distributing function f' with associated probability measure P'_p, then the posterior distributing function of $\tilde{p}$ at p, given H_r^n, is

$$f''(p|H_n^r) = Cp^r(1-p)^{n-r}f'(p) \tag{11.6a}$$

where

$$C = 1\Big/\int_0^1 p^r(1-p)^{n-r}\,\mathrm{d}P'_p. \tag{11.6b}$$

The proofs of (11.4) and (11.5) are immediate consequences of Bayes' Theorem as expressed in (10.15) and (10.18) with these identifications: $\tilde{p}$ plays the role of $\tilde{s}$ and the event H_r^n plays the role of the event $(\tilde{z} = z^*)$.

Two remarks are now appropriate. First, we wish to emphasize the point that the posterior distributing function of $\tilde{p}$ given H_r^n depends solely on the prior and on H_r^n and in *no way depends* on whether the decision maker (a) decided to take n observations and happened to observe a particular sequence with r Ss, or (b) decided to observe the process until r Ss appeared and happened to observe a particular sequence where the rth S occurred on the nth trial, or (c) decided to observe the process until interrupted by the telephone and happened to observe the particular sequence H_r^n.

Second, we feel that the focus of any theory of "statistical inference" should be directed toward the general objective of indicating how one should revise prior probability assessments in light of sample evidence to arrive at posterior probability assessments. In this sense, we feel that this section has enunciated the central theoretical message of statistical inference for the special case of sampling from a Bernoulli process.

11.3.3 Posterior Distribution of $\tilde{p}$: Simple Numerical Examples

Discrete Case Let the unknown parameter $\tilde{p}$ of a Bernoulli process be initially assigned a mf

$$f'(p) = \begin{cases} .6 & \text{if} \quad p = .3, \\ .4 & \text{if} \quad p = .7, \\ 0 & \text{if} \quad p \neq .3 \text{ or } .7. \end{cases}$$

Let 12 observations result in 8 Ss and 4 Fs in a particular sequence labelled H_8^{12}. Then the revised mf for $\tilde{p}$ given H_8^{12} is

$$f''(p|H_n^r) = \begin{cases} C(.3)^8(1-.3)^4(.6), & \text{if} \quad p = .3, \\ C(.7)^8(1-.7)^4(.4), & \text{if} \quad p = .7, \\ 0, & \text{if} \quad p \neq .3, .7, \end{cases}$$

where

$$C = 1/[(.3)^8(.7)^4(.6) + (.7)^8(.3)^4(.4)].$$

Thus

$$P(\tilde{p} = .7|H_8^{12}) = f''(.7|H_8^{12}) = \frac{(.7)^8(.3)^4(.4)}{(.3)^8(.7)^4(.6) + (.7)^8(.3)^4(.4)} = .95,$$

and

$$p(\tilde{p} = .3|H_8^{12}) = .05.$$

The numerical results of this example might seem surprising to you! Ward Edwards, a psychologist, concocted this example to show that most subjects seriously underestimate, from an intuitive point of view, the implications of sample evidence.

Continuous Case Let the unknown parameter $\tilde{p}$ of a Bernoulli process be initially assigned a df

$$f'(p) = 6p(1-p);$$

let 12 observations result in 8 Ss and 4 Fs in a particular sequence labelled H_8^{12}. Then the revised df for $\tilde{p}$ at p given H_8^{12} is

$$f''(p|H_8^{12}) = Cp^8(1-p)^4 6p(1-p) = C''p^9(1-p)^5,$$

where the constant C'' is a normalizing factor such that the area under $f''(\cdot|H_8^{12})$ from $0 \leq p \leq 1$ is 1; i.e.,

$$C'' = 1\bigg/\int_0^1 p^9(1-p)^5\,dp.$$

11.3.4 The Likelihood Function

We now specialize the discussion in section 10.3.3 about the likelihood function to the case of the Bernoulli model. In a purely formal manner we define the *likelihood function of p for given H_r^n* by

$$L(p|H_r^n) \equiv P(H_r^n|\tilde{p} = p) = p^r(1-p)^{n-r}. \tag{11.7}$$

The reader should keep in mind that the likelihood function $L(\cdot|H_r^n)$ is *not* a probability density function; for example, in general

$$\int_0^1 L(p|H_r^n)\,dp \neq 1.$$

In terms of the likelihood function the posterior distributing function is expressible as

$$f''(p|H_r^n) = CL(p|H_r^n)f'(p), \tag{11.8}$$

where C is a normalizing constant which depends on H_r^n but not on p. In terms of the proportionality symbol we can rewrite (11.8) as

$$f''(p|H_r^n) \propto L(p|H_r^n)f'(p). \tag{11.9}$$

In words: The posterior distributing function of $\tilde{p}$ given H_r^n is proportional to the product of the likelihood function and the prior distributing function.

At this point we merely call to the reader's attention that the likelihood function $L(\cdot|H_r^n)$, apart from a constant, is shaped like a beta density function with parameters $\rho = r + 1$, $\upsilon = n + 2$ (see (9.12) and figures 9.1, 9.2, and 9.3).

11.3.5 "Gentle" Prior Distributions

From formula (11.9) it is quite apparent how to draw qualitative conclusions about the shape of the posterior distributing function $f''(p|H_r^n)$ in two extreme cases. If, as in figure 11.1A, L is *gentle* or slowly changing

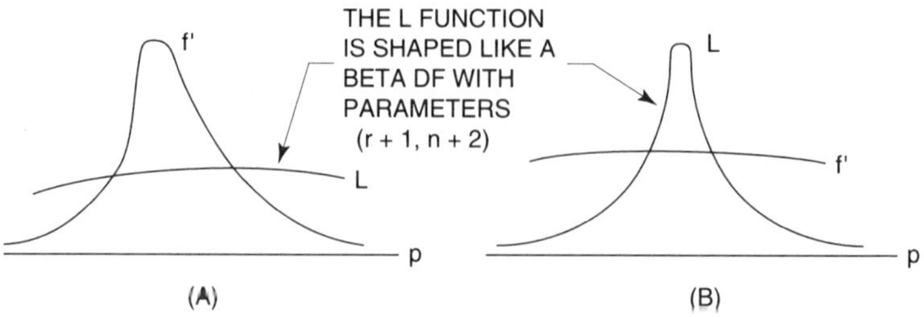

Figure 11.1
"Gentle" likelihood (A) or prior (B)

where f' is rapidly changing, then the shape of their product will largely be determined by the prior distributing function f'. If, as in figure 11.1B, f' is *gentle* or slowly changing where L is rapidly changing, then the shape of their product will largely be determined by the likelihood function L. As r and n increase, then, as was indicated in figure 9.2, the function L becomes very steep in the neighborhood of $p = r/n$ and eventually for any density function f' that is not too "spiky" the function L "takes over" in the sense that it alone essentially determines the shape of the posterior. This is exactly what we should expect.

11.4 The Beta Family of Priors[3]

11.4.1 Introduction

In the remaining sections of this chapter we shall consider the case where the unknown parameter $\tilde{p}$ of a Bernoulli process is given a prior density function in the so-called beta family. We remind the reader that this family has two adjustable parameters ρ and υ and by appropriately choosing these parameters one can obtain prior densities of a wide variety of shapes. This makes it possible in many situations to choose a beta prior density which more or less matches one's prior judgments about $\tilde{p}$. Furthermore, if $\tilde{p}$ is given a beta prior density and if a particular sequence of r successes and $n - r$ failures is observed, then the *posterior density of $\tilde{p}$ is also beta* and there is a very simple formula relating the prior parameters, the observed pair of statistics $(r, n - r)$, and the posterior parameters. We first show how to work with betas (section 11.4.2); then we investigate how sensitive the selection of a prior beta is as far as posterior assessments are concerned (section 11.4.3 and 11.4.4); finally, we show how to select parameters of a beta in order to fit judgments (section 11.5).

11.4.2 Prior to Posterior within the Beta Family

The beta family of prior distributions is the most convenient to use when working with a Bernoulli process because of the following simple but important theorem.

Theorem If the prior df of $\tilde{p}$ is beta with parameters (r', n') then observation of a particular sequence H_r^n of r successes in n trials leads to a *posterior* distribution of $\tilde{p}$ which is also beta with parameters

$$r'' = r' + r, \qquad n'' = n' + n. \tag{11.10}$$

3. The material in the remainder of this chapter uses the results in section 9.3 on the beta distribution.

Proof If $\tilde{p}$ has a prior beta (r', n'), then

$$f'(p) = C_1 p^{r'-1}(1-p)^{n'-r'-1}$$

where C_1 is a suitable constant. By (11.4), we then have

$$f''(p|H_r^n) = Cp^r(1-p)^{n-r}C_1p^{r'-1}(1-p)^{n'-r'-1}$$

$$= C_2 p^{(r+r')-1}(1-p)^{(n+n')-(r+r')-1},$$

where $C_2 = C \cdot C_1$. But this df is a beta df with parameters $(r' + r, n' + n)$ as was to be shown.

Example In the first example of section 11.3.3, $\tilde{p}$ was given a prior beta df with parameters (2, 4). We now know that after observing H_8^{12}, the posterior of $\tilde{p}$ is beta with parameters $(2 + 8, 4 + 12)$ or (10, 16); that is,

$$f''(p|H_8^{12}) = Cp^{10-1}(1-p)^{16-10-1},$$

which agrees, of course, with our previous result.

Observe the cumulative nature of these results for successive observations. If we start with a beta (2, 4) and observe H_8^{12}, we get a new beta df with parameters (10, 16). If we now take an additional sample of 15 observations and get 9 Ss then our revised beta df will have parameters $(10 + 9, 16 + 15)$ or (19, 31). Notice that we could couple the two samples together to form one sample of the type H_{17}^{27}, and if this is used to modify (2, 4), we once again end up with (19, 31).

Not only is it easy to revise a beta prior df in the light of sample results from a Bernoulli process to arrive at a posterior beta df, but it is then possible to use existing tables of the beta df (cf. section 9.3.2) to find posterior probabilities for such events as $(\tilde{p} \leq p_0)$, $(\tilde{p} \geq p_0)$, $(p_1 \leq \tilde{p} \leq p_2)$; furthermore, the integrals of some simple functions taken with respect to a beta df lead to results which are tabulated (cf. section 9.3.3 on expectations), and this will be important in the next chapter when we turn our attention to decision problems using beta df's.

11.4.3 Sensitivity of Posterior Distributions to Prior Parameters

In most if not all situations where decision theory is applied in practice, the responsible decision maker will have a very hard time deciding on the exact expression of his prior judgments concerning $\tilde{p}$—or concerning *any* rv whose value will determine the consequence of an act. Even specifying exact values for two or three quartiles will in general be difficult enough, let alone any specification of further details. Further difficulties may easily arise when an attempt is made to simplify analysis by using a member of a convenient family of functions, such as the beta in the case we are now

Table 11.1
Judgmental prior distributions

Distribution number	Parameters		Quartiles		Moments	
	r'	n'	$p'_{.5}$	$p'_{.75}$	$\bar{p}'$	$\breve{p}'$
1	2	2	.20	.30	.22	.017
2	1	4	.20	.37	.25	.038
3	4	12	.32	.42	.33	.017
4	2	6	.32	.45	.33	.032

studying, to represent the decision maker's quantified judgments; for it will generally be true that no member of a two-parameter family will agree exactly with three or more specifications (such as quartiles) expressed by the decision maker.

There is no single, generally acceptable way around these difficulties. The decision maker must either resolve his decision problem by using direct, unaided intuition or else decide exactly what prior distribution he is *willing to take as a basis for action.* In many situations, however, the difficulties we are discussing may be completely negligible because any prior distribution which the decision maker is willing even to consider adopting can be shown to lead to results that are the same for all practical purposes as the results of any other prior distribution he would be willing to consider. In such situations all the decision maker really has to do is to choose a prior distribution which agrees approximately with his *roughly formulated* judgments about $\tilde{p}$ (or any other rv on which consequences depend).

The situations in which the *exact* specification of the decision maker's judgments is likely to be unnecessary are those in which the analysis of the decision problem will rest, not directly on the judgmental distribution, but on a posterior distribution which combines a substantial amount of sample or experimental evidence with the original judgmental distribution. We shall proceed by first looking at two specific examples and then discussing in a more general way what we mean by "substantial" sample evidence.

Consider a decision maker faced with a problem involving a Bernoulli process and suppose that when first asked for his judgment concerning $\tilde{p}$ she answers that she would put the median somewhere between .20 and .30 and would put the third quartile at a value not less than .10 or more than .15 above the median, but to be more precise would be very painful indeed. In table 11.1 and figure 11.2 we show parameters and certain characteristics of four beta distributions corresponding roughly to the "limits" imposed by the decision maker, and it is immediately apparent

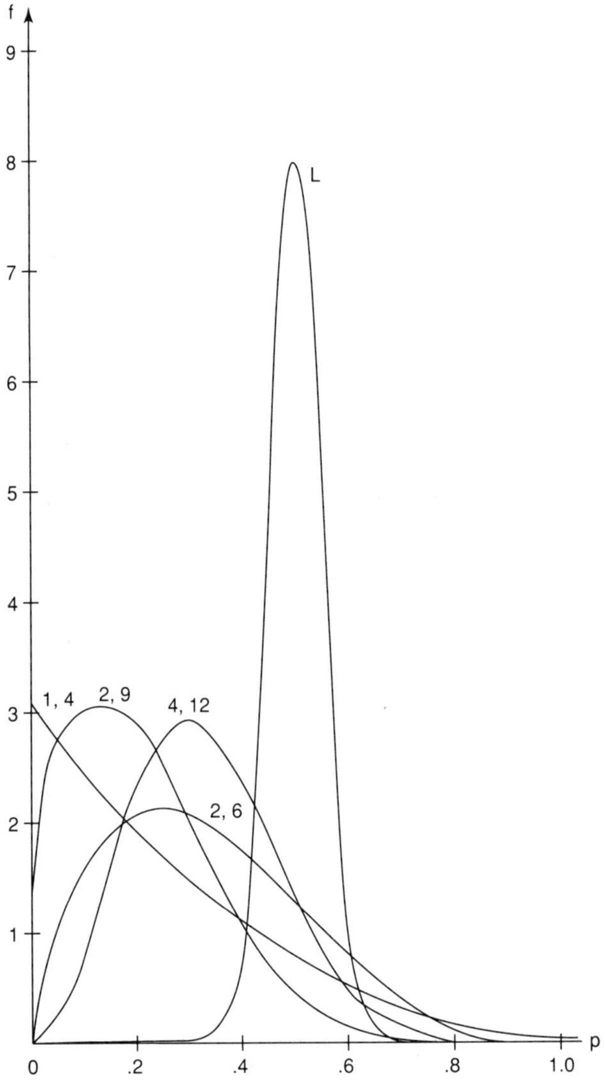

Figure 11.2
Four beta priors and likelihood for $n = 100$, $r = 50$

Table 11.2
Disbributions posterior to $n=100$, $r=50$

Distribution number	Parameters		Parameters		Moments	
	r''	n''	$p''_{.5}$	$p''_{.75}$	$\bar{p}''$	$\breve{p}''$
1	52	109	.48	.51	.48	.0023
2	51	104	.49	.52	.49	.0024
3	54	112	.48	.51	.48	.0022
4	52	106	.49	.52	.49	.0023

that these distributions might well have seriously different implications for action if an act were to be selected directly on the basis of the chosen distribution.

Suppose, however, that action does not have to be based entirely on this distribution because after assigning it the decision maker has observed the process during 100 trials, 50 of which were successes. In table 11.2 we show the posterior distributions corresponding to the priors of table 11.1, and it is immediately apparent that there is *exceedingly little practical difference between any two of these distributions.*

To understand these results, go back to section 11.3.4 and then consider figure 11.2 pertaining to the example just analyzed. Bayes' theorem in the form (11.8) says that, given any prior density of $\tilde{p}$, such as any one of the four in figure 11.2, we can plot the shape of the corresponding posterior density by selecting a large number of p's, for each one reading $f'(p)$ and $L(p|H_{50}^{100})$ from the appropriate curves in figure 11.2, and plotting the *products* $f'(p)L(p|_{50}^{100})$ against p. Inspection of the figure then shows immediately that, *regardless* of which prior f is used in this process, (1) outside the interval [.35,.65], the products $f'(p)L(p|H_{50}^{100})$ will be essentially 0 because the likelihood factor L is essentially 0 outside this interval; (2) inside the interval [.35,.65], the shape of the product curve will be almost entirely determined by the shape of the L curve because the *variation* in the height of this curve across the interval is so much greater than the variation in the height of any of the f' curves. *Absolute* height does not matter, because restoration of the constant of proportionality in Bayes' theorem will automatically rescale every product curve (posterior density) so that the area under it is 1.

The conclusion that emerges from our argument is therefore this:

If the prior distribution is "gentle" relative to the likelihood function, then the posterior distribution is largely determined by the likelihood function.

In our particular example, we would get essentially the same posterior distribution from *any* prior density whose variation across [.35,.65] was

Table 11.3

Distribution number	Prior parameters		Posterior parameters		Posterior moments	
	r'	n'	r''	n''	$\bar{p}''$	$\breve{p}''$
1	.1	2	.1	102	.001	.00001
2	1	2	1	102	.01	.0001

no greater than that of the four f curves in figure 11.2, provided the prior probability of the outside of this interval is not so enormous compared to the prior probability of the interval as to counterbalance the fact that L is so small outside the interval.

It is very tempting to try to simplify this principle by saying that the posterior will be largely determined by the sample if n is large relative to n', but unfortunately this is not necessarily true. Suppose for example that we have a sample with $r = 0$, $n = 100$, and two potential priors with parameters $r' = .1$, $n' = 2$, and $r' = 1$, $n' = 2$ respectively. The corresponding posteriors are shown in table 11.3, and it is immediately apparent that the two posteriors will *not* be equivalent in most applications.

What *can* be asserted about beta priors is the following: Let r'_0 and $(n'_0 - r'_0)$ be the *largest* values the decision maker would be willing even to consider, and let $(r'_0 - \delta)$ and $(n'_0 - r'_0 - \varepsilon)$ be the *smallest*. First, if both (1) δ is very small relative to r, and (2) ε is very small relative to $(n - r)$, then it will in general not be worth the decision maker's while to spend much effort on determination of the *exact* r' and n' which best express his judgments. Second, if both (1) r'_0 is very small relative to r, and (2) $(n'_0 - r'_0)$ is very small relative to $(n - r)$, then for posterior analysis the problem of choosing any specific r' and n' can usually be suppressed altogether by simply setting $r'' = r$ and $n'' = n$. This does not amount to saying that the decision maker adopts a beta prior distribution with $r' = n' = 0$, since no such thing exists; it amounts rather to saying that if the "true" *posterior* distribution would have r'' virtually equal to r and n'' virtually equal to n, we can save a great deal of bother with virtually no loss of useful accuracy by setting the posterior parameters $r'' = r$ and $n'' = n$ without bothering to specify the *exact prior* distribution *at all.*

11.4.4 The Problem of "No Prior Information"

Having seen that under certain circumstances it does not matter too much whether or not the prior distribution on which an analysis is based matches the decision maker's judgments exactly, we are ready to take up what is in a sense a diametrically opposite problem, namely the problem that arises when the decision maker feels that he cannot assign *any* prior distribution to $\tilde{p}$ because he has no information on which to base such a distribution.

It is perhaps inherent in human nature that a great deal of thought should have been expended in attempts to show that some one particular prior distribution of $\tilde{p}$ objectively represents "complete ignorance" about $\tilde{p}$, but the upshot of all the discussion is that certainly no such distribution exists and almost certainly the expression "complete ignorance" is devoid of real meaning. As to the distribution, the usual suggestion has been that if we know nothing about p, we "should" treat all possible ps as "equally likely"—more accurately, that we should treat all subintervals of equal length in $[0, 1]$ as equally likely, thus implying that the distribution of $\tilde{p}$ should be rectangular on $[0, 1]$.

This suggestion may seem appealing at first sight, but it breaks down as soon as we examine it a little more closely. It is purely arbitrary, although often very convenient, to characterize a Bernoulli process by the long-run ratio p of successes to trials; we could just as legitimately characterize it by the long-run ratio $\rho \equiv 1/p$ of trials to successes. Now if we are in a state of "complete ignorance" about p, we are certainly in a state of "complete ignorance" about $\rho \equiv 1/p$; and if "complete ignorance" implies a rectangular distribution, then we must assign rectangular distributions to both $\tilde{p}$ and $\tilde{\rho}$; but this is impossible, as can easily be seen. If $\tilde{p} \in [0, \frac{1}{2}]$ is as likely as $\tilde{p} \in [\frac{1}{2}, 1]$, this clearly implies that $\tilde{\rho} = 1/p \in [1, 2]$ is as likely as $\tilde{\rho} \in [2, \infty)$, but these two equally likely intervals for $\tilde{\rho}$ are *not* of equal length. In other words, $\tilde{p}$ and $\tilde{\rho}$ *cannot* have mutually consistent rectangular distributions, and we must therefore abandon the idea that rectangular distributions express "complete ignorance"—or for that matter, any other state of mind that applies equally to $\tilde{p}$ and $\tilde{\rho}$.

We conclude that although there is no "correct" way of translating "ignorance" about a true p into a particular prior distribution of $\tilde{p}$, the decision maker *can* assess the distribution of $\tilde{p}$ very roughly when any distribution he would be willing to consider is "gentle" relative to the likelihood function of a sample which has already been taken. When this condition is not met, the analysis of a decision problem may very well be very sensitive to changes in the judgmental distribution of $\tilde{p}$, and the decision maker will have to accept this fact and live with it.

11.5 Selection of a Distribution to Express Judgments about $\tilde{p}$

Let us now return to the decision maker who, in order to analyze a concrete decision problem, wishes to assign a distribution to some unknown quantity $\tilde{p}$ which in his opinion can have any value from 0 to 1. Although he must ultimately specify $P(\tilde{p} \leq p)$ for all p in $[0, 1]$, he does not have to do this directly, and in most situations he will find it easier not to do it directly.

In many—although not all—practical applications it will be possible to represent the decision maker's probability assignments in a way completely satisfactory *to him* by means of a beta density function with suitably chosen values for the parameters ρ and υ. The family of curves corresponding to the beta formula (9.12) with all possible values of the parameters ρ and υ is in fact remarkably rich; the reader can get some idea of this richness from figure 9.1. Some members of the family are U, J, or L shaped, concentrating the probability towards either end or both ends of $[0, 1]$; others are humped, concentrating the probability in some interior part of the interval. Curves of any of these shapes may be very "tight," putting most of the probability in a small subinterval, or very "loose," spreading the probability out more broadly. Among the latter, the beta family includes the rectangular density, which makes all subintervals of equal length equally likely; among the former, it includes members which can put any desired probability however large on any desired subinterval however small.

In section 11.5.1 we discuss ways whereby a decision maker can assess a left-tail cumulative distribution for $\tilde{p}$. In section 11.5.2 we indicate how such an assessed cumulative distribution can be approximated in a simple manner by a beta df. We do not, however, formalize the important question of whether this approximation is "good enough" for further analysis. In section 11.5.3 we give examples to help give the reader some feeling for the adequacy of such beta approximations.

11.5.1 Assessment of a Left-Tail Cumulative Distribution for $\tilde{p}$

At this point we suggest the reader reread the discussion in section 7.6, "Probability Assessments for a RV," and specialize that discussion by letting the unknown parameter $\tilde{p}$ of a Bernoulli process play the role of the rv $\tilde{\theta}$. For our present purposes, section 7.6.1 on fitting by use of judgmental fractiles is most relevant. In summary, the advice given there suggests that the decision maker should subdivide the interval $[0, 1]$, the range of possible values of $\tilde{p}$, into two equally likely intervals, and then successively subdivide these intervals in turn into two equally likely subintervals, and so forth. By this procedure the decision maker can generate points on his assessed left-tail cumulative function for $\tilde{p}$ of the form (p_k, k) where $k = \frac{1}{2}, \frac{1}{4}, \frac{3}{4}, \frac{1}{8}, \ldots$. By plotting these points and fairing a curve among them, the decision maker can assess a curve of $P(\tilde{p} \leq p)$ plotted against p.

In the exercises to this chapter the reader is asked to assess left-tail cumulative distributions for $\tilde{p}$ for various interpretations of $\tilde{p}$.

11.5.2 Fitting a Beta Density by Moments

From an assessed left-tail distribution for the unknown parameter $\tilde{p}$ of a Bernoulli process it is not difficult to compute approximately the expectation $\bar{p}$ and the variance $\breve{p}$ of $\tilde{p}$. Once $\bar{p}$ and $\breve{p}$ have been determined, it is then a simple task to select that member of the beta family which has that mean and variance. In particular, from (9.16) we get

$$\upsilon = \frac{\bar{p}(1-\bar{p})}{\breve{p}} - 1, \qquad \rho = \upsilon\bar{p}. \tag{11.11}$$

In order to calculate $\bar{p}$ and $\breve{p}$ from an assessed left-tail cumulative function we suggest two approaches.

First Method

From the assessed curve read off fractiles $p_{.05}, p_{.15}, \ldots, p_{.85}, p_{.95}$ where p_k is such that $P[\tilde{p} \leq p_k] = k$. Then, approximately,

$$\bar{p} \doteq \tfrac{1}{10}[p_{.05} + p_{.15} + \cdots + p_{.85} + p_{.95}],$$

and

$$\breve{p} \doteq \tfrac{1}{10}[p^2_{.05} + p^2_{.15} + \cdots + p^2_{.85} + p^2_{.95}] - \bar{p}^2.$$

Instead of using 10 fractiles the formulas for use with n fractiles would be

$$\bar{p} \doteq \frac{1}{n} \textstyle\sum_{j=0}^{n-1} p_{(j+0.5)/n}$$

and

$$\breve{p} \doteq \frac{1}{n} \textstyle\sum_{j=0}^{n-1} p^2_{(j+0.5)/n} - \bar{p}^2.$$

Second Method

Divide the interval $[0, 1]$ into n equally spaced intervals by points $1/n$, $2/n, \ldots, (n-1)/n$. Select the midpoint $(j-0.5)/n$ of the interval $(j-1)/n$ to j/n and concentrate the mass of

$$P\left(\tilde{p} \leq \frac{j}{n}\right) - P\left(\tilde{p} \leq \frac{j-1}{n}\right)$$

at this point. The mean and variance of this discrete distribution is then

$$\bar{p} \doteq \frac{1}{n} \textstyle\sum_{j=1}^{n} \frac{j-0.5}{n} \left\{P\left(\tilde{p} \leq \frac{j}{n}\right) - P\left(\tilde{p} \leq \frac{j-1}{n}\right)\right\},$$

and

$$\check{p} \doteq \frac{1}{n}\sum_{j=1}^{n}\left(\frac{j-0.5}{n}\right)^2\left\{P\left(\tilde{p}\le\frac{j}{n}\right)-P\left(\tilde{p}\le\frac{j-1}{n}\right)\right\}-\bar{p}^2.$$

11.5.3 Fitting a Beta Distribution Directly to Quartiles

Instead of fairing a graphical left-tail distribution for $\tilde{p}$ and computing moments, we can try to fit the beta to the original fractiles. Since the beta family has only two adjustable parameters, it will not be possible in general to find a member of the family that agrees *exactly* with more than two of the decision maker's judgmental fractiles, but in at least very many cases it will be possible to find a satisfactory compromise.

The tables of fractiles of the beta distribution at the end of the book will be of help in looking for a suitable member of the family; a starting point for the search can also be obtained using the following approximation. Let p_k be the kth fractile of a beta distribution; let

$$a_k \equiv \{[p_{.5}(1-p_k)]^{1/2}-[p_k(1-p_{.5})]^{1/2}\}^2. \tag{11.12}$$

The parameters of the beta distribution are then given approximately by

$$\rho = cp_{.5}+\tfrac{1}{3} \quad \text{and} \quad \upsilon = c+\tfrac{2}{3} \tag{11.13}$$

where c is determined according to one of the three cases below:

Case 1 Given $p_{.50}$ and $p_{.25}$: $c = .112/a_{.25}$. (11.14a)

Case 2 Given $p_{.50}$ and $p_{.75}$: $c = .112/a_{.75}$. (11.14b)

Case 3 Given $p_{.75}$, $p_{.50}$, and $p_{.25}$: $c = .056\left[\frac{1}{a_{.25}}+\frac{1}{a_{.75}}\right]$. (11.14c)

These approximations are derived from the fact that if $\tilde{p}$ is distributed according to a beta density with parameters ρ and υ, then the rv

$$\tilde{z} = 2\{[\tilde{p}(\upsilon-\rho-\tfrac{1}{3})]^{1/2}-[(1-\tilde{p})(\rho-\tfrac{1}{3})]^{1/2}\}$$

has approximately a so-called standardized Normal distribution, which we shall meet later on and study in great detail.

Illustration If $\rho = 2$ and $\upsilon = 9$, then from the beta fractile tables,

$p_{.25} = .1206,\qquad p_{.50} = .2011,\qquad p_{.75} = .3027.$

Suppose we now reverse the problem, given $p_{.25}$, $p_{.50}$, and $p_{.75}$ as above to find ρ and υ by use of the approximations (11.14). Fitting to the .25 and .50 fractiles, (i.e., using (11.14a)),

$c = 9.38, \qquad \rho \doteq 2.22, \qquad \upsilon \doteq 10.05;$

fitting to the .75 and .50 fractiles, (i.e., using (11.14b)),

$c = 8.27, \qquad \rho \doteq 2.00, \qquad \upsilon \doteq 8.94;$

fitting to all three fractiles $p_{.25}$, $p_{.50}$, and $p_{.75}$, (i.e., using (11.14c)),

$c = 8.82, \qquad \rho \doteq 2.10, \qquad \upsilon \doteq 9.47.$

Exercises

1. Consider an urn with a proportion p of balls marked S and a proportion $1 - p$ marked F. Assume that balls are drawn successively from the urn with replacements after each drawing. Let S_i and F_i denote respectively the event that the ith trial or drawing results in an S or an F. Assume that regardless of the past outcomes you feel that the next drawing is canonical: all balls are "equally likely" to be drawn. For this experiment argue that the fundamental system of probability assignments given in (11.1) is appropriate.

2. a. From this interpretation of a Bernoulli process argue that

   $f_b(k|n, p) = f_b(n - k|n, 1 - p).$

   b. From (a) show that

   $F_b(r|n, p) = G_b(n - r|n, 1 - p)$

   and

   $G_b(r|n, p) = F_b(n - r|n, 1 - p).$

3. In a Bernoulli process the rv $(\tilde{n}|1, p)$ can be thought of as the *waiting* time for the first success. For the purposes of this problem call this rv $\tilde{n}_1$.

   a. Argue directly (without use of (9.27)) that

   $P(\tilde{n}_1 = n) = (1 - p)^{n-1}p,$

   $P(\tilde{n}_1 > n) = (1 - p)^n.$

   b. From the above result, show that

   $P(\tilde{n}_1 > n + m|\tilde{n}_1 > m) = P(\tilde{n}_1 > n),$

   and interpret this result.

   c. Let $\tilde{v}$ be a rv with range set $\{1, 2, 3, \ldots\}$. Assume for any $m \geq 1$ and $n \geq 1$

   $P(\tilde{v} > n + m|\tilde{v} > m) = P(\tilde{v} > n).$

   Show that $\tilde{v}$ must then have a mf of the form

   $P(\tilde{v} = n) = (1 - p)^{n-1}p$

   for some p.

   Outline of Proof Let $G(a) = P(\tilde{v} > a)$. Show $G(n + m) = G(n)G(m)$. Show $G(n + 1) = G(1)G(n) = [G(1)]^{n+1}$. Observe that $P(\tilde{v} = n) = G(n - 1) - G(n)$. Conclude proof.

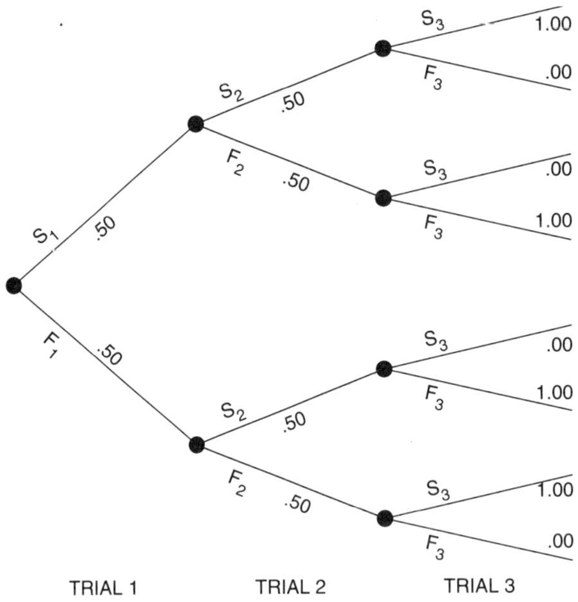

Figure 11E.1

4. Imagine a process which at each trial produces a digit from 0 to 9, and imagine that after each trial the process can be adjusted, if needed, in such a manner that regardless of the past outcomes all 10 possibilities are equally likely in your opinion. The process described above can be thought of as generating an infinite decimal $0.a_1a_2a_3 \ldots$ is the outcome of trial i for $i = 1, 2, \ldots$.

   a. What is the probability that the process generates an infinite decimal that falls in the interval $[0, b]$ (where $0 \leq b \leq 1$)?

   b. Let b itself be expressible as an infinite decimal $0.b_1b_2b_3 \ldots$. Show that the probability that it will take more than n trials to determine whether the generated number will be in $[0, b]$ or not is $1/10^n$.

5. a. Consider an urn containing 6 balls marked S and 4 balls marked F and let repeated drawings be made from this urn *without* replacement. The event that the ith drawing (trial) results in S will be denoted by S_i, and similarly for F_i. Assume that at each trial the ball is canonically selected from the set of balls remaining in the urn.
   From the formula

   $$P(S_2) = P(S_1)P(S_2|S_1) + P(F_1)P(S_2|F_1),$$

   verify that

   $$P(S_2) = P(S_1) = .6.$$

   b. Without the use of any formulas, argue from a commonsense point of view that

   $$P(S_i) = .6, \quad \text{for} \quad i = 1, 2, \ldots, 10.$$

   c. Do these 10 trials constitute a segment of a Bernoulli process? If not, why not?

6. Consider a process defined in terms of the tree diagram in figure 11E.1 and show that with this process.

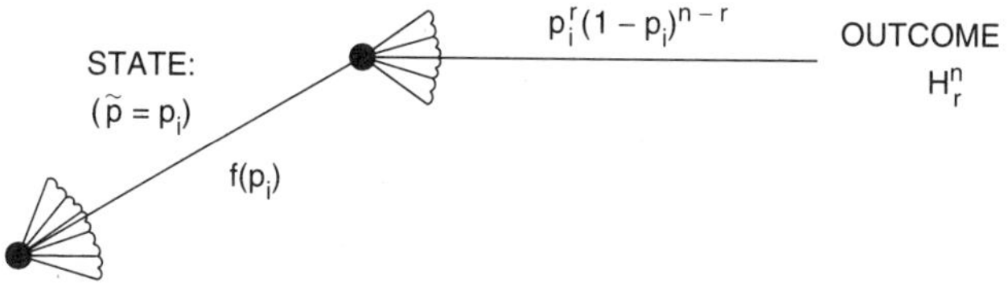

Figure 11E.2

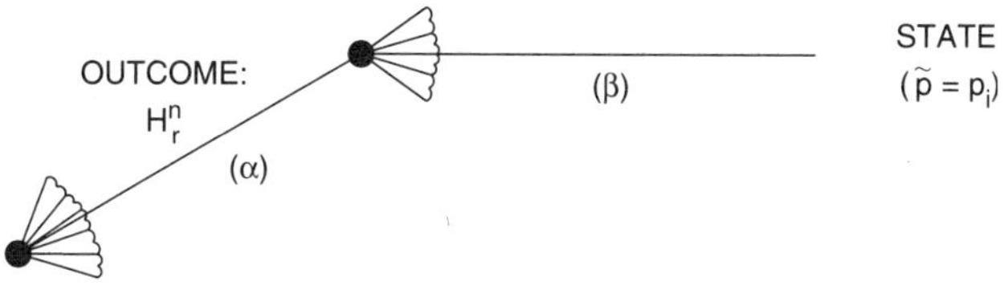

Figure 11E.3

$P(S_1) = P(S_2) = P(S_3) = .50.$

$P(S_2|S_1) = P(S_2|F_1) = .50.$

$P(S_3|S_1) = P(S_3|F_1) = .50.$

$P(S_3|S_2) = P(S_3|F_2) = .50.$

Is this a segment of a Bernoulli process? If not, why not?

7. The primary purpose of this exercise is to help the reader relate the material in section 11.3 with the discussion in chapter 6, especially the part concerned with assigning probabilities to the decision tree.

Suppose the unknown parameter $\tilde{p}$ of a Bernoulli process must be one of the values $p_1, \ldots, p_m$. Let f be the mf for the rv $\tilde{p}$ so that $P(\tilde{p} = p_i) = f(p_i)$. Let H_r^n denote some particular sequence of r Ss and $(n - r)$ Fs. We then have the tree shown in figure 11E.2.

From these assignments complete the joint assignments in the two-way table of table 11E.1.

Write down a formula for entries (a), (b), (c), and (d). Now "flip the tree" and indicate what probabilistic entries should stand in lieu of (α) and (β) in figure 11E.3.

Table 11.E.1
State

Outcomes	$(\tilde{p}=p_1)$	. . .	$(\tilde{p}=p_i)$	. . .	$(\tilde{p}=p_m)$	Marginal
⋮	⋮		⋮		⋮	⋮
H_r^n	(a)	. . .	(b)	. . .	(c)	(d)
⋮	⋮		⋮		⋮	⋮
Marginal	$f(p_1)$	. . .	$f(p_i)$	. . .	$f(p_m)$	1

8. A production process is adjusted daily and then tested. The output of the process in a given day acts like a Bernoulli process where the proportion p of defective items depends on the quality of two critical adjustments A and B according to the following table:

State	Probability of the state	Resulting process p
A good, B good	.6	.00
A good, B bad	.2	.05
A bad, B good	.1	.10
A bad, B bad	.1	1.00
	1.0	

For this process a sample of $n = 3$ items are taken; let $\tilde{r}$ denote the number of defective items in the sample.

a. Give the conditional mf of $\tilde{r}$ for each of the four values of p.

b. Exhibit the joint table (4×4) of state-outcome probabilities.

c. Give the conditional mf of $\tilde{p}$ given $\tilde{r} = 0$. Repeat for $\tilde{r} = 1, 2, 3$.

9. Suppose the parameter of a Bernoulli process can either be p_1 or p_2. Let P_1 be the prior probability that $(\tilde{p} = p_1)$ and let $P_2 = 1 - P_1$ be the prior probability of $(\tilde{p} = p_2)$. For a given particular history H_r^n show that the posterior probability of p_1 is

$$P(\tilde{p} = p_1 | H_r^n) = \frac{P_1}{\lambda P_1 + P_2}$$

where

$$\lambda = \frac{p_1^r(1 - p_1)^{n-r}}{p_2^r(1 - p_2)^{n-r}} = \frac{L(p_1)}{L(p_2)}$$

See (11.7) for the definition of L; the expression for λ (or its reciprocal) is called the "likelihood ratio."

Show that the prior odds in favor of $(\tilde{p} = p_1)$ are $P_1 : P_2$, and that after observing H_r^n the posterior odds are $\lambda P_1 : P_2$.

10. For $\rho > 1$ and $\upsilon > \rho + 1$ show that the function $f_\beta(p|\rho, \upsilon)$ has a maximum at $(\rho - 1)/(\upsilon - 2)$. [We therefore say that the *modal value* of $\tilde{p}$ is $(\rho - 1)/(\upsilon - 2)$.]

11. Let p be the proportion of families in the U.S. whose total stockholdings as of today are worth more than $25,000. Based on your present information, assess a judgmental distribution for this $\tilde{p}$ by giving your judgmental fractiles $p_{.50}, p_{.25}, p_{.75}, p_{.125}, p_{.375}, p_{.625}, p_{.875}$. Based on these fractiles find $\bar{p}$ and $\check{p}$ and then ρ and υ for a fitted beta distribution.

12. This exercise will involve your judgmental evaluations of the reactions of individuals to the question, "Over the past month would you say that you consumed more bourbon than scotch or more scotch than bourbon?" where possible answer are (i) more bourbon; (ii) more scotch; (iii) about the same; (iv) have not drunk either.

Let p be the conditional proportion of doctors in Boston who would answer (i) (more bourbon) among those that answer (i) or (ii).

a. Assess judgmental fractiles $p_{.50}, p_{.25}, p_{.75}$ and fit a beta distribution to these fractiles.

b. Suppose a sample of doctors are now drawn and of the 12 that answered (i) or (ii) 4 chose (i). What effect would this information have on your prior distribution? Posterior to this information what are your revised fractiles $p_{.50}, p_{.25}, p_{.75}$?

13. Let the parameter $\tilde{p}$ of a Bernoulli process be given a beta distribution with parameters $\rho = 7$ and $\upsilon = 18$. Give the probabilities of the following events

a. S_1,

b. S_2 given F_1,

c. S_3 given $F_1 F_2$,

d. S_4 given $F_1 F_2 S_3$,

e. S_5 given $F_1 F_2 S_3 F_4$.

14. In a trade union with 50,000 members in a given city, a random sample of 300 union members were asked if they favored using \$50,000 of the union's reserve funds to build a swimming pool for union members and their families. A total of 175 responded favorably, 85 responded unfavorably and the remaining 40 refused to answer or held no opinion. Let p be the proportion of the entire 50,000 union members who would respond favorably to this identical question. Argue why it might be reasonable in this case for one to assume that currently the unknown $\tilde{p}$ is beta distributed with parameters $r'' = 175$ and $n'' = 300$.

(Later on in this book you will learn how to compute (very quickly) the probability that $\tilde{p}$ lies in any given interval when the parameters of the beta are large and when their ratio is not close to 0 or to 1.)

15. Let the prior density of the parameter $\tilde{p}$ of a Bernoulli process be proportional to $\sin(2\pi p)$.

a. Give the posterior density for $r = 1$, $n = 4$.

b. What beta distribution has the same mean and variance as the actual prior and what posterior would it give for $r = 1$, $n = 4$?

c. Compare the posterior distributions in (a) and (b).

d. How would the results in (a)–(c) change for $r = 100$, $n = 400$?

16. In an approximate analysis of Bernoulli data,

a. What would be the advantages of choosing an approximating beta prior to have the same first two derivatives as the actual prior at r/n?

b. If one approximated the actual prior by a discrete distribution, what would happen for large n? How could one avoid this?

17. R out of N individuals or items have a certain property. From this population, n are drawn at random without replacement and scored S if they have the property, F otherwise.

a. Given R and N, what is the probability of a history H_r^n of the n observations?

b. In (a), what is the probability that S occurs exactly r times?

c. If R is unknown but N is known, what family of distributions of R might serve as the beta family does for a Bernoulli process?

12 Terminal Analysis: Opportunity Loss and the Value of Perfect Information

12.1 Introduction

We now turn to the terminal-action problem of choosing an act in situations where the consequence of one or more of the available acts depends on the value s of a random variable $\tilde{s}$ which may be thought of as expressing the true *state* of the world. *Any* problem of this sort can be solved by assigning a *utility* value $u_t(a, s)$ to the consequence of every act a given every state s, computing the expected utility

$$\bar{u}_t(a) \equiv Eu_t(a, \tilde{s})$$

of every act, and selecting the act which maximizes $\bar{u}_t$. (The subscript t is mnemonic for "terminal.") In those situations where consequences can be scaled in terms of a suitable numeraire, let $v_t(a, s)$ be the *value* of this numeraire corresponding to the choice of act a when state s is true; provided that expected value is a valid guide to action, the problem may be solved by computing

$$\bar{v}_t(a) \equiv Ev_t(a, \tilde{s})$$

for every a, and then selecting the a which maximizes $\bar{v}_t$. In some situations it is easier to work with negative values or *costs* rather than with values themselves. Let $c_t(a, s)$ be the cost corresponding to the (a, s) pair; provided that expected cost is a valid guide to action, the problem may be solved by computing

$$\bar{c}_t(a) = Ec_t(a, \tilde{s})$$

for every a, and then selecting the a which minimizes $\bar{c}_t$. In practice, the numeraire is often money itself, and the reader might wish to think in these terms throughout this chapter.

Our primary objective in this chapter is to examine several common types of decision problems and develop standard methods of analysis that apply to these problems when value or cost *is* a valid guide to action. Our first step, however, will be to introduce and interpret one additional economic quantity, *opportunity loss*, which is meaningful whenever value or cost is meaningful and which brings out certain features of a decision problem more clearly than does value or cost.

12.2 Opportunity Loss and the Value of Perfect Information

12.2.1 Opportunity Loss

Even though we choose the best possible act in the light of the information available before the fact, this act will often turn out "wrong" after the fact in the sense that some other act would have yielded a better consequence than the act actually chosen. Witness the case where a person takes out term insurance on his life for a given period and then fails to die. This, of course, is no criticism of the soundness of the original decision; such things are bound to happen when a decision has to be made on the basis of less than perfect information. It does mean, however, that in problems where consequences are measured by (monetary) *value* there is a particular interest to the *loss* which may be *incurred because of the imperfection of our information.* Such losses will be called *opportunity losses* because they represent the difference between the value we actually realize and the greater value we had the opportunity of realizing; of if we measure the consequence of our chosen act in terms of cost, they represent the difference between the cost we actually incur and the lesser cost we had the opportunity of incurring. Observe that an *opportunity* loss may be suffered even when an act results in a profit rather than a loss in the accounting sense. In this book, *the word* "*loss*" *will be used only in the sense of* "*opportunity loss,*" whether or not we repeat the word "opportunity" on every occasion. If an act results in costs which exceed revenues, we shall call the difference a "negative value," not a "loss."

Before defining opportunity loss formally, we digress to introduce some notation. Let there be a set A of acts a, a set S of possible states s, and a value function v_t with real values $v_t(a, s)$. Then *for any one particular* s there is a whole set of values $v_t(a, s)$, *one for every* a in A, and the greatest of these values will be denoted by $\max_a v_t(a, s)$.[1]

Observe carefully that while the quantity $\max_a v_t(a, s)$ will in general depend on *which particular* s is chosen from S, it does not depend on the choice of any particular a because it is evaluated by choosing the greatest of the quantities $v_t(a, s)$ as evaluated for *all* a. We may therefore say that $\max_a v_t(a, s)$ is a function of s alone, the a being "maxed out," just as we may say that $Ev_t(a, \tilde{s})$ is a function of a alone, $\tilde{s}$ being "expected out."

In our application, $\max_a v_t(a, s)$ is of course the greatest value the decision maker can possibly realize given the particular event $\tilde{s} = s$; and we can therefore write for the opportunity loss of any *particular* act a, given $\tilde{s} = s$,[2]

$$l_t(a, s) \equiv \max_a v_t(a, s) - v_t(a, s). \tag{12.1a}$$

1. Throughout this chapter we shall assume that even if A is infinite, the maximum value is achieved.

2. In (12.1a) the symbol "a" in the expression $\max_a v_t(a, s)$ is a dummy variable and we just as well could have written $\max_\alpha v_t(\alpha, s)$. A similar situation holds in (12.1b).

Table 12.1

(A) Value table for inventory example

d = number demanded	q = number stocked 0	1	2	3
0	0*	−2	−4	−6
1	0	+3*	+1	−1
2	0	+3	+6*	+4
3+	0	+3	+6	+6*

(B) Loss table for inventory example

d = number demanded	q = number stocked 0	1	2	3
0	0	2	4	6
1	3	0	2	4
2	6	3	0	2
3+	9	6	3	0

If a_s is the optimal act a for s, i.e., if $v_t(a_s, s) = \max_a v_t(a, s)$, then

$$l_t(a, s) = v_t(a_s, s) - v_t(a, s).$$

If we are working in terms of costs $c_t(a, s) = -v_t(a, s)$, this definition obviously yields the formula

$$l_t(a, s) = c_t(a, s) - \min_a c_t(a, s). \tag{12.1b}$$

If a_s is the optimal act for s, that is, if $c_t(a, s) = \max_a c_t(a_s, s)$, then

$$l_t(a, s) = c_t(a, s) - c_t(a_s, s).$$

Example A retailer pays \$2 per unit of a certain item and sells it for \$5 per unit. The item is stocked at the beginning of each day; if not sold by the end of the day it spoils and becomes a total loss. If we let q denote the act "stock q units" and let $\tilde{d}$ denote the random variable "number of units demanded," the monetary value of any act q given any event $\tilde{d} = d$ is

$$v_t(q, d) = -2q + 5\min\{q, d\}.$$

If there is no limit on the number of units the retailer can stock, then obviously v_t is maximized for given d by choosing $q = d$, that is, by stocking the number of units demanded, so that

$$\max_q v_t(q, d) = v_t(d, d) = 3d.$$

The opportunity loss of any act q given any event $\tilde{d} = d$ is therefore by (12.1a)

$$l_t(q, d) = 3d - (-2q + 5\min\{q, d\}).$$

If the retailer can stock at most 3 units, the *values* for this problem are as shown in table 12.1A and the *opportunity losses* are as shown in table 12.1B, where 3+ means "3 or more." In the *value* table, an asterisk is placed beside the greatest entry in each *row*, that is, beside $\max_q v_t(q, d) =$

$v_t(d, d)$; the reader should observe that each *row* in the *loss* table is constructed by subtracting each entry in the corresponding row in the value table from the starred entry in that row, in accordance with (12.1a).

12.2.2 Expected Opportunity Loss

If $\tilde{s}$ is a rv, then for any particular act a the loss $l_t(a, \tilde{s})$ is a rv and we shall write for its expectation

$$\bar{l}_t(a) \equiv El_t(a, \tilde{s}). \tag{12.2}$$

Combining this definition with the definition (12.1) of $l_t(a, s)$ we have

$$\bar{l}_t(a) = v_t^* - \bar{v}_t(a) \tag{12.3a}$$

where

$$v_t^* \equiv E \max_a v_t(a, \tilde{s}). \tag{12.3b}$$

We call the reader's attention to the fact that, as our notation implies, v_t^* is a definite number or "constant" which does not depend on either a or s—the a has been "maxed out" for every particular s and the s has then been "expected out." The quantity v_t^* could also be expressed as

$$v_t^* = Ev_t(a_{\tilde{s}}, \tilde{s}),$$

where a_s is the optimal act for state s.

Formulas (12.2) and (12.3) offer us the choice of two alternative methods for computing $\bar{l}_t(a)$ in any problem. We can either evaluate $l_t(a, s)$ for all (a, s) and then use (12.2), or else evaluate $v_t(a, s)$ for all (a, s), compute $\bar{v}_t(a)$ for all a, and then use (12.3). We also have, by (12.3), that for any two acts a' and a'',

$$\bar{v}_t(a') - \bar{v}_t(a'') = \bar{l}_t(a'') - \bar{l}_t(a'). \tag{12.4}$$

From either (12.3) or (12.4) it is immediately apparent that in any decision problem *the act that minimizes expected opportunity loss maximizes expected value.*

Example Suppose that in the inventory problem described by table 12.1 the retailer assigns to the rv $\tilde{d}$ (demand) the mass function f shown in table 12.2. Then for the particular act $q = 2$ we have

$$\bar{v}_t(2) = \$[-4(.2) + 1(.4) + 6(.3) + 6(.1)] = \$2.00,$$

$$\bar{l}_t(2) = \$[4(.2) + 2(.4) + 0(.3) + 3(.1)] = \$1.90, \qquad \text{[by (12.2)]}$$

$$v_t^* = \$[0(.2) + 3(.4) + 6(.3) + 9(.1)] = \$3.90, \qquad \text{[by 12.3b)]}$$

Table 12.2
Mass function for inventory example

d	$f(d)$
0	.2
1	.4
2	.3
3	.1
	1.0

and the reader can verify that given *any two* of these results we could compute the third by use of formula (12.3a).

Computational methods making direct use of the losses $l_t(a, s)$ are of interest primarily because in many problems it is much easier to evaluate the loss of every (a, s) combination than it is to evaluate the value of every (a, s) combination. In an inventory problem it may be easy, for example, to determine that an opportunity loss of \$3.87 will be incurred if 8 units are stocked when only 7 are demanded, whereas determination of the true value of stocking 8 and selling 7 may be much harder to determine because it involves certain costs, such as the cost of placing an order, which are difficult to determine and yet really irrelevant because they do not depend on the number of units ordered or sold.

We warn the reader, however, that sometimes direct determination of $l_t(a, s)$ is exceedingly tricky but determination of $v_t(a, s)$ is straightforward even if tedious. In cases where every relevant value is straightforward and monetary, $v_t(a, s)$ can always be found by simply writing down and summing all the cash flows which will occur if a is chosen and $\tilde{s} = s$ occurs, whereas direct evaluation of $l_t(a, s)$ involves exclusion of all cash flows which depend only on s and not on a.

12.2.3 The Value of Perfect Information

A particular interest attaches to the opportunity loss of the *optimal* act, the act that maximizes the decision maker's expected value $\bar{v}_t$ or minimizes his *expected* opportunity loss $\bar{l}_t$. Denoting this act by a^o, we may say that the perfect information that the true state is s would have a value of $l_t(a^o, s)$ to the decision maker because it would lead him to change his choice of an act from a^o to a_s and thereby avoid the loss $l_t(a^o, s)$. We therefore can interpret $l_t(a^o, s)$ as the *conditional value of the perfect information* that $\tilde{s} = s$.

It follows that the *expected* loss of the optimal act, $\bar{l}_t(a^o) = El_t(a^o, \tilde{s})$ can be interpreted as either (1) expected loss due to the imperfection of the decision maker's present information, or (2) the *expected value of perfect information* (EVPI) about the true value s.

It is true, of course, that the decision maker usually cannot in fact obtain perfect information about the true state s, but the EVPI is nevertheless of great practical interest. The decision maker can often obtain additional *imperfect* information about s (by experimentation, sampling, and so on), and he may be well advised to consider doing this before he decides on a specific terminal act. Whether or not it is worthwhile to obtain such information depends on whether its value exceeds its cost; and while calculation of the cost is usually easy, calculation of the value may be difficult. It is obvious, however, that the *value of imperfect information cannot exceed the value of perfect information*, and for this reason knowledge of the usually easily calculated EVPI may be of great help. If the EVPI is *less* than the cost of any real information which seems in common sense likely to be useful, it is clear that the decision maker need not worry further but should proceed immediately to choose the act which seems best given his existing information. The converse, of course, is not true. Even though the EVPI is very high, it is not certain that real information can be obtained at a cost less than its value; the need for further calculations cannot be avoided in this case.

Prior Expected Value of Action Posterior to Perfect Information

By (12.3) we may write

$$\text{EVPI} = v_t^* - \bar{v}_t(a^o), \qquad \text{where} \qquad v_t^* \equiv E \max_a v_t(a, \tilde{s}). \tag{12.5}$$

The term $\bar{v}_t(a^o)$ is of course simply the expected value of the optimal act; we shall now interpret the term v_t^*.

To do so, let us imagine a most fortunate decision maker who knows *now* that he *will be* told the true value s of $\tilde{s}$ *before* he has actually to choose an act a. If this person is told that $\tilde{s}$ has a particular value s, he will of course choose a so as to maximize his value and will therefore realize $\max_a v_t(a, s)$ or $v_t(a_s, s)$. The expectation v_t^* of this quantity is accordingly the monetary value he can now "expect" to realize, given that he will be told the true s before he chooses a; therefore, we shall call v_t^* the *prior expected value of action posterior to perfect information*. The EVPI can then by (12.5) also be interpreted as the difference between this quantity and the expected value of acting optimally on the basis of the *existing* information.

From a mathematical point of view it is instructive to rewrite the expression for EVPI in (12.5) as

$$\text{EVPI} = E \max_a v_t(a, \tilde{s}) - \max_a E v_t(a, \tilde{s}),$$

which brings out the point very clearly that the operators E and $\max_a$ are not commutative (i.e., that $E \max_a$ is not $\max_a E$).

Example Consider once again the inventory problem described in table 12.1 and let $\tilde{d}$ have the mass function given in table 12.2. Then using the formulas

$$\bar{v}_t(q) = Ev(q, \tilde{d}) = \textstyle\sum_{d=0}^{3} v_t(q, d) f(d),$$

$$\bar{l}_t(q) = El_t(q, \tilde{d}) = \textstyle\sum_{d=0}^{3} l_t(q, d) f(d),$$

the reader can easily verify the following calculations:

q	0	1	2	3
$\bar{v}_t(q)$	\$0.00	\$2.00	\$2.00	\$0.50
$\bar{l}_t(q)$	\$3.90	\$1.90	\$1.90	\$3.40

From these calculations, we observe that $\bar{v}_t(q) + \bar{l}_t(q) = v_t^*$ for all q, agreeing with (12.3a). Furthermore, we see that the optimal stock $q^o = 1$ or 2, and EVPI = \$1.90. If, for example, the retailer could buy on consignment (stock enough to cover any demand, return all unsold items and pay only for items used), then this privilege would be worth an additional \$1.90 to him.

12.3 Two-Action Problems with Linear Value

12.3.1 Introduction

One of the more common types of business decision problems involves choice between just *two* available acts, the (monetary or other) value of each of which is a *linear* function of some random variable. Thus in order to produce some new item, the ultimate sales of which are unknown, a businessman may have to purchase one or the other of two special-purpose machines, the first of which costs only \$10,000 but requires \$5 of direct labor per piece produced, while the second costs \$40,000 but requires only \$2 of direct labor per piece. If the product is to be sold for \$10 each and if the businessman takes contribution to overhead as his value criterion for measuring results, then letting $\tilde{s}$ denote the rv "sales in units" we have for the value functions of the two available acts

$$v_t(a_1, s) = \$(10 - 5)s - \$10{,}000,$$

$$v_t(a_2, s) = \$(10 - 2)s - \$40{,}000.$$

Before proceeding to the analysis of the class of problems typified by this example, we suggest that the reader review the notation used for the

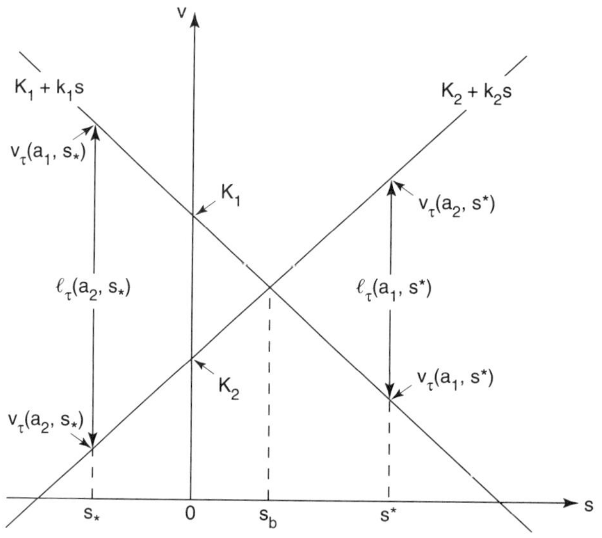

Figure 12.1
Linear terminal value and loss functions for two acts

two linear loss functions introduced in (8.25a) of section 8.4.2. These two functions will be of great convenience in expressing some of our results.

12.3.2 Analysis of Two-Action Problems with Linear Value

Let there be two acts $\{a_1, a_2\}$, let there be a rv $\tilde{s}$, and let

$$v_t(a_i, s) = K_i + k_i s, \qquad i = 1, 2, \tag{12.6}$$

where K_i and k_i are constants not depending on s. Assume that *each* of the inequalities

$$v_t(a_1, s) > v_t(a_2, s),$$

$$v_t(a_2, s) > v_t(a_1, s),$$

holds for *some* values of s, so that the two value functions can be graphed as *intersecting* somewhere, as shown in figure 12.1. No generality is lost by this assumption, since if, for example, $v_t(a_1, s) \le v_t(a_2, s)$ over *all* of S, then elimination of a_1 from further consideration would clearly cost the decision maker nothing. Since this assumption obviously implies that $k_1 \ne k_2$, we may further assume without loss of generality that the acts are numbered so that

$$k_1 < k_2, \tag{12.7}$$

thus making the labelling in figure 12.1 valid for all problems in the class

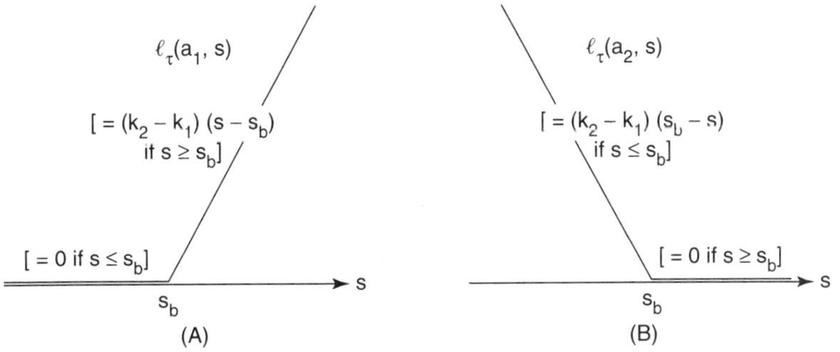

Figure 12.2
Linear terminal loss functions for two acts

we are considering and simplifying the statement of results valid for all such problems.

Now defining the intersection point or *breakeven* value

$$s_b \equiv \frac{K_1 - K_2}{k_2 - k_1}, \tag{12.8}$$

we leave the following five simple assertions (exercise 4) for the reader:

1. $\left.\begin{matrix} a_1 \\ a_2 \end{matrix}\right\}$ is optimal given $\tilde{s} = s$ if $s \left\{\begin{matrix} \leq \\ \geq \end{matrix}\right\} s_b$; (12.9)

2. $\bar{v}_t(a_i) = v_t(a_i, \bar{s}) = K_i + k_i\bar{s}$, where $\bar{s} \equiv E(\tilde{s})$; (12.10)

3. $\left.\begin{matrix} a_1 \\ a_2 \end{matrix}\right\}$ is optimal under uncertainty if $\bar{s} \left\{\begin{matrix} \leq \\ \geq \end{matrix}\right\} s_b$; (12.11)

4. $l_t(a_1, s) = (k_2 - k_1)\max\{0, s - s_b\}$,
   $l_t(a_2, s) = (k_2 - k_1)\max\{0, s_b - s\}$; (12.12)

5. $\bar{l}_t(a_1) = (k_2 - k_1)L^{(r)}(s_b)$, where $L^{(r)}(s_b) \equiv E\max\{0, \tilde{s} - s_b\}$,
   $\bar{l}_t(a_2) = (k_2 - k_1)L^{(l)}(s_b)$, where $L^{(l)}(s_b) \equiv E\max\{0, s_b - \tilde{s}\}$. (12.13)

The EVPI or expected loss of the optimal act under uncertainty can be evaluated from (12.11) and (12.13); the prior expected value of action posterior to perfect information can then be found via (12.5), by adding the EVPI to the expected value of the optimal act under uncertainty. The functions $l_t(a_1, \cdot)$ and $l_t(a_2, \cdot)$ as given in (12.12) are plotted in figure 12.2.

An analysis of the example given in 12.3.1 which motivated this section is deferred to the exercises at the end of this chapter.

12.3.3 Application to a Beta-Distributed $\tilde{p}$

Now let the role of $\tilde{s}$ be played by a rv $\tilde{p}$ having a beta distribution with parameters (ρ, υ) examples of practical situations in which such a model might apply will be found in the exercises. It is left (exercise 7) for the reader to show that

$$\left.\begin{matrix} a_1 \\ a_2 \end{matrix}\right\} \text{is optimal under uncertainty} \quad \text{if} \quad \frac{\rho}{\upsilon} \left\{\begin{matrix} \leq \\ \geq \end{matrix}\right\} p_b, \tag{12.14}$$

and that by (12.13) and (9.18),

$$\begin{aligned} \bar{l}_t(a_1) &= (k_2 - k_1)[\bar{p}G_\beta(p_b|\rho + 1, \upsilon + 1) - p_b G_\beta(p_b|\rho, \upsilon)], \\ \bar{l}_t(a_2) &= (k_2 - k_1)[p_b F_\beta(p_b|\rho, \upsilon) - \bar{p}F_\beta(p_b|\rho + 1, \upsilon + 1)], \end{aligned} \tag{12.15}$$

where $\bar{p} = \rho/\upsilon$, so that the EVPI can be evaluated by use of tables of beta tail areas.

12.4 Finite-Action Problems with Linear Value[3]

Another interesting class of practical decision problems consists of problems that are identical to the ones discussed in the previous section except that there are more than two possible acts. Thus the manufacturer of the example at the beginning of section 12.3.1 may have to choose among any number r of available machines. In this section we shall give algebraic results for the general case accompanied by a graphical illustration for the case $r = 3$; the reader who has trouble understanding any formula should start by convincing himself that in the case $r = 2$ it reduces to the results of the previous section and should then take the case $r = 3$ and obtain from the formula the results shown graphically in figure 12.3.

Let there be r acts $\{a_1, \ldots, a_i, \ldots, a_r\}$, let there be a rv $\tilde{s}$ and let

$$v_t(a_i, s) = K_i + k_i s, \qquad i = 1, 2, \ldots, r, \tag{12.16}$$

where K_i and k_i are constants not depending on s. Assume without loss of generality that each of the inequalities

$$v_t(a_i, s) > v_t(a_j, s), \quad \text{all } i \neq j,$$

holds for *some* values of s, so that the r value functions can be graphed in the way indicated for $r = 3$ in figure 12.3; and assume further without loss

3. The contents of this section are not required in any subsequent section.

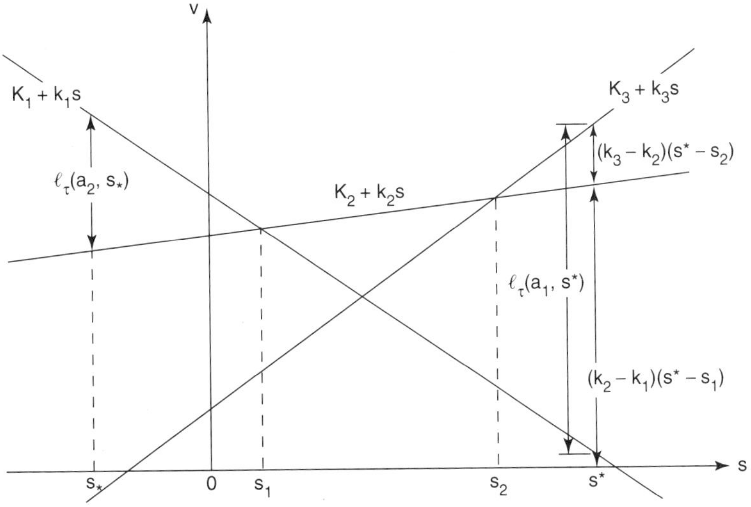

Figure 12.3
Linear terminal value and loss functions for three acts

of generality that

$$k_1 < k_2 < \ldots < k_r. \tag{12.17}$$

Now defining the $(r - 1)$ *breakeven values*

$$s_i \equiv \frac{K_i - K_{i+1}}{k_{i+1} - k_i} \qquad i = 1, 2, \ldots, r - 1, \tag{12.18a}$$

and the two auxiliary symbols

$$s_0 \equiv -\infty \qquad s_r \equiv +\infty \tag{12.18b}$$

we have as immediate generalizations of (12.9) through (12.11) that

$$a_i \text{ is optimal given } \tilde{s} = s \quad \text{if} \quad s_{i-1} \le s \le s_i, \tag{12.19}$$

$$\bar{v}_t(a_i) = v_t(a_i, \bar{s}) = K_i + k_i\bar{s}, \tag{12.20}$$

$$a_i \text{ is optimal } \textit{under uncertainty} \quad \text{if} \quad s_{i-1} \le \bar{s} \le s_i. \tag{12.21}$$

Exercise 8 at the end of the chapter concerns the generalization of (12.12):

$$l_t(a_i, s) = \textstyle\sum_{j=1}^{i-1} (k_{j+1} - k_j)\max\{(s_j - s), 0\}$$
$$\qquad + \textstyle\sum_{j=i}^{r-1} (k_{j+1} - k_j)\max\{0, (s - s_j)\}; \tag{12.22}$$

the exercise contains suggestions for understanding as well as for proving this formula. From this result, by treating s as a rv and taking expectations, we have the generalization of (12.13):

$$\bar{l}_t(a_i) = \sum_{j=1}^{i-1} (k_{j+1} - k_j)L^{(l)}(s_j) + \sum_{j=i}^{r-1} (k_{j+1} - k_j)L^{(r)}(s_j). \qquad (12.23)$$

The EVPI or expected loss of the optimal act under uncertainty can be evaluated from (12.21) and (12.23); the prior expected value of action posterior to perfect information can then be found, via (12.5), by adding the EVPI to the expected value of the optimal act under uncertainty.

12.5 Point Estimation

In the remainder of this chapter we shall consider decision problems which have the following structure: A decision maker has already assigned a distributing function to some unknown quantity of interest $\tilde{s}$ and he now wishes to choose a single number a to come "close" (in a sense to be described) to the true value of $\tilde{s}$. If he chooses the number a and $\tilde{s} = s$, he suffers an opportunity loss of $l_t(a, s)$. We assume that if his choice a agrees with s, then his loss is zero—that is, $l_t(s, s) = 0$. In problems of this kind we shall say that the number a is a *point estimate* of the unknown quantity $\tilde{s}$.

There are two categories of point estimation problems that we shall now describe. The first is rather straightforward and needs little explanation; the second is more involved and therefore needs some discussion.

Choice of a Real Act

This category of problem can best be illustrated by the simple example of a retailer who sells a perishable commodity and must decide on a specific, *real*, physical quantity a to stock of this quantity given her assessed evaluation for the unknown demand $\tilde{s}$ for this quantity. If she stocks a and $\tilde{s} = s$, she will suffer some opportunity loss $l_t(a, s)$. This concrete problem is in sharp contrast to the following category of problems.

Choice of a Summary Measure

In a great many situations a decision maker—say a business person, a researcher, or a scientist—wants additional information on the value of some unknown quantity, not because he is at the moment of choosing among a number of definite, well-defined "terminal" acts whose values depend on this quantity, but simply to guide his thinking in some general problem area. To give a simple example, a soap manufacturer who is thinking about developing and marketing a new detergent designed especially for use in automatic dishwashers may want to get some idea of the number of homes equipped with automatic dishwashers long before his thinking reaches the stage where he is ready even to specify his possible terminal acts, let alone to say exactly how the profitability of each act depends on the number in question.

Until the decision maker has completely specified his terminal acts, he will want to work primarily if not exclusively with an *estimate* of the quantity in which he is interested rather than with a *probability distribution* of this quantity. He will make rough calculations in which he treats the estimated number of homes equipped with dishwashers as if this estimate were a true value even though he knows that the estimate is almost certainly in error by some amount and that before making any *final* decision he may have to take formal account of his uncertainty about the true number. For the present, therefore, he is faced with the decision problem of *choosing the best possible estimate* of the unknown quantity. He will in general be well advised also to evaluate the *loss* he can "expect" to incur because of the possible errors in this estimate, because if this expected loss is high he may do better to obtain more information (for example, through a sample survey) before making and using *any* estimate.

In such situations there is obviously no "objective" way of evaluating the loss that will result if the decision maker uses a certain estimate a when the true value of the unknown quantity is some other number s; however, the decision maker *can* decide what value he subjectively places on any error, and in general it will be much easier for him to do this than to decide directly whether or not his existing information is adequate or should be augmented at a cost.

Another type of situation where a point estimate is often needed is the very common case where the number of unknown quantities is so great that the decision maker cannot practically take full formal account of all the uncertainties that he would like to introduce in his analysis; instead of using the full probability distribution of some "subsidiary" uncertain quantity he might choose some summary measure of this distribution—such as the mean, median, or other fractile—and use this summary measure *as if* it were the true value of the uncertain quantity. Usually this procedure will entail some loss of efficiency but the excuse is that this is counterbalanced by the simplification of the ensuing analysis. It is important in these situations to choose the proper summary measure, to investigate the possible loss of efficiency in using this abbreviated form of analysis, and to determine whether it is economically desirable to gather more information about this subsidiary uncertain quantity before assigning a summary measure.

In many situations an appropriate summary measure can be chosen such that there is absolutely no loss of efficiency involved in analyzing a given terminal-action problem; that is, treatment of this summary measure as if it were the true value of the quantity would lead to exactly the same *course of action* that would be chosen if an analysis were based on the complete distribution. Such a summary measure will be called a *certainty equivalent.*

In the remaining sections we shall analyze point estimation problems with different loss structures. In section 12.6 we show that for a quadratic loss structure the *mean* of the distributing function of $\tilde{s}$ is the appropriate point estimate or summary measure; in section 12.7 we show that for a particular, symmetrical linear loss structure the *median* is appropriate, and for other, asymmetrical linear cases some other fractile is appropriate; in section 12.8 we show that for a so-called zero-one loss structure the *mode* is appropriate.

12.6 Infinite-Action Problems with Quadratic Loss

12.6.1 Introduction

In many situations of the sort described in section 12.5 the decision maker will feel that the seriousness of estimating a when s is the true value (1) depends only on the *difference* $|s - a|$, not on a or s individually, and (2) is virtually negligible when $|s - a|$ is small but increases "geometrically" rather than "arithmetically" as $|s - a|$ increases. In such cases it will often be possible to represent the loss of an error $|s - a|$ by $k_t(s - a)^2$; the value of the constant k_t can be determined if needed by asking the decision maker to decide how much he would be willing to pay for exact knowledge of s if he were to be told for free that his best estimate a is one unit from the true s but had to pay cash to find out whether s is greater or less than a.

12.6.2 Expected Loss, Optimal Act, and EVPI

Formally, let $\tilde{s}$ be a rv, let the set of available acts (estimates) be the set of all real numbers, and let

$$l_t(a, s) = k_t(s - a)^2. \tag{12.24}$$

Then we leave as an exercise (exercise 9) that

$$\bar{l}_t(a) = k_t[\breve{s} + (\bar{s} - a)^2], \tag{12.25}$$

where $\breve{s}$ and $\bar{s}$ are respectively the variance and mean of $\tilde{s}$, from which it follows immediately that the optimal act a^o is given by

$$a^o = \bar{s} \tag{12.26}$$

and that the EVPI is

$$\bar{l}_t(a^o) = k_t \check{s}. \tag{12.27}$$

Observe that if the possible values of $\tilde{s}$ are discrete, a^o is *not* necessarily equal to some possible value of $\tilde{s}$. If, on the other hand, the set of available acts is restricted to coincide with the discrete possible values of $\tilde{s}$, in other words if the "estimate" must for some reason be equal to a possible value of $\tilde{s}$, then by (12.25) the optimal act is whichever a is closest to $\bar{s}$ and the EVPI is obtained by substituting this a into (12.25).

12.6.3 Application to a Beta Distribution $\tilde{p}$

Now let the role of $\tilde{s}$ be played by a rv $\tilde{p}$ having a beta distribution with parameters (ρ, υ) in terms of the example in section 12.5, the decision maker might think in terms of the fraction $\tilde{p}$ of all U.S. households owning an automatic dishwasher. The reader is asked to show (exercise 11) that $a^o = \rho/\upsilon$ and that the EVPI is

$$\bar{l}_t(a^o) = k_t \frac{\rho(\upsilon - \rho)}{\upsilon^2(\upsilon + 1)} = k_t \frac{\bar{p}(1 - \bar{p})}{\upsilon + 1}. \tag{12.28}$$

12.7 Infinite-Action Problems with Linear Loss

12.7.1 Introduction

We now consider situations like those in section 12.6 except that loss is proportional to the "error" $|s - a|$ itself rather than to its square; the constant of proportionality may or may not be the same when $s > a$ as it is when $s < a$. One source of such loss structures is estimation problems of the kind described in section 12.5 when the decision maker feels that the harm done by an error is proportional to the error rather than to its square; another source is the so-called "newsboy" class of inventory problems, typified by the example described in section 12.2.1.

12.7.2 Expected Loss

Let $\tilde{s}$ be a rv, let the available acts be the set of all real numbers, and let

$$l_t(a, s) = \begin{cases} k_u(s - a) & \text{if} \quad a \leq s, \\ k_o(a - s) & \text{if} \quad a \geq s. \end{cases} \tag{12.29a}$$

(Notice that k_o is the loss when the act a is 1 unit *over* the true value s while k_u is the loss when a is 1 unit *under* s.) The loss function as given in (12.29a)

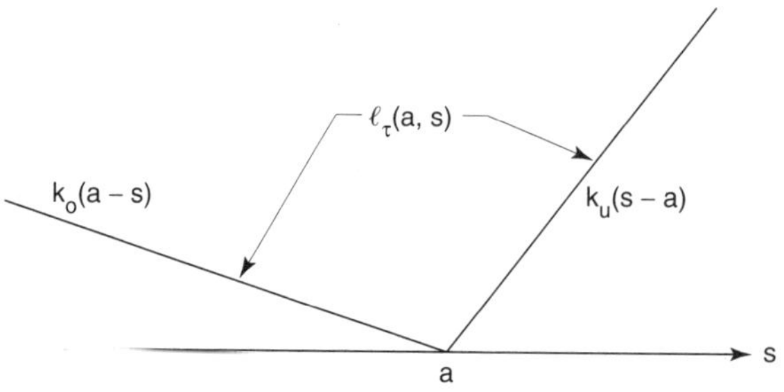

Figure 12.4
Piecewise linear terminal loss function for infinite-action problem

is plotted in figure 12.4. The reader is cautioned not to confuse the infinite-action problem under discussion here with the two-action problem with linear loss structure considered in section 12.3.2. Compare, for example, figures 12.2 and 12.4.

Expression (12.29a) can also be expressed in the alternative form

$$l_t(a, s) = k_u \max\{0, s - a\} + k_o \max\{0, a - s\}. \tag{12.29b}$$

When the loss is given as in (12.29) it follows immediately from (8.14), (8.13b), and the definitions (8.23) of linear-loss functions that

$$\begin{aligned} \bar{l}_t(a) &= E[k_u \max\{0, \tilde{s} - a\} + k_o \max\{0, a - \tilde{s}\}] \\ &= k_u E[\max\{0, \tilde{s} - a\}] + k_o E[\max\{0, a - \tilde{s}\}] \\ &= k_u L^{(r)}(a) + k_o L^{(l)}(a). \end{aligned} \tag{12.30}$$

12.7.3 The Optimal Act

When the rv $\tilde{s}$ is *continuous*, it is easy to find the act which minimizes the expected loss (12.30). If we define the *critical ratio*

$$k \equiv \frac{k_u}{k_u + k_o}, \tag{12.31}$$

the reader is asked to show (exercise 14) that (12.30) is minimized by setting a equal to the *k'th fractile* of the distribution of $\tilde{s}$; in other words, the optimal act a^o is defined by

$$P(\tilde{s} \le a^o) = k. \tag{12.32}$$

When the rv $\tilde{s}$ is *discrete*, the problem is a little trickier; however, if we define the critical ratio as in (12.31) above, the reader is asked to show (exercise 15) that *if* the kth fractile of the distribution of $\tilde{s}$ is unique (cf.

section 7.2.7), the optimal act is equal to this fractile, while if the kth fractile is not unique, then any act that is equal to any kth fractile is optimal. In algebraic notation, any act a^o that satisfies

$$P(\tilde{s} \leq s)\begin{cases} \leq k & \text{if} \quad s < a^o, \\ \geq k & \text{if} \quad s \geq a^o, \end{cases} \tag{12.33}$$

is an optimal act.

In *estimation* problems with losses of type (12.29), the constants k_o and k_u are often equal—the decision maker feels that overestimating is neither more nor less serious than underestimating. In such cases the critical fractile given by (12.32) or (12.33) is the (or a) *median* of the distribution of $\tilde{s}$, not the mean. In the case that k_u is larger than k_o, it is more serious to underestimate than to overestimate by a given amount; the quantity k is then larger than $\frac{1}{2}$ and the optimal estimate is a point in the right tail of the distribution (i.e., to the right of the median). The reverse holds if k_u is smaller than k_o.

12.7.4 Expected Loss of an Optimal Act

When the general expression (12.30) for the expected loss of an arbitrary act is evaluated for an optimal act as defined by (12.32) or (12.33), it reduces to the form

$$\bar{l}_t(a^o) = k_u E^{(r)}(a^o) - k_o E^{(l)}(a^o), \tag{12.34}$$

where $E^{(r)}$ and $E^{(l)}$ are respectively the right and left partial expectations defined in (8.20). The reader is asked to prove this result in exercise 17.

Hint Use $L^{(r)}(a) = E^{(r)}(a) - G(a)$ and $F(a^o) = k$.

12.7.5 Application to a Beta-Distributed $\tilde{p}$

Now let the role of $\tilde{s}$ be played as in section 12.6.3 by a rv $\tilde{p}$ having a beta distribution with parameters (ρ, υ). The reader is asked to show (exercise 17) that if the parameters ρ and υ are integral, the expression (12.34) for the expected loss of the *optimal* act can be reduced to the form

$$\bar{l}_t(a^o) = (k_u + k_o)\frac{\rho(\upsilon - \rho)}{\upsilon^2} f_b(\rho \mid a^o, \upsilon), \tag{12.35}$$

which is very convenient for practical evaluation of the loss. When ρ and υ are not both integral, $f_b(\rho \mid a^o, \upsilon)$ is strictly speaking not defined; but because both the binomial function and the beta function are well behaved, $\bar{l}_t(a^o)$ can still be evaluated by (12.35) with interpolation in tables of f_b.

12.8 Classification with a Zero-One Loss Structure

12.8.1 Introduction

The classes of problems considered in sections 12.6 and 12.7 above are of great practical importance; the classes of problems treated in the present section are interesting more because of their simplicity than because of their real importance in practice.

As an example, consider a personnel manager who must assign a new employee to one of several jobs each requiring quite different talents and who believes that if the employee is at first assigned to a job for which he is not suitable, he will ultimately be transferred to the correct job. Under these circumstances the personnel manager might feel that the economic loss occasioned by first assigning the employee to the wrong job will be the same regardless of both the particular job to which the employee is first assigned and the particular job for which he is really suitable, even though the economic *value* of the employee to the company depends on the job he is really suited to fill. Then letting s_i denote the event that the employee is really suited to the ith job and letting a_j denote the act of initially assigning him to the jth job, the loss and value tables for the personnel manager's decision problem will be as shown in table 12.3, where L denotes the loss due to incorrect initial assignment while V_i denotes the value of suitably filling the ith job.

12.8.2 Expected Loss and Optimal Act

Formally, let there be m acts $\{a_1, \ldots, a_m\}$, let there be a random variable $\tilde{s}$ with possible values $\{s_1, \ldots, s_m\}$ and mass function f, and let

$$l_t(a_j, s_i) = \begin{cases} 0 & \text{if} \quad i = j, \\ L & \text{if} \quad i \neq j; \end{cases} \tag{12.36}$$

then it is easily proved that

$$\bar{l}_t(a_j) = L[1 - f(s_j)] \tag{12.37}$$

Table 12.3

Loss table

	a_1	a_2	. . .	a_m
s_1	0	L	. . .	L
s_2	L	0	. . .	L
. . .	. . .	. . .	. . .	. . .
s_m	L	L	. .	0

Value table

	a_1	a_2		a_m
s_1	V_1	$V_1 - L$	. . .	$V_1 - L$
s_2	$V_2 - L$	V_2	. . .	$V_2 - L$
. . .	. . .	. . .	. . .	. . .
s_m	$V_m - L$	$V_m - L$	. . .	V_m

and that a_j is optimal under uncertainty if and only if $f(s_j) \geq f(s_i)$ for all $i \neq j$. In ordinary English, choose the act with the greatest probability of being right; if there are several acts with equal greatest probability, choose any one of them.

We leave to the reader as an exercise the following generalization of the above problem: Let $\tilde{s}$ have a distributing function f which is either a df or a mf; for any point estimate a (a real number) of $\tilde{s}$, let

$$l_t(a, s) = \begin{cases} 0 & \text{if} \quad |a - s| < \Delta, \\ L & \text{if} \quad |a - s| \geq \Delta, \end{cases}$$

where Δ is some preassigned positive number. The problem is to find a^o and EVPI.

12.9 Comparison of Summary Measures

Let $\tilde{s}$ have a distributing function f. Questions are often raised such as what is the "best" summary measure of the distribution of f. Is it the modal value (i.e., the most likely)? the mean? the median? or possibly some other fractile? Our unequivocal answer is that *if* a summary measure must be given—*and in most reporting cases it is not clear that a single summary measure should be given*—the appropriate choice *depends on the loss structure!* In section 12.8 it was appropriate to use the modal value; in section 12.6 it was the mean; in section 12.7 with $k_u = k_o$ it was the median and for $k_u \neq k_o$ it was the kth fractile where $k = k_u/(k_u + k_o)$. For problems with other loss structures, still other summary measures would be called for.

Exercises

1. For exercise 4 of chapter 6 assume that a decision maker feels that EMV is a valid guide to action. For convenience we repeat the value table here.

State	Act a_1	Act a_2	Probability of state
s_1	+\$400	−\$50	.8
s_2	−\$200	+\$1,000	.2
			1.0

a. Compute $\bar{v}(a_1)$, $\bar{v}(a_2)$ and find a^o.

b. Exhibit the opportunity loss table and compute $\bar{l}_t(a_1)$ and $\bar{l}_t(a_2)$.

c. Find and interpret the EVPI.

d. Compute the prior expected value of action posterior to perfect information.

e. For this example, verify (12.3a) and (12.4).

f. If a single drawing is made from the urn and the decision maker recomputes the EVPI, will it be the same as the original EVPI or larger or smaller? Why? [Make no computations.]

g. Compute the revised EVPI given that the drawing is made and the ball is (1) red; (2) black.

2. Over a considerable period of time a manufacturer has used a certain automatic machine for production of part A-11-Z in runs of 5000 pieces. At the beginning of each run, the machine is taken down for servicing and replacement of worn tools and then is set up by the operator. Experience has shown that when the machine is properly set up, the fraction defective in a run will be very close to .01, but experience has also shown that the operator's setups are somewhat unreliable; sometimes the fraction defective has gone as high as .25. A fraction defective of .01 can be guaranteed by having the operator's setup checked and, if need be, adjusted by an expert mechanic, but the time required when this has been done in the past has cost \$6 per setup on the average. On the other hand, the entire output has to go directly to assembly because screening would be prohibitively expensive, and experience has shown that although so-called defectives are perfectly functional, the difficulties encountered in fitting them into an assembly cause delays costing \$.04 per defective on the average.
A new run is about to be made and the manufacturer must decide whether or not to make use of the expert mechanic's services. Assume purely as an exercise that he assigns to the random variable "fraction defective" the mass function shown in the table below.

Fraction defective	mf
.01	.7
.05	.1
.15	.1
.25	.1
	1.0

a. Is EMV likely to be a valid criterion of choice in this problem?

b. Assuming that EMV *is* valid, find the optimal act and compute EVPI.

3. The marketing manager of a company that has developed a new product hesitates to put it into production because sales volume may not be sufficient to cover the cost of tooling up for production, let alone to make any contribution to overhead. Tooling costs \$100,000, each unit of the product will cost \$7 for raw materials and direct labor, and competitive conditions are such that the product will have to be priced at \$12 if it is placed on the market. Assume purely as an exercise that the marketing manager assigns to the random variable "demand" the mass function shown in the following table:

Demand	mf
10,000	.2
20,000	.4
30,000	.3
40,000	.1
	1.0

a. Is EMV likely to be a valid criterion for choice in this problem?

b. Assuming that EMV *is* valid, find the optimal act and compute the EVPI.

4. Prove (12.9) through (12.13).

5. Complete the analysis of the example given in section 12.3.1. Assume that the businessman has assigned the following mf to the rv s, the number of units sold:

s	$P(\tilde{s} = s)$
7,000	.10
8,000	.15
9,000	.25
10,000	.20
11,000	.15
12,000	.10
13,000	.05

Draw a graph analogous to figure 12.1 and follow through the calculations outlined in section 12.3.2. (Assume the EMV is a valid criterion for choice.)

6. Using the notation of section 12.3.2, for exercise 3, identify parameters K_1, k_1, K_2, k_2, s_b. Compute $L^{(r)}(s_b)$ and $L^{(l)}(s_b)$ and use (12.13) to find the EVPI.

7. a. Prove (12.14) and (12.15).
Hint Use (9.16) and (9.18).

b. For the two-action, linear-value problem with a beta distributed $\tilde{p}$, let $k_2 = 10^4$, $k_1 = 0$, $p_b = .4$, $\rho = 3$, $\upsilon = 10$. Use (12.15) and (9.15) to find the EVPI.

8. [Verification of (12.22).] Show that:

a. If s lies in the interval $[s_{i-1}, s_i]$ then all summands in (12.22) are zero and $l_t(a_i, s) = 0$.

b. If $s_{\upsilon-1} \leq s \leq s_\upsilon$ where $s_\upsilon < s_{i-1}$, then a_υ is best in this interval and

$$
\begin{aligned}
l_t(a_i, s) &= v_t(a_\upsilon, s) - v_t(a_i, s) \\
&= [v_t(a_\upsilon, s) - v_t(a_{\upsilon+1}, s)] \\
&\quad + [v_t(a_{\upsilon+1}, s) - v_t(a_{\upsilon+2}, s)] \\
&\quad\ \vdots \\
&\quad + [v_t(a_{i-1}, s) - v_t(a_i, s)] \\
&= (k_{\upsilon+1} - k_\upsilon)(s_\upsilon - s) \\
&\quad + (k_{\upsilon+2} - k_{\upsilon+1})(s_{\upsilon+1} - s) \\
&\quad\ \vdots \\
&\quad + (k_i - k_{i-1})(s_{i-1} - s) \\
&= \textstyle\sum_{j=\upsilon}^{i-1} (k_{j+1} - k_j)(s_j - s) \\
&= \textstyle\sum_{j=1}^{i-1} (k_{j+1} - k_j)\max\{(s_j - s), 0\}.
\end{aligned}
$$

This agrees with (12.22) for $s_{\upsilon-1} \leq s \leq s_\upsilon$ since all summands in the second sum of (12.22) are zero.

c. If $s_{\upsilon-1} \leq s \leq s_\upsilon$ for $s_{\upsilon-1} \geq s_i$ then proceed in a manner analogous to (b).

9. Verify (12.25) through (12.27). (See exercise 4 of chapter 8.)

10. The soap manufacturer of the example in section 12.5 decides that perfect information that would lead to a correction of 100,000 units in his best guess would be worth $100 to him regardless whether this correction would lead to an upward or downward revision of his best guess; a 200,000 unit correction would be worth $400 to him; a 300,000 unit correction would be worth $900 to him; and so forth. Assuming purely as an exercise that he assigns to $\tilde{s}$ the measure shown in the table below, find the optimal estimate and the expected loss of using this estimate without obtaining further information.

s	$P(\tilde{s} = s)$
800,000	.3
1,000,000	.4
1,200,000	.2
1,400,000	.1
	1.0

11. Verify (12.28).

12. In a given region there are 4,000,000 households and an unknown proportion p of these have an automatic dishwasher. In 500 households chosen at random there are 47 dishwashers. If s is the true number of households in this region that have dishwashers and a is the estimate, assume that the loss is given by

$$l_t(s, s) = \$.00001\,(a - s)^2.$$

On the basis of the sample survey what is the best estimate a and what would perfect information be worth at this point?

13. a. Consider the inventory example introduced in section 12.2.1 and summarized in tables 12.1 and 12.2. Apply the theory developed in section 12.7 to this problem.

b. Let $\tilde{s}$ have a df f and let

$$L^{(r)}(a) = \int_a^{\infty} (s - a) f(a)\, ds,$$

$$L^{(l)}(a) = \int_{-\infty}^{a} (a - s) f(s)\, ds.$$

Show that

$$\frac{d}{da} L^{(r)}(a) = -G(a);$$

$$\frac{d}{da} L^{(l)}(a) = F(a).$$

14. Verify (12.32).
Hint Differentiate expression for $\bar{l}_t(a)$ in (12.30) and use results of exercise 13.

15. Verify (12.33) as follows. Let a' and a'' be such that $a' < a''$ and $P(a' < \tilde{s} < a'') = 0$. Show that

a. $$l_t(a'', s) - l_t(a', s) = \begin{cases} k_o(a'' - a') & \text{if} \quad s \le a', \\ k_u(a' - a'') & \text{if} \quad s \ge a''. \end{cases}$$

b. $E[l_t(a'', \tilde{s}) - l_t(a', \tilde{s})] = (a'' - a')[-k_u + (k_o + k_u)F(a')]$.

c. $$\bar{l}_t'(a'') \begin{vmatrix} > \\ = \\ < \end{vmatrix} \bar{l}_t'(a') \iff F(a') \begin{vmatrix} > \\ = \\ < \end{vmatrix} \frac{k_u}{k_u + k_o} \equiv k.$$

Consider the two cases shown in figure 12E.1.

d. In case 1 show that if $a' < a^*$ or if $a' > a^*$, then a' cannot be optimal. Therefore a^* is optimal.

e. In case 2 show that if $a' < a_1^*$ or if $a' > a_2^*$, then a' cannot be optimal. Show that for all a^* between a_1^* and a_2^* the loss $\bar{l}_t'(a^*)$ is constant. Therefore any a^* such that $a_1^* \le a^* \le a_2^*$ is optimal.

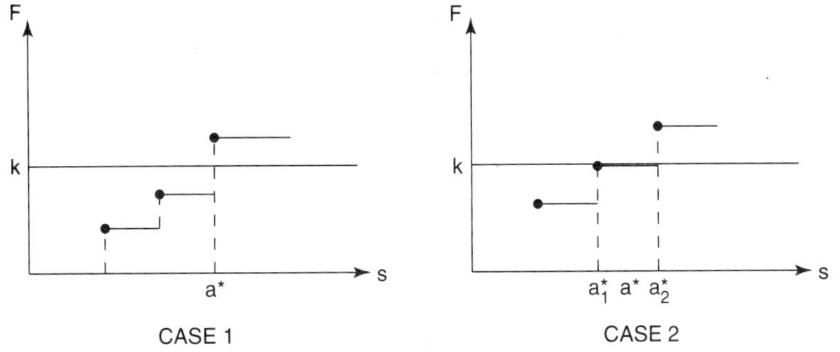

Figure 12E.1

16. Consider an inventory problem described by the following data:

k_1: cost per item stocked,
k_2: revenue per item sold,
k_3: scrap value per item stocked and not sold.

Defining

q: amount stocked,
d: demand;

assume that

$v_t(q,d) = -k_1 q + k_2 \min\{q,d\} + k_3 \max\{q-d,0\}.$

Show first that

a. $\max\{q-d,0\} = q - \min\{q,d\}$,

and then substituting (a) into the expression for $v_t(q,d)$,

b. $v_t(q,d) = (-k_1 + k_3)q + (k_2 - k_3)\min\{q,d\}$.

Show further that

c. $\bar{v}_t(q) = Ev_t(q,\tilde{d}) = (-k_1 + k_3)q + (k_2 - k_3)[E^{(l)}(q) + qP(\tilde{d} > q)]$,

d. $\bar{v}_t(q+1) - \bar{v}_t(q) = (-k_1 + k_3) + (k_2 - k_3)P(\tilde{d} \geq q+1)$,

e. $\bar{v}_t(q+1) > \bar{v}_t(q) \quad \Leftrightarrow \quad P(\tilde{d} \geq q+1) > \dfrac{k_1 - k_3}{k_2 - k_3}.$

17. Verify (12.34) and (12.35).

18. For the generalization suggested in section 12.8.2, find a^o and the EVPI.

19. *Reservation Policy*. In making reservations for a service with fixed capacity, as in hotel reservations or airplane reservations, it is customary for managers to let the number of reservations exceed capacity because not all customers "show." With this problem in mind, we consider the following model and associated decision problem. Let

n_0: number of available places,
n: number of reservations made (this number is the decision variable),
k_u: opportunity loss per place not occupied,
k_0: opportunity loss per customer with reservation who "shows" and for whom no place is available,
p: probability that any given customer with reservation will "show."

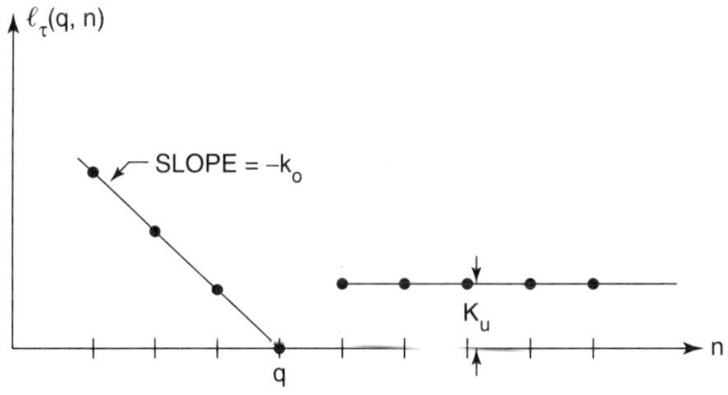

Figure 12E.2

Assumption If n reservations are made, the unknown number who "show" is the binomial rv $(\tilde{r}|n, p)$.

Suppose that n reservations have been made, where $n > n_0$, and that a request is made for the $(n + 1)^{\text{th}}$ reservation. Let act a_1 be "make this reservation" and act a_2 be "do not make this reservation"; let state s_1 be "this customer would show" and state s_2 be "this customer would not show." Complete details of the following reasoning:

a. If s_2, then $a_1 \sim a_2$. Hence a_1 and a_2 need only be compared given s_1.

b. If s_1, then a_1 has expected loss ________________.

c. If s_1, then a_2 has expected loss ________________.

d. Hence $a_1 \sim a_2$ if and only if ________________.

e. Therefore reservations should be made as long as ________________.

20. *Scrap Allowance.* A manufacturer who contracts to delivery exactly r good pieces of a specialized item will usually produce a larger number of pieces to allow for the possibility of defectives. Assume that the production process can be represented as a Bernoulli process where the probability at each trial of producing a good piece is p. Even though in fact the process will be terminated at some trial n, we can imagine it as potentially continuing indefinitely, and therefore we can let the Pascal rv $(\tilde{n}|r, p)$ represent the as yet unknown number of trials that would be required to get r good pieces. If the manufacturer schedules q pieces into production on the (first) run, then

i. If $\tilde{n} = n < q$, he only needed to schedule n pieces and he has suffered an opportunity loss through processing $(q - n)$ unneeded pieces. We assume in this exercise that this loss is directly proportional to the number of unneeded pieces,

$$l_t(a, n) = k_0(q - n), \qquad n \leq q.$$

ii. If $\tilde{n} = n > q$, the number of good pieces actually produced on the first run is smaller than the number required and some kind of opportunity loss is incurred. In this exercise we assume that the manufacturer will incur a fixed cost K_u in scheduling and setting up for a rerun, and we simplify the analysis by assuming that this is the *only* additional cost he will incur, so that

$$l_t(q, n) = K_u \qquad n > q.$$

(Actually, there may be overage or underage losses on the second run also, but in most cases these potential losses will be unimportant *relative* to the scheduling and setup cost K_u.)

On these assumptions the complete loss function l_t has the graph shown in figure 12E.2.

Note The losses are defined at integer values of n. The lines are drawn only as guides to the eye.

Show that

a. $\bar{l}_t(q) = El_t(q, \tilde{n}) = k_O L^{(1)}_{Pa}(q|r, p) + K_u G_{Pa}(q + 1|r, p)$.

b. $l_t(q + 1, n) - l_t(q, n) = \begin{cases} k_O & \text{if} \quad n \leq q, \\ -K_u & \text{if} \quad n = q + 1. \end{cases}$

c. $\bar{l}_t(q + 1) - \bar{l}_t(q) = k_O F_{Pa}(q|r, p) - K_u f_{Pa}(q + 1|r, p)$.

d. Given that the qth piece has been scheduled, the $(q + 1)$th piece should also be scheduled if

$$\frac{F_{Pa}(q|r, p)}{f_{Pa}(q + 1|r, p)} \leq \frac{K_u}{k_O}.$$

13 Paired Random Variables

13.1 Introduction: Definition of a Paired Random Variable

13.1.1 Paired Quantities and Values

In many situations we are interested in *paired* unknown or variable quantities. Thus a sample survey designed to obtain information bearing on factors influencing movie attendance may try to learn from each person interviewed both (1) the number of dollars spent last week on movie tickets, and (2) the number of hours spent last week in watching television. We could of course think of these two quantities as separate though possibly related entities, but it is often better to think of them as a *single entity* described by *two numbers*, and we shall take that point of view in this chapter. We shall consider such a survey as obtaining a series of values of an unknown quantity (dollars, hours); if a particular person spent 2 dollars and 12 hours we shall say that on this occasion the unknown quantity had the value (2, 12). Observe that a value like (2, 12) is an *ordered* pair in the sense that (12, 2) has the quite different meaning of 12 dollars and 2 hours.

In this chapter we extend the results developed in chapters 7 and 8, which dealt with a single random variable, to the case where we are concerned with the joint properties of a pair of random variables.

In section 13.1 we generalize the definition of a single random variable to the case of a pair of rv's. In section 13.2 we consider the case where each of the unknown quantities (random variables) can assume only a discrete set of values; we call this the *discrete* case. In section 13.3 we assume that one of the quantities is discrete but the other can take on a continuum of possible values; we call this the *mixed* case. Finally in section 13.4 we assume each of the unknown quantities can take on a continuum of possible values; we call this the *continuous* case. In later sections we develop results which hold for all three of these cases.

13.1.2 Definition of a Paired Random Variable

In section 7.1.6 we have defined an "interval" on the real line as any set of points of the form $(-\infty, b)$, $(-\infty, b]$, (a, b), $(a, b]$, $[a, b)$, $[a, b)$, $[a, \infty)$, or (a, ∞) where $a \leq b$. When dealing with a single rv $\tilde{x}$ we assumed that every event of the form $\tilde{x} \in I$, where I is an interval, had an associated P-measure.

When dealing with a *paired rv* $(\tilde{x}, \tilde{y})$ we shall assume that *all events of the form* $(\tilde{x} \in I', \tilde{y} \in I'')$, *where* I' *and* I'' *are intervals, have associated* P-*measures.*

When dealing with a single rv we invoked a *nullity assumption* (cf. section 7.1.5) to rule out certain pathologies. The nullity assumption for $\tilde{x}$ and $\tilde{y}$ individually implies the following

Nullity Assumption Consider two sequences of intervals

$I_1^{(1)} \supset I_2^{(1)} \supset \ldots \supset I_n^{(1)} \supset \ldots$

and

$I_1^{(2)} \supset I_2^{(2)} \supset \ldots \supset I_n^{(2)} \supset \ldots$

where there exists no point (x, y) such that ($x \in I_n^{(1)}$ and $y \in I_n^{(2)}$ for all n)—that is, whereas n goes to infinity the set $I_n^{(1)} \times I_n^{(2)}$ becomes smaller and in the limit vanishes. Then

$$\lim_{n\to\infty} P(\tilde{x} \in I_n^{(1)}, \tilde{y} \in I_n^{(2)}) = 0.$$

As a consequence of the Nullity Assumption we can easily prove:

a. $\lim_{\substack{x\to\infty \\ y\to\infty}} P(\tilde{x} \le x, \tilde{y} \le y) = 1;$ (13.1a)

b. $\lim_{x\to-\infty} P(\tilde{x} \le x, \tilde{y} \le y) = \lim_{y\to-\infty} P(\tilde{x} \le x, \tilde{y} \le y) = 0;$ (13.1b)

c. $\lim_{x\to\infty} P(\tilde{x} \le x, \tilde{y} \le y) = P(\tilde{y} \le y);$ (13.1c)

d. $\lim_{y\to\infty} P(\tilde{x} \le x, \tilde{y} \le y) = P(\tilde{x} \le x);$ (13.1d)

e. The expression $P(\tilde{x} \le x, \tilde{y} \le y)$ treated as a function of x (or of y) is continuous from the right.

13.2 Discrete Paired Random Variables

13.2.1 Definition of a Discrete Paired Random Variable

The paired rv $(\tilde{x}, \tilde{y})$ is said to be a *discrete* paired rv if there exists a denumerable set X with elements $x_1, \ldots x_i, \ldots$ and a denumerable set Y with elements $y_1, \ldots y_j, \ldots$ such that for all x and y,

$$P(\tilde{x} \le x, \tilde{y} \le y) = \sum_{\substack{x_i \le x \\ y_j \le y}} P(\tilde{x} = x_i, \tilde{y} = y_j), \tag{13.2}$$

where the sum is taken over all (x_i, y_j) pairs in $X \times Y$ for which both $x_i \le x$ and $y_j \le y$.

13.2.2 Joint Mass Function

A real-valued function f of two real arguments will be called a *joint mass function* if for some discrete set X and some discrete set Y,

Table 13.1

$\tilde{x}$ \ $\tilde{y}$	y_1	...	y_j	...	Total
x_1	$f(x_1, y_1)$	...	$f(x_1, y_j)$	...	$f_x(x_1)$
⋮	⋮		⋮		⋮
x_i	$f(x_i, y_1)$	...	$f(x_i, y_j)$	...	$f_x(x_i)$
⋮	⋮		⋮		⋮
Total	$f_y(y_1)$	...	$f_y(y_j)$	...	1.00

$$f(x, y)\begin{Bmatrix} \geq \\ = \end{Bmatrix} 0 \quad \text{for all } (x, y)\begin{Bmatrix} \in \\ \notin \end{Bmatrix} X \times Y, \tag{13.3a}$$

and

$$\sum f(x, y) = 1, \tag{13.3b}$$

where the sum is understood to be taken over all (x, y) pairs in $X \times Y$.

Schematic Representation

If f is a joint mf, then schematically all values of such a joint mf can be represented by the entries in the body of a table like table 13.1; the entries in the right and lower margins will be explained in a moment.

13.2.3 Joint MF of a Discrete Paired RV

If $(\tilde{x}, \tilde{y})$ is a discrete paired rv and f is defined by

$$f(x, y) \equiv P(\tilde{x} = x, \tilde{y} = y),$$

then the reader can verify that f is a joint mf.

Conversely, if f is a joint mf and if we define a measure P by

$$P(\tilde{x} \leq x, \tilde{y} \leq y) \equiv \sum_{\substack{x_i \leq x \\ y_j \leq y}} f(x_i, y_j),$$

then the paired rv $(\tilde{x}, \tilde{y})$ with this measure P is a discrete paired rv.

In either of these cases we shall say that f is the joint mf of the discrete paired rv $(\tilde{x}, \tilde{y})$.

13.2.4 Marginal Mass Functions

If f is the joint mf of a rv (x, y) with range $(X \times Y)$, the functions f_x and f_y defined by

$$f_x(x_i) \equiv \textstyle\sum_j f(x_i, y_j), \qquad x_i \in X, \tag{13.4a}$$

$$f_y(y_j) \equiv \textstyle\sum_i f(x_i, y_j) \qquad y_j \in Y, \tag{13.4b}$$

will be called the *marginal* mass functions of the rv's $\tilde{x}$ and $\tilde{y}$ respectively. Observe that $f_x(x_i)$ is the sum of all entries in the ith row of table 13.1 and that $f_y(y_j)$ is the sum of all entries in the jth column of table 13.1, from which it follows that

$$\textstyle\sum_j f_y(y_j) = \sum_i f_x(x_i) = 1.$$

The name "marginal" comes from the fact that the values of f_x and f_y appear in the margins of tables like table 13.1. The meaning of "marginal" in the context of probability has no connection with the meaning in such phrases as "marginal cost."

Observe that if $(\tilde{x}, \tilde{y})$ has a joint mf f, then

$$P(x = x_i) = f_x(x_i), \quad \text{and} \quad P(y = y_j) = f_y(y_j).$$

Notation

As regards our notation for marginal mf's, the *subscript* x in $f_x(x_i)$ indicates that we are dealing with the particular *function* f_x, while the *argument* x_i indicates that we want the function *evaluated* for the particular number x_i. That the notation is not redundant is clear from the fact that $f_x(1)$ has one clear meaning and $f_y(1)$ has another but $f(1)$ has no meaning at all.

In the sequel we shall have occasion to use the symbols $f_x(x)$ and $f_y(y)$, which seem a bit strange at first glance. The subscripts x and y on f refer to the random variables $\tilde{x}$ and $\tilde{y}$, whereas the arguments x and y refer to typical or generic values of these rv's. A purist might prefer the symbols $f_{\tilde{x}}(x)$ and $f_{\tilde{y}}(y)$, but for typographical purposes we prefer to drop the tilde symbol on subscripts.

In (13.4a) and (13.4b) we employed subscript notation such as x_i and y_j. In later sections, in order to bring out the analogy between the discrete and continuous cases, we occasionally drop subscripts, and in this notation (13.4a) and (13.4b) would be expressed in the form

$$f_x(x) = \textstyle\sum_y f(x, y), \qquad x \in X,$$

$$f_y(y) = \textstyle\sum_x f(x, y), \qquad y \in Y.$$

13.2.5 Conditional Mass Functions

The function $f_{x|y_j}$ defined by

$$f_{x|y_j}(x_i) \equiv \frac{f(x_i, y_j)}{f_y(y_j)}, \qquad f_y(y_j) > 0, \tag{13.5a}$$

will be called the *conditional mf of* $\tilde{x}$ *given* $\tilde{y} = y_j$; observe that $f_{x|y_j}$ is *not defined* for y_j such that $f_y(y_j) = 0$.

Referring back to table 13.1 the values of $f_{x|y_j}$ can be calculated *by dividing every entry in the j'th column of the table by the sum of those entries.*

Similarly the function $f_{y|x_i}$ defined by

$$f_{y|x_i}(y_j) \equiv \frac{f(x_i, y_j)}{f_x(x_i)}, \qquad f_x(x_i) > 0, \tag{13.5b}$$

will be called the *conditional mf of* $\tilde{y}$ *given* $\tilde{x} = x_i$. Its values can be calculated by dividing every entry in the *i'th row* of table 13.1 by the sum of those entries.

We can restate (13.5a) and (13.5b) in the form

$$f(x_i, y_j) = f_x(x_i) f_{y|x_i}(y_j) = f_y(y_j) f_{x|y_j}(x_i). \tag{13.5c}$$

As far as notation is concerned, once again, though the purist might prefer the symbols $f_{\tilde{x}|y_j}(x_i)$ and $f_{\tilde{y}|x_i}(y_j)$, for typographical purposes we prefer not to use the tilde symbol on subscripts. In any event the reader should check that he understands such symbols as $f_{x|3}(4)$ and $f_{y|2}(5)$. An example to be given in the next subsection will illustrate this notation.

Conditional Probability

From the formula for conditional probability

$$P(V|W) = \frac{P(V \cap W)}{P(W)}, \qquad P(W) > 0,$$

we have

$$\begin{aligned} P(\tilde{x} = x_i | \tilde{y} = y_j) &= \frac{P(\tilde{x} = x_i, \tilde{y} = y_j)}{P(\tilde{y} = y_j)} \\ &= \frac{f(x_i, y_j)}{f_y(y_j)} \\ &= f_{x|y_j}(x_i). \end{aligned}$$

In a similar manner, we also obtain

$$P(\tilde{y} = y_j | \tilde{x} = x_i) = f_{y|x_i}(y_j).$$

Thus the definition (13.5) of conditional mf fulfills the implication of the term: *The rv* $\tilde{x}$, *conditional on the event* $(\tilde{y} = y_j)$, *has the mf* $f_{x|y_j}(\cdot)$. Sometimes we shall call this the mf for the rv $(\tilde{x}|y_j)$. In particular, observe that for any y_j the function $f_{x|y_j}(\cdot)$ is a mf defined on X. (X is the "range" of the

Table 13.2

$\tilde{x}$ \ $\tilde{y}$	0	1	2	Total
0	.07	.22	.15	.44
1	.30	.14	.12	.56
Total	.37	.36	.27	1.00

Table 13.3

(A) Conditional mf of $\tilde{x}$ given y

$\tilde{x}$ \ $\tilde{y}$	0	1	2
0	7/37	22/36	15/27
1	30/37	14/36	12/27
Total	1	1	1

(B) Conditional mf of $\tilde{y}$ given x

$\tilde{x}$ \ $\tilde{y}$	0	1	2	Total
0	7/44	22/44	15/44	1
1	30/56	14/56	12/56	1

rv $\tilde{x}$ and the "domain" of its mf marginal or conditional.) For any x_i the function $f_{y|x_i}(\cdot)$ is a mf defined on Y; sometimes we shall call this the mf for the rv $(\tilde{y}|x_i)$.

13.2.6 Examples

Example 1 Let $(\tilde{x}, \tilde{y})$ have the joint mf given in table 13.2.
To illustrate the notation introduced above, observe the following

$$f(0,0) = .07, \qquad f(1,2) = .12,$$

$$f_x(0) = .44, \qquad f_x(1) = .56,$$

$$f_y(0) = .37, \qquad f_y(1) = .36, \qquad f_y(2) = .27,$$

$$f_{x|1}(0) = \tfrac{.22}{.36}, \qquad f_{y|1}(0) = \tfrac{.30}{.56}.$$

In table 13.3 we exhibit the conditional mf of $\tilde{x}$ given each of the values of y and the conditional mf of $\tilde{y}$ given each of the values of x. Table 13.3 is obtained directly from table 13.2 by use of formula (13.5).

Example 2 Let X and Y each consist of the set of positive integers and let f be defined by

$$f(x,y) = \begin{cases} (\frac{1}{2})^{x+y+1}y, & \text{if} \quad (x,y) \in X \times Y, \\ 0, & \text{if} \quad (x,y) \notin X \times Y. \end{cases}$$

The reader is asked (exercise 3) to show that

$$f_x(x) = \sum_{y=1}^{\infty} f(x, y) = (\tfrac{1}{2})^x, \qquad x = 1, 2, \ldots,$$

$$f_y(y) = \sum_{x=1}^{\infty} f(x, y) = (\tfrac{1}{2})^{y+1} y, \qquad y = 1, 2, \ldots,$$

$$\sum_{x=1}^{\infty} f_x(x) = \sum_{y=1}^{\infty} f_y(y) = 1,$$

$$f_{x|y}(x) \equiv \frac{f(x, y)}{f_y(y)} = (\tfrac{1}{2})^x,$$

$$f_{y|x}(y) \equiv \frac{f(x, y)}{f_x(x)} = (\tfrac{1}{2})^{y+1} y.$$

In this case the conditional mf's are the same as the marginal mf's; $\tilde{x}$ and $\tilde{y}$ are independent.

13.3 Mixed Paired Random Variables

13.3.1 Definition of a Mixed Paired Random Variable

In many situations we must deal with an unknown or variable quantity whose values are ordered pairs of real numbers only one of which must be taken from some discrete set of numbers while the other may be taken from a nondenumerable set. Thus, for example, we may be interested simultaneously in the paired quantity consisting of (1) the fraction defective p which a certain machine would produce if its present condition were to remain unaltered during an infinitely long production run, and (2) the number r of defectives which the machine will produce in a particular finite run of, say, $n = 100$ pieces; in this case p may be any number in the interval $[0, 1]$ while r is confined to the discrete set $\{0, 1, \ldots, 100\}$. Or we may be interested in the paired quantity whose first component is p as defined above but whose second component is the number n of pieces which must now be produced in order to obtain, say, exactly $r = 100$ good pieces. In this case p may as before be any number in $[0, 1]$, while n is confined to the discrete set $\{100, 101, \ldots\}$.

In what follows x denotes a value taken from *any* nondenumerable set, not necessarily the interval $[0, 1]$, and y denotes a value from *any* discrete set, not necessarily either $\{0, 1, \ldots, n\}$ or $\{1, 2, \ldots\}$.

The paired rv $(\tilde{x}, \tilde{y})$ is said to be a *mixed* paired rv if there exists a denumerable set Y with elements $y_1, \ldots, y_i, \ldots$ such that

a. $$P(\tilde{x} \le x, \tilde{y} \le y) = \sum_{y_i \le y} P(\tilde{x} \le x, \tilde{y} = y_i) \tag{13.6}$$

and

b. the expression $P(\tilde{x} \le x, \tilde{y} = y_i)$ is expressible as an integral from $-\infty$ to x of some nonnegative function (which depends on i), for all $y_i \in Y$; this implies that (but is not implied by) $P(\tilde{x} \le x, \tilde{y} = y_i)$ treated as a function of x is continuous.

13.3.2 Joint DM Functions

A real-valued function f of two real arguments will be called a (joint) density-mass function (dmf) if for some discrete Y

$$f(x, y) = 0, \qquad y \notin Y, \tag{13.7a}$$

$$f(x, y_i) \ge 0, \qquad y_i \in Y, \tag{13.7b}$$

$$\int_{-\infty}^{\infty} f(x, y_i)\, dx \quad \text{exists}, \quad y_i \in Y, \tag{13.7c}$$

$$\int_{-\infty}^{\infty} [\textstyle\sum_i f(x, y_i)]\, dx = 1. \tag{13.7d}$$

It can be shown by advanced calculus that if these conditions hold, then

$$\textstyle\sum_i \left[\int_{-\infty}^{\infty} f(x, y_i)\, dx\right] = 1. \tag{13.7e}$$

Example Let f be defined by

$$f(x, y) \equiv 2x^y(1 - x), \qquad \begin{matrix} 0 \le x \le 1 \\ y = 1, 2, \ldots; \end{matrix}$$

this definition is to be understood as implying that $f(x, y) = 0$ unless both x and y are in the specified sets. The reader is asked to show (exercise 5) that

$$\int_{-\infty}^{\infty} f(x, y)\, dx = \int_0^1 f(x, y)\, dx = \frac{2}{(y + 1)(y + 2)},$$

so that (13.7c) is satisfied, and

$$\int_{-\infty}^{\infty} [\textstyle\sum_{y=1}^{\infty} f(x, y)]\, dx = \int_0^1 2x\, dx = 1,$$

so that (13.7d) is also satisfied and f is a dmf.

13.3.3 Joint DM Function of a Mixed Paired Random Variable

If $(\tilde{x}, \tilde{y})$ is a mixed paired rv where $\tilde{y}$ has all of its mass on the denumerable set Y and if f is a function of two real variables such that for all $y_i \in Y$ and all x,

$$P(\tilde{x} \le x, \tilde{y} = y_i) = \int_{-\infty}^{x} f(t, y_i)\, dt$$

(note that t is merely a dummy variable of integration), and $f(x, y) = 0$ for $y \notin Y$, then f is a joint dmf. Observe in this case that if f is continuous at x, then

$$f(x, y_i) = \frac{d}{dx} P(\tilde{x} \le x, \tilde{y} = y_i).$$

Conversely, if f is a joint dmf and if we define a measure P by

$$P(\tilde{x} \le x, \tilde{y} \le y) = \sum_{y_i \le y} \int_{-\infty}^{x} f(t, y_i)\, dt,$$

then the paired rv $(\tilde{x}, \tilde{y})$ with this measure P is a mixed paired rv.

In either of these cases we shall say that f is the joint dmf of the mixed paired rv $(\tilde{x}, \tilde{y})$.

13.3.4 Marginal Functions

If f is the dmf of a rv $(\tilde{x}, \tilde{y})$, then the function f_x defined by

$$f_x(x) \equiv \textstyle\sum_i f(x, y_i) \qquad (13.8a)$$

will be called the *marginal density function of the rv* $\tilde{x}$, and the function f_y defined by

$$f_y(y_i) \equiv \int_{-\infty}^{\infty} f(x, y_i)\, dx, \qquad y_i \in Y, \qquad (13.8b)$$

will be called the *marginal mass function of the rv* $\tilde{y}$.

Example Let f be defined by

$$f(x, y) \equiv 2x^y(1 - x), \qquad \begin{array}{l} 0 < x < 1, \\ y = 1, 2, \ldots. \end{array}$$

As part of the discussion of this example in section 13.3.2, it has already been shown that

$$f_x(x) = 2x, \qquad 0 < x < 1,$$

$$f_y(y_i) = \frac{2}{(y_i + 1)(y_i + 2)}, \qquad y = 1, 2, \ldots.$$

Marginal Probability

It is left to the reader (exercise 10) to prove from (13.1) that

$$P(x_1 \le \tilde{x} \le x_2) = \int_{x_1}^{x_2} f_x(x)\, dx, \qquad x_1 \le x_2, \qquad (13.9a)$$

$$P(\tilde{y} = y_i) = f_y(y_i), \qquad y_i \in Y, \qquad (13.9b)$$

and that $\tilde{x}$ and $\tilde{y}$ are proper rv's.

13.3.5 Conditional Functions

The function $f_{x|y_i}$ defined by

$$f_{x|y_i}(x) \equiv \frac{f(x, y_i)}{f_y(y_i)}, \qquad f_y(y_i) > 0, \tag{13.10a}$$

will be called the *conditional density function of $\tilde{x}$ given $\tilde{y} = y_i$*; the function $f_{y|x_0}$ defined by

$$f_{y|x_0}(y_i) \equiv \frac{f(x_0, y_i)}{f_x(x_0)}, \qquad f_x(x_0) > 0, \tag{13.10b}$$

will be called the *conditional mass function of $\tilde{y}$ given $\tilde{x} = x_0$*.

We can restate (13.10a) and (13.10b) as

$$f(x, y_i) = f_x(x) f_{y|x}(y_i) = f_y(y_i) f_{x|y_i}(x). \tag{13.10c}$$

Example Let $(\tilde{x}, \tilde{y})$ have the dmf and marginal df and mf of the example in section 13.3.4. Then for any $y \in Y$

$$f_{x|y}(x) = \frac{2x^y(1 - x)}{2[(y + 1)(y + 2)]^{-1}} = x^y(1 - x)(y + 1)(y + 2),$$

and for any $x \in (0, 1]$

$$f_{y|x}(y) = \frac{2x^y(1 - x)}{2x} = x^{y-1}(1 - x).$$

Conditional Probability

Let $(\tilde{x}, \tilde{y})$ be a mixed paired rv with joint dmf f. We now wish to relate the conditional mf's and df's introduced above in a purely formal manner with conditional probability statements.

Case 1 **$(\tilde{x} \mid y_i)$** Let y_i be such that $P(\tilde{y} = y_i) > 0$. Then, for any x,

$$\begin{aligned} P(\tilde{x} \leq x \mid \tilde{y} = y_i) &= \frac{P(\tilde{x} \leq x, \tilde{y} = y_i)}{P(\tilde{y} = y_i)} \\ &= \frac{\int_{-\infty}^{x} f(t, y_i)\, dt}{f_y(y_i)} \\ &= \int_{-\infty}^{x} \frac{f(t, y_i)}{f_y(y_i)}\, dt \\ &= \int_{-\infty}^{x} f_{x|y_i}(t)\, dt. \end{aligned}$$

From this we conclude that *the rv* $\tilde{x}$, *conditional on the event* $(\tilde{y} = y_i)$, *has the df* $f_{x|y_i}$. We will not need the case where $P(\tilde{y} = y_i) = 0$.

Case 2 **($\tilde{y} \mid x$)** We may wish to assign a conditional measure to $\tilde{y}$ under the *hypothesis* that $\tilde{x}$ has some particular exact value x. In chapter 10 we considered this problem and came to the conclusion that $P(\tilde{y} = y_i | \tilde{x} = x)$ *must* be assigned in such a way that for all x^*

$$P(\tilde{x} \le x^*, \tilde{y} = y_i) = \int_{-\infty}^{x^*} P(\tilde{y} = y_i | \tilde{x} = x) f_x(x)\, dx. \tag{13.11}$$

But the left-hand side can also be expressed as

$$P(\tilde{x} \le x^*, \tilde{y} = y_i) = \int_{-\infty}^{x^*} f(x, y_i)\, dx. \tag{13.12}$$

Now if (13.11) and (13.12) are to hold for all x^*, then for (almost[1]) every value x_0 we must have

$$P(\tilde{y} = y_i | \tilde{x} = x_0) f_x(x_0) = f(x_0, y_i),$$

or

$$P(\tilde{y} = y_i | \tilde{x} = x_0) = \frac{f(x_0, y_i)}{f_x(x_0)} \equiv f_{y|x_0}(y_i). \tag{13.13}$$

From this we can assert that *the rv* $\tilde{y}$, *conditional on the hypothesis* $(\tilde{x} = x_0)$, *has the mf* $f_{y|x_0}$.

It still remains an open question whether $f_{y|x_0}(y_i)$ is the appropriate conditional assignment to make to the event $(\tilde{y} = y_i)$ if $\tilde{x}$ is observed to fall in an interval $x_0 - \delta \le \tilde{x} \le x_0 + \delta$, for a "small" value of δ. The following argument shows that under reasonable regularity conditions the answer is yes:

$$P(\tilde{y} = y_i | x_0 - \delta \le \tilde{x} \le x_0 + \delta) = \frac{P(x_0 - \delta \le \tilde{x} \le x_0 + \delta, \tilde{y} = y_i)}{P(x_0 - \delta \le \tilde{x} \le x_0 + \delta)}$$

$$= \frac{\int_{x_0-\delta}^{x_0+\delta} f(x, y_i)\, dx}{\int_{x_0-\delta}^{x_0+\delta} f_x(x)\, dx}.$$

1. Since a function under an integral sign can be arbitrarily changed on a set of measure zero without altering the evaluation of any integral, the sophisticated reader might bear in mind that strictly speaking the protecting phrase "almost everywhere" should appear almost everywhere in this chapter. We shall slight all such refinements to avoid confusing most of our intended audience; the deficiency can easily be supplied by our more mathematically erudite readers.

Now if $f_x(x_0) > 0$, and both f_x and $f(\cdot, y_i)$ are continuous at x_0, then it can be shown that

$$\lim_{\delta \to 0} P(\tilde{y} = y_i | x_0 - \delta \le \tilde{x} \le x_0 - \delta) = \frac{f(x_0, y_i)}{f_x(x_0)} \equiv f_{y|x_0}(y_i). \tag{13.14}$$

From this we conclude that if (a) $f_x(x_0) > 0$ and is continuous at x_0, and if (b) $f(x_0, y_i)$ is continuous at x_0 as a function of x for each y_i, then the rv $\tilde{y}$, conditional upon learning that $\tilde{x}$ is (approximately) x_0, has the (approximate) mf $f_{y|x_0}$.

13.4 Continuous Paired Random Variables

13.4.1 Notion of a Continuous Paired Random Variable

In many situations we must deal with an unknown or variable quantity whose values are ordered pairs of real numbers (x, y) both of which may be taken from a continuum of possible values. In order to avoid special formulas for special cases, we shall take the range of such a quantity to be the set of *all* pairs of real numbers, even though the real numbers may include some impossible as well as possible values of x and y.

We shall give a formal definition of a *continuous* paired rv in terms of the existence of a joint df (to be defined). From an informal point of view, however, the rv $(\tilde{x}, \tilde{y})$ is roughly speaking a *continuous* paired rv if the expression $P(\tilde{x} \le x, \tilde{y} \le y)$, treated as a function of the two real variables x and y, has for almost every (x, y) continuous mixed partial derivatives; that is, if the function is "smooth" except at certain troublesome spots which are not "too badly misbehaved."

13.4.2 Joint Density Function

A real-valued function f of two real arguments will be called a joint density function (df) if

$$f(x, y) \ge 0, \tag{13.15a}$$

$$\int_{-\infty}^{\infty} f(x, y)\,dx \quad \text{and} \quad \int_{-\infty}^{\infty} f(x, y)\,dy \quad \text{exist,} \tag{13.15b}$$

$$\int_{-\infty}^{\infty}\int_{-\infty}^{\infty} f(x, y)\,dx\,dy = 1. \tag{13.15c}$$

It can be shown that if these conditions hold, then

$$\int_{-\infty}^{\infty}\int_{-\infty}^{\infty} f(x, y)\,dy\,dx = 1. \tag{13.15d}$$

13.4.3 Joint Density Function of a Continuous Paired Random Variable

The rv $(\tilde{x}, \tilde{y})$ is said to be a *continuous* paired rv if there exists a joint df f such that for all x and y,

$$P(\tilde{x} \le x, \tilde{y} \le y) = \int_{-\infty}^{x} \int_{-\infty}^{y} f(t, u)\, du\, dt. \tag{13.16}$$

(Here t and u are merely dummy variables of integration.)

Observe that if f is continuous at the point (x, y), then

$$\frac{\partial^2}{\partial x\, \partial y} P(\tilde{x} \le x, \tilde{y} \le y) = \frac{\partial^2}{\partial y\, \partial x} P(\tilde{x} \le x, \tilde{y} \le y) = f(x, y). \tag{13.17}$$

13.4.4 Marginal Functions

If f is the joint df of the rv $(\tilde{x}, \tilde{y})$ then the function f_x defined by

$$f_x(x) \equiv \int_{-\infty}^{\infty} f(x, y)\, dy \tag{13.18a}$$

will be called the *marginal df of the rv* $\tilde{x}$, and the function f_y defined by

$$f_y(y) \equiv \int_{-\infty}^{\infty} f(x, y)\, dx \tag{13.18b}$$

will be called the *marginal df of the rv* $\tilde{y}$.

Marginal Probability

It is left (exercise 11) for the reader to prove from (13.1) that

$$P(x_1 \le x \lesssim x_2) = \int_{x_1}^{x_2} f_x(x)\, dx, \qquad x_1 \le x_2, \tag{13.19a}$$

$$P(y_1 \le \tilde{y} \le y_2) = \int_{y_1}^{y_2} f_y(y)\, dy, \qquad y_1 \le y_2, \tag{13.19b}$$

and that $\tilde{x}$ and $\tilde{y}$ are proper continuous rv's.

13.4.5 Conditional Functions

The function $f_{x|y_0}$ defined by

$$f_{x|y_0}(x_0) \equiv \frac{f(x_0, y_0)}{f_y(y_0)}, \qquad f_y(y_0) > 0, \tag{13.20a}$$

will be called the *conditional df of* $\tilde{x}$ *given* $\tilde{y} = y_0$, and the function $f_{y|x_0}$ defined by

$$f_{y|x_0}(y_0) \equiv \frac{f(x_0, y_0)}{f_x(x_0)}, \qquad f_x(x_0) > 0, \tag{13.20b}$$

will be called the *conditional df of* $\tilde{y}$ *given* $\tilde{x} = x_0$. Expressions (13.20a) and (13.20b) can be restated in the form

$$f(x_0, y_0) = f_x(x_0) f_{y|x_0}(y_0) = f_y(y_0) f_{x|y_0}(x_0). \tag{13.20c}$$

Conditional Probability

Let $(\tilde{x}, \tilde{y})$ be a continuous paired rv with joint df f. We now wish to relate the conditional df's introduced above in a purely formal manner with conditional probability statements.

We may wish to assign a conditional measure $\tilde{x}$ under the *hypothesis* that $\tilde{y}$ has some particular exact value y. In chapter 10 we considered this problem and came to the conclusion that $P(\tilde{x} \le x^* | \tilde{y} = y)$ must be assigned in such a way that for all y^*

$$P(\tilde{x} \le x^*, \tilde{y} \le y^*) = \int_{-\infty}^{y^*} P(\tilde{x} \le x^* | \tilde{y} = y) f_y(y)\, dy. \tag{13.21}$$

But the left-hand side of (13.21) can also be expressed as

$$P(\tilde{x} \le x^*, \tilde{y} \le y^*) = \int_{-\infty}^{y^*} \left[\int_{-\infty}^{x^*} f(x, y)\, dx \right] dy. \tag{13.22}$$

Now if (13.21) and (13.22) are to hold for all y^*, then for (almost) every value y_0 we must have

$$P(\tilde{x} \le x^* | \tilde{y} = y_0) f_y(y_0) = \int_{-\infty}^{x^*} f(x, y_0)\, dx,$$

or

$$P(\tilde{x} \le x^* | \tilde{y} = y_0) = \int_{-\infty}^{x^*} \frac{f(x, y_0)}{f_y(y_0)}\, dx = \int_{-\infty}^{x^*} f_{x|y_0}(x)\, dx, \tag{13.23}$$

provided that $f_y(y_0) > 0$. From this we conclude that if $f_y(y_0) > 0$, *the rv* $\tilde{x}$, *conditional on the hypothesis* $(\tilde{y} = y_0)$, *has the df* $f_{x|y_0}$. Interchanging the roles of $\tilde{x}$ and $\tilde{y}$ we conclude that *if* $f_x(x_0) > 0$, *the rv* $\tilde{y}$, *conditional on the hypothesis* $(\tilde{x} = x_0)$, *has the df* $f_{y|x_0}$.

It still remains an open question whether $f_{x|y_0}$ is the appropriate conditional df for the rv $\tilde{x}$ if $\tilde{y}$ is observed to fall in the interval $y_0 - \delta \le \tilde{y} \le y_0 + \delta$ for a "small" value of δ. The following argument shows that under reasonable regularity conditions the answer is yes:

$$P(\tilde{x} \le x^* | y_0 - \delta \le \tilde{y} \le y_0 + \delta) = \frac{P(\tilde{x} \le x^*, y_0 - \delta \le \tilde{y} \le y_0 + \delta)}{P(y_0 - \delta \le \tilde{y} \le y_0 + \delta)}$$

$$= \frac{\int_{y_0-\delta}^{y_0+\delta} \int_{-\infty}^{x^*} f(x, y)\, dx\, dy}{\int_{y_0-\delta}^{y_0+\delta} f_y(y)\, dy}.$$

Now if $f_y(y_0) > 0$, if $f_y(\cdot)$ is continuous at y_0, and if $f(x, \cdot)$ is uniformly continuous at y_0 for all x, then it can be shown that

$$\lim_{\delta \to 0} P(\tilde{x} \le x^* | y_0 - \delta \le \tilde{y} \le y_0 + \delta) = \int_{-\infty}^{x^*} f_{x|y_0}(x)\, dx, \tag{13.24}$$

from which we conclude that *the rv $\tilde{x}$, conditional upon learning that $\tilde{y}$ is (approximately) y_0, has the (approximate) df $f_{x|y_0}$*. A similar result is obtained by interchanging the roles of $\tilde{x}$ and $\tilde{y}$.

13.5 Independence

Let $(\tilde{x}, \tilde{y})$ be a paired rv. By the definition of independence (5.5) the two events $(\tilde{x} \le x_0)$ and $(\tilde{y} \le y_0)$ are independent if and only if

$$P(\tilde{x} \le x_0, \tilde{y} \le y_0) = P(\tilde{x} \le x_0) P(\tilde{y} \le y_0). \tag{13.25}$$

We now define the *random variables* $\tilde{x}$ and $\tilde{y}$ to be *independent* if and only if (13.25) holds for *all* x_0 and y_0.

Theorem Let $(\tilde{x}, \tilde{y})$ be a paired rv with distributing function f.[2] The rv's $\tilde{x}$ and $\tilde{y}$ are independent if and only if the following three equivalent conditions are met:

$$f(x_0, y_0) = f_x(x_0) f_y(y_0), \tag{13.26a}$$

$$f_{x|y_0}(x_0) = f_x(x_0), \qquad \text{for} \quad f_y(y_0) > 0, \tag{13.26b}$$

$$f_{y|x_0}(y_0) = f_y(y_0), \qquad \text{for} \quad f_x(x_0) > 0. \tag{13.26c}$$

Proof From the definitions of f, f_x, f_y, $f_{x|y}$, and $f_{y|x}$ it is immediate that (13.26a) implies (13.26b) and (13.26c). If $f_y(y_0) > 0$, then clearly (13.26b) implies (13.26a); if $f_y(y_0) = 0$, then $f(x_0, y_0) = 0$ so that in either case (13.26b) implies (13.26a). Similarly (13.26c) implies (13.26a). Now (13.25) asserts that

2. When dealing with paired random variables, we use the term *distributing* function to refer to a joint mf, a joint dmf, or a joint df.

$$\int_{-\infty}^{x_0}\int_{-\infty}^{y_0} f(x, y)\,dx\,dy = \left[\int_{-\infty}^{x_0} f_x(x)\,dx\right]\left[\int_{-\infty}^{y_0} f_y(y)\,dy\right]$$

for *all* (x_0, y_0). But this implies that

$$\int_{-\infty}^{x_0}\int_{-\infty}^{y_0} [f(x, y) - f_x(x)f_y(y)]\,dx\,dy = 0$$

for all (x_0, y_0), which implies the integrand equals 0, or that $f(x_0, y_0) = f_x(x_0)f_y(y_0)$, showing (13.25) implies (13.26a). It remains to show that (13.26a) implies (13.25) which follows from the argument

$$\begin{aligned} P(\tilde{x} \le x_0, \tilde{y} \le y_0) &= \int_{-\infty}^{x_0}\int_{-\infty}^{y_0} f(x, y)\,dx\,dy = \int_{-\infty}^{x_0}\int_{-\infty}^{y_0} f_x(x)f_y(y)\,dx\,dy \\ &= \int_{-\infty}^{x_0} f_x(x)\,dx \int_{-\infty}^{y_0} f_y(y)\,dy \\ &= P((\tilde{x} \le x_0)P(\tilde{y} \le y_0). \end{aligned}$$

Remarks Expressed in words, (13.26b) says that the knowledge that $\tilde{y} = y_0$ does not alter the distributing function for $\tilde{x}$. Similarly, expression (13.26c) asserts that knowledge that $\tilde{x} = x_0$ does not alter the distributing function for $\tilde{y}$.

13.6 Indirect Assessment of Joint Distributions

Although it is instructive to think of the joint distribution of a paired rv $(\tilde{x}, \tilde{y})$ as basic and to think of the marginal and conditional distributions of $\tilde{x}$ and $\tilde{y}$ as being derived from the joint distribution, this is rarely a practical method for *assessing* a joint distribution. Much more commonly we actually:

1. assign a marginal distribution to one of the two variables, say $\tilde{x}$;
2. assign a conditional distribution to $\tilde{y}$ for every x in the range of $\tilde{x}$;
3. use these to compute the joint distribution;
4. use the joint distribution to compute the marginal of $\tilde{y}$ and the conditionals of $\tilde{x}$ given every y in the range of $\tilde{y}$.

13.6.1 Computation of the Joint Distribution

If we have assigned a marginal mf or df f_x to $\tilde{x}$, and if for every x we have assigned a conditional mf or df $f_{y|x}$ to $\tilde{y}$, then by definition of this latter function

Table 13.4

(A)

$\tilde{x}$ \ $\tilde{y}$	0	1	
0	.25	.25	.50
1	.25	.25	.50
	.50	.50	1.00

(B)

$\tilde{x}$ \ $\tilde{y}$	0	1	
0	.10	.40	.50
1	.40	.10	.50
	.50	.50	1.00

$$f(x, y) = f_x(x) f_{y|x}(y) \tag{13.27a}$$

where f is the joint mf, df, or dmf as the case may be. The same procedure applies of course when x and y are interchanged:

$$f(x, y) = f_y(y) f_{x|y}(x). \tag{13.27b}$$

Observe that we *cannot* in general determine the joint distribution if all that we have to work with is the *marginal* of $\tilde{x}$ and the *marginal* of $\tilde{y}$; tables 13.4A and 13.4B show two entirely different joint distributions both having exactly the same marginals.

If $\tilde{x}$ and $\tilde{y}$ are *independent*, then their marginal distributions do suffice to determine their joint distribution; for in this case

$$f_{x|y} = f_x \text{ for all } y, \quad \text{and} \quad f_{y|x} = f_y \text{ for all } x,$$

so that we can substitute a marginal mf or df for the conditional called for in (13.27).

13.6.2 Marginal Distributions and Bayes' Formula

In the analysis of many decision problems what we will want for computation of expected values of acts will be f_y and/or $f_{x|y}$ for one or more ys; we will have no interest in the joint distribution as such. We have in mind a situation where we could observe y if we wished but the profitability of the available acts depends on x, which we cannot observe. In the notation and terminology of chapter 6, x is the "state of the world" s and y is the outcome z of an experiment e. In the case of the Bernoulli Process x is the process parameter p. The prior distribution of $\tilde{x}$ is the marginal distribution of $\tilde{x}$, so f_x is the *prior distributing function* of $\tilde{x}$. The conditional distribution of $\tilde{y}$ given x has distributing function $f_{y|x}$, so the *likelihood function* is $f_{y|x}(y)$ regarded as a function of x. The posterior distribution of $\tilde{x}$ is the conditional distribution of $\tilde{x}$ given y, so $f_{x|y}$ is the *posterior distributing function* of $\tilde{x}$. The posterior distribution of $\tilde{x}$ depends on y, so for *preposterior analysis*, which occurs before y is observed and indeed is concerned with whether to observe y, we need the marginal distribution of $\tilde{y}$.

(Since y determines the posterior distribution of $\tilde{x}$, the parameters of this distribution, or posterior parameters, are functions of y and hence the *prior distribution of the posterior parameters* is obtainable directly from the marginal distribution of $\tilde{y}$. In the case that y itself serves as the parameter of the posterior distribution of $\tilde{x}$, the marginal distribution of $\tilde{y}$ is the prior distribution of the posterior parameter.) The formulas we are about to give apply to any interpretation of $\tilde{x}$ and $\tilde{y}$, but one motivation for them lies in the kind of situation just described.

If in such a situation what we originally have to work with is f_x and $f_{y|x}$ for all x—and we cannot make do with less—we can obtain f_y from the *formulas for marginal mf's and df's*:

$$f_y(y) = \begin{cases} \sum_i f_x(x_i) f_{y|x_i}(y), & \tilde{x} \text{ discrete,} \\ \int_{-\infty}^{\infty} f_x(x) f_{y|x}(y)\, dx, & \tilde{x} \text{ continuous,} \end{cases} \tag{13.28}$$

which follow directly on substituting (13.27a) in the appropriate (discrete or continuous) definition of f_y. We can then obtain $f_{x|y}$ from *Bayes' formula for conditional mf's and df's*,

$$f_{x|y}(x) = \frac{f_x(x) f_{y|x}(y)}{f_y(y)}, \tag{13.29}$$

which follows directly on substituting (13.27a) in the appropriate definition of $f_{x|y}$. This latter formula is often more usefully thought of in the form

$$f_{x|y}(x) \propto f_x(x) f_{y|x}(y),$$

the suppressed denominator being regarded merely as a scale factor which must be chosen such that

$$\textstyle\sum_X f_{x|y}(x) \qquad \text{or} \qquad \int_{-\infty}^{\infty} f_{x|y}(x)\, dx$$

equals unity.

13.7 Expectations

13.7.1 Definition of the Expectation of a Function of Two Random Variables

In section 8.2.3 we showed that if φ is a real-valued function of a single real argument, if $\tilde{x}$ is a rv, and if the rv $\tilde{y}$ is defined by $\tilde{y} = \varphi(\tilde{x})$, then the expectation of $\tilde{y}$ can be represented either as

$$\bar{y} \equiv E(\tilde{y}) = \int y\, dP_y \tag{13.30a}$$

or as

$$\bar{y} \equiv E(\tilde{y}) = E[\varphi(\tilde{x})] = \int \varphi(x)\, dP_x, \tag{13.30b}$$

where P_y and P_x represent respectively the probability measures on Y and X. In section 8.2.3 we used (13.30a) as the definition of $E(\tilde{y})$ and proved the equivalence of (13.30a) and (13.30b) for the case where φ was reasonably "well behaved." If $\tilde{x}$ has a distributing function f, then (13.30b) can be rewritten as

$$E[\varphi(\tilde{x}) = \begin{cases} \sum_X \varphi(x) f(x), & f \text{ is a mf,} \\ \int_R \varphi(x) f(x)\, dx, & f \text{ is a df,} \end{cases} \tag{13.30c}$$

and we can say that the number $E[\varphi(\tilde{x})]$ is the *expectation of* φ *with respect to* f. In this section we shall generalize expression (13.30c) to the case where φ is a real-valued function of *two* real arguments. The symbol $\int_R$ means that the integration is over the real line R, that is, $\int_R \equiv \int_{-\infty}^{\infty}$.

Let φ be a real-valued function of two real arguments and let $(\tilde{x}, \tilde{y})$ be a paired rv with distributing function f. We shall now define the *expectation of* φ *wrt* f for the cases where f is a mf, df, and dmf.

1. Discrete Case Let f be the mass function of a rv $(\tilde{x}, \tilde{y})$ with discrete range $(X \times Y)$. The expectation of φ wrt f is defined to be

$$E\varphi((\tilde{x}, \tilde{y}) \equiv \textstyle\sum_{X \times Y} \varphi(x, y) f(x, y) \tag{13.31a}$$

$$= \textstyle\sum_X [\sum_Y \varphi(x, y) f(x, y)] \tag{13.31b}$$

$$= \textstyle\sum_Y [\sum_X \varphi(x, y) f(x, y)], \tag{13.31c}$$

provided that the sum in (13.31a) converges absolutely—that is, provided that when φ is replaced by $|\varphi|$ on the right-hand side of (13.31a), the sum still converges.

2. Continuous Case Let f be the density function of a rv $(\tilde{x}, \tilde{y})$. Then the expectation of φ wrt f is defined to be

$$E\varphi(\tilde{x}, \tilde{y}) \equiv \int_R \int_R \varphi(x, y) f(x, y)\, dx\, dy \tag{13.32a}$$

$$\int_R \int_R \varphi(x, y) f(x, y)\, dy\, dx, \tag{13.32b}$$

provided that both iterated integrals converge absolutely, in which case it is shown in books on advanced calculus that they are equal. If *both* fail to converge absolutely, we shall say that the expectation does not exist; for other cases, we refer the reader to advanced works on probability.

3. Mixed Case Let f be the dmf of a rv $(\tilde{x}, \tilde{y})$ with range $(R \times Y)$ where Y is discrete. Then the expectation of φ wrt f is defined to be

$$E\varphi(\tilde{x}, \tilde{y}) \equiv \int_R [\textstyle\sum_Y \varphi(x, y) f(x, y)]\, dx \tag{13.33a}$$

$$\textstyle\sum_Y \left[\int_R \varphi(x, y) f(x, y)\, dx\right], \tag{13.33b}$$

provided that (1) the integral in (13.33a) converges absolutely, and (2) the integral in (13.33b) converges absolutely for every y in Y, in which case it can be shown by advanced calculus that (13.33a) and (13.33b) are equal. If both conditions fail, we shall say that the expectation does not exist; for other cases, we refer the reader to advanced works on probability.

13.7.2 Conditional Expectation

Let $(\tilde{x}, \tilde{y})$ be a rv and let $f_{x|y_0}$ be the conditional mf or df of $\tilde{x}$ given the particular value y_0 of $\tilde{y}$.

Let $\varphi(\tilde{x}, \tilde{y})$ be a real-valued function of $(\tilde{x}, \tilde{y})$, fix $\tilde{y}$ at the particular value y_0, and let $\varphi(\tilde{x}, y_0)$ denote the resulting function of $\tilde{x}$ alone, y_0 being considered a "constant" in the definition of this function.

The expectation of $\varphi(\tilde{x}, y_0)$ taken with respect to the "univariate" mf or df $f_{x|y_0}$ will be called the *conditional expectation* of the "bivariate" function φ *given* y_0 and will be denoted by $E_{x|y_0}\varphi(\tilde{x}, y_0)$. The conditional expectation of φ given some particular value x_0 of $\tilde{x}$, denoted by $E_{y|x_0}\varphi(x_0, \tilde{y})$, is similarly defined.

Now letting y denote *any* value of $\tilde{y}$, observe that:

1. $E_{x|y}\varphi(\tilde{x}, y)$ depends on y because both the value of φ and the conditional mf or df of $\tilde{x}$ depend on y.

2. $E_{x|y}\varphi(\tilde{x}, y)$ does *not* depend on x because the x has been "expected out."

Example 1 Let $(\tilde{x}, \tilde{y})$ be a rv with mf defined by table 13.2 so that the conditional mf's of $\tilde{x}$ and $\tilde{y}$ are given by table 13.3, and let $\varphi(\tilde{x}, \tilde{y}) = 2x + 3y$. Then

$$E_{x|0}\varphi(\tilde{x}, 0) = \tfrac{7}{37}(0 + 0) + \tfrac{30}{37}(2 + 0) = \tfrac{60}{37},$$

$$E_{x|1}\varphi(\tilde{x}, 1) = \tfrac{22}{36}(0 + 3) + \tfrac{14}{36}(2 + 3) = \tfrac{136}{36},$$

$$E_{x|2}\varphi(\tilde{x}, 2) = \tfrac{15}{27}(0 + 6) + \tfrac{12}{27}(2 + 6) = \tfrac{187}{27}.$$

Example 2 Let $(\tilde{x}, \tilde{y})$ be a rv with the dmf of the example in section 13.3.4 so that the conditional df of $\tilde{x}$ and the mf of $\tilde{y}$ are

$$f_{x|y}(x) = x^y(1-x)(y+1)(y+2),$$

$$f_{y|x}(y) = x^{y-1}(1-x),$$

as shown in the example in section 13.3.5, and let φ be defined by $\varphi(x, y) = x^2 y$. The reader is asked to show (exercise 13) that

$$E_{x|y}\varphi(\tilde{x}, y) = \frac{y(y+1)(y+2)}{(y+3)(y+4)},$$

$$E_{y|x}\varphi(x, \tilde{y}) = \frac{x^2}{1-x}.$$

Conditional Expectation of a Function of One Variable

It is obvious in principle that the definition of conditional expectation applies even though the value of the function φ does not actually depend on one of its two arguments, but we shall pause a moment to look at the implications in this case.

To be specific, consider the case where the value of φ does not depend on y, so that we could write

$$\varphi(x, y) = \psi(x).$$

1. If we expect this function wrt the conditional mf or df of $\tilde{y}$ *given* x, the function is simply a constant; and therefore by the usual formula for the expectation of a constant,

$$E_{y|x}\psi(\tilde{x}) = \psi(x). \tag{13.34}$$

2. If we expect wrt the conditional mf or df of $\tilde{x}$ given y, then even though the *function* does not depend on y, the *mf or df* in general will depend on y, and therefore $E_{x|y}\psi(\tilde{x})$ *will depend on* y.

13.7.3 Marginal Expectation

Let $(\tilde{x}, \tilde{y})$ be a rv, let f_x be the marginal mf or df of $\tilde{x}$, and let ψ be a real-valued function of $\tilde{x}$. The expectation of ψ wrt f_x will be called the marginal expectation of ψ and will be denoted by $E_x\psi(\tilde{x})$. The marginal expectation of a function of $\tilde{y}$ is similarly defined.

Observe that *marginal* expectation is meaningful only for functions of *one* variable. Consider a function φ whose value depends on *both* x and y. In order to obtain its expectation wrt f_x, say, we must evaluate it for every possible x, and we can do so only by substituting a numerical value for y or else by regarding y itself as a fixed number; but at the same time the mf of df f_x would in general not be valid for any fixed y.

13.7.4 Iterated Expectation

In most situations the most convenient way of evaluating the expectation of a function φ wrt the mf, df, or dmf of a rv $(\tilde{x}, \tilde{y})$ is by iterated expectation following one of the two formulas

$$E\varphi((\tilde{x}, \tilde{y}) = E_x E_{y|x} \varphi((\tilde{x}, \tilde{y}) \tag{13.35a}$$

$$= E_y E_{x|y} \varphi(\tilde{x}, \tilde{y}) \tag{13.35b}$$

which will be justified as soon as we have explained their meaning. Taking (13.35a) as an example, we first evaluate the expectation of φ wrt $f_{y|x}$ for all x, thus obtaining the conditional expectation $E_{y|x}\varphi(x,\tilde{y})$ which is a function of x alone; we then evaluate the expectation of *this* function wrt f_x. Under (13.35b) the procedure is the same with x and y interchanged.

To justify formulas (13.35) we shall prove (13.35a) for the case where the rv $(\tilde{x}, \tilde{y})$ has a joint mass function, leaving the other cases to the reader (exercise 14). To do so we write

$$
\begin{aligned}
E\varphi(\tilde{x}, \tilde{y}) &= \textstyle\sum_{X \times Y} \varphi(x, y) f(x, y) && \text{(by definition of } E\text{)} \\
&= \textstyle\sum_X [\sum_Y \varphi(x, y) f(x, y)] && \text{(by (13.31b))} \\
&= \textstyle\sum_X [\sum_Y \varphi(x, y) f_{y|x}(y) f_x(x)] && \text{(by (13.27a))} \\
&= \textstyle\sum_X [\sum_Y \varphi(x, y) f_{y|x}(y)] f_x(x) && \\
&= \textstyle\sum_X [E_{y|x} \varphi(x, \tilde{y})] f_x(x) && \text{(by definition of } E_{y|x}\text{)} \\
&= E_x E_{y|x} \varphi(\tilde{x}, \tilde{y}) && \text{(by definition of } E_x\text{).}
\end{aligned}
$$

Example 1 Let $(\tilde{x}, \tilde{y})$ be a rv with mf defined by table 13.2 so that the marginal mf of $\tilde{y}$ is given by the bottom margin of that table; and let φ be defined by $\varphi(x, y) = 2x + 3y$, so that $E_{x|y}\varphi(\tilde{x}, y)$ is given for all y by example 1 of section 13.7.2. Then

$$
\begin{aligned}
E\varphi(\tilde{x}, \tilde{y}) &= E_y E_{x|y} \varphi(\tilde{x}, \tilde{y}) \\
&= .37(\tfrac{60}{37}) + .36(\tfrac{136}{36}) + .27(\tfrac{186}{27}) = 3.82.
\end{aligned}
$$

Example 2 Let $(\tilde{x}, \tilde{y})$ be a rv with the dmf of the example in section 13.3.4, so that the marginal df of $\tilde{x}$ is given by

$$f_x(x) = 2x, \qquad 0 < x < 1,$$

and let φ be defined by $\varphi(x, y) = x^2 y$, so that

$$E_{y|x}\varphi(x, \tilde{y}) = \frac{x^2}{1 - x},$$

as indicated previously. Then

$$E\varphi(\tilde{x}, \tilde{y}) = E_x E_{y|x} \varphi(\tilde{x}, \tilde{y}) = \int_0^1 \frac{2x^3}{1-x} dx$$

and the reader should observe that the expectation does *not exist* because this improper integral does not converge.

13.7.5 Expectation of Functions of One of Two Jointly Distributed RVs

Let $(\tilde{x}, \tilde{y})$ be a rv distributed by f and let ψ be a real-valued function of $\tilde{x}$ alone. The expectation of ψ wrt f is defined by (13.31), (13.32), or (13.33) in exactly the same way that the expectation of a function φ of both variables is defined, since we did not assume in those definitions that the value of φ actually depended on y—or for that matter, on *either* x or y. Compare the fact that if a is a constant, $E(a)$ was considered well defined in the univariate case.

The expectation of ψ wrt f is of course in general quite different from the *conditional* expectation of ψ wrt either $f_{x|y}$ or $f_{y|x}$, which we discussed in section 13.7.2. It is, however, exactly the *same* as the *marginal* expectation of ψ wrt f_x, which we discussed in section 13.7.3. Remember that since ψ is a function of $\tilde{x}$, it has no marginal expectation wrt $f_y(\cdot)$. For by (13.35a) and (13.34)

$$E\psi(\tilde{x}) = E_x E_{y|x} \psi(\tilde{x}) = E_x \psi(\tilde{x}). \tag{13.36a}$$

For actual computations, it turns out, perhaps surprisingly at first sight, that formula (13.35b) is often very convenient even when applied to a function of $\tilde{x}$ alone:

$$E\psi(\tilde{x}) = E_y E_{x|y} \psi(\tilde{x}). \tag{13.36b}$$

Computing $E_x \psi(\tilde{x})$ wrt f_x involves one step instead of two; but it may be easier to take two steps, first evaluating $E_{x|y} \psi(\tilde{x})$ as a function of y and then expecting this function wrt f_y.

13.8 Mean, Variance, Covariance, and Correlation

13.8.1 Mean of One of Two Jointly Distributed RVs

If $\tilde{x}$ is a rv with a mass or density function, then by definition the mean or expectation of $\tilde{x}$ is the expectation of the function $\psi(\tilde{x}) = x$ wrt the mf or df of $\tilde{x}$. If $(\tilde{x}, \tilde{y})$ is a rv, then $\tilde{x}$ may have both a marginal mf or df f_x and a family of conditional mf's or df's $f_{x|y}$ given y; and $\tilde{x}$ will have a mean or expectation corresponding to each of these mf's or df's.

1. We define the *conditional* mean or expectation of $\tilde{x}$ *given* y to be

$$\bar{x}_y \equiv E_{x|y}(\tilde{x}). \tag{13.37}$$

2. We define the *marginal* mean or expectation of $\tilde{x}$ to be

$$\bar{x} \equiv E_x(\tilde{x}). \tag{13.38}$$

From (13.36a) we see that the "marginal" expectation of $\tilde{x}$ is the same thing as "the" expectation of $\tilde{x}$ wrt the joint distribution of $(\tilde{x}, \tilde{y})$,

$$E_x(\tilde{x}) = E(\tilde{x}); \tag{13.39}$$

and from (13.36b) we then obtain a result often useful in computation:

$$\bar{x} = E(\tilde{x}) = E_y E_{x|y}(\tilde{x}) = E_y(\bar{x}_{\tilde{y}}). \tag{13.40}$$

A word of explanation about the notation employed in (13.40) might be helpful. In evaluating the expression $E_{x|y}(\tilde{x})$, we first think of y as being a fixed but arbitrary number and take the expectation of $\tilde{x}$ with respect to the conditional distributing function of $\tilde{x}$ given $\tilde{y} = y$; by the notation of (13.37) we get the number $\bar{x}_y$ which depends on the value of y; we now shift our orientation and think of y and $\bar{x}_y$ as rv's $\tilde{y}$ and $\bar{x}_{\tilde{y}}$ respectively; finally, we take the expectation of the rv $\bar{x}_{\tilde{y}}$ wrt the marginal distributing function of $\tilde{y}$.

Example Let $(\tilde{x}, \tilde{y})$ have the mf of table 13.2 so that f_x and f_y are given by table 13.2 and $f_{x|y}$ is given for all y by table 13.3A. Then

$$E_x(\tilde{x}) = 0(.44) + 1(.56) = .56;$$

$$E_{x|0}(\tilde{x}) = 0(\tfrac{7}{37}) + 1(\tfrac{30}{37}) = \tfrac{30}{37},$$

$$E_{x|1}(\tilde{x}) = 0(\tfrac{22}{36}) + 1(\tfrac{14}{36}) = \tfrac{14}{36},$$

$$E_{x|2}(\tilde{x}) = 0(\tfrac{15}{27}) + 1(\tfrac{12}{27}) = \tfrac{12}{27},$$

$$E_y E_{x|y}(\tilde{x}) = \tfrac{30}{37}(.37) + \tfrac{14}{36}(.36) + \tfrac{12}{27}(.27) = .56.$$

13.8.2 Variance of One of Two Jointly Distributed RVs

If $\tilde{x}$ is a rv with mf or df, then the variance of $\tilde{x}$ is the expectation of the function $\psi(x) = (x - \bar{x})^2$ wrt the mf or df of $\tilde{x}$. If $(\tilde{x}, \tilde{y})$ is a rv, there will be a variance corresponding to the marginal mf or df and a variance corresponding to each conditional mf or df.

1. We define the *conditional* variance of $\tilde{x}$ *given* y to be

$$\check{x}_y \equiv V_{x|y}(\tilde{x}) \equiv E_{x|y}(\tilde{x} - \bar{x}_y)^2. \tag{13.41}$$

2. We define the *marginal* variance of $\tilde{x}$ to be

$$\check{x} \equiv V_x(\tilde{x}) \equiv E_x(\tilde{x} - \bar{x})^2. \tag{13.42}$$

From (13.36a) we have

$$V_x(\tilde{x}) = E(\tilde{x} - \bar{x})^2 \equiv V(\tilde{x}); \tag{13.43}$$

then from (13.36b) we can derive a result frequently useful in computations:

$$\begin{aligned} V(\tilde{x}) &\equiv E_y V_{x|y}(\tilde{x}) + V_y E_{x|y}(\tilde{x}) \\ &= E_y(\check{x}_{\tilde{y}}) + V_y(\bar{x}_{\tilde{y}}). \end{aligned} \tag{13.44a}$$

In words: the total variance of $\tilde{x}$ is the sum of (1) the average variance of $\tilde{x}$ given y, and (2) the variance of the average $\tilde{x}$ given y.

The proof of (13.44a) is given below after we make some remarks about notation and illustrate (13.44a) by a simple numerical example.

Notation

In (13.44a) the symbols $\check{x}_{\tilde{y}}$ and $\bar{x}_{\tilde{y}}$ represent certain quantities or rv's since $\tilde{y}$ is a rv. Instead of placing the tilde on the y, in the sequel we shall write these expressions as $\check{\tilde{x}}_y$ and $\tilde{\bar{x}}_y$ which emphasize the interpretation that we are treating the quantities $\check{x}_y$ and $\bar{x}_y$ as certain quantities. In this new notation we shall write (13.44a) as

$$V(\tilde{x}) = E_y(\check{\tilde{x}}_y) + V_y(\tilde{\bar{x}}_y). \tag{13.44b}$$

Now since $E(\tilde{u})$ is written as $\bar{u}$, and $V(\tilde{u})$ as $\check{u}$, we can rewrite (13.44b) in the condensed form

$$\check{x} = \bar{\check{\tilde{x}}}_y + \check{\tilde{\bar{x}}}_y. \tag{13.44c}$$

Example Let $(\tilde{x}, \tilde{y})$ again have the mf of table 13.2. Then using the results of the previous example:

$$V_x(\tilde{x}) = (0 - .56)^2(.44) + (1 - .56)^2(.56) = .2464,$$

$$V_{x|0}(\tilde{x}) = (0 - \tfrac{30}{37})^2(\tfrac{7}{37}) + (1 - \tfrac{30}{37})^2(\tfrac{30}{37}) = .1537,$$

$$V_{x|1}(\tilde{x}) = (0 - \tfrac{14}{36})^2(\tfrac{22}{36}) + (1 - \tfrac{14}{36})^2(\tfrac{14}{36}) = .2377,$$

$$V_{x|2}(\tilde{x}) = (0 - \tfrac{12}{27})^2(\tfrac{15}{27}) + (1 - \tfrac{12}{27})^2(\tfrac{12}{27}) = .2469,$$

$$E_y V_{x|y}(\tilde{x}) = .1537(.37) + .2377(.36) + .2469(.27) = .2090,$$

$$V_y E_{x|y}(\tilde{x}) = (\tfrac{30}{37} - .56)^2(.37) + (\tfrac{14}{36} - .56)^2(.36) + (\tfrac{12}{27} - .56)^2(.27) = .0375,$$

$$V(\tilde{x}) = .2090 + .0375 = .2465,$$

which differs by .0001 from our first result because of rounding errors.

Proof of (13.44)

$V(\tilde{x}) = E(\tilde{x} - \bar{x})^2 = E_y E_{x|y}(\tilde{x} - \bar{x})^2.$

Substituting herein

$$(\tilde{x} - \bar{x})^2 = (\tilde{x} - \tilde{\bar{x}}_y + \tilde{\bar{x}}_y - \bar{x})^2$$
$$= (\tilde{x} - \tilde{\bar{x}}_y)^2 + (\tilde{\bar{x}}_y - \bar{x})^2 + 2(\tilde{x} - \tilde{\bar{x}}_y)(\tilde{\bar{x}}_y - \bar{x}),$$

we obtain

$$V(\tilde{x}) = A + B + C$$

where

$$A = E_y E_{x|y}(\tilde{x} - \tilde{\bar{x}}_y)^2 = E_y(\tilde{\bar{x}}_y),$$
$$B = E_y E_{x|y}(\tilde{\bar{x}}_y - \bar{x})^2 = E_y(\tilde{\bar{x}}_y - \bar{x})^2 = V_y(\tilde{\bar{x}}_y),$$
$$C = E_y[E_{x|y}(\tilde{x} - \tilde{\bar{x}}_y)](\tilde{\bar{x}}_y - \bar{x}) = E_y[0(\tilde{\bar{x}}_y - \bar{x})] = 0.$$

The proof is completed by adding $A + B + C$.

13.8.3 Covariance and Correlation[3]

In what follows $(\tilde{x}, \tilde{y})$ may be a discrete, mixed, or continuous paired rv.

The *covariance* of $\tilde{x}$ and $\tilde{y}$ is defined to be the quantity

$$V(\tilde{x}, \tilde{y}) \equiv E[(\tilde{x} - \bar{x})(\tilde{y} - \bar{y})] \equiv V(\tilde{y}, \tilde{x}) \tag{13.45a}$$

where $\bar{x}$ and $\bar{y}$ are the marginal means of $\tilde{x}$ and $\tilde{y}$. The reader may prove (exercise 15) the alternative formulas

$$\begin{aligned} V(\tilde{x}, \tilde{y}) &\equiv E[(\tilde{x} - \bar{x})\tilde{y}] \\ &= E(\tilde{x}\tilde{y}) - \bar{x}\bar{y}. \end{aligned} \tag{13.45b}$$

Observe that the covariance of $\tilde{x}$ with itself is simply the (marginal) variance of $\tilde{x}$:

$$V(\tilde{x}, \tilde{x}) = E(\tilde{x} - \bar{x})^2 \equiv V(\tilde{x}).$$

The *linear correlation* of x and y is defined to be the quantity

$$\rho(x, y) \equiv \frac{V(\tilde{x}, \tilde{y})}{[V(\tilde{x})V(\tilde{y})]^{1/2}}. \tag{13.46}$$

3. The material in sections 13.8.3 and 13.8.4, although basic, will not be used until chapter 21.

Table 13.5

		Range of $\tilde{x}$			
		-1	0	1	
Range	0	.25	0	.25	.50
of $\tilde{y}$	1	0	.25	0	.50
		.25	.50	.25	

The rv's $\tilde{x}$ and $\tilde{y}$ are said to be *uncorrelated* if and only if $\rho(\tilde{x}, \tilde{y}) = 0$, implying $V(\tilde{x}, \tilde{y}) = 0$. The fact that $\tilde{x}$ and $\tilde{y}$ are uncorrelated by no means implies that they are independent; an example of dependence without correlation is shown in table 13.5. The correlation $\rho(\tilde{x}, \tilde{y})$ measures the degree of linear association between $\tilde{x}$ and $\tilde{y}$ and its direction, in a sense made precise in exercises 26 and 27.

13.8.4 Regression

We have already defined the conditional expectation $\bar{y}_x = E_{y|x}(\tilde{y})$ of $\tilde{y}$ given $\tilde{x} = x$; it depends on x. Considered as a function of x, $\bar{y}_x$ is called the *regression function* of $\tilde{y}$ on $\tilde{x}$; the regression function of $\tilde{x}$ on $\tilde{y}$ is similarly defined but it is *not* the same function; it is $\bar{x}_y$ treated as a function of the argument y.

If $\bar{y}_x$ has the same value for all $x \in X$, then $\tilde{x}$ and $\tilde{y}$ are uncorrelated. For by (13.45),

$$V(\tilde{x}, \tilde{y}) \equiv E[(\tilde{x} - \bar{x})(\tilde{y} - \bar{y})] = E_x E_{y|x}[(\tilde{x} - \bar{x})(\tilde{y} - \bar{y})]$$

$$= E_x(\tilde{x} - \bar{x}) E_{y|x}(\tilde{y} - \bar{y})$$

$$= E_x(\tilde{x} - \bar{x})(\tilde{\bar{y}}_x - \bar{y}).$$

Now if $\tilde{\bar{y}}_x$ has the same value for all x, this value must be $\bar{y}$; therefore the right-hand side of the above equation vanishes for all x; therefore, $V(\tilde{x}, \tilde{y}) = 0$ as was to be proved.

Observe that the above italicized assertion goes only one way. It does not say that $V(\tilde{x}, \tilde{y}) = 0$ implies the constancy of the regression function of $\tilde{y}$ on $\tilde{x}$. It says the converse. The example in table 13.5 shows that $V(\tilde{x}, \tilde{y})$ can be equal to zero when the regression function is *not* constant. Since on the other hand *independence* obviously implies that $\bar{y}_x$ does not depend on x, we have the nonreversible implications

independence $\Rightarrow$ constant regression functions $\Rightarrow$ no correlation.

13.8.5 Linear Functions of Two Random Variables

Let the function φ be defined on $X \times Y$ by

$$\varphi(x, y) \equiv a + bx + cy. \tag{13.47a}$$

Then

$$E\varphi(\tilde{x}, \tilde{y}) = a + bE(\tilde{x}) + cE(\tilde{y}), \tag{13.47b}$$

$$V\varphi(\tilde{x}, \tilde{y}) = b^2 V(\tilde{x}) + c^2 V(\tilde{y}) + 2bcV(\tilde{x}, y). \tag{13.47c}$$

Proof of (13.47) The proof of (13.47b) is easy and should be supplied by the reader (exercise 16). To prove (13.47c) we write

$$\begin{aligned} V(\varphi) \equiv E(\tilde{\varphi} - \bar{\varphi})^2 &= E(a + b\tilde{x} + c\tilde{y} - a - b\bar{x} - c\bar{y})^2 \\ &= E(b[\tilde{x} - \bar{x}] + c[\tilde{y} - \bar{y}])^2 \\ &= E[b^2(\tilde{x} - \bar{x})^2 + c^2(\tilde{y} - \bar{y})^2 + 2bc(\tilde{x} - \bar{x})(\tilde{y} - \bar{y})] \end{aligned}$$

which equals the right-hand side of (13.47c).

For the special case where $\varphi(x, y) = x + y$ we obtain the important results:

$$E(\tilde{x} + \tilde{y}) = E(\tilde{x}) + E(\tilde{y}), \quad \text{(general)}, \tag{13.48a}$$

$$V(\tilde{x} + \tilde{y}) = V(\tilde{x}) + V(\tilde{y}) + 2V(\tilde{x}, \tilde{y}), \quad \text{(general)}, \tag{13.48b}$$

$$V(\tilde{x} + \tilde{y}) = V(\tilde{x}) + V(\tilde{y}), \quad (\text{if} \quad V(\tilde{x}, \tilde{y}) = 0). \tag{13.48c}$$

13.8.6 Distributing Function for a Sum of Two Independent RVs

Let $\tilde{x}$ have distributing function f_x; let $\tilde{y}$ have distributing function f_y; let $\tilde{x}$ and $\tilde{y}$ be independent; let

$$\tilde{z} = \tilde{x} + \tilde{y}; \tag{13.49}$$

let g be the distributing function of $\tilde{z}$.

Case 1 If f_x and f_y are both mf's, then g is a mf and

$$g(z) = \textstyle\sum_x f_y(z - x) f_x(x). \tag{13.50a}$$

Case 2 If f_x and f_y are both df's, then g is a df and

$$g(z) = \int_{-\infty}^{\infty} f_y(z - x) f_x(x)\, dx. \tag{13.50b}$$

The expression on the right-hand side of (13.50)—whichever case may be appropriate—is called the *convolution* of f_y and f_x, sometimes written as

$(f_x * f_y)(z)$, i.e., $g = f_x * f_y$.

We shall give the proof of (13.50b) and leave the easier proof of (13.50a) to the reader (exercise 23).

Proof We have

$$
\begin{aligned}
P(\tilde{z} \le z) &= P(\tilde{x} + \tilde{y} \le z) \\
&= \int_{-\infty}^{\infty} P(\tilde{x} + \tilde{y} \le z \mid \tilde{x} = x) f_x(x)\, dx && \text{[by (10.7b)]} \\
&= \int_{-\infty}^{\infty} P(\tilde{y} \le z - x \mid \tilde{x} = x) f_x(x)\, dx \\
&= \int_{-\infty}^{\infty} P(\tilde{y} \le z - x) f_x(x)\, dx && \text{[by independence]} \\
&= \int_{-\infty}^{\infty} \left[\int_{-\infty}^{z-x} f_y(y)\, dy \right] f_x(x)\, dx.
\end{aligned}
$$

Now make a change of variable $w = y + x$, $\tilde{x} = x$, obtaining

$$
\begin{aligned}
P(\tilde{z} \le z) &= \int_{-\infty}^{\infty} \left[\int_{-\infty}^{z} f_y(w - x)\, dw \right] f_x(x)\, dx \\
&= \int_{-\infty}^{z} \left[\int_{-\infty}^{\infty} f_y(w - x) f_x(x)\, dx \right] dw.
\end{aligned}
$$

Differentiating with respect to z, we obtain

$$
g(z) \equiv \frac{d}{dz} P(\tilde{z} \le z) = \int_{-\infty}^{\infty} f_y(z - x) f_x(x)\, dx,
$$

as was to be shown.

Exercises

1. Consider an urn which contains 10 balls each marked with a pair of numbers (x, y). The pairs are: $(0, 5)$, $(0, 4)$, $(3, 2)$, $(3, 4)$, $(5, 2)$, $(5, 7)$, $(8, 1)$, $(10, 4)$, $(10, 4)$, $(10, 5)$. A ball is drawn canonically from the urn; denote its as yet unknown "value" by $(\tilde{x}, \tilde{y})$ Exhibit
   a. the joint mass function f of the (paired) rv $(\tilde{x}, \tilde{y})$,
   b. the marginal mass function f_x,
   c. the marginal mass function f_y,
   d. the conditional mass function $f_{x|4}$,
   e. the conditional mass function $f_{y|0}$.
   f. Is the symbol $f(5)$ defined? If not, why not?

Table 13E.1

x	0	2	Total
$f_x(x)$	.6	.4	1

x	2	3	4	5	Total
$f_{y\|0}(y)$	.7	0	.3	0	1
$f_{y\|2}(y)$	0	.2	.3	.5	1

2. Suppose $(\tilde{x}, \tilde{y})$ is a discrete rv with f_x and $f_{y|x}$ as exhibited in table 13E.1.
   a. For what (x, y) pairs is $P[(\tilde{x}, \tilde{y}) = (x, y)] > 0$?
   b. Find $f_y(4)$, $f(2, 4)$, $f_{x|4}(0)$.

3. Verify the results of example 2 in section 13.2.6.
   Hints This problem needs the results of formulas (3.A) and (3.B) below. Writing

$$S = 1 + a + a^2 + \cdots a^r,$$

show that

$$S - aS = 1 - a^{r+1}$$

and that

$$S = \frac{1 - a^{r+1}}{1 - a}.$$

Next show that

$$1 + a + a^2 + \cdots = \frac{1}{1 - a} \quad \text{if} \quad -1 < a < 1. \tag{3.A}$$

Differentiate both sides of (3.A) to show that

$$1 + 2a + 3a^2 + \cdots = \frac{1}{(1 - a)^2} \quad \text{for} \quad -1 < a < 1. \tag{3.B}$$

4. In a production process the fraction defective p depends on whether A and B are correct. Assume that in the light of past records the following assessments are reasonable:

State	Probability	Resulting process p
A nondef., B nondef.	.6	.00
A nondef., B def.	.2	.05
A def., B nondef.	.1	.10
A def., B def.	.1	1.00
	1.0	

From this process a sample of $n = 3$ items are taken; let $\tilde{r}$ denote the number of defective items. Assuming that the process can legitimately be represented by the Bernoulli model:

a. Give the conditional mass function of $\tilde{r}$ for each of the 4 values of p.
b. Exhibit the joint mass function of $(\tilde{p}, \tilde{r})$.
c. Find the conditional mass function $f_{p|1}$.

5. In the example of section 13.3.2 the mass density function

$$f(x, y) = 2x^y(1 - x), \qquad \begin{array}{l} 0 \le x \le 1, \\ y = 1, 2, \ldots \end{array}$$

was considered.

a. Verify that

$$f_y(y) = \int_0^1 f(x, y)\, dx = \frac{2}{(y + 1)(y + 2)}.$$

b. Verify that $\sum_{y=1}^{\infty} \dfrac{2}{(y + 1)(y + 2)} = 1.$

Hint $\dfrac{1}{(y + 1)(y + 2)} = \dfrac{1}{y + 1} - \dfrac{1}{y + 2}.$

c. Using the results of exercise 3 verify that

$f_x(x) = \sum_{y=1}^{\infty} f(x, y) = 2x \quad$ for $\quad 0 \le x \le 1.$

Draw the density function f_x.

d. Verify that

$$f_{y|x}(y) = x^{y-1}(1 - x)$$

and interpret the $(\tilde{y}|x)$ with mass function $f_{y|x}$.

6. Consider the paired rv $(\tilde{p}, \tilde{r})$ where $\tilde{p}$ has a marginal density which is beta with parameters (2, 5): that is,

$$f_p(p) = f_\beta(p|2, 5) = \frac{4!}{1!\,2!} p(1 - p)^2 = 12p(1 - p)^2,$$

and the conditional mass function of $\tilde{r}$ given $\tilde{p} = p$ has a binomial mass function with parameters $(10, p)$; that is,

$$f_{r|p}(r) = f_b(r|10, p) = \frac{10!}{r!(10 - r)!} p^r(1 - p)^{10-r}.$$

a. Show that the joint density-mass function is given by

$$f(p, r) = \frac{(12)10!}{r!(10 - r)!} p^{r+1}(1 - p)^{12-r}.$$

b. Show that

$$P(\tilde{r} = 3) = f_r(3) = \frac{(4)(9)(8)}{(14)(13)(11)}.$$

Hint $f_r(3) = \int_0^1 f_b(3|10, p) f_\beta(p|2, 5)\, dp.$

c. Find the conditional density of $\tilde{p}$ given $\tilde{r} = 3$, that is, the density of $(\tilde{p}|\tilde{r} = 3)$.

Hint $f_{p|3}(p) \equiv \dfrac{f(p, 3)}{f_r(3)}.$

7. Consider the rv $(\tilde{p}, \tilde{r})$ where

$f_p(p) = f_\beta(p|1, 2) \qquad$ (i.e., a rectangular density)

and

$$f_{r|p}(r) = f_b(r|n, p) = \frac{n!}{r!(n - r)!} p^r(1 - p)^{n-r}.$$

Table 13E2

x \ y	-1	0	2	
0	.2	0	0	.2
1	0	.2	.3	.5
3	.1	0	.2	.3
	.3	.2	.5	1.0

Table 13E.3

x \ y	-1	0	2	
0	.67	.00	.00	$f_{x\|y}(x)$
1	.00	1.00	.64	
3	.33	.00	.40	
Total	1.00	1.00	1.00	
$f_y(y)$	.30	.20	.50	
$E_{x\|y}(\tilde{x})$	1.00	1.00	1.80	→ Mean = 1.40, Variance = .16
$E_{x\|y}(\tilde{x}^2)$	3.00	1.00	4.20	→ Mean = 3.20
$V_{x\|y}(\tilde{x})$	2.00	.00	.96	→ Mean = 1.08

a. Show that

$$P(\tilde{r} = r) = f_r(r) = \frac{1}{n+1} \quad \text{for} \quad r = 0, 1, \ldots, n$$

and interpret this result.

b. Show that

$$f_{p|r}(p) = f_\beta(p|r + 1, n + 2).$$

8. Let $(\tilde{x}, \tilde{y})$ have the joint mass function shown in table 13E.2. Verify the formulas:

$$E(y) = E_x E_{y|x}(\tilde{y}), \quad E(\tilde{y}^2) = E_x E_{y|x}(\tilde{y}^2), \quad V(\tilde{y}) = E_x V_{y|x}(\tilde{y}) + V_x E_{y|x}(\tilde{y}).$$

We demonstrate in table 13E.3 how this verification can be exhibited for the case where x and y are interchanged.

First observe that $E(\tilde{x}) = 1.40$, $E(\tilde{x}^2) = 3.20$, and $V(\tilde{x}) = 1.24$. Observe that

$$E(\tilde{x}) = E_y E_{x|y}(\tilde{x}),$$

$$E(\tilde{x}^2) = E_y E_{x|y}(\tilde{x}^2),$$

$$V(\tilde{x}) \neq E_y V_{x|y}(\tilde{x}),$$

$$V(\tilde{x}) = E_y V_{x|y}(\tilde{x}) + V_y E_{x|y}(\tilde{x}).$$

9. Show that if $x_2 > x_1$ and $y_2 > y_1$, then $P(x_1 < \tilde{x} \leq x_2,\ y_1 < \tilde{y} \leq y_2) = P(\tilde{x} \leq x_2, \tilde{y} \leq y_2) - P(\tilde{x} \leq x_1, \tilde{y} \leq y_2) - P(\tilde{x} \leq x_2, \tilde{y} \leq y_1) + P(\tilde{x} \leq x_1, \tilde{y} \leq y_1)$.

10. Prove (13.9).

11. Prove (13.19).

12. Let $f(x, y) = xe^{-x(y+1)}$, $0 \le x < \infty$, $0 \le y < \infty$. Show that:

a. $f_x(x) = e^{-x}$;
b. $f_y(y) = (y +)^{-2}$;
c. $\int_0^\infty \int_0^\infty f(x, y)\, dy\, dx = 1$;
d. $E(\tilde{x}) = \int_0^\infty xf(x)\, dx = 1$;
e. $E_{x|y}(\tilde{x}) = \int_0^\infty xf_{x|y}(x)\, dx = \int_0^\infty x^2(y+1)^2 e^{-x(y+1)}\, dx = \dfrac{2}{y+1}$;
f. $E(\tilde{x}) = E_y E_{x|y}(\tilde{x}) = \int_0^\infty 2(y+1)^{-3}\, dy = 1$.

13. Verify the conditional expectation exhibited in example 2 of section 13.7.2.

14. Prove formulas (13.35) for the case where the rv $(\tilde{x}, \tilde{y})$ has a joint df and a joint dmf.

15. Prove (13.45b): $V(\tilde{x}, \tilde{y}) = E(\tilde{x}\tilde{y}) - \bar{x}\bar{y}$.

16. For a discrete, mixed, or continuous rv $(\tilde{x}, \tilde{y})$ prove (13.47b):

$E(a + b\tilde{x} + c\tilde{y}) = a + bE(\tilde{x}) + cE(\tilde{y})$.

17. Let $f_1(\cdot)$ and $f_2(\cdot)$ be univariate density functions and let $f(\cdot, \cdot)$ be defined by

$f(x, y) = f_1(x)f_2(y)$.

Show $f(\cdot, \cdot)$ is a joint density function.

18. Prove: $\tilde{x}$ and $\tilde{y}$ are uncorrelated if and only if $E(\tilde{x}\tilde{y}) = \bar{x}\bar{y}$.

19. In the example given by table 13.5 show that the regression of $\tilde{y}$ on $\tilde{x}$ is a constant but the regression of $\tilde{x}$ on $\tilde{y}$ is not a constant.

20. If $\tilde{y} = \tilde{x}$ what is $V(\tilde{x}, \tilde{y})$? For this special case, use formula (13.47) to find $V(\tilde{x} - \tilde{y})$ and $V(\tilde{x} + \tilde{y})$.

21. If $\tilde{x}$ and $\tilde{y}$ are correlated find a formula for the constant b such that $\tilde{x}$ and $z = \tilde{y} - b\tilde{x}$ are uncorrelated.

22. Let $(\tilde{r}, \tilde{p})$ be a (paired) rv where the conditional distribution of $\tilde{r}$ given $\tilde{p} = p$ is binomial with parameter (n, p) and $\tilde{p}$ has a nondegenerate distribution. Define

$$\tilde{\varepsilon} \equiv \frac{\tilde{r}}{n} - \tilde{p},$$

and show that $\tilde{\varepsilon}$ and $\tilde{p}$ are uncorrelated but dependent.

Hint Consider $E_{\varepsilon|p}(\tilde{\varepsilon})$ and $V_{\varepsilon|p}(\tilde{\varepsilon})$.

23. Prove (13.50a).

24. The following problems are concerned with estimation with quadratic loss.

a. Suppose y is an unknown number that we wish to estimate. If we estimate y by the number a, let our opportunity loss be given by $l(a, y) = (y - a)^2$. If $\tilde{y}$ is treated as a rv with an assessed distribution then show

$a^o = E(\tilde{y}) = \bar{y}$ and EVPI $= El(a^o, \tilde{y}) = V(\tilde{y}) = \breve{y}$.

b. If $\tilde{x}$ and $\tilde{y}$ are jointly distributed show that posterior to observing $\tilde{x} = x$,

$a_x^o = E_{y|x}(\tilde{y}) = \bar{y}_x$ and $E_{y|x} l(a^o, \tilde{y}) = V_{y|x}(\tilde{y}) = \breve{y}_x$.

25. Assume $\tilde{x}$ and $\tilde{y}$ are jointly distributed in such a manner that the regression function of $\tilde{y}$ on $\tilde{x}$ is linear, that is,

$$\bar{y}_x = E_{y|x}(\tilde{y}) = a + bx. \quad \text{(A)}$$

Show in this case that

$$\bar{y}_x = \bar{y} + \frac{v_{21}}{v_{11}}(x - \bar{x}) \tag{B}$$

where

$$v_{21} = V(\tilde{y}, \tilde{x}) = V(\tilde{x}, \tilde{y}) \quad \text{and} \quad v_{11} = V(\tilde{x}) = V(\tilde{x}, \tilde{x}).$$

Hint

i. From (A) we have

$$\bar{y} = E(\tilde{y}) = E_x E_{y|x}(\tilde{y}) = E_x(a + b\tilde{x}) = a + b\bar{x},$$

or

$$(\bar{y}_x - \bar{y}) = b(x - \bar{x}). \tag{C}$$

ii. Multiplying both sides of (C) by $(x - \bar{x})$, treating $\tilde{x}$, $\tilde{y}$, and $y_{\tilde{x}}$ as rv's, and taking expectations gives

$$E[(\bar{y}_{\tilde{x}} - \bar{y}) + (\tilde{y} - \bar{y})](\tilde{x} - \bar{x})] = bv_{11}. \tag{D}$$

Now the left-hand side of (D) can be written as

$$E\{[(\bar{y}_{\tilde{x}} - \bar{y}) + (\tilde{y} - \bar{y})](\tilde{x} - \bar{x})\} = E[(\bar{y}_{\tilde{x}} - \bar{y})(\tilde{x} - \bar{x})] + v_{21}.$$

Writing E as $E_x E_{y|x}$ show that

$$E[(\bar{y}_{\tilde{x}} - \bar{y})(\tilde{x} - \bar{x})] = 0.)$$

(This problem says that if the regression of $\tilde{y}$ and $\tilde{x}$ is linear the regression line passes through the point $(\bar{x}, \bar{y})$ with slope $b = v_{21}/v_{11}$.)

26. (*Continuation of 25*). Let $v_{22.1} = E_x V_{y|x}(\tilde{y})$. If the regression of $\tilde{y}$ on $\tilde{x}$ is linear show that

$$v_{22.1} = v_{22} - \frac{v_{21}^2}{v_{11}} = \frac{v_{22}v_{11} - v_{21}^2}{v_{11}} = v_{22}[1 - \rho^2(\tilde{x}, \tilde{y})].$$

Hint Use the result

$$V(\tilde{y}) = V_x E_{y|x}(\tilde{y}) + E_x V_{y|x}(\tilde{y})$$

together with (B) of exercise 25.

27. (*Linear Decision Rules*).

a. If the regression of $\tilde{y}$ on $\tilde{x}$ is not linear, the best (squared error) estimate of $\tilde{y}$ given $\tilde{x} = x$ is not necessarily of the form $a + bx$. We can, however, formulate the problem of choosing a and b to minimize $E[\tilde{y} - (a + b\tilde{x})]^2$.

Show that

$$\begin{aligned} E[\tilde{y} - (a + b\tilde{x})]^2 &= E[(\tilde{y} - \bar{y}) - b(\tilde{x} - \bar{x}) + (\bar{y} - b\bar{x} - a)]^2 \\ &= v_{22} - 2bv_{21} + b^2 v_{11} + (\bar{y} - b\bar{x} - a)^2, \end{aligned}$$

since all other cross-product terms have expectation zero. Show that $E[\tilde{y} - (a + b\tilde{x})]^2$ is minimized by taking:

$$a = \bar{y} - b\bar{x} \quad \text{and} \quad b = v_{21}/v_{11}.$$

b. Show that

$$E\left[\tilde{y} - \bar{y} - \frac{v_{21}}{v_{11}}(\tilde{x} - \bar{x})\right]^2 = \frac{v_{22}v_{11} - v_{21}^2}{v_{11}}.$$

14 Preposterior Analysis: The Value of Sample Information

14.1 Introduction

Having learned in chapter 12 how to analyze certain problems of choice between terminal acts when value (and hence cost or loss) is a valid guide to action, we are now ready to attack the problem of deciding under these same conditions whether we *should* choose a terminal act on the basis of the information currently at hand or should instead defer the choice until more information has been obtained by sampling or experimentation. This problem can of course arise whether or not any current information was itself obtained from a sample already taken or an experiment already performed.

In chapter 6 we formulated a class of decision problems in terms of a four-move game where the decision maker was required at move 1 to choose an experiment (e) and at move 3 to choose a terminal act (a). We indicated in that chapter that this class of problems could be analyzed conceptually by the algorithm of backwards induction (or dynamic programming). In the present chapter we shall obtain further results for the special case where the consequence of any path (e, z, a, s) through the decision flow diagram can be described completely enough for practical purposes by the algebraic *sum* of one quantity which depends only on (a, s) and another quantity which depends only on (e, z); in this situation the economics of the problem can be thought of as being decomposed in an additive manner between a terminal-action part and a sampling or experimental part.

14.2 Basic Assumptions: Linear Preference; Additive Terminal and Sampling Values

We saw in chapter 6 that when *value* or its negative, *cost*, is a valid guide to action, the entire analysis can be carried out in terms of value or cost in place of utility. We shall assume throughout this chapter that value *is* a valid guide to action, and our method of analysis will be based either on the use of value or cost or else on the derived quantity *opportunity loss* that was introduced in chapter 12.

14.2.1 Terminal Value and Sampling Cost

Let $v(e, z, a, s)$ denote the value of performing a particular experiment e, observing a particular outcome z, and choosing a particular terminal act a, when the true state of the world is s. When expected value is a valid guide to action, it will usually be true that $v(e, z, a, s)$ consists of the *difference* between two separate parts: (1) the *terminal value* $v_t(a, s)$ that results from taking act a when the true state is s, and (2) the *sampling cost* $c_s(e, z)$

incurred by performing the experiment e which results in the outcome z. (Note that the subscript s in c_s refers to "sample" and not to "state." Frequently this cost will depend only on e and not on z, but to see that it *can* depend on z, consider the example of destructive sampling, where the cost of testing any given number of pieces depends, in part, on the number of good pieces destroyed.) We shall assume throughout this chapter that value *can* be decomposed in this way, so that

$$v(e, z, a, s) = v_t(a, s) - c_s(e, z) \tag{14.1}$$

In order to be able to work in terms of loss as well as in terms of value or cost, we first define $l_t(a, s)$ by (12.1): It is the difference between the *terminal* value of the act that is optimal *in the given state s* and the *terminal* value of the act a. We then define

$$l(e, z, a, s) = l_t(a, s) + c_s(e, z). \tag{14.2}$$

It is sometimes helpful to think of $l(e, z, a, s)$ as the difference between the terminal value $v_t(a_s, s)$ of choosing the act a_s, which is optimal given the true state s, and the value $[v_t(a, s) - c_s(e, z)]$ for the whole sequence (e, z, a, s).

14.3 The General Method of Analysis

14.3.1 Review of Posterior Analysis

Let e denote any one, particular, *proposed* experiment. *If* it is conducted, then *after* its outcome z is known, the decision maker's first step will be to revise her original distribution of $\tilde{s}$ to take account of the new information z; denote this revised distribution of $\tilde{s}$ by $P_{s|z}$ to display the dependence on z.

Having computed her revised measure $P_{s|z}$, the decision maker's next step is to use it to evaluate all the available acts via one of the two indices:

$$\bar{v}_t''(a, z) \equiv E_{s|z} v_t(a, \tilde{s}), \qquad \bar{l}_t''(a, z) \equiv E_{s|z} l_t(a, \tilde{s}) \tag{14.3}$$

where the double prime denotes *posterior* and implies that the expectation is taken with respect to the posterior distribution $P_{s|z}$ rather than the prior distribution P_s. Observe that because $P_{s|z}$ depends on z, *the two indices depend on* z; this accounts for the second argument of the functions $\bar{v}_t''$ and $\bar{l}_t''$.

Having evaluated all the available acts, the decision maker next selects the act which maximizes $\bar{v}_t''$ or minimizes $\bar{l}_t''$. This act will be denoted a_z^o to display the fact that the *optimal act depends on z* because the index by which it is chosen depends on z. Formally, a_z^o is defined by

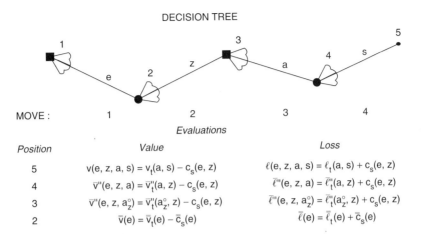

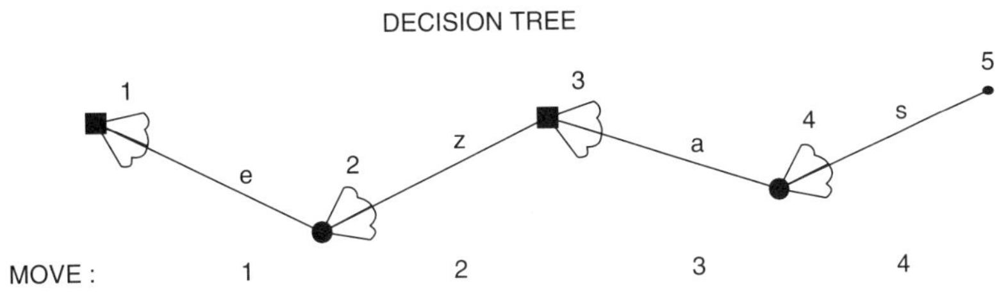

Evaluations

Position	*Value*	*Loss*
5	$v(e, z, a, s) = v_t(a, s) - c_s(e, z)$	$\ell(e, z, a, s) = \ell_t(a, s) + c_s(e, z)$
4	$\bar{v}''(e, z, a) = \bar{v}_t''(a, z) - c_s(e, z)$	$\bar{\ell}''(e, z, a) = \bar{\ell}_t''(a, z) + c_s(e, z)$
3	$\bar{v}''(e, z, a_z^o) = \bar{v}_t''(a_z^o, z) - c_s(e, z)$	$\bar{\ell}''(e, z, a_z^o) = \bar{\ell}_t''(a_z^o, z) + c_s(e, z)$
2	$\bar{\bar{v}}(e) = \bar{\bar{v}}_t(e) - \bar{\bar{c}}_s(e)$	$\bar{\bar{\ell}}(e) = \bar{\bar{\ell}}_t(e) + \bar{\bar{c}}_s(e)$

Figure 14.1
Choice of experiment and terminal act

$$\left.\begin{aligned} \bar{v}_t''(a_z^o, z) &\geq \bar{v}_t''(a, z) \\ \bar{l}_t''(a_z^o, z) &\leq \bar{l}_t''(a, z) \end{aligned}\right\} \quad \text{for all } a. \tag{14.4}$$

Finally, having selected the optimal act, the decision maker can evaluate his *net* "position" by computing one of the two indices

$$\begin{aligned} \bar{v}''(e, z, a_z^o) &\equiv \bar{v}_t''(a_z^o, z) - c_s(e, z), \\ \bar{l}''(e, z, a_z^o) &\equiv \bar{l}_t''(a_z^o, z) + c_s(e, z). \end{aligned} \tag{14.5}$$

14.3.2 Preposterior Analysis

We now turn to the decision maker's position *before* the proposed experiment e is actually conducted and hence *before* its outcome z is known. (See figure 14.1.) At this point e results in a lottery whose value $\bar{v}''(e, z, a_z^o)$ depends on an uncertain event $(\tilde{z} = z)$, just as a terminal act a results in a lottery whose value $v_t(a, s)$ depends on an uncertain event $(\tilde{s} = s)$. To evaluate the lottery associated with a, the decision maker assigns a distribution to $\tilde{s}$ and then computes the *expected* value $Ev_t(a, \tilde{s})$ or loss $El_t(a, \tilde{s})$ of a; she can evaluate the lottery associated with e in exactly the same way, by assigning a distribution to $\tilde{z}$ and then computing the *expected value*

$$\bar{\bar{v}}(e) \equiv E\bar{v}''(e, \tilde{z}, a_z^o) \tag{14.6a}$$

or alternatively the *expected loss*

$$\bar{\bar{l}}(e) \equiv E\bar{l}''(e, \tilde{z}, a_z^o). \tag{14.6b}$$

Computationally, it will almost always be easier to evaluate separately the expected cost of *sampling*[1]

$$\bar{\bar{c}}_s(e) \equiv E c_s(e, \tilde{z}) \tag{14.7}$$

and the expected value or loss of *terminal action*

$$\bar{\bar{v}}_t(e) \equiv E\bar{v}_t''(a_z^o, \tilde{z}), \qquad \bar{\bar{l}}_t(e) \equiv E\bar{l}_t''(a_z^o, \tilde{z}), \tag{14.8}$$

and then to use one of the formulas

$$\begin{aligned} \bar{\bar{v}}(e) &= \bar{\bar{v}}_t(e) - \bar{\bar{c}}_s(e), \\ \bar{\bar{l}}(e) &= \bar{\bar{l}}_t(e) + \bar{\bar{c}}_s(e), \end{aligned} \tag{14.9}$$

which follow directly from (14.6) and (14.5).

If *only one* experiment e is under consideration, the decision problem can now be solved by simply comparing the expected value of e with the expected value of optimal terminal action *without* sampling, that is, with the expected value of the act a^o that is optimal under the *current* or prior distribution of $\tilde{s}$; alternatively, the comparison can be made in terms of cost or loss. If the decision maker has available a *choice* of experiments, she must evaluate them all, select the one which maximizes $\bar{\bar{v}}$ or minimizes $\bar{\bar{l}}$, and then compare this selected experiment with no experiment at all.

In order to avoid continual repetition of this two-stage description of the decision procedure, we define

$$\left.\begin{aligned} \bar{v}'(a^o) &\equiv \text{expected value} \\ \bar{l}'(a^o) &\equiv \text{expected loss} \end{aligned}\right\} \text{of } \textit{immediate} \text{ optimal action,}$$

the prime denoting expectation wrt the prior distribution and the absence of a subscript on a^o denoting that it does not depend on any sample outcome; we then define the *null* experiment e_0 for which

$$\bar{\bar{v}}(e_0) \equiv \bar{\bar{v}}_t(e_0) = \bar{v}'(a^o), \qquad \bar{\bar{l}}(e_0) \equiv \bar{\bar{l}}_t(e_0) = \bar{l}'(a^o). \tag{14.10}$$

We can then say in one sentence that the decision maker's objective is to select the experiment (possibly e_0) that maximizes $\bar{\bar{v}}$ or minimizes $\bar{\bar{l}}$.

14.3.3 Expected Value of Sample Information

In chapter 12 we usually found it more instructive to look at the expected value of *perfect information* as such than to look at the expected value of

1. Although the expression for $\bar{\bar{c}}_s(e)$ arises from a single expectation operation, we prefer to use the double bar to keep this symbol parallel to $\bar{\bar{v}}_t(e)$

acting optimally after receiving perfect information; and in the same way we shall often find it instructive to look at the expected value of *experimental information* as such.

For any experiment or sample e, we define the *expected value of the sample information* or EVSI to be

$$\begin{aligned} I(e) &\equiv \bar{v}_t(e) - \bar{v}_t(e_0) = E\bar{v}_t''(a_z^o, \tilde{z}) - \bar{v}_t'(a^o) \\ &= \bar{\bar{l}}_t(e_0) - \bar{\bar{l}}_t(e) = \bar{l}_t'(a^o) - E\bar{l}_t''(a_z^o, \tilde{z}) \end{aligned} \tag{14.11}$$

It is the amount by which we "expect" our *terminal* value to be increased or our *terminal* loss to be decreased by the information that will be obtained from the sample.

In some types of problems another way of looking at EVSI is also helpful. If after performing the experiment e the decision maker were to adhere, regardless of the outcome z, to the act a^o that was optimal under the prior distribution, the experiment would clearly be worthless. Its value arises from the fact that for at least *some* outcomes z the decision maker will *alter* her choice of act and thereby increase her expected terminal value or decrease her expected terminal loss. As viewed at the time the change of act is made, the increase in value due to the change is

$$\bar{v}_t''(a_z^o, z) - \bar{v}_t''(a^o, z) = \bar{l}_t''(a^o, z) - \bar{l}_t''(a_z^o, z); \tag{14.12a}$$

as viewed before the experiment is conducted, the *expectation* of the increase in value is

$$\begin{aligned} I(e) &= E[\bar{v}_t''(a_z^o, \tilde{z}) - \bar{v}_t''(a^o, \tilde{z})] \\ &= E[\bar{l}_t''(a^o, \tilde{z}) - \bar{l}_t''(a_z^o, \tilde{z})]. \end{aligned} \tag{14.12b}$$

To prove that this formula is equivalent to the *definition* (14.11) of $I(e)$, we have only to observe that

$$\begin{aligned} E[\bar{v}_t''(a_z^o, \tilde{z}) - \bar{v}_t''(a^o, \tilde{z})] &= E\bar{v}_t''(a_z^o, \tilde{z}) - E\bar{v}_t''(a^o, \tilde{z}) \\ &= E\bar{v}_t''(a_z^o, \tilde{z}) - v_t'(a^o), \end{aligned}$$

the last step following from the fact, proved in chapter 12, that the *unconditional expectation* of any quantity is equal to the *expectation of its conditional expectation*—that is,

$$E\bar{v}_t''(a_z^o, \tilde{z}) = E_z E_{s|z} v_t(a^o, \tilde{s}) = Ev_t(a^o, \tilde{s}) = \bar{v}_t'(a^o).$$

14.3.4 Expected Net Gain of Sampling

The EVSI is of course the *gross* value of the information; to get the *net* gain we must subtract the cost of acquiring the information. We therefore define for any e the *expected net gain of sampling* or ENGS to be

$$G(e) \equiv I(e) - \bar{c}_s(e). \tag{14.13}$$

Equivalently, as the reader can easily show, it is the amount by which we can expect *overall value* to be increased or *total loss* to be decreased by the proposed sample or experiment:

$$\begin{aligned} G(e) &= \bar{v}(e) - \bar{v}(e_0) \\ &= \bar{\bar{l}}(e_0) - \bar{\bar{l}}(e). \end{aligned} \tag{14.14}$$

14.4 Sampling from a Bernoulli Process

14.4.1 Terminal Analysis

In this section we shall specialize the discussion of the preceding sections of this chapter to the case where the experiment (or sampling) consists of taking observations from a Bernoulli process with unknown parameter p. We shall, however, keep the economic structure (i.e., v_t, l_t, and c_s functions) completely general.

We shall assume that prior to the experiment to be analyzed the rv $\tilde{p}$ is assessed to have a mf or df f'. The experiment e and outcome z is equivalent, in this case, to a history H_r^n of a particular sequence of r successes in n trials. Posterior to observing the sample H_r^n the revised distributing function for $\tilde{p}$ is given by (11.9):

$$f''(p|H_r^n) \propto L(p|H_r^n)f'(p), \tag{14.15a}$$

where

$$L(p|H_r^n) \equiv p^r(1-p)^{n-r}. \tag{14.15b}$$

Letting $v_t(a, p)$ represent the terminal value of using act a when $(\tilde{p} = p)$, we would then have

$$\bar{v}''[a, (r, n)] = E_{p|r,n}v_t(a, \tilde{p}), \tag{14.16}$$

where for typographical reasons we replace H_r^n by (r, n). Depending on whether f' were a mf or a df, we would have

$$E_{p|r,n}v_t(a, \tilde{p}) = \begin{cases} \sum_i v_t(a, p_i)f''(p_i|H_r^n), & (f' \text{ discrete}), \\ \int_0^1 v_t(a, p)f''(p|H_r^n)\,dp, & (f' \text{ continuous}). \end{cases} \tag{14.17}$$

The problem of terminal analysis is then to choose for each (r, n) an act $a_{r,n}^o$ which maximizes $\bar{v}_t''$. Of course, from (14.15) and (14.17), we see that the choice of the optimal act also depends on the form of v_t and on f'.

Note that for terminal analysis the particular order of Ss and Fs in the history H_r^n is immaterial—assuming, of course, that the Bernoulli model applies. All that matters are the values of r and n. In our technical vernacular we say that the pair (r, n) is a *sufficient statistic* in the sense that the posterior distributing function for $\tilde{p}$ depends on the experimental evidence only through the pair (r, n). (The concept and recognition of sufficient statistics are more important in classical than Bayesian statistics, because Bayesian analysis automatically employs sufficient statistics. See also the appendix to chapter 20.)

Beta Prior

If the prior distributing function for $\tilde{p}$ is a beta df with parameters (r', n') and a history H_r^n is observed, then by (11.10) the posterior df of $\tilde{p}$ is beta with parameters (r'', n'') where $r'' = r' + r$ and $n'' = n' + n$. In this case, (14.17) specializes to

$$E_{p|r,n} v_t(a, \tilde{p}) = \int_0^1 v_t(a, p) f_\beta(p \mid r'', n'')\, dp, \tag{14.18}$$

and for a given act a, the quantity $\bar{v}_t''$ depends on the prior parameters (r', n') and the experimental outcome (r, n) only through the posterior parameters (r'', n'').

14.4.2 Preposterior Analysis: Binomial Sampling[2]

We now consider (at move 1 of the decision tree) the proposed experiment which consists of observing a *predetermined number n of trials*, so that the only element in the outcome (at move 2) that is both relevant and uncertain is the number of successes $\tilde{r}$. In this case we shall depart slightly from strictly logical rigor and say that the outcome is $\tilde{z} = \tilde{r}$ rather than $\tilde{z} = (\tilde{r}, n)$. The uncertainties in this situation then involve the paired rv $(\tilde{p}, \tilde{r})$. At move 2 on the decision tree we need the *marginal* mf for the rv $\tilde{r}$, and at move 4 on the decision tree we need the set of conditional distributing functions for $\tilde{p}$ given $\tilde{r} = r$ for $r = 0, 1, \ldots, n$. We have already discussed how to get these conditional distributions and we now turn our attention to the marginal distribution for $\tilde{r}$.

Our first task will be to derive an assessment for the *conditional mf for* $\tilde{r}$ *given* p. From these conditional mf's (one for each p) and the marginal distributing function for $\tilde{p}$, we then can use the procedure developed in the previous chapter to determine the marginal mf of $\tilde{r}$.

---

2. The results of sections 9.4.1 and 9.6.1 will be used in this subsection and should be reviewed.

Conditional Distribution of $\tilde{r}$ Given p

In n Bernoulli trials with parameter p, the unknown number of successes $\tilde{r}$ has a *binomial* mf with parameter (n, p); that is,

$$P(\tilde{r} = r|n, p) = f_b(r|n, p)$$
$$= C_r^n p^r(1 - p)^{n-r}. \tag{14.19}$$

Proof Conditional on knowing p, the probability of getting r successes in n trials in any one particular order is $p^r(1 - p)^{n-r}$; therefore, the probability of getting r successes in n trials in any order whatsoever is $Np^r(1 - p)^{n-r}$, where N is the total number of different ways of arranging r successes and $(n - r)$ failures. Exercise 2 at the end of the chapter gives a series of steps which lead to the conclusion that

$$N = C_r^n \equiv \frac{n!}{r!(n - r)!},$$

and the proof is now complete.

This type of experiment where the number of trials n is preassigned is called *binomial* sampling because the conditional distribution of $(\tilde{r}|n, p)$ is binomial.

Marginal Distribution of $\tilde{r}$

In n Bernoulli trials where the parameter $\tilde{p}$ has a prior distributing function f', the probability of getting r successes is given by

$$P(\tilde{r} = r|n) = \begin{cases} \sum_i C_r^n p_i^r(1 - p_i)^{n-r}f'(p_i), & (f' \text{ discrete}), \quad (14.20\text{a}) \\ \int_0^1 C_r^n p^r(1 - p)^{n-r}f'(p)\,dp, & (f' \text{ continuous}). \quad (14.20\text{b}) \end{cases}$$

Marginal Distribution of $\tilde{r}$ with a Beta Prior

In n Bernoulli trials where the prior df of the parameter $\tilde{p}$ is beta with parameters (r', n'), the unknown number of successes $\tilde{r}$ has a hyperbinomial mf with parameters (r', n', n); that is,

$$P(\tilde{r} = r|n) = f_{hb}(r|r', n', n). \tag{14.21}$$

Proof By (14.20b) and (9.35)

$$P(\tilde{r} = r|n) = \int_0^1 f_b(r|n, p)f_\beta(p|r', n')\,dp$$
$$= f_{hb}(r|r', n', n),$$

■

A formula for f_{hb} is given in (9.34). This formula is complicated enough to require machine computation for all but very small values of n.

Preposterior Analysis

If (at move 1) a binomial sample of size n is chosen and (at move 2) r successes are observed, then the evaluation (at move 3) for the optimal act $a^o_{r,n}$ is given by $\bar{v}_t''[a^o_{r,n}, (r, n)]$. Before the number of successes is observed, $\tilde{r}$ must be treated as a rv; by (14.8) we have to evaluate (at move 2)

$$\begin{aligned} \bar{\bar{v}}_t(n) &= E\bar{v}_t''[a^o_{\tilde{r},n}, (\tilde{r}, n)] \\ &= \textstyle\sum_{r=0}^{n} \bar{v}_t''[a^o_{\tilde{r},n}, (r, n)]P(\tilde{r} = r|n). \end{aligned} \tag{14.22}$$

The *expected cost of sampling*, defined by (14.7), is given by

$$\bar{\bar{c}}_s(n) = Ec_s(n, \tilde{r}) = \textstyle\sum_{r=0}^{n} c_s(n, r)P(\tilde{r} = r|n). \tag{14.23}$$

From (14.22) and (14.23) we obtain $\bar{\bar{v}}(n) = \bar{\bar{v}}_t(n) - \bar{\bar{c}}_s(n)$ and the remaining task is to choose n to optimize $\bar{\bar{v}}$.

14.4.3 Preposterior Analysis: Pascal Sampling[3]

We now consider (at move 1 of the decision tree) the proposed experiment which consists of observing the process until a *predetermined number of r successes occur*, so that the only element in the outcome (at move 2) that is both relevant and uncertain is the number of trials $\tilde{n}$ it takes to get r successes. In this case we shall depart slightly from strictly logical rigor and say that the outcome is $\tilde{z} = \tilde{n}$ rather than $\tilde{z} = (r, \tilde{n})$. The uncertainties in this situation then involve the paired rv $(\tilde{p}, \tilde{n})$. At move 2 on the decision tree we need the marginal mf of the rv $\tilde{n}$ and we now propose to derive this distribution.

Our first task will be to derive an assessment for the *conditional mf for $\tilde{n}$ given p*. From these conditional mf's (one for each p) and the marginal distributing function for $\tilde{p}$, we then can use the procedures developed in the previous chapter to determine the marginal mf of $\tilde{n}$.

Conditional Distribution of $\tilde{n}$ Given p

In a Bernoulli process with known parameter p, the unknown number of trials $\tilde{n}$ that are needed to obtain the rth success is a rv that has a *Pascal* mf with parameter (r, p); that is

$$\begin{aligned} P(\tilde{n} = n|r, p) &= f_{Pa}(n|r, p) \\ &= C^{n-1}_{r-1} p^r(1 - p)^{n-r}. \end{aligned} \tag{14.24}$$

---

3. The results of sections 9.5.1 and 9.6.2 will be used in this subsection and should be reviewed.

Proof Conditional on knowing p, the probability of getting r successes in n trials in any one particular order is $p^r(1-p)^{n-r}$; therefore the probability of getting the rth success on the nth trial in any order whatsoever is $Np^r(1-p)^{n-r}$, where N is the total number of different ways of arranging $(r-1)$ successes in the first $(n-1)$ trials; hence, $N = C_{r-1}^{n-1}$. The proof is now complete.

This type of experiment where the number of successes is predetermined is called *Pascal* sampling because the conditional distribution of $(\tilde{n}|r,p)$ is Pascal.

Marginal Distribution of $\tilde{n}$

In a Bernoulli process where the parameter $\tilde{p}$ has a prior distributing function f', the probability that the rth success occurs on the nth trial is given by

$$P(\tilde{n}=n|r) = \begin{cases} \sum_i C_{r-1}^{n-1} p_i^r(1-p_i)^{n-r} f'(p_i), & (f' \text{ discrete}), \quad (14.25a) \\ \int_0^1 C_{r-1}^{n-1} p^r(1-p)^{n-r} f'(p)\,dp, & (f' \text{ continuous}). \quad (14.25b) \end{cases}$$

Marginal Distribution of $\tilde{n}$ with a Beta Prior

In a Bernoulli process where the prior df of the parameter $\tilde{p}$ is beta with parameters (r', n') the unknown number of trials that are required to obtain r successes is a rv $\tilde{n}$ which has a *hyperpascal* mf with parameters (r', n', r); that is,

$$P(\tilde{n}=n|r) = f_{hp}(n|r', n', r). \tag{14.26}$$

Proof By (14.25b) and (9.38)

$$\begin{aligned} P(\tilde{n}=n|r) &= \int_0^1 f_{Pa}(n|r,p) f_\beta(p|r',n')\,dp \\ &= f_{hp}(n|r',n',r), \end{aligned}$$

■

A formula for f_{hp} is given in (9.37). This formula is complicated enough to require machine computation for all but very small values of n.

Preposterior Analysis

If (at move 1) a Pascal sample of "size" r is chosen (i.e., the process is to be observed until the rth success) and (a mdve 2) n trials are observed, then the evaluation (at move 3) for the optimal act $a^o_{r,n}$ is given by $\bar{v}''_t[a^o_{r,n}, (r,n)]$. Before the number of trials is observed, $\tilde{n}$ must be treated as a rv and by (14.8) we have the evaluation (at move 2) of

$$\bar{\bar{v}}_t(r) = E\bar{v}''[a^o_{r,n}, (r, \tilde{n})]$$
$$= \sum_{n-r}^{\infty} \bar{v}_t''[a^o_{r,n}, (r, n)] P(\tilde{n} = n|r). \tag{14.27}$$

The *expected cost of sampling*, defined by (14.7), is given by

$$\bar{\bar{c}}_s(r) = Ec_s(r, \tilde{n}) = \sum_{n=r}^{\infty} c_s(r, n) P(\tilde{n} = n|r). \tag{14.28}$$

From (14.27) and (14.28) we obtain $\bar{\bar{v}}(r) = \bar{\bar{v}}_t(r) - \bar{\bar{c}}_s(r)$ and the remaining task is to choose r to optimize $\bar{\bar{v}}$.

14.5 The Infinite-Action Problem with Quadratic Loss

14.5.1 General Analysis

As a first example of the application of the general principles of preposterior analysis, let us take infinite-action problems with quadratic loss. Terminal analysis for this class of problems was examined in section 12.6.

Let $\tilde{s}$ be the unknown state (a real number), let the set of available acts (estimates) be the set of all real numbers, and let

$$l_t(a, s) \equiv k_t(s - a)^2.$$

Let the prior mean and variance of $\tilde{s}$ be denoted respectively by $\bar{s}'$ and $\breve{s}'$; after observing ($\tilde{z} = z$), let the posterior mean and variance of $\tilde{s}$ be denoted respectively by $\bar{s}_z''$ and $\breve{s}_z''$. We showed in section 12.6.2 that:

a. The optimal act under prior information is $a^o = \bar{s}'$.

b. The EVPI is given by $\bar{l}_t'(a^o) = k_t \breve{s}'$.

c. The optimal act posterior to observing $\tilde{z} = z$ is $a_z^o = \bar{s}_z''$.

d. The posterior EVPI after observing $\tilde{z} = z$ is $\bar{l}_t''(a_z^o, z) = k_t \breve{s}_z''$.

By (14.11) the EVSI of a particular experiment e is given by

$$I(e) \equiv \bar{\bar{l}}_t(e_0) - \bar{\bar{l}}_t(e) = \bar{l}_t'(a^o) - E\bar{l}_t''(a_{\tilde{z}}^o, \tilde{z})$$
$$= k_t(\breve{s}' - E\breve{s}_{\tilde{z}}''). \tag{14.29a}$$

From the discussion in section 13.8.2 we can rewrite (14.29a) as

$$I(e) = k_t[V(\tilde{s}) - E_z V_{s|z}(\tilde{s})]$$
$$= k_t(\breve{s}' - \bar{\breve{s}}'') = k_t \breve{\bar{s}}''. \tag{14.29b}$$

In words this says that the EVSI is k_t times the prior variance of the as yet unknown posterior mean.

Table 14.1

Possible values of $\tilde{r}$	0	1	2
Marginal mf of $\tilde{r}$: $P(\tilde{r}=r\,|\,2)$	3/6	2/6	1/6
Posterior parameters (r'', n'')	(1, 5)	(2, 5)	(3, 5)
Posterior mean: $\bar{p}''$	1/5	2/5	3/5
Posterior variance: $\breve{p}''$	2/75	3/75	3/75

14.5.2 The RVs $\tilde{\bar{p}}''$ and $\tilde{\breve{p}}''$ for Binomial Sampling with a Beta Prior

Example Since we think at this point the reader's intuition will be considerably helped by keeping a simple example in mind, let us consider the following special problem. Consider a Bernoulli process where the unknown parameter $\tilde{p}$ has a beta df with parameters $(r', n') = (1, 3)$ so that $\bar{p}' = r'/n' = 1/3$ and $\breve{p}' = \bar{p}'(1 - \bar{p}')/(n' + 1) = 1/18$. Let a binomial sample be chosen from this process with $n = 2$. From (14.21) and (9.35) we obtain the marginal mf of the rv $\tilde{r}$ that is exhibited in the second row of the table. For each pair of the posterior parameters (r'', n'') in the third row, we exhibit the posterior mean

$$\bar{p}'' = \frac{r''}{n''}$$

in the fourth row and the posterior variance

$$\breve{p} = \frac{\dfrac{r''}{n''}\left(1 - \dfrac{r''}{n''}\right)}{n'' + 1}$$

in the fifth row.

In this example, after $n = 2$ has been chosen but before $\tilde{r} = r$ has been observed, the as-yet-unknown posterior mean can be treated as a rv $\tilde{\bar{p}}''$. The mf of the rv $\tilde{\bar{p}}''$ can be observed from lines 2 and 4 in table 14.1. We have

$$P(\tilde{\bar{p}}'' = \tfrac{1}{5}) = \tfrac{3}{6}, \qquad P(\tilde{\bar{p}}'' = \tfrac{2}{5}) = \tfrac{2}{6}, \qquad P(\tilde{\bar{p}}'' = \tfrac{3}{5}) = \tfrac{1}{6}.$$

The expectation and variance of the rv $\tilde{\bar{p}}''$ are given by

$$E(\tilde{\bar{p}}'') = (\tfrac{1}{5} \times \tfrac{3}{6}) + (\tfrac{2}{5} \times \tfrac{2}{6}) + (\tfrac{3}{5} \times \tfrac{1}{6}) = \tfrac{1}{3},$$

and

$$V(\tilde{\bar{p}}'') = \breve{\bar{p}}'' = [(\tfrac{1}{5})^2(\tfrac{3}{6}) + (\tfrac{2}{5})^2(\tfrac{2}{6}) + (\tfrac{3}{5})^2(\tfrac{1}{6})] - (\tfrac{1}{3})^2$$
$$= 1/45.$$

In a similar manner, we can consider the as yet unknown posterior variance $\tilde{\breve{p}}''$. The mf of this rv can be observed from lines 2 and 5 in table 14.1. We have

$$P(\tilde{\breve{p}}'' = \tfrac{2}{75}) = \tfrac{3}{6}, \qquad P(\tilde{\breve{p}}'' = \tfrac{3}{75}) = \tfrac{2}{6} + \tfrac{1}{6} = \tfrac{3}{6}.$$

The expectation of the $\tilde{\breve{p}}''$ is given by

$$E(\tilde{\breve{p}}'') = \bar{\breve{p}}'' = (\tfrac{2}{75} \times \tfrac{3}{6}) + (\tfrac{3}{75} \times \tfrac{3}{6}) = \tfrac{1}{30}.$$

From these calculations, observe that

$$E(\tilde{\bar{p}}'') = E(\tilde{p}) = \bar{p}' \tag{14.30a}$$

and

$$\breve{p}' = \check{\bar{p}}'' + \bar{\breve{p}}'', \tag{14.30b}$$

which agree with the theoretical results in (13.10) and (13.44c).

With this example as background we now state our main results for this subsection.

Let the parameter $\tilde{p}$ of a Bernoulli process have a beta df with parameters (r', n'), and let a binomial sample of size n be chosen. Then

$$E(\tilde{\bar{p}}'') = \bar{p}', \tag{14.31a}$$

$$V(\tilde{\bar{p}}'') \equiv \check{\bar{p}}'' = \frac{n}{n' + n}\breve{p}', \tag{14.31b}$$

$$E(\tilde{\breve{p}}'') \equiv \bar{\breve{p}}'' = \frac{n'}{n + n'}\breve{p}'. \tag{14.31c}$$

Proof Expression (14.31a) follows immediately from (13.40) once we rewrite (14.31a) in the less elliptical form:

$$E(\tilde{\bar{p}}'') = E_r(\bar{p}''_{\tilde{r}}) = E_r E_{p|r}(\tilde{p}) = E(\tilde{p}).$$

To prove (14.31b) we first observe that

$$\text{(A)} \quad V(\tilde{\bar{p}}'') = V\left[\frac{r' + \tilde{r}}{n' + n}\right] = \frac{1}{(n' + n)^2} V(\tilde{r}), \quad \text{[by (11.10) and section 8.3.4]}$$

and

$$\begin{aligned} V(\tilde{r}) &= V_p E_{r|p}(\tilde{r}) + E_p V_{r|p}(\tilde{r}) && \text{[by (13.44)]} \\ &= V_p(n\tilde{p}) + E_p[n\tilde{p}(1 - \tilde{p})] && \text{[by (9.24)]} \\ &= n^2\breve{p}' + n\bar{p}' - nE_p(\tilde{p}^2) \\ &= n^2\breve{p}' + n\bar{p}' - n[\breve{p}' + \bar{p}'^2] && \text{[by (8.19)]} \end{aligned}$$

$$= \breve{p}'(n^2 - n) + np'(1 - \bar{p}')$$

$$= \breve{p}'(n^2 - n) + n(n' + 1)\breve{p}' \qquad \text{[by (9.16)]}$$

$$\text{(B)} \qquad = \breve{p}'n(n' + n).$$

Substituting (B) into (A) gives (14.31b).

To prove (14.31c) we use the identity

$$\breve{p}' = \breve{\bar{p}}'' + \check{\bar{p}}'',$$

which gives

$$\breve{\bar{p}}'' = \breve{p}' - \check{\bar{p}}'' = \breve{p}' - \frac{n}{n + n'}\breve{p}' = \frac{n'}{n + n'}\breve{p}'.$$

This completes the proof.

Behavior of $\tilde{\bar{p}}''$ and $\breve{\tilde{\bar{p}}}''$ as n Increases

From (14.31a) we see that the mean of the rv $\tilde{\bar{p}}''$ remains fixed at $\bar{p}'$ as n increases. From (14.31b) we see that the variance of $\tilde{\bar{p}}''$ *increases as n increases and approaches $\breve{p}'$ in the limit.* This last remark must be thoroughly understood because it is crucial for many things we shall do throughout the remainder of this book. We shall argue heuristically that this is what should be expected. If n is small, the unknown posterior mean $\tilde{\bar{p}}''$ cannot differ very much from the prior mean, regardless of the outcome of $\tilde{r}$, since for small n the prior distribution will count most heavily in the posterior distribution of $\tilde{p}$. This means that for small n, the value of $\check{\bar{p}}''$ will be small; for the extreme case $n = 0$, the "posterior" mean is the prior mean $\bar{p}'$ and therefore $\check{\bar{p}}''$ is zero in agreement with (14.31b). For large n, however the sample value of $\tilde{r}$ can drastically alter the prior distribution of $\tilde{p}$, so that the posterior mean $\tilde{\bar{p}}''$ can swing through a wide range which means that $\check{\bar{p}}''$ will be large for large n. But how large? If n is chosen to be very large, then clearly the posterior distribution of $\tilde{p}$ will be centered very tightly about the "true" p value, so that $\bar{p}''$ will be close to the true p value; therefore for very large n, the probabilities of the events $(\tilde{p} < p_0)$ and $(\tilde{\bar{p}}'' \leq p_0)$ should be practically the same for all values of p_0. This says that as n increases the left-tail probability $P(\tilde{\bar{p}}'' \leq p_0)$ should approach $P(\tilde{p} \leq p_0)$ or that the rv $\tilde{\bar{p}}''$ should become more and more like the rv $\tilde{p}$. From this argument we should expect that $\check{\bar{p}}''$ should approach $\breve{p}'$ as n increases.

Do not confuse $\check{\bar{p}}''$ and $\breve{\bar{p}}''$. As n increases, one would expect the posterior distribution of $\tilde{p}$ to become tighter and tighter, which means the mf of the rv $\tilde{\bar{p}}''$ would tend to be more and more concentrated about zero. Therefore one would expect $\breve{\bar{p}}''$ to approach zero as n increases.

Finally, observe that, since

$$\check{p}' = \check{\check{p}}'' + \check{\bar{p}}''$$

for all n, it follows that as $\check{\bar{p}}''$ goes to zero, $\check{\check{p}}''$ must go to $\check{p}'$.

14.5.3 EVSI and Optimal Sample Size: Binomial Sampling with Beta Prior

Specializing the results of section 14.5.1 to the case where the unknown parameter $\tilde{p}$ of a Bernoulli process is given a beta df with parameters (r', n') and a binomial sample of size n is chosen, we get from (14.29b) and (14.31b)

$$I(n) = k_t(\check{p}' - \check{\bar{p}}'') = k_t\check{\check{p}}'' = k_t\check{p}'\frac{n}{n + n'}, \tag{14.32a}$$

where

$$\check{p}' = \frac{\bar{p}'(1 - \bar{p}')}{n' + 1}, \qquad \bar{p}' = \frac{r'}{n'}. \tag{14.32b}$$

Observe that $I(0) = 0$ and that

$$\lim_{n \to \infty} I(n) = k_t\check{p}' = \text{EVPI}. \tag{14.33}$$

Expected Net Gain of Sampling

If the cost of observing n trials is a linear function of n and does not depend on r, that is,

$$c_s(n, r) = K_s + k_s n$$

where K_s and k_s are respectively the fixed and variable costs of sampling, then by (14.13) the expected net gain of sampling, ENGS, is

$$G(n) = k_t\check{p}'\frac{n}{n' + n} - (K_s + k_s n). \tag{14.34}$$

(See figure 14.2.)

Optimal Sample Size

The reader is asked to show (exercise 6) that in this case the sample size n^o that maximizes expected net gain is given by

$$n^o + n' = \left[\frac{k_t n'}{k_s}\check{p}'\right]^{1/2} \tag{14.35}$$

provided that (1) n^o as given by this formula is positive and (2) $G(n^o)$ as given by (14.34) is positive; if either condition fails, the optimal sample size is 0.

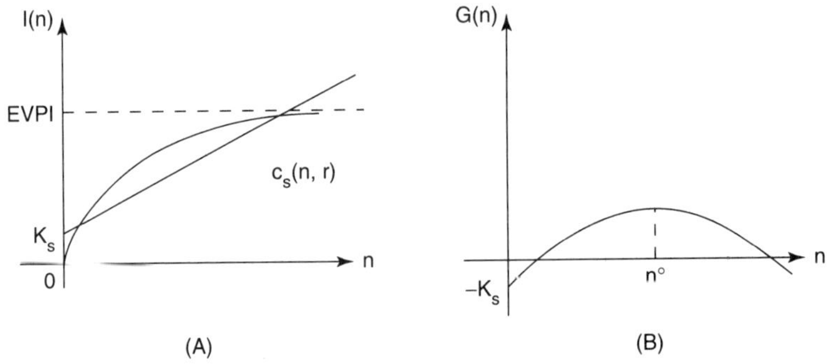

Figure 14.2
Expected value of sample information and expected net gain of sampling

14.6 The Infinite-Action Problem with Linear Loss

14.6.1 General Analysis

As a second example of the application of the general principles of preposterior analysis, let us take infinite-action problems with linear loss. Terminal analysis for this class of problems was examined in section 12.7.

Let $\tilde{s}$ be the unknown state (a real number); let the set of available acts be the set of all real numbers; let

$$l_t(a, s) = \begin{cases} k_u(s - a) & \text{if} \quad a \leq s, \\ k_O(a - s) & \text{if} \quad a \geq s; \end{cases}$$

let

$$k \equiv \frac{k_u}{k_u + k_O};$$

let s'_k be the kth fractile of the prior distributing function of $\tilde{s}$; after observing $(\tilde{z} = z)$, let $s''_k(z)$ be a kth fractile of the posterior distributing function of $\tilde{s}$. We showed in section 12.7 that

a. The optimal act under prior information is $a^o = s'_k$.

b. The EVPI is given by

$$\bar{l}'_t(a^o) = k_u E_s^{(r)}(s'_k) - k_O E_s^{(l)}(s'_k),$$

where $E_s^{(r)}$ and $E_s^{(l)}$ are respectively the right and left partial expectation operators [cf. (8.20)] taken wrt the distributing function of $\tilde{s}$.

c. The optimal act, posterior to observing $\tilde{z} = z$ is $a_z^o = s''_k(z)$

d. The posterior EVPI after observing $\tilde{z} = z$ is

$$\bar{l}_t''(a_z^o, z) = k_u E_{s|z}^{(r)}[s_k''(z)] - k_0 E_{s|z}^{(l)}[s_k''(z)],$$

where $E_{s|z}^{(r)}$ and $E_{s|z}^{(l)}$ are respectively the right and left partial expectation operators taken wrt the distributing function of $(\tilde{s}|z)$.

By (14.11) the EVSI of a particular experiment e is given by

$$I(e) = \bar{l}_t(e_0) - \bar{l}(e) = \bar{l}_t'(a^o) - E\bar{l}_t''(a_z^o, \tilde{z}). \tag{14.36}$$

Unfortunately, in most examples, including binomial sampling, the expression $E\bar{l}_t''(a_z^o, \tilde{z})$ is not very tractable. In chapter 16, however, we shall show that for the most important class of problems considered in this book—that is, sampling from a so-called Normal population—a simple analytical expression can be obtained for $I(e)$.

14.6.2 The Intractable Binomial Case

Specializing the results of section 14.6.1 to the case where the unknown parameter $\tilde{p}$ of a Bernoulli process is given a beta df with parameters (r', n') and where the binomial sample of size n is chosen, we get from (12.35) that

$$\bar{l}_t'(a^o) = (k_u + k_0)\bar{p}'(1 - \bar{p}')f_b(r'|n', p_k'),$$

where $\bar{p}' = r'/n'$ and p_k' is the kth fractile of the beta df with parameters (r', n'); also

$$\bar{l}_t''[a_{r,n}^o, (r, n)] = (k_u + k_0)\bar{p}''(1 - \bar{p}'')f_b(r''|n'', p_k'')$$

where $r'' = r' + r$, $n'' = n' + n$, $\bar{p}'' = r''/n''$, and p_k'' is the kth fractile of the beta df with parameters (r'', n'').

In preposterior analysis where n is predetermined, we must evaluate

$$E\bar{l}_t''[a_{\tilde{r},n}^o, (\tilde{r}, n)] = (k_u + k_0)E[\tilde{\bar{p}}''(1 - \tilde{\bar{p}}'')f_b(\tilde{r}''|n'', \tilde{p}_k'')],$$

which is unfortunately analytically unpleasant. In the Normal case discussed in chapter 16, two of the three arguments in the function analogous to f_b are rv's that are coordinated in such a way as to make it a *constant.* We will therefore be able to analyze that case fully and show how it can serve as an excellent approximation for the binomial sampling problem.

14.7 The Two-Action Problem with Linear Value

14.7.1 General Analysis

As our third example of the application of the general principles of preposterior analysis, let us take the two-action problem with linear

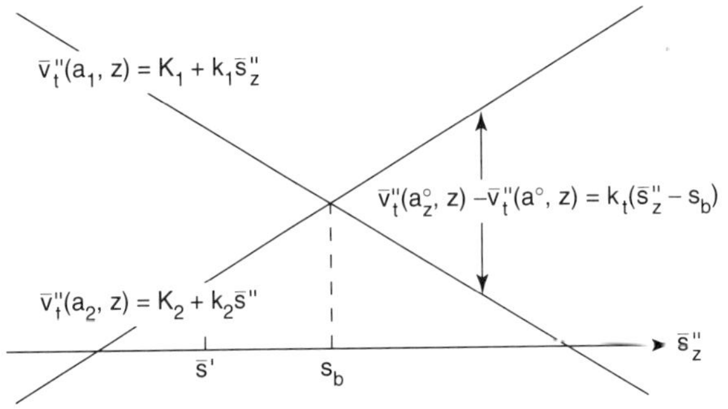

Figure 14.3
Two-action problem with linear value

economic structure. Terminal analysis for this class of problems was examined in section 12.3.

Let $\tilde{s}$ be the unknown state (a real number); let a_1 and a_2 be the two acts; let

$$v_t(a_i, s) = K_i + k_i s, \qquad i = 1, 2,$$

where $k_1 < k_2$; let $k_t = k_2 - k_1$; let $s_b = (K_1 - K_2)/(k_2 - k_1)$; let $\bar{s}'$ and $\bar{s}_z''$ be respectively the prior mean and the posterior mean after $(\tilde{z} = z)$ is observed. We showed in section 12.3 that:

a. The optimal act under prior information is

$$a^o = \begin{cases} a_1 & \text{if} \quad \bar{s}' \le s_b, \\ a_2 & \text{if} \quad \bar{s}' \ge s_b. \end{cases}$$

b. The EVPI is given by

$$\bar{l}_t'(a^o) = \begin{cases} k_t L_s^{(r)}(s_b) & \text{if} \quad \bar{s}' \le s_b, \\ k_t L_s^{(l)}(s_b) & \text{if} \quad \bar{s}' \ge s_b, \end{cases}$$

where $L_s^{(r)}$ and $L_s^{(l)}$ are respectively the right and left linear loss functions for the rv $\tilde{s}$.

c. The optimal act, posterior to observing $\tilde{z} = z$, is

$$a_z^o = \begin{cases} a_1 & \text{if} \quad \bar{s}'' \le s_b, \\ a_2 & \text{if} \quad \bar{s}'' \ge s_b. \end{cases}$$

To find EVSI, $I(e)$, we shall use (14.12). Suppose that the mean $\bar{s}'$ of the *prior* distribution is to the left of s_b as shown in figure 14.3, so that the optimal act a^o under the *prior* distribution is a_1. *If* the experiment is performed, then after z is known the decision maker will choose the act whose graph in figure 14.3 is highest at the abscissa corresponding to the mean $\bar{s}''_z$ of the *posterior* distribution of $\tilde{s}$, implying that:

1. If $\bar{s}''_z \leq s_b$, he will choose the same act a_1 that he would have chosen if no experiment had been performed and will realize no gain in terminal value:

$$\bar{v}''_t(a^o_z, z) - \bar{v}''_t(a^o, z) = 0 \quad \text{if} \quad \bar{s}''_z \leq s_b. \tag{14.37a}$$

2. If $\bar{s}''_z > s_b$, he *will* choose a_2 instead of a_1 and thereby increase his terminal value by the amount

$$\begin{aligned} \bar{v}''_t(a^o_z, z) - \bar{v}''_t(a^o, z) &= K_2 + k_2\bar{s}''_z - K_1 - k_1\bar{s}''_z \\ &= k_t(\bar{s}''_z - s_b) \quad \text{if} \quad \bar{s}''_z \geq s_b, \end{aligned} \tag{14.37b}$$

the second step following from the definition of s_b. Applying the same argument to the case where $\bar{s}'$ is to the right of s_b, the reader is asked to show (exercise 10) that

$$\bar{v}''_t(a^o_z, z) - \bar{v}''_t(a^o, z) = \begin{cases} k_t(\bar{s}''_z - s_b)^+ & \text{if} \quad \bar{s}' \leq s_b, \\ k_t(s_b - \bar{s}''_z)^+ & \text{if} \quad \bar{s}' \geq s_b, \end{cases} \tag{14.38}$$

where the symbol $w^+ \equiv \max\{0, w\}$.

Substituting this last result in formula (14.12b) for the EVSI we have

$$I(e) = \begin{cases} k_t E(\tilde{\bar{s}}'' - s_b)^+ = k_t L^{(r)}_{\tilde{\bar{s}}''}(s_b) & \text{if} \quad \bar{s}' \leq s_b, \\ k_t E(s_b - \tilde{\bar{s}}'')^+ = k_t L^{(l)}_{\tilde{\bar{s}}''}(s_b) & \text{if} \quad \bar{s}' \geq s_b, \end{cases} \tag{14.39}$$

where the linear-loss functions, defined in (8.23), are taken with respect to the distributing function of the rv $\tilde{\bar{s}}''$, that is, the as yet unknown posterior mean. Remember that the posterior mean is unknown since the outcome $\tilde{z}$ of the experiment e is unknown. In fuller notation we could replace the symbol $\tilde{\bar{s}}''$ by $\bar{s}''_{\tilde{z}}$ but we would rather have the reader think conceptually about the as yet unknown posterior mean and suppress its dependence on $\tilde{z}$.

The reader should compare (14.39) with the formula for the expected value of *perfect* information and observe that $\tilde{\bar{s}}''$ plays exactly the same role in determining EVSI that $\tilde{s}$ plays in determining EVPI. He should remember, however, that this parallelism is completely dependent on the parallelism between

$$v(a_i, s) = K_i + k_i s \quad \text{and} \quad \bar{v}''_t(a_i, z) = K_i + k_i\bar{s}''_z,$$

and that such parallelism will in general exist only when $v(a, s)$ is *linear* in s.

It is important to observe that if the distributing function of $\tilde{\tilde{s}}''$ is tight, as it will be in the case of a weak experiment, then $I(e)$ will be small; as the efficacy of the experiment increases the distributing function of $\tilde{\tilde{s}}''$ will spread out and $I(e)$ will increase, though not beyond EVPI, of course.

14.7.2 EVSI and Optimal Sample Size for Binomial Sampling with Beta Prior

Specializing the results of section 14.7.1 to the case where the unknown parameter $\tilde{p}$ of a Bernoulli process is given a beta df with parameters (r', n') and a binomial sample of size n is chosen, we get from (14.39) that

$$I(n) = \begin{cases} k_t \sum_{r=0}^{n} \left(\dfrac{r' + r}{n' + n} - p_b \right)^+ f_{hb}(r|r', n', n), & \text{if} \quad \bar{p}' \le p_b, \\ k_t \sum_{r=0}^{n} \left(p_b - \dfrac{r' + r}{n' + n} \right)^+ f_{hb}(r|r', n', n), & \text{if} \quad \bar{p}' \ge p_b. \end{cases} \tag{14.40}$$

It is shown in *ASDT* that $I(n)$ can be restated in the form

$$I(n) = \begin{cases} k_t[\bar{p}' G_{hb}(r^+|r' + 1, n' + 1, n) - p_b G_{hb}(r^+|r', n', n)], & \text{if} \quad \bar{p}' \le p_b, \\ k_t[p_b F_{hb}(r^-|r', n', n) - \bar{p}' F_{hb}(r^-|r' + 1, n' + 1, n)], & \text{if} \quad \bar{p}' \ge p_b, \end{cases} \tag{14.41}$$

where

$r^+ \equiv$ least integer greater than $n'' p_b - r'$,

and

$r^- \equiv$ greatest integer less than $n'' p_b - r'$.

$I(n)$ can be computed recursively, in the sense that the computations made for $I(n)$ are used as a basis for evaluation of $I(n + 1)$, and so forth.

The Shape of the EVSI Function

The function $I(n)$ typically has a shape as shown in figure 14.4. For values of n below some value n_1 say, the experiment is not powerful enough to change the appropriateness of the optimal prior action, regardless of the outcome of $\tilde{r}$. For example, if $r' = 1$, $n' = 7$, and $p_b = .41$, then $a^o = a_1$. For $n = 1, 2$, or 3 it is not possible to obtain a value of r such that $\bar{p}'' > .41$; hence $I(n) = 0$ for $n \le 3$. If $n = 4$ and $r = 4$, then $\bar{p}'' = 5/11 > .41$ and accordingly $I(4) > 0$. The function $I(n)$ increases monotonically and approaches the EVPI as an asymptote. The scalloping effect is caused by the jerkiness of the expression for r^+ and r^- needed in (14.41).

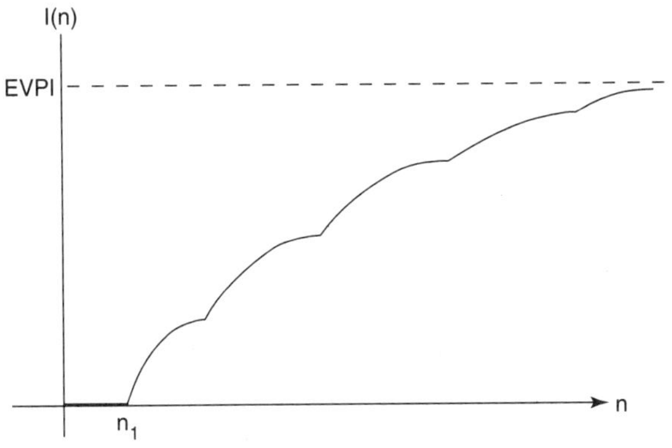

Figure 14.4
Expected value of sample information

14.8 Sequential Sampling

As a final example of preposterior analysis, we analyze a situation where the sampling rule is not restricted to being either binomial or Pascal but is completely flexible: after each observation you can decide whether to continue sampling or stop and make a terminal decision. The terminal decision problem we consider is the same two-action problem with linear value as in the previous section, and the sampling cost is k_s per observation. The observations come from a Bernoulli process with unknown p. Suppose you assign a beta distribution to $\tilde{p}$ a priori. After any sequence of observations $\tilde{p}$ will again have a beta distribution, but with new parameters. Thus in the space of beta parameter points (r', n'), the observations can be viewed as moving you from point to point, each observation increasing n' by one and either leaving r' unchanged or increasing it by one also. That is, you move from (r',n') to either $(r', n' + 1)$ or $(r' + 1, n' + 1)$. Once you have reached any particular beta distribution, the problem is essentially the same, whatever combination of prior density and observations led there, and in particular, sampling cost already incurred is sunk and need not be taken into account in choosing a strategy from there on. Thus the essential problem is to determine the *continuation region*, the set of beta parameter points (r', n') at which sampling should be continued. (For an example, see figure 14.5.) The *stopping region*, where sampling should not be continued, consists of two *decision regions*, where the optimum procedure is to stop sampling and choose a_1 or a_2. In what follows, these terms apply only to the optimum procedure; for example, the "continuation region" means the (Bayes) optimum continuation region.

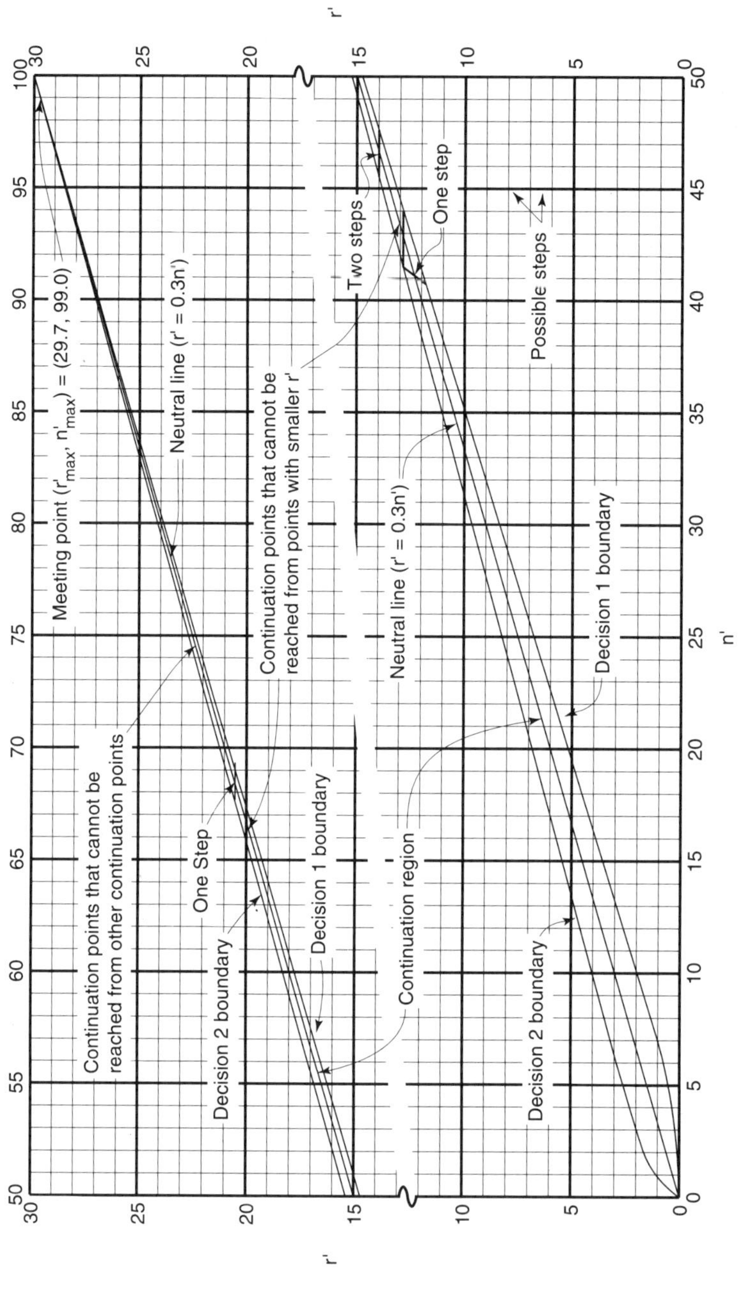

Figure 14.5
Bayes continuation region for Bernoulli process

Treat r' and n' as continuous (though each could be restricted to a grid of values with integer spacing). Let

$$v_t(a_2, p) - v_t(a_1, p) = k_t(p - p_b) \tag{14.42}$$

where p_b is the break-even value and the acts are numbered so that $k_t > 0$. The optimum terminal act is a_1 if at the time of stopping $\bar{p}' < p_b$. It is a_2 if $\bar{p}' > p_b$. Since $\bar{p}' = r'/n'$, we may describe this by saying that there is a *neutral line* $r' = n'p_b$ in the (r', n') space and that the two acts are equally good on this line, a_1 is preferable below it, and a_2 is preferable above it.

The continuation region is bounded, since the EVPI is less than the cost of even a single observation if n' is sufficiently large, regardless of the value r' (exercise 23).

For each n', it can be shown (Sobel [1953]) that the values of r' in the continuation region, if any, form an interval and the optimum procedure requires continuation in the interior, a_1 below the lower endpoint, and a_2 above the upper endpoint. The boundary of the continuation region therefore consists of two *decision boundaries* between it and the two decision regions, one above and one below the neutral line. The two decision boundaries must meet at a point on the neutral line. At this *meeting point*, the ENGS for a sample of size 1 is 0 (exercise 24a). It can be deduced (exercise 24b) that the meeting point is $(r'_{\max}, n'_{\max})$ where

$$n'_{\max} = (k_t/k_s)p_b(1 - p_b) - 1, \qquad r'_{\max} = n'_{\max}p_b. \tag{14.43}$$

The continuation region and the value of the optimum procedure can now be obtained by backward induction as follows. Let $V(r', n')$ be the value of the optimum sequential procedure starting at the point (r', n') all past costs leading to the state position (r', n') are sunk. Since we can only move from (r', n') to $(r' + 1, n' + 1)$ (with probability r'/n') or to $(r', n' + 1)$ (with complimentary probability) we can fully determine the value of $V(r', n')$ if we already know the values $V(r', n' + 1)$ and $V(r' + 1, n' + 1)$. In particular, by backward induction

$$V(r', n') = \max\{EV_t(a_1, \tilde{p}), EV_t(a_2, \tilde{p}), EV(\tilde{r}'', n' + 1) - k_s\}, \tag{14.44}$$

where

$$EV(\tilde{r}'', n' + 1) = \frac{r'}{n'}V(r' + 1, n' + 1) + \frac{n' - r'}{n'}V(r', n' + 1), \tag{14.45}$$

and where the expectation is taken with respect to the beta distribution with parameters (r', n'). Hence if we know $V(r, n')$ for all r and some value of n' we can quickly compute $V(r, n)$ for all (r, n) where $n < n'$. The choice a_1, a_2, or continuation is optimum according as the first, second, or third term in the braces in (14.44) is largest. The first two terms are specified by the terminal economics. For $n' > n'_{\max}$, the third term cannot be largest, so we can get the induction started. Charts of the continuation region for a variety of break-even values p_b and cost ratios k_t/k_s are given by Lindley and Barnett (1965).

From the condition that one should not continue when the EVPI $\leq k_s$, one obtains a presumably rather crude bound on the largest n' in the continuation region. This is enough to permit starting the backward induction, but it is more efficient to make use of the exact value of $n'_{\max}$ given by (14.43). Still more efficient, however, is to make use of the curious feature that a large part of the continuation region is inaccessible from earlier parts. More specifically, there are continuation points r', n' which cannot be reached by any sequence of observations keeping one in the continuation region starting from any continuation point (r, n) with $r < r'$ and $n - r < n' - r'$. (See figure 14.5.) This means that the inaccessible part of the continuation region need not be considered in calculating the accessible part by backward induction, provided the inaccessible part has been identified somehow. It turns out that for small k_s/k_t (when the continuation region is large), the maximum accessible n' is only 37%–50% of $n'_{\max}$, and an easily calculated bound is available which exceeds this only slightly (Pratt, 1966). The analysis is intricate, but starts from the following idea. On the boundary of the region where at most one further observation should be taken, the EVSI for a sample of size $n = 1$ is exactly k_s. The equations are (exercise 26a)

$$k_s = k_t\left(\frac{r' + 1}{n' + 1} - p_b\right)\frac{r'}{n'} \quad \text{for} \quad \frac{r'}{n'} \leq p_b, \tag{14.46}$$

$$k_s = k_t\left(p_b - \frac{r'}{n' + 1}\right)\frac{n' - r'}{n'} \quad \text{for} \quad \frac{r'}{n'} \geq p_b. \tag{14.47}$$

It follows that these are the equations of the decision boundaries from the meeting point back as far as the first point at which an observation can carry you from a solution of one equation to a solution of the other. The value of n' at which this happens is $\min\{p_b, 1 - p_b\}n'_{\max}$ plus an amount which is bounded no matter how large $n'_{\max}$ is (exercise 26b).

A variation of this problem that is easier to analyze is the case of sequential sampling with a prescribed truncation value N; for example, sample sequentially up to a maximum of 100 observations. In this case, if the initial starting distribution is beta (r_0, n_0), then the backward induction can start at $n_0 + N$ with terminal analysis. The EVSI of the sampling plan is often insensitive to the value of N. A lot of power can be gained from using a sequential plan even with surprisingly low truncation values.

Exercises

1. Consider once again exercise 4 of chapter 6 and assume the decision maker is an EMV'er. Using this problem find numerical values for each symbolic expression introduced in section 14.3. For example, give values for

$v_t(a, s)$	$\bar{v}_t''(a_z^o, z)$	$\bar{\bar{l}}(e)$
$l_t(a, s)$	$\bar{l}_t''(a_z^o, z)$	$\bar{c}_s(e)$
$c_s(e, z)$	$\bar{v}''(e, z, a_z^o)$	$\bar{\bar{v}}_t(e)$
$\bar{v}_t''(a, z)$	$\bar{l}''(e, z, a_z^o)$	$\bar{\bar{l}}_t(e)$
$\bar{l}_t''(a, z)$	$\bar{\bar{v}}(e)$	$I(e)$
		$G(e)$

[Suggestion for organizing the work: First display the decision tree and record $v_t(a, s)$, $l_t(a, s)$, and $c_s(e, z)$ at the tips of the tree. Now work backwards keeping v_t, l_t and c_s separate.]

2. Given n different objects and r different boxes where $r \leq n$, let

$P_r^n \equiv$ number of ways of placing exactly one object in each of the r boxes,

$C_r^n \equiv$ number of ways of selecting r different objects from the n different objects without arranging them.

Prove the following:

a. $P_r^n = n(n-1)\ldots(n-r+1)$.

Hint How many choices of objects do you have for the first box? After filling the first, how many choices do you have for the second box? Etc.

b. $P_r^r = r(r-1)\ldots(1) \equiv r!$

c. $P_r^n = C_r^n \cdot P_r^r$.

d. $C_r^n = \dfrac{n!}{r!(n-r)!}$

e. From the context, argue that $C_n^n = 1$ and therefore it is natural to define $0! \equiv 1$.

3. Let $\tilde{p}$ have a beta prior with parameters $(1, 2)$; that is, let $\tilde{p}$ have a rectangular prior. Show that the marginal sampling distribution of $\tilde{r}$ is given by $f_{hb}(r|1, 2, n) = 1/n + 1$ for $r = 0, 1, \ldots n$; and argue why this is an intuitively plausible result.

4. Repeat all the calculations of the example in section 14.5.2, only with a sample of size $n = 3$.

5. In an infinite act (estimation type) problem let

$l_t(a, p) = 10^5(p - a)^2$.

If $\tilde{p}$ is beta with parameters $(r', n') = (2, 5)$ find:

a. the optimal act a^o and EVPI;

b. the prior expected loss of optimal action taken posterior to a binomial sample of size $n = 5$;

c. the expected value of information, $I(5)$, in a binomial sample of size 5.

6. Verify (14.35).

7. The proportion p of individuals in the population that have attribute X is unknown. Suppose that on the basis of a pilot sample $\tilde{p}$ is given a beta density with parameters $(r', n') = (23, 85)$. If the problem is to estimate p where the loss

$l_t(a, p) = 10^8(a - p)^2$,

and where the cost of a binomial sample of size is $(100 + 2n)$, then for a given n find:

a. the prior expected loss of action taken posterior to sample information;

b. the expected value of sample information;

c. the expected net gain of sampling.

d. Find the n^o which maximizes the expected net gain of sampling.

8. a. Let $\tilde{p}$ be beta with parameters $(r', n') = (2, 5)$. Let $\tilde{r}$ be the number of successes in a binomial sample of size $n = 4$, and show that the marginal mf of $\tilde{r}$ is given by

$$f_r(r) = f_{hb}(r|2, 5, 4) = \frac{(r+1)(6-r)(5-r)}{140}$$

or

r	0	1	2	3	4	Total
$f_r(r)$	30/140	40/140	36/140	24/140	10/140	1

b. Suppose we wish to estimate p where

$$l_t(a, p) = \begin{cases} 400(p - a) & \text{if} \quad a \leq p, \\ 100(a - p) & \text{if} \quad a \geq p. \end{cases}$$

Verify and complete the following table:

r	0	1	2	3	4
$f_r(r)$	30/140	40/140	36/140	24/140	10/140
a_r^o	.3304	.4621	.5837	.6968	.8014
$\bar{l}_t''(a_r^o, r)$					

Hint Use the results of section 14.6.2 and F_β tables.

c. Find the prior expected loss of action taken posterior to the sample information.

d. Find a^o and $\bar{l}_t'(a^o)$.

e. Find EVSI for binomial sampling with $n = 4$.

9. If the prior distribution of $\tilde{p}$ is beta with parameters (r', n') and if a binomial sample of size n is taken but $\tilde{r}$ is not as yet disclosed, then we have seen from (14.31) that the rv $\tilde{\breve{p}}''$ has a mf where:

$$E(\tilde{\breve{p}}'') = \breve{p}'$$

and

$$V(\tilde{\breve{p}}'') = \breve{\breve{p}}'' = \frac{n}{n' + n}\breve{p}'.$$

a. If $n = 0$ show that $V(\tilde{\breve{p}}'') = 0$ and interpret the result.

b. What happens to the variance of the distribution of $\tilde{\breve{p}}''$ as the sample size n increases?

c. What happens to the mean of the distribution of $\tilde{\breve{p}}''$ (the as yet unknown variance of the posterior distribution of $\tilde{p}$) as n increases?

10. Verify (14.38).

11. Consider a two-act problem with linear value where the unknown state proportion $\tilde{p}$ has a beta prior distribution with parameters $(r', n') = (5, 11)$. Let

$$v_t(a_1, p) = 3{,}000\, p,$$

and

$v_t(a_2, p) = -6{,}000 + 13{,}000\, p.$

a. Show $a^o = a_1$ and $\bar{v}_t'(a^o) = 3{,}000\, \bar{p}' = ?$

b. Find $\bar{l}_t'(a^o)$. Interpret this figure.

c. For a binomial sample of size $n \leq 4$, argue that the EVSI must be 0.

Hint Show $a_r^o = a_1$ for all r if $n \leq 4$.

d. Consider a binomial sample of size $n = 39$. For what range of values for $\tilde{r}$ will the optimal act still be a_1?

e. For any value of r let

$$\bar{p}'' = \frac{r' + r}{n' + n} = \frac{5 + r}{11 + 39} = \frac{5 + r}{50}.$$

Argue that the expected value of the optimal act posterior to observing r is

$3{,}000\, \bar{p}'' + 10{,}000 \max\{0, \bar{p}'' - .60\}.$

f. If $\tilde{r}$ is as yet unknown then $\tilde{\bar{p}}''$ is as yet unknown; show that the prior expected value of action taken posterior to a binomial sample of size n is given by

$$E[3{,}000\, \tilde{\bar{p}}'' + 10{,}000 \max\{0, \tilde{\bar{p}}'' - .60\}]$$

$$= 3{,}000\, E(\tilde{\bar{p}}'') + 10{,}000\, E \max\{0, \tilde{\bar{p}}'' - .60\}$$

$$= 3{,}000\, \bar{p}' + 10{,}000\, L_{\tilde{\bar{p}}''}^{(r)}(.60 | 5, 11, 39).$$

g. Show that the expected value of information in a binomial sample of size n is therefore

$$I(n) = 10{,}000\, L_{\tilde{\bar{p}}''}^{(r)}(.60) = 10{,}000\, E \max\left\{0, \frac{5 + \tilde{r}}{50} - .60\right\}$$

$$= 10{,}000 \sum_{r=25}^{39} (.02r - .50) f_{hb}(r | 5, 11, 39).$$

h. From (14.39) show that

$$I(39) = 10{,}000[\tfrac{5}{11} G_{hb}(26 | 6, 12, 39) = .60\, G_{hb}(26 | 5, 11, 39)].$$

12. (*Continuation of Exercise 13.24*)
Before $\tilde{x}$ is observed, show that the expected value of sample (i.e., x) information is given by

$$\text{EVSI} = V(\tilde{y}) - E_x V_{y|x}(\tilde{y}) = V_x E_{y|x}(\tilde{y}).$$

13. (*Continuation of 13.26*)
If the regression of $\tilde{y}$ on $\tilde{x}$ is linear and the opportunity loss is that of exercise 13.24, show that

$$\frac{\text{EVSI}}{\text{EVPI}} = \frac{V_{21}^2}{V_{11} V_{22}} = [\rho(\tilde{x}, \tilde{y})]^2.$$

14. (*Continuation of 13.27*)

a. If the regression of $\tilde{y}$ on $\tilde{x}$ is not linear, but if one is restricted to a linear decision rule, then show that for squared error loss

$$\frac{\text{EVSI}}{\text{EVPI}} = [\rho(\tilde{x}, \tilde{y})]^2.$$

b. Show that the linear decision rule $a + b\,x$ which is best in the foregoing sense has positive slope b if $\rho(\tilde{x}, \tilde{y})$ is positive, slope 0 if $\rho(\tilde{x}, \tilde{y}) = 0$, and negative slope if $\rho(\tilde{x}, \tilde{y})$ is negative.

15. There is a list of N^* potential customers for a product. Each of these customers can only buy one unit of the product. If any customer is contacted there is an unknown probability $\tilde{p}$ that he will purchase the product. The customers can be contacted in two stages, a sampling stage and a main stage. If a sample of n is taken, the decision whether or not to contact the remainder $(N^* - n)$ of the customers will be based on the number of affirmative answers in the sample.

In the sampling stage let the cost of contacting n customers be $(K_s + c_s n)$ and let the revenue be π_s per success.

In the main stage let the cost of contacting $(N^* - n)$ customers be $[K_s + c_t(N^* - n)]$ and let the revenue be π_t per success.

Let $\tilde{p}$ be given a beta density with parameter (r', n').

a. Show that if a sample of size n is taken and r successes obtained then the remainder of the population should be contacted if and only if

$$\bar{p}'' > v(n)$$

where

$$\bar{p}'' \equiv \frac{r' + r}{n' + n} \quad \text{and} \quad v(n) \equiv \frac{K_t + c_t(N^* - n)}{\pi_t(N^* - n)}.$$

b. Let $V(n, r)$ denote the expected revenue if a sample of size n is taken, r successes are observed, and an optimal policy is then followed. Show that

$$V(n, r) = -K_s - nc_s + r\pi_s + \{-K_t + (N^* - n)[-c_t + \bar{p}''\pi_t]\}^+$$

where

$$\{x\}^+ \equiv \max(x, 0).$$

c. If n is determined but r is still unknown then the expected net revenue (ENR) is defined as

$$V^*(n) \equiv E_r V(n, \tilde{r}).$$

Show that

$$V^*(n) = -K_s + n(\bar{p}'\pi_s - c_s) + (N^* - n)\pi_t E\{\tilde{\bar{p}}'' = v(n)\}^+.$$

Note $V^*(n)$ can be computed recursively very efficiently.

d. If $K_t = 0$, then show that

$$V^*(n) = -K_s + n(\bar{p}'\pi_s - c_s) + (N^* - n)\pi_t L_{\bar{p}''}^{(r)}(c_t/\pi_t).$$

e. When $K_t \neq 0$, the function $V^*(n)$ might look as shown in figure 14E.1. Explain the linear behavior when n is small, the scalloping behavior for intermediate values of n, and the linear behavior for large values of n.

16. In problem 17 of chapter 11, suppose that the N individuals or items were drawn from a Bernoulli process with unknown p having a beta prior distribution.

a. If r successes are observed in a sample of n drawn without replacement from the N, what is the posterior distribution of the remaining $N - n$?

b. What is the marginal distribution of the posterior parameters?

c. How could you update these results to apply to a second sample after observing a first sample?

d. How could you carry out an analysis comparable to (a)–(c) without introducing the "latent" or "hyper-" parameter p?

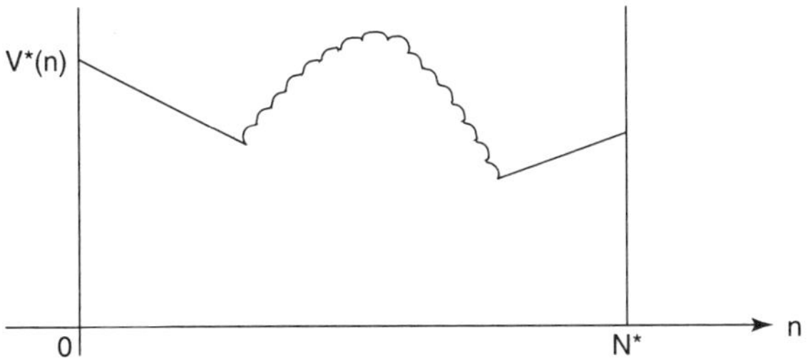

Figure 14E.1

16. The number of births each day at the County Small Community Hospital is equally likely to be 0, 1, 2, 3, 4, or 5 (the capacity of the maternity unit). A friend had a baby girl there recently and her doctor remarked that all babies born there that day were girls. What is the chance that the maternity unit was at capacity that day?

17. A production process produces good and defective items. When it is "in control," it behaves like a Bernoulli process with probability $p = .99$ of a good item on each trial. When it is "out of control," it behaves like a Bernoulli process with an unknown p which stays fixed until the production process is readjusted. The distribution of p for an "out of control" process is uniform on the interval $(0, .99)$. A sample of 8 items has been inspected. The third was defective and the other 7 were good.

a. If the process was "in control" throughout, what was the probability of observing this outcome?

b. If the process was "out of control" throughout, what was the probability (marginal on p) of observing this outcome?

Suppose that *a priori* the probability was 6/7 that the process would be "in control" throughout and 1/7 that it would be "out of control" throughout.

c. What is now the probability that the process is "in control?"

d. What is now the distribution of the process parameter p?

e. What is now the probability that the next item will be good?

f. A readjustment will be made after 100 more items. An extra readjustment can be made earlier at an additional cost K. After readjustment, the process will remain "in control" for at least 100 items. Inspection costs c per item and defectives cost d per item. Describe how you would go about deciding which items to inspect and when to readjust.

18. The XYZ Company is considering a new process for manufacturing plastic widgets. The crucial parameter is the proportion p_1 of defectives which would be produced in the long run by the new process. No direct measurements on this proportion are available, but biased measurements can be made (at considerable expense) by modifying the raw material now being used and using the modified material in the present process. To avoid intolerable burdens on the control of operations, it must be decided next week whether to make such a modification, and if so, how much of the raw material to modify. All modified material must be used, as the supply is just sufficient for production requirements.

XYZ has decided to analyze the problem under the following assumptions, at least to begin with: The new process is Bernoulli with parameter p_1. Modifying the raw material used in the present process would result in a Bernoulli process with parameter p_2. Raw material used per widget is constant, so the sampling problem is essentially how many widgets to make using the modified material, if any. The prior distribution of $\tilde{p}_2$ is beta with mean .008 and variance $(.004)^2$. The distribution of $\tilde{p}_1$ given p_2 (before or after sampling) has mean $E(\tilde{p}_1|p_2) = 1.1\, p_2$ and variance $V(\tilde{p}_1|p_2) = (.06\, p_2)^2$. The gain in value due to introducing the new process would be

$10^5 - 10^7\ p_1$. XYZ wishes to maximize expected value. The cost of sampling for a sample of size n with r defectives is $150 + .08n + 9r$.

a. What are the beta parameters of the prior distribution of $\tilde{p}_2$? What is its density?

b. What are now the mean and variance of $\tilde{p}_1$?

c. If no sampling is done, should the new process be introduced?

d. What is the expected cost of sampling for a sample of size 500?

e. If a sample of size 500 were decided upon and it turned out that 8 widgets out of the 500 were defective, what would the distribution of $\tilde{p}_2$ then be?

f. In the situation of (e), should the new process be introduced?

g. Indicate how the problem of choosing an optimal sample size can be reduced to a problem considered in the text for the course.

19. Two urns each contain a very large number of balls. Three quarters of the balls in urn I and one quarter of the balls in urn II are orange, the rest are black.

a. An urn is picked at random and balls drawn from it at random until the first black ball appears. This turns out to be the third ball drawn. What is the probability that the urn picked was urn I?

b. Suppose that you will receive $100 if you guess correctly the color of the next ball drawn (and you will receive nothing otherwise). What is your best guess and what is its expected monetary value?

c. What is the expected value of sample information for a further sample of size 2 before guessing in (b)?

d. If, in (a), balls had been drawn until the second black appeared and this turned out to be the fifth ball, what would be the probability that the urn was urn I?

e. Give an intuitive argument why the answer to (d) should be greater than, equal to, or less than the answer to (a).

f. Urn II is replaced by an urn whose proportion orange has a beta distribution with parameters 1 and 4 (mean 1/4 and variance 3/80). What is now the answer to (a)?

g. Does the intuitive argument in (e) still apply? Why or why not?

20. When the Managerial Economics Group at HBS has a lunchtime seminar in a lounge, free box lunches are provided. Prof. P has attended 6 such occasions this year, and only once were his favorite cookies provided. Assume that the occasions form a Bernoulli process with unknown parameter p representing the chance of Prof. P's favorite cookies.

a. Prof. P's prior distribution at the beginning of the year was uniform on p. What is his probability now that his favorite cookies will be provided the next time he attends? (He is, of course, a completely consistent Bayesian.)

b. For what proper beta prior distributions of p would his probability now of favorite cookies next time be 1/6?

c. Prof. P suddenly recalls that not only were his favorite cookies provided only once, but twice there were no cookies at all. Might this change his probability of favorite cookies next time? Why or why not? (Perhaps he is not a completely consistent Bayesian after all.)

d. How could the analysis be expanded to take the additional information properly into account?

e. Prof. P's secretary, Ms. X, must order lunches for the next time. She will, of course, order Prof. P's favorite cookies—she always does—but to order is not to receive. She is, however, concerned about how many lunches to order. Data on attendance are given in table A. Lunches cost $8 each. When there aren't enough, much bad temper, brouhaha, and disruption of the afternoon's work ensues. To avoid this, if it were possible, Ms. X would be willing to pay about $100.00 per lunchless attendee (out of HBS funds). Do an analysis leading to a recommended number of lunches to order.

Table A

Lunch number	Number attending
1	6
2	13
3	14
4	20
5	11
6	8
7	16
8	9
9	13
10	12
11	12
Mean	12.18
S.D.	3.84

Table B
(size of mailing list unknown)

Lunch number	Number attending	Number responding "Yes"	"No"
1	6	2	38
2	13	5	42
3	14	3	26
4	20	5	33
5	11	3	28
6	8	2	25
7	16	5	25
8	9	4	27
9	13	4	17
10	12	3	45
11	12	6	44

21. The success probability p of a Bernoulli process has prior density $3p^2$, $0 < p < 1$. Two acts are available. Act 1 has terminal value $200p$. Act 2 has terminal value 190.

a. Is the prior distribution of p a beta distribution?

b. Could the prior density have resulted from a uniform prior distribution of p at some previous time and some observations between then and now? If so, what observations? If not, why not?

c. What is the optimum act now?

d. The process will be observed until the first failure occurs. Suppose it occurs on the nth trial. What will the posterior distribution of p be?

e. What is the probability (now) that the first failure will occur after the $(n - 1)$th trial?

f. What is the probability that the first failure will occur on the nth trial?

g. What is the expected number of trials until the first failure?

h. What will the optimum act be a posteriori, as a function of n?

i. What is the probability (now) that the optimum act a posteriori will differ from the currently optimum act?

j. What is the expected value of sample information?

k. If each observation costs c, what is the expected net gain of sampling?

l. Describe a sequential sampling plan that dominates the plan under discussion.

22. a. Draw a decision tree for the sequential sampling problem of section 14.8 and relate it to the kind of diagram used there.

b. Show that for any prior distribution, beta or not, the same tree structure and diagram apply, although the probabilities are different.

23. Show that the EVPI $\to 0$ as $n' \to \infty$ uniformly in r' (but not in the economic parameters) for each of the problems considered in this chapter.

24. a. In section 14.8, show that the decision boundaries meet the neutral line in a common point where the ENGS for a sample of size 1 is 0.

b. Derive formulas for r' and n' at this point.

25. a. Show that the continuation region and opportunity loss in section 14.8 depend only on $v_t(a_2, p) - v_t(a_1, p)$ and k_s/k_t although the actual value function V depends on all the quantities individually.

b. Write the induction equations in a form that exploits this, specifically, assuming $v_t(a_1, p) = 0$ and $v_t(a_2, p) = (p - p_b)$. How would the general solution relate to this case?

26. a. Derive the equations for the locus of points (r', n') where the ENGS of a sample of size 1 is 0 in the two-action problem with linear value.

b. Argue that these equations give the decision boundaries in section 14.8 for $n' > \min\{p_b, 1 - p_b\}n'_{\max} + C$ where C is bounded.

CASES

C1 Acme Automatic Machine Company

The Acme Automatic Machine Company manufacturers a variety of screw-machine parts which are used in final assembly of its product. Part number 684 is a grooved cylindrical shaft used in an assembly with very close tolerances. The part is produced for inventory in lots of 5,000, amounting to a day's run of one machine. Considerable difficulty is being experienced in holding dimensional tolerances on this part, and defectives are causing serious losses. Time studies show that the interference with a smooth assembly operation caused by each defective reaching the assembly department costs roughly \$0.25 in addition to the \$0.15 cost of reworking the part in the shop.

Exact records of numbers of defectives on previous production runs have not been kept, but on the basis of discussions with the assembly foreman, the production manager, Mr. Paul O'Brien, estimates that when the machine is set up and then run in the normal manner there are less than 6% defectives 50% of the time, 6% to 8% defectives 25% of the time, and over 8% defectives 25% of the time. Some experimentation has shown that by extremely careful gauging and adjustment after setup, the machine can be made to produce 5% defectives with virtual certainty, but this extremely careful adjustment increases the setup cost by \$50 for labor and machine downtime. Mr. O'Brien is considering both the possibility of having every lot 100% inspected before stocking it in inventory and the possibility of using sample inspection to decide what to do. His studies show that an inspector paid \$3.00 an hour can inspect 100 pieces per hour.

a. Define the cost and loss functions for the four possible acts: normal adjustment followed by screening, normal adjustment not followed by screening, special adjustment followed by screening, special adjustment not followed by screening. Are any of these acts "inadmissible" even without consideration of the fraction defective that may result from any particular normal setup?

b. Putting yourself in the role of Mr. O'Brien's engineer for statistical quality control, select a beta distribution for process fraction defective after normal setup that you would be willing to submit to Mr. O'Brien as a basis for selection of an act.

c. Assuming that preference is linear in money, what act is optimal on the basis of your proposed distribution? What is the EVPI?

d. The process is set up by the "normal" procedure, 100 pieces are produced and inspected as a sample before proceeding with the actual production run, and ten defectives are found in the sample. Which of the four acts listed in (a) should be taken with respect to the 5000 pieces still to be produced on the production run? What is the EVPI at this point?

e. At the indicated rate of \$0.03 variable sampling cost per piece, what is the optimal sample size?

C2 Robinson Abrasive Company

The Robinson Abrasive Company manufactured a wide variety of grinding wheels for industrial use. These wheels were subject to extreme stresses; and since breakage could result in severe damage to machinery and injury to machine operators, the company was anxious to maintain high-quality output and subjected the wheels to rigorous testing procedures.

The first step in the manufacture of a grinding wheel was to mix bonding material, abrasive, and water until a smooth uniform mixture was obtained and then pour the mixture into molds which were allowed to dry for a period of several days. The dried wheels were then placed on a shaving machine and turned to the desired dimension. After bushings had been inserted, the wheels were loaded into a large kiln and baked for several hours at a very high temperature. Finally the finished product was tested for hardness, toughness, and strength; the strength test consisted of rotating the wheel inside a protective steel sheet at a speed 50% greater than the maximum speed which would be used under ordinary operating conditions.

Failure of finished wheels in the strength test could be due to a variety of causes. The bonding material itself was of variable quality, and sometimes a substantial number of wheels in a single batch would fail because the cohesive strength of the material was inadequate. Although he could not be completely sure of the reason for some of the individual failures, the quality-control supervisor believed that the fraction defective due to raw material tended to be under 2% in about 70% of all batches, between 2% and 5% in 20% of all batches, and over 5% in only the remaining 10% of all batches.

In September 1955, the research department announced that it had developed and had available for immediate use in manufacturing a new bonding material which was much stronger than the old. Wheels made of this material were no better or worse than wheels made of the old material which succeeded in passing inspection, but the failures due to the raw material were completely eliminated and the company intended to purchase no more material of the old kind. At this time the company had on hand enough of the old bonding material to make 1000 grinding wheels 36 inches in diameter; and since there was no test which would give a reliable measurement of the strength of this material other than actually using it to produce finished wheels, the superintendent raised the question whether it ought to be scrapped in order to avoid the risk of wasting money in processing wheels which might fail on final test.

The cost of processing plus the cost of the materials other than the bonding material amounted to $15 per wheel, but enough new bonding material to produce one thousand 36-inch wheels would cost $1,000 and the quality-control supervisor suggested that the batch of old material should be tested by actually using some of it to make finished wheels before a decision was reached to accept or reject the remainder. They would then be given the regular strength test, and the decision to accept or reject the remainder of the batch of material would be based on the outcome of this test.

a. Define two acts, one involving use of the old material and one involving scrapping the old material, such that the *costs* of one or both of the acts depend on the quality of the old material but the number of *good wheels produced* does *not* depend on this quality.

b. Select a beta distribution suitable for the fraction defective due to the remaining batch of raw material.

c. Assuming that preference is linear in money, which of the two acts defined in (a) is optimal under the distribution selected in (b)? What is the EVPI?

d. If a sample of 10 wheels is produced and one defective is found, which act is optimal as regards the remainder of the old batch of raw material? What is the EVPI?

e. Supposing it costs $50 to set up a test of the old material and $4.00 per wheel, how many wheels should be produced on a test basis? Ignore the resulting reduction in the material remaining.

C3 Smith Novelty Company

The Smith Novelty Company engaged in the business of selling unusual novelty and gift items by direct mail. It used a single mailing list for all offers; the list had been built up and weeded out over many years and currently consisted of about 30,000 "good prospects," almost all of whom had purchased on two or more occasions.

A large part of Smith's business was in items imported from Europe, where a buyer was permanently stationed. The ordinary procedure was for the buyer to find some item which he believed suitable for the company's business and contract for a lot which was shipped to Smith in the United States in a single shipment. When the merchandise was received, the company would prepare and send out a special mailing. The company was convinced that it was necessary to give a strong "special bargain" flavor to these mailings and therefore invariably restricted sales to "one to a customer."

The chief hazards in Smith's business were two: the risk of being left with a large quantity of unsold merchandise when response to a mailing was poor, and the risk of being short when response to a mailing was unusually good. When merchandise was left over, it was usually wholesaled off to retail bargain outlets at a considerable loss. On the other hand, Mr. James Smith, the owner of the company, felt that a very serious goodwill cost was incurred by unfilled customer orders in a business such as his, and when demand exceeded the contract quantity he usually tried to secure additional merchandise off the shelf even if the cost to him of such merchandise was higher than the price paid by the customer.

Smith had been thinking for some time about ways of reducing these losses and had finally concluded that at least in some cases it would be possible and might be profitable to sample his mailing list before ordering any specific quantity from the foreign supplier; the quantity ordered would then be set to correspond with the estimate made from the sample. Doing this would not be altogether simple, however: customers on the sample list would not be wiling to wait three or four months before receiving their merchandise, and the company could not tolerate disgruntled customers because of the importance of repeat business. It would be necessary, therefore, to make two importations: one of a quantity sufficient to anticipate the demand from the sample mailing, and then another to anticipate the demand from the main mailing. Since the initial importation would have to be purchased from the manufacturer's regular stocks at a higher price than that which would be obtained when buying a single contract quantity, and since per-unit shipping costs would be higher on the small quantity, there would be a very real cost involved in the sampling operation.

In June 1955, the buyer sent over a sample of a blue enameled Dutch skillet which Mr. Smith thought would be an excellent buy. Housewares of this general category had been offered before, and sales had ranged from about 1,000 to somewhat over 3,000 units. Smith thought that if this skillet were offered at $3, the sales would be somewhere in this general range but he could not tell just where; if he had to bet, he would give even money that sales would be at least 1,500 units, and he thought there was 1 chance in 4 that they would actually exceed 2,000 units.

The skillet could be bought from the manufacturer's stock in small quantities at his retail price of $2.75; delivery to the company's premises in the United States by parcel post would cost an additional $0.75 per skillet. In a contract quantity and a single shipment by ocean freight the cost would be about $1.50 including delivery. Postage and handling on the mail orders would average about $0.50 per sale. Smith believed that skillets remaining unsold after the mailing could be salvaged for about $1.10 each, net of expenses.

a. Select a beta distribution that Smith might be willing to assign to the *fraction* of all customers that will order.

b. Assuming that Smith's utility is linear in money, what order quantity is optimal on the basis of the distribution selected in (a)? What is the EVPI?

c. If Smith sends a sample mailing to 200 of his customers and 10 of them order a skillet, what act is optimal and what is the EVPI?

d. What is the optimal size of a sample mailing?

C4 Science Books, Inc.

The following problem faces the president of Science Books, Inc., a book club of 45,000 members which sells paperback reprints of scientific books by direct mail only. Immediately after learning that he could obtain the rights to a certain book, the president calculated that production would involve a fixed cost of $3,000 (payment for the rights and the original plates, setup of the presses, etc.), a fixed cost of \$50 for preparing the announcement to the members, a variable cost of \$0.15 for mailing this announcement, plus a variable cost of \$0.65 per book (paper, ink, labor, etc.). The club's regular pricing policy called for pricing the book at \$1.95 plus cost of mailing, so that there would be a gross margin of \$1.30 on each book produced and sold. If the book were to be produced, the actual press run would not be made until after it had been offered to the members and time had been allowed for all orders to be received. There was thus no problem of over or underproduction; the only problem was whether the number of orders received would at least equal the number required to cover the fixed costs and break even.

The club had already reprinted ten books on subjects of roughly the same level of difficulty and roughly the same level of general appeal as the one concerning which a decision must now be reached; the fraction of all members who ordered on the ten different occasions was .039, .139, .311, .051, .350, .104, .113, .407, .038, and .198. This evidence, however, did not seem to the president to constitute a really adequate basis for a decision, and he was therefore weighing the idea of actually sampling his membership. He could do so by designing the mailing piece that would actually be used if he decided to publish the book and then sending a certain number of copies as if he had actually decided to publish; the resulting orders could be filled with hard-cover copies of the original edition that he could buy in a bookstore for \$8.45 each. The cost of designing the mailing piece and producing the mat would be about \$50; each mailing involved a variable cost of about \$0.15 for printing, addressing, stuffing, and postage.

Note If a mailing piece is made up for the sample, it can be used also for the mailing to the general membership so that the \$50 fixed charge is not incurred twice.

Should a sample be taken and if so, how large?

15 Poisson Process

15.1 The Poisson Model with Known Parameter

15.1.1 Introduction*

Consider such phenomena as (1) the arrival of customers for service, where the "customers" to be served can be such diverse entities as potential buyers arriving at a store counter, mechanics arriving at a tool crib, airplanes arriving at a runway for takeoffs or landings, ships arriving at docks; (2) the departure of such customers from service; (3) the occurrence of accidents, breakdowns, births, divorces, and so forth.

We shall describe such processes by recording the successive times an event of the type under consideration occurs. Starting from a given time, which we agree to call $t = 0$, the process can be described by the sequence of times $t_1, t_2, \ldots, t_i, \ldots$ where t_i is the time of the ith occurrence. We shall assume that events are so defined that two events cannot occur simultaneously. We let $t_0 = 0$ and define $z_i = t_i - t_{i-1}$ for $i = 1, 2, \ldots$, so that z_i can be interpreted as the time between the ith and the $(i-1)$th occurrence or the interarrival time of the ith occurrence.

We shall assume that before the process is observed the occurrence times t_i and the interarrival times z_i are uncertain and accordingly can be treated as random variables $\tilde{t}_i$ and $\tilde{z}_i$. For the process to be of the so-called *Poisson* type means by definition that the rv's $\tilde{z}_1, \tilde{z}_2, \ldots$ are *independent and identically distributed* (iid), each with df

$$f_e(z \mid \lambda) = \lambda e^{-\lambda z}, \qquad z > 0, \lambda > 0. \tag{15.1}$$

This is known as the *exponential* df with parameter λ. (See section 9.10.) It has mean $1/\lambda$ and variance $1/\lambda^2$, by (9.96) and (9.97) respectively. The parameter λ will be called the *intensity* of the process and will play a role that is analogous to the parameter p of the Bernoulli process.

Sections 15.1.2 and 15.1.4 discuss two assumptions each of which leads to the exponential df. Section 15.1.3 summarizes and formalizes the definition of the Poisson process. Section 15.1.5 relates the Poisson and Bernoulli processes. Section 15.1.6 introduces the prior distribution that is convenient to use when λ is unknown. A preview of the rest of the chapter is given in section 15.1.7.

15.1.2 The Exponential Distribution

A very important property of a Poisson process is that each interarrival time $\tilde{z}$ satisfies

* Sections 9.10 and 9.11 should be reviewed in preparation for this chapter. The contents of this chapter are not used subsequently.

$$P(\tilde{z} > \xi + z | \tilde{z} > \xi) = P(\tilde{z} > z). \tag{15.2}$$

This says that the conditional probability that more than z *additional* "minutes" will elapse before the next event is independent of the number ξ of minutes that have already elapsed since the last event. This implies in turn that the distribution of the number of minutes from any arbitrarily chosen point of time to the next event is the same as the distribution of the number of minutes between two adjacent events.

To show that the independence of past history asserted by (15.2) follows from (15.1), we write

$$P(\tilde{z} > \xi + z | \tilde{z} > \xi) = \frac{\int_{\xi+z}^{\infty} e^{-\lambda u} \lambda \, du}{\int_{\xi}^{\infty} e^{-\lambda u} \lambda \, du} = \frac{e^{-\lambda(\xi+z)}}{e^{-\lambda\xi}} = e^{-\lambda z} = P(\tilde{z} > z).$$

Conversely, this independence of past history is a *unique* property of the Poisson process among all processes with continuous, iid interarrival times. The rest of this subsection is devoted to proving this.

Let $G(z)$ denote an as yet undetermined right-tail cumulative function for which (15.2) holds, that is,

$$\frac{G(\xi + z)}{G(\xi)} = G(z), \qquad G(0) = 1, \qquad G(\infty) = 0.$$

If we define

$$h(a) \equiv \log G(a),$$

these conditions imply that

$$h(\xi + z) = h(z) + h(\xi)$$

for all positive z and ξ. It then follows from the lemma below that $h(\cdot)$ must be of the form

$$h(z) = -\lambda z$$

for some $\lambda \geq 0$. Consequently

$$G(z) = e^{-\lambda z}$$

and since $G(\infty) = 0$, the parameter $\lambda > 0$. The result (15.1) then follows from the fact that the density is

$$-\frac{d}{dz} G(z) = \lambda e^{-\lambda z}.$$

Lemma Let h be a real-valued function defined on the interval $[0, \infty]$ such that

(1) $h(\xi + z) = h(\xi) + h(z)$ for all ξ, z,

(2) h is monotonic nonincreasing in x.

Then h is of the form

$h(z) = -\lambda z$ for some $\lambda \geq 0$.

Note The identification numbers on the extreme left are used for this lemma only.

Proof Using (1) to write

$h(mz) = h([m-1]z + z) = h([m-1]z) + h(z)$,

we get for integer m

(3) $h(mz) = mh(z)$.

Using (3) to write for integer n

$h(z) = h(n[\frac{1}{n}z]) = nh(\frac{1}{n}z)$,

we get

(4) $h(\frac{1}{n}z) = \frac{1}{n}h(z)$.

From (3) and (4) we have for integer m and n

(5) $h(\frac{m}{n}z) = \frac{m}{n}h(z)$.

Letting $z = 1$ and $h(1) = -\lambda$ we get from (5) that for any positive rational y

(6) $h(y) = -\lambda y$.

Since h is nonincreasing by hypothesis, $\lambda \geq 0$; since h is monotonic, (6) is true for all positive real y.

15.1.3 Definition of a Poisson Process

We now summarize and formalize the preceding subsections by giving a formal definition of a Poisson process.

Consider a process which generates "events" or "occurrences" at times $\tilde{t}_1, \tilde{t}_2, \ldots$; let $t_0 \equiv 0$ and let $\tilde{z}_i \equiv \tilde{t}_i - \tilde{t}_{i-1}$ for $i = 1, 2, \ldots$. The process is said to be a *Poisson process with parameter* λ if the rv's $\tilde{z}_1, \tilde{z}_2, \ldots$ are independent, and each has the common df $f_e(\cdot|\lambda)$.

In the light of the discussion of section 15.1.2, we can think of the Poisson process as characterized by the following condition. For any given time t the distribution of the waiting time until the next occurrence does *not* depend on the history of the process—that is, on the time t, on the number of occurrences before time t, or on the time of the last occurrence.

Generalizing the Role of Time

Although we defined the Poisson process in terms of an underlying *time* continuum it is sometimes appropriate to interpret the process in terms of an underlying *spatial* continuum, as illustrated in the following example.

Consider a machine which insulates electric wire and which produces pinhole defects here and there. After carefully investigating the process on several previous days and failing to discover any "assignable cause" for defects—any cause that produces defects in predictable places—the decision maker feels that, as far as today's run is concerned, he would at any position assign a distribution to the uncertain *distance* until the next defect, which is independent of the distance from the last defect or the number or placement of the earlier defects.

15.1.4 An Alternate Characterization

For a Poisson process with parameter λ the probability of obtaining at least one occurrence in time t to $t + \Delta$ is, by (15.2),

$$\int_0^\Delta \lambda e^{-\lambda z}\,dz = 1 - e^{-\lambda\Delta} = 1 - \left[1 - \lambda\Delta + \frac{(\lambda\Delta)^2}{2!} + \ldots\right]$$

$$= \lambda\Delta + \{\text{terms of higher order}\}.$$

The parameter λ can now be directly but somewhat imprecisely interpreted as follows: for a Poisson process with parameter λ, the probability that there will be an occurrence in the next *small* time interval Δ is approximately $\lambda\Delta$. From this interpretation it should now be clear why λ is called the "intensity" of the process.

Using this interpretation of λ let us now investigate the probability of obtaining *no* occurrences in time t to $t + T$, where T is not necessarily assumed to be small. Dividing this interval into a large number n of equally spaced subintervals, the probability of no occurrence in any particular one of these subintervals is approximately

$$1 - \frac{\lambda T + a(n)}{n}$$

where $a(n)$ is a "correction-for-approximation" term and is such that $\lim_{n\to\infty} a(n)/n = 0$. Since these n events are independent in a Poisson process, the probability of *no* occurrence in time t to $t + T$ is given by

$$\lim_{n\to\infty}\left[1-\frac{\lambda T+a(n)}{n}\right]^n = e^{-\lambda T},$$

which agrees with the expression $G_e(T|\lambda)$ given in (9.94).

We now give an alternate characterization of a Poisson process with parameter λ. It is a process which generates occurrences from time to time and is such that for any given time t and *any past history of occurrences before* t,

1. the probability of a single occurrence in time t to $t + \Delta$ is $\lambda\Delta + o(\Delta)$, and

2. the probability of more than one occurrence in time t to $t + \Delta$ is $o(\Delta)$, where $o(\Delta)$ denotes any expression such that $o(\Delta)/\Delta \to 0$ as $\Delta \to 0$.

15.1.5 An Approximating Bernoulli Process

A Poisson process with parameter λ can be approximated or simulated by a Bernoulli process. To do so, choose some time interval Δ that is sufficiently small so that up to the approximation one is willing to tolerate, the probability of two or more occurrences in any particular interval is negligible and can be ignored. Now consider a Bernoulli process with parameter $\lambda\Delta$, which generates occurrences (successes) or nonoccurrences (failures). If the kth Bernoulli trial yields an occurrence, then this is interpreted as an occurrence in time period $k\Delta - \Delta$ to $k\Delta$, and similarly for nonoccurrences.

15.1.6 The Gamma-1 and the Poisson Distributions

In an analysis of the Poisson process with a known parameter λ, two rv's play a central role: (1) the rv $\tilde{t}_r$, which denotes the time until the rth occurrence, and (2) the rv $\tilde{r}_t$, which denotes the number of occurrences in a time period t. In this chapter starting from section 15.2 we shall be concerned with the case where λ is unknown. In prior to posterior analysis we shall not make any use of the distributions of $\tilde{t}_r$ or of $\tilde{r}_t$; in preposterior analysis, however, it will be helpful to have these distributions.

As we shall soon see, the distributions of the rv's $\tilde{t}_r$ and $\tilde{r}_t$ are closely related and either one of these distributions can be obtained from the other. We shall first obtain the distribution of $\tilde{t}_r$ from which we shall derive the distribution of $\tilde{r}_t$. For the sake of completeness and because it is instructive, we shall also independently derive the distribution of $\tilde{r}_t$ and from this derive the distribution of $\tilde{t}_r$.

We shall show that:

$\tilde{t}_r$ is a gamma-1 rv with parameter (r, λ)

and

$\tilde{r}_t$ is a Poisson rv with parameter $t\lambda$.

Proofs[1] In deriving the distribution of $\tilde{t}_r$ we shall need the following lemma.

Lemma If the rv's $\tilde{y}_1, \tilde{y}_2, \ldots, \tilde{y}_n$ are independent and if $\tilde{y}_i$ has a gamma-1 df with parameter (ρ_i, τ), then the rv

$$\tilde{s} \equiv \tilde{y}_1 + \tilde{y}_2 + \cdots + \tilde{y}_n$$

is a gamma-1 rv with parameter $(\sum_{i=0}^{n} \rho_i, \tau)$.

Proof We prove the result for $n = 2$. The extension to an arbitrary n then follows by a simple induction argument. From the formula (13.49) for the df of the sum of two independent rv's, we get for $n = 2$ that the df $g(\cdot)$ of $\tilde{s} = \tilde{y}_1 + \tilde{y}_2$ is given by

$$\begin{aligned} g(s) &= \int_0^s f_{\gamma 1}(s - y_1 | \rho_2, \tau) f_{\gamma 1}(y_1 | \rho_1, \tau)\, dy_1 \\ &= \int_0^s \frac{e^{-(s-y_1)\tau}[(s - y_1)\tau]^{\rho_2 - 1}}{(\rho_2 - 1)!} \tau \frac{e^{-y_1\tau}(y_1\tau)^{\rho_1 - 1}}{(\rho_1 - 1)!} \tau\, dy_1 \\ &= \frac{e^{-s\tau}}{(\rho_1 + \rho_2 - 1)!} \int_0^s \frac{(\rho_1 + \rho_2 - 1)!}{(\rho_1 - 1)!(\rho_2 - 1)} (s\tau - y_1\tau)^{\rho_2 - 1}(y_1\tau)^{\rho_1 - 1}\tau^2\, dy_1 \\ &= \frac{e^{-s\tau}(s\tau)^{\rho_1 + \rho_2 - 1}\tau}{(\rho_1 + \rho_2 - 1)!} \int_0^s \frac{(\rho_1 + \rho_2 - 1)!}{(\rho_1 - 1)!(\rho_2 - 1)!} \left(1 - \frac{y_1}{s}\right)^{\rho_2 - 1} \left(\frac{y_1}{s}\right)^{\rho_1 - 1} \frac{1}{s} dy_1. \end{aligned}$$

Substituting herein

$$x = y_1/s, \qquad dx = dy_1/s,$$

we obtain

$$\begin{aligned} g(s) &= \frac{e^{s\tau}(s\tau)^{\rho_1 + \rho_2 - 1}\tau}{(\rho_1 + \rho_2 - 1)!} \int_0^1 \frac{(\rho_1 + \rho_2 - 1)!}{(\rho_1 - 1)!(\rho_2 - 1)!} x^{\rho_1 - 1}(1 - x)^{\rho_2 - 1}\, dx \\ &= f_{\gamma 1}(s | \rho_1 + \rho_2, \tau) F_\beta(1 | \rho_1, \rho_1 + \rho_2) = f_{\gamma 1}(s | \rho_1 + \rho_2, \tau). \end{aligned}$$ ■

Distribution of $\tilde{t}_r$

As before, denote the interarrival times by $\tilde{z}_1, \tilde{z}_2, \ldots$. We then have

$$\tilde{t}_r = \tilde{z}_1 + \tilde{z}_2 + \cdots + \tilde{z}_r.$$

1. The reader might choose at this point to skip the proofs in the remainder of the subsection and proceed directly to section 15.1.7.

The rv's $\tilde{z}_1, \ldots, \tilde{z}_r$ are independent and each has the df

$f_e(z|\lambda) = f_{\gamma 1}(z|1, \lambda)$.

Hence, by the above lemma, $\tilde{t}_r$ *has a gamma-1 df with parameter* (r, λ).

Distribution of $\tilde{r}_t$ Derived from the Distribution of $\tilde{t}_r$

Since there will be fewer than r events in length of time t if and only if the length of time until the rth event is greater than t,

$$P(\tilde{r}_t < r) = P(\tilde{t}_r > t) = G_{\gamma 1}(t|r, \lambda),$$

from which it follows that

$$P(\tilde{r}_t = r) = P(\tilde{r}_t < r + 1) - P(\tilde{r}_t < r) = G_{\gamma 1}(t|r + 1, \lambda) - G_{\gamma 1}(t|r, \lambda),$$

and by the lemma given immediately below we conclude that

$$P(\tilde{r}_t = r) = \frac{e^{-\lambda t}(\lambda t)^r}{r!} \equiv f_p(r|\lambda t). \tag{15.3}$$

Lemma

$$G_{\gamma 1}(t|r + 1, \lambda) = \frac{e^{-\lambda t}(\lambda t)^r}{r!} + G_{\gamma 1}(t|r, \lambda). \tag{15.4}$$

Proof Starting from

$$G_{\gamma 1}(t|r + 1, \lambda) = \int_t^\infty \frac{e^{-\lambda u}(\lambda u)^r}{r!} \lambda \, du$$

we integrate by parts as follows:

differentiating $\frac{(\lambda u)^r}{r!}$, we have $\frac{(\lambda u)^{r-1}}{(r-1)!} \lambda \, du$;

integrating $e^{-\lambda u} \lambda \, du$, we have $-e^{-\lambda u}$;

and combining the above, we get

$$G_{\gamma 1}(t|r + 1, \lambda) = \left. \frac{e^{-\lambda u}(\lambda u)^r}{r!} \right|_t^\infty + \int_t^\infty \frac{e^{-\lambda u}(\lambda u)^{r-1}}{(r-1)!} \lambda \, du,$$

from which the lemma follows. ■

Very shortly we shall make use of the following corollary to the above lemma.

Corollary For integral r,

$$G_{\gamma 1}(t|r, \lambda) = \sum_{j=0}^{r-1} \frac{e^{-\lambda t}(\lambda t)^j}{j!}. \tag{15.5}$$

Proof Using the lemma successively gives

$$G_{\gamma 1}(t|r,\lambda) = \frac{e^{-\lambda t}(\lambda t)^{r-1}}{(r-1)!} + G_{\gamma 1}(t|r-1,\lambda)$$

$$= \sum_{j=r-2}^{r-1} \frac{e^{-\lambda t}(\lambda t)^j}{j!} + G_{\gamma 1}(t|r-2,\lambda)$$

$$\vdots$$

$$= \sum_{j=1}^{r-1} \frac{e^{-\lambda t}(\lambda t)^j}{j!} + G_{\gamma 1}(t|1,\lambda)$$

$$= \sum_{j=0}^{r-1} \frac{e^{-\lambda t}(\lambda t)^j}{j!}.$$ ■

Direct Derivation of the Distribution of $\tilde{r}_t$

Consider the alternate characterization of the Poisson process given in section 15.1.4 and let $P_r(t)$ denote the probability of exactly r successes in length of time t. We then have, for $r = 0$,

$$P_0(t+\Delta) = P_0(t)[1 - \lambda\Delta - o(\Delta)]$$

or

$$\frac{P_0(t+\Delta) - P_0(t)}{\Delta} = -\lambda P_0(t) - \frac{o(\Delta)}{\Delta},$$

and taking limits as $\Delta \to 0$, we have

$$\frac{d}{dt} P_0(t) = -\lambda P_0(t). \tag{15.6}$$

From this requirement on P_0 and the initial condition that $P_0(0) = 1$, we conclude that

$$P_0(t) = e^{-\lambda t}. \tag{15.7}$$

For $r > 1$, we have

$$P_r(t+\Delta) = P_r(t)[1 - \lambda\Delta - o(\Delta)] + P_{r-1}(t)\lambda\Delta + o(\Delta) \tag{15.8}$$

or

$$\frac{P_r(t+\Delta) - P_r(t)}{\Delta} = -\lambda P_r(t) + \lambda P_{r-1}(t) + o(\Delta)/\Delta,$$

and taking limits as $\Delta \to 0$, we have

$$\frac{d}{dt}P_r(t) = -\lambda P_r(t) + \lambda P_{r-1}(t). \tag{15.9}$$

Now let $r = 1$ and substitute the value of P_0. From the differential requirement on P_1 and the initial condition that $P_1(0) = 0$, we conclude that

$$P_1(t) = e^{-\lambda t}(\lambda t).$$

Now let $r = 2$ and substitute the value of P_1. From the differential requirement on P_2 and the initial condition that $P_2(0) = 0$, we conclude that

$$P_2(t) = e^{-\lambda t}\frac{(\lambda t)^2}{2}.$$

Following this same procedure we get

$$P_3(t) = e^{-\lambda t}\frac{(\lambda t)^3}{3}$$

and finally we can verify by induction that

$$P(\tilde{r}_t = r) \equiv P_r(t) = \frac{e^{-\lambda t}(\lambda t)^r}{r!} \equiv f_P(r|\lambda t). \tag{15.10}$$

Distribution of $\tilde{t}_r$ Derived from the Distribution of $\tilde{r}_t$

As we argued before, since there will be fewer than r events in length of time t if and only if the length of time until the rth event is greater than t,

$$P(\tilde{t}_r > t) = P(\tilde{r}_t < r) = \textstyle\sum_{j=0}^{r-1} \dfrac{e^{-\lambda t}(\lambda t)^j}{j!}$$

From (15.5) we therefore conclude that

$$P(\tilde{t}_r > t) = G_{\gamma 1}(t|r, \lambda). \tag{15.11}$$

15.1.7 Preview of the Chapter

The remaining sections of this chapter will deal with the case where the parameter λ is unknown. In section 15.2 we examine the sampling distribution of a Poisson process which runs for a period of time t conditional upon a given value of λ. Next the likelihood function for a given sample outcome is considered and it is shown that the likelihood function depends on the sample outcome only through the pair (r, t) where r is the number of occurrences in time t; in this sense the pair (r, t) is a "sufficient" summary statistic for the sample outcome. (The appendix to chapter 20 further discusses sufficiency.)

In section 15.3 we apply Bayes' Theorem to find the posterior df of $\tilde{\lambda}$ corresponding to a given prior df of $\tilde{\lambda}$ after the process has been observed to run for a period of time t. As in the discussion of section 11.3.5 for the Bernoulli process we shall see that the shape of the posterior df is given by the product of the likelihood function L and the prior df f'. If f' is gentle, then, as we have seen before, the posterior df will approximately be the likelihood function suitably scaled so that the area under it is unity.

Recall that in sampling from a Bernoulli process, if the prior df of $\tilde{p}$ is taken from a beta family, the posterior df is also in the beta family and there is a simple algebraic formula connecting the prior parameters (r', n'), the sufficient statistics (r, n), and the posterior parameters (r'', n''). In section 15.4 we show an analogous result for sampling from a Poisson process: if a priori $\tilde{\lambda}$ is gamma-1, then there is a simple algebraic formula connecting the prior parameters (r', t'), the sufficient statistics (r, t) of the sample, and the posterior parameters (r'', t'').

In section 15.5 we investigate the sensitivity of the posterior df of $\tilde{\lambda}$ to the choice of the prior. Once again we bring up the provocative notion of "complete ignorance" and criticize its indiscriminate use. In section 15.6 we give the *un*conditional sampling distribution of $\tilde{r}$ and the distribution of the as yet unknown posterior mean $\tilde{\bar{\lambda}}''$ corresponding to a sample-observation period t, which is needed for preposterior analysis. In section 15.7 we consider terminal and preposterior analyses for decision problems which involve the unknown intensity of a Poisson process. In sections 15.8, 15.9, and 15.10 we specialize to our three prototype decision problems: infinite-action with quadratic loss, infinite-action with linear loss, and two-action with linear values. In section 15.11 we show how to select parameters of a gamma-1 df in order to fit judgments. Section 15.12 discusses the Poisson approximation of a Bernoulli process with small p.

15.2 Conditional Sampling Distributions

15.2.1 Conditional Probability of Sample Outcome Given λ

We consider a Poisson process with parameter λ and denote the sequence of times of occurrence by $t_1, t_2, \ldots$ and the successive interarrival times by $z_1, z_2, \ldots$.

We shall prove in this subsection that if we observe a Poisson process with *known* intensity parameter λ for a period of time t, the probability that there will be exactly r occurrences with interarrival times "approximately" equal to $z_1, z_2, \ldots, z_r$ is

$$P\{\tilde{z}_1 \doteq z_1, \ldots, \tilde{z}_r \doteq z_r, \tilde{z}_{r+1} > \zeta | \lambda\} = \Delta^r \lambda^r e^{-\lambda t}, \qquad (15.12a)$$

where Δ is some very small number and we use the symbol $\tilde{z}_i \doteq z_i$ to mean $z_i - \frac{\Delta}{2} \leq \tilde{z}_i \leq z_i + \frac{\Delta}{2}$ and where ζ is defined to be the number such that

$$t = z_1 + \cdots + z_r + \zeta. \tag{15.12b}$$

Observe that the probability in (15.12a) depends on $(z_1, \ldots, z_r, \zeta)$ only through the numbers (r, t).

Discussion and Proof of (15.12) Although the unknown outcomes $\tilde{z}_1$, $\tilde{z}_2, \ldots$ are continuous rv's, we shall assume that we can only observe or determine their values to a fixed number of decimal places. This assumption not only is realistic but also enables us to avoid discussing the theory of joint density functions for several rv's at this point.

Let $z_1, z_2, \ldots, z_r$ be numbers which all terminate at the kth decimal place (i.e., which are of the form $y + a_1 10^{-1} + a_2 10^{-2} + \cdots + a_k 10^{-k}$ where y is an integer and where a_is are integers from 0 to 9 inclusive), and let $\Delta \equiv 10^{-k}$. The probability that $\tilde{z}_i$ is observed to be z_i (rounding to the kth decimal place) for a given λ is

$$P\left(z_i - \frac{\Delta}{2} \leq z_i \leq z_i + \frac{\Delta}{2}\middle|\lambda\right) = \int_{z_i-(\Delta/2)}^{z_i+(\Delta/2)} f_e(w|\lambda)\,dw \quad .$$

$$= \Delta f_e(z_i|\lambda) + [\text{terms of higher order than } \Delta].$$

The event that $(z_i - \frac{\Delta}{2} \leq \tilde{z}_i \leq z_i + \frac{\Delta}{2})$ will be written as $\tilde{z}_i \doteq z_i$ and since in the sequel all terms of higher order will eventually be ignored, we have for all practical purposes

$$P(\tilde{z}_i \doteq z_i|\lambda) = \Delta f_e(z_i|\lambda). \tag{15.13a}$$

We now assume that we have observed that $\tilde{z}_1 \doteq z_1, \tilde{z}_2 \doteq z_2, \ldots, \tilde{z}_r \doteq z_r$, and finally that $\tilde{z}_{r+1} > \zeta$ (i. e., the $(r+1)$th interarrival time has not occurred on or before a time interval of ζ). Now the conditional probability, given λ that the process will generate an interval of length $\tilde{z} > \zeta$ is

$$\int_{\zeta}^{\infty} e^{-\lambda u}\lambda\,du = e^{-\lambda\zeta}. \tag{15.13b}$$

Since the rv's are conditionally independent given λ, we have from (15.13)

$$P(\tilde{z}_1 \doteq z_1, \ldots, \tilde{z}_r \doteq z_r, \tilde{z}_{r+1} > \zeta|\lambda) = \Delta^r \prod_{i=1}^{r} f_e(z_i|\lambda)e^{-\lambda\zeta}, \tag{15.14}$$

substituting the analytical expression for f_e we get

$$P(\tilde{z}_1 \doteq z_1, \ldots, \tilde{z}_r \doteq z_r, z_{r+1} > \zeta|\lambda) = \Delta^r\lambda^r e^{-\lambda t}, \tag{15.15a}$$

where

$$t = z_1 + \cdots + z_r + \zeta. \tag{15.15b}$$

In words this says, among other things, that if we observe the process for a period of time t, the probability that there will be exactly r occurrences with interarrival times approximately equal to $z_1, z_2, \ldots, z_r$ does *not* depend on the particular values of $z_1, z_2, \ldots, z_r$, but only on the number r.

15.2.2 Likelihood Function of λ

The expression $P(\tilde{z}_1 \doteq z_1, \ldots, \tilde{z}_r \doteq z_r, \tilde{z}_{r+1} > \zeta | \lambda)$ can be looked at in two ways: when viewed as a function of $z \equiv (z_1, \ldots, z_r, \zeta)$ for a fixed λ, it is called the joint probability function at z for λ; when viewed as a function of λ for a fixed z it is called the *likelihood* of λ for the sample outcome z and written $L(\lambda|z)$. From (15.12) we observe that by (9.102)

$$L(\lambda|z) = K \frac{e^{-\lambda t}(\lambda t)^r}{r!} t = K f_{\gamma 1}(\lambda | r + 1, t), \tag{15.16a}$$

where

$$K \equiv \Delta^r r! t^{-(r+1)} \tag{15.16b}$$

does not depend on the parameter λ. We therefore conclude that the likelihood function $L(\cdot|z)$ for a given sample z when plotted as a function of λ is merely a constant times a gamma-1 df with parameter $(r + 1, t)$. The shapes of some gamma-1 df's are exhibited in figure 9.8.

15.3 Posterior Distribution of $\tilde{\lambda}$

15.3.1 The Posterior as a Product of the Likelihood Function and the Prior

Let the prior distributing function of $\tilde{\lambda}$ be denoted by f', which we assume is quite general for the time being; let the posterior distributing function of $\tilde{\lambda}$ given $z = (z_1, \ldots, z_r, \zeta)$ be denoted by $f''(\lambda|z)$. Then by Bayes' theorem (10.21) we obtain

$$f''(\lambda|z) \propto L(\lambda|z) f'(\lambda), \tag{15.17}$$

which says that the shape of the posterior distributing function is given by the product of the likelihood function and the prior distributing function. From (15.16) this becomes

$$f''(\lambda|z) = C' f_{\gamma 1}(\lambda | r + 1, t) f'(\lambda) \tag{15.18}$$

where C' is a function of z but *not* of λ.

15.3.2 The Posterior for a "Gentle" Prior

From (15.18) we observe that if the prior df f' is "flat" or fairly "gentle," then $f''(\lambda|z)$ will have approximately the same shape as $f_{\gamma 1}(\lambda|r+1, t)$. From figure 9.8 we see that for a fixed value of r/t, as t increases the likelihood function $f_{\gamma 1}(\lambda|r+1, t)$ becomes tighter and tighter and therefore, from a comparative point of view, the prior df f' can be thought of as becoming more and more gentle with respect to the likelihood function as t increases.

15.3.3 Sufficiency of the Statistic (r, t)

Because the expression (15.18) for the posterior distributing function of $\tilde{\lambda}$ depends on the sample outcome $z = (z_1, \ldots, z_r, \zeta)$ only through the number of occurrences r and the total time $t = z_1 + \cdots + z_r + \zeta$ the process is observed, the pair (r, t) is a *sufficient* description of the sample outcome of a Poisson process. We shall also say that the pair (r, t) is the *sufficient statistic* of the sample. As far as making inferences or decisions about λ is concerned, a statistician who is given full information about the sample outcome $(z_1, \ldots, z_r, \zeta)$ is no better off than a statistician who is only given the summary information (r, t)—provided, and this proviso is crucial, that it is known that the observations $(z_1, \ldots, z_r, \zeta)$ are the outcome of a Poisson process with unknown parameter λ.

15.4 The Gamma-1 Family of Priors

15.4.1 Introduction

In the remaining sections of this chapter we shall consider the case where the unknown parameter $\tilde{\lambda}$ of a Poisson process is given a prior density function in the gamma-1 family. We remind the reader that this family has two adjustable parameters ρ and τ and that by appropriately choosing these parameters one can obtain prior densities of a wide variety of shapes. This makes it possible in many situations to choose a gamma-1 prior which matches more or less one's prior judgments about $\tilde{\lambda}$. Furthermore, if $\tilde{\lambda}$ is given a gamma-1 prior density, then after observing the outcome of a Poisson process the posterior density will also be in the gamma-1 family.

15.4.2 Prior to Posterior within the Gamma-1 Family

The gamma-1 family of prior distributions is most convenient to use when working with a Poisson process because of the following simple but important theorem:

Theorem If the prior df of $\tilde{\lambda}$ is gamma-1 with parameters (r', t') and if observation of a particular outcome of a Poisson process results in r occurrences in an interval of time t, then the posterior df of $\tilde{\lambda}$ is also gamma-1 with parameters

$$r'' = r' + r \quad \text{and} \quad t'' = t' + t. \tag{15.19}$$

Proof By (15.18) we have

$$f''(\lambda|z) = C' f_{\gamma 1}(\lambda|r + 1, t) f_{\gamma 1}(\lambda|r', t')$$

$$= C' \frac{e^{-\lambda t}(\lambda t)^r}{r!} t \frac{e^{-\lambda t'}(\lambda t')^{r'-1}}{(r' - 1)!} t' = C'' e^{-\lambda(t'+t)} \lambda^{r'+r-1},$$

where C'' is a factor which does not depend on λ. Since the area under $f''(\cdot|z)$ must be unity, the constant C'' according to (9.102) must be

$$C'' = \frac{(t' + t)^{r'+r}}{(r' + r - 1)!}$$

and the proof is complete.

Not only is it easy to revise a gamma-1 prior df in the light of sample results from a Poisson process, but it is then possible to use existing tables of the standardized gamma df (section 9.11.2) to find posterior probabilities for such events as $(\tilde{\lambda} \leq \lambda_0)$, $(\lambda_1 \leq \tilde{\lambda} \leq \lambda_2)$; furthermore, the expectations of some simple functions taken with respect to a gamma-1 df lead to results which are easily computed and even tabulated (section 9.11.3), and this will be of great importance when we turn our attention to decision problems that depend on the unknown parameter of a Poisson process.

15.5 Sensitivity of Posterior Distributions to Prior Parameters of the Family

15.5.1 Qualitative Conclusions

The points we wish to make in this section agree so closely in philosophy and in technical details with the discussion in sections 11.4.3 and 11.4.4 on sensitivity issues in the Bernoulli process that the reader is directed at this point merely to reread those sections and substitute "Poisson" for "Bernoulli," $\tilde{\lambda}$ for $\tilde{p}$, and t for n. Some of the numbers in the examples will change because we are dealing with a gamma-1 df instead of a beta df, but all the qualitative conclusions will remain. For sake of emphasis, however, we explicitly point out the following:

Situations in which the *exact* specification of the decision maker's judgments is likely to be unnecessary are those in which the analysis of the decision problem will rest not directly on the judgmental distribution but on a posterior distribution that combines a substantial amount of sample or experimental evidence with the judgmental distribution.

In the case where t is much larger than t' the posterior may be largely determined in shape by r' if r is small. Hence, it is *not* generally correct to assert that the posterior will be largely determined by the sample if t is large relative to t'.

Although there is no "correct" way of translating "complete ignorance" about a true λ into a particular prior distribution of $\tilde{\lambda}$, the decision maker (DM) *can* assess the distribution of $\tilde{\lambda}$ very roughly when any distribution the DM would be willing to consider is "gentle" relative to the likelihood function of a sample which has already been taken. When this condition is *not* met, the analysis of a decision problem may very well be sensitive to changes in the judgmental distribution of $\tilde{\lambda}$, and the DM will have to accept this fact and live with it.

15.5.2 Limiting Behavior of the Prior Distribution

It is interesting to investigate the limiting behavior of a gamma-1 df with parameter (r', t') when both r' and t' approach zero. If we hold r'/t' equal to some constant value c, say, and if we let both r' and t' approach zero, then by (9.109) the mean $\bar{\lambda}'$ of $\tilde{\lambda}$ remains fixed at c, and by (9.110) the variance $\breve{\lambda}'$ of $\tilde{\lambda}$ approaches infinity. Furthermore, in this case it is not difficult to show (cf. *ASDT*, p. 278) that the probability under df $f_{\gamma 1}(\cdot|r', t')$ becomes more and more concentrated toward $\lambda = 0$; more precisely, for any value λ_0, however small,

$$\lim_{\left\{\substack{r'\to 0\\ t'\to 0\\ r'/t'=c}\right\}} F_{\gamma 1}(\lambda_0|r', t') = 1. \tag{15.20}$$

Intuitively, these results mean that as r' and t' approach zero in a fixed proportion, more and more mass is concentrated near $\lambda = 0$ and smaller and smaller amounts of remaining mass are distributed further and further away from $\lambda = 0$ which accounts for the fact that $\breve{\lambda}' \to \infty$.

Suppose now that $\tilde{\lambda}$ is given a gamma-1 prior with parameters (r', t') and a sufficient statistic (r, t) is observed. By (15.19) the posterior parameters are $r'' = r' + r$ and $t'' = t' + t$. If $r' \to 0$ and $t' \to 0$, then $r'' \to r$ and $t'' \to t$. If, on the other hand, a flat prior[2] is chosen, then by (15.18) $r'' = r + 1$ and $t'' = t$. It is not immediately apparent how to account for the

2. Strictly speaking a flat prior from 0 to ∞ is not well defined. To circumvent this point, consider rectangular prior from 0 to Λ and then let $\Lambda \to \infty$. As $\Lambda \to \infty$, the *posterior* df of $\tilde{\lambda}$ approaches a gamma-1 df with parameter $(r + 1, t)$.

difference of the "+1" term in the expression for r''. The following observation is helpful in this regard: for any two values λ_1 and λ_2 it can readily be shown that

$$\lim_{\substack{r' \to 0 \\ t' \to 0}} \frac{f_{\gamma 1}(\lambda_1 | r', t')}{f_{\gamma 1}(\lambda_2 | r', t')} = \frac{\lambda_2}{\lambda_1}, \tag{15.21}$$

so that as far as prior to posterior analysis is concerned the effect of letting $r' \to 0$ and $t' \to 0$ is like choosing the function $1/\lambda$ as the prior df f' in the expression (15.18). This accounts for the "+1" (or "−1", depending on your orientation).

15.6 Preposterior Distribution Theory

15.6.1 Poisson and Gamma Sampling

If a sample is taken from a Poisson process in such a way that the value of the statistic t is predetermined and the value of $\tilde{r}$ is left to chance, the sampling will be called *Poisson*. In other words, Poisson sampling consists of observing the process over a predetermined amount of time, length, or other dimension, and counting the number of events which occur. The analogous kind of sampling for the Bernoulli process was called *binomial* sampling.

If a sample is taken from a Poisson process in such a way that the value of the statistic r is predetermined and the value of $\tilde{t}$ is left to chance, the sampling will be called *gamma*. In other words, gamma sampling consists of observing the process until the rth event occurs and measuring the time, length, or other dimension which "elapses" up to this point. The analogous kind of sampling for the Bernoulli process was called *Pascal* sampling.

In the remaining part of this chapter we shall consider only the case of Poisson sampling. The distribution theory for gamma sampling can be found in *ASDT*, section 10.2.

In preposterior analysis where a "sample size" t is prescribed, we shall require the *marginal* mf of the as yet unknown sufficient statistic $\tilde{r}$; this is needed for an analysis of moves 1 and 2 on the decision tree (see figure 6.1).

15.6.2 Distribution of $\tilde{r}$

Conditional Distribution of $\tilde{r}$ Given λ

If a sample of size t is drawn by Poisson sampling from a Poisson process with a given λ, the conditional distribution of $\tilde{r}$, as shown in section 15.1.6, is Poisson with parameter λt:

$$P(\tilde{r} = r|\lambda, t) = f_P(r|\lambda t) \equiv \frac{e^{-\lambda t}(\lambda t)^r}{r!}. \tag{15.22}$$

Unconditional Distribution of $\tilde{r}$

If a sample of size t is drawn by Poisson sampling from a Poisson process whose intensity is a random variable $\tilde{\lambda}$ having a gamma-1 density with parameter (r', t'), the unconditional distribution of $\tilde{r}$ is *negative-binomial* with parameter $(t/(t + t'), r')$, as defined by (9.126):

$$\begin{aligned} P(\tilde{r} = r|r', t', t) &= f_{nb}\left(r\,\middle|\,\frac{t}{t + t'}, r'\right) \\ &\equiv \frac{(r + r' - 1)!}{r!(r' - 1)!}\left(\frac{t}{t + t'}\right)^r \left(\frac{t'}{t + t'}\right)^{r'}. \end{aligned} \tag{15.23}$$

Proof Since

$$P(\tilde{r} = r|r', t', t) = \int_0^\infty f_P(r|\lambda t) f_{\gamma 1}(\lambda|r', t')\, d\lambda,$$

the result follows from (9.127).

15.6.3 Probabilistic Prediction

We now pose and answer the following problem: Consider a Poisson process with unknown intensity λ; let $\tilde{\lambda}$ be given a gamma-1 prior df with parameter (r', t'); let the process be observed to give r_1 occurrences in time t_1. What is the distribution of the unknown number of occurrences $\tilde{r}_2$ in the next period of time t_2?

The problem posed above has a simple answer in terms of the distribution theory we have already developed. After the sample has been observed to yield the sufficient statistic (r_1, t_1) the parameters of the df of $\tilde{\lambda}$ are updated from (r', t') to $(r' + r_1, t' + t_1)$. Now as far as the future of the process is concerned the current distribution of $\tilde{\lambda}$ is gamma-1 with parameter $(r' + r_1, t' + t_1)$ and the problem merely asks for the unconditional (or marginal) distribution of the unknown number of occurrences in a Poisson sample of size t_2. We conclude therefore that the distribution of $\tilde{r}_2$ is negative-binomial with parameter $(t_2/(t' + t_1 + t_2), r' + r_1)$.

Finally, we remark that section 9.13.3 contains formulas for the expectation, variance, partial expectation, and linear-loss integrals of a negative-binomial rv, and that these formulas may be of considerable use in analyzing a decision problem where losses depend on the uncertain number of occurrences in a Poisson process.

15.6.4 Distribution of $\tilde{\tilde{\lambda}}''$

If the prior distribution of $\tilde{\lambda}$ is gamma-1 with parameter (r', t') and if a sample then yields a sufficient statistic (r, t), formulas (15.19) and (9.109) show that the mean of the posterior distribution of $\tilde{\lambda}$ will be

$$\bar{\lambda}'' = \frac{r''}{t''} = \frac{r + r'}{t + t'}. \tag{15.24}$$

It follows that when the value of the $\tilde{r}$ to be obtained by Poisson sampling is still unknown and $\bar{\tilde{\lambda}}''$ is therefore a random variable, the distribution of $\tilde{\tilde{\lambda}}''$ can be obtained from the unconditional distribution (15.23) of $\tilde{r}$. Solving for r and substituting in (15.23) we have

$$P\{\tilde{\tilde{\lambda}}'' = \lambda | r', t'; t\} = f_{nb}\left(r_\lambda \middle| \frac{t}{t + t'}, r'\right), \quad r_\lambda = \lambda t'' - r'. \tag{15.25}$$

Then recalling that the argument of f_{nb} is integer-valued although its parameters are continuous we have by (9.132) that cumulative probabilities under the distribution of $\tilde{\tilde{\lambda}}''$ may be obtained from tables of the beta function by use of the relations:

$$P\{\tilde{\tilde{\lambda}}'' \leq \lambda | r', t'; t\} = F_{nb}\left(r_\lambda \middle| \frac{t}{t + t'}, r'\right) = G_\beta\left(\frac{t}{t + t'} \middle| r^- + 1, r' + r^- + 1\right),$$

$$P\{\tilde{\tilde{\lambda}}'' \geq \lambda | r', t'; t\} = G_{nb}\left(r_\lambda \middle| \frac{t}{t + t'}, r'\right) = F_\beta\left(\frac{t}{t + t'} \middle| r^+, r' + r^+\right), \tag{15.26a}$$

where

$$r^- \equiv \text{greatest integer} \leq \lambda t'' - r',$$
$$r^+ \equiv \text{least integer} \geq \lambda t'' - r'. \tag{15.26b}$$

The mean, partial expectation, and variance of this distribution of $\tilde{\tilde{\lambda}}''$ are

$$E(\tilde{\tilde{\lambda}}'' | r', t'; t) = \frac{r'}{t'} = E(\tilde{\lambda} | r', t') \equiv \bar{\lambda}', \tag{15.27a}$$

$$E^{(l)}_{\tilde{\tilde{\lambda}}''}(\lambda | r', t', t) = \bar{\lambda}' G_\beta\left(\frac{t}{t + t'} \middle| r^- + 1, r' + r^- + 2\right), \tag{15.27b}$$

$$V(\tilde{\tilde{\lambda}}'' | r', t'; t) = \frac{t}{t + t'} \frac{r'}{t'^2} = \frac{t}{t + t'} V(\tilde{\lambda} | r', t'). \tag{15.27c}$$

It follows at once from (15.26) and (15.27b) that the linear-loss integrals under this distribution of $\tilde{\bar{\lambda}}''$ are given by

$$L^{(l)}_{\bar{\lambda}''}(\lambda|r',t',t) \equiv \textstyle\sum_{z\leq\lambda}(\lambda - z)P\{\tilde{\bar{\lambda}}'' = z|r',t';t\}$$

$$= \lambda G_\beta\left(\frac{t}{t+t'}\middle| r^- + 1, r' + r^- + 1\right) - \bar{\lambda}' G_\beta\left(\frac{t}{t+t'}\middle| r^- + 1, r' + r^- + 2\right), \tag{15.28a}$$

and

$$L^{(r)}_{\bar{\lambda}''}(\lambda|r',t',t) \equiv \textstyle\sum_{z\geq\lambda}(z - \lambda)P\{\tilde{\bar{\lambda}}'' = z|r',t';t\}$$

$$= \bar{\lambda}' F_\beta\left(\frac{t}{t+t'}\middle| r^+, r' + r^+ + 1\right) - \lambda F_\beta\left(\frac{t}{t+t'}\middle| r^+, r' + r^+\right). \tag{15.28b}$$

Proof Formula (15.27a) follows immediately from (13.40). To prove formula (15.27b) we write the definition

$$E^{(l)}_{\bar{\lambda}''}(\lambda) \equiv \textstyle\sum_{\bar{\lambda}''\leq\lambda}\bar{\lambda}''P(\bar{\lambda}'')$$

and then substitute (15.24) for $\bar{\lambda}''$ and replace the probability of $\bar{\lambda}''$ by the probability (15.23) of r. We thus obtain

$$E^{(l)}_{\bar{\lambda}''}(\lambda) = \sum_{r\leq r^-}\frac{r+r'}{t+t'}\frac{(r+r'-1)!}{r!(r'-1)!}\frac{t^r t'^{r'}}{(t+t')^{r+r'}}$$

$$= \frac{r'}{t'}\sum_{r\leq r^-}\frac{(r+r')!}{r!r'!}\frac{t^r t'^{r'+1}}{(t+t')^{r+r'+1}} = \bar{\lambda}' F_{nb}\left(r^-\middle|\frac{t}{t+t'}, r'+1\right).$$

Formula (15.27b) then follows by (15.26).

To prove formula (15.27c) for the variance we make use of the fact that, by (15.24)

$$\tilde{\bar{\lambda}}'' = \frac{\tilde{r}}{t''} + \text{constant}$$

is a linear function of $\tilde{r}$, so that

$$V(\tilde{\bar{\lambda}}'') = \frac{1}{t''^2}V(\tilde{r}|r',t';t).$$

Formula (15.27c) is obtained by substituting herein from (9.134)

$$V(\tilde{r}|r',t';t) = r'\frac{t/(t+t')}{[t'/(t+t')]^2} = r'\frac{t/t''}{(t'/t'')^2} = \frac{r't''t}{t'^2}.$$

15.7 Terminal and Preposterior Analysis

15.7.1 Notation

Having developed the necessary distribution theory for a Poisson process with unknown intensity λ we now turn our attention to decision problems where the unknown state parameter is λ.

In chapter 14 we let $v(e, z, a, s)$ denote the value of performing experiment e, observing a particular outcome z, and choosing a particular terminal act a, when the true state of the world is s. In this chapter we specialize our notation letting $v(t, r, a, \lambda)$ denote the value of observing that a Poisson process in time t yields r occurrences, and of choosing a particular terminal act a when the true unknown state parameter is λ. We shall define $l(t, r, a, \lambda)$ in an analogous manner and, corresponding to (14.1) and (14.2), we shall write

$$v(t, r, a, \lambda) = v_t(a, \lambda) - c_s(t, r), \tag{15.29a}$$

and

$$l(t, r, a, \lambda) = l_t(a, \lambda) + c_s(t, r). \tag{15.29b}$$

The subscript t here is our usual designation for "terminal," not the time variable.

15.7.2 Terminal Analysis

If $\tilde{\lambda}$ is given a prior gamma-1 df with parameter (r', t') then the analogue of (14.3) becomes

$$\bar{v}_t''(a, (t, r)) = E_{\lambda|t,r} v_t(a, \tilde{\lambda}) = \int_0^\infty v_t(a, \lambda) f_{\gamma 1}(\lambda | r'', t'')\, d\lambda, \tag{15.30a}$$

$$\bar{l}_t''(a, (t, r)) = E_{\lambda|t,r} l_t(a, \tilde{\lambda}) = \int_0^\infty l_t(a, \lambda) f_{\gamma 1}(\lambda | r'', t'')\, d\lambda, \tag{15.30b}$$

where (r'', t'') is given in (15.19).

15.7.3 Preposterior Analysis

If $\tilde{\lambda}$ is given a prior gamma-1 df with parameter (r', t') then the analogue of (14.8) becomes

$$\bar{v}_t(t) = E\bar{v}_t''(a^o_{t,\tilde{r}}, (t, \tilde{r})) = \textstyle\sum_r \bar{v}_t''(a^o_{t,r}, (t, r)) f_{nb}\left(r \middle| \frac{t}{t + t'}, r'\right), \tag{15.31a}$$

and

$$\bar{\bar{l}}_t(t) = E\bar{l}_t''(a_{t,\tilde{r}}, (t, \tilde{r})) = \sum_r \bar{l}_t''(a_{t,r}^o, (t, r)) f_{nb}\left(r \middle| \frac{t}{t + t'}, r'\right). \tag{15.31b}$$

In the following sections we shall indicate how expressions (15.30) and (15.31) simplify when we consider our three prototype decision problems: infinite-action with quadratic loss, infinite-action with linear loss, two-action with linear value. In those special cases we shall investigate EVSI, ENGS, and the optimal sample size.

15.8 The Infinite-Action Problem with Quadratic Loss

15.8.1 Terminal Analysis

Let $\tilde{\lambda}$ be the unknown parameter of a Poisson process; let the set of available acts (estimates) be the set of real numbers; let

$$l_t(a, \lambda) \equiv k_t(a - \lambda)^2; \tag{15.32}$$

let the prior and posterior parameters of the gamma-1 rv $\tilde{\lambda}$ be (r', t') and (r'', t'') respectively. From section 12.6.2 we obtain:

a. The optimal act under prior information is $a^o = \bar{\lambda}' = r'/t'$.

b. The EVPI is given by $\bar{l}_t'(a^o) = k_t \check{\lambda}' = k_t r'/(t')^2$.

c. The optimal act, posterior to observing (r, t) is $a_{t,r}^o = \bar{\lambda}'' = (r' + r)/(t' + t)$.

d. The posterior EVPI after observing (r, t) is $\bar{l}_t''(a_{t,r}^o, (t, r)) = k_t \check{\lambda}'' = k_t(r' + r)/(t' + t)^2$.

15.8.2 Preposterior Analysis

Expected Value of Sample Information

From (14.30) and (15.27c) the EVSI is given by

$$I(t) = k_t \check{\bar{\lambda}}'' = \frac{t}{t + t'} k_t \check{\lambda}', \tag{15.33}$$

which is identical to the corresponding expression (14.32a) in binomial sampling except that t replaces n and $\check{\lambda}'$ replaces $\check{p}'$.

Observe that $I(0) = 0$ and that

$$\lim_{t \to \infty} I(t) = k_t \check{\lambda}' = \text{EVPI}. \tag{15.34}$$

Expected Net Gain of Sampling

If the cost of observing the process for time t is a linear function of t and does not depend on r,

$$c_s(t, r) = K_s + k_s t, \tag{15.35}$$

where K_s and k_s are respectively the fixed and variable costs of sampling, then by (14.13) the expected net gain of sampling, ENGS, is

$$G(t) = k_t \breve{\lambda}' \frac{t}{t + t'} - (K_s + k_s t). \tag{15.36}$$

Figure 14.2, which plots G against n for the binomial case, can also be interpreted for the present case after n is replaced by t.

Optimal Sample Size

The sample size (sampling time) that maximizes ENGS satisfies

$$t^o + t' = \left[\frac{k_t t'}{k_s} \breve{\lambda}'\right]^{1/2} \tag{15.37}$$

provided (1) that t^o as given by this formula is positive and (2) that $G(t^o)$ as given by (15.36) is positive; if either condition fails, the optimal sample size is 0. The proof of this assertion is exactly the same as the proof of the corresponding result in the binomial case, formula (14.35), which was left as an exercise for the reader.

15.9 The Infinite-Action Problem with Linear Loss

15.9.1 Terminal Analysis

Let $\tilde{\lambda}$ be the unknown parameter of a Poisson process; let the set of available acts (estimates) be the set of all real numbers; let

$$l_t(a, \lambda) \equiv \begin{cases} k_u(\lambda - a) & \text{if} \quad a \leq \lambda, \\ k_o(a - \lambda) & \text{if} \quad a \geq \lambda; \end{cases} \tag{15.38}$$

let $\tilde{\lambda}$ be given a gamma-1 df with parameter (r', t').

Prior Analysis

From (12.33) and (12.34), the optimal act a^o under prior information is the kth fractile λ'_k of the gamma-1 df of $\tilde{\lambda}$ where $k = k_u/(k_u + k_o)$. Symbolically,

$$a^o = \lambda'_k, \quad \text{where} \quad F_{\gamma 1}(\lambda'_k | r', t') = k. \tag{15.39}$$

We shall now prove the following result: the EVPI is given by

$$\bar{l}_t'(a^o) = (k_u + k_O)\check{\lambda}' f_{\gamma 1}(\lambda_k' | r' + 1, t'), \tag{15.40}$$

which can also be written as

$$\bar{l}_t'(a^o) = (k_u + k_O)\frac{r'}{t'} f_P(r' | \lambda_k' t'). \tag{15.41}$$

Proof From (12.36) we have that

$$\bar{l}_t'(a^o) = k_u E_{\gamma 1}^{(r)}(\lambda_k' | r', t') - k_O E_{\gamma 1}^{(l)}(\lambda_k' | r', t'),$$

and by (9.111) and (9.112) this becomes

$$\bar{l}_t'(a^o) = k_u \frac{r'}{t'} G_\gamma(t'\lambda_k' | r' + 1) - k_O \frac{r'}{t'} F_\gamma(t'\lambda_k' | r' + 1).$$

Now by (15.4) and (15.39)

$$\begin{aligned} G_\gamma(t'\lambda_k' | r' + 1) &= G_{\gamma 1}(\lambda_k' | r' + 1, t') \\ &= \frac{e^{-\lambda_k' t'}(\lambda_k' t')^{r'}}{r'!} + G_{\gamma 1}(\lambda_k' | r', t') \\ &= \frac{e^{-\lambda_k' t'}(\lambda_k' t')^{r'}}{r'!} + \frac{k_O}{k_u + k_O}. \end{aligned}$$

From this we obtain

$$F_\gamma(t'\lambda_k' | r' + 1) = -\frac{e^{-\lambda_k' t'}(\lambda_k' t')^{r'}}{r'!} + \frac{k_u}{k_u + k_O}.$$

Substitution gives

$$\begin{aligned} \bar{l}_t'(a^o) &= (k_u + k_O)\frac{r'}{t'}\frac{e^{-\lambda_k' t'}(\lambda_k' t')^{r'}}{r'!} + \left[k_u \frac{k_O}{k_u + k_O} - k_O \frac{k_u}{k_u + k_O}\right] \\ &= (k_u + k_O)\frac{r'}{t'}\frac{e^{-\lambda_k' t'}(\lambda_k' t')^{r'}}{r'!}. \end{aligned}$$

From this expression, (15.40) and (15.41) follow immediately.

Posterior Analysis

After the Poisson process has been observed to give r occurrences in time t, the prior parameters are updated from (r', t') to (r'', t''), and the optimal act and posterior EVPI are given by (15.39), (15.40), and (15.41) where all the single primes are merely replaced by double primes.

15.9.2 Preposterior Analysis

Unfortunately the preposterior analysis of the estimation problem with linear losses is not analytically tractable for Poisson sampling. The difficulty is similar to the one encountered in section 14.6.2 where we discussed the same problem for binomial sampling.

It is shown in *ASDT*, pp. 202–204, that the preposterior analyses of the estimation problem with linear losses is analytically tractable for the case of gamma sampling (i.e., where r is predetermined and $\tilde{t}$ is left to chance). It is shown there that if $\tilde{\lambda}$ is given a gamma-1 prior df with parameter (r', t'), and if the loss structure is given by (15.38), then the experimental design which observes the process until the rth occurrence has an EVSI of

$$I(r) = (k_u + k_0)\frac{r'}{t'} f_P(r' + r|\lambda^*), \tag{15.42a}$$

where λ^* is such that

$$F_\gamma(\lambda^*|r' + r) = k_u/(k_u + k_0). \tag{15.42b}$$

By tracing out the function $I(r)$ and comparing this with the cost of sampling, it is not difficult to find the optimal sample size r^o.

15.10 The Two-Action Problem with Linear Loss

15.10.1 Terminal Analysis

Let $\tilde{\lambda}$ be the unknown intensity of a Poisson process; let a_1 and a_2 be the available acts; let

$$v_t(a_i, \lambda) = K_i + k_i\lambda, \qquad i = 1, 2,$$

where $k_2 > k_1$; let $k_t = k_2 - k_1$; let $\lambda_b = (K_1 - K_2)/(k_2 - k_1)$; let the prior and posterior parameters of the gamma-1 rv $\tilde{\lambda}$ be (r', t') and (r'', t'') respectively. From the results of section 12.3 we conclude that:

a. The optimal act under prior information is

$$a^o = \begin{cases} a_1 & \text{if} \quad \bar{\lambda}' = r'/t' \le \lambda_b, \\ a_2 & \text{if} \quad \bar{\lambda}' = r'/t' \ge \lambda_b. \end{cases} \tag{15.43}$$

b. The EVPI is given by

$$\bar{l}_t'(a^o) = \begin{cases} k_t L_{\gamma 1}^{(r)}(\lambda_b|r', t') & \text{if} \quad \bar{\lambda}' \le \lambda_b, \\ k_t L_{\gamma 1}^{(l)}(\lambda_b|r', t') & \text{if} \quad \bar{\lambda}' > \lambda_b, \end{cases} \tag{15.44}$$

and from (9.113) and (9.114), $L_{\gamma 1}^{(l)}$ and $L_{\gamma 2}^{(r)}$ can be evaluated from cumulative probabilities of the gamma distribution.

c. The optimal act posterior to observing (r, t) is

$$a_{r,t}^{o} = \begin{cases} a_1 & \text{if} \quad \bar{\lambda}'' = r''/t'' \leq \lambda_b, \\ a_2 & \text{if} \quad \bar{\lambda}'' = r''/t'' \geq \lambda_b. \end{cases} \tag{15.45}$$

15.10.2 Preposterior Analysis

If the Poisson process is to be observed for time t, then by (14.39) the expected value of sample information (EVSI) is given by

$$I(t) = \begin{cases} k_t E \max\{0, \tilde{\bar{\lambda}}'' - \lambda_b\} & \text{if} \quad \bar{\lambda}' \leq \lambda_b, \\ k_t E \max\{0, \lambda_b - \tilde{\bar{\lambda}}''\} & \text{if} \quad \bar{\lambda}' \geq \lambda_b. \end{cases} \tag{15.46}$$

or in terms of linear-loss integrals by

$$I(t) = \begin{cases} k_t L_{\tilde{\bar{\lambda}}''}^{(r)}(\lambda_b | r', t', t) & \text{if} \quad \bar{\lambda}' \leq \lambda_b, \\ k_t L_{\tilde{\bar{\lambda}}''}^{(l)}(\lambda_b | r', t', t) & \text{if} \quad \bar{\lambda}' \geq \lambda_b. \end{cases} \tag{15.47}$$

From (15.28), these linear-loss integrals can be evaluated by means of cumulative probability tables of the beta distribution.

By tracing out the function $I(t)$ and comparing this with the cost of observing the process it is not difficult to find the optimal sample "size" t^o.

15.11 Selection of a Distribution to Express Judgments about $\tilde{\lambda}$

What we have to say about the selection of a distribution to express judgments about $\tilde{\lambda}$ is quite analogous to what we said in section 11.5 on the selection of a distribution to express judgments about the unknown parameter $\tilde{p}$ of a Bernoulli process. We suggest the reader review section 11.5 at this time.

Before asserting a distribution of $\tilde{\lambda}$ it is important to have in mind a clear interpretation of the intensity parameter λ. We feel that it is not too helpful to think of λ as the value such that the probability of an occurrence in a small interval of time Δ is approximately $\lambda\Delta$. Instead, the interpretation for λ we suggest keeping in mind is based on the fact that for a given λ the rv $(\tilde{r}/t)$ has a conditional expectation of λ and a conditional standard deviation that approaches 0 as t approaches ∞. (This last assertion follows since $V(r/t | \lambda) = (\lambda t)/t^2 = \lambda/t$.) Therefore one can think of λ as the anticipated limiting value of (r/t) as $t \to \infty$.

In section 11.5.1 we discussed the assessment of a left-tail cumulative distribution for $\tilde{p}$ by successively dividing intervals into two judgmentally equally likely subintervals. The same procedure is recommended for the assessment of the uncertain intensity parameter $\tilde{\lambda}$ of a Poisson process.

Fitting a Gamma-1 Density by Moments

From an assessed left-tail distribution for the unknown parameter $\tilde{\lambda}$ of a Poisson process it is not difficult to compute approximately the expectation $\bar{\lambda}$ and the variance $\check{\lambda}$ of $\tilde{\lambda}$. The two methods for computing these values that are suggested in section 11.5.2 are also applicable in the present case. Once $\bar{\lambda}$ and $\check{\lambda}$ have been determined, it is then a simple task to select that member of the gamma-1 family which has that mean and variance. Using ρ and τ to represent the parameters of the gamma-1 family of density functions, by (9.109) and (9.110) we get

$$\tau = \bar{\lambda}/\check{\lambda} \quad \text{and} \quad \rho = \bar{\lambda}\tau. \tag{15.48}$$

Fitting a Gamma-1 Density Directly to Quartiles

Instead of fairing a graphical left-tail distribution for $\tilde{\lambda}$ and computing moments, we can try to fit a gamma-1 distribution to some of the original fractiles. Since the gamma-1 family has only two adjustable parameters, it will not be possible in general to find a member of the family that agrees *exactly* with more than two of the decision maker's judgmental fractiles, but in many cases it will be possible to find a satisfactory compromise.

Let λ_k be the kth fractile of a gamma-1 distribution. We shall indicate how the parameter (ρ, τ) of a gamma-1 distribution can be approximately chosen given the pair $\lambda_{.50}$ and $\lambda_{.25}$, or the pair $\lambda_{.50}$ and $\lambda_{.75}$, or given all three quantities $\lambda_{.25}$, $\lambda_{.50}$, and $\lambda_{.75}$. Let

$$a_k \equiv (\sqrt{\lambda_k} - \sqrt{\lambda_{.5}})^2 \tag{15.49}$$

The parameters of the gamma-1 distribution are then given approximately by

$$\rho = \lambda_{.50}\tau + .25, \tag{15.50}$$

where τ is determined according to one of the three cases below:

Case 1—Given $\lambda_{.50}$ and $\lambda_{.25}$ $\quad \tau = .112/a_{.25}$. (15.51a)

Case 2—Given $\lambda_{.50}$ and $\lambda_{.75}$ $\quad \tau = .112/a_{.75}$. (15.51b)

Case 3—Given $\lambda_{.25}$, $\lambda_{.50}$, and $\lambda_{.75}$ $\quad \tau = .056\left(\dfrac{1}{a_{.25}} + \dfrac{1}{a_{.75}}\right)$. (15.51c)

These approximations are derived from the fact that if $\tilde{\lambda}$ is distributed according to a gamma-1 df with parameter (ρ, τ), then the rv

$$\tilde{u} = \sqrt{4\tau\tilde{\lambda}} - \sqrt{4\rho - 1}$$

has approximately a so-called standardized Normal distribution, which we shall soon meet and study in great detail.

Illustration If $\rho = 4$ and $\tau = 10$, then using the relationship

$$k_0 = F_{\gamma 1}(\lambda_k | \rho, \tau) = F_{\gamma}(\lambda_k \tau | \rho) = I\left(\frac{\tau\lambda_k}{\sqrt{\rho}}, \rho - 1\right),$$

we find (by Pearson's Tables of the Incomplete Γ-Function or later relatives) that

$$\lambda_{.25} = .2532, \qquad \lambda_{.50} = .3672, \qquad \lambda_{.75} = .5110.$$

Suppose we now reverse the problem: Given $\lambda_{.25}$, $\lambda_{.50}$, and $\lambda_{.75}$ as above to find ρ and τ by use of the approximations (15.51). Fitting to the .50 and .25 fractiles (i.e., using (15.51a)),

$$a_k = .0106, \qquad \tau \doteq 10.6, \qquad \rho \doteq 4.14;$$

fitting to the .50 and .75 fractiles (i.e., using (15.51b)),

$$a_k = .0119, \qquad \tau \doteq 9.41, \qquad \rho \doteq 3.71;$$

fitting to all three fractiles $\lambda_{.25}$, $\lambda_{.50}$, and $\lambda_{.75}$ (i. e., using (15.51c)),

$$\tau \doteq 10.0, \qquad \rho \doteq 3.92.$$

15.12 Use of the Poisson Process as an Approximation to a Bernoulli Process with Small *p*

15.12.1 Heuristic Analysis

A Bernoulli process with a parameter p of small magnitude can often be conveniently analyzed in terms of an associated Poisson process. To understand how this relationship comes about, first let us consider a Poisson process with parameter λ and divide time into equal small discrete periods of length Δ. Let us say that a *success* occurs on the ith *trial* if and only if there is at least one occurrence of the Poisson process during the ith interval of time. Then clearly the related process which generates successes and failures (i.e., nonsuccesses) is a Bernoulli process where the constant probability of a success on each trial is

$$p = 1 - P\{\text{no occurrences}\} = 1 - e^{-\lambda\Delta} = \lambda\Delta - \frac{(\lambda\Delta)^2}{2!} + \frac{(\lambda\Delta)^3}{3!} - \dots$$

If $\lambda\Delta$ is small, then as in section 15.1.4, two conclusions follow: first, p can be taken approximately equal to $\lambda\Delta$, and second, the chance of two or more occurrences in the same interval Δ will be miniscule—on the order of $(\lambda\Delta)^2$—which means that there will be a close correspondence between Poisson process and the associated Bernoulli process. Still under the assumption that $\lambda\Delta$ is small, we would expect that in time period $T = n\Delta$ the probability of getting exactly r occurrences, which by (15.3) is $f_P(r|\lambda T)$, would be approximately equal to getting r successes in T/Δ Bernoulli trials with parameter $p = \lambda\Delta$, which is $f_b(r|\lambda\Delta, T/\Delta)$; symbolically,

$$f_P(r|\lambda T) \doteq f_b(r|\lambda\Delta, T/\Delta).$$

More formally, we would expect that if we let $\Delta \to 0$ and hold T fixed so that $n = T/\Delta$ increases, then

$$f_P(r|\lambda T) = \lim_{\Delta \to 0} f_b(r|\lambda\Delta, T/\Delta). \tag{15.52}$$

The reader is invited as an exercise to prove (15.52) starting from the analytical forms of f_b and f_P.

Now let us change our orientation. Suppose we start by considering a Bernoulli process with a parameter p which is very small. We now can imagine a Poisson process with a parameter λ and suppose that the time axis is broken up into short intervals of length Δ where $\lambda\Delta = p$. From the above discussion it should now be intuitively clear that this Poisson process, when discretized in this manner, "approximates" the given Bernoulli process; in particular, we would have, among other relationships,

$$f_b(r|p, n) \doteq f_P(r|pn), \tag{15.53}$$

where the parameter pn of f_P can be thought of as the product of the intensity parameter (p/Δ) and the length of time $n\Delta$ that the process is observed. It is often helpful to think of Δ as equal to 1 so that $\lambda = p$, and the length of time the process is observed is equal to n.

15.12.2 Analysis of a Bernoulli Process with a Small but Unknown p

Let $\tilde{p}$ be the unknown parameter of a Bernoulli process and suppose that the prior distribution of $\tilde{p}$ is concentrated near 0. Let $\tilde{p}$ be given a beta prior df with parameter (r', n') where r' is small with respect to n'. We then have

$$\bar{p}' = r'/n',$$

and

$$\breve{p}' = \frac{r'}{n'^2} \frac{(n' - r')}{(n' + 1)} \doteq \frac{r'}{n'^2}.$$

In this case it is convenient to think of p as the intensity λ of a Poisson process and to assign to $\tilde{\lambda}$ a gamma-1 prior df with the same mean and variance as the beta distribution. Setting $t' = n'$, the appropriate parameter of the associated gamma-1 df of $\tilde{\lambda}$ is (r', t'). We can now proceed to analyze the related Poisson process instead of the original Bernoulli process.

Illustration In *ASDT*, p. 132, there is an analysis of the following two-action, linear-loss problem originally posed by Sittig (1951).

An acceptance lot contains 500 brush spindles for floor polishers. Acceptance of a defective ultimately leads to loss of the part to which it is welded; this part costs 3.90 guilders. A rejected lot is screened at a cost of .079 guilders per piece; sampling inspection costs this same amount per piece. The terminal costs (treated as if they were incurred on the whole lot rather than on only the uninspected portion) are

$$\text{cost of acceptance} = K_1 + k_1 p = 3.90 \times 500p = 1950p,$$

$$\text{cost of rejection} = K_2 + k_2 p = 0.79 \times 500 = 39.5;$$

and from these we can compute

$$k_t = |k_2 - k_1| = |0 - 1950| = 1950, \; p_b = \frac{39.5}{1950} = .020256.$$

The beta prior distribution of $\tilde{p}$ has parameter $(1, 45.45)$, which means that $\bar{p}' = 1/45.45 = .022$.

The EVSI function $I(n)$ and the net gain function $G(n)$ were investigated by means of a computer program for optimal binomial sampling and it was determined by this means that $n^o = 32$ and $G(n^o) = 5.80$ guilders.

We first propose to use the Poisson approximation, by letting $\tilde{\lambda} = \tilde{p}$ and choosing a prior gamma-1 df for $\tilde{\lambda}$ with parameter $(1, 45.45)$, in order to compute $G(32)$ and to compare it with the value of 5.80 guilders. From (15.47) we have that

$$I(t) = k_t L_{\bar{\lambda}''}^{(l)}(\lambda_b | r', t', t),$$

and from (15.28) we get

$$I(t) = k_t \left[\lambda_b G_\beta \left(\frac{t}{t+t'} \middle| r^- + 1, r' + r^- + 1 \right) - \bar{\lambda}' G_\beta \left(\frac{t}{t+t'} \middle| r^- + 1, r' + r^- + 2 \right) \right]$$

where

$$r^- = \text{greatest integer} \leq \lambda_b t'' - r'.$$

Substituting

$k_t = 1950, \lambda_b = p_b = .020256, t = 32, t' = 45.45, r' = 1, r^- = 0, \bar{\lambda}' = .022,$

we get

$I(32) = 1950[.020256\, G_\beta(.413|\,1,2) - .022\, G_\beta(.413|\,1,3)] = 8.40,$

and

$G(32) = I(32) - 32 \times (.079) = 5.87,$

which is in close agreement with the exact result of 5.80 guilders obtained by the computer program for binomial sampling.

The computer program for binomial sampling computes $I(n)$ and $G(n)$ recursively in steps of one unit starting from $n = 1$. Although the program is very fast, in some situations it is necessary to investigate sample sizes in the thousands and computational time can be excessive. Using the Poisson approximation, however, it is possible with the aid of beta or binomial tables to calculate directly, without even using a computer, values of $I(t)$ for any value of t. We can easily imagine quality control problems where it is only possible to sample items in aggregates of one thousand and in such situations a Poisson analysis would be extremely convenient.

16 Normal Process with Known Variance

16.1 The Normal Data-Generating Process

16.1.1 Introduction*

Many real-world processes of great practical importance can be described in terms of the following model: There is some physical quantity μ, which is not known with certainty; in order to gain additional information about μ, repeated measurements or observations $z_1, z_2, \ldots$, are taken, where the zs tend, in some loose sense, to fall in a haphazard manner about the true μ. More precisely, we shall assume that

$$z_i = \mu + \varepsilon_i, \qquad i = 1, 2, \ldots, \tag{16.1}$$

where the ε_i's can be viewed as errors of measurement or as contributions from factors left uncontrolled or unspecified. These ε terms are treated as rv's $\tilde{\varepsilon}_i, \tilde{\varepsilon}_2, \ldots$, and in this chapter we shall start our analysis of this problem by imposing very stringent assumptions on these rv's, which, of course, severely limit the applicability of the model. In later chapters we shall relax these assumptions and thereby extend the applicability of the model.

In this and the two following chapters we shall assume that the rv's $\tilde{\varepsilon}_i$, $\tilde{\varepsilon}_2, \ldots$ are:

a. *independent*, in the sense that the conditional distributing function for $\tilde{\varepsilon}_i$ given $(\tilde{\varepsilon}_1 = \varepsilon_1), \ldots, (\tilde{\varepsilon}_{i-1} = \varepsilon_{i-1})$, does not depend on $\varepsilon_1, \ldots, \varepsilon_{i-1}$, for all i;

b. *identically distributed*, in the sense that the rv's $\tilde{\varepsilon}_1, \tilde{\varepsilon}_2, \ldots$ have the same distributing function;

c. *Unbiased*, in the sense that $E(\tilde{\varepsilon}_i) = 0$ for all i.

We shall use the notation:

$$V(\tilde{\varepsilon}) \equiv \upsilon, \qquad \sigma \equiv \sqrt{\upsilon}, \qquad h \equiv 1/\upsilon. \tag{16.2}$$

In this and the following chapter we shall assume that each $\tilde{\varepsilon}_i$ is a *Normal* rv with parameter $(0, \upsilon)$. In this chapter we assume υ is *known*; in the next chapter we assume υ is *unknown*. In chapter 23B on biassed measurements we shall drop the assumption that $E(\tilde{\varepsilon}_i) = 0$ for all i, and assume that $E(\tilde{\varepsilon}_i) = \beta$ for all i, where β is unknown and where our judgments about $\tilde{\beta}$ and $\tilde{\mu}$ are intertwined.

16.1.2 A Model of Simple Sampling

Consider a population consisting of a collection of elements and suppose that to each element there is associated a unique number. For example,

* The material of section 9.7 should be reviewed in preparation for this chapter.

the population may consist of individuals in the United States who filed an income tax return for a particular year and to each individual (element) there is associated the amount of his tax. As another example, the population may consist of a list of customers and we may be concerned with the amount each customer has spent on a given commodity in a specified period. To keep a neutral interpretation in mind, let us consider an urn containing a collection of balls, each of which is marked with some number. Let μ be the average of all the numbers in this population.

From this population (or urn) an element (or ball) is selected canonically; let the resulting number be z_1. This element is then returned to the population and a second canonical drawing is made resulting in the number z_2. This process is continued and by this means a sequence of numbers $z_1, z_2, \ldots$ is generated.

Let ε_i be defined implicitly by (16.1); that is, let $\varepsilon_i = z_i - \mu$. Before the process is observed, the as yet unknown values can be thought of as a sequence of rv's $\tilde{z}_1, \tilde{z}_2, \ldots$ with an associated sequence of as yet unknown deviations $\tilde{\varepsilon}_1, \tilde{\varepsilon}_2, \ldots$. These $\tilde{\varepsilon}$ rv's are (a) independent, (b) identically distributed, and (c) unbiased. Hence we observe that a model of simple sampling leads to a data-generating process like the one we discussed in the previous subsection.

16.1.3 Definition of an Independent Normal Process

Formally, we shall deal in this chapter exclusively with processes generating rv's $\tilde{z}_1, \tilde{z}_2, \ldots$ where

$$\tilde{z}_i = \mu + \tilde{\varepsilon}_i, \qquad i = 1, 2, \ldots, \tag{16.3}$$

where the rv's $\varepsilon_1, \varepsilon_2, \ldots$ are independent, each having the same Normal df with parameter $(0, \upsilon)$; that is,

$$\tilde{\varepsilon}_i \sim f_N(\varepsilon_i | 0, \upsilon) \qquad i = 1, 2, \ldots. \tag{16.4}$$

Such a process will be called an *Independent Normal* process; the quantities μ and υ will be called the *parameters of the process* just as p was called the parameter of a Bernoulli process. In this chapter we shall assume that υ is a known number but that μ is unknown. We assume that the zs are observable, but as long as μ is unknown the εs remain unobservable.

From (16.3) and (16.4), *conditional on* μ, the rv's $\tilde{z}_1, \tilde{z}_2, \ldots$ are independent, each having the same Normal df with parameter (μ, υ); that is,

$$(z_i | \mu) \sim f_N(z_i | \mu, \upsilon) \qquad i = 1, 2, \ldots. \tag{16.5}$$

If $\tilde{\mu}$ is treated as a rv, then we *cannot* treat the rv's $\tilde{z}_1, \tilde{z}_2, \ldots$ as independent from an *unconditional* point of view. This is because the distribution of $\tilde{z}_{n+1}$ depends on the observed values of $z_1, \ldots, z_n$ since these observations affect our judgment about $\tilde{\mu}$ and therefore our judgment about $\tilde{z}_{n+1}$.

16.1.4 Assumption of Known Variance

In the general case, both the process mean μ and the process variance v will be the unknown quantities. In this chapter, however, we shall assume that the *process variance is known even though the process mean is not*. Such a situation can easily arise where, for example, tool wear may cause a drift in the mean diameter of the pieces produced by a machine without affecting the variability of the individual diameters about the mean. Even more frequently, the long-run μ of the measurements that could be generated by some measuring device is unknown because it is being used for its natural purpose of measuring an unknown dimension, but the variance v of these measurements *is* known because the device has previously been calibrated by making a large number of measurements of a known standard.

Even in cases where v is unknown, we shall see in the following chapters that there are situations where it is expedient to treat v as if it were some known particular value; in some of these situations it will be prudent to make a sensitivity study of this procedure by investigating the implications of several different plausible values of v for the given problem at hand.

16.1.5 Preview of the Chapter

The first problem that we shall study in this chapter is the following basic problem of statistical inference. After assigning a prior distribution to the unknown mean $\tilde{\mu}$ of an Independent Normal process with known variance v, and after observing the values $(z_1, \ldots, z_n)$ of n rv's generated by the process, the decision maker now wishes to revise his distribution of $\tilde{\mu}$ in accordance with the information contained in these observations. The broad structure of this part of the chapter parallels that of chapter 11 on the Bernoulli Process.

In section 16.2, we examine the sampling distribution of n observations conditional on given values of μ and v. Next the likelihood function corresponding to a sample $z_1, z_2, \ldots, z_n$ is considered and it is shown that the likelihood function depends on the sample outcomes $z_1, z_2, \ldots, z_n$ only through their sample mean $m = \sum_i z_i/n$ so that a "sufficient" summary of the sample outcomes is given by the pair (m, n).

In section 16.3 we apply Bayes' Theorem to find the posterior df of $\tilde{\mu}$ corresponding to a given prior df f' of $\tilde{\mu}$ after a sample $z_1, z_2, \ldots, z_n$ is observed. As in the discussion of section 11.3.5 for the Bernoulli process we shall see that the shape of the posterior df is given by the product of the likelihood function L and the prior df f'. If f' is gentle, then, as we have seen before, the posterior df will be approximately the likelihood function, suitably scaled so that the area under it is unity.

Recall that in sampling from a Bernoulli process, if the prior df of $\tilde{p}$ is taken from the beta family, then the posterior df is also in the beta family, and there is a simple algebraic formula connecting the prior parameters (r', n'). In section 16.4 we show an analogous result for sampling from a Normal Process: If $\tilde{\mu}$ is given a *Normal* prior df, then the posterior df of μ is *also Normal*, and there is a simple algebraic formula connecting the prior parameters $(\bar{\mu}', \breve{\mu}')$, the sufficient statistics (m, n) of the sample, and the posterior parameters $(\bar{\mu}'', \breve{\mu}'')$.

In section 16.5 we investigate the sensitivity of the posterior df of $\tilde{\mu}$ to the choice of the prior. Once again we bring up the enticing notion of "complete ignorance" and criticize its indiscriminate use.

In section 16.6 we give the unconditional sampling distribution of $\tilde{m}$ and the distribution of the as yet unknown posterior mean $\tilde{\bar{\mu}}''$ corresponding to a sample of size n, which is needed for preposterior analysis.

In section 16.7 we consider terminal and preposterior analysis for decision problems which involve the unknown mean of a Normal process.

In the remaining sections we specialize to our three prototype decision problems: infinite-action with quadratic loss, infinite-action with linear loss, and two-action with linear value.

16.2 Conditional Sampling Distributions

16.2.1 Conditional Probability of Sample Outcomes Given μ, v

We shall assume that although the unknown outcomes $\tilde{z}_1, \tilde{z}_2, \ldots$ are continuous rv's we can only observe or determine these values to a fixed number of decimal places. We feel that this assumption is realistic, and it enables us to avoid discussing at this point the theory of joint density functions for several rv's.

Let $z_1, z_2, \ldots, z_n$ be numbers that all terminate at the kth decimal place (i.e., which are of the form $y + a_1 10^{-1} + a_2 10^{-2} + \cdots + a_k 10^{-k}$ where y is an integer and where the a_i's are integers from 0 to 9 inclusive), and let $\Delta \equiv 10^{-k}$. The probability that $\tilde{z}_i$ is observed to be z_i (rounding to the kth decimal place) for a given μ is

$$P\left(z_i - \frac{\Delta}{2} \leq \tilde{z}_i \leq z_i + \frac{\Delta}{2} \middle| \mu\right) = \int_{z_i - \Delta/2}^{z_i + \Delta/2} f_N(t|\mu, v)\, dt$$

$$= \Delta f_N(z_i|\mu, v) + [\text{terms of order higher than } \Delta].$$

The event that $(z_i - \frac{\Delta}{2} \le \tilde{z}_i \le z_i + \frac{\Delta}{2})$ will be written as $(\tilde{z}_i \doteq z_i)$, and since in the sequel all terms of higher order will eventually be ignored, we have for all practical purposes

$$P(\tilde{z}_i \doteq z_i | \mu) = \Delta f_N(z_i | \mu, \upsilon). \tag{16.6}$$

Since the rv's $\tilde{z}_1, \tilde{z}_2, \ldots, z_n$ are conditionally independent given μ, we have

$$P(\tilde{z}_1 \doteq \tilde{z}_1, \ldots, \tilde{z}_n \doteq z_n | \mu) = \Delta^n \prod_{i=1}^{n} f_N(z_i | \mu, \upsilon). \tag{16.7}$$

We shall put this result in a much more convenient form by showing that if we define the sample *mean*

$$m \equiv \frac{1}{n} \textstyle\sum_i z_i, \tag{16.8}$$

then (16.7) can be written in the form

$$P(\tilde{z}_1 \doteq z_1, \ldots, \tilde{z}_n \doteq z_n | \mu) = \Delta^n K f_N(m | \mu, \upsilon/n), \tag{16.9a}$$

where

$$K \equiv (2\pi)^{-(1/2)(n-1)} e^{-(1/2)\sum_i (z_i - m)^2/\upsilon} \upsilon^{-(1/2)(n-1)} n^{-(1/2)} \tag{16.9b}$$

is a constant that does not involve the unknown μ.

Proof of (16.9) To prove that (16.7) is equivalent to (16.9) we have

$$\begin{aligned}\prod_{i=1} f_N(z_i | \mu, \upsilon) &= \prod_{i=1} (2\pi)^{-1/2} e^{-(1/2)(z_i - \mu)^2/\upsilon} \upsilon^{-1/2} \\ &= (2\pi)^{-(1/2)n} e^{-(1/2)\sum_i (z_i - \mu)^2/\upsilon} \upsilon^{-(1/2)n}.\end{aligned}$$

Analyzing the exponent of e, we get

$$\begin{aligned}\textstyle\sum_i (z_i - \mu)^2 &= \textstyle\sum_i (z_i - m + m - \mu)^2 \\ &= \textstyle\sum_i (z_i - m)^2 + \sum_i (m - \mu)^2 + 2\sum_i (z_i - m)(m - \mu)\end{aligned}$$

and observe (1) that the last term on the right vanishes because $\sum_i (z_i - m) = nm - nm = 0$ by the definition of m, and (2) that $\sum_i (m - \mu)^2 = n(m - \mu)^2$, so that

$$\textstyle\sum_i (z_i - \mu)^2 = \sum_i (z_i - m)^2 + n(m - \mu)^2.$$

Making this substitution in the exponent we obtain (16.9). ∎

16.2.2 Likelihood Function of μ

The expression $P(\tilde{z}_1 \doteq z_1, \ldots, \tilde{z}_n \doteq z_n | \mu)$ can be looked at in two ways: When viewed as a function of $z = (z_1, \ldots, z_n)$ for a fixed μ, it is called the

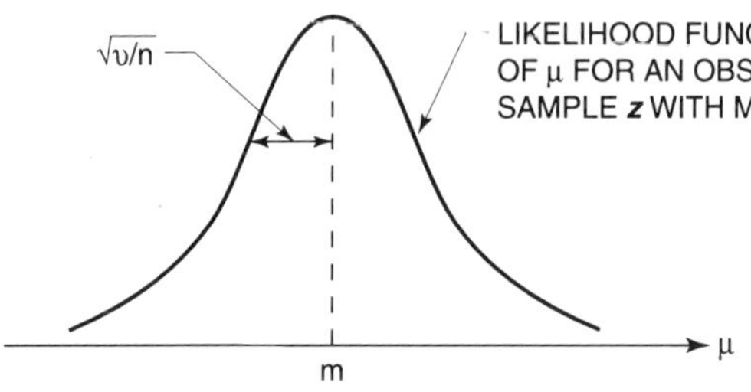

Figure 16.1
Normal likelihood

joint probability function at z for μ; when viewed as a function of μ for a fixed z it is called the *likelihood* of μ for the sample outcome z, and written $L(\mu|z)$. From (16.9) we observe that

$$L(\mu|z) = \Delta^n K(2\pi)^{-1/2}e^{-(1/2)(m-\mu)^2 n/\upsilon}(n/\upsilon)^{1/2} \tag{16.10}$$

where K depends on z *but not on* μ. Now since we are looking at L as a function of μ for a fixed z it is natural to switch the roles of m and μ in (16.9a) to obtain

$$L(\mu|z) = \Delta^n K f_N(\mu|m, \upsilon/n). \tag{16.11}$$

Observe carefully what has happened here: expressions (16.11) and (16.9a) are the same when written out in analytical form.

We therefore conclude that the likelihood function $L(\cdot|z)$ for a given sample z when plotted as a function of μ is merely a constant $\Delta^n K$ (depending on z) times a Normal df with mean m and variance υ/n (see figure 16.1). At this point in the argument it is important *not* to think of $L(\cdot|z)$ as a posterior df of μ.

16.3 Posterior Distribution of $\tilde{\mu}$

16.3.1 The Posterior as a Product of the Likelihood Function and the Prior

Let the prior distributing function of $\tilde{\mu}$ be denoted by f', which we leave quite general for the time being; let the posterior distributing function of $\tilde{\mu}$ given $z = (z_1, \ldots, z_n)$ be denoted by $f''(\mu|z)$. Then by Bayes' Theorem (10.21) we obtain

$$f''(\mu|z) \propto L(\mu|z)f'(\mu), \tag{16.12}$$

which says that the shape of the posterior distributing function is given by the product of the likelihood function and the prior distributing function. From (16.11) this becomes

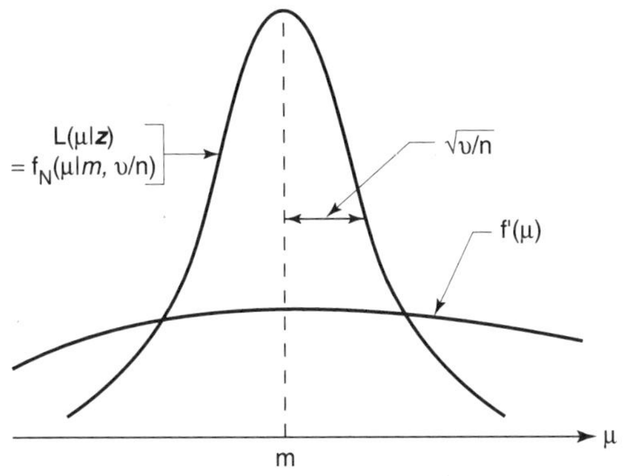

Figure 16.2
Normal likelihood and "gentle" prior

$$f''(\mu|z) = C'f_N(\mu|m, \upsilon/n)f'(\mu) \tag{16.13}$$

where C' is a function of z and not of μ; recall that $m = \sum_{i=1}^{n} z_i/n$.

16.3.2 Approximate Normality of the Posterior for a "Gentle" Prior

From figure 16.2 we see that as long as the prior df $f'(\mu)$ is "gentle" in the vicinity of $\mu = m$, the posterior df $f'(\mu|z)$ will be of the approximate shape of $L(\mu|z)$ in the vicinity of $\mu = m$, which means that $f''(\mu|z)$ will be approximately the same shape as $f_N(\mu|m, \upsilon/n)$ near $\mu = m$. Observe that as n increases the likelihood function $f_N(\mu|m, \upsilon/n)$ becomes tighter and tighter and it is reasonable to expect that for "large" n the prior df $f'(\mu)$ will be reasonably gentle over an interval which extends a few standard deviations $\sqrt{\upsilon/n}$ on either side of the sample mean. This observation can be summarized of the following rather vague proposition:

For "large" samples the posterior df of $\tilde{\mu}$ is Normal with a mean equal to the sample mean and a variance equal to the sampling variance of individual observations divided by the sample size. Symbolically, for "large" n,

$$f''(\mu|z) \doteq f_N(\mu|m, \upsilon/n).$$

The test for what "large" means can only be answered in terms of the variability in the height of the prior df $f'(\mu)$ over the interval $[m - k\sqrt{\upsilon/n}, m + k\sqrt{\upsilon/n}]$ for values of k on the order of 2 or 3. In very loose terms the reader should observe that the "degree of gentleness" of a prior df needs to be thought of in terms of the shape of the prior df in relationship to the tightness of the likelihood function and where this likelihood function happens to be centered. Suppose, for example, that $\upsilon = 4$, $n = 100$, and $m = 32$. Then the likelihood function is centered at 32 and $\sqrt{\upsilon/n} = .2$. If the prior distribution is such that it is reasonably gentle over the interval from 31.2 to 32.8, say, (i.e., four $\sqrt{\upsilon/n}$-units on either side of 32), then without further ado we can treat the posterior of $\tilde{\mu}$ as approximately Normal with parameters (32, 4/100). (Cf. sections 11.3.5 and 11.4.3 for the parallel discussion of the Bernoulli process.)

16.3.3 Sufficiency of the Sample Mean When υ Is Known

Because the expression (16.13) for the posterior distributing function of $\tilde{\mu}$ depends on the sample observations $(z_1, \ldots, z_n)$ only through their mean m and the number of observations n, the pair (m, n) are the *sufficient statistics* of the sample. As far as making inferences or decisions about μ is concerned, a statistician who is given information about all the sample outcomes $z_1, z_2, \ldots, z_n$ is no better off than a statistician who is only given the summary information (m, n)—provided, and this is crucial, that it is known that the observations $z_1, z_2, \ldots, z_n$ are outcomes of independent, identically distributed, Normal rv's with unknown mean μ and *known* variance υ. (See also the appendix to chapter 20.)

16.4 Posterior Analysis When the Prior Distribution of $\tilde{\mu}$ Is Normal

16.4.1 Normality of the Posterior Distribution

Suppose now that the *prior* distribution which the decision maker assigns to $\tilde{\mu}$ is *Normal*, so that we may write

$$f'(\mu) = f_N(\mu|\bar{\mu}', \breve{\mu}') \tag{16.14}$$

where the parameters $\bar{\mu}'$ and $\breve{\mu}'$ represent definite numbers chosen by the decision maker. We shall show that:

> If the prior distribution of the mean $\tilde{\mu}$ of an Independent Normal process is Normal and the process variance is known, then the posterior distribution of $\tilde{\mu}$ is also Normal.

This is the reason why it is extremely convenient to represent the decision maker's prior judgments by a Normal distribution rather than by a distribution of any other type; it was for an analogous reason that we found it very convenient in problems involving a Bernoulli $\tilde{p}$ to represent the decision maker's judgments concerning $\tilde{p}$ by a beta distribution rather than by one of any other type.

The assertion above is formalized in the form of the following

Theorem Let $z = (z_1, \ldots, z_n)$ be the sample from an Independent Normal process with known variance υ and unknown mean μ; let m be the sample mean; let $\tilde{\mu}$ be given a Normal prior df with mean $\bar{\mu}'$ and variance $\breve{\mu}'$. Then the posterior df of $\tilde{\mu}$ given z is given by

$$f''(\mu|z) = f_N(\mu|\bar{\mu}'', \breve{\mu}''), \tag{16.15a}$$

where

$$\bar{\mu}'' = \frac{(1/\breve{\mu}')\bar{\mu}' + (n/\upsilon)m}{(1/\breve{\mu}') + (n/\upsilon)}, \qquad \breve{\mu}'' = \frac{1}{(1/\breve{\mu}') + (n/\upsilon)}. \tag{16.15b}$$

Proof Substituting the specific form of the prior df of $\tilde{\mu}$ in (16.13) gives

$$\begin{aligned} f''(\mu|z) &= C' f_N(\mu|m, \upsilon/n) f_N(\mu|\bar{\mu}', \breve{\mu}') \\ &= C'' e^{-(1/2)S} \end{aligned}$$

where

$$S = \frac{(\mu - m)^2}{\upsilon/n} + \frac{(\mu - \bar{\mu}')^2}{\breve{\mu}'},$$

and C'' is a function of known values such as z, υ/n, $\breve{\mu}'$ but *not* of μ; therefore C'' may be treated as a constant for our present purposes. Expanding S, we obtain

$$\begin{aligned} S &= \frac{n}{\upsilon}[\mu^2 - 2\mu m + m^2] + \frac{1}{\breve{\mu}'}[\mu^2 - 2\mu\bar{\mu}' + \bar{\mu}'^2] \\ &= \mu^2\left[\frac{n}{\upsilon} + \frac{1}{\breve{\mu}'}\right] - 2\mu\left[\frac{n}{\upsilon}m + \frac{1}{\breve{\mu}'}\bar{\mu}'\right] + \left\{\begin{matrix}\text{terms not} \\ \text{involving } \mu\end{matrix}\right\} \\ &= \left[\frac{n}{\upsilon} + \frac{1}{\breve{\mu}'}\right]\left[\mu - \frac{\frac{n}{\upsilon}m + \frac{1}{\breve{\mu}'}\bar{\mu}'}{\frac{n}{\upsilon} + \frac{1}{\breve{\mu}'}}\right]^2 + \left\{\begin{matrix}\text{terms not} \\ \text{involving } \mu\end{matrix}\right\} \\ &= \frac{1}{\breve{\mu}''}(\mu - \bar{\mu}'')^2 + \left\{\begin{matrix}\text{terms not} \\ \text{involving } \mu\end{matrix}\right\}, \end{aligned}$$

where $\bar{\mu}''$ and $\breve{\mu}''$ are given in (16.15b). Hence we get

$$f''(\mu|z) = C''' e^{-(1/2)((\mu - \bar{\mu}'')^2/\breve{\mu}''}$$

and C''' must be $(2\pi\breve{\mu}'')^{-1/2}$ because this is the normalizing constant that makes the area under the right-hand side of the above equation equal to 1. This completes the proof of the theorem.

16.4.2 Interpretation of the Parameters of the Posterior Distribution of $\tilde{\mu}$

We denote the *precision* of any rv $\tilde{x}$ by $H(\tilde{x})$ and define it to be the reciprocal of the variance; in other words, $H(\tilde{x}) \equiv 1/V(\tilde{x})$. In our present problem we may write for the precisions of the prior and posterior distributions of $\tilde{\mu}$

$$H(\tilde{\mu}) = \breve{\mu}'^{-1}, \qquad H(\tilde{\mu}|m) = \breve{\mu}''^{-1}; \tag{16.16}$$

and when υ is known we shall show in section 16.6 that the precision of the conditional distribution of $\tilde{m}$ given μ is

$$H(\tilde{m}|\mu) = n/\upsilon. \tag{16.17}$$

Substituting (16.16) and (16.17) in formulas (16.15) for the parameters of the posterior distribution of $\tilde{\mu}$ we obtain

$$\bar{\mu}'' = \frac{H(\tilde{\mu})\bar{\mu}' + H(\tilde{m}|\mu)m}{H(\tilde{\mu}) + H(\tilde{m}|\mu)},$$
$$\breve{\mu}''^{-1} \equiv H(\tilde{\mu}|m) = H(\tilde{\mu}) + H(\tilde{m}|\mu). \tag{16.18}$$

The *posterior mean* is a *weighted average* of the prior mean $\bar{\mu}'$ and the mean m of the sample, the weights being the precisions of the prior distribution of $\tilde{\mu}$ and the conditional or sampling distribution of $\tilde{m}$ given μ; the *posterior precision* is simply the *sum* of the prior and sampling precisions.

In light of these observations, it becomes very tempting to think of $H(\tilde{\mu})$, $H(\tilde{m}|\mu)$, and $H(\tilde{\mu}|m)$ as measuring the *quantity of information* about $\tilde{\mu}$ that is contained respectively in the prior, sampling, and posterior distributions of $\tilde{\mu}$; and the temptation becomes even stronger when we observe that by (16.17) the sampling precision $H(\tilde{m}|\mu) = n/\upsilon$ is directly proportional to the number of observations in the sample. Such an interpretation of precision as quantity of information can in fact be very suggestive, and we shall use it from time to time; the reader must, however, always remember that, even under our Normality assumptions, such an interpretation is *at most* suggestive; in certain types of decision problems a prior distribution with $H(\tilde{\mu})$ extremely small may represent an *extremely important judgment* about $\tilde{\mu}$ even if it represents "very little information" about $\tilde{\mu}$.

There is still another very suggestive way to interpret formulas (16.15b) and (16.18). Let us define a number n' such that

$$n' = \upsilon/\breve{\mu}' \quad \text{or} \quad \breve{\mu}' = \upsilon/n'; \tag{16.19}$$

in terms of this definition, (16.15b) can be rewritten in the form

$$\bar{\mu}'' = \frac{n'\bar{\mu}' + nm}{n' + n}, \qquad \breve{\mu}'' = \frac{\upsilon}{n + n'}. \tag{16.20}$$

The parameter n' can be interpreted therefore as the "fictitious sample size" or equivalent number of sample observations that describes the amount of information implicit in the prior distribution.

16.5 Sensitivity of the Posterior to the Prior

16.5.1 Negligible Prior Information

Examining formulas (16.18) for the posterior mean and precision of $\tilde{\mu}$, we can see at once that if we hold the prior and sample means and the sample precision fixed but let the prior precision decrease toward 0 (i.e., let the prior variance $\breve{\mu}'$ increase without bound), then the posterior mean, variance, and precision respectively approach m, v/n, and n/v. Specifically,

$$\text{if} \left\{ \begin{matrix} \breve{\mu}' \to \infty \\ \text{or} \\ H(\mu) \to 0 \end{matrix} \right\}, \quad \text{then} \quad \left\{ \begin{matrix} \bar{\mu}' \to m \\ \breve{\mu}'' \to v/n \\ \text{and} \\ H(\mu|m) \to n/v \end{matrix} \right\}. \tag{16.21}$$

What is more important, we can also see at once from (16.18) that even if the prior precision is not strictly 0, the posterior parameters will have *very nearly* the values given by (16.21) whenever the prior precision is *small relative to the sample precision.* This fact can be quite useful in reducing or eliminating the considerable effort required to make a really careful assessment of a judgmental prior distribution of $\tilde{\mu}$. If the decision maker feels uncertain about the *exact values* she would want to assign to $\bar{\mu}'$ and $H(\tilde{\mu}) = \breve{\mu}'^{-1}$ but is nevertheless certain that the *highest* value she would even consider giving to $H(\tilde{\mu})$ is very small relative to the precision $H(\tilde{m}|\mu)$ of some *sample already at hand,* then in most problems she can spare herself further bother and either (1) choose *any* plausible values for $\bar{\mu}'$ and $\breve{\mu}'$, or even (2) decide to adopt a posterior distribution of $\tilde{\mu}$ with the parameters given by (16.21) and simply forget about evaluating and incorporating her prior judgments. If the decision maker does choose the latter alternative, it is suggestive to say that she has decided that she considers her "prior information" about μ to be "negligible in comparison with the information contained in the sample." (See the discussion of "gentle" prior distributions in section 16.3.2.)

16.5.2 "Uniform Prior Distributions"

If we examine what happens to the *prior* rather than the posterior distribution as $H(\tilde{\mu})$ approaches zero keeping $\bar{\mu}'$ fixed, we find that the prior density approaches a horizontal straight line. More precisely, for any two finite intervals I_1 and I_2 of the same length the ratio of the probability that $\tilde{\mu}$ lies within interval I_1 to the probability that it lies within interval I_2 approaches unity, so that we can say that the prior distribution approaches a *uniform* distribution over the real line.

For this reason a decision to neglect $\bar{\mu}'$ and $H(\tilde{\mu})$ and adopt a *posterior* distribution with parameters $\bar{\mu}'' = m$ and $H(\tilde{\mu}|m) = H(\tilde{m}|\mu)$ is sometimes called "adopting a uniform prior distribution," but the terminology is extremely misleading. As $H(\tilde{\mu})$ approaches 0, that is, as $\breve{\mu}'$ approaches ∞, the probability that $\tilde{\mu}$ lies within any specified bounded interval approaches 0, no matter how large the interval may be. This implies that as $H(\tilde{\mu})$ approaches 0 the odds at which the decision maker would bet that $\tilde{\mu}$ lies *outside* any specified bounded interval increase without bound. We leave it to the reader to try to imagine an interpretation of $\tilde{\mu}$ such that a reasonable decision maker would bet at odds of 10^{100} to 1 that $\tilde{\mu}$ is either greater than 10^{100} or less than -10^{100}. If a reasonable decision maker does not treat $H(\tilde{\mu})$ as 0 in computing a *posterior* distribution, it is purely and simply because the *posterior* distribution thus computed makes sense and not because he accepts any of the implications concerning the *prior* distribution. (See section 16.3.2 on "gentle" priors.)

"Total Ignorance"

One still occasionally hears uniform distributions defended as such on the grounds (1) that the decision maker may be "totally ignorant" about the value of $\tilde{\mu}$, and (2) that if he is, then he "should" treat all possible values of $\tilde{\mu}$ as equally likely—more precisely, he should assign equal probability to intervals of equal length.

Even on purely logical grounds, this argument is flatly untenable. If the expression "total ignorance" means anything at all, then surely total ignorance about $\tilde{\mu}$ implies total ignorance about $\tilde{\mu}^2$ and vice versa; unfortunately, it is simply impossible to assign equal probability to all values of $\tilde{\mu}$ and at the same time to assign equal probability to all values of $\tilde{\mu}^2$. Suppose, for example, that we say that it just as likely that $\tilde{\mu}$ is between 0 and 1 as it is that $\tilde{\mu}$ is between 1 and 2. This necessarily implies that $\tilde{\mu}^2$ is as likely to be between 0 and 1 as it is to be between 1 and 4; therefore, values of $\tilde{\mu}^2$ between 0 and 1 are three times as likely on the average as values between 1 and 4. As a second example, if $\tilde{\mu}$ is given a rectangular distribution from $\mu = -10^6$ to $\mu = 10^6$, then the probability that $-1 \leq 1/\tilde{\mu} \leq 1$ is .9999 to four significant figures. Does this represent total ignorance?

Thus even if a person responsible for a decision feels himself to be in a state of total ignorance about the value of $\tilde{\mu}$, there is no "objective" way of assigning prior probabilities. He must make up his own mind—he must place his own bets—and where there is no sample evidence available, it is these bets which will be crucial for the decision. *Prior information or prior betting odds can be neglected only when substantial sample evidence is available.*

16.5.3 Non-Normal Prior Distribution

Now that we have seen that the exact numerical values of the parameters of the prior distribution are of little importance when $H(\tilde{m}|\mu)$ is large, let us look briefly at the effect of the exact *shape* of the prior distribution on the posterior distribution when $H(\tilde{m}|\mu)$ is large. In figure 16.3A we show two contrasting prior distributions which we take as examples:

1. A *Normal* prior distribution with mean $\bar{\mu}' = 1$ and variance $\breve{\mu}' = 1$.

2. An *exponential* prior distribution with the same mean and variance as the Normal.

The exponential distribution is about as violently non-Normal as any smooth distribution can be: it is J-shaped rather than symmetric, and it actually assigns 0 probability to all negative values of the random variable $\tilde{\mu}$.

In the remaining four graphs of figure 16.3 we compare the *posterior* distributions corresponding to these two prior distributions after samples of four different sizes have been taken. In all four cases we assume that the process variance $v = 1$ and that the observed value of the sample mean $m = 1$; it is *only* the sample size n that differs from case to case. In figure 16.3B we see that if the sample consists of just one observation, there is a very substantial difference between the two posterior distributions; in figure 16.3C we see that the difference would still be quite large if $n = 4$. By the time $n = 9$, however, the difference is becoming much smaller (figure 16.3D), and it is *very* small for $n = 25$ (figure 16.3E). With a sample of 50 or more the difference would be completely negligible for almost all practical purposes.

Although figure 16.3 is only a study of a special case, the general nature of the conclusions derived from it hold for *any* prior density which is positive and reasonably smooth in the vicinity of the observed sample mean m, as can easily be seen from (16.13) and the discussion in section 16.3.2.

16.6 Preposterior Distribution Theory

In preposterior analysis where a sample size n is prescribed, we shall require the marginal df of the as yet unknown sufficient statistic $\tilde{m}$; this is needed for an analysis of moves 1 and 2 on the decision tree (figure 14.1). In this section we shall show that the marginal df of $\tilde{m}$ is Normal, and that the as yet unknown posterior mean $\tilde{\bar{\mu}}''$ is also Normal. We start off by first investigating the conditional df of $\tilde{m}$ given μ.

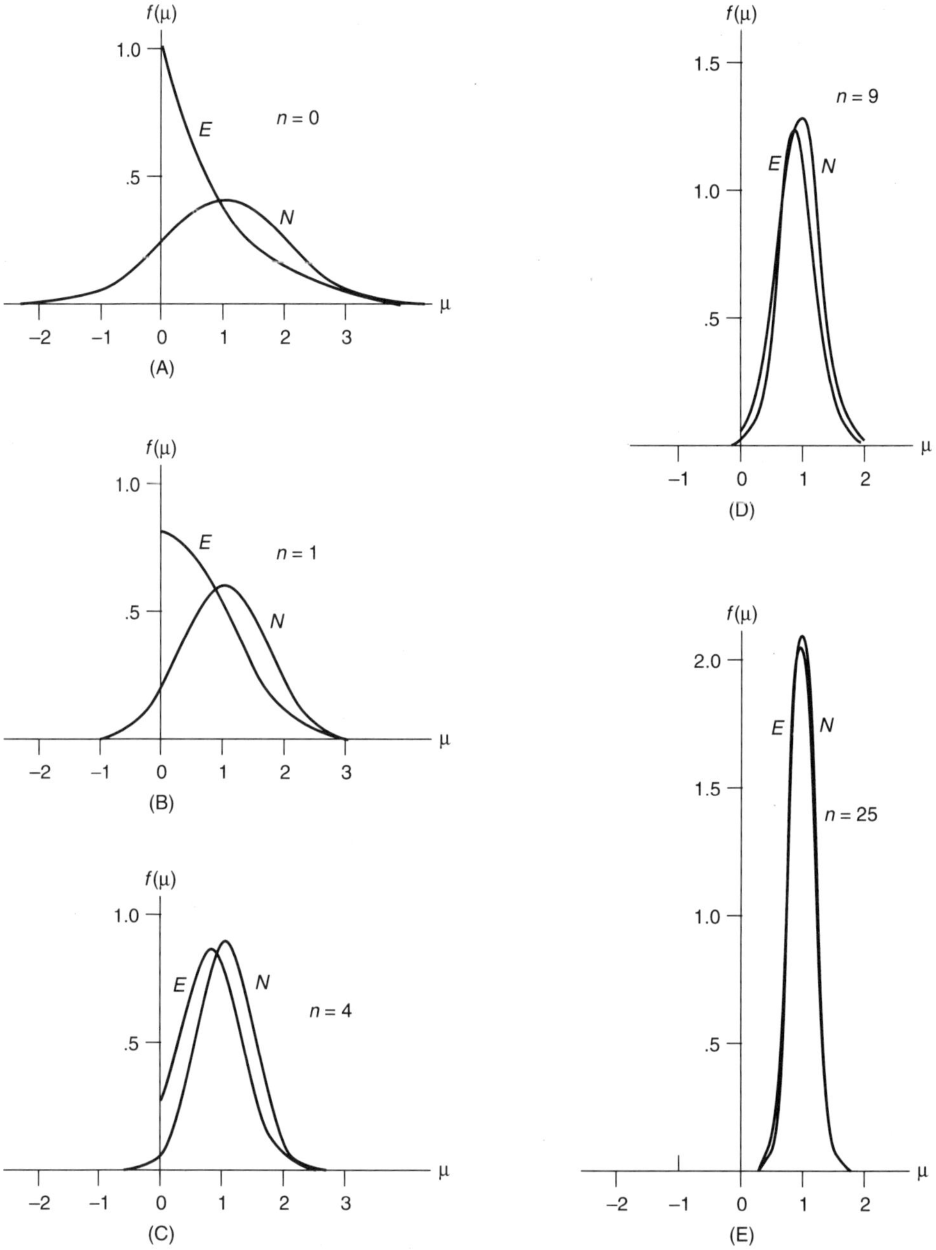

Figure 16.3
Posterior distributions corresponding to Normal and exponential prior distributions

16.6.1 Sums of Independent Normal RV's and the Conditional Normality of $(\tilde{m}|\mu)$

The following theorem is of basic importance not only in this subsection but in many of the following chapters:

Theorem Let $\tilde{x}_1, \tilde{x}_2, \ldots, \tilde{x}_n$ be independent Normal rv's where $\tilde{x}_i$ has the mean $\bar{x}_i$, and variance $\check{x}_i$, for $i = 1, 2, \ldots, n$; let

$$\tilde{S}_n = \tilde{x}_1 + \tilde{x}_2 + \cdots + \tilde{x}_n. \tag{16.22}$$

Then $\tilde{S}_n$ is a Normal rv with mean

$$\bar{S}_n = \bar{x}_1 + \bar{x}_2 + \cdots + \bar{x}_n, \tag{16.23a}$$

and variance

$$\check{S}_n = \check{x}_1 + \check{x}_2 + \cdots + \check{x}_n. \tag{16.23b}$$

Proof We shall first prove the result for the special case where $n = 2$ and $\bar{x}_1 = \bar{x}_2 = 0$; we shall then drop the assumption that $\bar{x}_1 = \bar{x}_2 = 0$; finally we shall extend the result to arbitrary n.

Special Case Where n = 2, $\bar{x}_1 = \bar{x}_2 = 0$ For typographic ease let $\tilde{z} = \tilde{x}_1 + \tilde{x}_2$, $\check{x}_i \equiv v_i$, $\sqrt{v_i} \equiv \sigma_i$. From (13.49), which gives a formula for the df of the sum of two independent rv's, we get

$$\begin{aligned}
g(z) &= \int_{-\infty}^{\infty} f_N(z - x_1|0, v_2) f_N(x_1|0, v_1)\, dx_1 \\
&= \int_{-\infty}^{\infty} \frac{1}{\sqrt{2\pi\sigma_2}} e^{-(1/2)((z-x_1)^2/v_2)} \frac{1}{\sqrt{2\pi\sigma_1}} e^{-(1/2)((x_1^2/v_1)}\, dx_1 \\
&= \frac{1}{2\pi\sigma_1\sigma_2} \int_{-\infty}^{\infty} e^{-(1/2)S}\, dx_1,
\end{aligned}$$

where

$$\begin{aligned}
S &= \frac{(z - x_1)^2}{v_2} + \frac{x_1^2}{v_1} \\
&= \frac{v_1(z^2 - 2x_1 z + x_1^2) + v_2 x_1^2}{v_1 v_2} \\
&= \frac{v_1 + v_2}{v_1 v_2}\left[x_1^2 - \frac{2x_1 v_1 z}{v_1 + v_2} + \frac{v_1 z^2}{v_1 + v_2}\right] \\
&= \frac{v_1 + v_2}{v_1 v_2}\left[\left(x_1 - \frac{v_1 z}{v_1 + v_2}\right)^2 - \frac{v_1^2 z^2}{(v_1 + v_2)^2} + \frac{v_1 z^2}{v_1 + v_2}\right] \\
&= \frac{v_1 + v_2}{v_1 v_2}\left(x_1 - \frac{v_1 z}{v_1 + v_2}\right)^2 + \frac{z^2}{v_1 + v_2}.
\end{aligned}$$

Hence,

$$g(z) = \frac{1}{\sqrt{2\pi}\sqrt{v_1 + v_2}} e^{-(1/2)(z^2/(v_1+v_2))} \int_{-\infty}^{\infty} \frac{1}{\sqrt{2\pi}} \sqrt{\frac{v_1 + v_2}{v_1 v_2}}$$

$$\cdot e^{-(1/2)[(v_1+v_2)/v_1 v_2][x_1 - v_1 z/(v_1+v_2)]^2} dx_1$$

$$= f_N(z|0, v_1 + v_2) \int_{-\infty}^{\infty} f_N\left(x_1 \middle| \frac{v_1 z}{v_1 + v_2}, \frac{v_1 v_2}{v_1 + v_2}\right) dx_1$$

$$= f_N(z|0, v_1 + v_2),$$

which concludes the proof for this special case.

***Special Case Where n* = 2** We now drop the restriction that $\bar{x}_1 = \bar{x}_2 = 0$. We have

$$\tilde{z} = [(\tilde{x}_1 - \bar{x}_1) + (\tilde{x}_2 - \bar{x}_2)] + (\bar{x}_1 + \bar{x}_2)$$

and from the above special case the df of the rv $[(\tilde{x}_1 - \bar{x}_1) + (\tilde{x}_2 - \bar{x}_2)]$ is $f_N(\cdot|0, \check{x}_1 + \check{x}_2)$. But since the sum of a Normal rv and a constant is a Normal rv (left as an exercise), this concludes the proof of this special case and the proof of the theorem for $n = 2$.

Extension to Arbitrary n From the above case $\tilde{x}_1 + \tilde{x}_2$ is Normal with mean $(\bar{x}_1 + \bar{x}_2)$ and variance $(\check{x}_1 + \check{x}_2)$. Since the rv's $(\tilde{x}_1 + \tilde{x}_2)$ and $\tilde{x}_3$ are independent Normal rv's, the above result enables us to conclude that $(\tilde{x}_1 + \tilde{x}_2) + \tilde{x}_3$ is a Normal rv with mean $(\bar{x}_1 + \bar{x}_2) + \bar{x}_3$ and variance $(\check{x}_1 + \check{x}_2) + \check{x}_3$. This process can now obviously be repeated for any number of independent Normal summands. More formally, if the theorem is true for $n = k$, it is true for $n = k + 1$, because

$$\tilde{S}_{k+1} = \tilde{S}_k + \tilde{x}_{k+1}$$

and the above result applies. This concludes the proof of the theorem.

We now propose to use the above theorem to prove the following

Theorem If m is the mean of n observations $(\tilde{z}_1, \tilde{z}_2, \ldots, \tilde{z}_n)$ generated by an Independent Normal process with mean μ and variance v, then the conditional distribution of $\tilde{m}$ given μ and v is Normal with mean μ and variance v/n. Symbolically,

$$(\tilde{m}|\mu) \sim f_{m|\mu}(m) = f_N(m|\mu, v/n). \tag{16.24}$$

Proof For a given μ and v, the rv's $\tilde{z}_1, \tilde{z}_2, \ldots, \tilde{z}_n$ are independent Normal rv's with common mean μ and common variance v. Hence by the previous theorem, for a given μ and v, the rv

$$\tilde{S}_n \equiv \tilde{z}_1 + \tilde{z}_2 + \cdots + \tilde{z}_n,$$

is Normal with mean $n\mu$ and variance nv. Symbolically,

$$(\tilde{S}_n|\mu) \sim f_N(S_n|n\mu, nv).$$

Now it is left to the reader to complete the proof by showing that, for a given μ and v, the rv

$$\tilde{m} \equiv \tilde{S}_n/n$$

is Normal with mean $n\mu/n$ and variance nv/n^2. ■

16.6.2 Unconditional Normality of $\tilde{m}$

In this section we show the following:

If the prior distribution of $\tilde{\mu}$ is Normal, then the as yet unknown sample mean from an Independent Normal process with known variance v and unknown mean μ is Normal.

This assertion is formalized in the form of the following

Theorem For a given μ let the rv's $\tilde{z}_1, \tilde{z}_2, \ldots, \tilde{z}_n$ be independent, identically distributed (iid) Normal rv's with mean μ and variance v; let $\tilde{\mu}$ be Normal with mean $\bar{\mu}'$ and variance $\breve{\mu}'$; let

$$\tilde{m} = \textstyle\sum_{i=1}^n \tilde{z}_i/n.$$

Then the df of $\tilde{m}$ is given by

$$f_m(m) = f_N(m|\bar{\mu}', \breve{\mu}' + v/n). \tag{16.25}$$

Proof By (13.18) and (13.20),

$$\begin{aligned} f_m(m) &= \int_{-\infty}^{\infty} f_{m|\mu}(m) f_\mu(\mu)\, d\mu \\ &= \int_{-\infty}^{\infty} f_N(m|\mu, v/n) f_N(\mu|\bar{\mu}', \breve{\mu}')\, d\mu \\ &= C \int_{-\infty}^{\infty} e^{-(1/2)S}\, d\mu, \end{aligned}$$

where

$$S = \frac{n}{v}(m-\mu)^2 + \frac{1}{\breve{\mu}'}(\mu - \bar{\mu}')^2,$$

and C is a factor which does not depend on μ. Expanding S, we get

$$S = \frac{1}{\breve{\mu}''}(\mu - \bar{\mu}'')^2 + \frac{1}{\breve{\mu}' + \upsilon/n}(m - \bar{\mu}')^2$$

where $\bar{\mu}''$ and $\breve{\mu}''$ are defined in (16.15b). Substituting,

$$f_m(m) = C'e^{-(1/2)(1/(\breve{\mu}'+\upsilon/n))(m-\bar{\mu}')^2} \int_{-\infty}^{\infty} f_N(\mu|\bar{\mu}'', \breve{\mu}'')\, d\mu$$

$$= f_N(m|\bar{\mu}', \breve{\mu}' + \upsilon/n).$$

Alternate Proof Since $\tilde{\mu}$ and $(\tilde{m} - \tilde{\mu})$ are independent Normal rv's, and

$$\tilde{m} = \tilde{\mu} + (\tilde{m} - \tilde{\mu}),$$

it follows from the first theorem in section 16.6.1 that $\tilde{m}$ is Normal with mean $(\bar{\mu}' + 0)$ and variance $(\breve{\mu}' + \upsilon/n)$. ■

16.6.3 Normality of $\tilde{\bar{\mu}}''$

If υ is known, if the prior df of $\tilde{\mu}$ is Normal with parameters $(\bar{\mu}', \breve{\mu}')$ and if a sample from an Independent Normal process yields sufficient statistics (m, n) then by (16.15b) the posterior mean is given by

$$\bar{\mu}'' = a + bm \tag{16.26a}$$

where

$$a = \frac{(1/\breve{\mu}')\bar{\mu}'}{(1/\breve{\mu}') + (n/\upsilon)}, \qquad b = \frac{n/\upsilon}{(1/\breve{\mu}') + (n/\upsilon)}. \tag{16.26b}$$

If a sample of size n is proposed by m has not as yet been observed, then the sample mean is a rv $\tilde{m}$ and also the posterior mean is a rv $\tilde{\bar{\mu}}''$, where

$$\tilde{\bar{\mu}}'' = a + b\tilde{m}. \tag{16.27}$$

Since $\tilde{m}$ has been shown to be *un*conditionally Normal, it follows that $\tilde{\bar{\mu}}''$ is *Normal* and we shall show that

$$E(\tilde{\bar{\mu}}'') = \bar{\mu}' \tag{16.28}$$

and

$$V(\tilde{\bar{\mu}}'') \equiv \breve{\bar{\mu}}'' = \breve{\mu}' \frac{\breve{\mu}'}{\breve{\mu}' + \upsilon/n} = \breve{\mu}' - \breve{\mu}'', \tag{16.29a}$$

where

$$\breve{\mu}'' = \frac{1}{(1/\breve{\mu}') + (n/\upsilon)}. \tag{16.29b}$$

Proof There are two ways of showing these results. First, from (16.27)

$$E(\tilde{\bar{\mu}}'') = a + bE(\tilde{m}), \qquad V(\tilde{\bar{\mu}}'') = b^2 V(\tilde{m}),$$

and then we use (16.26b) and (16.25). Second, from general theory we know that

$$\bar{\mu}', = E(\tilde{\mu}) = E_m E_{\mu|m}(\tilde{\mu}) = E(\tilde{\bar{\mu}}''),$$

which establishes (16.28), Also from general theory

$$\breve{\mu}' = \breve{\bar{\mu}}'' + \bar{\breve{\mu}}'';$$

now from (16.15b) we know that $\breve{\mu}''$ does *not* depend on m and therefore $\breve{\mu}''$ is not unknown once n has been chosen; hence $\bar{\breve{\mu}}'' = \breve{\mu}''$ and we obtain

$$\breve{\bar{\mu}}'' = \breve{\mu}' - \breve{\mu}''.$$

Substituting the value for $\breve{\mu}''$ as given in (16.15b) and repeated in (16.29b) we obtain (16.29a). ■

Observe that as n *increases* from 0 to ∞, $\breve{\mu}''$ *decreases* from $\breve{\mu}'$ to 0, and $\breve{\bar{\mu}}''$ increases from 0 to $\breve{\mu}'$.

16.6.4 Probabilistic Prediction

We now pose and answer the following problem. Consider an Independent Normal process with unknown mean μ and known variance υ; let $\tilde{\mu}$ be given a Normal prior df with parameter $(\bar{\mu}', \breve{\mu}')$. After observing the outcomes $z_1, z_2, \ldots, z_n$, what is the conditional df of the next rv $\tilde{z}_{n+1}$?

The problem posed above has a simple answer in terms of the distribution theory we have already developed. After the sample $z_1, z_2, \ldots, z_n$ is observed the parameters of the df of $\tilde{\mu}$ are updated from $(\bar{\mu}', \breve{\mu}')$ to $(\bar{\mu}'', \breve{\mu}'')$. Now as far as the $(n + 1)$th observation is concerned, the prior distribution of $\tilde{\mu}$ can be taken as Normal with parameter $(\bar{\mu}'', \breve{\mu}'')$ and the problem merely asks for the marginal distribution of the mean of a future sample of size one. But the marginal df of $\tilde{m}$ is known to be Normal with a mean equal to the prior mean (which in this case is the updated mean $\bar{\mu}''$) and a variance equal to the sum of the prior variance (which in this case is the updated variance $\breve{\mu}'' = \upsilon/(n' + n)$) and the sampling variance (which in this case is $\upsilon/1$). We conclude therefore that, for given values z_1, $z_2, \ldots, z_n$, *the conditional df of* $\tilde{z}_{n+1}$ *is Normal with mean* $\bar{\mu}''$, *and variance* $\upsilon[1/(n' + n) + 1]$.

There is another instructive way of looking at this problem. Keeping in mind that $\tilde{\mu}$ can be treated as a rv, we have

$$\tilde{z}_{n+1} = \tilde{\mu} + \tilde{\varepsilon}_{n+1},$$

Table 16.1
[*Model.* Let $\tilde{\varepsilon}_i$ be iid, Normal $(0, \upsilon)$; let $\tilde{z}_i = \mu + \tilde{\varepsilon}_i$; let $\tilde{m} \equiv \sum_{i=1}^{n} \tilde{z}_i / n$]

RV	Type	Mean	Variance
$\tilde{\varepsilon}_i$	Normal	0	υ
$\tilde{z}_i \| \mu$	Normal	μ	υ
$\tilde{m} \| \mu$	Normal	μ	υ / n
$\tilde{\mu}$	Normal	$\bar{\mu}'$	$\breve{\mu}' = \upsilon / n'$
$\tilde{\mu} \| m$	Normal	$\bar{\mu}'' = \frac{n'\bar{\mu}' + nm}{n' + n}$	$\breve{\mu}' = \frac{\upsilon}{n + n'}$
$\tilde{m}$	Normal	$\bar{\mu}'$	$\upsilon\left[\frac{1}{n'} + \frac{1}{n}\right]$
$\tilde{\bar{\mu}}''$	Normal	$\bar{\mu}'$	$\bar{\mu}'' = \upsilon\left[\frac{1}{n'} - \frac{1}{n + n'}\right]$
			$= \breve{\mu}' \frac{n}{n + n'}$
$\tilde{z}_{n+1} \| z_1, \ldots, z_n$	Normal	$\bar{\mu}''$	$\upsilon\left[\frac{1}{n' + n} + 1\right]$

wherc the rv's $\tilde{\mu}$ and $\tilde{\varepsilon}_{n+1}$ are independent. After observing $z_1, \ldots, z_n$, the current distribution of $\tilde{\mu}$ is Normal with parameter $(\bar{\mu}'', \breve{\mu}'')$; the df of $\tilde{\varepsilon}_{n+1}$ is Normal with parameter $(0, \upsilon)$. Hence the df of $\tilde{z}_{n+1}$ is Normal with a mean $\bar{\mu}''$ and a variance of $\breve{\mu}'' + \upsilon$.

16.6.5 Summary of Distribution Theory

The distribution theory we have developed in this chapter is summarized in table 16.1.

16.7 Terminal and Preposterior Analyses

16.7.1 Notation

Having developed the necessary distribution theory for an Independent Normal process with unknown mean μ and known variance υ, we now turn our attention to decision problems where the unknown state parameter is μ.

In chapter 14 we let $v(e, z, a, s)$ denote the value of performing experiment e, observing a particular outcome z, and choosing a particular terminal act a, when the true state of the world is s. In the remainder of this chapter we specialize our notation and let $v(n, m, a, \mu)$ denote the value of choosing a fixed size sample of size n from an Independent Normal process, observing a particular sufficient statistic (the sample mean) m, and choosing a particular terminal act a, when the true unknown parameter is μ. We shall define $l(n, m, a, \mu)$ in an analogous manner, and corresponding to (14.1) and (14.2) we shall write

$$v(n, m, a, \mu) = v_t(a, \mu) - c_s(n, m), \tag{16.31a}$$

and

$$l(n, m, a, \mu) = l_t(a, \mu) + c_s(n, m). \tag{16.31b}$$

16.7.2 Terminal Analysis

If $\tilde{\mu}$ is given a prior Normal df with parameter $(\bar{\mu}', \breve{\mu}')$, then the analogue of (14.3) becomes

$$\bar{v}_t''(a, (n, m)) \equiv E_{\mu|n,m} v_t(a, \tilde{\mu})$$

$$= \int_{-\infty}^{\infty} v_t(a, \mu) f_N(\mu | \bar{\mu}'', \breve{\mu}'')\, d\mu, \tag{16.32a}$$

$$\bar{l}_t''(a, (n, m)) \equiv E_{\mu|n,m} l_t(a, \tilde{\mu})$$

$$= \int_{-\infty}^{\infty} l_t(a, \mu) f_N(\mu | \bar{\mu}'', \breve{\mu}'',)\, d\mu, \tag{16.32b}$$

where $(\bar{\mu}'', \breve{\mu}'')$ is given by (16.15b).

Observe that in terminal analysis $a^o_{n,m}$ depends on the parameter $(\bar{\mu}'', \breve{\mu}'')$ in exactly the same way that the optimal act a^o, prior to observing (n, m), depends on the parameter $(\bar{\mu}', \breve{\mu}')$. Observe also that the expressions $\bar{v}_t''(a^o_{n,m}, (n, m))$ and $\bar{l}_t''(a^o_{n,m}, (n, m))$ depend on (n, m) only through the parameter $(\bar{\mu}'', \breve{\mu}'')$.

16.7.3 Preposterior Analysis

If $\tilde{\mu}$ is given a prior Normal df with parameter $(\bar{\mu}', \breve{\mu}')$, then the analogue of (14.8) becomes

$$\bar{\bar{v}}_t(n) \equiv E\bar{v}_t''(a^o_{n,\tilde{m}}, (n, \tilde{m}))$$

$$= \int_{-\infty}^{\infty} \bar{v}_t''(a^o_{n,m}, (n, m)) f_N(m | \bar{\mu}', \breve{\mu}' + v/n)\, dm, \tag{16.33a}$$

and

$$\bar{\bar{l}}_t(n) \equiv E\bar{l}_t''(a^o_{n,\tilde{m}}, (n, \tilde{m}))$$

$$= \int_{-\infty}^{\infty} \bar{l}_t''(a^o_{n,\tilde{m}}, (n, m)) f_N(m | \bar{\mu}', \breve{\mu}' + v/n)\, dm. \tag{16.33b}$$

In the remaining sections of this chapter we shall indicate how expressions (16.32) and (16.33) simplify when we consider our three prototype decision problems: infinite-action with quadratic loss, infinite-action with linear loss, two-action with linear value. In these special cases we shall investigate EVSI, ENGS, and the optimal sample size.

16.8 Infinite-Action Problems with Quadratic Loss

16.8.1 Terminal Analysis

Let $\tilde{\mu}$ be the unknown parameter of an independent Normal process; let the set of available acts (estimates) be the set of all real numbers; let

$$l_t(a, \mu) \equiv k_t(a - \mu)^2; \tag{16.34}$$

let the prior and posterior parameters of the Normal rv $\tilde{\mu}$ be $(\bar{\mu}', \breve{\mu}')$ and $(\bar{\mu}'', \breve{\mu}'')$ respectively. From section 12.6.2 we obtain:

a. The optimal act under prior information is $a^o = \bar{\mu}'$.

b. The EVPI is given by $\bar{l}_t'(a^o) = k_t \breve{\mu}'$.

c. The optimal act, posterior to observing (n, m) is $a^o_{n,m} = \bar{\mu}''$, where $\bar{\mu}''$ is given in (16.15b).

d. The posterior EVPI after observing (n, m) is $\bar{l}_t''(a^o_{n,m}, (n, m)) = k_t \breve{\mu}''$, where $\breve{\mu}''$ is given in (16.15b).

16.8.2 Preposterior Analysis

Expected Value of Sample Information

From (14.29b) and table 16.1, the EVSI is given by

$$I(n) = k_t \breve{\bar{\mu}}'' = k_t \breve{\mu}' \frac{n}{n + n'} \tag{16.35}$$

which is identical to the corresponding expression (14.32a) in binomial sampling except that $\breve{p}'$ is replaced by $\breve{\mu}'$.

Observe that $I(0) = 0$ and that

$$\lim_{n \to \infty} I(n) = k_t \breve{\mu}' = \text{EVPI}. \tag{16.36}$$

Expected Net Gain of Sampling

If the cost of a sample of size n is a linear function of n and does not depend on m,

$$c_s(n, m) = K_s + k_s n,$$

where K_s and k_s are respectively the fixed and variable costs of sampling, then by (14.13) the expected net gain of sampling (ENGS) is

$$G(n) = k_t \breve{\mu}' \frac{n}{n + n'} - (K_s + k_s n). \tag{16.37}$$

Figure 14.2 which plots $G(n)$ against n for the binomial case can also be interpreted directly for the present case.

Optimal Sample Size

The sample size that maximizes ENGS is n^o given by

$$n^o + n' = \left[\frac{k_t n'}{k_s} \breve{\mu}'\right]^{1/2} \tag{16.38}$$

provided (1) that n^o as given by this formula is positive and (2) that $G(n^o)$ as given by (16.37) is positive; if either condition fails, the optimal sample size is 0. The proof is identical to the one required for (14.35). (See exercise 14.6.)

16.9 The Infinite-Action Problem with Linear Loss

16.9.1 Terminal Analysis

Let $\tilde{\mu}$ be the unknown parameter of an independent Normal process; let the set of possible acts (estimates) be the set of all real numbers; let

$$l_t(a, \mu) = \begin{cases} k_u(\mu - a) & \text{if} \quad a \le \mu, \\ k_0(a - \mu) & \text{if} \quad a \ge \mu; \end{cases} \tag{16.39}$$

let $\tilde{\mu}$ be given a Normal df with parameter $(\bar{\mu}', \breve{\mu}')$.

Prior Analysis

From (12.31) and (12.32), the optimal act a^o under prior information is the kth fractive μ_k' of the Normal df of $\tilde{\mu}$ where $k = k_u/(k_u + k_0)$. Symbolically,

$$a^o = \mu_k' \qquad \text{where} \qquad F_N(\mu_k' | \bar{\mu}', \breve{\mu}') = k. \tag{16.40}$$

We shall now prove the following result: The EVPI is given by

$$\bar{l}_t'(a^o) = k_t \ddot{\mu}' \tag{16.41a}$$

where

$$\ddot{\mu}' \equiv (\breve{\mu}')^{1/2}, \tag{16.41b}$$

$$k_t \equiv (k_u + k_0) f_{N^*}(u_k), \tag{16.41c}$$

and u_k is the kth fractile of the standardized Normal distribution; that is,

$$F_{N^*}(u_k) = k = \frac{k_u}{k_u + k_0}. \tag{16.41d}$$

Proof From (12.34), EVPI is given by

$$\bar{l}_t'(a^o) = k_u E_N^{(r)}(\mu_k'|\bar{\mu}', \breve{\mu}') - k_0 E_N^{(l)}(\mu_k'|\bar{\mu}', \breve{\mu}');$$

by (9.62), (9.63), and (9.58), after defining

$$u_k' \equiv \frac{\mu_k' - \bar{\mu}'}{\ddot{\mu}'}, \qquad \ddot{\mu}' \equiv (\breve{\mu}')^{1/2},$$

we obtain

$$\bar{l}_t'(a^o) = k_u[\bar{\mu}' G_{N^*}(u_k') + \ddot{\mu}' f_{N^*}(u_k')] - k_0[\bar{\mu}' F_{N^*}(u_k') - \ddot{\mu}' f_{N^*}(u_k')].$$

But since by (9.57)

$$F_{N^*}(u_k') = F_N(\mu_k'|\bar{\mu}', \breve{\mu}') = k,$$

we get

$$\bar{l}_t'(a^o) = k_u[\bar{\mu}'(1-k) + \ddot{\mu}' f_{N^*}(u_k')] - k_0[\bar{\mu}' k - \ddot{\mu}' f_{N^*}(u_k')]$$
$$= (k_u + k_0) f_{N^*}(u_k')\ddot{\mu}',$$

where the term $\bar{\mu}'[k_u(1-k) - k_0 k]$ vanishes because of the definition of k. Finally, since the value of μ_k' is such that $F_{N^*}(u_k') = k$ and does not depend on $(\bar{\mu}', \breve{\mu}')$ we drop the prime. This completes our proof.

Posterior Analysis

After a sample size n has been observed and the prior parameters have been updated to $(\bar{\mu}'', \breve{\mu}'')$, the choice of the optimal act is similar to the previous case; we obtain

$$a_{n,m}^o = \mu_k'' \quad \text{where} \quad F_N(\mu_k''|\bar{\mu}'', \breve{\mu}'') = k. \tag{16.42}$$

The posterior EVPI is given by

$$\bar{l}_t''(a_{n,m}^o, (n,m)) = k_t \ddot{\mu}'' \tag{16.43}$$

where $\ddot{\mu}'' = (\breve{\mu}'')^{1/2}$ and k_t is defined as in (16.41c).

16.9.2 Preposterior Analysis

Expected Value of Sample Information

By (14.11) and (16.19) the EVSI for a sample of size n is given by

$$I(n) = \bar{l}_t'(a^o) - E\bar{l}_t''(a_{n,\tilde{m}}^o, (n, \tilde{m}))$$
$$= k_t(\ddot{\mu}' - \ddot{\mu}'') \tag{16.44a}$$
$$= k_t \sigma[(n')^{-1/2} - (n' + n)^{-1/2}], \tag{16.44b}$$

where $\sigma^2 = v$.

Expected Net Gain of Sampling and Optimal Sample Size

If the cost of sampling is linear, so that $c_s(n, m) = K_s + k_s n$, then the ENGS is expressible as

$$G(n) = k_t \sigma[(n')^{-1/2} - (n' + n)^{-1/2}] - K_s - k_s n. \tag{16.45}$$

It is left to the reader to show as an exercise that the sample size that maximizes ENGS is n^o given by

$$n^o + n' = \left[\frac{k_t \sigma}{2k_s}\right]^{2/3} \tag{16.46}$$

provided (1) that n^o as given by this formula is positive, and (2) that $G(n^o)$ as given by (16.45) is positive; if either condition fails, the optimal sample size is 0.

16.10 The Two-Action Problem with Linear Value

16.10.1 Terminal Analysis

Let $\tilde{\mu}$ be the unknown parameter of an Independent Normal process; let a_1 and a_2 be the available acts; let

$$v_t(a_i, \mu) = K_i + k_i \mu, \qquad i = 1, 2, \tag{16.47}$$

where $k_2 > k_1$; let $k_t = k_2 - k_1$; let $\mu_b = (K_1 - K_2)/(k_2 - k_1)$; let the prior and posterior parameters of the Normal rv $\tilde{\mu}$ be $(\bar{\mu}', \breve{\mu}')$ and $(\bar{\mu}'', \breve{\mu}'')$ respectively. From the results of section 12.3 we conclude that

a. The optimal act under prior information is

$$a^o = \begin{cases} a_1 & \text{if} \quad \bar{\mu}' \leq \mu_b, \\ a_2 & \text{if} \quad \bar{\mu}' \geq \mu_b. \end{cases} \tag{16.48}$$

b. The EVPI is given by

$$\bar{l}_t'(a^o) = \begin{cases} k_t L_N^{(r)}(\mu_b | \bar{\mu}', \breve{\mu}') = k_t \ddot{\mu}' L_{N^*}(D') & \text{if} \quad \bar{\mu}' \leq \mu_b \\ k_t L_N^{(l)}(\mu_b | \bar{\mu}', \breve{\mu}') = k_t \ddot{\mu}' L_{N^*}(D') & \text{if} \quad \bar{\mu}' \geq \mu_b \end{cases} \tag{16.49a}$$

where

$$\ddot{\mu}' \equiv (\breve{\mu}')^{1/2} \quad \text{and} \quad D' \equiv |\bar{\mu}' - \mu_b| / \ddot{\mu}'. \tag{16.49b}$$

c. The optimal act posterior to observing (n, m) is

$$a_{n,m}^o = \begin{cases} a_1 & \text{if} \quad \bar{\mu}'' \leq \mu_b, \\ a_2 & \text{if} \quad \bar{\mu}'' \geq \mu_b. \end{cases} \tag{16.50}$$

16.10.2 Preposterior Analysis: EVSI and ENGS

We shall show that the EVSI for a sample of size n is given by

$$I(n) = k_t \sigma_n^* L_{N^*}(D_n^*), \tag{16.51a}$$

where

$$\sigma_n^* \equiv (\breve{\mu}'')^{1/2} \tag{16.51b}$$

and

$$D_n^* \equiv \frac{|\bar{\mu}' - \mu_b|}{\sigma_n^*}; \tag{16.51c}$$

an expression for $\breve{\mu}''$ is given in table 16.1, and is repeated here for the reader's convenience:

$$\breve{\mu}'' = v\left(\frac{1}{n'} - \frac{1}{n' + n}\right) = \breve{\mu}' \frac{n}{n' + n}. \tag{16.51d}$$

The subscript n on σ_n^* and D_n^* is used to emphasize the point that both of these values depend on n.

Proof From (14.39), we obtain

$$I(n) = \begin{cases} k_t E(\tilde{\bar{\mu}}'' - \mu_b)^+ & \text{if} \quad \bar{\mu}' \leq \mu_b, \\ k_t E(\mu_b - \tilde{\bar{\mu}}'')^+ & \text{if} \quad \bar{\mu}' \geq \mu_b, \end{cases}$$

where once again we remind the reader that $w^+ \equiv \max\{0, w\}$. Since $\tilde{\bar{\mu}}''$ is a Normal rv with parameter $(\bar{\mu}', \breve{\mu}'')$, for the case $\bar{\mu}' \leq \mu_b$, we have by (9.66)

$$\begin{aligned} E(\tilde{\bar{\mu}}'' - \mu_b)^+ &= L_N^{(r)}(\mu_b | \bar{\mu}', \breve{\mu}'') \\ &= \sigma_n^* L_{N^*}\left(\frac{\mu_b - \bar{\mu}'}{\sigma_n^*}\right) = \sigma_n^* L_{N^*}(D_n^*), \end{aligned}$$

where σ_n^* and D_n^* are given respectively in (16.51b) and (16.51c). This proves (16.51a) for $\bar{\mu}' \leq \mu_b$. In an analogous manner, for the case $\bar{\mu}' \geq \mu_b$, we have by (9.65),

$$\begin{aligned} E(\mu_b - \tilde{\bar{\mu}}'')^+ &= L_N^{(\ell)}(\mu_b | \bar{\mu}', \breve{\mu}'') \\ &= \sigma_n^* L_{N^*}\left(-\frac{\mu_b - \bar{\mu}'}{\sigma_n^*}\right) = \sigma_n^* L_{N^*}(D_n^*) \end{aligned}$$

which proves (16.51a) for $\bar{\mu}' \geq \mu_b$.

The ENGS of the proposed new sample is the EVSI less the cost of sampling, so that on the assumptions of this chapter

$$G(n) = k_t \sigma_n^* L_{N^*}(D_n^*) - K_s - k_s n, \tag{16.52}$$

where σ_n^* and D_n^* are defined by (16.51b) and (16.51c).

16.10.3 Behavior of ENGS When $K_s = 0$

In the two classes of decision problems considered earlier in this chapter we were able to write the ENGS of a new sample in a form that made the behavior of the ENGS with n immediately apparent, and hence we were able to proceed immediately to the problem of finding the value n^o of n which maximizes the ENGS. In our present problem, on the contrary, formula (16.52) for the ENGS is too complicated to let us proceed in this manner, and therefore in this section we shall discuss the general behavior of the ENGS and defer to the next section the problem of actually finding the optimal sample size. *We restrict our initial discussion to the case where the fixed element K_s in sampling cost is 0*; subsequently we shall make the easy generalization to the case where $K_s > 0$.

The function G in which we are now interested is defined by

$$G(n) = k_t \sigma_n^* L_{N^*}(D_n^*) - k_s n, \tag{16.53}$$

where σ_n^* and D_n^* are defined by (16.51). This function is formally identical to the function v^* defined by (5.38) on p. 115 of *ASDT*, and we simply summarize here the results obtained on pp. 115–21 of *ASDT*.[1]

Our first step is to examine the limit approached by the EVSI—the first term on the right of (16.53)—as n increases, and to do so we first recall that

$$\sigma_n^* = \breve{\mu}' \left(\frac{n}{n + n'} \right)^{1/2}, \qquad D_n^* = \frac{|\bar{\mu}' - \mu_b|}{\sigma_n^*}.$$

From these formulas it is immediately apparent that as $n \to \infty$ the function σ_n^* approaches $\breve{\mu}'$ monotonically from below, so that D_n^* approaches

$$D' = \frac{|\bar{\mu}' - \mu_b|}{\breve{\mu}'}$$

monotonically from above, and $L_{N^*}(D_n^*)$ approaches $L_{N^*}(D')$ monotonically from below; therefore, it follows at once that

1. The necessary identifications with *ASDT* notation are

$$H = 1/v^*, \qquad n' = v^*/V_\infty^*.$$

$$\lim_{n \to \infty} I(n) = k_t \breve{\mu}' L_{N^*}(D') = \text{EVPI}. \tag{16.54}$$

This result agrees, of course, with the intuitive feeling that as the size of a prospective sample increases, the expected value of sample information to be obtained from it increases and approaches the expected value of perfect information.

In later chapters where we discuss so-called "biased" sampling, we shall show that as the sample size n increases, σ_n^* will increase and approach a limit σ_∞^* which will be less than $\breve{\mu}'$; also D_n^* will decrease and approach a limit D_∞^*; and $I(n)$ will increase and approach a limit $I(\infty)$ where

$$I(\infty) \equiv k_t \sigma_\infty^* L_{N^*}(D_\infty^*).$$

Because of the presence of "bias," it will turn out that $I(\infty) <$ EVPI. We now want to write the remainder of the chapter in such a manner that it will also be applicable when we consider the important case of biased sampling. *Hence, from now on we shall use the symbol* D_∞^* *instead of* D' but as far as this chapter is concerned, $D_\infty^* = D'$.

Having made the observation (16.54), we can easily determine, by taking the first and second derivatives of G wrt n, that as n runs from 0 to infinity, G and its components I and $k_s n$ must behave in one of the ways illustrated in figure 16.4.

1. If $D_\infty^* = 0$, then the EVSI has infinite slope at the origin and is everywhere concave from below; since the cost of sampling is proportional to n, the ENGS rises to a unique maximum and then declines monotonically.

We can rationalize this by saying that when $D_\infty^* = 0$, the prior mean $\bar{\mu}'$ is exactly equal to the breakeven value μ_b, implying that (a) without sampling there is an even chance that the chosen act will be wrong, and thus (b) even a very small sample can make a worthwhile reduction in the risk of wrong decision.

2. If $D_\infty^* > 0$, then the EVSI has zero slope at the origin and one inflection point to the right of the origin, implying that the ENGS has negative slope $-k_s$ at the origin and one inflection point. Further investigation shows that, for any given D_∞^*, there exists a critical value λ_c of the quantity

$$\lambda \equiv \frac{(\breve{\mu}')^{3/2}}{v} \cdot \frac{k_t}{k_s} \tag{16.55}$$

such that

a. If $\lambda > \lambda_c$, then the ENGS has a (negative) local minimum followed by a positive local maximum, after which it decreases monotonically;

b. If $\lambda < \lambda_c$, then the ENGS is negative for all $n > 0$; it has either a negative local maximum or no local maximum at all.

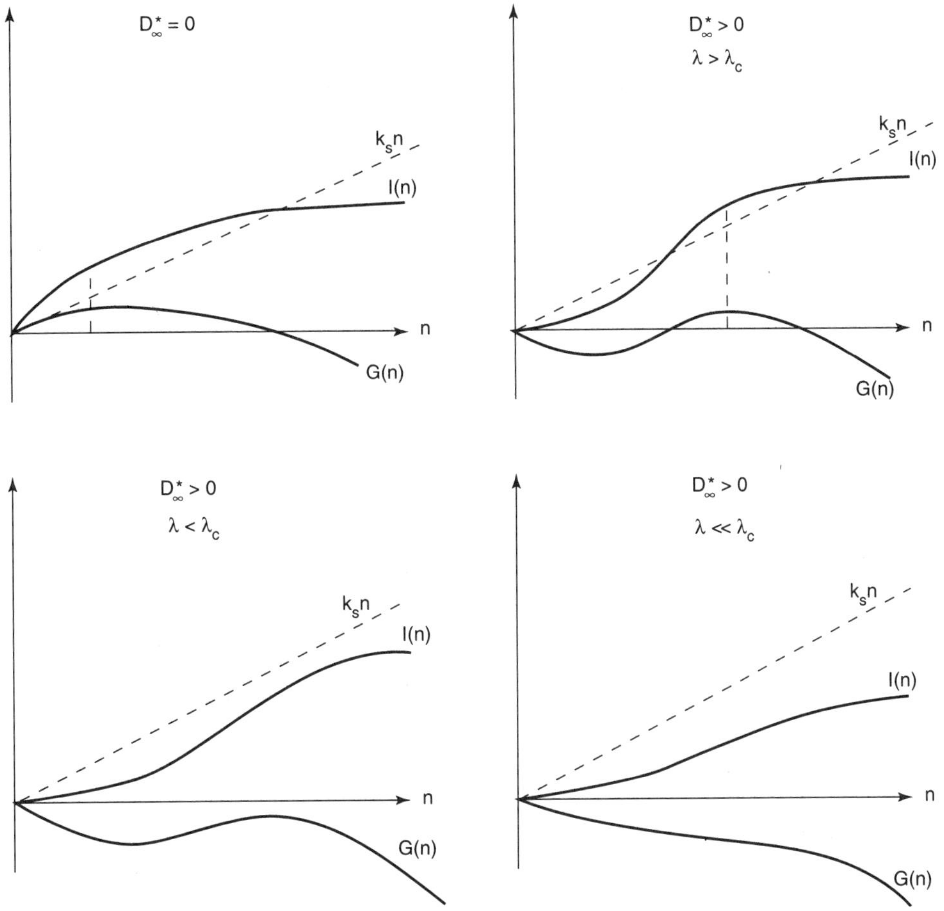

Figure 16.4
Possible behaviors of EVSI

The cube root Z_c of the critical ratio λ_c is graphed against D^*_∞ in figure 16.5, and in the light of this graph we can rationalize the behavior of the ENGS for $D^*_\infty > 0$ as follows. The fact that $D^*_\infty > 0$ implies $\bar{\mu}' \neq \mu_b$ so that the prior distribution definitely favors one of the two acts and the chance that a very small sample will lead to a posterior which favors the other act is too small to make taking the sample worthwhile. Whether larger samples can have a good enough chance of reversing the choice of act to be worth their cost depends on a comparison between the "decisiveness" of the prior distribution as measured by D^*_∞ and the "riskiness" of terminal action relative to the cost of sampling as measured by the ratio $\lambda = Z^3$. Observe that if we measure μ in units of $\upsilon^{1/2} \equiv \sigma$ and money in units of k_s, the formula for λ reduces to

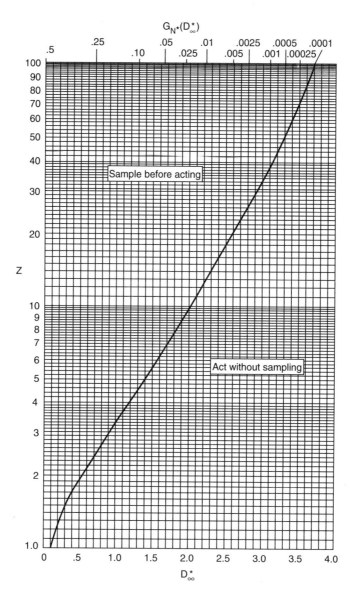

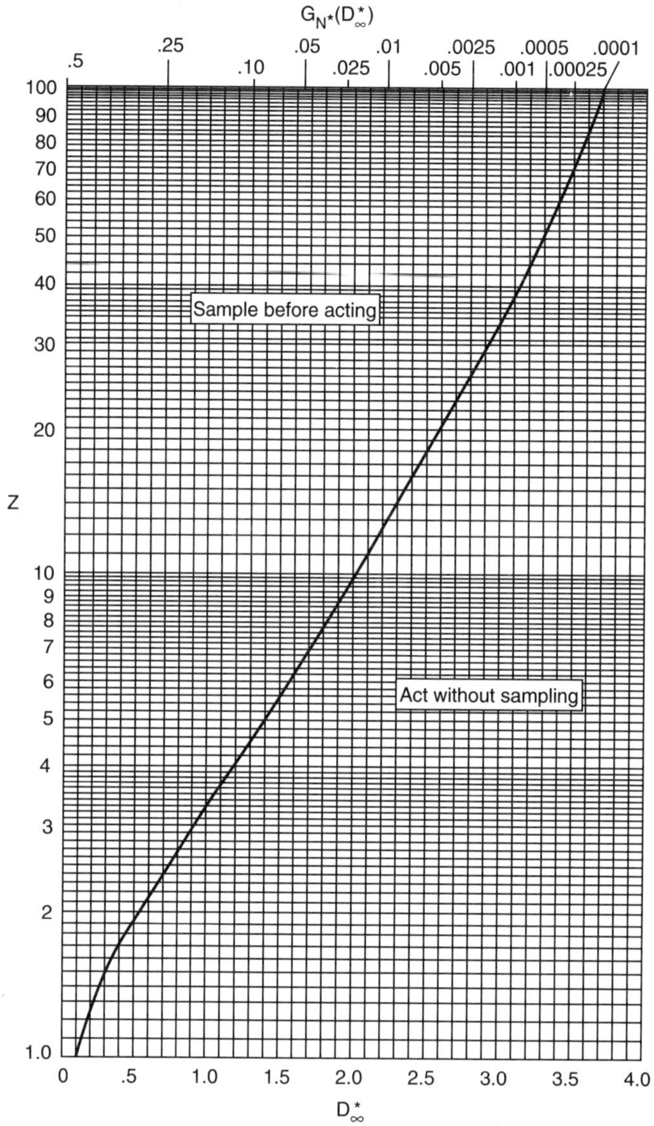

Figure 16.5
Critical ratio for sampling

$$\lambda = (\breve{\mu}')^{3/2} k_t;$$

hence an increase in either $\breve{\mu}'$ or k_t amounts to an increase in the riskiness of terminal action, and the critical ratio $\lambda_c = Z_c^3$ is an increasing function of D_∞^*.

16.10.4 Optimal Sample Size and Maximal Net Gain When $K_s = 0$

The ENGS as defined by (16.53) above for the case $K_s = 0$ depends on the "variable" n and on six "parameters": on k_t and k_s explicitly, on $\breve{\mu}'$ and υ through σ_n^* and on μ_b and $\bar{\mu}'$ through D_n^*. The value of the optimal n^o which maximizes G therefore depends on six quantities, and if it depended on each one of them "individually," so to speak, it would be hopeless to try to tabulate optimal sample size as a function of the parameters. It is obvious, however, that some simplification is possible (e.g., the optimal sample size will clearly depend only on the ratio of k_t to k_s and not on either k_t or k_s individually); and analysis shows that a great deal more simplification of this same sort is possible.

The "essential" parameters of the problem are in fact only two in number; the quantity $D_\infty^* = D'$ defined by (16.49b) and the quantity λ defined by (16.55). To see this we need only define the *standardized sample size*

$$\rho \equiv \frac{\breve{\mu}'}{\upsilon} n \tag{16.56}$$

and the "dimensionless" ENGS

$$G^*(\rho) \equiv \frac{\breve{\mu}'}{k_s \upsilon} G(n). \tag{16.57}$$

If in the formula (16.53) for $G(n)$ we express σ_n^*, D_∞^*, and n in terms of λ, D_∞^* and ρ, and if we substitute the result in (16.57), we can arrive by straightforward algebraic reduction at the result

$$G^*(\rho) = \lambda \theta_\rho L_{N^*}(D_\infty^*/\theta_\rho) - \rho, \quad \text{where} \quad \theta_\rho \equiv \left(\frac{\rho}{\rho + 1}\right)^{1/2}. \tag{16.58}$$

In checking these results the reader should first verify that $\theta_\rho = \sigma_n^*/\breve{\mu}'$. Clearly the ρ^o which maximizes G^* depends only on λ and D_∞^*. This reduction simplifies both computer programming and tabulation.

Table of Optimal Sample Size

The computations which would be required to find the ρ^o which maximizes G^* as given by (16.58) and thus to find the n^o which maximizes G as given by (16.53) are very burdensome, but the desired results can easily be found by use of the table on pages 1 and 2 of table MT-9, which can be found at the end of this book, and which shows

$$R \equiv \log \rho^o \tag{16.59}$$

as a function of $D = D_\infty^*$ and

$$\Lambda \equiv \log \lambda, \tag{16.60}$$

all logs being to base 10.

To use the table, we first compute

$$\Lambda = \tfrac{3}{2}\log \breve{\mu}' + \log k_t - \log \upsilon - \log k_s,$$
$$D_\infty^* = \frac{|\bar{\mu}' - \mu_b|}{\ddot{\mu}'}. \tag{16.61}$$

(For convenience a short table of logarithms can be found at the back of this book.) We then enter the table in the column for D_∞^* and the row for Λ, read R from the table, and compute

$$n^o = \text{anti}\log(R + \log \upsilon - \log \breve{\mu}'). \tag{16.62}$$

A zero in the body of the table indicates that the optimal sample size is 0, that is, that λ is less than the critical value λ_c for the D_∞^* in question. A minus sign in front of any logarithm (either Λ or R) indicates that the *entire logarithm* is negative, not just the characteristic (the portion preceding the decimal). If the user of the table computes, for example, $\Lambda = 8.8723 - 10$, he must convert this to $\Lambda = -1.227$ before entering the table. If he reads $R = -0.9614$ in the table, he must convert this to $R = 9.0386 - 10$ before continuing his calculations. For Λ too large to appear in the table, use the approximation (which is actually an upper bound) $R = \frac{1}{2}\Lambda + \varphi(D)$ where φ(phi) is given at the bottom of each column.

Table of Maximal Net Gain

Once the optimal sample size has been determined, the ENGS of a sample of this size could easily be determined by calculating σ_n^* for this n and then using (16.53), but it can be determined still more easily by using the table on pages 3 and 4 of MT-9, which shows directly as a function of D_∞^* and Λ the quantity

$$\Gamma = \log G^*(\rho^o), \tag{16.63}$$

the logarithm of the standardized net gain of the sample which is optimal for the given D_∞^* and Λ.

To use the table, we first compute the quantities called for by (16.61), then enter the table with D_∞^* and Λ, read Γ from the table, and compute

$$G(n^o) = \text{anti}\log(\Gamma + \log \upsilon + \log k_s - \log \breve{\mu}'). \tag{16.64}$$

A zero in the body of the table or a minus sign in front of a logarithm (either Λ or Γ) has the same meaning as in the table of optimal sample size. For Λ too large to appear in the table, use the approximation (which is actually an upper bound) $\Gamma \doteq \Lambda + \psi(D)$ where ψ(psi) is given at the bottom of each column.

16.10.5 ENGS and Optimal Sample Size When $K_s > 0$

If taking a sample involves not only a cost $k_s n$ that is proportional to the sample size but also nonzero fixed cost K_s that is independent of sample size, then clearly:

1. The ENGS for $K_s = 0$ which was computed and graphed against n in section 16.10.3 above is reduced by the *same* amount K_s for all n except $n = 0$.
2. If ENGS with $K_s = 0$ is negative for all $n > 0$, ENGS with $K_s > 0$ will be negative for all $n > 0$.
3. If ENGS with $K_s = 0$ has a positive local maximum at $n^o > 0$, ENGS with $K_s > 0$ will have a local maximum at this same n^o but this local maximum may be negative.

It follows immediately that optimal sample size when $K_s > 0$ can be determined by the following two-step procedure:

1. Determine the sample size n^o which would be optimal if K_s were 0;
2. If n^o as thus determined is not 0, compute $G(n^o)$ to determine whether it is positive, in which case the optimal sample size is n^o, or negative, in which case the optimal sample size is 0. The value of $G(n^o)$ can easily be found by using pages 3 and 4 of MT-9 to determine what it would be if K_s were 0 and then subtracting the actual value of K_s.

16.10.6 Numerical Illustration

Let μ be the unknown parameter of an Independent Normal process; let a_1 and a_2 be the two available acts; let

$$v_t(a_1, \mu) = K_1 + k_1\mu = \$100{,}000 + \$10{,}000\mu,$$

$$v_t(a_2, \mu) = K_2 + k_2\mu = \$55{,}000 + \$25{,}000\mu.$$

From the above we identify

$$K_1 = \$100{,}000, \qquad k_1 = \$10{,}000,$$

$$K_2 = \$55{,}000, \qquad k_2 = \$25{,}000.$$

We can now compute

$$k_t \equiv k_2 - k_1 = \$25{,}000 - \$10{,}000 = \$15{,}000,$$

$$\mu_b \equiv (K_1 - K_2)/(k_2 - k_1) = (\$100{,}000 - \$55{,}000)/\$15{,}000 = 3.0.$$

We shall consider two values of the fixed sampling cost K_s:

(a) $K_s = 0$,

(b) $K_s = \$16{,}000$,

and three possible values of the variable sampling cost k_s:

(a) $k_s = \$1{,}500$,

(b) $k_s = \$15$,

(c) $k_s = \$.00015$.

Now let $\bar{\mu}' = 9$ and $\breve{\mu}' = \upsilon = 100$. From (16.48) we have that the optimal act is a_2 since $9 > 3$. From (16.49) we find the EVPI:

$$\begin{aligned} \bar{l}_t(a^o) = k_t L_N^{(l)}(\mu_b|\bar{\mu}', \breve{\mu}') &= k_t \breve{\mu}' L_{N^*}(D') \\ &= 15{,}000(10)L_{N^*}(.6) \\ &= 15{,}000(10)(.1687) \\ &= 25{,}305. \end{aligned}$$

Now suppose we take a sample of 100 and observe a sample mean of 10. By (16.15b)

$$\bar{\mu}'' = \frac{(\frac{1}{100})9 + (\frac{100}{100})10}{\frac{1}{100} + \frac{100}{100}} = 9.990,$$

$$\breve{\mu}'' = \frac{1}{\frac{1}{100} + \frac{100}{100}} = .990.$$

By (16.50) a_2 is still the optimal act posterior to the sample.

To calculate the EVSI of a sample of 100, we first find

$$n' = \frac{100}{100} = 1,$$

$$\breve{\mu}'' = 100\left(\frac{100}{101}\right) = 99.009,$$

$$\sigma_n^* = \sqrt{99.009} = 9.95,$$

$$D_n^* = \frac{6}{9.95} = .6030.$$

Now from (16.51a)

$$I(100) = (15{,}000)(9.95)L_{N^*}(.6030) \doteq 25{,}059.$$

Thus, the EVSI is less than the EVPI by only 25,305 − 25,059 = \$246. The ENGS is $G(100) = 25{,}059 - 100k_s$.

We now wish to compute the optimal sample size. We first consider the case where $K_s = 0$. From (16.55) we have that

$$\lambda = \frac{(100)^{3/2}}{100} \times \frac{15{,}000}{k_s} = 150{,}000/k_s.$$

From (16.61) we have for each of the three different variable sampling costs:

(a) $\Lambda = \log_{10}(150{,}000/1{,}500) = 2.0,$

(b) $\Lambda = \log_{10}(150{,}000/15) = 4.0,$

(c) $\Lambda = \log_{10}(150{,}000/.00015) = 9.0.$

From (16.61) we also have that

$$D_\infty^* = .6.$$

To find the optimal sample size, we use table MT-9, pages 1 and 2. For each of the first two cases:

(a) $R = .5113,$

(b) $R = 1.6018.$

For the case $\Lambda = 9.0$, we use the approximation

$$R < \tfrac{1}{2}\Lambda + \varphi(D),$$

where $\varphi(D)$ is the last entry in each column. In our case

$$R < 4.5 - .3891 = 4.1109.$$

From (16.62), we can now compute n^o for each case:

(a) $\log n^o = 0.5113,$

$$n^o = 3;$$

(b) $\log n^o = 1.6018,$

$$n^o = 40;$$

(c) $\log n^o = 4.1109,$

$$n^o = 12{,}909.$$

To find the expected net gain of the optimal sample, we use pages 3 and 4 of table MT-9. For the first two cases:

(a) $\Gamma = 0.9796,$

(b) $\Gamma = 3.2057.$

For the case $\Lambda = 9.0$, we use the approximation

$$\Gamma < \Lambda + \psi(D),$$

where $\psi(D)$ is the last entry in each column. In our case

$$\Gamma < 9.0 - .7730 = 8.2270.$$

From (16.64) we can compute the ENGS for each case:

(a) $\log G(n^o) = 0.9796 + 3.1761 = 4.1557,$

$$G(n^o) \doteq 14{,}310;$$

(b) $\log G(n^o) = 3.2057 + 1.1761 = 4.3818,$

$$G(n^o) \doteq 24{,}088;$$

(c) $\log G(n^o) = 8.2270 - 3.8239 = 4.4031,$

$$G(n^o) \doteq 25{,}300.$$

When $K_s = \$16{,}000$, we see that in cases (b) and (c), the optimal sample size would remain the same; to find ENGS subtract 16,000 from the value given above. In case (a), since subtracting 16,000 gives a negative ENGS, both n^o and ENGS $= 0$.

16.11 Effect of Nonoptimal Sample Size

Some interesting general results concerning the unnecessary loss which results from taking a sample of nonoptimal size is given in this section for the special case where there is no uncertainty about bias and no fixed element K_s in sampling cost and where the optimal sample size is not zero.

We remind the reader that the symbol $\bar{l}(n)$ defined in (14.9) can be interpreted as the *total expected loss of a sample of size n*, which includes

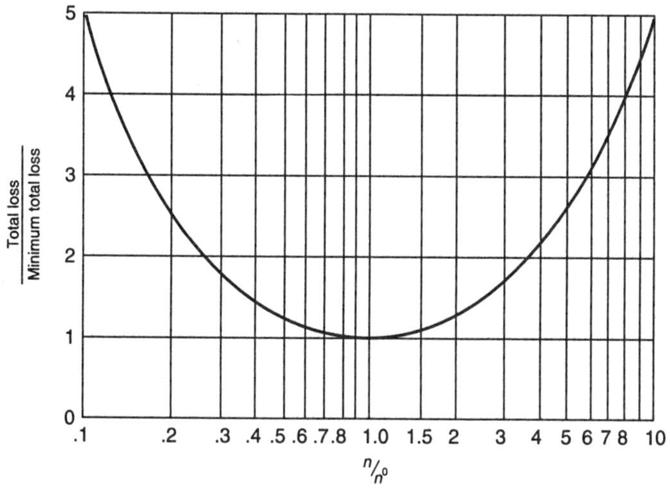

Figure 16.6
Effect of nonoptimal sample size

the sum of the cost of sampling (i.e., $k_s n$) and the expected loss due to the terminal action after the sample is taken (i.e., the prior expectation of the posterior optimal loss). If n^o is the optimal n, then by definition

$$\bar{\bar{l}}(n^o) < \bar{\bar{l}}(n).$$

It can be shown (cf. Antelman 1965) that *in any of the three classes of decision problems considered in this chapter*

$$\frac{\bar{\bar{l}}(n)}{\bar{\bar{l}}(n^o)} \le \frac{1}{2}\left(\frac{n}{n^o} + \frac{n^o}{n}\right). \tag{16.65}$$

The expression on the right-hand side of (16.65) is graphed in figure 16.6, and it is immediately apparent that a moderate error in sample size is of no practical importance whatever: A sample which is 10 per cent above or below optimum cannot increase total expected loss by as much as 6/10 of 1 percent; a sample which is 20% above or below optimum cannot increase total expected loss by more than 2.5%. What is more, even these very low maximum effects are actually approached only in extreme cases; in most problems that occur in common practice the effect of nonoptimal sample size is very substantially less than the limit given by (16.65). Observe on the other hand that substantial departures from optimal sample size *may* have serious effects; a sample which is half or twice what it ought to be *may* increase total expected loss by as much as 25%, and total expected loss may be more than doubled if the sample is a fourth of or four times the optimal size.

Exercises

1. Let $\tilde{\mu}$ be the rv denoting the average demand in the population for product X and assume that $\tilde{\mu}$ has a Normal df with mean 103 and variance 100.

a. If the estimate of μ is a, let the loss be given by

$$l_t(a,\mu) = 10^3(a-\mu)^2.$$

What is the optimal a^o, and $\bar{l}_t'(a^o)$ or EVPI?

b. If the estimate of μ is a, let the loss be given by

$$l_t(a,\mu)\begin{cases}10^3(\mu-a) & \text{if} \quad \mu \geq a,\\ 5\times 10^2(a-\mu) & \text{if} \quad a > \mu.\end{cases}$$

What is the optimal a^o, and $\bar{l}_t'(a^o)$ or EVPI?

c. In a two-action problem with linear value let the breakeven value be $\mu_b = 100$ and let

$$l_t(a_1,\mu) = 10^5 \max\{0, \mu - \mu_b\},$$

$$l_t(a_2,\mu) = 10^5 \max\{0, \mu_b - \mu\}.$$

What is the optimal a^o, and $\bar{l}_t'(a^o)$ or EVPI?

2. *Competitive Sealed Bidding.* A given property (or commodity, contract, etc.) is to be sold to the company with the highest sealed bid. The research department of XYZ Company has given the following report:

i. If our company obtains the property, the resulting monetary flows are uncertain but we figure that the cash equivalent (i.e., selling price) of the property should be V^*.

ii. The unknown maximum bid of our competitors is the rv $\tilde{\mu}$ which is assessed to have the df f, and left-tail cumulative F.

iii. EMV is a valid guide to action.

iv. Any further analysis our company makes about the sealed bid we should enter should not change our probability assessment in (ii).

a. If company XYZ bids a where $a < V^*$, show that their expected profitability is

$$\bar{v}_t(a) = (V^* - a)F(a).$$

b. Show that the optimal bid a^o satisfies the following condition:

$$V^* - a^o = \frac{F(a^o)}{f(a^o)} \quad \text{or} \quad \frac{1}{V^* - a^o} = \frac{f(a^o)}{F(a^o)}.$$

c. Show that for any a, the opportunity loss $l_t'(a,s)$ is graphed as in figure 16E.2.

d. Show that the EVPI

$$\bar{l}_t'(a^o) = L^{(l)}(V^*) - (V^* - a^o)F(a^o).$$

e. In the special case that $\tilde{\mu}$ has a Normal df with mean $\bar{\mu}'$ and standard deviation $\ddot{\mu}'$, if we define u^o and u^* by

$$u^o = \frac{a^o - \bar{\mu}'}{\ddot{\mu}'}, \qquad u^* = \frac{V^* - \bar{\mu}'}{\ddot{\mu}'},$$

show that u^o is such that

$$\frac{1}{u^* - u^o} = \frac{f_{N^*}(u^o)}{F_{N^*}(u^o)}.$$ (The function f_{N^*}/F_{N^*} is plotted in figure 16E.1.)

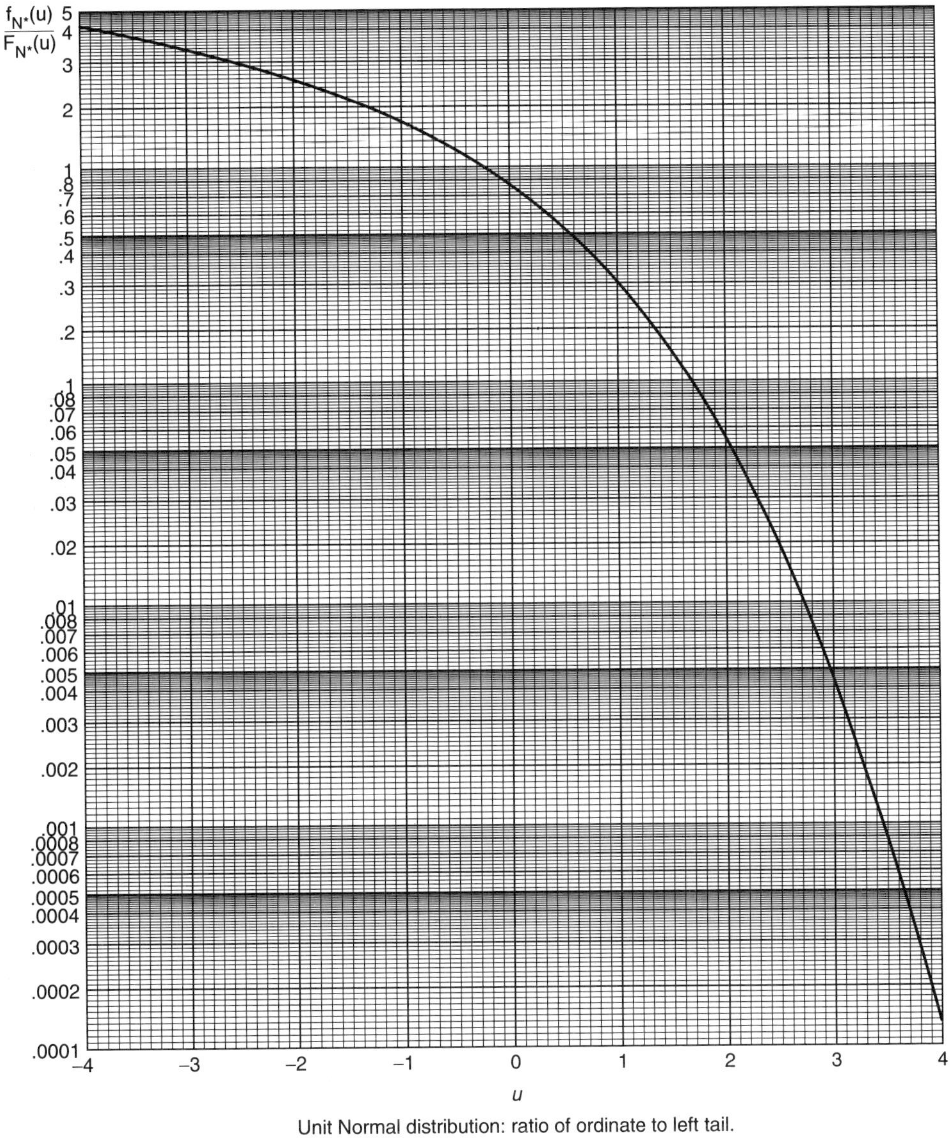

Figure 16E.1
Ratio of Normal ordinate to left tail

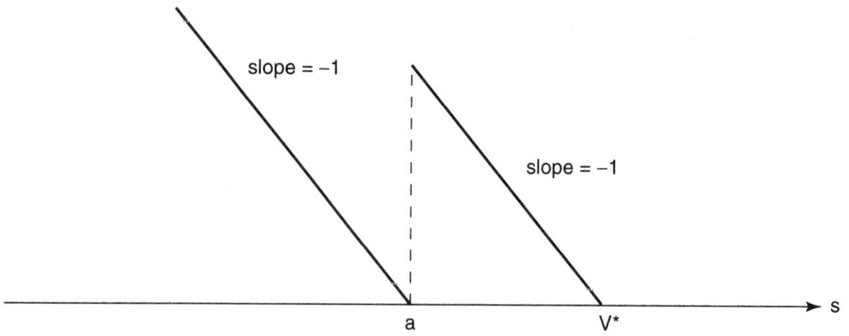

Figure 16E.2

f. Find a^o, $\bar{v}_t'(a^o)$, $\bar{l}_t'(a^o)$ for

$V^* = 100{,}000, \qquad \bar{\tilde{\mu}}' = 80{,}000, \qquad \ddot{\mu}' = 10{,}000.$

g. Repeat for

$V^* = 100{,}000, \qquad \bar{\tilde{\mu}}' = 100{,}000, \qquad \ddot{\mu}' = 10{,}000.$

h. Show that in the Normal case

$$a^o \begin{bmatrix} < \\ > \end{bmatrix} \begin{matrix} \bar{\mu}' \\ \bar{\mu}' \end{matrix} \quad \text{if} \quad \frac{V^* - \bar{\mu}'}{\ddot{\mu}'} \begin{bmatrix} < \\ > \end{bmatrix} \begin{matrix} 1/(2f_{N^*}(0)) \doteq 1.25, \\ 1.25. \end{matrix}$$

3. *Scrap Allowance*. Let $\tilde{\mu}$ represent demand for a given item and a represent the amount stocked. Assume that if the stock exceeds demand the opportunity loss is given by $k_0(a - \mu)$. If, however, demand exceeds stock it necessitates an extra trip and there is a flat penalty of K_u regardless of the amount of underage.

a. For a given a, show that the expected loss is given by

$\bar{l}_t(a) = k_0 L^{(l)}(a) + K_u G(a).$

b. To find the optimal stock a^o, differentiate to get

$$\frac{d}{da}\bar{l}_t(a) = k_0 F(a) - K_u f(a),$$

(see exercise 13, chapter 12), and setting this derivative equal to zero, show that the optimal a^o satisfies

$$\frac{f(a^o)}{F(a^o)} = \frac{k_0}{K_u}.$$

(See exercise 20, chapter 12.)

c. If $\tilde{\mu}$ is Normal $(\bar{\mu}', \ddot{\mu}')$, defining u^o by $a^o = \bar{\mu}' + u^o\ddot{\mu}'$, show that

$$\frac{f_{N^*}(u^o)}{F_{N^*}(u^o)} = \ddot{\mu}'\frac{k_0}{K_u}.$$

d. Find a^o and $\bar{l}_t(a^o)$ for the following numbers:

$\tilde{\mu}$ is Normal (1000, 400),

$k_0 = 2, \qquad K_u = 50.$

e. Repeat for $\tilde{\mu}$ and k_0 as in (d) but $K_u = 400$.

4. Timid Corporation of USA has a single contract written in a foreign currency, to deliver a large piece of U.S.-manufactured equipment in Naples, for which it will receive 2 billion lire (2×10^9 liras) 90 days hence. Timid Corporation does its accounting in U.S. dollars and is quite concerned about the possible fluctuation in the dollar value of the lira. Timid's treasurer's considered subjective distribution for the dollar value of one lira 90 days hence is Normal with mean M and variance V. His utility for the dollar value of the payment the company receives is $-ce^{-cx}$.

   a. What is the treasurer's certainty equivalent for the 2 billion lire payment? (You may use the fact that $Ee^{t\tilde{u}} = e^{(1/2)t^2}$ if $\tilde{u}$ has a unit Normal distribution.)

   b. "Forward markets" in lire exist. The treasurer can contract now to sell any number of lire 90 days hence at d dollars per lira. How many should he sell? What is the resulting certainty equivalent?

   c. Suppose there is also a fixed fee in a forward market transaction, independent of the size of the transaction. Is it approximately or exactly valid to subtract this fixed fee from the certainty equivalent calculated in (b)? Why or why not?

   d. How would the fee in (c) affect your answer to (b) if the subtraction in (c) is treated as valid?

   e. Timid Corporation actually faces other risks. Would the analysis necessarily be changed by considering them as well? Why or why not?

   f. Show that, if $d < M$, then for any "reasonable" utility function the treasurer should sell less than the full 2 billion lire. (Cf. appendix 3.)

5. Suppose that Mr. Waterman has the utility function given in chapter 4, and that it applies no matter how much he gains or loses, that any investment he makes must be sold on April 1, 1970, and that neither the Norwood nor Prescott deal is available.

   a. What is Mr. Waterman's certainty equivalent for an investment whose after-tax return is Normally distributed with mean 6.75 and variance 250?

   b. Suppose Mr. Waterman can buy any number of whole or fractional units of such an investment. How many units should he buy if no other investment is available?

   c. Suppose that a second investment is also available whose after-tax return is independent of the first and is Normal with mean 6.25 and variance 300. How many units of each of the two investments should Mr. W. buy?

   d. What are the certainty equivalents of Mr. Waterman's investments in (b) and (c)?

17 Normal Process with Unknown Variance

In the present chapter we shall continue to restrict our attention to situations where the decision maker's interest is in the mean μ of an Independent Normal process, but we shall consider the case where the process variance υ is also unknown. Even if the decision maker is *directly* interested only in μ and not in υ (because the utilities of the acts among which he wishes to choose depend only on μ and not on υ), his uncertainty about υ will prevent him from going from a prior to a posterior distribution of $\tilde{\mu}$ in the simple way described in the last chapter. Because the sample likelihood (16.10) depends on υ as well as on μ, the parameters (16.15) specify the *conditional* posterior distribution *given* υ and this is obviously not what is required when an act must be chosen in the absence of knowledge of υ.

The way out in this example is simple enough in principle. The decision maker has only to assign a *joint* prior df to $\tilde{\mu}$ and $\tilde{\upsilon}$, obtain the *joint* posterior df of $\tilde{\mu}$ and $\tilde{\upsilon}$ by applying a bivariate analogue of Bayes' formula, and then compute the *marginal* (posterior) df of $\tilde{\mu}$ from the joint df by the standard procedure discussed in chapter 13 on paired random variables.

The material of sections 9.8 and 9.9 is relevant to this chapter. For detailed analysis, see *ASDT* and Bracken and Schleifer (1964). We caution the reader that the third argument of the Normal density f_N in these references is the *precision* of the process whereas in this book it is the *variance* of the process.

17.1 Introduction

The first problem that we shall study in this chapter is the following basic problem of statistical inference. After assigning a joint df of $\tilde{\mu}$ *and* $\tilde{\upsilon}$, and after observing the values $(z_1, \ldots, z_n)$ of n rv's generated by the process, we obtain the joint posterior df of $\tilde{\mu}$ and $\tilde{\upsilon}$ by applying a bivariate case of Bayes' formula and then compute the marginal (posterior) df of $\tilde{\mu}$ from the joint df by the standard procedure discussed in chapter 13 on paired random variables.

In section 17.2, we examine the sampling distribution of n observations conditional on given values of μ and υ. Next the likelihood function corresponding to a sample $z_1, \ldots, z_n$ is considered and it is shown that the likelihood function depends on the sample outcomes $z_1, \ldots, z_n$ only through their sample mean, m, and variance, v, so that a "sufficient" summary of the sample outcomes is given by the triple (m, v, n). (In the appendix to chapter 20, we discuss "sufficiency" in greater detail.)

In section 17.3 we apply Bayes' theorem to find the posterior df of $(\tilde{\mu}, \tilde{\upsilon})$ corresponding to a given prior df of $(\tilde{\mu}, \tilde{\upsilon})$ after the sample $(z_1, \ldots, z_n)$ is observed.

In section 17.4 we present a specific updating result for sampling from a Normal Process: if $(\tilde{\mu}, \tilde{v})$ is given a Normal-Inverted-Gamma prior df (to be defined), then the posterior df of $(\tilde{\mu}, \tilde{v})$ is also Normal-Inverted-Gamma, and there is a simple algebraic formula connecting the prior parameters (m', n', v', ν'), the sufficient statistics (m, n, v) of the sample, and the posterior parameters (m'', n'', v'', ν'').

In section 17.5 we investigate the sensitivity of the marginal posterior df of $\tilde{\mu}$ to the choice of the prior. Once again we bring up the provocative notion of "complete ignorance" and criticize its indiscriminate use.

In section 17.6 we give the conditional and unconditional sample distribution of $(\tilde{m}, \tilde{v})$ and the unconditional distribution of $\tilde{m}$ and $\tilde{v}$ respectively. We also give the df of the as yet unknown posterior mean, $\tilde{\tilde{\mu}}''$, and variance, $\tilde{\breve{\mu}}$, corresponding to a sample of size n, which is needed for preposterior analysis. We conclude this section with some remarks about the predictive distribution of $\tilde{z}_{n+1}$.

In section 17.7 we consider terminal and preposterior analysis for decision problems that involve the unknown mean and variance of a Normal process.

In section 17.8 we briefly mention some other approaches that could be used to analyze prior-to-posterior analysis of $\tilde{\mu}$ when $\tilde{v}$ is also unknown.

17.2 Conditional Sampling Distributions

17.2.1 Conditional Probability of Sampling Outcomes Given μ, v

We have already seen in chapter 16 that the likelihood of observation z_1, $z_2, \ldots, z_n$ for an Independent Normal data-generating process is

$$(2\pi)^{-(1/2)n} e^{-(1/2v)\sum(z_i-\mu)^2} v^{-(1/2)n}. \tag{17.1}$$

If we now define the statistics

$$m \equiv \frac{1}{n}\sum z_i \tag{17.2a}$$

$$v \equiv \frac{1}{n-1}\sum (z_i - m)^2, \tag{17.2b}$$

then we have, as at (16.9), omitting higher-order terms:

$$P(\tilde{z}_1 \doteq z_1, \ldots, \tilde{z}_n \doteq z_n | \mu, v)$$

$$= \Delta^n (2\pi)^{-(1/2)n} e^{-(1/2v)(n-1)v-(1/2)(n/v)(m-\mu)^2} v^{-(1/2)n}$$

$$= \Delta^n K f_N\left(m \middle| \mu, \frac{v}{n}\right) f_{\gamma 2}\left(v \middle| \frac{1}{v}, n-1\right) \tag{17.3}$$

where

$$K \equiv (2\pi)^{-(1/2)(n-1)} n^{1/2} \Gamma(\tfrac{1}{2}(n-1)) \tfrac{1}{2}(n-1)^{-(1/2)(n-1)} v^{1-(1/2)(n-1)} \tag{17.4}$$

and f_N and $f_{\gamma 2}$ are defined by (9.48) and (9.68) respectively. Note that K is a constant that does not involve the unknowns μ and υ.

Proof of (17.3) We use

$$\sum (z_i - \mu)^2 = \sum (z_i - m + m - \mu)^2$$
$$= \sum (z_i - m)^2 + \sum (m - \mu)^2 + 2\sum (z_i - m)(m - \mu).$$

By the definition of m, we have

$$\sum (z_i - m) = mn - nm = 0,$$

so that

$$\sum (z_i - \mu)^2 = \sum (z_i - m)^2 + n(m - \mu)^2$$
$$= v(n-1) + n(m - \mu)^2.$$

Making this substitution, we get (17.3).

17.2.2 Likelihood Function of (μ, υ)

The expression $P(\tilde{z}_1 \doteq z_1, \ldots, \tilde{z}_n \doteq z_n | \mu, \upsilon)$ can be looked at in two ways: when viewed as a function of $z = (z_1, \ldots, z_n)$ for fixed μ and υ, it is called the joint probability function at z for μ and υ; when viewed as a function of μ and υ for a fixed z, it is called the likelihood of (μ, υ) for the sample outcome z and written $f_{Ni\gamma}(\mu, \upsilon | m, v, n, n-1)$, that is,

$$f_{Ni\gamma}(\mu, \upsilon | m, v, n, n-1) = \Delta^n K f_N(\mu | m, \upsilon/n) f_{i\gamma}(\upsilon | v, n-1) \tag{17.5a}$$

where the Inverted-Gamma-2 density $f_{i\gamma}$ satisfies

$$f_{i\gamma}(\upsilon | v, n-1) \equiv f_{\gamma 2}\left(\frac{1}{\upsilon} \middle| v, n-1\right). \tag{17.5b}$$

Notice that K depends on z but not on μ and υ.

(*Remark on Notation:* In *ASDT* the authors parameterize the unknowns of the generating distribution by the mean, μ, and the *precision*, h, which is defined as the reciprocal of the variance (i. e., $h \equiv 1/\upsilon$). In *ASDT* the likelihood function of (μ, h) given the sample is called Normal-Gamma. Here, since we are using υ and not h, we are forced to talk about a Normal-Inverted-Gamma Distribution. In keeping somewhat with *ASDT* notation we do not choose to write $f_{i\gamma 2}$ and $f_{Ni\gamma 2}$ in (17.5b and a), but that would have been perfectly reasonable. We apologize for the inconsistency.)

17.3 Posterior Distribution of $(\tilde{\mu}, \tilde{v})$

17.3.1 The Joint Posterior as a Product of the Likelihood Function and the Joint Prior

Let the joint prior distributing function of $(\tilde{\mu}, \tilde{v})$ be denoted by f'; let the joint posterior distributing function of $(\tilde{\mu}, \tilde{v})$ given $z = (z_1, \ldots, z_n)$ be denoted by $f''(\mu, v|z)$. Then by Bayes' theorem (10.21) we have

$$f''(\mu, v|z) \sim f_{Ni\gamma}(\mu, v|m, v, n, n-1)f'(\mu, v), \tag{17.6}$$

which says that the shape of the posterior distributing function is given by the product of the likelihood function and the prior distributing function. From (17.5) this becomes

$$f''(\mu, v|z) = C'f_{Ni\gamma}(\mu, v|m, v, n, n-1)f'(\mu, v) \tag{17.7}$$

where C' is a function of z and not of μ and v; recall that $m = \sum z_i/n$ and $v = \sum (z_i - m)^2/(n-1)$.

17.3.2 Sufficiency of the Sample Mean and Variance

Because the expression (17.7) for the joint posterior distributing function of $(\tilde{\mu}, \tilde{v})$ depends on the sample observations $(z_1, \ldots, z_n)$ only through their mean, m, variance, v, and the number of observations n, the triplet (m, n, v) are the sufficient statistics of the sample. As far as making inferences or decisions about (μ, v) is concerned, a statistician who is given information about all the sample outcomes $z_1, \ldots, z_n$ is no better off than a statistician who is only given the summary information (m, n, v), provided that the observations $z_1, \ldots, z_n$ are known to be outcomes of independent, identically distributed Normal rv's with unknown mean μ and unknown variance v.

17.4 Posterior Analysis When the Joint Prior Distribution of $(\tilde{\mu}, \tilde{v})$ is Normal-Inverted-Gamma

17.4.1 Joint Posterior Distribution

Suppose now that the prior distribution which the decision maker assigns to $(\tilde{\mu}, \tilde{v})$ is Normal-Inverted-Gamma so that we may write

$$f'(\mu, v) = f'_{Ni\gamma}(\mu, v|m', v', n', v'), \tag{17.8}$$

where the parameters m', v', n', v' represent definite numbers chosen by the decision maker. We shall show that:

If the prior distribution of the mean $\tilde{\mu}$ and variance $\tilde{\upsilon}$ of an Independent Normal process is Normal-Inverted-Gamma then the posterior distribution of $(\tilde{\mu}, \tilde{\upsilon})$ is also Normal-Inverted-Gamma.

Theorem Let $z = (z_1, \ldots, z_n)$ be the sample from an Independent Normal process with unknown mean μ and variance υ. Let m and v be the sample mean and variance respectively. Let $(\tilde{\mu}, \tilde{\upsilon})$ be given a Normal-Inverted-Gamma prior distribution with parameters m', v', n', ν'. Then the posterior distribution of $(\tilde{\mu}, \tilde{\upsilon})$ given z is given by

$$f''_{Ni\gamma}(\mu, \upsilon | m'', n'', v'', \nu'') = C' f_N\left(\mu | m'', \frac{\upsilon}{n''}\right) f_{i\gamma}(\upsilon | v'', \nu''), \tag{17.9}$$

where

$$m'' = \frac{n'm' + nm}{n' + n}, \tag{17.10a}$$

$$n'' = n' + n, \tag{17.10b}$$

$$v'' = \frac{[\nu' v' + n'm'^2] + [\nu v + nm^2] - n''m''^2}{[\nu' + \delta(n')] + [\nu + \delta(n)] - \delta(n'')}, \tag{17.10c}$$

$$\nu'' = [\nu' + \delta(n')] + [\nu + \delta(n)] - \delta(n''), \tag{17.10d}$$

$$\delta(n) = \begin{cases} 0 & \text{if} \quad n = 0, \\ 1 & \text{if} \quad n > 0. \end{cases} \tag{17.10e}$$

Proof of (17.10) Let the prior density of $(\tilde{\mu}, \tilde{\upsilon})$ be

$$f'_{Ni\gamma}(\mu, \upsilon | m', n', v', \nu') = f'_N\left(\mu | m', \frac{\upsilon}{n'}\right) f_{i\gamma}(\upsilon | v', \nu'). \tag{17.11}$$

Multiplying the prior density (17.11) by the likelihood function (17.5) and dropping the constant, we have

$$e^{-(1/2)(v'\nu'/\upsilon)-(1/2)n'(\mu-m')^2/\upsilon}\upsilon^{-((1/2)\nu'+(1/2)\delta(n')-1)}e^{-(1/2)(v\nu/\upsilon)-(1/2)n(m-\mu)^2/\upsilon}$$

$$\cdot\, \upsilon^{-((1/2)\nu+(1/2)\delta(n))}.$$

We observe first that the posterior exponent of υ^{-1} will be

$$\tfrac{1}{2}\nu' + \tfrac{1}{2}\delta(n') - 1 + \tfrac{1}{2}\nu + \tfrac{1}{2}\delta(n)$$

$$= \tfrac{1}{2}[\nu' + \delta(n') + \nu + \delta(n) - \delta(n'')] + \tfrac{1}{2}\delta(n'') - 1,$$

which by (17.6d) can be written

$$\tfrac{1}{2}\nu'' + \tfrac{1}{2}\delta(n'') - 1,$$

in agreement with the exponent of υ^{-1} in (17.7).

We next observe that the posterior exponent of e will be $-(1/2)(S/\upsilon)$ where

$$S \equiv v'\upsilon' + n'[\mu - m']^2 + v\upsilon + n[\mu - m]^2$$

$$= v'\upsilon' + n'm'^2 + v\upsilon + nm^2 - (n'm' + nm)^2/(n' + n)$$

$$+ (n' + n)[\mu - (n'm' + nm)/(n' + n)]^2.$$

Using (17.10b), our last result can be written

$$S = (v'\upsilon' + n'm'^2 + v\upsilon + nm^2 - n''m''^2) + n''(\mu - m'')^2,$$

and by (17.10d) this becomes

$$v''\upsilon'' + n''(\mu - m'')^2,$$

in agreement with the exponent of e in (17.7).

Remark The likelihood function of (μ, υ), given the sample observations treated as a function of (μ, υ), is a Normal-Inverted-Gamma distribution with really three parameters: m, υ, n. In (17.5), however, we write it with four parameters, $f_{Ni\gamma}(\mu, \upsilon | m, \upsilon, n, n-1)$ where the fourth parameter, which we shall call v, is really just $(n - 1)$. When we consider the prior on $(\tilde{\mu}, \tilde{\upsilon})$, for tractability we use $f_{Ni\gamma}(\mu, \upsilon | m', \upsilon', n', v')$ but no longer do we restrict v' to be $(n' - 1)$. This provides us with extra versatility, since often in practice, a priori we might have more (or less) knowledge about υ than about μ. For example, we might have already observed samples from another data-generating process with a different mean μ but with the same unknown variance υ. By freeing v' from n' we can reflect this asymmetry in a priori information.

17.4.2 Marginal Distribution of $\tilde{\upsilon}$

If the joint distribution of the random variable $(\tilde{\mu}, \tilde{\upsilon})$ is Normal-Inverted-Gamma as defined by (17.8), the marginal distribution of $\tilde{\upsilon}$ is Inverted-Gamma-2 as defined by

$$D(\upsilon | m, \upsilon, n, v) = f_{i\gamma}(\upsilon | \upsilon, v). \tag{17.12}$$

It follows immediately that (see *ASDT* (7.58))

$$E(\tilde{\upsilon} | m, \upsilon, n, v) = \upsilon \sqrt{\frac{v}{2}} \left(\frac{1}{2}v - \frac{3}{2}\right)! \bigg/ \left(\frac{1}{2}v - 1\right)!, \tag{17.13a}$$

$$V(\tilde{\upsilon} | m, \upsilon, n, v) = \upsilon^2 \frac{v}{v - 2}. \tag{17.13b}$$

17.4.3 Marginal Distribution of $\tilde{\mu}$

If the joint distribution of $(\tilde{\mu}, \tilde{v})$ is Normal-Inverted-Gamma as defined by (17.8), then the marginal distribution of $\tilde{\mu}$ is the Student distribution (as defined in (9.73)):

$$D(\mu|m, v, n, \nu) = f_S(\mu|m, n/v, \nu). \tag{17.14}$$

This is easily proved by (9.77). Notice that the marginal distribution of $\tilde{\mu}$ depends on all four parameters of the joint distribution of $(\tilde{\mu}, \tilde{v})$.

17.4.4 Interpretation of the Parameters of the Marginal Distribution of $\tilde{\mu}$

The mean and variance are given by (9.84) and (9.85):

$$E(\tilde{\mu}|m, v, n, \nu) = \bar{\mu} = m, \tag{17.15a}$$

$$V(\tilde{\mu}|m, v, n, \nu) = \breve{\mu} = \frac{v}{n}\frac{\nu}{\nu - 2}. \tag{17.15b}$$

From (17.10a) we know that the posterior mean is a weighted average of the prior mean m' and the mean m of the sample, the weights being the "fictitious sample size" n' and real sample size n. The posterior variance is inversely proportional to the sum of the fictitious and real sample sizes, with an adjustment factor $\nu/(\nu - 2)$ reflecting the uncertainty about v/v.

17.5 Sensitivity of the Posterior to the Prior

17.5.1 Negligible Prior Information

From the results above for the marginal posterior distribution of $\tilde{\mu}$, we can see at once that if we hold the prior and sample means and sample variance fixed but let n' and ν' decrease toward 0 , that is, let the prior become flat, then the posterior mean and variance of $\breve{\mu}$ approach m and $(v/n)(\nu/(\nu - 2))$ respectively:

$$\text{if } n' \to 0 \text{ and } \nu' \to 0 \text{ then } \bar{\mu}'' \to m \text{ and } \breve{\mu}'' \to \frac{v}{n}\frac{\nu}{\nu - 2}. \tag{17.16}$$

What is more important, we can also see at once from (17.10) and (17.15) that even if the prior ν' and n' are not strictly 0, the posterior parameters will have very nearly the values given by (17.16) whenever the prior n' and ν' are small relative to the sample size n. This fact can greatly reduce the care required in judgmental prior assessment. As long as the decision maker feels certain that the highest values he would even consider giving to n' and ν' are very small relative to the sample size already at hand, then in most problems he can either (1) choose any plausible values for n' and ν' or even (2) decide to adopt a posterior distribution of $\breve{\mu}$ with the parameters given by (17.16) and simply forget about evaluating and incorporating his prior judgments. If the decision maker does choose the latter alternative, it is suggestive to say that he has decided that his "prior information" about μ is "negligible in comparison with the information contained in the sample." As in section 16.5.2, however, this by no means constitutes "total ignorance," but rather a definite judgment with some extreme prior implications that are, however, "swamped" by the data.

17.5.2 Limiting Behavior of the Prior Distribution

From (17.15) we can see that as $n \to 0$ both the conditional and marginal distributions of $\breve{\mu}$ become increasingly uniform over $-\infty < \mu < +\infty$, and their variances become infinite, although their means remain fixed at m.

As $\nu \to 0$, the conditional distribution of $\tilde{\mu}$ given v is not affected; the variance of the marginal distribution of $\tilde{\mu}$ becomes infinite but the distribution does not become uniform: the ratio of the density at any two points μ_1 and μ_2 approaches $|\mu_2 - m|/|\mu_1 - m|$ (see *ASDT*, chapter 11).

17.5.3 Assessment of a Reasonable Normal-Inverted-Gamma Prior Distribution

One way to assess a Normal-Inverted-Gamma Distribution for $(\tilde{\mu}, \tilde{v})$ is to assess a marginal distribution for $\tilde{v}$, and then a conditional distribution for $\tilde{\mu}$ given a modal value of $\tilde{v}$. Indeed to assess a distribution of $\tilde{v}$ it might be easier to think about $\sigma \equiv v^{1/2}$, the standard deviation of the process. If we knew μ, roughly half the z_i observations should eventually fall in the interval $[\mu - \frac{2}{3}\sigma, \mu + \frac{2}{3}\sigma]$.

Let's take the case of heights of a random sample of adult males. Without looking at any data a reasonable guess might be a mean of 69 inches and a σ-value of 3 inches. If we were told the mean were 69 we might think it would be an even money bet that half the adult males would have a height between 67 and 71 inches; it would be an even money bet that 95% of the males would fall between 63 and 74 inches.

We now can go after $\tilde{\mu}$ assuming $v = 3^2 = 9$. It might be reasonable to assign to $\tilde{\mu}$ a conditional Normal distrib tion of $m' = 69$ and a standard deviation of say 1, or $\breve{\mu}' = 1^2 = 1$ and since $\breve{\mu}' = v/n'$ and $v = 9$ we conclude n' is about 9. Hence we may start with a prior of $(m', n', v', \nu') = (69, 9, 9, 15)$.

Of course we are not sure of that ballpark value of 3 for σ. We could set the median, $\sigma_{.50}$, at 3 and ask ourselves reasonable values of $\sigma_{.25}$ and $\sigma_{.75}$. Our guesses at $\sigma_{.25}$ and $\sigma_{.75}$ were 2.5 and 3.5 respectively. Now using figure 17.1 (a reproduction of figure 7.5 of *ASDT*) we conclude that $\nu' = 20$ approximately.

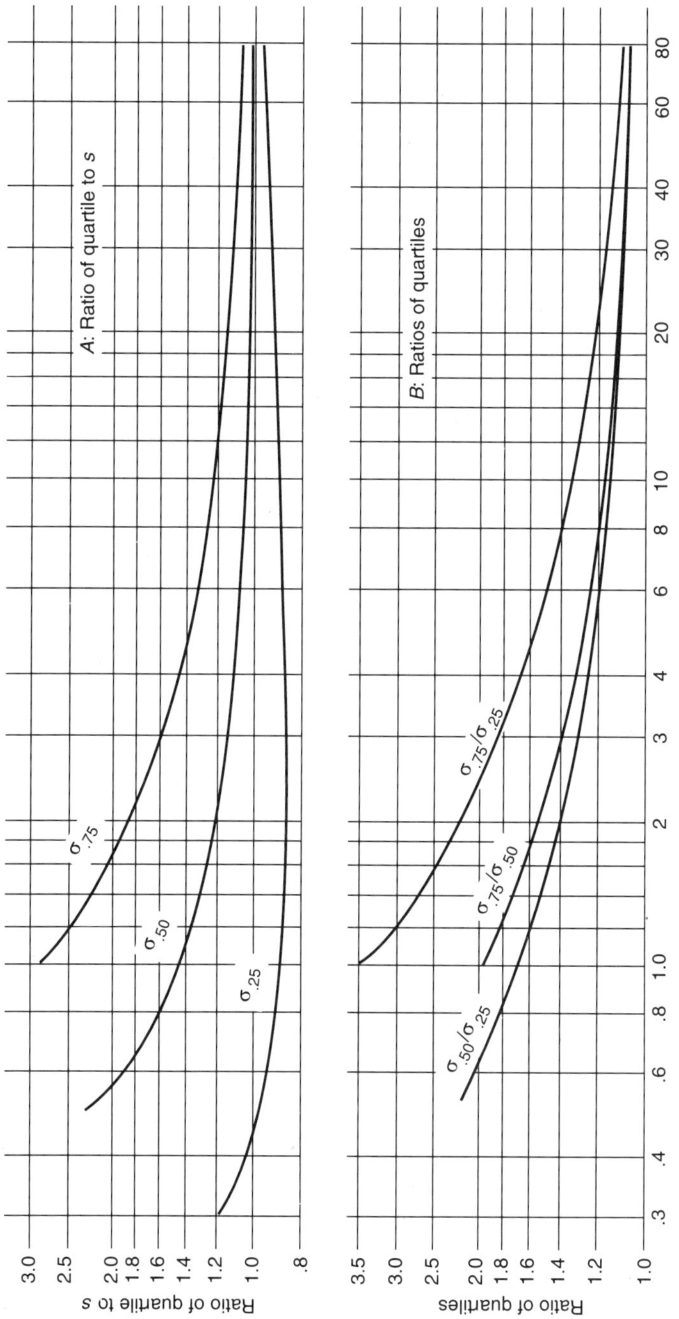

Figure 17.1
Quartiles of the cumulative inverted-gamma-2 function

17.6 Preposterior Distribution Theory

In this section we assume throughout that a sample with prespecified sample size $n > 0$ is to be taken from an Independent Normal process, whose parameter $(\tilde{\mu}, \tilde{v})$ has a proper Normal-Inverted-Gamma distribution with parameter (m', n', v', r'). The fact that the distribution is proper implies that v', n', $r' > 0$.

17.6.1 Conditional Joint Distribution of $(\tilde{m}, \tilde{v} | \mu, v)$

For a given value of the process parameter (μ, v), the conditional joint distribution of the statistic $(\tilde{m}, \tilde{v})$ is the product of the independent densities of $\tilde{m}$ and $\tilde{v}$:

$$D(m, v | \mu, v, n, r) = f_N(m | \mu, v/n) f_{\gamma 2}(v | 1/v, r). \tag{17.17}$$

This is easy to prove using (17.5).

17.6.2 Unconditional Joint Distribution of $(\tilde{m}, \tilde{v})$

If the parameter $(\tilde{\mu}, \tilde{v})$ of the process is treated as having a Normal-Inverted-Gamma density of type (17.9), the unconditional joint distribution of the statistic $(\tilde{m}, \tilde{v})$ will have the density

$$D(m, v | m', v', n', \nu', n, \nu)$$

$$= \int_{-\infty}^{\infty} \int_{0}^{\infty} f_N(m | \mu, v/n) f_{\gamma 2}\left(v \middle| \frac{1}{v}, \nu\right) f_{Ni\gamma}(\mu, v | m', n', v', \nu') \, d\mu \, dv$$

$$\sim \frac{(\nu v)^{(1/2)\nu - 1}}{(\nu' v' + \nu v + n_u [m - m']^2)^{(1/2)\nu n}}, \tag{17.18a}$$

where v', n', $\nu' > 0$, and

$$n_u \equiv \frac{n' n}{n' + n}, \qquad \frac{1}{n_u} = \frac{1}{n'} + \frac{1}{n}, \tag{17.18b}$$

$$\nu'' = \nu' + \nu + 1.$$

Proof See *ASDT*, chapter 11.

17.6.3 Unconditional Distribution (Marginal) of $\tilde{m}$ and $\tilde{v}$

From the unconditional joint distribution (17.17) of $(\tilde{m}, \tilde{v})$, we can obtain two distributions of $\tilde{m}$, both unconditional as regards the parameter (μ, v). The first is also unconditional as regards v; its density is

$$D(m|m', v', n', \nu'; n, \nu) = f_S(m|m', n_u/v', \nu') \tag{17.19}$$

The second is conditional on v even though unconditional as regards (μ, v); its density is

$$D(m|m', v', n', \nu'; n, \nu, v) = f_S(m|m', n_u/U, \nu' + \nu) \tag{17.20}$$

where

$$U \equiv \frac{\nu' v' + \nu v}{\nu' + \nu}.$$

In the same way the joint distribution of $(\tilde{m}, \tilde{v})$ implies two distributions of $\tilde{v}$. Marginally as regards $\tilde{m}$, the statistic $\tilde{v}$ has the Inverted-Beta-2 density

$$D(v|m', v', n', \nu'; n, \nu) = f_{i\beta 2}(v|\tfrac{1}{2}\nu, \tfrac{1}{2}\nu', \nu' v'/\nu); \tag{17.21}$$

while conditional on m, the density of $\tilde{v}$ is

$$D(v|m', v', n', \nu'; n, \nu, m) = f_{i\beta 2}\left(v|\tfrac{1}{2}\nu, \tfrac{1}{2}(\nu' + 1), \frac{\nu' v' + M}{\nu}\right), \tag{17.22}$$

where

$$M \equiv n_u(m - m')^2.$$

Proof See *ASDT*, chapter 11.

17.6.4 Distribution of $\tilde{\bar{\mu}}''$

The mean $\bar{\mu}''$ of the posterior distribution of $\tilde{\mu}$, by (17.15a), is equal to the parameter m'' of the distribution, so that the prior distribution of $\tilde{\bar{\mu}}''$ is obtained by merely substituting $\bar{\mu}''$ for m'' in the (marginal) density of $\tilde{m}''$ obtained from formulas (17.19) and (17.10a):

$$D(\bar{\mu}''|m', v', n', \nu'; n, \nu) = f_S(\bar{\mu}''|m', n^*/v', \nu'), \tag{17.23a}$$

where

$$n^* \equiv \frac{n + n'}{n} n', \qquad \frac{1}{n^*} = \frac{1}{n'} - \frac{1}{n''}. \tag{17.23b}$$

It then follows that

$$\begin{aligned} E(\tilde{\bar{\mu}}''|m', v', n', \nu'; n, \nu) &= m' = E(\tilde{\mu}|m', n', v', \nu'), \qquad \nu' > 1, \\ V(\tilde{\bar{\mu}}''|m', v', n', \nu'; n, \nu) &= \frac{v'}{n^*} \frac{\nu'}{\nu' - 2}, \qquad \nu' > 2. \end{aligned} \tag{17.24}$$

17.6.5 Distribution of $\tilde{\breve{\mu}}''$

The variance of the posterior distribution of $\tilde{\mu}$ will be

$$V(\tilde{\mu}|m'', v'', n'', v'') \equiv \breve{\mu}'' = \frac{v''}{n''}\frac{\nu''}{\nu''-2}, \qquad \nu'' > 2, \tag{17.25}$$

where $\tilde{v}''$ and therefore $\tilde{\breve{\mu}}''$ are random variables. This formula permits us to obtain the distribution of $\tilde{\breve{\mu}}''$ from the (unconditional) distribution of $\tilde{v}''$:

$$P\{\tilde{\breve{\mu}}'' < \breve{\mu}''|m', v', n', \nu'; n, \nu\} = F_{i\beta 1}\left(\breve{\mu}''\frac{n''[\nu''-2]}{\nu''}\middle|\frac{1}{2}\nu', \frac{1}{2}\nu'', \frac{\nu' v'}{\nu''}\right). \tag{17.26}$$

The expected value of the kth power of $\tilde{\breve{\mu}}''$ under this distribution is

$$E(\tilde{\breve{\mu}}''^k|m', v', n', \nu'; n, \nu) = \left[\frac{\nu' v'}{n''(\nu''-2)}\right]^k \frac{(\frac{1}{2}\nu''-1)!(\frac{1}{2}\nu'-1-k)!}{(\frac{1}{2}\nu''-1-k)!(\frac{1}{2}\nu'-1)!}$$

$$= \breve{\mu}'^k\left[\frac{n'(\nu'-2)}{n''(\nu''-2)}\right]^k \frac{(\frac{1}{2}\nu''-1)!(\frac{1}{2}\nu'-1-k)!}{(\frac{1}{2}\nu''-1-k)!(\frac{1}{2}\nu'-1)!}. \tag{17.27}$$

Important special cases are

$$E(\tilde{\breve{\mu}}''|m', v', n', \nu'; n, \nu) = \frac{v'}{n''}\frac{\nu'}{\nu'-2} = \frac{n'}{n''}\breve{\mu}', \tag{17.28}$$

$$E(\sqrt{\tilde{\breve{\mu}}''}|m', v', n', \nu'; n, \nu) = \sqrt{\frac{n'}{n''}\breve{\mu}'}\exp\left[-\frac{3}{8}\left(\frac{1}{\frac{1}{2}\nu'-1} - \frac{1}{\frac{1}{2}\nu''-1}\right)\right]. \tag{17.29}$$

For detailed discussion, see *ASDT*, chapter 11.

17.6.6 Probabilistic Prediction

We now consider an Independent Normal process with unknown mean μ and variance v; let $(\tilde{\mu}, \tilde{v})$ be given a Normal-Inverted-Gamma prior distribution with parameters (m', n', v', ν'). After observing the outcomes $(z_1, \ldots, z_n)$ with sufficient statistics (m, v, n), the posterior of (μ, v) remains Normal-Inverted-Gamma with parameters (m'', n'', v'', ν''). What is the *predictive* distribution of the next, as yet unknown, $\tilde{z}_{n+1}$?

We have

$$\tilde{z}_{n+1} = \tilde{\mu} + \tilde{\varepsilon}_{n+1}$$

where $\tilde{\varepsilon}_{n+1}$ is Normal with mean 0 and variance $\tilde{v}$. *Conditional* on v, the random variables $\tilde{\mu}$ and $\tilde{\varepsilon}_{n+1}$ have independent Normal distributions and therefore their sum is also Normal (conditional on v being given). Integrating out v using the posterior marginal distribution of $\tilde{v}$ (an inverted-gamma-2 distribution with parameters (v'', ν'')), we conclude that $\tilde{z}_{n+1}$ has a Student distribution. In particular using (9.77) we have

$$D(z_{n+1}|m, n', v', \nu', m, n, v)$$
$$= \int_0^\infty f_N\left(z_{n+1}|m'', v\left(\frac{1}{n''}+1\right)\right) f_{i\gamma}(v|v'', \nu'')\,dv$$
$$= f_S\left(z_{n+1}|m'', \frac{1}{v''}\frac{n''}{n''+1}, \nu''\right). \tag{17.30}$$

It is easy to verify that the same result is obtained from (17.19) by updating the prior distribution and regarding z_{n+1} as the mean of a new sample of size 1.

17.7 Terminal and Preposterior Analysis

17.7.1 Notation

Having developed the necessary distribution theory for an Independent Normal process with unknown mean μ and variance v, we now turn our attention to decision problems where the economically relevant unknown state parameter is μ.

We define $V(n, m, v, a, \mu)$ as the value of choosing a fixed-size sample of size n from an Independent Normal process, observing a particular sufficient statistic (the sample mean and variance) m and v, and choosing a particular terminal act a, when the true unknown parameter is μ. We define $l(n, m, v, a, \mu)$ in an analogous manner, and corresponding to (14.1) and (14.2), we write

$$V(n, m, v, a, \mu) = V_t(a, \mu) - c_s(n, m, v), \tag{17.31}$$

and

$$l(n, m, v, a, \mu) = l_t(a, \mu) + c_s(n, m, v). \tag{17.32}$$

17.7.2 Terminal Analysis

If $(\tilde{\mu}, \tilde{v})$ is given a prior Normal-Inverted-Gamma df with parameter (m', n', v', ν'), then we know the marginal df of $\tilde{\mu}$ is $f_S(\tilde{\mu}|m', n'/v', \nu')$. Hence, the analogue of (14.3) becomes

$$\bar{V}_t''(a, (m, n, v)) \equiv E_{\mu|n,m,v} V_t(a, \tilde{\mu})$$
$$= \int_{-\infty}^{\infty} V_t(a, \mu) f_S(\mu|m'', v''/n'', \nu'')\,d\mu; \tag{17.33}$$

and

$$\bar{l}_t''(a,(m,n,v)) \equiv E_{\mu|n,m,v} l_t(a,\mu)$$

$$= \int_{-\infty}^{\infty} l_t(a,\mu) f_S(\mu|m'',v''/n'',v'')\,d\mu, \tag{17.34}$$

where m'', v'', n'', v'' are given by (17.10).

Observe that in terminal analysis $a^o_{n,m,v}$ depends on the parameter (m'',n'',v'',v'') in exactly the same way that the optimal act a^o, prior to observing (n,m,v), depends on the parameter (m',n',v',v').

17.7.3 Preposterior Analysis

If $(\tilde{\mu},\tilde{v})$ is given a prior Normal-Inverted-Gamma df with parameter (m',n',v',v') then the prior df of $(\tilde{m},\tilde{v})$ is defined by (17.18a). We have

$$\bar{\bar{V}}_t(n) \equiv E\bar{V}_t''(a^o_{n,\tilde{m},\tilde{v}},(n,\tilde{m},\tilde{v}))$$

$$= c\iint_{-\infty}^{\infty} \bar{V}_t''(a^o_{n,m,v},(n,m,v))\frac{(vv)^{(1/2)r-1}}{(v'v'+vv+n_u[m-m']^2)^{(1/2)vn}}\,dm\,dv, \tag{17.35}$$

and

$$\bar{\bar{l}}_t(n) \equiv E\bar{l}_t''(a^o_{n,\tilde{m},\tilde{v}},(n,\tilde{m},\tilde{v}))$$

$$= c'\iint_{-\infty}^{\infty} \bar{l}_t''(a^o_{n,m,v},(n,m,v))\frac{(vv)^{(1/2)r-1}}{(v'v'+vv+n_u[m-m']^2)^{(1/2)vn}}\,dm\,dv, \tag{17.36}$$

where c and c' are constant.

17.8 Infinite-Action Problems with Quadratic Loss

We shall consider the optimal sample size problem with quadratic loss only. For others, see *ASDT.*

17.8.1 Terminal Analysis

Let $\tilde{\mu}$ be the unknown parameter of an Independent Normal process; let the set of available acts (estimates) be the set of all real numbers; let

$$l_t(a,\mu) \equiv K_t(a-\mu)^2;$$

let the prior and posterior mean and variance of the rv $\tilde{\mu}$ be $(\bar{\mu}',\breve{\mu}')$ and $(\bar{\mu}'',\breve{\mu}'')$. From section 12.6.2, we have:

a. The optimal act under prior information is $a^o = \bar{\mu}'$;

b. The EVPI is given by $\bar{l}_t'(a^o) = K_t \breve{\mu}'$;

c. The optimal act, posterior to observing (n, m, v) is $a^o_{n,m,v} = \bar{\mu}''$;

d. The posterior EVPI after observing (n, m, v) is

$$\bar{l}_t''(a^o_{n,m,v}, (n, m, v)) = K_t \breve{\mu}'',$$

where $\bar{\mu}''$ and $\breve{\mu}''$ are given by (17.13).

17.8.2 Preposterior Analysis

Expected Value of Sample Information

From (14.29b) and (17.24) the EVSI is given by

$$I(n) = k_t \breve{\bar{\mu}}'' = k_t \frac{v'}{n^*} \frac{\nu'}{\nu' - 2}, \tag{17.37}$$

where

$$n^* = \frac{n + n'}{n} n'.$$

Observe that $I(0) = 0$ and that

$$\lim_{n \to \infty} I(n) = k_t \frac{v'}{n'} \frac{\nu'}{\nu' - 2} = k_t \breve{\mu}' = \text{EVPI}.$$

Expected Net Gain of Sampling

If the cost of a sample of size n is a linear function of n and does not depend on m and v,

$$c_s(n, m, v) = K_s + k_s n, \tag{17.38}$$

where K_s and k_s are respectively the fixed and variable costs of sampling, then by (14.13) the expected net gain of sampling (ENGS) is

$$G(n) = k_t \frac{v'}{n^*} \frac{\nu'}{\nu' - 2} - (K_s + k_s n). \tag{17.39}$$

Optimal Sample Size

The sample size that maximizes ENGS is n^o given by

$$(n^o + n') = \left[\frac{k_t \nu' v'}{k_s(\nu' - 2)}\right]^{1/2} \tag{17.40}$$

provided (1) that n^o as given by this formula is positive and (2) that $G(n^o)$ as given by (17.39) is positive; if either condition fails, the optimal sample size is 0.

17.9 Alternate Approaches

17.9.1 Review of What Was Done: The Fully Bayesian Analysis

We posited a data-generating process that yields observations $\tilde{z}_1, \ldots, \tilde{z}_n$ that are iid, each Normally distributed with unknown mean $\tilde{\mu}$ and variance $\tilde{v}$. The likelihood of $z_1, \ldots, z_n$ as a function of (μ, v) is a constant times a Normal-Inverted-Gamma (two) density and if we use a Normal-Inverted Gamma prior on $(\tilde{\mu}, \tilde{v})$ the posterior remains in the same family. In the Normal-Inverted-Gamma family, the conditional distribution of $\tilde{\mu}$ given v is Normal and the marginal on $\tilde{v}$ is inverted gamma (two); the marginal on $\tilde{\mu}$ is Student. Observe also that $\tilde{\mu}$ and $\tilde{v}$ are dependent rvs and that they would also be dependent even if we assessed independent prior distributions for $\tilde{\mu}$ and $\tilde{v}$.

The sufficient statistics of the sample are (m, v, n) and updating from (m', v', n', v') through $(m, v, n, n - 1)$ is simply done. In a conceptually straightforward manner, given n, we obtained the distribution of $(\tilde{m}, \tilde{v})$, marginal with respect to $\tilde{\mu}$ and $\tilde{v}$,which opened up the possibility of getting the preposterior distribution of $\tilde{\tilde{\mu}}''$ and $\tilde{\tilde{\mu}}''$. We also obtained the predictive distribution of $\tilde{z}_{n+1}$ given $(m', v', n', v', m, v, n)$ which was shown to be a Student distribution.

Given the prior and posterior distributions of $\tilde{\mu}$ and $\tilde{v}$, terminal analysis is straightforward and now no more complicated than for the case of a known v. It was routine to find optimal sample sizes for the quadratic loss case with with linear sampling costs but the analysis becomes messy and hence was omitted for the two-action linear loss problem. All in all the theory is reasonably operational. A sticky point is perhaps the assessment of a joint prior for $(\tilde{\mu}, \tilde{v})$.

17.9.2 A Simple Pragmatic Alternative: A Bayesian/Classical Mixture

We can simplify and cut corners. If our task is merely to report a posterior distribution of $\tilde{\mu}$ based on a reasonable size sample, we could treat v as a nuisance parameter, estimate its value by, say, the maximum likelihood method—which in this case means estimating v by $\hat{v} = v(n - 1)/n$ as shown in (19.5b) to follow—and then we can make believe that v was known at the outset to equal $\hat{v}$ and proceed using the prior-to-posterior analysis on $\tilde{\mu}$ given in the previous chapter. The posterior of $\tilde{\mu}$ will then be Normal

Table 17.1
Discretized prior distribution of $(\tilde{\mu}, \tilde{\upsilon})$

	υ_1	...	υ_j	...	υ_J		Marginal
μ_1	f'_{11}	...	f'_{1j}	...	f_{1J}		$f'_{1.}$
$\vdots$	$\vdots$		$\vdots$		$\vdots$		
μ_i	f'_{i1}	...	f'_{ij}	...	f'_{iJ}		$f'_{i\cdot}$
$\vdots$	$\vdots$		$\vdots$		$\vdots$		
μ_I	f'_{I1}	...	f'_{Ij}	...	f'_{IJ}		$f'_{I\cdot}$
							$\downarrow$
Marginal	$f'_{.1}$		$f'_{.j}$	...	$f'_{.J}$	$\rightarrow$	1.0

instead of Student and this would show up in a slightly tighter posterior distribution for $\tilde{\mu}$. The approximation is not bad for samples of reasonable size (say $n \geq 20$).

Of course, this trick of point-estimating the nuisance parameter will not help us if our task is to do preposterior analysis for $\tilde{\mu}$. But in many inference problems a sample size might have been predetermined by operational convenience and if so, posterior reporting on $\tilde{\mu}$ using a classical point estimate of $\tilde{\upsilon}$ is not a bad idea.

17.9.3 Discrete Approximations Using Spreadsheet Analysis

With a computer we could use discrete approximations to update a prior on $(\tilde{\mu}, \tilde{\upsilon})$. For example, we could do the following: (a) Discretize the distribution of $\tilde{\mu}$ by I values (say, $I = 50$): $\mu_1, \ldots, \mu_i, \ldots, \mu_I$; (b) discretize $\tilde{\upsilon}$ by J values (say, $J = 20$): $\upsilon_1, \ldots, \upsilon_j, \ldots, \upsilon_J$; it will help if the values of the μ_i and υ_j are each equally spaced; (c) assign a prior discrete probability distribution to (μ_i, υ_j) pairs—perhaps using a formula. You may wish to make the prior discrete distribution on $\tilde{\mu}$ and $\tilde{\upsilon}$ independent (but the posteriors will be dependent, nevertheless). Denoting the prior probability of $(\tilde{\mu} = \mu_i, \tilde{\upsilon} = \upsilon_j)$ by f'_{ij} the prior distribution can be depicted in a spreadsheet format (table 17.1).

As a word of caution, check the spreadsheet to make sure $\sum_{ij} f'_{ij} = 1$, or close to it. In the table we use the natural notation $f'_{i.} = \sum_j f'_{ij}$ for the marginal probability of μ_i and $f'_{.j} = \sum_i f_{ij}$ for the marginal probability of υ_j.

Now observe the sample $z_1, \ldots, z_n$ and compute the sufficient statistics (m, υ). From (17.3), ignoring constants, let

$$L_{ij} = e^{-(1/2\upsilon_j)(n-1)}\upsilon^{-(1/2)(n/\upsilon_j)(m-\mu_i)^2}\upsilon_j^{-(1/2)n}$$

be the likelihood of (m, υ) at (μ_i, υ_j) and display this in table 17.2. This is

Table 17.2
Likelihood of (m, v) at (μ_i, v_j)

	v_1	...	v_j	...	v_J
μ_1	L_{11}	...	L_{1j}	...	L_{1J}
$\vdots$	$\vdots$		$\vdots$		$\vdots$
μ_i	L_{i1}	...	L_{ij}	...	L_{iJ}
$\vdots$	$\vdots$		$\vdots$		$\vdots$
μ_I	L_{I1}	...	L_{Ij}	...	L_{IJ}

Table 17.3
Product of prior and likelihood (cell by cell)

	v_1	...	v_j	...	v_J	
μ_1	$f'_{11} \times L_{11}$	...	$f'_{1j} \times L_{1j}$	...	$f'_{1J} \times L_{1J}$	
$\vdots$	$\vdots$		$\vdots$		$\vdots$	
μ_i	$f'_{i1} \times L_{i1}$	...	$f'_{ij} \times L_{ij}$	...	$f'_{iJ} \times L_{iJ}$	
$\vdots$	$\vdots$		$\vdots$		$\vdots$	
μ_I	$f'_{I1} \times L_{I1}$	...	$f'_{Ij} \times L_{Ij}$	...	$f'_{IJ} \times L_{IJ}$	
						K

Note: $K = \sum_{ij} f'_{ij} \times L_{ij}$

Table 17.4
Discretized posterior distribution

	v_1	...	v_j	...	v_J		Marginal
μ_1	f''_{11}	...	f''_{1j}	...	f''_{1J}		$f''_{1\cdot}$
$\vdots$	$\vdots$		$\vdots$		$\vdots$		
μ_i	f''_{i1}	...	f''_{ij}	...	f''_{iJ}		$f''_{i\cdot}$
$\vdots$	$\vdots$		$\vdots$		$\vdots$		
μ_I	f''_{I1}	...	f''_{Ij}	...	f''_{IJ}		$f''_{I\cdot}$
							↓
Marginal	$f''_{\cdot 1}$		$f''_{\cdot j}$	...	$f''_{\cdot J}$	→	1.0

(Note: $f''_{ij} \equiv f'_{ij} \times L_{ij}/K$.)

really simple to do. Check that the discretization was fine enough so that the values L_{ij} capture the shape of the likelihood function.

Next in table 17.3, multiply the prior times the likelihood to get

$$f''_{ij} \times K = f'_{ij} L_{ij}$$

where

$$K = \sum_{ij} f'_{ij} L_{ij}.$$

To get the posterior in table 17.4, divide each of the entries in table 17.3 by the normalizing factor K. The (i, j)th entry is now the posterior of (μ_i, υ_j) and labeled f''_{ij}. The marginals are labeled $f''_{i.}$ and $f''_{.j}$.

This is easy to do and might be quite satisfactory for prior-to-posterior analysis. It is a lot harder to push this discretization technique to handle preposterior analysis.

18 Large Sample Theory

18.1 The Central Limit Theorem

18.1.1 Sums of Independent, Identically Distributed RV's

Let $\tilde{x}_1$, $\tilde{x}_2$, ... be a sequence of independent, identically distributed (iid) rv's, with common left-tail cumulative function F; that is, let

$$P(a < \tilde{x}_{n+1} \leq b | \tilde{x}_1 = x_1, \ldots, \tilde{x}_n = x_n) = F(b) - F(a) \tag{18.1}$$

for all n, a, b, x_1, ..., x_n. Let $\bar{x}$ and $\check{x}$ denote the common mean and variance of these rv's.

Standardized Sums

Define

$$\tilde{T}_n \equiv \tilde{x}_1 + \cdots + \tilde{x}_n \quad \text{and} \quad \tilde{M}_n \equiv \tilde{T}_n/n. \tag{18.2}$$

From (13.48) we have that

$$E(\tilde{T}_n) = n\bar{x}, \qquad V(\tilde{T}_n) = [S(\tilde{T}_n)]^2 = n\check{x} \tag{18.3a}$$

$$E(\tilde{M}_n) = \bar{x}, \qquad V(\tilde{M}_n) = [S(\tilde{M}_n)]^2 = \check{x}/n. \tag{18.3b}$$

As n increases we see that the distribution of the rv $\tilde{T}_n$ does not stabilize: if $\bar{x} > 0$, then $E(\tilde{T}_n)$ becomes increasingly large with n and the distribution of $\tilde{T}_n$ becomes *more and more dispersed.* For the rv $\tilde{M}_n$, on the other hand, $E(\tilde{M}_n)$ remains stable at $\bar{x}$ and $V(\tilde{M}_n)$ diminishes at the rate of $1/n$.

We now define the standardized sums of $\tilde{x}_1, \tilde{x}_2, \ldots, \tilde{x}_n$ to be

$$\tilde{u}_n \equiv \frac{\tilde{T}_n - E(\tilde{T}_n)}{S(\tilde{T}_n)}. \tag{18.4}$$

The reader can easily verify that $\tilde{u}_n$ is also expressible as

$$\tilde{u}_n = \frac{\tilde{M}_n - E(\tilde{M}_n)}{S(\tilde{M}_n)} \tag{18.5}$$

and that

$$E(\tilde{u}_n) = 0, \qquad V(\tilde{u}_n) = 1. \tag{18.6}$$

Although the mean and variance of $\tilde{u}_n$ do not change with n, the distribution of $\tilde{u}_n$ does change in general with n. For example, for two numbers $a < b$, in general

$$P(a \leq \tilde{u}_i \leq b) \neq P(a \leq \tilde{u}_j \leq b), \quad \text{where} \quad i \neq j$$

(notice the *inequality*). The remarkable fact is that regardless of the common distributing function of the rv's $\tilde{x}_i$, just so long as $\bar{x}$ and $\check{x}$ exist, the *distributions of $\tilde{u}_1$, $\tilde{u}_2$, ... tend more and more toward the standardized Normal distribution.* This assertion, known as the *central limit theorem*, is probably the single most important result in the theory of probability and statistics. This section is devoted to the development of that result.

18.1.2 Behavior of Sums of Bernoulli RVs

If we arbitrarily assign the "value" 1 to a "success" and the "value" 0 to a "failure," then the outcome of any one trial of a Bernoulli process with known parameter p can be thought of as a *random variable* $\tilde{x}$ with mf f defined by

$$f(x) = \begin{cases} p & \text{if} \quad x = 1, \\ 1 - p & \text{if} \quad x = 0. \end{cases} \tag{18.7}$$

Since the successive trials are independent by the definition of a Bernoulli process (section 11.2), we may consider the outcomes of any n Bernoulli trials as a set of n iid rv's $(\tilde{x}_1, \ldots, \tilde{x}_n)$ with mf's given by (18.7).

The reader is asked to prove as an exercise that the mean and variance of any one of the $\tilde{x}$'s are

$$\bar{x} \equiv E(\tilde{x}) = p, \qquad \check{x} \equiv V(\tilde{x}) = p(1 - p). \tag{18.8}$$

From this result and (18.3) we have at once that if we denote the *sum* of the n $\tilde{x}$'s by

$$\tilde{r}_n \equiv \textstyle\sum_{i=1}^{n} \tilde{x}_i, \tag{18.9}$$

then

$$\bar{r}_n \equiv E(\tilde{r}_n) = np, \qquad \check{r}_n \equiv V(\tilde{r}_n) = np(1 - p). \tag{18.10}$$

(These same results were obtained by a different argument as (9.24); also (18.8) could be obtained from (9.24) by considering the special case $n = 1$.) The *standardized sum* of the n $\tilde{x}$'s will be denoted by

$$\tilde{u}_n \equiv \frac{\tilde{r}_n - \bar{r}_n}{\ddot{r}_n} = \frac{\tilde{r}_n - np}{\sqrt{np(1 - p)}} = \frac{\dfrac{\tilde{r}_n}{n} - p}{\sqrt{\dfrac{p(1 - p)}{n}}}. \tag{18.11}$$

For any given p, we can obtain a sequence of rv's $\tilde{r}_n$ and $\tilde{u}_n$ and a sequence of corresponding mass functions by letting n increase from 1 to ∞. For $p = .5$, the mf's of $\tilde{r}_n$ for $n = 10$, 20, and 50 are shown in the three graphs on the right-hand side of figure 18.1, and the mf's of $\tilde{u}_n$ for the same three values of n are shown on the right-hand side of figure 18.2. In both series of graphs the mass at any possible r_n or u_n is represented, not by

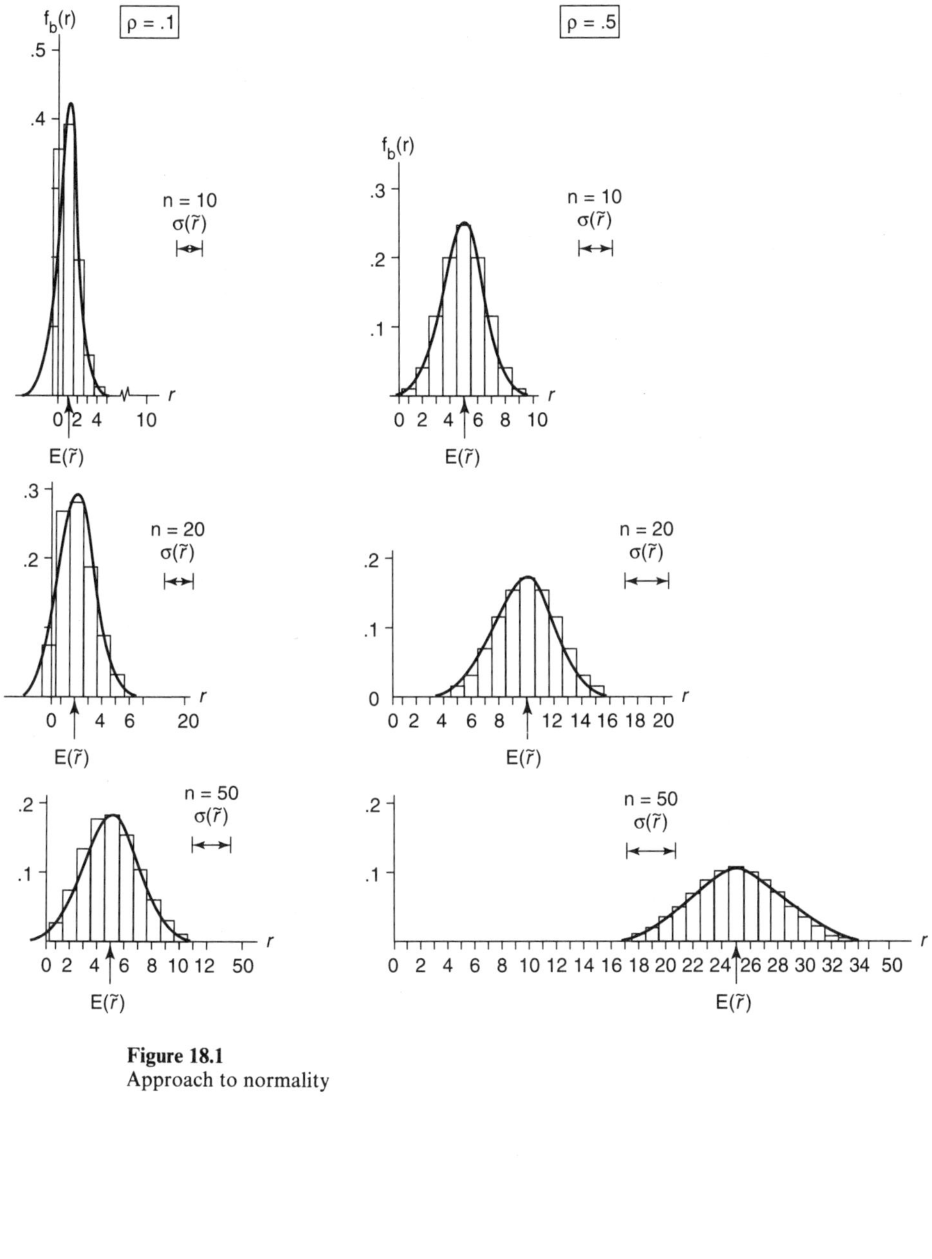

Figure 18.1
Approach to normality

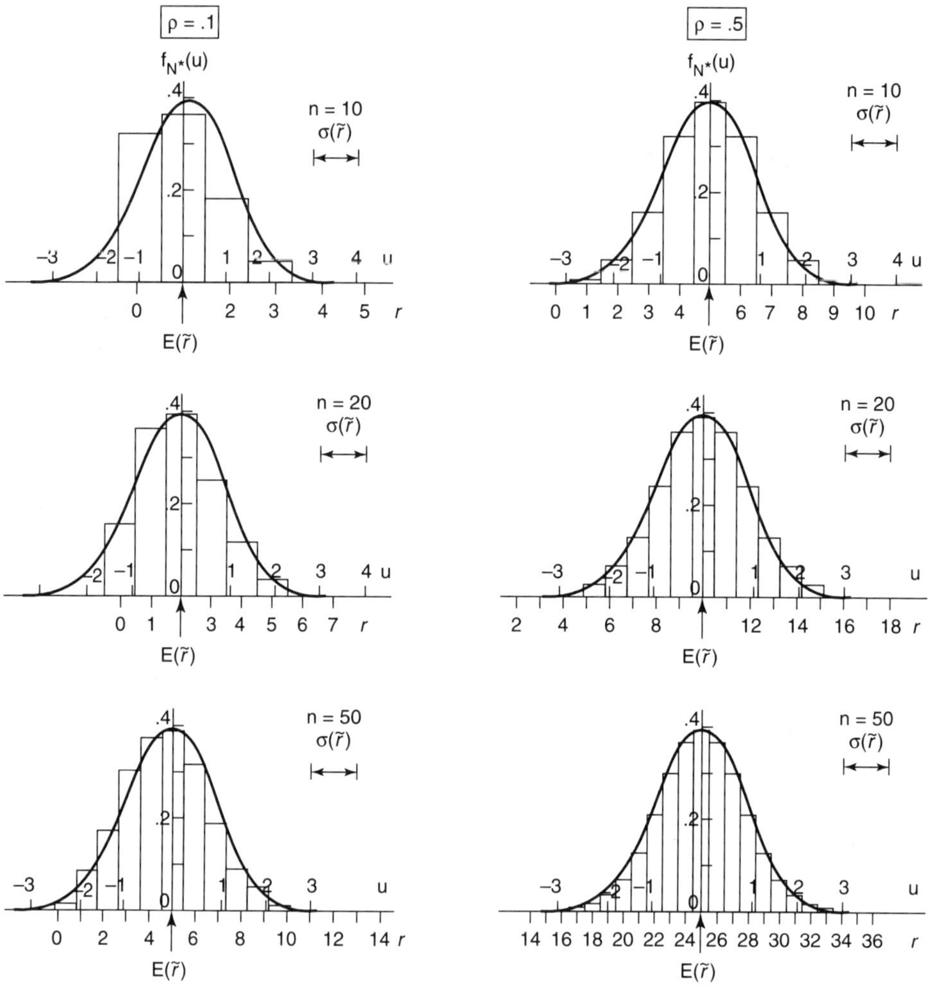

Figure 18.2
Standardized approach to normality

the height of a line, but by the *area* of a bar; in both series there is superimposed upon each graph a Normal density having the same mean and variance as the mass function.

Inspecting the three graphs for $p = .5$ in figure 18.1, we see that as n increases, the mass function of $\tilde{r}_n$ in some sense becomes more and more like the corresponding Normal density, but because the distributions are successively wider and flatter, it is hard to see exactly what is happening. The implications of the three graphs for $p = .5$ in figure 18.2 are much clearer: The Normal density is fixed because $\tilde{u}_n$ has mean 0 and variance 1 regardless of the value of n, and it is very clear that *as n increases, the histogram of the mf of $\tilde{u}_n$ approaches the unit Normal density.*

Similar sets of graphs for $p = .1$ are shown on the left-hand sides of figures 18.1 and 18.2, and again the phenomenon appears; as n increases, the histogram of the *standardized* sum $\tilde{u}_n$ approaches the unit Normal density. The only difference is that the approach is slower when $p = .1$ than when $p = .5$.

18.1.3 Behavior of Sums of Exponential RVs

Now consider a set of r iid continuous rv's $(\tilde{x}_1, \ldots, \tilde{x}_r)$ each of which has the exponential density function f defined by

$$f(x) = e^{-\lambda x}\lambda, \qquad \begin{cases} 0 \le x \le \infty, \\ 0 \le \lambda \le \infty. \end{cases} \tag{18.12}$$

The distribution of the sum

$$\tilde{t}_r \equiv \textstyle\sum_{i=1}^{r} \tilde{x}_i \tag{18.13}$$

of r such rv's is given in chapter 15, and the density function of the standardized sum

$$\tilde{u}_r \equiv \frac{\tilde{t}_r - \bar{t}_r}{\ddot{t}_r} \tag{18.14}$$

is graphed for several values of r from 1 to 25 in figure 18.3. It is apparent on inspection of this figure that we are in the presence of essentially the same phenomenon that we observed in the Bernoulli case. Even though the df of an individual exponential rv is violently non-Normal, the df of the standardized sum of r exponential rv's approaches the unit Normal df as r increases.

18.1.4 Formal Statement of the Central Limit Theorem

The really amazing generality of this phenomenon is expressed by the *central limit theorem* which we now state:

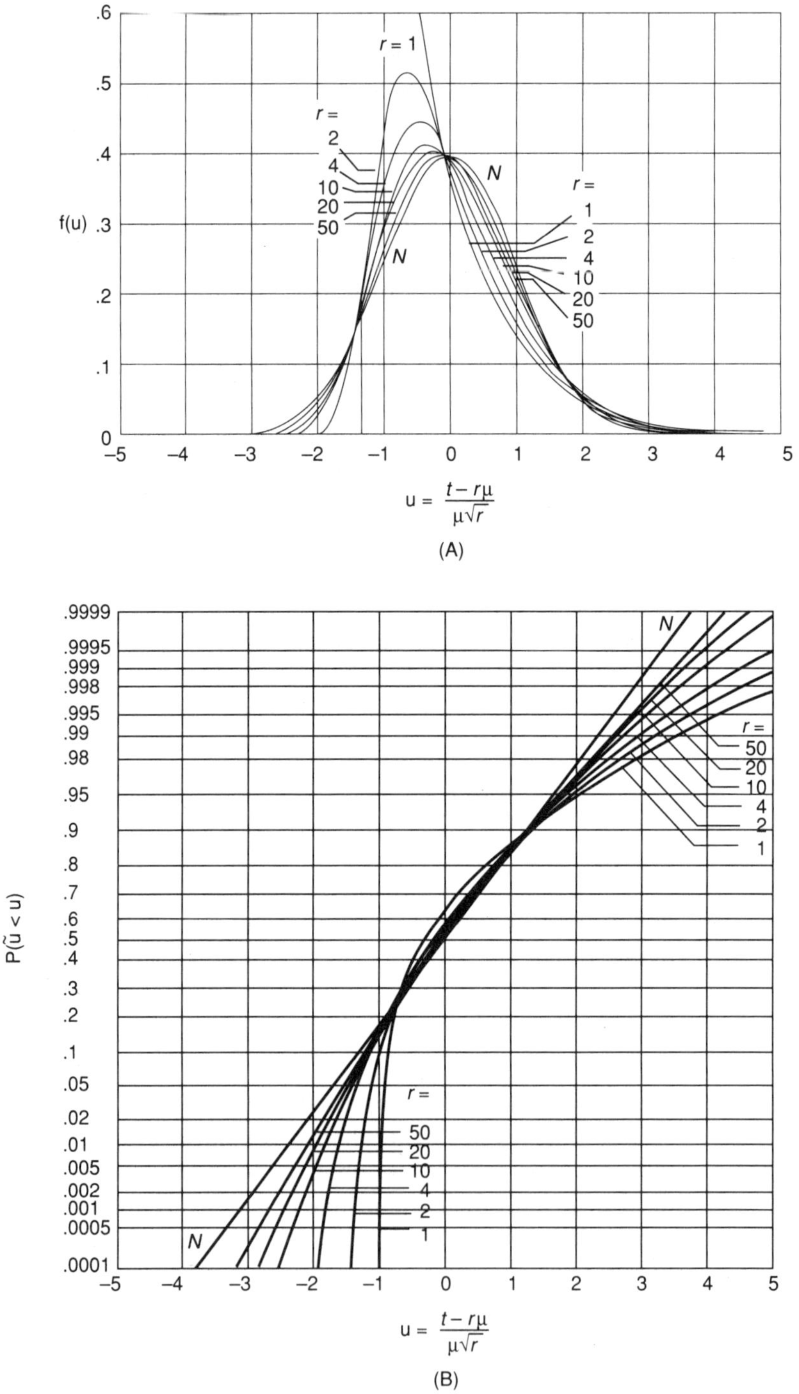

Figure 18.3
Gamma distributions with Normal approximations

Let $(\tilde{x}_1, \ldots, \tilde{x}_n)$ be iid rv's with finite mean and variance, let $\tilde{u}_n$ be their standardized sum. Then for any number a,

$$\lim_{n\to\infty} P(\tilde{u}_n \leq a) = F_{N^*}(a). \tag{18.15}$$

A proof of a slightly restricted version of this theorem is given in section 18.1.5.

For "large" n, (18.15) becomes

$$P\left\{\frac{\tilde{T}_n - n\bar{x}}{\sqrt{n\check{x}}} \leq a\right\} \doteq F_{N^*}(a), \tag{18.16}$$

where the sign $\doteq$ is read "approximately equal to." Hence, for any number b,

$$\begin{aligned} P(T_n \leq b) &= P\left\{\frac{\tilde{T}_n - n\bar{x}}{\sqrt{n\check{x}}} \leq \frac{b - n\bar{x}}{\sqrt{n\check{x}}}\right\} \\ &\doteq F_{N^*}\left(\frac{b - n\bar{x}}{\sqrt{n\check{x}}}\right) = F_N(b \mid n\bar{x}, n\check{x}), \end{aligned} \tag{18.17}$$

and we can assert that $\tilde{T}_n$ is approximately Normal with mean $n\bar{x}$ and variance $n\check{x}$. The reader is asked to show as an exercise that in an analogous manner $\tilde{M}_n$ is approximately Normal with mean $\bar{x}$ and variance $\check{x}/n$.

It should be pointed out that the central limit theorem just stated does *not* imply, for instance, that the *density* function of $\tilde{u}_n$ (if it has one) approaches the unit Normal density function as in figure 18.3, or that the expectation of an arbitrary function of $\tilde{u}_n$ approaches the expectation of the same function of a unit Normal rv. Further theorems exist, but to go into them would take us far afield without completely closing the gap, since the theorems we really need are not yet fully developed. We really need theorems about the likelihood function, and bounds on the errors. General theorems now available are too weak to justify fully the approximations we shall make except for very large n. Accordingly we shall content ourselves with pointing out on the one hand the closeness of the Normal approximation in special cases and on the other hand, the generality of the theorem just stated. In what follows, however, we shall without further comment act as if the distribution of $\tilde{T}_n$ or $\tilde{M}_n$ or $\tilde{u}_n$ is Normal to a sufficient approximation for our purposes, whatever they may be.

18.1.5 Proof of the Central Limit Theorem

In this section we shall prove the central limit theorem for the special case where the rv's $\tilde{x}_1, \tilde{x}_2, \ldots$ have a finite third moment, that is, where $E[|\tilde{x}_i|^3]$ is finite. A similar but somewhat more elaborate proof can be given requiring only that $E[\tilde{x}_i^2]$ be finite. (See Trotter, 1959.) Usual proofs make use of theorems on Fourier transforms which are beyond the level of mathematical sophistication required for this book.

We shall first need the following lemma.

Lemma Let $\tilde{x}_1, \tilde{x}_2, \ldots$ be iid rv's with finite third moments, let $\tilde{u}_n$ denote the standardized sum of the first n rv's, let $\tilde{u}$ be unit Normal, and let φ be any function with a continuous, bounded third derivative. Then

$$\lim_{n\to\infty} E[\varphi(\tilde{u}_n)] = E[\varphi(\tilde{u})].$$

Proof We shall assume in the proof that the common distribution of the $\tilde{x}_i$ has mean 0 and variance 1; extension to the general case is trivial.

Let $\tilde{y}_1, \ldots, \tilde{y}_n$ be unit Normal rv's that are independent of each other and of the $\tilde{x}_i$'s and define

$$\text{(1a)} \quad D_n \equiv E[\varphi(n^{-1/2} \textstyle\sum_i \tilde{x}_i) - \varphi(n^{-1/2} \textstyle\sum_i \tilde{y}_i)];$$

from (16.22) and (16.23) it follows that $n^{-1/2} \sum_i \tilde{y}_i$ is itself a unit Normal rv, and therefore the lemma can be rewritten in the form

$$\text{(1a)} \quad \lim_{n\to\infty} D_n = 0.$$

If now we define

$$\text{(2a)} \quad \tilde{z}_i \equiv n^{-1/2}[\textstyle\sum_{j=1}^{i-1} \tilde{y}_j + \textstyle\sum_{j=i+1}^{n} \tilde{x}_j]$$

and verify that

$$\tilde{z}_1 + n^{-1/2}\tilde{x}_1 = n^{-1/2} \textstyle\sum_i \tilde{x}_i,$$

and

$$\tilde{z}_n + n^{-1/2}\tilde{y}_n = n^{-1/2} \textstyle\sum_i \tilde{y}_i,$$

while

$$\tilde{z}_i + n^{-1/2}\tilde{y}_i = \tilde{z}_{i+1} + n^{-1/2}\tilde{x}_{i+1}, \qquad i = 1, 2, \ldots, n-1,$$

we see that (1a) can be written as a "collapsing series"

$$D_n = E \textstyle\sum_i [\varphi(\tilde{z}_i + n^{-1/2}\tilde{x}_i) - \varphi(\tilde{z}_i + n^{-1/2}\tilde{y}_i)];$$

and by reversing the order of summation and integration we obtain

$$\text{(2b)} \quad D_n = \textstyle\sum_i E[\varphi(\tilde{z}_i + n^{-1/2}\tilde{x}_i) - \varphi(\tilde{z}_i + n^{-1/2}\tilde{y}_i)].$$

We next expand each term in the sum in (2b) by using Taylor's theorem in the form

$$\varphi(z + t) = \varphi(z) + t\varphi'(z) + \tfrac{1}{2}t^2\varphi''(z) + \tfrac{1}{6}t^3\varphi'''(\zeta(t)),$$

where $\zeta(t)$ is some point in $[z, z + t]$, thus obtaining

(3a) $D_n = \sum_i E(\tilde{A}_i + \tilde{B}_i)$

where

(3b) $\tilde{A}_i = n^{-1/2}(\tilde{x}_i - \tilde{y}_i)\varphi'(\tilde{z}_i) + \tfrac{1}{2}n^{-1}(\tilde{x}_i^2 - \tilde{y}_1^2)\varphi''(\tilde{z}_i),$

(3c) $\tilde{B}_i = \tfrac{1}{6}n^{-3/2}[\tilde{x}_i^3\varphi'''(\zeta(n^{-1/2}\tilde{x}_i)) - \tilde{y}_i^3\varphi'''(\zeta(n^{-1/2}\tilde{y}_i))].$

Now because the $\tilde{x}$'s are independent of the $\tilde{y}$'s by assumption, we have by (2a) that $\tilde{x}_i$ and $\tilde{y}_i$ are independent of $\tilde{z}_i$; it then follows from (3b) and the formula for the expectation of the product of independent rv's that

$$E(\tilde{A}_i) = n^{-1/2}[E(\tilde{x}_i) - E(\tilde{y}_i)]E\varphi'(\tilde{z}_i)$$
$$+ \tfrac{1}{2}n[E(\tilde{x}_i^2) - E(\tilde{y}_i^2)]E\varphi''(\tilde{z}_i);$$

since by assumption

$$E(\tilde{x}_i) = E(\tilde{y}_i) = 0 \quad \text{and} \quad E(\tilde{x}_i^2) = E(\tilde{y}_i^2) = 1,$$

it follows that

(4) $E(\tilde{A}_i) = 0.$

Denoting the bound on φ''' by c, we have by (3c)

(5) $|\tilde{B}_i| \le n^{-3/2}[c|\tilde{x}_i^3| + c|\tilde{y}_i^3|],$

and hence by (3a) and (4)

(6) $|D_n| \le \dfrac{cn^{-3/2}}{6}\sum_i E[|\tilde{x}_i^3| + |\tilde{y}_i^3|]$

$$= \frac{cn^{-1/2}}{6}[E|\tilde{x}_i^3| + E|\tilde{y}_i^3|]$$

from which (1b) follows immediately. ■

Using the lemma just proved, we can now prove the central limit theorem for the case where the $\tilde{x}_i$ have a finite third moment by simply letting φ be a function with a continuous, bounded third derivative such that

$\varphi(t) = 1$	for	$t \le a,$
$0 < \varphi(t) < 1$	for	$a < t < a + h,$
$\varphi(t) = 0$	for	$a + h \le t.$

Defining

(1) $F^{(n)}(a) \equiv P[n^{-1/2} \sum_i x_i \le a]$

(2) $F_{N^*}(a) \equiv P[\tilde{u} \le a]$,

we have at once that, for any a and h,

(3) $F^{(n)}(a) \le E\varphi(n^{-1/2} \sum_i \tilde{x}_i)$,

(4) $E\varphi(\tilde{u}) \le F_{N^*}(a + h)$.

Now by the previous lemma, for any ε, we can find n_0 such that

(5) $E\varphi(n^{-1/2} \sum \tilde{x}) < E\varphi(\tilde{u}) + \frac{1}{2}\varepsilon, \qquad n \ge n_0$;

because F_{N^*} is a continuous function, for any ε, we could have chosen h when defining φ so that

(6) $F_{N^*}(a + h) < F_{N^*}(a) + \frac{1}{2}\varepsilon$.

We thus have that for any ε and $n \ge n_0$

(7) $F_N(a) \le E\varphi(n^{-1/2} \sum_i \tilde{x}_i)$ [by (3)]

$< E\varphi(\tilde{u}) + \frac{1}{2}\varepsilon$ [by (5)]

$< F_{N^*}(a + h) + \frac{1}{2}\varepsilon$ [by (4)]

$< F_{N^*}(a) + \varepsilon$ [by (6)];

and since we can easily establish by a similar argument that

(8) $F^{(n)}(a) > F_{N^*}(a) - \varepsilon$,

the central limit theorem follows. ■

18.1.6 Purely Empirical Application of the Central Limit Theorem

Besides approximating the distribution of a sum of a known number of independent rv's with identical distributions, the Normal distribution can sometimes approximate the distribution of a rv which can be considered as the sum of an unknown number of only more or less independent rv's with not necessarily identical distributions. If, for example, we have a fairly long record of weekly usage of some replacement part, we may find that the frequency distribution of this weekly usage can be very closely fitted by a Normal curve. Much more often, we find that the frequency distribution of the lengths of pieces turned out by an automatic machine is very nearly Normal, or that the frequency distribution of repeated measurements of a single physical quantity is very nearly Normal.

When we do observe Normality or near-Normality in such situations, we can usually "explain" it by arguing that the variability in the observed quantity is due, not to the operation of one or two factors each of which has a really substantial effect on the observed quantity, but to the simultaneous operation of a very large number of factors each of which has only a very small effect. Such an "explanation" not only makes common sense but can be related to extended versions of the central limit theorem which say that as more and more rv's are added to a sum, the distribution of the sum will under certain conditions approach Normality even though the rv's are not identically distributed or even completely independent. We shall not formally discuss the application of the central limit theorem to such phenomena, however, because formal analysis is of no practical use since we gain nothing by appealing to the theorem when we do not know how many rv's we are summing.

The *only* way, then, of deciding whether an empirical process will generate approximate Normally distributed part-usages, dimensions, or measurements of a particular dimension is actually to examine the historical output of the particular process in question; we warn the reader that the output of real physical processes is much more often very far from than really close to Normal. The easiest way of examining the output is to plot the *cumulative* historical distribution on what is known as "Normal probability paper," the grid of which is such that a Normal cumulative distribution plots as a straight line. (Figure 18.3B shows such plots of standardized gamma and normal distributions.) We would also point out that even though in a given circumstance we might be convinced that the output of a real physical process is different from Normal, we still might choose to treat the process as if it were Normal, because (1) the analysis might be hopelessly involved otherwise, and (2) the losses attributable to this misspecification of a distribution might be known not to be serious.

18.2 Normal Approximation to Mathematically Well-Defined Distributions

Many of the rv's encountered in practice are in fact sums of iid rv's, and the importance of the Normal distribution is due essentially to the fact that, as indicated by the central limit theorem, the distribution of such sums can be approximated by the Normal distribution provided that the number of iid variables included in the sum is large enough. To use the approximation, we simply compute the true mean and variance of the sum and then treat the sum *as if* it were in fact a Normal rv with that mean and variance.

Applications of the Normal approximation fall into two broad categories:

1. Cases where the "true" distribution of a rv is mathematically well defined and a Normal approximation is used only because it is analytically more tractable or because existing tables do not give a required numerical probability.

2. Cases where the "true" distribution of a rv would be extremely difficult if not impossible to determine and use of a Normal approximation is for practical purposes the *only* available method of solving a decision problem.

In this section we make some remarks on the former and more technical category on which there is extensive literature; the remainder of the chapter will deal with the latter category.

18.2.1 Approximation of Binomial Probabilities

When a *discrete* rv is treated as if it were Normal, certain special problems arise which can easily be explained by taking a binomial rv as an example. Looking at the graphs in figure 18.2, observe again that what approaches a Normal density function is the *histogram* of the mass function, in which the mass attached to each possible value r of the rv $\tilde{r}$ is represented by the *area* of a bar whose base extends from $(r - \frac{1}{2})$ to $(r + \frac{1}{2})$.

Cumulative Probabilities

In diagrams like those just cited, the probability $P(\tilde{r} \geq r)$ is represented by the area in the histogram to the right of the point $(r - \frac{1}{2})$ on the horizontal axis, *not* by the area to the right of the point r itself; and it follows that we should take as the Normal approximation to $P(\tilde{r} \geq r)$ the area under the corresponding Normal curve to the right of $(r - \frac{1}{2})$ rather than to the right of r. Algebraically, the approximation is

$$G_b(r|n, p) \doteq G_{N^*}(u), \tag{18.18a}$$

where in terms of

$$\bar{r} = np, \qquad \ddot{r} \equiv S(\tilde{r}) = [np(1-p)]^{1/2}, \tag{18.18b}$$

we define

$$u \equiv \frac{(r - \frac{1}{2}) - \bar{r}}{\ddot{r}} \qquad \left(\text{and } not \quad u \equiv \frac{r - \bar{r}}{\ddot{r}}\right).$$

The procedure for finding other cumulative binomial probabilities is very similar, except that we do not always *add* $\frac{1}{2}$ to the specified value r:

Whether we add or subtract the $\frac{1}{2}$ which takes us from the center of a bar to the edge depends on (1) which tail we want and (2) whether the bar for the specified value r is included in the tail or excluded from it. *In case of doubt, sketch a few bars of the histogram.*

Individual Probabilities

In principle, we can use the Normal approximation to a binomial probability $P(\tilde{r} = r)$ by approximating $P(\tilde{r} \geq r)$ and $P(\tilde{r} \geq r + 1)$ and subtracting the latter quantity from the former; it is easier to proceed as follows. The probability $P(\tilde{r} = r)$ is represented by the area of the corresponding bar in graphs like those in figures 18.1 and 18.2 and in the *non*standardized graphs in figure 18.1 (*not* 18.2); this bar has *width* 1 and *height* approximately equal to the ordinate of the corresponding *non*standardized Normal curve at the *midpoint* of the bar. Since this Normal curve has mean $\bar{r}$ and standard deviation $\ddot{r}$, it follows from (9.56) that its ordinate at the point r is $(1/\ddot{r})f_{N^*}(u)$ where $u = (r - \bar{r})/\ddot{r}$ and hence that

$$f_b(r|n, p) \doteq \frac{1}{\ddot{r}} f_{N^*}(u) \tag{18.19a}$$

where

$$u = \frac{r - \bar{r}}{\ddot{r}}, \qquad \bar{r} = np, \qquad \ddot{r} = [np(1 - p)]^{1/2}. \tag{18.19b}$$

When we approximate *individual* binomial probabilities in this way, there is no trouble with $\pm\frac{1}{2}$.

How Large Is Large Enough?

The central limit theorem says that the error in the Normal approximation to any probability involving a sum of iid rv's will be negligible provided that the number of rv's in the sum is "large enough," but says nothing whatsoever about how large "large enough" is. The assertion

$$\lim_{n \to \infty} P(\tilde{u}_n \leq a) = F_{N^*}(a)$$

means simply that, given any number ε however small, and given any particular number a, there exists *some* (large) number n_0 such that

$$|P(\tilde{u}_n \leq a) - F_{N^*}(a)| \leq \varepsilon \quad \text{if} \quad n \geq n_0;$$

the theorem does not tell us how large n_0 *is* for given ε and a.

What is worse, the n_0 required for given ε and *a depends on the distribution of the individual rv's being summed*: the accuracy of the Normal approximation to the distribution of the sum of any particular number n of iid rv's depends on the distribution of the individual rv's. We have already observed in the graphs of figures 18.1 and 18.2 that the binomial distribution approaches the Normal more slowly when $p = .1$ than when $p = .5$, and while the Normal approximation is fairly good for n even as small as 10 when $p = .5$, it can be shown to be quite bad for n even as large as 100 when $p = .01$.

18.2.2 Approximation of Beta Probabilities

In this section we shall indicate how the Normal tables can be used most simply to approximate beta tail probabilities. (See also chapter 9 and references given in section 9.1.)

From (9.15) and (18.18), we obtain

$$F_\beta(p|\rho, \nu) = G_b(\rho|\nu - 1, p) \doteq G_{N^*}(u) \tag{18.20a}$$

where

$$u = \frac{(\rho - \frac{1}{2}) - (\nu - 1)p}{\sqrt{(\nu - 1)p(1 - p)}}. \tag{18.20b}$$

This approximation is especially good if p is not near 0 or 1 and ν is large.

Example From (18.20)

$$F_\beta(.3|7, 26) \doteq G_{N^*}(u) \qquad \text{where} \qquad u = \frac{6.5 - 25(.3)}{\sqrt{(25)(.3)(.7)}} = -0.436.$$

From the Normal tables $G_{N^*}(-0.436) = 1 - G_{N^*}(.436) = .6686$. From beta tables the exact value of $F_\beta(.3|7, 26)$ is .6593.

If $\tilde{p}$ has a beta df with parameters $(r + 1, n + 2)$ where r and n are "reasonably" large, then we shall show that $\tilde{p}$ is approximately Normal with mean r/n and variance $(r/n)(1 - r/n)/n$ as follows:

Starting with a rectangular prior for $\tilde{p}$ (i.e., a beta prior with parameters $r' = 1, n' = 2$) after observing r successes in n trials the posterior df of $\tilde{p}$ has been shown to be beta with parameters $(r + 1, n + 2)$. We also know that the posterior df is the product of the likelihood function $L(p) = f_b(r|n, p)$ (treated as a function of p) and the prior df. Thus we have, using (18.19),

$$\begin{aligned} f_\beta(p|r + 1, n + 2) &= CL(p)f_\beta(p|1, 2) \\ &= Cf_b(r|n, p)1 \\ &\doteq C\frac{1}{S(\tilde{r})}e^{-(1/2)((r-np)/(\sqrt{np(1-p)}))^2} \\ &\doteq C\frac{1}{\sqrt{2\pi}}e^{-(1/2)((p-r/n)/(\sqrt{p(1-p)/n}))^2}\frac{1}{\sqrt{p(1-p)/n}}. \end{aligned}$$

Now for large r and n the above function of p is highly concentrated about r/n, and therefore for p in the vicinity of r/n we can use the approximation

$$\frac{p(1-p)}{n} \doteq \frac{\frac{r}{n}\left(1-\frac{r}{n}\right)}{n}.$$

We therefore obtain

$$f_\beta(p|r+1, n+2) \doteq f_N\left(p\left|\frac{r}{n}, \frac{r}{n}\left(1-\frac{r}{n}\right)\right/n\right) \tag{18.21}$$

as we wished to show.

Example Using the above approximation, if $\tilde{p}$ has a beta df with parameters (10, 27) then $\tilde{p}$ is approximately normal with mean $9/25 = .36$ and variance $.36(.64/25) = .009216$. In the table below we compare some fractiles of the beta df with parameters (10, 27) with the corresponding fractiles of the Normal df with parameters (.36, .009216). We observe that the approximation is not too far off even for this modest size of n.

Fractile α	.05	.25	.50	.75	.95
p_α based on beta (10, 27)	.2257	.3058	.3671	.4315	.5262
p_α based on Normal approximation	.203	.296	.360	.424	.517

18.3 Introduction to Large Sample Theory: On the Intractability of Multiparameter Processes

In the remainder of this chapter we shall restrict our attention to situations in which the decision maker's interest is in the *mean* of some data-generating process (e.g., the population mean when the data-generating process is a result of simple sampling from this population), but we shall consider situations that differ from those considered in preceding chapters because we shall no longer assume a particular form for the conditional sampling distributions, for reasons to be explained shortly. We shall obtain results that are valid only when the sample is "large" in a sense to be made more precise as we go along; hence the name of this chapter.

Hitherto we have examined the use of sample evidence only in the case where the evidence was generated by a mathematically well-defined process with one or two unknown parameters; in these cases we saw that correct use of the sample evidence was very simple indeed. All that we had to do was assign a prior distribution to the unknown parameters, work out the likelihood of the sample given any possible values of the parameters, and then apply Bayes' formula to obtain the posterior distribution of the parameters. We even found that if the prior distribution was chosen from an appropriate family of distributions, the posterior would remain in this same family, thus very appreciably simplifying the analysis.

In the great majority of important applied decision problems, however, the correct use of sample evidence is by no means so simple as this, essentially because an exact specification of the process which generates the data would involve *many* unknown parameters, and all these parameters would become involved in the analysis.

Suppose, for example, that a decision maker is interested in the mean amount μ of low-sudsing detergent "carried in stock" by individual households, and suppose that in order to learn more about this quantity she draws a sample of households and determines the stock on hand in each household in the sample. Letting $\tilde{z}_i$ denote the amount on hand in the ith household, our problem is to choose a mathematical formula containing some definite number of parameters such that, if the values of these parameters were known, the formula would describe with reasonable accuracy the long-run frequency distribution of the $\tilde{z}_i$s that would be obtained if the sampling process were continued indefinitely. To make the discussion more concrete, let us imagine that we *will* learn the true frequency distribution of the $\tilde{z}_i$s by taking an extremely large sample, and that our problem is to select *now* a family of mathematical functions—that is, a *formula* with a certain number of adjustable parameters—rich enough for us to be sure that when we *do* learn the true distribution of the $\tilde{z}_i$s we will be able to fit it by specifying appropriate numerical values for the parameters of our chosen formula.

It is quite clear from the outset that a function with just two parameters cannot possibly be flexible enough to be sure of giving a reasonably good fit to the true distribution of the $\tilde{z}_i$s. If, for example, we were to choose the Normal function $f_N(z_i|\mu, \upsilon)$, we would be able to adjust its location by adjusting the parameter μ and its dispersion by adjusting the parameter υ, but no matter what we did the curve would remain symmetric, and we have every reason to think that the frequency distribution we are trying to fit will *not* be symmetric. A large fraction of the z_is will have the value 0, and the distribution of the remainder may very well have a tail extending quite far to the right because there will be a few consumers who like to buy detergent in very large quantities at bargain prices.

Obviously, then, we must choose a function with *at least* three or four adjustable parameters if we are to feel at all certain of being able to describe just the main features of the main body of the distribution, the size of the cluster about zero, the length and size of the right tail, and so forth.

Suppose, however, that we do find a four-parameter family of curves which looks to us so flexible that some member is bound to give a good representation of the true distribution of the $\tilde{z}_i$s, suppose that one of these four parameters represents the mean μ in which the decision maker is really interested, and denote the other three parameters by α, β, and γ. When we come really to use this model of the data-generating process in actual practice, we will *not* be dealing with a sample so large that all we have to do is to fit the curve to the data. We will be in essentially the same situation that we are when we want to learn something about the mean μ of an Independent Normal process with unknown variance υ, except that now we will have *three* nuisance parameters (α, β, and γ) instead of just one (υ). We will be unable to apply Bayes' formula to $\tilde{\mu}$ by itself because the sample likelihood will depend on α, β, and γ as well as μ; therefore, the decision maker will have to assign a *joint* prior distribution to *all four* parameters, obtain their joint posterior distribution, and then compute the marginal posterior distribution of $\tilde{\mu}$.

Although this approach is conceptually absolutely straightforward and simple, it would be extremely difficult to apply it in most practical situations: When a decision maker assigns a probability distribution to the process *mean*, he has a real feeling for the "meaning" of the quantity in question and therefore his judgments about the possible values of this quantity will have real meaning. The same thing may be true when he expresses judgments about the *variance* of an Independent Normal process. Although he may find it hard to think about process variance as such, he probably can internalize the meaning of, say, the average absolute difference between the individual $\tilde{z}_i$s and their mean; if he gives us his quantified judgments about the possible values of *this* quantity, we can by routine calculations translate them into quantified judgments about the possible values of $\tilde{\upsilon}$. If, however, the model we are using contains more than two unknown parameters, it will be very difficult to express each of them in a way the decision maker can really understand, and even more difficult to express all of them in a way which makes his judgments about one parameter independent of his judgments about the others. If, for example, one parameter determines the variance of the process while another in some sense determines its asymmetry and thus has something to do with the length of the long right tail, it is very likely that no ordinary man will be able to internalize what these parameters really mean separately and thus to express meaningful judgments about their possible values.

It is true, of course, that if the sample is "large enough," the decision maker may feel that any prior information he may have that bears on any of the parameters describing the process is negligible relative to the information contained in the sample; if so, then just as in the case of a single unknown parameter the posterior distribution of all the parameters may be obtained by simply rescaling the sample likelihood function. Even so, the result may be sensitive to the parameterization, especially when the number of parameters is large. Furthermore, we will still almost certainly have very serious computational difficulties in obtaining and using the (marginal) posterior distribution of the decision parameter $\tilde{\mu}$; if we are going to neglect prior information and be satisfied with more or less good approximations in any case, we will in general be well advised to use a far simpler method of obtaining approximate solutions, which we shall now describe.

18.4 Use of the Sample Mean as a Summary Statistic

18.4.1 The Normal Approximation to the Likelihood of μ Given m

From the central limit theorem we know that the mean of a sample from a process generating iid observations will have a distribution which approaches Normality as the size of the sample increases provided only that the variance of the values generated by the process is finite—the proposition is independent of the "shape" of the distribution of the individual observations generated by the process. We also know that if the *process* mean and variance are respectively μ and υ, then the mean and variance of the *sample* mean $\tilde{m}$ are respectively μ and υ/n, again regardless of the values of any other parameters that may be involved in a complete description of the process.

These two facts taken together imply (1) that if the *sample size* is "*large enough*," the conditional df of the sample mean $\tilde{m}$ given μ will be quite accurately given by $f_N(m|\mu, \upsilon/n)$, and (2) that if the *process variance* υ is *known*, then we can revise a prior distribution of $\tilde{\mu}$ to take account of the information contained in the sample mean m by simply substituting $f_N(m|\mu, \upsilon/n)$ in Bayes' formula. The result will of course be identical to the result we would obtain if the process were independent Normal—if the prior distribution of $\tilde{\mu}$ is Normal with parameters $\bar{\mu}'$ and $\breve{\mu}'$, the posterior distribution will be Normal with parameters $\bar{\mu}''$, $\breve{\mu}''$, where

$$\bar{\mu}'' = \frac{n'\bar{\mu}' + nm}{n' + n}, \qquad \breve{\mu}'' = \frac{\upsilon}{n' + n}$$

and where n' is defined in such a manner that

$$\breve{\mu}' = \upsilon/n' \qquad (\text{or} \quad n' \equiv \upsilon/\breve{\mu}').$$

We conclude therefore that if (1) we wish to act as if υ were known, (2) we decide to ignore the information in the sample other than the sample mean, and (3) the sample size is "large" so that $(\tilde{m}|\mu)$ can be taken as Normal with mean μ and variance υ/n, then the results of chapter 16 on the Independent Normal process with known variance υ can be applied without modification. Indeed, this is the principal reason why we spent so much time developing the results of chapter 16.

18.4.2 Loss of Information

Observe carefully the difference between the logic underlying this result when it is obtained for an Independent Normal process and the logic underlying the same result obtained for any other process. In the former case, we saw in section 16.3.3 that the sample mean was *sufficient* when υ was known, so that use of the sample mean led to *exactly* the same posterior distribution that was obtained by using the complete sample likelihood and thus could be said to utilize *all* the information about μ that was contained in the sample. When on the contrary we base a posterior distribution of $\tilde{\mu}$ on the mean of a sample from a process of unspecified form, we cannot assert that we are using all the information in the sample—we are simply using the information contained in the sample mean.

The only way to find out whether the sample mean *does* summarize all the information about μ that is contained in the entire sample is actually to specify a complete model of the data-generating process of the sort discussed in the previous section, and then to write down the joint likelihood of the sample observations in accordance with this model. The sample mean m is sufficient for μ, that is, it contains *all* the relevant information about μ in the sample, if and only if this joint likelihood can be factored into two parts, one of which *does not depend on* μ and therefore cancels out in Bayes' formula, while the other (a) depends on *no unknown parameters* other than μ, and (b) depends on the sample observations *only through* m. The extent to which we "lose information" by using the sample mean instead of the complete sample depends on the extent to which these conditions are violated and the violations affect the conceptually correct analysis described in section 18.3.

In almost all practical situations, such an analysis of the extent to which information is lost by use of the sample mean instead of the complete sample, even if feasible, would not be worth the trouble.

Example The following example illustrates the possible loss of efficiency that can arise from basing an inference about μ solely on the sample mean m. As a model of the data-generating process let us assume that

$$\tilde{z}_i = \mu + \tilde{\varepsilon}_i$$

where the $\tilde{\varepsilon}_i$s are iid rv's, each having a rectangular distribution from -10 to $+10$; that is,

$$\tilde{\varepsilon} \sim f(\varepsilon) = \begin{cases} 1/20 & \text{if} \quad -10 \le \varepsilon \le 10, \\ 0 & \text{otherwise.} \end{cases}$$

By example 4 of section 18.3.2 we have

$$\upsilon = \breve{\varepsilon} = (20)^2/12 = 33.33.$$

Suppose a sample of 4 observations is taken; labelling these in order of increasing size $z_{[1]}, z_{[2]}, z_{[3]}, z_{[4]}$, let

$$z_{[1]} = 61, \qquad z_{[2]} = 65, \qquad z_{[3]} = 70, \qquad z_{[4]} = 79,$$

and

$$m = \tfrac{1}{4}(z_{[1]} + \cdots + z_{[4]}) = 68.75.$$

To calculate the likelihood of μ based on m alone, we first observe that $(\tilde{m}|\mu)$ has mean μ, variance $\upsilon/4 = 8.33$, and is symmetrically, unimodally distributed about μ with a bell-shaped distribution. It is not unreasonable in this case to use the Normal approximation and get for the likelihood

$$l_1(\mu|m) \propto f_N(\mu|68.75, 8.33).$$

Now let us calculate the full likelihood of μ based on $z_{[1]}, z_{[2]}, z_{[3]}, z_{[4]}$ under the full assumption that the $\tilde{\varepsilon}$s are rectangularly distributed. We obtain

$$l_2(\mu|z_{[1]}, \ldots, z_{[4]}) \propto \begin{cases} C & \text{if} \qquad z_{[4]} - 10 \le \mu \le z_{[1]} + 10 \\ 0 & \text{otherwise,} \end{cases}$$

where C is a constant. This means that for the observed (hypothetical) data the true likelihood l_2 is constant for μ values between 69 and 71 inclusive. In figure 18.4 we plot the approximate likelihood function l_1 based on the sample mean and the true likelihood function l_2 based on the full information in the sample. Remembering that to find the posterior distribution of $\tilde{\mu}$ we must multiply the likelihood function of μ with the prior distributing function of $\tilde{\mu}$ and then normalize, we see how serious an error we can make if we use l_1 instead of l_2. Furthermore, it is important to emphasize that this error arises because in this case the sample mean is a pitifully inadequate summary of the sample information, and that this serious error has very little to do with the inadequacy of the Normal approximation to the distribution of the mean of four iid, rectangular rv's.

The above example is purposely an extreme case. In situations where the distribution of $\tilde{\varepsilon}$ is unimodal and does not cut off sharply at the ends

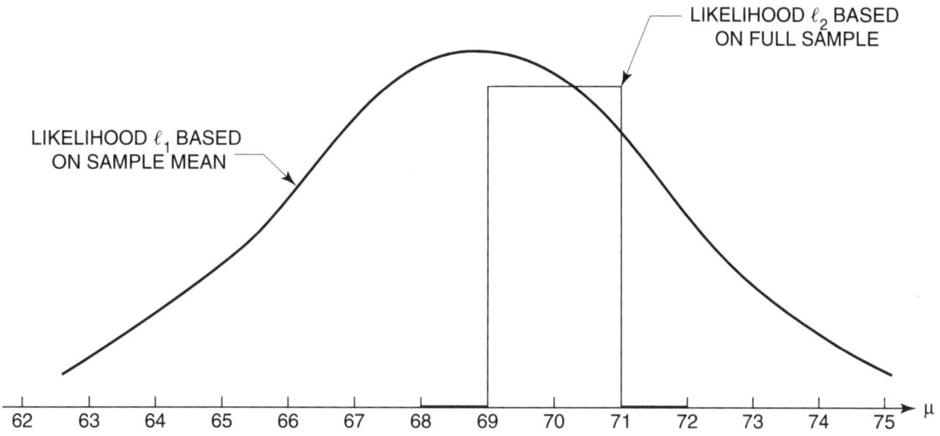

Figure 18.4
Approximate and true likelihood of rectangular sample

(as in the case of the rectangular distribution), the sample mean is usually a pretty good summary statistic of the sample for the purpose of making a Bayesian inference about $\tilde{\mu}$. The assumption that $\tilde{\varepsilon}$ is rectangular, let alone with known range, is not even close to realistic in any practical problem we have ever heard of.

18.4.3 Normality of the Sample Mean

Granted that we are ready to discard that part of the sample information about μ which is not contained in the sample mean m, when can we legitimately treat the sample mean as if it were Normally distributed?

Strictly speaking, the only way in which we can really decide how accurate the Normal approximation is in any particular case is to do exactly what we did in section 18.1 when we first discussed the central limit theorem and the use of Normal approximations, namely, assign a specific distribution to the individual observations and then work out the true distribution of their sum or mean. The procedure would be far more complex in the present case, however, because the "exact" distribution would involve not only the process mean μ and variance v but also some additional unknown nuisance parameters, and the conditional distribution of $\tilde{m}$ might approach Normality rapidly for some values of these nuisance parameters, slowly for other values.

Both empirical and theoretical analyses have shown that the effect of skewness (in the population distribution) on the Normality of the sample mean is much more serious than the effect of rectangularity—for many purposes it might be rather unsafe to use the Normal approximation for small samples from a highly skewed population.

18.4.4 Estimation of the Process Variance

Although we rarely if ever really know the variance of the population and therefore of $\tilde{m}$ (given μ) *exactly*, we very often know enough about the variance υ to treat it as if it were known exactly when costs will depend only on the value of μ. Exact knowledge of υ is not very critical when the cost-determining random variable is $\tilde{\mu}$ because uncertainty about υ has only a "second-order" effect on the posterior distribution of $\tilde{\mu}$.

Before we attempt to analyze the case where υ is unknown and the case where the distributions of the $\tilde{\varepsilon}$s are not necessarily Normally distributed, let us first review some of the conclusions of chapter 17 for the case of Normally distributed $\tilde{\varepsilon}$s. When both μ and υ are unknown and when the $\tilde{\varepsilon}$s are Normally distributed, we showed that the sample $(z_1, \ldots, z_n)$ can be summarized without loss of sample information by the triplet (m, v, n) where

$$m \equiv \frac{1}{n} \sum_i z_i \quad \text{and} \quad v \equiv \frac{1}{n-1} \sum_i (z_i - m)^2 \tag{18.22}$$

(i.e., the triplet (m, v, n) is "sufficient"). Furthermore, we showed that, given any μ, υ pair, the random variables $\tilde{m}$ and $\tilde{v}$ are *independent*. For a full analysis of this problem, we showed that the decision maker must assign a *joint* prior distribution to $\tilde{\mu}$ and $\tilde{\upsilon}$, obtain a joint posterior distribution to $\tilde{\mu}$ and $\tilde{\upsilon}$ (based on the prior distribution and the sufficient statistic (m, v, n)), and then compute the *marginal* (posterior) distribution of $\tilde{\mu}$ from the joint density by the standard procedure for computing marginal from conditional densities.

In the case that the joint prior distribution of $\tilde{\mu}$ and $\tilde{\upsilon}$ is Normal-gamma, we showed that the posterior distribution of $\tilde{\mu}$ has a Student distribution whose posterior parameters depend on the prior parameters and on the sufficient statistic (m, v, n); let us label this distribution simply by $f_S''(\mu)$. Now instead of calculating the distribution f_S'' suppose we use the following procedure for generating an approximate posterior distribution: (1) compute the statistic v, ignoring for the time being m; (2) treat the unknown $\tilde{\upsilon}$ as if it were v for certain; (3) assign a Normal prior to $\tilde{\mu}$ in agreement with the conditional prior distribution of $\tilde{\mu}$ given that $\tilde{\upsilon} = v$, a prior that by (17.6) will be $f_N(\mu | m', v/n')$; and (4) calculate the posterior distribution of $\tilde{\mu}$ based on the above prior and on the statistic (m, n) using Normal theory with known variance $\upsilon = v$. This posterior distribution will be $f_N(\mu | \bar{\mu}'', \breve{\mu}'')$ where

$$\bar{\mu}'' = \frac{n'm' + nm}{n' + n}, \qquad \breve{\mu}'' = \frac{v}{n' + n}. \tag{18.23}$$

We showed in chapter 17 that, provided n is large, $f_N(\mu|\bar{\mu}'', \breve{\mu}'')$ is an excellent approximation for $f_S''(\mu)$.

Based on the above result we are now prepared to suggest a procedure for arriving at a posterior distribution of $\tilde{\mu}$ after observing a "large" sample $(z_1, \ldots, z_n)$ when υ is unknown and when the $\tilde{z}$s (or the $\tilde{\varepsilon}$s) are not necessarily Normal.

Letting f' and f'' represent respectively the prior and posterior distributing function of $\tilde{\mu}$, we propose that f'' be approximated by

$$f''(\mu|m, v, n) \propto f_N(\mu|m, v/n)f'(\mu). \tag{18.24}$$

This approximation is tantamount to treating the expression $f_N(\mu|m, v/n)$ as an "approximate likelihood function" of μ based on the sample statistic (m, v, n). This approximate likelihood function is analytically identical to the expression $f_N(m|\mu, v/n)$, which is the distribution of the random variable $(\tilde{m}|\mu, \upsilon)$ when $\upsilon = v$.

It is instructive to view the above procedure from two slightly different points of view. Suppose that someone other than the decision maker computes the quantities m and v. On the basis of the v information alone let the decision maker select a point estimate of the "subsidiary" uncertain quantity υ. Call this point estimate $\hat{\upsilon}$. For large samples it is reasonable to let $\hat{\upsilon} = v$ since it can be shown that for any given data-generating process with a true variance υ, the sampling distribution of $\tilde{v}$ will have υ as its mean, that is,

$$E(\tilde{v}|\upsilon) = \upsilon, \tag{18.25}$$

and the variance of this distribution will approach zero with increasing sample size, that is,

$$\lim_{n\to\infty} V(\tilde{v}|\upsilon) = 0. \tag{18.26}$$

In the vernacular of classical statistics, the sample statistic v is an *unbiased* estimate of υ, because of (18.25), and *consistent* (in squared error), because of (18.26). Treating $\hat{\upsilon}$ as if it were the true value υ, the decision maker is now prepared to process the m information. Letting $f'(\mu)$ be the distribution function of $\tilde{\mu}$ before the m information is processed (but after v is processed), and assuming that the conditional distribution of $\tilde{m}$ given μ is approximately Normal with parameter $(\mu, \hat{\upsilon}/n)$, the posterior distribution of $\tilde{\mu}$ after observing m is by Bayes' theorem

$$f''(\mu) \propto f_N(m|\mu, \hat{\upsilon}/n)f'(\mu).$$

An alternate rationalization for the use of (18.24) can be explained as follows: When υ is known, use is made of the fact that the rv $\tilde{m}$ is approximately Normal $(\mu, \upsilon/n)$ or equivalently that the rv

$$\tilde{u} \equiv \frac{\tilde{m} - \mu}{\sqrt{\upsilon/n}} \tag{18.27}$$

is unit Normal, that is, $E(\tilde{u}) = 0$ and $V(\tilde{u}) = 1$. When υ is unknown, it is reasonable to examine the rv

$$\tilde{t} \equiv \frac{\tilde{m} - \mu}{\sqrt{\tilde{\upsilon}/n}} \tag{18.28}$$

and attempt to argue that for large n, $\tilde{t}$ is also approximately unit Normal. If this can be substantiated, then the likelihood of μ given $t = (m - \mu)/\sqrt{\upsilon/n}$ will be $f_N(\mu|m, \upsilon/n)$ and (18.24) follows.

From (18.27) and (18.28),

$$\tilde{t} = \left(\frac{\tilde{\upsilon}}{\upsilon}\right)^{-1/2} \tilde{u}, \tag{18.29}$$

and it is now intuitively clear that, regardless of the distribution of the $\tilde{\varepsilon}$s (or of the $\tilde{z}_i$'s given μ), for any μ the distribution of $\tilde{t}$ approaches unit Normal as n increases. For as n increases $\tilde{u}$ approaches unit Normal and the distribution of $(\tilde{\upsilon}/\upsilon)$ becomes more and more tightly concentrated around its expected value 1. To get a little better feel for the magnitudes of these approximations it can be shown, in agreement with (18.25) and (18.26), that

$$E\left(\frac{\tilde{\upsilon}}{\upsilon}\right) = 1 \tag{18.30}$$

and

$$V\left(\frac{\tilde{\upsilon}}{\upsilon}\right) = \frac{2}{n-1} + \frac{\gamma_2}{n} \tag{18.31}$$

where γ_2 depends on the distribution of the individual $\tilde{\varepsilon}$s. For example $\gamma_2 = 0$ for a Normal distribution. Since data-generating processes encountered in actual practice have γ_2s ranging from about -1 to about $+6$ the variance of $(\tilde{\upsilon}/\upsilon)$ ranges from about $1/n$ to about $8/n$.

As an example, suppose $\gamma_2 = 2$ and $n = 25$ so that $V(\tilde{\upsilon}/\upsilon) \doteq 4/25$ and $S(\tilde{\upsilon}/\upsilon) \doteq 2/5$. In a situation of this kind it would not be unreasonable to obtain a sample value of υ/υ such as .5 and then $(\upsilon/\upsilon)^{-1/2} = \sqrt{2} \doteq 1.4$, which is quite a sizable multiplication factor in (18.29).

It must also be pointed out that the two rv's on the right-hand side of (18.29) are *dependent* except when the individual $\tilde{\varepsilon}_i$s are Normal, hence it is quite possible in a given case for there to be a tendency for $(v/\upsilon)^{-1/2}$ to be large whenever $\tilde{u}$ happens to be large. This is troublesome to say the least.

If the individual $\tilde{\varepsilon}_i$s are not exactly Normal but roughly so, then everything works out nicely: (m, v, n) effectively squeezes out almost all the information about μ in the sample, $\tilde{u}$ will be approximately Normal, the two rv's on the right-hand side of (18.29) will be practically independent and finally γ_2 will be 0. Under the assumption that $\tilde{\varepsilon}_i$s are Normal it is not difficult to show that $\tilde{t}$ has the unit Student density function with $n - 1$ degrees of freedom and for n above 20 or so the rv $\tilde{t}$ is practically unit Normal.

If the individual $\tilde{\varepsilon}_i$s may have highly skewed distributions, we can only conclude that there may be quite serious errors involved in treating v as if it were the true υ and using (18.24)—unless, of course, n is very large (say on the order of 100 or more). When the $\tilde{\varepsilon}_i$s are possibly skewed and n is small the only way we know how to proceed is to assign a model to these $\tilde{\varepsilon}_i$s and use a full Bayesian procedure. Of course, in this case we will use more of the sample $z_1, \ldots, z_n$ than merely the inadequate summary (m, v, n). Also if we use a full Bayesian procedure, then the exact distribution of $\tilde{t}$ (given μ) does not enter formally into the analysis and its distribution is only of interest when comparing the full analysis with the approximate procedure given by (18.24).

19 Statistical Analysis in Normal Form

19.1 Comparison of Extensive-Form and Normal-Form Analyses

19.1.1 Analysis in Extensive Form

Let us consider again the general decision problem first posed and analyzed in chapter 6. The problem was defined in terms of six ingredients: (1) a set of possible terminal acts, (2) a set of possible "states of the world," (3) a set of possible experiments, (4) a set of potential outcomes of all experiments, (5) a utility function, and (6) a probability measure. The general decision problem was posed as a game between the decision maker and chance (playing nonstrategically), and the game was pictorially represented as a decision tree. The analysis proceeded by first mapping out the tree; second, assigning utilities at the tips of the tree; third, assigning unconditional probabilities to outcomes z on move 2 and assigning conditional probabilities to states s given z on move 4; and fourth, proceeding with the backward induction by the averaging-out-and-folding-back process. This procedure for analyzing a decision problem will be called the *extensive form of analysis.* We introduce a name for this type of analysis at this point because we shall shortly compare it with another mode of analysis.

There are a few salient features of the analysis in extensive form that we now wish to recall in order to facilitate this comparison between the two modes of analysis.

1. The analysis by backwards induction first examines the choice of an optimal act a_z^o for each outcome z; this requires knowledge of the utility function u and the probability measure $P_{s|z}$ which in most situations (e.g., the imperfect tester) is derived from the measures P_s and $P_{z|s;e}$. Note that both the utility function (or value or loss functions) and the prior probability measure P_s are introduced at the very first step of the analysis.

2. The final product of the extensive form of analysis can be thought of as the description of an optimal *strategy* consisting of two parts:

a. A prescription of the experiment e^o which should be performed.

b. A *decision rule* prescribing for every possible outcome z of the chosen e the optimal terminal act a_z^o.

The whole decision rule for the optimal e can be simply "read off" from the results of that part of the analysis which determined the optimal a_z^o for every z in Z. (We remark incidentally that these same results also enable us to read off the optimal decision rule to accompany any other e in E, even though the e in question is not itself optimal.)

19.1.2 Decision Rules

The *normal form of analysis*, which we are now about to examine, also has as its end product the description of an optimal strategy, and it arrives at the same optimal strategy as the extensive form of analysis, but it arrives there by a different route. Instead of first determining the optimal act a_z^o for every possible outcome z, and thus implicitly defining the optimal decision rule for any e, the normal form of analysis starts by explicitly considering every possible decision rule for a given e and then choosing the optimal decision rule for that e. After this has been done for all e in E, the optimal e is selected exactly as in the extensive form of analysis.

Definition In any situation where a terminal act a is to be chosen after an experiment e has been performed and its outcome z is known, a *decision rule* d is a rule that prescribes for every possible z an act a which shall be taken if that z is observed. In mathematical language, a decision rule is a function d which assigns to every $z \in Z$ an $a \in A$.

Example 1 (The Imperfect Tester) From figure 6.4, the optimal decision rule d^o for experiment e_1 is the one that prescribes a_1 if z_1 occurs and a_2 if z_2 occurs; in functional notation, $d^o(z_1) = a_1$ and $d^o(z_2) = a_2$. The other possible decision rules for e_1 in the example are:

d_1 where $d_1(z_1) = a_1, \quad d_1(z_2) = a_1,$

d_2 where $d_2(z_1) = a_2, \quad d_2(z_2) = a_2,$

d_3 where $d_3(z_1) = a_2, \quad d_3(z_2) = a_1.$

Example 2 If a binomial sample of size n is to be taken from a Bernoulli process and if the prior distribution of $\tilde{p}$ is beta with parameters r' and n', the optimal rule for estimating p under quadratic loss is

$$d^o(r) = \frac{r' + r}{n' + n} \quad \text{for } r = 0, 1, \ldots, n.$$

19.1.3 Analysis in Normal Form

If the decision maker chooses a particular e and a particular rule d for that e, and if chance chooses a particular pair (z, s), the decision maker's act as prescribed by the rule will be $a = d(z)$ and his preference index will be $u(e, z, d(z), s)$; however, *before* the experimental outcome z has been observed, $u(e, \tilde{z}, d(\tilde{z}), \tilde{s})$ is a random variable because both $\tilde{z}$ and $\tilde{s}$ are random variables. For a particular strategy choice (e, d) there is associated a lottery whose consequence depends on the unknown pair $(\tilde{z}, \tilde{s})$.

The decision maker's objective is therefore to choose the strategy (e, d) which maximizes his utility value

$$\bar{u}^*(e,d) \equiv E_{s,z;e}u(e,\tilde{z},d(\tilde{z}),\tilde{s}) \tag{19.1}$$

for the resulting lottery; the expectation operator $E_{s,z;e}$ is taken with respect to the joint probability measure $P_{s,z;e}$. This double expectation, just like a double summation or a double integration, can be accomplished by iterated expectation, and the iterated expectation can be carried out in either order: We can first expect over $\tilde{s}$ holding z fixed (using probability measure $P_{s|z;e}$) and then over $\tilde{z}$ (using $P_{z;e}$); or we can first expect over $\tilde{z}$ holding s fixed (using $P_{z|s;e}$), and then over s (using P_s). In the normal form of analysis it is customary to use the latter iteration and we shall therefore proceed here in this manner.

If e and d are given and s is held fixed, then by taking the expectation of $u(e,\tilde{z},d(\tilde{z}),s)$ with respect to the conditional measure $P_{z|s;e}$, we obtain

$$\bar{u}^*(e,d|s) = E_{z|s;e}u(e,\tilde{z},d(\tilde{z}),s), \tag{19.2}$$

which will be called the *conditional* utility evaluation of (e,d) *for a given state s*. Next, expecting over s with respect to P_s, we obtain

$$\bar{\bar{u}}^*(e,d) = E_s\bar{u}^*(e,d|\tilde{s}) = E_sE_{z|s;e}u(e,\tilde{z},d(\tilde{z}),\tilde{s}). \tag{19.3}$$

As we have seen numerous times before, whenever it is appropriate to work in terms of expected value, cost, or loss it is not necessary and certainly not convenient to transform these quantities into utility values. We shall therefore carry over our symbolism in an obvious fashion: $\bar{v}^*(e,d|s)$ and $\bar{\bar{v}}^*(e,d)$ for "value"; $\bar{c}^*(e,d|s)$ and $\bar{\bar{c}}^*(e,d)$ for cost; $\bar{\ell}^*(e,d|s)$ and $\bar{\bar{\ell}}^*(e,d)$ for loss.

Example 1 (continued) For the Imperfect Tester example (see figure 6.4), letting $d^o(z_1) = a_1$ and $d^o(z_2) = a_2$, we have in terms of costs (see section 6.3.2),

$$\begin{aligned}
\bar{c}^*(e_1,d^o|s_1) &= c(e_1,z_1,a_1,s_1)P(\tilde{z}=z_1|\tilde{s}=s_1;e_1) \\
&\quad + c(e_1,z_2,a_2,s_1)P(\tilde{z}=z_2|\tilde{s}=s_1;e_1) \\
&= 10(.7) + 45(.3) = 20.5, \\
\bar{c}^*(e_1,d^o|s_2) &= c(e_1,z_1,a_1,s_2)P(\tilde{z}=z_1|\tilde{s}=s_2;e_1) \\
&\quad + c(e_1,z_2,a_2,s_2)P(\tilde{z}=z_2|\tilde{s}=s_2;e_1) \\
&= 110(.2) + 45(.8) = 58, \\
\bar{\bar{c}}^*(e,d^o) &= \bar{c}^*(e,d|s_1)P(\tilde{s}=s_1) + \bar{c}^*(e,d|s_2)P(\tilde{s}=s_2) \\
&- 20.5(.7) + 58(.3) = 31.75;
\end{aligned}$$

since d^o is optimal for e_1, the value of $\bar{c}(e, d^o)$ must agree with the entry at the e_1-node of figure 6.4.

Choice of a Decision Rule

As regards any strategy pair (e, d), the normal form of analysis consists of evaluating $\bar{u}^*(e, d)$ by means of (19.2) and (19.3). As regards an experiment e, the normal form of analysis consists in evaluating $\bar{u}^*(e, d)$ for a class of different ds, selecting the d^* which maximizes $\bar{u}^*(e, d)$ for ds in this class and then assigning to the experiment the value

$$\bar{u}_0^*(e) \equiv \max_d \bar{u}^*(e, d) = \bar{u}^*(e, d^*).$$

If the truly optimal decision rule d^o happens to be among the class of ds that are compared, then of course the comparison will select $d^* = d^o$ and $\bar{u}_0^*(e)$ will be equal to the value $\bar{u}'(e)$ obtained by the extensive form of analysis; but we can be sure of these results only if either (1) we evaluate *every possible d*, or else (2) we can in some way prove without actual evaluation that d^o must be a member of a certain family of ds and then evaluate every member of this family.

Quite obviously normal-form analysis will often be less convenient than extensive-form analysis, and most of this book is therefore based on extensive-form analysis. Normal-form analysis may however be of interest for one or more of three quite different reasons.

1. In some problems we may be unable to carry out a complete preposterior analysis and thus be sure of arriving at the truly optimal d^o, but we *may* be able to evaluate a number of different ds by normal-form analysis. In such a situation we will in general do better to choose the best of the ds we *can* evaluate rather than to choose a d at random. Such problems, however, will not be encountered in this book.

2. In many situations the conditional distribution of $\tilde{z}$ given s is easy to assess and "objective" in the sense that almost all reasonable people will more or less agree on this distribution, but the utility function u and especially the prior distribution of $\tilde{s}$ may be very difficult to assess and highly subjective in the sense that reasonable people will differ widely in their assessments. If we use extensive-form analysis in such a situation, the very first step in the analysis requires use of the highly subjective prior distribution (in order to compute the posterior distribution that is required to find a_z^o), whereas with normal-form analysis the initial steps rest only on the objective conditional distribution of $\tilde{z}$ given s; and the most subjective element, the prior distribution, comes in only at the end. It is argued that we should carry out formal analysis only as far as the data entering the calculations are objective and thus avoid building an analysis

on the sands of subjective assessments; we answer that it is possible to go only so far by means of a completely objective analysis and this falls far short of prescribing an appropriate strategy for experimentation and action for the decision maker. This gap must be bridged by one means or another. Some objectivists feel that rather than resorting to subjective assessments various ad hoc objective conventions should be employed; this we feel (in de Finetti's imagery) amounts to taking away the sands (of subjective assessments) and building upon the void. There are those who are most reluctant to introduce subjective assessments at the beginning of an analysis but who might be willing to do so at the end of the analysis; this we feel is often a matter of taste and tactics but the resulting answer will be the same no matter where given subjective assessments are inserted. Finally, there are those who believe the objective analysis should be carried as far as possible and that the gap should be bridged by subjective judgment but in an informal rather than a formal manner; this we feel is a reasonable attitude but it is often in this very area that decision makers are in most need of formal guidance. It will be the purpose of the remainder of this chapter and chapter 20 to examine these controversial issues.

3. In chapter 20 we shall discuss some of the principal differences and similarities between the so-called Bayesian approach to statistical problems—the point of view of this book—and the more widely used, traditional, classical, orthodox approach to these problems. It will be especially convenient in examining these partially opposing viewpoints to use the normal form of analysis.

19.2 Infinite-Action Problems

As a first example of a specific application of normal-form analysis, consider a decision maker who wishes to estimate an unknown s after performing an experiment e which will result in outcome z; the reader can think of s as the mean of a population of heights and of z as the mean height in a sample from this population, or he can think of s as the long-run fraction defective p generated by some process and of z as the fraction defective r/n in a sample of the output of this process.

19.2.1 No Losses, No Prior

Suppose first that although the decision maker is perfectly willing to assess the conditional distribution of $\tilde{z}$ given any possible s, he feels that it would be extremely difficult for him either to assess a meaningful distribution of $\tilde{s}$ or to assign a value to the loss which will result from any given error in the estimate of s, and he therefore wishes to base the estimate exclusively on the observed z and whatever can be deduced from the conditional distribution of $\tilde{z}$ given s. Two different basic approaches to this problem have been proposed and will now be examined.

1. Maximum Likelihood Estimation

The first proposed solution is very simple: Take as the estimate of s that value which maximizes the likelihood for the given observed z. In the mathematical notation let $L(s|z)$ be the likelihood of s for given z—that is, it is the probability (or density) at $\tilde{z} = z$ given s; then the maximum likelihood decision rule (or "estimator") attaches to each z the estimate $\hat{s}$ defined by

$$L(\hat{s}|z) \geq L(s|z) \quad \text{for all } s. \tag{19.4}$$

Whenever we wish to exhibit explicitly the dependence of $\hat{s}$ on z we shall write $\hat{s}_z$. The reader should keep in mind that $\hat{s}$ is not only that *state* which maximizes the likelihood but also must be thought of as the *act* which the maximum likelihood decision rule attaches to the observed z.

If for a given z there is more than one value of s that maximizes the likelihood, then the maximum likelihood estimate is not unique. This possibility occurs rarely in practice and will be ignored hereafter.

The reader is asked to show (exercise 1) that if s is the parameter p of a Bernoulli process, then whether the sampling is binomial or Pascal, the maximum likelihood estimate of p is $\hat{p} = r/n$. If in a given context we were more interested in the parameter $\tau = 1/p$ than in the parameter p, then the likelihood of the sample would be given by

$$L(\tau|r, n) = \left(\frac{1}{\tau}\right)^r \left(1 - \frac{1}{\tau}\right)^{n-r}$$

and the likelihood would be maximized by $\hat{\tau} = 1/\hat{p} = n/r$. This example illustrates the following more general principle of maximum likelihood estimation.

Let s and S be two alternate parametrizations of a given state variable and let s and S be related in a one-to-one manner by the function $S = h(s)$. If $\hat{s}_z$ is the maximum likelihood estimate of s for a given z, then the maximum likelihood estimate of S for a given z is $\hat{S}_z = h(\hat{s}_z)$.

Thus, for example, in a Bernoulli process the maximum likelihood estimate of $\log p$, based on a sample with sufficient statistic (r, n), would be $\log \hat{p}$ or $\log (r/n)$.

To help motivate the next point, we remark now that the reader is asked to show (exercise 1) that if s is the parameter (μ, v) of a Normal process, then the (μ, υ) pair that maximizes the likelihood for the sample observation $z = (x_1, \ldots, x_n)$ is $(\hat{\mu}, \hat{\upsilon})$, where

$$\hat{\mu} = m \equiv \sum x_i/n, \tag{19.5a}$$

and

$$\hat{\upsilon} = \frac{1}{n}\sum (x_i - m)^2. \tag{19.5b}$$

By *definition* we would then say that m is a maximum likelihood estimate of μ and that $\sum (x_i - m)^2/n$ is a maximum likelihood estimate of υ. We also remark that if (θ, ω) is an alternate parametrization, where (θ, ω) is one-to-one related to (μ, υ), by the functions $\theta = g_1(\mu, \upsilon)$, $\omega = g_2(\mu, \upsilon)$, then the maximum likelihood estimates of θ and ω are $\hat{\theta} = g_1(\hat{\mu}, \hat{\upsilon})$ and $\hat{\omega} = g_2(\hat{\mu}, \hat{\upsilon})$ respectively.

Definition Suppose the state parameter is represented in terms of k components, that is, $s = (s_1, \ldots, s_k)$. If s has a maximum likelihood estimate $\hat{s} = (\hat{s}_1, \ldots, \hat{s}_k)$, then $\hat{s}_i$ is the maximum likelihood estimate of s_i; $(\hat{s}_i, \hat{s}_j)$ is the maximum likelihood estimate of (s_i, s_j); and so forth.

From a Bayesian point of view, if we think of s as a rv $\tilde{s}$, and if $\tilde{s}$ has a gentle prior distribution, then the maximum likelihood estimate $\hat{s}$ is the *mode* of the posterior distribution of $\tilde{s}$. If the likelihood is suitably symmetric, $\hat{s}$ will also be (approximately) the posterior mean and median. We wish to point out, however, that we have already met examples (e.g., the Bernoulli case where $r = 0$ or n, and the Poisson case with small r) where the likelihood is highly skewed.

2. Comparative Performance of Estimators

The other, quite different approach to the problem of choosing a "point estimator" consists of considering what would happen if the *same experiment e* were to be performed repeatedly and if on each occasion the *same decision rule* or estimator were to be used to compute an estimate $\hat{s}_z = d(z)$, the *true s remaining fixed* during the entire process. Since we know the conditional distribution of $\tilde{z}$ given s for every s, we can compute for every s the (conditional) distribution of the estimates $\hat{s}_{\tilde{z}} = d(\tilde{z})$ which would result from repeated use of any given decision rule or estimator d; the second basic approach to the problem of estimation without losses or priors consists of examining these conditional distributions for every proposed estimator d and choosing the d whose distributions have the nicest properties.

2a. Unbiasedness

It has often been asserted that a very nice property for an estimator to have is absence of "systematic error," that is, absence of a tendency to generate estimates which are either too high or too low *in the long run.* There are, of course, various ways of measuring or defining such a tendency. Thus we might say that an estimator has systematic error if repeated estimates of the same true s tend to *average out* higher or lower than s, or alternatively we might say that an estimator has systematic error if *more than half* of the estimates tend to be above or below s, and so forth. The former criterion is by far the most frequently applied in practice, and is therefore the only one we shall study in this book.

Let $h(s)$ be any real-valued function of a state variable s. (For example, if s is a single number, then $h(s)$ might be $\sqrt{s}$, s^2, $\log s$, and so on; if s represents a pair of numbers (s_1, s_2), then $h(s)$ might be $1/s_1^2$, $\log s_2$, $\sqrt{s_1^2 + s_2^2}$, and so on.) An estimator d is called *unbiased for* $h(s)$ if

$$E_{z|s} d(\tilde{z}) = h(s) \qquad \text{for all } s; \tag{19.6}$$

that is, if the *long-run average* of repeated estimates of the same true quantity $h(s)$ would be exactly equal to $h(s)$ whatever the value of s may be.[1]

With respect to estimators of the parameter p of a Bernoulli process, the reader can show (exercise 2) that: (1) if the sampling is binomial (fixed n), the estimator (for p)

$$d_b(r) = \frac{r}{n} \tag{19.7}$$

is unbiased, whereas (2) if the sampling is Pascal (fixed r), the estimator

$$d_{Pa}(n) = \frac{r-1}{n-1} \tag{19.8}$$

is unbiased for $r \geq 2$, and is also unbiased for $r = 1$ provided that we assign the value 1 to the indeterminate quantity 0/0 which results when $\tilde{n} = 1$. Note that observing a Bernoulli process until the occurrence of the first success and counting the trials up to this point requires us to estimate either $\hat{p} = 0$, or $\hat{p} = 1$ if we wish to use an unbiased procedure. The maximum likelihood estimate, on the contrary, would be $1/n$.

1. The interested reader can find articles in the literature on "median-unbiased" estimators which generate estimates such that in the long run exactly half the estimates will be above $h(s)$ and half below.

Consider a data generating process with a state parameter s (possibly multidimensional) that generates observations $\tilde{x}_1, \tilde{x}_2, \ldots$. For a given s, the rv's $\tilde{x}_1, \tilde{x}_2, \ldots$ are independent and identically distributed. Let μ and υ represent respectively the (population) mean and variance of these rv's. Of course, the true μ and υ depend on the true parameter s. We shall show that if exactly n observations $x_1, \ldots, x_n$ are taken from this process, then

$$m \equiv \frac{1}{n}\sum x_i \qquad \text{is an unbiased estimate of } \mu, \tag{19.9a}$$

and

$$\mathrm{v} \equiv \frac{1}{n-1}\sum (x_i - m)^2 \qquad \text{is an unbiased estimate of } \upsilon, \tag{19.9b}$$

and this result is completely *independent of the particular form of the likelihood function.*

Proof Expression (19.9a) follows immediately from the equalities

$$E(\tilde{m}|s) = E\left[\frac{1}{n}\sum \tilde{x}_i|s\right] = \frac{1}{n}\sum E(\tilde{x}_i|s) = \frac{1}{n}n\mu = \mu.$$

To prove (19.9b), we start with the identity

$$\begin{aligned}\sum (x_i - \mu)^2 &= \sum [(x_i - m) + (m - \mu)]^2 \\ &= \sum (x_i - m)^2 + n(m - \mu)^2,\end{aligned}$$

from which we get

$$\begin{aligned}E(\mathrm{v}|s) &= E\left\{\frac{1}{n-1}[\sum (\tilde{x}_i - \mu)^2 - n(\tilde{m} - \mu)^2]|s\right\} \\ &= \frac{1}{n-1}\sum E[(\tilde{x}_i - \mu)^2|s] - \frac{n}{n-1}E[(\tilde{m} - \mu)^2|s] \\ &= \frac{1}{n-1}n\upsilon - \frac{n}{n-1}\frac{\upsilon}{n} = \upsilon.\end{aligned}$$ ■

The estimate $m = \sum x_i/n$ is just one of an entire class of unbiased estimates for μ. The reader is asked to show as an exercise that $\sum a_i x_i$, where $\sum a_i = 1$ is an unbiased estimate of μ. This raises the natural question of how best to choose an estimator from a class of unbiased estimators which leads to our next topic.

2b. Minimum Variance

In problems where there exists more than one unbiased estimator it is common to consider small variance of the estimator as an additional nice property. Remembering that the distributions we are considering are all *conditional* distributions of $d(\tilde{z})$ *given* s, it is clear that one estimator d' may have smaller variance than another estimator d'' for some s but larger variance for others. An unbiased estimator d^* is said to have *uniformly* minimum variance, which is a *very* nice property, if the variance $d^*(\tilde{z})$ given s is smaller than that of any other unbiased estimator $d(\tilde{z})$ given s, no matter which s is chosen; that is, if

$$V[d^*(z)|s] \leq V[d(\tilde{z})|s] \qquad \text{for all } s.$$

We indicated above that if n independent observations $x_1, \ldots, x_n$ are taken from a population with unknown mean μ, then $\sum a_i x_i$, where $\sum a_i = 1$ is an unbiased estimate of μ. Now for a given state variable s, the conditional variance of this estimator is given by

$$V(\sum a_i \tilde{x}_i|s) = \sum V(a_i \tilde{x}_i|s) = v \sum a_i^2,$$

which does not depend on s or on the form of the likelihood function. To find the uniformly minimum variance unbiased estimator in this class, we must minimize $\sum a_i^2$ subject to the condition that $\sum a_i = 1$. We shall now show that, unsurprisingly, this is accomplished by letting $a_i = 1/n$ for all i.

Proof Let $a_i = 1/n + \varepsilon_i$ so that $\sum a_i = 1$ can be rewritten as $\sum \varepsilon_i = 0$. Now

$$\sum a_i^2 = \sum \left(\frac{1}{n} + \varepsilon_i\right)^2 = \frac{1}{n} + \sum \varepsilon_i^2,$$

where the last equality makes use of the condition $\sum \varepsilon_i = 0$. Hence the minimum occurs by letting $\varepsilon_i = 0$ or $a_i = 1/n$, for all i.

We summarize:

In the class of linear unbiased estimators of μ (i.e., those of the form $\sum a_i x_i$) the sample mean has uniformly minimum variance.

The above proposition can be generalized as follows. Consider the model

$$\tilde{x}_i = \mu + \tilde{\varepsilon}_i, \qquad i = 1, \ldots, n, \tag{19.10}$$

where $E(\tilde{\varepsilon}_i) = 0$, $V(\tilde{\varepsilon}_i) = v_i$ (note the dependence on i), and where the $\tilde{\varepsilon}_i$s are independent rv's. We do not assume any particular functional forms for the distributions of the $\tilde{\varepsilon}_i$s. The problem is to estimate the unknown parameter μ from the observations $x_1, x_2, \ldots, x_n$. As before, it is clear that $\sum a_i x_i$ is an unbiased estimator of μ provided that $\sum a_i = 1$. (Why?) The conditional variance of the estimator $\sum a_i x_i$ is $\sum a_i^2 v_i$. Hence we are led to the following.

Problem Choose $a_1, \ldots, a_n$ to minimize $\sum a_i^2 v_i$ subject to the condition that $\sum a_i = 1$. The answer is given by $a_i = c/v_i$, where c is such that $\sum a_i = 1$ or $1/c = \sum 1/v_i$.

Proof For readers who know the principle of Lagrangians this is a simple exercise. We offer the following remarks for others. Let $a_1, \ldots, a_n$ be any particular choice of as such that $\sum a_i = 1$, and let $T \equiv \sum a_i^2 v_i$. Consider transferring a small amount Δ from a_i to a_j while keeping all the other as fixed. Let T^* be the resulting index. Then, by algebra,

$$T^* - T = 2\Delta(a_j v_j - a_i v_i) + \Delta^2(v_i + v_j),$$

and it is clear that it is possible to make $T^* < T$ if $a_j v_j \neq a_i v_i$. Hence the appropriate choice of as must be such that $a_j v_j = a_i v_i$ for all i, j, which implies the solution we stated above.

We summarize:

For the model given in (19.10), the linear unbiased estimator of μ that has uniformly minimum variance is

$$\frac{\sum x_i/v_i}{\sum 1/v_i}.$$

Observe that it would not make sense to look for an estimator with very small variance without at the same time placing some other requirement such as unbiasedness on the estimator. For consider the estimator or decision rule in a binomial sample which says simply, "Estimate $p = \frac{1}{2}$ regardless of the sample outcome." This estimator has strictly zero variance, and yet it obviously is not to be seriously considered.

Unbiasedness from the Bayesian Point of View

Let s be the state parameter, let z be the outcome of the experiment, and let $d(z)$ be an unbiased estimator of s; then

$$E_{z|s}[d(\tilde{z}) - s] = 0 \qquad \text{for all } s.$$

Now let us treat the state parameter as a rv $\tilde{s}$ having a prior distribution. In this case it is natural to define the conditional bias of d for a given z by

$$\beta(z) \equiv E_{s|z}[d(z) - \tilde{s}],$$

where $E_{s|z}$ denotes the expectation operator for $\tilde{s}$ after observing z. Of course, even though d is unbiased, $\beta(z)$ is not generally equal to zero. It is true, however, that the conditional bias of d for a given z when "expected out" over the *marginal* distribution of $\tilde{z}$ is zero, that is,

$$E_z\beta(\tilde{z}) = E_z E_{s|z}[d(\tilde{z}) - \tilde{s}] = 0.$$

This follows since

$$E_z E_{s|z}[s(\tilde{z}) - \tilde{s}] = E[d(\tilde{z}) - \tilde{s}] = E_s E_{z|s}[d(\tilde{z}) - \tilde{s}] = 0.$$

Estimation of Functions of s

We have already remarked in another context that a Bernoulli process can just as legitimately be characterized by the long-run ratio $\tau = 1/p$ of trials to successes as by the long-run ratio p of successes to trials, and a decision maker may perfectly well be directly interested in τ and an estimate of τ rather than in p and an estimate of p. More generally, he may be interested in some function h of s and in an estimate of $h(s)$ rather than in s itself.

In general, our knowledge of expectations of functions of a random variable leads to the following proposition. If d is an unbiased estimator of s and h is some function of s, then (1) if h is *linear*, $h(d)$ is an unbiased estimator of $h(s)$, but (2) if h is *not linear*, then it is only in extremely unusual circumstances that $h(d)$ is an unbiased estimator of $h(s)$. As specific examples, let s be the parameter p of a Bernoulli process, let the sampling be binomial so that $d(r) \equiv r/n$ is an unbiased estimator of p, and consider two functions h_1 and h_2 respectively defined by

$$\begin{aligned} h_1(p) &= \alpha + \beta p \quad \text{so that} \quad h_1[d(r)] = \alpha + \beta r/n, \\ h_2(p) &= 1/p \quad \text{so that} \quad h_2[d(r)] = n/r. \end{aligned} \tag{19.11}$$

The estimator $h_1(d)$ is an unbiased estimator of $h_1(p)$, but the estimator $h_2(d)$ is *not* an unbiased estimator of $h_2(p)$. As another example observe that in (19.9b) we asserted that v is an unbiased estimate of $\upsilon = \sigma^2$. It does *not* follow that $\sqrt{\text{v}}$ is an unbiased estimate of $\sqrt{\upsilon} = \sigma$. Indeed, $E(\sqrt{\text{v}}) < \sqrt{\upsilon}$ by section 4.2.5.

Nonexistence of Unbiased Estimators

If our decision maker wants an unbiased estimator of $\tau = 1/p$, it can be obtained by using Pascal sampling and the estimator

$$d'(n) = \frac{n}{r}, \tag{19.12}$$

as the reader can prove (exercise 10). If, however, the sampling is *binomial*, then, as the reader can prove (exercise 9), *no unbiased estimator of $\tau = 1/p$ exists.*

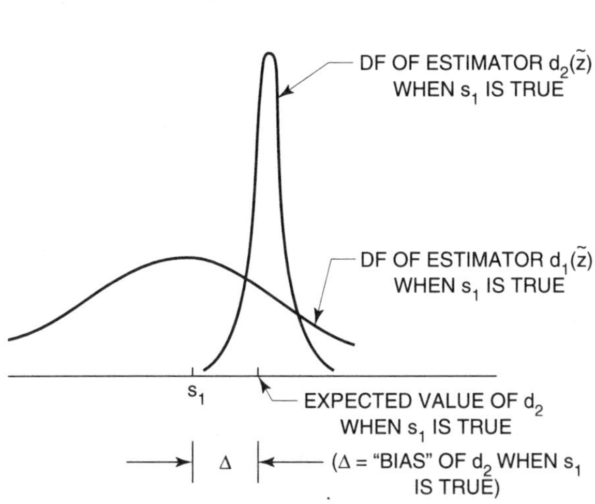

Figure 19.1
Choice of estimator

This latter situation is not at all exceptional: there are very many problems in which there is *no* unbiased estimator of a given quantity. There are other cases where an unbiased estimator of a given quantity s exists but where the estimator is clearly inappropriate. For example, suppose it is known that an unknown quantity s must by necessity fall in the interval from s_* to s^*. There are examples where the only unbiased estimator d is such that for some values of z, the estimate $d(z)$ falls outside the interval s_* to s^*. Clearly, if for some z, $d(z) < s_*$, then one is better off to estimate s by s_* than by a value less than s_*. But when this modification is made the decision rule is no longer unbiased.

Impossibility of Correcting for Bias

Let d_1 and d_2 be two estimators of an unknown quantity s; for a given value s_1, let the df's of rv's $d_1(\tilde{z})$ and $d_2(\tilde{z})$ be given as in figure 19.1. Let

$$E_{z|s_1} d_1(\tilde{z}) = s_1,$$

and

$$E_{z|s_1} d_2(\tilde{z}) = s_1 + \Delta,$$

so that d_1 is unbiased at s_1 and d_2 has a bias of Δ at s_1. Even though d_2 is biased at s_1 the distribution of estimates is much closer to s_1 for d_2 than it is for d_1, and for this reason d_2 might be preferred from the vantage point of s_1.

The question naturally arises: Why not subtract the quantity Δ from $d_2(z)$ for all z? It is true that in this case

$$E_{z|s_1}[d_2(\tilde{z}) - \Delta] = s_1,$$

but the bias of d_2 generally *depends on* s_1 and making a correction for s_1 will generally be at the expense of making the bias worse at other s values.

Choice of an Experiment

So far we have dealt only with the choice of an estimator to use after some particular sample or experiment e has been conducted; there remains the problem of deciding what experiment to conduct if any. Thus in the Bernoulli case we must decide whether to use binomial or Pascal or some other kind of sampling, and we must then decide on the size of the sample.

With neither losses nor priors to guide us, about all that we *can* do is to select a variety of reasonable-looking designs and sizes and then for each one plot against p some measure or measures of the conditional distribution of the chosen estimator given s. If the chosen estimator is unbiased, we might plot simply the conditional variance of d given s; if it is not unbiased, we might also plot the conditional bias, that is, the difference between the true s and the conditional mean $E_{z|s}d(\tilde{z})$ of the estimator, or we might plot instead the mean squared error. By comparing the various curves or pairs of curves, one for each proposed experiment, and keeping in mind the cost in money, time, and effort of each experiment, the decision maker must arrive at a choice of some one particular experiment. To make this choice without introduction of losses and priors seems to us to be asking a great deal of unaided intuition.

19.2.2 Losses, No Prior

The notion that the better of two unbiased estimators is the one with the lesser variance quite naturally suggests that it might be interesting to compare *all* estimators by looking at the extent to which the estimates they generate "tend" to be "close" to the true s. Just like systematic error, "closeness" can be measured in various ways—for example, by the magnitude of the difference between $\hat{s}$ and s, or by the square of this difference; and similarly the "tendency" can be defined as the long-run average closeness, the long-run fraction of estimates meeting a certain standard of closeness, and so on. The most commonly used measures of "closeness" are the two we have mentioned, $|\hat{s} - s|$ and $(\hat{s} - s)^2$, and almost the only commonly used definition of "tendency" is the long-run average; so that we would cover most of the ground if we examined for each estimator being considered the two quantities

$$E_{z|s}|\hat{s}_{\tilde{z}} - s| = E_{z|s}|d(\tilde{z}) - s| \tag{19.13a}$$

and

$$E_{z|s}[\hat{s}_{\tilde{z}} - s]^2 = E_{z|s}[d(\tilde{z}) - s]^2. \tag{19.13b}$$

Observe as regards the second of these quantities that

$$E_{z|s}[d(\tilde{z}) - s]^2 = V_{z|s}d(\tilde{z}) + [E_{z|s}d(\tilde{z}) - s]^2;$$

for a given s, the measure (19.13b) is thus equal to the sampling variance of an *unbiased* estimator but this measure is greater than the variance of a *biased* estimator by the square of the bias.

We now observe, however, that the measures (19.13a) and (19.13b) are exactly the quantities we would compute as the first step in a normal-form analysis—compare (19.2)—if the decision maker were to tell us that the *loss* of an error $(\hat{s} - s)$ were $|\hat{s} - s|$ or $(\hat{s} - s)^2$ respectively. We can therefore avoid a duplicate discussion of what is essentially the same problem by proceeding *as if* the decision maker had told us either (1) that

$$l_t(\hat{s}, s) \equiv l_t[d(z), s] = k_t|d(z) - s|, \tag{19.14}$$

or else (2) that

$$l_t(\hat{s}, s) \equiv l_t[d(z), s] = k_t[d(z) - s]^2, \tag{19.15}$$

where k_t can be interpreted as dollars per unit of error if the decision maker is willing to specify such a constant but can be simply set equal to 1 and disregarded if the decision maker so prefers.

Our present objective is thus to evaluate the *conditional* expectation *given* s of the two loss functions (19.14) and (19.15). We shall do this for the particular case of a Bernoulli process with binomial sampling and for the particular family of estimators d defined by

$$d(r) = \frac{r + \alpha}{n + \beta} \tag{19.16}$$

where α and β are constants that can be chosen at the decision maker's pleasure. Observe that the family contains the estimator r/n which is both maximum-likelihood and minimum-variance unbiased in the Bernoulli binomial case. We start with quadratic rather than linear loss because quadratic loss is both easier to analyze and more commonly used in practice.

1. Quadratic Loss

The reader can show (exercise 11) that if

$$l_t(\hat{p}, p) = l_t[d(r), p] = k_t[d(r) - p]^2, \tag{19.17}$$

then for d given in (19.16)

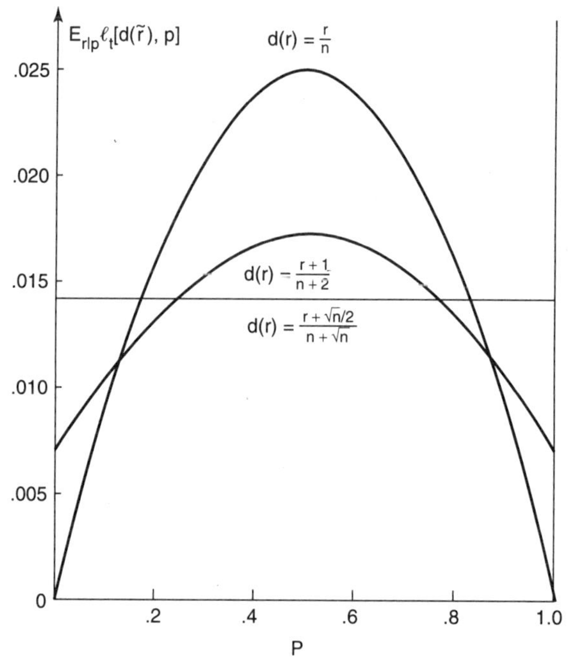

Figure 19.2
Expected loss of three estimators

$$E_{r|p}l_t[d(r), p] = k_t\frac{np(1-p) + (\alpha - \beta p)^2}{(n+\beta)^2}. \tag{19.18}$$

The conditional expected loss of three selected estimators in the family (19.16) is graphed against p in figure 19.2 for the sample size $n = 10$, and it is immediately apparent that the problem of choice even among only these three estimators is by no means trivial. Each of them is best for certain values of p, worst for others, and intermediate for still others.

The reason for choosing the particular three estimators shown in figure 19.2 is simply that they possess special features, namely:

a. r/n is the maximum-likelihood and the minimum-variance-unbiased estimator, as we have already remarked.

b. The conditional expected loss of $(r + 1)/(n + 2)$ *averaged over* p (the area under the curve) is less than that of any other estimator.

c. The *maximum* conditional expected loss of $(r + \frac{1}{2}\sqrt{n})/(n + \sqrt{n})$ (the "peak" of the curve) is less than the maximum for any other estimator.

We warn the reader, however, not to jump to conclusions on the basis of these properties. In particular, a statement that $(r + 1)/(n + 2)$ is better than other estimators *because* its average conditional expected loss is less than that of any other estimator amounts, as we shall see in section 19.2.3 below, to assuming that the decision maker has assigned a rectangular prior distribution to $\tilde{p}$; our present objective is to see how the decision maker can choose a decision rule *without* assigning a prior distribution to $\tilde{p}$.

2. Symmetric Linear Loss

The reader can show (exercise 12) that if

$$l_t(\hat{p}, p) = l_t[d(r), p] = k_t|d(r) - p|, \tag{19.19}$$

then for any d of the form $d(r) = (r + \alpha)/(n + \beta)$

$$\frac{1}{k_t} E_{r|p} l_t[d(\tilde{r}), p] = \left[p - \frac{\alpha}{n + \beta}\right][1 - 2G_b(r^*|n, p)]$$

$$- \frac{np}{n + \beta}[1 - 2G_b(r^* - 1|n - 1, p)] \tag{19.20a}$$

where G_b is the right-tail binomial cumulative function and

$$r^* \equiv (n + \beta)p - \alpha. \tag{19.20b}$$

(Remember that G_b is well defined for nonintegral arguments and for arguments outside the interval $[0, n]$.)

A graph similar to figure 19.2 could be prepared to show the conditional expected loss of selected estimators, but since it is not clear what we should do with such a graph after we have it, we shall spare the trouble.

Choice of an Experiment

Even though it is not very clear how to use conditional expected loss to select a decision rule or estimator d for use in conjunction with a given e, conditional expected loss *can* be of considerable help in *limiting the range* of e's to be considered provided that the decision maker actually assigns a value to the loss constant k_t. To see how, suppose that the decision maker has decided that loss as measured in dollars is

$$l_t[d(r), p] = k_t[d(r) - p]^2, \tag{19.21}$$

that he has decided to use the estimator r/n, so that conditional expected loss as given by (19.18) is

$$E_{r|p} l_t[d(\tilde{r}), p] = k_t \frac{p(1 - p)}{n}, \tag{19.22}$$

and that all that remains is to settle on the sample size n when the cost of sampling as measured in dollars is

$$\bar{c}(n) = k_s n. \tag{19.23}$$

Then, whatever the true p may be, the decision maker's "total" loss (relative to estimating $\hat{p} = p$ without sampling) is

$$T(n, p) = k_t \frac{p(1 - p)}{n} + k_s n. \tag{19.24}$$

In figure 19.3 we graph $T(n, p)/k_t$ against p for $k_t/k_s = 1{,}600$ and various n and we observe at once that for any given p (except 0 and 1), $T(n, p)$ first decreases and then increases as n increases. As long as there is *some* p for which $T(n, p)$ is decreasing, it is just as hard to decide whether an increase in n is worthwhile as it was to decide between various possible ds in figure 19.2. In our present problem, however, we ultimately get to a point where $T(n, p)$ increases with n for all p, and here we really know we have gone too far.

The *maximum admissible* sample size n is the largest n such that a decrease in n would increase $T(n, p)$ for some p.[2] The reader can show (exercise 13) that if loss is quadratic as given by (19.21), sampling cost is linear as given by (19.23), and the estimator is r/n, so that $T(n, p)$ is given by (19.24), then

$$\text{Maximum admissible } n = \tfrac{1}{2}\sqrt{k_t/k_s}. \tag{19.25}$$

Similar expressions can, of course, be obtained for other losses, sampling costs, and estimators.

19.2.3 Losses and Prior

Suppose now that after carefully examining a chart like figure 19.2 the decision maker decides that after all he *Does* really think that p is substantially less likely to be, say, outside the interval [.25,.75] than it is to be inside this interval and therefore concludes that upon reflection he does not really fancy the maximum-likelihood minimum-variance-unbiased estimator r/n which has very high conditional expected loss inside the interval in question. Suppose further that this initial conclusion leads him after further reflection to decide that perhaps a very good way of choosing one estimator among the infinitely many possible estimators would be to de-

2. The maximum admissible sample size is also the *smallest* n such that an *increase* in n would *increase* $T(n, p)$ for all p.

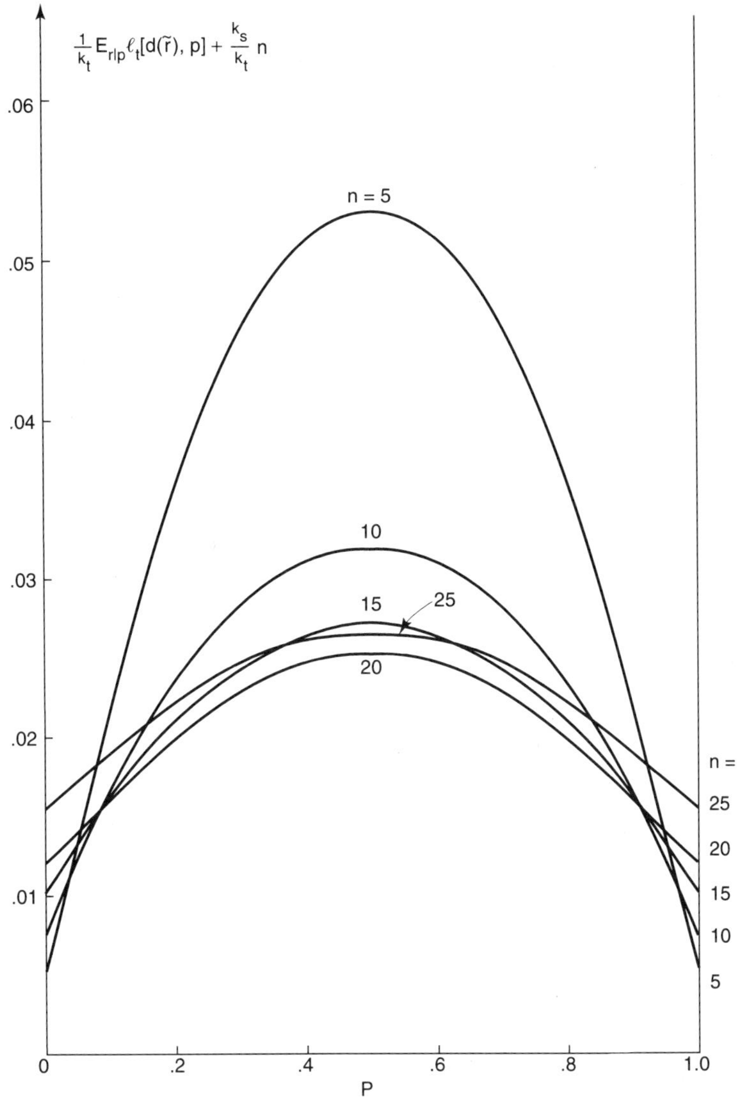

Figure 19.3
Total expected loss

cide on *weights* that roughly express the relative importance he attaches to conditional expected loss in various ranges of p, use these weights to compute the *weighted-average loss* of each estimator, and then choose the estimator whose weighted-average loss is least.

Now in mathematical notation the weights assigned by the decision maker to various ranges of p define a weighting function w of p, and the weighted-average loss of any d can be expressed by

$$\frac{1}{W}\int_0^1 E_{r|p} l_t[d(\tilde{r}), p]\, w(p)\, dp, \tag{19.26a}$$

where

$$W \equiv \int_0^1 w(p)\, dp. \tag{19.26b}$$

We will obviously get exactly the same result if we rescale the weights by defining a new weighting function f_p by

$$f_p(p) = \frac{1}{W} w(p) \tag{19.27a}$$

and then compute the weighted average

$$\int_0^1 E_{r|p} l[d(\tilde{r}), p]\, f_p(p)\, dp. \tag{19.27b}$$

The function f_p, however, has all the properties that by (7.13) define a *probability density function*, and therefore the "weighted-average loss" (19.27) is identical to the *unconditional expected loss*

$$\bar{l}_t^*(e, d) = E_p E_{r|p} l_t[d(\tilde{r}), \tilde{p}] \tag{19.28}$$

which we obtain by treating f_p as the judgmental prior density of $\tilde{p}$.

Suppose then specifically that the decision maker decides to compare estimators of a Bernoulli p with binomial sampling by selecting the estimator with the lowest weighted-average or unconditional expected loss, and suppose that he gives us a weighting function w to use in the computations. Once we have "normalized" this function in the way defined by (19.27a), we must (in consultation with the decision maker) decide whether to use the rough weights exactly as he gives them to us or to smooth them out and possibly represent them by some curve chosen from a convenient family of mathematically defined curves.

In the remainder of this section we shall assume that the decision maker does decide that he is willing to choose his estimator in accordance with weights which can be represented by a *beta* density with parameters r' and n'. We shall also assume throughout that the sampling is to be *binomial*.

1. Quadratic Loss

If the decision maker adopts a quadratic loss function of type (19.17) so that the *conditional* expected loss of any estimator in the family defined by $d(r) = (r + \alpha)/(n + \beta)$ is given by (19.18), then as the reader can show as an exercise the *unconditional* expected loss with a binomial sample of size n is

$$\bar{l}_t^*(n, d) = k_t \frac{(nn' + \beta^2)\breve{p}' + (\alpha + \beta\bar{p}')^2}{(n + \beta)^2} \tag{19.29a}$$

where

$$\bar{p}' = \frac{r'}{n'}, \qquad \breve{p}' = \frac{r'(n' - r')}{n'^2(n' + 1)}. \tag{19.29b}$$

The best rule in the particular family being considered may now be found by routine minimization techniques. The reader may show (exercise 14) that (19.29a) is minimized when $\alpha = r'$ and $\beta = n'$, implying that the best rule in the family being considered is

$$d(r) = \frac{r + r'}{n + n'}. \tag{19.30}$$

We know of course by the results of posterior analysis in section 12.6.2 that this rule is the best of *all possible* rules under quadratic loss.

2. Symmetric Linear Loss

If the decision maker adopts a symmetric linear loss function of type (19.19) so that the *conditional* expected loss of any estimator in the family defined by $d(r) = (r + \alpha)/(n + \beta)$ is given by (19.20) then as the reader can show as an exercise the *unconditional* expected loss with a binomial sample of size n is given by a formula identical to (19.20) except that the binomial cumulative functions $G_b(\cdot\,|n, p)$ are replaced by hyperbinomial cumulative functions $G_{hb}(\cdot\,|r', n', n)$.

Again we could find the best rule in the family in question by routine minimization techniques, but we shall not do so because we already know by the results of section 12.7.3 that the truly optimal estimator

$$d^o(r) = p''_{1/2}, \qquad \text{where} \qquad F_\beta(p''_{1/2}|r' + r, n' + n) \equiv \tfrac{1}{2} \tag{19.31}$$

is not a member of the family we have evaluated. This optimal estimator is of so strange a form to anyone who looks first at *conditional* loss given p and only later at averages over p that it is highly improbable that it would ever be discovered through such an approach. It is true, of course, that if someone writes the normal-form evaluation of a *general* d,

$$E_p E_{r|p} l_t[d(\tilde{r}), \tilde{p}] = \int_0^1 \textstyle\sum_{r=0}^{n} |d(r) - p| f_b(r|n, p) f_\beta(p|r', n')\, dp, \tag{19.32}$$

it might occur to him that he could find the optimal estimator by reversing the order of summation and integration, carrying out the integration only, and then finding the optimal $d^o(r)$ *for each* r before he sums; but this amounts exactly to doing the analysis in extensive rather than normal form and *can be done only if the prior distribution of* $\tilde{p}$ *is brought into the statement of the problem at the beginning.*

19.3 Two-Action Problems with Breakeven Values

In a great many decision problems there are two possible acts a_1 and a_2 and an unknown state s such that the decision maker would prefer a_1 if he knew s to be less than or equal to some fixed value s_b but would prefer a_2 if he knew s to be greater than s_b. Such an attitude will of course exist if the two acts have monetary values that are *linear* in s, but it will also exist when the two acts have nonlinear monetary value or utility functions provided that these functions "cross" at only one value s_b of s; and the decision maker will often hold such an attitude even without having assigned any specific monetary value or utility function to the two acts.

19.3.1 Decision Rules

In a problem of this kind, if an experiment e is to be conducted and its outcome z is to be used as a basis for choice between a_1 and a_2, then all possible values of z must be partitioned into just two sets Z_1 and Z_2 and the decision rule must be of the form

$$d(z) = \begin{cases} a_1 & \text{if} \quad z \in Z_1 \\ a_2 & \text{if} \quad z \in Z_2. \end{cases} \tag{19.33}$$

There exists a good deal of literature on the nature of Z_1 and Z_2 in the general case, but for the purposes of this book we shall do much better to omit general discussion and turn immediately to the specific case where the role of s is played by the parameter p of a Bernoulli process and the sampling is either binomial or Pascal. The results of this special case can be easily generalized to all other cases that we shall encounter.

Assume then that p is the parameter of a Bernoulli process and that a_1 is preferable if $p \le p_b$ while a_2 is preferable if $p \ge p_b$. It is quite obvious that if the sampling is binomial, the optimal decision rule will be of the general form

$$d(r) = \begin{cases} a_1 & \text{if} \quad r \le c, \\ a_2 & \text{if} \quad r > c, \end{cases} \tag{19.34}$$

for some integral value of c, while if the sampling is Pascal, the optimal rule will be of the general form

$$d(n) = \begin{cases} a_1 & \text{if} \quad n \ge c, \\ a_2 & \text{if} \quad n < c. \end{cases} \tag{19.35}$$

The problem of choosing a rule d for given e thus reduces to one of choosing a *critical value* c.

19.3.2 No Losses, No Prior

The way in which any decision rule of type (19.34) or (19.35) will perform *if* the process parameter has any particular value p can be described by computing the *conditional* probability *given* p that the rule will lead to the *wrong* act, that is, to the act which is *not* preferred for that p. Thus if the sampling is binomial,

$$P(\text{error}|p) = \begin{cases} P[d(\tilde{r}) = a_2|p] = G_b(c+1|n,p) & \text{if} \quad p \le p_b, \\ P[d(\tilde{r}) = a_1|p] = F_b(c|n,p) & \text{if} \quad p > p_b. \end{cases} \tag{19.36}$$

A curve showing the probability of error for *all* p will be called the *error characteristic* of the decision rule d.

Example A manufacturer must decide whether to proceed with a production run using the setup made by the regular operator of the machine or to have the setup checked and if need be readjusted by an expert mechanic at extra cost. The manufacturer believes that the machine as set up by the operator will behave as a Bernoulli process with some unknown fraction defective p and that if p had a value greater than $p_b = .04$ it would pay to readjust the setup (act a_2), whereas if p had a value less than .04 it would pay to leave the setup alone (act a_1). In figure 19.4 error characteristics are shown for rules based on binomial sampling with $n = 75$ and various critical values of c; in figure 19.5 error characteristics are shown for several n values.

Choice of a Decision Rule for Given e

If the sample design and sample size have already been fixed, then the choice of a decision rule amounts simply to the choice of a critical value c. The reader can readily ascertain by inspection of the curves in figure 19.4 and formula (19.36) above that if sampling is binomial, then an increase in c decreases the probability of making a wrong decision *if* p has any value less than or equal to p_b but only at the cost of increasing the probability of

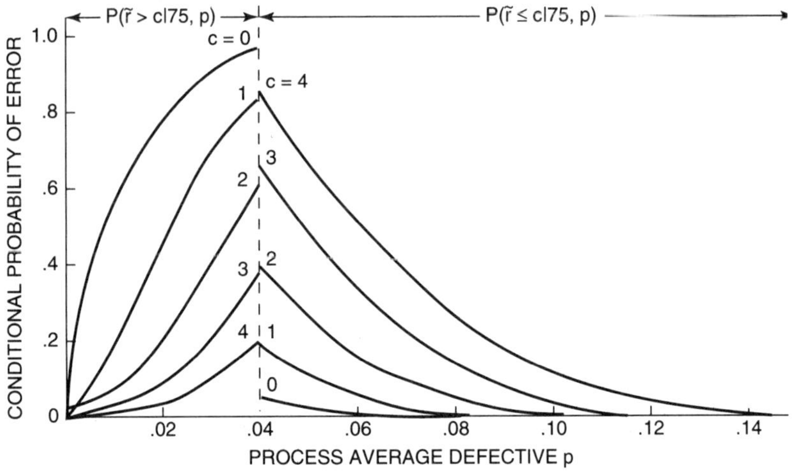

Figure 19.4
Error characteristics for different critical values

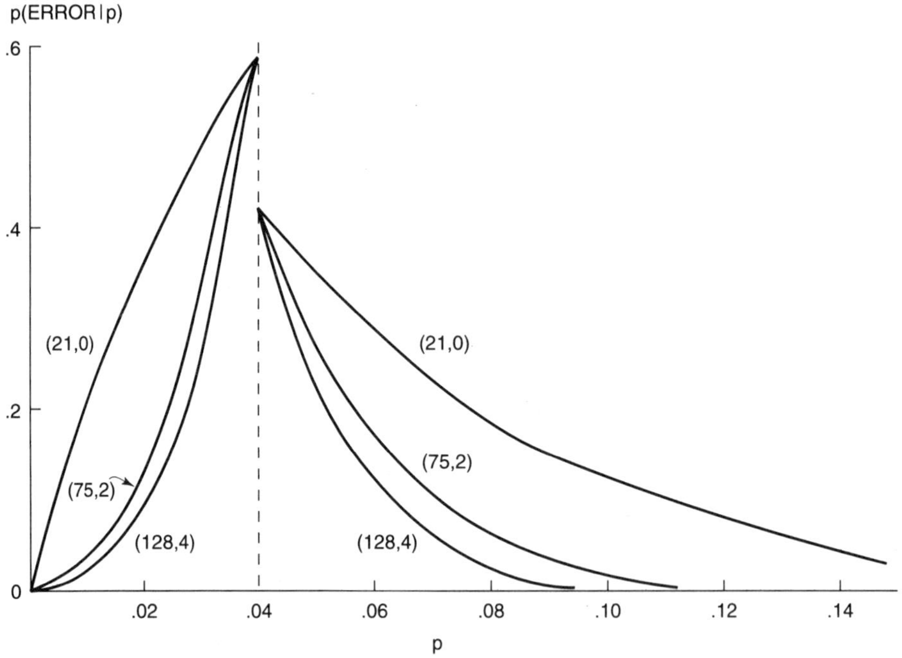

Figure 19.5
Error characteristics for different sample sizes

making a wrong decision *if* p has any value greater than p_b; then, comparing (19.35) leads to a similar statement concerning a rule based on Pascal sampling. Even more generally, comparing (19.33), one can see that in *any* two-action problem where the sample design and sample size have already been fixed, a decrease in the probability of making a wrong decision if s has any value less than or equal to s_b can be obtained only at the cost of an increase in the probability of making a wrong decision if s has any value greater than s_b.

If neither losses nor prior distributions are to be introduced into the problem, the decision maker must choose a critical value c by simply comparing curves like those in figure 19.4. It is sometimes suggested that the choice may be made by dopting some one of the following rules.

1. Choose the c which comes closest to giving a 50-50 chance to both acts if p actually has the breakeven value p_b. (In the above example for $n = 75$, this would be $c = 2$.)

2a. Set some upper limit α on the probability of making a wrong decision if p has *any* value greater than p_b and then subject to this constraint choose the c which gives the lowest probability of making a wrong decision if p has any value less than or equal to p_b. (If we set $\alpha = .20$ for the case graphed in figure 19.4, the constraint says that c must be either 1 or 0 and we then choose $c = 1$ in order to minimize the probability of error for $p \leq p_b$.)

2b. Same as (2a) except that the limit α is placed on the conditional probability of error for $p \leq p_b$ and the subsequent minimization is for $p > p_b$.

3a. Like (2a) except that instead of putting a limit α on the probability of error given *any* $p > p_b$, the decision maker first selects a value p^* which is just far enough above p_b to make a choice of a_1 instead of a_2 a "serious" error in his judgment and then places the limit α on the probability of error if $p \geq p^*$. (If in the case graphed in figure 19.4 the decision maker decides that choosing a_1 is a serious error only if $p \geq .06$ and sets a limit $\alpha = .20$ on the probability of error if $p \geq .06$, he is constrained to use $c = 0$, 1, or 2, and he then chooses $c = 2$ in order to minimize the probability of error for $p \leq p_b = .04$.)

3b. Like (3a) except that the decision maker reverses the roles of a_1 and a_2, chooses a p_* *below* p_b, and proceeds accordingly.

4. The decision maker selects a value of $p^* > p_b$ as in (3a), and a value of $p_* < p_b$ as in (3b) with the added restriction that in his view an error at p_* is equally as serious as an error at p^*. Choose the c which makes the larger of the error probabilities at p_* and p^* as small as possible.

It is up to the decision maker to decide, by reflecting on the circumstances of his problem, whether he will choose c by inspection of complete error characteristics or by one of these "shortcut" methods; if he chooses to use a shortcut method, it is again up to him to specify α and, if he uses method (3), to specify p_* or p^*; if he uses method (4) he must specify both p_* and p^*. Without the use of losses, there exists no method of analysis that can aid him in his choice.

Choice of an Experiment

In figure 19.5 we show error characteristics for $p_b = .04$ and three different binomial sample sizes, the decision rule or critical value c being chosen for each sample size in such a way that all three rules have almost exactly the same probability of a wrong decision given p at p_b; the probability of a wrong decision decreases for *all* p (except $p = 0$ and 1). It is obvious, furthermore, that such a result can be obtained in the general case: except for minor discrepancies near p_b or s_b due to the fact that r or z is discrete, we can always reduce the conditional probabilities of error for *all* p or s by increasing the sample size and adjusting c appropriately.

The decision maker can thus choose his experiment by looking at the probabilities of error shown by curves like those in figure 19.5 while keeping in mind the cost in time, money, and effort of each increase in sample size. The following shortcut has also been suggested and can be used if the decision maker wishes to do so. First, specify the value p_* which is just far enough *below* p_b to make a choice of a_2 a "serious" error if in fact $p = p_*$, and specify a limit α on the probability of wrong decision given any $p \leq p_*$. Next, specify the value p^* which is just far enough *above* p_b to make a choice of a_1 a "serious" error if in fact $p = p^*$, and specify a limit β on the probability of wrong decision given any $p \geq p^*$. Finally, through the binomial tables, find a pair (n, c) whose error characteristic comes as close as possible to satisfying these conditions, that is, which comes as close as possible to satisfying

$$G_b(c + 1|n, p_*) = \alpha, \qquad F_b(c|n, p^*) = \beta.$$

If the decision maker does decide to use this shortcut, he must rely on his own judgment in selecting p_*, p^*, α, and β, since without the use of losses there exists no method of analysis that can aid him in his choice. It may turn out, of course, that this procedure will result in an n which represents an intolerable cost in money, time or effort. If so, the decision maker is free to pick a new p_*, p^*, α, and β and try again.

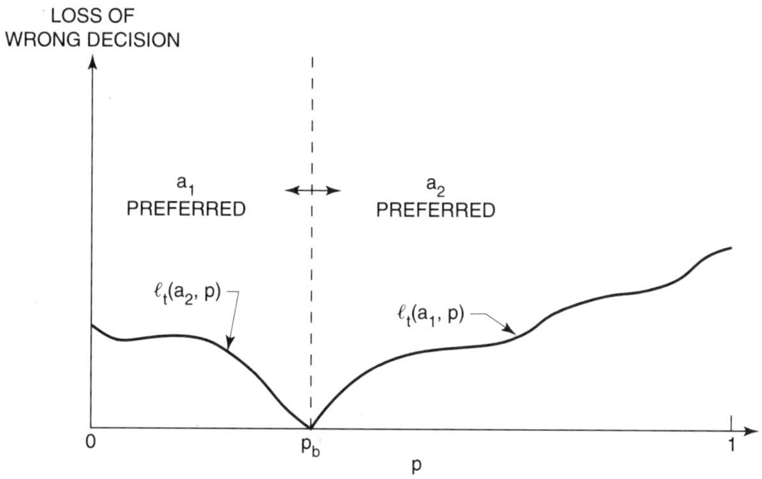

Figure 19.6
Possible terminal loss function

19.3.3 Losses, No Prior

Suppose now that for both acts a_1 and a_2 and every p the decision maker can assign a value $l_t(a_i, p)$ to the loss which will result from choosing a_1 if p is true. The *conditional expected loss* of any decision rule d given p can then be computed from the standard formula

$$E_{r|p} l_t[d(\tilde{r}), p] = l_t(a_1, p) P[d(\tilde{r}) = a_1 | p] + l_t(a_2, p) P[d(\tilde{r}) = a_2 | p], \qquad (19.37)$$

but the fact that there are only two possible acts permits us to simplify this formula and make it more comprehensible. Since the loss of the optimal act for any p is zero by the definition of loss, and since by hypothesis a_1 is optimal for $p \leq p_b$ while a_2 is optimal for $p > p_b$, only one of the two terms on the right-hand side of (19.37) can be nonzero for any p, and the conditional expected loss given any p can be thought of as simply the product of (1) the loss of the *wrong* decision given p, and (2) the conditional probability given p that the decision rule will lead to the *wrong* decision. If the losses are plotted as in figure 19.6, then in principle the conditional expected loss of any rule d given any particular p can be calculated by (1) reading from figure 19.6 the loss that will occur if the wrong act is chosen when p has that particular value, (2) reading from the appropriate error characteristic the conditional probability, given that p, that the rule in question will lead to the wrong decision, and (3) multiplying these two quantities together.

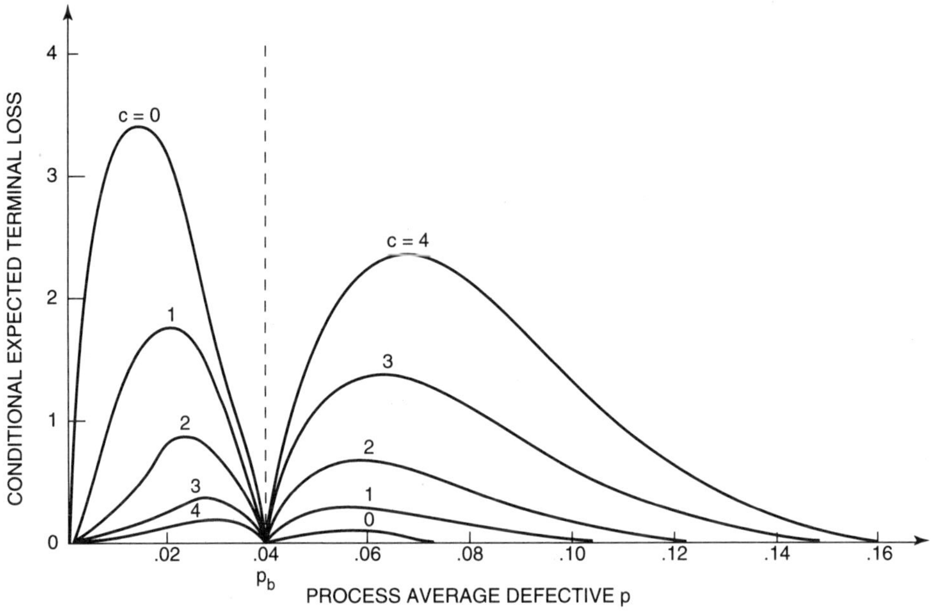

Figure 19.7
Conditional expected terminal loss for different critical values

Linear Losses

If the decision maker assigns the loss functions

$$l_t(a_1, p) = k_t \max\{0, p - p_b\},$$
$$l_t(a_2, p) = k_t \max\{p_b - p, 0\}, \tag{19.38}$$

which correspond to assigning linear value functions to the two acts—compare (12.12)—then for binomial sampling the expression (19.37) for conditional expected loss reduces to

$$E_{r|p} l_t[d(\tilde{r}), p] = \begin{cases} k_t(p_b - p)G_b(c + 1|n, p) & \text{if} \quad p \le p_b, \\ k_t(p - p_b)F_b(c|n, p) & \text{if} \quad p > p_b. \end{cases} \tag{19.39}$$

In figure 19.7 the reader will find curves of conditional expected loss for $p_b = .04$, $k_t = 200$, and binomial sampling with the same sample size n and critical values c for which the error characteristics were shown in figure 19.4. The "butterfly" shape of these curves is characteristic for most practical problems with losses of type (19.38) and sampling distributions ordinarily encountered in practice; the reader should confirm that it is reasonable for any such curve to approach 0 at the extreme left, at p_b, and at the extreme right, and to have peaks between 0 and p_b and between p_b and 1.

Choice of a Decision Rule for Given *e*

Comparison of curves for any two values of c shows immediately that a change in c decreases conditional expected loss given any p (except 0 or 1) on one side of p_b but only at the cost of increasing conditional expected loss given any p on the other side of p_b. If a decision rule d, that is, a critical value c, is to be chosen for a *given* experiment e, the decision maker who does not wish to assign a prior distribution to $\tilde{p}$ must choose by inspection of curves like the ones under discussion. It has been suggested that she *may* want to choose the curve whose *worst* conditional expected loss is lower than the *worst* conditional expected loss of any other curve—this would be the curve for $c = 2$ in figure 19.7—but whether or not she wants to accept this "minimax-loss" or "minimax-regret" solution is up to her to decide.

Choice of an Experiment

If the type and/or size of experiment is not predetermined, then any set of es can be compared by first choosing the decision rule or critical value which would be used *if* each of the es in question were to be performed and then plotting for each (e, d) combination, as a function of s, the conditional expected total loss given s,

$$\bar{l}^*(e, d|s) = E_{z|s} l_t[d(\tilde{z}), s] + E_{z|s} c_s(e, \tilde{z}); \tag{19.40}$$

the word "conditional" is included since the evaluation is for a given s, and the word "expected" is included since the rv $\tilde{z}$ is "expected out." If the role of s is played by a Bernoulli p, the role of z will be played by r if sampling is binomial or by n if sampling is Pascal. In figure 19.8 we show curves of total loss for a situation with $p_b = .04$, $k_t = \$200$, $c_s(n, r) = .1n$, and the binomial sample sizes and decision rules whose error characteristics were shown in figure 19.5 above.

19.3.4 Losses and Prior

If the decision maker assigns to p a weighting function $w(p)$ describing the *importance* that the decision maker attaches to the way in which a rule will behave given each possible value of p, then any two decision rules can be compared by computing the *weighted-average* height of their curves of conditional expected loss. We have seen in section 19.2.3, however, that such a procedure is exactly equivalent to assigning a "prior" density function to $\tilde{p}$ and computing the unconditional expected loss

$$\bar{\bar{l}}_t^*(e, d) = E_p E_{r|p} l_t[d(\tilde{r}), \tilde{p}]. \tag{19.41}$$

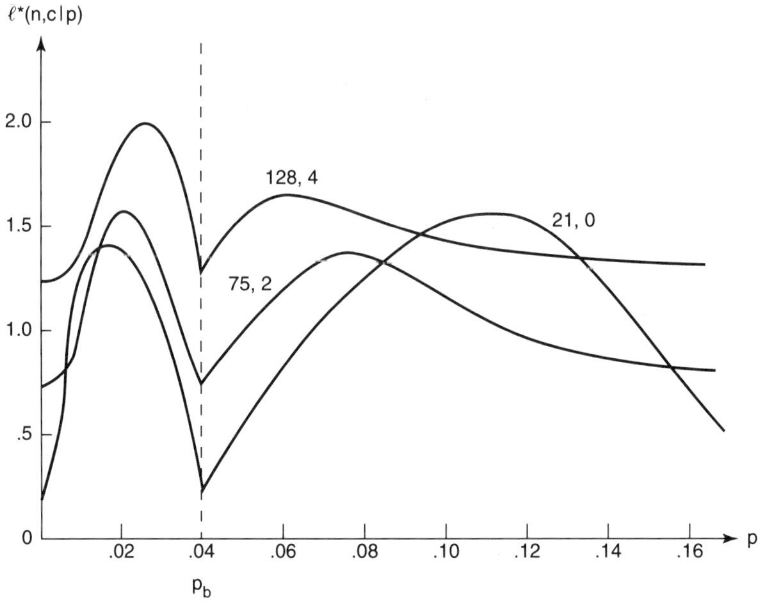

Figure 19.8
Conditional expected terminal loss for different sample sizes

Without repeating the discussion in section 19.2.3 of *choice* of a weighting function, let us simply assume that the decision maker chooses a beta density with parameters r' and n', and let us also assume that sampling will be binomial, so that the number of observations n describes e the critical value c describes d. If in addition the losses assigned to the two acts are of type (19.38), so that the conditional expected loss of any c is given by (19.39), then by (19.41) the unconditional expected loss is given by

$$\frac{1}{k_t}\bar{\bar{l}}_t^*(n,c) = \int_0^{p_b} (p_b - p) G_b(c+1|n,p) f_\beta(p|r',n')\,dp$$
$$+ \int_{p_b}^{1} (p - p_b) F_b(c|n,p) f_\beta(p|r',n')\,dp. \qquad (19.42)$$

To find the optimal c for given n we could evaluate this integral in terms of the cumulative hyperbinomial function, which is easy, and then optimize by looking at first differences with respect to r, which is clumsy. It will be more instructive, however, to proceed in another way, which amounts in effect to evaluating (n,c) by extensive rather than normal-form analysis. Compare the similar device used at the end of section 19.2.3

The reader can verify (exercise 16) that, by substituting $1 - F_b(c)$ for $G_b(c+1)$ and reversing the order of summation and integration, we may write (19.42) in the form

$$\frac{1}{k_t}\bar{l}_t^*(n,c) = \int_0^{p_b} (p_b - p) f_\beta(p|r',n')\,dp - \textstyle\sum_{r=0}^{c} (p_b - \bar{p}_r'') f_{hb}(r|n',n',n) \tag{19.43}$$

where

$$\bar{p}_r'' \equiv \frac{r'+r}{n'+n}.$$

If now $\bar{p}' \geq p_b$, we can interpret the first term on the right of (19.43) as the expected loss of *immediate* terminal action, without sampling, whereupon the second term represents the expected value of the sample information *given that this information is to be exploited via a decision rule with critical value c.*

Regardless of the interpretation, the best critical value c^o is obviously the one which maximizes the second term on the right of (19.43) and thus minimizes $\bar{l}_t^*(n,c)$, and c^o is easy to find. Remembering that $\bar{p}_r''$ increases with r, we see on inspection of the summand that the rth term in the sum will increase the sum if r is small enough to make $\bar{p}_r''$ less than p_b but will decrease the sum if r is large enough to make $\bar{p}_r''$ greater than p_b.

From this it follows that

$$c^o = \text{maximum integer} \leq p_b(n'+n) - r'; \tag{19.44}$$

hence

$$r \begin{Bmatrix} \leq \\ > \end{Bmatrix} c^o \quad \text{implies} \quad \bar{p}_r'' \begin{Bmatrix} \leq \\ > \end{Bmatrix} p_b \tag{19.45}$$

and this result is exactly equivalent to the result we obtained by preposterior analysis, namely

$$a_r^o = \begin{Bmatrix} a_1 \\ a_2 \end{Bmatrix} \quad \text{if} \quad \bar{p}_r'' \begin{Bmatrix} \leq \\ \geq \end{Bmatrix} p_b. \tag{19.46}$$

19.3.5 Nuisance Parameters

Consider the case where $\tilde{x}_1, \ldots, \tilde{x}_n$ are independent rv's drawn from a Normal population with unknown mean μ and known variance υ. The normal mode of analysis for two-action problems of the kind we have been considering in this book is straightforward and parallels the treatment we gave for binomial sampling. When υ is unknown, however, the analysis becomes more complex. In this case υ would be termed a "nuisance" parameter and the epithet is well chosen.

Assume then that (μ, υ) is the parameter of an independent Normal process and that a_1 is preferable if $\mu \leq \mu_b$ while a_2 is preferable if $\mu > \mu_b$. As done previously, define

$$m \equiv \sum x_i/n,$$

$$\mathrm{v} = \sum (x_i - m)^2/(n - 1).$$

If d is a decision rule that assigns to each (m, v) outcome an act a_1 or a_2, then for a given μ the conditional probability that d will lead to an error will depend not only on μ but also on υ. Therefore we cannot plot the probability of an error against the relevant single parameter μ as was done in figure 19.4 for the Bernoulli case. We could, of course, plot the error as a function of (μ, υ) but this would require a surface in three-space. Imagine what a complex task it would then be to choose among error characteristic surfaces or among conditional expected total loss surfaces!

There is a special decision rule that must be mentioned because of its important role in classical (i.e., non-Bayesian) statistics. Let the statistic t be defined by

$$t = \frac{m - \mu_b}{\sqrt{\mathrm{v}/n}}. \tag{19.47}$$

It can be shown that the conditional distribution of $\tilde{t}$ given (μ, υ) depends only on (μ, υ) through the quantity $\delta \equiv (\mu - \mu_b)/\sqrt{\upsilon}$, which is called the noncentrality parameter; furthermore, for $\mu = \mu_b$, the distribution of $\tilde{t}$ does not depend on υ and is the standardized Student distribution we discussed in section 9.9. Observe hattif in the definition of t the statistic v were replaced by the parameter υ, then for a given μ the modified $\tilde{t}$ would have a Normal distribution. A decision rule commonly employed for this problem is given by

$$d(m, \mathrm{v}) = \begin{cases} a_1 & \text{if} \quad t \leq c, \\ a_2 & \text{if} \quad t > c, \end{cases} \tag{19.48}$$

where t is given by (19.47) and c is the cutoff value that controls the error performance of the rule. For a decision rule in this class the contour lines where the probability of making an error is constant are on any ray emerging from the point $(\mu_b, 0)$, as shown in figure 19.9. Notice that on any ray the value of the noncentrality parameter δ is constant.

One of the difficulties of this analysis for most economic decision problems is that although the probability of making an error does not change along a ray in figure 19.9, the loss incurred in making such an error does

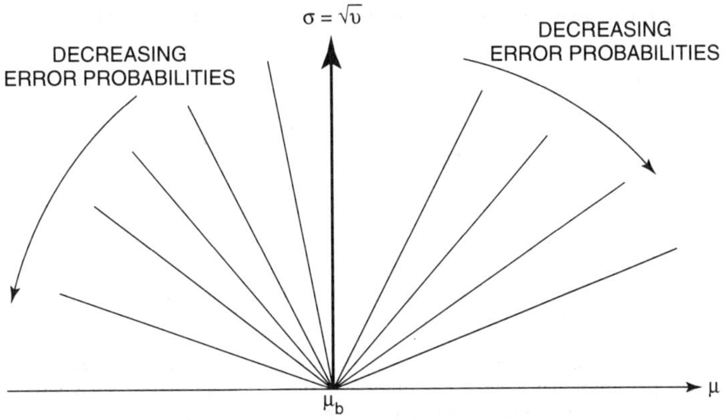

Figure 19.9
Normal error-probability contours

change. This certainly is the case where the loss is directly proportional to $|\mu - \mu_b|$ or to $(\mu - \mu_b)^2$, independent of the value of υ. Thus (19.48) with a constant cutoff value c would ordinarily be far from optimum.

Exercises

1. a. For a binomial sample of size n, the probability that $\tilde{r} = r$ is

$$P(\tilde{r} = r|n, p) = C_r^n p^r(1 - p)^{n-r}.$$

Show that the value of p that maximizes this probability for a given (r, n) is $\hat{p} = r/n$.

b. In Pascal sampling where r is preassigned, the probability that $\tilde{n} = n$ is

$$P(\tilde{n} = n|r, p) = C_{r-1}^{n-1} p^r(1 - p)^{n-r}.$$

Show that $\hat{p} = r/n$ maximizes this probability.

c. Show that if (μ, υ) is the parameter of a Normal process, then the (μ, υ) pair that maximizes the likelihood for an observed sample $z = (x_1, \ldots, x_n)$ is $(\hat{\mu}, \hat{\upsilon})$, where

$$\hat{\mu} = m \equiv \sum x_i/n,$$

and

$$\hat{\upsilon} = \frac{1}{n}\sum (x_i - m)^2.$$

d. In (c), show that the likelihood for an observed $\hat{\upsilon}$ depends only on υ and is maximum at $\upsilon = n\hat{\upsilon}/(n - 1)$. (The change from (c) to (d) is perhaps paradoxical. See David, Stone, and Zidek 1973.)

2. Assume that p is the parameter of a Bernoulli process. Show that if the sampling is binomial (fixed n), the estimator

$$d_b(r) = r/n$$

is unbiased, whereas if thc sampling is Pascal (fixed r), the estimator

$$d_{Pa}(n) = \frac{r-1}{n-1}$$

is unbiased for $r \geq 2$, and also for $r = 1$ if we assign the value 1 to the indeterminate quantity 0/0 which results when $\tilde{n} = 1$.

3. Suppose the parameter λ is unknown and for any given λ the rv $\tilde{x}$ has the density

$$f(x|\lambda) = e^{-\lambda x}\lambda.$$

Show that if $\tilde{x} = 3$ is observed, the λ-value that maximizes the likclihood of the sample result is $\lambda = \frac{1}{3}$.

4. For a binomial sample of size n, the maximum likelihood procedure estimates r/n for the unknown p if $\tilde{r} = r$ is observed. Show that no matter what p is, the conditional expected value of the estimator $\tilde{r}/n$ given p is p, that is,

$$E\left[\frac{\tilde{r}}{n}\middle| p\right] = p \quad \text{for all } p.$$

5. For a binomial sample of size $n = 4$ exhibit the conditional sampling distribution of estimator $\tilde{r}/n$ of p when $p = .5, .4, .2, .1$ (fill in the blanks in table 19E.1).

Values of r/n	.00	.25	.50	.75	1.00
$P\left[\frac{\tilde{r}}{n} = \frac{r}{n}\middle| p = .5\right]$					
$P\left[\frac{\tilde{r}}{n} = \frac{r}{n}\middle| p = .4\right]$					
$P\left[\frac{\tilde{r}}{n} = \frac{r}{n}\middle| p = .3\right]$					
$P\left[\frac{\tilde{r}}{n} = \frac{r}{n}\middle| p = .2\right]$					
$P\left[\frac{\tilde{r}}{n} = \frac{r}{n}\middle| p = .1\right]$					

6. Repeat exercise 4 for estimator $(\tilde{r} + 3)/(n + 6)$.

7. Compare the estimators of exercises 5 and 6 for $p = .5, .4, .2, .1$.

8. Consider the estimator of p which ignores the sample observations and estimates the value 1/2 for p no matter what $\tilde{r}$ is. Compare this estimator with the estimator $\tilde{r}/4$ for a binomial sample of size 4.

9. In a binomial sample of size $n = 2$ consider the estimator $d(\tilde{r})$ where the numbers $d(0)$, $d(1)$, and $d(2)$ are to be determined shortly to satisfy some requirement.

a. Show that

$$E[d(\tilde{r})|p] = d(0)(1-p)^2 + 2d(1)p(1-p) + d(2)p^2$$
$$= p^2[d(2) - 2d(1) + d(0)] + p[-2d(0) + 2d(1)] + d(0).$$

b. Show that $E[d(\tilde{r})|p] = p$, for all p, if and only if $d(0) = 0$, $d(1) = \frac{1}{2}$ and $d(2) = 1$. Interpret this result.

c. Show that $E[d(\tilde{r})|p] = p^2$, for all p, if and only if $d(0) = 0$, $d(1) = 0$ and $d(2) = 1$. Interpret. Observe that the unbiased estimator of p^2 is *not* the square of the unbiased estimator of p.

d. Show that $d(0)$, $d(1)$, and $d(2)$ cannot be chosen so that $E[d(\tilde{r})|p] = 1/p$, or $\sqrt{p}$, or $\log p$, for all p. Interpret and generalize.

10. Show that a decision maker who wants an unbiased estimator of $\tau = 1/p$ can obtain one by using Pascal sampling and the estimator $d'(n) = n/r$.

11. Verify (19.18), conditional expected quadratic loss.

12. Verify (19.20), conditional expected absolute error.

13. Verify (19.25), maximum admissible n.

14. Verify (19.29) and (19.30), best linear estimator.

15. Show that if the decision maker adopts a symmetric linear loss function of type (19.19) so that the *conditional* expected loss of any estimator in the family defined by $d(r) = (r + \alpha)/(n + \beta)$ is given by (19.20) then the *unconditional* expected loss with a binomial sample of size n is given by a formula identical to (19.20) except that the binomial cumulative functions $G_b(\cdot|n, p)$ are replaced by hyperbinomial cumulative functions $G_{hb}(\cdot|r', n', n)$.

16. Verify (19.43).

17. Let s be an unknown parameter that can take on one of the values $(-4, -1, 0, 1, 2)$. Since s is not directly observable an experiment is conducted which can result in one of the four possible z outcomes $(10, 20, 30, 40)$ where the conditional probability of each z outcome for each s value is given in the table below.

Sample	Possible state s				
outcome z	-4	-1	0	1	2
10	.6	.3	.2	.1	.0
20	.3	.4	.3	.2	.2
30	.1	.2	.3	.5	.4
40	.0	.1	.2	.2	.4
	1.0	1.0	1.0	1.0	1.0

a. What is the maximum likelihood estimate of s given $\tilde{z} = 10$? $\tilde{z} = 20$? $\tilde{z} = 30$? $\tilde{z} = 40$?

b. Denoting the maximum likelihood rule or estimator by d_1, compute

$l^*(d_1, s) \equiv E_{z|s}|d_1(\tilde{z}) - s|^2$

for $s = -4, -1, 0, 1, 2$.

c. Let d_2 be the rule where $d_2(10) = -1$, $d_2(20) = -5$, $d_2(30) = 1$, $d_2(40) = 1.5$. Compare the conditional expected loss functions of d_1 and d_2 using quadratic loss.

d. If d_3 were an unbiased estimator of s then what system of linear equations would the four numbers $d_3(10)$, $d_3(20)$, $d_3(30)$, and $d_3(40)$ have to satisfy?

e. For any decision rule d and any s let

$l^*(d|s) \equiv E_{z|s}[d(\tilde{z}) - s]^2.$

Let d_4 be the decision rule which minimizes the expression

$2l^*(d|-4) + 1l^*(d|-1) + 4l^*(d|0) + 3l^*(d|2).$

What is $d_4(20)$?
Hint Think about priors, posteriors, etc.

18. Using the data of exercise 9 suppose there are two possible acts a_1 and a_2 where a_1 is preferred if $s < 0$ and a_2 is preferred if $s \geq 0$.

a. Let d_1 be such that

$$d_1(z) \equiv \begin{cases} a_1 & \text{if} \quad z \in \{10, 20\} \\ a_2 & \text{if} \quad z \in \{30, 40\}. \end{cases}$$

What is the probability that d_1 will lead to an error for $s = -4$? $s = -1$? $s = 0$? $s = 1$? $s = 2$?

b. Repeat for d_2 where

$$d_2(z) \equiv \begin{cases} a_1 & \text{if} \quad z = 10 \\ a_2 & \text{if} \quad z \in \{20, 30, 40\}. \end{cases}$$

c. Assume that the seriousness of an error depends on the value of s. In particular, let the losses be as follows:

Value of s	-4	-1	0	1	2
Conditional loss of choosing the wrong act	100	10	5	20	40

Let $l^*(d|s)$ represent the conditional expected loss of rule d when s is true. Find $l^*(d_1|s)$ for all values of s. Repeat for d_2.

d. Describe how you would find the decision rule d_3 which would minimize the following index:

$$1l^*(d|-4) + 2l^*(d|-1) + 2l^*(d|0) + 4l^*(d|1) + 1l^*(d|2).$$

19. In a lot of 10,000 items the proportion p of defective items is unknown. If a defective item is not corrected before its insertion in a piece of electronic equipment an extra cost of \$2.00 will be incurred. Each item, however, can be hand-checked at a cost of \$0.10 per item and experience has shown that .80 of the defective items are corrected but .01 of the non-defective items are inadvertently damaged in the inspection process in a manner that the inspector does not suspect. The problem arises whether the lot of items should be accepted (a_1) or rejected and hand-checked (a_2).

a. Show that the expected cost of acceptance given p is

$$10{,}000 \times 2p = 20{,}000p.$$

b. Show that the expected cost of rejection given p is

$$\begin{aligned} &10{,}000[(.10) + (.20)p(2) + (1 - p)(.01)(2)] \\ &\quad = 10{,}000[.12 + .38p] = 1{,}200 + 3{,}800p. \end{aligned}$$

c. Show that if $p \leq p_b \doteq .074$ then the lot should be accepted outright but if $p > p_b$ then each item should be hand-checked.

d. Since p is unknown, a binomial sample of size $n = 20$ is taken and the decision maker decides to reject the lot if and only if the number of defectives $\tilde{r}$ is greater than $c = 1$. The inspection process is infallible and entails a cost of \$1 per item inspected, and all items inspected are perfectly adjusted. Plot (carefully) on a piece of graph paper the conditional probability that this decision rule will lead to an error for each of the following values of p: .01, .02, .03, .04, .05, .06, .08, .10, .15, and .20 and fair in a smooth curve.

e. Repeat this error analysis for $c = 0$ and 2.

f. Show that after inspection the conditional losses are given by:

$$l_t(a_1, p) = \begin{cases} 0 & \text{if} \quad p \leq p_b = .074 \\ 9{,}980(1.62)(p - p_b) & \text{if} \quad p > p_b, \end{cases}$$

and

$$l_t(a_2, p) = \begin{cases} 9{,}980(1.62)(p_b - p) & \text{if} \quad p \le p_b \\ 0 & \text{if} \quad p > p_b. \end{cases}$$

Draw these two conditional loss functions on the same piece of graph paper as used for parts d and e.

g. For each of the three decision rules plot on a separate piece of graph paper, using a different vertical scale, the conditional expected losses for p values: .01, .02, .03, .04, .05, .06, .08, .10, .15, and .20 and fair in a smooth curve (the "butterflies").

h. Repeat all parts for decision rules $(n = 50, c = 3)$, $(n = 50, c = 4)$, $(n = 50, c = 5)$.

i. Plot the total conditional expected loss functions for each of the six decision rules considered thus far.

j. Which of these six rules should the decision maker choose if he decides to give each of the following 10 intervals equal weight: [0,.009], (.009,.019], (.019,.030], (.030,.042], (.042,.056], (.056,.074], (.074,.096], (.096,.127], (.127,.177], (.177,1]?

20. Let $\mathscr{D}(e)$ be the class of all decision rules for experiment e. In the following exercise all decision rules are assumed to belong to $\mathscr{D}(e)$ for the same e which is held fixed.

Definition Decision rule d_1 dominates d_2 if $\bar{u}^*(e, d_1|s) \ge \bar{u}^*(e, d_2|s)$ for all s and $>$ holds for some s, or equivalently, in loss terms,

$$\bar{l}^*(e, d_1|s) \le \bar{l}^*(e, d_2|s),$$

for all s and $<$ holds for some s.

Definition Decision rule d^* is *admissible* if d^* is *not* dominated by any $d \in \mathscr{D}(e)$.

a. Show that d^* is admissible if and only if for any $d \in \mathscr{D}(e)$, there exists an s such that

$$\bar{l}^*(e, d^*|s) < \bar{l}^*(e, d|s).$$

b. Let the set of states S be finite and denote these states by $\{s_1, s_2, \ldots, s_n\}$. For a given prior distribution P' where $P'(s_i) > 0$ for all i (note the strict inequality!), let d^* be the optimal rule; that is, let d^* be such that

$$\sum \bar{l}^*(e, d^*|s_i)P'(s_i) \le \sum \bar{l}^*(e, d|s_i)P'(s_i)$$

for all $d \in \mathscr{D}(e)$. Show that d^* is admissible.

21. For the loss structure

$$l_t(\hat{p}, p) = (p - \hat{p})^2$$

show that

$$d^*(r) = \frac{r + \sqrt{n}/2}{n + \sqrt{n}}$$

is the minimax estimator, that is,

$$\max_p E_{\tilde{r}|p} l_t[d^*(\tilde{r}), p] \le \max_p E_{\tilde{r}|p} l_t[d(\tilde{r}), p]$$

for any estimator d.
Hint Use the fact that d^* is optimal for a beta prior with parameter $(\sqrt{n}/2, \sqrt{n})$ and that $E_{\tilde{r}|p} l_t[d^*(\tilde{r}), p]$ does not depend on p. Now argue contrapositively; i.e., "Suppose d^* were not minimax; then there would exist a d^{**} such that ..."

22. In estimating a Bernoulli parameter p it is sometimes appropriate to consider an error of a given magnitude more seriously if p is close to 0 or to 1 than if p is nearer to $\frac{1}{2}$. In those circumstances it is convenient to use the loss structure

$$l_t(\hat{p}, p) = \frac{(p - \hat{p})^2}{p(1 - p)}.$$

a. Show that the maximum likelihood decision rule $\hat{d}(r) = r/n$ is such that

$$E_{r|p} l_t[\hat{d}(\tilde{r}), p] = \frac{1}{n} \quad \text{for all } p.$$

b. Show that $\hat{d}$ is optimal against a rectangular prior distribution for this loss structure.

c. From (a) and (b) argue that for this loss structure $\hat{d}$ is a minimax estimator in the sense that

$$\max_p E_{r|p} l_t[\hat{d}(\tilde{r}), p] \le \max_p E_{r|p} l_t[d(\tilde{r}), p]$$

for any decision rule d.

23. Let $x_1, x_2, \ldots, x_n$ be n observations taken from a Normal distribution with *known* mean μ and unknown variance υ.

a. Show that the maximum likelihood estimate and the unbiased estimate of υ are both given by

$$w = \frac{1}{n} \sum (x_i - \mu)^2.$$

b. Consider the loss structure

$$l_t(\hat{\upsilon}, \upsilon) = (\hat{\upsilon} - \upsilon)^2.$$

Now for this class of estimators of the form

$$d_\lambda(\tilde{x}) = \lambda \sum (\tilde{x}_i - \mu)^2,$$

where λ is an arbitrary number, show that for any υ

$$E_{\tilde{x}|\upsilon} l_t[d_\lambda(\tilde{x}), \upsilon]$$

is minimized by letting $\lambda = 1/(n + 2)$ and that

$$E_{\tilde{x}|\upsilon} \left[\frac{1}{n + 2} \sum (x_i - \mu)^2 - \upsilon \right]^2 = \frac{2\upsilon^2}{n + 2}.$$

Hint First, use the fact that

$$\frac{d}{d\lambda} E_{x|\upsilon} l_t[d_\lambda(\tilde{x}), \upsilon] = E_{x|\upsilon} \frac{d}{d\lambda} l_t[d_\lambda(\tilde{x}, \upsilon)];$$

second, using the fact that $E_{x_i|\mu}(x_i - \mu)^4 = 3\upsilon^2$, show that

$$E[\sum (x_i - \mu)^2]^2 = n(n + 2)\upsilon^2.$$

24. Let the set of states be $S = \{s_1, s_2\}$; let the set of outcomes of an experiment e be $Z = \{z_1, \ldots, z_m\}$; denote $P(\tilde{z} = z_i | s_j)$ by p_{ij} for $i = 1, \ldots, m$ and $j = 1, 2$; let there be two acts a_1 and a_2 and assume that the loss structure is given by

		ACT	
		a_1	a_2
State	s_1	0	A
	s_2	B	0

where $A > 0$, $B > 0$. A randomized decision rule δ assigns to each outcome z_i a probability δ_i that act a_2 will be accepted; thus if z_i is observed and $\delta_i = 1$, then a_2 is chosen.

a. Show that if s_1 is true, the probability that decision rule δ will lead to an error is

$$\alpha(\delta) = \sum p_{i1}\delta_i.$$

b. Show that if s_2 is true the probability that decision rule δ will lead to an error is

$$\beta(\delta) = \sum p_{i2}(1 - \delta_i) = 1 - \sum p_{i2}\delta_i.$$

c. Suppose we now pose the following problem: Given a value α^*, choose a decision rule δ to minimize $\beta(\delta)$ subject to the constraint $\alpha(\delta) \le \alpha^*$. Show that this problem is equivalent to the special linear programming problem: Choose nonnegative values δ_1, $\delta_2, \ldots, \delta_m$ subject to the linear inequalities

$$\delta_i \le 1, \qquad i = 1, \ldots, m,$$

and

$$\sum p_{i1}\delta_i \le \alpha^*,$$

to maximize the linear form

$$\sum p_{i2}\delta_i.$$

d. Show that the solution to the problem posed in (c) can be characterized as follows: Define $\lambda_i \equiv p_{i2}/p_{i1}$ and for convenience of notation relabel the zs such that $\lambda_1 \ge \lambda_2 \ge \cdots \ge \lambda_m$. With this ordering let i_0 be such that

$$\sum_{j=1}^{i_0-1} p_{j1} \le \alpha^* < \sum_{j=1}^{i_0} p_{j1}.$$

Choose $\delta_i = 1$ for all $i < i_0$, let δ_{i_0} be such that

$$\sum_{j=1}^{i_0-1} p_{j1} + \delta_{i_0} p_{i_0 1} = \alpha^*,$$

and let $\delta_i = 0$ for all $i > i_0$.

e. Let $B(\alpha^*)$ denote the minimum value of $\beta(\delta)$ when δ is constrained such that $\alpha(\delta) \le \alpha^*$. Using the notation of (d), show that

$$\frac{d}{d\alpha^*} B(\alpha^*) = -\lambda_{i_0}.$$

(For readers who know the theory of linear programming, show that λ_{i_0} is the dual variable corresponding to the primal inequality $\sum p_{i1}\delta_i \le \alpha^*$.)

f. A *likelihood ratio rule* (l.r.r.) with index k is defined to be a rule such that $\delta_i = 1$ if $\lambda_i > k$, $\delta_i = 0$ if $\lambda_i < k$, and δ_i is arbitrary (i.e., not prescribed) if $\lambda_i = k$. Observe that in (d) the optimal rule is a l.r.r. with index λ_{i_0}. Now let the states have prior probabilities $P'(s_1) = \pi'_1$ and $P'(s_2) = \pi'_2 = 1 - \pi'_1$. Show that the rule that minimizes

$$\pi'_1 A\alpha(\delta) + \pi'_2 B\beta(\delta)$$

is a l.r.r. rule with index $\pi'_1 A/(\pi'_2 B)$. Establish this result by substituting for the expression for $\alpha(\delta)$ and $\beta(\delta)$ and minimizing.

g. Obtain the same result as in part (f) by an extensive-form analysis. That is, argue that if z_i is observed the posterior probabilities of the states are

$$\pi''_{1i} \equiv P(s_1|z_i) = \frac{p_{i1}\pi'_1}{p_{i1}\pi'_1 + p_{i2}\pi'_2},$$

$$\pi''_{i2} \equiv P(s_2|z_i) = \frac{p_{i2}\pi'_2}{p_{i2}\pi'_2 + p_{i1}\pi'_1};$$

then find the expected loss with each act and choose accordingly.

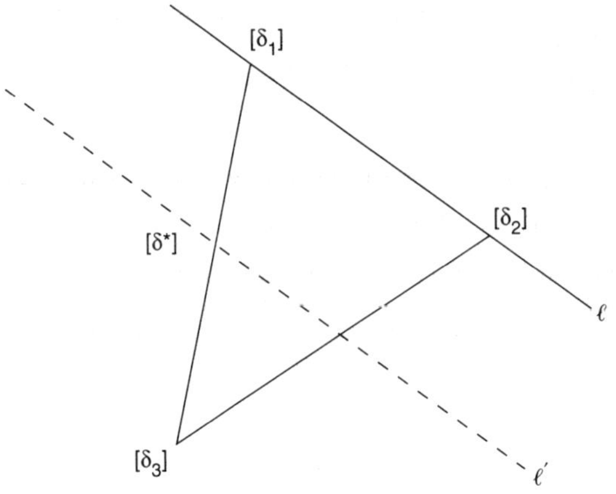

Figure 19E.1

h. Show that any l.r.r rule with index $0 < k < \infty$ minimizes $\pi'_1 A\alpha(\delta) + \pi'_2 B\beta(\delta)$ for some value of π'_1. Interpret.

25. Consider once again the two-state, two-action problem given in the previous exercise. Any decision rule δ can be characterized by its error performance $[\alpha(\delta), \beta(\delta)]$, which can be plotted as a point (α, β) in two-space. Let R denote the set of achievable (α, β) points. A basic problem is: How should the decision maker select the best (α, β) pair from R? Leaving aside the question of achievability for the moment, let us first examine the question of preferences and indifferences in the α, β plane.

a. Show that indifference curves in the (α, β) plane that are not straight are *not* reasonable.
Hint Suppose that δ' yields (α', β'), δ'' yields (α'', β'') and that δ' is indifferent to δ''; that is, $(\alpha', \beta') \sim (\alpha'', \beta'')$, so that both points are on a common indifference curve. Now argue that $[(\alpha' + \alpha'')/2, (\beta + \beta'')/2)]$ should be on the *same* indifference curve.
Second-order Hint Consider the strategy of tossing a coin, heads you take δ', and tails you take δ''.

b. Let l be an indifference line in the α, β plane and let (α^*, β^*) be a point not on l. Argue that the indifference line through (α^*, β^*) should be parallel to l.
Hint In the accompanying figure denote (α, β) points by their associated decision rules; thus δ^* gives rise to (α^*, β^*), δ_i gives rise to (α_i, β_i). Let δ_i be as chosen in the figure, and assume that δ^* is indifferent to a decision rule that gives a p chance at δ_1 and a $(1 - p)$ chance at δ_3, for a suitably chosen p. Now argue that therefore δ^* should also be indifferent to a decision rule that gives a p chance at δ_2 and a $(1 - p)$ chance at δ_3, for the *same p value*, and show that this latter decision rule has an (α, β) which lies on a line l' that is parallel to l and passes through (α^*, β^*).

c. Show that the family of indifference lines can be expressed in the form

$$p_1\alpha + p_2\beta = \text{constant},$$

where $p_1 \geq 0$, $p_2 \geq 0$, $p_1 + p_2 = 1$, and that along any contour line the substitution rate

$$\frac{d\beta}{d\alpha} = -\frac{p_1}{p_2}.$$

d. Argue from (a), (b), (c), and exercise 24 that instead of posing the decision problem in terms of minimizing $\beta(\delta)$ subject to a condition $\alpha(\delta) \leq \alpha^*$, it is more meaningful to set up a desired substitution rate between β and α and to use an l.r.r. rule with the absolute value of this substitution rate as the cutoff index.

26. You are offered the chance to bet \$10 on the flip of a coin that in all likelihood is biased. The rules are that you can call heads or tails but before you decide which choice to make, you are allowed n preliminary tosses with this coin at a cost of $c\ n$. Assume that outcomes of repeated tosses can be thought of as a Bernoulli process where the long-run proportion of heads is p.

Let d_n be the decision rule which uses n preliminary tosses and calls H if the number of heads is at least $n/2$. For rule d_n plot the conditional expected gain from d_n for a given p as a function of p.

Show that the procedure that maximizes the minimum gain is d_0.

If $\tilde{p}$ is beta $(1, 2)$ and $c = .01$ what is the optimal d_n?

Appendix: Statistical Decision Theory from an Objectivistic Viewpoint

The purpose of this appendix is to define certain concepts arising naturally in objectivistic (non-Bayesian) approaches to decision problems.

The Basic Problem

We follow the notation of chapter 6. We posit the existence of a pre-specified:

i. Set of *States*, $S = \{s\}$

ii. Set of *terminal acts*, $A = \{a\}$

iii. Set of possible *experiments*, $E = \{e\}$

iv. Set of potential outcomes of all experiments, $Z = \{z\}$

v. Utility function u, where $u(e, z, a, s)$ is the decision maker's utility value for the path (e, z, a, s).

vi. Set of conditional probability measures $P_{z|e,s}$ for the rv $\tilde{z}$ given (e, s). In this objectivistic analysis we do not assume a (prior) probability measure over S.

Let $D = \{d\}$ be the set of *decision rules* for experimentation and action. Thus d specifies an experiment e_d, and depending on the outcome z, specifies an action $d(z)$. The central problem is to characterize "desirable" decision rules, d.

For any decision rule d, let

$$u(d, s) \equiv E_{z|s} u(e_d, \tilde{z}, d(\tilde{z}), s).$$

We assume throughout that all expectations exist and are finite. For a given d, we define the *performance profile* of d as the function $u(d, \cdot)$ on S.

Admissibility and Complete Classes

Definitions One decision rule *dominates* another if it is as good in every state s and better in at least one state. Specifically, d_1 dominates d_2 if $U(d_1, s) \geq U(d_2, s)$ for all s, with inequality for some s. A decision rule is *inadmissible*, or *dominated*, if there is an available decision rule which dominates it. It is *admissible*, or *nondominated*, otherwise, that is, if no available decision rule dominates it. In economic theory an admissible rule is often called an *efficient* rule or a *Pareto-efficient* rule. A class of decision rules is *complete* if every available decision rule outside the class is dominated by at least one rule in the class.

One of the principal problems in objectivistic decision theory is to characterize a minimal complete class of decision rules. As an example, consider the case of a data-generating process that yields i.i.d. observations $(\tilde{z}_1, \ldots, \tilde{z}_n)$ each with a Normal distribution with unknown mean μ and variance v; let A comprise two actions $\{a_1, a_2\}$ with linear loss, and where a_1 is preferred if and only if μ is greater than some breakeven value μ_b. A complete class of decision rules might be of the following form: take a sample of size n; compute the sample mean, m, and choose a_1 if and only if $m \geq c$. The class of rules of form (n, c) can be shown to be complete.

In the absence of a compactness condition (in Euclidean space compact $\equiv$ [closed and bounded]) there may be no admissible decision rules.

Representation in Euclidean Space

When there are only finitely many states s, we may represent the situation as follows. Suppose there are r states, $s_1, s_2, \ldots, s_r$. For any decision rule d, define an r-dimensional utility vector $\boldsymbol{u}$ whose components are the utility values arising in the r states:

$$\boldsymbol{u} = [U(d, s_1) \ldots U(d, s_r)]^t.$$

where the superscript t means *transpose* of the row vector. In this case $\boldsymbol{u}$ is a column vector. The original setup is essentially equivalent to the following. Nature chooses an integer i, $1 < i \leq r$. In ignorance of i, you choose a utility vector $\boldsymbol{u}$ from the set of available utility vectors. Your utility value is then u_i, the ith component of $\boldsymbol{u}$. The one inequivalence between this and the original setup is that different decision rules can correspond to the same point $\boldsymbol{u}$. This happens, however, only when your utility value for these rules is the same in every state, in which case they are essentially equivalent.

In this representation, $\boldsymbol{u}$ dominates $\boldsymbol{v}$ if $\boldsymbol{u}$ is the northeast of $\boldsymbol{v}$, that is, $u_i \geq v_i$ for all i and $\boldsymbol{u} \neq \boldsymbol{v}$. (For illustration where $r = 2$, see figure 19.10A.) An available $\boldsymbol{u}$ is inadmissible if there is an available $\boldsymbol{w}$ northeast of it, and admissible otherwise (see figure 19.10B, C). A subset of the set of available $\boldsymbol{u}$s is *complete* if every available $\boldsymbol{u}$ is southwest of some member of the subset.

The set of decision rules whose associated vectors are on the darkened boundary of figure B is a complete class; and since no subset is also complete, it is a minimal complete class.

Mixed Strategies and Convexity

Suppose two decision rules have utility vectors $\boldsymbol{u}$ and $\boldsymbol{v}$, and consider the *mixed strategy* of selecting $\boldsymbol{u}$ (or the corresponding decision rule) with probability α and $\boldsymbol{v}$ with probability $1 - \alpha$, this selection being made independently of all other events in the problem. (See figure 19.10D.) This strategy has utility vector $\alpha\boldsymbol{u} + (1 - \alpha)\boldsymbol{v}$. This is a vector on the straight line segment with endpoints $\boldsymbol{u}$ and $\boldsymbol{v}$. As α ranges from 0 to 1, every vector on this segment is obtained.

Assumption We assume henceforth that any such probability mixture of two available strategies is also available. Then the set of available utility vectors $\boldsymbol{u}$ is convex, as in the figures depicted.

Remarks (1) Starting with a set of "pure strategies" and mixing as above gives strategies which are mixtures of two pure strategies. Mixing these gives mixtures of four pure strategies, etc. Any utility vector obtainable by any amount of mixing can be obtained by mixing $r + 1$ or fewer of the initial "pure" strategies. (2) In a situation where the decision rule involves a choice of terminal act for each possible outcome z of an experiment, one might consider choosing a terminal act according to some probability distribution, after observing z. Under the previous assumption, however, this does not enlarge the set of available utility vectors $\boldsymbol{u}$: mixing after observing z does not accomplish anything which cannot also be accomplished by mixing whole decision rules.

Relation among Concepts

The first relation we shall mention follows immediately from the definitions.

Theorem 1 All admissible decision rules are in every complete class.

The converse is not even close to true, since a complete class can include any decision rule whatever. Note also that, in the absence of suitable "compactness," some inadmissible decision rules may not be dominated by any admissible rule but only by other inadmissible rules. Thus the class of admissible decision rules may not be complete. It follows from Theorem 1, however, that if the class of admissible rules is complete then it is a minimal complete class, and conversely, if there is a minimal complete class then it is the class of admissible rules. In this case, the dominance idea leads to consideration of exactly the class of admissible strategies, no more no less.

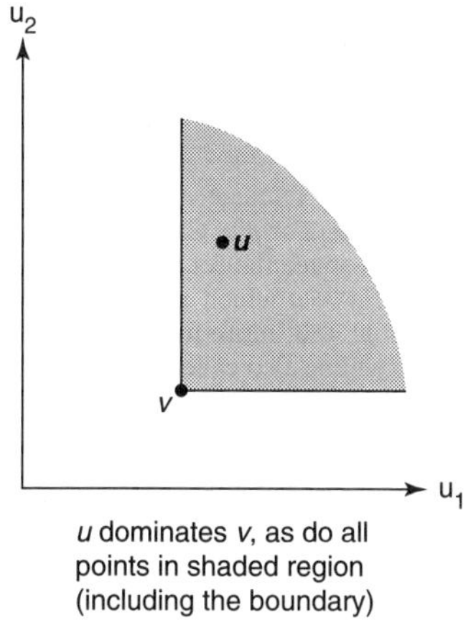

Figure 19.10A

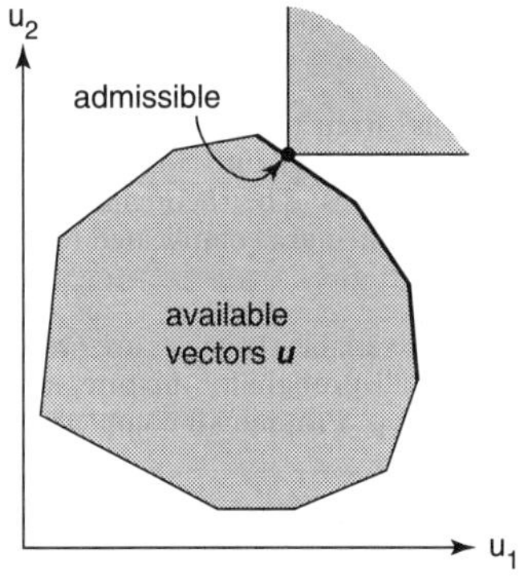

Figure 19.10B

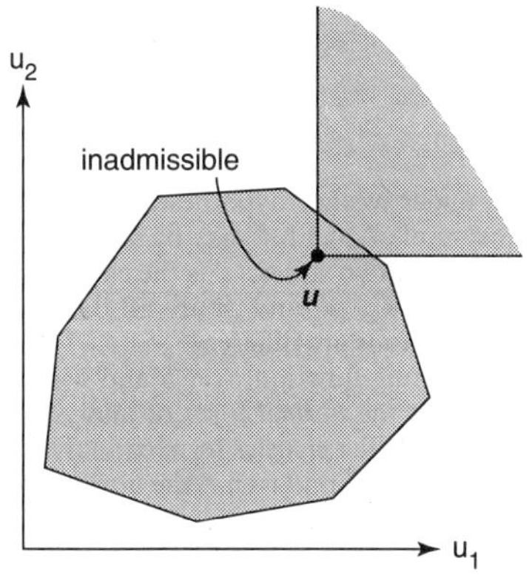

Figure 19.10C

Bayes Rules and Complete Classes

Keep in mind that thus far we have not resorted to the use of any prior probability distribution over S.

Let the state space be of dimension r so that the available vectors are points in Euclidean r-space. In a purely formal way introduce a weighting vector $\boldsymbol{p} = [p_1 \dots p_r]$, where $p_i \geq 0$, and $\sum p_i = 1$ and evaluate available $\boldsymbol{u}$s by the index $\sum p_i u_i$ or $\boldsymbol{p}'\boldsymbol{u}$. Call this the expected utility of $\boldsymbol{u}$ with respect to the weighting vector $\boldsymbol{p}$. In the u-space the set of $\boldsymbol{u}$s which yield a common value of $\boldsymbol{p}'\boldsymbol{u}$ is a hyperplane. (See figure 19.10E.) A $\boldsymbol{u}$ which maximizes $\boldsymbol{p}'\boldsymbol{u}$ will be called "Bayes" with respect to the weighting function $\boldsymbol{p}$; and, more fully, any decision rule whose associated performance index $u(d, \cdot)$ is "Bayes" will be also called a Bayes rule. Thus a Bayes strategy with respect to $\boldsymbol{p}$ maximizes $\boldsymbol{p}'\boldsymbol{u}$ among available utility vectors $\boldsymbol{u}$. For fixed $\boldsymbol{p}$, as a function of $\boldsymbol{u}$, the contours of $\boldsymbol{p}'\boldsymbol{u}$ are parallel hyperplanes perpendicular to $\boldsymbol{p}$. (See figure E.) The hyperplanes where $\boldsymbol{p}'\boldsymbol{u}$ has larger values lie above those where it has smaller values. Thus an available utility vector $\boldsymbol{v}$ is a Bayes strategy with respect to $\boldsymbol{p}$ if and only if all available utility vectors $\boldsymbol{u}$ lie on or below the hyperplane through $\boldsymbol{v}$ perpendicular to $\boldsymbol{p}$.

We are now prepared for Theorem 2.

Theorem 2 If the number of states is finite, then

$$\mathscr{B}_+ \subset \mathscr{A} \subset \mathscr{B}$$

where $\mathscr{A}$ is the set of all admissible decision rules, $\mathscr{B}$ is the set of all Bayes rules, and $\mathscr{B}_+$ is the set of all decision rules which are Bayes with respect to some distribution attaching positive probability to every state.

This theorem and the next two are "obvious" from the geometric representations. (See figure 19.10G.) The geometrical ideas can be translated into algebraic/analytic terms to provide rigorous proofs, for which see the references. The theorems can be extended to infinitely many states, but the conditions then required are complicated to state, though not very restrictive.

Theorem 3 If the number of states is finite, if all available strategies are probability mixtures of some one finite set of decision rules, and if all probability mixtures of these rules are available (as assumed above), then $\mathscr{B}_+ = \mathscr{A}$ and is a (minimal) complete class. (See figure 19.10H.)

In this case, the set of available utility vectors is a closed, bounded, convex polyhedron.

The next theorem involves topological considerations and hence will be stated only in terms of the vector representation. It involves the closure of $\mathscr{B}_+$, that is, $\mathscr{B}_+$ together with its limit points.

Theorem 4 If the number of states is finite and if the set of available utility vectors is closed, bounded, and (as assumed above) convex, then

$$\mathscr{B}_+ \subset \mathscr{A} \subset [\text{closure of } \mathscr{B}_+] \subset \mathscr{B}$$

and $\mathscr{A}$ is a (minimal) complete class.

This relates admissible to Bayes rules under weaker hypotheses than Theorem 3. Under these weaker hypotheses, $\mathscr{B}_+$, $\mathscr{A}$, the closure of $\mathscr{B}_+$, and $\mathscr{B}$ may be all different, regardless of the number of states, except that if there are just two states, $\mathscr{A}$ is the closure of $\mathscr{B}_+$. See figure 19.10I for an example with two states where $\mathscr{B}_+$, $\mathscr{A}$, and $\mathscr{B}$ are all different; figure 19.10J depicts an example with three states where all four are different.

Suppose we agree on a (normalized) weighting function over S and wish to find its associated Bayes decision rule. We can use either the *normal* form of analysis, which uses the weighting function at the end of the analysis, or the *extensive* form of analysis, which uses the weighting function at the beginning. In particular, for a given e, the normal form involves the process:

$$\max_d E_s E_{z|s} u(e, z, d(\tilde{z}), s),$$

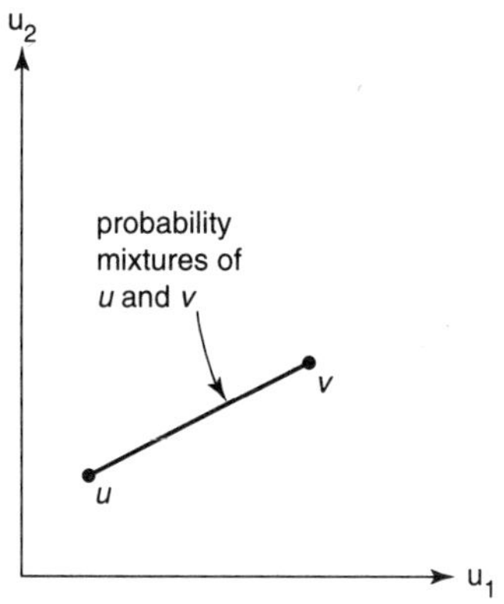

Figure 19.10D

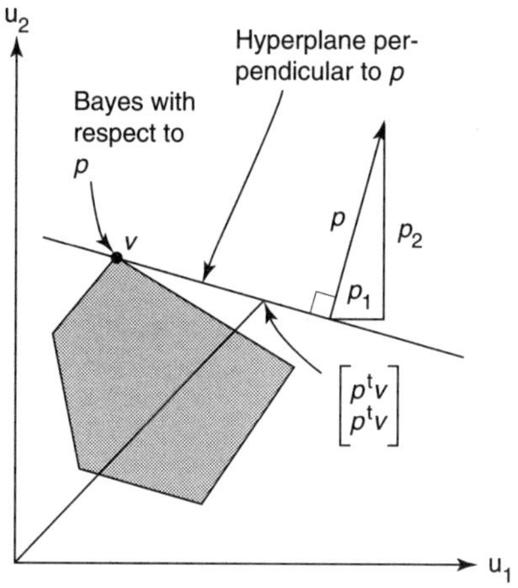

Figure 19.10E

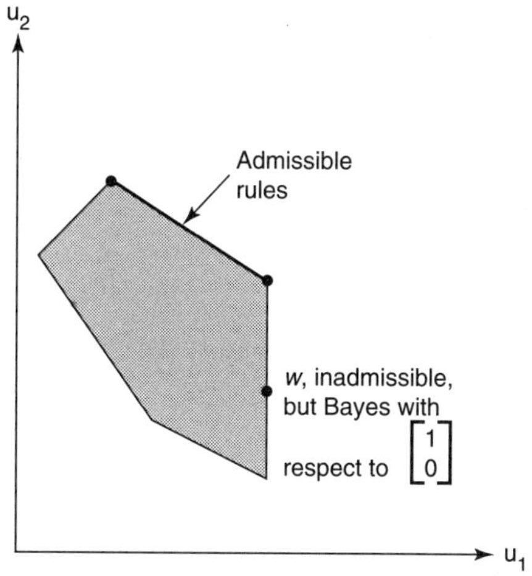

Figure 19.10F

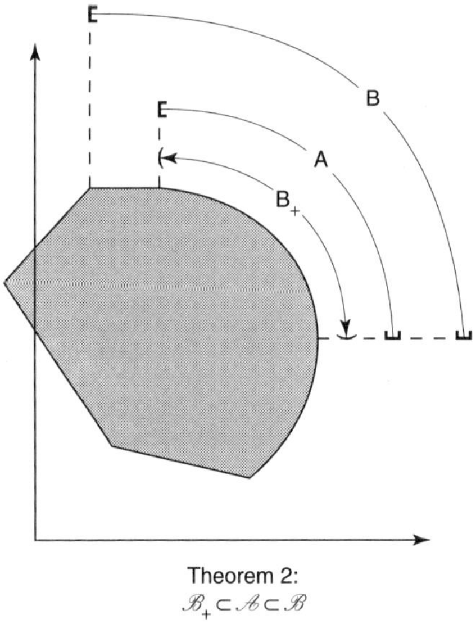

Figure 19.10G

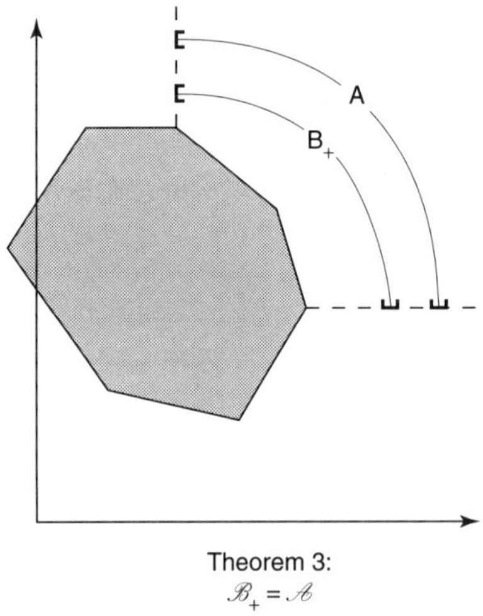

Figure 19.10H

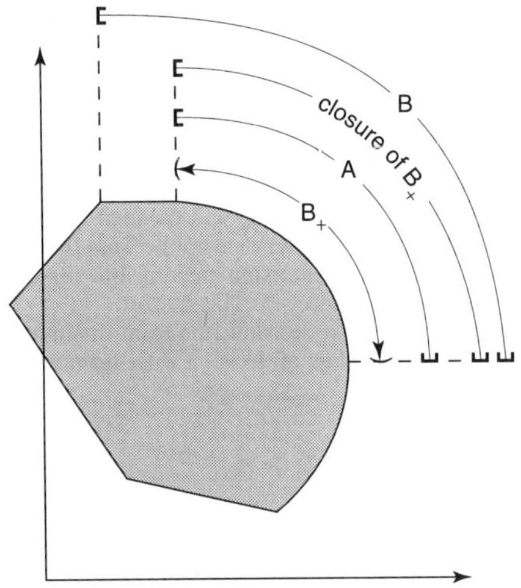

Theorem 4:
$\mathscr{B}_+ \subset \mathscr{A} \subset$ closure of $\mathscr{B}_+ \subset \mathscr{B}$
Example of $\mathscr{B}_+ \neq \mathscr{A} \neq \mathscr{B}$

Figure 19.10I

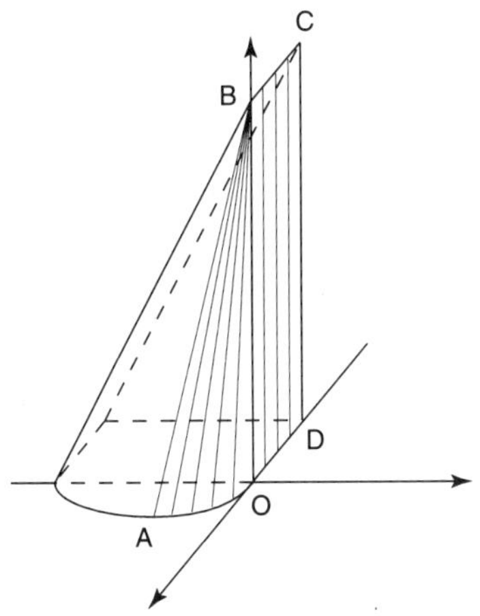

Example of $\mathscr{B}_+ \neq \mathscr{A} \neq$ closure of $\mathscr{B}_+ \neq \mathscr{B}$
in 3 dimensions (after Blackwell and Girschick, 1954)

$\mathscr{B}_+$ = surface region OAB excluding all edges
$\mathscr{A}$ = OAB including edges OA and AB with points A and B but not O
closure of $\mathscr{B}_+$ = OAB including all edges and vertices
$\mathscr{B}$ = OABCD including all edges and vertices

Figure 19.10J

where $E_{z|s}$ uses the conditional distribution of $\tilde{z}$ given s; the extensive form involves the process:

$$E'_z \max_{d|z} E''_{s|z} u(e, z, d(z), s),$$

where $E''_{s|z}$ involves the posterior df of $\tilde{s}$, given z, and E'_z involves the marginal distribution of $\tilde{z}$. Both yield the same result. In practice it often is easier to find the optimum, d, using the extensive form of analysis. So a lot of time and energy is expended by objectivists using various prior-to-posterior distributions to find Bayes rules, not because they believe in using these prior, normalized weighting functions for decision making but for characterizing a minimal (or close to minimal) complete class of decision rules.

But now how does the objectivist decide on a decision rule from the (minimal) complete class of decision rules? There may be a huge class of decision rules from which to choose a "best" member. That's our next topic.

Choice of a Decision Rule for the Complete Class

We shall describe three ways to proceed to choose a "best" rule from the minimal complete class.

Choose the Weighting Function as a Prior Judgmental Distribution and Treat it Seriously

This is the preferred alternative we subjectivists espouse. Our reasons for this "rational" choice were given in chapters 2 and 3.

Use of Minimax Decision Rules

A decision rule d is *maximin* if it maximizes the $\min_s u(d, s)$ over all decision rules. Since in most presentations of statistical decision theory loss or disutilities are featured, the roles of max and min are interchanged and a decision rule will be said to be *minimax* if it minimizes the $\max_s l(d, s)$ over all decision rules—where we use l mnemonic for loss. Even though we shall stick with u, we shall succumb to the usual terminology and refer to the rule, which is really maximin, as the "minimax rule."

We can think of the decision problem as a two-person game between the decision maker, who controls d, and "nature," who "controls" s. Corresponding to the joint choice of d and s, the payoff to the decision maker is $u(d, s)$.

The geometry of minimax can be described as follows: Let T_z be the set of vectors $\boldsymbol{u}$ with no component smaller than z, that is, $T_z = \{\boldsymbol{u} : u_i \geq z \text{ for all } i\}$. T_z is a corner-shaped region with vertex at $[z \cdots z]^t$. (See figure 19.10K.) As z varies, T_z slides along the equiangular line through the origin. Slide T_z along this line (from a high value of z downwards) until it just touches the set of available vectors $\boldsymbol{u}$. Then T_z is a just touching corner set. Call this value z^* and label T_{z^*} by T^*. For this T^*, no available vector can be interior to T^*, and an available vector is minimax if and only if it is on the boundary of T^*. (See figures 19.10L, M, and N.)

Two-Person Zero-Sum Games

Suppose that the state s is chosen by an opposing player instead of neutral nature. Suppose further that the rules of the game are such that what you win your opponent loses and vice versa and that you and your opponent both have linear utility functions. (If it happened in some other way that your utility for any possible outcome is the negative of your opponent's, that would suffice.) Such a situation is called a two-person zero-sum game. If your opponent is sophisticated enough, then we shall see in Theorem 5 that there is a natural sense in which it is optimum for you to use a minimax rule (and for her to use a rule which is minimax from her point of view).[3]

---

3. If we departed from the standard terminology, we would prefer to say that you would choose a maximin rule and your opponent would choose her minimax rule (in terms of your payoffs).

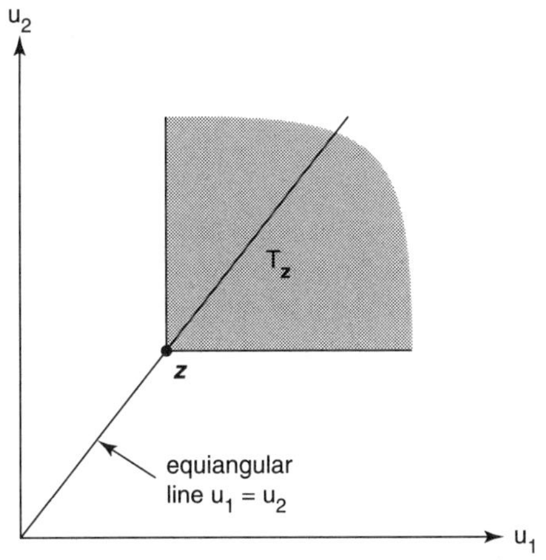

Figure 19.10K

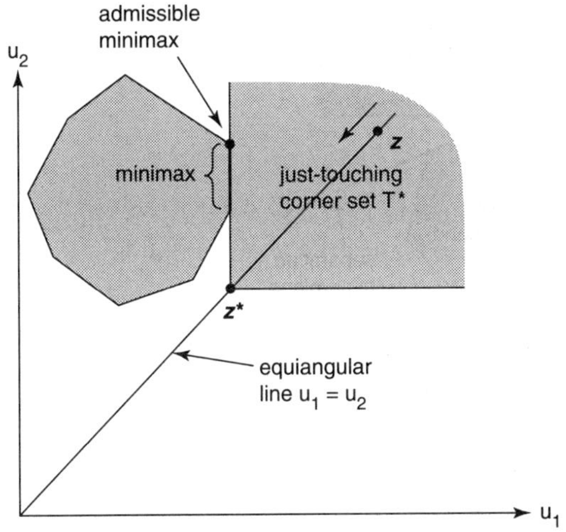

Figure 19.10L

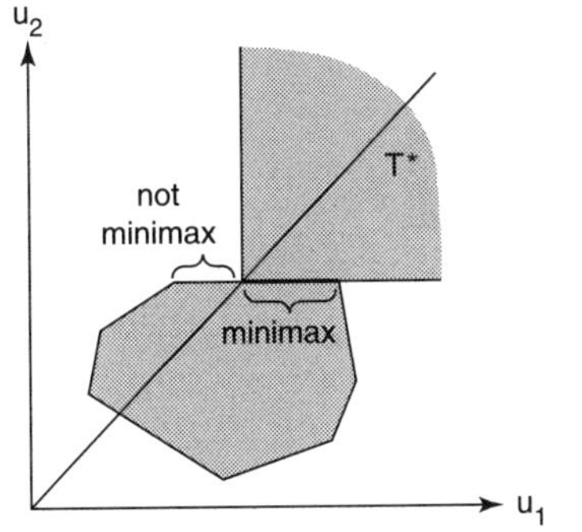

Figure 19.10M

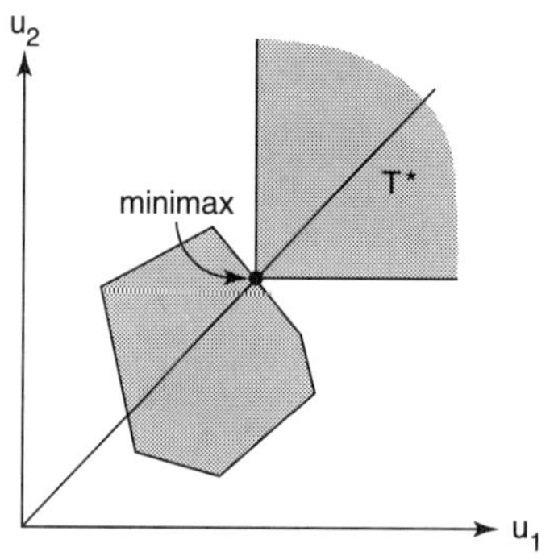

Figure 19.10N

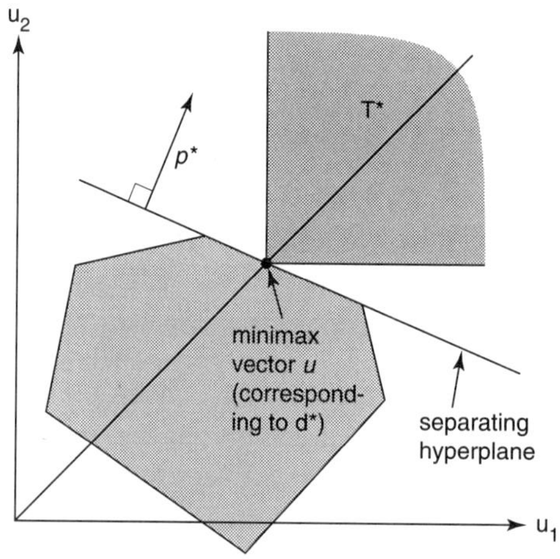

Figure 19.10O

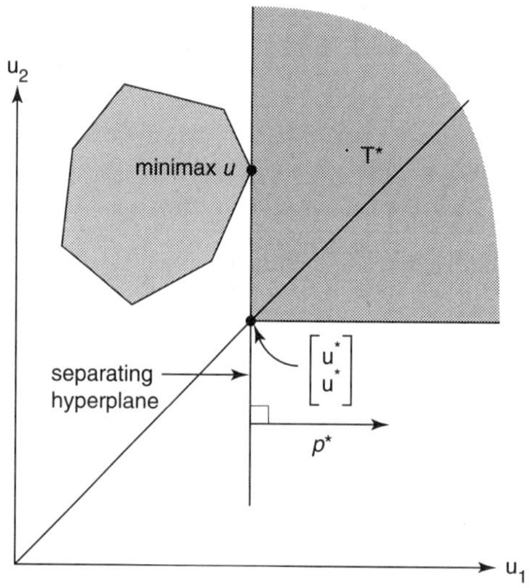

Figure 19.10P

We now state the fundamental theorem of two-person zero-sum games, known as the Minimax Theorem.

Theorem 5 Under the hypotheses of Theorem 3 or 4, there is a decision rule d^* and a probability distribution $\boldsymbol{p}^*$ over states such that

(1) $U(d^*, s) \geq u^* \geq E[U(d, \tilde{S})\}$

for all s and d, where $\tilde{S}$ has distribution $\boldsymbol{p}^*$ and

(2) $u^* = \max_d \min_s U(d, s) = E\{U(d^*, \tilde{S})\}$.

A decision rule d^* is minimax if and only if it satisfies the left inequality in (1) for all s. For every minimax rule d^* and every $\boldsymbol{p}^*$ satisfying the right inequality in (1) for all d, both (1) and (2) hold and d^* is Bayes with respect to $\boldsymbol{p}^*$.

Theorem 5 says that you can guarantee yourself expected utility at least u^* using d^* and nature can prevent you from having expected utility more than u^* by using $\boldsymbol{p}^*$, which is thus a *least favorable* distribution for nature from your point of view. Just as d^* is minimax and is Bayes with respect to $\boldsymbol{p}^*$, if nature's utility is the negative of yours, then $\boldsymbol{p}^*$ is minimax for nature and is a Bayes rule for nature with respect to d^*. Thus, in a two-person zero-sum game between sophisticated players, each should presumably use a minimax rule: you can thereby guarantee yourself at least u^* no matter what your opponent does, while she can be sure to hold you to u^* no matter what you do.

The essential step in the geometric proof of Theorem 5 is to construct a hyperplane separating the set of all available utility vectors $\boldsymbol{u}$ from the just touching corner set T^* (or, strictly, the interior of T^*) and let $\boldsymbol{p}^*$ be a perpendicular to the hyperplane. The decision rule d^* can be any minimax rule, that is, any available $\boldsymbol{u}$ in T^*. In figure 19.10O there is a unique separating hyperplane; all $\boldsymbol{u}$ vectors on the segment from A to B are Bayes with respect to $\boldsymbol{p}^*$. Figure 19.10P depicts the case where $\boldsymbol{p}^*$ places zero weight on state s_2; in this case the minimax rule does not have equal payoffs for all states. In figure 19.10N the separating hyperplane and therefore the least favorable distribution $\boldsymbol{p}^*$ is not unique. In figure 19.10L the vector $\boldsymbol{u}$ on the line segment A to B are all minimax but only A is admissible. In figure 19.10M some of the rules that are Bayes with respect to the least favorable distribution are minimax but others are not.

Minimax rules do not require the assessment by the decision maker of a judgmental probability distribution over the set of states, S. In this sense minimax rules are objective. They also have the property that they are Bayes rules with respect to a least favorable weighting distribution. But if this least favorable weighting distribution is judgmentally implausible, then doing best against it may be unappealing. Luce and Raiffa (1957, pp. 315–16) cite a case where the least favorable distribution puts all its weight on a single state (in a continuum of states) and thereby discourages the accumulation of experimental evidence (no matter how slight the cost!) to dispel this prior judgment.

Minimax Regret Rules

Minimax *regret* rules, a variation of minimax rules, have been introduced in the faint hope that it would generally lead to a satisfactory rule in ordinary decision situations without the use of subjective probabilities. Unfortunately, it too leads to unappealing rules in many situations. These rules violate the principle of irrelevant alternatives. Examples can be concocted where d^* is the optimal (i.e., minimax regret) rule but d^* although still available is no longer optimal when the class of decision rules is restricted to a smaller class. For example, in a given problem the best sample size might be 35, but if the sample size is restricted to less than 50, then the optimum (i.e., minimax regret rule) can shift to 25.

Formally, we define the *regret* ($R(d, s)$ as the opportunity loss (in units of utility) for using decision rule d when the state is s, by

$R(d, s) \equiv \max_D u(D, s) - u(d, s)$.

The rule d^* is a minimax regret rule if it minimizes the maximum regret, that is,

$\min_d \max_s R(d, s)$ occurs at d^*.

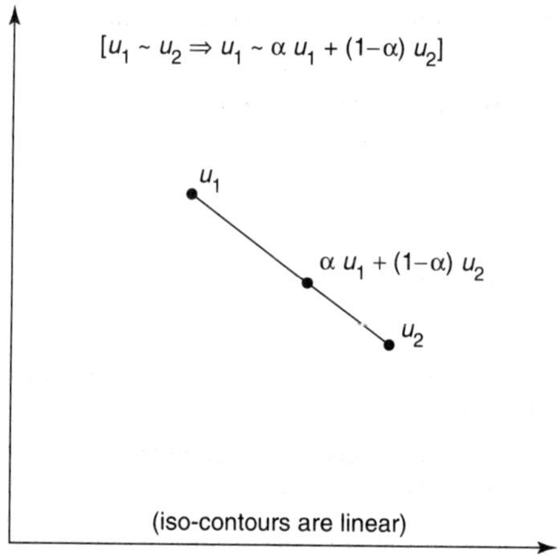

Figure 19.10Q

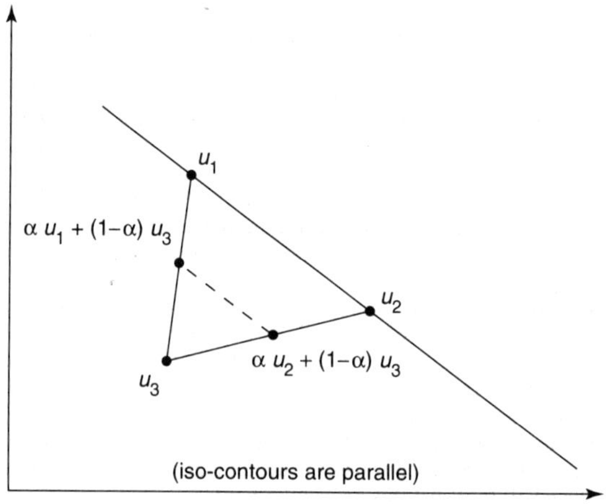

Figure 19.10R

Indifference Contours

Suppose that there are r states and the available $\boldsymbol{u}$s form a closed, bounded set in Euclidean r-space. Let our task be to choose a "best" $\boldsymbol{u}$ from this available set. When we introduce a weighting vector $\boldsymbol{p}$ and minimize $\boldsymbol{p}'\boldsymbol{u}$, we implicitly are assuming that equal-utility contours (or indifference contours) are parallel hyperplanes. But why should we restrict ourselves to such an indifference structure? Akin to the Neyman-Pearson theory, for example, we might impose a restriction on some components and subject to this we may wish to maximize a weighted average of the other components. Or we may wish to impose some lexicographic ordering: first worry about the performance on state s_1; if ties, look at state s_2; if ties on s_1 and s_2, look at s_3; etc. Or, as in elementary books in economics, we may choose to use nonlinear contours. Since the measurement on each component is assumed in our case to be in utility units, we assert that *indifference curves should be parallel hyperplanes*, and once that rationalization is accepted it is not difficult to argue for the use of a subjective prior weighting distribution.

Roughly the argument for linearity of contours goes as follows: if $\boldsymbol{u}_1$ and $\boldsymbol{u}_2$ are equally desirable, so should the mixed (randomized) rule be that selects $\boldsymbol{u}_1$ with probability α and $\boldsymbol{u}_2$ with probability $(1 - \alpha)$. But this means that

$$\boldsymbol{u}_1 \sim \boldsymbol{u}_2 \Rightarrow \boldsymbol{u}_1 \sim [\alpha\boldsymbol{u}_1 + (1 - \alpha)\boldsymbol{u}_2], \qquad 0 \leq \alpha \leq 1.$$

and therefore the indifference contours must be linear. (See figure 19.10Q.) Now if $\boldsymbol{u}_1 \sim \boldsymbol{u}_2$, we also deem it reasonable (as in the substitution axiom of chapter 3) that

$$\boldsymbol{u}_1 \sim \boldsymbol{u}_2 \Rightarrow [\alpha\boldsymbol{u}_1 + (1 - \alpha)\boldsymbol{u}_3] \sim [\alpha\boldsymbol{u}_2 + (1 - \alpha)\boldsymbol{u}_3] \quad \text{for all } \boldsymbol{u}_3.$$

This implies that indifference hyperplanes must be parallel. (See figure 19.10R.) This argument is spelled out more systematically for $r = 2$ as exercise 25 of chapter 19.

20 Classical Methods

Many people do not accept the axioms on which this book is based. It is useful to know something about the methods they have developed, both because these methods are in widespread use and because they are often interpretable and useful from our point of view.

20.1 Models and "Objective" Probabilities

We have examined problems almost entirely in what is called the Bayesian framework. We may observe a rv $\tilde{z}$, say. The state of nature, insofar as it is unobservable but relevant, is described by a rv $\tilde{s}$, say. We assess the prior distribution of $\tilde{s}$ and the conditional distribution of $\tilde{z}$ given s for each s. This determines the joint distribution of $(\tilde{z}, \tilde{s})$:

$$f(z, s) = f'(s)f(z \mid s). \tag{20.1}$$

From this, the conditional distribution of any quantity of interest related to $\tilde{s}$ can be obtained for each observed z.

"Classical" and "Bayesian" statisticians talking about the same problem define z and s the same way, except for personal differences unrelated to the classical/Bayesian distinction; that is, everyone lets z and s stand for the same real-world quantities. However, *the only probabilities classical statisticians admit into the discussion are conditional probabilities given s.*

In the Bayesian view there is no difference in principle between conditional probabilities given s and any other probabilities: all probabilities of interest can be given judgmental interpretations, all distributions can be obtained once one has the joint probability distribution of the quantities relevant to the problem, and this joint distribution may be assessed in whatever way is most convenient. In practice, however, a Bayesian will almost always assess the marginal distribution of $\tilde{s}$ and the conditional distribution of $\tilde{z}$ given s. Furthermore, the assessment that will cost him effort and require him to exercise his "judgment" is the marginal distribution of $\tilde{s}$, the "prior distribution." Generally he will settle on the conditional distribution of $\tilde{z}$ given s, the "sampling distribution," with little thought and few qualms. A committee of Bayesians might argue and substantially disagree about the marginal distribution of $\tilde{s}$, but the conditional distribution of $\tilde{z}$ given s would often be taken so much for granted by everyone that it would never be mentioned. Thus, in practice, even for Bayesians there is something special about probabilities conditional on s, namely that people generally agree on what they are. (This comes about partly because s is usually redefined if necessary so that the description of the state of nature includes a resolution of any matter subject to disagreement, for instance the value of an unknown variance.)

Classical statisticians are willing to talk about only "objective" probabilities. To the extent that "objective" means "agreed upon by most people who pretend to understand the problem," the foregoing remarks already indicate why this means that classical methods are restricted to probabilities conditional on s. Generally an "objective probability" is defined less superficially, as an empirically verifiable limiting relative frequency in repeated identical trials. We shall not enter here into the difficulties of defining "empirical verification" or "repeated identical trials" without using the concept of probability that is being defined, nor into the modifications required to handle a nonrepeatable series of dependent trials as in Markov chains and economic time series. Suffice it to say that in practice, probabilities conditional on s are in some sense more objective than others; classical statisticians are willing to call these and only these "probabilities," and Bayesians will attach the same values to these probabilities as classical statisticians but will also attach values to other probabilities that are in no sense objective but are matters of judgment.

We do not assert that either Bayesian or classical statisticians are committed in principle to operate within the particular framework assumed above, the z, s model. However, in practice both do, and within this framework the basic distinction between them boils down to that described above, and all other differences stem from this one.

Actually, nothing said so far constitutes any necessary reason why classical and Bayesian statisticians should not make the same decisions when the chips are down. Classical principles do not suffice to determine a decision procedure, but leave the choice in small or large part to judgment. The Bayesian method of bringing judgment to bear is conspicuously absent from classical statistics textbooks but is not actually incompatible with any avowed principles of classical statisticians. In theory, then, revision of terminology could remove the differences. Bayesians would have to call all probabilities other than those conditional on s by some other name, work in "normal" rather than "extensive" form (see chapter 19), and describe decision procedures in ways that would seem unnatural in order to satisfy classical statisticians, who place primary emphasis on matters of secondary concern to a Bayesian. This would be cumbersome but possible. Similarly, classical statisticians could behave Bayesianly without committing legally provable heresy. In fact, however, they do not. Their procedures and tables are not designed to be used Bayesianly, and it would be most unnatural from their point of view to use them that way. Their descriptions of their procedures and the atmosphere surrounding them are such as to discourage Bayesian behavior. Only a very sophisticated person could follow the classical school of statistics and still behave approximately Bayesianly. Thus there are substantial differences in the behavioral implications of classical and Bayesian statistics as they have developed.

For anything short of an actual terminal decision, the question becomes one of summarizing the available evidence concerning s, and the difference in point of view precludes any possibility of philosophic or conceptual agreement. Thus one might expect even greater discrepancy between Bayesian and classical summaries of evidence than between their terminal actions. In practice, this turns out not to be true. Several kinds of classical statements of evidence, when *misinterpreted* in a natural and almost inevitable way, become good approximations to Bayesian posterior statements. With this possibility in mind, we next discuss the three main forms of classical inference in turn.

20.2 Point Estimation

As we pointed out earlier there are two basically different problems that generally fall under the heading of "point estimation." First, there is the case of the bona fide infinite-action problem, such as how much inventory to stock given an unknown demand and given a clearly defined loss structure. Second, there is the case where the investigator does not have a well-structured terminal action problem in mind but where instead she merely wishes to get some "feeling" for some unknown quantity s. For example, in preliminary planning she might want to get some representative or ballpark figure that she might treat for the time being as certain.

Most discussions in the classical statistical literature have the second category of problems in mind. These discussions invariably mention the dangers involved in presenting just a single point estimate and they argue the importance of accompanying this isolated best guess with some hedging statement about the "variability" of this estimate. How this is done from the classical point of view will be the subject matter of this section and the next.

In order for a user of a statistical report to know how much to rely on a point estimate of a given relevant parameter, it is customary to give along with the point estimate its (estimated) standard deviation. For example, in a research report one might read, "Based on our research findings, the average demand in the target population of Brand X is 180 ± 20 pounds." First, what does this mean to a classical statistician? If we let μ be the true population average, let z represent the statistical evidence and let $d(z)$ be the estimate of μ for the observed z, then in strictly orthodox terms this means

a. z is such that $d(z) = 180$, and

b. for any given μ, before z is observed the rv $d(\tilde{z})$ has a conditional standard deviation of 20 pounds, that is,

$S[d(\tilde{z})|\mu] = 20.$

(We are assuming here that the conditional standard deviation of $d(\tilde{z})$ for a given μ does not depend on μ; we shall return to this point later.)

If the assertion quoted from the research report is based on a large sample, then because of the pervasive effect of the central limit theorem the rv $d(\tilde{z})|\mu$ will probably be approximately Normal; to make the ensuing issues clear, let us assume that this is the case. Most users of statistics—we are not talking about professional statisticians now—who have had some training in classical statistics interpret "180 ± 20" in the following terms: The odds are 1 : 1 (i.e., it is equally likely) that μ will be below 180 or above; the odds are roughly 2 : 1 that μ will lie between 160 and 200; the odds are roughly 95 : 5 that μ will lie between 140 and 220. This interpretation, of course, runs counter to the entire philosophy of classical statistics since these assertions are probability statements about μ based on the sample outcome, and as we said before and repeat once again: in classical statistics, it is only permissible to make probability statements about sample outcomes for given values of population parameters.

The classicist would argue that it is meaningless to say there is a 2 to 1 chance that μ lies in the interval 160 to 200; it either does or doesn't! If it does, the probability is 1, and if it doesn't, the probability is 0. He would point out that μ is a fixed number, albeit unknown, and is not subject to a frequency interpretation of probability, and that when one assigns a probability to an unknown parameter value, one is slipping from the objective into the subjective realms. The Bayesian, of course, while agreeing with this evaluation, would not consider the "subjectivity" tag as a liability but as one of those inevitabilities that are inherent in the problem. The classicist would argue that it is not necessary to resort to a subjective interpretation, since a perfectly valid, objective, frequency-based interpretation can be given to the research report's "180 ± 20." The Bayesian would respond that the classicist can indeed couch his reports in objective terms, but that these reports, if literally interpreted, are not relevant for the problem at hand, and this being the case, are more often than not misinterpreted by the consumer. True, many of these misinterpretations are rather innocuous, but both classicists and Bayesians would concur that they are sometimes harmful; moreover, the differences of viewpoint must be clearly understood because they permeate the entire field of statistical inference and decision and greatly influence both the kinds of problems that are investigated and the analyses of those problems.

To help bring out the differences of viewpoints more clearly, suppose now that after receiving the report that the average demand for brand X is 180 $\pm$ 20 pounds, management wants to know how much of Brand X to stock and they determine that their losses are lincar, with a cost of underage, $k_u = \$400$ per pound of μ, and a cost of overage, $k_0 = \$100$ per pound of μ. The Bayesian would now think of the average demand as a rv $\tilde{\mu}$ and argue that for terminal analysis it is optimal to stock for an average demand that is the $k_u/(k_u + k_0)$ or .80 fractile of his current distribution of $\tilde{\mu}$. If, on the basis of the research report, it is reasonable to assume that $\tilde{\mu}$ is Normal with mean 180 and standard deviation 20—this depends, of course, on whether the sample of the research report swamps his prior judgment—then he would use the .80 fractile of this distribution. The classicist, faced with this same problem, would proceed in an entirely different manner. First of all he would put aside the sample that actually was observed and pose the problem: What stocking procedure should he follow for each of the potential outcomes of the experiment that could have occurred but did not? In other words, even though he already knows the outcome of the experiment, he must put himself in the position he was in before he observed the sample and employ a normal-form analysis (see chapter 19) in order to decide on an appropriate decision rule. The chosen decision rule tells him what to do for any sampling outcome and therefore, in particular, it would tell him what to do for the outcome that in fact was observed. We also emphasize here a point that should not be overlooked and that was fully discussed in chapter 19: there is no "objectively" correct way of choosing a "best" decision rule in the normal mode of analysis. In summary, we feel that the classical statistical report, which gives an estimate together with its standard deviation, when it is interpreted according to strict classical tenets, cannot be conveniently used as a step in the formal analysis of a terminal action problem.

Now let us return to a point that we brushed over too quickly. Suppose that $d(z)$ is an estimate of μ. In practice, the conditional standard deviation of the estimator $d(\tilde{z})$ for a given μ *depends on* μ (and perhaps on some nuisance parameters besides). Thus, for example, suppose we wish to estimate the parameter of p of a Bernoulli process and the process has been observed to give 4 successes in 25 trials. The maximum likelihood estimate is $d(4) = 4/25 = .16$, and for a given p the standard deviation of the estimator $\tilde{r}/25$ is $\sqrt{p(1-p)/25}$, which depends on p. (As an aside, we remark that if $r = 4$ were preassigned and $\tilde{n}$, left to chance, turned out to be 25, then the standard deviation of the estimator $4/\tilde{n}$ would not be $\sqrt{p(1-p)/25}$.) As an approximation, however, we could, in turn, give an estimate of this unknown standard deviation; this is usually accomplished by substituting $d(z)$ for μ, which in this case means substituting .16 for p to give

$\sqrt{.16(.84)/25} = .0733$. The estimate of p would then be reported as $.16 \pm .0733$. Of course, we are not too sure of the number .0733, since it is itself an estimate, and we could attempt to give an indication of the reliability of this estimate. But this line of attack sets up an infinite regression and leads into a hopeless maze.

One last word of advice to Bayesians: If in a report of statistical evidence an estimate of s is given in the form $A \pm B$ and if *you think it appropriate* to assume that for a given s the estimator $d(\tilde{z})$ is approximately Normally distributed about s with a standard deviation of B, then it is a simple matter to introduce your own prior on $\tilde{s}$ and get your own posterior based on the report $A \pm B$. If your prior is diffuse relative to the report $A \pm B$, then your posterior distribution for $\tilde{s}$ is Normal with mean A and standard deviation B.

20.3 Confidence Intervals

We indicated in the last section that merely reporting one specific number as a best estimate of a value of an unknown quantity (parameter) of interest is not very informative since any such estimate will almost certainly differ by some amount from the true value and the user of the estimate will want some indication of its reliability. A classical solution to this problem is to report a band of possible values of the unknown quantity rather than a single value and in addition to quote a number which purports to measure the "confidence" that the user may place in the proposition that the true value actually lies within the reported band or "interval."

We shall first give a classical interpretation of confidence intervals; second, we shall sketch two methods for generating such intervals; third, we shall indicate a relation between confidence interval statements and posterior probability statements; and finally, we shall briefly describe some of the inadequacies inherent in the confidence-interval procedure.

20.3.1 Formal Interpretation of a Confidence Interval

To keep the discussion concrete, consider the following typical example of a confidence-interval statement:

On the basis of our sampling experiments, the proportion of our customers who prefer package X over Y lies between .34 and .46 with confidence .95.

If we let p denote the true proportion of such customers, then an elliptic form of this statement can be expressed in the symbolic form:

$$.34 \leq p \leq .46 \quad \text{with confidence } .95.$$

What does such a statement mean according to orthodox classical tenets? Certainly, it does *not* mean that the posterior probability that $\tilde{p}$ lies in the interval [.34, .46] is .95. It means that:

1. Before the particular sample was observed, the statistician selected the confidence level .95—he could have chosen any other value.

2. Before the particular sample was observed, he selected a decision rule, d, which associates to each sample outcome z a lower number $d_l(z)$ and upper number $d_u(z)$, where the rule is designed such that

$$P_{z|p}(d_\ell(\tilde{z}) \leq p \leq d_u(\tilde{z})) = .95 \qquad \text{for all } p. \tag{20.2}$$

In frequency terms, this means that if independent repetitions of this same experiment were made, and if p were held fixed at some value p_0, say, then in the long run the proportion of intervals that would include p_0 would be .95.

3. A particular outcome z_0 was in fact observed, and for this value $d_l(z_0) = .34$, $d_u(z_0) = .46$.

The classical statistician would say that the true p either lies in the interval [.34, .46] or it does not, so that the *probability* that $.34 \leq p \leq .46$ is either 1 or 0. "However," he would add, "the procedure I had in mind for generating such statements is such that in a large number of independent situations my batting average for generating correct statements would be .95; so draw your own conclusions in this particular case."

20.3.2 Two Techniques for Generating Confidence Intervals

We illustrate the first technique by a simple example. Let $\tilde{x}_1, \ldots, \tilde{x}_n$ be the as yet unknown outcomes of an Independent Normal data-generating process with unknown mean μ and known variance v. Let the associated sample mean be denoted by $\tilde{m}$. Let γ be the preselected confidence level. Since for any μ the rv $(\tilde{m} - \mu)/\sqrt{v/n}$ has a standardized Normal distribution, we have

$$P_{m|\mu}\left(-k \leq \frac{\tilde{m} - \mu}{\sqrt{v/n}} \leq k\right) = \gamma, \tag{20.3}$$

where k is such that the area from $-k$ to $+k$ under the standardized Normal distribution is γ. Now (20.3) can be rewritten in the form

$$P_{m|\mu}(\tilde{m} - k\sqrt{v/n} \leq \mu \leq \tilde{m} + k\sqrt{v/n}) = \gamma \qquad \text{for all } \mu. \tag{20.4}$$

Hence, if we let $d_l(\tilde{m}) = \tilde{m} - k\sqrt{v/n}$ and $d_u(\tilde{m}) = \tilde{m} + k\sqrt{v/n}$, then for any μ the probability of getting an $\tilde{m}$ such that μ lies in the interval

$[d_l(\tilde{m}), d_u(\tilde{m})]$ is γ. If now a particular sample mean m is observed, then the classicist would report

$$\text{“}m - k\sqrt{v/n} \le \mu \le m + k\sqrt{v/n} \quad \text{with confidence } \gamma.\text{”}$$

The reader should observe that in this case the Bayesian would assign a posterior probability of γ to this interval—provided, of course, his prior distribution for $\tilde{\mu}$ were diffuse. Symbolically, the Bayesian counterpart of (20.4) is

$$P_{\mu|m}(m - k\sqrt{v/n} \le \tilde{\mu} \le m + k\sqrt{v/n}) = \gamma. \tag{20.5}$$

Generalizing from this example, one common technique for generating a confidence interval for a parameter s is to devise an appropriate function of the parameter s and the sample outcome z—call it $h(s, z)$, say—such that the conditional distribution of $h(s, \tilde{z})$ given s has a functional form that is independent of s, which would allow us to write down an expression analogous to (20.3). Furthermore, h must be chosen in an ingenious enough manner to allow us to rewrite the analogue of (20.3) in the form

$$P_{z|s}(d_l(\tilde{z}) \le s \le d_u(\tilde{z})) = \gamma \quad \text{for all } s,$$

which is the analogue of (20.4).

The second technique will be explained in an abstract setting but the discussion will be simpler if we assume that the rv $\tilde{z}|s$ has a continuous distribution. For each possible value of s, select a subset of possible outcomes $Z(s)$ such that

$$P_{z|s}(\tilde{z} \in Z(s)) = \gamma \quad \text{for all } s. \tag{20.6}$$

In terms of this collection of selections, we can now generate a confidence statement. For any observation z define the subset of parameter values $S(z)$ to be such that $s \in S(z)$ if and only if $z \in Z(s)$, that is,

$$S(z) = \{s | z \in Z(s)\}. \tag{20.7}$$

If z is observed, then we assert that "$s \in S(z)$ with confidence γ." Mathematically, this means that

$$P_{z|s}(s \in S(\tilde{z})) = \gamma \quad \text{for all } s. \tag{20.8}$$

This follows from (20.7) and (20.6) since

$$P_{z|s}(s \in S(\tilde{z})) = P_{z|s}(\tilde{z} \in Z(s)) = \gamma \quad \text{for all } s.$$

It is easy to see what is going on in terms of figure 20.1. In the (z, s) plane—this is only a symbolic representation since z or s may be multidimensional—a band of values is selected such that for any given s_0 the

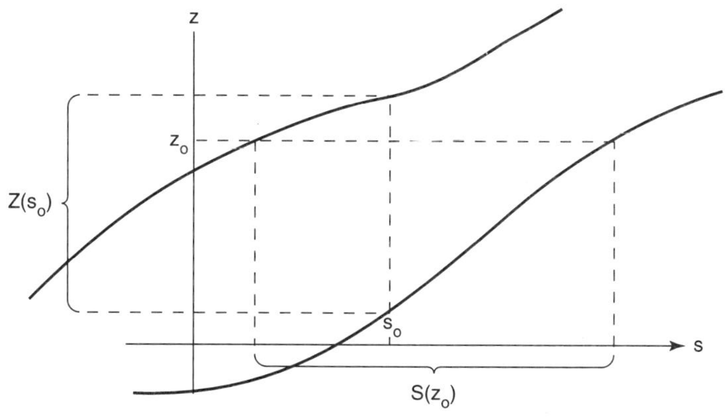

Figure 20.1
Probability and confidence regions

conditional *probability* that $\tilde{z}$ falls in a vertical slice at s_0 (i.e., in $Z(s_0)$) is γ; it then follows that for any z_0 the *confidence* that s falls in a horizontal slice at z_0 (i.e., in $S(z_0)$) is γ.

Notice that nothing is unique about this constructive procedure.

If the rv $\tilde{z}|s$ is not continuous, then for any given γ it may not be possible to select $Z(s)$ to satisfy (20.6) exactly. In this case, two alternative procedures can be followed. One is to choose $Z(s)$ such that

$$P_{z|s}(\tilde{z} \in Z(s)) \geq \gamma \qquad \text{for all } s, \tag{20.9}$$

and then define $S(z)$ as in (20.7); one can assert that $s \in S(z)$ with a confidence of *at least* γ. The second alternative is to conduct an auxiliary experiment that generates an unknown outcome $\tilde{u}$ (e.g., draw a "random" number from the interval 0 to 1) where the distribution of $\tilde{u}$ is continuous and does not depend on s; and then for each s, to select a subset $Z^*(s)$ of pairs (z, u)—that is $Z^*(s)$ is a subset of the Cartesian product of the spaces associated with $\tilde{z}$ and $\tilde{u}$—in such a manner that

$$P_{z,u|s}((\tilde{z}, \tilde{u}) \in Z^*(s)) = \gamma \qquad \text{for all } s. \tag{20.10}$$

Corresponding to the observed outcome (z, u) we can then assert with confidence γ that s belongs to the set

$$S(z, u) = \{s|(z, u) \in Z^*(s)\}. \tag{20.11}$$

The second alternative is called a *randomized* confidence set and although it generates mathematically correct statements most classicists would not employ this technique since they feel that the outcome of u should not influence any inference statement about s. (We, of course, would concur with this reasoning and later on we use an extended version of this argument to show that any inference procedure for s should be based solely on the likelihood function of s for the given observation. Incidentally, confidence intervals do not, in general, satisfy this requirement.)

20.3.3 Confidence Intervals and Posterior Probabilities

The classical explanation of confidence procedures is that they make statements of the form "s is in $S(z)$" by a method that has probability γ of making true statements (the probability being realized as a relative frequency in independent repetitions of the same experiment in the same state of nature). However, in the classical view s is not a rv so no probability can be attached to the truth of any *particular* confidence statement for any *particular* observed z. Unfortunately, in any substantive problem one is interested not in the method of making statements but in s. Furthermore, when you say that you have made a statement by a method that has probability γ of making correct statements, almost everyone will think that your statement has probability γ of being correct. Classical statisticians explain carefully that this is wrong, but they offer no other psychologically feasible way of thinking about the uncertainty of a particular confidence statement. It seems to us that even some of the best orthodox statisticians seem unable to avoid giving this impression if they attempt an explanation at all.

Let us first illustrate, by an admittedly extreme example, why it may be drastically incorrect to equate a confidence level with a posterior probability. Suppose that we are concerned with the proportion p of individuals in a population that have a given attribute X. Let us base our confidence interval for p on the outcome of a number $\tilde{z}$ that is drawn at random from a rectangular distribution over the interval 0 to 1, where the outcome of $\tilde{z}$ has nothing whatsoever to do with p, according to the following ridiculous recipe:

if $z < .025$, assert that p is negative;
if $.025 \leq z \leq .975$, assert that p lies in the interval 0 to 1 inclusive;
if $z > .975$, assert that p is greater than 1.

Now it is trivial to verify that, no matter what the true p is, the procedure for making statements is such that in the long run .95 of the statements will be true. Thus, following this logic, if we observe for example that $z = .452\ldots$, we are entitled to say: "Based on the particular outcome of the experiment, the true p lies in the interval from 0 to 1 inclusive with confidence .95." This is a mathematically correct statement but certainly no one in his right mind would confuse this statement with a betting odds statement. The whole point of this exercise is to impress upon the reader the fact that although a confidence statement has a valid long-run frequency interpretation, something additional has to be added before it is legitimate to think of a particular confidence statement in terms of betting odds or posterior probability statements.

Suppose now that a classicist uses a confidence procedure that associates to each z a set $S(z)$ such that

$$P_{z|s}(s \in S(\tilde{z})) = \gamma \qquad \text{for all } s. \tag{20.12}$$

Now suppose that you are a Bayesian with a given prior distribution on $\tilde{s}$. If z is observed and the confidence set $S(z)$ determined, then you, as a Bayesian, would assign the posterior probability $\gamma^*(z)$ to this set, where

$$\gamma^*(z) = P''_{s|z}(\tilde{s} \in S(z)). \tag{20.13}$$

Although $\gamma^*(z)$ is, in general, different from γ, it is true that

$$E_z \gamma^*(z) = \gamma. \tag{20.14}$$

This follows since

$$E_z \gamma^*(\tilde{z}) = E_z P''_{s|z}(\tilde{s} \in S(\tilde{z})) = P_{s,z}(\tilde{s} \in S(\tilde{z}))$$
$$= E'_s P_{z|s}(\tilde{s} \in S(\tilde{z})) = \gamma.$$

To help explain the meaning of this result, suppose a classicist says to a Bayesian, "I have observed an outcome z, but I won't disclose it to you. I also have written down a statement $s \in S(z)$ with confidence .95, but I won't disclose the form $S(z)$ takes. Could you as a Bayesian assign a probability to the assertion that $s \in S(z)$?" In the light of the above result the answer is "Yes, the probability is γ." The Bayesian would add though, "But as soon as you tell me something about z or $S(z)$ then the probability that I would associate to the statement will change."

The following example partially illustrates the above discussion and also plays a central role in classical statistics. Suppose that a sample from an Independent Normal process with unknown μ and υ is sufficiently summarized by the mean $m = 100$, the sampling standard deviation $s = 12$, and the sample size $n = 9$. Suppose that prior to taking the sample, the investigator is very vague about μ and he thinks that υ is about $(24)^2$ or 576, but is not quite sure. Now a well-known classical result states,

"$m - ks/\sqrt{n} \leq \mu \leq m + ks/\sqrt{n}$ with confidence γ,"

where k is chosen such that the area from $-k$ to $+k$ under the standardized Student distribution with $\nu = n - 1$ degrees of freedom is γ. In our example if γ is .95, then k is 2.3 and the particular assertion becomes

(A) "$100 - 2.3(4) \le \mu \le 100 + 2.3(4)$ with confidence .95."

If s were 48 instead of 12 (i.e., twice our rough prior judgmental estimate of σ instead of half of this estimate), then the confidence interval statement would be

(B) "$100 - 2.3(16) \le \mu \le 100 + 2.3(16)$ with confidence .95."

Keeping in mind that $\tilde{m}$ and $\tilde{s}$ are conditionally independent for any (μ, υ) pair, certainly one would want to assign a much higher posterior probability to the interval in (B) than to the interval in (A)—after all, the interval in (B) is *four times* as wide as the interval in (A).

20.3.4 Further Criticisms of Confidence Intervals

A feature of confidence regions which is particularly disturbing is the fact that the confidence level must be selected in advance and the region we then look at is imposed by chance and may not be at all one we are interested in. Imagine the plight of a manager who exclaims, "I understand [does he?] the meaning that the demand for XYZ will lie in the interval 973 to 1374 with confidence .90. However, I am particularly interested in the interval 1300 to 1500. What confidence can I place on that interval?" Unfortunately, this question *cannot* be answered. Of course, however, it is possible to give a posterior probability to that particular interval—or any other—based on the sample data and on a codification of the manager's prior judgments.

Another particularly disturbing feature of confidence regions is the fact that they severely circumscribe the choice of the quantity to be estimated. For example, suppose that the state parameter is given by a pair of values (s_1, s_2) and that it is possible to make the statement that (s_1, s_2) lies in a particular region of the plane with confidence γ. It also may be possible to make a confidence assertion about some quantity t which is a particular function of s_1 and s_2. However, because of the substantive issues involved in a given analysis, one might be particularly interested in another quantity w that is also a particular function of s_1 and s_2. How disappointing it is to be told that it is not possible to make any confidence statement at all about w. This is a case where the methodology forces an investigator to make precise "objective" statements about tangential issues. We consider this serious indeed. Using the Bayesian approach this difficulty does not arise. If a posterior probability distribution is given to $(\tilde{s}_1, \tilde{s}_2)$, then one can always obtain (by numerical means, if need be) the probability distribution of any function of $(\tilde{s}_1, \tilde{s}_2)$.

The theory of confidence intervals has been devised to satisfy an important demand: to report sample information on the value of some unknown quantity in an informative manner when the person reporting the information does not necessarily know how the information will ultimately be used or when he knows that the same information will be used in many different ways by many different people. In such a situation it is important to bear in mind how consumers of this report could use it. Could a confidence-interval report on a quantity s be used in the formal analysis of a terminal decision problem where the uncertainty in question is this same quantity s? Only indirectly by unscrambling the report to get at the underlying statistics—but this very often loses valuable information.

20.4 Testing Hypotheses

20.4.1 Definitions and Introductory Remarks

In the first quarter of the twentieth century statisticians viewed their task as one of establishing the truth or falsity of statements or "hypotheses" rather than to show how to choose among acts. An important achievement of the theory now called classical was to recognize that the establishment of ultimate truth is not an achievable goal for mere human endeavor and that the real problem of statistics is to aid in choice among acts under uncertainty, but the language of "hypotheses" remains as a historical residue. In this section we shall adopt and explain this classical language.

One special, but very common, type of problem is that in which a choice must be made between just two hypotheses, and in such problems the procedure by which the choice is made is commonly called a "test" of one of the hypotheses against the other. The hypothesis that is "tested" is usually called the "null" hypothesis while the other is called the "alternate" hypothesis, and the choice is said to be between *acceptance* and *rejection* of the *null* hypothesis rather than between acceptance of one hypothesis and acceptance of the other. *Rejection* of the null hypothesis when it is actually true is said to be an *error of the first kind* or of Type I; *acceptance* of the null hypothesis when it is actually false is said to be an *error of the second kind* or of Type II.

Let us once again work in the framework where we may observe a sample outcome z from the sample space Z of possible outcomes, and where the state of nature is described by a parameter s from the set S of all possible states. A null hypothesis is now usually identified with some prescribed subset H_0 of S, and a test of H_0 at some preassigned level α partitions Z into an acceptance region A and a rejection region R where

$$P_{z|s}(\text{rejection}) = P_{z|s}(\tilde{z} \in R) \leq \alpha \qquad \text{for all } s \in H_0. \tag{20.15}$$

The *exact level* of a test is the smallest α for which (20.15) holds, that is,

$$\alpha = \max P_{z|s}(\tilde{z} \in R) \quad \text{for} \quad s \in H_0. \tag{20.16}$$

Hence the exact level of a test is merely the maximum probability of making an error of the first kind. For any $s_0 \notin H$, the quantity $P_{z|s_0}(\tilde{z} \in A)$ is called the *power* of the test at alternative s_0 and is merely the probability of making an error at s_0.

If the observed outcome $z \in R$, then the result is said to be "significant" or "significant at level α"; if $z \in A$, then the result is said to be "nonsignificant" or "nonsignificant at level α." "Significance" leads to rejection of the null hypothesis and "nonsignificance" to acceptance of the null hypothesis.

This asymmetric usage of language is due to the belief widely held among statisticians that in almost all two-action problems that require statistical analysis one of the two hypotheses will be of such a nature that the consequence of rejecting it when true is much more serious than the consequence of accepting it when false—in other words, the truth of one of the two hypotheses is to be given a very strong benefit of any doubt that may exist, and attention is to be focussed on this fact by calling this favored hypothesis the "tested" or the "null" hypothesis—the actual name "null" is another historical residue and will be explained in section 20.4.3.

As an example, consider the problem of deciding whether or not a certain batch of some drug contains impurities that make it poisonous. The two hypotheses are "the drug is poisonous" and "the drug is not poisonous," and the former is called the null hypothesis because an error made when the former hypothesis is true is more serious than an error made when the latter hypothesis is true.

Another example might help to highlight the innuendoes of this highly suggestive vernacular. A research industrial psychologist conjectures that management can increase productivity by following a certain prescribed selection and training process that depart from current practice. There are skeptics who believe otherwise. To convince others, as well as herself, the psychologist devises an index for individual productivity, ascertains that under current practice the average productivity index is μ_0, and performs an experiment to investigate the average productivity index under the alternate selection and training procedures. It is considered good practice for the investigator to play devil's advocate with herself and to set up the null hypothesis that her research conjecture is false, which in this case means to set up the null hypothesis that the average index μ with the new technique is less than or equal to μ_0. She should then test her null hypothesis at some preassigned significance level α, such as .05 or .01. Naturally she hopes that the experiment will yield "significant" results, that the null hypothesis will be rejected, and that her research conjecture will be thereby substantiated. The smaller the significance level she chooses the more demanding is the test and the more impressive her conclusion appears to be—provided, of course, her results are significant. We shall discuss this example further in the next section because there are a host of subtleties that should not be overlooked.

Many papers in research journals present experimental evidence that purportedly supports or substantiates some given theory. There is always the danger that some of these experimental results are not the consequence of some meaningfully underlying "truth" but are purely artifactual and have arisen by chance. Some feel that there is a need to control the floodgates of contributions and to dampen the enthusiasm of well-intentioned but naive researchers by adopting a uniform standard of acceptance in journals. One such standard would be to require each experimenter to state a null hypothesis, to use a test procedure at some standardized level such as $\alpha = .05$, and to obtain experimentally significant results. "If all papers," so the argument goes, "that are published in our journal are significant at the .05 level, then, at least, the reader knows that at most .05 of the papers can be wrong in the long run." The fallacy in this reasoning can be brought out clearly by the following extreme case. Suppose that 1,000 researchers in a given area make 1,000 different research conjectures, all of which happen in fact to be false; if they all test their experiments at the .05 level it is not unreasonable that approximately 50 of them will yield significant results. This output of tested and proven results should fill several issues of a given journal. We are not implying by citing this example that our journals are full of errors but rather we are bringing out the well-recognized but often overlooked point that if a consumer reads an article which obtains significant results at the .05 level, he cannot infer that this paper is one of a category of papers that have at least a .95 relative frequency of being true. We also do not wish to imply by this example that a Bayesian approach could easily s rmount the difficulty of optional selection in the reporting of experimental data. As far as establishing criteria of acceptance in journals is concerned, we feel that any uniform policy, such as requiring a .05 level of significance, is particularly naive as will become evident in the ensuing discussion.

20.4.2 Testing a One-Sided Null Hypothesis

We now consider the special but very important case where $\theta = h(s)$ is a real-valued function of s, where the null hypothesis is of the form $\theta \leq \theta_0$ for some preassigned θ_0, and where the test of this null hypothesis is based on some statistic $\tilde{T} = g(\tilde{z})$, say. For example, θ may be a population mean μ and $\tilde{T}$ could be the sample mean $\tilde{m}$; or θ may be the Bernoulli parameter

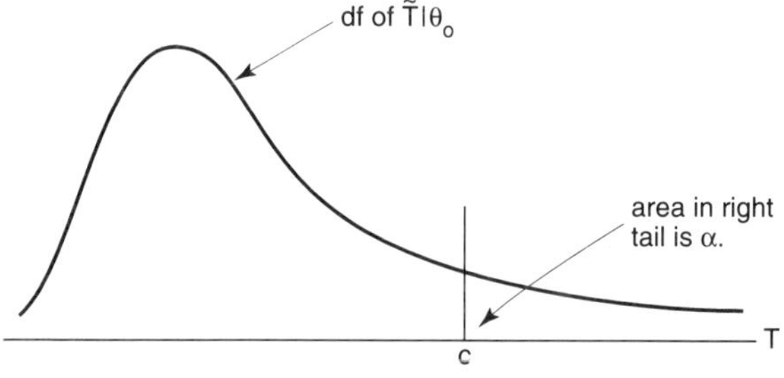

Figure 20.2
Significance level and critical value

p and $\tilde{T}$ could be the number $\tilde{r}$ of successes in n trials. If large values of $\tilde{T}$ are more likely to occur when θ is large, then it is natural to use an upper-tailed test based on $\tilde{T}$ that rejects the null hypothesis if $\tilde{T} \geq c$ and accepts it otherwise, where c is an adjustable cutoff value. The value c is related to the exact level α of the test by the relation

$$\max_{H_0} P_{z|s}(\tilde{T} \geq c) = \alpha, \tag{20.17}$$

where $\max_{H_0}$ is understood to mean that the maximum is to be taken over all s such that $\theta \equiv h(s) \leq \theta_0$. Typically the maximum probability of rejection under the null hypothesis occurs at θ_0 and is the same for all s with $h(s) = \theta_0$, that is,

$$\alpha = P_{z|s}(\tilde{T} \geq c) \quad \text{for} \quad \theta \equiv h(s) = \theta_0. \tag{20.18}$$

This means that c is such that the area to the right of c under the conditional distribution of $\tilde{T}$ given θ_0 is α (see figure 20.2). Suppose now that the statistic T_0 is observed. If $T_0 \leq c$ then the result is not significant at level α; if $T_0 > c$ then the result is significant at level α. There are some orthodox purists who argue that a level α should be chosen and all that should be reported is whether the observed T_0 falls below c or above c. For an honest-to-goodness terminal action problem that is all that counts. In most cases where tests of hypotheses are used, however, the terminal action problem is not all this clear cut and for reporting purposes it is nice to know how far T_0 falls below c or above c. One common way of reporting this information is to report the level at which the observed T_0 is "just significant"; this is traditionally called the *P-value* for T_0, and labelling this by $\alpha^*(T_0)$, we have

$$\text{P-value for } T_0 \equiv \alpha^*(T_0) \equiv P_{T|\theta_0}(\tilde{T} \geq T_0). \tag{20.19}$$

Thus if the P-value for a particular T_0 were .0347, then for any $\alpha > .0347$ the results would be significant and for any $\alpha < .0347$ the results would be nonsignificant.

Relation of a P-value to a Posterior Probability

Now let us suppose that θ is a translation parameter determining the distribution of $\tilde{T}$, in the sense that the conditional distribution of $(\tilde{T} - \tilde{\theta})$ does not depend on θ. In this case the rv's $(\tilde{T} - \tilde{\theta})$ and $\tilde{\theta}$ are independent from a Bayesian point of view, and if the prior distribution of $\tilde{\theta}$ is diffuse, then we show below that the *P-value for* T_0 *is exactly the conditional probability that* $\tilde{\theta} \leq \tilde{\theta}_0$ *given* T_0, that is,

$$P_{\theta|T_0}(\tilde{\theta} \leq \theta_0) = \alpha^*(T_0). \tag{20.20}$$

Proof We have

$$\begin{aligned}\alpha^*(T_0) &= P(\tilde{T} \geq T_0 | \tilde{\theta} = \theta_0) = P(\tilde{T} - \theta_0 \geq T_0 - \theta_0 | \tilde{\theta} = \theta_0)\\ &= P(\tilde{T} - \tilde{\theta} \geq T_0 - \theta_0 | \tilde{\theta} = \theta_0)\\ &= P(\tilde{T} - \tilde{\theta} \geq T_0 - \theta_0)\end{aligned}$$

where the last equality follows since $\tilde{T} - \tilde{\theta}$ is independent of $\tilde{\theta}$. We shall show shortly that since $\tilde{T} - \tilde{\theta}$ and $\tilde{\theta}$ are independent and $\tilde{\theta}$ is diffuse, that $\tilde{T} - \tilde{\theta}$ and $\tilde{T}$ are also independent. Using this assertion we can continue with our stream of equalities and obtain

$$\begin{aligned}\alpha^*(T_0) &= P(\tilde{T} - \tilde{\theta} \geq T_0 - \theta_0)\\ &= P(\tilde{T} - \tilde{\theta} \geq T_0 - \theta_0 | \tilde{T} = T_0)\\ &= P(T_0 - \tilde{\theta} \geq T_0 - \theta_0 | \tilde{T} = T_0)\\ &= P(\tilde{\theta} \leq \theta_0 | \tilde{T} = T_0).\end{aligned}$$

It remains to show that $\tilde{T} - \tilde{\theta}$ and $\tilde{T}$ are independent, which can be accomplished by arguing that the expression

$$P(T_1 \leq \tilde{T} \leq T_2 | \tilde{T} - \tilde{\theta} = a)$$

does not depend on a. Now

$$\begin{aligned}P(T_1 \leq \tilde{T} \leq T_2 | \tilde{T} - \tilde{\theta} = a) &= P(T_1 \leq \tilde{\theta} + a \leq T_2 | \tilde{T} - \tilde{\theta} = a)\\ &= P(T_1 - a \leq \tilde{\theta} \leq T_2 - a)\end{aligned}$$

since $\tilde{\theta}$ is independent of $\tilde{T} - \tilde{\theta}$. But now since $\tilde{\theta}$ is assumed diffuse or flat this last expression does not depend on a, and the proof is complete.

In figure 20.3 we indicate the relation between a P-value and the posterior probability that the null hypothesis is true for the special case where θ is the population mean μ of a Normal process with known variance and $\tilde{T}$ is $\tilde{m}$. Let m_0 be the observed sample mean. It is important to emphasize

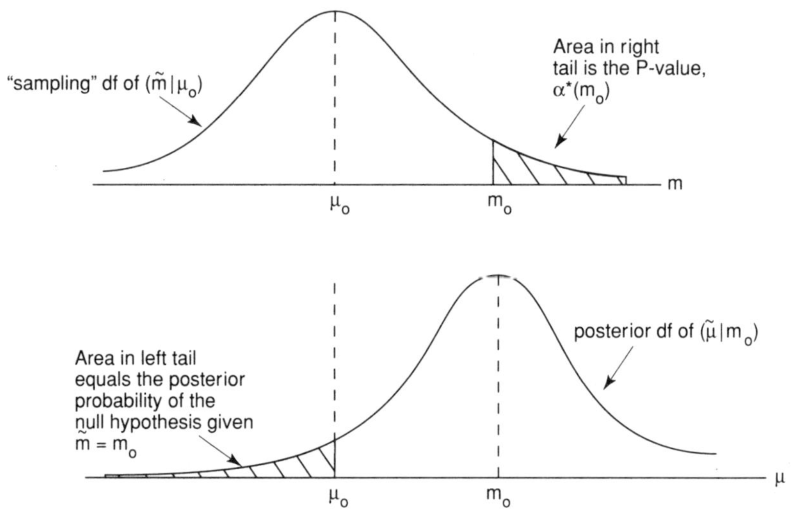

Figure 20.3
P-value and posterior probability of the null hypothesis

that the P-value can only be equated to the posterior probability that the null hypothesis is correct if the prior on $\tilde{\theta}$ is diffuse, and a diffuse prior on an infinite range (as above) can be at best an approximation. If one has strong prior feelings about $\tilde{\theta}$ then the foregoing does not apply (unless the sample information is large relative to the prior information).

Significance, Meaningfulness, and Sample Size

Suppose as a research scientist you wish to show that $\mu > \mu_0$ and accordingly you set up the null hypothesis that $\mu \leq \mu_0$. As far as the meaningfulness of your theory is concerned, would you rather that the sample results show significance at (A) a P-value of .06, say, based on a sample size 15, or at (B) a P-value of .02, say, based on a sample of size 100? In an informal polling we found that most empirical researchers argue that alternative B is better since it is more impressive to get a lower P-value and obviously a larger sample is better than a smaller sample. But the issue is not all this clear-cut, as is shown in figure 20.4. With the same kind of sampling in both cases, the posterior distribution of $\tilde{\mu}$ based on a large sample will be tighter than that based on a small sample. Although curve A has a larger area to the left of μ_0, the researcher may justifiably be quite excited by the results of A and quite let down by the results of B. It depends, of course, on his loss structure.

As far as reporting of statistical evidence is concerned, the above illustration points out the inadequacies of just reporting a P-value—and reporting significance or nonsignificance at a predetermined α-level is even

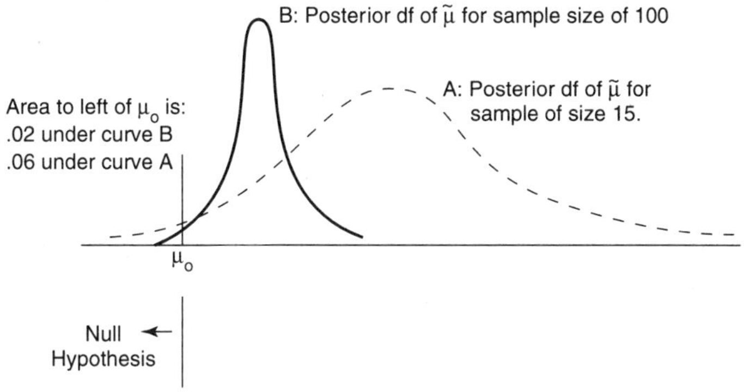

Figure 20.4
Effect of sample size

less informative. In addition to the P-value the sophisticated consumer must also keep in mind the sample size and the efficacy of the sample. This is not easy to do even for the professional statistician.

Suppose now a test has been made of the null hypothesis $\mu \leq \mu_0$ and the results yield a P-value of .14. Not a very impressive result. To a Bayesian this means, assuming he had a diffuse prior on $\tilde{\mu}$ before the sample, that his current assessment of the probability that $\tilde{\mu} > \mu_0$ is .86. Now since the posterior distribution of $\tilde{\mu}$ will become tighter and tighter about the true μ with increasing sample size, he can now give 86 to 14 odds that an additional sample will yield significant results at any preassigned significance level (say $\alpha = .001$) provided the sample size is sufficiently large.

Setting a Significance Level for a Bona Fide Two-Action Problem

Consider the specific two-action problem of whether to switch from a process with known yield μ_0 to a new process with unknown yield $\tilde{\mu}$. Here it is customary to test the null hypothesis $\mu \leq \mu_0$ and switch if it is rejected, setting α low enough to allow for the fact that switching would be expensive, which makes rejecting when $\mu \leq \mu_0$ the more serious of the two kinds of error. The Bayesian procedure, if the utilities are linear in μ, is to find the breakeven value μ_b and switch if the mean of the posterior distribution on $\tilde{\mu}$ exceeds μ_b, but not otherwise. At least in this problem, using a natural null hypothesis (not depending on changeover costs) and allowing for the greater seriousness of one kind of error by setting a conventionally small α like .05 will not lead to the optimal procedure except by remarkable coincidence or remarkable intuition in the choice of α. We feel that if a classical analysis must be made in such a problem, then it would be far better to test the null hypothesis $\mu \leq \mu_b$ at level .50 than to test the null hypothesis $\mu \leq \mu_0$ at level .05 or .01. We have heard some statisticians retort to this advice that it is not always easy to find μ_b since this might entail a complex economic analysis and some intangibles might also have to be taken into account. To this we reply that if a decision maker cannot decide which of two actions he should adopt *when μ is known*, then he clearly is not prepared to analyze the problem when he is uncertain about μ.

A more sophisticated analysis of the two-action problem that also includes sample size considerations is given in chapter 19 on Normal-form analysis. Recall that in this mode of analysis the prior distribution on $\tilde{s}$ (or on $\tilde{\mu}$) is not brought into play until the very last step and the analysis up to that point follows acceptable classical tenets.

20.4.3 Testing a Two-Sided Null Hypothesis

Suppose as above that $\theta = h(s)$ is a real-valued function of s and $T = g(z)$ is a real-valued function of the sample outcome z, and for convenience that $\tilde{T}$ is a continuous rv. A test rejecting when $\tilde{T} \le c_1$ or $\tilde{T} \ge c_2$ and accepting otherwise is called a two-tailed test based on $\tilde{T}$. If large values of $\tilde{T}$ are likely to occur when θ is large and small values when θ is small, and if the null hypothesis is $\theta = \theta_0$, then it is natural to use a two-tailed test based on $\tilde{T}$. Usually the two critical values c_1 and c_2 are adjusted so that

$$P_{T|s}(\tilde{T} \le c_1) = P_{T|s}(\tilde{T} \ge c_2) = \tfrac{1}{2}\alpha, \quad \text{for} \quad h(s) = \theta_0, \tag{20.21}$$

the test statistic T typically being chosen so that the distribution of $\tilde{T}$ given s is the same for all values of s such that $h(s) = \theta_0$.

It is perfectly possible to have unequal probabilities in the two tails. It is also possible to make two-tailed tests of null hypotheses of the form $\theta_0 \le \theta \le \theta_1$. In practice, these possibilities are rarely used, and we shall not discuss them further.

We return to the typical case (20.21). Then the two-tailed test at level α rejects if either one-tailed test at level $\frac{1}{2}\alpha$ would reject. Therefore the P-value of the two-tailed test, the largest α at which z is significant, is twice the P-value of the one-tailed test having the smaller P-value. We may regard the upper-tailed test as a test of $\theta \le \theta_0$, and the lower-tailed test as a test of $\theta \ge \theta_0$. Recalling the interpretation of the P-value for a one-tailed test we find that, in typical circumstances,

> the P-value or level at which z is just significant by a two-tailed test of the null hypothesis $\theta = \theta_0$ is approximately *twice* the posterior probability that $\tilde{\theta}$ lies on the opposite side of θ_0 from that suggested by the observations.

The "typical circumstances" include the assumption that $\tilde{\theta}$ is a priori diffusely distributed. If one is testing $\theta = \theta_0$ because a priori $\tilde{\theta}$ seems likely to be near θ_0 (or $= \theta_0$), then the foregoing interpretation of the P-value does not apply, unless the sample information is large relative to the strength of the prior feeling.

Notice that the P-value bears no special relation to the posterior probability that $\tilde{\theta}$ is near θ_0, that is, to

$$P_{s|z}\{|\tilde{\theta} - \theta_0| \leq \delta\}, \tag{20.22}$$

where δ is chosen so that $|\tilde{\theta} - \theta_0| \leq \delta$ means $\tilde{\theta}$ is near θ_0 for practical purposes. There is no classical counterpart to the probability (20.22). One could invent a test of the null hypothesis $|\theta - \theta_0| \leq \delta$ or a test of the null hypothesis $|\theta - \theta_0| \geq \delta$, but the result of neither test would give an approximation to (20.22).

We remark that the P-value of a two-tailed test is not itself, except by coincidence, an approximation to any posterior probability of interest. It is often approximately the posterior probability that $\tilde{\theta}$ is as near $\hat{\theta}$ as θ_0 is, that is $P_{s|z}\{\theta_0 \leq \tilde{\theta} \leq 2\hat{\theta} - \theta_0\}$, where $\hat{\theta}$ is some reasonable estimate of $\tilde{\theta}$. There is no obvious reason why anyone should be interested in this particular interval, however.

The only interesting, generally applicable Bayesian interpretation of a two-tailed P-value that we know of is that given previously, which involves dividing the two-tailed P-value in half. This amounts to choosing which one-tailed test to make on the basis of the data, which is utter heresy by classical dogma.

We now divide our further discussion of two-tailed tests into two cases depending on whether it is reasonable a priori to think that θ is *exactly* θ_0.

Case 1 $P'(\tilde{\theta} = \theta_0) = 0$. Consider the following two thumbnail sketches of problems:

a. The aim is to test whether a given coin is "fair" or not. If we let p be the long-run proportion of heads in repeated tosses, then a commonly formulated problem is to test the null hypothesis that p is exactly equal to $\frac{1}{2}$.

b. The aim is to ascertain whether the average score of males on a given psychological test is different from that of females. Letting μ_M and μ_F denote respectively the average scores of males and females in the population, a commonly formulated problem is to test the null hypothesis that $\mu_M = \mu_F$, or equivalently the null hypothesis that $\Delta \equiv \mu_M - \mu_F = 0$.

It is unreasonable, from a priori grounds, to think that p will be exactly .500 in problem (a) or that Δ will be exactly 0.00 in problem (b). From a literal point of view it does not make sense to test such extreme hypotheses. We know a priori that the alternative hypothesis is true and therefore, for any significance level that is chosen, the null hypothesis will have to be rejected if the sample size is sufficiently large. But if we know this beforehand, why sample? A famous quotation by Joseph Berkson (1938) emphasizes this point in another context. Berkson was concerned with a test of the extreme null hypothesis that a given body of data was drawn from a population which is exactly Normally distributed:

> I believe that an observant statistician who has had any considerable experience with applying the chi-square test repeatedly will agree with my statement that, as a matter of observation, when the numbers in the data are quite large, the *P*'s tend to come out small. Having observed this, and on reflection, I make the following dogmatic statement, referring for illustration to the normal curve: "If the normal curve is fitted to a body of data representing any real observations whatever of quantities in the physical world, then if the number of observations is extremely large—for instance, on the order of 200,000—the chi-square *P* will be small beyond any usual limit of significance."
>
> This dogmatic statement is made on the basis of an extrapolation of the observation referred to and can also be defended as a prediction from *a priori* considerations. For we may assume that it is practically certain that any series of real observations does not actually follow a normal curve *with absolute exactitude* in all respects, and no matter how small the discrepancy between the normal curve and the true curve of observations, the chi-square *P* will be small if the sample has a sufficiently large number of observations in it.
>
> If this is so, then we have something here that is apt to trouble the conscience of a reflective statistician using the chi-square test. For I suppose it would be agreed by statisticians that a large sample is always better than a small sample. If, then, we know in advance the *P* that will result from an application of a chi-square test to a large sample, there would seem to be no use in doing it on a smaller one. But since the result of the former test is known, it is no test at all!

To see how a classicist might defend testing the null hypothesis $\theta = \theta_0$ when he would agree that $P'(\tilde{\theta} = \theta_0) = 0$, let us consider the situation of problem (b). Let the experiment consist of taking an equal number of males and females, let m_M and m_F denote respectively the sample means for male and female subjects, and let $d = m_M - m_F$. Assume that for any μ_M, μ_F the conditional distribution of $\tilde{d}$ is Normal with mean $\Delta = \mu_M - \mu_F$ and choose units such that the conditional variance of $\tilde{d}$ is 1. Now suppose the actual experiment yields a value $d = 1.88$. Under a two-tailed test of the extreme null hypothesis $\Delta = 0$ this result would be just significant at level .06. After looking at the data one might be tempted to test the null hypothesis that $\Delta \leq 0$. If this were done the results would be just significant at level .03. Now the classicist would argue that if d were negative he would want to test $\Delta \geq 0$ and *not* $\Delta \leq 0$ and this must be taken into consideration; hence what is relevant for him is the probability

$$P(\tilde{d} \geq 1.88 | \tilde{d} \geq 0 \quad \text{and} \quad \Delta = 0)$$

and this probability has the value .06 and not .03. He would add that when he reports that the value $d = 1.88$ is just significant at level .06 for the null hypothesis $\Delta = 0$, he is also saying that the value $d = 1.88$ is just significant at level .06 for the null hypothesis $\Delta \leq 0$ allowing for the fact that he chose this hypothesis to test on the basis of the data itself. We repeat that for a Bayesian with a diffuse prior on $\tilde{\Delta}$ the posterior probability that $\tilde{\Delta} \leq 0$ given $d = 1.88$ is .03 and not .06. The Bayesian would argue that the classicist would do better in this situation to select a one-sided hypothesis on the basis of the data and report significance without trying to compensate for this selection of which hypothesis to test. Needless to say, the classicist does not agree, since this procedure would destroy the frequency interpretation of the significance level.

Case 2 $P'(\tilde{\theta} = \theta_0) > 0$. As an example of a situation where we really do want to know whether a parameter is or is not exactly equal to some specified value, consider the problem of deciding whether or not an individual is gifted with extrasensory perception. An experiment might be conducted by tossing a coin repeatedly, on each toss allowing a "sender" to see how the coin falls and then asking a "receiver" in the next room to say which face is up. In this problem one hypothesis will be that the sender has no effect on the receiver and that the receiver's guesses are right or wrong purely by chance; the other hypothesis will be that the receiver's guesses *are* affected by what the sender sees and therefore that the receiver will do either better than chance or, conceivably, worse than chance if the astral wires are crossed. Letting p denote the long-run fraction of correct guesses, we shall follow traditional practice and take as our null hypothesis: $p = \frac{1}{2}$. We note in passing that it is this kind of problem that explains the word "null": the null hypothesis asserts that the sender has *no* effect on the receiver.

In this example it is reasonable to allow $0 < P'(\tilde{p} = .500\ldots) < 1$. In these circumstances D. V. Lindley (1957), shows that if we denote the null hypothesis $p = .500\ \ldots$ by H_0, then the following two phenomena can occur simultaneously:

i. a two-tailed significance test for H_0 reveals significance at, say, the .05 level;

ii. the posterior probability of H_0, given the sample results, for quite small prior probabilities of H_0 is as high as .95.

As Lindley says, "Clearly the common-sense interpretations of (i) and (ii) are in direct conflict. The phenomenon is fairly general with significance tests [of extreme null hypotheses] and casts doubts on the meaning of a significance level in some circumstances."

Let us now illustrate for a special case how these results could arise. For the prior probability distribution let us place a mass of π' on the null hypothesis, $H_0: p = .500 \ldots$, and let us distribute the remaining mass of $1 - \pi'$ uniformly over the interval from 0 to 1. (It is possible to obtain the results we are after for any other continuous prior distribution for the remaining mass of $1 - \pi'$, but the analysis will be more difficult.) In a binomial sample of size n let us assume that the number of successes r is such that

$$\frac{r - \frac{n}{2}}{\sqrt{n}/2} = 1.96, \tag{20.23}$$

so that by the Normal approximation the result has a two-tailed P-value of .05. The conditional probability of observing this result is

a. $\frac{2}{\sqrt{n}} f_{N*}(1.96)$ if H_0 is true;

b. $\frac{1}{n+1}$ if H_0 is false.

(Result (a) follows from the Normal approximation and (b) from the fact that all $n + 1$ outcomes of a binomial experiment of size n are marginally equally likely if the prior on $\tilde{p}$ is uniform.) Hence the posterior probability of H_0, given that (r, n) satisfies (20.23), is

$$\begin{aligned} \pi'' &= \frac{\pi' 2 f_{N*}(1.96)/\sqrt{n}}{\pi' 2 f_{N*}(1.96)/\sqrt{n} + (1 - \pi')/(n + 1)} \\ &= \frac{1}{1 + k\sqrt{n}/(n + 1)}, \end{aligned} \tag{20.24}$$

where

$$k = \frac{1 - \pi'}{2\pi' f_{N*}(1.96)}.$$

From (20.24) it follows that for a sample result with a P-value of .05, the posterior probability π'' of H_0 is an increasing function of the sample size n and approaches 1 in the limit no matter how small π' is (as long as it is positive). (If the mass of $1 - \pi'$ were distributed not uniformly but continuously, then (20.24) would remain approximately valid with a different expression for k.) Since the posterior probability varies strikingly with n for a fixed significance level, merely reporting a significance level can be a quite misleading summary of what the experimental evidence has to say about the null hypothesis. This is not to say that sophisticated classical statisticians cannot make appropriate allowances for sample sizes, but think of the poor unsuspecting consumer!

20.5 Tests of Significance as Sequential Decision Procedures

In the classical theory, a test of significance is *not* a procedure for deciding whether or not to postpone terminal action; it is a procedure for choosing between terminal acts. Tests of significance, however, were used long before the current classical theory of such tests was developed, and the original purpose of these tests was entirely different from their purpose according to classical theory. This original purpose was to decide whether or not the sample evidence already at hand was or was not adequate to reject some null hypothesis, and the alternative to rejection of the null hypothesis was not acceptance of the null hypothesis—it was "suspension of judgment." Since "suspension of judgment" means identically the same thing as deciding to collect more information before reaching *any* terminal decision, this amounts to saying that tests of significance were originally conceived of as *sequential* rather than single-sample decision procedures.

An experimenter who has obtained data which support some interesting hypothesis may withhold publication because the data are not "statistically significant," but he will rarely conclude that he must now and forever discard this hypothesis from his mind as the classical theory would require him to do. On the contrary, he will continue to regard his hypothesis as probable though "not proved," and if he can obtain the required funds he will almost certainly go on to conduct another experiment to obtain additional evidence in its support.

Consider, for example, a situation involving two terminal acts, one better when $\theta > 0$, the other when $\theta < 0$. One common way to decide whether the information at hand is enough or further sampling should be done is to make a two-tailed test of the null hypothesis $\theta = \theta_0$, and if it cannot be rejected at level α (say .05) sample further. This procedure leads to two questions: (a) What assurance will one have that θ is on the side of θ_0 it appears to be on when sampling is stopped? (b) Is this a sensible sample rule?

As regards (a), if each test is made on the combined data to date, at level α, then the posterior probability of a wrong act will typically be half of the P-value at the time of stopping and hence at most $\frac{1}{2}\alpha$. Notice, however, that a conscientious classical statistician would presumably feel obliged to allow for the fact that he was testing more than once. How he would wind up doing so is problematical, but any allowance would lead to a quite different relation between α and any posterior probability. In actuality, this stopping rule, when used at all, is used not premeditatively but casually, without any allowance, so we will not pursue the allowance further here. In the next section we shall consider the general problem of optional stopping.

As regards (b), the stopping rule under discussion must be far from optimal because it takes no account of how far θ appears to be from θ_0 or how the loss of a wrong terminal act varies with θ. If many observations have been taken without obtaining significance, then the posterior distribution of $\tilde{\theta}$ will be concentrated near θ_0 so that in typical problems the expected loss of an immediate decision (i.e., EVPI) will be small, yet the rule calls for continuing to sample just as much as it does after a few observations have been taken without obtaining significance, when the expected loss of an immediate decision (again, EVPI) is much larger and the probability is much greater that a small number of additional observations will change the optimal terminal act (i.e., will have a large EVSI).

20.6 The Likelihood Principle and Optional Stopping

Bayesian methods satisfy the *likelihood principle*: If, in a given situation, two random variables are observable, and if the value x of the first and the value y of the second give rise to the same likelihood function, then observing the value x of the first and observing the value y of the second are equivalent in the sense that they should give the same inference, analysis, conclusion, decision, action, or anything else. Stated alternatively, if s is the state parameter, and if experiment e results in outcome z, with likelihood function $l(s|z)$, then any information about e over and above the likelihood function is irrelevant for inferences about s. Thus, for example, if a Bernoulli process results in r successes in n trials, it has the likelihood function $p^r(1-p)^{n-r}$ and as far as inferences about p are concerned, it is irrelevant whether either n or r was predetermined, or whether the experimenter was interrupted after the nth trial because the baby was crying. Classical statistical methods do not satisfy the likelihood principle: tests of significance, confidence intervals, and unbiassed estimation—to name the most important—violate it. The classicist feels that the experimental frame of reference—which, in particular, would supply conditional probability assessments for other sample outcomes that in fact did not occur—cannot and should not be ignored.

The difference of viewpoints can be illustrated in an example Pratt gives while discussing a paper by Birnbaum (1962):

An engineer draws a random sample of electron tubes and measures the plate voltages under certain conditions with a very accurate volt-meter, accurate enough so that measurement error is negligible compared with the variability of the tubes. A statistician examines the measurements, which look normally distributed and vary from 75 to 99 volts with a mean of 87 and a standard deviation of 4. He makes the ordinary normal analysis, giving a confidence interval for the true mean. Later he visits the engineer's laboratory, and notices that the volt-meter reads only as far as 100, so the population appears to be "censored." This necessitates a new analysis, if the statistician is orthodox. However, the engineer says he has another meter, equally accurate over 100. This is a relief to the orthodox statistician, because it means the population was effectively uncensored after all. But the next day the engineer telephones and says, "I just discovered my high-range volt-meter was not working the day I did the experiment you analyzed for me." The statistician ascertains that the engineer would not have held up the experiment until the meter was fixed, and informs him that a new analysis will be required. The engineer is astounded. He says, "But the experiment turned out just the same as if the high-range meter had been working. I obtained the precise voltages of my sample anyway, so I learned exactly what I would have learned if the high-range meter had been available. Next you'll be asking about my oscilloscope."

I agree with the engineer. If the sample has voltages under 100, it doesn't matter whether the upper limit of the meter is 100, 1000, or 1 million. The sample provides the same information in any case. And this is true whether the end-product of the analysis is an evidential interpretation, a working conclusion, a decision, or an action.

If the point of view expressed here is formalized and pushed to its logical conclusion, it implies the likelihood principle. Allan Birnbaum in his very penetrating paper, "Foundations of Statistical Inference," (1962) convincingly demonstrates this principle in another way. He first formalizes the *Principle of Conditionality*, which we restate as follows:

Let s be an unknown state and let $e_1, e_2, \ldots, e_n$ be n experiments which can be performed and which bear information about s. Let e^* be a mixture experiment, which consists in adopting e_i with canonical probability p_i (where $\sum_i p_i = 1$). If the outcome of the auxiliary canonical device leads to performance of experiment e_h and outcome z_h is observed, then the "evidential meaning" of (e_h, z_h) should not in any way depend on the overall structure of e^*. Birnbaum then shows that the Principle of Conditionality implies (and is implied by) the *Likelihood Principle.* There are many orthodox statisticians who are not willing to adopt all the axioms leading to the Bayesian point of view, but who are nevertheless inclined to adopt the Principle of Conditionality. But once they make this leap, the basic cornerstones of orthodox statistics are no longer of fundamental importance; they can only be resurrected as convenient approximations of concepts that are more fundamental in character.

The Principle of Conditionality is somewhat related to our basic behavioral assumptions 4 and 5 of chapters 2 and 3.

Many classical statisticians are particularly concerned about the implications of the likelihood principle for the sequential analysis of decision problems and for the problem of *optional stopping.* The likelihood principle asserts the *irrelevance of the stopping rule* regardless of how dependent the observations are permitted to be or how vaguely circumscribed their distribution may bc.

Is it legitimate, to take an extreme example, for a scrupulously honest but otherwise misguided Bayesian, in sampling from a Normal population, to decide that she would like to make an assertion such as "$\mu \leq 0$ with probability at least .95" and then to sample until she can either make the statement (based on a diffuse prior) or exhaust her patience in so trying? Suppose at the 11,347th trial she is in a position to make that assertion. If *you* were diffuse to begin with, would you now give at least 95 to 5 odds that $\mu \leq 0$ when you know what optional stopping procedure the experimenter had in mind? At first examination it might appear that sooner or later the experimenter will be able to make the statement and therefore since it is bound to happen, no information is obtained when it does happen! But it is not true that if μ is positive, the assertion can always be made eventually. It is true that a small *positive* value of μ can be chosen so that the probability of eventually making the statement is arbitrarily large, say above .99. This observation, however, is only a red herring and should not deter you from the inescapable mathematical conclusion that as far as the validity of the assertion is concerned, the stopping rule is completely irrelevant.

The irrelevance of the stopping rule can be clarified by recapitulating Birnbaum's argument for this case, where the argument applies particularly beautifully and convincingly.

Consider a situation in which random variables $\tilde{x}_1, \tilde{x}_2, \ldots$ could be observed, and consider two stopping rules (one perhaps having fixed sample size) under which it would be possible to observe the values $x_1, \ldots, x_n$ and stop. Let outcomes 1 and 2 be the occurrence of $x_1, \ldots, x_n$ under the first and second rules respectively when the rule has been chosen in the ordinary way. Let 1′ and 2′ be the same except that the rule has been chosen by flipping a fair coin.

Step A $1' \leftrightarrow 1$, $2' \leftrightarrow 2$

Explanation It is usually felt that one ought to proceed on the basis of the stopping rule actually used, that is, that 1′ is equivalent to 1 and 2′ is equivalent to 2 for whatever purposes the observations and analysis are being made. We denote such equivalence by $\leftrightarrow$. Formally step A uses the Principle of Conditionality.

Step B $1' \leftrightarrow 2'$

Explanation Upon learning that 1′ or 2′ has occurred but not which, the conditional probability that the first stopping rule was used is one-half, whatever may be the joint distribution of $\tilde{x}_1, \tilde{x}_2, \ldots$. Hence nothing additional can be inferred about the unknown state parameter from knowledge of whether the outcome was $1'$ or whether it was $2'$. This means that $1'$ is equivalent to $2'$. (In classical vernacular, it is *sufficient* to know that $1'$ or $2'$ occurred without knowing which.)

Step C $1 \leftrightarrow 2$

Explanation From steps A and B, and transitivity (i.e., if α has the same evidential meaning as β, and if β has the same evidential meaning as γ, then α has the same evidential meaning as γ), it follows that the occurrence of $x_1, \ldots, x_n$ under the first stopping rule (i.e., outcome 1) is equivalent to its occurrence under the second stopping rule, (i.e., outcome 2). This completes the argument.

20.7 Further Uses of Tests of Hypotheses

In practice, significance tests are used for a variety of other purposes in statistical analyses; among them, we shall sketch only three, since full descriptions would take us too far afield.

20.7.1 To Simplify Description

Suppose output depends on two factors, such as type of equipment and operator's years of education. Describing and interpreting the situation is much easier if the effects of equipment and education are additive (equipment type i and education level j gives average output $\mu_{ij} = \alpha_i + \beta_j$ for some constant α_i and β_j) than if they interact (μ_{ij} cannot be so written.) Exact additivity surely fails, but an additive approximation may be "close enough." What is "close enough" in data? Is it appropriate to test the null hypothesis of additivity when we know additivity does not exist?

20.7.2 To Improve Analysis

In the previous situation, if one restricts oneself to classical or diffuse-prior estimates, then it is better to use an additive model when the nonadditivity appears to be small and a nonadditive model otherwise, than to use either an additive or a nonadditive model regardless. How should one choose (or compromise) based on the data? More generally, if we suspect that a parameter is small and the data tell us little about it, we may do better to make it 0, effectively leaving it out, than to include it and use either a classical mode of analysis or a Bayesian analysis with a "nonprejudicial" diffuse-prior distribution.

In complicated models with lots of parameters where the sample data do not effectively swamp a reasonable prior, it is important to set a prior responsibly. But this may be hard to do. A pragmatic compromise may be to choose a simpler model (which sets some parameters at zero) with diffuse priors, because now the data may be efficacious enough to tolerate such inaccurate priors.

20.7.3 To Justify the Model

One may plan to base an analysis on a model incorporating additivity (just discussed) or Normality (Berkson's concern above). If the model is inadequate, a more complicated model and analysis will be needed. What data require the more complicated treatment?

In a wide variety of problems, classical approaches have yielded useful models and statistics and valuable insights, but "objective" significance levels are related unclearly if at all to the issues at hand, as classical statisticians like Berkson have themselves recognized. Unfortunately the issues are complex and difficult and defy both "objective" and operational Bayesian resolution. A subjective (Bayesian) resolution may be possible conceptually but far too intractable to implement in practice.

Appendix: Outline of Some Aspects of Sufficient Statistics

For each of the processes we have discussed in detail (Bernoulli, Poisson, and Normal), we noted that the analysis depended only on a small number of "sufficient" statistics, beyond which the full history or set of observations was not needed. Because this simplification occurred automatically, further discussion was unnecessary. From a broader perspective, however, one wants to know when it will occur, and the concept of sufficiency is very important in classical statistics, where nothing is automatic, and in all sorts of theoretical, mathematical, and methodological discussions. We sketch here some essential aspects of sufficiency and related concepts, without rigor or proofs.

1. Sufficiency

Suppose a probability model for the observable quantity $\tilde{x}$ given the state parameter θ and a prior distribution of $\tilde{\theta}$ have been specified. For example, θ might be the parameter p of a Bernoulli process and x the particular history observed according to some specified sampling rule such as (i) take exactly 10 observations, or (ii) stop after the 17th success or 4th failure, whichever occurs first. The prior distribution of $\tilde{\theta}$ could then be some member of the beta family, or any other specified distribution on $[0, 1]$.

Let $y = y(x)$ be a function of x, such as $y(x) = (r, n)$ in the Bernoulli example, where r is the number of successes and n the number of observations in the history x. (In general x, y, and θ may be vectors.) A natural Bayesian definition of "y is sufficient for x" is

A. (Bayesian Sufficiency) The distribution of $\tilde{\theta}$ given $\tilde{x} = x$ is the same as that given $\tilde{y} = y$ for all x. (Here x and y must correspond, that is, $y = y(x)$.)

For example, the distribution of the Bernoulli process parameter $\tilde{p}$ given any history x is the same as that given (r, n) for the r and n implied by x (verification below). This is true for all prior distributions, but as we shall see, true for one implies true for all here, so the distinction between them is minor.

Another natural B yesian definition, fortunately equivalent, is that y indexes (parameterizes) the posterior distributions:

B. (Sufficient Parameterization) The distribution of $\tilde{\theta}$ given x depends only on $y(x)$.

For example, the distribution of $\tilde{p}$ given any history x depends only on (r, n). If your intuition says (A) and (B) are obviously equivalent, you are correct, but you should write out a proof.

Two equivalent analytical conditions, the second already famous in classical statistics, are

C. (Form of Posterior) The mass or density function of $\tilde{\theta}$ given x is a function of θ and $y(x)$.

D. (Neyman Factorization) The mass or density function of $\tilde{x}$ given θ is a function of x times a function of $y(x)$ and θ.

We now illustrate and verify (A)–(D) in the Bernoulli case where x is the particular history observed, $\theta = p$, and $y(x) = (r, n)$. The model has mass function

$$f(x|\theta) = \delta(x)\theta^r(1-\theta)^{n-r}$$

where $\delta(x) = 1$ if x is consistent with the sampling rule and $\delta(x) = 0$ otherwise. Thus the Neyman factorization (D) clearly holds. For any prior density $f_0(\theta)$, the posterior density

$$f(\theta|x) \propto f_0(\theta)\theta^r(1-\theta)^{n-r},$$

which is a function of θ and (r, n) and hence has the form (C). The posterior distribution of $\tilde{\theta}$ depends only on (r, n) which is therefore a sufficient parameter (B).

The mass function of (r, n) given θ is

$$f((r,n)|\theta) = N(r,n)\theta^r(1-\theta)^{n-r}$$

where $N(r, n)$ is the number of histories consistent with the sampling rule and with (r, n). The posterior density given (r, n) is

$$f(\theta|(r,n)) \propto f_0(\theta)\theta^r(1-\theta)^{n-r}.$$

This is the same as $f(\theta|x)$, which verifies the definition of Bayesian sufficiency (A).

Condition (D) is to be understood as holding for all θ where the prior mass or density function of $\tilde{\theta}$ is positive. Since conditions (A)–(C) are equivalent, these conditions also depend on the prior mass or density function of $\tilde{\theta}$ only through where it is positive, although the actual posterior distributions mentioned in (A)–(C) depend on the actual prior distribution.

Sometimes a definition is used requiring (A)–(C) to hold for all prior distributions. They do so if they hold for any one prior mass or density function that is positive at all values of θ. This definition is therefore a special case of the definition using a single prior. Indeed it is equivalent if one takes as the range of θ the region where the prior mass or density function of $\tilde{\theta}$ is positive, which one might as well do.

The Neyman factorization criterion (D) was invented for the classical definition of "y is sufficient for x," namely

E. (Classical Sufficiency) The distribution of $\tilde{x}$ given y and θ depends on y alone.

In the Bernoulli example, this says that the distribution of x given (r, n) and p is the same for all p, so intuitively (?) x is not providing any information about p beyond that provided by (r, n). Giving this intuition concrete form, a specific reason for adopting definition (E), in the classical framework, is that it is equivalent to

F. (Model Reproducibility) Given $\tilde{y}$ alone, one can define a random variable $\tilde{X}$ such that the distribution of $\tilde{X}$ given θ is the same as the distribution of $\tilde{x}$ given θ for all θ.

This implies that the operating characteristics of any procedure depending on x can be duplicated knowing y alone, by applying the procedure to $\tilde{X}$.

In the Bernoulli example, classical sufficiency (E) is verified by calculating

$$f(x|(r,n),\theta) = \frac{f(x,(r,n)|\theta)}{f((r,n)|\theta)} = \frac{\delta(x,r,n)}{N(r,n)}$$

where $\delta(x, r, n) = 1$ if x is consistent with the sampling rule and with (r, n), and $\delta(x, r, n) = 0$ otherwise. To reproduce the model (F), one observes (r, n) and then sets $\tilde{X} = x$ with probability $\delta(x, r, n)/N(r, n)$, that is, chooses at random one of the $N(r, n)$ histories that could have produced (r, n) under the sampling rule.

The equivalence of all six conditions in general is easy to prove once the concepts are fully understood. The equivalence requires that the range of θ in (D)–(F) coincide with the region where the prior mass or density function of $\tilde{\theta}$ is positive in (A)–(C). This says the model is what the prior distribution effectively permits, so it is a natural requirement under which to compare definitions of sufficiency, and we assume it implicitly throughout.

The reader is invited to verify each of the conditions (A)–(F) for the Normal model with known variance when $y = (m, n)$ where m is the sample mean, and for unknown variance when y is suitably defined.

2. Closure under Sampling

Suppose that the observable quantities $\tilde{z}_1, \tilde{z}_2, \ldots$ form an independent random process with mass or density function $f_{z|\theta}(z|\theta)$, that is, the model specifies that, given θ, the $\tilde{z}_i$ are independently, identically distributed with this mass or density function. (Most of what follows would be much more complicated to state for nonindependent models.) A family of distributions for $\tilde{\theta}$ is called *closed under sampling* if the posterior distribution of $\tilde{\theta}$ belongs to the family whenever the prior distribution belongs to the family, whatever the observations $z_1 \ldots z_n$ may be. (The quantity $\tilde{x}$ of the previous section would be the vector of observations actually made under some specific sampling rule, but in the following discussion, sampling can continue indefinitely.)

For a Bernoulli process with parameter θ, the family of beta distributions for $\tilde{\theta}$ is closed under sampling. So is the family of beta distributions with integer parameters (i.e. densities of the form $\theta^{\rho-1}(1-\theta)^{\sigma-1}/B(\rho,\sigma)$ with ρ and σ positive integers). So are some non-beta families, as we shall see. The Bernoulli model, not the beta family, is crucial here.

Let F_0 be any particular prior distribution of $\tilde{\theta}$ and consider the family of all posterior distributions which can arise from the prior distribution F_0 as the observations vary, that is, as n and $z_1, \ldots, z_n$ vary. The reader should verify that this family is closed under sampling. We shall call it the family generated by F_0.

For the Bernoulli process, a uniform prior distribution generates the family of beta distributions with integer parameters. To motivate the next point, we note that this family can be parameterized by the sufficient statistic (r, n) by identifying $\rho = r + 1$, $\sigma = n - r + 1$. The prior density $\theta^{-1/2}(1-\theta)^{-1/2}/\pi$ generates the family with ρ and σ each a positive half-integer, that is, $\frac{1}{2}$ less than a positive integer. It can be parameterized by (r, n) by identifying $\rho = r + \frac{1}{2}$, $\sigma = n - r + \frac{1}{2}$. The prior density $(\pi/2)\sin(\pi\theta)$ generates the family of non-beta densities $K(a,b)\theta^a(1-\theta)^b\sin(\pi\theta)$ where a and b are nonnegative integers and

$$K(a,b) = 1 \Big/ \int_0^1 \theta^a(1-\theta)^b \sin(\pi\theta)\,d\theta.$$

This family is also closed under sampling, and can be parameterized by (r, n) by identifying $a = r$, $b = n - r$. Similar comments apply to any prior density. The significant feature of these families is that their parameter is two-dimensional—no matter how many observations are made, the distribution of $\tilde{\theta}$ remains within a family described by a parameter of fixed dimension—and the sufficient statistic (r, n) can serve as the parameter. This is true for the family generated by any prior F_0 whatever. (Technically it is difficult to define rigorously the minimum number of dimensions required to describe a statistic or parameterize a family of distributions, especially when integer restrictions are present, but this does not negate our positive statements or intuition.)

Returning to the general case, let F_0 be any prior distribution. If, for each n, the statistic $y_n = y_n(z_1, \ldots, z_n)$ is sufficient for $z_1, \ldots, z_n$, then the family generated by F_0 can be parameterized by y_n. (Assume throughout that n is a component of y_n.) In particular, if the dimension of y_n never exceeds k, then the family can be parameterized by a k-dimensional parameter. We thus have a k-parameter family of distributions which is closed under sampling.

Note that this possibility is a property of the model and not of the prior distribution F_0. It depends on whether the model admits a k-dimensional sufficient statistic (including n in the statistic). It does not depend on the choice of F_0.

If F_0 is replaced by an r parameter family $\mathscr{F}_0$ of distributions, then the union of the families generated by all F_0 in $\mathscr{F}_0$ is itself a family closed under sampling. It can be parameterized by a $(k + r)$-dimensional parameter if the model admits a k-dimensional sufficient statistic y_n. The dimension can of course be less than $k + r$; for instance, it is r if $\mathscr{F}_0$ is closed under sampling to begin with, like the beta family for the Bernoulli process.

3. Dimension of Sufficient Statistics. Generalized Exponential Models

The full vector of observations $z_1, \ldots, z_n$ is of course a sufficient statistic for each n. This sufficient statistic has dimension n, however, which obviously grows inconveniently as the number of observations increases. When do simpler sufficient statistics exist? Unfortunately only in quite special circumstances. For independent random process models, it is a remarkable fact that under certain regularity conditions, reduction of the dimension is possible if and only if the mass or density function has the *generalized exponential* form

$$f_{z|\theta}(z|\theta) = C(\theta)h(z)\exp\{\textstyle\sum_{j=1}^{k} \lambda_j(\theta)T_j(z)\}.$$

Though special, this form allows more flexibility than it may appear through choices of the functions h, λ_j, and T_j. (C is then determined by integration.) The reader should verify that the Normal density, the Poisson mass function, and the mass function for Bernoulli trials have this form; for the latter

$$C(\theta) = 1 - \theta, \qquad \lambda_1(\theta) = \log\frac{\theta}{1-\theta}, \qquad T_1(z) = z,$$

$k = 1$, and $h(z) = 1$ for $z = 0, 1$; $h(z) = 0$ otherwise.

It is easy to apply the Neyman factorization criterion (D) to the generalized exponential form and show that, for every n, a $(k + 1)$-dimensional sufficient statistic for $z_1, \ldots, z_n$ is

$$y_n(z_1, \ldots, z_n) = (n, \textstyle\sum_{v=1}^{n} T_1(z_v), \ldots, \sum_{v=1}^{n} T_k(z_v)).$$

Note the dimension of y_n does not depend on n. What is surprising is the converse: if, for even one n, a sufficient statistic of dimension less than n exists for $z_1, \ldots, z_n$ under an independent random process model satisfying certain regularity conditions, then the model must be of the generalized exponential form (with respect to some measure). The important regularity condition is that the set of zs where $f_{z|\theta}(z|\theta) > 0$ does not depend on θ. Dropping this condition allows as additional possibilities families of rectangular distributions and generalizations such as $f_{z|\theta}(z|\theta) = C(\theta)h(z)$ if $\theta_1 < z < \theta_2$ and $f_{z|\theta}(z|\theta) = 0$ otherwise, where the sample minimum and maximum are sufficient; and models that combine these with the generalized exponential form. The other regularity conditions are smoothness requirements without which we are in exotic terrain.

All this means that streamlined types of closure under sampling, updating (combining samples), and so on, essentially occur only in one well-known class of models where they can be reduced to particular simple forms. In all other cases the full sample is needed. The variety one might expect and enjoy does not exist.

4. Updating

If $y' = y_n(z_1, \ldots, z_n)$ is sufficient for the first n observations and $y'' = y_m(z_{n+1}, \ldots, z_{n+m})$ is sufficient for the next m observations, then $y = (y', y'')$ is sufficient for the whole set of $n + m$ observations. (The reader should prove this.) However, the dimension of y is the sum of the dimensions of y' and y''.

The generalized exponential form allows updating by simple addition. In the Bernoulli process, for example, let $y' = (r_1, n)$ and $y'' = (r_2, m)$ where r_1 and r_2 are the numbers of successes in the first n and the next m observations. Then $y = y' + y'' = (r_1 + r_2, n + m)$ is the updating rule. The same rule extends to y_n as defined above in the general case, namely

$$y_{n+m}(z_1, \ldots, z_{n+m}) = y_n(z_1, \ldots, z_n) + y_m(z_{n+1}, \ldots, z_{n+m}).$$

Other statistics may be more natural for other reasons, but less simple to update. Think, for example, how the sample mean and standard deviation update. The sample minimum and maximum are also easy to update.

A sufficient statistic y_n defined for each n may not be updatable at all if it includes unnecessary information, but of course there is no reason to do so within the framework of the model. An example would be $y_n = (r, n, z_n - z_1)$ for a Bernoulli process.

The updating of prior distributions needs no separate discussion, since it amounts to the updating of sufficient statistics. We emphasize again that the complexity of the updating rule depends primarily on the model, secondarily on the choice of sufficient statistic, and not at all fundamentally on the prior or family of priors used.

21 Multivariate Random Variables

21.1 Introduction: Definition of a Multivariate Random Variable

21.1.1 Multivariate Quantities and Values

In most practical situations we are interested simultaneously in several unknown or variable quantities. For instance, when contemplating a market test of a new product, we might want to consider at least the following quantities: the sales of the new product in each of several stores in the test area in each of several weeks; the sales of similar products in these and other stores in the same weeks; and the total national sales of the new product that would be obtained in the first year if the product were marketed nationally with a certain marketing strategy. If we are interested in r quantities simultaneously, we could of course think of them as r separate though possibly related entities, but in this chapter we shall think of them as a *single entity* described by r numbers. As in chapter 13, which dealt with paired rv's, we will keep track of which numerical value applies to which quantity by keeping the r quantities in the same order throughout any discussion. Thus, we will be dealing with an r-variate quantity, each possible value of which is an *ordered* r-tuple.

Many (but not all) aspects of the joint distribution of several rv's appear clearly in the bivariate case. For fuller discussion of these aspects than is given in this chapter, the reader may refer to chapter 13. The organization of this chapter closely follows that of chapter 13. Section 21.1 contains the formal definition of a multivariate rv. In sections 21.2, 21.3, and 21.4 we consider successively the cases where the component rv's are all discrete, some discrete and some continuous, or all continuous; we call these the *discrete*, *mixed*, and *continuous* cases respectively. Later sections develop results which hold for all three of these cases.

21.1.2 Notation

Let $\tilde{z}_1, \tilde{z}_2, \ldots, \tilde{z}_r$ be rv's with which we wish to deal simultaneously. As indicated above, we shall work in terms of the ordered r-tuple $(\tilde{z}_1, \tilde{z}_2, \ldots, \tilde{z}_r)$. Sometimes it is more convenient to use instead the $r \times 1$ vector[1]

$$\tilde{\mathbf{z}} = [\tilde{z}_1 \tilde{z}_2 \ldots \tilde{z}_r]^t = \begin{bmatrix} \tilde{z}_1 \\ \tilde{z}_2 \\ \vdots \\ \tilde{z}_r \end{bmatrix}.$$

1. Vector and matrix notation and operations are explained in appendix 2. We shall often write column vectors as transposed row vectors for typographical economy.

It makes no essential difference whether r-tuples or $r \times 1$ vectors are used, and we shall not state every formula in both notations, nor shall we apologize every time we switch from one notation to the other.

The generic values of $\tilde{z}$ will be denoted by $(z_1, z_2, \ldots, z_r)$ or $z = [z_1 z_2 \ldots z_r]'$. Thus the event

$$(\tilde{z}_1 = z_1, \tilde{z}_2 = z_2, \ldots, \tilde{z}_r = z_r)$$

may also be written

$$(\tilde{z}_1, \tilde{z}_2, \ldots, \tilde{z}_r) = (z_1, z_2, \ldots, z_r)$$

or

$$[\tilde{z}_1 \tilde{z}_2 \ldots \tilde{z}_r]' = [z_1 z_2 \ldots z_r]'$$

or simply

$$\tilde{z} = z.$$

We define inequality of vectors and r-tuples in such a way that the last sentence remains true when $=$ is replaced by $\leq$.

21.1.3 Definition of a Multivariate RV

Any unknown r-tuple $(r \geq 1)$ of real quantities $(\tilde{z}_1, \tilde{z}_2, \ldots, \tilde{z}_r)$ will be called a *multivariate rv* or simply a *rv* if each component $\tilde{z}_i$ is a real rv and if probability assessments can also be made for all events of the form

$$(\tilde{z}_1 \in I_1, \tilde{z}_2 \in I_2, \ldots, \tilde{z}_r \in I_r)$$

where $I_1, I_2, \ldots, I_r$ are intervals on the real line.

It follows immediately from the definition that if $(\tilde{z}_1, \tilde{z}_2, \ldots, \tilde{z}_r)$ is a multivariate rv, then any sub-tuple, such as $(\tilde{z}_2, \ldots, \tilde{z}_r)$ or $(\tilde{z}_1, \tilde{z}_3, \tilde{z}_4)$ or $(\tilde{z}_{r-1})$ is also a rv.

Using the Nullity Assumption for the component rv's $\tilde{z}_i$, we can easily prove[2]:

a. $P(\tilde{z}_1 \leq z_1, \tilde{z}_2 \leq z_2, \ldots, \tilde{z}_r \leq z_r) \to 1$

if $z_1 \to \infty$, $z_2 \to \infty$, …, and $z_r \to \infty$; (21.1a)

b. $P(\tilde{z}_1 \leq z_1, \tilde{z}_2 \leq z_2, \ldots, \tilde{z}_r \leq z_r) \to 0$

if $z_1 \to -\infty$ or $z_2 \to -\infty$ … or $z_r \to -\infty$; (21.1b)

---

2. The Nullity Assumption of section 13.1.2 is equivalent to the assumption that $\tilde{x}$ and $\tilde{y}$ each satisfy the Nullity Assumption of chapter 7.

c. $P(\tilde{z}_1 \leq z_1, \ldots, \tilde{z}_i \leq z_i, \ldots, \tilde{z}_r \leq z_r)$

$\rightarrow P(\tilde{z}_1 \leq z_1, \ldots, \tilde{z}_{i-1} \leq z_{i-1}, \tilde{z}_{i+1} \leq z_{i+1}, \ldots, \tilde{z}_r \leq z_r)$

if $z_i \rightarrow \infty$; (21.1c)

d. The expression $P(\tilde{z}_1 \leq z_1, \tilde{z}_2 \leq z_2, \ldots, \tilde{z}_r \leq z_r)$ treated as a function of any z_i is continuous from the right.

21.2 Discrete Multivariate RV's

21.2.1 Definition of a Discrete Multivariate RV

A multivariate rv $(\tilde{z}_1, \ldots, \tilde{z}_r)$ is said to be a *discrete* multivariate rv if there exist discrete sets $Z_1, \ldots, Z_r$ of real numbers such that for all $z_1, \ldots, z_r$,

$$P(\tilde{z}_1 \leq z_1, \ldots, \tilde{z}_r \leq z_r) = \sum_{x_1 \leqq z_1} \cdots \sum_{x_r \leqq z_r} P(\tilde{z}_1 = x_1, \ldots, \tilde{z}_r = x_r),$$

$$x_1 \in Z_1, \ldots, x_r \in Z_r, \qquad (21.2)$$

where $x_1, \ldots, x_r$ are dummy variables of summation and where the sum is taken over all r-tuples $(x_1, \ldots, x_r)$ in $Z_1 \times \cdots \times Z_r$ for which $x_1 \leq z_1, \ldots$ $x_r \leq z_r$. In similar summations hereafter, it is to be understood that the dummy variables belong to $Z_1, \ldots, Z_r$ as appropriate, even if this is not explicitly mentioned.

21.2.2 Joint Mass Function

A real-valued function f of r real arguments will be called a *joint mass function* if, for some discrete sets $Z_1, \ldots, Z_r$,

$$f(z_1, \ldots, z_r) \begin{Bmatrix} \geq \\ = \end{Bmatrix} 0 \quad \text{for all } (z_1, \ldots, z_r) \begin{Bmatrix} \in \\ \notin \end{Bmatrix} Z_1 \times \cdots \times Z_r \qquad (21.3a)$$

and

$$\sum f(z_1, \ldots, z_r) = 1,$$

where the sum is understood to be taken over all r-tuples $(z_1, \ldots, z_r)$ in $Z_1 \times \cdots \times Z_r$.

21.2.3 Joint MF of a Discrete Multivariate RV

If $(\tilde{z}_1, \ldots, \tilde{z}_r)$ is a discrete multivariate rv and f is defined by

$$f(z_1, \ldots, z_r) \equiv P(\tilde{z}_1 = z_1, \ldots, \tilde{z}_r = z_r),$$

then the reader can verify that f is a joint mf.

Conversely, if f is a joint mf and if we define P by

$$P[(\tilde{z}_1,\ldots,\tilde{z}_r)\in S] = \sum_{(z_1,\ldots,z_r)\in S} f(z_1,\ldots,z_r),$$

then P is a probability measure and the multivariate rv $(\tilde{z}_1,\ldots,\tilde{z}_r)$ with this measure P is a discrete multivariate rv.

In either of these cases we shall say that f is the joint mf of the discrete multivariate rv $(\tilde{z}_1,\ldots,\tilde{z}_r)$.

Display of the Joint Mass Function in the Finite Case

When Z_1, ..., Z_r are finite, the joint mass function of $\tilde{z}_1$, ..., $\tilde{z}_r$ can be displayed in the form of a list, no matter what r may be. This is illustrated for the special case of four two-valued rv's in table 21.1 at the end of this section. Alternative forms of display with additional features will be given for the same example shortly.

21.2.4 Marginal Mass Functions

Suppose $(\tilde{z}_1,\ldots,\tilde{z}_r)$ is a discrete rv with joint mass function f. Then by exercise 1, $\tilde{z}_1$ is a discrete rv with mass function f_1, where

$$f_1(z_1) = P(\tilde{z}_1 = z_1) = \sum_{z_2,\ldots,z_r} f(z_1,z_2,\ldots,z_r) \qquad \text{for all } z_1. \tag{21.4}$$

We shall call f_1 the *marginal mass function* of $\tilde{z}_1$. The marginal mass functions of $\tilde{z}_2$, ..., $\tilde{z}_r$ are similarly defined. Hereafter such statements concerning symmetric relations are taken for granted.

Under the same circumstances, $(\tilde{z}_1,\tilde{z}_2)$ is a discrete paired rv with joint mass function $f_{1,2}$, where

$$\begin{aligned} f_{1,2}(z_1,z_2) &= P(\tilde{z}_1 = z_1, \tilde{z}_2 = z_2) \\ &= \sum_{z_3,\ldots,z_r} f(z_1,z_2,z_3,\ldots,z_r) \qquad \text{for all } z_1,\, z_2. \end{aligned} \tag{21.5}$$

We shall call $f_{1,2}$ the *marginal mass function* of $(\tilde{z}_1,\tilde{z}_2)$, or the *joint mass function* of $\tilde{z}_1$ and $\tilde{z}_2$ *marginal on* $\tilde{z}_3,\ldots,\tilde{z}_r$. Marginal mass functions such as $f_{1,2,3}$ or $f_{4,5,6,8}$ are similarly defined and related to the joint mass function f. The word *marginal* merely supplies emphasis and could be omitted from the expression "marginal mass function" without changing its meaning.

For a multivariate rv, such as $(\tilde{x},\tilde{\mu},\tilde{\xi})$ whose component rv's do not have numerical suffixes, we shall use letter suffixes on marginal mf's, as in chapter 13. Thus $f_{x,\mu}$ denotes the (joint) mf of $\tilde{x}$ and $\tilde{\mu}$, marginal on all other rv's.

The display in table 21.2, at the end of the section, not only shows the joint mass function of $\tilde{z}_1$, $\tilde{z}_2$, $\tilde{z}_3$, and $\tilde{z}_4$ for the example of table 21.1 but also shows the marginal mass functions of $\tilde{z}_1$, $\tilde{z}_3$, $(\tilde{z}_1,\tilde{z}_2)$ and $(\tilde{z}_3,\tilde{z}_4)$ and makes the marginal mf's of $\tilde{z}_2$ and $\tilde{z}_4$ very easy to compute. Still another form of display is the tree in figure 21.1, which shows directly the joint mass function and the marginal mf's of $(\tilde{z}_1, \tilde{z}_2, \tilde{z}_3)$, $(\tilde{z}_1, \tilde{z}_2)$, and $\tilde{z}_1$.

Vector Notation

Let $\tilde{z}_1, \tilde{z}_2, \ldots, \tilde{z}_r$ be considered as a $r \times 1$ vector $\tilde{\mathbf{z}}$. Now partition $\tilde{\mathbf{z}}$ into $\tilde{\mathbf{z}}_1$ and $\tilde{\mathbf{z}}_2$:

$$\tilde{\mathbf{z}} = [\tilde{z}_1 \ldots \tilde{z}_p \vdots \tilde{z}_{p+1} \ldots \tilde{z}_r]^t = [\tilde{\mathbf{z}}_1^t \tilde{\mathbf{z}}_2^t]^t. \tag{21.6}$$

When we are using vector notation, f_1 will denote the marginal mass function of $\tilde{\mathbf{z}}_1$, so that f_1 in vector notation is identical in meaning to $f_{1,2,\ldots,p}$ in scalar notation. In vector notation we then have

$$f_1(\mathbf{z}_1) = P(\tilde{\mathbf{z}}_1 = \mathbf{z}_1) = \textstyle\sum_{\mathbf{z}_2} f(\mathbf{z}_1, \mathbf{z}_2) \tag{21.7}$$

where the summation is over all $\mathbf{z}_2$, that is, over all $z_{p+1}, \ldots, z_r$, and where we use the somewhat informal notation $f(\mathbf{z}_1, \mathbf{z}_2)$ instead of the formal but unwieldy $f([\mathbf{z}_1^t \mathbf{z}_2^t]^t)$. Equation (21.7) reduces to (21.5) when $p = 2$, that is, when $\tilde{\mathbf{z}}_1 = [\tilde{z}_1 \tilde{z}_2]^t$, and to similar equations for other values of p. For $p = 1$, $\mathbf{z}_1$ is actually scalar, that is, $\tilde{\mathbf{z}}_1 = \tilde{z}_1$, and equation (21.7) reduces to (21.4). In fact, (21.7) may be considered a completely general formula for any marginal mass function, in view of the possibility of renumbering the components of $\tilde{\mathbf{z}}$.

21.2.5 Conditional Mass Functions

Let $(\tilde{z}_1, \ldots, \tilde{z}_r)$ be a discrete rv with mass function f. Then by exercise 1, conditional on the event $(\tilde{z}_2 = z_2, \ldots, \tilde{z}_r = z_r)$ the rv $\tilde{z}_1$ is a discrete rv with mf $f_{1|2,\ldots,r}(\cdot \mid z_2, \ldots, z_r)$, where

$$f_{1|2,\ldots,r}(z_1 \mid z_2, \ldots, z_r) \equiv \frac{f(z_1, \ldots, z_r)}{f_{2,\ldots,r}(z_2, \ldots, z_r)} \tag{21.8}$$

for all $z_2, \ldots, z_r$ such that $f_{2,\ldots,r}(z_2, \ldots, z_r) > 0$. We shall call $f_{1|2,\ldots,r}(\cdot \mid z_2, \ldots, z_r)$ the *conditional mass function* of $\tilde{z}_1$ *given* $z_2, \ldots, z_r$. The subscripts on f indicate the rv whose distribution concerns us, then the rv's whose values we are conditioning on, while the arguments denote the values of these rv's in the same order. We could not do without the subscripts because when we substitute numerical values for the arguments z_1 and $z_2, \ldots, z_r$, the subscripts tell us what rv's the numerical values apply to: $f_{1|2}(7|3)$ and $f_{2|1}(7|3)$ have different meanings.

Similarly, *given* that $\tilde{z}_3 = z_3, \ldots, \tilde{z}_r = z_r$, the *conditional (joint) mass function* of $\tilde{z}_1$ and $\tilde{z}_2$ is $f_{1,2|3,\ldots,r}(\cdot \mid z_3, \ldots, z_r)$, where

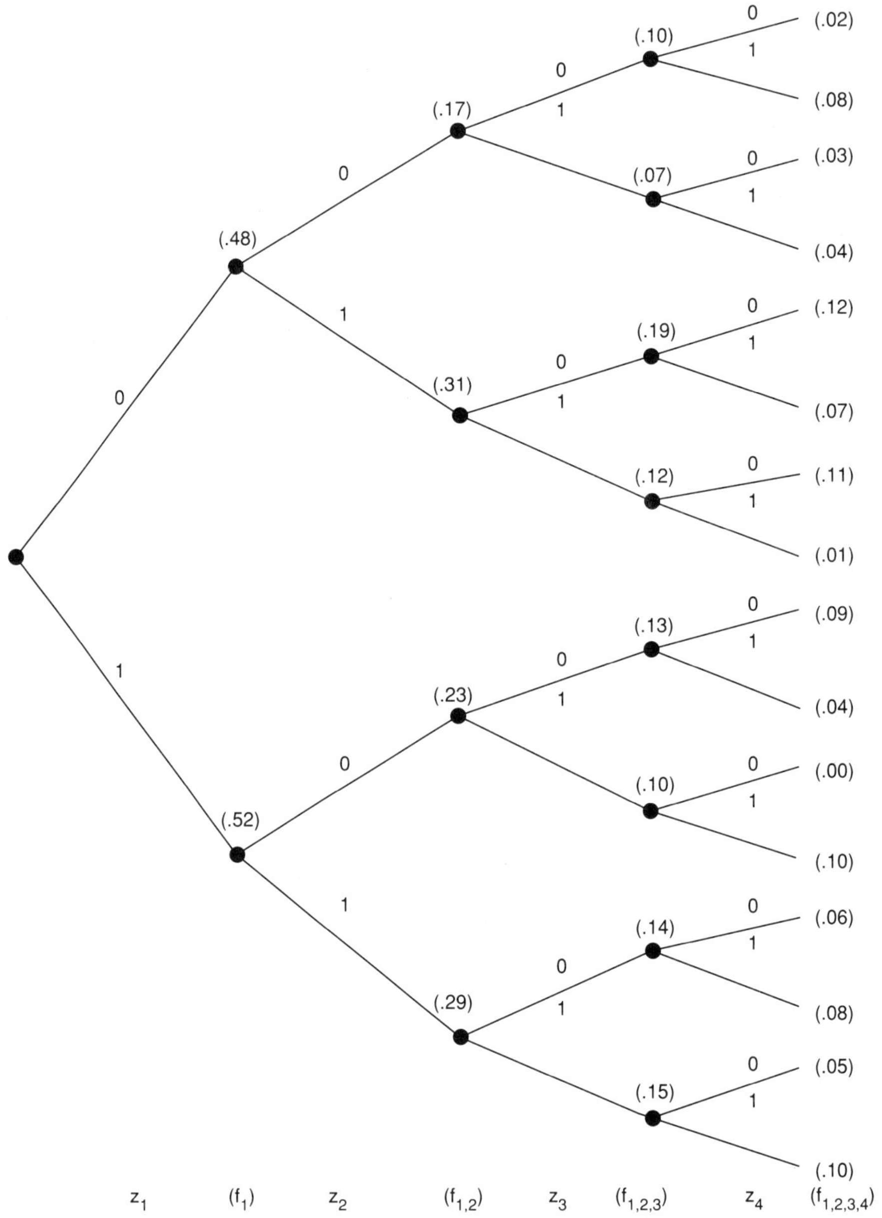

Figure 21.1
Probability tree

$$f_{1,2|3,\ldots,r}(z_1, z_2 | z_3, \ldots, z_r) \equiv \frac{f(z_1, \ldots, z_r)}{f_{3,\ldots,r}(z_3, \ldots, z_r)} \tag{21.9}$$

for all $z_3, \ldots, z_r$ such that $f_{3,\ldots,r}(z_3, \ldots, z_r) > 0$. Other conditional mass functions such as $f_{3,5|1,2,4}$ are similarly defined.

Vector Notation

Let the $r \times 1$ rv $\tilde{z}$ be partitioned into two vectors $\tilde{z}_1$ and $\tilde{z}_2$ as in (21.6) and let f_2 denote the marginal (joint) mass function of $\tilde{z}_2$. Then the *conditional mass function* of $\tilde{z}_1$ given z_2 is $f_{1|2}(\cdot | z_2)$, where

$$f_{1|2}(z_1 | z_2) \equiv \frac{f(z_1, z_2)}{f_2(z_2)} = \frac{f(z)}{f_2(z_2)} \tag{21.10}$$

for all z_2 such that $f_2(z_2) > 0$. By renumbering the components of $\tilde{z}$ as necessary, we may take (21.10) as a completely general formula for the conditional mass function of any rv or set of rv's given a specified value or set of values of any other rv or set of rv's.

From the joint mass function of table 21.2, the reader should derive the two conditional mass functions in table 21.3, and from figure 21.1, the two conditional mass functions is table 21.4.

21.2.6 Conditional-Marginal Mass Functions

We are frequently interested in the mass function of some variable(s) conditional on some other variable(s) but marginal as regards yet some other variable(s). Formally, let $\tilde{z}$ be partitioned

$$\tilde{z} = [\tilde{z}_1^t \tilde{z}_2^t \tilde{z}_3^t]^t,$$

let f_2 be the marginal mass function of $\tilde{z}_2$, and let $f_{1,2}$ be the marginal mass function of $(\tilde{z}_1, \tilde{z}_2)$. Then the conditional mass function of $\tilde{z}_1$ given $\tilde{z}_2 = z_2$ is $f_{1|2}(\cdot | z_2)$, where

$$f_{1|2}(z_1 | z_2) \equiv \frac{f_{1,2}(z_1, z_2)}{f_2(z_2)} = P(\tilde{z}_1 = z_1 | \tilde{z}_2 = z_2) \tag{21.11}$$

for all z_2 such that $f_2(z_2) > 0$. Technically we are in the same situation as in the previous subsection, but when we wish to emphasize that all this is marginal as regards $\tilde{z}_3$, we shall call $f_{1|2}(\cdot | z_2)$ the mass function of $\tilde{z}_1$ conditional on $\tilde{z}_2 = z_2$ but marginal as regards $\tilde{z}_3$, or the conditional-marginal mass function of $\tilde{z}_1$ given $\tilde{z}_2 = z_2$ and marginal on $\tilde{z}_3$. From table 21.2 the reader should obtain the mass function in table 21.5a, which is marginal as regards $\tilde{z}_4$, and from figure 21.1 he should obtain the mass function in table 21.5b, which is marginal as regards (z_3, z_4).

Table 21.1

z_1	z_2	z_3	z_4	$f(z_1, z_2, z_3, z_4)$
0	0	0	0	.02
0	0	0	1	.08
0	0	1	0	.03
0	0	1	1	.04
0	1	0	0	.12
0	1	0	1	.07
0	1	1	0	.11
0	1	1	1	.01
1	0	0	0	.09
1	0	0	1	.04
1	0	1	0	.00
1	0	1	1	.10
1	1	0	0	.06
1	1	0	1	.08
1	1	1	0	.05
1	1	1	1	.10
				1.00

Table 21.2

z_1	z_2	z_3:	0		1		$f_{1,2}$	f_1
		z_4	0	1	0	1		
0	0:		.02	.08	.03	.04	.17	.48
	1:		.12	.07	.11	.01	.31	
1	0:		.09	.04	.00	.10	.23	.52
	1:		.06	.08	.05	.10	.29	
$f_{3,4}$:			.29	.27	.19	.25		
f_3:			.56		.44			1.00

Table 21.3a

z_4	$f_{4\|1,2,3}(z_4\|0, 1, 1)$
0	.11/.12
1	.01/.12
	1

Table 21.3b

z_2	z_3	$f_{2,3\|1,4}(z_2, z_3\|0, 1)$
0	0	.08/.20
0	1	.04/.20
1	0	.07/.20
1	1	.01/.20
		1

Table 21.4a

z_4	$f_{4\|1,2,3}(z_4\|1, 0, 0)$
0	.09/.13
1	.04/.13
	1

Table 21.4b

z_3	z_4	$f_{3,4\|1,2}(z_3, z_4\|0, 1)$
0	0	.12/.31
0	1	.07/.31
1	0	.11/.31
1	1	.01/.31
		1

Table 21.5a

z_1	z_2	$f_{1,2\|3}(z_1, z_2\|1)$
0	0	(.03 + .04)/.44
0	1	(.11 + .01)/.44
1	0	(.00 + .10)/.44
1	1	(.05 + .10)/.44
		1

Table 21.5b

z_2	$f_{2\|1}(z_2\|0)$
0	.17/.48
1	.31/.48
	1

21.3 Mixed Multivariate Random Variables

The concept of a mixed paired rv discussed in section 13.3 can be generalized to a mixed multivariate rv $\tilde{z}$. All essential features of the distribution of a mixed multivariate rv are present in either the mixed bivariate case (section 13.3), the discrete multivariate case (section 21.2), or the continuous multivariate case (section 21.4, to follow). Accordingly, and because we will not make any use of it, the mixed multivariate casc will not be discussed in detail. The formulas for the marginal, conditional, and conditional-marginal density-mass functions (which sometimes reduce to mass or density functions) are like those in the discrete and continuous cases.

21.4 Continuous Multivariate RV's

21.4.1 Introduction

In many situations we wish to deal simultaneously with several continuous real rv's. This calls for a generalization, to be carried out now, of section 13.4, which concerned a pair of continuous real rv's. Again, we shall avoid special formulas for special cases by taking the range of each real rv to be *all* real numbers. A continuous multivariate rv will be defined formally in terms of a joint density function. Informally, however, we may say that a multivariate rv $(\tilde{z}_1, \ldots, \tilde{z}_r)$ is continuous if $P(\tilde{z}_1 \leq z_1, \ldots, \tilde{z}_r \leq z_r)$ is a "sufficiently smooth" function of $z_1, \ldots, z_r$.

21.4.2 Joint Density Function

A real-valued function f of r real arguments will be called a joint density function (df) if

$$f(z_1, \ldots, z_r) \geq 0 \qquad \text{for all } z_1, \ldots, z_r; \tag{21.12a}$$

$$\int_{-\infty}^{\infty} f(z_1, \ldots, z_r)\, dz_i \qquad \text{exists for all } z_1, \ldots, z_{i-1}, z_{i+1}, \ldots, z_r \text{ and all } i; \tag{21.12b}$$

$$\int_{-\infty}^{\infty} \cdots \int_{-\infty}^{\infty} f(z_1, \ldots, z_r)\, dz_1 \ldots dz_r = 1. \tag{21.12c}$$

It can be shown that if these conditions hold, then the integral of f over all arguments in any order is 1, that is (21.12c) holds whatever the order of integration.

21.4.3 Joint Density Function of a Continuous Multivariate RV

The rv $(\tilde{z}_1, \ldots, \tilde{z}_r)$ is said to be a *continuous* multivariate rv if there exists a joint df f such that, for all $z_1, \ldots, z_r$,

$$P(\tilde{z}_1 \leq z_1, \ldots, \tilde{z}_r \leq z_r) = \int_{-\infty}^{z_1} \cdots \int_{-\infty}^{z_r} f(x_1, \ldots, x_r)\, dx_r \cdots dx_1. \tag{21.13a}$$

(Here $x_1, \ldots, x_r$ are dummy variables of integration and the notation of the integral follows the usual convention that the innermost integral sign carries the limits of the innermost variable of integration.) The function f is called the *joint density function of the rv* $(\tilde{z}_1, \ldots, \tilde{z}_r)$. In vector notation, (21.13a) may be written:

$$P(\tilde{z} \leq z) = \int \cdots \int_{x \leq z} f(x)\, dx. \tag{21.13b}$$

If f is continuous at the point z, then

$$\frac{\partial^r}{\partial z_1 \ldots \partial z_r} P(\tilde{z} \leq z) = f(z). \tag{21.14}$$

It follows from (21.13) that

$$P(\tilde{z} \in S) = \int \cdots \int_{S} f(z)\, dz \tag{21.15}$$

for all "reasonable" sets S. This in turn implies that if f is continuous at the point z and S_z is a set contained in a small sphere about z and having volume $\mathrm{Vol}(S_z)$, then we have the approximate equality

$$P(\tilde{z} \in S_z) \doteq f(z)\, \mathrm{Vol}(S_z) \tag{21.16a}$$

and the limiting relation

$$f(z) = \lim \frac{P(\tilde{z} \in S_z)}{\mathrm{Vol}(S_z)}, \tag{21.16b}$$

where the limit is to be taken as the radius of the smallest sphere about z containing S_z approaches 0. This says that $f(z)$ can be interpreted as the amount of probability per unit volume for $\tilde{z}$ near z.

21.4.4 Marginal Density Functions

Suppose $(\tilde{z}_1, \ldots, \tilde{z}_r)$ is a continuous multivariate rv with density function f. Then by exercise 18, $\tilde{z}_1$ is a continuous rv with density function f_1, called the *marginal density function* of $\tilde{z}_1$, where

$$f_1(z_1) = \int \cdots \int f(z_1, z_2, \ldots, z_r)\, dz_2 \cdots dz_r \tag{21.17}$$

is obtained by integrating out all variables except z_1. Furthermore, $(\tilde{z}_1, \tilde{z}_2)$ is a continuous rv with marginal density function $f_{1,2}$, where

$$f_{1,2}(z_1, z_2) = \int \cdots \int f(z_1, z_2, z_3, \ldots, z_r)\, dz_3 \cdots dz_r. \tag{21.18}$$

In general, and in vector notation, if $\tilde{z} = [\tilde{z}_1^t \tilde{z}_2^t]^t$ has density f, then $\tilde{z}_1$ has marginal density f_1, where

$$f_1(z_1) = \int f(z_1, z_2)\, dz_2. \tag{21.19}$$

21.4.5 Conditional Density Functions

Let $\tilde{z} = [\tilde{z}_1 \ldots \tilde{z}_r]^t$ be a continuous rv with density function f. Partition $\tilde{z}$ in the form $\tilde{z} = [\tilde{z}_1^t \tilde{z}_2^t]^t$. Then by exercise 19, as in the bivariate case (section 13.4.5), conditional on the hypothesis $\tilde{z}_2 = z_2$ the rv $\tilde{z}_1$ is a continuous rv with df $f_{1|2}(\cdot|z_2)$, called the *conditional density function* of $\tilde{z}_1$ *given* $\tilde{z}_2 = z_2$, where

$$f_{1|2}(z_1|z_2) = \frac{f(z_1, z_2)}{f_2(z_2)}, \tag{21.20a}$$

provided that $f_2(z_2) > 0$. This defines the conditional density functions expressed in non-vector notation as $f_{1|2,\ldots,r}(\cdot|z_2, \ldots, z_r)$, $f_{1,2|3,\ldots,r}(\cdot, \cdot|z_3, \ldots, z_r)$, and so on, where $f_{1|2,\ldots,r}(\cdot|z_2, \ldots, z_r)$ is the conditional density function of $\tilde{z}_1$ given $\tilde{z}_2 = z_2$, $\ldots$, $\tilde{z}_r = z_r$, and so on.

21.4.6 Conditional-Marginal Density Functions

Suppose $\tilde{z}$ is a continuous multivariate rv with df f and let $\tilde{z}$ be partitioned into three parts, $\tilde{z} = [\tilde{z}_1^t \tilde{z}_2^t \tilde{z}_3^t]^t$. Then the conditional density function of $\tilde{z}_1$ given $\tilde{z}_2 = z_2$, but marginal as regards $\tilde{z}_3$, is $f_{1|2}(\cdot|z_2)$, where

$$f_{1|2}(z_1|z_2) = \frac{f_{1,2}(z_1, z_2)}{f_2(z_2)}, \tag{21.20b}$$

provided that $f_2(z_2) > 0$. Technically nothing new is involved here, as $f_{1|2}$ has already been defined from the joint density of $(\tilde{z}_1, \tilde{z}_2)$, but sometimes it is helpful to use phraseology emphasizing that this is marginal as regards $\tilde{z}_3$.

21.5 Independence

21.5.1 Independence of Two Multivariate RV's

Let $\tilde{z}_1$ and $\tilde{z}_2$ be multivariate rv's and let $\tilde{z} = [\tilde{z}_1^t \tilde{z}_2^t]^t$. By the definition of independence (5.5), the two events $(\tilde{z}_1 \leq z_1)$ and $(\tilde{z}_2 \leq z_2)$ are independent if and only if

$$P(\tilde{z}_1 \leq z_1, \tilde{z}_2 \leq z_2) = P(\tilde{z}_1 \leq z_1)P(\tilde{z}_2 \leq z_2). \tag{21.21}$$

We now define the rv's $\tilde{z}_1$ and $\tilde{z}_2$ to be independent if and only if (21.21) holds for all z_1 and z_2.

If $\tilde{z}_1$ and $\tilde{z}_2$ are independent rv's, then the two events $\tilde{z}_1 \in S_1$ and $\tilde{z}_2 \in S_2$ are independent not just for S_1 and S_2 of such a form that (21.21) applies but for almost all arbitrary sets S_1 and S_2. We shall not prove this in general, but when $\tilde{z}$ is discrete, mixed, or continuous, it follows easily from the first part of the following theorem (exercise 25).

Theorem Let $\tilde{z} = [\tilde{z}_1^t \tilde{z}_2^t]^t$ be a multivariate rv with distributing function f.[3] The rv's $\tilde{z}_1$ and $\tilde{z}_2$ are independent if and only if the following three equivalent conditions are met:

$$f(z_1, z_2) = f_1(z_1)f_2(z_2) \quad \text{for all } z_1, z_2; \tag{21.22a}$$

$$f_{1|2}(z_1|z_2) = f_1(z_1) \quad \text{for all } z_1, z_2 \text{ with } f_2(z_2) > 0; \tag{21.22b}$$

$$f_{2|1}(z_2|z_1) = f_2(z_2) \quad \text{for all } z_1, z_2 \text{ with } f_1(z_1) > 0. \tag{21.22c}$$

The last two conditions say that the distributing function of $\tilde{z}_1$ is the same whether or not the value of $\tilde{z}_2$ is known. The proof of the theorem is exactly like that in the bivariate case (section 13.5) and is omitted.

In non-vector notation, the definition following (21.21) says that the multivariate rv $(\tilde{z}_1, \ldots, \tilde{z}_p)$ and the multivariate rv $(\tilde{z}_{p+1}, \ldots, \tilde{z}_r)$ are independent if the events $(\tilde{z}_1 \leq z_1, \ldots, \tilde{z}_p \leq z_p)$ and $(\tilde{z}_{p+1} \leq z_{p+1}, \ldots, \tilde{z}_r \leq z_r)$ are independent for all $z_1, \ldots, z_p, z_{p+1}, \ldots, z_r$. Condition (21.22a) is

$$f(z_1, \ldots, z_r) = f_{1,\ldots,p}(z_1, \ldots, z_p)f_{p+1,\ldots,r}(z_{p+1}, \ldots, z_r) \quad \text{for all } z_1, \ldots, z_r.$$

Conditions (21.22b) and (21.22c) can be rewritten similarly (exercise 25). It is often convenient, instead of referring carefully to multivariate rv's, to say that the set of rv's $(\tilde{z}_1, \ldots, \tilde{z}_p)$ and the set of rv's $(\tilde{z}_{p+1}, \ldots, \tilde{z}_r)$ are independent. This does not mean that the rv's $\tilde{z}_1, \ldots, \tilde{z}_p$ are independent of one

3. As in the bivariate case, a distributing function is defined to be a mf, dmf, or df.

another or that $\tilde{z}_{p+1}, \ldots, \tilde{z}_r$ are independent of one another. It means that the two sets are independent of each other. In this respect, it is clearer to say that the set of rv's $(\tilde{z}_1, \ldots, \tilde{z}_p)$ is independent of the set of rv's $(\tilde{z}_{p+1}, \ldots, \tilde{z}_r)$, though this phraseology does not reflect of the symmetry of the independence relation and one could equally well say that the set $(\tilde{z}_{p+1}, \ldots, \tilde{z}_r)$ is independent of the set $(\tilde{z}_1, \ldots, \tilde{z}_p)$.

21.5.2 Marginal and Conditional Independence

Let $\tilde{z}_1$, $\tilde{z}_2$, and $\tilde{z}_3$ be three multivariate rv's and let $\tilde{z} = [\tilde{z}_1^t \tilde{z}_2^t \tilde{z}_3^t]^t$. Suppose $\tilde{z}$ has distributing function f.

The relation between $\tilde{z}_1$ and $\tilde{z}_2$ now gives us *two* cases to consider. (1) We may look at the *marginal* joint distribution of $(\tilde{z}_1, \tilde{z}_2)$ and ask whether $\tilde{z}_1$ and $\tilde{z}_2$ are independent under this distribution; or (2) we may look at the conditional joint distribution of $(\tilde{z}_1, \tilde{z}_2)$ *given* a particular value z_3 of $\tilde{z}_3$ and ask whether $\tilde{z}_1$ and $\tilde{z}_2$ are independent under *this* distribution.

The rv's $\tilde{z}_1$ and $\tilde{z}_2$ are said to be *marginally independent* if they are independent in their *marginal joint distribution.* By (21.22a), this is equivalent to

$$f_{1,2}(z_1, z_2) = f_1(z_1) f_2(z_2) \qquad \text{for all } z_1,\ z_2, \tag{21.23}$$

where $f_{1,2}$ is the marginal joint distributing function of $(\tilde{z}_1, \tilde{z}_2)$, marginal as regards $\tilde{z}_3$, and f_1 and f_2 are the marginal distributing functions of $\tilde{z}_1$ and $\tilde{z}_2$. Condition (21.23) is also equivalent to each of the conditions (21.22b) and (21.22c) where now $f_{1|2}$ is the distributing function of $\tilde{z}_1$ conditional on z_2 but marginal on $\tilde{z}_3$, and similarly for $f_{2|1}$. As usual, the word "marginal" supplies an emphasis which is often helpful, but it would be possible to suppress all reference to it: technically, "independent" and "marginally independent" are equivalent.

The rv's $\tilde{z}_1$ and $\tilde{z}_2$ are said to be *conditionally independent given a particular value* z_3 of $\tilde{z}_3$ if they are independent in their *conditional joint distribution given* z_3. Applying (21.22) to this conditional distribution shows that each of the following conditions is equivalent to the statement that $\tilde{z}_1$ and $\tilde{z}_2$ are conditionally independent given $\tilde{z}_3 = z_3$:

$$f_{1,2|3}(z_1, z_2 | z_3) = f_{1|3}(z_1 | z_3) f_{2|3}(z_2 | z_3) \qquad \text{for all } z_1,\ z_2; \tag{21.24a}$$

$$f_{1|2,3}(z_1 | z_2, z_3) = f_{1|3}(z_1 | z_3) \qquad \text{for all } z_1,\ z_2 \text{ with } f_{2|3}(z_2 | z_3) > 0; \tag{21.24b}$$

$$f_{2|1,3}(z_2 | z_1, z_3) = f_{2|3}(z_2 | z_3) \qquad \text{for all } z_1,\ z_2 \text{ with } f_{1|3}(z_1 | z_3) > 0. \tag{21.24c}$$

Finally, $\tilde{z}_1$ and $\tilde{z}_2$ are said to be *conditionally independent* (*given* $\tilde{z}_3$) if they are conditionally independent given z_3 for every z_3. This is equivalent to each of the conditions (21.24) with the addition of the requirement "for all z_3" to each, that is, with "for all z_1, z_2" changed to "for all z_1, z_2, z_3" in each case.

Table 21.6a

		$f_{1,2\mid 3}(z_1, z_2\mid z_3)$			
z_1	z_3:	0		1	
	z_2:	0	1	0	1
0		$\frac{1}{16}$	$\frac{3}{16}$	$\frac{4}{9}$	$\frac{2}{9}$
1		$\frac{3}{16}$	$\frac{9}{16}$	$\frac{2}{9}$	$\frac{1}{9}$

Table 21.6b

		$f_{1,2}(z_1, z_2)$	
z_1	z_2:	0	1
0		$\frac{73}{288}$	$\frac{59}{288}$
1		$\frac{59}{288}$	$\frac{97}{288}$

Conditional Independence Does Not Imply Marginal Independence

As one example, consider the three rv's $\tilde{z}_1$, $\tilde{z}_2$, and $\tilde{z}_3$, each of which has range [0, 1] and let the *conditional* joint mass functions of $(\tilde{z}_1, \tilde{z}_2)$ *given* $\tilde{z}_3 = 0$ and *given* $\tilde{z}_3 = 1$ be as shown in table 21.6a. It is easy to verify that $\tilde{z}_1$ and $\tilde{z}_2$ are independent given either $\tilde{z}_3 = 0$ or $\tilde{z}_3 = 1$; given $\tilde{z}_3 = 0$, for example, we see that there is probability 1/4 that $\tilde{z}_1 = 0$ regardless of whether $\tilde{z}_2 = 0$ or 1, and so forth. Suppose, however, that we assign probability 1/2 to each of the two possible values of $\tilde{z}_3$ and then compute the marginal joint mass function of $(\tilde{z}_1, \tilde{z}_2)$. This simply averages the two conditional probabilities shown in table 21.6a for each (z_1, z_2) pair; the marginal $P(\tilde{z}_1 = 0, \tilde{z}_2 = 0) = 1/2 \times 1/16 + 1/2 \times 4/9 = 73/288$, and so forth. The results are shown in table 21.6b, where it is obvious that $\tilde{z}_1$ and $\tilde{z}_2$ are *not* independent. The conditional probability that $\tilde{z}_1 = 1$ now increases when z_2 increases from 0 to 1, the ultimate reason being (loosely speaking) that increasing $\tilde{z}_3$ from 0 to 1 decreases the chances of the value 1 for *both* $\tilde{z}_1$ and $\tilde{z}_2$.

This is perhaps the simplest possible example of the phenomenon often known as "spurious correlation." To give a well-known example, the marriage rate is correlated with pig-iron production, the "reason" being of course that both are linked to general economic conditions. The correlation is entirely real, but it can be "explained" by other variables. This is not to suggest that correlation can be taken to imply causality whenever no such "explanation" is handy.

For another example, suppose $\tilde{z}_3$ is the long-run average daily yield of a production process and $\tilde{z}_1$ and $\tilde{z}_2$ are the yields on two different days. Then a large value of one day's yield, say $\tilde{z}_1$, suggests that the long-run average yield $\tilde{z}_3$ is large and hence that the other day's yield $\tilde{z}_2$ is large, so that $\tilde{z}_1$ and $\tilde{z}_2$ are not independent marginally on $\tilde{z}_3$. At the same time one *might* assess the daily yields $\tilde{z}_1$ and $\tilde{z}_2$ as independent conditional on the long-run average yield z_3, for any z_3; that is, one might assess $\tilde{z}_1$ and $\tilde{z}_2$ as conditionally independent given $\tilde{z}_3$. In particular, this assessment is implied if $\tilde{z}_1$ and $\tilde{z}_2$ are regarded as coming from a Normal process with mean $\tilde{z}_3$ and known variance (chapter 16). Though the term "spurious correlation" has seldom been used in this connection, one could perfectly well say that $\tilde{z}_1$ and $\tilde{z}_2$ are marginally correlated but that this correlation is "spurious" because it is "explained" by the fact that $\tilde{z}_1$ and $\tilde{z}_2$ are both related to $\tilde{z}_3$. The reason "spurious correlation" has seldom been used here is that in the frequency tradition of probability $\tilde{z}_3$ is not treated as a rv and only conditional distributions given z_3 are discussed, so that the marginal (joint) distribution of $\tilde{z}_1$ and $\tilde{z}_2$ is never mentioned.

Marginal Independence Does Not Imply Conditional Independence

As an example, let $\tilde{z}_1$ and $\tilde{z}_2$ be Bernoulli trials with known p (not 0 or 1) and let $\tilde{z}_3 = 0$ if $\tilde{z}_1 = \tilde{z}_2$ while $\tilde{z}_3 = 1$ otherwise. Then $\tilde{z}_1$ and $\tilde{z}_2$ are marginally independent by the definition of a Bernoulli process with known p. However, they are not independent given either $\tilde{z}_3 = 0$ or $\tilde{z}_3 = 1$; given $\tilde{z}_3 = 0$, for example, we see that $\tilde{z}_1 = 1$ has probability 1 given $\tilde{z}_2 = 1$, but has probability 0 given $\tilde{z}_2 = 0$, and so forth. The marginal and conditional distributions of $(\tilde{z}_1, \tilde{z}_2)$ are given in table 21.7 for $p = \frac{1}{2}$ (exercise 10), where we can see that, loosely speaking, the dependence between $\tilde{z}_1$ and $\tilde{z}_2$ goes in one direction when $\tilde{z}_3 = 0$, in the other when $\tilde{z}_3 = 1$, and exactly cancels out marginally over $\tilde{z}_3$.

21.5.3 Functions of Independent RV's

Theorem Let $\tilde{z}_1$ and $\tilde{z}_2$ be independent rv's and let $\tilde{y}_1$ be a function of $\tilde{z}_1$ and $\tilde{y}_2$ a function of $\tilde{z}_2$, that is, $\tilde{y}_1 = y_1(\tilde{z}_1)$ and $\tilde{y}_2 = y_2(\tilde{z}_2)$; then $\tilde{y}_1$ and $\tilde{y}_2$ are independent.

Proof $\tilde{y}_1 \in S_1$ if and only if $\tilde{z}_1 \in S_1'$ where S_1' is the set of all z_1 such that $y_1(z_1) \in S_1$; similarly $\tilde{y}_2 \in S_2$ if and only if $\tilde{z}_2 \in S_2'$. Therefore

$$\begin{aligned} P\{\tilde{y}_1 \in S_1, \tilde{y}_2 \in S_2\} &= P\{\tilde{z}_1 \in S_1', \tilde{z}_2 \in S_2'\} \\ &= P\{\tilde{z}_1 \in S_1'\}P\{\tilde{z}_2 \in S_2'\} = P\{\tilde{y}_1 \in S_1\}P\{\tilde{y}_2 \in S_2\}, \end{aligned} \tag{21.25}$$

Table 21.7a

		$f_{1,2\mid 3}(z_1, z_2\mid z_3)$			
z_1	z_3:	0		1	
	z_2:	0	1	0	1
0		$\frac{1}{2}$	0	0	$\frac{1}{2}$
1		0	$\frac{1}{2}$	$\frac{1}{2}$	0

Table 21.7b

		$f_{1,2}(z_1, z_2)$	
z_1	z_2:	0	1
0		$\frac{1}{4}$	$\frac{1}{4}$
1		$\frac{1}{4}$	$\frac{1}{4}$

where the second equality follows from the first sentence of the second paragraph of section 21.5.1. Since S_1 and S_2 are arbitrary, this shows that $\tilde{y}_1$ and $\tilde{y}_2$ satisfy the definition of independence.

As a special case, suppose that (1) $\tilde{z}_1$ and $\tilde{z}_2$ are independent, (2) $\tilde{y}_1$ consists of some of the elements of $\tilde{z}_1$, and (3) $\tilde{y}_2$ consists of some of the elements of $\tilde{z}_2$; then $\tilde{y}_1$ and $\tilde{y}_2$ are independent marginally as regards the elements of $\tilde{z}_1$ and $\tilde{z}_2$ not included in $\tilde{y}_1$ and $\tilde{y}_2$. That is, if

$$\tilde{z}_1 = \begin{bmatrix} \tilde{y}_1 \\ \tilde{x}_1 \end{bmatrix}, \qquad \tilde{z}_2 = \begin{bmatrix} \tilde{y}_2 \\ \tilde{x}_2 \end{bmatrix} \tag{21.26}$$

and $\tilde{z}_1$ is independent of $\tilde{z}_2$, then $\tilde{y}_1$ is independent of $\tilde{y}_2$ marginally on $\tilde{x}_1$ and $\tilde{x}_2$. As a special case of this, *if a rv is independent of some set of rv's, it is independent of any subset of that set.*

21.5.4 Pairwise and Mutual Independence

Let $\tilde{z}_1, \ldots, \tilde{z}_r$ be rv's having a joint distribution, that is, let $(\tilde{z}_1, \ldots, \tilde{z}_r)$ be a multivariate rv. (Each $\tilde{z}_i$ may be either univariate or multivariate.) We shall call $\tilde{z}_1, \ldots, \tilde{z}_r$ *pairwise independent* if $\tilde{z}_i$ and $\tilde{z}_j$ are *marginally* independent for *every* i, j with $1 \leq i \leq j \leq r$. We shall call $\tilde{z}_1, \ldots, \tilde{z}_r$ *mutually independent* if $\tilde{z}_i$ is independent of the remainder jointly for every i (that is, if $\tilde{z}_1$ is independent of $(\tilde{z}_2, \ldots, \tilde{z}_r)$, $\tilde{z}_2$ is independent of $(\tilde{z}_1, \tilde{z}_3, \ldots, \tilde{z}_r)$, and so on). These two kinds of independence must be distinguished, as they are *not* equivalent (see below). Both are properties of the *set* of rv's $(\tilde{z}_1, \ldots, \tilde{z}_r)$, though we will often say that $\tilde{z}_1, \ldots, \tilde{z}_r$ are pairwise or mutually independent instead of saying that the set $(\tilde{z}_1, \ldots, \tilde{z}_r)$ is.

Theorem The rv's $\tilde{z}_1, \ldots, \tilde{z}_r$ with joint distributing function f are mutually independent if and only if

$$f(z_1, z_2, \ldots, z_r) = f_1(z_1)f_2(z_2)\cdots f_r(z_r) \qquad \text{for all } z_1, z_2, \ldots, z_r. \tag{21.27}$$

Proof For $r = 2$, this theorem follows from the theorem of section 21.5.1, which also implies that $\tilde{z}_1$ is independent of $(\tilde{z}_2, \ldots, \tilde{z}_r)$ if and only if

$$f(z_1, z_2, \ldots, z_r) = f_1(z_1)f_{2,\ldots,r}(z_2, \ldots, z_r) \qquad \text{for all } z_1, z_2, \ldots, z_r. \tag{21.28}$$

Suppose now that (21.27) holds. Integrating or summing it over z_1 gives

$$f_{2,\ldots,r}(z_2, \ldots, z_r) = f_2(z_2), \ldots, f_r(z_r) \qquad \text{for all } z_2, \ldots, z_r. \tag{21.29}$$

Substituting this in (21.27) gives (21.28). Therefore $\tilde{z}_1$ is independent of $(\tilde{z}_2, \ldots, \tilde{z}_r)$. Similarly $\tilde{z}_i$ is independent of the remainder jointly for every i. Thus (21.27) implies mutual independence. Suppose, conversely $\tilde{z}_1, \ldots, \tilde{z}_r$ are mutually independent, and suppose the theorem has been proved for $r - 1$. Then (21.28) holds; and (21.29) holds as well, since $\tilde{z}_2, \ldots, \tilde{z}_r$ are mutually independent, being a subset of a mutually independent set $\tilde{z}_1, \ldots, \tilde{z}_r$. Substituting (21.29) in (21.28) gives (21.27). Therefore, by mathematical induction, mutual independence implies (21.27). This completes the proof.

Mutual Independence Implies Pairwise Independence

This is simply a special case of the proposition, proved in section 21.5.3, that if a rv is independent of some set of rv's (all $\tilde{z}_j$ except $\tilde{z}_i$ in our present application), it is independent of any subset of that set ($\tilde{z}_j$ in our present application).

Pairwise Independence Does Not Imply Mutual Independence

As an example, let $\tilde{z}_1$ and $\tilde{z}_2$ be Bernoulli trials with $p = \frac{1}{2}$ and let $\tilde{z}_3 = 0$ if $\tilde{z}_1 = \tilde{z}_2$, while $\tilde{z}_3 = 1$ otherwise. The reader should verify that (1) $\tilde{z}_1$, $\tilde{z}_2$, and $\tilde{z}_3$ are pairwise independent, but (2) *no* $\tilde{z}_i$ is independent of the other two jointly. (See exercise 10.)

21.6 Indirect Assessment of Joint Distributions

For the same reason as in section 13.6, one often wants to start with the marginal distribution of a rv $\tilde{z}_1$ and the conditional distribution of a rv $\tilde{z}_2$ given z_1 for each z_1 and proceed from there. Throughout this section we allow $\tilde{z}_1$ and $\tilde{z}_2$ to be univariate or multivariate, we let

$$\tilde{z} = \begin{bmatrix} \tilde{z}_1 \\ \tilde{z}_2 \end{bmatrix},$$

and we assume that $\tilde{z}$ has distributing function f.

21.6.1 Determination of the Joint Distribution

If f_1 and $f_{2|1}$ are given, then f is determined by

$$f(z) = f(z_1, z_2) = f_1(z_1)f_{2|1}(z_2|z_1) \quad \text{for all } z_1, z_2. \tag{21.30}$$

Thus we see that

> the joint distributing function of r scalar random variables is completely determined if we are given (1) the marginal (joint) distributing function of any p of the rv's, and (2) the conditional (joint) distributing function of the remaining $(r - p)$ rv's for every possible set of values of the first p.

Notice that the joint distribution of $\tilde{z}_1$ and $\tilde{z}_2$ is in general *not* completely determined if we are given merely the marginal (joint) distributions of $\tilde{z}_1$ and $\tilde{z}_2$. The point was illustrated in section 13.6.1 for the case where $\tilde{z}_1$ and $\tilde{z}_2$ are both scalar.

21.6.2 Marginal Distributions and Bayes' Formula

Since (1) the marginal distributing function of $\tilde{z}_1$, together with a complete set of conditional distributing functions of $\tilde{z}_2$ given each z_1, completely determines the joint distributing function of $\tilde{z}_1$ and $\tilde{z}_2$, and (2) the joint distributing function of $\tilde{z}_1$ and $\tilde{z}_2$ completely determines the marginal and conditional distributing functions of all possible vector combinations of the scalar components of $\tilde{z} = [\tilde{z}_1^t \, \tilde{z}_2^t]^t$, it is clear that

> the marginal of $\tilde{z}_1$ and the conditionals of $\tilde{z}_2$ given z_1 completely determine the marginal of $\tilde{z}_2$ and the conditional of $\tilde{z}_1$ given z_2.

Computationally, given f_1 and $f_{2|1}$, we obtain f_2 from the formula

$$f_2(z_2) = \begin{cases} \sum_{z_1} f_1(z_1)f_{2|1}(z_2|z_1) & \text{if } \tilde{z}_1 \text{ is discrete,} \\ \int f_1(z_1)f_{2|1}(z_2|z_1)\,dz_1 & \text{if } \tilde{z}_1 \text{ is continuous,} \end{cases} \tag{21.31}$$

which follows directly on substituting (21.30) in (21.7) or (21.19). We can then obtain $f_{1|2}$ from Bayes' formula for conditional mf's and df's

$$f_{1|2}(z_1|z_2) = \frac{f_1(z_1)f_{2|1}(z_2|z_1)}{f_2(z_2)}, \tag{21.32}$$

which follows directly on substituting (21.30) in (21.10) or (21.20). Bayes' formula is often more usefully thought of in the form

$$f_{1|2}(z_1|z_2) \propto f_1(z_1)f_{2|1}(z_2|z_1), \tag{21.33}$$

the suppressed denominator being regarded merely as a scale factor which must be chosen such that

$$\sum_{z_1} f_{1|2}(z_1|z_2) \quad \text{or} \quad \int f_{1|2}(z_1|z_2)\,dz_1$$

equals unity.

21.7 Expectations

21.7.1 Definition of the Expectation of a Function of Several RV's

Let $\tilde{z}$ be a multivariate rv and let $\tilde{y} = \varphi(\tilde{z})$ be a real-valued function of $\tilde{z}$. Then the distribution $\tilde{y}$ is induced by φ from that of $\tilde{z}$, and the expectation $E(\tilde{y})$ has been defined in (8.10) in terms of the distribution of $\tilde{y}$. As in sections 8.2.3 and 13.7.1, however, we need not obtain the distribution of $\tilde{y} = \varphi(\tilde{z})$ to compute its expectation. Let $\tilde{z}$ have distributing function f and define the expectation of φ with respect to f to be

$$E\varphi(\tilde{z}) = \begin{cases} \sum_z \varphi(z) f(z) & \textit{if} \quad \tilde{z} \quad \text{is discrete,} \\ \int \varphi(z) f(z)\,dz & \text{if} \quad \tilde{z} \quad \text{is continuous,} \end{cases} \tag{21.34}$$

provided the sum or integral converges absolutely, that is, provided it converges when $\varphi(z)$ is replaced by $|\varphi(z)|$. (The definition for $\tilde{z}$ mixed is similar.) The expectation of φ with respect to f is identical to the expectation of $\tilde{y} = \varphi(\tilde{z})$ with respect to the induced distribution of $\tilde{y}$. The proof of this equivalence is discussed further in section 8.2.3.

21.7.2 Conditional Expectation

Let $\tilde{z}$ be a rv with distributing function f as before, but now suppose some elements of $\tilde{z}$ are given. Specifically, suppose $\tilde{z} = [\tilde{z}_1^t\, \tilde{z}_2^t]^t$ and it is given that $\tilde{z} = z_2$. Then $\tilde{z}_1$ becomes a rv with conditional distributing function $f_{1|2}(\cdot|z_2)$. Let $\tilde{\varphi} = \varphi(\tilde{z}) = \varphi(\tilde{z}_1, \tilde{z}_2)$ be a real-valued function of $\tilde{z}$ and consider $\varphi(\tilde{z}_1, z_2)$ as a function of $\tilde{z}_1$ alone resulting from fixing $\tilde{z}_2$ at the value z_2.

The expectation of $\varphi(\tilde{z}_1, z_2)$ taken with respect to the conditional distribution of $\tilde{z}_1$ given z_2 will be called the *conditional expectation* of φ *given* z_2. It will be denoted in any of a number of self-explanatory ways, such as

$$E_{1|2}\varphi(\tilde{z}_1, z_2) \quad \text{or} \quad E_{1|2}\{\varphi(\tilde{z}_1, \tilde{z}_2)|z_2\} \quad \text{or} \quad E_{z_1|z_2}\varphi(\tilde{z}_1, z_2).$$

The conditional expectation of φ given the values of any of the elements of $\tilde{z}$ is similarly defined.

As in the bivariate case (section 13.7.2), $E_{1|2}\varphi(\tilde{z}_1, z_2)$ does not depend on z_1 because z_1 has been "expected out," but it does depend on z_2 because both the value of φ and the conditional distribution of $\tilde{z}_1$ depend on z_2. If φ is a function of z_1 alone, say

$$\varphi(z_1, z_2) = \psi(z_1) \quad \text{for all } z_1, z_2,$$

then its conditional expectation given z_2 still depends on z_2 because the conditional distribution of $\tilde{z}_1$ does; that is, $E_{1|2}\{\psi(\tilde{z}_1)|z_2\}$ depends on z_2.

21.7.3 Marginal Expectation

Let $\tilde{z}$ be a multivariate rv with distributing function f and let ψ be a real-valued function of some of the elements of $\tilde{z}$; say ψ is a function of $\tilde{z}_1$ where $\tilde{z} = [\tilde{z}_1^t \tilde{z}_2^t]^t$. Then the expectation of ψ with respect to f_1 will be called the *marginal expectation* of ψ and will be denoted by $E_1\psi(\tilde{z}_1)$. It equals the expectation of ψ with respect to f. Thus the expectation of ψ with respect to f, the marginal expectation of ψ (with respect to f_1), and the expectation of $\tilde{y} = \psi(\tilde{z}_1)$ (with respect to the induced distribution of $\tilde{y}$) are all identical. The meaning of the expectation in question is the same, whatever it is called. The different terms merely suggest different contexts and different methods of computation.

21.7.4 Iterated Expectation

It is often convenient to evaluate the unconditional expectation of $\varphi(\tilde{z})$ by evaluating its conditional expectation given every possible value of some elements of $\tilde{z}$ and then evaluating the (unconditional) expectation of this conditional expectation. In symbols, if $\tilde{z} = [\tilde{z}_1^t \tilde{z}_2^t]^t$, then

$$E\varphi(\tilde{z}_1, \tilde{z}_2) = E_{z_2}E_{z_1|z_2}\varphi(\tilde{z}_1, \tilde{z}_2) = E_2E_{1|2}\varphi(\tilde{z}_1, \tilde{z}_2). \tag{21.35}$$

Of course, $\tilde{z}_2$ may be replaced by any set of elements of $\tilde{z}$ and $\tilde{z}_1$ by the remainder. It is left to the reader to show (exercise 21) that if $\tilde{z}$ is discrete or continuous, these formulas follow directly from (21.30) and (21.34) respectively and the definitions of the expectations involved.

21.8 Mean and Variance of a Vector RV

21.8.1 Marginal and Conditional Means

Let $\tilde{z}$ be a $(r \times 1)$ rv. The mean or expectation of $\tilde{z}$ is defined and denoted by

$$E(\tilde{z}) \equiv E\begin{bmatrix} \tilde{z}_1 \\ \vdots \\ \tilde{z}_r \end{bmatrix} \equiv \begin{bmatrix} E(\tilde{z}_1) \\ \vdots \\ E(\tilde{z}_r) \end{bmatrix} \equiv \begin{bmatrix} \bar{z}_1 \\ \vdots \\ \bar{z}_r \end{bmatrix} \equiv \bar{z}. \tag{21.36}$$

Now suppose $\tilde{z}$ is partitioned: $\tilde{z} = [\tilde{z}_1^t \tilde{z}_2^t]^t$. Since $\tilde{z}_1$ is a rv on its own, its mean is defined by (21.36) applied to $\tilde{z}_1$ in place of $\tilde{z}$. Since the relevant distribution of $\tilde{z}_1$ is marginal as regards $\tilde{z}_2$, we will sometimes speak of the *marginal mean* of $\tilde{z}_1$ instead of simply the mean of $\tilde{z}_1$, but they are identical.

It is convenient to note that when the mean of $\tilde{z}$ is partitioned in the same way as $\tilde{z}$, the components are the marginal means of $\tilde{z}_1$ and of $\tilde{z}_2$:

$$E\begin{bmatrix}\tilde{z}_1\\ \tilde{z}_2\end{bmatrix} = \begin{bmatrix}E(\tilde{z}_1)\\ E(\tilde{z}_2)\end{bmatrix}, \qquad \text{or equivalently} \qquad \bar{z} = \begin{bmatrix}\bar{z}_1\\ \bar{z}_2\end{bmatrix}. \tag{21.37}$$

That is, $\bar{z}_1$ as defined by partitioning $\bar{z}$ is identical to the mean $\bar{z}_1$ of $\tilde{z}_1$ as defined by (21.36).

The *conditional mean* of $\tilde{z}_1$ given z_2 is defined as the expectation of $\tilde{z}_1$ under the conditional distribution of $\tilde{z}_1$ given z_2. It is a vector whose elements are the conditional means of the elements of $\tilde{z}_1$ given z_2. It will be written in any of a number of self-explanatory ways, such as

$$E_{z_1|z_2}(\tilde{z}_1) \quad \text{or} \quad E_{1|2}(\tilde{z}_1|z_2) \quad \text{or} \quad \bar{z}_{1|2}(z_2).$$

Applying (21.35) to each element of $\tilde{z}_1$ gives

$$E(\tilde{z}_1) = E_{z_2}E_{z_1|z_2}(\tilde{z}_1) = E_2 E_{1|2}(\tilde{z}_1|\tilde{z}_2) = E_2[\bar{z}_{1|2}(\tilde{z}_2)]. \tag{21.38}$$

This formula is useful for both computation and theory. It says, for instance, that the (prior) expectation of the posterior mean of a rv equals the prior mean of that rv.

21.8.2 Mean of a Matrix of RV's

It is convenient for some manipulations to generalize the previous subsection from vectors to matrices. We define the mean of a $(m \times n)$ matrix $\tilde{\mathbf{y}}$ whose elements are real rv's $\tilde{y}_{ij}$ to be the matrix of means $\bar{y}_{ij}$:

$$\bar{\mathbf{y}} \equiv E(\tilde{\mathbf{y}}) \equiv \begin{bmatrix}\bar{y}_{11} & \bar{y}_{12}\cdots\bar{y}_{1n}\\ \bar{y}_{21} & \bar{y}_{22}\cdots\bar{y}_{2n}\\ \vdots & \vdots \quad \vdots\\ \bar{y}_{m1} & \bar{y}_{m2}\cdots\bar{y}_{mn}\end{bmatrix}. \tag{21.39}$$

In the case $n = 1$, this reduces to (21.36). As in (21.37), the mean of a submatrix of $\tilde{\mathbf{y}}$ is the corresponding submatrix of $\bar{\mathbf{y}}$. The conditional mean of $\tilde{\mathbf{y}}$ given the value x of a rv $\tilde{x}$ is denoted $E_{y|x}(\tilde{\mathbf{y}})$ and is the matrix of conditional means $E_{y|x}(\tilde{y}_{ij})$. Applying (21.25) to each element of $\tilde{\mathbf{y}}$ shows that the mean is again the mean of the conditional mean:

$$E(\tilde{\mathbf{y}}) = E_x E_{y|x}(\tilde{\mathbf{y}}|\tilde{x}). \tag{21.40}$$

It is often useful to know that the mean of a sum is the sum of the means, and that the mean of a nonrandom matrix multiple of a random matrix is the same multiple of the mean of the random matrix. Explicitly (exercise 26):

$$E(\tilde{\mathbf{y}} + \tilde{\mathbf{w}}) = E(\tilde{\mathbf{y}}) + E(\tilde{\mathbf{w}}) = \bar{\mathbf{y}} + \bar{\mathbf{w}}; \tag{21.41}$$

$$E(\mathbf{a}\tilde{\mathbf{y}}) = \mathbf{a}E(\tilde{\mathbf{y}}) = \mathbf{a}\bar{\mathbf{y}}; \qquad E(\tilde{\mathbf{y}}\mathbf{a}) = E(\tilde{\mathbf{y}})\mathbf{a} = \bar{\mathbf{y}}\mathbf{a}. \tag{21.42}$$

These formulas may also be interpreted as saying that the expectation operation can be interchanged with addition and with multiplication by a nonrandom matrix.

21.8.3 Marginal and Conditional Variances

The *variance* (or *variance matrix*) of a $(r \times 1)$ rv $\tilde{z}$ is defined and denoted by

$$V(\tilde{z}) \equiv \check{\mathbf{z}} = \begin{bmatrix} \check{z}_{11} & \check{z}_{12} \cdots \check{z}_{1r} \\ \check{z}_{21} & \check{z}_{22} \cdots \check{z}_{2r} \\ \vdots & \vdots \quad\quad \vdots \\ \check{z}_{r1} & \check{z}_{r2} \cdots \check{z}_{rr} \end{bmatrix}, \tag{21.43}$$

where for all i and j

$$\check{z}_{ij} \equiv V(\tilde{z}_i, \tilde{z}_j) \equiv E(\tilde{z}_i - \bar{z}_i)(\tilde{z}_j - \bar{z}_j), \tag{21.44a}$$

which is the *covariance* of $\tilde{z}_i$ and $\tilde{z}_j$ (section 13.8.3). For $i = j$, we see that the diagonal elements of $\check{\mathbf{z}}$ are the variances

$$\check{z}_{ii} \equiv V(\tilde{z}_i, \tilde{z}_i) = E(\tilde{z}_i - \bar{z})^2 \equiv V(\tilde{z}_i). \tag{21.44b}$$

A compact and theoretically useful formula for the variance of $\tilde{z}$, which uses the notation of the previous subsection and which the reader is invited to verify, is

$$V(\tilde{z}) \equiv E[(\tilde{z} - \bar{z})(\tilde{z} - \bar{z})^t]. \tag{21.45}$$

If $\tilde{z} = [\tilde{z}_1^t \tilde{z}_2^t]^t$, the variance of $\tilde{z}_1$ is sometimes referred to as the *marginal variance* of $\tilde{z}_1$ to emphasize that it is a property of the marginal distribution of $\tilde{z}_1$.

Let $\tilde{z} = [\tilde{z}_1^t \tilde{z}_2^t]^t$ where $\tilde{z}_1$ is $(p \times 1)$ and let $V(\tilde{z})$ be partitioned as

$$V(\tilde{z}) \equiv \check{\mathbf{z}} = \begin{bmatrix} \check{\mathbf{z}}_{11} \check{\mathbf{z}}_{12} \\ \check{\mathbf{z}}_{21} \check{\mathbf{z}}_{22} \end{bmatrix} \tag{21.46}$$

where $\check{\mathbf{z}}_{11}$ is $(p \times p)$ (from which it follows that $\check{\mathbf{z}}_{12}$ is $p \times (r - p)$, etc.). Then (exercise 22)

$$\check{\mathbf{z}}_{ij} = V(\tilde{z}_i, \tilde{z}_j) \equiv E[(\tilde{z}_i - \bar{z}_i)(\tilde{z}_j - \bar{z}_j)^t] \quad \text{for } i, j = 1, 2, \tag{21.47}$$

where $V(\tilde{z}_i, \tilde{z}_j)$ is defined by the second equality and is called the *covariance* of $\tilde{z}_i$, $\tilde{z}_j$. (If $\tilde{z}_i$ and $\tilde{z}_j$ are actually real rv's, this reduces to the earlier definition.) Note that $V(\tilde{z}_1, \tilde{z}_2)$ is not $V([z_1^t z_2^t]^t) = V(\tilde{z})$ but only its upper right corner.

For $i = j$, (21.47) becomes

$$\check{\mathbf{z}}_{ii} = V(\tilde{z}_i, \tilde{z}_i) = V(\tilde{z}_i) = \check{\mathbf{z}}_i,$$

so that the variance matrices of $\tilde{z}_1$ and $\tilde{z}_2$ are simply the upper left and lower right corners of the variance matrix of $\tilde{z}$. In general, if a rv consists, like $\tilde{z}_1$, of some of the elements of $\tilde{z}$, then its variance matrix consists, like $\check{\mathbf{z}}_1$, of the corresponding rows and columns of $\check{\mathbf{z}}$, and thus can be read off from $\check{\mathbf{z}}$.

The *conditional variance* of $\tilde{z}_1$ *given* z_2 is defined as the variance of $\tilde{z}_1$ under the conditional distribution of $\tilde{z}_1$ given z_2. Specifically, it is denoted and defined by

$$V_{1|2}(\tilde{z}_1 | z_2) = V_{z_1|z_2}(\tilde{z}_1) = \check{\mathbf{z}}_{1|2}(z_2)$$

$$= E_{z_1|z_2}\{[\tilde{z}_1 - E_{1|2}(\tilde{z}_1 | z_2)][\tilde{z}_1 - E_{1|2}(\tilde{z}_1 | z_2)]^t\}. \qquad (21.48)$$

Formula (13.44) generalizes to (exercise 24)

$$V(\tilde{z}_1) = E_{z_2} V_{z_1|z_2}(\tilde{z}_1) + V_{z_2} E_{z_1|z_2}(\tilde{z}_1)$$

$$= E_2 V_{1|2}(\tilde{z}_1 | \tilde{z}_2) + V_2 E_{1|2}(\tilde{z}_1 | \tilde{z}_2)$$

$$= E_2[\check{\mathbf{z}}_{1|2}(\tilde{z}_2)] + V_2[\bar{z}_{1|2}(\tilde{z}_2)]. \qquad (21.49)$$

In words: The (marginal) variance of $\tilde{z}_1$ is the mean of its conditional variance *plus* the variance of its conditional mean.

Conditional covariance is defined and denoted in a similar way.

21.8.4 Regression

In section 21.8.1 we defined the conditional expectation of $\tilde{z}_1$ given $\tilde{z}_2 = z_2$. It depends on z_2, as the notations $\bar{z}_{1|2}(z_2)$ and $E_{1|2}(\tilde{z}_1 | z_2)$ clearly indicate. Considered as a function of z_2, $\bar{z}_{1|2}(z_2) = E_{1|2}(\tilde{z}_1 | z_2)$ is called the *regression function* (or *regression*) of $\tilde{z}_1$ on $\tilde{z}_2$; the function (as distinct from its value at z_2) might be denoted $\bar{z}_{1|2}(\cdot)$ or $E_{1|2}(\tilde{z}_1 | \cdot)$. The regression function of $\tilde{z}_2$ on $\tilde{z}_1$ is similarly defined but it is not the same functional relationship: the relation between z_1 and z_2 given by $z_1 = E_{1|2}(\tilde{z}_1 | z_2)$ is not the same as that given by $z_2 = E_{2|1}(\tilde{z}_2 | z_1)$.

If the regression of $\tilde{z}_1$ on $\tilde{z}_2$ is constant, that is, if $E_{1|2}(\tilde{z}_1 | z_2)$ has the same value for all z_2, then $V(\tilde{z}_1, \tilde{z}_2) = \check{\mathbf{z}}_{12} = \mathbf{0}$, that is, the covariance of $\tilde{z}_1$ and $\tilde{z}_2$ is $\mathbf{0}$. (The proof is like that in the bivariate case, section 13.8.4.)

Since, furthermore, independence obviously implies that $E_{1|2}(\tilde{z}_1|z_2)$ does not depend on z_2, we have

independence $\Rightarrow$ constant regression functions $\Rightarrow$ no correlation.

The implications cannot be reversed, as we have already seen in the bivariate case (section 13.8.4).

Now let $\tilde{z}$ be partitioned $[\tilde{z}_1^t \tilde{z}_2^t \tilde{z}_3^t]^t$. Then $[\tilde{z}_1^t \tilde{z}_2^t]^t$ is a rv, and the regression function of $\tilde{z}_1$ on $\tilde{z}_2$ has just been defined to be $E_{1|2}(\tilde{z}_1|\cdot)$, that is, $E_{1|2}(\tilde{z}_1|z_2)$ considered as a function of z_2. Since this is the mean of $\tilde{z}_1$ conditional on z_2 but marginal as regards $\tilde{z}_3$, it will sometimes be called the *marginal regression function* of $\tilde{z}_1$ on $\tilde{z}_2$.

The *conditional regression function* of $\tilde{z}_1$ on $\tilde{z}_2$, conditional on $\tilde{z}_3 = z_3$, is $E_{1|2,3}(\tilde{z}_1|\cdot, z_3)$, that is $E_{1|2,3}(\tilde{z}_1|z_2, z_3)$ considered as a function of z_2. Observe that this is the mean of $\tilde{z}_1$ conditional on *both* z_2 and z_3 considered as a function of z_2 for fixed z_3.

21.8.5 Correlation

Let $\tilde{z}$ be partitioned $[\tilde{z}_1 \tilde{z}_2 \tilde{z}_3^t]^t$ as in the previous section except that now $\tilde{z}_1$ and $\tilde{z}_2$ are scalar rv's. The correlation between $\tilde{z}_1$ and $\tilde{z}_2$ is defined as in (13.46) except that now we must specify whether we mean correlation with respect to (1) the marginal joint distribution of $(\tilde{z}_1, \tilde{z}_2)$ or (2) the conditional joint distribution of $(\tilde{z}_1, \tilde{z}_2)$ given a particular value z_3 of $\tilde{z}_3$.

The *marginal* or *zero-order* correlation (or simply the correlation) between $\tilde{z}_1$ and $\tilde{z}_2$ is defined with respect to their marginal joint distribution:

$$\rho_{1,2} \equiv \frac{\check{z}_{12}}{(\check{z}_{11}\check{z}_{22})^{1/2}}. \tag{21.50}$$

The *conditional* correlation between $\tilde{z}_1$ and $\tilde{z}_2$ given z_3 is the correlation of $\tilde{z}_1$ and $\tilde{z}_2$ under their conditional joint distribution given z_3:

$$\rho_{1,2|3}(z_3) \equiv \frac{\check{z}_{1,2|3}(z_3)}{[\check{z}_{1,1|3}(z_3)\check{z}_{2,2|3}(z_3)]^{1/2}}. \tag{21.51}$$

Observe that, as the notation emphasizes, the conditional variances, covariance, and correlation of $\tilde{z}_1$ and $\tilde{z}_2$ are all functions of z_3, *not* of z_1 or z_2.

21.9 Linear Transformations: Characteristics of a Variance Matrix

21.9.1 Mean and Variance of a Linear Transformation

Let $\tilde{z} = [\tilde{z}_1 \tilde{z}_2 \ldots \tilde{z}_r]^t$ have mean $\bar{z}$ and variance $\check{\mathbf{z}}$ and let $\tilde{y} = a + \mathbf{b}\tilde{z}$ (21.52a)

where

$$\boldsymbol{a} = \begin{bmatrix} a_1 \\ a_2 \\ \cdot\cdot \\ a_q \end{bmatrix}, \qquad \mathbf{b} = \begin{bmatrix} b_{11} & b_{12}\dots b_{1r} \\ b_{21} & b_{22}\dots b_{2r} \\ \dots & \dots & \dots \\ b_{q1} & b_{q2}\dots b_{qr} \end{bmatrix}, \tag{21.52b}$$

and q may be less than, equal to, or greater than r. Then

$$\bar{y} = \boldsymbol{a} + \mathbf{b}\bar{z}, \tag{21.53a}$$

$$\check{\mathbf{y}} = \mathbf{b}\check{\mathbf{z}}\mathbf{b}^t. \tag{21.53b}$$

Proof (21.53a) follows from (21.41) and (21.42). To prove (21.53b), we need simply apply (21.45) to $\tilde{y}$, substitute (21.52a) and (21.53a) therein, and then apply (21.42), obtaining

$$\check{\mathbf{y}} = E[(\tilde{y} - \bar{y})(\tilde{y} - \bar{y})^t] = E[\{\mathbf{b}(\tilde{z} - \bar{z})\}\{\mathbf{b}(\tilde{z} - \bar{z})\}^t]$$

$$= E[\mathbf{b}(\tilde{z} - \bar{z})(\tilde{z} - \bar{z})^t\mathbf{b}^t] = \mathbf{b}[E(\tilde{z} - \bar{z})(\tilde{z} - \bar{z})^t]\mathbf{b}^t = \mathbf{b}\check{\mathbf{z}}\mathbf{b}^t.$$

Formula (21.53b) includes many other formulas as special cases. For $q = 1$, for example, it gives the variance of a real-valued linear function of $\tilde{z}_1, \dots, z_r$:

$$V(a + b_1\tilde{z}_1 + \dots + b_r\tilde{z}_r) = \textstyle\sum_{i=1}^{n} b_i^2 V(\tilde{z}_i) + 2\sum_{i=1}^{n}\sum_{j=1}^{i-1} b_i b_j V(\tilde{z}_i, \tilde{z}_j). \tag{21.54}$$

This in turn reduces to (13.47c) when $r = 2$. For $q > 1$, the element $\check{y}_{12}$ of $\check{\mathbf{y}}$ is the covariance of two different real-valued linear functions of $\tilde{z}_1, \dots, \tilde{z}_r$, so (21.53b) includes a formula for such a covariance.

21.9.2 Characteristics of a Variance Matrix

Let $\check{\mathbf{z}}$ be the variance matrix of a rv $\tilde{z}$. Then the matrix $\check{\mathbf{z}}$ is symmetric, that is $\check{z}_{ij} = \check{z}_{ji}$ for all i, j. This follows immediately from (21.44a). Furthermore, we shall prove below that the matrix $\check{\mathbf{z}}$ is

1. positive-semidefinite, and
2. positive-definite unless $P(\boldsymbol{b}^t\tilde{z} = a) = 1$ for some vector $\boldsymbol{b} \neq \boldsymbol{0}$ and some real number a.

The definitions of positive-semidefinite and positive-definite are given in appendix 2. What $P(\boldsymbol{b}^t\tilde{z} = a) = 1$ with $\boldsymbol{b} \neq \boldsymbol{0}$ means is that all the P-measure is concentrated on a hyperplane of dimension $r - 1$ (or less) in the r-dimensional z-space, namely the hyperplane consisting of all z such that $\boldsymbol{b}^t z = a$. This is a degenerate case: the rv's $\tilde{z}_1, \dots, \tilde{z}_r$ are functionally related. More specifically, if $P(\boldsymbol{b}^t\tilde{z} = a) = 1$ and $b_1 \neq 0$, then solving

$\boldsymbol{b}^t\tilde{\boldsymbol{z}} = a$ for $\tilde{z}_1$ we see that

$$\tilde{z}_1 = \frac{1}{b_1}(a - b_2\tilde{z}_2 - \cdots - b_r\tilde{z}_r) \qquad \text{with probability one.} \tag{21.55}$$

This says that $\tilde{z}_1$ is (with probability one) a linear function of $\tilde{z}_2, \ldots, \tilde{z}_r$ (or a constant, if $b_2 = \cdots = b_r = 0$). If $b_1 = 0$, we can make the same statement with 1 and i interchanged for any i such that $b_i \neq 0$; there must be some $b_i \neq 0$ if $\boldsymbol{b} \neq \boldsymbol{0}$.

Proof We will now prove that a variance matrix $\check{\mathbf{z}}$ has the properties stated at 1 and 2 above. Replacing $\mathbf{b}$ by $\boldsymbol{b}^t$ in (21.53b) and recalling that the variance of a real rv is nonnegative, we find

$$\boldsymbol{b}^t\check{\mathbf{z}}\boldsymbol{b} = V(\boldsymbol{b}^t\tilde{\boldsymbol{z}}) \geq 0 \qquad \text{for all } \boldsymbol{b}.$$

Therefore $\check{\mathbf{z}}$ is positive-semidefinite (by definition) and positive-definite as well unless $\boldsymbol{b}^t\check{\mathbf{z}}\boldsymbol{b} = \boldsymbol{0}$ for some $\boldsymbol{b} \neq \boldsymbol{0}$. The case $\boldsymbol{b}^t\check{\mathbf{z}}\boldsymbol{b} = V(\boldsymbol{b}^t\tilde{\boldsymbol{z}}) = 0$ is possible only if $\boldsymbol{b}^t\tilde{\boldsymbol{z}}$ is constant with probability one.

21.9.3 Density Function of a Nonsingular Linear Transformation

Let $\tilde{\boldsymbol{z}}$ be a continuous rv with density function f and let $\tilde{\boldsymbol{y}}$ be defined by

$$\tilde{\boldsymbol{y}} = \boldsymbol{a} + \mathbf{b}\tilde{\boldsymbol{z}} \tag{21.56a}$$

where $\mathbf{b}$ is nonsingular. Then $\mathbf{b}^{-1}$ exists and

$$\tilde{\boldsymbol{z}} = \mathbf{b}^{-1}(\tilde{\boldsymbol{y}} - \boldsymbol{a}). \tag{21.56b}$$

We shall show that $\tilde{\boldsymbol{y}}$ has a density function g given by

$$g(\boldsymbol{y}) = f(\mathbf{b}^{-1}[\boldsymbol{y} - \boldsymbol{a}])|\det \mathbf{b}|^{-1} \tag{21.57}$$

where $|\det \mathbf{b}|$ is the absolute value of the determinant of $\mathbf{b}$. Notice that the point at which f is evaluated in (21.57) is the $\boldsymbol{z}$ corresponding to $\boldsymbol{y}$ by (21.56).

Proof We have, by (21.56) and (21.15),

$$P(\tilde{\boldsymbol{y}} \leq \boldsymbol{y}) = P(\boldsymbol{a} + \mathbf{b}\tilde{\boldsymbol{z}} \leq \boldsymbol{y}) = \int_{\boldsymbol{a}+\mathbf{b}\boldsymbol{z} \leq \boldsymbol{y}} f(\boldsymbol{z})\, d\boldsymbol{z}.$$

Since the change of variable $\boldsymbol{z} = \mathbf{b}^{-1}(\boldsymbol{x} - \boldsymbol{a})$ has Jacobian

$$\frac{\partial(\boldsymbol{z})}{\partial(\boldsymbol{x})} = \det \left\| \frac{\partial z_i}{\partial x_j} \right\| = \det(\mathbf{b}^{-1}) = (\det \mathbf{b})^{-1},$$

we obtain upon making this change of variable

$$P(\tilde{y} \leq y) = \int_{x \leq y} f(\mathbf{b}^{-1}[x - a])|\det \mathbf{b}|^{-1}\, dx,$$

by advanced calculus. It follows by (21.13) or (21.14) that the last integrand is the density function of $\tilde{y}$.

Exercises

1. Interpret and verify (21.4), (21.5), and (21.8).

2. For the joint distribution given by table 21.1 exhibit tables for the following:
   a. $f_2(z_2)$ $f_4(z_4)$, $f_{1,3}(z_1, z_3)$, $f_{2,4}(z_2, z_4)$.
   b. $f_{1,4|2,3}(z_1, z_4|1, 1)$.
   c. $f_{1,4|3}(z_1, z_4|1)$.

3. Figure 21.1 gives the distribution of $\tilde{z}_1$, $(\tilde{z}_1, \tilde{z}_2)$, $(\tilde{z}_1, \tilde{z}_2, \tilde{z}_3)$, and $(\tilde{z}_1, \tilde{z}_2, \tilde{z}_3, \tilde{z}_4)$, that is, it gives the mass functions f_1, $f_{1,2}$, $f_{1,2,3}$, and $f_{1,2,3,4}$. Make a similar tree diagram for the same $(\tilde{z}_1, \tilde{z}_2, \tilde{z}_3, \tilde{z}_4)$ giving the distribution of $\tilde{z}_1$ and the conditional distributions of $\tilde{z}_2$ given z_1, of $\tilde{z}_3$ given (z_1, z_2), and of $\tilde{z}_4$ given (z_1, z_2, z_3) that is, give f_1, $f_{2|1}$, $f_{3|1,2}$, and $f_{4|1,2,3}$.

4. Let $\tilde{z} = [\tilde{z}_1 \tilde{z}_2 \tilde{z}_3]'$, $f_1(0) = .6$, $f_1(1) = .4$ and let the joint distributions of $\tilde{z}_2$ and $\tilde{z}_3$ given z_1 be given in the following tables:

Table 21E.1

z_2 \ z_3	$f_{2,3|1}(z_2, z_3|0)$: 0	1
0	.4	.1
1	.2	0
2	.1	.2

Table 21E.2

z_2 \ z_3	$f_{2,3|1}(z_2, z_3|1)$: 0	1
0	0	.1
1	.2	3
2	.2	.2

Find the distribution of $\tilde{z}_3$ and the conditional distributions of $\tilde{z}_2$ given z_3 and $\tilde{z}_1$ given (z_3, z_2) and exhibit them in a tree diagram.

5. a. Verify table 21.3 from table 21.2.

   b. Verify table 21.4 from figure 21.1.

6. Let $(\tilde{z}_1, \tilde{z}_2, \tilde{z}_3)$ have the joint mf given in the following table.

	$f(z_1, z_2, z_3)$			
z_2:	0		1	
z_1 / z_3:	0	1	0	1
0:	$\frac{4}{192}$	$\frac{12}{192}$	$\frac{24}{192}$	$\frac{24}{192}$
1:	$\frac{17}{192}$	$\frac{15}{192}$	$\frac{39}{139}$	$\frac{57}{192}$

Show that:

a. All pairs $(\tilde{z}_i, \tilde{z}_j)$, $i \neq j$, are marginally independent;

b. No pair $(\tilde{z}_i, \tilde{z}_j)$, $i \neq j$, is conditionally independent given the value of the third rv;

c. No $\tilde{z}_i$ is independent of the remaining pair;

d. The rv's $\tilde{z}_1$, $\tilde{z}_2$, $\tilde{z}_3$ are pairwise independent but not mutually independent.

7. Let $\tilde{\mathbf{z}} = [\tilde{z}_1 \tilde{z}_2 \tilde{z}_3]^t$ be such that

$$E(\tilde{\mathbf{z}}) = \begin{bmatrix} 4.0 \\ 2.0 \\ -1.6 \end{bmatrix} \quad \text{and} \quad V(\tilde{\mathbf{z}}) = \begin{bmatrix} 9.0 & 2.0 & 0 \\ 2.0 & 1.0 & -.25 \\ 0 & -.25 & 4.0 \end{bmatrix}.$$

Let $\tilde{\mathbf{x}} = [\tilde{z}_1 \tilde{z}_3]^t$. Exhibit $E(\tilde{\mathbf{x}})$ and $V(\tilde{\mathbf{x}})$.

8. Consider a population of schoolchildren and for each child let z_1 denote the child's age, z_2 intellectual level, and z_3 physical level. A child drawn at random will have an unknown triplet $\tilde{\mathbf{z}} = [\tilde{z}_1 \tilde{z}_2 \tilde{z}_3]^t$ which we can treat as a (vector) rv. Argue that $\tilde{z}_2$ and $\tilde{z}_3$ are highly correlated, but conditional on z_1, rv's $\tilde{z}_2$ and $\tilde{z}_3$ are practically uncorrelated. Can you think of other sets of three variables that exhibit this same property?

   If $\tilde{z}_2$ and $\tilde{z}_3$ are highly correlated but if this correlation largely disappears when the population is stratified by any value of $\tilde{z}_1$ then one often says that $\tilde{z}_1$ is an "explanatory" variable which accounts for the relation between $\tilde{z}_2$ and $\tilde{z}_3$. Can we conclude that $\tilde{z}_1$ is a causal determinant of $\tilde{z}_2$ and $\tilde{z}_3$? Is it in your examples?

9. Think of a real-world example where $\tilde{z}_1$ and $\tilde{z}_2$ are practically uncorrelated but become highly correlated given a value of z_3. Think of two variables that tend to go in the same direction for a low value of a third variable and tend to go in opposite directions for a high value of this third variable.

10. Let a fair coin be tossed twice. Let $z_i = 1$ or 0 depending on whether the ith toss is heads or tails respectively ($i = 1, 2$). Let $z_3 = 0$ or 1 depending on whether the first two tosses match or not.

    a. Show that $\tilde{z}_1$, $\tilde{z}_2$, and $\tilde{z}_3$ are pairwise independent.

    b. Show that no $\tilde{z}_i$ is independent of the other two jointly.

    c. Verify table 21.7.

11. Let the rv's $\tilde{z}_1$, $\tilde{z}_2$, and $\tilde{z}_3$ each have range $\{0, 1\}$ and let the *conditional* joint mass functions of $(\tilde{z}_1, \tilde{z}_2)$ *given* that $\tilde{z}_3 = 0$ and given that $\tilde{z}_3 = 1$ be as follows:

		$f_{1,2\|3}(z_1, z_2 \| z_3)$			
	z_3:	0		1	
z_1	z_2:	0	1	0	1
0:		$\frac{1}{8}$	$\frac{3}{8}$	$\frac{3}{8}$	$\frac{1}{8}$
1:		$\frac{3}{8}$	$\frac{1}{8}$	$\frac{1}{8}$	$\frac{3}{8}$

a. Show that $\tilde{z}_1$ and $\tilde{z}_2$ are not conditionally independent given either $\tilde{z}_3 = 0$ or $\tilde{z}_3 = 1$.

b. Show that if each possible value of $\tilde{z}_3$ has probability $\frac{1}{2}$, then $\tilde{z}_1$ and $\tilde{z}_2$ are marginally independent.

c. Are $\tilde{z}_1$ and $\tilde{z}_2$ marginally independent if $P(\tilde{z}_3 = 0) = \frac{1}{4}$, $P(\tilde{z}_3 = 1) = \frac{3}{4}$?

12. Give tables corresponding to tables 21.7a and 21.7b in the case of an arbitrary known p.

13. Let $\tilde{z}_1, \tilde{z}_2, \tilde{z}_3$ and $\tilde{z}_4$ be uncorrelated rv's each with mean 0 and variance 1. Let

$$\tilde{y}_1 = -3 + 2\tilde{z}_2$$

$$\tilde{y}_2 = 4 + 1\tilde{z}_1 + 3\tilde{z}_2$$

$$\tilde{y}_3 = 5 + 8\tilde{z}_1 - 5\tilde{z}_3.$$

a. In finding the distribution of $\tilde{\boldsymbol{y}} = [\tilde{y}_1 \tilde{y}_2 \tilde{y}_3]'$ is it necessary to use the characteristics of $\tilde{z}_4$? What if $\tilde{z}_4$ were correlated with $\tilde{z}_1, \tilde{z}_2$ and $\tilde{z}_3$?

b. Find $\bar{\boldsymbol{y}}$ and $\check{\mathbf{y}}$.

14. a. Let $\tilde{\boldsymbol{z}} = [\tilde{z}_1 \tilde{z}_2 \tilde{z}_3]'$ have mean and variance:

$$\bar{\boldsymbol{z}} = [3.0\ 3.2\ 3.5]' \text{ and } \check{\mathbf{z}} = \begin{bmatrix} 8 & 1 & 8 \\ 1 & 9 & 6 \\ 8 & 6 & 20 \end{bmatrix}.$$

Let

$$\tilde{y}_1 = \tilde{z}_1$$

$$\tilde{y}_2 = a\tilde{z}_1 + \tilde{z}_2$$

$$\tilde{y}_3 = b\tilde{z}_1 + c\tilde{z}_2 + \tilde{z}_3$$

and choose a, b, c such that $\tilde{y}_1, \tilde{y}_2$, and $\tilde{y}_3$ are uncorrelated.
Hint

$$\check{y}_{12} = a\check{z}_{11} + \check{z}_{12}$$

$$\check{y}_{13} = b\check{z}_{11} + c\check{z}_{12} + \check{z}_{13}$$

$$\check{y}_{23} = ab\check{z}_{11} + (ac + b)\check{z}_{12} + a\check{z}_{13} + c\check{z}_{22} + \check{z}_{23}$$

$$= a(b\check{z}_{11} + c\check{z}_{12} + \check{z}_{13}) + b\check{z}_{12} + c\check{z}_{22} + \check{z}_{23}.$$

b. Find $\bar{\boldsymbol{y}}$ and $\check{\mathbf{y}}$.

c. Let

$$\tilde{\boldsymbol{x}} = \boldsymbol{a} + \mathbf{b}\tilde{\boldsymbol{z}}$$

and find $\boldsymbol{a}$ and $\mathbf{b}$ such that $\bar{\boldsymbol{x}} = [0, 0, 0]'$ and $\check{\mathbf{x}} = \mathbf{I}$, the identity matrix.

15. Given rv's $\tilde{z}_1, \tilde{z}_2, \ldots, \tilde{z}_{25}$, what is meant by the symbol $\rho_{3,13|2,4,7}(8.2, 1.7, -16.0)$?

16. (A problem involving sequential experimentation for diagnosis.) An item must be classified into one of two categories. Let s_i be the state that the item truly belongs to the ith category and let a_i be the act of classifying the item into the ith category ($i = 1, 2$). The profitability of the consequences associated with different act-state pairs is as follows:.

		Act	
		a_1	a_2
State	s_1	\$300	\$100
	s_2	-500	50

Let the prior probability of s_1 be $P(s_1) = .8$.

The decision maker has at his disposal three possible diagnostic tests, T_1, T_2, and T_3. Each test when applied will give one of two possible responses, which are coded by the symbols 0 or 1. These tests have been used extensively in the past and on the basis of this experience the following table has been prepared. (Let $\tilde{z}_i$ be the outcome of test T_i.)

Values of			Conditional probability of (z_1, z_2, z_3) given	
z_1	z_2	z_3	s_1	s_2
0	0	0	.02	.22
0	1	0	.03	.25
1	1	0	.05	.21
1	1	1	.07	.23
0	0	1	.08	.02
0	1	1	.07	.01
1	0	0	.35	.04
1	0	1	.33	.02

The question arises whether we should use all the diagnostic tests, use some of them, or use them sequentially in some order (the choice of the second test, if any, depending on the result of the first test). Let the cost of administering tests T_1, T_2, and T_3, respectively, be \$15, \$25, and \$20, respectively. Assume that at most one test can be applied at a time. Assume that because of time delays there is an additional \$5 cost if two tests are used and \$10 if three tests are used.

This problem can now be analyzed. Rather than go through all the arithmetic, outline in reasonable detail how you would proceed. Be prepared to discuss your strategy for analysis.

In principle, could the following happen? Among the three tests, T_2 is better than either T_1 or T_3 when taken separately but in a sequential design T_2 may not be used?

17. Show that if $\tilde{z}_1, \ldots, \tilde{z}_r$ are (a) pairwise or (b) mutually independent, the same is true of any subset.

18. Show that if $\tilde{z}$ has density f then

a. $\tilde{z}_1$ has density f_1 given by (21.17);

b. $\tilde{z}_1$ has density f_1 given by (21.19).

19. Show that if $\tilde{z}$ has density f then, conditional on the hypothesis $\tilde{z}_2 = z_2$, the rv $\tilde{z}_1$ has density $f_{1|2}(\cdot|z_2)$ given by (21.20a).

20. Prove that the expectation of φ wrt f as given by (21.34) equals the expectation of $\tilde{y} = \varphi(\tilde{z})$ wrt the induced distribution of $\tilde{y}$ in the case that $\tilde{z}$ is discrete.

21. Prove that the mean equals the mean of the conditional mean, (21.35), for

a. $\tilde{z}$ discrete,

b. $\tilde{z}$ continuous.

22. Show that partitioning $V(\tilde{z})$ gives $V(\tilde{z}_1)$, $V(\tilde{z}_2)$ and the covariances $V(\tilde{z}_1, \tilde{z}_2)$ and $V(\tilde{z}_2, \tilde{z}_1)$ as asserted by (21.47).

23. Show that $V(\tilde{z}_1, \tilde{z}_2)$ is the transpose of $V(\tilde{z}_2, \tilde{z}_1)$.

24. Show that the variance equals the mean of the conditional variance plus the variance of the conditional mean, (21.49).

25. Show that (21.22) implies that the events $\tilde{z}_1 \in S_1$ and $\tilde{z}_2 \in S_2$ are independent in (a) the discrete case; (b) the continuous case.

26. a. Provc (21.41).
 b. Prove (21.42).

27. An item is either satisfactory ($\tilde{z}_1 = 1$) or unsatisfactory ($\tilde{z} = 0$). It must be either accepted (a_1) or rejected (a_2). The opportunity loss of accepting an unsatisfactory item is \$400. The opportunity loss of rejecting a satisfactory item is \$100. Before acting, the decision maker can, if desired, observe the value of a discrete rv $\tilde{z}_2$ at a cost of \$10, or a discrete rv $\tilde{z}_3$ at a cost of \$15, or both at a cost of \$25. Past experience with these items indicates that the joint mass function of $(\tilde{z}_1, \tilde{z}_2, \tilde{z}_3)$ is as follows.

z_1	z_2	z_3	$f(z_1, z_2, z_3)$
0	0	0	.01
0	0	1	.02
0	1	0	.04
0	1	1	.03
1	1	1	.90

 a. Give the marginal mass functions of f_1, f_2, and f_3.
 b. Give the marginal joint mass function of $(\tilde{z}_1, \tilde{z}_2)$.
 c. Give the marginal joint mass function of $(\tilde{z}_1, \tilde{z}_3)$.
 d. Give the conditional mass function of $\tilde{z}_1$ given z_2 for each possible z_2.
 e. Give the conditional mass function of $\tilde{z}_1$ given z_3 for each possible z_3.
 f. Give the conditional mass function of $\tilde{z}_1$ given (z_2, z_3) for each possible pair (z_2, z_3).
 g. What is the optimum act without observation?
 h. What possible observations would lead to a change of act?
 i. What is the EVSI for observing $\tilde{z}_2$? $\tilde{z}_3$? both?
 j. What is the optimum choice of observation?

28. Suppose that $(\tilde{z}_1, \tilde{z}_2, \tilde{z}_3)$ are discrete random variables with range $-1, 0, 1$ and $\tilde{z}_2$ and $\tilde{z}_3$ are conditionally independent given z_1. Suppose the marginal mass function of $\tilde{z}_1$ and the conditional mass functions of $\tilde{z}_2$ given z_1 and $\tilde{z}_3$ given z_1 are as follows:

		$f_{2\|1}(z_2\|z_1)$			$f_{3\|1}(z_3\|z_1)$		
z_1	$f_1(z_1)$	$z_2 = -1$	$z_2 = 0$	$z_2 = 1$	$z_3 = -1$	$z_3 = 0$	$z_3 = 1$
-1	.3	.5	.5	0	.6	0	.4
0	.2	.2	.6	.2	.5	0	.5
1	.5	0	.5	.5	.4	0	.6

 a. Give the marginal mass function of $\tilde{z}_2$.
 b. Give the marginal mass function of $\tilde{z}_3$.
 c. Give the marginal mass function of $\tilde{z}_2 + \tilde{z}_3$.
 d. Consider a decision maker with total assets of \$5 million and utility function $u(x) = \sqrt{x}$, where x is total assets in millions of dollars. He has two investment opportunities; one would yield $\tilde{z}_2$ million dollars net and the other would yield $\tilde{z}_3$ million dollars net. He may accept neither, one, or both. Give directions for calculating what action he should take. You need not carry out the calculation.

29. A ticket is for sale which entitles its holder to a prize. The prize depends on an unknown number $\tilde{x}$ and on a choice which must be made by the ticket-holder before x is revealed. The following table gives the prize (in \$10,000 units) in each possible situation.

	Choice 1	Choice 2	Choice 3
$x = 0$	0	2	5
$x = 1$	5	4	1

Also for sale is information as to the value of two other unknown quantities $\tilde{y}$ and $\tilde{z}$. (Information on $\tilde{y}$ and $\tilde{z}$ separately is not available.)

Consider a decision maker with assets 5 who has assessed $P(\tilde{x} = 0) = .4$ and $P(\tilde{x} = 1) = .6$, along with the following conditional probabilities.

	y:	2	2	3	3
	z:	4	5	4	5
$P(\tilde{y} = y, \tilde{z} = z \mid \tilde{x} = 0)$		.1	.1	.2	.6
$P(\tilde{y} = y, \tilde{z} = z \mid \tilde{x} = 1)$		.2	.6	.2	0

Suppose first that the decision maker has linear utility for assets.

a. If the decision maker were given the ticket, which choice should he make in the absence of information about y and z?

b. What is his cash equivalent for the ticket if he does not buy y or z information?

c. What is the maximum amount he should be willing to pay for the ticket if he does not buy y or z information?

d. If he buys the ticket, does the maximum amount he should be willing to pay to learn the value of $\tilde{y}$ and $\tilde{z}$ depend on the price he pays for the ticket?

e. If he pays 2 for the ticket, what is the maximum amount he should then be willing to pay to learn the value of $\tilde{y}$ and $\tilde{z}$?

f. Now answer the same questions supposing the decision maker's utility function for assets is $u(x) = -1/x$.

30. Let $\tilde{X} = \tilde{x} - \bar{x}$, $\tilde{Y} = \tilde{y} - \bar{y}$. Prove:

a. $E(\tilde{x}\tilde{y}) = \bar{x}\bar{y} + V(\tilde{x}, \tilde{y})$.

b. $V(\tilde{x}\tilde{y}) = \bar{x}^2\check{y} + \bar{y}^2\check{x} + 2\bar{x}\bar{y}V(\tilde{x}, \tilde{y}) + 2\bar{x}E(\tilde{X}\tilde{Y}^2) + 2\bar{y}E(\tilde{X}^2\tilde{Y}) + V(\tilde{X}\tilde{Y})$.

c. $E(\tilde{X}\tilde{Y}^2) = V(\tilde{X}, \tilde{Y}^2)$.

d. $V(\tilde{X}\tilde{Y}) = E(\tilde{X}^2\tilde{Y}^2) - [V(\tilde{x}, \tilde{y})]^2$

$$= \check{x}\check{y}(1 - \rho^2) - V(\tilde{X}^2, \tilde{Y}^2)$$

where ρ is the correlation between $\tilde{x}$ and $\tilde{y}$.

e. If $\tilde{x}$ and $\tilde{y}$ are independent, then

$$V(\tilde{x}, \tilde{y}) = \bar{x}^2\check{y} + \bar{y}^2\check{x} + \check{x}\check{y}.$$

f. Any "raw moment" (expectation of a product of powers of $\tilde{x}$ and $\tilde{y}$) can be expressed in terms of $\bar{x}$, $\bar{y}$, and "central moments" (expectations of products of powers of $\tilde{X}$ and $\tilde{Y}$).

22 The Multivariate Normal Distribution

Continuous bivariate and multivariate rv's were defined in sections 13.4 and 21.4, respectively. Basically, they are rv's that have a joint density function. This chapter introduces the most convenient and widely used multivariate density function. It is a natural generalization of the univariate Normal density function, whose convenience and usefulness are already clear from chapters 16–18. The multivariate Normal distribution is flexible enough to be very serviceable as a prior distribution. Furthermore, when a univariate or multivariate Normal prior is joined to a Normal data-generating process, all the probability theory can be expressed naturally in terms of the multivariate Normal distribution. Thus chapter 16 already involved the multivariate Normal distribution, though we avoided introducing it explicitly there. However, we will need it in more complicated situations.

The rest of this book will use the multivariate Normal distribution in a variety of practical problems; this chapter defines the distribution and describes its main properties, playing a role here like that of section 9.7 in the univariate case. We shall often treat the bivariate case separately, and many readers may find it helpful to specialize to the bivariate case still more often. In fact, some may wish to think only of the bivariate case the first time they read this chapter. A separate chapter on the bivariate Normal distribution would, however, be almost word for word the same as this chapter.

22.1 The Unit Spherical Multivariate Normal Distribution

22.1.1 Definition of a Unit Spherical Multivariate Normal RV

We shall say that a multivariate rv $(\tilde{u}_1, \ldots, \tilde{u}_r)$ is *unit spherical Normal* if $\tilde{u}_1, \ldots, \tilde{u}_r$ are mutually independent, unit Normal rv's. The reason for the term "spherical" will become evident shortly.

22.1.2 Density Function

If $(\tilde{u}_1, \ldots, \tilde{u}_r)$ is unit spherical Normal, then it has a joint density function f_{N*} which we shall call the *unit spherical multivariate Normal density function* and which is given by (exercise 1)

$$f_{N*}(\boldsymbol{u}) = (2\pi)^{-(1/2)r} e^{-(1/2)\boldsymbol{u}^t \mathbf{I} \boldsymbol{u}}, \qquad -\infty < \boldsymbol{u} < \infty. \tag{22.1}$$

The quadratic form in the exponent is

$$\boldsymbol{u}^t \mathbf{I} \boldsymbol{u} = u_1^2 + u_2^2 + \cdots + u_r^2. \tag{22.2}$$

The **I** is superfluous and could be dropped, but we retain it for formal similarity with more general formulas to be obtained later.

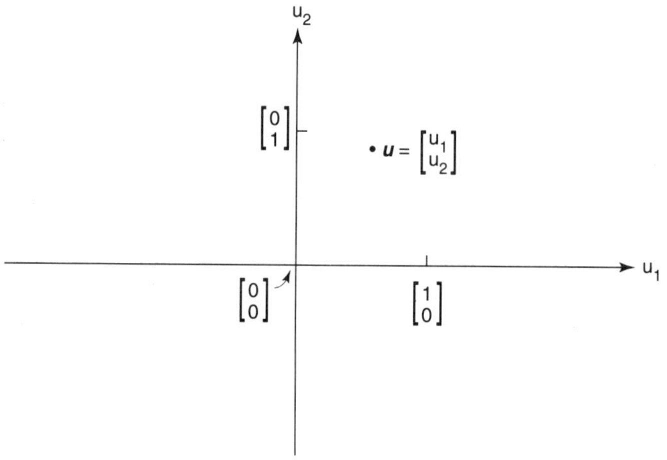

Figure 22.1
(u_1, u_2)-plane

The unit spherical bivariate Normal density function is given by (22.1) with $r = 2$. In non-matrix notation it is

$$f_{N^*}(u_1, u_2) = \frac{1}{2\pi} e^{-(1/2)(u_1^2 + u_2^2)}. \tag{22.3}$$

22.1.3 Mean and Variance Matrix

Let $(\tilde{u}_1, \ldots, \tilde{u}_r)$ be unit spherical multivariate Normal. Then each $\tilde{u}_i$ is (marginally) unit Normal and therefore by (9.59) and (9.60)

$$E(\tilde{u}_i) \equiv \bar{u}_i = 0, \qquad V(\tilde{u}_i) \equiv \breve{u}_i = 1 \qquad \text{for all } i. \tag{22.4a}$$

Furthermore, since $\tilde{u}_1, \ldots, \tilde{u}_r$ are mutually (and hence pairwise) independent and since independence implies zero covariance,

$$V(\tilde{u}_i, \tilde{u}_j) \equiv \breve{u}_{ij} = 0 \qquad \text{for all } i, j, i \neq j. \tag{22.4b}$$

We summarize this in matrix notation by writing

$$E(\tilde{\boldsymbol{u}}) \equiv \bar{\boldsymbol{u}} = \boldsymbol{0}, \qquad V(\tilde{\boldsymbol{u}}) \equiv \breve{\mathbf{u}} = \mathbf{I}. \tag{22.4c}$$

22.1.4 Graphic Representation in the Bivariate Case

Let a sheet of paper represent the (u_1, u_2) plane as in figure 22.1, and visualize the density $f_{N*}(u_1, u_2)$ at the generic point (u_1, u_2) as a height above the paper. This height, which is given by formula (22.3), is a continuous function of the coordinates u_1, u_2. Thus we can represent the entire density function as a smooth surface of varying height above the paper.

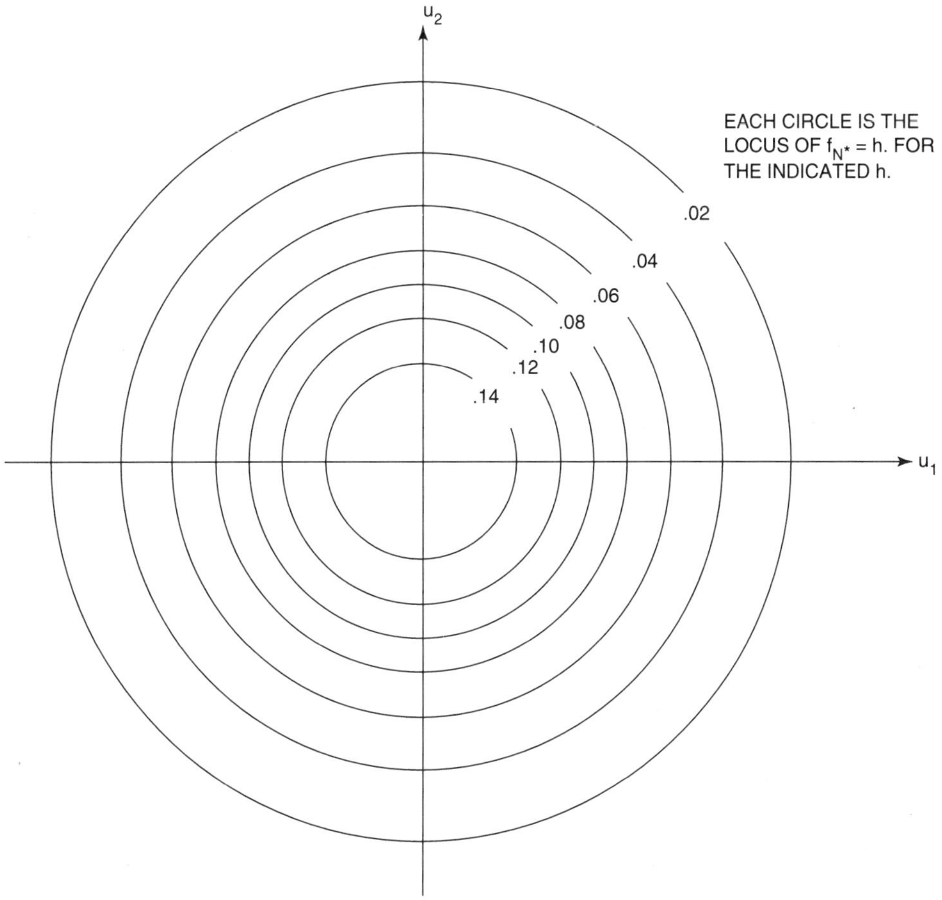

Figure 22.2
Contours of unit-spherical bivariate Normal density

This amounts to a graph of $f_{N^*}(u_1, u_2)$ and it requires three dimensions for the same reason that graphing a function of one variable requires two dimensions.

The density function or, equivalently, the density surface can be represented in two dimensions instead of three by using contours. One represents a hill in a two-dimensional contour map by selecting a number of fixed heights and for each one drawing on the map a curve running through all the points where the hill has the height in question. In exactly the same way, figure 22.2 shows the curve running through all the points where $f_{N^*}(u_1, u_2)$ has a specified value, for each of a number of specified values. The contours are circles because if we select any particular value h and look for the locus of all points (u_1, u_2) such that

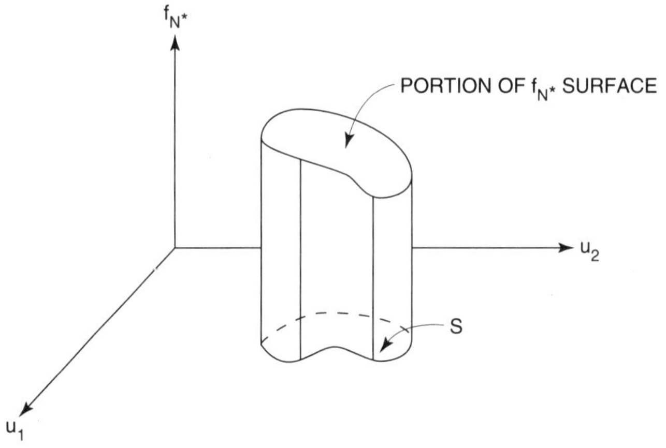

Figure 22.3
Probability as volume under density surface

$$f_{N^*}(u_1, u_2) \equiv \frac{1}{2\pi} e^{-(1/2)(u_1^2+u_2^2)} = h, \tag{22.5a}$$

this is the same thing as looking for all points (u_1, u_2) such that

$$u_2^1 + u_2^2 = -2\log(2\pi h), \tag{22.5b}$$

and these points lie on a circle of radius $\sqrt{-2\log(2\pi h)}$ about the origin. (For $h > 1/(2\pi)$, the locus is empty, that is, no points (u_1, u_2) satisfy (22.5), because $f_{N^*}(u_1, u_2) \leq f_{N^*}(0, 0) = 1/(2\pi)$.) In the r-variate case, a similar argument shows that the contours of f_{N^*} are the surfaces of concentric r-dimensional spheres.

The probability that $(\tilde{u}_1, \tilde{u}_2)$ lies within any particular region S in the (u_1, u_2) plane can be thought of as the volume under the density surface over the region in question, as sketched in figure 22.3. Analytically, the probability in question can be written

$$P[(\tilde{u}_1, \tilde{u}_2) \in S] = \iint_S f_{N^*}(u_1, u_2)\, du_1\, du_2. \tag{22.6}$$

22.1.5 Computation of Probabilities

Numerical Integration

The probability that a unit spherical Normal rv $\tilde{\mathbf{u}}$ (of any dimension) lies in a region S is

$$P(\tilde{\mathbf{u}} \subset S) = \int_S f_{N^*}(\mathbf{u})\, d\mathbf{u} \tag{22.7}$$

Only for very special regions S can this be evaluated in closed form. In principle, it can always be computed by numerical integration. In practice, although $f_{N^*}(\boldsymbol{u})$ is easy to compute, the numerical integration is not easy to do accurately, because $f_{N^*}(\boldsymbol{u})$ is very nonlinear, decreasing rapidly relative to its size as $\boldsymbol{u}$ gets far from $\boldsymbol{0}$. Computer packages handle various special cases.

Tables Even for regions of special shapes, tabulation is difficult because of the number of variables involved. There are, however, tables for certain regions in the bivariate and trivariate cases. For references, see Greenwood and Hartley (1962). A reference to one important set of tables of the bivariate unit spherical Normal distribution and instructions for their use are given in *ASTD*, section 8.1.2.

Simulation Since a unit spherical Normal rv $\tilde{\boldsymbol{u}}$ is simply an r-tuple of independent unit Normal real rv's, the probability that $\tilde{\boldsymbol{u}}$ belongs to any region S can be simulated by generalizing independent unit Normal random numbers, taking successive sets or r of these numbers, treating the first number of each set as u_1, the second as u_2, etc., and for each set determining whether $\boldsymbol{u} = (u_1, \ldots, u_r)$ is inside or outside S.

22.2 The General Nonsingular Multivariate Normal Distribution

Let $(\tilde{u}_1, \ldots, \tilde{u}_r)$ be unit spherical Normal and suppose each of a number of rv's z_i is a linear function of $\tilde{u}_1, \ldots, \tilde{u}_r$; that is, in matrix notation, suppose that $\tilde{\boldsymbol{z}} = \boldsymbol{a} + \mathbf{b}\tilde{\boldsymbol{u}}$ for some vector $\boldsymbol{a}$ and some matrix $\mathbf{b}$. Any such rv $\tilde{\boldsymbol{z}}$ will be called multivariate Normal, and we shall describe the distribution of all such rv's in the course of this chapter. It is convenient to consider first the case when the $\tilde{z}_i$'s jointly are related in a one-to-one manner with the $\tilde{u}_i$'s jointly, that is, $\tilde{\boldsymbol{z}}$ is a one-to-one function of $\tilde{\boldsymbol{u}}$. This is equivalent to $\mathbf{b}$ being a square, nonsingular matrix. It is also convenient not to start by deriving the distribution of $\boldsymbol{a} + \mathbf{b}\tilde{\boldsymbol{u}}$ for $\mathbf{b}$ nonsingular and $\tilde{\boldsymbol{u}}$ unit spherical Normal, but instead to introduce the distribution in its own right and later show, among other things, that it can be regarded as arising in this way.

22.2.1 The Nonsingular Multivariate Normal Density Function, Mean, and Variance

The function f_N defined by

$$f_N(z|\boldsymbol{M}, \mathbf{V}) = (2\pi)^{-(1/2)r} e^{-(1/2)(z-\boldsymbol{M})^t \mathbf{V}^{-1}(z-\boldsymbol{M})} (\det \mathbf{V})^{-1/2}, \tag{22.8}$$

where

z is $(r \times 1)$, $\boldsymbol{M}$ is $(r \times 1)$, $\mathbf{V}$ is $(r \times r)$ and positive-definite, will be called the *nonsingular multivariate* (or *r-variate*) *Normal density function with mean* $\boldsymbol{M}$ *and variance* $\mathbf{V}$ (or *parameters* $\boldsymbol{M}$ *and* $\mathbf{V}$), and any rv with this density will be called nonsingular multivariate Normal with mean $\boldsymbol{M}$ and variance $\mathbf{V}$. This terminology presupposes certain facts which, along with some other important properties, will be stated now and proved later.

1. $f_N(\cdot|\boldsymbol{M},\mathbf{V})$ is a density function with mean $\boldsymbol{M}$ and variance $\mathbf{V}$. Furthermore, given any $(r \times 1)$ $\boldsymbol{M}$ and any $(r \times r)$ positive-definite $\mathbf{V}$, there is exactly one nonsingular multivariate Normal density function with mean $\boldsymbol{M}$ and variance $\mathbf{V}$.

2. $f_N(z|\boldsymbol{0},\mathbf{I}) = f_{N^*}(z)$ for all z, that is, the multivariate Normal density with mean $\boldsymbol{0}$ and variance $\mathbf{I}$ is the unit spherical multivariate Normal density.

3. The nonsingular r-variate Normal densities are exactly those densities which arise by a nonsingular linear transformation from a unit spherical r-variate Normal density. Specifically:

a. If $\tilde{\boldsymbol{u}}$ is unit spherical r-variate Normal and

$$\tilde{z} = \boldsymbol{a} + \mathbf{b}\tilde{\boldsymbol{u}}, \qquad \boldsymbol{a}(r \times 1), \qquad \mathbf{b}(r \times r) \text{ nonsingular,} \tag{22.9a}$$

then $\tilde{z}$ is nonsingular multivariate Normal with mean and variance

$$\boldsymbol{M} = E(\tilde{z}) = \bar{z} = \boldsymbol{a}, \qquad \mathbf{V} = V(\tilde{z}) = \check{\mathbf{z}} = \mathbf{b}\mathbf{b}^t. \tag{22.9b}$$

b. If $\tilde{z}$ is nonsingular r-variate Normal with mean $\boldsymbol{M}$ and variance $\mathbf{V}$ and $\mathbf{b}$ is any $(r \times r)$ solution (there are many) of

$$\mathbf{b}\mathbf{b}^t = \mathbf{V} = \check{\mathbf{z}}, \tag{22.10a}$$

then $\mathbf{b}$ is nonsingular, $\tilde{\boldsymbol{u}} = \mathbf{b}^{-1}(\tilde{z} - \boldsymbol{M})$ is unit spherical r-variate Normal, and

$$\tilde{z} = \boldsymbol{M} + \mathbf{b}\tilde{\boldsymbol{u}}. \tag{22.10b}$$

4. If $\tilde{z}$ is nonsingular r-variate Normal and $\tilde{\boldsymbol{y}}$ is a nonsingular linear transformation of $\tilde{z}$, then $\tilde{\boldsymbol{y}}$ is nonsingular r-variate Normal. Specifically, if

$$\tilde{\boldsymbol{y}} = \boldsymbol{a} + \mathbf{b}\tilde{z}, \qquad \boldsymbol{a}(r \times 1), \qquad \mathbf{b}(r \times r) \text{ nonsingular,} \tag{22.11a}$$

then $\tilde{\boldsymbol{y}}$ is nonsingular r-variate Normal with mean and variance

$$\bar{\boldsymbol{y}} = \boldsymbol{a} + \mathbf{b}\bar{z}, \qquad \check{\boldsymbol{y}} = \mathbf{b}\check{\mathbf{z}}\mathbf{b}^t. \tag{22.11b}$$

Remarks To bring out the close resemblance between the multivariate density (22.8) and the univariate density (9.48), we observe that in both cases it is the *inverse* of the variance that appears in the exponent. Furthermore, the restriction $V > 0$ in the univariate case corresponds to the restriction V positive-definite in the multivariate case.

There are, of course, any number of nonsingular multivariate Normal rv's with mean $\boldsymbol{M}$ and variance $\mathbf{V}$, but there is only one multivariate Normal distribution with $\boldsymbol{M}$ and variance $\mathbf{V}$. If the rv $\tilde{z} = (\tilde{z}_1, \ldots, \tilde{z}_r)$ has mean $\boldsymbol{M}$ and nonsingular variance $\mathbf{V}$ and *if $\tilde{z}$ is multivariate Normal*, then $\boldsymbol{M}$ and $\mathbf{V}$ determine the density of $\tilde{z}$, and it is given by (22.8). It is possible that $\tilde{z}_1, \ldots, \tilde{z}_r$ can be Normal individually (i.e., marginally Normal) without being multivariate Normal; in this case $\boldsymbol{M}$ and $\mathbf{V}$ do not determine the joint distribution of $\tilde{z}_1, \ldots, \tilde{z}_r$.

Property 3a is a special case of property 4: If $\tilde{z}$ has mean $\boldsymbol{0}$ and variance $\mathbf{I}$ in property 4, then it is unit spherical Normal like $\tilde{\boldsymbol{u}}$ in property 3a and $\tilde{\boldsymbol{y}}$ in property 4 plays the role of $\tilde{z}$ in property 3a.

The transformation (22.10b) is not unique, since it is possible to find an infinity of matrices $\mathbf{b}$ satisfying (22.10a); compare the fact that the analogous univariate transformation (9.51) could contain a $\pm$ sign in the denominator. On the other hand, the absolute value of the determinant of $\mathbf{b}$ is unique, since (22.9b) implies $\det \mathbf{b} = \pm\sqrt{\det \mathbf{V}}$, corresponding to $\pm\sqrt{\mathbf{V}}$ in the univariate case (see also exercise 3).

Proof Property 2 is immediate, since substitution of $\boldsymbol{0}$ for $\boldsymbol{M}$ and $\mathbf{I}$ for $\mathbf{V}$ in (22.8) gives (22.1).

Formula (22.11b) is simply a repetition of (21.53) and (22.9b) in a special case.

We next complete the proof of property 3a. The density of $\tilde{z}$ in property 3a can be obtained from that of $\tilde{\boldsymbol{u}}$ by applying (21.53) to (22.1). This replaces the exponent of (22.1) by

$$(\mathbf{b}^{-1}[z - \boldsymbol{a}])^t\mathbf{I}(\mathbf{b}^{-1}[z - \boldsymbol{a}]) = (z - \boldsymbol{a})^t(\mathbf{b}^{-1})^t\mathbf{I}(\mathbf{b}^{-1})(z - \boldsymbol{a})$$

$$= (z - \boldsymbol{a})^t(\mathbf{b}\mathbf{b}^t)^{-1}(z - \boldsymbol{a}) = (z - \boldsymbol{M})^t\mathbf{V}^{-1}(z - \boldsymbol{M})$$

and multiplies (22.1) by the factor $|\det \mathbf{b}|^{-1}$. Since $\det(\mathbf{V}) = \det(\mathbf{b})\det(\mathbf{b}^t) = [\det \mathbf{b}]^2$, this factor can also be written

$$|\det \mathbf{b}|^{-1} = (\det \mathbf{V})^{-1/2}.$$

Thus the density of $\tilde{z}$ is of the form (22.8) with $\boldsymbol{M} = \boldsymbol{a} = \bar{z}$ and $\mathbf{V} = \mathbf{b}\mathbf{b}^t = \check{\mathbf{z}}$. Furthermore, $\mathbf{V} = \mathbf{b}\mathbf{b}^t$ is positive-definite by A2.7, Theorem 3. Thus we have proved property 3a.

We have also proved property 1, at least for all $\boldsymbol{M}$ and $\mathbf{V}$ of the form (22.9b). But all $(r \times 1)$ vectors $\boldsymbol{M}$ and all positive-definite $(r \times r)$ matrices $\mathbf{V}$ are of the form (22.9b), since $\boldsymbol{a}$ can be any $(r \times 1)$ vector and $\mathbf{b}$ any nonsingular $(r \times r)$ matrix in (22.9b), and any positive-definite matrix $\mathbf{V}$ is of the form $\mathbf{b}\mathbf{b}^t$ with $\mathbf{b}$ nonsingular, by A2.7, Theorem 7.

Property 4 can now be proved just as property 3a was. Alternatively, since we have already shown that $\tilde{z}$ has the same density as a nonsingular linear transformation of a unit spherical Normal rv $\tilde{\boldsymbol{u}}$, say as $\boldsymbol{\alpha} + \boldsymbol{\beta}\tilde{\boldsymbol{u}}$, we can conclude immediately that $\tilde{y}$ has the same density as $\boldsymbol{a} + \mathbf{b}(\boldsymbol{\alpha} + \boldsymbol{\beta}\tilde{\boldsymbol{u}}) = \boldsymbol{a} + \mathbf{b}\boldsymbol{\alpha} + \mathbf{b}\boldsymbol{\beta}\tilde{\boldsymbol{u}}$, which is also a nonsingular linear transformation of $\tilde{\boldsymbol{u}}$ and is therefore nonsingular Normal by property 3a.

Only property 3b remains to be proved. We have already noted that there is a solution $\mathbf{b}$ of (33.10a); in fact, by exercise 3, there are many. The rv $\tilde{\boldsymbol{u}} = \mathbf{b}^{-1}(\tilde{z} - \boldsymbol{M}) = -\mathbf{b}^{-1}\boldsymbol{M} + \mathbf{b}^{-1}\tilde{z}$ is a nonsingular linear transformation of $\tilde{z}$ and therefore nonsingular bivariate Normal by property 4, and it is unit spherical since it has mean $\boldsymbol{0}$ and variance $\mathbf{I}$, as the reader can verify by straightforward calculation (exercise 2).

22.2.2 Independence

If $\tilde{z}_1$ and $\tilde{z}_2$ are independent nonsingular univariate or multivariate Normal rv's, not necessarily of the same dimension, then their joint distribution is nonsingular multivariate Normal with

$$\boldsymbol{M} = \begin{bmatrix} \bar{z}_1 \\ \bar{z}_2 \end{bmatrix}, \qquad \mathbf{V} = \begin{bmatrix} \check{z}_1 & 0 \\ 0 & \check{z}_2 \end{bmatrix}. \tag{22.12}$$

In particular, $\mathbf{V}_{12} = V(\tilde{z}_1, \tilde{z}_2) = \mathbf{0}$. Conversely, if $\tilde{z} = (\tilde{z}_1, \tilde{z}_2) = [\tilde{z}_1^t \tilde{z}_2^t]^t$ is nonsingular multivariate Normal and if the covariance $\mathbf{V}_{12} = \check{z}_{12} = V(\tilde{z}_1, \tilde{z}_2) = 0$, then $\tilde{z}_1$ and $\tilde{z}_2$ are independent Normal rv's. Note that it is part of the assumption of this last statement that $\tilde{z}_1$ and $\tilde{z}_2$ are *jointly* Normal. Normality of $\tilde{z}_1$ and $\tilde{z}_2$ individually is not enough: $\tilde{z}_1$ and $\tilde{z}_2$ may be marginally Normal with covariance $\mathbf{0}$ but still not independent and not jointly Normal. An extreme example is given in exercise 5.

The statements of the previous paragraph can be summarized as follows.

Theorem The rv's $\tilde{z}_1$ and $\tilde{z}_2$ are independent and marginally nonsingular Normal if and only if they are jointly nonsingular Normal and $V(\tilde{z}_1, \tilde{z}_2) = \mathbf{0}$.

The proof is exercise 4.

It follows from the preceding theorem (exercise 31) that

Theorem If $\tilde{z}_1$ and $\tilde{z}_2$ are jointly nonsingular Normal, then $\tilde{z}_1$ and $\tilde{z}_2 - \check{\mathbf{z}}_{21}\check{\mathbf{z}}_{11}^{-1}\tilde{z}_1$ are independent, nonsingular Normal rv's.

The rv $\tilde{z}_2 - \check{\mathbf{z}}_{21}\check{\mathbf{z}}_{11}^{-1}\tilde{z}_1$ may seem to have appeared from nowhere, but if one seeks a matrix $\mathbf{c}$ such that $\tilde{z}_1$ and $\tilde{z}_2 + \mathbf{c}\tilde{z}_1$ have covariance $\mathbf{0}$, one finds immediately that $\mathbf{c} = -\check{\mathbf{z}}_{21}\check{\mathbf{z}}_{11}^{-1}$ (exercise 6b). In the case of univariate $\tilde{z}_1$ and z_2, this was done in exercise 21.14a

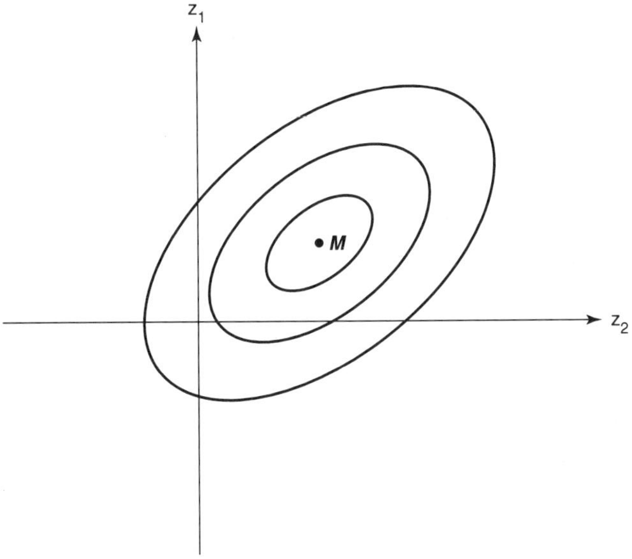

Figure 22.4
Elliptical density contours

22.2.3 Contours

Consider first the bivariate case. If we wish to represent a nonsingular bivariate Normal density function by means of a contour map on the (z_1, z_2) plane, we observe that (22.8) will be constant if the quadratic form in the exponent is constant. Letting $\mathbf{H} = \mathbf{V}^{-1}$, we have for this quadratic form

$$(z - \boldsymbol{M})^t \mathbf{V}^{-1}(z - \boldsymbol{M})$$

$$= H_{11}(z_1 - M_1)^2 + 2H_{12}(z_1 - M_1)(z_2 - M_2) + H_{22}(z_2 - M_2)^2. \quad (22.13)$$

H is positive-definite because it is the inverse of a positive-definite matrix. Therefore this form is constant along an *ellipse* with center $(M_1, M_2) = \boldsymbol{M}$. In figure 22.4 we show such ellipses of constant density.

In the r-variate case, a contour is again a locus of points z for which (22.8) is constant and hence for which the quadratic form $(z - \boldsymbol{M})^t \mathbf{V}^{-1}(z - \boldsymbol{M})$ appearing in the exponent of (22.8) is constant. This quadratic form is again positive-definite, and the surface on which a positive-definite quadratic form is constant is called an ellipsoid. (It is a linear transformation of a sphere.) Thus we find that the contours of a nonsingular, multivariate Normal density function are ellipsoids all having the same center $\boldsymbol{M}$ and the same shape and orientation (but, though it is irrelevant here, not the same foci).

22.2.4 Computation of Probabilities

The probability that a nonsingular, multivariate Normal rv $\tilde{z}$ lies in a region S can be reduced to the unit spherical case (see section 22.1.5), but it can rarely be expressed in closed form or calculated easily by numerical integration. Often one will want to resort to simulation. An r-variate Normal rv $\tilde{z}$ with mean $\bar{z} = M$ and nonsingular variance $\check{\mathbf{z}} = \mathbf{V}$ can, by property 3a of section 22.2.1, be simulated as follows. Find a $\mathbf{b}$ such that $\mathbf{b}\mathbf{b}^t = \mathbf{V}$. Generate independent unit Normal random numbers, say $u_1, u_2, \ldots$. Take successive sets of r of these numbers and form vectors $\boldsymbol{u}^{(1)}, \boldsymbol{u}^{(2)}, \ldots$, that is, let $\boldsymbol{u}^{(1)} = [u_1 u_2 \ldots u_r]^t$, $\boldsymbol{u}^{(2)} = [u_{r+1} u_{r+2} \ldots u_{2r}]^t$, and so on. For each $\boldsymbol{u}^{(i)}$, compute the corresponding

$$z^{(i)} = M + \mathbf{b}\boldsymbol{u}^{(i)}. \tag{22.14}$$

Then the $z^{(i)}$ simulate $\tilde{z}$, that is $\tilde{z}^{(1)}, \tilde{z}^{(2)}, \ldots$ are independent, r-variate Normal rv's each with mean M and variance $\mathbf{V}$.

In the bivariate case, one matrix $\mathbf{b}$ which satisfies the requirement is suggested by the second theorem of section 22.2.2 and is given by

$$\begin{aligned} b_{11} &= V_{11}^{1/2} = \ddot{z}_1, & b_{12} &= 0, \\ b_{21} &= V_{12} V_{11}^{-1/2} = \frac{\check{z}_{12}}{\ddot{z}_1}, & b_{22} &= (V_{22} - V_{12}^2 V_{11}^{-1})^{-1/2}. \end{aligned} \tag{22.15}$$

It is easily verified (exercise 7) that this $\mathbf{b}$ satisfies $\mathbf{b}\mathbf{b}^t = \mathbf{V}$.

22.3 Marginal and Conditional Distributions

22.3.1 Marginal and Conditional Distributions of a Given Joint Distribution

Let the rv $\tilde{z}$ be nonsingular r-variate Normal with parameters M and $\mathbf{V}$; let the rv and the parameters be partitioned

$$\tilde{z} = \begin{bmatrix} \tilde{z}_1 \\ \tilde{z}_2 \end{bmatrix}, \qquad M = \begin{bmatrix} M_1 \\ M_2 \end{bmatrix}, \qquad \mathbf{V} = \begin{bmatrix} \mathbf{V}_{11} & \mathbf{V}_{12} \\ \mathbf{V}_{21} & \mathbf{V}_{22} \end{bmatrix}, \tag{22.16}$$

where $\tilde{z}_1$ and M_1 are $p \times 1$ and $\mathbf{V}_{11}$ is $p \times p$ (from which the remaining dimensions can be deduced). Regarding the marginal and conditional distributions of $\tilde{z}_1$ and $\tilde{z}_2$ we shall prove the following results.

The *marginal* distribution of $\tilde{z}_i$ is nonsingular Normal with parameters

$$E(\tilde{z}_i) \equiv \bar{z}_i = M_i, \qquad V(\tilde{z}_i) \equiv \check{z}_i = \mathbf{V}_{ii}, \qquad i = 1, 2. \tag{22.17}$$

The *conditional* distribution of $\tilde{z}_i$ given that $\tilde{z}_j$ has some particular value z_j is *nonsingular Normal* with parameters

$$E(\tilde{z}_i|z_j) = \boldsymbol{M}_i + \mathbf{V}_{ij}\mathbf{V}_{jj}^{-1}(z_j - \boldsymbol{M}_j), \tag{22.18a}$$

$$V(\tilde{z}_i|z_j) = \mathbf{V}_{ii} - \mathbf{V}_{ij}\mathbf{V}_{jj}^{-1}\mathbf{V}_{ji}, \quad i = 1, j = 2 \quad \text{or} \quad i = 2, j = 1. \tag{22.18b}$$

In the bivariate case, these results say that if $\tilde{z}_1$ and $\tilde{z}_2$ are jointly Normal real rv's, then they are marginally Normal (with their marginal means and variances as parameters) and the conditional distribution of $\tilde{z}_1$ given $\tilde{z}_2 = z_2$ is Normal with mean and variance

$$E(\tilde{z}_1|z_2) = \bar{z}_1 + \frac{\check{z}_{12}}{\check{z}_{22}}(z_2 - \bar{z}_2), \qquad V(\tilde{z}_1|z_2) = \check{z}_1 - \frac{\check{z}_{12}^2}{\check{z}_{22}}. \tag{22.19}$$

The conditional distribution of $\tilde{z}_2$ given z_1 is the same with the subscripts 1 and 2 interchanged.

Note that, by (22.18a), the conditional mean of $\tilde{z}_i$ given z_j depends *linearly* on z_j, that is, the regressions of $\tilde{z}_1$ on $\tilde{z}_2$ and of $\tilde{z}_2$ on $\tilde{z}_1$ are linear. Note also that, by (22.18b), the conditional variance of $\tilde{z}_i$ given z_j, which could in principle depend on z_j, is here a constant.

Certain of these formulas take a particularly suggestive form when expressed in terms of the inverses of the variances involved. Let the inverse of a variance (matrix) be called a *precision* (matrix). Let the precision matrix of $\tilde{\mathbf{z}}$ be $\mathbf{H}$; that is, let

$$\mathbf{H} = \check{\mathbf{z}}^{-1} = \mathbf{V}^{-1}. \tag{22.20}$$

Partition $\mathbf{H}$ as $\mathbf{V}$ is partitioned in (22.16):

$$\mathbf{H} = \begin{bmatrix} \mathbf{H}_{11} & \mathbf{H}_{12} \\ \mathbf{H}_{21} & \mathbf{H}_{22} \end{bmatrix} \quad \text{where} \quad \mathbf{H} \text{ is } p \times p. \tag{22.21}$$

Then by (A2.12)

$$\mathbf{V}_{ii}^{-1} = \mathbf{H}_{ii} - \mathbf{H}_{ij}\mathbf{H}_{jj}^{-1}\mathbf{H}_{ji},$$

$$\mathbf{H}_{ii}^{-1} = \mathbf{V}_{ii} - \mathbf{V}_{ij}\mathbf{V}_{jj}^{-1}\mathbf{V}_{ji},$$

$$\mathbf{V}_{ij}\mathbf{V}_{jj}^{-1} = -\mathbf{H}_{ii}^{-1}\mathbf{H}_{ij}, \qquad i = 1, j = 2 \text{ or } j = 1, i = 2. \tag{22.22}$$

Notice that $\mathbf{H}_{11}$ is *not* the precision of $\tilde{z}_1$, since $\mathbf{H}_{11} \neq \mathbf{V}_{11}^{-1}$. In fact, comparison of (22.22) and (22.18) reveals that $\mathbf{H}_{11}$ is the inverse of $V(\tilde{z}_1|z_2)$, that is, $\mathbf{H}_{11}$ is the precision of the conditional distribution of $\tilde{z}_1$ given z_2. Thus partitioning the precision matrix of $\tilde{z}$ does not give the marginal precisions of $\tilde{z}_1$ and $\tilde{z}_2$, as partitioning a variance matrix gives marginal variances. However, *if $\tilde{z}$ is Normal,* partitioning the precision matrix of $\tilde{z}$ gives the conditional precision of $\tilde{z}_1$ given z_2 and that of $\tilde{z}_2$ given z_1. In terms of precision matrices, the marginal and conditional means and variances (22.17) and (22.18) can be written by (22.22) as

$$E(\tilde{z}_i) = M_i,$$

$$H(\tilde{z}_i) \equiv [V(\tilde{z}_i)]^{-1} = \mathbf{H}_{ii} - \mathbf{H}_{ij}\mathbf{H}_{jj}^{-1}\mathbf{H}_{ji},$$

$$E(\tilde{z}_i|z_j) = M_i - \mathbf{H}_{ii}^{-1}\mathbf{H}_{ij}(z_j - M_j),$$

$$H(\tilde{z}_i|z_j) \equiv [V(\tilde{z}_i|z_j)]^{-1} = \mathbf{H}_{ii}, \qquad i = 1, j = 2 \quad \text{or} \quad j = 1, i = 2. \tag{22.23}$$

Thus, if $\tilde{z}_1$ and $\tilde{z}_2$ are jointly Normal, $\mathbf{H}_{ii}$ can be interpreted as the precision of our information about $\tilde{z}_i$ when we know z_j, while $\mathbf{V}_{ii}^{-1} = \mathbf{H}_{ii} - \mathbf{H}_{ij}\mathbf{H}_{jj}^{-1}\mathbf{H}_{ji}$ can be interpreted as the precision of our information about $\tilde{z}_i$ when we do not know z_j. Knowledge of z_j contributes an amount $\mathbf{H}_{ij}\mathbf{H}_{jj}^{-1}\mathbf{H}_{ji}$ to the precision of our information about $\tilde{z}_i$ and reduces the variance of $\tilde{z}_i$ by an amount $\mathbf{V}_{ij}\mathbf{V}_{jj}^{-1}\mathbf{V}_{ji} = VE(\tilde{z}_i|\tilde{z}_j)$. Notice that these amounts are matrices unless $\tilde{z}_i$ is scalar.

Proof We shall now derive the marginal and conditional distributions of $\tilde{z}_1$ and $\tilde{z}_2$ when jointly $\tilde{z} = [\tilde{z}_1^t \, \tilde{z}_2^t]^t$ is nonsingular Normal with mean M and variance $\mathbf{V}$. According to the second theorem of section 22.2, the rv's $\tilde{z}_1$ and

$$\tilde{e} \equiv \tilde{z}_2 - \mathbf{V}_{21}\mathbf{V}_{11}^{-1}\tilde{z}_1 \tag{22.24}$$

are independent, nonsingular Normal. Their means and variances are (exercise 31)

$$E(\tilde{z}_1) = M_1, \qquad V(\tilde{z}_1) = \mathbf{V}_{11},$$

$$E(\tilde{e}) = M_2 - \mathbf{V}_{21}\mathbf{V}_{11}^{-1}M_1, \qquad V(\tilde{e}) = \mathbf{V}_{22} - \mathbf{V}_{21}\mathbf{V}_{11}^{-1}\mathbf{V}_{12}. \tag{22.25}$$

It follows that $\tilde{z}_1$ is marginally nonsingular Normal with mean M_1 and variance $\mathbf{V}_{11}$, satisfying (22.17) for $i = 1$. It also follows by the definition of independence that the conditional distribution of $\tilde{e}$ given $\tilde{z}_1 = z_1$ is the same as its marginal distribution, which is Normal with the mean and variance just given. It follows that the conditional distribution of

$$\tilde{z}_2 = \tilde{e} + \mathbf{V}_{21}\mathbf{V}_{11}^{-1}\tilde{z}_1, \tag{22.26}$$

given that $\tilde{z}_1 = z_1$ is nonsingular Normal with mean and variance

$$E(\tilde{z}_2|z_1) = E(\tilde{e}|z_1) + \mathbf{V}_{21}\mathbf{V}_{11}^{-1}z_1 = M_2 + \mathbf{V}_{21}\mathbf{V}_{11}^{-1}(z_1 - M_1),$$

$$V(\tilde{z}_2|z_1) = V(\tilde{e}|z_1) = \mathbf{V}_{22} - \mathbf{V}_{21}\mathbf{V}_{11}^{-1}\mathbf{V}_{12}, \tag{22.27}$$

satisfying (22.18) for $i = 1$, $j = 2$. Interchanging the subscripts 1 and 2 completes the proof

A somewhat longer but more straightforward method of obtaining these results is to complete the square in the exponent of (22.8) regarded as a function of z_1 and then to observe that (22.8) can be factored into a Normal density function of z_1 with mean depending on z_2, times a Normal density function of z_2. Details can be found in *ASTD*, section 8.2.1.

22.3.2 Indirect Assessment of Joint Distributions

For the reasons explained in section 13.6, instead of starting with the joint distribution of $\tilde{z}_1$ and $\tilde{z}_2$, we will often start with the marginal distribution of $\tilde{z}_1$ and the conditional distribution of $\tilde{z}_2$ given z_1 for each z_1 and proceed from there. This subsection and the next one approach the multivariate Normal distribution in this manner.

Suppose that $\tilde{z}_1$ is nonsingular Normal with mean $\bar{z}_1$ and variance $\check{\mathbf{z}}_1$. Suppose further that the conditional distribution of $\tilde{z}_2$ given z_1 is *Normal* for each z_1, with mean depending *linearly* on z_1 and *constant* nonsingular variance, say,

$$E(\tilde{z}_2|z_1) = \boldsymbol{a} + \mathbf{b}z_1, \tag{22.28a}$$

$$V(\tilde{z}_2|z_1) = \mathbf{c}, \tag{22.28b}$$

where $\boldsymbol{a}$, $\mathbf{b}$, and $\mathbf{c}$ are constant matrices of appropriate orders and $\mathbf{c}$ is positive-definite. Then we shall prove that $\tilde{z} = [\tilde{z}_1^t \tilde{z}_2^t]^t$ is nonsingular Normal with mean and variance

$$\boldsymbol{M} = \bar{z} = \begin{bmatrix} \bar{z}_1 \\ \bar{z}_2 \end{bmatrix} = \begin{bmatrix} \bar{z}_1 \\ \boldsymbol{a} + \mathbf{b}\bar{z}_1 \end{bmatrix}. \tag{22.29a}$$

$$\mathbf{V} = \check{\mathbf{z}} = \begin{bmatrix} \check{\mathbf{z}}_1 & \check{\mathbf{z}}_1\mathbf{b}^t \\ \mathbf{b}\check{\mathbf{z}}_1 & \mathbf{b}\check{\mathbf{z}}_1\mathbf{b}^t + \mathbf{c} \end{bmatrix}. \tag{22.29b}$$

This may be considered a converse to section 22.3.1 where we proved that if $\tilde{z}$ is Normal, then the marginal and conditional distributions of $\tilde{z}_1$ and $\tilde{z}_2$ are Normal. As we pointed out in section 22.3.1 the conditional means and variances (22.18) are always of the form (22.28). For the converse result of this section, it is essential to assume this form as part of the hypothesis.

Proof It is easily verified by (22.17) and (22.18) that if $\tilde{z}$ is Normal with mean and variance (22.29), then it has the specified marginal and conditional distribution, and since these determine the joint distribution, $\tilde{z}$ must have this Normal distribution.

Alternative Proof Let

$$\tilde{e} = \tilde{z}_2 - a - \mathbf{b}\tilde{z}_1. \tag{22.30}$$

The conditional distribution of $\tilde{e}$ given z_1 is Normal with mean and variance

$$\bar{e} = 0, \qquad \check{\mathbf{e}} = \mathbf{c}. \tag{22.31}$$

Since this conditional distribution does not depend on z_1, it follows that $\tilde{e}$ is independent of $\tilde{z}_1$ and is marginally Normal with this mean and variance. Now

$$\tilde{z} = \begin{bmatrix} 0 \\ a \end{bmatrix} + \begin{bmatrix} \mathbf{I} & \mathbf{0} \\ \mathbf{b} & \mathbf{I} \end{bmatrix} \begin{bmatrix} \tilde{z}_1 \\ \tilde{e} \end{bmatrix}. \tag{22.32}$$

Therefore $\tilde{z}$ is Normal; its mean is easily computed and its variance is

$$\check{\mathbf{z}} = \begin{bmatrix} \mathbf{I} & \mathbf{0} \\ \mathbf{b} & \mathbf{I} \end{bmatrix} \begin{bmatrix} \check{\mathbf{z}}_1 & 0 \\ \mathbf{0} & \mathbf{c} \end{bmatrix} \begin{bmatrix} \mathbf{I} & \mathbf{b}^t \\ \mathbf{0} & \mathbf{I} \end{bmatrix}, \tag{22.33}$$

which gives (22.29b) when multiplied out.

22.3.3 Indirect Assessment of Marginal and Conditional Distributions

Suppose, as in the previous subsection, that $\tilde{z}_1$ is marginally nonsingular Normal and that $\tilde{z}_2$ is conditionally nonsingular Normal given $\tilde{z}_1$ with mean and variance (22.28). Then it follows immediately from the result of the previous subsection that $\tilde{z}_2$ is marginally nonsingular Normal with mean and variance

$$E(\tilde{z}_2) = a + \mathbf{b}\bar{z}_1, \qquad V(\tilde{z}_2) = \mathbf{b}\check{\mathbf{z}}_1\mathbf{b}^t + \mathbf{c}, \tag{22.34}$$

which can be read off from (22.29).[1] It also follows that the conditional distribution of $\tilde{z}_1$ given z_2 is Normal with mean and variance that (as we prove below) can be written

$$E(\tilde{z}_1 | z_2) = \mathbf{H}''^{-1}[\mathbf{H}'\bar{z}_1 + \mathbf{b}^t\mathbf{c}^{-1}(z_2 - a)], \tag{22.35a}$$

$$V(\tilde{z}_1 | z_2) = \mathbf{H}''^{-1}, \tag{22.35b}$$

where

$$\mathbf{H}' = \check{\mathbf{z}}_1^{-1}, \qquad \mathbf{H} = \mathbf{b}^t\mathbf{c}^{-1}\mathbf{b}, \qquad \mathbf{H}'' = \mathbf{H}' + \mathbf{H}. \tag{22.35c}$$

---

1. Formulas (22.34) and (22.29) can also be easily obtained by use of (21.38) and (21.49), but the latter formulas do not imply the Normality of $\tilde{z}_2$.

We write the conditional mean and variance in this particular way for the following reason. (See also the analogous explanation of (16.18); the *validity* of the formulas is of course neither contingent on nor proved by such explanations.) Suppose $\tilde{z}_1$ is a state parameter and $\tilde{z}_2$ is observable. Then the prior distribution of $\tilde{z}_1$ is its marginal distribution, so $\mathbf{H}' = \check{\mathbf{z}}_1^{-1}$ is the prior precision of $\tilde{z}_1$, that is, the inverse of the prior variance of $\tilde{z}_1$. Furthermore, the posterior distribution of $\tilde{z}_1$ is its conditional distribution given z_2, so $\mathbf{H}'' = [V(\tilde{z}_1|z_2)]^{-1}$ is the posterior precision of $\tilde{z}_1$. Thus the symbols $\mathbf{H}'$ and $\mathbf{H}''$ accord with the convention that primes denote priors and double primes posteriors and with the convention that the letter H denotes precision. The definition of the unprimed matrix $\mathbf{H}$ was chosen so that it could be interpreted as the sampling precision in the sense that the posterior precision is the sum of the prior precision and the sampling precision, that is, $\mathbf{H}'' = \mathbf{H}' + \mathbf{H}$. Note that this $\mathbf{H}$ differs from the $\mathbf{H}$ of (22.20) and (22.21).

For future reference we mention also that by exercise 36 the marginal distribution of the conditional mean $E(\tilde{z}_1|z_2)$, which is the unconditional distribution of the posterior mean in the situation just discussed, is Normal with mean

$$E[E(\tilde{z}_1|\tilde{z}_2)] \equiv E_2[E_{1|2}(\tilde{z}_1|\tilde{z}_2)] = \bar{z}_1 \tag{22.36a}$$

and variance

$$V(E[\tilde{z}_1|\tilde{z}_2)] \equiv V_2(E_{1|2}[\tilde{z}_1|\tilde{z}_2]) = \mathbf{H}'^{-1} - \mathbf{H}''^{-1} = \mathbf{H}''^{-1}\mathbf{H}\check{\mathbf{z}}_1. \tag{22.36b}$$

Proof of (22.35) By (22.18) and (22.29a)

$$E(\tilde{z}_1|z_2) = \bar{z}_1 + \mathbf{V}_{12}\mathbf{V}_{22}^{-1}(z_2 - \bar{z}_2) = (\mathbf{I} - \mathbf{V}_{12}\mathbf{V}_{22}^{-1}\mathbf{b})\bar{z}_1 + \mathbf{V}_{12}\mathbf{V}_{22}^{-1}(z_2 - \boldsymbol{a}).$$

Now by (22.29b)

$$\mathbf{V}_{12}\mathbf{V}_{22}^{-1} = \check{\mathbf{z}}_1\mathbf{b}^t(\mathbf{b}\check{\mathbf{z}}_1\mathbf{b}^t + \mathbf{c})^{-1} = (\mathbf{b}^t\mathbf{c}^{-1}\mathbf{b} + \check{\mathbf{z}}_1^{-1})^{-1}\mathbf{b}^t\mathbf{c}^{-1} = \mathbf{H}''^{-1}\mathbf{b}^t\mathbf{c}^{-1}, \tag{22.37}$$

where the second equality is equivalent to

$$(\mathbf{b}^t\mathbf{c}^{-1}\mathbf{b} + \check{\mathbf{z}}_1^{-1})\check{\mathbf{z}}_1\mathbf{b}^t = \mathbf{b}^t\mathbf{c}^{-1}(\mathbf{b}\check{\mathbf{z}}_1\mathbf{b}^t + \mathbf{c}), \tag{22.38}$$

which is seen to be true when multiplied out. It follows that

$$\mathbf{I} - \mathbf{V}_{12}\mathbf{V}_{22}^{-1}\mathbf{b} = \mathbf{H}''^{-1}(\mathbf{H}'' - \mathbf{b}^t\mathbf{c}^{-1}\mathbf{b}) = \mathbf{H}''^{-1}(\mathbf{H}'' - \mathbf{H}) = \mathbf{H}''^{-1}\mathbf{H}'. \tag{22.39}$$

Substituting, we obtain

$$E(\tilde{z}_1|z_2) = \mathbf{H}''^{-1}\mathbf{H}'\bar{z}_1 + \mathbf{H}''^{-1}\mathbf{b}^t\mathbf{c}^{-1}(z_2 - \boldsymbol{a}), \tag{22.40}$$

which gives (22.35a). Furthermore, by (22.18) and (22.29b)

$$V(\tilde{z}_1|z_2) = \mathbf{V}_{11} - \mathbf{V}_{12}\mathbf{V}_{22}^{-1}\mathbf{V}_{21}$$
$$= (\mathbf{I} - \mathbf{V}_{12}\mathbf{V}_{22}^{-1}\mathbf{b})\check{\mathbf{z}}_1 = \mathbf{H}''^{-1}\mathbf{H}'\check{\mathbf{z}}_1 = \mathbf{H}''^{-1}, \tag{22.41}$$

which is (22.35b).

Alternative Proof of (22.35) Using (22.33) and the easily verified fact that

$$\begin{bmatrix} \mathbf{I} & \mathbf{0} \\ \mathbf{b} & \mathbf{I} \end{bmatrix}^{-1} = \begin{bmatrix} \mathbf{I} & \mathbf{0} \\ -\mathbf{b} & \mathbf{I} \end{bmatrix} \tag{22.42}$$

and the transpose of this relation, we obtain

$$\begin{bmatrix} \mathbf{H}_{11} & \mathbf{H}_{12} \\ \mathbf{H}_{21} & \mathbf{H}_{22} \end{bmatrix} \equiv \check{\mathbf{z}}^{-1} = \begin{bmatrix} \mathbf{I} & \mathbf{b}^t \\ \mathbf{0} & \mathbf{I} \end{bmatrix}^{-1} \begin{bmatrix} \check{\mathbf{z}}_1 & \mathbf{0} \\ \mathbf{0} & \mathbf{c} \end{bmatrix}^{-1} \begin{bmatrix} \mathbf{I} & \mathbf{0} \\ \mathbf{b} & \mathbf{I} \end{bmatrix}^{-1}$$
$$= \begin{bmatrix} \mathbf{I} & -\mathbf{b}^t \\ \mathbf{0} & \mathbf{I} \end{bmatrix} \begin{bmatrix} \mathbf{H}' & \mathbf{0} \\ \mathbf{0} & \mathbf{c}^{-1} \end{bmatrix} \begin{bmatrix} \mathbf{I} & \mathbf{0} \\ -\mathbf{b} & \mathbf{I} \end{bmatrix} = \begin{bmatrix} \mathbf{H}'' & -\mathbf{b}^t\mathbf{c}^{-1} \\ -\mathbf{c}^{-1}\mathbf{b} & \mathbf{c}^{-1} \end{bmatrix}. \tag{22.43}$$

By (22.23) this gives (22.35b) immediately and

$$E(\tilde{z}_1|z_2) = \bar{z}_1 + \mathbf{H}''^{-1}\mathbf{b}^t\mathbf{c}^{-1}(z_2 - a - \mathbf{b}^t\bar{z}_1)$$
$$= \mathbf{H}''^{-1}[\mathbf{H}''\bar{z}_1 + \mathbf{b}^t\mathbf{c}^{-1}(z_2 - a) - \mathbf{H}\bar{z}_1]$$
$$= \mathbf{H}''^{-1}[\mathbf{H}'\bar{z}_1 + \mathbf{b}^t\mathbf{c}^{-1}(z_2 - a)], \tag{22.44}$$

which is (22.35a). Note that because we are using the definition (22.35c) of $\mathbf{H}$, we avoided denoting $\check{\mathbf{z}}^{-1}$ by $\mathbf{H}$ as in (22.20) and (22.21).

22.3.4 Bivariate Normal Regression and Correlation

Let $(\tilde{z}_1, \tilde{z}_2)$ be bivariate Normal. We have already stressed that the regression of $\tilde{z}_1$ on $\tilde{z}_2$, namely $E(\tilde{z}_1|z_2)$ considered as a function of z_2, is linear. In other words, since we are now in two dimensions, it is a straight line. The regression of $\tilde{z}_2$ on $\tilde{z}_1$ is, of course, also a straight line.

It is instructive to work in terms of the "standardized" rv's

$$\tilde{u}_1 = \frac{\tilde{z}_1 - \bar{z}_1}{\ddot{z}_1}, \qquad \tilde{u}_2 = \frac{\tilde{z}_2 - \bar{z}_2}{\ddot{z}_2}, \tag{22.45}$$

obtained from $\tilde{z}_1$ and $\tilde{z}_2$ by first subtracting the marginal means $\bar{z}_1$ and $\bar{z}_2$ and then dividing by the marginal standard deviations $\ddot{z}_1$ and $\ddot{z}_2$. The "standardized" rv's $\tilde{u}_1$ and $\tilde{u}_2$ are marginally unit Normal and, furthermore, jointly Normal with mean and variance (exercise 37)

$$\bar{\mathbf{u}} = \begin{bmatrix} 0 \\ 0 \end{bmatrix}, \qquad \check{\mathbf{u}} = \begin{bmatrix} 1 & \rho \\ \rho & 1 \end{bmatrix}, \tag{22.46}$$

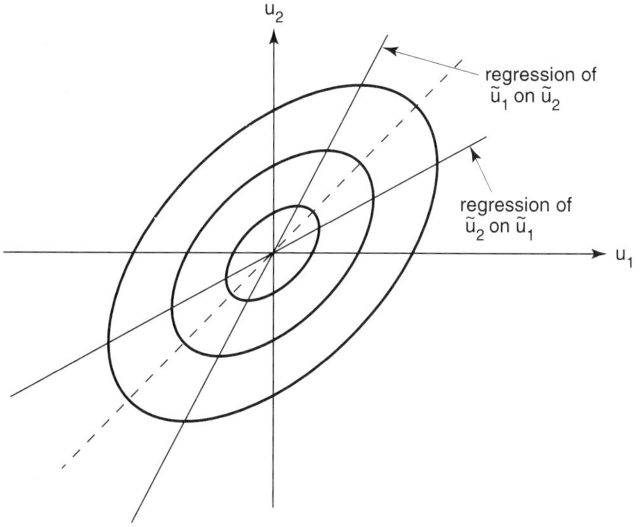

Figure 22.5
Regression lines

where

$$\rho = \frac{\check{z}_{12}}{\ddot{z}_1 \ddot{z}_2} \equiv \rho(\tilde{z}_1, \tilde{z}_2) \equiv \rho(\tilde{z}_2, \tilde{z}_1); \tag{22.47}$$

ρ is the (*linear*) *correlation* of $\tilde{z}_1$ and $\tilde{z}_2$, originally defined by (13.46). Either by (22.19) and straightforward algebra, or by application of (22.19) to $(\tilde{u}_1, \tilde{u}_2)$, we can write the regression lines as

$$E(\tilde{u}_1|u_2) = \frac{E(\tilde{z}_1|z_2) - \bar{z}_1}{\ddot{z}_1} = \rho \frac{z_2 - \bar{z}_2}{\ddot{z}} \equiv \rho u_2 \tag{22.48a}$$

and, interchanging the subscripts 1 and 2,

$$E(\tilde{u}_2|u_1) = \frac{E(\tilde{z}_2|z_1) - \bar{z}_2}{\ddot{z}_2} = \rho \frac{z_1 - \bar{z}_1}{\ddot{z}_1} \equiv \rho u_1. \tag{22.48b}$$

In words, this says that the regression of each "standardized" rv on the other is a straight line through the origin having slope ρ. Recall that $-1 \leq \rho \leq 1$ by exercise 13.26. (This also follows from an interpretation of ρ^2 given later in this subsection.) Figure 22.5 shows the regression lines (and some density contours) for a value of ρ between 0 and 1. It is left to the reader to sketch a corresponding figure for a value of ρ between 0 and -1.

Observe the following points:

1. Because the rv's $\tilde{u}_1$ and $\tilde{u}_2$ have the same marginal variance, the projection of the distribution on the u_1 axis is identical to its projection on the u_2 axis.

2. For the same reason, the major axis of the density contour ellipses has slope 45° for any value of $\rho > 0$ and slope $-45°$ for any value of $\rho < 0$. It goes through the origin.

3. The regression line of $\tilde{u}_2$ on $\tilde{u}_1$ makes the same angle with the u_1 axis that the regression line of $\tilde{u}_1$ on $\tilde{u}_2$ makes with the u_2 axis. Thus the two regression lines are *symmetric to each other about the major axis of the ellipses*, but they are *not the same line* (unless $\rho = \pm 1$). Both lines go through the origin.

4. The density contours are vertical at the points where they cross the regression line of $\tilde{u}_2$ on $\tilde{u}_1$ and horizontal where they cross the regression line of $\tilde{u}_1$ on $\tilde{u}_2$. The regression line of $\tilde{u}_2$ on $\tilde{u}_1$ is in fact the locus of points where the contours are vertical and the regression line of $\tilde{u}_1$ on $\tilde{u}_2$ is the locus of points where the contours are horizontal.

5. If $\rho = 0$, then the regression lines coincide with the axes, the ellipses are circles, and $\tilde{u}_1$ and $\tilde{u}_2$ are *independent*. Notice, as pointed out in section 22.2.2, that (a) zero correlation *together with joint Normality* implies independence, and (b) zero correlation *without joint Normality* does not imply independence.

6. If the correlation were ± 1, the regression lines would coincide with the major axis of the ellipses and the ellipses would shrink to the major axis; the distribution would not be nonsingular Normal because each $\tilde{u}_i$ would be constrained to be equal to the other. See also section 22.4, especially subsections 22.4.3 and 22.4.5.

Inasmuch as $\tilde{u}_1$ and $\tilde{u}_2$ are related to the unstandardized rv's $\tilde{z}_1$ and $\tilde{z}_2$ by (22.45), the foregoing statements are indirectly statements about $\tilde{z}_1$ and $\tilde{z}_2$. It is fairly straightforward to obtain from them similar statements applying directly to $\tilde{z}_1$ and $\tilde{z}_2$. We shall give the main points, but leave the details to the reader. First, if the variances $\check{z}_1$ and $\check{z}_2$ are equal, then statements 1–6 apply to $\tilde{z}_1$ and $\tilde{z}_2$ without essential change. Second, if $\check{z}_1 \neq \check{z}_2$ but $\bar{z}_1$, $\bar{z}_2$, $\check{z}_1$, and $\check{z}_2$ are kept fixed while ρ varies, then:

1. The projections of the distribution of $(\tilde{z}_1, \tilde{z}_2)$ on the z_1 and z_2 axes do not vary with ρ.

2. Let rectangles with sides parallel to the axes be circumscribed about the density contour ellipses. These rectangles do not vary with ρ. However, the major axis of the ellipses is not a diagonal of the rectangles and does vary with ρ.

3. The regression line of $\tilde{z}_2$ on $\tilde{z}_1$ is more nearly horizontal and that of $\tilde{z}_1$ on $\tilde{z}_2$ more nearly vertical than the relevant diagonal of the rectangles. The regression lines go through the mean $(\bar{z}_1, \bar{z}_2)$ but are not the same (unless $\rho = \pm 1$).

4. The regression lines are again the loci of points where the contours are vertical and horizontal.

5. If $\rho = 0$, then the regression lines are parallel to the axes and $\tilde{z}_1$ and $\tilde{z}_2$ are independent.

6. If ρ were ± 1, the regression lines would coincide, the ellipses would shrink to a line, and the distribution would not be nonsingular Normal.

Observe carefully that these statements concern only *jointly Normally* distributed rv's $\tilde{z}_1, \tilde{z}_2$.

Misunderstandings about the following two points are common.

The Regression Effect

Suppose, for convenience, that the variances $\tilde{z}_1$ and $\tilde{z}_2$ are the same. Then by (22.48), for any given value of z_1, $\tilde{z}_2$ has a tendency to fall nearer to its mean than z_1 is to its mean, and vice versa. This is called the "regression effect." Thus sons of tall fathers tend to be shorter than their fathers, while sons of short fathers tend to be taller than their fathers. This is sometimes interpreted incorrectly as implying a continual tendency toward the average as time progresses. But it is also true that fathers of tall sons tend to be shorter than their sons while fathers of short sons tend to be taller than their sons, and this sounds as though the trend in time is away from the average. The two statements may equally well be phrased as follows, in which form they appear to prove nothing interesting: Tall fathers tend to be taller than their sons and short fathers shorter than their sons; tall sons tend to be taller than their fathers and short sons shorter than their fathers. A tendency of each given member of a population to move nearer the average does not imply that the population is becoming more concentrated around the average. In fact, if this tendency does not exist, the population must become less concentrated. Specifically, let the earlier and later values be z_1 and z_2 respectively: if $E(\tilde{z}_2|z_1) = z_1$ for all z_1, then by (13.44)

$$V(\tilde{z}_2) = EV(\tilde{z}_2|\tilde{z}_1) + V(\tilde{z}_1) > V(\tilde{z}_1) \tag{22.49}$$

except in the trivial case that $\tilde{z}_2 = \tilde{z}_1$ with probability one.

The Lines of "Best Fit"

It is sometimes asked what line "best fits" the joint distribution of (z_1, z_2), or what line the distribution "clusters most closely" around. It is dangerous to think in such terms, because different criteria of "best fit" or "closest clustering" lead to different lines and the differences are by no means small in practice. Consider jointly Normal $(\tilde{z}_1, \tilde{z}_2)$. If the "best fit" minimizes the expectation of the squared vertical deviation, then the regression of $\tilde{z}_2$ on $\tilde{z}_1$ "fits best"; if, however, it minimizes the expectation of the squared horizontal deviation, then the regression of $\tilde{z}_1$ on $\tilde{z}_2$ "fits best" (exercise 38). If $\tilde{z}_1$ and $\tilde{z}_2$ both enter the definition of "best fit" in a similar way in some sense, then some other line will result. If $\tilde{z}_1$ and $\tilde{z}_2$ have equal means and equal variances, then it is clear from figure 22.5 that the line $z_1 = z_2$ will "fit best" for essentially any definition treating $\tilde{z}_1$ and $\tilde{z}_2$ alike, regardless of how large the correlation between $\tilde{z}_1$ and $\tilde{z}_2$ is; that is, the distribution of $(\tilde{z}_1, \tilde{z}_2)$ *clusters most closely* around the *same* line regardless of what the two regression lines may be (provided they have positive slope. If they have negative slope, the distribution of $(\tilde{z}_1, \tilde{z}_2)$ clusters most closely around $z_1 = -z_2$.) In short, a regression line should *not* be thought of as a line of "best fit" in any general sense.

Interpretation of Correlation as Reduction of Variance

Let $\tilde{z}_1$ and $\tilde{z}_2$ be jointly Normal. The marginal variance of $\tilde{z}_1$ is $\check{z}_1$, while by (22.19) the conditional variance of $\tilde{z}_1$ given z_2 is $(\check{z}_{11} - \check{z}_{12}^2/\check{z}_{22})$; thus *knowledge of z_2 reduces the variance of the distribution of $\tilde{z}_1$* by the amount $\check{z}_{12}^2/\check{z}_{22}$. This latter expression can by (22.47) be written in the form $\rho^2\check{z}_{11}$, and therefore we may regard ρ^2 as a measure of the *proportional amount* by which knowledge of z_2 reduces the variance of $\tilde{z}_1$, or the proportion of the variance of $\tilde{z}_1$ "explained" or "removed" by regression on $\tilde{z}_2$. This statement has been proved only for jointly Normal $(\tilde{z}_1, \tilde{z}_2)$, but it can easily be proved whenever the regression of $\tilde{z}_1$ on $\tilde{z}_2$ is linear and the conditional variance of $\tilde{z}_1$ given z_2 is the same for all values of z_2. Of course, the subscripts 1 and 2 could be interchanged throughout. (See exercise 12.25 and 13.26.)

In this situation, it is surprising how large the correlation has to be before the variance of one variable is reduced substantially by knowledge of the other. If this correlation is 5% ($\rho = .05$), then only $\frac{1}{4}$ of 1% of the variance is explained by regression, that is, the conditional variance is 99.75% of the marginal variance. If the correlation is 10%, then 1% of the variance is explained by regression. The correlation must be over 31% before even 10% of the variance is explained by regression. A correlation of 50% corresponds to a regression explaining 25% of the variance. The corresponding figures for the standard deviation are even smaller, and it is the standard deviation, not the variance, that "scales" the distribution. A correlation of 60% corresponds to a regression explaining only 20% of the standard deviation. Remembering that the correlation is the slope of the

Table 22.1
Proportional reduction in variance and standard deviation

Correlation	ρ	0	.05	.10	.30	.50	.70	.90	.95	1.00
Variance reduction	ρ^2	0	.0025	.010	.090	.25	.49	.81	.90	1.00
Std. dev. reduction	$1-\sqrt{1-\rho^2}$	0	.0013	.005	.046	.13	.29	.56	.69	1.00

Note: $[\breve{z}_2 - V(\tilde{z}_2|z_1)]/\breve{z}_2 = \rho^2$ and $[\ddot{z}_2 - S(\tilde{z}_2|z_1)]/\ddot{z}_2 = 1-\sqrt{1-\rho^2}$.

regression line when the variances $\breve{z}_1$ and $\breve{z}_2$ are the same, and proportional to it otherwise, we see that the conditional variance (or standard deviation) will be substantially smaller than the marginal only when the regression line is relatively far from constant. The situation is summarized in table 22.1.

22.4 Linear Transformations and Singular Distributions

22.4.1 Introduction

We have seen (property 4 of section 22.2.1) that a nonsingular linear transformation of a nonsingular Normal rv is nonsingular Normal. We shall now see what happens when we make other linear transformations. We shall find that we sometimes obtain a so-called "singular Normal" rv, and we shall discuss the corresponding distribution briefly. We shall then find that making further linear transformations creates no new problems.

22.4.2 Transformation Having Full Row Rank of a Nonsingular RV

We note first that certain linear transformations do not lead us away from the nonsingular Normal distribution.

Theorem Let $\tilde{\boldsymbol{z}}$ be nonsingular s-variate Normal and let

$$\tilde{\boldsymbol{y}} = \boldsymbol{a} + \mathbf{b}\tilde{\boldsymbol{z}} \tag{22.50}$$

where $\mathbf{b}$ is $(r \times s)$ of rank r. Then $\tilde{\boldsymbol{y}}$ is nonsingular r-variate Normal.

If $r = s$, this is just property 4 of section 22.2.1. If $r > s$, then $\mathbf{b}$ cannot be of rank r. The only other possibility is $r < s$. To illustrate this possibility, suppose $s > 1$ and $r = 1$, so that

$$\tilde{y} = a + b_1\tilde{z}_1 + b_2\tilde{z}_2 + \cdots + b_s\tilde{z}_s \tag{22.51}$$

is univariate. Then the hypothesis of the theorem is that $\tilde{\boldsymbol{z}}$ is nonsingular, multivariate Normal and that the b_i are not all 0; the conclusion is that $\tilde{y}$ is nonsingular, univariate Normal, that is, $\tilde{y}$ is Normal with positive variance. As a special case, let $a = 0, b_1 = 1, b_2 = \cdots = b_s = 0$: Then $\tilde{y} = \tilde{z}_1$ and the theorem states that the marginal distribution of one of several jointly nonsingular Normal rv's is nonsingular Normal. As another special case, let $a = 0$, $b_1 = b_2 = \cdots = b_s = 1$; then $\tilde{y} = \tilde{z}_1 + \tilde{z}_2 + \cdots + \tilde{z}_s$. Therefore a sum of jointly nonsingular Normal rv's is nonsingular Normal. The subcase when $\tilde{z}_1, \tilde{z}_2, \ldots, \tilde{z}_s$ are mutually independent is the theorem of section 16.6.1.

Proof of the Theorem The theorem has already been proved except when $r < s$. In this case, let

$$\tilde{y}^* = \begin{bmatrix} \tilde{y} \\ \tilde{\eta} \end{bmatrix} = \begin{bmatrix} a \\ 0 \end{bmatrix} + \begin{bmatrix} \mathbf{b} \\ \boldsymbol{\beta} \end{bmatrix} \tilde{z}. \tag{22.52}$$

where $\boldsymbol{\beta}$ is chosen so that $[\mathbf{b}^t \quad \boldsymbol{\beta}^t]^t$ is square and nonsingular. The distribution of $\tilde{y}^*$ is nonsingular Normal by section 22.2.1, and therefore the (marginal) distribution of $\tilde{y}$ is nonsingular Normal by section 22.3.1.

22.4.3 The Singular Normal Distribution

Suppose now that $\tilde{y}$ is defined by (22.50) where $\tilde{z}$ is nonsingular s-variate Normal and $\mathbf{b}$ is $(r \times s)$ of rank $p < r$. Then $\tilde{y}$ is not nonsingular Normal, since its variance $\check{\mathbf{y}} = \mathbf{b}\check{\mathbf{z}}\mathbf{b}^t$ is singular. (Actually, $\check{\mathbf{y}}$ is $(r \times r)$ of rank p.) We shall call the distribution of $\tilde{y}$ *singular Normal*. Note that $\tilde{y}$ satisfies one or more linear restrictions with probability one, that is, $P(c^t\tilde{y} = d) = 1$ for some $c \neq 0$ and some d (exercise 39).

The singular Normal distribution has many properties like those of the nonsingular Normal distribution. In particular:

1. For any $(r \times 1)$ M and any $(r \times r)$ positive-semidefinite, singular $\mathbf{V}$, there is a singular Normal distribution with mean M and variance $\mathbf{V}$.

2. The singular Normal distribution is determined by its mean and variance. That is, if two singular Normal rv's have the same mean and variance then they have the same distribution, though of course they need not be the same rv and they may arise in entirely different ways.

These two facts and the corresponding facts for the nonsingular Normal distribution mean that we may speak without ambiguity of "the" Normal distribution with mean M and variance $\mathbf{V}$, since there is always exactly one such distribution; the distribution is singular or nonsingular according as $\mathbf{V}$ is singular or nonsingular. (Of course, M and $\mathbf{V}$ must be a possible mean and variance, that is, $\mathbf{V}$ must be positive-semidefinite and M must be $(r \times 1)$ if $\mathbf{V}$ is $(r \times r)$.)

3. The marginal distributions of a singular Normal distribution are Normal. They may be singular or nonsingular.

4. The rv's $\tilde{y}_1$ and $\tilde{y}_2$ are independent and marginally Normal and at least one of them is singular if and only if they are jointly singular Normal and $V(\tilde{y}_1, \tilde{y}_2) = \mathbf{0}$.

The singular Normal counterpart of some other nonsingular Normal properties is less straightforward to state. For example, the singular Normal distribution does not have a density in the ordinary sense, and discussion of the conditional distributions (which are Normal) comes up against inverses of possibly singular matrices in (22.18). We have no need to go into such matters in this book, however. Since any singular Normal rv is related to some nonsingular Normal rv by a transformation of the form (22.50), it follows that any problem involving a singular distribution can be solved in terms of variables having a nonsingular distribution.

Proof The proof of properties 1, 3, and 4 is left to the reader (exercise 40). We shall now prove property 2. Suppose $\tilde{y}$ is of the form (22.50) where $\tilde{z}$ is nonsingular Normal and we know what $\bar{y} = a + \mathbf{b}\bar{z}$ and $\check{y} = \mathbf{b}\check{\mathbf{z}}\mathbf{b}^t$ are, but we do not know a, $\mathbf{b}$, $\bar{z}$, and $\check{\mathbf{z}}$ individually. We must show that the distribution of $\tilde{y}$ is nonetheless determined. Subtracting $\bar{y} = a + \mathbf{b}\bar{z}$ from (22.50), we see that it suffices to show that if $\tilde{y} = \mathbf{b}\tilde{z}$ where $\tilde{z}$ is nonsingular Normal with mean 0, then the distribution of $\tilde{y}$ is determined by $\check{\mathbf{y}} = \mathbf{b}\check{\mathbf{z}}\mathbf{b}^t$. Without loss of generality we may assume that the first p rows of $\mathbf{b}$ are linearly independent and the remainder are linear combinations of these. Partitioning accordingly, we have

$$\tilde{y} = \begin{bmatrix} \tilde{y}_1 \\ \tilde{y}_2 \end{bmatrix} = \begin{bmatrix} \mathbf{b}_1\tilde{z} \\ \mathbf{b}_2\tilde{z} \end{bmatrix}, \qquad \check{\mathbf{y}} = \begin{bmatrix} \check{\mathbf{y}}_{11} & \check{\mathbf{y}}_{12} \\ \check{\mathbf{y}}_{21} & \check{\mathbf{y}}_{22} \end{bmatrix} = \begin{bmatrix} \mathbf{b}_1\check{\mathbf{z}}\mathbf{b}_1^t & \mathbf{b}_1\check{\mathbf{z}}\mathbf{b}_2^t \\ \mathbf{b}_2\check{\mathbf{z}}\mathbf{b}_1^t & \mathbf{b}_2\check{\mathbf{z}}\mathbf{b}_2^t \end{bmatrix}. \tag{22.53}$$

By section 22.4.2, $\tilde{y}_1$ is nonsingular Normal and hence its distribution is determined by its mean, which is 0, and its variance, which is $\check{\mathbf{y}}_{11}$. Since the rows of $\mathbf{b}_2$ are linear combinations of the rows of $\mathbf{b}_1$, we have, for some $\mathbf{c}$,

$$\mathbf{b}_2 = \mathbf{c}\mathbf{b}_1, \qquad \tilde{y}_2 = \mathbf{c}\tilde{y}_1.$$

It remains to show that the appropriate partitioning and the matrix $\mathbf{c}$ can be determined from $\check{\mathbf{y}}$. The appropriate partitioning is determined by the fact that the first p rows of $\check{\mathbf{y}}$ are linearly independent and the remainder are linear combinations of them, namely

$$[\check{\mathbf{y}}_{21} \quad \check{\mathbf{y}}_{22}] = [\mathbf{c}\check{\mathbf{y}}_{11} \quad \mathbf{c}\check{\mathbf{y}}_{12}] = \mathbf{c}[\check{\mathbf{y}}_{11} \quad \check{\mathbf{y}}_{12}].$$

Furthermore, $\check{y}_{21} = \mathbf{c}\check{y}_{11}$ determines $\mathbf{c} = \check{\mathbf{y}}_{21}\check{\mathbf{y}}_{11}^{-1}$. This completes the proof.

22.4.4 Transformations of Singular RV's and Transformations of Transformations

Let $\tilde{z}$ be an $(s \times 1)$ Normal rv, singular or nonsingular, and let $\tilde{y}$ be defined by

$$\tilde{y} \equiv \mathbf{bcd}\cdots\mathbf{k}\tilde{z}, \tag{22.54}$$

where the matrices $\mathbf{b}, \mathbf{c}, \ldots, \mathbf{k}$ may be of any dimensionality provided only that they are conformable and that $\mathbf{k}$ has s columns. It is obvious from the results of the preceding sections that $\tilde{y}$ is r-variate Normal, where r is the number of rows of $\mathbf{b}$, and that $\tilde{y}$ is singular or nonsingular according as

$$\check{\mathbf{y}} = (\mathbf{bcd} \cdots \mathbf{k})\check{\mathbf{z}}(\mathbf{bcd} \cdots \mathbf{k})^t \tag{22.55}$$

is singular or nonsingular. Recall that the rank of a product cannot exceed the lowest rank of any individual factor. Therefore $\tilde{y}$ is singular if any one of $\mathbf{b}, \mathbf{c}, \mathbf{d}, \ldots, \mathbf{k}$ has rank less than r, in particular if $\mathbf{b}$ is not of full row rank. It is also singular if $\check{\mathbf{z}}$ has rank less than r, in particular if $\tilde{z}$ has lower dimension than $\tilde{y}$, or if they have the same dimension and $\tilde{z}$ is singular. Adding constant vectors at each stage [like $\boldsymbol{a}$ in (22.50)] would not affect the foregoing statement.

Let us return to the case

$$\tilde{y} = \boldsymbol{a} + \mathbf{b}\tilde{z} \tag{22.56}$$

where $\tilde{y}$ and $\boldsymbol{a}$ are $(r \times 1)$, $\mathbf{b}$ is $(r \times s)$, and $\tilde{z}$ is a $(s \times 1)$ Normal rv. Whether or not $\tilde{z}$ is singular, $\tilde{y}$ is Normal with mean and variance

$$\bar{y} = \boldsymbol{a} + \mathbf{b}\bar{z}, \qquad \check{\mathbf{y}} = \mathbf{b}\check{\mathbf{z}}\mathbf{b}^t, \tag{22.57}$$

and is singular or nonsingular according as $\check{\mathbf{y}} = \mathbf{b}\check{\mathbf{z}}\mathbf{b}^t$ is singular or nonsingular. When $s < r$, that is, $\tilde{z}$ has smaller dimension than $\tilde{y}$, $\tilde{y}$ is singular. When $s = r$, $\tilde{y}$ is nonsingular if and only if $\mathbf{b}$ is nonsingular and $\tilde{z}$ is nonsingular. When $s > r$, $\tilde{y}$ is singular if $\mathbf{b}$ does not have full row rank, and $\tilde{y}$ is nonsingular if $\mathbf{b}$ has full row rank and $\tilde{z}$ is nonsingular, but $\tilde{y}$ may be either singular or nonsingular if $\mathbf{b}$ has full row rank and $\tilde{z}$ is singular (exercise 18).

22.4.5 Geometry of Linear Transformations of a Nonsingular RV[2]

Let $\tilde{z}$ be a nonsingular Normal rv and let $\tilde{y} = \boldsymbol{a} + \mathbf{b}\tilde{z}$. Some insight, especially into the singular Normal distribution, can be gained from a geometric view of the situation. For this purpose, there is no real loss of generality in taking $\boldsymbol{a} = \boldsymbol{0}$, so that

$$\tilde{y} = \mathbf{b}\tilde{z}. \tag{22.58}$$

Bivariate Case Let us consider first the case when $\mathbf{b}$ is 2×2, that is, $\tilde{y}$ and $\tilde{z}$ are both bivariate. Then (22.58) can be written as

$$\begin{bmatrix} \tilde{y}_1 \\ \tilde{y}_2 \end{bmatrix} = \tilde{z}_1 \begin{bmatrix} b_{11} \\ b_{21} \end{bmatrix} + \tilde{z}_2 \begin{bmatrix} b_{12} \\ b_{22} \end{bmatrix}. \tag{22.59}$$

2. This subsection is optional.

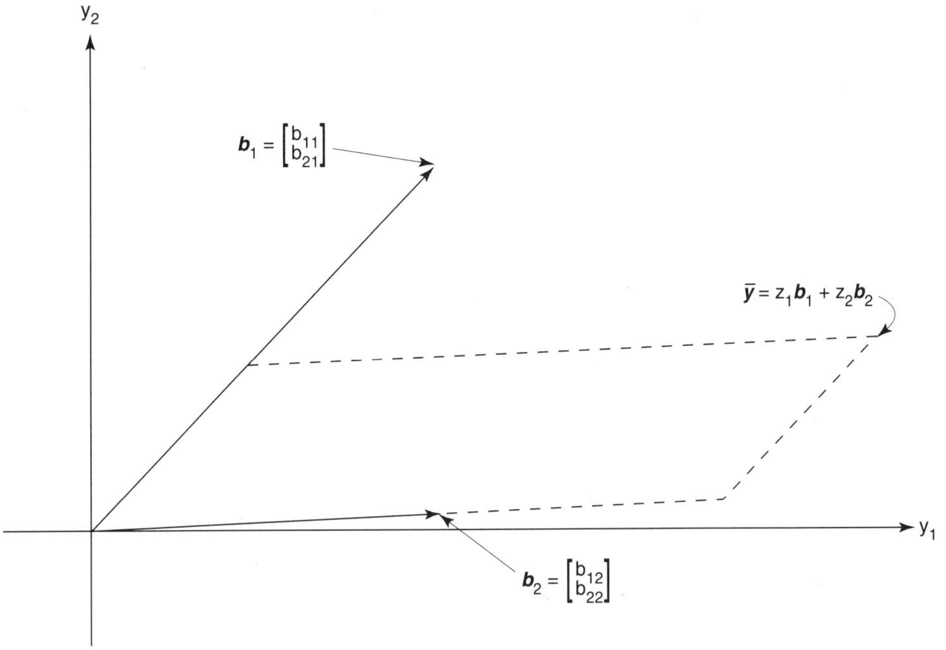

Figure 22.6
Linear combinations of two two-dimensional vectors (rank 2)

Thus we can regard $\tilde{\boldsymbol{y}}$ as a random linear combination of the columns **b**, the first column being weighted by $\tilde{z}_1$ and the second by $\tilde{z}_2$.

If **b** has rank 2, then its columns considered as two-dimensional vectors span the whole two-dimensional space, as shown in figure 22.6. Since there is a nonzero density assigned to every set of weights $(\tilde{z}_1, \tilde{z}_2)$, there is also a nonzero density attached to every point $\boldsymbol{y}$ in the (y_1, y_2) plane, that is, $\tilde{\boldsymbol{y}}$ has a nonsingular distribution.

If, on the other hand, **b** has rank 1, then its columns span a one-dimensional space, and hence lie on a single line, as in figure 22.7. Whatever weights are attached to these columns, the weighted sum $\boldsymbol{y}$ will lie on this line; points off the line are impossible. Therefore, when **b** is of rank 1, (a) $\tilde{y}_1$ and $\tilde{y}_2$ are linear functions of each other, but (b) at least one of them is a bona fide random variable, and that random variable is Normal by section 22.4.2. (It is permitted that $\boldsymbol{b}_1$ and $\boldsymbol{b}_2$ lie along one of the axes in figure 22.7; in this case $\tilde{y}_1$ or $\tilde{y}_2$ is 0. It is also permitted that $\boldsymbol{b}_1$ and $\boldsymbol{b}_2$ point in opposite directions along the same line, or that one of them be $\boldsymbol{0}$.)

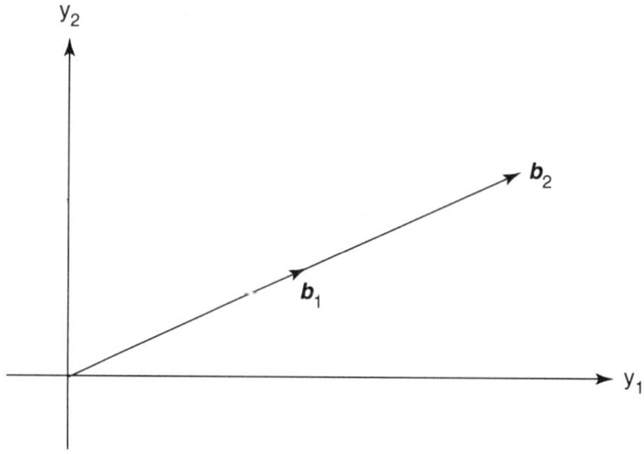

Figure 22.7
Two two-dimensional vectors with rank 1

If **b** has rank 0, then **b** = **0**, in which case $\tilde{y}$ is *0*.

The foregoing remarks remain true with only slight changes if **b** is $2 \times s$, that is, if $\tilde{y}$ is bivariate and $\tilde{z}$ is s-variate. We leave these changes to the reader, remarking only that if **b** is 2×1, then the case that **b** has rank 2 cannot occur.

The General Case Now suppose **b** is $(r \times s)$, where r and s are arbitrary. Then $\tilde{y}$ and the columns of **b** are $(r \times 1)$ vectors, and $\tilde{y} = \mathbf{b}\tilde{z}$ can be considered a random linear combination of the columns of **b**, the first column being weighted by $\tilde{z}_1$, the second by $\tilde{z}_2, \ldots,$ and the last by $\tilde{z}_s$. We are assuming that $\tilde{z}$ is nonsingular, so that there is a nonzero density assigned to every set of weights z. If **b** has rank r, then the columns of **b** span the entire r-dimensional space and there will be a nonzero density assigned to every point $y = [y_1 \ldots y_r]^t$ in the y space.

Now suppose that **b** is of *rank p*, where $0 < p < r$. This implies that $s - p$ of the columns of **b** are linear combinations of the other p columns, and thus that all s columns together span a space of only $p < r$ dimensions. *All* linear combinations y of the columns of **b** must lie within this p-dimensional subspace of the r-dimensional space in which a point y is defined.

This implies that when **b** is of rank p where $0 < p < r$, it is possible (1) to find p components of $\tilde{y}$ which are (a) linearly independent, and (b) bona fide random variables with a nonsingular Normal distribution, and then (2) to express the remaining $r - p$ components as linear functions of these p. (This is also evident from the proof in section 22.4.3.)

22.5 Some Comments on the Assessment of Multivariate Priors

22.5.1 Introduction

In most real decision problems, the state variable is multivariate, or at least it is natural to think of it as multivariate. Analysis of such problems calls for the assessment of a multivariate prior distribution. In this section we shall make some comments on such assessments, especially on the assessment of bivariate and multivariate Normal prior distributions.

An unrestricted *uni*variate distribution, that is, a univariate distribution not restricted to any particular analytical form, can be assessed with a reasonable expenditure of mental effort. To make a similarly detailed assessment of the distribution of a bivariate rv $(\tilde{z}_1, \tilde{z}_2)$, one might first assess the distribution of $\tilde{z}_1$ and then assess the conditional distributions of $\tilde{z}_2$ given z_1 for an appropriate collection of values of z_1. The number of values of z_1 used cannot be too small or the bivariate distribution will not be at all well pinned down, and each value used requires a separate assessment of a univariate distribution for $\tilde{z}_2$ given z_1, entailing many assessments. A similar difficulty would arise in any approach to assessing an unrestricted bivariate distribution, and as the number of rv's increases beyond two, the amount of assessment required increases exponentially. Thus, unless some consideration such as independence justifies the assumption of a special structure, a multivariate prior distribution will in practice have to be chosen from some reasonably flexible but restricted analytically convenient family of distributions. Even in the univariate case this was desirable; in the multivariate case it is almost essential, and the multivariate Normal family of distributions is, more often than any other, the most convenient, sufficiently flexible family.

The authors have discovered by experience that to learn much about the practical assessment of multivariate priors or to provide convincing support for abstract statements on the subject, one must consider realistic problems at considerable length. This is not the place for extensive discussion of realistic problems, however. Accordingly, we shall simply give some indications of realistic assessment problems for the reader to think about in the exercises and provide some comments based on our own experience, without supporting them, in the rest of this section.

22.5.2 Some Methods of Assessment of Prior Distributions

We note first of all that no two assessment problems are exactly alike. Two problems with much the same real-world framework may call for entirely different assessment methods. No more is a particular method of assessment always called for by a particular sampling model or any other mathematical feature of the situation. At the same time, two problems with entirely different real-world frameworks and apparently entirely different mathematical structures may turn out to call for similar methods of assessment. Also, the quantities it is natural to introduce because of the economics of a business problem or the mathematical features of the situation are usually not the best ones for direct probability judgments. To obtain satisfying assessments it is essential to banish all preconceptions and to think directly about the quantities whose distribution one can most comfortably assess. From their distribution one can then deduce the distribution of quantities that are of interest for other reasons.

We shall now summarize in an abstract way some of the ideas that have emerged from concrete assessment problems. The following list is not supposed to be in any sense a complete list of assessment methods, nor is only one method on the list supposed to apply in any given situation: the methods listed are neither collectively exhaustive nor mutually exclusive. It is not feasible to structure the practical problems of assessment so completely that they can sensibly be handled by a "routine."

1. First get any relevant information that is available essentially free. It is often easier to make assessments conditional on this information than without it. If this conditional assessment proves hard to make, you can always imagine yourself back in the situation you would have been in before getting the information and process the information by Bayes' formula. The latter requires much more assessment. You must assess the distribution of the state of nature without (that is, marginal on) the information (be careful to expunge the information in your imagination when making this assessment); you also must assess the conditional distribution of the information given the state of nature. This assessment is typically difficult to make for the kind of information that is available free, though it is usually easy to make for the kind of information that is collected for the purpose at hand according to a deliberate plan and at appreciable expense.

2. If available information applies directly to a set of rv's $\tilde{y}$, express the rv's $\tilde{z}$ of interest as functions of $\tilde{y}$ and some other rv's $\tilde{w}$. Assess the marginal distribution of $\tilde{y}$ and the conditional distribution of $\tilde{w}$ given y for every y. This determines the joint distribution of $\tilde{y}$ and $\tilde{w}$ and hence the distribution of $\tilde{z}$, since $\tilde{z}$ is a function of $(\tilde{y}, \tilde{w})$.

3. Express the rv's $\tilde{z}$ of interest as functions of some other rv's $\tilde{w}_1, \tilde{w}_2, \ldots$ which are judged to be independent and whose distributions can comfortably be assessed. This determines the joint distribution of $\tilde{w}_1, \tilde{w}_2, \ldots$ and hence the distribution of $\tilde{z}$. When this can be done, it is usually very satisfying psychologically, because it avoids the difficulties of dependent assessments.

4. To apply the idea of method 3 in the context of method 2, choose $\tilde{w}$ so that $\tilde{w}_1, \tilde{w}_2, \ldots$ and $\tilde{y}$ are mutually independent, and then proceed.

5. If the rv's of interest can be regarded as random drawings from a large real population, assess the joint distribution of the population mean $\tilde{M}$ and one or more parameters describing the shape of the population. This joint distribution and the judgment of random drawing suffice to determine the distribution of the rv's of interest.

6. Introduce a probability model of how the rv's of interest arose, and assess the distribution of the parameters of the model. The distribution of the rv's of interest is then determinable as a marginal distribution. Method 5 is a special case of this.

7. To assess a relationship (as between demand and price), assume it is of a reasonably simple yet flexible form (such as a line) and assess the parameters of the assumed form. This is similar to method 6.

8. It may facilitate thinking about an assessment problem to introduce underlying parameters (such as a population mean) even when they seem superfluous.

9. It may help to reparametrize, that is, to introduce new parameters which are in one-to-one relation with the parameters of interest but easier to think about (such as $\frac{1}{2}[z_1 + z_2]$ and $z_2 - z_1$).

10. Exploit any symmetry in your judgments.

11. Consider what effect certain data would have. Especially if you have had some experience in analyzing data, it may be possible to infer a satisfactory prior distribution by assessing how you would feel if presented with certain evidence, or how much evidence it would take to change your opinion in a certain way. To some extent this begs the question, though—after all, one of the purposes of formal analysis is to be more accurate about the effect of data on prior opinions.

12. Generate fictitious data that you regard as "equivalent" to your prior. Compute your prior by combining the fictitious data with a "diffuse" prior. This is subject to the same danger as method 11.

13. To assess a bivariate Normal prior, once you have made all the transformations that will help, it is necessary to determine five parameters. Various possibilities and pitfalls are described in the next subsection. Multivariate Normal assessments are discussed briefly thereafter.

14. Use a hierarchical scheme like that discussed in section 22.5.4 below.

22.5.3 Assessment of Bivariate Normal Distributions

In this subsection we shall comment on the problem of assessing the joint distribution of $\tilde{z}_1$ and $\tilde{z}_2$ on the assumption that it is bivariate Normal (or adequately represented thereby). We assume also that we have made any helpful transformations, so that it is $\tilde{z}_1$ and $\tilde{z}_2$ we want to think directly about.

A bivariate Normal distribution has five distinct parameters, so five distinct determinations are needed, but there are various possibilities. Notice that not all determinations are distinct. For example, the mean of $\tilde{z}_2$ is the same as the conditional mean of $\tilde{z}_2$ given that $\tilde{z}_1$ equals its mean, $E(\tilde{z}_2) = E_{2|1}(\tilde{z}_2|\bar{z}_1)$, so assessing both will give a check on consistency but will not provide two of the five distinct determinations needed. The same goes for $V(\tilde{z}_2|z_1)$ at two values of z_1.

Minimal Sets of Assessments

The following assessment schemes just determine a bivariate Normal distribution.

1. If $\tilde{z}_1$ and $\tilde{z}_2$ are judged to be independent, then it suffices to assess their marginal means and standard deviations. Assessing conditional means and standard deviations is equivalent, since they are the same as the marginal means and standard deviations under independence.

2. Assess the marginal mean and standard deviation of $\tilde{z}_1$, the conditional mean of $\tilde{z}_2$ at two values of z_1, and the conditional standard deviation of $\tilde{z}_2$ given z_1 (say, given that $\tilde{z}_1 = \bar{z}_1$). Assessing the marginal mean of $\tilde{z}_2$ is equivalent to assessing the conditional mean of $\tilde{z}_2$ given that $\tilde{z}_1 = \bar{z}_1$.

3. Assess the marginal means and standard deviations of $\tilde{z}_1$ and $\tilde{z}_2$ and the conditional standard deviation of $\tilde{z}_2$ given z_1.

4. Assess the marginal means and standard deviations of $\tilde{z}_1$ and $\tilde{z}_2$ and $E(\tilde{z}_2|z_1)$ at some $z_1 \neq \bar{z}_1$. The latter may be replaced by an assessment of the slope of the regression of $\tilde{z}_2$ on $\tilde{z}_1$.

5. Assess the marginal means and standard deviations of $\tilde{z}_1$ and $\tilde{z}_2$ and the marginal standard deviation of $\tilde{z}_2 - \tilde{z}_1$. Replacing the latter by $S(\tilde{z}_2 - \tilde{z}_1|z_1)$ gives method 3 again, because $S(\tilde{z}_2 - \tilde{z}_1|z_1) = S(\tilde{z}_2|z_1)$. This is mentioned here because it is easy to be confused about whether you are assessing the standard deviation of $\tilde{z}_2 - \tilde{z}_1$ marginally or conditionally on $\tilde{z}_1$. (The two are not the same, though they are approximately the same in the special circumstances discussed in the last paragraph of this subsection.)

If you use one of these methods, you will almost always want to compute the remaining marginal and conditional means and standard deviations of $\tilde{z}_1$ and $\tilde{z}_2$ and sometimes those of $\tilde{z}_2 - \tilde{z}_1$ and/or $\frac{1}{2}(\tilde{z}_2 + \tilde{z}_1)$, to make sure the values obtained are reasonable. When you do, you may be in for a surprise, as we shall now see.

Difficulties

In some situations, especially those where one's judgment of $\tilde{z}_1$ and $\tilde{z}_2$ is symmetric so that in particular $E(\tilde{z}_1) = E(\tilde{z}_2)$ and $V(\tilde{z}_1) = V(\tilde{z}_2)$, it is easy to think that

a. $E(\tilde{z}_2|z_1) = z_1$,

b. $E(\tilde{z}_1|z_2) = z_2$;

that is, if one knew either variable this would be the "best prediction" of the other. But the two assertions (a) and (b), or either one of them and $V(\tilde{z}_1) = V(\tilde{z}_2)$, imply that $\tilde{z}_1 = \tilde{z}_2$ *for sure* (i.e., with probability one). Thus an innocuous-looking assessment may imply an extreme conclusion that we did not intend and do not believe. Although any method of assessment has pitfalls, this indicates that assessing conditional means is *very* tricky, though it is not obvious that assessing conditional standard deviations is much less tricky. It is hard to account properly in one's mind for the "regression effect" and the multiplicity of lines of "best fit" discussed in section 22.3.4. But it is also hard to account properly for the relation between the slopes of the regression lines and the conditional standard deviations, given in table 22.1. Simply remembering to avoid the mistake represented by (a) and (b) above by no means removes these difficulties. That such an extreme mistake is so easy to make merely points up the magnitude of the difficulties.

Overdetermined Assessments

Since assessment of the joint distribution of $\tilde{z}_1$ and $\tilde{z}_2$ is so tricky (except when they are judged independent), it seems unsafe to rely entirely on a minimal set of assessments. A possibility mentioned earlier is to assess a minimal set and then compute some consequences to be sure they are reasonable. If they are, splendid, but if they are not, it is not fully clear how to proceed. Another possibility is to make enough assessments to overdetermine the distribution and hope they are consistent. Again it is splendid if they are but unclear what should be done if they are not. In either case, once the inconsistencies are revealed, presumably sufficient psychoanalysis will lead to a catharsis in which all is reconciled. Although this may be a satisfactory way to get one's own joint distributions, it does not seem a feasible way to elicit those of others.

The following procedure seems more feasible for use with others, and it may even be preferable for one's own use: Present the distribution-assessor with *compatible sets* of assessments and let him pick a *set*. (One presumably will want to get into the right ballpark before drawing up the list.) While this procedure undoubtedly has merit if properly applied, it by no means justifies tossing any old type of assessment into the list, leaving the assessor to decide which ones deserve substantial weight as he picks his compatible set; the same thing applies to the alternative method of explicitly asking the assessor which types of assessment he feels most comfortable about and then "taking off the top" just enough to determine the distribution. If the assessor does feel sure that $E(\tilde{z}_2|z_1) = z_1$ and $E(\tilde{z}_1|z_2) = z_2$, for example, we will get an absurd result because in effect we asked the assessor to be his own probabilist. Until more information is available on the reliability of all kinds of lay assessments, we will just have to use unaided judgment in selecting the questions we ask the assessor in practice.

The Standard Deviation of the Difference[3]

The possibility of assessing the variance matrix of a jointly Normal pair $(\tilde{z}_1, \tilde{z}_2)$ by assessing the standard deviations of $\tilde{z}_1$, $\tilde{z}_2$, and $\tilde{\delta} = \tilde{z}_2 - \tilde{z}_1$ was mentioned earlier (method 5 near the beginning of this subsection). This might be natural, for instance, in a situation involving an uncertain bias (section 16.1.1, exercise 22.15, chapter 23B below), with $\tilde{z}_1$ the parameter of interest, $\tilde{z}_2$ the process mean of the biased observations, and $\tilde{\delta}$ the bias. Often, however, it is hard to distinguish judgmentally between the marginal standard deviation of $\tilde{\delta}$ and its conditional standard deviation given $\tilde{z}_1$ or $\tilde{z}_2$. All three cannot be exactly the same, but if they were approximately the same it would be unimportant to distinguish among them. For the marginal standard deviation $S(\tilde{\delta})$ and the conditional standard deviation $S(\tilde{\delta}|z_i)$ to be approximately the same means that their difference is small as a proportion of $S(\tilde{\delta})$. But this proportion is just the proportion of the standard deviation of $\tilde{\delta}$ removed by regression on $\tilde{z}_i$, discussed at the end of section 22.3.4, namely,

$$\frac{S(\tilde{\delta}) - S(\tilde{\delta}|z_i)}{S(\tilde{\delta})} = 1 - \sqrt{1 - \rho^2(\tilde{\delta}, \tilde{z}_i)}, \qquad i = 1, 2,$$

where the equality is exercise 41. We are asking, then, that this quantity be small. In view of the inequalities (which we leave as an exercise)

$$\frac{1}{2}\rho^2 \leq 1 - \sqrt{1 - \rho^2} \leq \frac{\rho^2}{2 - \rho^2} \leq \rho^2,$$

it is equivalent to ask that the squared correlation of $\tilde{\delta}$ and $\tilde{z}_i$ be small. Since we are assuming joint Normality, this is equivalent to asking that $\tilde{\delta}$

3. The rest of this subsection is optional.

be approximately independent of $\tilde{z}_i$, $i = 1, 2$. In view of the joint Normality and the fact that $\tilde{\delta} = \tilde{z}_2 - \tilde{z}_1$, it is impossible for $\tilde{\delta}$ to be exactly independent of $\tilde{z}_1$ and $\tilde{z}_2$ individually. It can nevertheless be approximately independent of each individually.

In short, for $\tilde{z}_1$ and $\tilde{z}_2$ *jointly Normal* and $\tilde{\delta} = \tilde{z}_2 - \tilde{z}_1$, it is unimportant to distinguish the marginal distribution of $\tilde{\delta}$ from its conditional distribution given z_i if and only if any one of the following three equivalent conditions holds:

(ia) $\tilde{\delta}$ and $\tilde{z}_i$ are approximately independent;

(ib) the squared correlation of $\tilde{\delta}$ and $\tilde{z}_i$ is small;

(ic) $S(\tilde{\delta})$ and $S(\tilde{\delta}|z_i)$ differ little relatively.

We may be willing to make a judgment on one of these points directly. If not, we may want to make use of the fact that these conditions hold for both $\tilde{z}_1$ and $\tilde{z}_2$ if and only if both

(ii) $S(\tilde{\delta})$ is small relative to $S(\tilde{z}_1)$ or $S(\tilde{z}_2)$; and

(iii) $S(\tilde{z}_1) - S(\tilde{z}_2)$ is small in absolute value relative to $S(\tilde{\delta})$.

We also point out that it is not enough to suppose that $S(\tilde{\delta})$ is small relative to both $S(\tilde{z}_1)$ and $S(\tilde{z}_2)$.

Proof From $\tilde{z}_2 = \tilde{z}_1 + \tilde{\delta}$ and $\tilde{z}_1 = \tilde{z}_2 - \tilde{\delta}$, we obtain

$$\check{z}_2 = \check{z}_1 + \check{\delta} + 2\ddot{z}_1\ddot{\delta}\rho_1 \tag{22.60a}$$

$$\check{z}_1 = \check{z}_2 + \check{\delta} - 2\ddot{z}_2\ddot{\delta}\rho_2 \tag{22.60b}$$

where

$$\rho_i = \rho(\tilde{z}_i, \tilde{\delta}), \qquad i = 1, 2. \tag{22.61}$$

Suppose first that ρ_1^2 and ρ_2^2 are small. Subtracting (22.60b) from (22.60a), we obtain after a little algebra

$$\frac{\ddot{z}_2 - \ddot{z}_1}{\ddot{\delta}} = \frac{\rho_1\ddot{z}_1 + \rho_2\ddot{z}_2}{\ddot{z}_1 + \ddot{z}_2}. \tag{22.62}$$

Adding (22.60a) and (22.60b), we obtain after a little more algebra

$$\ddot{\delta} = \rho_2\ddot{z}_2 - \rho_1\ddot{z}_1. \tag{22.63}$$

It follows from (22.62) and (22.63) that if ρ_1^2 and ρ_2^2 are small, then (ii) and (iii) hold.

To prove the converse, let $\varepsilon_1 - \ddot{\delta}/\ddot{z}_1$ and $\varepsilon_2 = (\ddot{z}_1 - \ddot{z}_2)/\ddot{\delta}$. Solving (22.60a), we obtain

$$\rho_1 = \frac{\check{z}_2 - \check{z}_1 - \check{\delta}}{2\ddot{z}_1\ddot{\delta}} = -\frac{(\ddot{z}_2 + \ddot{z}_1)\varepsilon_2}{2\ddot{z}_1} - \frac{\varepsilon_1}{2}. \tag{22.64a}$$

Since

$$\ddot{z}_2 = \ddot{z}_1 - \varepsilon_2\ddot{\delta} = \ddot{z}_1(1 - \varepsilon_1\varepsilon_2), \tag{22.64b}$$

we have

$$\rho_1 = -\tfrac{1}{2}(1 - \varepsilon_1\varepsilon_2)\varepsilon_2 - \tfrac{1}{2}\varepsilon_2 - \tfrac{1}{2}\varepsilon_1 = -\varepsilon_2 - \tfrac{1}{2}\varepsilon_1 + \tfrac{1}{2}\varepsilon_1\varepsilon_2^2. \tag{22.65a}$$

Solving (22.60b), we obtain similarly

$$\begin{aligned}\rho_2 &= \frac{\check{z}_2 - \check{z}_1 + \check{\delta}}{2\ddot{z}_2\ddot{\delta}} \\ &= \frac{-(\ddot{z}_2 + \ddot{z}_1)\varepsilon_2 + \ddot{z}_1\varepsilon_1}{2\ddot{z}_2} \\ &= -\frac{\varepsilon_2}{2} + \frac{\varepsilon_1 - \varepsilon_2}{2(1 - \varepsilon_1\varepsilon_2)}.\end{aligned} \tag{22.65b}$$

It follows from (22.65) that if ε_1 and ε_2 are small, then ρ_1^2 and ρ_2^2 are small. This completes the proof.

22.5.4 Assessment of Multivariate Normal Distributions

In theory, a k-variate Normal prior can be assessed simply by assessing the joint distribution of each pair of rv's. More specifically, if the marginal means and variances have been assessed, then all that is needed to determine a multivariate Normal distribution is the covariances, and the covariance between any two of the rv's can be assessed in various ways as indicated in section 22.5.3.

Several new difficulties arise, however.

1. The number of covariances to be assessed may be so large that the assessment becomes too costly in time. Our formal decision-theoretic apparatus takes no account of the cost of thought.

2. The assessed variance matrix may not turn out to be positive-semidefinite.

3. The assessments may have unexpected consequences. In particular, they may imply that some linear combination of the rv's has much smaller variance than we think reasonable. This will be illustrated below. In a way, (2) is an extreme case of (3).

If some structure can be given the distribution, the multivariate assessment problem may become much more tractable. One example would be the case that the rv's are judged independent. Another would be a sampling model (section 22.5.2, method 5). Still another would be a hierarchical structure like that described below.

Variance of a Linear Combination

If you assess a number r of "factors" or "treatment effects" $\tilde{z}_i$ as independently Normal with mean μ and variance σ^2, it follows that you are assessing the average effect $\sum \tilde{z}_i/r$ as Normal with mean μ and variance σ^2/r. For r large, this implies you are nearly certain that the average effect is practically equal to μ, which may not accord with your judgment. This particular difficulty is easily avoided by treating the average effect as an underlying rv with some reasonable distribution, as in the sampling model (section 22.5.2, method 5), but it raises the question whether, in more complicated situations, some more complicated function of the parameters might unwittingly be assumed overly well known.

Hierarchical Assessment

A natural approach to the selection of an investment portfolio is to assess the joint distribution of the market prices of various securities (stocks, bonds, etc.) at the end of an investment period of some arbitrary length, and then select the investment mix whose distribution is "best." (The definition of "best" obviously reflects preference judgments rather than probability assessments, and will not be discussed here.) In practice, there are so many available securities that directly assessing the joint distribution of all their prices is infeasible, whether or not it would otherwise be the best strategy. Instead, the following indirect method of assessment seems very natural in connection with security prices. We will interpret the rv's we introduce in terms of this problem. There is nothing inherent in the method, however, that restricts it to the investment problem. It may well be useful in entirely different problems having nothing to do with securities or investments of any kind. Indeed it generalizes the standard factor-analytic model for mental-test data.

Suppose you want to assess the joint distribution of r rv's $\tilde{z}_1, \ldots, \tilde{z}_r$ (prices of r securities six months hence). Suppose you can find a smaller number of rv's $\tilde{y}_1, \ldots, \tilde{y}_k$ (economic and stock indices, etc.) such that you would regard $\tilde{z}_1, \ldots, \tilde{z}_r$ as conditionally independent given $\tilde{y}_1, \ldots, \tilde{y}_k$. (Given various indices, including a utility stock index, you might regard utility stock prices as independent, etc.) Assess the conditional mean and standard deviation of each $\tilde{z}_i$ given $y_1, \ldots, y_k$; under joint Normality of all the rv's, the conditional means must be linear in $y_1, \ldots, y_k$ and the conditional standard deviations constant. (The conditional means of the utility stocks might depend linearly on the utility index alone, etc.) Under

Normality and the conditional independence mentioned earlier, the assessment of the conditional means and standard deviations of the $\tilde{z}_i$ individually suffices to determine the conditional joint distribution of $\tilde{z}_1, \ldots, \tilde{z}_r$. Assessment of the joint distribution of $\tilde{y}_1, \ldots, \tilde{y}_k$ (marginal on $\tilde{z}_1, \ldots, \tilde{z}_r$) will now determine the joint distribution of all the $\tilde{y}$s and $\tilde{z}$s and therefore the joint distribution of the $\tilde{z}$s (marginal on the ys).

Assessing the conditional distribution of the $\tilde{z}$s given the $\tilde{y}$s and the marginal joint distribution of the $\tilde{y}$s may be easier than the original problem of assessing the distribution of the $\tilde{z}$s because (a) it requires assessment of only the r conditional means and the r conditional standard deviation of the individual $\tilde{z}$s and the $\frac{1}{2}k(k+1)$ variances and covariances of the $\tilde{y}$s rather than the $\frac{1}{2}r(r+1)$ variances and covariances of the zs; (b) the ys (indices) are easier to think about than the $\tilde{z}$s (individual securities); (c) one may want to use historical data about the conditional behavior of the $\tilde{z}$s given the $\tilde{y}$s in assessing the distribution of the $\tilde{z}$s given the $\tilde{y}$s, but it is almost impossible to bring such data in when the $\tilde{y}$s are not introduced. If the two-step assessment is not easier than the original one, there is of course no point in introducing the $\tilde{y}$s.

In assessing the joint distribution of $\tilde{y}_1, \ldots, \tilde{y}_k$, it may be worthwhile to take still another step of the same kind: introduce $\tilde{x}_1, \ldots, \tilde{x}_m$ such that $\tilde{y}_1, \ldots, \tilde{y}_i, \ldots, \tilde{y}_k$ are conditionally independent given $x_1, \ldots, x_m$; assess the conditional distribution of each $\tilde{y}_i$ given $x_1, \ldots, x_m$; this together with the conditional independence determines the conditional joint distribution of $\tilde{y}_1, \ldots, \tilde{y}_k$; assess the (marginal) joint distribution of $\tilde{x}_1, \ldots, \tilde{x}_m$; this determines the joint distribution of all the $\tilde{x}$s and $\tilde{y}$s and thus the joint distribution of the $\tilde{y}$s (marginal on the $\tilde{x}$s).

Obviously this hierarchical scheme can be carried to as many levels as desired. Furthermore, in a particular problem it may be helpful to tighten or loosen the structure. For example, $\tilde{z}_1, \ldots, \tilde{z}_r$ might not be conditionally independent given $y_1, \ldots, y_k$ but instead subsets might be conditionally independent of each other and the conditional distribution of each subset might have a special structure. For example, $(\tilde{z}_1, \ldots, \tilde{z}_{10})$ might be conditionally independent of $(\tilde{z}_{11}, \ldots, \tilde{z}_r)$, $\tilde{z}_{11}, \ldots, \tilde{z}_r$ conditionally independent, and $\tilde{z}_1, \ldots, \tilde{z}_{10}$ conditionally independent except for the constraint

$$c_1\tilde{z}_1 + \cdots + c_{10}\tilde{z}_{10} = y_1.$$

(Suppose, for instance, y_1 is a stock index and $\tilde{z}_1, \ldots, \tilde{z}_{10}$ are the stocks comprising the index.) The meaning of "independent except for a constraint" is discussed below.

An example of a tightening of the structure would be that the conditional mean of each $\tilde{z}_i$ given $y_1, \ldots, y_k$ depends on only one of the ys. For instance, the conditional means of $\tilde{z}_1, \ldots, \tilde{z}_{10}$ might depend only on y_1, of $\tilde{z}_{11}, \ldots, \tilde{z}_{20}$ only on y_2, and so on, that is

$$E(\tilde{z}_i | y_1, \ldots, y_k) = a_i + b_i y_1, \qquad i = 1, \ldots, 10,$$

$$E(\tilde{z}_i | y_1, \ldots, y_k) = a_i + b_i y_2, \qquad i = 11, \ldots, 20,$$

and so on.

Independence Except for a Constraint[4]

A set of rv's $\tilde{z}_1, \ldots, \tilde{z}_r$ satisfying the constraint

$$\boldsymbol{c}^t\tilde{\boldsymbol{z}} = \textstyle\sum_1^r c_i \tilde{z}_i = c_0 \tag{22.66}$$

will be called independent except for this constraint if the conditional distribution of $(\tilde{z}_1, \ldots, \tilde{z}_{j-1})$ given $z_j, \ldots, z_r$ depends only on $c_j z_j + \cdots + c_r z_r$, and similarly for any other division of the $\tilde{z}$s into two sets. If the $\tilde{z}$s are jointly Normal, they are independent except for the constraint (22.66) for some c_0 if and only if $E(\tilde{z}_i | z_j, \ldots, z_r)$ depends only on $c_j z_j + \cdots + c_r z_r$ for $i < j$ and similarly for any $\tilde{z}_i$ and any subset of the zs excluding z_i; and this in turn is equivalent to the condition that the variance matrix $\mathbf{V}$ of $\tilde{\boldsymbol{z}}$ can be written in the form

$$V_{ii} = d_i - kc_i^2 d_i^2, \tag{22.67a}$$

$$V_{ij} = -kc_i d_i c_j d_j, \qquad i \neq j, \tag{22.67b}$$

where $d_1, \ldots, d_r$ are nonnegative constants and

$$k = 1/\textstyle\sum_1^r c_i^2 d_i. \tag{22.67c}$$

These conditions are natural considering that if $\tilde{z}_1, \ldots, \tilde{z}_r$ are independent and Normal with $V(\tilde{z}_i) = d_i$, then the conditional distribution of $\tilde{z}_1, \ldots, \tilde{z}_r$ given $\boldsymbol{c}^t\tilde{\boldsymbol{z}} = y$ satisfies (22.67) and $\tilde{z}_1, \ldots, \tilde{z}_r$ satisfy the definition of conditionally independent except for the constraint $\boldsymbol{c}^t\tilde{\boldsymbol{z}} = y$. Furthermore, any variance matrix satisfying (22.67) can arise in this way.

Proofs

1. If $\tilde{\boldsymbol{z}}$ is Normal with $V(\tilde{\boldsymbol{z}}) = \mathbf{D} = \text{diag}(d_i)$, then the conditional variance of $\tilde{\boldsymbol{z}}$ given $\boldsymbol{c}^t\tilde{\boldsymbol{z}} = y$ is

$$\begin{aligned} V(\tilde{\boldsymbol{z}} | y) &= \mathbf{D} - \mathbf{V}(\tilde{\boldsymbol{z}}, \tilde{y})[V(\tilde{y})]^{-1}\mathbf{V}(\tilde{y}, \tilde{\boldsymbol{z}}) \\ &= \mathbf{D} - \mathbf{D}\boldsymbol{c}(\boldsymbol{c}^t\mathbf{D}\boldsymbol{c})^{-1}\boldsymbol{c}^t\mathbf{D}, \end{aligned} \tag{22.68}$$

4. The rest of this subsection is optional.

which satisfies (22.67), since

$$c^t\mathbf{D}c = \textstyle\sum_1^r c_i^2 d_i = k^{-1}, \tag{22.69a}$$

$$\mathbf{D}cc^t\mathbf{D} = [d_i c_i c_j d_j]. \tag{22.69b}$$

2. If $\tilde{z}$ satisfies the constraint (22.66) and is Normal with $V(\tilde{z}) = \mathbf{V}$ given by (22.67) or equivalently by

$$\mathbf{V} = \mathbf{D} - k\mathbf{D}cc^t\mathbf{D}, \tag{22.70}$$

then to show that $\tilde{z}_1, \ldots, \tilde{z}_r$ are independent except for the constraint (22.66) we need show only that $E(\tilde{z}_1 | z_2)$ depends only on $c_2^t z_2$ and similarly for any other division of $\tilde{z}_1, \ldots, \tilde{z}_r$ into two sets. Now,

$$E(\tilde{z}_1 | z_2) = \bar{z}_1 + \mathbf{V}_{12}\mathbf{V}_{22}^{-1}(z_2 - \bar{z}_2) \tag{22.71a}$$

where

$$\mathbf{V}_{12} = -k\mathbf{D}_1 c_1 c_2^t \mathbf{D}_2, \tag{22.71b}$$

$$\mathbf{V}_{22} = \mathbf{D}_2 - k\mathbf{D}_2 c_2 c_2^t \mathbf{D}_2. \tag{22.71c}$$

Showing that $E(\tilde{z}_1 | z_2)$ depends only on $c_2^t z_2$ therefore amounts to showing $\mathbf{V}_{12}\mathbf{V}_{22}^{-1} = bc_2^t$ for some vector b, or equivalently that

$$\mathbf{V}_{12} = bc_2^t\mathbf{V}_{22}. \tag{22.72}$$

This is indeed true, since

$$bc_2^t\mathbf{V}_{22} = b(1 - kc_2^t\mathbf{D}_2 c_2)c_2^t D_2, \tag{22.73a}$$

which equals $\mathbf{V}_{12}$ if

$$\begin{aligned} b &= -k(1 - kc_2^t\mathbf{D}_2 c_2)^{-1}\mathbf{D}_1 c_1 \\ &= -(c_1^t\mathbf{D}_1 c_1)^{-1}\mathbf{D}_1 c_1. \end{aligned} \tag{22.73b}$$

3. Now suppose that $\tilde{z}_1, \ldots, \tilde{z}_r$ satisfy the constraint (22.66), are jointly Normal, and are independent except for the constraint. We wish to show that $\mathbf{V} = \mathbf{V}(\tilde{z})$ can be written in the form (23.67). We have by (22.66)

$$0 = V(\tilde{z}, c^t\tilde{z}) = \mathbf{V}c \tag{22.74}$$

and, since the $\tilde{z}$'s are independent except for the constraint, by (22.72)

$$\begin{aligned} V_{1j} &= a_2 w_{2j}, \\ V_{2j} &= b_2 w_{2j}, \end{aligned} \qquad j > 2, \tag{22.75}$$

where b in (22.72) is now $[a_2 b_2]^t$ and $c_2^t\mathbf{V}_{22} = w_2$. Similarly

$$\begin{aligned} V_{1j} &= a_i w_{ij}, \\ V_{ij} &= b_i w_{ij}, \end{aligned} \qquad i \neq 1; \qquad j \neq 1, i. \tag{22.76}$$

Neglecting the possibility of 0's, we then find by (22.76) and (22.75) that

$$\frac{V_{ij}}{V_{1j}} = \frac{b_i}{a_i} = \frac{V_{i2}}{V_{12}}, \qquad i \neq 1, \qquad j \neq 1, i; \tag{22.77}$$

$$\frac{V_{i2}}{V_{i1}} = \frac{V_{2i}}{V_{1i}} = \frac{b_2}{a_2}, \qquad i > 2. \tag{22.78}$$

Substituting (22.78) in (22.77) gives

$$V_{ij} = \frac{V_{i2} V_{1j}}{V_{12}} = \frac{b_2}{a_2 V_{12}} V_{1i} V_{1j}, \qquad 1 < j < i, \tag{22.79}$$

and the same holds for $1 < i < j$ by symmetry. Defining r and $\boldsymbol{e}$ by

$$r \equiv (b_2/a_2) V_{12}, \tag{22.80a}$$

$$e_1 \equiv 1/r, \tag{22.80b}$$

$$e_i \equiv V_{1i}, \qquad i > 1 \tag{22.80c}$$

we see that $V_{ij} = r e_i e_j$ for $i \neq j$, and therefore that

$$\mathbf{V} = \mathbf{D} + r\boldsymbol{e}\boldsymbol{e}^t \tag{22.81}$$

where $\mathbf{D} = \text{diag}(d_i)$ is diagonal.

4. We conclude the proof begun in step 3 by showing that if $\mathbf{V}$ satisfies (22.81) and (22.74) then it satisfies (22.67) with the same definition of d_i, a fact of some interest in itself. It follows from (22.81) and (22.74) that

$$d_i c_i + r e_i \boldsymbol{e}^t \boldsymbol{c} = 0. \tag{22.82}$$

Defining k in accordance with (22.67c) and using (22.82), we obtain

$$k = (\textstyle\sum_1^r c_i^2 d_i)^{-1} = -r^{-1}(\boldsymbol{e}^t\boldsymbol{c})^{-2}. \tag{22.83}$$

By (22.82) and (22.83)

$$r e_i e_j = r(r\boldsymbol{e}^t\boldsymbol{c})^{-2} c_i d_i c_j d_j = -k c_i d_i c_j d_j, \tag{22.84}$$

and this, with (22.81) implies (22.67a) and (22.67b).

Exercises

1. a. Using tables of the univariate unit Normal distribution, compute the probability that the unit spherical bivariate Normal rv $\tilde{\boldsymbol{u}}$ lies in the region R_1 in figure 22E.1.

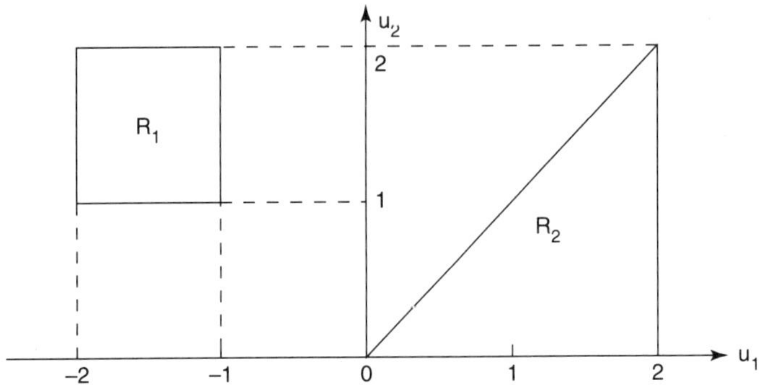

Figure 22E.1
Two regions

b. Repeat above for region R_2.
Hint Use the symmetry properties of the unit spherical bivariate Normal distribution.

c. For $\tilde{\boldsymbol{u}}$ as above find

$$P\left(\frac{1}{2} \le \frac{\tilde{u}_2}{\tilde{u}_1} \le 1\right), \qquad \tilde{u}_1 \ge 0.$$

2. Prove the assertion of section 22.2.1 that if $\tilde{z}$ has mean $\boldsymbol{M}$ and nonsingular variance $\mathbf{V} = \mathbf{b}\mathbf{b}^t$ where $\mathbf{b}$ is square, then $\mathbf{b}$ is nonsingular and $\tilde{\boldsymbol{u}} = \mathbf{b}^{-1}(\tilde{z} - \boldsymbol{M})$ has mean $\boldsymbol{0}$ and variance $\mathbf{I}$. (This does not require Normality.)

3. a. Prove that if $\mathbf{V}$ is nonsingular, $\mathbf{b}\mathbf{b}^t = \mathbf{V}$, $\mathbf{B} = \mathbf{b}\mathbf{P}$, and $\mathbf{P}$ is orthogonal, then $\mathbf{B}\mathbf{B}^t = \mathbf{V}$.

   b. Prove that if $\mathbf{V}$ is $(r \times r)$ positive-definite then there is a one-to-one correspondence between the $(r \times r)$ orthogonal matrices $\mathbf{P}$ and the square matrices $\mathbf{B}$ such that $\mathbf{B}\mathbf{B}^t = \mathbf{V}$.

4. Prove the assertions of section 22.2.2 that (a) if $\tilde{z}_1$ and $\tilde{z}_2$ are independent nonsingular Normal rv's then they are jointly nonsingular bivariate Normal with the mean and variance given in (22.12); (b) if $\tilde{z}$ is nonsingular bivariate Normal with $\check{\mathbf{z}}_{12} = 0$ then $\tilde{z}_1$ and $\tilde{z}_2$ are independent nonsingular Normal rv's.

5. Let $\tilde{z}_1$ be univariate unit Normal, $\tilde{w}$ be independent of $\tilde{z}_1$ with $P(\tilde{w} = 1) = P(\tilde{w} = -1) = \frac{1}{2}$, and $\tilde{z}_2 = \tilde{w}\tilde{z}_1$. Show that $\tilde{z}_1$ and $\tilde{z}_2$ are marginally Normal and uncorrelated but not independent and not jointly Normal.

6. a. Without using the results of section 22.3, prove that if $\tilde{z}$ is nonsingular, bivariate Normal with variance $\mathbf{V}$, then $\tilde{z}_1$ and $\tilde{z}_2 - V_{21}V_{11}^{-1}\tilde{z}_1$ are independent Normal with the means and variances given in (22.25).

   b. Prove that if $\tilde{z}_1$ and $\tilde{z}_2 + \mathbf{c}\tilde{z}_1$ have covariance $\mathbf{0}$, then $\mathbf{c} = -\check{\mathbf{z}}_{21}\check{\mathbf{z}}_{11}^{-1}$.

7. Prove the assertion of section 22.2.4 that if $\tilde{z}$ is bivariate with variance $\mathbf{V}$ then $\mathbf{b}\mathbf{b}^t = \mathbf{V}$ for

$$\mathbf{b} = \begin{bmatrix} V_{11}^{1/2} & 0 \\ V_{12}V_{11}^{-1/2} & (V_{22} - V_{12}^2 V_{11}^{-1})^{1/2} \end{bmatrix}.$$

8. Let $\tilde{z}$ be bivariate Normal with

$$\bar{\tilde{z}} = \begin{bmatrix} 1 \\ 2 \end{bmatrix}, \qquad \check{\mathbf{z}} = \begin{bmatrix} 2 & 1 \\ 1 & 3 \end{bmatrix},$$

and let $\tilde{y}$ be defined by

$\tilde{y} = \mathbf{b}\tilde{z}.$

Specify completely the distribution of $\tilde{y}$ when

a. $\mathbf{b} = \begin{bmatrix} 1 & 2 \\ 2 & 3 \end{bmatrix}$,

b. $\mathbf{b} = \begin{bmatrix} 1 & 2 \\ 2 & 4 \end{bmatrix}$,

c. $\mathbf{b} = [1 \quad 2]$.

d. Find $\boldsymbol{M}$ and $\mathbf{b}$ such that $\tilde{z} = \boldsymbol{M} + \mathbf{b}\tilde{\boldsymbol{u}}$ where $\tilde{z}$ is the above rv and where $\tilde{\boldsymbol{u}}$ is unit spherical bivariate Normal.

9. Let $\tilde{z}$ be bivariate Normal with

$$\bar{z} = [22, \quad 47]^t, \qquad \breve{\mathbf{z}} = \begin{bmatrix} 13 & 11 \\ 11 & 17 \end{bmatrix}.$$

a. Find the marginal distributions of $\tilde{z}_1$ and $\tilde{z}_2$.

b. Find the conditional distribution of $\tilde{z}_1$ given that $\tilde{z}_2 = 33.7$ and the conditional distribution of $\tilde{z}_2$ given that $\tilde{z}_1 = 26$.

c. Find the regression functions of $\tilde{z}_2$ on $\tilde{z}_1$ and $\tilde{z}_1$ on $\tilde{z}_2$.

d. Supposing that you wish to simulate the distribution of $\tilde{z}$, give precise numerical instructions for generating a sequence $z^{(1)}, z^{(2)}, \ldots$ using a table of unit Normal random numbers.

Hints Use parts (a) and (b). Alternatively, find $\mathbf{b}$ such that $\mathbf{b}\mathbf{b}^t = \breve{\mathbf{z}}$.

10. Let $\tilde{\mu}$ be Normal with mean $\bar{\mu}'$ and variance $\breve{\mu}'$. Let $\tilde{m}$ given μ be Normal with mean μ and variance υ/n. Using the results of this chapter, prove that

a. $[\tilde{m} \quad \tilde{\mu}]^t$ is bivariate Normal with mean and variance

$$\boldsymbol{M} = \begin{bmatrix} \bar{\mu}' \\ \bar{\mu}' \end{bmatrix}, \qquad \mathbf{V} = \begin{bmatrix} \breve{\mu}' + \upsilon/n & \breve{\mu}' \\ \breve{\mu}' & \breve{\mu}' \end{bmatrix}.$$

b. The marginal distribution of $\tilde{m}$ is Normal with mean $\bar{\mu}'$ and variance $\breve{\mu}' + \upsilon/n$.

c. The conditional distribution of $\tilde{\mu}$ given m is Normal with mean $\bar{\mu}'' = [(\upsilon/n)\bar{\mu}' + \breve{\mu}'m]/[\breve{\mu}' + \upsilon/n]$ and variance $\breve{\mu}'' = \breve{\mu}'(\upsilon/n)/(\breve{\mu}' + \upsilon/n)$.

d. Compare these results with those of chapter 16.

11. In the previous problem, let $\bar{\mu}' = 50$, $\breve{\mu}' = 25$, $\upsilon = 25$, $n = 5$. Find

a. The conditional distribution of $\tilde{m}$ given that $\tilde{\mu} = 56$.

b. The marginal distribution of $\tilde{m}$.

c. The conditional distribution of $\tilde{\mu}$ given that $\tilde{m} = 56$.

d. The marginal distribution of $\tilde{\mu}$.

e. The distribution of $\tilde{\bar{\mu}}''$.

12. Let there be two acts a_1 and a_2 with utilities

$$u(a_1, \mu) = 0, \qquad u(a_2, \mu) = -88 + 2\mu.$$

Given the distributions specified in the previous exercise, evaluate

a. EVPI if $\tilde{m}$ is not observed.

b. EVSI.

c. EVPI if $\tilde{m} = 56$ is observed.

13. A population of individuals is partitioned into two strata. We are given that 37% of the population belongs to stratum 1. We are concerned with the population mean μ of a certain characteristic. Let μ_1 and μ_2 be the population means of strata 1 and 2 respectively. Since μ, μ_1, and μ_2 are unknown they are to be treated as rv's. The decision maker now assigns to $\tilde{\mu}_1$ a Normal distribution with mean 46 and variance 16, assigns to $(\tilde{\mu}_2 - \tilde{\mu}_1)$ a Normal distribution with mean 4 and variance 9, and considers $\tilde{\mu}_1$ and $(\tilde{\mu}_2 - \tilde{\mu}_1)$ to be independent. Give:

a. The joint distribution of $\tilde{\mu}_1$ and $(\tilde{\mu}_2 - \tilde{\mu}_1)$.

b. The joint distribution of $\tilde{\mu}_1$ and $\tilde{\mu}_2$.

c. The distribution of $\tilde{\mu}_2$ marginal as regards $\tilde{\mu}_1$.

d. The conditional distribution of $\tilde{\mu}_1$ given μ_2.

e. The regression of $\tilde{\mu}_1$ on $\tilde{\mu}_2$.

f. The distribution of the population mean $\tilde{\mu}$.

g. Show that $\tilde{\mu}_2$ and $(\tilde{\mu}_1 - \tilde{\mu}_2)$ are not independent.

h. Find c such that $\tilde{\mu}_2$ and $(\tilde{\mu}_1 - c\tilde{\mu}_2)$ are independent.

14. (*Continuation of exercise 13*) Assume that a sample of 20 observations is taken from stratum 2; the sample mean m_2 is 56 and the sample standard deviation s_2 is 10. (Assume that stratum 2 has population standard deviation 10 so that the calculations done for exercise 11 can be used.)

a. Would observing a sample from stratum 2 change the odds at which someone who already knew the true value of $\tilde{\mu}_2$ would bet on the value of $\tilde{\mu}_1$?

b. Find the joint distribution of $\tilde{\mu}_1$ and $\tilde{\mu}_2$ posterior to observing $m_2 = 56$.
Remark This problem *can* be done using only the bivariate Normal with the help of part (a). One method also uses part (b) of exercise 13. The problem can be done more straightforwardly with the trivariate Normal.

c. Find the posterior distribution of the grand mean $\tilde{\mu}$ of the whole population.

15. We can introduce the notion of bias into our model of chapter 16 by letting $\tilde{\mu} = \tilde{\xi} + \tilde{\beta}$, where $\tilde{\xi}$ is the unknown true value and $\tilde{\beta}$ is the unknown bias. Suppose that $\tilde{\xi}$, $\tilde{\beta}$, and $\tilde{\varepsilon}$ (as before, the unknown true sample error) are independent Normal a priori, with means and variances

$$\bar{\xi}' = 48, \qquad \bar{\beta}' = 2, \qquad \bar{\varepsilon}' = 0,$$

$$\breve{\xi}' = 20, \qquad \breve{\beta}' = 5, \qquad \breve{\varepsilon}' = 100.$$

a. Find the joint distribution of $\tilde{\xi}$ and $\tilde{\mu} \equiv \tilde{\xi} + \tilde{\beta}$.

b. Find the marginal distribution of $\tilde{\mu}$ and conditional distribution of $\tilde{\xi}$ given μ.

c. Assuming that m is the sample mean of a sample of 20, find the distribution of $\tilde{\mu}$ posterior to observing that $m = 56$.

d. Find the posterior joint distribution of $\tilde{\xi}$ and $\tilde{\mu}$.
Remark This *can* be done using only the bivariate Normal by the same kind of trick suggested in exercise 14b.

e. Find the posterior joint distribution of $\tilde{\xi}$ and $\tilde{\beta}$.

16. a. Consider two production processes one with average yield μ_1 and one with average yield μ_2. Assume that a bivariate Normal prior has been assessed for $\tilde{\boldsymbol{\mu}} = [\tilde{\mu}_1 \tilde{\mu}_2]^t$. Now a sample of size n_i is taken from process i and statistics m_i (sample mean) and s_i (sample standard deviation) are observed ($i = 1, 2$). Assuming that the distribution of $\tilde{m}_i$ given $[\mu_1 \mu_2]^t$ is Normal with mean μ_i and variance s_i^2/n_i, indicate in principle (not in detail!) how you would find the posterior distribution of $\tilde{\boldsymbol{\mu}}$.
Remark This, like exercises 14 and 15, *can* be done using the bivariate Normal only.

b. Discuss the following statement: "It is the difference between the ... means [of sample from two populations] which supplies information on the difference between the two population means."

17. In a two-action problem let w_i be the profitability, in units of thousands of dollars, of act $a_i (i = 1, 2)$. A detailed analysis leads to a joint distribution on $\tilde{\mathbf{w}} = [\tilde{w}_1 \tilde{w}_2]^t$ which is Normal with

(a) mean, $\bar{\mathbf{w}} = [25 \quad 30]$

and

(b) variance, $\breve{\mathbf{W}} = \begin{bmatrix} 100 & 200 \\ 200 & 900 \end{bmatrix}.$

a. If the decision maker wishes to maximize expected profitability, which is the optimal act and what is the expected value of perfect information?

b. If the decision maker wishes to maximize expected utility where the utility value of w (in thousands of dollars) is given by

$u(w) = 1 - e^{-.02w},$

then which act should be chosen?
Hint

$$\int_{-\infty}^{\infty} e^{tx} f_N(x|\mu, \sigma^2)\, dx = e^{t\mu + (1/2)t^2\sigma^2}.$$

18. Let $\tilde{\mathbf{z}}$ be singular bivariate Normal and $\tilde{y} = \mathbf{b}\tilde{\mathbf{z}}$ univariate Normal. Show by example that $\tilde{y}$ may be either singular or nonsingular.

19. A certain rapidly growing corporation has a large turnover in its workforce. Due to ongoing plant expansion and the high turnover, there is an almost continuous process of screening and selecting from among the many workers applying for employment.

In the past, prospective employees have filed application forms with the corporation's personnel office. These forms were designed to obtain information concerning the applicant's address, age, education, previous employment and experience, marital status, and so forth. By evaluating this information with respect to various well-established criteria, the personnel office was able to eliminate certain applications from further consideration. The applicants who survived this screening process were scrutinized further, mainly by means of an interview, and employment was offered to those surviving this second screening process.

Recent examination of the firm's hiring policies has disclosed that the second stage screening possesses little or no discriminating ability—in other words, an objective measure of ultimate job performance of those hired as a result of the current screening procedure behaves as if these employees were randomly selected from among those surviving the first screening.

The corporation is considering and has investigated an aptitude-testing program to improve their selection process and thereby raise the average ultimate job performance of those workers hired. If such a testing procedure were to be adopted, it would replace the second-stage interviewing procedure currently used.

Aptitude test scores (x) of applicants surviving the initial screening and objective measures (y) of their ultimate job performances if hired are scaled in such a way that they are known to have a joint bivariate Normal distribution with $E(\tilde{x}) = 0$, $V(\tilde{x}) = 1$, $E(\tilde{y}) = \mu$, $V(\tilde{y}) = \sigma^2$, and $V(\tilde{x}, \tilde{y}) = \rho\sigma > 0$, where μ and σ and ρ are known numbers.

In the past, a fraction p of all applicants who survived the first screening were hired. This selection ratio, p, is to be maintained on the average in the future.

An index of the "value" of a decision not to hire any particular applicant is zero, while that of a decision to hire him may be taken as y, the measure of his ultimate performance. Notice that y may be negative.

a. Show that if applying the old interview technique is really equivalent to random selection with probability of hiring equal to p, then the expected index of the value of a single decision made by this process is $p\mu$.

b. Argue that the optimal procedure using the test is to accept all individuals whose x score is greater than or equal to x_p, where

$$G_{N^*}(x_p) = p.$$

c. If the incremental cost of administering the aptitude test is c per person tested, where c is measured in index units, show that the expected index of value of a single optimal decision made on the basis of the aptitude test score is

$$p\mu + \rho\sigma f_{N^*}(x_p) - c.$$

Hint for Part (c) Show that $E(\tilde{y}|x) = \mu + \rho\sigma x$; then show that the expected index of value of a single decision made on the basis of the aptitude score is

$$\int_{x_p}^{\infty} (\mu + \rho\sigma x) f_{N^*}(x)\, dx - c.$$

d. Demonstrate that the net gain of testing, i.e., the difference between the expected indices of value found in parts (a) and (c) above, is $\rho\sigma f_{N^*}(x_p) - c$. Show this difference is maximized if the selection ratio, p, is equal to one-half.

e. If the corporation were to consider two competing aptitude tests, each having the *same* incremental cost, should the test having the higher correlation of test score x with the index of value or ultimate job performance y be preferred? Why?

f. In most contexts, as the number of applicants increases it is reasonable to assume that the selection ratio p will decrease. Show that *if the test must be administered either to all applicants or to none*, then as p decreases from 1/2 the net gain per applicant of testing decreases, and if p is below some value then this test should *not* be administered.

If it is permissible to test some of the applicants without testing them all, it might be desirable to choose a subset of individuals (say at random) and then administer the test to this subset. Why?

g. Suppose we have an unlimited pool of applicants and we wish to select roughly n applicants (say, $n = 500$). Next suppose that we choose any arbitrary selection ratio p, choose n/p applicants at random, and test them using the selection ratio p. Show that the expected net gain of testing is

$$\bar{g}(p) = \frac{n}{p}[\rho\sigma f_{N^*}(x_p) - c] \quad \text{where} \quad G_{N^*}(x_p) \equiv p.$$

Defining $\bar{g}^*(p) \equiv \bar{g}(p)/nc$, show that

$$\bar{g}^*(p) = \frac{Af_{N^*}(x_p) - 1}{p}, \quad \text{where} \quad A = \frac{\rho\sigma}{c}.$$

h. The problem now is to choose the value p^o of p that maximizes $\bar{g}^*(p)$. Show that

$$p^o = G_{N^*}(u^o), \quad \text{where} \quad L_{N^*}(u^o) \equiv \frac{c}{\rho\sigma},$$

by showing that

$$\frac{d}{dp}\bar{g}^*(p) = \frac{A[x_p p - f_{N^*}(x_p)] - 1}{p^2} = \frac{A[x_p G_{N^*}(x_p) - f_{N^*}(x_p)] + 1}{p^2}$$

$$= -\frac{AL_{N^*}(x_p) + 1}{p^2}.$$

Hint Observe that

$$G_{N^*}(x_p) = p$$

and that differentiating both sizes with respect to p yields

$$-f_{N^*}(x_p)\frac{d}{dp}(x_p) = 1.$$

i. Suppose in this problem that instead of merely having to maintain some selection ratio p on the average, the corporation has N applicants surviving the initial screening (these N may be assumed to be a random sample from the population of all such applicants) and exactly n of these must be hired to fill existing job vacancies, where n and N are small numbers. If the testing procedure is used, which applicants should be hired? Explain how a simulation technique might be used to evaluate the expected index of value of selection based upon the aptitude test scores.

20. Let a_1 and a_2 be the two terminal acts, let $-\infty < \mu < \infty$ be the unknown state parameter, and let the terminal payoffs be given by

$$u_t(a_i, \mu) = K_i + k_i\mu, \qquad i = 1, 2.$$

Define μ_b by

$$u_t(a_1, \mu_b) = u_t(a_2, \mu_b)$$

and let

$$k_t \equiv |k_1 - k_2|.$$

Assume that $\mu_b = 100$ and that $k_t = 10{,}000$.

In this problem we shall be concerned with the problem of nonresponse to a simple mail questionnaire. To this end let us assume that if the questionnaire were to be distributed to the entire population then a proportion π_1 would answer and a proportion $\pi_2 = 1 - \pi_1$ would not. Denote the population mean rates amongst responders and nonresponders by μ_1 and μ_2 respectively. We then have

$$\mu = \pi_1\mu_1 + \pi_2\mu_2.$$

Prior to the experiment, $(\tilde{\mu}_1, \tilde{\mu}_2)$ is given a joint Normal distribution as follows:

(a) $\tilde{\mu}_1$ is given a prior with mean $\bar{\mu}'_1 = 110$ and variance $\breve{\mu}'_{11} = 81$.

(b) $\tilde{\mu}_2$ given μ_1 is given a prior Normal distribution with conditional mean $\mu_{2|1} = 4 + 0.9\mu_1$ and conditional variance 49.

A sample of 1,000 questionnaires were distributed and 700 responses were obtained with a sample mean

$$m_1 = \textstyle\sum_{i=1}^{700} x_i/700 = 102.7$$

and sample variance

$$s_1^2 = \frac{1}{699}\textstyle\sum_{i=1}^{700}(x_i - 102.7)^2 = (70)^2.$$

Assuming that the sampling variance among nonrespondents is very close to s_1^2, should the nonrespondents be interviewed and if so how many? Assume that it costs $10 to interview a nonrespondent.

21. Let $\tilde{y} = [\tilde{y}_1 \tilde{y}_2 \tilde{y}_3]^t$ have a (trivariate) Normal distribution with mean

$$\bar{y} = [22 \quad 47 \quad 38]^t$$

and variance

$$\breve{y} = \begin{bmatrix} 13 & 11 & 7 \\ 11 & 17 & 19 \\ 7 & 19 & 42 \end{bmatrix}.$$

a. Find the conditional distribution of $\tilde{y}_3$ given that $\tilde{y}_1 = y_1$, and specialize to the case $y_1 = 24$.

b. Find the conditional distribution of $\tilde{y}_3$ given that $\tilde{y}_2 = y_2$, and specialize to the case $y_2 = 43$.

c. Find the conditional distribution of $\tilde{y}_3$ given that $\tilde{y}_1 = y_1$ and $\tilde{y}_2 = y_2$, and specialize to the case $y_1 = 24$ and $y_2 = 43$.

d. Find

i. $V(\tilde{y}_3)$

ii. $V(\tilde{y}_3|y_1)$,

iii. $V(\tilde{y}_3|y_2)$

iv. $V(\tilde{y}_3|y_1, y_2)$.

e. If you had to predict the value of $\tilde{y}_3$ (with squared error loss), find how much you would pay for

i. y_1 information;

ii. y_2 information;

iii. y_1 and y_2 information;

iv. y_2 information given that $y_1 = 25$;

v. y_1 information given that $y_2 = 53$.

f. How would (e) change if you had to predict $\tilde{y}_3$ with absolute error loss?

22. (*Multiple Correlation*). Let $\tilde{z}_1$ and $\tilde{\mathbf{z}}_2 = [\tilde{z}_2 \tilde{z}_3 \cdots \tilde{z}_r]^t$ be jointly distributed, not necessarily Normally. Let $T(\tilde{\mathbf{z}}_2)$ represent a function of $\tilde{\mathbf{z}}_2$ and for simplicity denote the scalar rv $T(\tilde{\mathbf{z}}_2)$ by $\tilde{T}$. We shall be concerned with the expression

$$\frac{E(\tilde{z}_1 - \bar{z}_1)^2 - E_T E_{z_1|T}(\tilde{z}_1 - \tilde{T})^2}{E(\tilde{z}_1 - \bar{z}_1)^2} \tag{22.85}$$

which we can interpret as the ratio EVSI/EVPI where $\tilde{T}$ is an estimator of $\tilde{z}_1$ under quadratic loss. The maximum of expression (22.85) taken over all $\tilde{T} = T(\tilde{\mathbf{z}}_2)$ will be denoted by $\eta^2_{1\cdot 2,\ldots,r}$ or more briefly by $\eta^2_{1\cdot 2}$ and will be called the multiple (nonlinear) correlation of $\tilde{z}_1$ against $\tilde{\mathbf{z}}_2$. The maximum of expression (22.68) taken over all T of the form $T(\mathbf{z}_2) = b_1 + \mathbf{b}^t\mathbf{z}_2 = b_1 + \sum_{j=2}^r b_j z_j$ will be denoted by $\rho_{1\cdot 2,\ldots,r} \equiv \rho^2_{1\cdot 2}$ and will be called the multiple (linear) correlation of $\tilde{z}_1$ against $\tilde{\mathbf{z}}_2$.

a. Show that $\eta^2_{1\cdot 2} \geq \rho^2_{1\cdot 2}$.

b. Show that

$$E_T E_{z_1|T}(\tilde{z}_1 - \tilde{T})^2 = V(\tilde{z}_1 - \tilde{T}) + (\bar{z}_1 - \bar{T})^2. \tag{22.86}$$

c. Show that in both maximization problems leading to $\eta^2_{1\cdot 2}$ and $\rho^2_{1\cdot 2}$, $T(\mathbf{z}_2)$ should be chosen so that $\bar{T} = \bar{z}_1$.

d. Show that

$$\eta^2_{1\cdot 2} = \max_T \frac{V(\tilde{z}_1) - V(\tilde{z}_1 - \tilde{T})}{V(\tilde{z}_1)}, \quad \text{for } \tilde{T} \equiv T(\tilde{\mathbf{z}}_2) \text{ unrestricted,} \tag{22.87}$$

and

$$\rho^2_{1\cdot 2} = \max_T \frac{V(\tilde{z}_1) - V(\tilde{z}_1 - \tilde{T})}{V(\tilde{z}_1)}, \quad \text{for } \tilde{T} \equiv T(\tilde{\mathbf{z}}_2) \text{ linear.} \tag{22.88}$$

e. Show that

$$\eta^2_{1\cdot 2} = \frac{V(\tilde{z}_1) - E_{z_2} V_{z_1|z_2}(\tilde{z}_1)}{V(\tilde{z}_1)} = \frac{V_{z_2} E_{z_1|z_2}(\tilde{z}_1)}{V(\tilde{z}_1)} \tag{22.89}$$

f. Show that if $V_{z_1|z_2}(\tilde{z}_1)$ does not depend on z_2, the so-called "homoskedastic" case, then

$$\eta^2_{1\cdot 2} = \frac{V_1 - V_{1|2}}{V_1}, \quad \text{where} \quad \begin{aligned} V_1 &\equiv V(\tilde{z}_1), \\ V_{1|2} &\equiv V_{z_1|z_2}(\tilde{z}_1) \text{ all } z_2. \end{aligned} \tag{22.90}$$

g. Show that if the regression function is linear, i.e., if

$$\bar{z}_{1|2}(z_2) = E_{z_1|z_2}(\tilde{z}_1) = b_1 + \textstyle\sum_{j=1}^r b_j z_j = b_1 + \boldsymbol{b}^t \boldsymbol{z}_2,$$

then $\eta^2_{1\cdot 2} = \rho^2_{1\cdot 2}$. (This holds, for instance, if $\tilde{z}_1$ and $\tilde{\boldsymbol{z}}_2$ are jointly Normal.)

h. To develop further the analysis for $\rho^2_{1\cdot 2}$ whether or not $\bar{z}_{1|2}(z_2)$ is linear, show that the linear $T(\boldsymbol{z}_2)$ that minimizes $V[\tilde{z}_1 - T(\tilde{\boldsymbol{z}}_2)]$ in (22.88) is

$$T^*(\tilde{\boldsymbol{z}}_2) = \bar{z}_1 + \mathbf{V}_{12}\mathbf{V}_{22}^{-1}(\tilde{\boldsymbol{z}}_2 - \bar{\boldsymbol{z}}_2) = \bar{z}_1 + \boldsymbol{b}^{*t}(\tilde{\boldsymbol{z}}_2 - \bar{\boldsymbol{z}}_2), \tag{22.91}$$

where

$$\mathbf{V} = \begin{bmatrix} V_{11} & \mathbf{V}_{12} \\ \mathbf{V}_{21} & \mathbf{V}_{22} \end{bmatrix}, \qquad \begin{aligned} V_{11} &= V(\tilde{z}_1) \text{ is } (1 \times 1), \\ \mathbf{V}_{22} &= \mathbf{V}(\tilde{\boldsymbol{z}}_2) \text{ is } [(r-1) \times (r-1)], \end{aligned}$$

and $\boldsymbol{b}^{*t} \equiv \mathbf{V}_{12}\mathbf{V}_{22}^{-1}$.

i. Show that $V[\tilde{z}_1 - T^*(\tilde{\boldsymbol{z}}_2)] = V_{11} - \mathbf{V}_{12}\mathbf{V}_{22}^{-1}\mathbf{V}_{21}$.

j. Show that $\rho^2_{1\cdot 2} = \dfrac{\mathbf{V}_{12}\mathbf{V}_{22}^{-1}\mathbf{V}_{21}}{V_{11}}$.

Observe that if $\tilde{\boldsymbol{z}}_2 = \tilde{z}_2$ (i.e., $\tilde{\boldsymbol{z}}_2$ is a univariate rv) then V_{11}, V_{12}, V_{21}, and V_{22} are all scalars and $\rho^2_{1\cdot 2}$ is just the square of the ordinary linear correlation of $\tilde{z}_1$ and $\tilde{z}_2$, i.e., $V^2_{12}/V_{11}V_{22}$.

23. a. (*Partial Correlation*). Define the partial correlation $\rho_{1,2.3} = \dfrac{\rho_{1,2} - \rho_{1,3}\rho_{2,3}}{\sqrt{1-\rho^2_{2,3}}\sqrt{1-\rho^2_{1,3}}}$.

If $[\tilde{z}_1\tilde{z}_2\tilde{z}_3]^t$ is nonsingular Normal, show that the conditional correlation $\rho_{1,2|3}$ of $\tilde{z}_1$ and $\tilde{z}_2$ given that $\tilde{z}_3 = z_3$ does not depend on the particular value of z_3 and equals $\rho_{1,2|3}$.

Hint Use (22.18) to show that the conditional covariance of $\tilde{z}_i$ and $\tilde{z}_j$ given that $\tilde{z}_3 = z_3$ is

$$V(\tilde{z}_i, \tilde{z}_j | \tilde{z}_3 = z_3) = \check{z}_{ij|3} = \check{z}_{ij} - \check{z}_{i3}\check{z}_{3j}\check{z}_{33}^{-1}, \qquad \begin{cases} i = 1, 2, \\ j = 1, 2. \end{cases}$$

b. Show that $\rho_{1,2.3} = 0 \Leftrightarrow \rho_{1,2} = \rho_{1,3}\rho_{2,3}$.

c. What is $\rho_{1,3|2}$ for exercise 21?

24. Let $\tilde{z}_1$, $\tilde{z}_2$, $\tilde{z}_3$, $\tilde{z}_4$, and $\tilde{z}_5$ be independent, identically distributed random variables, each Normal with mean μ and variance σ^2. Define the random variables $\tilde{m}$, $\tilde{M}$, and $\tilde{w}$ as follows:

$$\tilde{m} \equiv \min\{\tilde{z}_1, \tilde{z}_2, \tilde{z}_3, \tilde{z}_4, \tilde{z}_5\},$$

$$\tilde{M} \equiv \max\{\tilde{z}_1, \tilde{z}_2, \tilde{z}_3, \tilde{z}_4, \tilde{z}_5\}.$$

$$\tilde{w} \equiv \tilde{M} - \tilde{m}.$$

Describe exactly how you could use simulation to estimate for each of these three rv's:

a. The mean of its distribution,

b. The variance of its distribution,

c. The .65 fractile of its distribution,

and describe exactly how you would decide in each case when you had made enough Monte Carlo trials.

25. Let there be three possible acts a_i, $i = 1, 2, 3$; let the profit of a_i be μ_i; and let $\tilde{\boldsymbol{\mu}} = [\tilde{\mu}_1 \tilde{\mu}_2 \tilde{\mu}_3]^t$ be Normal with mean and variance

$$\bar{\boldsymbol{\mu}} = \begin{bmatrix} 3.0 \\ 3.2 \\ 3.5 \end{bmatrix}, \qquad \check{\boldsymbol{\mu}} = \begin{bmatrix} 8 & 0 & 8 \\ 0 & 9 & 6 \\ 8 & 6 & 20 \end{bmatrix} = \begin{bmatrix} 2 & 0 & 2 \\ 0 & 3 & 0 \\ 0 & 2 & 4 \end{bmatrix} \begin{bmatrix} 2 & 0 & 0 \\ 0 & 3 & 2 \\ 2 & 0 & 4 \end{bmatrix}.$$

Assume that utility for money is linear.

a. Find the optimal act and its expected utility;

b. Explain exactly how you could compute the EVPI.

26. a. Let $(\tilde{x}_1, \tilde{x}_2, \ldots, \tilde{x}_n)$ represent an uncertain monetary flow where $\tilde{x}_i$ is the payment (possibly negative) to be obtained in the ith period. Show that its present value (PV) given by $\tilde{y} \equiv \sum_{j=1}^{n} \rho^j \tilde{x}_j$ has mean $\bar{y} = \sum_{j=1}^{n} \rho^j \bar{x}_j$ and variance $\check{y} = [\rho^1 \rho^2 \ldots \rho^n] \check{\mathbf{x}} [\rho^1 \rho^2 \ldots \rho^n]^t = \sum \rho^{i+j} \check{x}_{ij}$.
If $\tilde{\boldsymbol{x}}$ is multivariate Normal, show that $\tilde{y}$ is Normal.

b. Suppose

$$\tilde{x}_{t+1} = \tilde{x}_t + \tilde{\varepsilon}_{t+1} \qquad t = 0, 1, 2, \ldots, n-1$$

where $\tilde{x}_0$ is a given constant A, and where the $\tilde{\varepsilon}_t$s are independent Normal with mean 0 and variance v. Show that $\tilde{\boldsymbol{x}}$ is multivariate Normal, $\bar{x}_t = A$, $\check{x}_t = tv$, and

$$V(\tilde{x}_{t+k}, \tilde{x}_t) = tv \qquad \text{for } k \geq 0.$$

c. For the model of part (b) exhibit $\check{\mathbf{x}}$.

d. Show for (b) that $\rho_{t-1,t+1 \cdot t} = 0$, where partial correlation is defined in exercise 23.

27. Let $\tilde{\boldsymbol{z}} = [\tilde{z}_1 \tilde{z}_2 \ldots \tilde{z}_n]^t$ have a variance matrix that has constant value down the main diagonal and another constant value off the main diagonal, that is,

$$\check{z}_{ii} = a \qquad \text{for all } i,$$

and

$$\check{z}_{ij} = b \qquad \text{for all } i \neq j.$$

a. Show that $\rho_{ij} = b/a$, if $i \neq j$.

b. Show that $\rho_{i,j \cdot k} = b/(a+b)$, if i, j, k are distinct.

c. If $\tilde{T} \equiv \sum_{i=1}^{n} \tilde{z}_i$ is a constant, i.e., $V(\tilde{T}) = 0$, then show

$$b = \frac{a}{n-1}.$$

d. Show that $a < b(n-1)$ is impossible.

28. A certain rv $\tilde{m}$ is Normal with mean M and variance V. The conditional distribution of $\tilde{\boldsymbol{y}}$ given that $\tilde{m} = m$ is Normal with mean $[m \ldots m]^t$ and variance $v\mathbf{I}$.

a. Find the mean and variance of the distribution of $\tilde{\boldsymbol{y}} = [\tilde{y}_1 \ldots \tilde{y}_n]^t$.

b. Is $\tilde{\boldsymbol{y}}$ marginally Normal?

29. Suppose that $\tilde{\boldsymbol{z}} = [\tilde{z}_1 \tilde{z}_2 \tilde{z}_3 \tilde{z}_4]^t$ is Normally distributed and

i. $\tilde{z}_1$ has mean 14 and variance 25,

ii. $\tilde{z}_2 | z_1$ has mean $z_1 + 2$ and variance 9,

iii. $\tilde{z}_3$ and $\tilde{z}_4$ are conditionally independent given z_1 and z_2, each with mean $.8z_2 + 1$ and variance 2.25.

Find the mean and variance of $\tilde{\boldsymbol{z}}$.

30. Suppose that $\tilde{z}_1$ and $\tilde{z}_2$ are jointly Normal rv's with $E(\tilde{z}_1) = 10$, $E(\tilde{z}_2) = 11$, $V(\tilde{z}_1) = 3$, $V(\tilde{z}_2) = 3$, $V(\tilde{z}_1, \tilde{z}_2) = 2$. Suppose that, given $\tilde{z}_1 = z_1$ and $\tilde{z}_2 = z_2$, $\tilde{z}_3$ and $\tilde{z}_4$ are independent Normal rv's with $E(\tilde{z}_3|z_1, z_2) = z_2$, $E(\tilde{z}_4|z_1, z_2) = 0$, $V(\tilde{z}_3|z_1, z_2) = 2$, $V(\tilde{z}_4|z_1, z_2) = 2$.

    a. Give the mean and variance of $\tilde{\boldsymbol{z}} = [\tilde{z}_1 \tilde{z}_2 \tilde{z}_3 \tilde{z}_4]^t$.

    b. What is the distribution of $\tilde{\boldsymbol{z}}$?

    c. Is $\tilde{z}_3$ independent of $(\tilde{z}_1, \tilde{z}_2)$?

    d. Is $\tilde{z}_4$ independent of $(\tilde{z}_1, \tilde{z}_2, \tilde{z}_3)$?

    e. What is the conditional distribution of $\tilde{z}_1$ given $\tilde{z}_3 = 12$?

31. (*Multivariate Case of Exercise 6.*) Suppose $\tilde{\boldsymbol{z}} = [\tilde{\boldsymbol{z}}_1^t \tilde{\boldsymbol{z}}_2^t]^t$ is nonsingular multivariate Normal. Without using the results of section 22.3, show that

    a. $\check{\mathbf{z}}_{11}$ is nonsingular.

    b. $\tilde{\boldsymbol{z}}_1$ and $\tilde{\boldsymbol{z}}_2 - \check{\mathbf{z}}_{21}\check{\mathbf{z}}_{11}^{-1}\tilde{\boldsymbol{z}}_1$ are independent Normal rv's.

32. (*Singular Variance Matrix.*) Suppose that $\tilde{\boldsymbol{z}}$ is a $(r \times 1)$ rv, not necessarily Normal, that the first p rows of $\check{\mathbf{z}}$ are linearly independent, and that the remaining rows are linear combinations of these, so that $\check{\mathbf{z}}$ is of rank p. Partition $\check{\mathbf{z}}$ as

$$\check{\mathbf{z}} = \begin{bmatrix} \check{\mathbf{z}}_{11} & \check{\mathbf{z}}_{12} \\ \check{\mathbf{z}}_{21} & \check{\mathbf{z}}_{22} \end{bmatrix}, \quad \text{where} \quad \begin{matrix} \check{\mathbf{z}}_{11} \text{ is } (p \times p), \\ \check{\mathbf{z}} \text{ is } (r \times r). \end{matrix}$$

    Prove the following (each step is short and uses an earlier one):

    a. There is a matrix $\mathbf{b}$ such that

$$\check{\mathbf{z}} = \begin{bmatrix} \mathbf{I} \\ \mathbf{b} \end{bmatrix} [\check{\mathbf{z}}_{11} \quad \check{\mathbf{z}}_{12}].$$

    b. $V(\tilde{\boldsymbol{z}}_2 - \mathbf{b}\tilde{\boldsymbol{z}}_1) = \mathbf{0}$.

    c. There is a vector $\boldsymbol{a}$ such that $P(\tilde{\boldsymbol{z}}_2 = \boldsymbol{a} + \mathbf{b}\tilde{\boldsymbol{z}}_1) = 1$.

    d. Conversely, if $P(\tilde{\boldsymbol{z}}_2 = \boldsymbol{a} + \mathbf{b}\tilde{\boldsymbol{z}}_1) = 1$, then the rank of $\check{\mathbf{z}}$ is at most the dimension of $\boldsymbol{z}_1$.

    e. If $\check{\mathbf{z}}$ has rank p, then there are p elements of $\tilde{\boldsymbol{z}}$ such that the remainder are linear functions of these p with probability one, but fewer than p would not suffice.

33. Suppose that $\tilde{z}_1, \tilde{z}_2, \tilde{z}_3$ are jointly Normal and that $\tilde{z}_1$ and $\tilde{z}_2$ are independent marginally on $\tilde{z}_3$ and that $\tilde{z}_1$ and $\tilde{z}_3$ are independent marginally on $\tilde{z}_2$.

    a. Is $\tilde{z}_1$ independent of the pair $(\tilde{z}_2, \tilde{z}_3)$?

    b. What if joint Normality is not assumed?

34. Let $\tilde{z}$ be a scalar Normal rv and let $\tilde{\boldsymbol{y}} = \boldsymbol{a} + \mathbf{b}\tilde{z}$ where $\boldsymbol{a}$ and $\mathbf{b}$ are 2×1. Describe the distribution of $\tilde{\boldsymbol{y}}$.

35. Suppose that the real rv's $\tilde{z}_1$ and $\tilde{z}_2$ are not necessarily Normal but the regressions of $\tilde{z}_1$ on $\tilde{z}_2$ and of $\tilde{z}_2$ on $\tilde{z}_1$ are linear. Show that:

    a. The regression lines are given by (22.48).

    b. Both regression lines go through the point $(\bar{z}_1, \bar{z}_2)$.

    c. The regression line of $\tilde{z}_2$ on $\tilde{z}_1$ is more nearly horizontal and that of $\tilde{z}_1$ on $\tilde{z}_2$ more nearly vertical than the line

$$\frac{z_2 - \bar{z}_2}{\ddot{z}_2} = \pm \frac{z_1 - \bar{z}_1}{\ddot{z}_1}$$

    where the $+$ is to be used if $\rho \geq 0$, the $-$ if $\rho \leq 0$.

    These results may be compared with property 3 of section 22.3.4 and exercise 13.25.

36. Prove (22.36).

37. Prove (22.46).

38. Prove the assertion made in the middle of section 22.3.4, namely, that if the "best fit" minimizes the expectation of the squared vertical deviation, then the regression of $\tilde{z}_2$ on $\tilde{z}_1$ "fits best"; if, however, it minimizes the expectation of the squared horizontal deviation, then the regression of $\tilde{z}_1$ on $\tilde{z}_2$ "fits best."

39. Prove the assertion made in the last line of the first paragraph of section 22.4.3.

40. Prove properties 1, 3, and 4 of section 22.4.3.

41. Prove the equality contained in the last part of section 22.5.3, namely,

$$\frac{S(\tilde{\delta}) - S(\tilde{\delta}|z_i)}{S(\tilde{\delta})} = 1 - \sqrt{1 - \rho^2(\tilde{\delta}, \tilde{z}_i)}, \qquad i = 1, 2.$$

The following exercises give thumbnail sketches of several (mostly oversimplified) situations. In each case, unless otherwise stated, the exercise is to discuss how a decision maker might reasonably go about assigning a distribution for the relevant unknown quantities, under some reasonable assumption about the information at hand.

42. *Sales of a Product in Two (or More) Stores.* A company is deciding whether to market a new consumer product, and if so how to package and promote it. Some possible decisions are: do not market the product; market the product, packaging and promoting it in the way some vice president's spouse or secretary thinks most appealing; run an experiment of a size and design to be determined and do what seems best after the experiment. Typical experiments would involve many variables whose joint distribution would have to be assessed to determine the EVSI. Do not attempt now to discuss such an experiment in full, but let $\tilde{z}_1$ and $\tilde{z}_2$ be the long-run average sales of the product in two particular stores with particular packaging and promotion. Consider assessing the joint distribution of $(\tilde{z}_1, \tilde{z}_2)$ assuming no information about the stores except that they are of roughly the same size and type.

43. *Effect of Package Material on Sales.* In the same situation as the preceding exercise, let $\tilde{y}_1$ and $\tilde{y}_2$ be the long-run average nationwide sales of the product with a particular type of promotion and two package materials, say glass and tin. Consider assessing $(\tilde{y}_1, \tilde{y}_2)$.

44. *Demand Curve for Excursion Fare.* Harvard Student Agencies is considering offering a charter flight to Paris, leaving Boston the Saturday before Christmas and returning the Sunday after January 1. Their decision whether to do so and if so at what price depends on the demand that there would be at various prices. They have not previously offered winter charters, but last year they offered a group fare of \$319 on a regular flight on the corresponding days and obtained a group of 53. The only other relevant information is that their summer charters have carried 1,088, 1,208, 1,355, 1,447, and 1,563 passengers in the past five years, at various dates and rates, and the actual demand was a little higher. The average rate was about \$280 every summer and promotional methods remained essentially the same. The problem is to assess the distribution for the winter charter at prices from \$100 to \$280, assuming it is promoted in the same way that the group fare was promoted last year.

45. *Demand Curve for Light Bulbs.* A light bulb manufacturer is considering changing the price of light bulbs. His decision depends on how many he could sell at various prices.

46. *Effect of Level of Detailing on Urban and Rural Drug Sales.* A drug company is considering doubling its detailing (missionary selling to doctors) on a prescription drug. It can do so in urban areas only, rural areas only; both; or neither. An experiment is contemplated. The decision maker needs to assess the joint distribution of $\tilde{z}_1$

and $\tilde{z}_2$, the increase in sales that would result from doubling urban and rural detailing respectively. Currently 1/3 of attempts to contact urban doctors and 2/3 of attempts to contact rural doctors are successful. The only other information readily available is that another company increased overall sales of a similar drug 10% by doubling its detailing everywhere.

47. *Repeat and Switch Probabilities for a Drug.* A drug company has an unusually successful over-the-counter unadvertised headache remedy called Obecalp. It is considering making it into a proprietary drug with hardhitting promotion. Currently sales are small but increasing nicely and customer loyalty is unusually high. The probability of repeat is about .5; that is, of the people buying Obecalp at any given time, about one-half buy it again the next time they buy a headache remedy. The probability of repeat for a typical advertised product is about .25. Introducing advertising will change the image of Obecalp and may reduce its appeal to its present users, but it may turn Obecalp into a real success on a large scale rather than a real success on a small scale. The probability of repeat will presumably drop from .5, but perhaps not as low as .25, and the probability of use by a current nonuser will presumably increase greatly.

Supposing the company does promote Obecalp, let p_1 be the probability a person buying Obecalp on one occasion will buy it again on the next and let p_2 be the probability a person buying some other drug on one occasion will buy Obecalp on the next. That is, p_1 is the conditional probability that a person buying a headache remedy will buy Obecalp given that the last time he bought a headache remedy he bought Obecalp, and p_2 is the probability he will buy Obecalp given that he bought something else last time. From p_1 and p_2 and certain reasonable assumptions, it is possible to calculate what sales would be if Obecalp were promoted. To make rational decisions, however, the decision maker must assess a joint distribution of $\tilde{p}_1$ and $\tilde{p}_2$. Of course, one could assess the distribution of sales directly, but it is more natural, especially in view of the information available, to assess $\tilde{p}_1$ and $\tilde{p}_2$.

48. *True Value and Bias.* Suppose observations or measurements can be made on a quantity whose "true value" is ξ. Let μ be the long-run average that would be obtained in an infinite number of observations or measurements with the observation or measurement process in its present condition. The bias $\beta \equiv \mu - \xi$ is assumed to be fixed as long as the observation or measurement process remains "in its present condition," but may vary from one set of conditions to the next.

Can you think of a situation in which it would be natural to assign distributions directly to $\tilde{\mu}$ and $\tilde{\beta}$? To $\tilde{\xi}$ and $\tilde{\beta}$? What if $\tilde{\xi}$ is unemployment in the target population and $\tilde{\mu}$ is unemployment in a repeatedly sampled population? What if $\tilde{\xi}$ is the actual fraction of Democratic votes for some office in some year and $\tilde{\mu}$ is the fraction of some sampled population who would have responded "Democratic" if drawn into the sample?

Can you think of a situation in which $\tilde{\beta}$ might be judged to be independent of $\tilde{\mu}$? Independent of $\tilde{\xi}$? What about selection or nonresponse bias in a sample?

Can you think of a situation in which it would be natural to assess $\tilde{\mu}$ and $\tilde{\beta}$ directly but $\tilde{\xi}$ and $\tilde{\beta}$ independent?

49. *Job Times in PERT.* In complicated scheduling problems the program evaluation and review technique (PERT) approach requires assessing of the distribution of the length of time that will be required for each "task" or "activity" involved in the problem. Assuming that these times are independent, it is then possible to compute the distribution of the time required to complete all the tasks under any particular schedule. Comment on the method actually used to assess any particular task or activity, which is as follows: Someone knowledgeable about the particular task specifies a "most likely" value z_m, an "optimistic" value z_0, and a "pessimistic" value z_p for the elapsed time z that the task will require. Then $\tilde{z}$ is assigned a distribution with mean $(z_0 + 4z_m + z_p)/6$ and range (z_0, z_p) arising by linear transformation from a beta distribution with variance 1/36. That is, $(\tilde{z} - z_0)/(z_p - z_0)$ is assigned a beta distribution with mean $(z_p + 4z_m - 5z_0)/6(z_p - z_0)$ and variance 1/36, and therefore with parameters r, n determined by

$$\frac{r}{n} = \frac{z_p + 4z_m - 5z_0}{6(z_p - z_0)} = \frac{1}{6} + \frac{2}{3}\frac{z_m - z_0}{z_p - z_0},$$

$$\frac{r(n-r)}{n^2(n+1)} = \frac{1}{36}.$$

Note that z_m is not the mode of the resulting distribution of $\tilde{z}$.

The concepts of "optimistic," "most likely," and "pessimistic" elapsed times have to be explicated for the person who will specify them. Various definitions have been suggested, but definitions representing a useful consensus in the opinion of R. W. Miller (1962, p. 95) are as follows:

Optimistic: An estimate of the minimum time an activity will take, a result that can be obtained only if unusual good luck is experienced and everything "goes right the first time."

Most likely: An estimate of the normal time an activity will take, a result that would occur most often if the activity could be repeated a number of times under similar circumstances.

Pessimistic: An estimate of the maximum time an activity will take, a result that can occur only if unusually bad luck is experienced. It should reflect the possibility of initial failure and fresh start, but should not be influenced by such factors as "catastrophic events"—strikes, fires, power failures, and so on—unless these hazards are risks inherent in the activity.

50. *Life Expectancy of Men and Women.* Decision problems concerning retirement insurance plans require the assessment of the probability distribution of the average age at which people now aged 65 will die. Typical problems involve the averages for men and women separately, and their individual and joint prior distributions are needed. Average discounted age should really be used, but neglect discounting because it is hard to think about an average discounted age and because available data concern average age without discounting.

Let the life expectancy of men and women now 65 be $\tilde{z}_1$ and $\tilde{z}_2$ respectively. Discuss assessment of the joint distribution of $(\tilde{z}_1, \tilde{z}_2)$ in each of the following situations.

a. You have only the information that in 1950 the life expectancy at age 65 for men and women combined was 13.83 years while in 1850 it was 11.10 years.

b. You have only the information that in 1950 the life expectancy at 65 for men alone was 12.38.

c. You have only the information that in 1950 the life expectancy at 65 was 12.38 for males and 15.28 for females.

Note Insurance mortality tables give as the life expectancy of people now 65 a kind of composite average that involves the ages at death of people who were 65 at various years in the past and that is adjusted downward ("enriched") considerably as a safety margin. However, the hypothetical life expectancies given above for any calendar year are to be interpreted as the average time until death of people turning 65 in the calendar year in question. (The average for any calendar year cannot be exactly known until everyone who was 65 that year has died, but on reasonable assumptions it is essentially known when most have died.)

51. The Imprint Printing Company is considering putting out a special calendar featuring a recently deceased public figure. The calendars would cost \$.75 apiece to print and distribute, over and above a setup cost of \$25,000. Unsold calendars will be worthless. The relation of demand to the price charged by Imprint is unknown, but it has been decided that there is a "true" relationship representable to an adequate approximation as

"true demand" $= \alpha - \beta p$

where p is price in dollars and α and β are parameters that are unfortunately unknown. The joint distribution of $\tilde{\alpha}$ and $\tilde{\beta}$ has been assessed as jointly Normal with

$E(\tilde{\alpha}) = 50{,}000, \qquad E(\tilde{\beta}) = 12{,}000,$

$V(\tilde{\alpha}) = (10{,}000)^2, \qquad V(\tilde{\beta}) = (3{,}000)^2, \qquad \rho = -0.5,$

where ρ is the correlation between $\tilde{\alpha}$ and $\tilde{\beta}$. It is considered that the actual demand will differ from the "true demand" by a "random error" e:

actual demand = "true demand" + e

where $\tilde{e}$ is independent of $(\tilde{\alpha}, \tilde{\beta})$ and Normal with $E(\tilde{e}) = 0$, $V(\tilde{e}) = (1{,}000)^2$.

a. What is the distribution of actual demand at a price of $2.00?

b. If it is decided to put out the calendar at a price of $2.00, how many should be printed to maximize expected monetary value?

c. What is the expected profit in (b) if this is done?

d. What price should be chosen to maximize expected monetary value?

52. The Reverend Thomas Bayes preaches every Sunday in an unheated church. Two of his parishioners claim to be weather experts and each has a theory that leads to a forecast distribution of the Sunday maximum temperature. On January 19, 1991, Parishioner A's forecast for Sunday, January 20, is Normal with mean 28 and standard deviation 5, while B's is Normal with mean 34 and standard deviation 5 (all in degrees Fahrenheit). The Reverend is evenhanded (he doesn't favor either parishioner in the absence of evidence) and simpleminded (he can't conceive that both theories could be wrong). He needs to forecast the temperature to decide how many layers of underwear to put on.

a. What are the mean and variance of his forecast distribution?

b. What should his forecast be

i. for squared error loss?

ii. for absolute error loss?

iii. if the loss is u times the error for underestimates (he sweats) and $2u$ times the error for overestimates (he shivers)?

c. If the temperature turns out to be 32, what faith should he put in Parishioner A thereafter?

d. If history repeats itself on the next weekend (same forecasts, same temperature), what faith should he then put in Parishioner A?

e. In (d), if the forecasts for January 27 were made on January 19 rather than January 26, would the answer be affected? Why or why not?

53. Let X_i be an observation drawn from a Normal process $N(\mu_i, 1)$ for each $i = 1, 2, \ldots$. Let the μ_i in turn be drawn from a Normal process $N(\theta, \sigma^2)$ with known σ^2. Let θ have a flat prior distribution. The μ_i are not observed.

a. What is the joint distribution of $X_1, X_2, X_3, \mu_1, \mu_2, \mu_3$ given θ?

b. Let $Y = (X_1 + \cdots + X_n)/n$. What is the distribution of Y given θ?

c. What is the distribution of θ given Y?

d. Show that $(X_1 - Y, \ldots, X_n - Y)$ is conditionally independent of Y given θ.

e. Show that the distribution of θ given $X_1, \ldots, X_n$ is the same as the distribution of θ given Y.

f. What is the distribution of μ_{n+1} given $X_1, \ldots, X_n$?

g. What is the distribution of X_{n+1} given $\mu_{n+1}, X_1, \ldots, X_n$?

h. Show that $E\{\mu_{n+1} | X_1, \ldots, X_{n+1}\} = (\sigma^2 X_{n+1} + Z)/(\sigma^2 + 1)$ where $Z = (X_1 + \cdots + X_{n+1})/(n + 1)$.

i. What is the distribution of μ_{n+1} given $X_1, \ldots, X_{n+1}$?

j. Which of Tversky and Kahneman's (in Kahneman, Slovic, and Tversky, 1982) heuristics and biases does this relate to and how?

23A Choosing the Best of Several Processes

23.1 Introduction, Definitions, and Assumptions

A classical problem in statistics is to choose the "best" of several "treatments"—for instance, the best of several different fertilizers; the best amount to use of a given fertilizer; the best of several package designs for a commercial product; the best of several educational methods; and so forth. Additional information concerning the "quality" of any one of the treatments can often be obtained by sampling, so that the decision maker must decide (1) how large a sample (if any) to take on each of the various treatments, and (2) which of the treatments to choose after the various sample outcomes are known. In this chapter, we shall see how any such problem may be solved formally, under certain Normality assumptions and the assumption of linear value, which are explained precisely in this section. We then obtain the posterior probability distribution in section 23.2. Terminal decisions are discussed in section 23.3, and the expected value of perfect information in section 23.4. In section 23.5 we turn to preposterior analysis and discuss how to obtain the expected value of sampling information, the expected net gain of sampling, and the optimal sample sizes. The chapter concludes with an example.

In accordance with the usual terminology for the assumptions to be made shortly, we shall use the word *process* to denote a treatment, such as a fertilizer or a particular amount of a fertilizer, a package design, or a teaching method, and we shall use the term *process mean* to denote, for instance, the true long-run average crop per acre, unit sales per store per month, or test score achieved by all students. We shall denote by r the total number of processes among which a choice is to be made, by μ_i the ith process mean, by a_i the act which consists of choosing the ith process, and by v_i the value of a_i ($i = 1, \ldots, r$).

Assume that utility is linear in value and that the value of a_i depends solely and linearly on μ_i:

$$v_i = v_t(a_i, \boldsymbol{\mu}) = K_i + k_i \mu_i, \qquad i = 1, \ldots, r. \tag{23.1}$$

Assume further that the prior distribution of

$$\tilde{\boldsymbol{\mu}} \equiv [\tilde{\mu}_1 \ldots \tilde{\mu}_r]^t \tag{23.2}$$

is *nonsingular Normal* with mean $\bar{\boldsymbol{\mu}}'$ and variance $\check{\boldsymbol{\mu}}'$.

Now suppose that it is possible to make observations on the ith process, for instance, by using the ith fertilizer on a number of experimental plots, by trying out the ith package in a number of experimental stores, or by using the ith teaching method on a number of pupils. Letting n_i denote the number of observations on the ith process and m_i the mean of these observations, assume that, given $\boldsymbol{\mu}$, the m_i are *independently Normal* with means and variances

$$E(\tilde{m}_i|\boldsymbol{\mu}) \equiv \mu_i, \qquad V(\tilde{m}_i|\boldsymbol{\mu}) = v_i/n_i, \qquad i = 1,\ldots,r, \tag{23.3}$$

where the process variances v_i are assumed known. Then we are in the situation of (22.28) with

$$\tilde{z}_1 = \tilde{\boldsymbol{\mu}}, \qquad \tilde{z}_2 = \tilde{\boldsymbol{m}} = [\tilde{m}_1 \ldots \tilde{m}_r]^t, \tag{23.4a}$$

$$\boldsymbol{a} = \boldsymbol{0}, \qquad \mathbf{b} = \mathbf{I}, \qquad \mathbf{c} = \begin{bmatrix} v_1/n_1 & & 0 \\ & \ddots & \\ 0 & & v_r/n_r \end{bmatrix} \tag{23.4b}$$

if all processes are sampled. Similar formulas apply when not all processes are sampled (exercise 9).

The conditional distribution assumption of (23.3) will be satisfied if the observations on each process form an independent Normal process and the "measurement errors" of the processes are independent of one another, that is, if the rv's

$$\tilde{\varepsilon}_{ij} = \tilde{z}_{ij} - \tilde{\mu}_i, \qquad i = 1,\ldots,r; \qquad j = 1,\ldots,n_i$$

are mutually independent and Normal with mean 0 and variance v_i, where $\tilde{z}_{ij}$ is the jth observation on the ith process. In this case posterior distributions may be considered conditional on all observations made. The conditional distribution assumption of (23.3) will also be satisfied to a sufficient approximation for practical purposes if the $\tilde{\varepsilon}_{ij}$ are mutually independent and if, for each process actually sampled, n_i is large enough to permit reliance on the central limit effect. In this case, however, posterior distributions must be considered conditional on the means m_i only. See also section 18.4.

23.2 Posterior Analysis

The posterior distribution of $\tilde{\boldsymbol{\mu}}$ can now be obtained by (22.29). It is nonsingular Normal with mean $\bar{\boldsymbol{\mu}}''$ and variance $\breve{\boldsymbol{\mu}}''$, which can be obtained by computing

$$\mathbf{H}' = \breve{\boldsymbol{\mu}}'^{-1}, \tag{23.5a}$$

$$\mathbf{H} = \begin{bmatrix} n_1/v_1 & & 0 \\ & \ddots & \\ 0 & & n_r/v_r \end{bmatrix}, \tag{23.5b}$$

$$\mathbf{H}'' = \mathbf{H}' + \mathbf{H}, \tag{23.5c}$$

$$\bar{\boldsymbol{\mu}}'' = \mathbf{H}''^{-1}(\mathbf{H}'\bar{\boldsymbol{\mu}}' + \mathbf{H}\boldsymbol{m}), \tag{23.5d}$$

$$\breve{\boldsymbol{\mu}}'' = \mathbf{H}''^{-1}. \tag{23.5e}$$

All the formulas (23.5) hold even if some processes are not sampled (exercise 9; the definition of m_i for unsampled processes will not affect $\bar{\boldsymbol{\mu}}''$, but may as well be taken to be 0).

23.3 Values as a RV; Terminal Analysis

If $\tilde{\mu}_i$ is treated as a rv, then $\tilde{v}_i$ as defined by (23.1) is a rv:

$$\tilde{v}_i = K_i + k_i\tilde{\mu}_i, \qquad i = 1,\ldots,r. \tag{23.6a}$$

Since the $\tilde{\mu}_i$ are jointly Normal and the $\tilde{v}_i$ are linear functions of the $\tilde{\mu}_i$, the $\tilde{v}_i$ are also jointly Normal, with

$$\bar{v}_i = \bar{v}_t(a_i) = K_i + k_i\bar{\mu}_i, \qquad i = 1,\ldots,r. \tag{23.6b}$$

$$V(\tilde{v}_i, \tilde{v}_j) = k_i k_j \breve{\mu}_{ij}, \qquad i,j = 1,\ldots,r. \tag{23.6c}$$

We may write this in matrix notation as

$$\tilde{\boldsymbol{v}} = \boldsymbol{K} + \mathbf{k}\tilde{\boldsymbol{\mu}}, \tag{23.6d}$$

$$\bar{\boldsymbol{v}} = \boldsymbol{K} + \mathbf{k}\bar{\boldsymbol{\mu}}, \qquad \breve{\mathbf{v}} = \mathbf{k}\breve{\boldsymbol{\mu}}\mathbf{k}^t, \tag{23.6e}$$

where the vectors in question are defined as usual and

$$\mathbf{k} = \begin{bmatrix} k_1 & & 0 \\ & \ddots & \\ 0 & & k_r \end{bmatrix}. \tag{23.6f}$$

In *terminal analysis* our sole objective is to find the act with the greatest expected value. Letting $\bar{\boldsymbol{\mu}}'$ denote the mean of the current distribution of $\tilde{\boldsymbol{\mu}}$, whether or not this distribution is posterior to some sample already taken, we have only to compute the corresponding $\bar{\boldsymbol{v}}'$ and select the process i' which maximizes $\bar{v}_i' = K_i + k_i\bar{\mu}_i'$. Thus we define i' by

$$\bar{v}_{i'}' = \max_i \bar{v}_i'. \tag{23.7}$$

If more than one i maximizes $\bar{v}_i'$, any maximizing i' may be chosen.

23.4 Expected Value of Perfect Information

If we choose process i' because it maximizes expected value under our current distribution of $\tilde{\boldsymbol{\mu}}$ but some other treatment in fact has the greatest

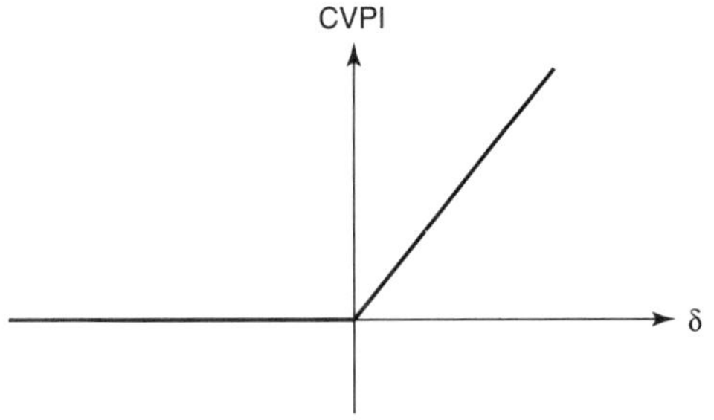

Figure 23.1A
Conditional value of perfect information (two processes)

value, we suffer an *opportunity loss* of amount equal to the difference between the value of treatment i' and the value of the act with the greatest value. This difference is therefore the conditional value of perfect information (CVPI)—the most we could *in hindsight* have afforded to pay for exact knowledge of all μ_i. We want now to evaluate the expectation of this loss or EVPI *before* we actually choose any process, since if the EVPI is large it is at least a strong indication that we might do better to get more information about $\boldsymbol{\mu}$ before making any terminal choice.

23.4.1 Formulation of CVPI

The value of the act with greatest value is

$$v_{\max} = \max\{v_1, \ldots, v_r\}. \tag{23.8}$$

The CVPI is the difference between this and the choice i' which *seems* best under the current distribution, that is,

$$\text{CVPI} = v_{\max} - v_{i'}. \tag{23.9}$$

If the process i' is *in fact* best, then $v_{i'} = v_{\max}$ and the CVPI $= 0$. If some other process is better than process i', then had we known $\boldsymbol{\mu}$ we would have chosen the process with the *greatest* superiority over process i' and the CVPI > 0.

The Case $r = 2$

If there are only two processes and

$$\bar{v}_2' = K_2 + k_2\bar{\mu}_2' > K_1 + k_1\bar{\mu}_1' = \bar{v}_1',$$

then $i' = 2$ and choice of process 2 will result in an opportunity loss of

$$\text{CVPI} = \begin{cases} 0 & \text{if} \quad v_1 \le v_2, \\ \delta = v_1 - v_2 & \text{if} \quad v_1 > v_2. \end{cases}$$

The CVPI is graphed as a function of δ in figure 23.1A.

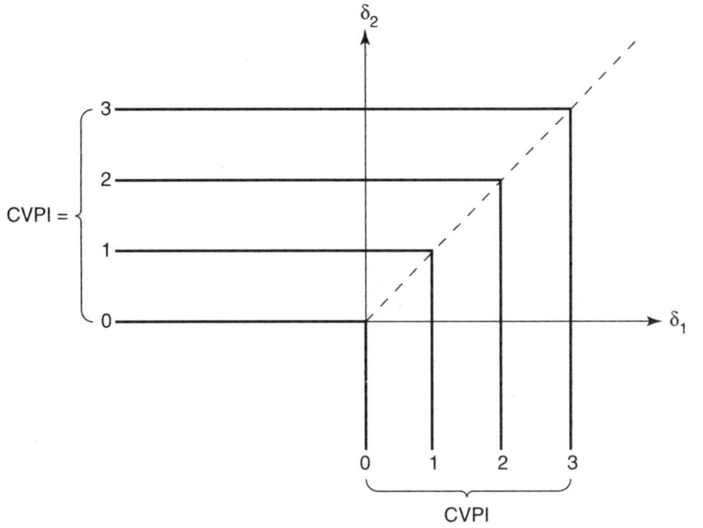

Figure 23.2A
Conditional value of perfect information, contours (three processes)

The Case of $r = 3$

(Optional.) If there are three processes and $\bar{v}'_3$ is greater than either $\bar{v}'_1$ or $\bar{v}'_2$, then $i' = 3$ and choice of process 3 will result in an opportunity loss or

$$\text{CVPI} = \begin{cases} 0 & \text{if} \quad v_1 \text{ and } v_2 \text{ both} \le v_3, \\ \delta_1 \equiv v_1 - v_3 & \text{if} \quad v_1 \ge \text{both } v_2 \text{ and } v_3, \\ \delta_2 \equiv v_2 - v_3 & \text{if} \quad v_2 \ge \text{both } v_1 \text{ and } v_2. \end{cases}$$

The contours of constant CVPI are graphed in figure 23.2A, where the following facts should be observed: (1) CVPI is 0 everywhere in the third quadrant (where both δs are negative, implying that v_3 is greater than both v_1 and v_2). (2) CVPI is equal to δ_2 everywhere in the second quadrant and in half of the first (where δ_2 is both positive and greater than δ_1, implying that v_2 is greater than both v_1 and v_3). (3) In the fourth quadrant and the other half of the first, the previous statement applies with subscripts 1 and 2 interchanged.

23.4.2 Computation of EVPI by Monte Carlo

By the definition of (23.9) of the CVPI given any particular $\boldsymbol{v}$, the EVPI is

$$\text{EVPI} = E[\tilde{v}_{\max} - \tilde{v}_{i'}] = E[\max_i \tilde{v}_i - \tilde{v}_{i'}], \tag{23.10}$$

where the expectation is with respect to the distribution of $\tilde{\boldsymbol{v}}$, which is Normal with mean and variance given by (23.6). We can therefore Monte Carlo the EVPI by the following procedure.

1. Find a $\boldsymbol{\beta}$ such that $\boldsymbol{\beta}\boldsymbol{\beta}^t = \check{\mathbf{v}}' = \mathbf{k}\check{\boldsymbol{\mu}}'\mathbf{k}^t$;

2. Generate a sequence $\boldsymbol{u}^{(1)}, \ldots, \boldsymbol{u}^{(j)}, \ldots$ of unit spherical Normal vectors each consisting of as many independent scalar Normal numbers as $\boldsymbol{\beta}$ has columns;

3. For each $\boldsymbol{u}^{(j)}$ compute the corresponding

$$\boldsymbol{v}^{(j)} = \bar{\boldsymbol{v}}' + \boldsymbol{\beta}\boldsymbol{u}^{(j)};$$

4. For each $\boldsymbol{v}^{(j)}$ compute the corresponding CVPI which we denote by

$$x_j = \max_i v_i^{(j)} - v_{i'}^{(j)}.$$

5. Thinking of the CVPI computed at the jth stage as the jth x drawn from a population of xs, from time to time use *all x's drawn to date* to make the estimates

$$x_* = \frac{1}{n}\textstyle\sum_j x_j \qquad \text{of the population mean (EVPI),}$$

$$s^2 = \frac{1}{n-1}\textstyle\sum_j (x_j - x_*)^2, \qquad \text{of the population variance,}$$

$$s^2/n \qquad \text{of the variance of } \tilde{x}_*.$$

6. Stop when s^2/n is "small enough."

Note Since $E[\tilde{v}_{\max} - \tilde{v}_{i'}] = E[\tilde{v}_{\max}] - \bar{v}_{i'}$, one could evaluate $E[\tilde{v}_{\max}]$ by Monte Carlo, instead of $E[\tilde{v}_{\max} - \tilde{v}_{i'}]$. This would eliminate the subtraction at the fourth step. Actually, it is even better to Monte Carlo the distribution of the $r-1$ differences $\tilde{\delta}_i = \tilde{v}_i - \tilde{v}_{i'}$, $i \neq i'$.

23.4.3 Analytical Evaluation of EVPI When $r = 2$

When there are only two processes, it is possible to evaluate EVPI analytically, and this is easier than Monte Carlo. If $\bar{v}_2' > \bar{v}_1'$, so that $i' = 2$, then we superimpose the distribution of $\tilde{\delta} = \tilde{v}_1 - \tilde{v}_2$ on figure 23.1A, obtaining figure 23.1B. We leave it to the student to prove (exercise 8a) that

$$\text{EVPI} = \ddot{\delta}' L_{N^*}(D'), \tag{23.11a}$$

where

$$\ddot{\delta}'^2 = \check{\delta}' = k_1^2\check{\mu}_{11}' + k_2^2\check{\mu}_{22}' - 2k_1k_2\check{\mu}_{12}', \tag{23.11b}$$

$$D' = |\bar{\delta}'/\ddot{\delta}'| = |\bar{v}_1' - \bar{v}_2'|/\ddot{\delta}'. \tag{23.11c}$$

If $\bar{v}_1' < \bar{v}_2'$, so that $i' = 1$, formula (23.11) still holds, as it remains the same when 1 and 2 are interchanged.

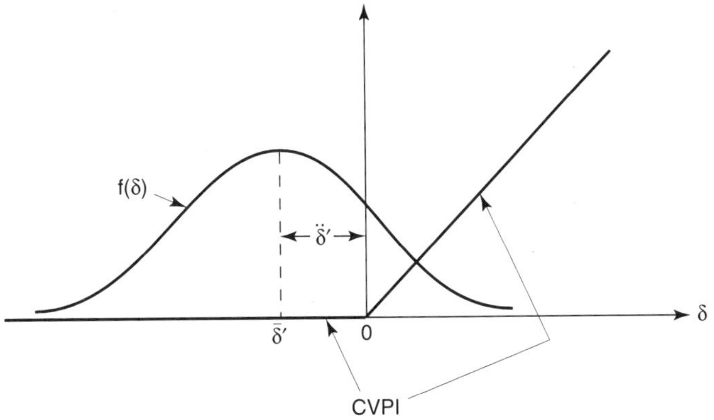

Figure 23.1B
CVPI and probability density (two processes)

23.4.4 Bounds on the EVPI When $r > 2$

(Note: this subsection is optional.) When $r > 2$ the exact EVPI cannot be calculated analytically, but we can obtain upper and lower bounds analytically. Letting

$$\tilde{\delta}_i = \tilde{v}_i - \tilde{v}_{i'}, \qquad i = 1, \ldots, r, \tag{23.12}$$

and noting that $\delta_{i'} = 0$, we have by (23.10) that

$$\text{EVPI} = E[\max_i \tilde{\delta}_i] = E[\max_i \max\{\tilde{\delta}_i, 0\}]. \tag{23.13}$$

It follows at once that a *lower* bound is provided by

$$\text{EVPI} \geq \max_i E[\max\{\tilde{\delta}_i, 0\}], \tag{23.14a}$$

while an *upper* bound is provided by

$$\text{EVPI} \leq E[\max\{\tilde{\delta}^1, 0\}] + E[\max\{\tilde{\delta}_2, 0\}] + \cdots + E[\max\{\tilde{\delta}_r, 0\}]. \tag{23.14b}$$

These bounds are analytic inasmuch as

$$E[\max\{\tilde{\delta}_i, 0\}] = \ddot{\delta}_i' L_{N*}(D_i'), \qquad i \neq i', \tag{23.15a}$$

where

$$\ddot{\delta}_i'^2 = \check{\delta}_i' = k_i^2 \check{\mu}_{ii}' + k_{i'}^2 \check{\mu}_{i'i'} - 2k_i k_{i'} \check{\mu}_{ii'}, \tag{23.15b}$$

$$D_i' = -\bar{\delta}_i'/\ddot{\delta}_i' = (\bar{v}_{i'} - \bar{v}_i)/\ddot{\delta}_i', \qquad i \neq i'. \tag{23.15c}$$

Note that $\bar{v}_{i'} - \bar{v}_i \geq 0$ by definition and that $E[\max\{\tilde{\delta}_{i'}, 0\}] = 0$.

The meaning of these two formulas will perhaps be clearer if we look at the case $r = 3$, $i' = 3$, as shown in figure 23.2B, where the density contours

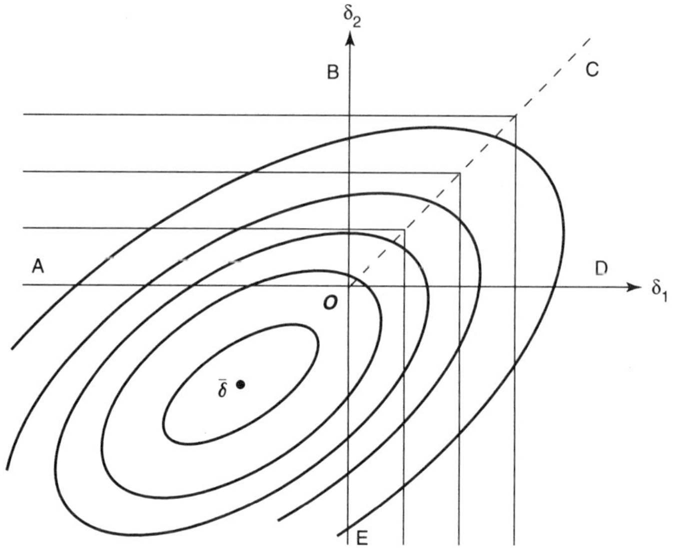

Figure 23.2B
CVPI and probability density contours (three processes)

of $\tilde{\delta}_1, \tilde{\delta}_2$) are superimposed on the loss contours of figure 23.2A. Recall that $\tilde{\delta}_3 = 0$ if $i' = 3$. From the figure we observe that:

1. The *exact* EVPI is obtained according to (23.13) by adding the (partial) expectation of $\tilde{\delta}_2$ over the region AOC and the expectation of $\tilde{\delta}_1$ over the region COE.

2. The quantity $E \max\{\tilde{\delta}_1, 0\}$ is the expectation of $\tilde{\delta}_1$ over the entire half plane to the right of the δ_2 axis and is less than the EVPI by the sum of (1) the expectation of $\tilde{\delta}_2$ over the region AOB and (2) the expectation of $(\tilde{\delta}_2 - \tilde{\delta}_1)$ over the region BOC. The quantity $E \max\{\tilde{\delta}_2, 0\}$ is similarly less than the EVPI, so that (23.14a) clearly provides a lower bound.

3. On the other hand, (23.14b) exceeds the EVPI by the sum of (1) the expectation of $\tilde{\delta}_1$ over BOC and (2) the expectation of $\tilde{\delta}_2$ over COD.

23.5 The Distribution of $\tilde{\bar{v}}''$ and EVSI

Suppose now that we are free but not obliged to perform a single experiment (or an additional experiment) before making any definitive choice of process, and suppose that this experiment would consist in taking n_1 observations on process 1, n_2 on process 2, and so on. Relative to this proposed new experiment our current distribution of $\tilde{\mu}$ will be called a prior distribution with mean and variance $\bar{\mu}'$ and $\breve{\mu}'$, even though this distribution may be posterior to some experiment already performed; double-primed quantities will refer to the posterior distribution of $\tilde{\mu}$ that will result from the new experiment if it is performed.

23.5.1 Formulation of the CVSI

As before, let process i' be the one having the greatest expected value under the *prior* distribution of $\tilde{\mu}$,

$$\bar{v}'_{i'} = \max_i \bar{v}'_i. \tag{23.16}$$

If the experiment is conducted, resulting in a vector of sample means $\boldsymbol{m} = [m_1, \ldots, m_n]^t$, this will modify the prior distribution of $\tilde{\mu}$ into a posterior distribution and will thereby modify each $\bar{v}'_i$ into a generally different $\bar{v}''_i$. It is possible that the outcome $\boldsymbol{m}$ will be such that process i' still seems best, that is,

$$\bar{v}''_{i'} = \max_i \bar{v}''_i;$$

if so the experiment has been valueless because the same process would have been chosen and the same value achieved if the experiment had never been performed. It is also possible, however, that the outcome $\boldsymbol{m}$ will be such that one or more $\bar{v}''_i$ are greater than $\bar{v}''_{i'}$; if so, we will switch our choice to the best of these, process i'' where i'' is defined by

$$\bar{v}''_{i''} = \max_i \bar{v}''_i; \tag{23.17}$$

and the experiment will have increased our expected value by the difference $\bar{v}''_{i''} - \bar{v}''_{i'}$. This difference is therefore the conditional value of the sample information or CVSI given the particular sample outcome $\boldsymbol{m}$. Thus we have

$$\text{CVSI} = \bar{v}''_{i''} - \bar{v}''_{i'} = \bar{v}''_{\max} - \bar{v}''_{i'}. \tag{23.18}$$

Comparing (23.18) with (23.9) we see that *the CVSI function is formally identical to the CVPI function.* Graphs of CVSI when $r = 2$ and 3 and $i' = r$ can be obtained from figures 23.1 and 23.2 respectively by simply relabelling them CVSI instead of CVPI and changing the definitions to $\delta = \bar{v}''_1 - \bar{v}''_2$, $\delta_1 = \bar{v}''_1 - \bar{v}''_3$, $\delta_2 = \bar{v}''_2 - \bar{v}''_3$.

23.5.2 Computation of EVSI

Since we are evaluating the experiment *before* it is performed, its outcome $\tilde{\boldsymbol{m}}$ is a rv, consequently the $\tilde{\bar{v}}''$ which it will produce is a rv, and consequently the CVSI as given by (23.18) is a rv. Notice that both $\tilde{\bar{\boldsymbol{v}}}''$ and $\tilde{i}''$ are random. What we need in order to evaluate the experiment before it is performed is the (prior) *expected value* of the CVSI or

$$\text{EVSI} \equiv E[\tilde{\tilde{v}}''_{\max} - \tilde{\tilde{v}}''_{i'}] \equiv E[\max_i \tilde{\tilde{v}}''_i - \tilde{\tilde{v}}''_{i'}], \tag{23.19}$$

and in order to compute this expected value we must first obtain the distribution of $\tilde{\tilde{\mathbf{v}}}''$.

By (23.6e), $\tilde{\tilde{\mathbf{v}}}''$ is a linear transformation of $\tilde{\tilde{\boldsymbol{\mu}}}''$. By section 22.3.2, (22.29), and (23.5), $\tilde{\tilde{\boldsymbol{\mu}}}''$ is Normal with

$$E(\tilde{\tilde{\boldsymbol{\mu}}}'') = \bar{\boldsymbol{\mu}}', \qquad V(\tilde{\tilde{\boldsymbol{\mu}}}'') = \breve{\boldsymbol{\mu}}' - \breve{\boldsymbol{\mu}}'' = \mathbf{H}''^{-1}\mathbf{H}\breve{\boldsymbol{\mu}}'. \tag{23.20}$$

It follows immediately that $\tilde{\tilde{\mathbf{v}}}''$ is Normal with

$$E(\tilde{\tilde{\mathbf{v}}}'') = \boldsymbol{K} + \mathbf{k}\bar{\boldsymbol{\mu}}' = \bar{\mathbf{v}}', \tag{23.21a}$$

$$V(\tilde{\tilde{\mathbf{v}}}'') = \mathbf{k}(\breve{\boldsymbol{\mu}}' - \breve{\boldsymbol{\mu}}'')\mathbf{k}^t = \mathbf{k}\mathbf{H}''^{-1}\mathbf{H}\breve{\boldsymbol{\mu}}'\mathbf{k}^t. \tag{23.21b}$$

Given these results the EVSI can be computed with respect to the distribution of $\tilde{\tilde{\mathbf{v}}}''$ in exactly the same way that EVPI can be computed with respect to the distribution of $\tilde{\mathbf{v}}$, as can bounds like those in section 23.4.4.

23.5.3 Sampling Some of the Processes

Sections 23.5.1 and 23.5.2 apply whether or not samples are taken from all of the r processes. If samples are to be taken from only $p < r$ of the r processes, we see by (23.5d) that the distribution of $\tilde{\tilde{\boldsymbol{\mu}}}''$ is *singular* Normal, being confined to a p-dimensional subspace of the r-dimensional space on which a point $\boldsymbol{\mu}$ is defined. The mean and variance of $\tilde{\tilde{\boldsymbol{\mu}}}''$ and $\tilde{\tilde{\mathbf{v}}}''$ are still given by (23.20) and (23.21), however, and we can still find a $\boldsymbol{\beta}$ such that $\boldsymbol{\beta}\boldsymbol{\beta}^t = V(\tilde{\tilde{\mathbf{v}}}'')$. The only difference singularity makes in the Monte Carlo procedure for evaluating the EVSI is that $\boldsymbol{\beta}$ can be chosen to have only p columns and the unit-spherical Normal random variables that must be generated will therefore consist of only p independent scalar Normal numbers.

23.5.4 ENGS and Optimal Sample Sizes

If the sampling and terminal costs are additive, then the expected net gain of sampling is the EVSI minus the expected cost of sampling. The ENGS is a function of the sample sizes $n_1, n_2, \ldots, n_r$. The optimal sample sizes are, of course, those which maximize the ENGS. In general they cannot be obtained analytically but only by search. This is true even if the sampling cost is linear, say

$$\sum K_{si} + k_{si} n_i, \tag{23.22}$$

where the sum is over those i for which $n_i > 0$. Note that for each set of sample sizes tried in the search, to obtain the ENGS, the EVSI must first be computed, by Monte Carlo in general.

If there are only two processes and the sampling cost is linear, then the optimal sample sizes and optimal ENGS can be obtained analytically, as we shall see in chapter 23C. In the case of an arbitrary number of processes and linear sampling costs, one can search using a computer program that includes the Monte Carlo evaluation of the EVSI.

23.6 A Numerical Example

A chemical manufacturer wishes to choose one of three possible processes for producing a certain product; the criterion of choice is to be expected monetary profit. The chosen process will definitely be used for one year, after which the entire question will be examined again; accordingly, the manufacturer wishes any investments in fixed assets required by the choice of process to be considered as expense in this year. If process A is used, it will be possible to produce 110 batches during the year, with materials and labor costing \$500 per batch; for process B, the corresponding figures are 100 batches at \$600 per batch; for process C, 90 batches at \$700 per batch. Processes B and C require no equipment not already available, but if process A is used, it will be necessary to invest \$7,500 in a special mixer. The product sells for \$1 per pound. Ten pilot-plant experiments have been conducted on each of the three processes in order to determine their yields; the means of the indicated yields are 950 lbs./batch for process A, 1,000 for B, and 1,150 for C. Management feels that in comparison with this experimental evidence all other information concerning the yields is of negligible weight. Further experiments can be conducted at a cost of \$100 each for process A, \$110 for B, and \$120 for C. Letting x denote the yield of a single experimental trial multiplied by a factor converting it into an estimate of the yield of a batch of full production size, these experiments have indicated that the standard deviation of $\tilde{x}$ is 50 lbs./batch for any one of the three processes. The experiments are considered to be unbiassed in the sense that the average of $\tilde{x}$ over an infinite number of experiments on any process would be equal to the full-scale mean yield of that process.

Since management wishes to treat its outside or judgmental information as negligible in comparison with the experimental results already obtained, we have as the expected yields per batch of the three processes

A: 950,

B: 1,000,

C: 1,150.

From these we can compute the expected profits:

$$\begin{aligned} &\text{A:}\quad 110(\$950 - \$500) - \$7{,}500 = \$42{,}000,\\ &\text{B:}\quad 100(\$1{,}000 - \$600) \qquad\qquad = 40{,}000,\\ &\text{C:}\quad 90(\$1{,}150 - \$700) \qquad\qquad\;\; = 40{,}500. \end{aligned}$$

Defining

$\mu_1 \equiv$ yield of process A,

$\mu_2 \equiv$ yield of process B,

$\mu_3 \equiv$ yield of process C,

we are now ready to formalize the statement of the problem in the framework of this chapter. With all monetary amounts in units of \$100, the economic structure is described by (23.1) with $r = 3$ and

$$K_1 = -110 \times 5 - 75 = -625, \qquad k_1 = 1.1,$$

$$K_2 = -100 \times 6 = -600, \qquad k_2 = 1.0,$$

$$K_3 = -90 \times 7 = -630, \qquad k_3 = .9.$$

Regarding the data-generating process, we may treat as known for all practical purposes

$$\upsilon_1 = \upsilon_2 = \upsilon_3 = 50^2.$$

As regards the prior distribution of $\tilde{\boldsymbol{\mu}}$, we have already seen that

$$\bar{\boldsymbol{\mu}}' = [950 \quad 1{,}000 \quad 1{,}150]^t.$$

Since the manufacturer wishes to treat any judgmental information he may have as negligible in comparison with information obtained from the experiments already conducted, the marginal variance of each of the $\tilde{\mu}$s is simply $50^2/10 = 250$ and the covariances are all 0:

$$\breve{\boldsymbol{\mu}}' = \mathbf{H}'^{-1} = \begin{bmatrix} 250 & 0 & 0 \\ 0 & 250 & 0 \\ 0 & 0 & 250 \end{bmatrix}.$$

From these results we can compute (23.6b)

$$\bar{\upsilon}_1' = K_1 + k_1 \bar{\mu}_1' = 420,$$

$$\bar{\upsilon}_2' = K_2 + k_2 \bar{\mu}_2' = 400,$$

$$\bar{\upsilon}_3' = K_3 + k_3 \bar{\mu}_3' = 405,$$

results already obtained above.

Terminal Analysis

If the manufacturer is to choose one of the three processes without further experimentation, he will simply choose process 1 (that is, A) because it maximizes his expected monetary value. Thus $t' = 1$.

Bounds on the EVPI

To bound the EVPI by the method of section 23.4.4 we compute

$\check{\delta}'_2 = (1.0)^2 250 + (1.1)^2 250 - 0 = 552.5, \qquad \ddot{\delta}'_2 = 23.51,$

$\check{\delta}'_3 = (\ .9)^2 250 + (1.1)^2 250 - 0 = 505.0, \qquad \ddot{\delta}'_3 = 22.47;$

$D'_2 = (420 - 400)/23.51 = .8507, \qquad D'_3 = (420 - 405)/22.47 = .6676;$

$E[\max\{\tilde{\delta}_2, 0\}] = \ddot{\delta}'_2 L_{N^*}(D'_2) = 23.51 \times .1099 = 2.584,$

$E[\max\{\tilde{\delta}_3, 0\}] = \ddot{\delta}'_3 L_{N^*}(D'_3) = 22.47 \times .1509 = 3.391.$

Since $i' = 1$, $\delta_1 = 0$, and $E \max\{\tilde{\delta}_1, 0\} = 0$, so (23.14) becomes

$\text{EVPI} \geq \max\{2.584, 3.391\} = 3.391 \qquad (= \$339.10),$

$\text{EVPI} \leq 2.584 + 3.391 \qquad = 5.975 \qquad (= \$597.50).$

Since a single additional observation on just one of the three processes will cost from \$100 to \$120 depending on the process, it seems obvious that the expected net gain of further experimentation will almost certainly be negative for all possible experiments; at best it can be a negligible positive amount. The commonsense conclusion is to choose process 1 without further ado. The calculations in the remainder of this analysis are given solely for illustration.

By use of the Monte Carlo methods of 23.4.2 and 23.5.2, the following values were obtained.

EVPI = \$485;

$$\text{EVSI} = \begin{cases} \$163 & \text{for} \quad n_1 = 8,\ n_2 = 8,\ n_3 = 8, \\ \$201 & \text{for} \quad n_1 = 9,\ n_2 = 9,\ n_3 = 9, \\ \$220 & \text{for} \quad n_1 = 10,\ n_2 = 10,\ n_3 = 10, \\ \$225 & \text{for} \quad n_1 = 15,\ n_3 = 8,\ n_3 = 6. \end{cases}$$

If additional observations on process 1 cost \$4 each, on process 2 cost \$8 each, and on process 3 cost \$4 each, with no set-up costs, then a search program yields roughly optimal sample sizes

$n_1^o = 15, \qquad n_2^o = 8, \qquad n_3^o = 6$

and ENGS = \$85.

Exercises

1. a. Specialize section 23.2 to the case $r = 1$ and compare results with section 16.4.

   b. Specialize section 23.3 to the case where $\check{\boldsymbol{\mu}}'$ is diagonal and observe that each process can be handled separately or independently.

2. a. Let $\tilde{\boldsymbol{\mu}} = [\tilde{\mu}_1 \tilde{\mu}_2]^t$ be nonsingular Normal with mean and variance

$$\bar{\boldsymbol{\mu}}' = [10 \quad 13]^t,$$

$$\breve{\boldsymbol{\mu}}' = \begin{bmatrix} 20 & -14 \\ -14 & 10 \end{bmatrix}.$$

Given $\boldsymbol{\mu}$, assume that the jth drawing from the ith process is given by

$$\tilde{x}_{ij} = \mu_i + \tilde{\varepsilon}_{ij} \qquad \begin{matrix} i = 1, 2, \\ j = 1, 2, \ldots, \end{matrix}$$

where the $\tilde{\varepsilon}_{ij}$ are independent and Normally distributed, each with mean 0 and let

$$\breve{\varepsilon}_{ij} = \begin{cases} 0 \\ 16 \end{cases} \text{if} \quad \begin{matrix} i = 1 \\ i = 2 \end{matrix} \qquad \text{for all } j.$$

For these data, show that

$$\upsilon_1 = 9, \qquad \upsilon_2 = 16,$$

and that

$$\mathbf{H}' \equiv \breve{\boldsymbol{\mu}}'^{-1} = \begin{bmatrix} 2.5 & 3.5 \\ 3.5 & 5.0 \end{bmatrix}.$$

b. If $n_1 = 24$ and $n_2 = 36$ observations are taken from processes 1 and 2, respectively, show that given $\boldsymbol{\mu}$, the vector of sample means $\tilde{\boldsymbol{m}} = [\tilde{m}_1 \tilde{m}_2]^t$ is Normal with mean $\boldsymbol{\mu}$ and precision (inverse variance) $\mathbf{H}$ where

$$\mathbf{H} = \begin{bmatrix} 8/3 & 0 \\ 0 & 9/4 \end{bmatrix}.$$

c. For the $\mathbf{H}$ as given in (b) and the data of (a) compute the posterior variance and precision of $\tilde{\boldsymbol{\mu}}$. Observe that in this case these quantities depend on $\mathbf{H}$ and not on the observed $\boldsymbol{m}$. In particular, show that the posterior precision is given by

$$\mathbf{H}'' = \frac{1}{12}\begin{bmatrix} 62 & 42 \\ 42 & 87 \end{bmatrix}$$

and the posterior variance by

$$\mathbf{H}''^{-1} = \frac{12}{3630}\begin{bmatrix} 87 & -42 \\ -42 & 62 \end{bmatrix} = \begin{bmatrix} .29 & -.14 \\ -.14 & .20 \end{bmatrix}.$$

d. Verify that for the $\mathbf{H}$ as given in (b) the as yet unknown posterior mean $\tilde{\bar{\boldsymbol{\mu}}}''$ is nonsingular Normal with mean $\bar{\boldsymbol{\mu}}'$ and variance

$$V(\tilde{\bar{\boldsymbol{\mu}}}'') = \breve{\boldsymbol{\mu}}' - \breve{\boldsymbol{\mu}}'' = \begin{bmatrix} 19.71 & -13.86 \\ -13.86 & 9.80 \end{bmatrix}.$$

e. If the observed sample mean vector is $\boldsymbol{m} = [9 \quad 14]^t$ then show that the posterior distribution of $\tilde{\boldsymbol{\mu}}$ is Normal with mean

$$\bar{\boldsymbol{\mu}}'' = \mathbf{H}''^{-1}[\mathbf{H}'\bar{\boldsymbol{\mu}}' + \mathbf{H}\boldsymbol{m}]$$

$$= [9.0 \quad 13.1]^t.$$

3. a. In exercise 2, modify (b) so that $n_1 = 24$ and $n_2 = 0$—that is, observations are taken from only the first process. For this experimental design describe the preposterior distribution of $\tilde{\bar{\boldsymbol{\mu}}}''$.

b. If the mean of the sample is $m_1 = 9$, then find the posterior distribution of $\tilde{\boldsymbol{\mu}}$.

4. Let $\tilde{\boldsymbol{\mu}} = [\tilde{\mu}_1 \tilde{\mu}_2]^t$ be bivariate Normal with mean $\bar{\boldsymbol{\mu}}'$ and variance $\breve{\boldsymbol{\mu}} = [\breve{\mu}'_{ij}]$ where $\breve{\mu}'_{12} = \breve{\mu}'_{21} \neq 0$. A sample with mean vector $\tilde{\boldsymbol{m}} = [\tilde{m}_1 \tilde{m}_2]^t$ is drawn in such a way that the conditional distribution of $\tilde{\boldsymbol{m}}$ given $\boldsymbol{\mu}$ is Normal with mean $\boldsymbol{\mu}$ and variance

$$V(\tilde{\boldsymbol{m}}|\boldsymbol{\mu}) = \begin{bmatrix} \sigma_1^2/n_1 & 0 \\ 0 & \sigma_2^2/n_2 \end{bmatrix}$$

where σ_1 and σ_2 are known. Letting ρ'' denote the *posterior* correlation between $\tilde{\mu}_1$ and $\tilde{\mu}_2$, show that $|\rho''|$ decreases as n_1 and n_2 increase and interpret this result.

5. a. For the case $r = 2$ (two processes) verify formulas (23.11).

b. Find the EVPI for the following numerical values

$$r = 2; \qquad \bar{\mu}'_1 = 90, \qquad \bar{\mu}'_2 = 100;$$

$$\breve{\boldsymbol{\mu}}' = \begin{bmatrix} 100 & 64 \\ 64 & 100 \end{bmatrix};$$

$$K_1 = -100, \qquad k_1 = 10; \qquad K_2 = -150; \qquad k_2 = 9.$$

6. a. Defining $\tilde{\delta}_i$ as in (23.12) prove formulas (23.15).

b. Discuss the justification of the step leading from (23.13) to (23.14a), namely:

$$E[\max_i \max\{\tilde{\delta}_i, 0\}] \geq \max_i E[\max\{\tilde{\delta}_i, 0\}].$$

c. For any numbers $\delta_1, \ldots, \delta_r$ argue that

$$\max\{\delta_1, \delta_2, \ldots, \delta_r\} \leq \max\{\delta_1, 0\} + \max\{\delta_2, 0\} + \cdots + \max\{\delta_r, 0\}.$$

and from this justify (23.14b).

d. Use (23.14) to find bounds for the EVPI for the following numerical values:

$$r = 3; \qquad \bar{\mu}'_1 = 100; \qquad \bar{\mu}'_2 = 80; \qquad \bar{\mu}' = 90;$$

$$\breve{\boldsymbol{\mu}}' = \begin{bmatrix} 225 & 0 & 144 \\ 0 & 100 & 0 \\ 144 & 0 & 225 \end{bmatrix};$$

$$K_1 = K_2 = K_3 = 0; \qquad k_1 = k_2 = k_3 = 1000.$$

7. a. Let $u_1, u_2, \ldots, u_r$ be independent Normal rv's each with mean 0 and variance 1. Let

$$\lambda_r \equiv E[\max\{u_1, u_2, \ldots, u_r\}].$$

The quantity $2\lambda_r$ is tabulated in Pearson and Hartley (1966, table 27) to 5 decimal places for $r = 2(1)500(10)1000$. Here are some values of λ_r:

r	2	3	4	5	10	50	100	1000
λ_r	.56419	.84628	1.02938	1.16297	1.86748	2.24907	2.50759	3.24143

For the problem under discussion in this chapter, show that if $\bar{v}'_1 = \cdots = \bar{v}'_r$ $(= d$ say$)$ and if $\breve{\mathbf{v}}' = a^2\mathbf{I}$ then

$$\text{EVPI} = a\lambda_r.$$

Hint In this case show that

$$\text{EVPI} = E[\max\{(\tilde{v}_1 - d), (\tilde{v}_2 - d), \ldots, (\tilde{v}_r - d)\}].$$

8. (*Alternate Derivation of the EVSI Formula*) Let $\mathbf{H}$ represent the experimental design and $\boldsymbol{m}$ the outcome of the experiment so that $(\boldsymbol{m}, \mathbf{H})$ sufficiently summarizes the sample results. Note that:

i. Given $(\boldsymbol{m}, \mathbf{H})$ the posterior expected payoff is

$$\max_i E_{v_i|\boldsymbol{m}, \mathbf{H}}(\tilde{v}_i) = \max_i \bar{v}''_{i|\boldsymbol{m}},$$

where we suppress the $\mathbf{H}$ from the abbreviated notation

$$\bar{v}''_{i|\boldsymbol{m}} \equiv E_{v_i|\boldsymbol{m}, \mathbf{H}}(\tilde{v}_i).$$

ii. Given $\mathbf{H}$, where $\tilde{\boldsymbol{m}}$ is as yet unknown, the prior expectation of the posterior expected payoff is

$$E_{\boldsymbol{m}|\mathbf{H}}\{\max_i \bar{v}''_{i|\tilde{\boldsymbol{m}}}\}.$$

iii. The prior expected payoff is $\bar{v}'_{i'}$, where i' is such that

$$\bar{v}'_{i'} \geq \bar{v}'_i \qquad \text{for all } i.$$

Show that the EVSI, which by definition is the difference between the prior expectation of the posterior expected payoff and the prior expected payoff, is given by

$$E_{\boldsymbol{m}|\mathbf{H}}[\max_i\{\bar{v}''_{i|\tilde{\boldsymbol{m}}} - \bar{v}''_{i'|\tilde{\boldsymbol{m}}}\}].$$

9. Instead of selecting the best of r processes, suppose the problem is to choose none or at most one of the r processes—the idea being that none of the processes would be chosen if it were known that $v_i \leq 0$ for all i. Is the model analyzed in this chapter flexible enough to handle this variation? If so, how?

10. a. In the case $r = 2$ suppose there is budgetary constraint on the amount to be spent for further sampling. In particular, suppose n_1 and n_2 must be chosen to satisfy the requirements

$$\text{(A)} \quad k_{s1}n_1 + k_{s2}n_2 = K_s^*, \qquad n_1 \geq 0, \qquad n_2 \geq 0,$$

where k_{s1}, k_{s2}, and K_s^* are prespecified. Show that the optimal allocation of sampling effort (for problem considered in this chapter) is to choose n_1 and n_2 satisfying (A) that minimizes the posterior variance of $\tilde{\delta} = \tilde{v}_1 - \tilde{v}_2$.

b. Show that the posterior variance of $\tilde{\delta}$ is given by

$$\frac{k_1^2 H''_{22} + 2k_1k_2H'_{12} + k_2^2 H''_{11}}{H''_{11}H''_{22} - H'^2_{12}}$$

where

$$H''_{11} = H'_{11} + H_{11} \quad \text{and} \quad H''_{22} = H'_{22} + H_{22}.$$

Remark In chapter 23C on stratified sampling we shall "solve" the analytical problem posed in this exercise.

11. Schlaifer (1956, chapter 32) discusses the problem of the comparison of two unknown quantities. In his text, however, the machinery for a full bivariate Normal analysis is not developed. Using the notation of the present chapter, Schlaifer proceeds as follows: He puts independent priors on $\tilde{\mu}_1$ and $\tilde{\mu}_2$ and obtains from these a prior on

$$\tilde{\delta} \equiv \tilde{v}_1 - \tilde{v}_2 = k_1\tilde{\mu}_1 - k_2\tilde{\mu}_1 + (K_1 - K_2);$$

letting m_i represent the sample mean of n_i observations from the ith process ($i = 1, 2$), he considers the statistic (a scalar)

$$m \equiv k_1 m_1 - k_2 m_2.$$

(Observe that the sampling distribution of $\tilde{m}$ given δ is Normal with mean δ and with known variance.) Based on the statistic m (and not on m_1 and m_2 separately) he then obtains the posterior of $\tilde{\delta}$ given m.

What are the inadequacies, if any, of this procedure?

23B Allowance for Uncertain Bias

23.7 The Problem of Bias

23.7.1 Introduction

In chapter 16 we introduced the concept of a Normal process with known variance and learned how to revise a prior distribution of the process mean $\tilde{\mu}$ using the information contained in a sample from the process. We also discussed terminal and preposterior analysis of three prototypical decision problems concerning $\tilde{\mu}$. In chapters 17 and 18 we saw that even when the process variance is unknown and the process is not Normal, we can still apply the results of chapter 16 to exploit the information contained in the *mean* of a sample provided that both the size of the sample and the number of degrees of freedom underlying the estimate of the process variance are large enough.

Unfortunately, there are few decision problems in which consequences depend *directly* on the process mean μ of a data-generating process. As a good example of the kind of *indirect* dependence that actually occurs in practice, consider a sample survey done to learn how much the average household spends per week on some class of products. An individual z_i in such a problem is the figure given by an individual respondent, μ can be interpreted as the mean of all the z_is which would be obtained by trying to interview one member of every household in the United States, and clearly μ is *not* the figure of real interest to the decision maker who is paying for the survey. What he wants to know is how much the average household *really* spends, where μ is what the average respondent *would say* the household spends; it would be most remarkable if these two averages happened to be exactly equal.

In situations of this kind, both the correct interpretation of a sample and the correct analysis of whether or not a sample is worth taking obviously depend on how uncertain the relation is between the quantity really of interest, which we shall call ξ from now on, and the quantity measurable with only "random" error, which we have already named μ. We shall therefore develop in this chapter methods for analyzing decision problems in which consequences depend on ξ and not on μ.

23.7.2 Informal Model of a Measuring Process

For clarity, we shall begin our discussion of bias by considering, not a relatively complex example of the kind just suggested, but a very simple example involving physical measurements. After presenting the required concepts, we shall show how to apply them to the apparently more complex problems in which we are primarily interested.

Consider therefore some simple physical measuring process (e.g., calipering or titration) and imagine that it could be used to make an *infinite number of measurements* of a *single, fixed quantity* (e.g., the length of a particular block of metal or the acidity of a particular lot of reagent) under *conditions* that are *fixed* in the sense that there is no apparent reason why any one particular measurement should be greater or less than any other particular measurement. Define

ξ: true value of quantity being measured,

z_i: value of the ith measurement,

μ: average of all the measurements.

Systematic Error or Bias

Experience tells us that we should expect in general that the *process mean* μ will *not* be equal to the *true value* ξ but will differ from it by some amount

$$\beta \equiv \mu - \xi \tag{23.23}$$

which is usually called the *systematic error* or *bias* of the measuring *process*. In many situations this systematic error will depend not only on the inherent characteristics of the measuring process as such but also on the conditions (operator, temperature, etc.) under which it is used. Saying that a set of measurements are made under constant conditions amounts therefore to saying that β is constant during any one set of measurements even though it may vary from set to set; this basic assumption (or better, definition) applies throughout our discussion.

Random Error

Experience also tells us that in general each *individual measurement* z_i will differ from the process mean μ by an amount

$$\varepsilon_i \equiv z_i - \mu \tag{23.24}$$

which is usually called the *random error* of the individual *measurement*. Because ε_i is defined as the difference between z_i and the long-run average μ of all z_is made under the same conditions, we have at once that

$$E(\tilde{\varepsilon}_i) = 0 \quad \text{for all } i, \tag{23.25}$$

by definition. We shall also make the assumption throughout that the random errors $\tilde{\varepsilon}_i$ are *independent* with *identical* distributions that *do not depend on* ξ or β. In particular, the variance of the $\tilde{\varepsilon}_i$ is assumed not to depend on ξ or β; it will be denoted by

$$V(\tilde{\varepsilon}_i) = v \quad \text{for all } i. \tag{23.26}$$

23.7.3 The Formal Model

The heuristic discussion above motivates the following formal statement. We shall in this chapter consider processes generating rv's $\tilde{z}_1, \ldots, \tilde{z}_i, \ldots$ according to the model

$$\tilde{z}_i = \xi + \beta + \tilde{\varepsilon}_i \qquad i = 1, 2, \ldots, \tag{23.27a}$$

where ξ and β are parameters and the $\tilde{\varepsilon}_i$ are iid with mean and variance

$$E(\tilde{\varepsilon}_i) = 0, \qquad V(\tilde{\varepsilon}_i) = \upsilon, \tag{23.27b}$$

which do not depend on ξ or β.

Observe that the model asserts that any measurement is the *sum* of (1) the "true value" of the quantity being measured, (2) the systematic error or bias of the measuring process, and (3) the random error of the individual measurement. Observe also in particular that the difference $z_i - \xi$ between a measurement and the true value does *not* enter the model *directly*.

23.7.4 Other Applications of the Model

Exactly the same model can be applied when ξ is not the true value of a single distinct physical entity but the average of a number of individual "true values." As an example, let ξ be the true consumption of instant coffee by the average U.S. household during the past year, let z_i be the response obtained when the ith household is drawn by some sampling process and one of its members is asked how much instant coffee the household consumed during the past year, and let μ denote the mean of an infinite number of z_is obtained by sampling in this manner "with replacement" (i.e., allowing the same household to be drawn more than once and simply using the previously obtained response over again each time the household is drawn.) Clearly an individual z_i will in general differ from the mean μ of all the z_is by some amount ε_i due purely to "sampling fluctuation"; and equally clearly the long-run average μ will almost certainly differ from the true mean consumption ξ by some amount β due to (1) systematic imperfections in the process by which individual households are drawn, (2) incorrect statements by those who respond, and (3) a possible difference between consumption in households where a response can be obtained and consumption in households where no response can be obtained.

The reader is urged to pay very particular attention to one point in this last example. The *true* consumption of an *individual* household does *not* enter the model explicitly. The only reference to true consumption is to the true average ξ across all households. Similarly the model makes no explicit reference to what in other contexts we might call the "response error," namely the difference between what the respondent says the household consumed and what the household actually consumed. The *systematic* error or bias $\beta = \mu - \xi$ contains the average of all such errors but it also contains much more (namely, discrepancies due to nonresponse and to imperfections in the sampling as such). Similarly the *random error* ε_i contains much more than the respondent's variable inexactitude, since it is the difference between the one response and the average of all responses.

23.7.5 Preview of the Chapter

Our first objective is to solve the following basic problem of statistical inference. After assigning a prior distribution to the true value $\tilde{\xi}$ and the bias $\tilde{\beta}$ and after observing the values of n rv's generated by the process, how should the decision maker revise the prior distribution? In particular, what is the posterior distribution of $\tilde{\xi}$? This is discussed in section 23.9. Once the posterior distribution of $\tilde{\xi}$ has been found, it is straightforward to find the optimal terminal act after observation.

Our second main objective is to find the optimal sample size to observe. A necessary preliminary is preposterior distribution theory, which is discussed in section 23.10. Then, in section 23.11, we discuss optimal sample size in our three prototypical decision problems.

In this chapter we shall also discuss situations in which it is possible to make not only biased observations, as above, but also unbiased observations, presumably at greater cost. Since the probability analysis is not appreciably simplified by assuming only biased observations are available, we shall allow from the outset for the possibility that unbiased observations may also be available. When we first come to economic analysis, however, in section 23.11, we shall consider only biased observations. Then, in section 23.12, we shall discuss optimal sample sizes when both biased and unbiased observations are available.

23.8 Probability Assumptions

23.8.1 Prior Distribution

Let ξ be the loss determining quantity, let β be the bias of a measuring process, and let $\mu = \xi + \beta$. We shall suppose that the decision maker's joint prior distribution for $\tilde{\xi}$ and $\tilde{\mu}$ can be adequately represented by a bivariate Normal distribution. If $(\tilde{\xi}, \tilde{\beta})$ or $(\tilde{\mu}, \tilde{\beta})$ is bivariate Normal, then so is $(\tilde{\xi}, \tilde{\mu})$, and the means and variances of the three pairs are simply related (exercise 1).

Under bivariate Normality, the prior distribution of $(\tilde{\xi}, \tilde{\mu})$ is determined by the prior means $\bar{\xi}'$ and $\bar{\mu}'$, the prior variances $\breve{\xi}'$ and $\breve{\mu}'$, and the prior covariance of $\tilde{\xi}$ and $\tilde{\mu}$, which we shall denote V'_{12}.

23.8.2 Conditional Sampling Distribution

We shall sometimes suppose that it is possible to observe a process with process mean ξ and process variance υ_1. Let m_1 be the sample mean of n_1 such unbiased observations. We shall always suppose that it is possible to observe another process with process mean $\mu = \xi + \beta$ and process variance υ_2. Let m_2 be the sample mean of n_2 such biased observations. A situation where only biased observations are available can be described simply by requiring that $n_1 = 0$. Similarly $n_2 = 0$ if observations are made only on the unbiased process. For the moment we permit but do not require either $n_1 = 0$ or $n_2 = 0$. We shall not bother to mention certain modifications of the assumptions which are appropriate if $n_1 = 0$ or $n_2 = 0$ either by choice or by necessity.

We assume first that each process variance υ_i can be treated as known. In effect, this means we must have available an estimate of υ_i based on enough degrees of freedom to allow us to treat this estimate as if it were the true value of υ_i. For an indication of the condition under which this assumption is legitimate, we refer the reader to the discussion of chapter 17.

Second, we assume for each process either that it is Normal or that its sample mean may be treated as Normal by virtue of the central limit effect. More specifically, we assume that the conditional distribution of $\tilde{m}_1$ given ξ may be treated as Normal with mean ξ and variance υ_1/n_1 and that the conditional distribution of $\tilde{m}_2$ given μ may be treated as Normal with mean μ and variance υ_2/n_2. Our posterior distributions and decision rules exploit all the information in the observations on a process if the process is Normal, but only the information in the sample mean if the central limit effect is being relied on. In either case, the posterior distribution is conditional on m_1 and m_2. If either process is Normal, conditioning on the actual observations from that process would not change the posterior distribution, nor would taking them into account change the optimal terminal decision or sample size.

Our final assumption is that the two processes are independent of each other in the sense that the conditional distribution of the observations from one process given the process mean would not be altered by knowledge of either the observations from the other process or the other process mean (or both). Equivalently, we assume that the "measurement errors" of the two processes are mutually independent, even between processes, and collectively independent of $(\tilde{\xi}, \tilde{\mu})$. This implies that (1) the conditional distribution of $\tilde{m}_1$ given (ξ, μ) is the same as the conditional distribution given ξ; (2) the conditional distribution of $\tilde{m}_2$ given (ξ, μ) is the same as its conditional distribution given μ; and (3) $\tilde{m}_1$ and $\tilde{m}_2$ are conditionally independent given (ξ, μ). It follows from this and the assumption of the previous paragraph that given (ξ, μ), the rv's $\tilde{m}_1$ and $\tilde{m}_2$ are independent and Normal with means ξ and μ and variance υ_1/n_1 and υ_2/n_2 respectively.

We point out that even if only biased observations are possible, we need implication (2) for the analysis to follow. That is, if we know the process mean μ, then the distribution of the biased observations is assumed unaltered by knowledge of the true value ξ in addition.

The following illustration of a situation in which the two processes are *not* independent of each other may clarify the aspect of the final assumption that is particularly relevant to implication (3). Let ξ be the average amount per U.S. household actually spent on new automobiles in a certain calendar year; let the ith biased measurement be the response obtained when the ith household is drawn by some sampling process and the head of the household is asked about buying intentions; and let the ith unbiased measurement be the amount actually spent by the *same* household, obtained by careful checking at the end of the year. However great the systematic error, or bias, may be, one may expect and would certainly not want to exclude the possibility that responses above the average response tend to be accompanied by spending above the average spending. If the two processes consist of measurements made on the same "sampling units," the analysis of this chapter will not apply. This does not mean it is a poor idea to make measurements of this kind. In fact, it may be an excellent idea; however, a different analysis will be required.

23.8.3 Summary of Probability Assumptions

We assumed in section 23.8.1 that the prior distribution of $(\tilde{\xi}, \tilde{\mu})$ is bivariate Normal with mean and variance

$$E\begin{bmatrix} \tilde{\xi} \\ \tilde{\mu} \end{bmatrix} = \begin{bmatrix} \bar{\xi}' \\ \bar{\mu}' \end{bmatrix}, \qquad V\begin{bmatrix} \tilde{\xi} \\ \tilde{\mu} \end{bmatrix} = \begin{bmatrix} \breve{\xi}' & V'_{12} \\ V'_{12} & \breve{\mu}' \end{bmatrix}. \tag{23.28}$$

The assumptions of section 23.8.2 imply that the conditional distribution of (m_1, m_2) given (ξ, μ) is bivariate Normal with mean and variance

$$E\left(\begin{bmatrix} \tilde{m}_1 \\ \tilde{m}_2 \end{bmatrix} \middle| \begin{bmatrix} \xi \\ \mu \end{bmatrix}\right) = \begin{bmatrix} \xi \\ \mu \end{bmatrix}, \qquad V\left(\begin{bmatrix} \tilde{m}_1 \\ \tilde{m}_2 \end{bmatrix} \middle| \begin{bmatrix} \xi \\ \mu \end{bmatrix}\right) = \begin{bmatrix} \upsilon_1/n_1 & 0 \\ 0 & \upsilon_2/n_2 \end{bmatrix}. \tag{23.29}$$

Notice that we are in the situation of (22.28) with

$$\tilde{z}_1 = [\tilde{\xi} \quad \tilde{\mu}]^t, \qquad \tilde{z}_2 = \tilde{\boldsymbol{m}} = [\tilde{m}_1 \quad \tilde{m}_2]^t, \tag{23.30a}$$

$$\boldsymbol{a} = \boldsymbol{0}, \qquad \mathbf{b} = \mathbf{I} \qquad \mathbf{c} = \begin{bmatrix} v_1/n_1 & 0 \\ 0 & v_2/n_2 \end{bmatrix}. \tag{23.30b}$$

The last two sentences hold if $n_1 > 0$ and $n_2 > 0$. If n_1 or n_2 is 0, similar but simpler formulas apply.

23.9 Posterior Distributions

Under the foregoing assumptions, the posterior distribution of $\tilde{\xi}$ and $\tilde{\mu}$ can be obtained by (22.35). Specifically, compute

$$\mathbf{H}' = \begin{bmatrix} H'_{11} & H'_{12} \\ H'_{12} & H'_{22} \end{bmatrix} = \begin{bmatrix} \breve{\xi}' & V'_{12} \\ V'_{12} & \breve{\mu}' \end{bmatrix}^{-1}, \tag{23.31a}$$

$$\mathbf{H} = \begin{bmatrix} n_1/v_1 & 0 \\ 0 & n_2/v_2 \end{bmatrix}, \tag{23.31b}$$

$$\mathbf{H}'' = \mathbf{H}' + \mathbf{H} = \begin{bmatrix} H'_{11} + n_1/v_1 & H'_{12} \\ H'_{12} & H'_{22} + n_2/v_2 \end{bmatrix}. \tag{23.31c}$$

Then $\tilde{\xi}$ and $\tilde{\mu}$ have a jointly Normal posterior distribution with mean and variance

$$\begin{bmatrix} \bar{\xi}'' \\ \bar{\mu}'' \end{bmatrix} = \mathbf{H}''^{-1}\left(\mathbf{H}'\begin{bmatrix} \bar{\xi}' \\ \bar{\mu}' \end{bmatrix} + \mathbf{H}\boldsymbol{m}\right), \tag{23.32a}$$

$$\mathbf{V}'' \equiv \begin{bmatrix} \breve{\xi}'' & V''_{12} \\ V''_{12} & \breve{\mu}'' \end{bmatrix} = \mathbf{H}''^{-1}, \tag{23.32b}$$

where V''_{12} is the posterior covariance of $\tilde{\xi}$ and $\tilde{\mu}$.

The joint distribution of $\tilde{\xi}$ and $\tilde{\mu}$ is useful for preposterior analysis of contemplated further samples, but for terminal decision on the basis of the present sample, only the marginal posterior distribution of $\tilde{\xi}$ is needed, since $\tilde{\xi}$ is Normal with mean and variance (exercise 2)

$$\bar{\xi}'' = \bar{\xi}' + \frac{1}{\det \mathbf{H}''}\left[\frac{n_1}{v_1} H''_{22}(m_1 - \bar{\xi}') - \frac{n_2}{v_2} H'_{12}(m_2 - \bar{\mu}')\right], \tag{23.33a}$$

$$\breve{\xi}'' = \frac{H''_{22}}{\det \mathbf{H}''} = \frac{1}{H''_{11} - H''^{-1}_{22} H'^{2}_{12}}, \tag{23.33b}$$

where

$$\det \mathbf{H}'' = H''_{11} H''_{22} - H'^{2}_{12}. \tag{23.34}$$

All these formulas hold even if $n_1 = 0$ or $n_2 = 0$ or both (exercise 3). The optimal terminal decision is simply that decision whose expected loss is least under the posterior distribution of $\tilde{\xi}$. The posterior expected loss can also be computed from the posterior distribution of $\tilde{\xi}$ only.

23.10 Preposterior Distributions

Suppose the sample sizes n_1 and n_2 have been prescribed but the sample means m_1 and m_2 are as yet unknown. Then $\tilde{m}_1$ and $\tilde{m}_2$ are rv's, and under the assumptions we have made, by the theory of section 22.3.2 and section 22.3.3, the marginal joint distribution of $(\tilde{m}_1, \tilde{m}_2)$ is Normal. Its mean and variance are given in exercise 4.

Consider next the expressions (23.32) for the posterior mean and variance of $(\tilde{\xi}, \tilde{\mu})$; all quantities in these expressions are known except $\tilde{\boldsymbol{m}} = [\tilde{m}_1 \tilde{m}_2]^t$. In particular, the posterior variance is known. Furthermore, the posterior mean $(\tilde{\bar{\xi}}'', \tilde{\bar{\mu}}'')$ is a linear function of $\tilde{\boldsymbol{m}}$, so its preposterior distribution is joint Normal (exercise 5).

The marginal joint distribution of $\tilde{\boldsymbol{m}}$ or of $(\tilde{\bar{\xi}}'', \tilde{\bar{\mu}}'')$ would be needed for problems involving more than one possible stage of sampling. At present, however, we are contemplating at most one stage of sampling, to be followed by a terminal decision. As pointed out in the previous section, only the marginal posterior distribution of $\tilde{\xi}$ is relevant to this terminal decision. Accordingly, for preposterior analysis, all we need is the prior (or "preposterior") distribution of the parameters of the posterior distribution of $\tilde{\xi}$. These parameters are $\bar{\xi}''$ and $\check{\xi}''$, given by (23.33). As already pointed out, $\check{\xi}''$ is known, and the distribution of the as yet unknown $\tilde{\bar{\xi}}''$ is Normal with mean and variance

$$E(\tilde{\bar{\xi}}'') = \bar{\xi}', \qquad V(\tilde{\bar{\xi}}'') \equiv \check{\bar{\xi}}'' = \check{\xi}' - \check{\xi}''. \tag{23.35}$$

These formulas are easily obtained by the second method used in the proof in section 16.6.3.

23.11 Economic Analysis, Biased Sampling Only

23.11.1 Preliminaries

We suppose in this section that observations are available on only one process, and that this process is biased. Specifically, we assume that we are in the situation discussed heretofore but that $n_1 = 0$ of necessity. The case of an unbiased process is a degenerate special case arising when $\tilde{\mu} = \tilde{\xi}$, and the reader should check that the results obtained agree with those of chapter 16 in this case.

As usual, we shall consider problems in which the loss, whose expectation we seek to minimize, is decomposable into a terminal loss plus a linear sampling cost. Specifically, we assume that the loss is

$$l_t(a, \xi) + c_s(n_2) \tag{23.36a}$$

where

$$c_s(n_2) = K_{s2} + k_{s2}n_2 \quad \text{if} \quad n_2 > 0, \tag{23.36b}$$

and $c_s(0) = 0$. We shall consider the three prototype decision problems: infinite-action with quadratic loss, infinite-action with linear loss, and two-action with linear value. Since $\tilde{\xi}$ is Normal at the time of decision, whether before or after sampling, the choice of optimal act is given by chapter 16 with ξ in place of μ. We shall therefore omit the choice of optimal act here.

The problem of preposterior analysis is to choose n_2. Since by (23.31c),

$$H''_{22} = H'_{22} + n_2/\upsilon_2, \qquad n_2 = \upsilon_2(H''_{22} - H'_{22}), \tag{23.37}$$

choosing a value of n_2 is equivalent to choosing a value of H''_{22}. In each problem we discuss, we shall give the optimal values of both n_2 and H''_{22}. Some derivations lead more immediately to the optimal H''_{22}, and use of H''_{22} sometimes simplifies the description as well. This is especially true in the next section, where both biased and unbiased observations are available.

23.11.2 The Infinite-Action Problem with Quadratic Loss

Let

$$l_t(a, \xi) = k_t(a - \xi)^2. \tag{23.38}$$

Then, as in section 16.8, the EVPI prior to observation is $k_t\breve{\xi}'$ while the EVPI posterior to observation is $k_t\breve{\xi}''$, so that the EVSI is $k_t(\breve{\xi}' - \breve{\xi}'')$ and the ENGS is

$$G(n_2) = k_t(\breve{\xi}' - \breve{\xi}'') - K_{s2} - k_{s2}n_2 \quad \text{if} \quad n_2 > 0, \tag{23.39}$$

and $G(0) = 0$. We shall show that the optimal choice of H''_{22} and n_2 is

$$H''^{o}_{22} = \frac{1}{H'_{11}}\left(|H'_{12}|\left[\frac{k_t}{k_{s2}\upsilon_2}\right]^{1/2} + H'^{2}_{12}\right), \tag{23.40a}$$

$$n^o_2 = \frac{1}{\breve{\mu}'}\left(|V'_{12}|\left[\frac{k_t\upsilon_2}{k_{s2}}\right]^{1/2} - \upsilon_2\right), \tag{23.40b}$$

provided (1) that n^o_2 as given by this formula is positive, or equivalently that $H''^{o}_{22} > H'_{22}$, and (2) that $G(n^o_2)$ as given by (23.39) is positive; if either condition fails, then the optimal sample size is 0.

Proof By (23.39)

$$\frac{dG(n_2)}{dn_2} = -k_t \frac{d\ddot{\xi}''}{dn_2} - k_{s2}. \tag{23.41}$$

Since $\ddot{\xi}''$, as given by (23.33b), depends on n_2 only through H''_{22} and H''_{22} is given by (23.37), we have that

$$\frac{d\ddot{\xi}''}{dn_2} = \frac{d\ddot{\xi}''}{dH''_{22}} \frac{dH''_{22}}{dn_2} = \frac{-H'^2_{12}}{(H''_{11}H''_{22} - H'^2_{12})^2} \frac{1}{\upsilon_2}. \tag{23.42}$$

Substituting this in (23.41) and using $H''_{11} = H'_{11}$, which follows from (23.31c) and the fact that $n_1 = 0$ here, we obtain by straightforward algebra the tentative optimal H''^o_{22} given by (23.40a). The corresponding formula for n^o_2 follows by (23.37) and more algebra. The remainder of the proof is left as an exercise (exercise 6).

23.11.3 The Infinite-Action Problem with Linear Loss

Let

$$l_t(a, \xi) = \begin{cases} k_u(\xi - a) & \text{if} \quad a \le \xi, \\ k_o(a - \xi) & \text{if} \quad a \ge \xi. \end{cases} \tag{23.43}$$

Then, as in section 16.9, the EVPI prior to observation is $k_t\ddot{\xi}'$ and the EVPI posterior to observation is $k_t\ddot{\xi}''$, where

$$k_t = (k_u + k_o) f_{N^*}(u_k), \tag{23.44a}$$

with u_k defined by

$$F_{N^*}(u_k) = \frac{k_u}{k_u + k_o}. \tag{23.44b}$$

Therefore the EVSI is $k_t(\ddot{\xi}' - \ddot{\xi}'')$ and the ENGS is

$$G(n_2) = k_t(\ddot{\xi}' - \ddot{\xi}'') - K_{s2} - k_{s2}n_2 \quad \text{if} \quad n_2 > 0, \tag{23.45}$$

and $G(0) = 0$. We shall show that setting the derivative of $G(n_2)$ equal to 0 gives the equation

$$H''^o_{22}(H'_{11}H''^o_{22} - H'^2_{12})^3 = \left(\frac{k_t H'^2_{12}}{2k_{s2}\upsilon_2}\right)^2. \tag{23.46}$$

The optimal choice of H''_{22} is the solution of H''^o_{22} of this equation and the optimal choice of n_2 is $n^o_2 = (H''^o_{22} - H'_{22})\upsilon_2$, provided (1) that this n^o_2 is positive, or equivalently that $H''^o_{22} > H'_{22}$, and (2) that $G(n^o_2)$ as given by (23.45) is positive; if either condition fails, then the optimal sample size is 0.
Note The rest of this subsection is optional.

Table 23.1
ψ as a function of x

x	.00	.01	.02	.03	.04	.05	.06	.07	.08	.09
.0	1.000	1.000	1.000	1.000	1.000	1.000	1.000	1.000	1.000	1.000
.1	1.000	1.000	1.000	1.000	.999	.999	.999	.999	.999	.999
.2	.998	.998	.998	.998	.997	.997	.997	.996	.996	.996
.3	.995	.995	.994	.994	.994	.993	.993	.992	.992	.991
.4	.990	.990	.989	.989	.988	.988	.987	.986	.986	.985
.5	.984	.984	.983	.983	.982	.981	.981	.980	.980	.979
.6	.978	.978	.977	.977	.976	.976	.975	.975	.975	.974
.7	.974	.973	.973	.973	.973	.973	.973	.973	.973	.973
.8	.973	.973	.973	.974	.974	.974	.975	.976	.977	.978
.9	.979	.980	.982	.983	.985	.987	.989	.991	.994	.997
1.0	1.000									

A computing aid for finding the tentative optima H''^{o}_{22} and n^{o}_{2} may be obtained as follows. It is easily verified by straightforward algebra that the quartic equation (23.46) may be put into the standard form

$$X^3(1 + dX) = 1 \tag{23.47}$$

by making the substitutions

$$H''^{o}_{22} = \frac{H'^2_{12}}{H'_{11}} + AX, \tag{23.48a}$$

$$d = \frac{H'_{11}}{H'^2_{12}} A = \left(\frac{\check{\mu}'\check{\xi}'}{V'^2_{12}} - 1\right)\check{\mu}' A, \tag{23.48b}$$

where

$$A = \left(\frac{k_t |H'_{12}|}{2k_{s2} v_2 H'_{11}}\right)^{2/3} = \left(\frac{k_t |V'_{12}|}{2k_{s2} v_2 \check{\mu}'}\right)^{2/3}. \tag{23.48c}$$

An approximate solution of (23.47) is

$$x = (1 + d)^{-1/4}. \tag{23.49}$$

Let us write the exact solution as

$$X = x\psi(x) \tag{23.50}$$

where $\psi(x)$ is a correction factor tabulated in table 23.1. Then the computing procedure is as follows.

1. Evaluate A by (23.48c) and d by (23.48b).
2. Evaluate x by (23.49) and $\psi(x)$ by table 23.1.

3. Evaluate X by (23.50) and the tentative optimum $H_{22}''^{o}$ by (23.48a) or the tentative optimum n_2^o by

$$n_2^o = \upsilon_2\left(AX - \frac{1}{\breve{\mu}'}\right). \tag{23.51}$$

Remarks The *definition* of the function $\psi(x)$ is that $X = x\psi(x)$, which satisfies (23.47) when d is related to x by (23.49), that is, when $d = x^{-4} - 1$. This means that $\psi(x)$ is defined by

$$x^3\psi^3(x) + (1 - x^4)\psi^4(x) = 1. \tag{23.52}$$

However, this is not useful for *tabulation* of $\psi(x)$. The tabulation was carried out by computing

$$\psi = (X^4 - X^3 + 1)^{1/4} \quad \text{and} \quad x = X/\psi \tag{23.53}$$

for various values of X and then interpolating to obtain ψ as a function of x. Equations (23.53) are obtained by simple algebra from (23.47), (23.49), and (23.50).

The approximation (23.49) is suggested by the following considerations. We are interested only in positive X, because of (23.48a) and the inequalities $A > 0$ and $H_{22}'' \geq H_{22}' \geq H_{12}'^2/H_{11}'$. (The last inequality follows from the positive-semidefiniteness of **H**.) There is just one positive solution X of (23.47) and this solution is a function of d with the following properties: X decreases from 1 to 0 as d increases from 0 to ∞; and $X \leq d^{-1/4}$ with approximate equality for large d, since $dX^4 \leq X^3(1 + dX) = 1$ with approximate equality for large d. A convenient function of d with these properties is $x = (1 + d)^{-1/4}$, which suggests the approximation (23.49).

It follows also that the correction factor ψ by which x must be multiplied to give the exact solution X of (23.47) is ≤ 1 and $= 1$ at $d = 0\,(x = 1)$ and at $d = \infty\,(x = 0)$. The correction factor could be tabulated as a function of d or of x; the latter is more convenient, mainly because it has range $[0, 1]$.

The reader may wonder why we did not tabulate directly the solution X of (23.47) in terms of d. One reason is that both d and X have wide ranges and this involves loss of accuracy when interpolating. A second reason is that the approach we did follow gives a reasonable approximation when the correction factor is omitted: this leads to an error in X and hence in $H_{22}''^{o} = H_{22}' + n_2/\upsilon_2$ of less than 3%, and the cost of irrationality of such an error is usually tiny.

Proof The equation (23.46) for the tentative optimum $H_{22}''^{o}$ is obtained by setting the derivative of $G(n_2)$ equal to zero. By (23.45)

$$\frac{dG(n_2)}{dn_2} = -k_t \frac{d\breve{\xi}''^{1/2}}{dn_2} - k_{s2} = -\tfrac{1}{2}k_t \breve{\xi}''^{-1/2} \frac{d\breve{\xi}''}{dn_2} - k_{s2}. \tag{23.54}$$

Substituting (23.42) and (23.33b) in (23.54) leads to (23.46) after a little algebra. The conditions under which the tentative optimum is a true optimum are left to exercise 7.

The justification of the computing procedure using table 23.1 has already been given, except for some algebra which we have left to the reader.

23.11.4 The Two-Action Problem with Linear Value

Let there be two available acts a_1 and a_2 with values

$$v_t(a_i, \xi) = K_i + k_i\xi, \qquad i = 1, 2, \quad k_1 \neq k_2, \tag{23.55}$$

and define

$$\xi_b \equiv \frac{K_1 - K_2}{k_2 - k_1}, \qquad k_t \equiv |k_2 - k_1|. \tag{23.56}$$

Then, as in section 16.10, the ENGS is

$$G(n_2) = k_t\sigma^* L_{N^*}(D^*) - K_{s2} - k_{s2}n_2 \quad \text{if} \quad n_2 > 0 \tag{23.57a}$$

where

$$\sigma^* \equiv S(\tilde{\bar{\xi}}'') = (\breve{\xi}' - \breve{\xi}'')^{1/2}, \tag{23.57b}$$

$$D^* \equiv \frac{|\bar{\xi}' - \xi_b|}{\sigma^*}. \tag{23.57c}$$

This can be proved either by imitating the proof in section 16.10.2 or by observing that the present problem is exactly the same as that of section 16.10 as regards EVSI. In particular, $\tilde{\xi}$ is Normal a priori and a posteriori, its posterior variance is not random, and its posterior mean $\tilde{\bar{\xi}}''$ is marginally Normal with mean $\bar{\xi}'$ and variance $\breve{\xi}'' - \breve{\xi}'$.

We want to maximize $G(n_2)$. It depends on n_2 through the variable sampling cost $k_{s2}n_2$ and through σ^* and D^*, which should perhaps have a subscript n_2. Now σ^{*2} can be seen by (23.33b) to be n_2 divided by a linear function of n_2, and D^* is a constant divided by σ^*. This was also the situation in section 16.10. Therefore the behavior of $G(n_2)$ and the analytical problem of maximizing it are essentially the same here as in section 16.10. It is merely a matter of relating the parameters of the two situations.

As n_2 increases from 0 to ∞, σ^* increases from 0 to

$$\sigma^*_\infty = [\breve{\xi}' - V'(\tilde{\xi}|\mu)]^{1/2} = \frac{V'_{12}}{\breve{\mu}'}; \tag{23.58}$$

also D^* decreases from ∞ to

$$D^*_\infty = \frac{|\bar{\xi}' - \xi_b|}{\sigma^*_\infty} = \frac{\breve{\mu}'}{V'_{12}}|\bar{\xi}' - \xi_b| \tag{23.59}$$

(except that if $\bar{\xi}' = \xi_b$ then $D^* = 0$ for all $n_2 > 0$); and the EVSI increases from 0 to

$$I(\infty) = k_t \sigma^*_\infty L_{N^*}(D^*_\infty). \tag{23.60}$$

The behavior of the ENGS $G(n_2)$ is as described in section 16.10 except that now

$$\lambda = \frac{|V'_{12}|\breve{\mu}' k_t}{\upsilon_2 k_{s2}}. \tag{23.61}$$

Reducing the analytical problem of maximizing $G(n_2)$ to the same standard form here as in section 16.10.4 is a matter of straightforward algebra, which gives

$$G(n_2) = \frac{k_{s2}\upsilon_2}{\breve{\mu}'} G^*(\rho) - K_s, \tag{23.62}$$

where

$$\rho = \frac{\breve{\mu}'}{\upsilon_2} n_2, \tag{23.63}$$

$$G^*(\rho) = \lambda\theta_\rho L_{N^*}(D^*_\infty/\theta_\rho - \rho), \quad \text{where} \quad \theta_\rho = \left(\frac{\rho}{\rho + 1}\right)^{1/2}. \tag{23.64}$$

This is the same function $G^*(\rho)$ that appeared in (16.58), so the tables described there apply here also. Specifically, compute D^*_∞ and

$$\Lambda = \log\lambda = \log|V'_{12}| + \tfrac{1}{2}\log\breve{\mu}' + \log k_t - \log\upsilon_2 - \log k_{s2}. \tag{23.65}$$

Then read the value of R from the table on pages 1 and 2 of table MT-9. A zero in the body of the table indicates that the optimal sample size is 0. Otherwise R is the logarithm of the maximizing ρ^o:

$$R = \log\rho^o. \tag{23.66}$$

Accordingly, the tentative optimum n_2^o can be computed by

$$n_2^o = \frac{\upsilon_2}{\breve{\mu}'}\,\text{antilog}\,R \tag{23.67}$$

The ENGS of a sample size n_2^o can be computed directly, but it is easier to use the table on pages 3 and 4 of MT-9. One can read from this table the value of

$$\Gamma = \log G^*(\rho^o), \tag{23.68}$$

and then compute

$$G(n_2^o) = \frac{k_{s2} v_2}{\breve{\mu}'} \text{antilog}\,\Gamma - K_s. \tag{23.69}$$

The optimal choice of n_2 is n_2^o provided that $G(n_2^o)$ is positive. Otherwise the optimal sample size is 0.

23.12 Economic Analysis, Biased and Unbiased Sampling

23.12.1 Preliminaries

We suppose in this section that observations are available on two processes, one biased and one unbiased. Specifically, we assume that the probability assumptions of section 23.8 are satisfied and that there is no restriction on the number n_1 of unbiased observations or the number n_2 of biased observations we may make. The posterior and preposterior distributions needed have already been obtained in sections 23.9 and 23.10.

As in section 23.11, we shall assume that the loss, whose expectation we seek to minimize, is decomposable into a terminal loss plus a sampling cost,

$$l_t(a, \xi) + c_s(n_1, n_2). \tag{23.70}$$

We shall suppose first that the cost of sampling is linear in the sample sizes and that there are no fixed (setup) costs, that is,

$$c_s(n_1, n_2) = k_{s1} n_1 + k_{s2} n_2. \tag{23.71}$$

The modification necessary when there are fixed costs of sampling will be discussed in section 23.12.6.

The problem of preposterior analysis is to choose n_1 and n_2. Since by (23.31c),

$$H''_{ii} = H'_{ii} + n_i/v_i, \qquad n_i = v_i(H''_{ii} - H'_{ii}), \qquad i = 1, 2, \tag{22.72}$$

choosing values of n_1 and n_2 is equivalent to choosing values of H''_{11} and H''_{22}. In each problem we discuss, we shall give the optimal values of both n_1, n_2 and H''_{11}, H''_{22}. The latter are more directly derived and permit somewhat simpler description of certain phenomena.

23.12.2 Optimal Allocation

Recall that the posterior distribution of the cost-determining parameter $\tilde{\xi}$ is Normal with mean $\bar{\xi}''$ and variance $\check{\xi}''$ given by (23.33). Before sampling, the posterior variance $\check{\xi}''$ is known, being determined by the sample sizes n_1 and n_2, but the posterior mean $\bar{\xi}''$ is not known and hence is a rv. By section 23.10, the distribution of $\tilde{\bar{\xi}}''$ before sampling is Normal with mean $\bar{\xi}'$ and variance $\check{\check{\xi}}'' = \check{\xi}' - \check{\xi}''$. We see, therefore, that the prior distribution of the posterior parameters depends on the sample sizes n_1 and n_2 only through $\check{\xi}''$.

A given $\check{\xi}''$ can be obtained by various combinations of n_1 and n_2. Whatever our decision problem and whatever $\check{\xi}''$ we use, we will clearly want to choose n_1 and n_2 to minimize the sampling cost $c_s(n_1, n_2)$ for this $\check{\xi}''$. The smaller $\check{\xi}''$ is, the larger the cost of obtaining it, so the minimum $c_s(n_1, n_2)$ will increase as $\check{\xi}''$ decreases. (See also exercise 8.) Therefore we may instead choose n_1 and n_2 to minimize $\check{\xi}''$ for a given sampling cost $c_s(n_1, n_2)$. This is more natural than the reverse procedure. Furthermore, the sampling budget is sometimes fixed by administrative considerations or fiat and $\check{\xi}''$ never is. In this subsection we shall therefore consider a fixed sampling budget and find the optimal allocation of this budget to n_1 and n_2 by minimizing $\check{\xi}''$. Once we have found those combinations of n_1 and n_2 that are efficient, that is, which minimize $\check{\xi}''$ for a given sampling cost and vice versa, we shall then turn to the problem of which efficient combination to use.

Notice that the optimal allocation depends only on the sampling cost function c_s and not on the terminal loss function l_t. The remaining optimization does depend on the terminal loss function, and will be carried out for our three prototypical decision problems in sections 23.12.3–23.12.5. The results on optimal allocation obtained here, however, apply regardless of the terminal loss function.

Consider, then, a fixed sampling budget

$$k_{s1} n_1 + k_{s2} n_2 = k^*. \tag{23.73a}$$

By (23.72), this is equivalent to

$$k_{s1} \upsilon_1 H''_{11} + k_{s2} \upsilon_2 H''_{22} = \text{constant}. \tag{23.73b}$$

Subject to this condition, we wish to minimize $\check{\xi}''$. By (23.33b), this is equivalent to maximizing

$$\check{\xi}''^{-1} = H''_{11} - H''^{-1}_{22} H'^{2}_{22}. \tag{23.74}$$

Notice that under the condition (23.73a), n_1 is a linear function of n_2 (and vice versa). Since also $n_1 \geq 0$ and $n_2 \geq 0$, the possible values of n_2 form an interval whose lower endpoint is $n_2 = 0$ and whose upper endpoint is the value of n_2 corresponding via (23.73a) to $n_1 = 0$. Equivalently, under (23.73b) H''_{22} determines H''_{11} linearly and the possible values of H''_{22} form an interval whose lower endpoint is $H''_{22} = H'_{22}$, corresponding to $n_2 = 0$, and whose upper endpoint corresponds to $H''_{11} = H'_{11}$, $n_1 = 0$.

Solving (23.73b) for H''_{11} in terms of H''_{22}, substituting in (23.74), and differentiating the result with respect to H''_{22} gives

$$\frac{d\breve{\xi}''^{-1}}{dH''_{22}} = -\frac{k_{s2}\upsilon_2}{k_{s1}\upsilon_1} + \frac{H'^2_{12}}{H''^2_{22}}, \tag{23.76}$$

which is,

$$\begin{aligned} &\text{positive for } H''_{22} < h^*, \\ &\text{negative for } H''_{22} > h^*, \end{aligned} \tag{23.77a}$$

where

$$h^* = |H'_{12}|\left(\frac{k_{s1}\upsilon_1}{k_{s2}\upsilon_2}\right)^{1/2}. \tag{23.77b}$$

There are now three possibilities, depending on whether h^* lies (A) below, (B) above, or (C) within the range of H''_{22}.

A. Allocating the entire sampling budget to unbiased observations, that is,

$$n_1 = k^*/k_{s1}, \qquad H''_{11} = H'_{11} + k^*/k_{s1}\upsilon_1, \tag{23.78a}$$

$$n_2 = 0, \qquad H''_{22} = H'_{22}, \tag{23.78b}$$

is optimal if $H'_{22} \geq h^*$, or equivalently if $\breve{\xi}' \geq |V'_{12}|(k_{s1}\upsilon_1/k_{s2}\upsilon_2)^{1/2}$. Then

$$\breve{\xi}'' = (H''_{11} - H''^{-1}_{22}H'^2_{12})^{-1} = \left(\frac{n_1}{\upsilon_1} + \frac{1}{\breve{\xi}'}\right)^{-1}. \tag{23.78c}$$

B. Allocating the entire sampling budget to biased observations, that is,

$$n_1 = 0, \qquad H''_{11} = H'_{11}, \tag{23.79a}$$

$$n_2 = k^*/k_{s2}, \qquad H''_{22} = H'_{22} + k^*/k_{s2}\upsilon_2, \tag{23.79b}$$

is optimal if this results in $H''_{22} \leq h^*$. Then

$$\breve{\xi}'' = (H'_{11} - H''^{-1}_{22}H'^2_{12})^{-1}. \tag{23.79c}$$

C. The allocation given by $H''_{22} = h^*$ is optimal if it is possible, that is,

$$n_1 = (k^* - k_{s2}n_2)/k_{s1}, \qquad H''_{11} = H'_{11} + n_1/\upsilon_1, \tag{23.80a}$$

$$n_2 = \upsilon_2(h^* - H'_{22}) \qquad H''_{22} = h^*, \tag{23.80b}$$

is optimal if it results in $n_1 \geq 0$, $n_2 \geq 0$. Then

$$\check{\xi}'' = (H''_{11} - h^*)^{-1}. \tag{23.80c}$$

To summarize, we compute H'_{11}, H'_{22}, and h^* from the prior variance matrix of $(\tilde{\xi}, \tilde{\mu})$ and the cost parameters. By sampling, we may increase H'_{11} and H'_{22} to H''_{11} and H''_{22}, at a cost. If possible, (C), we should sample the biased process just enough to make $H''_{22} = h^*$. This may be impossible either because (B) the sampling budget is too small, in which case we should sample the biased process only; or because (A) $H'_{22} > h^*$ to begin with, in which case we should sample the unbiased process only.

As the sampling budget increases, the optimal allocation behaves as follows. If $H'_{22} \geq h^*$, then only the unbiased process is sampled. If $H'_{22} < h^*$, then the biased process is sampled until H''_{22} reaches h^*, and thereafter the unbiased process is sampled.

Notice that if it is possible to make unbiased observations, then no matter how much cheaper biased observations may be, there is a limit to the number of biased observations that should be made. Beyond this limit, *all* money available for sampling should be allocated to unbiased observations.

23.12.3 The Infinite-Action Problem with Quadratic Loss

Let l_t be defined by (23.38). Then, by the argument of section 23.11.2, the ENGS is

$$G(n_1, n_2) = k_t(\check{\xi}' - \check{\xi}'') - k_{s1}n_1 - k_{s2}n_2. \tag{23.81}$$

Observe first that (a) if $H'_{22} \geq h^*$, then optimal allocation requires unbiased sampling only, putting us in the situation of section 16.8. The optimal choices in this case are therefore

$$n_1^o = \left(\frac{k_t \upsilon_1}{k_{s1}}\right)^{1/2} - \frac{\upsilon_1}{\check{\xi}'}, \qquad H''^o_{11} = \left(\frac{k_t}{k_{s1}\upsilon_1}\right)^{1/2} + \frac{H'^2_{12}}{H'_{22}}, \tag{23.82a}$$

$$n_2^o = 0, \qquad H''^o_{22} = H'_{22}, \tag{22.82b}$$

provided that n_1^o as given by this formula is positive. Otherwise the optimal sample sizes are both 0.

We shall now prove that (b) if $H'_{22} < h^*$, then the optimal choices are

$$n_1^o = \upsilon_1(H''^o_{11} - H'_{11}), \qquad H''^o_{11} = \left(\frac{k_t}{k_{s1}\upsilon_1}\right)^{1/2} + \frac{H'^2_{12}}{h^*}, \tag{23.83a}$$

$$n_2^o = \upsilon_2(h^* - H'_{22}), \qquad H''^o_{22} = h^*, \tag{22.83b}$$

provided that n_1^o as given by this formula is positive. Otherwise it is optimal to do only biased sampling ($n_1 = 0$) and the optimal amount of biased sampling to do is given in section 23.11.2.

We observe that the first sentence of (b) arises from case (C) of optimal allocation (section 23.12.2) and the second sentence from case (B).

Proof Optimal allocation requires either (B) $n_1 = 0$, in which case we are in the situation of section 23.11.2; or (C) $H''_{22} = h^*$. In the latter case, n_2 is fixed and

$$\frac{dG(n_1, n_2)}{dn_1} = -k_t \frac{d\check{\xi}''}{dn_1} - k_{s1}. \tag{23.84}$$

Since $\check{\xi}''$, as given by (23.33b), depends on n_1 only through H''_{11} and H''_{11} is given by (23.72), we have that

$$\frac{d\check{\xi}''}{dn_1} = \frac{d\check{\xi}''}{dH''_{11}} \frac{dH''_{11}}{dn_1} = -\frac{1}{(H''_{11} - H''^{-1}_{22} H'^2_{12})^2 \upsilon_1}. \tag{23.85}$$

Substituting this in (23.84) and using $H''_{22} = h^*$ we obtain by straightforward algebra the tentative optimum H''^o_{11} given by (23.83a). That we need not check the possibility (B) if this gives $n^o_1 \geq 0$ follows fairly easily from the fact that decreasing H''_{22} would increase the optimum H''_{11} for that fixed H''_{22}.

23.12.4 The Infinite-Action Problem with Linear Loss

Let l_t be defined by (23.43). Then, by the argument of section 23.11.3, the ENGS is

$$G(n_1, n_2) = k_t(\ddot{\xi}' - \ddot{\xi}'') - k_{s1} n_1 - k_{s2} n_2 \tag{23.86}$$

where k_t is defined by (23.44). Observe first that (a) i $H'_{2\natural} \geq h^*$, then optimal allocation requires unbiased sampling only, putting us in the situation of section 16.9. The optimal choices in this case are therefore

$$n^o_1 = \upsilon_1 \left[\left(\frac{k_t}{2k_{s1}\upsilon_1} \right)^{2/3} - \frac{1}{\check{\xi}'} \right], \qquad H''^o_{11} = \left(\frac{k_t}{2k_{s1}\upsilon_1} \right)^{2/3} + \frac{H'^2_{12}}{H'_{22}} \tag{23.87a}$$

$$n^o_2 = 0, \qquad H''^o_{22} = H'_{22}, \tag{23.87b}$$

providing that n^o_1 as given by this formula is positive. Otherwise the optimal sample sizes are both 0.

We shall now prove that (b) if $H'_{22} < h^*$, then the optimal choices are

$$n^o_1 = \upsilon_1(H''^o_{11} - H'_{11}), \qquad H''^o_{11} = \left(\frac{k_t}{2k_{s1}\upsilon_1} \right)^{2/3} + \frac{H'^2_{12}}{h^*}, \tag{23.88a}$$

$$n^o_2 = \upsilon_2(h^* - H'_{22}), \qquad H''^o_{22} = h^*, \tag{23.88b}$$

provided that n_1^o as given by this formula is positive. Otherwise it is optimal to do only biased sampling ($n_1 = 0$) and the optimal amount of biased sampling to do is given in section 23.11.3.

Again the first sentence of (b) arises from case (C) of optimal allocation (section 23.12.2) and the second sentence from case (B).

Proof Optimal allocation requires either (B) $n_1 = 0$, in which case we are in the situation of section 23.11.3; or (C) $H''_{22} = h^*$. In the latter case, n_2 is fixed and

$$\frac{dG(n_1, n_2)}{dn_1} = -k_t \frac{d\ddot{\xi}''}{dn_1} - k_{s1}. \tag{23.89}$$

By (23.85)

$$\frac{d\ddot{\xi}''}{dn_1} = \frac{1}{2}\ddot{\xi}''^{-1/2}\frac{d\check{\xi}''}{dn_1} = -\frac{1}{(H''_{11} - H''^{-1}_{22}H'^{2}_{12})^{3/2}\upsilon_1}. \tag{23.90}$$

Substituting this in (23.89) and using $H''_{22} = h^*$ we obtain by straightforward algebra the tentative optimum H''^{o}_{11} given by (23.88a). The remainder of the proof is like that in the previous subsection.

23.12.5 The Two-Action Problem with Linear Value

Let the economic problem be defined as in section 23.11.4. Then the ENGS is

$$G(n_1, n_2) = k_t \sigma^* L_{N^*}(D^*) - k_{s1} n_1 - k_{s2} n_2 \tag{23.91}$$

in the notation of (23.55)–(23.57). Observe first that (a) if $H'_{22} \geq h^*$, the optimal allocation requires unbiased sampling only ($n_2 = 0$), putting us in the situation of section 16.10. We have

$$G(n_1, 0) = \frac{k_{s1}\upsilon_1}{\ddot{\xi}'} G^*(\rho), \tag{23.92a}$$

where $G^*(\rho)$ is defined by (16.58) with

$$\rho = \frac{\ddot{\xi}'}{\upsilon_1} n_1, \tag{23.92b}$$

$$D^*_\infty = \frac{|\bar{\xi}' - \xi_b|}{\ddot{\xi}'}, \tag{23.92c}$$

$$\lambda = \frac{\ddot{\xi}'^3 k_t}{\upsilon_1 k_{s1}}. \tag{23.92d}$$

The optimal choice of n_1 can now be obtained with the help of the table on pages 1 and 2 of table MT-9, which gives the optimal choice of $R = \log \rho$ as a function of D_∞^* and $\Lambda = \log \lambda$. The optimal n_2 is 0, as already mentioned. The table on pages 3 and 4 of table MT-9 facilitates finding the ENGS of the optimal procedure. (The use of table MT-9 is discussed further in section 16.10. The relation of the notation of this section to that of section 16.10 must be borne in mind.)

We shall now prove that (b) if $H'_{22} < h^*$, then the optimal procedure is either to do only biased sampling ($n_1 = 0$) in which case the optimal amount of biased sampling to do is given in section 23.11.4, or to choose

$$n_2^o = \upsilon_2(h^* - H'_{22}), \qquad H''^o_{22} = h^*, \tag{23.93}$$

in which case

$$G(n_1, n_2^o) = \frac{k_{s1}\upsilon_1}{\ddot{\xi}'}\left[G^*(\rho) + H'^2_{12}\left(1 - \frac{H'_{22}}{h^*}\right)\right] \tag{23.94a}$$

where $G^*(\rho)$ is defined by (16.58) with

$$\rho = \frac{\ddot{\xi}'}{\upsilon_1} n_1 + |V'_{12}H'_{12}|\left(1 - \frac{H'_{22}}{h^*}\right), \tag{23.94b}$$

$$D_\infty^* = \frac{|\bar{\xi}' - \xi_b|}{\ddot{\xi}'}, \tag{23.94c}$$

$$\lambda = \frac{\ddot{\xi}'^3 k_t}{\upsilon_1 k_{s1}}. \tag{23.94d}$$

In the latter case, as in (a), the optimal choice of n_1 can now be obtained with the help of the table on pages 1 and 2 of table MT-9, and the table on pages 3 and 4 of table MT-9 facilitates finding the ENGS of the optimal procedure.

In general, one must compute $G(n_1, n_2)$ for each of the foregoing possibilities to determine which is better. However, if the ρ maximizing (23.94a) leads by (23.94b) to a negative value of n_1, then the value $n_1 = 0$ and the value of n_2 obtained in section 23.11.4 are optimal. Similarly, if the value of n_2 obtained in section 23.11.4 exceeds the value given in (23.93), then the n_2 given in (23.93) and the value of n_1 given by (23.94b) for the value of ρ maximizing (23.94a) are optimal.

Proof Optimal allocation gives either $n_1 = 0$ or (23.93). In the latter case, (23.94) can be obtained by straightforward algebra. The rest of the proof is simply a matter of the definition of table MT-9.

23.12.6 Fixed Sampling Costs

Fixed sampling costs (setup costs) are handled the same way in each of the problems just discussed. Suppose first that a fixed cost K_s is incurred unless $n_1 = n_2 = 0$, that is,

$$c_s(n_1, n_2) = k_{s1}n_1 + k_{s2}n_2 + K_s\delta(n_1 + n_2) \tag{23.95}$$

where

$$\delta(0) = 0 \quad \text{and} \quad \delta(n) = 1 \quad \text{if} \quad n > 0. \tag{23.96}$$

In this case the optimum (n_1, n_2) is the same as when $K_s = 0$ except that if this choice gives a negative ENGS when K_s is taken into account, then the optimal sample sizes are $n_1 = 0$, $n_2 = 0$. This applies also to situations in which sampling without (or with) bias is impossible so that necessarily $n_1 = 0$ (or $n_2 = 0$).

Suppose now that both kinds of sampling are possible and that in addition to a fixed cost for any sampling, there are separate fixed costs for the two kinds of sampling, that is

$$c_s(n_1, n_2) = k_{s1}n_1 + k_{s2}n_2 + K_s\delta(n_1 + n_2) + K_{s1}\delta(n_1) + K_{s2}\delta(n_2). \tag{23.97}$$

In this case the optimal choice is either (i) the same as when $K_s = K_{s1} = K_{s2} = 0$, or (ii) $n_1 = 0$ and the optimal n_2 for $n_1 = 0$, (iii) $n_2 = 0$ and the optimal n_1 for $n_2 = 0$, or (iv) $n_1 = n_2 = 0$. To determine which is actually optimal the ENGS must generally be computed for each possibility.

Exercises

1. Given the model $\mu = \xi + \beta$, show that if $(\tilde{\xi}, \tilde{\beta})$ or $(\tilde{\mu}, \tilde{\beta})$ is bivariate Normal, then so is $(\tilde{\xi}, \tilde{\mu})$. Given the mean and variance of any one pair, find the means and variances of the other two pairs.

2. Verify (23.33).

3. Verify that formulas (23.32) and (23.33) hold even if $n_1 = 0$ or $n_2 = 0$ or both, as asserted in section 23.9.

4. Find the mean and variance of the (marginal) joint distribution of $(\tilde{m}_1, \tilde{m}_2)$ given that n_1 and n_2 have been prescribed. (See section 23.10).

5. Find the mean and variance of the joint Normal preposterior distribution of $(\tilde{\tilde{\xi}}'', \tilde{\tilde{\mu}}'')$. (See the second paragraph of section 23.10).

6. Complete the proof given in section 23.11.2.

7. Find the conditions under which the tentative optimum H''_{22}, which is the solution of (23.46), is the true optimum.

8. For any sample plan $n = [n_1 n_2]'$ it is possible to compute the quantities $c_s(n)$ and $\breve{\xi}''$, the cost and the posterior variance respectively. The set

$$S \equiv \{(c_s(\boldsymbol{n}), \check{\xi}''): n_1 \geq 0, n_2 \geq 0\}$$

comprises all such possible pairs of joint evaluations. The efficient sampling plans are the southwest boundary of S in the diagram.

a. Argue that the lower boundary of S cannot have a horizontal linear section, that is, a section where the smallest $\check{\xi}''$ does not strictly decrease as c_s increases.

b. Argue that a given point $A = (c^*, v^*)$ on the efficient boundary of S is such that

$$\min\{\check{\xi}''(\boldsymbol{n}): c_s(\boldsymbol{n}) \leq c^*\} = v^*,$$

or

$$\min\{c_s(n): \check{\xi}''(\boldsymbol{n}) \leq v^*\} = c^*.$$

c. Give a plausibility argument for the proposition that there exists a $\lambda > 0$ such that

$$\min_{\boldsymbol{n} \geq 0} \{\check{\xi}''(\boldsymbol{n}) + \lambda c_s(\boldsymbol{n})\}$$

occurs at $\boldsymbol{n}^*$ where $[c_s(\boldsymbol{n}^*)\check{\xi}''(\boldsymbol{n}^*)] = [c^* v^*]$.

d. What is the relation of (c) to the Lagrange multiplier technique?

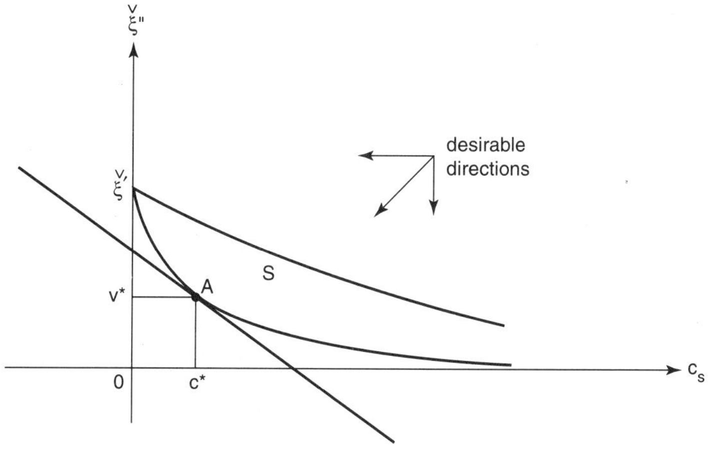

Figure 23E.1
Optimal allocation, problem of uncertain bias

9. Here is the skeleton outline of a potential problem for this chapter. Write an "armchair caselet" along the following lines. Management plans to market a new product next fall, in time for the Christmas season, with an extensive promotional campaign. The basic unknown is $\tilde{\xi}$, the average demand for the product. It is now spring and there is time to get sample information. However, the average demand $\tilde{\mu}$ for the product at this time of year is different from $\tilde{\xi}$. It is felt nevertheless that if management knew μ they would then be in a much better position to assess $\tilde{\xi}$. Management could proceed by putting a joint distribution on $(\tilde{\xi}, \tilde{\mu})$ and, given the economics of the problem, then deciding whether to get sample information on μ.

10. a. If $H'_{12} = 0$ then by (23.33b) $\check{\xi}''$ depends only on n_1 and not on n_2, that is, the size of the sample on the process with bias has no influence at all on the posterior variance of the cost-determining quantity. Give an intuitive explanation of this phenomenon.

b. Argue intuitively and show mathematically that if $\tilde{\xi}$ and $\tilde{\beta}$ are independent prior to sampling then they become dependent after a sample with $n_1 = 0, n_2 > 0$.

c. Argue intuitively and show mathematically that if $\tilde{\mu}$ and $\tilde{\beta}$ are independent prior to sampling then they remain independent after a sample with $n_1 = 0, n_2 > 0$.

11. Let μ and ξ be, respectively, the population average of reported and actual money spent on a given commodity, say liquor. (Another example would be time spent in watching television programs of a given kind.) In this chapter we discussed the possibility of taking observations either on ξ (at a high cost) or on μ (at a low cost) or on both. In some applications it is possible to take both types of observations *on the same individual*. Does the theory of this chapter cover this case? How would you go about exploiting the possibility of this type of sampling?

12. a. Intuitively one might expect that one would never want to measure with bias if measurements without bias are as cheap ($k_{s1} \leq k_{s2}$) and the unbiased measuring process has no larger variance ($v_1 \leq v_2$). Show that this conjecture is false, because the conditions $k_{s1} \leq k_{s2}$ and $v_1 \leq v_2$ do not suffice to guarantee that the optimality condition (A) in section 23.12.2 holds.

b. Show in particular that if $k_{s1} = k_{s2}$, $v_1 = v_2$, $\tilde{\xi}$ and $\tilde{\beta}$ are positively correlated, then the condition does not hold, so that optimal allocation requires $n_2 > 0$.

c. Argue intuitively that if $k_{s1} = k_{s2}$, $v_1 = v_2$, and $\beta = b\xi$ where b is a known number, then optimal allocation requires $n_1 = 0$ if $b > 0$ or $b < -2$ and $n_2 = 0$ if $-2 < b < 0$.

13. Suppose that $\tilde{\xi}$ is (a priori) Normal with mean 30 and variance 1/4, $\tilde{\beta}$ is Normal with mean 3 and variance .04, and $\tilde{\xi}$ and $\tilde{\beta}$ are independent. Suppose that there is a Normal process with process mean ξ and process variance 1 on which observations may be made at a cost of \$9 each, and a second Normal process with process mean $\xi + \beta$ and process variance 1 on which observations may be made at a cost of \$1 each.

a. Show that the variance of $\tilde{\xi}$ after n_1 observations on the first process and n_2 on the second would be $(25 + n_2)/(100 + 25n_1 + 29n_2 + n_1 n_2)$.

b. Show that an optimal pair of sample sizes (n_1, n_2) will never have $n_2 > 50$. (Here and hereafter, neglect the fact that n_1 and n_2 must be integers.)

c. Consider an infinite-action problem with $l_t(a, \xi) = 3600(a - \xi)^2$.

i. Show that the EVPI = 900.

ii. Show that the optimal sample sizes are $n_1 = 0$, $n_2 = 48$ (or 48.3).

iii. Show that for the optimal sample sizes, the ENGS = 676.

d. Consider an infinite-action problem with $l_t(a, \xi) = 3800(a - \xi)$ if $a \geq \xi$ and $l_t(a, \xi) = 1500(\xi - a)$ if $a \leq \xi$.

i. Show that the EVPI = 900.

ii. Show that the optimal sample sizes are $n_1 = 1$ (or .92), $n_2 = 50$.

iii. Show that for the optimal sample sizes, the ENGS = 455.8.

iv. Show that, if sampling from the first process were impossible, the optimal sample size would be $n_2 = 52$ (or 51.8).

e. Consider a two-action problem with

$$v_t(a_1, \xi) = -4725 + 900\xi, \qquad v_t(a_2, \xi) = -280{,}000 + 10{,}000\xi.$$

i. Show that the EVPI = 900.

ii. Show that the optimal sample sizes are $n_1 = 0$, $n_2 = 48$ (or 47.8).

iii. Show that for the optimal sample sizes, the ENGS = 686.

f. What is the cost of irrationality (decrease in ENGS) if the sample sizes $n_1 = 1$, $n_2 = 50$ are used in (c) and (e)?

14. In the previous problem it was assumed that the terminal decision was to be made at a date allowing only one round of sampling. Suppose that, after a round of sampling, a delay occurred postponing the decision sufficiently to permit another round of sampling, with the same sampling costs as before.

a. Give an argument why one should not sample on the second round in 13 (c) if the first-round sample sizes were optimal.

b. Give an argument why, if the first-round sample sizes in 13 (c) were smaller than optimal, one should sample on the second round so as to make the total sample sizes equal to the optimal one-round sample sizes.

c. Give an argument why, in 13 (c), among all choices of sample sizes for the two rounds, a procedure is optimal if and only if it gives total sample sizes equal to the optimal one-round sample sizes.

d. Do parts (a)–(c) for 13 (d) instead of 13 (c).

e. Give an argument why one might want to sample on the second round in 13 (e) even though the first-round sample sizes were the optimal one-round sample sizes.

f. Do you think that, in 13 (e), among all two-round sampling procedures, the optimal first-round sample sizes equal the optimal one-round sample sizes?

15. There are 100 first-graders in the local elementary school. You are interested in the number N who have two parents living at home. A prior distribution on the possible values of N (the integers 0 to 100) is a complicated beast, so you assess it indirectly. You treat the 100 first-graders as coming from a Bernoulli process with unknown parameter p (representing the fraction of hypothetical first-graders with two parents at home in the proverbial "long run"). Based on a combination of experience and judgment, you give p a mean of .6 and a standard deviation of .1 (variance .01). You treat p as beta-distributed.

a. What are the implied mean and variance of N?

b. In a sample of 20 of the 100 first-graders, 15 say they have two parents at home and 5 say they do not. Assume their answers are correct. What are now the mean and variance of N?

c. Assume instead that you know by experience that first-graders sometimes answer incorrectly, specifically, that the chance of an incorrect answer is .05 if a first-grader has two parents at home but is .15 otherwise. What is the answer to (b) on this assumption?

d. Now assume that you are not certain of the error rates .05 and .15, but you assess the two error rates as independent with these means. Either show that this uncertainty would not change the answer to (c) or show how to incorporate it into the formulation and analysis.

16. It is well known that, when asked about their utility bills, people tend to overestimate them. The people of East Moribund are presumably no exception. We are interested in the mean τ of the actual electric bills in East Moribund in 1984. Each household has an actual bill and a value it would report if asked. Let θ be the mean of the reported-if-asked bills for all households in East Moribund. Suppose that, a priori, τ is Normal with mean \$400 and standard deviation \$100 while $\theta - \tau$ is Normal with mean \$150 and standard deviation \$75 and independent of τ. A random sample of 100 households in East Moribund has produced a mean reported bill of \$510. A separate random sample of 10 households has a mean reported bill of \$485. In return for suitable bribes, the respondents in the second sample have looked up their actual bills and the mean actual bill in this sample turned out to be \$390. In the second sample, the standard deviation of the actual bills was \$125 and the correlation between actual and reported bills was .8. In the combined sample, the standard deviation of the reported bills was \$87.50. Assume that, given τ and θ, the joint distribution of actual and reported-if-asked bills for the population of East Moribund households is Normal with means τ and θ and standard deviations and correlation equal to the sample values.

a. What is the prior distribution of $\tilde{\theta}$?

b. Show, or argue from a known fact, that for data consisting of a sample of n households, the sample means of the actual and reported bills form a sufficient statistic.

c. Show that, in (b), given τ and θ, the joint distribution of the sample means is Normal with correlation .8. What are their standard deviations?

d. What is the posterior distribution of τ given the two samples? (If this problem is too time-consuming, lay out the calculation clearly. If you don't know how to do it for the two samples, do it for whichever sample you can.)

CASES

C1 Mar-Pruf Finishes, Inc.

Mar-Pruf Finishes, Inc., was a relatively small firm operating in a segment of the industrial-finishes market which was dominated by the American Paint and Lacquer Company. Mar-Pruf's research chemists had recently developed a product to compete with American's type A-1 lacquer and the company was trying to decide whether or not to put this product on the market. Preliminary market research had shown that although some firms considered the new Mar-Pruf product to be superior to American's A-1, the difference was not great enough to permit Mar-Pruf to charge a price appreciably higher than American's price of $8.75 per gallon. On the other hand, any attempt to seize American's market by charging a lower price was almost certain to produce a price war which American was sure to win because of its superior financial resources. It was clear that if the product was to be marketed at all it would have to be marketed at a price of $8.75 per gallon.

Mar-Pruf figured that if it installed the necessary equipment for economical manufacture of the new product it could realize a net contribution (selling price less variable cost of production, selling, and delivery) amounting to about $.40 per gallon. After considering the amount of time during which a customer could be expected to continue buying the product, Mar-Pruf's management had decided that the discounted present value of the whole stream of future contributions to be expected from a customer who was initially sold on the new product would be about $2 for each gallon-per-year of initial sales. In other words: Mar-Pruf "expected" to realize contributions with a present value of $20 from a customer who started buying at a rate of 10 gallons per year, $50 from a customer who started buying at a rate of 25 gallons per year, and so forth.

Mar-Pruf hesitated to enter the market with this new product because the total cost of installing and debugging the necessary equipment for volume manufacture plus the cost of the required introductory sales effort would amount to about \$600,000, so that unless a sales volume of \$600,000/\$2 = 300,000 gallons per year could be attained, the introduction of the product would result in a net loss. Mar-Pruf's market research had shown that there were about 10,000 firms who could be considered potential customers for the product, so that the break-even point could also be considered as achieving annual sales averaging 30 gallons per firm. Because of the considerable risk involved in the decision, Mar-Pruf's marketing-research department had drawn a sample of 100 of these 10,000 firms in such a way that each firm had an equal chance of being drawn, and had then dispatched salesmen to give free samples of the product to these firms and to ask whether they would buy if it were actually placed on the market and, if so, how much of it per year. The results of this survey are shown in simplified form in the table below.

Annual purchase rate	Number of firms
0	60
60	10
90	20
120	10

Before taking the consumer survey, the Mar-Pruf management had done its best to assess the market potential and had decided that the most likely average sales rate was 50 gallons per customer per year but that there was only a 50-50 chance that this estimate was within plus or minus 20 units of the true figure.

Before the consumer survey was taken, Mar-Pruf's management was asked whether they believed that customers on the average would actually buy as much as they said they would. Management responded that the average potential customer is almost certain to say that he will buy more than he will actually buy. Management guessed that the most likely average amount of overstating is 20 gallons per year but would not bet more than even money that this best guess is actually within 10 gallons per year of the true figure.

Mar-Pruf's management must now decide whether or not to go into production. One more round of consumer sampling is still possible but may not be worthwhile because according to the market-research department it costs \$25 on the average for a salesman to interview each customer.

Analyze!

C2 Grand Western Railroad

In January 1957, a number of American railroads were offering a special passenger tariff known as the "Family Fare Plan." There were some variations in the details from road to road, but basically the tariff provided that if a husband bought a round trip at the regular rate, his wife could buy a round trip at half price and his children could buy their round trips at still lower prices. A single ticket was issued to cover the transportation of the entire family.

There was great controversy among passenger officers of the various roads concerning the effect of the Family Fare Plan on revenue and profit, and the Grand Western Railroad was seriously considering abandoning it. A good deal of revenue was at stake: sales of Family Fare tickets amounted to about $4 million per year on the Grand Western, and if the same passengers had been carried at full fare this figure would have been nearly doubled. While the general passenger agent of the Grand Western believed that 90% of the passenger-miles sold under the special tariff would not have been sold at all under the normal tariff, the senior executives of the Grand Western knew that the general passenger agent of another railroad serving exactly the same major cities believed that about 90% of the passenger-miles sold under the special tariff *could* have been sold at regular fares.

The president of the Grand Western, O. L. Jones, was particularly puzzled by the fact that both his own GPA and the GPA of the other road based their contradictory statements on the results of surveys carried out by having ticket agents ask purchasers of Family Fare tickets whether or not they would have made the same trip if the special rates had not been in effect. Jones was inclined to believe that the samples taken by the two men were too small to be reliable; since there was no one among the road's personnel who was an expert in such matters, he called in a representative of a marketing-research agency specializing in consumer surveys and laid the problem before him. The agency representative answered that both the samples were so large that sampling error as such could not possibly account for more than 1 or 2 of the 80 percentage points of difference; he went on to assert that the real difficulty was that reliable answers to a question like the one asked of the ticket buyers could not possibly be obtained through hurried interviews conducted by ticket clerks under unfavorable conditions. Even if the Grand Western sample were extended to a 100% count, there would in his opinion be no more real knowledge than there was before any data were collected. He recommended that the railroad employ his agency to draw a small equal-probability sample of purchasers of Family Fare tickets and have the persons in the sample interviewed in their homes by really skilled interviewers.

The agency representative quoted a price for such a survey of \$1,000 for general expenses plus \$100 per family in the sample, explaining the high cost per head as due in part to the fees of the skilled interviewers and in part to the time and expense that would be incurred in securing interviews with people selected with equal probabilities among all persons who had travelled on Family Fare tickets during the preceding year. To Jones this implied that a sample large enough to give reliable results would be prohibitive in cost, but the agency representative argued that this was not necessarily true, and that in any case a good deal of useful information could be obtained by taking a very small pilot sample and analyzing its results. Since the total amount of Grand Western revenue at stake was substantial, Jones finally decided to contract with the marketing-research agency to interview a sample of 50 families at a cost of \$6,000.

Before taking the sample, the agency examined the available data on the values of the individual Family Fare tickets sold during the previous year and found that the large majority of the tickets were for short trips and actually accounted for only a small part of the total dollar sales: 80% of the dollars came from individual sales of \$150 and over. The railroad and the agency quickly agreed that the sample should be drawn exclusively from families who had paid over \$150 for their tickets, since it seemed very likely that the behavior of these families alone would determine whether the plan was profitable overall.

The pilot sample was promptly drawn and interviewed with the results show (in simplified form) in the table below. The figure shown in the column headed "effect of cancellation" was calculated by subtracting the amount which the family *actually* spent on its Family Fare ticket from the amount it *would* have spent travelling on the Grand Western if Family Fares had not been available.

Effect of cancellation	Number of families
−\$200	10
− 100	12
0	7
+ 100	16
+ 200	5
	50

When these results were in Jones was still unsure about what to do next. It was easy to calculate that the effect of cancellation of the plan on families in the sample would have been a reduction in revenue amounting to $600 in total or $12 per family on the average. Jones also knew that about 20,000 Family Fare tickets had been sold for amounts of $150 and over in the past year, so that *if* the $12 sample figure held for the entire population, about $240,000 would be lost in one year by abandoning the plan. The road's passenger-train schedules and consists were such that the reduction in passenger-miles travelled would have no effect on train costs, so that this loss of revenue was an out-and-out loss of that much net income.

Jones believed that conditions were changing so rapidly that the entire question would have to be examined again next year and therefore that there was no sense in projecting profit or loss farther than a year in advance, but he was seriously disturbed about basing his decision on a sample of only 50 families.

1. On the evidence of the pilot sample alone, what is the best course of action and what risk is involved?

2. Recompute your answers to (1), making the additional assumption that since Jones believes that most people do not really know what they will do until they do it, he would be willing to bet even money that the average dollar effect of cancellation as estimated by interviews would be at least $25 above or below the true effect of actual cancellation even if 100 per cent of the customers were included in the sample.

3. The marketing-research agency would be willing to conduct additional interviews according to this rate schedule:

Additional number of interviews	Total cost
50	$4,000
100	7,000
200	12,000
500	25,000

Should Jones ask the market research agency to conduct further interviews? If so, how many?

C3 Ace Supermarkets

Act I (October)

Mr. H. V. McCarthy, a buyer of fresh oranges for Ace Supermarkets, is preparing for the start of the new buying season. Following the general practice in the industry, McCarthy contracts to buy oranges while they are still on the trees. Usually the owner of an orange grove solicits offers from several buyers for the entire unharvested orange crop in the grove; after some negotiation between the buyers and the seller a fixed-price contract is signed with the buyer who has offered the highest price. If the fruit later turns out to be worth less than the contract price, the loss is taken solely by the buyer and his company; if the fruit turns out to be worth more than the contract price, the gain belongs entirely to the buyer and his company.

The only groves which are of real importance to McCarthy are groves of mature trees, at least 15 years old, that produce fruit in large quantity. From the casual impressions he has already received, McCarthy thinks that the fruit from an average tree in an average mature grove will be worth somewhere around \$10 this season and he would be willing to bet even money that it will be worth somewhere between \$9 and \$11. But these overall figures derived from general experience in the industry are of almost no use to McCarthy when he comes to evaluate any one particular grove, since there is great variation from grove to grove in condition of soil, type of tree, quality of care, and so forth. Consequently McCarthy's standard procedure is to make a survey of a large number of prospective sellers very early in the season, some time before the date at which the first contracts are signed, in order both to size up the general prospects for the orange crop and to locate what seem to him the best opportunities for actual offers to be made later on as Ace's requirements for fresh oranges become definite. The essential information that he wants from each grove in this survey is an estimate of the ultimate cash value of the fruit on the trees; when he comes to actual buying a little later on, these estimates will not only determine his choice of the sellers to whom he will make offers, but will also have substantial effect on the price he will offer to each, although of course he may resurvey a grove before he actually makes a firm offer.

McCarthy's first step in estimating the cash value of the fruit in a grove is to have one of his technical assistants estimate the actual amount of fruit on each of several trees in the grove. These quantity estimates are made with great care, by first determining the cross-sectional area (at the trunk) of all main branches on the tree, then selecting some of the branches and actually counting the oranges on them, and finally multiplying this count by the ratio of the cross-sectional area of all branches to the cross-sectional area of the counted branches. The wage cost of a quantity estimate of a single tree is therefore substantial, roughly \$5 per tree on the average.

After an assistant has delivered the quantity estimates for the selected trees in a grove, McCarthy converts them into estimates of cash values, bringing in all his information about current conditions in the market.

Over the years he has tried to improve his methods by keeping careful track of both his estimates of the cash value of the fruit on individual trees and the true average cash value per tree of the crop in those groves where he ultimately bought the crop; figures on the true cash value of the fruit on individual trees are not available. Originally his performance was very poor, as might be expected; but by analyzing and learning from his mistakes he has now arrived at a point where his value estimates average out almost exactly correct and a good half of his estimates for individual trees are within plus or minus $2 of the true average value per tree in the grove from which the trees were selected. As a result, he is beginning to ask himself whether his current practice of having quantity estimates made by his assistants for 5% of the trees in each grove is really unnecessarily expensive; his estimate of the total cash value of all the fruit in any particular grove might be adequately reliable even if it were based on a much smaller number of trees.

McCarthy feels that while some overestimates have no serious consequence at all there is about an even chance that overestimating the value of a grove by any given amount will lead to buying the crop at that same amount above its true value; he feels that underestimates are about equally serious because they may lead him to lose contracts that he could have signed under favorable conditions and thus force him to sign others under less favorable conditions.

1. For how many trees in a grove containing 2,000 mature trees should McCarthy have quantity estimates made by his assistants?

2. If he does have estimates made for the number of trees that you recommend, what opportunity loss should he expect to suffer through misestimation of the cash value of the crop in such a grove?

3. Should the number of trees for which quantity estimates are made be a fixed percentage of the total number of trees in a grove? If not, how should the number estimated vary with the number in the grove?

Act II (One Month Later)

Mr. McCarthy is now actively at work buying oranges for Ace Supermarkets and is currently preparing to bid on a large grove containing 5,000 mature trees. Another buyer has already offered a price amounting to $11.50 per tree but has definitely refused to go any higher, and the owner has told McCarthy that he will sign with McCarthy if McCarthy will offer him $11.55 per tree by next Monday; otherwise he will sign with the buyer who made the earlier offer of $11.50.

In his pre-season round of surveys McCarthy had studied this grove and an adjacent one belonging to the same owner and had intended to estimate the crops in the two groves in his usual manner. Unfortunately, the assistant assigned to the two jobs had fallen ill after completing his estimates for 39 trees in the other grove; as a result McCarthy recieved an estimate of $12.23 per tree for the adjacent grove but no formal estimate at all for the grove being offered at $11.55 per tree. The two groves looked much the same, but the grove being bid on seemed to have a generally less favorable exposure than the other, to the extent that McCarthy would be willing to bet 3 to 1 that its average value per tree is less than the other grove's and to bet even money that the difference would amount to at least $.50 per tree. Accordingly, McCarthy is thinking even at this late date of having estimates made of the quantity of fruit on each of several trees in the grove at issue; he could do this and still meet the owner's deadline by having one of his assistants do the work over the weekend, although this would mean paying Sunday rates amounting to $10 rather than $5 per tree and would also involve special travel and living expenses amounting to about $70.

1. If McCarthy does not have any quantity estimates made, should he offer $11.55 per tree?

2. What is the expected value of perfect information concerning the value of the fruit in the grove?

3. Should McCarthy have quantity estimates made, and if so for how many trees?

4. (a) If the optimal number of trees is *not* 0, what is the expected value of the information to be gained from an optimal survey? (b) If the optimal number of trees *is* 0, what is the expected value of the information to be gained from a survey of 10 trees?

5. Suppose that McCarthy takes a survey of 10 trees, whether or not this is optimal, and suppose that the average of the quantity estimates converted into dollar estimates is $11.50. Should he offer $11.55 per tree?

23C Stratification

23.13 Introduction: Stratified Sampling

23.13.1 Introduction

A problem of classical sampling theory is to draw a "stratified" sample from some population of items or individuals and then to "estimate" the population mean.[1] A more complete description of stratified sampling will be given shortly. Most of this chapter applies, however, not only to stratified sampling but more generally to any situation of the following sort. Suppose that there are r processes, on each of which observations may be made satisfying the same Normality assumptions as in chapter 23A. Instead of the economic structure of chapter 23A, however, we assume here that the value of any available act depends only on a certain linear combination of the process means $\mu_1, \ldots, \mu_r$, namely on

$$\mu = \boldsymbol{\pi}^t \boldsymbol{\mu} = \sum_{i=1}^{r} \pi_i \mu_i = \pi_1 \mu_1 + \pi_2 \mu_2 + \cdots + \pi_r \mu_r, \tag{23.101}$$

where $\pi_1, \ldots, \pi_r$ are known numbers. An example of a problem of this kind, other than stratified sampling, is that of sampling with or without bias, as discussed in section 23.12.1.

Before describing stratified sampling, we digress to recall the definitions of simple random sampling with and without replacement.

23.13.2 Simple Random Sampling with and without Replacement

Consider a population of N items or individuals. One obtains a *simple random sample with replacement* by making independent drawings from this population, each item having equal chance $1/N$ of being drawn each time. For the drawings to be independent, each item drawn must be replaced before the next drawing; think, for instance, of drawing balls from an urn. Sampling is usually done, however, without replacement of this sort. One obtains a *simple random sample without replacement* by making successive drawings on each of which, conditional on the previous drawings, each item not previously drawn has equal probability of being drawn. Then, if n is the sample size, all sets of n distinct members of the population are equally likely to be drawn. Note that distinct members of the population may nevertheless yield the same value of the characteristic being measured.

23.13.3 Stratified Random Sampling

Suppose that the population of interest is partitioned into r well-defined strata. (For instance, people may be partitioned into male and female, or

1. The treatment of Bayesian stratified sampling derives largely from Ericson (1963).

into "under 21," "between 21 and 65 inclusive," and "over 65.") A stratified sample is simply an independent set of simple random samples from the individual strata. We allow the possibility that some strata are not sampled at all. For strata that are sampled, all the items sampled are to make up one simple random sample (with or without replacement).

Suppose that we are interested in the mean μ of some numerical characteristic in some population that is or can be partitioned into r well-defined strata. If μ_i is the mean of this characteristic in the ith stratum, then the mean μ of the whole population is given by (23.101), that is, $\mu = \sum \pi_i \mu_i$, where π_i is the proportion of the population belonging to the ith stratum. We are assuming that the proportions $\pi_1, \ldots, \pi_r$ are known numbers. Here they also satisfy the extra condition $\pi_i \geq 0, \sum \pi_i = 1$.

23.14 Probability Assumptions

Returning to our more general framework, we make the following assumptions, also made in chapter 23A. First, letting μ_i be the ith process mean, we assume that the prior distribution of

$$\tilde{\boldsymbol{\mu}} = [\tilde{\mu}_1 \ldots \tilde{\mu}_r]^t \tag{23.102}$$

is *nonsingular Normal* with mean $\bar{\boldsymbol{\mu}}'$ and variance $\breve{\boldsymbol{\mu}}'$.

Second, letting n_i denote the number of observations made on the ith process and m_i the mean of these observations, we assume that given $\boldsymbol{\mu}$, the $\tilde{m}_i$ are *independently Normal* with means and variances

$$E(\tilde{m}_i | \boldsymbol{\mu}) = \mu_i, \qquad V(\tilde{m}_i | \boldsymbol{\mu}) = \upsilon_i / n_i, \qquad i = 1, \ldots, r, \tag{23.103}$$

where the process variances υ_i are assumed known. If not all processes are sampled, we make the same assumption about the m_i for those processes that are sampled. In cases where this assumption about the m_i is satisfied, the paragraph following (23.3) applies verbatim here.

In the case of stratified random sampling, μ_i has already been defined as the mean of the characteristic of interest in the ith stratum. Let m_i be the mean and n_i the size of the sample drawn from the ith stratum. Then given $\boldsymbol{\mu} = [\mu_1 \ldots \mu_r]^t$, the $\tilde{m}_i$ will be independently approximately Normal with means μ_i and variances υ_i / n_i, as required above, provided: (1) each sample *either* is drawn with replacement (unusual in practice) *or* is drawn without replacement but has small size compared to the stratum size (so that the "finite population correction" to the variance is negligible); (2) each sample mean is conditionally approximately Normal by virtue of either large sample size and the central limit effect or approximate Normality of the stratum from which it is drawn, or a combination of these. (If some strata are not sampled at all, then (1) and (2) need hold only in the strata that are sampled.)

23.15 Posterior Analysis and Terminal Decisions

23.15.1 Posterior Analysis

Under the probability assumptions of the previous section, we are in the situation of (22.18), just as we were in chapter 23A. As in section 23.2, the posterior distribution of $\tilde{\boldsymbol{\mu}}$ is nonsingular Normal with mean $\bar{\boldsymbol{\mu}}''$ and variance $\breve{\boldsymbol{\mu}}''$ that can be obtained by computing

$$\mathbf{H}' = \breve{\boldsymbol{\mu}}'^{-1} \tag{23.104a}$$

$$\mathbf{H} = \begin{bmatrix} n_1/v_1 & & 0 \\ & \ddots & \\ 0 & & n_r/v_r \end{bmatrix}, \tag{23.104b}$$

$$\mathbf{H}'' = \mathbf{H}' + \mathbf{H}, \tag{23.104c}$$

$$\bar{\boldsymbol{\mu}}'' = \mathbf{H}''^{-1}(\mathbf{H}'\bar{\boldsymbol{\mu}}' + \mathbf{H}\boldsymbol{m}), \tag{23.104d}$$

$$\breve{\boldsymbol{\mu}}'' = \mathbf{H}''^{-1}. \tag{23.104e}$$

In this chapter, however, we are specifically interested in $\tilde{\mu} = \sum \pi_i \tilde{\mu}_i$. Since $\tilde{\mu}$ is a linear function of $\tilde{\boldsymbol{\mu}}$ and the posterior distribution of $\tilde{\boldsymbol{\mu}}$ is multivariate Normal, the posterior distribution of $\tilde{\mu}$ is also Normal. Specifically, the posterior distribution of $\tilde{\mu}$ is univariate Normal with mean and variance

$$\bar{\mu}'' = \boldsymbol{\pi}^t \bar{\boldsymbol{\mu}}'' = \textstyle\sum_{i=1}^r \pi_i \bar{\mu}_i'', \tag{23.105a}$$

$$\breve{\mu}'' = \boldsymbol{\pi}^t \mathbf{H}''^{-1} \boldsymbol{\pi} = \textstyle\sum_{i=1}^r \sum_{j=1}^r \pi_i \pi_j \breve{\mu}_{ij}'', \tag{23.105b}$$

where $\bar{\boldsymbol{\mu}}''$, $\mathbf{H}''$, and $\breve{\boldsymbol{\mu}}$ are given by (23.104).

23.15.2 Terminal Decisions

Since the values of the available acts depend only on $\tilde{\mu}$ and the posterior distribution of $\tilde{\mu}$ is univariate Normal, the posterior terminal decision problems for the present situation reduce to univariate Normal terminal decision problems. If, for instance, there are two available acts and their values are linear in μ, then there will be a break-even value μ_b and one act will be chosen if $\bar{\mu}'' > \mu_b$, the other if $\bar{\mu}'' < \mu_b$. Since univariate Normal terminal decision problems have been discussed previously, they will not be considered further here.

The situation is the same for terminal decisions made without sampling. Before sampling, $\tilde{\mu}$ is Normal with mean and variance given by (23.105) with primes instead of double primes, and again we face a univariate Normal terminal decision problem.

23.16 Outline of the Rest of the Chapter

In the next section we shall turn to the problem of finding the optimal choice of the sample sizes $n_1, \dots, n_r$. Under the usual assumption about the sampling cost, or even a somewhat weaker assumption, we shall find as in chapter 23B that the relevant probability distributions depend on the sample sizes $n_1, \dots, n_r$ only through the posterior variance $\breve{\mu}''$ of the quantity $\tilde{\mu}$ of interest. Consequently we shall again be able to separate the problem into two parts. One is the allocation problem: How should $n_1, \dots, n_r$ be chosen to minimize the sampling cost for a given value of $\breve{\mu}''$, or, equivalently, to minimize $\breve{\mu}''$ for a given sampling budget? The optimal allocation does not depend on the nature of the terminal decision problem, and will be treated at some length. The remaining problem is to choose the value of $\breve{\mu}''$ or of the sampling budget. Here, of course, the terminal economics enter, and detailed analytical treatment is very complicated; we shall content ourselves with indicating the general nature of the solution and one or two of its special features.

For a diffuse prior, the optimal allocation takes a particularly simple form. The extra cost incurred by using some other allocation in this case can be expressed easily and suggestively. This is done in section 23.18.

Finally, in section 23.19, we compare stratified random sampling with simple random sampling.

23.17 Preposterior Analysis

23.17.1 Introduction

This section is concerned with the optimal choice of the sample sizes $n_1, \dots, n_r$. To make progress, we require some assumption about the economic structure of the problem. Let us make the assumption, on which most of the preposterior analysis in this book has been based, that utility is linear in value where value can be expressed as terminal value minus sampling cost. (See section 14.2.) In our present notation, this means that value can be written in the form

$$v(\boldsymbol{n}, \boldsymbol{m}, u, \boldsymbol{\mu}) - v_t(a, \mu) \quad c_s(\boldsymbol{n}, \boldsymbol{m}) \tag{23.106}$$

and that the optimal procedure maximizes expected value. (The terminal value depends only on $\mu = \boldsymbol{\pi}^t\boldsymbol{\mu} = \sum \pi_i \mu_i$ by the assumption of section 23.13.1.) The assumption just made entitles us to use such concepts as EVSI and ENGS.

We shall now show that the optimal procedure must allocate $n_1, \ldots, n_r$ in such a way as to minimize the expected sampling cost $\bar{c}_s(\boldsymbol{n}) \equiv Ec_s(\boldsymbol{n}, \tilde{\boldsymbol{m}})$ for given $\breve{\mu}''$, , or equivalently to minimize $\breve{\mu}''$ for given $\bar{c}_s(\boldsymbol{n})$. Then, in the next subsection, we shall consider the problem of finding the optimal allocation when the expected sampling cost $\bar{c}_s(\boldsymbol{n})$ is a linear function of $\boldsymbol{n}$.

Observe first that the a posteriori expected terminal loss of the optimal decision depends only on the economics of the terminal decision and on the posterior distribution of μ, which is Normal with mean $\bar{\mu}''$ and variance $\breve{\mu}''$. Accordingly, the EVSI depends only on the terminal decision economics and on the prior distribution of the posterior parameters $\tilde{\bar{\mu}}''$ and $\breve{\mu}''$.

The posterior variance $\breve{\mu}''$, given by (23.105b), is known before the sample is drawn. By (23.104) it depends only on the prior variance matrix $\breve{\boldsymbol{\mu}}'$ and the sample sizes $n_1, \ldots, n_r$, not on the sample means $m_1, \ldots, m_r$.

The posterior mean $\bar{\mu}''$ is not known before the sample is drawn. However, by (23.105) and (16.29a), the distribution of $\tilde{\bar{\mu}}''$ is Normal with mean and variance

$$E(\tilde{\bar{\mu}}'') = \bar{\mu}' = \sum \pi_i \bar{\mu}_i', \tag{23.107a}$$

$$V(\tilde{\bar{\mu}}'') = \breve{\mu}' - \breve{\mu}'', \tag{23.107b}$$

where $\breve{\mu}''$ is given by (23.105b) and $\breve{\mu}'$ by (23.105b) with primes in place of double primes.

It follows that the EVSI depends on the choice of sample sizes $n_1, \ldots, n_r$ only through $\breve{\mu}''$. For once $\breve{\mu}''$ is selected, the prior distribution of the posterior parameters is determined; the posterior variance is simply the selected $\breve{\mu}''$ (not a rv), while the posterior mean $\tilde{\bar{\mu}}''$ is Normal with mean $\bar{\mu}'$ and variance $\breve{\mu}' - \breve{\mu}''$, and $\bar{\mu}'$ and $\breve{\mu}'$ do not depend on the choice of $n_1, \ldots, n_r$.

Since the EVSI depends on $n_1, \ldots, n_r$ only through $\breve{\mu}''$, whatever our decision problem and whatever $\breve{\mu}''$ we select, we will want to choose $n_1, \ldots, n_r$ so as to obtain the selected value of $\breve{\mu}''$ at minimum expected sampling cost. Thus we can break up the problem of choosing $n_1, \ldots, n_r$ into two parts: choosing $\breve{\mu}''$, and choosing $n_1, \ldots, n_r$ to minimize expected sampling cost for a given $\breve{\mu}''$.

Minimizing expected sampling cost for given $\breve{\mu}''$ is essentially the same as minimizing $\breve{\mu}''$ for given expected sampling cost, and it is usually more natural to look at the problem in this way. Thus the problem of choosing $n_1, \ldots, n_r$ is broken into two parts: choosing the sampling budget (expected sampling cost), and choosing $n_1, \ldots, n_r$ to minimize $\breve{\mu}''$ for a given budget.

This conclusion remains valid, though the foregoing derivation does not, even if the assumption of linear utility is dropped, provided the sampling cost depends only on the sample sizes and not on the observations. Specifically, it is enough to assume that utility is an increasing function of value where value is expressible in the form (23.106) with $c_s(\boldsymbol{n}, \boldsymbol{m})$ a function of $\boldsymbol{n}$ alone. The proof in this case is left as an exercise.

23.17.2 Optimal Allocation

We saw in the previous subsection that, under certain assumptions, one part of the problem of choosing the sample sizes $n_1, \ldots, n_r$ is to minimize $\breve{\mu}''$ for a given sampling budget $\bar{c}_s(\boldsymbol{n})$, or to minimize the expected sampling cost $\bar{c}_s(\boldsymbol{n})$ for a given $\breve{\mu}''$. We have called this the "optimal allocation problem," because it is concerned with allocating a given sampling budget in such a way as to maximize the effectiveness of the sample (minimize $\breve{\mu}''$). This problem will be discussed in this subsection, under the assumption that the expected sampling cost is a linear function of the sample sizes. Notice that the optimal allocation depends on the prior distribution of $\tilde{\boldsymbol{\mu}}$ and the sampling costs, but not on the economics of the terminal decision problem. These economics play a role only in the remaining part of the problem of choosing $n_1, \ldots, n_r$, namely choosing the overall sampling budget (or $\breve{\mu}''$). This part of the problem is harder in some ways, but easier in that it is essentially one-dimensional. In any case, it can conveniently be discussed only after the allocation problem is solved, since it requires one to take account of the relation between $\breve{\mu}''$ and the sampling budget under optimal allocation.

Assume now that the expected cost of sampling is of the form

$$\bar{c}_s(\boldsymbol{n}) = \bar{c}_s(n_1, \ldots, n_r) = \textstyle\sum_{i=1}^{r} k_{si} n_i. \tag{23.108}$$

In particular, assume that there are no stage (i.e., fixed) costs. (The modifications required if there are stage costs are much the same as in problems discussed earlier.)

The allocation problem is to minimize $\breve{\mu}''$, which is given by (23.105b), subject to the constraint that $\bar{c}_s(\boldsymbol{n})$ has a specified value and that $n_1, \ldots, n_r$ be nonnegative integers. We omit henceforth the requirement that the n_i be integers; then the constraints are all linear in the n_i. We do not have a linear programming problem, however, because $\breve{\mu}''$, the quantity to be minimized (objective function), is not a linear function of the n_i. Fortunately, there are techniques for minimizing any well-behaved function subject to linear constraints, and $\breve{\mu}''$ is an eminently well behaved function as far as these techniques are concerned, its only drawback being that it is

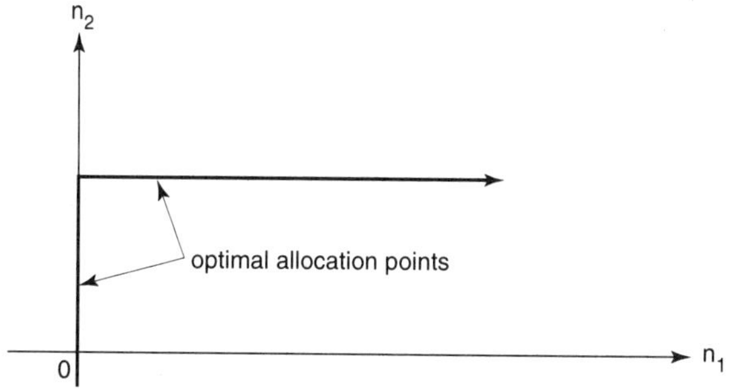

Figure 23.3
Optimal allocation, special case

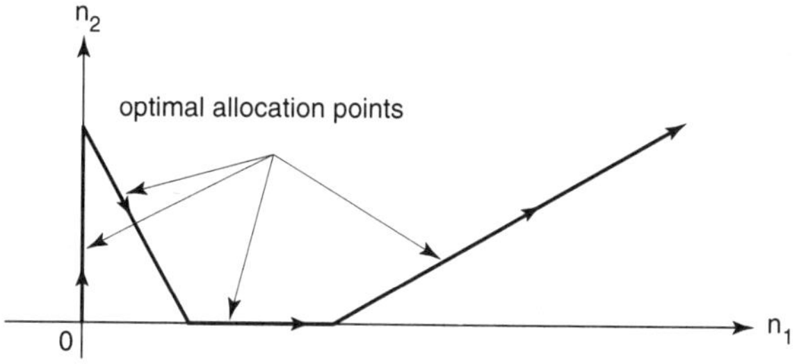

Figure 23.4
Optimal allocation, unusual case

not trivial to calculate. (Notice what must be done for each value of $\check{\mu}''$ calculated.) It can be shown that the optimal n_i are piecewise linear functions of the sampling budget. Examples are given in figure 23.3, which corresponds to the problem of chapter 23B, and in figure 23.4, which exhibits the curious but possible phenomenon that it may be optimal to sample entirely from one of two processes (strata) if the budget is small, entirely from the other if the budget is of intermediate size, and from both if the budget is large. A more typical situation is shown in figure 23.5.

We can go further analytically if, as we now assume, the $\tilde{\mu}_i$ are independent a posteriori. (This will be the case if and only if the $\tilde{\mu}_i$ are independent a priori.) Then the posterior variance matrix $\check{\boldsymbol{\mu}}''$ is diagonal, so is $\mathbf{H}''$, and

$$\check{\mu}''_{ii} = \check{\mu}''_i = (H''_{ii})^{-1}, \qquad \check{\mu}''_{ij} = 0, \qquad j \neq i = 1, \dots, r. \tag{23.109}$$

It follows that

$$\check{\mu}'' = \sum_{i=1}^{r} \frac{\pi_i^2}{H''_{ii}}. \tag{23.110}$$

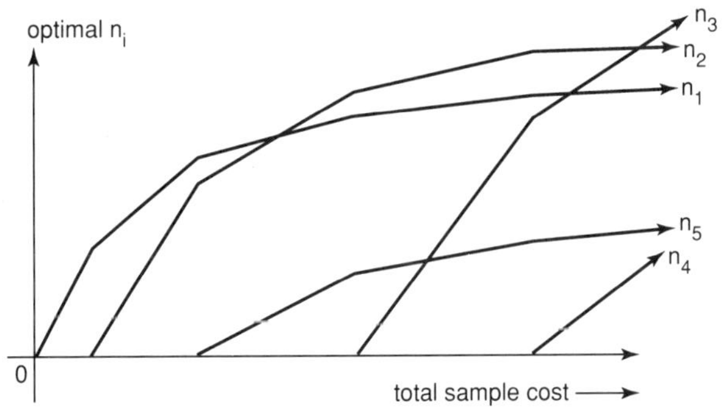

Figure 23.5
Optimal allocation, usual case

Recall that by (23.104)

$$H''_{ii} = H'_{ii} + n_i/\upsilon_i \qquad i = 1, \ldots, r. \tag{23.111}$$

Therefore choosing n_i is equivalent to choosing H''_{ii}. In terms of H''_{ii}, the constraints are that $H''_{ii} \geq H'_i (n_i \geq 0)$ and the sampling budget condition, which is that

$$\bar{\bar{c}}_s(\boldsymbol{n}) = \textstyle\sum_{i=1}^r k_{si}\upsilon_i H''_{ii} - \sum_{i=1}^r k_{si}\upsilon_i H'_{ii} \tag{23.112}$$

have a specified value. As we shall show a little later by the Lagrange multiplier technique, the minimum of (23.110) subject to the sampling budget condition that (23.112) have a particular value occurs at

$$H''^{o}_{ii} = \lambda|\pi_i|(k_{si}\upsilon_i)^{-1/2}, \qquad i = 1, \ldots, r, \tag{23.113a}$$

where the factor λ must be chosen to satisfy the sampling budget condition. The equation for λ may be written

$$\lambda \textstyle\sum |\pi_i|(k_{si}\upsilon_i)^{1/2} = \sum k_{si}\upsilon_i H'_{ii} + C, \tag{23.113b}$$

where C is the specified value of the sampling budget. The n_i corresponding to (23.113a) are

$$n_i^o = \lambda|\pi_i|(\upsilon_i/k_{si})^{1/2} - H'_{ii}\upsilon_i, \qquad i = 1, \ldots, r. \tag{23.113c}$$

Equations (23.113) therefore give the optimal allocation provided they give $H''^{o}_{ii} \geq H'_{ii}$, or equivalently $n_i^o \geq 0$, $i = 1, \ldots, r$.

If the prior is diffuse ($\mathbf{H}' = \mathbf{0}$) then these inequalities will certainly be satisfied. Notice that in this case the optimal allocation of the sample sizes is inversely proportional to the square root of the variable sampling cost, directly proportional to the process standard deviation of the ith process or stratum, and directly proportional to $|\pi_i|$, which is the proportion in the ith stratum in the situation of section 23.13.3.

If the prior is not diffuse (but the $\tilde{\mu}_i$ are independent a priori) then as long as the sampling budget C is large enough, (23.113) will still give $H''^o_{ii} \geq H'_{ii}$, $n^o_i \geq 0$, for all i and hence give the optimal allocation. As C decreases, λ decreases, and hence the n^o_i decrease; when one of the n^o_i becomes 0, then for all smaller C the corresponding stratum is not sampled and is omitted from (23.113a) and (23.113c) and from the sums in (23.113b); as C decreases further, further strata drop out in the same way. The ith stratum drops out when λ has decreased to

$$H'_{ii}(\upsilon_i k_{si})^{1/2}/|\pi_i|. \tag{23.114}$$

In this manner the optimal allocation for every possible sampling budget is obtained, in a convenient form for subsequent optimization of the budget. Notice that the optimal H''_{ii} and n_i are piecewise linear functions of the budget, which (as we asserted earlier) is true in general.

If the sampling budget is not to be chosen optimally but is fixed by external fiat, then one is really interested only in the optimal allocation for one particular budget. In this case one can cut corners a little in the foregoing procedure, proceeding instead as follows. First use (23.113) as it stands. If all $H''^o_{ii} \geq H'_{ii}$, $n^o_i \geq 0$, this is the solution. If some $H''^o_{ii} \leq H'_{ii}$, $n^o_i \leq 0$, then the optimal sample size for these processes (strata) is 0. In this case, use (23.113) again on the remaining processes, that is, omit from (23.113a) and (23.113c) and from the sums in (23.113b) all those values for i for which the first trial give $H''^o_{ii} \leq H'_{ii}$, $n^o_i \leq 0$. (The new value of λ will be smaller.) If all new $H''^o_{ii} \geq H'_{ii}$, $n^o_i \geq 0$, then this is the solution. If some new $H''^o_{ii} \leq H'_{ii}$, $n^o_i \leq 0$, then the optimal sample size for these processes is 0. In this case, use (23.113) again on the remaining processes, and so on, until all new $H''^o_{ii} \geq H'_{ii}$, $n^o_i \geq 0$. This procedure gives the optimal allocation for one specified budget more rapidly than that of the preceding paragraph, but is not as good for giving the optimal allocation for all budgets.

We conclude this section by proving that the allocation (23.113) is optimal provided it is legitimate, that is, provided $H''^o_{ii} \geq H'_{ii}$, $n^o_i \geq 0$. We shall not prove our assertions about what happens when (23.113) gives some $H''^o_{ii} < H'_{ii}$, $n^o_i < 0$.

Proof We are to choose H''_{ii} so as to minimize $\breve{\mu}''$, given by (23.110), subject to the constraint that $\bar{c}_s(\boldsymbol{n})$, given by (23.112), has a specified value. Introducing the Lagrange multiplier λ^*, we write

$$F = \breve{\mu}'' - \lambda^* \bar{c}_s(\boldsymbol{n}) = \sum \frac{\pi_i^2}{H''_{ii}} - \lambda^*[\sum k_{si}\upsilon_i H''_{ii} - \text{constant}]. \tag{23.115}$$

Setting the partial derivatives of F with respect to the H''_{ii} equal to zero, we find that

$$\frac{\partial F}{\partial H''_{ii}} = -\frac{\pi_i^2}{H''^2_{ii}} - \lambda^* k_{si} \upsilon_i = 0 \quad \text{for all } i. \tag{23.116}$$

Solving for H''_{ii} gives

$$H''_{ii} = (-\lambda^*)^{-1/2} |\pi_i| (k_{si}\upsilon_i)^{-1/2} \quad \text{for all } i, \tag{23.117}$$

where λ^* is to be determined so that $\bar{c}_s(\boldsymbol{n})$ has the required value. Therefore (23.117) minimizes $\breve{\mu}''$ subject to the constraint on $\bar{c}_s(\boldsymbol{n})$. Since (23.113a) is just (23.117) with $\lambda = (-\lambda^*)^{-1/2}$, the proof is complete.

23.17.3 Optimal Sampling Budget

Under certain assumptions, the problem of choosing the sample sizes $n_1, \ldots, n_r$ was shown, in section 23.17.1, to be separable into two parts, and one of these parts has just been discussed, namely how to allocate $n_1, \ldots, n_r$ optimally, so as to minimize $\breve{\mu}''$ for a given sampling budget, or to minimize the expected sampling cost for a given $\breve{\mu}''$. The remaining part of the problem is to choose the sampling budget. We shall now discuss briefly the nature of this problem under the assumptions made previously.

Consider first the case of a diffuse prior ($\mathbf{H}' = \mathbf{0}$). Then the optimal allocation is given by (23.113) as it stands. Under the optimal allocation we have that

$$\bar{c}_s(\boldsymbol{n}^o) = \lambda K, \qquad \breve{\mu}'' = K/\lambda, \tag{23.118a}$$

where

$$K = \textstyle\sum_{i=1}^r |\pi_i| (k_{si}\upsilon_i)^{1/2}. \tag{23.118b}$$

What remains to be chosen is the sampling budget, or equivalently $\breve{\mu}''$, or equivalently λ. It will be seen that this problem is mathematically exactly the same as that of choosing the optimal sample size λ to draw from an unbiased Normal process with known variance under similar circumstances. Specifically, suppose one can observe a Normal process with unknown process mean μ and known process variance K, the prior distribution of $\tilde{\mu}$ is diffuse, the sampling cost is K per observation, and the terminal decisions and loss functions are the same as in the actual problem. Then a sample of size λ will have exactly the same properties as are obtained in the present problem by the choice of λ under the optimal allocation (23.113); in particular, the sampling cost and posterior variance are given by (23.118a) in both cases. For our two prototypical estimation problems, the optimal λ can therefore be found as in sections 16.8 and 16.9. The details are left as an exercise.

If the prior is not diffuse (and even if there are stage costs) the worst that can happen is that there is a finite number of intervals on each of which $\bar{c}_s(\boldsymbol{n}^o)$ is a linear function of λ and $\breve{\mu}''$ is a linear function of $1/\lambda$, but that the linear functions vary from interval to interval. It can be seen from this that on each interval the mathematical problem is the same as that arising for the same terminal decision problem when the only sampling possible is on a Normal process with unknown bias. At worst, then, one has to solve one unknown bias problem for each interval and choose the best of these solutions. We will neither prove this nor pursue it in more detail here. Chapter 23B provides an example with two intervals.

It is not essential to the argument of the previous two paragraphs that λ enter in exactly the way that it does, or indeed that λ be mentioned at all. The essential points in the next-to-last paragraph are that under optimal allocation the expected sampling cost and the posterior variance $\breve{\mu}''$ are inversely proportional, and that the same relation arises in sampling from an unbiased Normal process. In the last paragraph, the essential points are that under optimal allocation the expected sampling cost and the posterior variance are piecewise "bilinearly" related, and that the same bilinear relations arise in sampling from biased Normal processes. (Two variables are said to be *bilinearly* related if a nonconstant linear function of one is inversely proportional to a nonconstant linear function of the other, or equivalently, if each is a quotient of two linear functions of the other but is not a linear function of the other.)

23.18 Nonoptimal Allocation (Diffuse Prior)

Under certain conditions, we obtained in section 23.17.2 the optimal allocation of the sample sizes $n_1, \ldots, n_r$ to minimize the expected sampling cost for a given $\breve{\mu}''$, or to minimize $\breve{\mu}''$ for a given expected sampling cost. In this section we shall be concerned with how much is lost by not using the optimal allocation. There are at least two reasons for considering this question. One is that the answer will give us some idea how carefully we need to make the assignments on which the optimal allocation is based. Another is that it is sometimes impossible to allocate optimally, for instance, when the same stratified sample is being used to obtain information about several characteristics of the population.

We make the same assumptions as in section 23.17.2 and in addition we assume that the prior is diffuse ($\mathbf{H}' = \mathbf{0}$). For convenience we also assume all $\pi_i \geq 0$; otherwise π_i must be replaced by $|\pi_i|$ in what follows. Then by (23.113c), the optimal allocation is $n_i^o = \lambda \pi_i \sigma_i k_{si}^{-1/2}$, where

$$\sigma_i = v_i^{1/2} \qquad (23.119)$$

is the ith process standard deviation. For any allocation $\boldsymbol{n}$, let b_i be defined by

$$n_i = n_i^o b_i = \lambda \pi_i \sigma_i k_{si}^{-1/2} b_i, \qquad i = 1, \dots, r. \tag{23.120}$$

Then $b_i = n_i / n_i^o$ is the misallocation factor by which the allocation n_i of (23.120) differs from the optimal allocation. In particular, $b_i = 1$ gives optimal allocation. Notice, however, that multiplying all b_i by a constant makes no essential difference, as this constant can be absorbed into λ. Accordingly, it is the extent to which the b_i differ from each other that really matters, not the extent to which they differ from 1. This will be evident in what follows.

Under the allocation (23.120) we have by (23.110), (23.111), (23.120), and (23.108) that

$$\breve{\mu}'' \bar{\bar{c}}_s(\boldsymbol{n}) = \textstyle\sum_{i=1}^r \pi_i \sigma_i k_{si}^{1/2} b_i^{-1} \sum_{j=1}^r \pi_j \sigma_j k_{sj}^{1/2} b_j. \tag{23.121a}$$

For later use, we note that this formula is unchanged if $n_i = n_i^o / b_i$ instead of $n_i^o b_i$, that is, if

$$n_i = \lambda \pi_i \sigma_i k_{si}^{-1/2} b_i^{-1}, \qquad i = 1, \dots, r. \tag{23.122}$$

Thus it is equally bad to misallocate by the factors $1/b_i$ as by the factors b_i.

Under the optimal allocation we have, by (23.121a) with $b_i = 1$, that

$$\breve{\mu}''^o \bar{\bar{c}}_s(\boldsymbol{n}^o) = (\textstyle\sum \pi_i \sigma_i k_{si}^{1/2})^2. \tag{23.121b}$$

The ratio of (23.121a) to (23.121b) is

$$\frac{\breve{\mu}'' \bar{\bar{c}}_s(\boldsymbol{n})}{\breve{\mu}''^o \bar{\bar{c}}_s(\boldsymbol{n}^o)} = \frac{\sum \pi_i \sigma_i k_{si}^{1/2} b_i^{-1} \sum \pi_j \sigma_j k_{sj}^{1/2} b_j}{(\sum \pi_i \sigma_i k_{si}^{1/2})^2}. \tag{23.123}$$

We shall comment on the interpretation of this formula and exemplify it shortly. First, however, we shall rewrite it in a way that makes the effect of the misallocation factors b_i easier to see. To this end, we let

$$a_i = \pi_i \sigma_i k_{si}^{1/2} b_i^{-1} \qquad \text{for all } i, \tag{23.124a}$$

and define a discrete rv $\tilde{b}$ with possible values $b_1, \dots, b_r$ having probabilities proportional to $a_1, \dots, a_r$; that is, we let

$$P(\tilde{b} = b_i) = a_i / \textstyle\sum a_j \qquad \text{for all } i. \tag{23.124b}$$

The rv $\tilde{b}$ thus defined has mean and mean square

$$\bar{b} = \frac{\sum a_i b_i}{\sum a_j}, \qquad E(\tilde{b}^2) = \frac{\sum a_i b_i^2}{\sum a_i}. \tag{23.125}$$

The rv $\tilde{b}$ is just an artificial construct introduced to give meaning to the algebraic expressions encountered here. In terms of $\tilde{b}$ we may write (23.121) and (23.123) as

$$\check{\mu}''\bar{\bar{c}}_s(\boldsymbol{n}) = (\textstyle\sum a_i)^2 E(\tilde{b}^2), \tag{23.126}$$

$$\check{\mu}''^{o}\bar{\bar{c}}_s(\boldsymbol{n}^o) = (\textstyle\sum a_i)^2 \bar{b}^2, \tag{23.127}$$

$$\frac{\check{\mu}''\bar{\bar{c}}_s(\boldsymbol{n})}{\check{\mu}''^{o}\bar{\bar{c}}_s(\boldsymbol{n}^o)} = \frac{E(\tilde{b}^2)}{\bar{b}^2}. \tag{23.128}$$

Furthermore, we have

$$\check{\mu}''\bar{\bar{c}}_s(\boldsymbol{n}) - \check{\mu}''^{o}\bar{\bar{c}}_s(\boldsymbol{n}^o) = (\textstyle\sum a_i)^2 V(\tilde{b}), \tag{23.129}$$

$$\frac{\check{\mu}''\bar{\bar{c}}_s(\boldsymbol{n}) - \check{\mu}''^{o}\bar{\bar{c}}_s(\boldsymbol{n}^o)}{\check{\mu}''^{o}\bar{\bar{c}}_s(\boldsymbol{n}^o)} = \frac{V(\tilde{b})}{\bar{b}^2}. \tag{23.130}$$

Notice that the right-hand sides of these formulas can be written in terms of the b_i and a_i and hence in terms of the b_i and π_i, σ_i, and k_{si}. However, the expressions given here convey more than the more elaborate algebraic expressions would. As a sidelight we point out that the fact that the right-hand side of (23.129) cannot be negative constitutes another proof of the fact that allocation proportional to $\pi_i \sigma_i k_{si}^{-1/2}$ is optimal when $\mathbf{H}' = \mathbf{0}$. This proof is easily extended to diagonal $\mathbf{H}'$.

The formulas above can be interpreted as follows. Formula (23.128), or equivalently (23.123), is the ratio of the posterior variances given by $\boldsymbol{n}$ and $\boldsymbol{n}^o$ if they have the same sampling cost. It is also the ratio of the sampling costs of $\boldsymbol{n}$ and $\boldsymbol{n}^o$ if they give the same posterior variance. Similarly, (23.129) implies that if $\boldsymbol{n}$ and $\boldsymbol{n}^o$ have the same sampling cost, say $\bar{\bar{c}}_s(\boldsymbol{n}) = \bar{\bar{c}}_s(\boldsymbol{n}^o) = C$, then the posterior variance $\check{\mu}''$ arising from $\boldsymbol{n}$ will exceed that arising from $\boldsymbol{n}^o$ by an amount equal to (23.129) divided by the common cost C. Also, if $\boldsymbol{n}$ and $\boldsymbol{n}^o$ give the same posterior variance $\check{\mu}''$, then $\boldsymbol{n}^o$ has smaller sampling cost than $\boldsymbol{n}$ by an amount equal to (23.129) divided by $\check{\mu}''$. Similarly, (23.130) is the factor by which the sampling cost of $\boldsymbol{n}$ exceeds that of $\boldsymbol{n}^o$ if they give the same posterior variance, and it is the factor by which the posterior variance obtained from $\boldsymbol{n}$ exceeds that obtained from $\boldsymbol{n}^o$ if they have the same sampling cost.

Recall that optimal allocation corresponds to the case that the b_i are all equal, and in particular that $V(\tilde{b}) = 0$. Formulas (23.129) and (23.130) reflect this. For example, (23.130) says that to achieve the same posterior variance with $\boldsymbol{n}$ as with $\boldsymbol{n}^o$ will cost more by a factor equal to the relative variance of the b_i. The extra cost will be relatively small or large according as the b_i vary little or much relative to their average size.

For any b_i, we may say that the advantage of the optimal allocation $\boldsymbol{n}^o$ over the allocation $\boldsymbol{n}$ given by (23.120) or (23.122) consists exactly of the elimination of the effect of differences among the b_i. Thus we can see what happens if we fail to take π_i, σ_i, and k_{si} all into account in the allocation. If we allocate n_i proportional to $\pi_i k_{si}^{-1/2}$, forgetting σ_i, we have (23.122) with $b_i = \sigma_i$, so the advantage of optimal allocation over allocation proportional to $\pi_i k_{si}^{-1/2}$ consists exactly of the elimination of the effect of differences among the σ_i. Similarly, if we allocate proportional to $\pi_i \sigma_i$, forgetting $k_{si}^{-1/2}$, we have (23.120) with $b_i = k_{si}^{1/2}$; allocating optimally instead would eliminate exactly the effect of differences among the k_{si}. Similarly, if we allocate proportional to $\sigma_i k_{si}^{-1/2}$, forgetting π_i, we have (23.122) with $b_i = \pi_i$; optimal allocation would eliminate exactly the effect of differences among the π_i.

This interpretation follows most directly from (23.128) or (23.130). For calculation, however, it is easier to use (23.123). Specifically, if we allocate proportional to $\pi_i k_{si}^{-1/2}$, forgetting σ_i, then we have (23.122) with $b_i = \sigma_i$ and hence, by (23.123),

$$\frac{\breve{\mu}''\bar{c}_s(\boldsymbol{n})}{\breve{\mu}''^{o}\bar{c}_s(\boldsymbol{n}^o)} = \frac{\sum \pi_i k_{si}^{1/2} \sum \pi_j k_{sj}^{1/2} \sigma_j^2}{(\sum \pi_i k_{si}^{1/2} \sigma_i)^2}. \tag{23.131}$$

If, for example, $r = 2$, $\pi_1 = \pi_2$, $k_{si} = k_{s2}$, and $\sigma_1 : \sigma_2 = 3:1$, then with $n_1 = n_2$ it costs 25% more to obtain the same $\breve{\mu}''$ as with the optimal allocation $n_1 : n_2 = 3:1$, since (23.131) equals

$$\frac{(1+1)(9+1)}{(3+1)^2} = 1.25.$$

Similarly, if we allocate proportional to $\pi_i \sigma_i$, forgetting $k_{si}^{-1/2}$, then we have (23.120) with $b_i = k_{si}^{1/2}$ and hence, by (23.123)

$$\frac{\breve{\mu}''\bar{c}_s(\boldsymbol{n})}{\breve{\mu}''^{o}\bar{c}_s(\boldsymbol{n}^o)} = \frac{\sum \pi_i \sigma_i \sum \pi_j \sigma_j k_{sj}}{(\sum \pi_i \sigma_i k_{si}^{1/2})^2}. \tag{23.132}$$

If, for example, $r = 2$, $\pi_1 = \pi_2$, $\sigma_1 = \sigma_2$, and $k_{s1} : k_{s2} = 1:2$, then with $n_1 = \mathrm{n}_2$ it costs 2.9% more to obtain the same $\breve{\mu}''$ as with the optimal allocation $n_1 : n_2 = 1 : 2^{-1/2} = 1 : 0.7071$, since (23.132) equals

$$\frac{(1+1)(1+2)}{(1+2^{1/2})^2} = 1.029.$$

Similarly, if we allocate proportional to $\sigma_i k_{si}^{-1/2}$, forgetting π_i, then we have (23.132) with $b_i = \pi_i$ and hence, by (23.123)

$$\frac{\breve{\mu}''\bar{c}_s(\boldsymbol{n})}{\breve{\mu}''^{o}\bar{c}_s(\boldsymbol{n}^o)} = \frac{\sum \sigma_i k_{si}^{1/2} \sum \sigma_j k_{sj}^{1/2} \pi_j^2}{(\sum \sigma_j k_{sj}^{1/2} \pi_j)^2}. \tag{23.133}$$

If, for example, $r = 2$, $\sigma_1 = \sigma_2$, $k_{s1} = k_{s2}$, and $\pi_1 : \pi_2 = 2:1$, then with

$n_1 = n_2$ it costs $\frac{1}{9}$ more to obtain the same $\breve{\mu}''$ as with the optimal allocation $n_1 : n_2 = 2:1$, since (23.133) equals

$$\frac{(1+1)(4+1)}{(2+1)^2} = \frac{10}{9}.$$

The effect of omitting two of the three factors in the optimal allocation is not the sum of the effects of omitting the two factors individually. In fact, it may be *better* to omit two factors than just one of the two, as the two factors may partially cancel each other. We will not go over the whole ground again for omission of each pair of factors, but only for one pair which will be of interest later.

If we allocate proportional to π_i, forgetting σ_i and $k_{si}^{-1/2}$, we have (23.122) with $b_i = \sigma_i k_{si}^{-1/2}$, and

$$\frac{\breve{\mu}''\bar{\bar{c}}_s(\boldsymbol{n})}{\breve{\mu}''^o\bar{\bar{c}}_s(\boldsymbol{n}^o)} = \frac{\sum \pi_i k_{si} \sum \pi_j \sigma_j^2}{(\sum \pi_i \sigma_i k_{si}^{1/2})^2}. \tag{23.134}$$

Optimal allocation would eliminate exactly the effect of differences among the $\sigma_i k_{si}^{-1/2}$. Notice that if k_{si} is proportional to σ_i^2, then $\sigma_i k_{si}^{-1/2}$ is constant, and allocation proportional to π_i is optimal and in particular better than allocation proportional to any two of the three factors π_i, σ_i, and $k_{si}^{-1/2}$. On the other hand, if the processes (strata) with large σ_i^2 have small k_{si} and vice versa, then the effects of differences among the σ_i and differences among the k_{si} are compounded and optimal allocation may be far better than allocation proportional to π_i. If, for example, $r = 2$, $\pi_1 = \pi_2$, $\sigma_1 : \sigma_2 = 3:1$, and $k_{s1} : k_{s2} = 1:2$, then with $n_1 = n_2$ it costs 54% more to obtain the same $\breve{\mu}''$ as with the optimal allocation $n_1 : \mathrm{n}_2 = 3 : 2^{-1/2} = 3 : 0.7071 = 4.243 : 1$, since (23.134) equals

$$\frac{(1+2)(9+1)}{(3+2^{1/2})^2} = 1.54.$$

Notice that the increase of 54% is far more than the sum of 25% (for $\sigma_1 : \sigma_2 = 3:1$, $k_{s1} = k_{s2}$) and 2.9% (for $k_{s1} : k_{s2} = 1:2$, $\sigma_1 = \sigma_2$).

23.19 Stratified Random Sampling versus Simple Random Sampling

In the foregoing analysis we had in mind particularly, though we seldom mentioned it explicitly, stratified random samples as described in section 23.13.3. We now consider them explicitly, and in particular consider the question, why stratify? Why not just take a simple random sample from the whole population?

23.19.1 General Discussion

There are generally four reasons or four related groups of reasons why gathering information about some population by means of a stratified random sample would be desirable. These are:

1. Administrative

In order to draw a simple random sample it is desirable to have an exhaustive listing of all the elements of the population. Such a list is called the *sampling frame.* Numbers are then assigned serially to the elements listed in the frame. A simple random sample is then obtained by drawing random numbers and including in the sample those population elements whose serial numbers correspond to the random numbers drawn.

It may happen that the sampling frame consists of several mutually exclusive lists corresponding to certain "natural" strata. Further, it may happen that no lists exist or only incomplete ones are available. In such cases it may be desirable to at least stratify the population into "listed" and "unlisted" groups. Stratification may be desirable in these cases because it often facilitates physically selecting the sample and gathering the sample data. Indeed, different sampling techniques may be appropriate in different strata. For example, simple random sampling may be appropriate in strata for which there exist complete lists, but other sampling techniques may be more appropriate for unlisted strata.[2]

Stratification may also be desirable when information is specifically wanted, not only on certain characteristics of the population as a whole, but also on smaller subgroups of the population. Stratification on the basis of these subgroups guarantees that a predetermined number of observations will be drawn from each of these groups, while under simple random sampling from the population these numbers are left to chance. Such a situation might arise in decision problems where the decision maker is faced with a different loss structure in each stratum.

2. Increased Sample Information

A second major class of reasons for using stratified sampling arises from the fact that the information provided by such a sample may greatly exceed that provided by a simple random sample of the same total size or having the same cost. Such an increase in sample information may be obtained if the population can be partitioned into relatively homogeneous

2. For a description of various other sampling techniques see: Hansen, Hurwitz, and Madow (1953, especially pp. 34–55) or Cochran (1977).

strata, meaning that the variability of the population items within any stratum is small, while the variability among the individual strata means is large. If a population can be so stratified, then the sampling variance for a properly selected stratified sample depends only on the small within-stratum variability, while that of a simple random sample will be larger, depending also on the between-strata variability. Further gains may be secured by drawing relatively larger samples from those strata having larger within-stratum variance.

3. Cost Reductions

A third reason for stratification arises from the potential savings in cost. First, as mentioned under (1) above, a stratified random sample may actually be administratively and physically easier to obtain and thus result in a lower cost. Also, if there are differences among the strata in the per-observation cost of sampling, then, as was shown earlier, by taking fewer observations in a stratum with a high sampling cost and more in a low-cost stratum one can often obtain the same sample information at a lower cost than would otherwise be obtainable.

4. Full Use of Prior Information

Finally, the decision maker may possess prior information concerning *individual stratum means*, having various amounts of information on different strata and on *relationships among stratum means.* Such prior information is most fully utilized if stratified sampling is undertaken. Greater posterior information will be obtained at the same or at a lower cost than under simple random sampling by using stratification and making full use of the prior information in determining the relative allocation of sampling effort among the various strata—for instance, by taking relatively more observations from a stratum about which the decision maker has little prior information, or even by not sampling at all from a stratum in which observations are expensive and prior information is large.

23.19.2 Posterior Variance

To compare stratified random sampling and simple random sampling quantitatively we need the posterior variance and the sampling cost for both kinds of sampling in the same situation. The posterior variance obtained from a stratified sample has already been derived. This subsection concerns the posterior variance that would be obtained by taking a simple random sample instead of a stratified one in the situation we have been discussing. This is a necessary preliminary to the comparison in the next subsection, which takes into account the sampling cost as well as the posterior variance.

Recall that we are concerned with the mean μ of some numerical characteristic in some population; that μ_i is the ith stratum mean; that σ_i is the ith stratum standard deviation; and that π_i is the proportion of the whole population belonging to the ith stratum.

We must distinguish two possibilities concerning the *analysis* of a simple random sample.

1. If we take the strata into account in the analysis, then the prior-posterior theory is the same as in stratified sampling. The difference is that we don't know in advance how large the sample sizes $n_1, \ldots, n_r$ will be. However,

$$E(\tilde{n}_i) = \pi_i n \quad \text{for all } i,$$

where n is the size of the sample random sample. Thus if n is fairly large we may expect in advance to get about the same posterior variance from a simple random sample as from a stratified random sample of the same total size with allocation proportional to stratum size, provided we take the strata into account in the analysis. For these reasons, simple random sampling with stratified analysis, that is, with strata taken into account in the analysis, will not hereafter be distinguished from stratified random sampling with allocation proportional to stratum size, and except where otherwise specified the term "simple random sampling" will presuppose the following method of analysis, *not* a stratified analysis.

2. If we do not know or do not keep track of which strata the observations fall in, then it is not possible to analyze the simple random sample like a stratified random sample. In fact we then have simply a random sample from a population with mean μ and some variance σ^2. This variance is (see exercise 8)

$$\sigma^2 = \sigma_w^2 + \sigma_b^2 \tag{23.135a}$$

where

$$\sigma_w^2 = \sum \pi_i \sigma_i^2, \qquad \sigma_b^2 = \sum \pi_i (\mu_i - \mu)^2. \tag{23.135b}$$

We can interpret σ_w^2 as the (average) "within-stratum variance" and σ_b^2 as the "between-strata variance." (Notice that σ_b^2 is just the variance of a discrete probability distribution with probability π_i at the point μ_i.) With this interpretation, (23.135a) says that the population variance is the sum of the within-stratum variance and the between-stratum variance.

Since we are assuming that $\tilde{\boldsymbol{\mu}}$ is multivariate Normal, we cannot very well assume that σ_b^2 is known, or therefore that σ^2 is known. Thus we are really in a situation similar to that of chapter 17. As in chapter 17, however, if the sample is at all large, it will provide an estimate $\hat{\sigma}^2$ of σ^2 and the posterior distribution of $\tilde{\mu}$ given the sample mean and $\hat{\sigma}^2$ will be almost the same as if σ^2 were known to be equal to $\hat{\sigma}^2$. In particular, if the prior distribution of $\tilde{\mu}$ is diffuse, then the posterior distribution of $\tilde{\mu}$ will be approximately Normal with mean equal to the sample mean and variance

$$\breve{\mu}'' = \frac{1}{n}\hat{\sigma}^2. \tag{23.136}$$

A stratified random sample of total size n with allocation proportional to stratum size will have $n_i = \pi_i\, n$ and hence, if the prior is diffuse, by (23.110) and (23.111)

$$\breve{\mu}'' = \frac{1}{n}\sum \pi_i \sigma_i^2 = \frac{1}{n}\sigma_w^2. \tag{23.137}$$

Accordingly, stratification proportional to stratum size (or taking the strata into account in the analysis) reduces the posterior variance by approximately

$$\frac{1}{n}\hat{\sigma}_b^2 \equiv \frac{1}{n}(\hat{\sigma}^2 - \sigma_w^2) \tag{23.138}$$

if the prior is diffuse and the sample not too small. Notice that $\hat{\sigma}_b^2$, as defined by (23.138), is an estimate of σ_b^2, since $\hat{\sigma}^2$ is an estimate of $\sigma_w^2 + \sigma_b^2$. Thus, as compared to a simple random sample *of the same size*, stratification proportional to stratum size eliminates the estimated effect of differences among the μ_i. Optimal allocation will further eliminate the effect of variability among the $\sigma_i k_{si}^{-1/2}$, as explained at (23.134). These two steps cannot be added up, however, as the first one equates sample size rather than sampling cost. More fundamentally, to compare the desirability of the two methods of sampling, we must consider sampling costs as well as posterior variances. We shall do so in the next subsection.

23.19.3 Preposterior Comparison

We now have formulas for the posterior variance under both simple and stratified random sampling in the same situation. The objective of this subsection is to take account of costs as well in comparing the two. However, there is one difficulty to be disposed of first.

In the situation we are discussing, before a simple random sample is drawn, the $\breve{\mu}''$ that will result is unknown, since σ^2 as given by (23.135) is unknown. Furthermore, if we operate in a purely formal way with a diffuse prior on $\tilde{\boldsymbol{\mu}}$, we find that the prior expected value of $\tilde{\breve{\mu}}''$ is infinite, $E(\tilde{\breve{\mu}}'') = \infty$. For most terminal decision problems, as conventionally expressed, this would lead to the conclusion that stratified random sampling is preferable no matter how much more expensive. This is unreasonable, and it is clear anyway that the diffuse prior on $\tilde{\boldsymbol{\mu}}$ will not ordinarily lead to a good approximation to the *prior* distribution of $\tilde{\mu}''$. However, all our statements concerning *posterior* analysis are approximately true provided we are dealing with sample sizes large enough so that the sample information will swamp the prior information. And often prior information that will be negligible a posteriori is at the same time not negligible for *preposterior* analysis, and is indeed considerable in view of the insensitivity of EVSI to uncertainty about σ^2 when $\tilde{\mu}$ is the cost-determining parameter. (Compare chapter 17.) Thus in many situations we will obtain a reasonable approximation if we set σ^2 as given by (23.135) equal to some "certainty equivalent" for preposterior analysis and yet assume that the posterior analysis will be based on a diffuse prior. Since the σ_i^2 have been assumed known all along, using a certainty equivalent for σ^2 amounts by (23.135) to using a certainty equivalent for σ_b^2.

On these grounds, for preposterior comparison of simple and stratified random sampling, let us assume that (1) the prior distribution of $\tilde{\mu}$ is diffuse enough and the sample large enough so that section 23.17 applies to stratified random sampling, and (2) the EVSI of the simple random sample is the same as if the prior distribution of $\tilde{\mu}$ were diffuse and σ^2 as given by (23.135) were known in advance. Assumption (2) means that for preposterior analysis of the simple random sampling we will take

$$\breve{\mu}'' = \frac{1}{n}\sigma^2 = \frac{1}{n}(\sigma_w^2 + \sigma_b^2) \tag{23.139}$$

and treat it as known in advance. And we can now compare simple and stratified random sampling merely by comparing the sampling costs of obtaining a specified value of $\breve{\mu}''$. Since it will turn out that the same method is better for all values of $\breve{\mu}''$, we will not need to discuss the economics of the terminal decision problem at all (exercise 9). Of course, the less well the assumptions we are using approximate the true situation, the less accurate our results will be. Under other assumptions, one could still compare the ENGS of simple and stratified random samples, but the calculation would be more difficult and involve terminal economics and the results would be more complicated and less perspicuous.

Under our assumptions, for simple random sampling we may use formula (23.139) for $\breve{\mu}''$ in preposterior analysis, treating σ_b^2 as known along with σ_w^2, which is known because the π_i and σ_i^2 are known. For stratified random sampling with $n_i = n\pi_i$ or simple random sampling with analysis taking account of the strata, we may use formula (23.137) for $\breve{\mu}''$. Suppose simple random sampling costs k_s per observation, while stratified sampling or analysis costs $\bar{k}_s = k_s + k_\Delta$ per observation in every stratum. Then by (23.137) and (23.139) stratifying proportional to π_i or taking the strata into account in the analysis is worth more than the incremental expense

k_Δ per observation if and only if

$$\frac{k_\Delta}{k_s} < \frac{\sigma_b^2}{\sigma_w^2}, \qquad (23.140)$$

that is, if and only if the proportional increase in cost per observation is less than the ratio of the "between-strata variance" σ_b^2 to the "average within-stratum variance" σ_w^2.

If simple random sampling costs k_s per observation while stratified random sampling with $n_i = n\pi_i$ (or simple random sampling with analysis taking account of the strata) costs k_{si} per observation in stratum i, the latter is preferable if and only if

$$\frac{\sum \pi_i k_{si}}{k_s} - 1 < \frac{\sigma_b^2}{\sigma_w^2}. \qquad (23.141)$$

Note that the left-hand side of (23.141) is the average proportional increase in expense per observation, $\sum \pi_i (k_{si} - k_s)/k_s = k_\Delta/k_s$, say. We can relate this paragraph to the previous one by letting $\bar{k}_s = \sum \pi_i k_{si}$, the average cost per observation of stratified random sampling with $n_i = n\pi_i$. Then $k_\Delta = \bar{k}_s - k_s$ as before, and (23.141) is the same as (23.140).

If one were really using a stratified random sample rather than taking account of the strata in analyzing a simple random sample, one would presumably allocate optimally rather than proportional to π_i. This will be different unless σ_i^2/k_{si} is constant. Stratified random sampling with optimal allocation is preferable to simple random sampling if and only if

$$[\sum \pi_i \sigma_i (k_{si}/k_s)^{1/2}]^2 < \sigma_w^2 + \sigma_b^2. \qquad (23.142)$$

Remember that σ_b^2 in formulas (23.140)–(23.142) is really only a certainty equivalent for σ_b^2 as given by (23.135b), and that formulas (23.140)–(23.142) are based on the assumptions that this certainty equivalent is adequate for *preposterior* analysis of simple random sampling, but that once the sample information is available it will swamp the prior information for either simple or stratified random sampling. As pointed out earlier, if these assumptions are not satisfied, one can still make a preposterior comparison of simple and stratified random sampling. In most situations, a comparison of this kind sufficiently accurate for practical purposes could be obtained fairly directly from results contained in this book. This would lead to complicated formulas different for each terminal decision problem in general. In any particular situation, the problem of which sampling method is preferable would be solved. The formulas would be too complicated, however, to reveal much about the general nature of the solution or to make them good illustrations of the methodology of this book. Accordingly we shall not derive them here.

Exercises

1. With the assumptions and notation of this chapter, suppose that there are two strata where

$$\boldsymbol{\pi} = [.75 \quad .25]^t, \qquad \bar{\boldsymbol{\mu}}' = [5 \quad 4]^t, \qquad \breve{\boldsymbol{\mu}}' = \begin{bmatrix} 4 & 2 \\ 2 & 3 \end{bmatrix};$$

let the stratum variances be $v_1 = 4$ and $v_2 = 6$. A stratified sample is drawn with $n_1 = 2$, $n_2 = 3$ and the resulting sample mean is

$$\boldsymbol{m} = [7.5 \quad 2.5]^t.$$

a. Find the prior distributions of $\tilde{\boldsymbol{\mu}}$ and $\tilde{\mu} = \boldsymbol{\pi}^t\tilde{\boldsymbol{\mu}}$.

b. Find the posterior distributions of $\tilde{\boldsymbol{\mu}}$ and $\tilde{\mu}$.

2. a. Let $\mu = \frac{1}{2}\mu_1 + \frac{1}{2}\mu_2$ and let the prior distribution of $\tilde{\boldsymbol{\mu}} = [\tilde{\mu}_1 \tilde{\mu}_2]^t$ be bivariate Normal with parameters

$$\bar{\boldsymbol{\mu}}' = [10 \quad 12]^t \quad \text{and} \quad \breve{\boldsymbol{\mu}}' = \begin{bmatrix} 10 & 3 \\ 3 & 4 \end{bmatrix}.$$

Consider an infinite-action problem in which, if a is chosen and μ is the "true value," the loss is given by

$$l_t(a, \mu) = 20(a - \mu)^2.$$

Find the optimal act $a^{o\prime}$ and the EVPI.

b. Suppose the decision maker considers drawing a stratified random sample of size $n_1 = 4$, $n_2 = 2$. Let the strata be Normal with variances $v_1 = 2$ and $v_2 = 4$. Let the cost of sampling be $k_{s1} = 6$ and $k_{s2} = 12$.

Find EVSI and ENGS for this sample. Is it worth sampling?

3. A decision maker must decide on the amount of product A to stock in order to meet his demand μ for the next period. The population of potential customers can be stratified as follows:

Stratum	:	1	2	3	4
Demand (unknown)	:	μ_1	μ_2	μ_3	μ_4
π_i	:	.36	.24	.30	.10
k_{si}	:	\$.64	\$.81	\$1.00	\$.49
$\sqrt{v_i}$	:	2,000	1,000	4,000	3,000

The loss per unit of overage is \$2, the loss per unit of underage is \$8. The decision maker possesses only negligible prior information about the μ's.

What is the optimal budget for sampling and how should this budget be allocated among the strata?

4. A retailer must order and stock some definite quantity of a new product A to meet an unknown demand μ. If the quantity she stocks is Q, then her

$$\text{Loss} = \begin{cases} \$.1(\mu - Q) & \text{if} \quad Q \le \mu, \\ \$.2(Q - \mu) & \text{if} \quad Q \ge \mu. \end{cases}$$

The retailer serves a large metropolitan area, embracing both a large city and its many suburbs. She knows that her competitors will also stock and sell the new product A.

In considering her stocking problem the retailer has divided the population of all potential consumers of product A into two groups: city consumers and suburban consumers. On the basis of past information concerning her share of the total market for products similar to A, she estimates that 8,000 "average" city consumers and 10,000 "average" suburban consumers will buy product A from her. In other words, letting μ_1 denote the unknown mean consumption per suburban consumer and μ_2 that per city consumer, she estimates that her total demand for product A will be

$$\mu = 10{,}000\mu_1 + 8{,}000\mu_2.$$

The retailer believes that a bivariate Normal distribution of $\tilde{\boldsymbol{\mu}}$ with mean and variance

$$\bar{\boldsymbol{\mu}}' = \begin{bmatrix} 40 \\ 50 \end{bmatrix}, \qquad \breve{\boldsymbol{\mu}}' = \begin{bmatrix} 200 & 100 \\ 100 & 200 \end{bmatrix},$$

adequately describes her prior information.

In order to obtain more information concerning the unknown mean consumption the retailer draws a sample of 50 suburban consumers and 36 city consumers and determines the consumption of product A for each member of each sample. The *mean* consumption in the two samples is

$$\boldsymbol{m} = \begin{bmatrix} m_1 \\ m_2 \end{bmatrix} = \begin{bmatrix} 54.0 \\ 38.6 \end{bmatrix}.$$

From the samples the following statistics were also computed:

$$s_1^2 = \tfrac{1}{49}\sum (x_i - 54.0)^2 = 1000, \qquad s_2^2 = \tfrac{1}{35}\sum (x_i - 38.6)^2 = 720.$$

The retailer was convinced that there was little or no bias in the sample observations.

a. What was the optimal stock level before sampling?

b. What was the expected value of perfect information before sampling?

c. After sampling, what is the optimal stock level? How much is perfect information worth now?

d. Suppose the retailer can obtain a further sample of 50 suburban customers at a cost of \$250. Would such a sample be worth taking?

5. We are interested in the mean μ of some characteristic in some population. A random sample of N_1 individuals is selected from the population, but because of refusals or not-at-homes, the value x of the characteristic of interest is obtained for only N_2 of the N_1 individuals originally selected. (Suppose, for example, $N_1 = 3{,}000$ and $N_2 = 2{,}000$.) We are afraid the nonrespondents may not be typical of the population as a whole, in which case we may have "nonresponse bias." Suppose that we also measure w, where w has possible values $w^{(1)}, \ldots, w^{(r)}$. Assume that from census data the proportion of individuals in each w-category is known. Indicate (a) how you would proceed to get a distribution on $\tilde{\mu}$ after sampling, (b) what assumptions you are making, (c) why it might be worthwhile to measure w even if there were no problems of "nonresponse bias."

6. Under the assumptions of section 23.17.2 and the additional assumption that the prior is diffuse ($\mathbf{H}' = \mathbf{0}$), show that, in the notation of chapters 23C and 16,

a. For the infinite-action problem with quadratic loss, the optimal sample sizes are $n_i^o = |\pi_i|(k_t v_i/k_{si})^{1/2}$, giving total sampling cost $\bar{c}_s(\boldsymbol{n}^o) = k_t^{1/2} K$ and posterior variance $\breve{\mu}'' = k_t^{-1/2} K$;

b. For the infinite-action problem with linear loss, the optimal sample sizes are $n_i^o = (k_t^2/4K)^{1/3}|\pi_1|(v_i/k_{si})^{1/2}$, giving total sampling cost $\bar{c}_s(\boldsymbol{n}^o) = (\tfrac{1}{2}k_t K)^{2/3}$ and posterior variance $\breve{\mu}'' = (2K^2/k_t)^{2/3}$.

c. What happens in the case of a two-action problem with linear value?

7. a. Under the original assumptions of section 23.17.1, consider any terminal decision problem and any family S of sampling plans. Let $\boldsymbol{n}^o$ be the optimal sampling plan, let $\boldsymbol{n}^*$ be the best plan in the family S, let $\boldsymbol{n}^a$ be the best plan in the family having the same $\breve{\mu}''$ as n^o, and let $\boldsymbol{n}^b$ be a plan with optimal allocation and the same $\breve{\mu}''$ as $\boldsymbol{n}^*$. Show that the ENGS of $\boldsymbol{n}^o$ exceeds that of $\boldsymbol{n}^*$ by at least $\bar{c}_s(\boldsymbol{n}^b) - \bar{c}_s(\boldsymbol{n}^*)$ and at most $\bar{c}_s(\boldsymbol{n}^a) - \bar{c}_s(n^o)$.

b. How much of the structure of the situation discussed in chapter 23C is essential in (a)?

8. Verify (23.135).
Hint Use (13.44).

9. Verify the assertion made after (23.139) that if we compute $\breve{\mu}''$ from (23.139) and treat it as if it were known in advance, we can compare simple and stratified random sampling merely by comparing sampling costs without having to discuss the terminal decision problem at all.

23D The Portfolio Problem

23.20 Introduction[1]

23.20.1 A General Mathematical Model

Many business decisions can be viewed as follows. If act a is chosen, a stream of cash flows will result, say $\tilde{z}_{1,a}, \tilde{z}_{2,a}, \ldots$, where $\tilde{z}_{t,a}$ is the cash flow in the time period t and where, in general, the $\tilde{z}_{t,a}$ are unknown and hence must be regarded as rv's. Thus a choice among acts is equivalent to a choice among streams of cash flows, where each stream is a sequence of jointly distributed rv's. The choice also needs to take account of the fact that a decision is not isolated, but is made in a context: its cash flows may be used for further investment, and other decisions which have been made and will be made have cash flow streams of their own. Utility is basically a function of the stream of total cash flows resulting from all decisions.

Substantial simplification in a decision problem occurs, at least conceptually, if we assume that (1) it can be treated as an isolated "small world" in itself, so that context can be ignored, and (2) every cash flow which could result from every possible act can be treated as occurring simultaneously. Under these assumptions utility need be assessed only on the cash flow at a single time, and only the cash flow from the decision at hand need be considered. The "small world" assumption is not essential to the simplification when utility is linear, which we have usually assumed, and it can perhaps be mitigated in other circumstances by taking context into account in the assessment of the utility function. The timing assumption is essential to this simplification, however. For if cash flows cannot be treated as occurring at the same time, then to solve an isolated decision problem, the decision maker must arrive at a utility function u defined on cash flow streams. He would then choose the act with maximum expected utility, that is, maximize

$$E[u(\tilde{z}_{1,a}, \tilde{z}_{2,a}, \ldots)]$$

with respect to a. The utility function u expresses the decision maker's attitude toward risk, the timing of cash flows, and their interaction.

In the general problem, when simultaneity cannot be assumed, as opposed to the special cases discussed in this book when it can, the context may be a simplifying rather than a complicating feature: it may enable one to use such concepts as cost of capital and marginal opportunity rate to eliminate the timing aspect of the problem. Whether such uses are well

1. The formulation of the portfolio problem and many of the results presented in this chapter were given by Markowitz (1959). Some of the results were given by Tobin (1958).

founded theoretically or effective practically will not be argued here. Let us hope so, however, because formidable difficulties arise when a decision problem of the general type formulated above is isolated or is so treated. To appreciate this, the reader is invited to consider assessing a utility function $u(z_1, z_2, \ldots)$ in the absence of any possibilities for raising or investing money. This is difficult whether $z_1, z_2, \ldots$ represent cash flows to a company or cash flows to an individual to be used for consumption only.

23.20.2 Special Cases

Some progress has been made on a number of special cases of the general problem posed above. Most of this book is concerned with situations where neither timing nor risk is important, that is, where the objective is to maximize expected monetary value and where all flows occur within a short enough span of time that they can be treated as simultaneous. Under these conditions, we could formally handle decisions with fairly complicated structures.

Linear programming ideas have been the basis for considerable progress on the special cases where timing is important but all flows are deterministic (that is, known with certainty), and the objective is to maximize a linear function of the cash flows up to a finite horizon time. Generalizations in the same spirit have been handled similarly. This line of work will not be discussed in this book.

In this chapter we shall discuss still another special case, where risk is important but timing is not. All flows will be treated as occurring simultaneously, eliminating the timing problems, but expected monetary value will not be taken as the criterion of utility. However, the available decisions and flows will have a fairly simple structure. Choosing a portfolio of securities is the practical problem best represented by the model discussed in this chapter.

23.20.3 The Portfolio Problem

We shall say that we have a portfolio problem if:

1. A finite number of investments are available;

2. The available capital can be divided up in any way among the investments;

3. All investments must be held for a certain period of time at the end of which they must be sold, or might as well be sold because the transaction cost of sale and repurchase is negligible;

4. The return per dollar on the ith investment does not depend on the amount invested in the ith or any other investment;

5. Utility is a function only of return on capital over the period of time in question.

For investments in securities, "return" would typically consist of dividends received plus end-of-period market value.

For the moment we assume that it is impossible to raise additional capital. Borrowing is considered in section 23.24.1. Let r be the number of investments available and let $\tilde{z}_i$ be the return per dollar of the ith investment, $i = 1, \ldots, r$. Since $\tilde{z}_i$ is not assumed to be known a priori, it is a rv. If the period of time of the investment is one year, a unit amount in the ith investment might typically have a return $\tilde{z}_i$ with, for example, mean $\bar{z}_i = 1.20$ and standard deviation $\ddot{z}_i = .30$.

The decision maker must choose the fraction of available capital to be invested in each investment. Thus an act may be viewed as a vector $\boldsymbol{\pi} = [\pi_1 \cdots \pi_r]^t$, where π_i is the fraction invested in the ith investment. We have

$$\pi_i \geq 0, \qquad \sum \pi_i = 1. \tag{23.151a}$$

(If some capital may be held as cash, we include cash as one of the possible investments.) The act $\boldsymbol{\pi}$ leads to an investment mix or portfolio whose return per dollar invested is

$$\tilde{Z} = \boldsymbol{\pi}^t \tilde{\boldsymbol{z}} = \sum \pi_i \tilde{z}_i. \tag{23.151b}$$

The optimal act π^o maximizes $Eu(\tilde{Z}) = Eu(\boldsymbol{\pi}^t \tilde{\boldsymbol{z}})$ where u is the decision maker's utility function for return.

23.21 Available Means and Standard Deviations

23.21.1 Mean and Standard Deviation of Return

It is natural to consider the mean and standard deviation of the return $\tilde{Z}$ of the portfolio $\boldsymbol{\pi}$. They are

$$E(\tilde{Z}) \equiv \bar{Z} = \boldsymbol{\pi}^t \bar{\boldsymbol{z}}, \tag{23.152a}$$

$$S(\tilde{Z}) \equiv \ddot{Z} = (\boldsymbol{\pi}^t \check{\boldsymbol{z}} \boldsymbol{\pi})^{1/2}, \tag{23.152b}$$

where $\bar{\boldsymbol{z}}$ and $\check{\boldsymbol{z}}$ are the mean vector and variance matrix of the rv $\tilde{\boldsymbol{z}}$ whose components are the returns $\tilde{z}_i$ on the individual investments. Notice that the standard deviation of a portfolio depends on the covariances between the returns of the individual investments as well as on their variances. Without some assumption, such as joint Normality of the returns $\tilde{z}_i$, we cannot assert that the mean and standard deviation of the portfolio return $\tilde{Z}$ determines its probability distribution or expected utility or, a fortiori, the corresponding portfolio; but formulas (23.152) apply nonetheless.

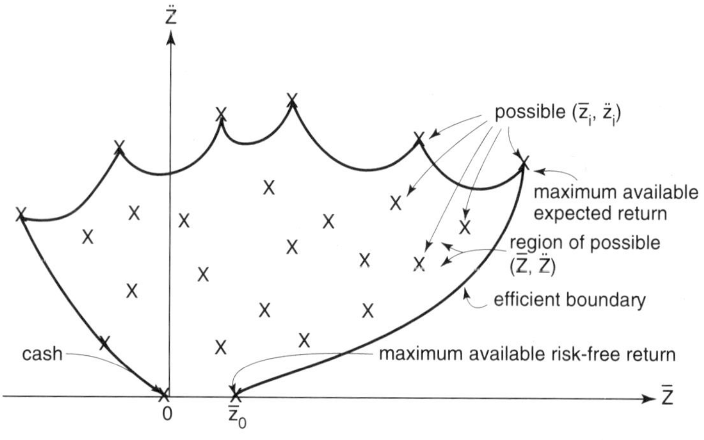

Figure 23.6
Region of possible means and standard deviations

23.21.2 The Region of Possible Means and Standard Deviations

It is useful to consider (see figure 23.6) the region of all possible points $(\bar{Z}, \ddot{Z})$ corresponding to possible portfolios. The points $(\bar{z}_i, \ddot{z}_i)$ are all possible. Suppose that $(\bar{Z}_1, \ddot{Z}_1)$ and $(\bar{Z}_2, \ddot{Z}_2)$ are possible, corresponding to $\boldsymbol{\pi}^{(1)}$ and $\boldsymbol{\pi}^{(2)}$ respectively. Then the portfolio $\boldsymbol{\pi} = \alpha\boldsymbol{\pi}^{(1)} + (1 - \alpha)\boldsymbol{\mu}^{(2)}$ is possible for any α, $0 \leq \alpha \leq 1$. It has return

$$\tilde{Z} = \alpha\tilde{Z}_1 + (1 - \alpha)\tilde{Z}_2 \tag{23.153}$$

with mean and standard deviation

$$\bar{Z} = \alpha\bar{Z}_1 + (1 - \alpha)\bar{Z}_2, \tag{23.154a}$$

$$\ddot{Z} = [\alpha^2\ddot{Z}_1^2 + (1 - \alpha)^2\ddot{Z}_2^2 + 2\alpha(1 - \alpha)\rho\ddot{Z}_1\ddot{Z}_2]^{1/2} \tag{23.154b}$$

where ρ is the correlation between $\tilde{Z}_1$ and $\tilde{Z}_2$. Since $-1 \leq \rho \leq 1$, we have

$$\ddot{Z} \leq \alpha\ddot{Z}_1 + (1 - \alpha)\ddot{Z}_2, \tag{23.155}$$

with equality if and only if $\rho = 1$, or $\ddot{Z}_1 = 0$, or $\ddot{Z}_2 = 0$, or $\alpha = 0$ or 1. Thus we see that as α varies between 0 and 1, $(\bar{Z}, \ddot{Z})$ sweeps out a curve of possible points connecting the points $(\bar{Z}_1, \ddot{Z}_1)$ and $(\bar{Z}_2, \ddot{Z}_2)$, and this curve lies below the straight line segment between these two points unless $\rho = 1$ or $\ddot{Z}_1 = 0$ or $\ddot{Z}_2 = 0$, in which case the curve is the straight line segment between the two points (figure 23.7). It follows that the region of all possible points $(\bar{Z}, \ddot{Z})$ is connected (all one piece) and convex from below, and that its boundary has a straight portion rising from the point corresponding to the largest available risk-free return $\bar{z}_o$, as long as some investment

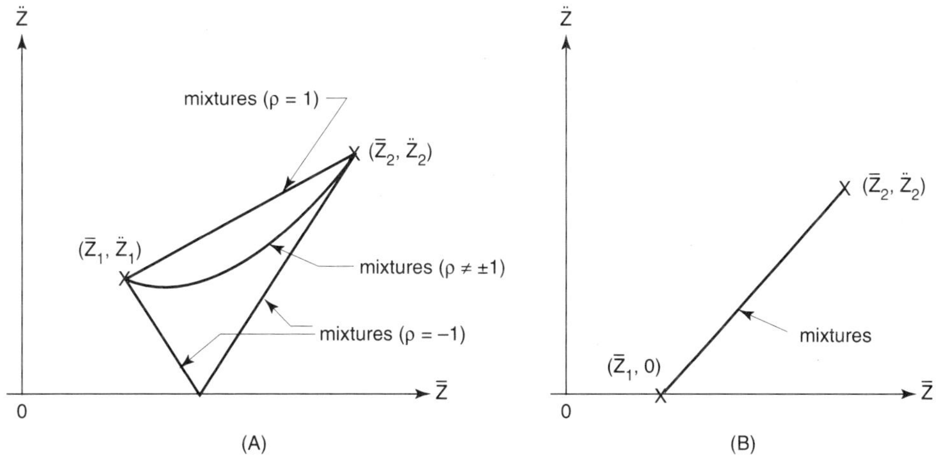

Figure 23.7
Mean and standard deviation of mixtures

has larger expected return $\bar{z}_i$ than the largest available risk-free return. (If there is no risk-free investment, then the efficient bounary in figure 23.6 will not extend to the horizontal axis, where $\ddot{Z} = 0$.) The statement is true even if the largest available risk-free return is not obtainable by investing in a single investment. This can happen, but only if the covariance matrix of those $\tilde{z}_i$ with $\ddot{z}_i > 0$ is singular. (See exercise 2.)

23.21.3 Efficient Points

A possible point $(\bar{Z}, \ddot{Z})$ will be called *efficient* if no other possible point $(\bar{Z}_1, \ddot{Z}_1)$ has $\bar{Z}_1 \geq \bar{Z}$ and $\ddot{Z}_1 \leq \ddot{Z}$. The efficient points form the lower right boundary of the set of possible points. The composition of a portfolio corresponding to an efficient point is unique as regards those investments with $\ddot{z}_i > 0$ unless the covariance matrix of these $\tilde{z}_i$ is singular (exercise 2), and it is unique as regards those investments with $\ddot{z}_i = 0$ unless more than one investment maximizes the return available risk-free. It should be understood, however, that the assumptions made so far do *not* guarantee that the optimal act gives an efficient point, as they do not even imply that the distribution of $\tilde{Z}$ is determined by its mean and standard deviation. (See also the end of section 23.21.1.)

23.22 Utility Determined by Mean and Standard Deviation

23.22.1 Preference among Normally Distributed Portfolios

Suppose now that the returns $\tilde{z}_i$ are jointly Normal. Then the return $\tilde{Z}$ of any portfolio is also Normal, and the probability distribution of $\tilde{Z}$ is determined by its mean and standard deviation. Therefore, the decision maker's utility for any portfolio is determined by the corresponding $(\bar{Z}, \ddot{Z})$ point. Since $\tilde{Z}$ has the distribution of $\bar{Z} + \ddot{Z}\tilde{w}$, where $\tilde{w}$ is unit Normal, the expected utility of $\tilde{Z}$ is

$$Eu(\tilde{Z}) - Eu(\bar{Z} + \ddot{Z}\tilde{w}) \equiv U(\bar{Z}, \ddot{Z}), \tag{23.156}$$

where the last equality defines U. Notice that utility u is a function of *return* measured as a *proportion of present capital.*

For any strictly increasing utility function u, we see immediately that

(a) $U(\bar{Z}, \ddot{Z})$ is strictly increasing in $\bar{Z}$ for fixed $\ddot{Z}$, that is, utility is strictly increasing toward the right in the $(\bar{Z}, \ddot{Z})$ plane.

Now suppose also that u is strictly risk averse. Then we shall show that

(b) $U(\bar{Z}, \ddot{Z})$ is strictly decreasing in $\ddot{Z}$ for fixed $\tilde{Z}$, that is, utility is strictly decreasing toward the top in the $(\bar{Z}, \ddot{Z})$ plane;

(c) If $U(\bar{Z}_1, \ddot{Z}_1) = U(\bar{Z}_2, \ddot{Z}_2)$ and $(\bar{Z}, \ddot{Z})$ is on the straight line segment between $(\bar{Z}_1, \ddot{Z}_1)$ and $(\bar{Z}_2, \ddot{Z}_2)$, say,

$$\bar{Z} = \alpha\bar{Z}_1 + (1 - \alpha)\bar{Z}_2, \qquad \ddot{Z} = \alpha\ddot{Z}_1 + (1 - \alpha)\ddot{Z}_2, \qquad 0 < \alpha < 1, \tag{23.157a}$$

then

$$U(\bar{Z}, \ddot{Z}) > U(\bar{Z}_1, \ddot{Z}_1) = U(\bar{Z}_2, \ddot{Z}_2). \tag{23.157b}$$

We may summarize (a)–(c) by saying that if u is strictly risk averse, then the indifference curves (i.e., equi-utility curves) in the $(\bar{Z}, \ddot{Z})$ plane are strictly increasing and concave, and utility increases toward the east and south, as in figure 23.8.

Suppose, for example, that u has constant positive risk aversion c, meaning

$$u(x) = -e^{-cx}. \tag{23.158}$$

This utility function has constant risk aversion in the sense that all preferences between risks are preserved under all changes in present capital, where the risks stay the same in dollars, not as a proportion of capital. (See exercise 5a.) The indifference curves corresponding to (23.158) are

$$\bar{Z} - \tfrac{1}{2}c\ddot{Z}^2 = \text{constant}, \tag{23.159}$$

by exercise 5b. Plotted in the $(\bar{Z}, \ddot{Z})$ plane, these curves are hyperbolas of equal width along the $\bar{Z}$-axis. (They are straight lines in the $(\bar{Z}, \check{Z})$ plane, of course.)

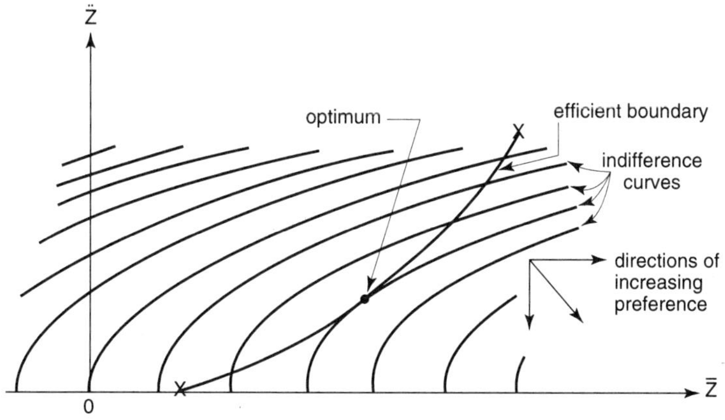

Figure 23.8
Indifference curves and efficient boundary

Since the indifference curves are concave and the region of possible $(\bar{Z}, \ddot{Z})$ points is convex from below, it follows that for any given strictly risk averse utility function, there is a unique, most desirable $(\bar{Z}, \ddot{Z})$ point. There could be more than one portfolio giving this point, but only under the special circumstances mentioned in section 23.21.3.

Proof of (b) and (c) Consider first any two points $(\bar{Z}_1, \ddot{Z}_1)$ and $(\bar{Z}_2, \ddot{Z}_2)$ and any $(\bar{Z}, \ddot{Z})$ satisfying (23.157a); by (23.156) and the concavity of u,

$$U(\bar{Z}, \ddot{Z}) = Eu(\alpha\bar{Z}_1 + (1-\alpha)\bar{Z}_2 + [\alpha\ddot{Z}_1 + (1-\alpha)\ddot{Z}_2]\tilde{w})$$
$$> \alpha Eu(\bar{Z}_1 + \ddot{Z}_1\tilde{w}) + (1-\alpha)Eu(\bar{Z}_2 + \ddot{Z}_2\tilde{w}). \tag{23.160a}$$

Expressing the right-hand side by means of (23.156), we obtain

$$U(\bar{Z}, \ddot{Z}) > \alpha U(\bar{Z}_1, \ddot{Z}_1) + (1-\alpha)U(\bar{Z}_2, \ddot{Z}_2). \tag{23.160b}$$

Part (c) follows immediately. Furthermore, for $\bar{Z}_2 = \bar{Z}_1$, $\ddot{Z}_1 > 0$, $\ddot{Z}_2 = 0$, (23.160b) gives

$$U(\bar{Z}_1, \alpha\ddot{Z}_1) > \alpha U(\bar{Z}_1, \ddot{Z}_1) + (1-\alpha)U(\bar{Z}_1, 0). \tag{23.161a}$$

By (23.156) and the concavity of u again

$$U(\bar{Z}_1, 0) = u(E\tilde{Z}_1) > Eu(\tilde{Z}_1) = U(\bar{Z}_1, \ddot{Z}_1). \tag{23.161b}$$

Applying this inequality to the previous one gives

$$U(\bar{Z}_1, \alpha\ddot{Z}_1) > U(\bar{Z}_1, \ddot{Z}_1) \tag{23.162}$$

which proves (b). Alternatively, (b) can be proved by differentiating $U(\bar{Z}, \ddot{Z})$ with respect to $\ddot{Z}$ (exercise 3).

23.22.2 Weakening the Normality Assumption[2]

How far do the essential points of the foregoing analysis hold without the assumption that the $\tilde{z}_i$ are jointly Normal? The following remarks are relevant here, though they do not completely answer the question. Bell (1991) gives further, complementary results.

1. Under quadratic utility u, the mean and standard deviation of the $\tilde{Z}$s do determine preferences among them, and (a)–(c) hold if u is strictly risk averse. The indifference curves are of the form (23.159), but for a different reason (exercise 7).

2. If two parameters of the distribution of $\tilde{Z}$ determine preferences among the $\tilde{Z}$s under the utility functions (23.158) with constant risk aversion c for all c in some nondegenerate interval, or a fortiori under all utility functions of any larger class, then the same two parameters determine the distribution of $\tilde{Z}$. This means one cannot generally plot utilities in two dimensions unless the family of distributions of $\tilde{Z}$s is a two-parameter family.

Proof If $\tilde{Z}_1$ and $\tilde{Z}_2$ are equally desirable under constant risk aversion c, then $Ee^{-c\tilde{Z}_1} = Ee^{-c\tilde{Z}_2}$. If this holds for all c in some nondegenerate interval, then by the uniqueness of Laplace transforms or moment-generating functions, $\tilde{Z}_1$ and $\tilde{Z}_2$ have the same distribution.

3. If the family of distributions of $\tilde{Z}$s is a two-parameter family, and includes at least two different risk-free returns, then the two parameters may be taken to be $\bar{Z}$ and $\ddot{Z}$, and $(\tilde{Z} - \bar{Z})/\ddot{Z}$ has the same distribution for all $\tilde{Z}$s with $\ddot{Z} > 0$. (The proof is omitted.)

4. If $(\tilde{Z} - \bar{Z})/\ddot{Z}$ has the same distribution for all $\tilde{Z}$'s with $\ddot{Z} > 0$, then (a)–(c) hold for all risk-averse utility functions.

Proof (23.156) holds, though $\tilde{w}$ may not be Normal. This is all that was used in the proof of (a)–(c).

5. If $(\tilde{Z} - \bar{Z})/\ddot{Z}$ has the same distribution for all $\tilde{Z}$s with $\ddot{Z} > 0$ and there are at least two independent $\tilde{Z}$'s with $\ddot{Z} > 0$, then the $\tilde{Z}$s are all Normal and the $\tilde{z}_i$ are jointly Normal.

Proof Let $\tilde{Z} = \alpha\tilde{Z}_1 + (1 - \alpha)\tilde{Z}_2$, $0 < \alpha < 1$, where $\tilde{Z}_1$ and $\tilde{Z}_2$ are independent with $\ddot{Z}_1 > 0$, $\ddot{Z}_2 > 0$. Let

$$\tilde{w} = (\tilde{Z} - \bar{Z})/\ddot{Z} \quad \text{and} \quad \tilde{w}_i = (\tilde{Z}_i - \bar{Z}_i)/\ddot{Z}_i, \qquad i = 1, 2. \tag{23.163}$$

Then $\tilde{w}_1$ and $\tilde{w}_2$ are independent and

$$\tilde{w} = b_1\tilde{w}_1 + b_2\tilde{w}_2, \tag{23.164a}$$

2. This subsection is optional.

where

$$b_1 = \alpha\ddot{Z}_1/\ddot{Z} \qquad b_2 = (1-\alpha)\ddot{Z}_2/\ddot{Z}. \tag{23.164b}$$

Furthermore, $\tilde{w}$, $\tilde{w}_1$, and $\tilde{w}_2$ have the same distribution. Letting

$$\varphi(t) = E[e^{t\tilde{w}}], \tag{23.165}$$

we therefore have

$$\varphi(t) = E[e^{t(b_1\tilde{w}_1 + b_2\tilde{w}_2)}] = E[e^{tb_1\tilde{w}_1}]E[e^{tb_2\tilde{w}_2}]$$
$$= \varphi(tb_1)\varphi(tb_2). \tag{23.166}$$

This holds for all t and all positive b_1 and b_2 with $b_1^2 + b_2^2 = 1$. Letting $x_1 = t^2 b_1$, $x_2 = t^2 b_2$, and

$$\psi(x) = \log\varphi(\sqrt{x}) \qquad \text{for } x > 0, \tag{23.167}$$

we may express (23.166) as

$$\psi(x_1 + x_2) = \psi(x_1) + \psi(x_2) \qquad \text{for } x_1 > 0, x_2 > 0, \tag{23.168}$$

and similarly for $x_1 < 0$, $x_2 < 0$. It follows that $\psi(x)$ is linear in x and hence that $\log\varphi(t)$ is linear in t^2. This implies that $\tilde{w}$ is Normal.

We know that $(\tilde{Z} - \bar{Z})/\ddot{Z}$ is Normal for every $\tilde{Z}$ with $\ddot{Z} > 0$. It follows that all $\tilde{Z}$s are Normal. It can be shown from this that the $\tilde{z}_i$ are jointly Normal. (The proof is omitted.)

6. If the hypothesis of remark 2, the second hypothesis of remark 3, and the second hypothesis of remark 5 all hold, then the $\tilde{z}_i$ are jointly Normal.

Proof This follows from remarks 2–5.

23.23 Finding Points on the Efficient Boundary

23.23.1 Introduction

The efficient points are those that minimize $\ddot{Z}$ for a specified $\bar{Z}$. An equivalent problem is to choose $\boldsymbol{\pi}$ so as to minimize

$$\ddot{Z}^2 = \check{Z} = \boldsymbol{\pi}^t \check{z} \boldsymbol{\pi} \tag{23.169}$$

subject to the constraints: $\pi_i \geq 0$ for $i = 1, \ldots, r$, $\sum \pi_i = 1$, and $\boldsymbol{\pi}^t\bar{z} = \bar{Z}$ has a specified value. This is a much-studied programming problem, which we shall not go into here. Nor shall we go into the modifications appropriate when one wishes, as one ordinarily does, to generate the whole efficient boundary rather than the single efficient point with a specified $\bar{Z}$. We shall, however, point out some situations in which only one programming

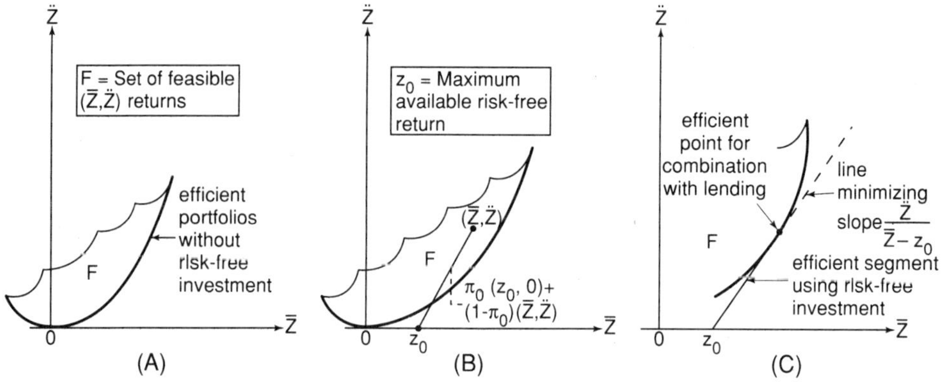

Figure 23.9
Efficient portfolios without and with lending

problem need be solved, discuss the modifications occurring when borrowing and/or short sales are permitted, and give the programming solutions when the nonnegativity constraints are not binding.

23.23.2 Constant Risk Aversion, Normal Returns

If u has constant positive risk aversion c and the $\tilde{z}_i$ are jointly Normal, then every portfolio $\tilde{Z}$ is Normal and by exercise 6 the optimal portfolio maximizes

$$\bar{Z} - \tfrac{1}{2}c\check{Z} = \boldsymbol{\pi}^t\bar{\boldsymbol{z}} - \tfrac{1}{2}c\boldsymbol{\pi}^t\check{\boldsymbol{z}}\boldsymbol{\pi}, \tag{23.170}$$

subject to the constraints $\pi_i \geq 0$ for $i = 1, \ldots, r$, and $\sum \pi_i = 1$. This is a single programming problem of almost the same type as in the previous subsection. The maximum cannot occur at $\ddot{Z} = 0$ (as long as some $\bar{z}_i$ exceeds the maximum available risk-free return).

23.23.3 Partly Risk-Free Portfolios

Suppose the return $\tilde{\boldsymbol{z}} = [\tilde{z}_1 \ldots \tilde{z}_r]^t$ is such that no risk-free portfolio can be obtained. The feasible set F of $(\bar{Z}, \ddot{Z})$ points that can be achieved by portfolio mixtures is depicted in figure 23.9A. Now assume there is available in addition a risk-free investment with mean z_0 (and standard deviation zero). By taking a mixture of this risk-free investment and any feasible point $(\bar{Z}, \ddot{Z})$, we can achieve points on the ray from $(z_0, 0)$ to $(\bar{Z}, \ddot{Z})$; see figure 23.9B. A typical mixture

$$\pi_0(z_0, 0) + (1 - \pi_0)(\bar{Z}, \ddot{Z})$$

with $0 < \pi_0 < 1$ is achieved by a portfolio that invests a proportion of assets π_0 in the risk-free investment (i.e., in lending) and a proportion

$(1 - \pi_0)$ in the portfolio that gives rise to $(\bar{Z}, \ddot{Z})$. If π_0 is negative, then money is borrowed at the risk-free rate z_0 and $(1 - \pi_0)$—an amount greater than 1—is invested in the portfolio $(\bar{Z}, \ddot{Z})$. In this case the ray from $(z_0, 0)$ to $(\bar{Z}, \ddot{Z})$ is extended beyond $(\bar{Z}, \ddot{Z})$. (See the dotted line in figure 23.9B.)

If a risk-free investment is available, then a previously efficient point such as b in figure 23.9C is no longer efficient because better points can be achieved by mixtures of $(z_0, 0)$ and point a in that figure.

The point a is characterized as the feasible point on the supporting tangent line to F. To find the point a in F we need to minimize the slope connecting the risk-free point and a point in F. More formally we must choose a portfolio $\boldsymbol{\pi}$ to minimize

$$\frac{(\boldsymbol{\pi}^t \check{\boldsymbol{z}} \boldsymbol{\pi})^{1/2}}{\boldsymbol{\pi}^t \bar{z} - z_0}. \tag{23.171}$$

In the financial literature, the reciprocal of (23.171) is called the "relative risk premium" of the portfolio $\boldsymbol{\pi}$. The tangent point a will be called the "Efficient Point (for combination) with Lending."

Our problem thus boils down to finding a vector $\boldsymbol{\pi} = [\pi_1 \ldots \pi_r]^t$ where $\pi_i \geq 0$ for $i = 1, \ldots, r$ and $\sum_{i=1}^{r} \pi_i = 1$, that minimizes (23.171), or equivalently, minimizes

$$\frac{\check{Z}}{(\bar{Z} - z_0)^2} = \frac{\boldsymbol{\pi}^t \check{\boldsymbol{z}} \boldsymbol{\pi}}{(\boldsymbol{\pi}^t \boldsymbol{b})^2}, \tag{23.172}$$

where

$$\boldsymbol{b} \equiv \begin{bmatrix} \bar{z}_1 - z_0 \\ \vdots \\ \bar{z}_i - z_0 \\ \vdots \\ \bar{z}_r - z_0 \end{bmatrix} = \bar{\boldsymbol{z}} - z_0 \boldsymbol{1}. \tag{23.173}$$

Now since we can multiply $\boldsymbol{\pi}$ by a positive constant and not change (23.172), we may drop the constraint $\sum_{i=1}^{r} \pi_i = 1$ and add the constraint $\boldsymbol{\pi}^t \boldsymbol{b} = d$ for any positive constant d. We choose $d = 1$.

Again summarizing, we wish to find a vector $\boldsymbol{\pi} = [\pi_1 \ldots \pi_r]$ that minimizes

$$\boldsymbol{\pi}^t \check{\boldsymbol{z}} \boldsymbol{\pi} \tag{23.174a}$$

subject to the condition $\pi_i \geq 0$ for $i = 1, \ldots, r$ and

$$\boldsymbol{\pi}^t \boldsymbol{b} = 1. \tag{23.174b}$$

We now can invoke the following lemma.

Lemma If $\mathbf{V}$ is positive-definite, then the minimum of $\boldsymbol{x}'\mathbf{V}\boldsymbol{x}$ subject to independent linear constraints $\mathbf{b}'\boldsymbol{x} = \boldsymbol{d}$ occurs at

$$\boldsymbol{x} = \mathbf{V}^{-1}\mathbf{b}\boldsymbol{\lambda} \tag{23.175a}$$

where

$$\boldsymbol{\lambda} = (\mathbf{b}'\mathbf{V}^{-1}\mathbf{b})^{-1}\boldsymbol{d}. \tag{23.175b}$$

The minimum is

$$\boldsymbol{d}'\boldsymbol{\lambda}. \tag{23.175c}$$

The proof follows very easily upon application of the Lagrange multiplier technique (exercise 4).

In specializing the Lemma to our case, the $\boldsymbol{d}$ and λ are scalars, $d = 1$, $\mathbf{b}$ is a vector, and we have

$$\boldsymbol{\pi} = \lambda \check{\mathbf{z}}^{-1}\boldsymbol{b}, \tag{23.176}$$

where

$$\lambda = 1/(\boldsymbol{b}'\check{\mathbf{z}}^{-1}\boldsymbol{b}), \tag{23.177}$$

and the minimum is λ.

Now recalling that we dropped the assumption that $\sum_{i=1}^{r} \pi_i = 1$, we conclude that the efficient portfolio for combination with lending is $\boldsymbol{\pi}^*$ where $\pi_j^* = \pi_j / \sum \pi_i$ and where $\boldsymbol{\pi}$ satisfies (23.176).

If it turns out that $\pi_i^* \geq 0$ for all $i = 1, \ldots, r$, then our problem is solved. If, however, some π_i turn out to be negative, then the story becomes more complicated since some π_i will then have to be set equal to zero and the problem must be restricted to a subset of investments.

23.23.4 The Capital Asset Pricing Model

Once again assume that in addition to r investments with return $\tilde{z} = [\tilde{z}_1 \ldots \tilde{z}_r]$, where $\check{\mathbf{z}}$ is non-singular, there is a risk-free investment with return z_0. Let's also make the heroic assumption that all investors—this can be weakened—have the same probability assessment for $\tilde{z}$ and they are all risk averse, but perhaps with different utility functions. Each investor will mix the same risk-free investment with the efficient point for combination with lending. Let us call this common portfolio used by all investors as $\boldsymbol{\pi}^* = [\pi_1^* \ldots \pi_r^*]'$. What happens if $\pi_i^* = 0$ for some i? In this case each investor will not use investment i in his or her optimum portfolio and accordingly, in a more dynamic world, the price of the investment would change in a manner to make each $\pi_i^* > 0$. Indeed it would change to make π_i^* the same fraction of the supply of security i for every i, so that the optimum portfolio is a share of the whole market. Without delving into equilibrium analysis, let us posit at this point that $\pi_i^* > 0$, for each i, and examine the necessary condition for an interior optimum (23.176), which can be rewritten as

$$\check{\boldsymbol{z}}\boldsymbol{\pi} = \lambda \boldsymbol{b}.$$

If we divide both sides by $\sum \pi_i$, we can re-express this as

$$\check{\boldsymbol{z}}\boldsymbol{\pi}^* = \lambda^* \boldsymbol{b} = \lambda^*(\bar{\boldsymbol{z}} - z_0 \boldsymbol{1}) \tag{23.178}$$

where $\lambda^* = \lambda / \sum \pi_i$. Now premultiplying both sides by $\boldsymbol{\pi}^{*t}$ we get

$$\boldsymbol{\pi}^{*t}\check{\boldsymbol{z}}\boldsymbol{\pi}^* = \lambda^*(\boldsymbol{\pi}^{*t}\bar{\boldsymbol{z}} - z_0),$$

or

$$\check{Z}^* = \lambda^*(\bar{Z}^* - z_0), \tag{23.179}$$

where $\check{Z}^*$ and $\bar{Z}^*$ are respectively the variance and mean of the efficient portfolio with lending, $\tilde{Z}^*$. Solving for λ^* in (23.179) and substituting this into (23.178), we get

$$\check{\boldsymbol{z}}\boldsymbol{\pi}^* = \frac{\check{Z}^*}{\bar{Z}^* - z_0}(\bar{\boldsymbol{z}} - z_0 \boldsymbol{1}). \tag{23.180}$$

and the ith equation in this set of r simultaneous equations is

$$\textstyle\sum_j \check{z}_{ij}\pi_j^* = \dfrac{\check{Z}^*}{\bar{Z}^* - z_0}(\bar{z}_i - z_0). \tag{23.181}$$

Now observing that

$$\textstyle\sum_j \check{z}_{ij}\pi_j^* = \operatorname{cov}(\tilde{z}_i, \tilde{Z}^*) = \rho_i^* \ddot{z}_i \ddot{Z}^* \tag{23.182}$$

(where ρ_i^* is the correlation of investment i with the optimum portfolio), we can re-express (23.181) as

$$\frac{\bar{z}_i - z_0}{\ddot{z}_i} = \rho_i^* \frac{\bar{Z}^* - z_0}{\ddot{Z}^*} \quad \text{for all } i, \tag{23.183a}$$

or

$$\mathrm{RRP}_i = \rho_i^* \mathrm{RRP}^* \quad \text{for all } i. \tag{23.183b}$$

In words, the relative risk premium of the ith stock is ρ_i^* times the relative risk premium of the efficient portfolio with lending. Another common way of re-expressing (23.183b) is

$$\bar{z}_i - z_0 = \beta_i(\bar{Z}^* - z_0), \quad \text{with} \quad \beta_i \equiv \rho_i^* \ddot{z}_i / \ddot{Z}^*. \tag{23.183c}$$

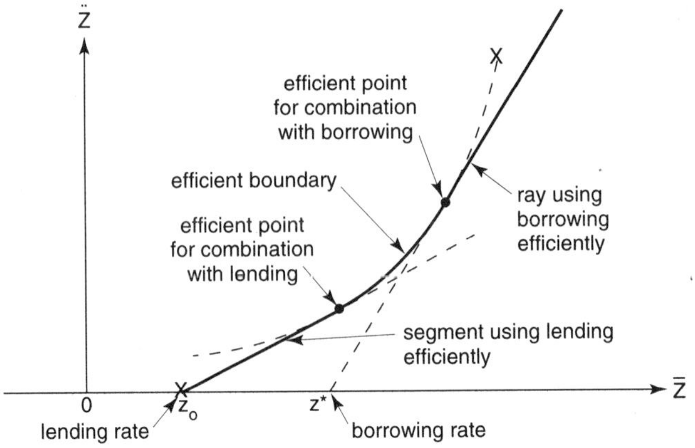

Figure 23.10
Efficient boundary with risk-free lending and borrowing

The Capital-Asset-Pricing Model (CAPM) asserts that

$$\tilde{z}_i - z_0 = \beta_i(\tilde{Z}^* - z_0) + \sigma_i\tilde{\varepsilon}_i \tag{23.184}$$

where $\tilde{\varepsilon}_1 \ldots \tilde{\varepsilon}_r$ are iid. rvs each with mean 0 and variance 1, and σ_i is the standard deviation of the component of $\tilde{z}_i$ independent of the market portfolio. In this case, $\tilde{Z}^*$ is interpreted as the market portfolio and β_i, the beta of the ith investment, is the slope of the regression line of $\tilde{z}_i$ on the market portfolio $\tilde{Z}^*$. Empirical beta values for different securities are published periodically in the financial literature and stock prices adjust roughly to make this model a plausible first approximation to reality.

23.24 Extensions

23.24.1 Borrowing

If, in addition to the previous assumptions, it is possible to borrow at the rate z^*, then borrowing an amount equal to t times the available capital and investing this and the original capital in $\tilde{Z}$ will yield a return

$$(1 + t)\tilde{Z} - tz^* \tag{23.185}$$

with

$$\text{mean} = \bar{Z} + t(\bar{Z} - z^*), \tag{23.186a}$$

$$\text{standard deviation} = \ddot{Z} + t\ddot{Z}. \tag{23.186b}$$

(We define z^* to include capital for comparability with $\tilde{Z}$, that is, the

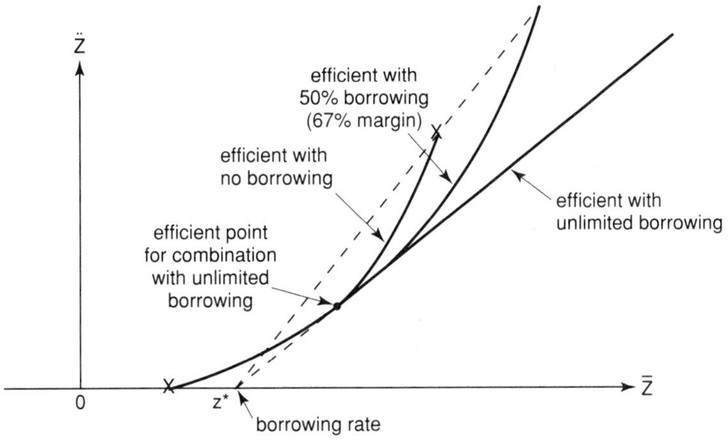

Figure 23.11
Efficient boundary with limited borrowing

interest rate is $z^* - 1$.) Thus, if the point $(\bar{Z}, \ddot{Z})$ is available, then so are all points on the ray extending from $(\bar{Z}, \ddot{Z})$ in a direction exactly opposite to $(z^*, 0)$ (figure 23.10). Borrowing at the rate z^* is like lending at the rate z^* except that the lending gives the straight line segment between $(z^*, 0)$ and $(\bar{Z}, \ddot{Z})$ while borrowing gives the extension beyond $(\bar{Z}, \ddot{Z})$.

If it is possible to borrow any amount at the rate z^*, then the outer portion of the efficient set will be a ray extending from a point obtained as in section 23.23.3 with z^* in place of z_0. We shall call this point efficient for combination with borrowing.

If it is possible to borrow only up to some limited amount at the rate z^*, then the ray will not extend indefinitely but will end at an easily determined point. In this case, the remainder of the efficient boundary with borrowing is obtained by borrowing the maximum possible amount and investing in points on the remainder of the efficient boundary without borrowing. (See figure 23.11.) That is, let $(\bar{Z}, \ddot{Z})$ be efficient without borrowing, with $\bar{Z} > z^*$, and let t be the maximum ratio of borrowing to capital. Then (23.186) gives an efficient point with borrowing.

If the borrowing rate z^* is the same as the maximum available risk-free return z_0, and if any amount may be borrowed at this rate, then the borrowing ray and the lending segment lie on the same line, and the efficient portfolio for combination with borrowing coincides with the efficient portfolio for combination with lending, so that only the single programming problem of section 23.23.3 need be solved. These conditions could hardly hold exactly, but might hold approximately in some circumstances. In particular, if the borrowing rate is constant up to some critical level of borrowing and the desired level of borrowing would be less than this critical level even without the limitation, then the limitation is not binding.

If the rate of interest depends on the amount borrowed or the investments made, then none of the foregoing analyses apply.

Exercises

1. Show that $S(\alpha\tilde{Z}_1 + (1-\alpha)\tilde{Z}_2) \leq \alpha S(\tilde{Z}_1) + (1-\alpha)S(\tilde{Z}_2)$ for $0 < \alpha < 1$, per (23.155), with equality only in the cases mentioned there.

2. Show that the returns $\tilde{z}_i$ with $\ddot{z}_i > 0$ have a singular variance matrix if, for portfolios made up of the corresponding investments, either (a) there is one with $\ddot{Z} = 0$, or (b) there are two different ones minimizing $\ddot{Z}$ for the same $\bar{Z}$.

3. Show that if u is strictly risk averse, then the derivative of $Eu(a + t\tilde{w})$ with respect to t is negative.

4. Derive formula (23.175) concerning the minimum of a positive definite quadratic form subject to linear constraints.
Hint Use Lagrange multipliers. An alternative, once the answer has been guessed, is to let $\boldsymbol{\Delta} = \boldsymbol{x} - \mathbf{V}^{-1}\mathbf{b}\boldsymbol{\lambda}$, where $\boldsymbol{\lambda}$ is given by (23.175b), and show that if $\mathbf{b}'\boldsymbol{x} = \boldsymbol{d}$, then $\mathbf{b}'\boldsymbol{\Delta} = 0$ and

$$\boldsymbol{x}'\mathbf{V}\boldsymbol{x} = \boldsymbol{\lambda}'\mathbf{b}'\mathbf{V}^{-1}\mathbf{b}\boldsymbol{\lambda} + \boldsymbol{\Delta}'\mathbf{V}\boldsymbol{\Delta}.$$

Remark Letting $\boldsymbol{y} = \boldsymbol{\beta}'\boldsymbol{x}$ where $\mathbf{V} = \boldsymbol{\beta}\boldsymbol{\beta}'$, we are minimizing the squared length of $\boldsymbol{y}$ subject to the constraints $(\boldsymbol{\beta}^{-1}\mathbf{b})'\boldsymbol{y} = \boldsymbol{d}$, that is, projecting $\boldsymbol{y}$ on a plane.

5. Let $u(x)$ be the decision maker's utility value for assets x. Assume $u(\cdot)$ is twice differentiable and denote the first and second derivative of u by u' and u'' respectively. As a measure of the concavity of u at the point x we define the function

$$r(x) \equiv -\frac{u''(x)}{u'(x)}.$$

(It can be shown that if

$$\tilde{z}_\Delta = \begin{bmatrix} +\Delta & \text{with probability} & \frac{1}{2}, \\ -\Delta & & \frac{1}{2}, \end{bmatrix}$$

so that $\bar{z}_\Delta = 0$, $\check{z}_\Delta = \Delta^2/2$, then the decision maker with assets x would pay an insurance premium of $\pi(x; \tilde{z}_\Delta)$ to unburden himself from $\tilde{z}_\Delta$ where

$$\lim_{\Delta \to 0} \frac{\pi(x; \tilde{z}_\Delta)}{\Delta^2/4} = r(x).$$

Hence $r(x)$ can be interpreted as a measure of *local risk aversion*. See also appendix 3.)

a. Show that (23.158) has constant positive risk aversion.

b. Verify (23.159).

6. Verify (23.170).

7. Let

$$u(x) = x - x^2/2c \quad \text{for} \quad x \leq c.$$

a. Show

$$Eu(\tilde{Z}) = \bar{Z} - \frac{1}{2c}[\bar{Z}^2 + \check{Z}].$$

b. Show that u has increasing (local) risk aversion, in other words that

$$r(x) \equiv -\frac{u''(x)}{u'(x)}$$

is a monotone increasing function of x. Comment on the reasonableness of u.

24 Normal Linear Regression with Known Variance

24.1 Definition of the Model

24.1.1 Introduction

Only a small proportion of practical problems can be satisfactorily represented by the models considered so far in this book; most are more complicated in structure. In this chapter we shall introduce a very flexible and general model that is extremely useful in practice and is perhaps the most widely used of all statistical models. It is general enough to include as special cases, for example, all the Normal models of earlier chapters of this book, and, as will become evident, it is flexible enough to represent without serious distortion many situations in which there is no good reason to postulate the model or even good reason not to.

In this section we shall first define and exemplify the simplest special case of the model that exhibits its essential features and then define and exemplify the general case. Analysis of the model will be given in sections 24.2–5. Section 24.1.5 gives a fuller outline of the chapter, which ends with two important, broader topics, model selection and causation.

24.1.2 A Special Case

The kind of situation we shall discuss is exemplified by the model

$$\tilde{y}_i = \beta_1 + \beta_2 x_i + \tilde{\varepsilon}_i, \tag{24.1}$$

where β_1 and β_2 are parameters whose values are unknown but remain fixed throughout, x_i is a known number on each trial but is not necessarily the *same* on each trial, and the $\tilde{\varepsilon}$s are independent Normal rv's all having mean 0 and variance υ.

The xs may be the values of rv's. For example, if the pairs $(\tilde{x}_i, \tilde{y}_i)$ are mutually independent and all have the same bivariate Normal distribution, then the foregoing model holds when the xs are known, that is, conditional on the xs. Specifically, if the bivariate Normal distribution has means $\bar{x}$ and $\bar{y}$, variances $\check{x}$ and $\check{y}$, and covariance V_{12}, then (24.1) holds with

$$\beta_1 = \bar{y} - \frac{V_{12}}{\check{x}}\bar{x}, \qquad \beta_2 = \frac{V_{12}}{\check{x}}, \tag{24.2a}$$

$$\upsilon = \check{y} - \frac{V_{12}^2}{\check{x}}. \tag{24.2b}$$

However, model (24.1) is much more general, as it makes no assumption about the distribution of the xs, or indeed whether they have one. And model (24.1) is itself only an example of the general model we will discuss.

Example Suppose that on New Year's Eve we are interested in the next day's noon temperature at the Rose Bowl. We might first look up the historical record of such temperatures. Treating them as observations on a Normal process, that is, using a Normal sampling model, we could make inferences about the next day's noon temperature. If, however, we are able to take account of the temperature in Pasadena on New Year's Eve, say at 6:00 p.m., we might gain a good deal by doing so. Suppose that we have obtained the historical record of these temperatures, and in addition we know the temperature in Pasadena this New Year's Eve. To make use of this additional information, we need a model. Let y_i be the noon temperature at the Rose Bowl on New Year's Day of year i, and let x_i be the previous day's temperature at 6:00 p.m. in Pasadena. Since we are interested in making inferences about $\tilde{y}_n$ and x_n and the previous history of the process, what is vital about the model is the conditional distribution of the $\tilde{y}$s given the xs. The model (24.1) would be a good possibility.

What if we wanted to take account also of the temperature in Pasadena on December 30 each year, say at 6:00 p.m.? Call these temperatures w_i. The obvious extension of (24.1) would be

$$\tilde{y}_i = \beta_1 + \beta_2 x_i + \beta_3 w_i + \tilde{\varepsilon}_i.$$

The natural generalization of this in turn will be given in the next subsection.

24.1.3 The General Normal Linear Regression Model and Assumptions

A Normal linear regression process is defined as a process generating independent scalar rv's $\tilde{y}_1, \ldots, \tilde{y}_i, \ldots$ according to the model

$$\tilde{y} = \textstyle\sum_{j=1}^{r} x_{ij}\beta_j + \tilde{\varepsilon}_i, \tag{24.3}$$

where the βs are parameters whose values remain fixed during an entire experiment or series of observations; the xs are known numbers or observed values of rv's and in general may vary from one observation to the next; and, given the βs and the xs and the *process variance* υ, the $\tilde{\varepsilon}$s are independent Normal rv's all having mean 0 and variance υ.

Usually (but not necessarily) $x_{i1} = 1$ for every i. This means that the term β_1 appears on the right hand side of (24.3) for every i. For instance, when $r = 2$ and $x_{i1} = 1$, the model (24.3) becomes

$$\tilde{y}_i = \beta_1 + \beta_2 x_{2i} + \tilde{\varepsilon}_i,$$

which is the same as (24.1) except that x_i of (24.1) is now x_{2i}.

The word *linear* in the definition refers to the linearity in the βs. It is this linearity that is important, not the linearity in the xs. The latter can be obtained simply by redefining the xs if necessary, as we shall see in examples shortly.

If we define the vectors

$$\boldsymbol{x}_i^t \equiv [x_{i1}\, x_{i2} \ldots x_{ir}], \tag{24.4}$$

$$\boldsymbol{\beta} \equiv [\beta_1\, \beta_2 \ldots \beta_r]^t, \tag{24.5}$$

then the model (24.3) of the ith observation can be written

$$\tilde{y}_i = \boldsymbol{x}_i^t \boldsymbol{\beta} + \tilde{\varepsilon}_i. \tag{24.6}$$

Since $\tilde{\varepsilon}_i$ is Normal with mean 0 and variance υ, it follows that $\tilde{y}_i$ is conditionally Normal with mean $\boldsymbol{x}_i^t \boldsymbol{\beta}$ and variance υ and density

$$f_N(y_i | \boldsymbol{x}_i^t \boldsymbol{\beta}, \upsilon) = (2\pi)^{-1/2} e^{-(1/2)(y_i - \boldsymbol{x}_i^t \boldsymbol{\beta})^2/\upsilon} \upsilon^{-1/2}. \tag{24.7}$$

If we further define

$$\tilde{\boldsymbol{y}} \equiv [\tilde{y}_1 \ldots \tilde{y}_n]^t, \tag{24.8a}$$

$$\mathbf{x} \equiv \begin{bmatrix} \boldsymbol{x}_1^t \\ \vdots \\ \boldsymbol{x}_n^t \end{bmatrix} \equiv \begin{bmatrix} x_{11} & \cdots & x_{1r} \\ \vdots & & \vdots \\ x_{n1} & \cdots & x_{nr} \end{bmatrix}, \tag{24.8b}$$

$$\tilde{\boldsymbol{\varepsilon}} \equiv [\tilde{\varepsilon}_1 \cdots \tilde{\varepsilon}_n]^t, \tag{24.8c}$$

then the model (24.3) for the set of n observations $\tilde{y}_1, \ldots, \tilde{y}_n$ can be written

$$\tilde{\boldsymbol{y}} = \mathbf{x}\boldsymbol{\beta} + \tilde{\boldsymbol{\varepsilon}}. \tag{24.9}$$

Since $\tilde{\boldsymbol{\varepsilon}}$ is Normal with mean $\boldsymbol{0}$ and variance $\upsilon\mathbf{I}$, by (24.7) and the conditional independence of $\tilde{y}_1, \ldots, \tilde{y}_n$, it follows that $\tilde{\boldsymbol{y}}$ is Normal with mean $\mathbf{x}\boldsymbol{\beta}$ and variance $\upsilon\mathbf{I}$ and density

$$f_N(\boldsymbol{y} | \mathbf{x}\boldsymbol{\beta}, \upsilon\mathbf{I}) = (2\pi)^{-(1/2)n} e^{-(1/2)(\boldsymbol{y} - \mathbf{x}\boldsymbol{\beta})^t(\boldsymbol{y} - \mathbf{x}\boldsymbol{\beta})/\upsilon} \upsilon^{-(1/2)n}. \tag{24.10}$$

The set of possible means $\mathbf{x}\boldsymbol{\beta}$ as $\boldsymbol{\beta}$ varies is a linear subspace of the n-dimensional $\boldsymbol{y}$-space; this is the fundamental linearity in the model.

We shall assume throughout that the process variance υ is known; this is discussed further in section 24.2.6. Unless specifically stated otherwise, we shall also assume that $\mathbf{x}$ is of rank r, implying $n \geq r$, and all xs which are observed values of rv's will be treated as given, that is, all distributions will be conditional on the observed xs. Thus, for instance, the marginal distribution of $\tilde{\boldsymbol{y}}$ which will be given is marginal on $\tilde{\boldsymbol{\beta}}$ but conditional on the xs. The prior distribution of $\tilde{\boldsymbol{\beta}}$ may equally well be regarded as marginal or conditional on the xs in the case that the xs are *uninformative* about the βs, meaning by definition that the conditional distribution of $\tilde{\boldsymbol{\beta}}$ given the xs is the same as the marginal distribution of $\tilde{\boldsymbol{\beta}}$. The contrary case of *informative* xs is probably best thought of as excluded, because the theory below is not what is needed in this case and is likely to be misleading, though technically it is correct conditional on all xs. Random xs are discussed further in section 24.5.

24.1.4 Examples

We describe below some situations in which the model (24.3) might be used. In some of them we do not set up the model in detail, but the reader may do so as an exercise. We also describe some situations in which the model is not adequate as it stands but requires extension in one way or another, illustrating some important sources of danger in its indiscriminate use.

Example 1 Stratified sampling (chapter 23C).

Example 2 Multivariate Normal $(\tilde{x}_i^t, \tilde{y}_i)$ (chapter 22).

Example 3 The lead broker for a syndicate bidding on a new municipal bond offering has data on previous offerings, namely the winning bid, highest losing bid, other bids, number of bids, size (total value) of the issue, quality rating by Moody (one of five levels from AAA to B), coupon rate to be paid by the municipality, and price at which the broker plans to offer the bonds to its customers. Bids, coupon rate, and reoffering price are expressed as equivalent yields (interest rates). The broker wants a forecast distribution of the highest competing bid to use in choosing its own bid. (See J. L. Jessup case.)

Example 4 The yield of a chemical reaction depends on the temperature at which it is run and on which of two catalysts A and B is used. For the ith batch, let y_i be the yield, $x_{i1} = 1$, $x_{i2} =$ the temperature, $x_{i3} = 1$ if catalyst A is used and 0 otherwise, $x_{i4} = 1$ if catalyst B is used and 0 otherwise; $r = 4$.

Example 5 In the previous example, if the yield is thought to depend quadratically on temperature, the model (24.3) can still be applied by letting $x_{i5} = x_{i2}^2 =$ the square of the temperature.

Example 6 What if, in the previous example, the dependence of yield on temperature is thought to differ between catalysts?

Example 7 An experiment on 10 treatments (Youden and Connor). Suppose the weather resistance of 10 varieties of paint is to be tested. An experiment could be done as follows. Cut each of five boards into quarters and apply each paint to two quarters, according to the following scheme. (The paints are denoted by the letters A–J).

A	B	E	F	H	I	J	C	D	G
C	D	G	A	B	E	F	H	I	J

After exposure of the boards to weathering for a certain time, measure the performance of each paint. (How to measure performance is a serious problem, but our concern with this problem here extends only to hoping that the measurement is not too tenuously related to economically important variables.) Painted boards differ greatly in how they weather. A model of the form (24.3) might be used with a β corresponding to each paint and a β corresponding to each board.

Example 8 Predict television viewing where the independent variables are (a) day of week, (b) time of day, (c) type of program, and (d) interaction among the first three variables. What other variables might you use, and how?

Example 9 A sample was drawn from a list of N shoe factories. For each factory in the sample, the number of machines of a certain type was counted in an on-site inspection. An inference about the total number of such machines in all factories was sought. For every factory there was available an estimate of the number of shoes produced in an earlier year by each of the three general types of production processes (which differ in their typical machine requirements). Let the number of machines of the relevant type in factory i be y_i, let $x_{i1} = 1$, and let the estimated numbers of shoes produced in factory i in the earlier year by the three types of production processes be x_{i2}, x_{i3}, and x_{i4}. Then model (24.3) might be reasonable, and the total number of machines of the relevant type in all factories would be

$$Y = \beta_1 N + \beta_2 X_2 + \beta_3 X_3 + \beta_4 X_4$$

where X_j is the total over all factories of x_{ij}, $j = 2, 3, 4$. When we have learned how to obtain the posterior distribution of $(\tilde{\beta}_1, \tilde{\beta}_2, \tilde{\beta}_3, \tilde{\beta}_4)$, we will be in a position to make an inference about $\tilde{Y}$. A scatter diagram of y_i versus $\bar{\beta}_1'' + \bar{\beta}_2'' x_{2i} + \bar{\beta}_3'' x_{3i} + \bar{\beta}_4'' x_{4i}$ cast serious doubt on the hypothesis of the model that all $\tilde{\varepsilon}_i$ have the same variance, however. Specifically, the variance seemed to be larger in the larger factories, as might have been expected if the question had been raised in advance.

Example 10 In the previous example, machines of more than one type were of interest. An analysis can be done for each type in the same way. However, the quantity of interest (for antitrust purposes) was the ratio of the total number of machines of one type in all factories to the total number of another type. An inference about this ratio must take account of the possibility that the $\tilde{\varepsilon}$s for the same factory for two machine types are not independent. This calls for an extension of the model to multivariate $\tilde{y}$s.

Example 11 Demands y_i in successive time periods might be thought to follow a model

$$\tilde{y}_i = \beta_1 + \beta_2 w_i + \beta_3 v_i + \beta_4 y_{i-1} + \tilde{\varepsilon}_i$$

where w_i and v_i are some variables that might "help predict" demand and where y_{i-1} is the demand in the previous time period. We can let $x_{i1} = 1$, $x_{i2} = w_i$, $x_{i3} = v_i$, and $x_{i4} = y_{i-1}$, and the foregoing equation will agree with (24.3). However, the assumptions of the model are violated. (How?) An extension to this case will be discussed later.

Example 12 In evaluating the effectiveness of cloud seeding, one would like to make an inference about what the rainfall in the target area would have been in the absence of seeding. A series of observations is available for successive storms (unseeded), giving the rainfall in the "target" area and a nearby "control" area not so near as to be affected by seeding. (The unit of a storm is not trivial to define, but this is less of a problem than one might think.) It is natural to use the model (24.1) with y_{i-1} = rainfall in the "target" area in the absence of seeding and x_i = rainfall in the "control" area during the ith storm. There is reason to fear, however, that the $\tilde{\varepsilon}_i$ are not independent but positively correlated at nearby times. Sometimes such a contingency can be handled by a model like that of Example 11.

Example 13 Calibrating a forecaster.

24.1.5 Outline of the Chapter

In this section we have introduced and exemplified the general Normal linear regression model. The rest of the chapter concerns inference and decision problems for this model. More specifically, section 24.2 gives first the prior-posterior analysis for a "gentle" prior. The complete probability analysis, prior-posterior and preposterior, is discussed in section 24.3 for a Normal prior distribution. The process variance v is assumed throughout to be known; some comments on this are made in section 24.2.6.

Sections 24.2 and 24.3 give the probability analysis only in abstract form. In section 24.4 we illustrate this formal theory by means of special cases.

We have permitted the xs to be observed values of rv's as long as they are all known at the time the theory is applied. When some are not known in advance, prior-posterior theory remains the same if interpreted correctly, but new preposterior theory is needed. The situation is explained in section 24.5, along with the closely related *autoregressive* case.

Choosing an adequate statistical model is a knotty problem in practical data analysis, with far too many ramifications to go into here. Section 24.6 discusses one aspect particularly relevant to the methods of this book, namely the relation between the Bayesian analysis of individual models and analysis assuming only that some one of the models holds. It goes on to sketch very briefly what happens when none of the posited models holds exactly. The theory given is not specific to regression models, but they represent the most prominent type of situation in this book where choice of model is a common problem in practice.

Often one is interested in causation—what happens if one or more xs are controlled or changed? But correlation does not imply causation. People's height and weight are highly correlated; either can be used to predict the other. Which regression depends on which prediction, but neither is causal. In section 24.7 we will discuss the additional assumptions needed to justify a causal interpretation of regression coefficients. Until then, β_j should be interpreted as the increase in y_i associated with a unit increase in x_{ij} in a statistical sense only. Even if an x can be controlled or changed, intervention to do so usually alters the statistical relationship.

24.2 "Gentle" Prior

24.2.1 Introduction

We shall now consider the posterior distribution that arises when the prior density of $\tilde{\boldsymbol{\beta}}$ is "gentle." More specifically, we shall compute the posterior distribution as if the prior density of $\tilde{\boldsymbol{\beta}}$ were constant over the entire range of $\boldsymbol{\beta}$. This cannot hold exactly, of course, but the resulting posterior is a good approximation to the posterior that would result from a carefully assessed prior when the latter is "gentle." The limitations of such a procedure are the same as in sections 16.3.2 and 16.5, to which the reader is referred for further discussion. We consider only prior-posterior theory because a "gentle" prior does not provide a good approximation for most preposterior purposes, leading to some meaningless marginal probability distributions and, except in special cases, to nonsensical choices of experiment. We remind the reader that we are assuming throughout that the process variance v is known, and that $\mathbf{x}$ is a known matrix of rank r.

24.2.2 Posterior Distribution

If the prior distribution of $\tilde{\boldsymbol{\beta}}$ is *diffuse*, that is, if the prior density of $\tilde{\boldsymbol{\beta}}$ is effectively a constant, then the posterior density of $\tilde{\boldsymbol{\beta}}$ is proportional to the likelihood (24.10) by Bayes' formula. As a function of $\boldsymbol{\beta}$, (24.10) is a constant times e raised to a power that is a quadratic function of $\boldsymbol{\beta}$. It follows, as we shall see, that the posterior density of $\tilde{\boldsymbol{\beta}}$ is Normal.

Alternatively, the diffuse prior on $\tilde{\boldsymbol{\beta}}$ may be considered a Normal distribution with precision $\mathbf{0}$. Since the conditional distribution of $\tilde{\boldsymbol{y}}$ given $\boldsymbol{\beta}$ is by (24.10) Normal with mean depending linearly on $\boldsymbol{\beta}$ and constant variance, it follows that $\tilde{\boldsymbol{y}}$ and $\boldsymbol{\beta}$ are jointly Normal, and therefore that the conditional (posterior) distribution of $\tilde{\boldsymbol{\beta}}$ given $\boldsymbol{y}$ is Normal. This approach will be used in section 24.3.

We shall presently show that the posterior density of $\tilde{\boldsymbol{\beta}}$ for a diffuse prior is that Normal density which, as a function of $\boldsymbol{\beta}$, is proportional to (24.10). So as to be able to find the mean and variance of this distribution (and for other purposes) we first *complete the square* in the exponent of (24.10) as follows:

$$(\boldsymbol{y} - \mathbf{x}\boldsymbol{\beta})^t(\boldsymbol{y} - \mathbf{x}\boldsymbol{\beta}) = \boldsymbol{\beta}^t\mathbf{x}^t\mathbf{x}\boldsymbol{\beta} - \boldsymbol{y}^t\mathbf{x}\boldsymbol{\beta} - \boldsymbol{\beta}^t\mathbf{x}^t\boldsymbol{y} + \boldsymbol{y}^t\boldsymbol{y}$$
$$= (\boldsymbol{\beta} - \boldsymbol{b})^t\mathbf{x}^t\mathbf{x}(\boldsymbol{\beta} - \boldsymbol{b}) + v, \qquad (24.11)$$

where

$$\boldsymbol{b} \equiv (\mathbf{x}^t\mathbf{x})^{-1}\mathbf{x}^t\boldsymbol{y}, \qquad (24.12a)$$

$$v \equiv \boldsymbol{y}^t\boldsymbol{y} - \boldsymbol{y}^t\mathbf{x}(\mathbf{x}^t\mathbf{x})^{-1}\mathbf{x}^t\boldsymbol{y}. \qquad (24.12b)$$

It is convenient to define the matrix

$$\mathbf{P} \equiv \mathbf{x}(\mathbf{x}^t\mathbf{x})^{-1}\mathbf{x}^t, \qquad (24.12c)$$

in terms of which (24.12b) becomes

$$v = \boldsymbol{y}^t(\mathbf{I} - \mathbf{P})\boldsymbol{y}. \qquad (24.12d)$$

Our assumption that $\mathbf{x}$ has rank r implies that $\mathbf{x}^t\mathbf{x}$ is nonsingular, so that its inverse, which appears in the preceding formulas, is defined; in the usual case $n > r$, and hence $\mathbf{P}$ is singular. $\mathbf{I} - \mathbf{P}$ is always singular (exercise 18).

Substituting (24.11) in (24.10) gives

$$f_N(\boldsymbol{y}|\mathbf{x}\boldsymbol{\beta}, v\mathbf{I}) = (2\pi)^{-(1/2)n}e^{-(1/2)(\boldsymbol{\beta}-\boldsymbol{b})^t\mathbf{x}^t\mathbf{x}(\boldsymbol{\beta}-\boldsymbol{b})/\upsilon}e^{-(1/2)v/\upsilon}\upsilon^{-(1/2)n}. \qquad (24.13)$$

We now see that if the prior density of $\tilde{\boldsymbol{\beta}}$ is simply a constant, then by Bayes' formula and (24.13), the posterior density of $\tilde{\boldsymbol{\beta}}$ is proportional to

$$e^{-(1/2)(\beta-b)^t \mathbf{H}(\beta-b)}, \tag{24.14a}$$

where

$$\mathbf{H} = \frac{1}{\upsilon}\mathbf{x}^t\mathbf{x}. \tag{24.14b}$$

The constant of proportionality is whatever is required to make the complete integral with respect to β equal to 1; comparing (24.14a) with (22.8) we see that this density is Normal and that

$$E(\tilde{\boldsymbol{\beta}}|y) = \boldsymbol{b}, \qquad V(\tilde{\boldsymbol{\beta}}|y) = \mathbf{H}^{-1}. \tag{24.14c}$$

This is therefore the posterior distribution of $\tilde{\boldsymbol{\beta}}$ for a diffuse prior.

24.2.3 Sufficient Statistics

Inspection of (24.13) reveals that whatever the prior distribution of $\tilde{\boldsymbol{\beta}}$ is, its posterior distribution will depend on $\boldsymbol{y}$ only through $\boldsymbol{b}$, that is $\boldsymbol{b}$ (in conjunction with $\mathbf{H}$) is a *sufficient statistic* in the sense of section 16.3.2 and the appendix to chapter 20. The distribution of $\tilde{\boldsymbol{b}}$ given $\boldsymbol{\beta}$ is nonsingular Normal with mean and variance (exercise 9)

$$E(\tilde{\boldsymbol{b}}|\boldsymbol{\beta}) = \boldsymbol{\beta}, \qquad V(\tilde{\boldsymbol{b}}|\boldsymbol{\beta}) = \mathbf{H}^{-1}. \tag{24.15}$$

An alternative sufficient statistic is $\mathbf{P}\boldsymbol{y}$. It must be sufficient because it determines $\boldsymbol{b}$, which is sufficient. In fact, $\boldsymbol{b}$ and $\mathbf{P}\boldsymbol{y}$ are one-to-one functions of one another, since by (24.12)

$$\boldsymbol{b} = (\mathbf{x}^t\mathbf{x})^{-1}\mathbf{x}^t\mathbf{P}\boldsymbol{y}, \tag{24.16a}$$

$$\mathbf{P}\boldsymbol{y} = \mathbf{x}\boldsymbol{b}. \tag{24.16b}$$

This sufficiency implies that for making inferences or decisions about $\tilde{\boldsymbol{\beta}}$ or about not-yet-observed $\tilde{y}$s, a statistician who knows all so-far-observed ys (and the corresponding xs) is no better off than a statistician who knows only $\boldsymbol{b}$ (and $\mathbf{H}$), *provided* the assumptions we have made are all satisfied, in particular, the assumptions that the $\tilde{\varepsilon}$s are independent, are Normal, have mean 0, and have known variance υ.

24.2.4 Least Squares Interpretation

For any $\boldsymbol{x}_i^t$ and any given estimate $\hat{\boldsymbol{\beta}}$ of $\boldsymbol{\beta}$ we can compute an *estimate* $\hat{y}_i$ by evaluating

$$\hat{y}_i = \boldsymbol{x}_i^t\hat{\boldsymbol{\beta}}. \tag{24.17}$$

The classical "theory of least squares" selects the estimate $\hat{\beta}$ in such a way as to minimize the sum of squared *errors*

$$\sum_i (y_i - \hat{y}_i)^2. \tag{24.18a}$$

To get (24.10) from (24.7) we have already implicitly made use of the fact that

$$\sum_i (y_i - \hat{y}_i) \equiv \sum_i (y_i - x_i^t \hat{\boldsymbol{\beta}})^2 = (\boldsymbol{y} - \mathbf{x}\hat{\boldsymbol{\beta}})^t(\boldsymbol{y} - \mathbf{x}\hat{\boldsymbol{\beta}}). \tag{24.18b}$$

It now follows from (24.11), since v does not depend on $\boldsymbol{\beta}$ and since $\mathbf{x}^t\mathbf{x}$ is positive-definite, that the minimizing $\hat{\boldsymbol{\beta}}$ in (24.18) is $\boldsymbol{b}$ uniquely. Thus the posterior mean $\boldsymbol{b}$ of $\tilde{\boldsymbol{\beta}}$ for a diffuse prior is also the "least squares" estimate of $\boldsymbol{\beta}$, the value that minimizes the classical sum of squares (24.18). Since the density (24.10) of $\tilde{\boldsymbol{y}}$ given $\boldsymbol{\beta}$, the *likelihood*, is a strictly decreasing function of the sum of squares (24.18), $\boldsymbol{b}$ is also the *maximum likelihood* estimate of $\boldsymbol{\beta}$, the value that maximizes the likelihood.

24.2.5 Interpretation as Projection[1]

As an aside, to be disregarded if it is not helpful, we remark that, given $\boldsymbol{\beta}$, the rv's $\mathbf{P}\tilde{\boldsymbol{y}}$ and $\tilde{\boldsymbol{y}} - \mathbf{P}\tilde{\boldsymbol{y}}$ are (independently) Normal with

$$E_{y|\beta}(\mathbf{P}\tilde{\boldsymbol{y}}) = \mathbf{P}\boldsymbol{x}\boldsymbol{\beta} = \mathbf{x}\boldsymbol{\beta} = E_{y|\beta}(\tilde{\boldsymbol{y}}), \tag{24.19a}$$

$$E_{y|\beta}(\tilde{\boldsymbol{y}} - \mathbf{P}\tilde{\boldsymbol{y}}) = \mathit{0}, \tag{24.19b}$$

$$V_{y|\beta}\begin{bmatrix} \mathbf{P}\tilde{\boldsymbol{y}} \\ \tilde{\boldsymbol{y}} - \mathbf{P}\tilde{\boldsymbol{y}} \end{bmatrix} = v\begin{bmatrix} \mathbf{P} \\ \mathbf{I} - \mathbf{P} \end{bmatrix}\begin{bmatrix} \mathbf{P} \\ \mathbf{I} - \mathbf{P} \end{bmatrix}^t = v\begin{bmatrix} \mathbf{P} & \mathbf{0} \\ \mathbf{0} & \mathbf{I} - \mathbf{P} \end{bmatrix}, \tag{24.19c}$$

by section 22.2, (24.10), and the formula

$$\mathbf{P} = \mathbf{P}^t = \mathbf{P}^2 = \mathbf{P}^t\mathbf{P}, \tag{24.20}$$

which follows by straightforward matrix algebra from (24.12c). The apparently magical facts that, given $\boldsymbol{\beta}$, the conditional mean of $\mathbf{P}\tilde{\boldsymbol{y}}$ is the same as that of $\tilde{\boldsymbol{y}}$ and that $\mathbf{P}\tilde{\boldsymbol{y}}$ and $\tilde{\boldsymbol{y}} - \mathbf{P}\tilde{\boldsymbol{y}}$ are conditionally independent given $\boldsymbol{\beta}$ are actually consequences of the fact that $\mathbf{P}\boldsymbol{y}$ is the projection of $\boldsymbol{y}$ on the linear space (plane through the origin) consisting of all possible vectors $\mathbf{x}\boldsymbol{\beta} = E(\tilde{\boldsymbol{y}}|\boldsymbol{\beta})$, hence $\mathbf{P}\boldsymbol{y}$ and $\boldsymbol{y} - \mathbf{P}\boldsymbol{y}$ are orthogonal (perpendicular). This follows from the least squares property of $\mathbf{P}\boldsymbol{y} = \mathbf{x}\boldsymbol{b}$. Related is the fact that v is the minimum of the sum of squared *errors* (24.18a) which is the square of the length of the perpendicular, $\boldsymbol{y} - \mathbf{P}\boldsymbol{y}$:

$$v = (\boldsymbol{y} - \mathbf{x}\boldsymbol{b})^t(\boldsymbol{y} - \mathbf{x}\boldsymbol{b}) = (\boldsymbol{y} - \mathbf{P}\boldsymbol{y})^t(\boldsymbol{y} - \mathbf{P}\boldsymbol{y}).$$

This is easily verified with the help of (24.16b) and (24.20); indeed, the relevant relation $(\mathbf{I} - \mathbf{P})^2 = \mathbf{I} - \mathbf{P}$ has already been used at (24.19c). See also section A2.10.

1. This subsection is optional.

24.2.6 Unknown Process Variance

Maximum Likelihood Estimation

If the process variance υ is unknown, as well as $\boldsymbol{\beta}$, then the maximum likelihood estimate of $(\upsilon, \boldsymbol{\beta})$ by definition maximizes (24.13) over both υ and $\boldsymbol{\beta}$. For any value of υ, the maximizing $\boldsymbol{\beta}$ is $\boldsymbol{b}$, as we have already seen. Substituting $\boldsymbol{b}$ for $\boldsymbol{\beta}$ in (24.13) gives

$$(2\pi)^{-(1/2)n} e^{-(1/2)\upsilon/\upsilon} \upsilon^{-(1/2)n}, \tag{24.21}$$

and the maximum of this over υ occurs at (exercise 19)

$$\upsilon = \frac{\upsilon}{n} = \frac{1}{n} \boldsymbol{y}^t(\mathbf{I} - \mathbf{x}(\mathbf{x}^t\mathbf{x})^{-1}\mathbf{x}^t)\boldsymbol{y}. \tag{24.22}$$

Therefore υ/n is the maximum likelihood estimator of υ.

Unbiased Estimation

It can be shown that the maximum likelihood estimator of υ has conditional mean, given $\boldsymbol{\beta}$ and υ,

$$E\left(\frac{\tilde{\upsilon}}{n} \middle| \boldsymbol{\beta}, \upsilon\right) = \frac{n-r}{n} \upsilon, \tag{24.23}$$

where r is the dimension of $\boldsymbol{\beta}$. On the other hand,

$$E\left(\frac{\tilde{\upsilon}}{n-r} \middle| \boldsymbol{\beta}, \upsilon\right) = \upsilon, \tag{24.24}$$

so $\tilde{\upsilon}/(n-r)$ is an *unbiased* estimator of υ. The desirable connotations of the word *unbiased* should not be taken too seriously, but if one were going to use always the same multiple of v to estimate υ, disregarding the prior distribution of υ and any information about υ that might be gleaned from the discrepancy between $\bar{\boldsymbol{\beta}}'$ and $\bar{\boldsymbol{\beta}}''$, then (24.24) suggests using $\tilde{\upsilon}/(n-r)$. Intuitively, dividing by $n-r$ rather than n allows on average for the "overfitting" due to using the r fitted values $\hat{\beta}_j$ that minimize (24.18b) rather than the unknown true values β_j. In fact, the distribution of $\tilde{\upsilon}$ given $(\boldsymbol{\beta}, \upsilon)$ depends only on υ and $n-r$, not n.

Bayesian Treatment

A full Bayesian treatment when υ is unknown would require a joint prior distribution of $\tilde{\upsilon}$ and $\tilde{\boldsymbol{\beta}}$, and the posterior distribution of $\tilde{\boldsymbol{\beta}}$ would depend not only on $\boldsymbol{b}$ and the prior distribution of $\tilde{\boldsymbol{\beta}}$ but also on v and the prior distribution of $\tilde{\upsilon}$. An analysis of this sort is given in *ASDT*, chapter 13. A similar analysis in the special case of a simple Normal process is given in chapter 17 of this book. As there, the posterior distribution of $\tilde{\boldsymbol{\beta}}$ (marginal on $\tilde{\upsilon}$) that the full analysis would give can be approximated, if $n - r$ is large, by using $v/(n - r)$ as a certainty equivalent for υ. This means: set $\upsilon = v/(n - r)$, treat it as known, and use the analysis of section 24.2.2 above or, more generally, section 24.3 below, taking as the prior for $\tilde{\boldsymbol{\beta}}$ the conditional prior distribution of $\tilde{\boldsymbol{\beta}}$ given υ at the value $\upsilon = v/(n - r)$.

24.3 Normal Prior

24.3.1 Introduction and Assumptions

We shall now assume that the prior distribution of $\tilde{\boldsymbol{\beta}}$ is nonsingular multivariate Normal. Under this assumption, the posterior distribution of $\tilde{\boldsymbol{\beta}}$ will be given in section 24.3.2 and various useful preposterior distributions in section 24.3.3. Section 24.3.4 discusses what happens when more than one sample is to be taken simultaneously. This actually "solves" certain classical inference problems and makes trivial the solution of certain decision problems, but we shall postpone all applications, even in abstract form, to subsequent sections. This section is concerned solely with the probability analysis of the situation.

Assume, then, that $\tilde{\boldsymbol{\beta}}$ is a priori nonsingular Normal with mean and variance

$$E(\tilde{\boldsymbol{\beta}}) = \bar{\boldsymbol{\beta}}', \qquad V(\tilde{\boldsymbol{\beta}}) = \breve{\boldsymbol{\beta}}'. \tag{24.25}$$

Recall that we have already assumed, at (24.10) that the conditional distribution of $\tilde{\boldsymbol{y}}$ given $\boldsymbol{\beta}$ is Normal with mean and variance

$$E(\tilde{\boldsymbol{y}}|\boldsymbol{\beta}) = \mathbf{x}\boldsymbol{\beta}, \qquad V(\tilde{\boldsymbol{y}}|\boldsymbol{\beta}) = \upsilon\mathbf{I}. \tag{24.26}$$

Notice that the conditional mean of $\tilde{\boldsymbol{y}}$ given $\boldsymbol{\beta}$ depends linearly on $\boldsymbol{\beta}$ while the conditional variance is constant. We are therefore in the situation of section 22.3.2, from which we can deduce the desired probability distributions.

24.3.2 Posterior Distribution of $\tilde{\boldsymbol{\beta}}$

By (22.35), the posterior distribution of $\tilde{\boldsymbol{\beta}}$, which is the conditional distribution of $\tilde{\boldsymbol{\beta}}$ given $\boldsymbol{y}$, is Normal with mean and variance

$$\bar{\boldsymbol{\beta}}'' \equiv E(\tilde{\boldsymbol{\beta}}|\boldsymbol{y}) = \mathbf{H}''^{-1}\left(\mathbf{H}'\bar{\boldsymbol{\beta}}' + \frac{1}{\upsilon}\mathbf{x}^t\boldsymbol{y}\right), \tag{24.27a}$$

$$\breve{\boldsymbol{\beta}}'' \equiv V(\tilde{\boldsymbol{\beta}}|\boldsymbol{y}) = \mathbf{H}''^{-1}, \tag{24.27b}$$

where

$$\mathbf{H}' \equiv \breve{\boldsymbol{\beta}}'^{-1}, \qquad \mathbf{H} \equiv \frac{1}{v}\mathbf{x}^t\mathbf{x}, \qquad \mathbf{H}'' \equiv \mathbf{H}' + \mathbf{H}. \tag{24.27c}$$

This $\mathbf{H}$ is the same as that defined in (24.14b). It is easily verified (exercise 10) that (24.27) reduces to (24.14c) when $\mathbf{H}' = \mathbf{0}$. Formula (24.27a) for $\bar{\boldsymbol{\beta}}''$ may be rewritten in the form (exercise 11)

$$\bar{\boldsymbol{\beta}}'' = \mathbf{H}''^{-1}(\mathbf{H}'\bar{\boldsymbol{\beta}}' + \mathbf{H}\boldsymbol{b}), \tag{24.27d}$$

where $\boldsymbol{b}$ is defined by (24.12a). This form looks prettier but is less convenient for calculation, because $\boldsymbol{b} = (\mathbf{x}^t\mathbf{x})^{-1}\mathbf{x}^t\boldsymbol{y}$ is harder to calculate than $\mathbf{x}^t\boldsymbol{y}$ and would not otherwise have to be calculated. The pretty looks are actually deceptive, because the matrix-weighted average (24.27d) need not lie between $\bar{\boldsymbol{\beta}}'$ and $\boldsymbol{b}$. In fact, given $\bar{\boldsymbol{\beta}}'$ and $\boldsymbol{b}$, for every $\bar{\boldsymbol{\beta}}''$ not on the line through them there exist positive definite $\mathbf{H}'$ and $\mathbf{H}$ satisfying (24.27d) (exercise 12).

24.3.3 Marginal Distributions

By (22.34), the marginal or unconditional distribution of $\tilde{\boldsymbol{y}}$ is nonsingular Normal with mean and variance

$$E(\tilde{\boldsymbol{y}}) = \mathbf{x}\bar{\boldsymbol{\beta}}', \qquad V(\tilde{\boldsymbol{y}}) = \mathbf{x}\breve{\boldsymbol{\beta}}'\mathbf{x}^t + v\mathbf{I}. \tag{24.28}$$

Therefore the marginal distribution of $\tilde{\boldsymbol{b}} = (\mathbf{x}^t\mathbf{x})^{-1}\mathbf{x}^t\tilde{\boldsymbol{y}}$ is nonsingular Normal with mean and variance (exercise 13).

$$E(\tilde{\boldsymbol{b}}) = \bar{\boldsymbol{\beta}}' \qquad V(\tilde{\boldsymbol{b}}) = \breve{\boldsymbol{\beta}}' + \mathbf{H}^{-1}. \tag{24.29}$$

By section 22.3.1, in particular equation (22.36), the marginal distribution of the as yet unknown posterior mean $\tilde{\bar{\boldsymbol{\beta}}}''$ is Normal with mean and variance

$$E(\tilde{\bar{\boldsymbol{\beta}}}'') = \bar{\boldsymbol{\beta}}', \qquad V(\tilde{\bar{\boldsymbol{\beta}}}'') = \breve{\boldsymbol{\beta}}' - \breve{\boldsymbol{\beta}}'' = \mathbf{H}''^{-1}\mathbf{H}\breve{\boldsymbol{\beta}}'. \tag{24.30}$$

24.3.4 Successive Samples

Suppose two sets of observations are made successively on the regression process. Let $\boldsymbol{y}_1$ be the observations of the first set and let $\mathbf{x}_1$ be the corresponding $\mathbf{x}$ matrix. Define $\boldsymbol{y}_2$ and $\mathbf{x}_2$ similarly for the second set. Note that $\boldsymbol{y}_1$ and $\boldsymbol{y}_2$ are in general vectors and not the scalars y_1 and y_2; they partition the whole set of observations $\boldsymbol{y}$ exactly as z_1 and z_2 partition z in (22.6). Similarly, $\mathbf{x}_1$ and $\mathbf{x}_2$ partition the $\mathbf{x}$ corresponding to $\boldsymbol{y}$, so that we have

$$\boldsymbol{y} = \begin{bmatrix} \boldsymbol{y}_1 \\ \boldsymbol{y}_2 \end{bmatrix}, \qquad \mathbf{x} = \begin{bmatrix} \mathbf{x}_1 \\ \mathbf{x}_2 \end{bmatrix}. \tag{24.31}$$

If the prior distribution of $\tilde{\beta}$ is Normal before either y_1 or y_2 is observed, then its posterior distribution after y_1 is observed can be computed by (24.27) with $\mathbf{x}_1$ and y_1 in place of $\mathbf{x}$ and y, it will be Normal. This posterior distribution given y_1 is, as far as y_2 is concerned, the prior distribution. That is, the prior distribution for looking forward is the same as the posterior distribution for looking back. The fact that, posterior to y_1 but prior to y_2, the distribution of $\tilde{\beta}$ is again Normal means that the situation is again of the same type as originally. In particular, if we take this distribution of $\tilde{\beta}$ as a prior distribution and use $\mathbf{x}_2$ and y_2 in place of $\mathbf{x}$ and y, then formula (24.27) for the posterior distribution of $\tilde{\beta}$ gives its posterior distribution conditional on y_1 and y_2, and formula (24.28) for the marginal distribution of $\tilde{y}$ gives the distribution of $\tilde{y}_2$ conditional on y_1 but marginal on $\tilde{\beta}$. Of course, the posterior distribution of $\tilde{\beta}$ given y_1 and y_2 could also be obtained by applying (24.27) to y, using the original prior distribution of $\tilde{\beta}$.

Specifically, for $j = 1, 2$, let $\bar{\beta}'_{(j)}$ and $\bar{\beta}''_{(j)}$ be the mean of $\tilde{\beta}$ just prior and just posterior to observation of $y_{(j)}$, and define the variances $\breve{\boldsymbol{\beta}}'_{(j)}$ and $\breve{\boldsymbol{\beta}}''_{(j)}$ similarly; let

$$\mathbf{H}'_{(j)} \equiv \breve{\boldsymbol{\beta}}'^{-1}_{(j)}, \qquad \mathbf{H}_{(j)} \equiv \frac{1}{v}\mathbf{x}_j^t\mathbf{x}_j, \qquad \mathbf{H}''_{(j)} \equiv \mathbf{H}'_{(j)} + \mathbf{H}_{(j)}. \tag{24.32}$$

The subscripts are included in parentheses when they do not denote a partitioning. The notation here, though heavy, is logical and avoids the ambiguity that would arise from the use of unsubscripted symbols.

We are assuming that the original prior distribution of $\tilde{\beta}$, before either y_1 or y_2 is observed, is Normal. In the present notation, it has mean $\bar{\beta}'_{(1)}$ and variance $\breve{\boldsymbol{\beta}}'_{(1)}$. By section 24.3.2, the distribution of $\tilde{\beta}$ posterior to y_1 but prior to y_2 is Normal with mean and variance

$$\bar{\beta}''_{(1)} = \bar{\beta}'_{(2)} = E(\tilde{\beta}|y_1) = \mathbf{H}''^{-1}_{(1)}\left(\mathbf{H}'_{(1)}\bar{\beta}'_{(1)} + \frac{1}{v}\mathbf{x}_1^t y_1\right), \tag{24.33a}$$

$$\breve{\boldsymbol{\beta}}''_{(1)} = \breve{\boldsymbol{\beta}}'_{(2)} = V(\tilde{\beta}|y_1) = \mathbf{H}''^{-1}_{(1)}, \tag{24.33b}$$

and the distribution of $\tilde{\beta}$ posterior to y_1 and y_2 is Normal with mean and variance

$$\bar{\beta}''_{(2)} = E(\tilde{\beta}|y_1, y_2) = \mathbf{H}''^{-1}_{(2)}\left(\mathbf{H}'_{(2)}\bar{\beta}'_{(2)} + \frac{1}{v}\mathbf{x}_2^t y_2\right), \tag{24.34a}$$

$$\breve{\boldsymbol{\beta}}''_{(2)} = V(\tilde{\beta}|y_1, y_2) = \mathbf{H}''^{-1}_{(2)}. \tag{24.34b}$$

Notice that

$$\mathbf{H}'_{(2)} = \breve{\boldsymbol{\beta}}'^{-1}_{(2)} - \mathbf{H}''_{(1)}, \tag{24.35}$$

so that all the quantities on the right-hand side of (24.34) are defined.

By section 24.3.3, the marginal distribution of $\tilde{y}_1$ before y_1 or y_2 is observed is Normal with mean and variance

$$E(\tilde{y}_1) = \mathbf{x}_1\bar{\boldsymbol{\beta}}'_{(1)}, \qquad V(\tilde{y}_1) = \mathbf{x}_1\check{\boldsymbol{\beta}}'_{(1)}\mathbf{x}_1^t + v\mathbf{I}, \tag{24.36}$$

and the marginal distribution of $\tilde{y}_2$ after y_1 has been observed, that is, the distribution of $\tilde{y}_2$ conditional on y_1 but marginal on $\tilde{\boldsymbol{\beta}}$, is Normal with mean and variance

$$E(\tilde{y}_2|y_1) = \mathbf{x}_2\bar{\boldsymbol{\beta}}'_{(2)} = \mathbf{x}_2\mathbf{H}''^{-1}_{(1)}\left(\mathbf{H}'_{(1)}\bar{\boldsymbol{\beta}}'_{(1)} + \frac{1}{v}\mathbf{x}_1^t y_1\right), \tag{24.37a}$$

$$V(\tilde{y}_{(2)}|y_1) = \mathbf{x}_2\check{\boldsymbol{\beta}}'_{(2)}\mathbf{x}_2^t + v\mathbf{I} = \mathbf{x}_2\mathbf{H}''^{-1}_{(1)}\mathbf{x}_2^t + v\mathbf{I}. \tag{24.37b}$$

If the original prior is diffuse ($\mathbf{H}'_{(1)} = \mathbf{0}$), then formulas (24.33), (24.34), and (24.37) continue to hold, but (24.36) becomes meaningless (exercise 20).

The posterior mean and variance of $\tilde{\boldsymbol{\beta}}$ after both y_1 and y_2 have been observed can be obtained either by two successive applications of (24.27), leading to (24.34), or by a simple application (24.27) to the combined set of observations $y = [y_1^t y_2^t]^t$. These two methods must agree, of course. To see the algebraic relation between them, note first that

$$\begin{aligned}\mathbf{H}''_{(2)} &= \mathbf{H}'_{(2)} + \mathbf{H}_{(2)} = \mathbf{H}''_{(1)} + \mathbf{H}_{(2)} \\ &= \mathbf{H}'_{(1)} + \mathbf{H}_{(1)} + \mathbf{H}_{(2)} = \mathbf{H}'_{(1)} + \frac{1}{v}\mathbf{x}_1^t\mathbf{x}_1 + \frac{1}{v}\mathbf{x}_2^t\mathbf{x}_2 \\ &= \mathbf{H}'_{(1)} + \frac{1}{v}\begin{bmatrix}\mathbf{x}_1\\ \mathbf{x}_2\end{bmatrix}^t\begin{bmatrix}\mathbf{x}_1\\ \mathbf{x}_2\end{bmatrix} = \mathbf{H}'_{(1)} + \frac{1}{v}\mathbf{x}^t\mathbf{x};\end{aligned} \tag{24.38a}$$

the last expression is exactly what a single application of (24.27c) gives. Note also that

$$\begin{aligned}\mathbf{H}''_{(2)}\bar{\boldsymbol{\beta}}''_{(2)} &= \mathbf{H}'_{(2)}\bar{\boldsymbol{\beta}}'_{(2)} + \frac{1}{v}\mathbf{x}_2^t y_2 = \mathbf{H}''_{(1)}\bar{\boldsymbol{\beta}}''_{(1)} + \frac{1}{v}\mathbf{x}_2^t y_2 \\ &= \mathbf{H}'_{(1)}\bar{\boldsymbol{\beta}}'_{(1)} + \frac{1}{v}\mathbf{x}_1^t y_1 + \frac{1}{v}\mathbf{x}_2^t y_2 = \mathbf{H}'_{(1)}\bar{\boldsymbol{\beta}}'_{(1)} + \frac{1}{v}\mathbf{x}^t y;\end{aligned} \tag{24.38b}$$

the last expression here is exactly what a single application of (24.27a) gives. Thus two successive applications of (24.27) amounts algebraically to partitioning $\mathbf{x}$ and y in the formulas

$$\mathbf{H}'' = \mathbf{H}' + \frac{1}{v}\mathbf{x}^t\mathbf{x}, \tag{24.39a}$$

$$\mathbf{H}''\bar{\boldsymbol{\beta}}'' = \mathbf{H}'\bar{\boldsymbol{\beta}}' + \frac{1}{v}\mathbf{x}^t y. \tag{24.39b}$$

More than two sets of observations can be processed successively in a similar way. The distribution of $\tilde{\beta}$ posterior to the jth set of observations can be obtained from its distribution posterior to the $j-1$st set (prior to the jth set) just as its distribution posterior to y_1, y_2 was obtained from its distribution posterior to y_1 (prior to y_2) at (24.34). As at (24.38), this amounts algebraically to adding successive values of $\mathbf{x}^t y/\upsilon$ starting with the initial value $\mathbf{H}'\bar{\beta}'$. At any stage, the two totals are the current $\mathbf{H}''$ and $\mathbf{H}''\bar{\beta}''$, from which $\bar{\boldsymbol{\beta}}''$ and $\breve{\boldsymbol{\beta}}''$ can be obtained. This totaling is computationally simpler than repeated use of the generalization of (24.34). Slightly simpler still is to start with the initial values

$$\mathbf{n}' \equiv \upsilon\mathbf{H}' \equiv \upsilon\breve{\boldsymbol{\beta}}'^{-1} \quad \text{and} \quad \boldsymbol{d}' \equiv \mathbf{n}'\bar{\boldsymbol{\beta}}' \tag{24.40a}$$

and to add to them respectively successive values of

$$\mathbf{n} \equiv \mathbf{x}^t\mathbf{x} \quad \text{and} \quad \boldsymbol{d} \equiv \mathbf{x}^t\boldsymbol{y}. \tag{24.40b}$$

If at any time the totals are $\mathbf{n}''$ and $\boldsymbol{d}''$, then the distribution of $\tilde{\beta}$ at that time (posterior to the past, prior to the future) is Normal with mean and variance

$$\bar{\boldsymbol{\beta}}'' = \mathbf{n}''^{-1}\boldsymbol{d}'', \qquad \breve{\boldsymbol{\beta}}'' = \upsilon\mathbf{n}''^{-1}. \tag{24.41}$$

24.4 Special Cases

24.4.1 Introduction

The foregoing theory can be exemplified in any of the situations of section 24.1.4. The reader should think about what probability questions might arise in those situations and how they could be handled with the help of the theory of sections 24.2 and 24.3. We shall illustrate the theory in another way here by developing certain special cases.

24.4.2 Forecasting

A classical problem of statistics is to forecast y_{n+1} on the basis of $y_1, \ldots, y_n$, under the model (24.3). It is assumed that the corresponding $\boldsymbol{x}$ vectors are all known, that is, that $\boldsymbol{x}_1^t, \ldots, \boldsymbol{x}_n^t, \boldsymbol{x}_{n+1}^t$ are known.

From our point of view, the problem is not well posed, since what is a good forecast depends on what is to be done with it. As far as *inference* about y_{n+1} is concerned, we can say that if the prior distribution of $\tilde{\beta}$ before observing any ys was Normal with mean $\bar{\beta}'$ and variance $\breve{\boldsymbol{\beta}}'$, then the conditional distribution of $\tilde{y}_{n+1}$ given $y = (y_1, \ldots, y_n)$ but marginal on $\tilde{\beta}$ is Normal with mean and variance

$$E(\tilde{y}_{n+1}|y) = \boldsymbol{x}_{n+1}^t\bar{\boldsymbol{\beta}}'', \qquad V(\tilde{y}_{n+1}|y) = \boldsymbol{x}_{n+1}^t\mathbf{H}''^{-1}\boldsymbol{x}_{n+1} + \upsilon, \tag{24.42}$$

where $\bar{\boldsymbol{\beta}}''$ and $\mathbf{H}''$ are given by (24.27) with $\boldsymbol{y} = [y_1 \ldots y_n]^t$ and $\mathbf{x} = [\boldsymbol{x}_1 \ldots \boldsymbol{x}_n]^t$. This follows from (24.37), or from (24.28) and the fact that at the time of forecasting we are in the same situation as originally except that the relevant quantities are $\boldsymbol{x}_{n+1}^t$, $\bar{\boldsymbol{\beta}}''$, and $\mathbf{H}''^{-1}$ in place of $\mathbf{x}$, $\bar{\boldsymbol{\beta}}'$, and $\check{\boldsymbol{\beta}}'$. We may interpret $V(\tilde{y}_{n+1}|\boldsymbol{y})$ as being the sum of two components: the variance $V(\tilde{\varepsilon}_{n+1}) = v$ attributable to the random error $\tilde{\varepsilon}_{n+1}$, which would be present even if we knew $\boldsymbol{\beta}$ exactly, and the variance $V_{\beta}[E(\tilde{y}_{n+1}|\tilde{\boldsymbol{\beta}})] = \boldsymbol{x}_{n+1}^t \mathbf{H}''^{-1} \boldsymbol{x}_{n+1}$ attributable to our uncertainty about $\tilde{\boldsymbol{\beta}}$, which would be present even if we knew that $\tilde{\varepsilon}_{n+1} = 0$.

If a "point forecast" (a single value) is required, it is natural to use $E(\tilde{y}_{n+1}|\boldsymbol{y})$. It should be clearly understood, however, as pointed out in section 12.5, that if a point forecast is to be used as a certainty equivalent, that is, if an act is to be chosen as if the point forecast were the true value of y_{n+1}, then the forecast should be chosen in such a way that treating it as a certainty will result in the optimal act. This means that the best point forecast depends on the structure of the terminal decision problem, and the naive formulation of the point forecasting problem rather puts the cart before the horse.

24.4.5 Setting Prior by Pilot Sample

Suppose one has taken a pilot sample on the regression process (24.3) with $\mathbf{x}'$ in place of $\mathbf{x}$ and has observed $\boldsymbol{y}'$. If one's prior before taking the pilot sample was diffuse, then the posterior after the pilot sample is Normal with mean and variance given by (24.14c) but with $\mathbf{x}'^t\mathbf{x}'/v = \mathbf{H}'$ in place of $\mathbf{H}$ and $\boldsymbol{b}' \equiv (\mathbf{x}'^t\mathbf{x}')^{-1}\mathbf{x}'^t\boldsymbol{y}'$ in place of $\boldsymbol{b}$. The posterior after the pilot sample, which is the prior for the next sample, is thus of exactly the form assumed above. That is, if one starts with a diffuse prior and takes a pilot sample, one will be in the position assumed in section 24.3.1, with $\bar{\boldsymbol{\beta}}' = \boldsymbol{b}'$ and $\check{\boldsymbol{\beta}}' = \mathbf{H}'^{-1}$. This is just the case $\mathbf{H}'_{(1)} = \mathbf{0}$ in section 24.3.4.

24.4.6 Regression on One Independent Variable

Consider the first linear regression model introduced, (24.1):

$$\tilde{y}_i = \beta_1 + \beta_2 x_i + \tilde{\varepsilon}_i.$$

This model is often used with x_i equal to the observed value of some measurement paired (and, one hopes, closely associated) with y_i. In this context, x_i is often called the *independent variable* and y_i the *dependent variable*. Often the underlying situation is fundamentally symmetric in x_i and y_i, which simply form an observed pair of measurements, like height and weight. The nonsymmetry of the terminology and of the way in which we are looking at the situation is nevertheless justified when the inference or decision problem we wish to solve is not symmetric in x and y. That is, we may have reason to be concerned with the dependence of y on x, but not with how x depends on anything; then it makes sense to regard y as a dependent variable and x as an independent variable. The guesser at the county fair forecasts weight from height (and other clues), not vice versa.

Suppose υ is known and β_1 and β_2 are a priori jointly Normal with means $\bar{\beta}'_1$ and $\bar{\beta}'_2$ and variance matrix $\breve{\boldsymbol{\beta}}'$ whose inverse is

$$\breve{\boldsymbol{\beta}}'^{-1} = \mathbf{H}' - \begin{bmatrix} H'_{11} & H'_{12} \\ H'_{21} & H'_{22} \end{bmatrix}. \tag{24.43}$$

Then the following facts may be shown as exercises (exercise 21):

1. The posterior distribution of $\tilde{\boldsymbol{\beta}}$ given $\boldsymbol{y} = [y_1 \dots y_n]^t$ is Normal with mean $\bar{\boldsymbol{\beta}}''$ and variance $\breve{\boldsymbol{\beta}}'' = \mathbf{H}''^{-1}$, where

$$\mathbf{H}'' = \begin{bmatrix} H'_{11} + \frac{n}{\upsilon} & H'_{12} + \frac{1}{\upsilon}\sum x_i \\ H'_{21} + \frac{1}{\upsilon}\sum x_i & H'_{22} + \frac{1}{\upsilon}\sum x_i^2 \end{bmatrix}, \tag{24.44a}$$

$$\bar{\boldsymbol{\beta}}'' = \mathbf{H}''^{-1} \begin{bmatrix} H'_{11}\bar{\beta}'_1 + H'_{12}\bar{\beta}'_2 + \frac{1}{\upsilon}\sum y_i \\ H'_{21}\bar{\beta}'_1 + H'_{22}\bar{\beta}'_2 + \frac{1}{\upsilon}\sum x_i y_i \end{bmatrix}. \tag{24.44b}$$

2. The average of a very large number of observations y all occurring with the same value of x would, with high probability, be very close to $\tilde{\beta}_1 + \tilde{\beta}_2 x$. This line is the so-called *true regression line.* Given $\boldsymbol{y} = [y_1 \dots y_n]^t$, the posterior distribution of $\tilde{\beta}_1 + \tilde{\beta}_2 x$ is Normal with

$$\text{mean} = \bar{\beta}''_1 + \bar{\beta}''_2 x, \qquad \text{variance} = \breve{\beta}''_1 + 2\breve{\beta}''_{12} x + \breve{\beta}''_2 x^2. \tag{24.45}$$

The quartiles of this posterior distribution are given for each x in a typical case in figure 24.1.

3. The conditional distribution of y_{n+1} given $\boldsymbol{y} = [y_1 \dots y_n]^t$, for $x_{n+1} = x$, is Normal with mean and variance

$$E(\tilde{y}_{n+1} | \boldsymbol{y}) = \bar{\beta}''_1 + \bar{\beta}''_2 x, \qquad V(\tilde{y}_{n+1} | \boldsymbol{y}) = \breve{\beta}''_1 + 2\breve{\beta}''_{12} x + \breve{\beta}''_2 x^2 + \upsilon. \tag{24.46}$$

The quartiles of this distribution are also given for each x in figure 24.1.

4. Let the prior distribution of $\tilde{\beta}_1$ and $\tilde{\beta}_2$ be diffuse ($\mathbf{H}' = \mathbf{0}$) and let

$$m_z \equiv \frac{1}{n}\sum z_i, \qquad s_{zz} \equiv \frac{1}{n}\sum (z_i - m_z)^2 = \frac{1}{n}\sum z_i^2 - m_z^2, \qquad \text{for } z = x, y; \tag{24.47a}$$

$$s_{xy} \equiv \frac{1}{n}\sum (x_i - m_x)(y_i - m_y) = \frac{1}{n}\sum x_i y_i - m_x m_y. \tag{24.47b}$$

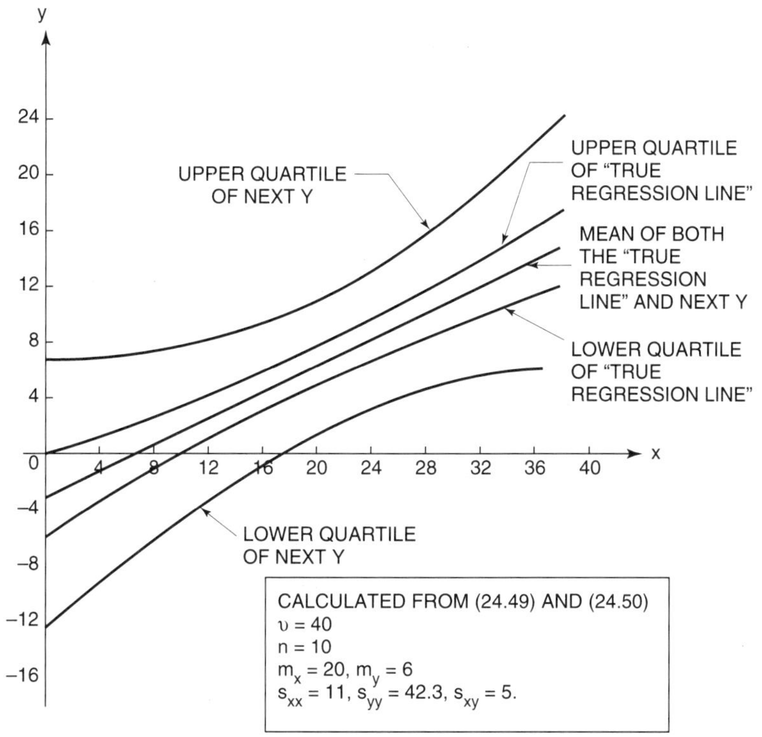

Figure 24.1
Quartiles of posterior and forecast distributions

Then the posterior means, variances, and covariance of $\tilde{\beta}_1$ and $\tilde{\beta}_2$ can be written

$$\bar{\beta}_1'' = b_1 = m_y - m_x \frac{s_{xy}}{s_{xx}}, \qquad \bar{\beta}_{12}'' = b_2 = \frac{s_{xy}}{s_{xx}}, \tag{22.48a}$$

$$\breve{\beta}_1'' = \frac{\upsilon}{n}\left(1 + \frac{m_x^2}{s_{xx}}\right), \qquad \breve{\beta}_{12}'' = -\frac{\upsilon m_x}{n s_{xx}}, \qquad \breve{\beta}_2'' = \frac{\upsilon}{n s_{xx}}. \tag{24.48b}$$

Furthermore, the posterior mean and variance of the *true regression line* $\tilde{\beta}_1 + \tilde{\beta}_2 x$ can be written

$$\text{mean} = m_y + \frac{s_{xy}}{s_{xx}}(x - m_x), \qquad \text{variance} = \frac{\upsilon}{n}\left(1 + \frac{[x - m_x]^2}{s_{xx}}\right), \tag{24.49}$$

and the mean and variance of $\tilde{y}_{n+1}$ given $\boldsymbol{y}$, for $x_{n+1} = x$, are similarly

$$E(\tilde{y}_{n+1} | \boldsymbol{y}) = m_y + \frac{s_{xy}}{s_{xx}}(x - m_x), \qquad V(\tilde{y}_{n+1} | \boldsymbol{y}) = \upsilon\left(1 + \frac{1}{n} + \frac{[x - m_x]^2}{n s_{xx}}\right). \tag{24.50}$$

24.5 Not All xs Known in Advance

24.5.1 Introduction

At the end of section 24.1.3 we stipulated that all xs that are observed values of rv's are to be treated as given. This stipulation remained in force throughout the subsequent theory. This means that all distributions heretofore have been conditional on all xs, or at least on all xs corresponding to ys which have been or may be observed.

Usually when xs are observed values of rv's, they are not all known in advance. Then the foregoing theory, though correct, is not obviously relevant. We shall see, however, that the theory actually is relevant provided the xs are *uninformative*, although additional theory is needed for preposterior analysis of sampling or observational plans. This is explained in the next subsection.

Section 24.5.3 clarifies the difficulties that arise when one attempts to apply the theory of this chapter to problems in which the xs are *informative*. Section 24.5.4 considers briefly the *autoregressive* case, which technically does not fit the linear regression model (24.3) as stated, but requires a slight extension of it.

24.5.2 Uninformative xs

Suppose first that each x_{ij} is either a constant or the observed value of a rv; that the linear regression model (24.3) or (24.9) holds; that $\tilde{\mathbf{x}}$, $\tilde{\boldsymbol{\beta}}$, and all the $\tilde{\varepsilon}$s are mutually independent; and that $\tilde{\boldsymbol{\beta}}$ and the $\tilde{\varepsilon}$s have the same distribution as before. In other words, conditional on the xs, the previous assumptions hold and $\bar{\boldsymbol{\beta}}'$, $\check{\boldsymbol{\beta}}'$, and υ do not depend on the xs.

The posterior distribution of $\tilde{\boldsymbol{\beta}}$, that is, the conditional distribution of $\tilde{\boldsymbol{\beta}}$ given $\boldsymbol{y}$ and $\mathbf{x}$, is obtained just as before, and is Normal with mean and variance (24.27). We have indicated that the prior distribution of $\tilde{\boldsymbol{\beta}}$ used in this calculation should be conditional on $\mathbf{x}$. But since $\tilde{\boldsymbol{\beta}}$ and $\tilde{\mathbf{x}}$ are independent, the distribution of $\tilde{\boldsymbol{\beta}}$ (marginal on $\tilde{\varepsilon}$) is the same marginal on $\tilde{\mathbf{x}}$ as conditional on $\tilde{\mathbf{x}}$. Therefore, once the judgment has been made that $\tilde{\boldsymbol{\beta}}$ is independent of $\tilde{\mathbf{x}}$, its prior distribution may be assessed marginally on $\tilde{\mathbf{x}}$ instead of conditionally on $\mathbf{x}$ if this is more comfortable, as it usually is. Again (24.14c) is an alternative formula for the case of a *diffuse* prior distribution of $\tilde{\boldsymbol{\beta}}$, and the likelihood function is still given by (24.14a). And again the prior-posterior analysis of successive samples can be carried out successively as in (24.32)–(24.35) or (24.40) and (24.41).

The conditional (sampling) distributions (24.10) and (24.15) are now the conditional distributions of $\tilde{\boldsymbol{y}}$ and of $\tilde{\boldsymbol{b}}$ given $\mathbf{x}$ as well as $\boldsymbol{\beta}$. Thus it is appropriate to rewrite (24.15) as

$$E(\tilde{\boldsymbol{b}}|\boldsymbol{\beta}, \mathbf{x}) = \boldsymbol{\beta}, \qquad V(\tilde{\boldsymbol{b}}|\boldsymbol{\beta}, \mathbf{x}) = \mathbf{H}^{-1} \equiv \upsilon(\mathbf{x}^t\mathbf{x})^{-1}. \tag{24.51}$$

It follows in particular that the mean of $\tilde{\boldsymbol{b}}$ conditional on $\boldsymbol{\beta}$ (but marginal on $\tilde{\mathbf{x}}$) is still $\boldsymbol{\beta}$, so that $\tilde{\boldsymbol{b}}$ is an *unbiased* estimate of $\boldsymbol{\beta}$, a matter of some interest to classical statisticians. However, the distribution of $\tilde{\boldsymbol{b}}$ conditional on $\boldsymbol{\beta}$ but marginal on $\tilde{\mathbf{x}}$ is not Normal in general, and its variance is $\upsilon E[(\tilde{\mathbf{x}}^t\tilde{\mathbf{x}})^{-1}]$.

The marginal distributions (24.28)–(24.30) are now the distributions of $\tilde{\boldsymbol{y}}$, $\tilde{\boldsymbol{b}}$, and $\tilde{\bar{\boldsymbol{\beta}}}''$ marginal on $\tilde{\boldsymbol{\beta}}$ but conditional on $\mathbf{x}$. Thus it is appropriate to rewrite (24.28) as

$$E(\tilde{\boldsymbol{y}}|\mathbf{x}) = \mathbf{x}\bar{\boldsymbol{\beta}}', \qquad V(\tilde{\boldsymbol{y}}|\mathbf{x}) = \mathbf{x}\check{\boldsymbol{\beta}}'\mathbf{x}^t + \upsilon\mathbf{I}. \tag{24.52}$$

Similarly, for successive sets of observations, (24.37) gives the distribution of $\tilde{\boldsymbol{y}}_2$ marginal on $\tilde{\boldsymbol{\beta}}$ but conditional on both $\mathbf{x}_2$ and $\mathbf{x}_1$ as well as $\boldsymbol{y}_1$. The special case (24.42) is therefore

$$\begin{aligned} E(\tilde{y}_{n+1}|\boldsymbol{y}, \mathbf{x}, \boldsymbol{x}_{n+1}^t) &= \boldsymbol{x}_{n+1}^t\bar{\boldsymbol{\beta}}'', \\ V(\tilde{y}_{n+1}|\boldsymbol{y}, \mathbf{x}, \boldsymbol{x}_{n+1}^t) &= \boldsymbol{x}_{n+1}^t\mathbf{H}''^{-1}\boldsymbol{x}_{n+1} + \upsilon. \end{aligned} \tag{24.53}$$

Such distributions of one or more ys given the corresponding xs (but marginal on $\tilde{\boldsymbol{\beta}}$) are what is needed for *forecasting* and decision problems about unknown ys, provided of course that the corresponding xs are known at the time of forecast or decision.

The foregoing marginal distributions are unfortunately not exactly what is typically needed for preposterior analysis of sampling or observational plans. When we are concerned with the desirability of a plan or with choosing among plans, the xs that are observed values of rv's are typically, almost by definition, not all observed in advance. Thus we need distributions marginal on $\tilde{\mathbf{x}}$, and such distributions are different from any of those discussed so far. The marginal distribution of $\tilde{\boldsymbol{y}}$, marginal on $\tilde{\mathbf{x}}$ as well as $\tilde{\boldsymbol{\beta}}$, can be simulated by simulating $\tilde{\mathbf{x}}$ and $\tilde{\boldsymbol{y}}|\mathbf{x}$, the latter being Normal with mean and variance (24.52). The marginal distribution of $\tilde{\boldsymbol{b}}$, $\tilde{\bar{\boldsymbol{\beta}}}''$, or the conditional value of sample information, can be simulated similarly. Thus preposterior analysis of sampling plans can be done by "Monte Carlo" simulation. Shortly, we shall give formulas for various marginal means and variances, but it should be remembered that even when these formulas can be evaluated analytically, the marginal distributions in question are not Normal in general. By (24.52) we can express the marginal mean and variance of $\tilde{\boldsymbol{y}}$ as

$$E(\tilde{\boldsymbol{y}}) = \bar{\mathbf{x}}'\bar{\boldsymbol{\beta}}', \qquad V(\tilde{\boldsymbol{y}}) = V(\tilde{\mathbf{x}}\bar{\boldsymbol{\beta}}') + E(\tilde{\mathbf{x}}\check{\boldsymbol{\beta}}'\tilde{\mathbf{x}}^t) + \upsilon\mathbf{I}. \tag{24.54a}$$

Similarly, we have the marginal means and variances

$$E(\tilde{b}) = \bar{\beta}', \qquad V(\tilde{b}) = \breve{\beta}' + E(\tilde{\mathbf{H}}^{-1}); \tag{24.54b}$$

$$E(\tilde{\bar{\beta}}'') = \bar{\beta}', \qquad V(\tilde{\bar{\beta}}'') = \mathbf{H}'^{-1} - E[(\mathbf{H}' + \tilde{\mathbf{H}})^{-1}]; \tag{24.54c}$$

$$E(\tilde{\breve{\beta}}'') = E[(\mathbf{H}' + \tilde{\mathbf{H}})^{-1}]. \tag{24.54d}$$

Notice that one cannot compute any of the expectations involving $\tilde{\mathbf{x}}$ or $\tilde{\mathbf{H}} = \tilde{\mathbf{x}}^t\tilde{\mathbf{x}}$ in (24.54) simply by substituting $\bar{\mathbf{x}}'$ for $\tilde{\mathbf{x}}$.

24.5.3 Informative x's[2]

Suppose again that each x_{ij} is either a constant or the observed value of a rv; that the linear regression model (24.3) or (24.9) holds; and that $(\tilde{\mathbf{x}}, \tilde{\beta})$ and all the εs are mutually independent. Now, however, we do not require $\tilde{\mathbf{x}}$ and $\tilde{\beta}$ to be independent. Thus the conditional distribution of $\tilde{\beta}$ given $\mathbf{x}$ may depend on $\mathbf{x}$, so that $\mathbf{x}$ is informative about $\tilde{\beta}$. The previously assumed distribution of $\tilde{\beta}$ is now assumed conditional on $\mathbf{x}$. Specifically, we assume that the conditional distribution of $\tilde{\beta}$ given $\mathbf{x}$ is Normal with mean $\bar{\beta}'$ and variance $\breve{\beta}'$, which are permitted to depend on $\mathbf{x}$. (We do not introduce notation indicating this dependence, because we are not going to discuss this case at any length.) As always, we assume that the $\tilde{\varepsilon}$s are Normal with mean 0 and known variance υ.

The posterior distribution of $\tilde{\beta}$, that is, the conditional distribution of $\tilde{\beta}$ given y and $\mathbf{x}$, is still Normal with mean and variance (24.27). Now, however, it is essential that the prior mean $\bar{\beta}'$ and variance $\breve{\beta}'$ used in this calculation be conditional on $\mathbf{x}$, as they were defined to be in the previous paragraph. The mean and variance of $\tilde{\beta}$ marginal on both $\tilde{\mathbf{x}}$ and $\tilde{y}$ cannot be used in (24.27). It would often be more natural to regard the distribution of $\tilde{\beta}$ marginal on both $\tilde{\mathbf{x}}$ and $\tilde{y}$ as the prior distribution; this is perfectly legitimate, and a correct calculation starting from this point would lead to the same result, but it would not be correct to use the mean and variance of this distribution in (24.27).

Subject to the same understanding about $\bar{\beta}'$ and $\breve{\beta}'$, the marginal distributions (24.28)–(24.30) are, as in the previous subsection, the distributions of $\tilde{y}$, $\tilde{b}$, and $\tilde{\bar{\beta}}''$ marginal on $\tilde{\beta}$ but conditional on $\mathbf{x}$, and in particular (24.52) holds.

Thus the formulas (24.27)–(24.30) for the posterior and marginal distributions therein can be preserved by suitable definition of $\bar{\beta}'$ and $\breve{\beta}'$. Unfortunately, this is of limited usefulness, and perhaps even dangerously misleading, since in general the distribution of $\tilde{\beta}$ changes whenever new xs are observed. This means that the prior-posterior analysis of successive

2. This subsection is optional.

samples cannot be done successively by (24.32)–(24.35) or (24.40) and (24.41); the conditional distribution of $\tilde{\boldsymbol{\beta}}$ given $(\boldsymbol{y}_1, \mathbf{x}_1)$ is not the same as that given $(\boldsymbol{y}_1, \mathbf{x}_1, \mathbf{x}_2)$; the distribution of $\tilde{\boldsymbol{y}}_2$ marginal on $\tilde{\boldsymbol{\beta}}$ but conditional on $\boldsymbol{y}_1$, $\mathbf{x}_1$, $\mathbf{x}_2$ is not given by (24.37); and the distribution of $\tilde{y}_{n+1}$ given $(\boldsymbol{y}, \mathbf{x}, \boldsymbol{x}_{n+1})$ is not given by (24.42). All these formulas are correct only under a very artificial and irrelevant interpretation, namely that all distributions including the original prior distribution are conditional on all xs corresponding to ys that will at some time be observed.

The remarks about conditional sampling distributions in the previous subsection, specifically the paragraph including (24.51), remain true here without change, except that the final expectation must be taken conditional on $\boldsymbol{\beta}$.

Preposterior analysis of sampling plans requires distributions not given in this chapter even in the case of uninformative xs. The situation here is similar with the added complication that the effect of the xs on the distribution of $\tilde{\boldsymbol{\beta}}$ must also be taken into account. Formulas (24.54) no longer hold.

24.5.4 Autoregressive Schemes

Consider the model

$$\tilde{y}_i = \tilde{y}_{i-1} + \tilde{\varepsilon}_i, \tag{24.55}$$

where y_0 is a constant and $\tilde{\varepsilon}_1$, $\tilde{\varepsilon}_2$, ... are independent Normal rv's with mean 0 and variance υ, as before. This model is formally much like those discussed earlier with $x_i = y_{i-1}$, but now the xs are not only random, they are determined by earlier ys. Such a situation is called *autoregressive* and is not covered by the earlier discussion, because $\tilde{\boldsymbol{\varepsilon}}$ is no longer independent of $\tilde{\mathbf{x}}$; indeed, $\tilde{\varepsilon}_i = \tilde{x}_{i+1} - \tilde{x}_i$.

More generally, we now assume that the $\tilde{y}_i$ follow the model (24.3) or (24.6), where x_{ij} may be a rv and even a function of $y_1, \ldots, y_{i-1}$, but the conditional distribution of $\tilde{\varepsilon}_i$ is Normal with mean 0 and variance υ given $\boldsymbol{\beta}$, $y_1, \ldots, y_{i-1}$, and $\boldsymbol{x}_1, \ldots, \boldsymbol{x}_i$, that is, given $\boldsymbol{\beta}$, the "history through time $i-1$," and $\boldsymbol{x}_i$. We assume further that the conditional distribution of $\tilde{\boldsymbol{\beta}}$ given $y_1, \ldots, y_{i-1}$ and $\boldsymbol{x}_1, \ldots, \boldsymbol{x}_i$ is the same as the conditional distribution of $\tilde{\boldsymbol{\beta}}$ given $y_1, \ldots, y_{i-1}$ and $\boldsymbol{x}_1, \ldots, \boldsymbol{x}_{i-1}$, that is, that $\boldsymbol{x}_i$ is informative about $\tilde{\boldsymbol{\beta}}$ only insofar as it depends on $y_1, \ldots, y_{i-1}$. (Conditions insuring this will not be spelled out here.) Then the posterior distribution of $\tilde{\boldsymbol{\beta}}$ given $(\boldsymbol{y}, \mathbf{x})$ is still Normal with mean and variance given by (24.27) and the conditional distribution of a single further observation $\tilde{y}_{n+1}$ given $(\boldsymbol{y}, \mathbf{x}, \boldsymbol{x}_{n+1})$ is still Normal with mean and variance given by (24.42). (This follows from the fact that if the observations are processed one at a time, we will get the same situation as before at each stage: conditional on $y_1, \ldots, y_i, \boldsymbol{x}_1, \ldots, \boldsymbol{x}_i$, we find that $\tilde{\boldsymbol{x}}_{i+1}$, $\tilde{\boldsymbol{\beta}}$, and $\tilde{\varepsilon}_{i+1}$ are independently distributed as in section 24.5.2, so the distribution of $\tilde{\boldsymbol{\beta}}$ conditional on $(y_{i+1}, \boldsymbol{x}_{i+1})$ in addition is the same as before, and the distribution of y_{i+1} conditional on $\boldsymbol{x}_{i+1}$ in addition—but marginal on $\tilde{\boldsymbol{\beta}}$—is the same as before. Alternatively, one may observe that the βs and the last y enter the likelihood in the same way as before, although the earlier ys enter in a much more complicated way.)

Though posterior analysis and forecasting of *one* new y are not changed, everything else is. Even the sampling distributions of $\tilde{\boldsymbol{y}}$ and $\tilde{\boldsymbol{b}}$ are changed, no longer being given by (24.10) and (24.15). Indeed now $E(\tilde{\boldsymbol{b}}|\boldsymbol{\beta}) \neq \boldsymbol{\beta}$ in general, so that $\tilde{\boldsymbol{b}}$ is a *biased* estimator of $\boldsymbol{\beta}$, a matter of considerable concern to some classical statisticians.

24.6 Choice among Models

In practical situations, it is common to consider a variety of statistical models that might fit or explain the data, and to choose among them somehow. For example, one might choose a regression model with y or $\log y$ as the dependent variable, at the same time choosing whether or not to include each potential explanatory variable x and what transformations of the included variables to make. While it would often be preferable from some points of view to adopt a "supermodel" incorporating all possibilities in a smooth way, it usually appears desirable as a practical matter to approach the problem as if one of the simpler models were correct. Reasons include the difficulty of interpreting complex models with many interrelated parameters and the difficulty of arriving at satisfactory methods of making statistical inferences about them. (For Bayesians, a multiplicity of parameters makes the prior distribution hard or impossible to assess responsibly but at the same time important, because the likelihood does not swamp it. For others, equally great difficulties arise in other forms. Exercise 24 hints at one.) We will not embark upon this general topic here, but limit ourselves to a few basic points about the Bayesian analysis of multiple models. Even in our limited framework, however, responsible prior assessment is a significant practical concern.

Theoretically, Bayesian analysis of multiple models is straightforward, closely related to and not much harder than Bayesian analysis of individual ones. In brief, suppose two or more statistical models for a set of observations z are under consideration. Then for purposes of Bayesian inference about which model is correct, the likelihood is simply the probability or density of z under each model, and the posterior probability of model i is proportional to the product of the prior probability and the likelihood of model i, by Bayes' formula. The posterior distribution of the parameters of model i, conditional on model i's being correct, is the same as when model i is the only model considered. Specifically, let $f_\theta^{(i)}(\theta^{(i)})$ be the prior density we would use for $\tilde{\theta}^{(i)}$, the vector of parameters of model i. Let $f_z^{(i)}(z) = E_{\theta^{(i)}} f(z|\tilde{\theta}^{(i)})$, the marginal density (or mass function) we would obtain for $\tilde{z}$ if we knew (or assumed) model i to be correct. Let p_i' be the prior probability we decide to attach to model i. Then the posterior probabilities p_i'' of the models are given by

$$p_1'' : p_2'' : p_3'' \ldots :: p_1' f_z^{(1)}(z) : p_2' f_z^{(2)}(z) : p_3' f_z^{(3)}(z) \ldots \tag{24.56}$$

according to Bayes' Theorem. Equivalently, $p_i'' = p_i' f_z^{(i)} / \sum_j p_j' f_z^{(j)}(z)$. Also the conditional posterior distribution of $\tilde{\theta}^{(i)}$ given z and given that model i holds is just the posterior distribution we would obtain for $\tilde{\theta}^{(i)}$ if we assumed model i to be correct.

We thus have a simple description of the prior-to-posterior analysis: the prior probabilities p_i are revised by (24.56) to give the posterior probabilities, and the conditional prior density $f_\theta^{(i)}(\theta^{(i)})$ of $\tilde{\theta}^{(i)}$ given model i is revised to give the conditional posterior density $f_{\theta|z}^{(i)}(\theta^{(i)}|z)$ of $\tilde{\theta}^{(i)}$ given model i by exactly the usual prior-to-posterior analysis for model i.

Preposterior analysis in this situation can be based on the marginal distribution of $\tilde{z}$, which has density

$$f_z(z) = p_1' f_z^{(1)}(z) + p_2' f_z^{(2)}(z) + \cdots. \tag{24.57}$$

In "forecasting" problems, one is ordinarily interested in the distribution of some future observations given the past observations but marginal on the parameters of the model, and here, marginal on which model holds. This distribution is, of course, the same as the marginal distribution of $\tilde{z}$ just discussed except that everything is posterior to the past observations. Specifically, the forecasting density of future observations $\tilde{z}_2$ given past observations z_1 is

$$f_{z|z}(z_2|z_1) = p_1'' f_{z|z}^{(1)}(z_2|z_1) + p_2'' f_{z|z}^{(2)}(z_2|z_1) + \cdots \tag{24.58}$$

where $f_{z|z}^{(i)}$ is the forecasting density under model i, which is, again, the marginal density of future observations under model i, computed posterior to the past observations. Fractiles, means, variances, and so on, of future observations can thus be obtained. The posterior probabilities of the models are automatically accounted for: there is no need to choose one model and proceed as if it were known to hold. In particular,

$$E(\tilde{z}_2|z_1) = p_1'' E^{(1)}(\tilde{z}_2|z_1) + p_2'' E^{(2)}(\tilde{z}_2|z_1) + \cdots. \tag{24.59}$$

Both posterior distributions and preposterior (or forecasting) distributions involve the marginal distribution of $\tilde{z}$ under each model, and this is ordinarily the most difficult part of the computation.

As $n \to \infty$, for random process models, under some regularity conditions, the posterior distribution concentrates on the true process distribution exponentially fast, that is, the posterior probability outside any neighborhood of the true process distribution approaches 0 exponentially fast. In large samples one can therefore afford to use comprehensive models—the truth will prevail anyway. Furthermore, if one does not do so, the effects of model misspecification may far exceed the statistical uncertainty while the analysis addresses only the latter. At the other extreme, in small samples, for reasonable models, misspecification error will ordinarily be small relative to sampling error, and a straightforward Bayesian approach will not be easy to improve upon even though it may be based on a somewhat misspecified model. The real difficulty is how rapidly to broaden or proliferate models as n increases when one wishes to balance misspecification and sampling error, especially since one must also allow for cognitive limitations in the assessment of prior distributions. (In non-Bayesian approaches, similar difficulties appear in a somewhat different guise, as do they if one is prepared to accept some misspecification error in the interest of simplicity per se, or "parsimony.")

We now sketch a simple heuristic way to derive and understand the foregoing and similar asymptotic results. If the true random process has density or mass function f_0, then the likelihood for an assumed function f can be seen by applying the law of large numbers to the logarithm of the likelihood to be (exercise 32)

$$e^{n\eta(f_0,f)+\text{remainder}} \tag{24.60}$$

where

$$\eta(f_0,f_0) = E_0\{\log f(\tilde{z})\}, \tag{24.61}$$

E_0 denoting expectation when $\tilde{z}$ has density f_0. The likelihood ratio of f to f_0 is therefore

$$e^{-nI(f_0,f)+\text{remainder}} \tag{24.62}$$

where

$$I(f_0,f) = \eta(f_0,f_0) - \eta(f_0,f) = E_0\{\log[f_0(\tilde{z})/f(\tilde{z})]\}. \tag{24.63}$$

(I is the Shannon-Wiener information of f with respect to f_0, except for a factor log 2 because the Shannon-Wiener information uses logs to the base 2.) If $f \neq f_0$, then $\eta(f_0,f_0) < \eta(f_0,f)$, that is, $I(f_0,f) > 0$ (exercise 33), so the likelihood ratio is exponentially small. As long as f_0 is "possible" a priori (every neighborhood of f_0 has positive prior probability), it follows that, as $n \to \infty$, the posterior mode and maximum likelihood estimate will approach f_0, and posterior probability will vanish exponentially fast except in a neighborhood of f_0. If several models are allowed and f_0 is possible under just one of them, then the posterior probability of all the others will vanish exponentially fast.

If f_0 is not possible under the model or models allowed, then the posterior mode and maximum likelihood estimate will approach the nearest f that is possible in the sense of minimizing $\eta(f_0, f)$, and the posterior distribution will concentrate in the neighborhood of f; if the nearest f is not unique or does not exist, the story is more complicated but similar. In any event, the sense of "nearest" generally differs from squared error or whatever other loss function might be natural or derivable from the economics in a particular practical situation. In such a case, uncritical use of Bayesian (or other likelihood) methods will lead asymptotically to a worse model than methods more robust to misspecification.

Although we shall not go further here, expanding the log likelihood to one more term in the neighborhood of f_0 and applying the central limit theorem leads to the asymptotic Normality of the maximum likelihood estimate with precision equal to Fisher's information.

Finally, we should emphasize that stating and proving the foregoing results rigorously under adequate regularity conditions is complicated and difficult, even conditional on f_0 as above. Results taking into account the fact that the "true" f_0 is itself uncertain undoubtedly hold but seem even more difficult to state and prove rigorously.

24.7 Causation

It is commonplace that correlation is not causation. Neighborhood police activity is associated with but does not cause crime. Siblings' heights do not influence each other. A better but more radical medical treatment may have worse results on average because it is applied to sicker patients. And this may be true even after correcting or otherwise allowing for all available variables because what the doctors and patients know is not all in the available data.

Difficulties in establishing causation do not mean, for example, that one should continue despite all evidence to attribute the apparent ill effects of smoking to omitted variables, let alone that one should attend only to evidence favoring one's prejudices and preconceived opinions. But they do imply that healthy skepticism is called for when seriously attempting to learn from complex data—and when reading simplistic analyses whether by journalists or experts. This is not the place for extended discussion, but we will give a brief introduction to some aspects of causality that are basic yet not widely understood or presented.

We will discuss only the kind of causal effects that are revealed by ideal experiments and directly relevant to decisions. About other kinds we will say only that they abound but should not be used causally or confused with the kind discussed here, because they do not have the same kind of interpretation, or any other everyday interpretation that we know of. To keep things as simple as possible, we shall focus on linear models, though models are irrelevant to the fundamental concepts, and we start with the case that all x variables are causal, though this case is rare in practice. We also ignore problems of inference from limited data, discussing when and how causal interpretation can be given to statistical relationships that are hypothetically known or estimated with negligible error; correlation does not become causation by becoming known. We discuss what a causal structure *is* before discussing statistical relationships, and we warn the reader that although the subject is not esoteric or mathematically difficult, the precise form of the concepts is unfamiliar and somewhat ticklish and nothing should be taken for granted.

24.7.1 Simple Causal Structures

The soufflé desserts offered by the Galloping Gourmet Restaurant are cooked to order, one at a time. Management is concerned with the effect of cooking time on the results, conveniently measured by the height of each soufflé. Suppose that, if the ith soufflé were cooked for x minutes, its height would be y_{xi}. For every soufflé these heights are defined for *all* potential cooking times x, regardless of what the actual cooking times happen to be or how they are chosen, whether by customers, management, the chef, or any other prescient or prankish process. We can think of the potential heights y_{xi} in the form of a table with a column for each soufflé and a row for each cooking time as follows, where we have included only integer cooking times from 20 to 30 minutes, but conceptually there could be a continuum of rows.

$y_{20,1}$	$y_{20,2}$	$y_{20,3} \cdots$
$y_{21,1}$	$y_{21,2}$	$y_{21,3} \cdots$
$y_{22,1}$	$y_{22,}$	$y_{22,3} \cdots$
$\vdots$	$\vdots$	$\vdots$
$y_{30,1}$	$y_{30,2}$	$y_{30,3} \cdots$

Although every element of this table is a potential observation, only one element in each column will actually occur. We assume that the choice of x in any column has no effect on the potential values in any other column; for instance, if the second soufflé is cooked for 22 minutes, its height will be exactly the same whether the first soufflé was cooked for 20 minutes or 30 minutes or any time in between. This assumption is sometimes described as no interference between units (soufflés), and it could fail if, for example, the chef uses the same oven for successive soufflés and is too casual about controlling its temperature. Other than this, the choice of x is unconstrained, inasmuch as the effect of this choice is what we want to learn; the chef's choices may depend on other observed or unobserved variables and may not be describable by any model, thereby frustrating our learning.

Assume that, for each x, the potential heights $\tilde{y}_{xi}$ for $i = 1, 2, 3, \ldots$ are independently, identically distributed according to a known process distribution $D(\tilde{y}_x)$. Then, in the absence of supplementary information, this is the height distribution we would face if we chose cooking time x for any soufflé i, and the long-run distribution we would obtain if we always chose x. In this situation we say that we have a simple casual structure $D(\tilde{y}_x)$. By supplementary information we mean information other than past values that might help predict $\tilde{y}_{xi}$, such as the size of the eggs or exact amount of some other ingredient in the ith soufflé, or the oven temperature, or the cooking times actually chosen by the chef which may themselves reflect additional information. For simplicity we assume independence across i for all x jointly, not merely each x individually. (Exercise 34 illustrates why.) We nevertheless allow and even expect statistical dependence across values of x for the same i: an unexpectedly fluffy batch would rise unexpectedly high at all cooking times. Such dependence has little role theoretically, however, because even if our main interest is what difference a change in x would make, we can never observe more than one value of x for a given i.

In general, then, we define a *simple causal structure* or *stochastic law* as follows. We have a set of potential treatments x and a probability distribution $D(\tilde{y}_x)$ for every x. For every x and $i = 1, 2, 3, \ldots$, we have potential observations $\tilde{y}_{xi}$ each of which has conditional distribution $D(\tilde{y}_x)$ given all $\tilde{y}_{xi}$ with $j < i$. For each i, one value of x is chosen somehow and $\tilde{y}_{xi}$ is realized for the chosen value of x, but this choice has no effect on any potential $\tilde{y}_{xj}$. Only the realized values y_{xi} are observed, along with the values of x chosen.

Remarks The index i could have a finite or infinite number of possible values. It could refer to a sequence of occasions, like successive soufflés, or to members of some finite set, like individuals in a population of interest or plots in an agricultural field. The independence condition could be stated symmetrically, and this would be more natural in static settings. The law may hold only under limited circumstances—for example, changing chefs might change $D(\tilde{y}_x)$. The treatments could be continuous (temperature) or discrete (number of eggs) and univariate (cooking time only) or multivariate (cooking time *and* temperature); in the latter case, the component variables are often called factors. The choice of treatment may be purely hypothetical—if the chef brooks no interference, for example. The treatment may be a selection rather than a manipulation—we cannot change anyone's gender or SAT score, but selecting more females or high scorers causes changes in course enrollments and academic performance. Incorporating supplementary information is possible but takes us beyond simple causal structures to the case discussed in section 24.7.6. Regardless, if the choice of x reflects unincorporated information, the conditional distribution of $\tilde{y}_{xi}$ given that x was chosen may differ from the structural distribution, as exemplified earlier and discussed later; a good chef beats any recipe.

24.7.2 Linear Models for Simple Causation

Linear models are often posited because they facilitate both estimation from finite data and understanding of complex relationships. They are also a good context in which to discuss some further aspects of causal structures and their relation to statistical association.

We call a simple causal structure $D(\tilde{y}_x)$ *linear* if x is a vector and $E(\tilde{y}_x)$ is linear in x, say $E(\tilde{y}_x) = \gamma_0 + \boldsymbol{\gamma}'\boldsymbol{x}$. In this case we can write

$$\tilde{y}_{xi} = \gamma_0 + \boldsymbol{\gamma}'\boldsymbol{x} + \tilde{u}_{xi} \tag{24.64}$$

where $E\tilde{u}_x = 0$ for all x. (Without this identifying restriction, the terms on the right-hand side would be ambiguous because we could add a linear function of x to $\tilde{u}_{xi}$ and subtract it from $\gamma_0 + \boldsymbol{\gamma}'\boldsymbol{x}$ without changing $\tilde{y}_{xi}$.) The structure's independence across i and possible dependence across x carry over to $\tilde{u}_{xi}$. The distribution of $\tilde{u}_x$, in particular its variance, may still depend on x and may also be modelled. Even if it does not, the value of $\tilde{u}_{xi}$ may depend on x.

A linear causal structure looks much like a regression model, but the realized observations may follow a regression process with entirely different coefficients if it follows one at all. For example, the chef may remove soufflés from the oven whenever they reach a height of 5 inches even though longer cooking would make them higher, or may cook larger batches longer, thereby adding "spurious" correlation. Because it is so easy to confuse causal and regression processes for the same data, and so important to distinguish them, we turn immediately to the question of when observed regression coefficients allow a causal interpretation.

24.7.3 Observability of a Simple Causal Structure

We start with the linear case (24.64). For each i, a treatment $\boldsymbol{x}_i$ is chosen somehow and the potential y_{xi} for $\boldsymbol{x} = \boldsymbol{x}_i$ is realized. Thus the observed process is

$$y_i = \gamma_0 + \gamma^t \boldsymbol{x}_i + u_i \tag{24.65}$$

where $y_i = y_{x_i i}$ and $u_i = u_{x_i i}$. This resembles the regression model (24.1) or (24.3) except that $\boldsymbol{x}_i$ and u_i are typically correlated. (The reader should think why in the various examples above.) This correlation makes the regression coefficients of y_i on $\boldsymbol{x}_i$ different from the structural coefficients γ. The difficulty of describing explicitly how $\boldsymbol{x}_i$ is chosen in many situations makes it difficult to define a process correlation between $\boldsymbol{x}_i$ and u_i, but does not reduce the difference between the regression and structural coefficients in the observed data. Regression will overstate the effect of cooking time if the chef cooks longer than average the soufflés likely to rise higher than average. It will understate the potency of a drug if the doctor prescribes stronger doses for sicker patients.

In the general case of a causal structure $D(\tilde{y}_x)$, we will be misled by the realized observations if a particular value of x has an especially great chance of being chosen when y_{xi} is especially large, or when y_{xi} is unusual in any other way. This leads us to say that a causal structure $D(\tilde{y}_x)$ is *observable* if, on every observation i, the choice of treatment is statistically independent of the *potential* values $\tilde{y}_{xi}$ for all x. This allows x_i to be deterministic, but not to be opportunistic. If this condition is satisfied, then the conditional distribution of the realized observation $\tilde{y}_{xi}$ given that $\tilde{x}_i = x$ is $D(\tilde{y}_x)$ for all x and i. In this case, the observations $\tilde{y}_i$ which received treatment x follow a random process whose process distribution is the structural distribution; if their number approaches infinity, their empirical distribution will approach the structural distribution; and statistical inferences about the random process will at the same time be inferences about the structure. In the linear case, for example, the structural coefficients will also be regression coefficients, and the methods of this chapter will apply if the $\tilde{u}_i$ satisfy the additional conditions imposed on the $\tilde{\varepsilon}_i$ earlier.

24.7.4 Randomized Experiments

It is sometimes possible to guarantee observability by carrying out a randomized experiment. For example, if four treatments are available, one might pick each with probability 1/4 independently of all else at every observation i. More commonly, the randomization is constrained, for example to equalize the number of times each treatment is used altogether, or even within blocks of observations. A still more elaborate possibility would be to assign ten treatments (paints) at random to the ten letters in example 7 of section 24.1.4 (a "balanced incomplete block" design). As long as the randomization is independent of the potential values $\tilde{y}_{xi}$, the observability condition will be satisfied. Of couse good experiments and analyses embody many other practices and considerations, but no amount of experimental control or analytical adjustment can provide the guarantee (and credibility) that actual randomization does.

24.7.5 Direct, Indirect, and Total Effects and Choice of Factors

Suppose that soufflés height obeys a linear causal structure with two factors, cooking time x_1 and oven temperature x_2, namely

$$\tilde{y}_{xi} = \lambda_0 + \lambda_1 x_1 + \lambda_2 x_2 + \tilde{u}_{xi} \tag{24.66}$$

where x is without subscript i because (24.58) is a causal structure. Suppose also that the way the chef sets oven temperature obeys a linear causal structure with one factor, cooking time x_1:

$$\tilde{x}_{2i} = \mu_0 + \mu_1 x_1 + \tilde{u}_{x_1 i} \tag{24.67}$$

Then soufflé height also obeys a linear causal structure with factor x_1, namely

$$\tilde{y}_{x_1 i} = \gamma_0 + \gamma_1 x_1 + \tilde{u}_{x_1 i} \tag{24.68}$$

where $\gamma_1 = \lambda_1 + \lambda_2 \mu_1$ and similarly for the other terms (exercise 36). The coefficient of x_1 is different in (24.68) than in (24.66): λ_1 in (24.66) is the effect of a one-minute change in cooking time with oven temperature held fixed, while γ_1 in (24.68) is the effect of a one-minute change in cooking time with oven temperature set in accordance with the causal structure (24.67) followed by the chef. One could think of γ_1 as a total effect made up of the direct effect λ_1 and the indirect effect $\lambda_2 \mu_1$. Of course the direct effects in the two-factor structure (24.66) would be total effects relative to a causal structure with yet more factors and a causal structure governing the determination of these factors from cooking time and oven temperature. Which causal structure is relevant, if any, depends on the decision to be made and whether the causal structure applies to that decision: λ_1 might be the effect of taking the soufflé out of the oven a minute earlier or later than the chef intended for the convenience of the waiter or customer, while γ_1 might be the effect if the chef decided in advance to shorten or lengthen the cooking time in anticipation of greater or less demand on oven capacity (exercise 37).

Neither γ_1 nor λ_1 is the effect of cooking time with everything else held fixed, not only because γ_1 is not λ_1 and λ_1 is not the coefficient of cooking time in a causal structure with more factors, but because everything else cannot be fixed: if oven temperature is fixed, then its deviation from the norm for the cooking time chosen cannot be fixed and vice versa. Thus "everything else fixed" is either ambiguous or impossible. Similarly the coefficient of cooking time in (24.66), and its interpretation, would change if the second factor, oven temperature, were replaced by its deviation from the norm (exercise 38a). And the disturbance u in a linear causal structure is not the combined effect of the excluded variables, which suffers from the same kind of ambiguity; it is rather the *remainder* of the combined effect of the excluded variables after the effect of the included factor variables on the excluded variables has been subtracted out (exercise 38d).

Coefficients in regressions on different sets of explanatory variables are related to one another by similar rules, but their interpretation is not causal: the coefficient of x_1 in a regression is the amount by which the expectation of y would be increased if x_1 happened to be one unit larger, all other included variables happened to be the same (which they ordinarily would not be), and all excluded variables were left free to vary as usual in the circumstances. Similarly the included terms include forecasts of the terms that would be added if excluded variables were added (exercise 39), and the residual ε is that part of the variation of y which cannot be forecasted (linearly) by the included explanatory variables when all other variables vary as usual.

Finally, of course, the particular causal structure relevant to the decision at hand need not be observable even if the variables in it have been observed. Regressions can always be run, but whether the coefficients are causal is extrinsic and cannot be determined by statistics alone. Observability requires either randomization or appeal to some worldview. We shall discuss this further after introducing the concept of concomitants, which greatly enlarge the possibilities for observability of effects of interest.

24.7.6 Causal Structures with Concomitants

The Galloping Gourmet's soufflés are actually of several sizes (for 1 to 6 people) and types (cheese, chocolate, Grand-Marnier, and catch-of-the-day). The chef adjusts cooking time and oven temperature according to batch size (at least). Clearly, then, neither the causal structure (24.66) nor the causal structure (24.68) will be observable: the choice of treatment is not statistically independent of the potential height y_x or disturbance u_x for a given treatment in either case, and the corresponding regressions will include "proxy" effects for batch size. We want to bring batch size into the story, but not as a factor because management cannot control it and the observability of its effect is arguable at best. Similarly, a patient's age, sex, and health status on arrival in the doctor's office are not factors under the doctor's control but may affect the choice and results of treatment. To incorporate such variables, we need to extend our concepts of causal structure and observability.

In addition to treatments x and potential observations y_{xi}, our purview now includes variables which we call *concomitants* and denote by z_{xi}. We define a *causal structure* or *stochastic law with concomitants* as follows. For every x and z we have a probability distribution $D(\tilde{y}_{xz})$ representing a conditional distribution of $\tilde{y}_x$ given z. For every x and $i = 1, 2, 3, \ldots$, we have potential observations y_{xi} and z_{xi}. The process generating the concomitants $\tilde{z}_{xi}$ is arbitrary, but $\tilde{y}_{xi}$ has conditional distribution $D(\tilde{y}_{xz})$ given $\tilde{z}_{xi} = z$ and given all $\tilde{y}_{xj}$, $\tilde{z}_{xj}$ with $j < i$. For each i, one value of x is chosen somehow and is realized for the chosen value of x, but this choice has no effect on any potential $\tilde{y}_{xj}$ or $\tilde{z}_{xj}$. Only the realized values y_{xi} and z_{xi} are observed, along with the values of x chosen. Interpretation of causal structures and observability is easier when concomitants are unaffected by the choice of treatment x, and this case is assumed in most of our examples and almost all of the literature, so the reader may wish to think about it first, and mentally replace z_{xi} by z_i. We call such concomitants *strict*.

If a stochastic law with concomitants holds, it tells us what distribution of $\tilde{y}$ we face if we choose x conditional on the concomitants z. Thus appropriate laws, when known and applicable, tell us the potential distribution of soufflé height if we choose a particular cooking time and oven temperature given a particular order size, and the distribution of patient response if we choose a particular treatment given the patient's age, sex, and other characteristics. These choices may depend on any concomitants known at the time of choice (implying strictness), as order size would be for soufflés made to order and many patient characteristics would be when a doctor prescribes treatment.

A causal stru ture with concomitants is, conditional on the concomitants, essentially a simple causal structure. Similarly, it will be observable if the observability condition for a simple causal structure holds conditional on the concomitants. Thus we say that a causal structure with concomitants $D(\tilde{y}_{xz})$ is *observable* if, on every observation i, the choice of treatment is conditionally independent of the potential values $\tilde{y}_{xi}$ given $\tilde{z}_{xi} = z$ for all x and z. This allows x_i to depend on z_{xi}, but not on other variables predictive of $\tilde{y}_{xi}$ given z_{xi}, whether causal or not. If this condition is satisfied, then the conditional distribution of the realized observation $\tilde{y}_{xi}$ given that $\tilde{x}_i = x$ and $\tilde{z}_{xi} = z$ is $D(\tilde{y}_{xz})$ for all x, z, and i. If the doctor's choice takes into account patient characteristics not included among the concomitants z_{xi}, and the doctor can predict the potential outcome of a given treatment better from z_{xi} and these characteristics than from z_{xi} alone, then observability does not hold.

24.7.7 Linear Causal Models with Concomitants

A causal structure with concomitants $D(\tilde{y}_{xy})$ is *linear* if x and z are vectors and $E(\tilde{y}_x|z)$ is linear in x and z, say $\gamma_0 + \boldsymbol{\gamma}^t\boldsymbol{x} + \boldsymbol{\lambda}^t\boldsymbol{z}$. In this case we can write

$$\tilde{y}_{xi} = \gamma_0 + \boldsymbol{\gamma}^t\boldsymbol{x} + \boldsymbol{\lambda}^t\boldsymbol{z}_i + \tilde{u}_{xi} \tag{24.69}$$

where $E(\tilde{u}_{xi}|\tilde{z}_{xi} = z) = 0$ for all x and z, the identifying restriction again making the representation unique. The coefficient vector γ has a causal interpretation: an element of γ is the expected (direct) effect of a unit change in the corresponding factor with the other factors held fixed and the concomitants allowed to vary as usual. (If the concomitants are not affected by the factors, the direct effect equals the total effect. Otherwise it is the part of the total effect not due to the effect of the factor on the concomitants.) The coefficients λ are process regression coefficients and cannot be interpreted causally.

The disturbance $\tilde{u}_{xi}$ can be interpreted as the *remainder* of the combined effect of the excluded variables after both (1) the part predictable by the concomitants and (2) the effects of the included factor variables on the excluded variables have been subtracted out. A linear causal structure with concomitants $D(\tilde{y}_{xz})$ is observable if, on each observation i, the choice of treatment is conditionally independent of the potential disturbance $\tilde{u}_{xi}$ given $\tilde{z}_{xi} = z$ for all x and z. The regression coefficients in observed data will coincide with the structural coefficients, enabling estimation of the full structural distribution from the regression residuals, under technically but not intuitively weaker conditions of no correlation.

24.7.8 Uses and Selection of Concomitants

In practical data analysis concomitant variables play many roles that are relevant to their inclusion or exclusion and may even lead to conflicting requirements (not to mention requirements for unobtainable data). In randomized experiments, strict concomitants—the only kind usually discussed—serve to refine a causal structure in two ways, the first more emphasized in textbooks, the second more fundamental.

1. Concomitants reduce random error or residual variance, at least on average. This sharpens both what the law says about any potential y and—as is important in finite data—the estimates of causal effects.

2. If interactions between factors and concomitants are present, they allow identification of different causal effects for different concomitant values. For example, taking sex as a concomitant in a suitable model enables one to investigate the possibility that a treatment is good for one sex and not the other, or to estimate the average effect of a treatment in a population having a different sex ratio than the data (exercise 41).

In observational data without randomization, concomitants serve even more fundamental purposes.

3. Concomitants may be needed for a causal structure to exist at all.

a. In many situations, concomitants are needed to account for variation that is too irregular to be represented reasonably by a process with independent, identically distributed residuals. Even if the definition of a causal structure were extended to other kinds of processes, some variables other than factors would still be needed.

b. Autocorrelated errors and lagged y's can often be accommodated by introducing suitable concomitants (exercise 42). Nevertheless, although the basic concpet of causality depends on some concept of repeatable conditions, extension beyond processes or models in which all randomness enters in independently, identically distributed form would be at least convenient and is perhaps fundamentally needed.

c. Trend *may* be an adequate proxy for unidentified excluded variables when, without concomitants, the independent, identically distributed repetitions required for a law could not exist in the face of drifts in the environment. Of course one cannot expect a trend to last forever, and true concomitants rather than a deterministic proxy would be preferable if available, but trend may be much better than nothing. Indeed an infinite number of repetitions is only a useful fiction anyway, often closer to the truth with trend than without.

4. Concomitants may be needed for observability of even a well-formulated law, as in the examples used to motivate the introduction of concomitants in section 24.7.6. We emphasize that concomitants need not themselves be causal in order to proxy well for omitted variables that affect both y and the choice of treatment x.

5. A variable whose values can (at least conceptually) be arbitrarily chosen may nevertheless be better classified as a concomitant. If it fails the condition for observability, its causal effect cannot be learned even from infinite data. If may still serve as a concomitant that makes other causal effects observable as long as it is allowed to take whatever value it naturally takes.

Finally, some points relevant to all causal analyses:

6. If a concomitant z is affected by factors, it must be included if what we want to learn is the effects given z and must be excluded if we want to learn the total effects. That is, a concomitant affected by factors is either defining or inadmissible, never optional. Of course one could obtain a total effect from direct and indirect effects by integrating out z or adding back its effect, but this is functionally equivalent to omitting z to begin with.

7. Concomitants may extend the range of circumstances in which a stochastic law applies, or increase our confidence in applying it, the range typically being much hazier for stochastic than deterministic laws. When extrapolating the effect of plant varicty on yield from the location where it was estimated to another with different rainfall, even if observability permits excluding rainfall we will be on much safer ground if we include it, and either estimate the interaction between plant variety and rainfall, however shakily, or establish that it is negligible, if we can. If rainfall varies little in the data, it may be useless or "statistically insignificant" as a concomitant, and we may claim fine "experimental control," but the extent to which we can extrapolate our findings on the basis of evidence rather than blind faith will be very limited.

8. If each i denotes a "unit" such as a soufflé or a patient and each treatment is applied to a set of units drawn at random from the population of interest, both observability and extrapolatability are guaranteed: observability because the choice of treatment for each i is random, extrapolatability because the units observed are a random sample from the population of interest. The latter is rare in practice: the soufflés and patients of interest have no chance of being in the sample because they lie in the future. Thus, even in the simplest case, what we think of as a comparative experiment is in practice almost always like a survey based on a nonrandom sample for each treatment. What makes the experiment comparative is not comparison of different treatments on the same unit i, but other aspects of the experimental design, such as "blocking," or applying more than one treatment to the same "experimental unit" or "unit of study" (which then is not the unit identified by i). Extrapolation almost always relies on models. Observability implies that the statistical and causal structures coincide in a model-free sense, and eliminates one of the most worrisome sources of bias, but it does not make the assumed form of the causal structure any better or worse, or more extrapolatable, than it is.

9. Choice of variables in statistical literature and practice has been heavily driven by problems of inference stemming from finitude of data and a desire for (over?)simplification. Too little attention has been paid to the usefulness of "statistically insignificant" variables in identifying significant real uncertainty in structural estimates or even dangerous extrapolation in passive forecasts, let alone to their real significance for the meaning of coefficients and their absolute necessity for observability. However, although the subject of balancing statistical and nonstatistical errors in practice is illuminated by the Bayesian point of view, it is too complex to go into here at any length. We limit ourselves to one last warning against unthinking adoption of conventional dicta and procedures:

10. A concomitant that substantially reduces bias in estimating the effect of a factor is likely to be highly correlated with the factor. Hence it is likely to contribute little to conventional measures of fit; it may well have a "statistically insignificant" coefficient; and including it is likely to increase the standard error of estimate of the factor's effect. Dropping such a concomitant merely conceals the bias and the true uncertainty about the effect.

24.7.9 Bayesian Causation

If a linear causal structure is not observable, the situation is a generalization of the unknown-bias model of chapter 23B (exercise 43). Treating the likelihood function of the regression coefficients b as if it were the likelihood of the causal coefficients c, even using a computer, will of course give neither *b*eans nor *c*orn but *s*uccotash (Pratt and Schlaifer, 1988, p. 49). The principles of prior-to-posterior analysis are the same as always: assess a joint prior distribution of b, c, and any other "nuisance" parameters in the model, update it by Bayes' formula, and integrate out b and the other nuisance parameters to obtain the posterior distribution of c. The data say a lot about b and nothing about the conditional distribution of c given b, so the aspect of the prior that remains important after observing the data is this conditional distribution. However, even it ordinarily has so many parameters of such obscurity as to defy reasonable judgmental assessment, and effort might better be spent on searching for adequate concomitants than on evaluating one's ignorance precisely.

Exercises

1. A process generates a sequence of rv's $\tilde{y}_1, \tilde{y}_2, \ldots, \tilde{y}_i, \ldots$ whose distributions are given by the model

$$\tilde{y}_i = \beta_1 x_i + \tilde{\varepsilon}_i, \qquad i = 1, 2, \ldots,$$

where β_1 is a parameter whose value remains fixed throughout the sequence of trials, x_i is a known number on each trial but is not necessarily the same on each trial, and the $\tilde{\varepsilon}$s are independent Normal rv's all having mean 0 and variance υ.

Using a table of Normal random numbers generate two sets of 5 successive ys which the process might have generated if on the first set of trials

$$\beta_1 = 2, \qquad \upsilon = 1,$$

on the second set of trials

$$\beta_1 = 10, \qquad \upsilon = 100,$$

while on *both* sets of trials

$$(x_1, x_2, x_3, x_4, x_5) = (0, 2, 6, -1, -3).$$

2. Consider the model

$$\tilde{y}_i = \beta_0 + \beta_1 x_i + \tilde{\varepsilon}_i, \qquad i = 1, 2, \ldots,$$

where the $\tilde{\varepsilon}$s are independent, Normal rv's with mean 0 and variance υ. Generate ys for the same x_i as in exercise 1 and

a. $\beta_0 = 1, \quad \beta_1 = 2, \quad \upsilon = 1;$

b. $\beta_0 = -1, \quad \beta_1 = 2, \quad \upsilon = 1;$

c. $\beta_0 = 20, \quad \beta_1 = 1, \quad \upsilon = 100.$

You may reuse the data generated in exercise 1.

3. Consider the model

$$\tilde{y}_i = \beta_0 + \beta_1 x_i + \beta_2 x_i^2 + \tilde{\varepsilon}_i, \qquad i = 1, 2, \ldots,$$

where the $\tilde{\varepsilon}$s are independent, Normal rv's with mean 0 and variance υ. Generate ys for the same x_i as in exercise 1 and

a. $\beta_0 = 1, \quad \beta_1 = 2, \quad \beta_2 = 1, \quad \upsilon = 1;$

b. $\beta_0 = 20, \quad \beta_1 = 1, \quad \beta_2 = 10, \quad \upsilon = 100.$

4. Consider the model

$$\tilde{y}_i = \beta_0 + \beta_1 x_i + \beta_2 e^{x_i} + \tilde{\varepsilon}_i, \qquad i = 1, 2, \ldots,$$

where the $\tilde{\varepsilon}$s are independent, Normal rv's with mean 0 and variance υ. Generate ys for the same x_i as in exercise 1 and

$$\beta_0 = -1, \quad \beta_1 = 2, \quad \beta_2 = 1, \quad \upsilon = 1.$$

5. Consider the model

$$\tilde{y}_i = \beta_0 + \beta_1 x_i + \beta_2 w_i + \tilde{\varepsilon}_i, \qquad i = 1, 2, \ldots,$$

where the $\tilde{\varepsilon}$s are independent, Normal rv's with mean 0 and variance υ. Generate ys for the same x_i as in exercise 1 and

$$(w_1, w_2, \ldots, w_5) = (0, 4, 36, 1, 9)$$

$$\beta_0 = 1, \quad \beta_1 = 2, \quad \beta_2 = 1, \quad \upsilon = 1.$$

Compare this with exercise 3(a).

6. Consider the model

$$\tilde{y}_i = \beta_0 + \beta_1 \tilde{y}_{i-1} + \beta_2(\tilde{y}_{i-1} - \tilde{y}_{i-2}) + \tilde{\varepsilon}_i,$$

where the $\tilde{\varepsilon}$s are independent, Normal rv's with mean 0 and variance υ. Assuming $y_0 = 0$, $y_1 = 5$, generate a set $y_2, y_3, \ldots, y_8$ which the process might have generated with

$$\beta_0 = 1, \quad \beta_1 = .7, \quad \beta_2 = .3, \quad \upsilon = 9.$$

With these parameters given (i.e., $\beta_0 = 1$, etc.), how could you use simulation to find the conditional distribution of $\tilde{y}_8$ given $y_0 = 0$, $y_1 = 5$?

7. We are concerned with the economic time series:

c_t = consumer expenditures per capita in time period t, $t = 0, 1, \ldots, 10$.

y_t = disposable income per capita in time period t, $t = 0, 1, \ldots, 10$.

z_t = investment expenditures per capita in time period t, $t = 0, 1, \ldots, 10$.

The values c_t, y_t, and z_t are so defined that, for all t,

(1) $\tilde{y}_t = \tilde{c}_t + z_t.$

We will explain now why we treat y_t and c_t as random but not z_t.

In trying to explain observable time series, one often takes the point of view that the z_t are given numbers (exogenous to the system) and that the y_t and c_t (endogenous to the system) adjust themselves (always satisfying (1)) so that consumption can be thought of as a linear function of disposable income—plus error. In particular, in addition to (1) we assume

(2) $\tilde{c}_t - \beta_0 + \beta_1 \tilde{y}_t + \tilde{e}_t,$

where $\tilde{e}_1, \tilde{e}_2, \ldots$ are independent, Normal rv's with mean 0 and variance v.

The parameters of this system are β_0, β_1, and v. The series $z_1, z_2, \ldots, z_{10}$ are manifest observables (i.e., given numbers).

To better understand the model, let us simulate data when the manifest numbers are:

$z_0 = 10,\quad z_1 = 10,\quad z_2 = 10,\quad z_3 = 12,\quad z_4 = 12,\quad z_5 = 20,\quad z_6 = 20,\quad z_7 = 20,$

$z_8 = 30,\quad z_9 = 30,\quad z_{10} = 30,$

and the parameters are

$\beta_0 = 3,\qquad \beta_1 = .4,\qquad v = 9.$

To generate y_1 and c_1 we proceed as follows. Get e_1 by choosing a number from a table of random Normal numbers with mean 0 and variance 1 and multiplying it by 3. Thus, if the random drawing is $-.623$ then $e_1 = -1.869$. Solve the equation system for y_1, c_1:

$y_1 = c_1 + 10$

$c_1 = 3 + .4y_1 - 1.869.$

We get $c_1 = 8.55$ and $y_1 = 18.55$.

Using your own simulated numbers generate pairs $(y_1, c_1), (y_2, c_2), \ldots, (y_{10}, c_{10})$. On good graph paper carefully plot y_t against z_t, c_t against z_t, and c_t against y_t.

Hint The easiest way to proceed is to express $\tilde{c}_t$ and $\tilde{y}_t$ each in terms of z_t and $\tilde{e}_t$. For example, from (1) and (2) we have:

(3) $\tilde{c}_t = \dfrac{\beta_0}{1-\beta_1} + \dfrac{\beta_1}{1-\beta_1} z_t + \dfrac{\tilde{e}_t}{1-\beta_1}$

and

(4) $\tilde{y}_t = \dfrac{\beta_0}{1-\beta_1} + \dfrac{1}{1-\beta_1} z_t + \dfrac{\tilde{e}_t}{1-\beta_1}.$

8. Consider the linear regression model

$\tilde{y}_i = \beta_1 + \beta_2 w_i + \tilde{\varepsilon}_i,$

where the $\tilde{\varepsilon}$s are independent, Normal rv's with mean 0 and variance v. Suppose $\tilde{\beta}_1$ and $\tilde{\beta}_2$ are a priori independent of the $\tilde{\varepsilon}$s and Normal with mean 0 and variance $\breve{\boldsymbol{\beta}}'$ whose inverse is

$$\breve{\boldsymbol{\beta}}'^{-1} = \mathbf{H}' = \begin{bmatrix} H'_{12} & H'_{12} \\ H'_{21} & H'_{22} \end{bmatrix}.$$

a. Show that the posterior distribution of $\tilde{\boldsymbol{\beta}}$ given $y = [y_1 \ldots y_n]^t$ is Normal with mean $\tilde{\beta}''$ and variance $\mathbf{H}''^{-1}$ where

$$\mathbf{H}'' = \begin{bmatrix} H'_{11} + n/v & H'_{12} + \sum_i w_i/v \\ H'_{21} + \sum_i w_i/v & H'_{22} + \sum_i w_i^2/v \end{bmatrix},$$

$$\bar{\boldsymbol{\beta}}'' = \mathbf{H}''^{-1}\begin{bmatrix} \sum_i y_i/v \\ \sum_i w_i y_i/v \end{bmatrix}.$$

b. If $\breve{\beta}'_{12} = 0$ and $\sum_i w_i = 0$ show that $\tilde{\beta}_1$ and $\tilde{\beta}_2$ are conditionally independent given $\boldsymbol{y}$ and that

$$\bar{\beta}''_1 = \frac{\sum_i y_i}{n + v/\breve{\beta}'_1}, \qquad \bar{\beta}''_2 = \frac{\sum_i w_i y_i}{\sum_i w^2 + v/\breve{\beta}'_2}.$$

c. Letting

$$m_w = \frac{1}{n}\sum_i w_i, \qquad m_y = \frac{1}{n}\sum_i y_i,$$

$$s_{ww} = \frac{1}{n}\sum_i (w_i - m_w)^2, \qquad s_{wy} = \frac{1}{n}\sum_i (w_i - m_w)(y_i - m_y),$$

$$s_{yy} = \frac{1}{n}\sum_i (y_i - m_y)^2,$$

show that if $\mathbf{H}' = \mathbf{0}$ then

$$V(\tilde{\beta}_1|\boldsymbol{y}) = \frac{v}{n}\left(1 + \frac{m_w^2}{s_{ww}}\right), \qquad V(\tilde{\beta}_2|\boldsymbol{y}) = \frac{v}{n s_{ww}},$$

$$E(\tilde{\beta}_1|\boldsymbol{y}) = m_y - m_x\frac{s_{wy}}{s_{ww}}, \qquad E(\tilde{\beta}_2|\boldsymbol{y}) = \frac{s_{wy}}{s_{ww}}.$$

9. Show that, given $\boldsymbol{\beta}$, $\tilde{\boldsymbol{b}}$ is nonsingular Normal with mean and variance (24.15).

10. Show that (24.27) reduces to (24.14c) when $\mathbf{H}' = 0$.

11. Show that (24.27a) for $\bar{\boldsymbol{\beta}}''$ may be rewritten in the form (24.27d).

12. Show that, given any $\bar{\boldsymbol{\beta}}'$ and $\boldsymbol{b}$, the set of possible posterior means $\bar{\boldsymbol{\beta}}''$ satisfying (24.27d) for some positive definite $\mathbf{H}'$ and $\mathbf{H}$ is:

a. the open line segment with endpoints $\bar{\boldsymbol{\beta}}'$ and $\boldsymbol{b}$ if $\mathbf{H}'$ is a scalar multiple of $\mathbf{H}$;

b. the open rectangular solid with corners $\bar{\boldsymbol{\beta}}'$ and $\boldsymbol{b}$ and edges parallel to the axes if $\mathbf{H}'$ and $\mathbf{H}$ are diagonal;

c. the open sphere with diameter $\bar{\boldsymbol{\beta}}'$, $\boldsymbol{b}$ if $\mathbf{H}'\mathbf{H} = \mathbf{H}\mathbf{H}'$
Hint Rotate part (b).

d. the ellipsoid $(\bar{\boldsymbol{\beta}}'' - \bar{\boldsymbol{\beta}}')^t\mathbf{H}(\bar{\boldsymbol{\beta}}'' - \boldsymbol{b}) < 0$ if $\mathbf{H}$ is fixed
Hint Show that, given vectors $\boldsymbol{a} \neq \boldsymbol{0}$ and $\boldsymbol{c}$, there exists a positive definite matrix $\mathbf{Q}$ such that $\mathbf{Q}\boldsymbol{a} = \boldsymbol{c}$ if and only if $\boldsymbol{a}^t\boldsymbol{c} > 0$. Let $a = \bar{\boldsymbol{\beta}}'' - \bar{\boldsymbol{\beta}}'$ and $c = \mathbf{H}(\boldsymbol{b} - \bar{\boldsymbol{\beta}}'')$. See Leamer (1978).

e. all points not on the line through $\bar{\boldsymbol{\beta}}'$ and $\boldsymbol{b}$ together with the segment of part (a) if $\mathbf{H}'$ and $\mathbf{H}$ are not further restricted.

13. Show that $\tilde{\boldsymbol{b}}$ is marginally Normal with mean and variance (24.29) under the assumptions of section 24.3.

14. Verify that the methods of section 24.3.4 for processing successive samples give the same posterior distribution as processing all the samples as one.

15. What appears to be the advantage of the experimental layout of example 7 in section 24.1.4 over the following layout?

1		2		3		4		5	
A	B	A	B	E	F	E	F	I	J
C	D	C	D	G	H	G	H	I	J

16. If (24.3) is satisfied with $g(\mathbf{x}, \boldsymbol{\beta})$ in place of $\mathbf{x}\boldsymbol{\beta}$, show that the xs can be redefined so that (24.3) holds as stated, provided that $g(\mathbf{x}, \boldsymbol{\beta})$ is linear in $\boldsymbol{\beta}$ for each $\mathbf{x}$.
Give an example showing that this is not always possible when $g(\mathbf{x}, \boldsymbol{\beta})$ is linear in $\mathbf{x}$ for each $\boldsymbol{\beta}$.

17. Describe how the model (24.3) may be used in those examples of section 24.1.4 that are not discussed in detail in the text.

18. Show that $(\mathbf{I} - \mathbf{P})$ in (24.12d) is always singular.

19. Verify (24.22).

20. Show that in section 24.3.4 if the original prior is diffuse ($\mathbf{H}'_{(1)} = 0$), then formulas (24.33), (24.34), and (24.37) continue to hold, but (24.36) becomes meaningless.

21. Verify assertions 1–4 at the end of section 24.4.6.

22. Specialize section 24.3.4 to the case of a single observation y_2 in the second set.

23. a. In figure 2.4.2, as $n \to \infty$, what is the order of magnitude of the spacing between the curves?

b. When does extrapolation to values of x far from m_x become dangerous, according to the formulas of section 24.4.6?

24. Consider a Normal linear regression model (24.3) with $\mathbf{H}' = \mathbf{0}$. Suppose observations $y_1, \ldots, y_n$ are made at $\boldsymbol{x}_1, \ldots, \boldsymbol{x}_n$. Show that

$$\text{Average}_x V(\boldsymbol{x}^t\tilde{\boldsymbol{\beta}} | \boldsymbol{y}, \mathbf{x}) = \frac{r}{n} v,$$

$$\text{Average}_{x_{n+1}} V(\tilde{y}_{n+1} | \boldsymbol{y}, \mathbf{x}, \boldsymbol{x}_{n+1}) = \left(\frac{r}{n} + 1\right) v,$$

where the first [second] Average is an arithmetic average over the values $\boldsymbol{x}_1, \ldots, \boldsymbol{x}_n$ for $\boldsymbol{x}[\boldsymbol{x}_{n+1}]$. Interpret the two equalities.

25. The SWEN News Company would like to improve its ordering policy for a weekly magazine called the *Saturday Inside News* (SIN.). It appears on Friday each week. Orders for any one issue must be made by noon on Monday of the week it is to appear. For almost a year, SWEN has been recording the number of copies of each issue sold by noon on the Monday after it appears. Total demand has not been recorded, partly because it is unknown at the time the next order must be made and partly because it never will be known if stockout occurs. However, total demand appears to average about 50% more than the demand by Monday noon, and as often as not to differ from this amount by 20 copies or more.
SWEN has been ordering 625 copies each week, but an improvement seems possible because weeks of high demand tend to cluster. Management does not feel it is worthwhile to attempt to predict demand on the basis of outside information, but would use a routine stocking policy based on the number of copies of the previous issue sold by Monday noon, if they would gain appreciably by doing so. Unsold copies cost SWEN 20 cents each, while stockouts cost 30 cents per copy in lost profits and nothing in good will, in the management's opinion.

Exhibit 24.1

t	y_t	t	y_t	t	y_t	t	y_t	t	y_t
0	400	10	214	20	334	30	433	40	438
1	457	11	288	21	372	31	373	41	479
2	381	12	286	22	408	32	413	42	480
3	392	13	394	23	424	33	410	43	471
4	392	14	420	24	431	34	413	44	377
5	368	15	335	25	432	35	389	45	287
6	351	16	356	26	506	36	433	46	400
7	298	17	375	27	489	37	420	47	411
8	226	18	363	28	389	38	392	48	406
9	247	19	339	29	421	39	466	49	431
								50	420

$\sum_0^{50} y_t = 19{,}820.$	$\sum_0^{49} y_t = 19{,}400.$	$\sum_0^{50} y_t = 19{,}420.$
$\sum_0^{50} y_t^2 = 7{,}910{,}132.$	$\sum_0^{49} y_t^2 = 7{,}733{,}752.$	$\sum_0^{50} y_t^2 = 7{,}750{,}152.$
$\sum_1^{50} y_t y_{t-1} = 7{,}690{,}265.$	$\sum_1^{50} y_t y_{t-1} = 7{,}507{,}465.$	
$(19{,}820)^2 = 392{,}832{,}400.$	$(19{,}400)^2 = 376{,}360{,}000.$	$(19{,}420)^2 = 377{,}136.400.$

Let y_t be the number of copies of the issue of week t sold by noon on the Monday after it appears. Assume that

$$\tilde{y}_t = \beta_1 + \beta_2 y_{t-1} + \tilde{\varepsilon}_t,$$

where the $\tilde{\varepsilon}_t$ are independent, Normal rv's with mean 0 and variance 1600.

a. Show that, for a diffuse prior, the distribution of $(\tilde{\beta}_1, \tilde{\beta}_2)$ given the data in exhibit 24.1 is Normal with

$$\text{mean} = \begin{bmatrix} 97 \\ 0.75 \end{bmatrix}, \qquad \text{variance} = \begin{bmatrix} 1198.1 & -3.0055 \\ -3.0055 & .0077462 \end{bmatrix}.$$

Some relevant and some irrelevant computations are given in exhibit 24.1.

Do the rest of the problem using this result even if you did not obtain it or did not attempt to.

b. What is the distribution of the next $\tilde{y}_t$ given the data?

c. What is the distribution of total demand for the next issue given the data? How many copies should be ordered?

d. If, more realistically, the variance of $\tilde{\varepsilon}_t$ were assumed to be unknown, how could one obtain an estimate adequate for this problem?

26. In controlled experimentation when we wish to predict or investigate the behavior of a criterion variable y (yield, say) from controlled variables $x_1, x_2, \ldots, x_k$ (e.g. temperature, time, etc.) it is often convenient to choose the xs to facilitate the estimation of parameters and to make the estimators statistically independent. To illustrate this point consider the model where

$$\tilde{y}_i = \beta_0 + x_{i1}\beta_1 + x_{i2}\beta_2 + x_{i3}\beta_3 + x_{i4}\beta_4 + \tilde{\varepsilon}_i.$$

The x levels are chosen (with awareness aforethought) as in the table following.

For example: x_1 may be temperature with the scale coded such that

$40°\text{C} = -1, \qquad 50°\text{C} = 0, \qquad 60°\text{C} = 1.$

Find the posterior distribution of the unknown coefficients $\tilde{\beta}_0, \ldots, \tilde{\beta}_4$ based on a diffuse prior.

Indicate *clearly* how to estimate v without carrying out all the numerical details. Assume that the $\tilde{\varepsilon}$s are independent, Normal, $E(\tilde{\varepsilon}_i) = 0$ and $V(\tilde{\varepsilon}_i) = v$ for all i.

Trial	*Chosen x Levels* 1	2	3	4	Observed ys
1	−1	−1	−1	−1	10
2	1	1	−1	−1	21
3	1	−1	1	−1	26
4	−1	1	1	−1	31
5	1	−1	−1	1	21
6	−1	1	−1	1	25
7	−1	−1	1	1	30
8	1	1	1	1	39
9	0	0	0	0	22
10	0	0	0	0	24
11	0	0	0	0	25
12	0	0	0	0	25

27. The Antler Auto Rental Company was given a sample of 40 tablets of a battery additive called DDA. The manufacturer of DDA claimed that it increased battery life by reducing sedimentation in the battery cells. The prescribed dose is one tablet per battery cell per year, and the tablets cost 10 cents each. The chemical name of DDA is too long to give here, but the man on whom the Antler Company relies in such matters said that there was no reason to suppose DDA would differ from earlier additives, which had had no noticeable effect, desirable or undesirable.

An informal test was run on a 12-cell battery which had been removed from service and whose 7th cell was defective. Two tablets (twice the prescribed dose) were placed in the second cell and two in the fourth cell, and the first six cells were given a tough bench test consisting of heavy charges and discharges alternately. (Cells 7–12 were disconnected for the test.) The battery was then taken apart and inspected. There was no evidence of undesirable chemical or physical effects of DDA in other respects than sedimentation. The sedimentation measurements are given in exhibit 24.2.

Mr. Deering, the president of Antler, and his chemical expert agreed that the evidence on sedimentation provided by a bench test was worthless as far as actual driving conditions are concerned, but since even a double dose of DDA didn't appear to do any harm, Mr. Deering decided to place the remaining 36 tablets in batteries in service. A year later these batteries were removed and taken apart. Again there was no evidence of undesirable effects in other respects than sedimentation. The sedimentation measurements and other information are given in exhibit 24.3.

Mr. Deering has found the information in exhibit 24.3 difficult to assimilate and has asked you to write a summary of the status of the DDA question. He does not want to assess any prior distributions until he has some idea whether it is worth the trouble, and anyway he would like to know what the data in exhibit 24.3 "say by themselves," separate from any subjective judgments.

You are preparing to write the summary Mr. Deering has requested. You may do parts (a) and (b) below separately or together, but if you do them together, be sure to indicate clearly which parts of your answer belong to (a) and which to (b).

Exhibit 24.2
Bench test of a single battery
(Cells 7–12 disconnected)

Cell no.	1	2	3	4	5	6
Sediment (oz.)	1.12	1.01*	1.37	1.26*	1.35	1.23

*Cell receiving DDA.

Exhibit 24.3
Sediment (oz.) in road test of nine batteries

Battery†									
No.	1	2	3	4	5	6	7	8	9
Age	10	15	9	8	11	4	8	7	12
Miles	22349	23664	19652	20646	17306	21741	19294	24149	16797
mpg	17.8	12.6	14.1	16.9	17.2	13.9	13.8	12.8	13.1
Cell #									
1	0.83*	1.14*	1.36*	0.32	1.25	1.43	1.12	0.01	1.19
2	1.18	1.05	1.19	1.21*	0.80*	0.90*	1.21	1.25	1.07
3	1.19	1.40	1.05	0.69	1.18	0.79	1.36*	1.36*	1.26*
4	0.85*	1.33*	1.32*	0.91	0.56	0.55	1.06	1.09	1.22
5	1.23	1.13	0.77	0.87*	0.88*	0.59*	0.79	0.94	1.25
6	1.17	1.10	0.90	0.90	0.89	0.96	1.06*	1.12*	0.90*
7	1.45*	1.31*	1.27*	1.30	1.10	0.87	0.94	1.32	1.40
8	1.20	0.98	1.22	0.68*	1.08*	0.76*	0.61	1.08	1.48
9	1.11	1.25	1.04	1.34	1.31	0.70	1.23*	1.36*	1.01*
10	0.86*	1.24*	1.07*	1.38	1.17	0.77	0.79	0.73	1.36
11	1.23	1.49	1.26	0.96*	1.10*	0.86*	0.99	0.86	0.84
12	0.75	1.28	0.97	0.93	1.05	0.56	1.07*	1.35*	1.20*

† Battery number for identification purposes only. Age is age of battery in months at beginning of test. Miles and mpg are miles traveled and miles per gallon during year of test. Batteries no. 1, 4, and 5 were in "compact" autos, remainder in low-priced, standard-size autos.
* Cell receiving DDA.

a. Write step-by-step computational instructions to your assistant, who understands mathematical notation (including matrix algebra) but knows no probability or statistics.

b. Explain for the benefit of someone who has read this text what the computations give which you requested in part (a).

28. Market Prognosticators, Inc. (MPI) has been retained by a supermarket chain to forecast sales (gross in the first two years) at a potential store site in West Moribund, Massachusetts. A variety of relevant demographic and other interesting characteristics are available. MPI has no Massachusetts sales data, but using data from other states, MPI has developed a regression relationship $y = \boldsymbol{x}'\boldsymbol{\beta} + \varepsilon$ where y = sales at a site, $\boldsymbol{x}$ is the vector of relevant characteristics, $\boldsymbol{\beta}$ is a vector of unknown parameters (regression coefficients), and ε is an "error" or "deviation" or "disturbance." Let the vector $\boldsymbol{y}$ and the matrix $\mathbf{x}$ denote the sales and characteristics data available from other states, arrayed in the usual way. Let $\boldsymbol{z}$ denote the relevant characteristics of the West Moribund site. Suppose MPI, at least in a "first-cut" analysis, is satisfied to use only the information in the data, to treat the errors ε as independent and Normal with common variance v, and to treat an estimate of v as if it were a known value of v. Illustrative data appear in exhibit 24.4, where $x_{i1} = 1$ on every observation, x_{i2} and x_{i3} have been "centered" for convenience, and no units are given because the data are disguised for confidentiality anyway. (Of course MPI actually used many more characteristics.) West Moribund's characteristics (for this illustration) are $z_1 = 1$, $z_2 = 2.1$, $z_3 = -3.4$.

Give formulas by which answers to the following questions can be calculated. If time permits, give numerical answers in (a)–(d) for the illustrative data. Where you do not give numerical answers, be as explicit as you can about how numerical answers could be calculated.

Exhibit 24.4

Observation	Sales	Characteristics								
Number	y_i	x_{i1}	x_{i2}	x_{i3}	y_i^2	$y_i x_{i2}$	$y_i x_{i3}$	x_{i2}^2	$x_{i2}x_{i3}$	x_{i3}^2
$i=1$	23	1	5	−2	529	115	−46	25	−10	4
2	18	1	1	−4	324	18	−72	1	−4	16
3	8	1	−2	3	64	−16	24	4	−6	9
4	20	1	1	−3	400	20	−60	1	−3	9
5	17	1	−1	−1	289	−17	−17	1	1	1
6	13	1	−4	1	169	−52	13	16	−4	1
7	10	1	−4	5	100	−40	50	16	−20	25
8	19	1	3	0	361	57	0	9	0	0
9	15	1	1	4	225	15	60	1	4	16
10	17	1	0	−3	289	0	−51	0	0	9
Totals	160	10	0	0	2750	100	−99	74	−42	90

a. Suppose MPI thinks sites in Massachusetts are like those anywhere else. What is its forecast distribution of sales at West Moribund?

b. MPI's clients understand only point forecasts, not distributions. If MPI uses squared error for its loss function, what should its point forecast be?

c. Actually MPI has experienced more *tsuris* (grief) for overestimating than underestimating sales. If MPI takes its loss to be $y - \hat{y}$ when its forecast $\hat{y}$ is less than actual sales y, but takes its loss to be $3(\hat{y} - y)$ when $\hat{y} \geqq y$, what should its point forecast be? (MPI would prefer two different nonlinear functions in the two cases, but even their hotshots couldn't come up with anything tractable.)

d. Suppose MPI wakes up and realizes that Massachusetts is not like anywhere else, and times have changed anyway. MPI describes the relevant relationship in Massachusetts at this time as $y = \boldsymbol{x}'\boldsymbol{\gamma} + \varepsilon$ and assumes that ε has the same distribution as before. It regards the amount $\boldsymbol{\delta} = \boldsymbol{\gamma} - \boldsymbol{\beta}$ by which the regression coefficients have changed as independent of $\boldsymbol{\beta}$ and Normally distributed. For illustration say $\boldsymbol{\delta}$ has

$$\text{Mean} = \begin{bmatrix} -1.1 \\ 4.7 \\ -1.3 \end{bmatrix} \text{ and variance} = \begin{bmatrix} 4 & -3 & 1 \\ -3 & 8 & -2 \\ 1 & -2 & 5 \end{bmatrix}.$$

With this view of the world, what is the forecast distribution of sales at West Moribund?

e. By some snooping, at the cost of some effort, delay, and risk to its reputation, MPI could obtain sales and characteristics data on two other Massachusetts sites. Suppose it did. What would the forecast distribution of sales at West Moribund then be?

f. What would the conditional value of this snooped information (CVSI) be, given the information obtained, under the loss function in part (b)? In part (c)? Would it depend on the snooped sales data? The snooped characteristics data?

g. What would the expected value of snooping information (EVSI) be under the two loss functions?

h. Forget snooping and Massachusetts's peculiarities and return to the assumptions of (a). It is possible, if not on the illustrative numbers then on others, that MPI's estimated loss due to forecasting error, as calculated in (b) and (c), would be smaller if it ignored all information on one characteristic and dropped this characteristic from the regression model. How can this paradox be explained?

29. Suppose we are given n observations on a Normal linear regression model

$$\tilde{y}_i = \boldsymbol{x}_i^t \boldsymbol{\beta} + \tilde{\varepsilon}_i$$

where the $\tilde{\varepsilon}_i$ are independent and $N(0, v)$ with v known. Suppose the prior distribution of $\tilde{\boldsymbol{\beta}}$ is assessed not directly but by way of some further parameters $\boldsymbol{\theta}$. Specifically, the distribution of $\tilde{\boldsymbol{\beta}}$ given $\boldsymbol{\theta}$ is $N(\mathbf{A}\boldsymbol{\theta}, \mathbf{W})$ where $\mathbf{A}$ and $\mathbf{W}$ are specified, while $\tilde{\boldsymbol{\theta}}$ is $N(\bar{\boldsymbol{\theta}}', \breve{\boldsymbol{\theta}}')$.

a. Give the joint distribution of $(\tilde{\boldsymbol{\beta}}, \tilde{\boldsymbol{\theta}})$.

b. Show that the posterior distribution of $\tilde{\boldsymbol{\beta}}$ is $N(\bar{\boldsymbol{\beta}}'', \breve{\boldsymbol{\beta}}'')$ where

$$\breve{\boldsymbol{\beta}}'' = v[\mathbf{x}^t\mathbf{x} + v(\mathbf{W} + \mathbf{A}\breve{\boldsymbol{\theta}}'\mathbf{A}^t)^{-1}]^{-1}$$

and

$$\bar{\boldsymbol{\beta}}'' = \breve{\boldsymbol{\beta}}''\left[\frac{1}{v}\mathbf{x}^t\boldsymbol{y} + (\mathbf{W} + \mathbf{A}\breve{\boldsymbol{\theta}}\mathbf{A}^t)^{-1}\mathbf{A}\bar{\boldsymbol{\theta}}'\right].$$

c. What is or how would you find the optimum estimate d of $\delta = \beta_1 - \beta_2$ (the difference between the first 2 components of $\boldsymbol{\beta}$) for the loss function $(d - \delta)^2$? For the loss function $|d - \delta|$? If you can't answer this question for estimation of δ, answer for estimation of β_1 instead.

d. Are the estimates in (c) admissible? (Remember to justify your answer.)

e. What is the distribution of $\tilde{y}_{n+1}$ if the first n observations are known and it is also known that $\boldsymbol{x}_{n+1} = z$?

f. Display $\mathbf{A}$ and $\mathbf{W}$ for the case that $\boldsymbol{\theta}$ is one-dimensional and the components of $\tilde{\boldsymbol{\beta}}$ given θ are independent and $N(\theta, \tau^2)$.

g. If time permits, simplify the expressions for $\breve{\boldsymbol{\beta}}''$ and $\bar{\boldsymbol{\beta}}''$ in this case.

30. Let $\tilde{y}_i = \beta_0 + \beta_1 x_{i1} + \beta_2 x_{i2} + \beta_3 x_{i3} + \tilde{\varepsilon}_i$ be a Normal linear regression process with known process variance 25. Suppose 30 observations have been made with

$$\sum_i \boldsymbol{x}_i \boldsymbol{x}_i^t = \begin{bmatrix} 30 & 0 & 0 & 0 \\ 0 & 15 & -11 & 0 \\ 0 & -11 & 48 & 0 \\ 0 & 0 & 0 & 8 \end{bmatrix} \qquad \sum_i \boldsymbol{x}_i y_i = \begin{bmatrix} 687 \\ 34 \\ -61 \\ 12 \end{bmatrix}$$

where $\boldsymbol{x}_i^t = [1 \quad x_{i1} x_{i2} x_{i3}]$. Please calculate to at least 3 significant places.

a. What is the posterior distribution of $\tilde{\boldsymbol{\beta}}$ if its prior distribution is "gentle?"

b. Assume henceforth that $\tilde{\beta}_0$, $\tilde{\beta}_1$, $\tilde{\beta}_2$ and $\tilde{\beta}_3$ are independently Normal a priori with means 27, 2.4, -1.1, and 1.4 and variances 0.4, 0.5, 0.2, and 0.8 respectively. What is their posterior distribution?

c. For which j, k are $\tilde{\beta}_j$ and $\tilde{\beta}_k$ independent a priori? For what multivariate Normal prior distributions would the same posterior independence hold?

d. What are the mean, variance, and three quartiles of the posterior distribution of $\tilde{\beta}_1$?

e. A new observation y_{31} will be made with $\boldsymbol{x}_{31}^t = [1 \quad 1 \quad 2 \quad -0.3]$. What is its forecast distribution?

f. What is the best "point forecast" $\hat{y}_{31}$ for the loss function $100(y_{31} - \hat{y}_{31})^2$? What is its expected loss?

g. Suppose two acts are available, one of which must be chosen before y_{31} is observed. Act 1 has value $1000 - 50y_{31}$ while act 2 has value $200 - 10y_{31}$. Which act should be chosen? What is its expected value?

h. What is the expected value of learning y_{31} before choosing an act? Of learning β_0, β_1, β_2, and β_3 but not y_{31}?

i. Suppose x_{i1} is a dummy variable (value 0 or 1) and the model above arose by taking (natural) logarithms in the model

$$\tilde{Y}_i = B_0 B_1^{x_{i1}} X_{i2}^{\beta_2} X_{i3}^{\beta_3} \tilde{E}_i,$$

that is, $\tilde{y}_i = \log \tilde{Y}_i$, $\beta_0 = \log B_0$, $\beta_1 = \log B_1$, $x_{i2} = \log X_{i2}$, $x_{i3} = \log X_{i3}$, and $\tilde{\varepsilon}_i = \log \tilde{E}_i$. Thus B_1 is the multiplicative effect of $x_{i1} = 1$ as compared to $x_{i1} = 0$. What are the mean, variance, and three quartiles of the posterior distribution of $\tilde{B}_1$?

j. What are the mean, variance, and three quartiles of the forecast distribution of $\tilde{Y}_{31}$ if $x_{31,1} = 0$, $X_{31,2} = 0.2$ and $X_{31,3} = 1.4$?

31. In preparation for deciding on his investments for the next period, Mr. Rich is undertaking to assess the joint distribution of next-period price changes $y_1, y_2, \ldots, y_n$ in a variety of stocks, bonds, real estate, and so on, that he might invest in. Rather than develop opinions about all the y_i directly, he has assessed a joint Normal distribution of the changes $x_1, x_2, \ldots, x_k$ in k economic indicators (unemployment, housing starts, etc.). He has used historical data to arrive at a regression of each y_i on these indicators and on a prediction z_i of y_i made by an advisory service to which he subscribes. Let these regressions be $\tilde{y}_i = a_i z_i + b_{i0} + b_{i1} x_1 + b_{i2} x_2 + \cdots + b_{ik} x_k + \tilde{\varepsilon}_i$. To start he assumes that the $\tilde{\varepsilon}_i$ are independently Normal with mean 0 and variances v_i.

a. What is the joint distribution of $\tilde{y}_1, \tilde{y}_2, \ldots, \tilde{y}_n$?

b. Are they independent?

c. How might Mr. Rich go about allocating his fortune to investments for the next period?

d. In fact one of the economic indicators is the Dow-Jones average, which is a weighted average of 30 of the stocks Mr. Rich might invest in. How might this affect his thinking or procedure?

32. Derive expression (24.60) for the asymptotic behavior of the log likelihood. What does the law of large numbers imply about the remainder?

33. Prove the information inequalities stated after (24.63).
Hint Use the concavity of the logarithm.

34. In section 24.7.3, let x have finitely many possible values.

a. Show that if the conditional probability that $\tilde{x}_i = x$ given y_{xi} and all observed values x_j, y_j with $j < i$ does not depend on y_{xi}, then the sequence of observed values $\tilde{y}_i$ for which $\tilde{x}_i = x$ is independently, identically distributed according to $D(\tilde{y}_x)$.

b. Arrange the possible values of x in some order and let Y_i be the vector of potential values y_{xi} arranged in the same order. Show that if $\tilde{x}_i$ is conditionally independent of $\tilde{Y}_i$ given all observed values x_j, y_j with $j < i$, then the hypothesis of part a is satisfied.

c. Show that the hypothesis in part b is technically stronger than the hypothesis in part a.

d. In the linear case, show that it is equivalent to substitute u_{xi} for y_{xi} in the hypothesis of part a and $\tilde{U}_i$ for $\tilde{Y}_i$ in the hypothesis of part b, where U_i is defined in the obvious way.

35. Let $\tilde{y}_{1,i}$ be independently, identically distributed for $i = 0, 1, 2, \ldots$. Let $\tilde{y}_{2,i} = \tilde{y}_{1,i-1}$ for all $i \geq 1$.

a. Show that the $\tilde{y}_{x,i}$, $i = 1, 2, \ldots$, are independent for each x and that the pairs $[\tilde{y}_{1,i}, \tilde{y}_{2,i}]$, $i = 1, 2, \ldots$, are identically distributed but not independent.

b. How can you exploit this to "beat the odds" in a sequence of trials i if you must choose $x_i = 1$ or 2 before the ith trial and you will observe and receive $\tilde{y}_{x_i,i}$ for the chosen x_i on each trial.

36. Assuming linear causal structures (24.66) and (24.67), derive (a) the coefficients and (b) the properties of $\tilde{u}$ in (24.68).

37. Why might or might not λ_1 and γ_1 have the causal interpretations proposed at the end of the paragraph containing (24.68)?

38. a. Rewrite the linear causal structure (24.66) in terms of the factors x_1 and x_3 where $x_3 = x_2 - \alpha_0 - \alpha_1 x_1$. (One could but need not interpret $\alpha_0 + \alpha_1 x_1$ as normal oven temperature and x_3 as deviation of x_2 from the norm.) Which coefficients in the two forms of the structure are the same and which are different?

b. What causal structure does (24.67) imply for x_3?

c. Show that the same structure (24.68) arises from (24.66) and (24.67) in the rewritten forms of (a) and (b) as from the original forms.

d. Interpret u in (24.68) in the light of (c).

39. Show that if $L(y; \boldsymbol{x}_1, \boldsymbol{x}_2) = b_0 + \boldsymbol{b}_1^t \boldsymbol{x}_1 + \boldsymbol{b}_2^t \boldsymbol{x}_2$ and $L(\boldsymbol{x}_2; \boldsymbol{x}_1)$ is linear, then $L(y; \boldsymbol{x}_1) = b_0 + \boldsymbol{b}_1^t \boldsymbol{x}_1 + \boldsymbol{b}_2^t L(\boldsymbol{x}_2; \boldsymbol{x}_1)$ for the following:

a. $L(y; \boldsymbol{x}) = E(\tilde{y} | \tilde{\boldsymbol{x}} = \boldsymbol{x})$;

b. $L(y; \boldsymbol{x})$ is the ordinary least squares regression of y on $\boldsymbol{x}$ in a given data set.

c. Interpret (b) in terms of projections.

d. Relate this to the "forecasts of the terms that would be added if excluded variables were added" mentioned near the end of section 24.7.5.

40. Let $\tilde{u}_x$ be defined for each x, let $\tilde{x}$ be chosen somehow (not necessarily independently of $\tilde{u}_x$) and let $\tilde{u} = \tilde{u}_{\tilde{x}}$.

a. Show that $\tilde{x}$ is independent of $\tilde{u}$ if and only if $D(\tilde{u}_x | \tilde{x} = x)$ is the same for all x.

b. Under observability ($\tilde{x}$ independent of $\tilde{u}_x$ for all x), show that $\tilde{x}$ is independent of $\tilde{u}$ if and only if $D(\tilde{u}_x)$ is the same for all x. (This precludes a heteroskedastic causal structure.)

c. Show that when a linear causal structure is observed as at (24.65), neither $\tilde{x}_i$ independent of $\tilde{u}_i$ nor observability implies the other, but each implies that $\tilde{x}_i$ is uncorrelated with $\tilde{u}_i$ and hence the regression and causal coefficients coincide.

41. Suppose that the mean response to a treatment at level x (possibly 0) is $a_1 + c_1 x$ for females and $a_2 + c_2 x$ for males.

a. Express this as a linear causal structure with sex as a concomitant.

b. Suppose the treatment is a prescription drug and, in the data, some doctors prescribe it more often or in higher doses for one sex than the other. Under what conditions, if any, is the structure observable?

c. Suppose the treatment is a food additive and the percentage of females among consumers differs from place to place. How can data from one place be used to estimate the average effect in another place?

42. Express each of the following situations as a linear causal structure with concomitants.

a. $\tilde{y}_{xi} = y_{i-1} + \gamma_0 + \boldsymbol{\gamma}^t \boldsymbol{x} + \tilde{u}_{xi}$ where $\tilde{u}_{xi}$ for $i = 1, 2, 3, \ldots$ are independently, identically distributed and $y_j = y_{x_j j}$ for all j.

b. The residuals in (24.56) are autocorrelated, namely $\tilde{u}_{xi} = r\tilde{u}_{i-1} + \tilde{e}_{xi}$ where the $\tilde{e}_{xi}$ for $i = 1, 2, 3, \ldots$ are independently, identically distributed.

43. a. How might the model (23.27) be generalized to a linear causal structure with Normal disturbances unobservable in the data?

b. What would the posterior distribution of the causal parameters be for a Normal prior distribution?

44. Given the type of data a firm might have on the characteristics of job applicants and the progress, productivity, and remuneration of those hired, how might you study whether the firm discriminates unfairly?

Appendix 1: The Terminology of Sets

A1.1 The General Idea of a Set

We assume that the reader understands what is meant by a *set* (or collection) of elements (or objects, things, entities, etc.). We assume for example that there is no ambiguity in such expressions as:

a. the set of positive integers from 5 to 25 inclusive,

b. the set of women in the United States aged 40 or more,

c. the set of households that used 100 or more ounces of instant coffee in the last calendar year.

For a set to be well defined it must be possible to determine in principle whether a given element of discourse does or does not belong to the set. Mathematically, if an element x belongs to a set V we shall write $x \in V$ (read: x belongs to V); if x does not belong to V we shall write $x \notin V$.

A1.2 Relations among Sets

A1.2.1 Definitions

In most applications we shall be concerned with some *universal* set that contains all the possible elements of our discourse and with various *subsets* of this universal set. Thus, for example, we may be concerned with the universal set of all households in the United States and a subset of households in which last year's reported taxable income was over $15,000. Certain symbols denoting sets, subsets, and relations among sets and subsets are defined in table A1.1.

From these definitions it follows immediately (as the reader should verify) that

$$\bar{U} = \varnothing, \qquad V \cup \bar{V} = U, \qquad V \cap \bar{V} = \varnothing.$$

Sets V and W are said to be *disjoint* if they have no element in common, that is, if $V \cap W = \varnothing$.

Table A1.1

Symbol	*Read as*	*Meaning*
U	Universal set	Set of all elements of discourse.
$\varnothing$	Empty set	Set containing no elements of U.
$V \subset W$	V is contained in W or W contains V	Every element of V belongs to W; or $x \in V \Rightarrow x \in W$.
$\bar{V}$	Complement of V	Set of all elements in U *not* belonging to V.
$V \cup W$	V union W	Set of all elements in V *or* in W (or in both).
$V_1 \cup V_2 \cup \cdots \cup V_m$	Union of $V_1, \ldots, V_m$	Set of all elements in *one or more* of $V_1, \ldots, V_m$.
$V \cap W$	V intersect W	Set of all elements *common* to V and W.
$V_1 \cap V_2 \cap \cdots \cap V_m$	Intersection of $V_1, \ldots, V_m$	Set of all elements *common* to $V_1, \ldots, V_m$.

A1.2.2 Pictorial Representation of Sets

In reasoning about sets it is often helpful to employ pictorial representations like figure A1.1, where each numbered dot represents an element and all the dots within the rectangle together constitute the universal set U. The reader should verify that the following descriptions of certain other sets agree with the figure:

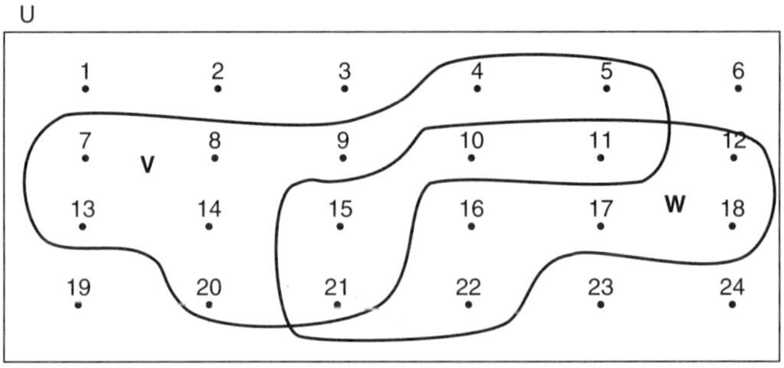

Figure A1.1
A universal set and two subsets

$W = \{10, 11, 12, 15, 16, 17, 18, 21, 22\},$

$V \cap W = \{10, 11, 15, 21\},$

$\overline{(V \cup W)} = \{1, 2, 3, 6, 19, 23, 24\};$

then identify some other sets such as $V \cup W$, $\bar{V}$, $\bar{V} \cap \bar{W}$, $\bar{V} \cup \bar{W}$, and determine that $V \cup W = \overline{(\bar{V} \cap \bar{W})}$.

A1.2.3 Partitions

A *collection of sets* $\{V_1, V_2, \ldots, V_m\}$ is said to *partition* a set Z if all of the following conditions hold:

$$V_i \subset Z, \qquad i = 1, 2, \ldots, m,$$

$$V_i \cap V_j = \varnothing, \qquad i \neq j,$$

$$V_1 \cup V_2 \cup \cdots \cup V_m = Z.$$

In other words, the Vs partition Z if (a) every V is included in Z, (b) the Vs are disjoint, and (c) the Vs taken together include every element in Z. Or more briefly, the Vs partition Z if (a) every element of Z is in one and only one V, and (b) no V contains any element outside of Z. As one example of a partition, the sets

$$V_1 = \{1, 3\}, \qquad V_2 = \{2, 4, 5\}, \qquad V_3 = \{0, 6\}$$

constitute a partition of the set

$$Z = \{0, 1, 2, 3, 4, 5, 6\}.$$

As another example, the set of all residents of the United States can be partitioned into {male, female}, or into {Catholic, Jewish, Protestant, other}, or into {under 20 years old, at least 20 but under 60, over 60}, and so forth.

If a collection of sets $\{V_1, V_2, \ldots, V_m\}$ partitions the *universal set* U, then we shall say the Vs are *mutually exclusive* (i.e., disjoint) and *collectively exhaustive.*

The following proposition concerning partitions can be easily verified by the reader.

Let $\{V_1, V_2, \ldots, V_m\}$ be a partition of the universal set U, and let X be any subset of U. Then

$$\{V_1 \cap X, V_2 \cap X, \ldots, V_m \cap X\}$$

is a partition of X.

Thus for example, let U be the set of all residents of the United States, let U be partitioned {male, female}, and let X be the set of all adult residents of the United States. Then {adult male, adult female} is a partition of X.

A1.3 Special Types of Sets: Notation

A1.3.1 Finite Sets

A set is called *finite* if it is possible, in principle, to count all of its elements; the set of all individuals on our planet is an example of a finite set. Since a finite set can be counted, it is possible to list its elements by starting with a first element and continuing the listing until a *last* element is reached. A finite set can be described by displaying all of its members between curly brackets, the order in which the members appear being irrelevant; thus the set of all positive integers from 1 to 4 inclusive can be written $\{1, 2, 3, 4\}$ or $\{3, 1, 2, 4\}$, and so forth.

A1.3.2 Denumerable Sets

A set is called denumerable (or denumerable or countable) if it is possible to devise a procedure for *listing* the members of the set such that every member of the set has a well-defined serial number, that is, a well-defined place in the listing, whether or not the listing ever terminates. The set can then be described by indicating a possible listing procedure within curly brackets. Thus the set $\{1, 2, 3, \ldots\}$ of all positive integers is denumerable, as are the set $\{-1, +1, -2, +2, \ldots\}$ of all positive and negative integers and the set

$$\{\tfrac{1}{2}; \tfrac{1}{3}, \tfrac{2}{3}; \tfrac{1}{4}, \tfrac{3}{4}; \tfrac{1}{5}, \tfrac{2}{5}, \tfrac{3}{5}, \tfrac{4}{5}; \tfrac{1}{6}, \ldots\}$$

of all proper fractions.

A1.3.3 Discrete Sets

The term *discrete set* is sometimes taken as synonymous with *denumerable set*, but in this book we use it in a more restrictive sense. A (denumerable) set of real numbers will be called discrete if there corresponds to each member of the set (a) a *next larger* member whenever there are *larger* members, and (b) a *next smaller* member whenever there are *smaller* members. If we think of the members of a set of real numbers as represented by points on a line, then the set is discrete if *each* member has (1) either no left-hand neighbor or a next left-hand neighbor, and (2) either no right-hand neighbor or a next right-hand neighbor. Thus the set $\{1, 2, 3, \ldots\}$ of all positive integers is discrete, as is the set $\{\tfrac{1}{1}, \tfrac{1}{2}, \tfrac{1}{3}, \ldots\}$; however, the set of all rational proper fractions is not discrete because, given any two rational fractions, we can construct an infinity of rational fractions *between* them, so that to every member of the set there corresponds a larger member but no *next* larger member.

A1.3.4 Cartesian Products

The *Cartesian product* of a finite collection of sets U_1, U_2, ..., U_m is a *single set*, denoted by $U_1 \times U_2 \times \ldots \times U_m$, comprising all elements of the form $(u_1, u_2, \ldots, u_m)$ where $u_1 \in U_1$, $u_2 \in U_2, \ldots, u_m \in U_m$. Thus, for example, if $U_1 = \{a, b, c\}$, $U_2 = \{\gamma, \delta)$, $U_m = \{2, 7\}$, then the set $U_1 \times U_2 \times U_3$ is given by the listing $\{(a, \gamma, 2), (a, \gamma, 7), (a, \delta, 2), (a, \delta, 7)\ (b, \gamma, 2), (b, \gamma, 7), (b, \delta, 2)\ (b, \delta, 7), (c, \gamma, 2), (c, \gamma, 7)\ (c, \delta, 2)\ (c, \delta, 7)\}$. It makes no difference in this example in what order these 12 elements are listed, but it *is* crucial not to interchange the ordering of symbols within an element. For example, $(b, \delta, 2)$ is an element of $U_1 \times U_2 \times U_3$ whereas $(\delta, 2, b)$ is *not* an element of $U_1 \times U_2 \times U_3$—it is an element of $U_2 \times U_3 \times U_1$.

A1.3.5 Intervals on the Real Line

An *interval on the real line* is the (in general nondenumerable) set of all real numbers between two specified numbers; the description of the interval must state whether or not each of the two boundary points is included in the set. If a and b are real numbers such that $b \geq a$, the set

$$[a, b] \equiv \{x: a \leq x \leq b\}$$

consisting of all real numbers from a to b *inclusive* is called a *closed* interval; the set

$$(a, b) \equiv \{x: a < x < b\}$$

of all real numbers from a to b *exclusive* is called an *open* interval; the sets

$$[a, b) \equiv \{x: a \leq x < b\},$$

$$(a, b] \equiv \{x: a < x \leq b\},$$

are half-open, the former being closed on the left and open on the right, and so forth.

The interval

$$[a, \infty) \equiv \{x: a \leq x\}$$

is the set of all real numbers greater than or equal to a, and the symbols (a, ∞), $(-\infty, a)$ and $(-\infty, a]$ are similarly defined. Symbols like $[a, \infty]$ and $(a, \infty]$ are meaningless.

The set of *all real numbers* can be denoted by $(-\infty, \infty)$. The set consisting of the *single real number* x can be considered to be a "degenerate" interval and denoted by $[x, x]$.

The *union* of any *finite* set of intervals may be called a *generalized interval.*

A1.3.6 *n*-tuples and *n*-dimensional Intervals

A group of n real numbers which taken together describe some *one entity* will be called an *n-tuple.* Thus a point on a plane with x and y axes can be described by a 2-tuple such as (x, y) or $(3, 7)$; a point in 3-dimensional space can be represented as a 3-tuple (x, y, z); and so forth. In an n-tuple the ordering of the numbers is important and in general if we permute the elements of the n-tuple we change the n-tuple. Observe that the n numbers in an n-tuple do not constitute a set, but we may think of *sets* of n-tuples.

If x_1, x_2, y_1, and y_2 are four real numbers such that $x_2 \geq x_1$ and $y_2 \geq y_1$, then the set of all 2-tuples (x, y) such that

$$x_1 \leq x \leq x_2 \quad \text{and} \quad y_1 \leq y \leq y_2$$

constitutes a (closed) *two-dimensional interval* or *interval in Euclidean 2-space.* The set can also be described in curly-bracket notation as

$$\{(x, y): x_1 \leq x \leq x_2 \quad \text{and} \quad y_1 \leq y \leq y_2\}.$$

Intervals in higher dimensional space are similarly defined; and any union of n-dimensional intervals will be called a generalized n-dimensional interval.

Appendix 2: Elements of Matrix Theory

A2.1 Definition of a Matrix

A $(m \times n)$ matrix is a rectangular array of real numbers

$$\mathbf{A} = \begin{bmatrix} a_{11} & \cdots & a_{1j} & \cdots & a_{1n} \\ \vdots & & \vdots & & \vdots \\ a_{i1} & \cdots & a_{ij} & \cdots & a_{in} \\ \vdots & & \vdots & & \vdots \\ a_{m1} & \cdots & a_{mj} & \cdots & a_{mn} \end{bmatrix}.$$

The *element* in row i and column j, or the element in position (i, j), is denoted by a_{ij}. The matrix $\mathbf{A}$ is also said to be of *order* $(m \times n)$, read "m by n". The ith row of $\mathbf{A}$ is the $(1 \times n)$ submatrix

$$[a_{i1} \cdots a_{ij} \cdots a_{in}],$$

and the jth column of $\mathbf{A}$ is the $(m \times 1)$ submatrix

$$\begin{bmatrix} a_{1j} \\ \vdots \\ a_{ij} \\ \vdots \\ a_{mj} \end{bmatrix}.$$

The matrix will often be symbolized in the more compact form

$$\mathbf{A} = [a_{ij}] \qquad \begin{cases} i = 1, \ldots, m, \\ j = 1, \ldots, n. \end{cases}$$

A2.1.1 Row and Column Vectors

An array with 1 row and n columns will also be referred to as a *row vector* of n components. An array with m rows and 1 column will be referred to as a *column vector* of m components.

A2.2 Operations on Matrices

A2.2.1 Addition and Scalar Multiplication

Let $\mathbf{A} = [a_{ij}]$ and $\mathbf{B} = [b_{ij}]$ be two given matrices. The expression $\mathbf{A} + \mathbf{B}$ is defined if and only if $\mathbf{A}$ and $\mathbf{B}$ have the same order, that is, the same number of rows and the same number of columns. If this is so, $\mathbf{A} + \mathbf{B}$ is a matrix $\mathbf{C} = [c_{ij}]$ where $c_{ij} \equiv a_{ij} + b_{ij}$. Symbolically:

$$[a_{ij}] + [b_{ij}] = [a_{ij} + b_{ij}] \qquad \begin{cases} i = 1, \ldots, m, \\ j = 1, \ldots, n. \end{cases} \tag{A2.1}$$

The *scalar product* of a real number k times a matrix $\mathbf{A}$ is defined by

$$k \cdot \mathbf{A} = \mathbf{A} \cdot k = [ka_{ij}], \qquad \begin{cases} i = 1, \ldots, m, \\ j = 1, \ldots, n; \end{cases} \tag{A2.1b}$$

that is, the product is a matrix of the same order as $\mathbf{A}$ where every element of $\mathbf{A}$ is multiplied by k.

The $(m \times n)$ *zero matrix* denoted by $\mathbf{0}$ or $[0]$ consists of all zero elements.

The matrix $-\mathbf{A}$ is understood to be $(-1)\mathbf{A}$, and $\mathbf{A} - \mathbf{B}$ is understood to be $\mathbf{A} + (-1)\mathbf{B}$.

If $\mathbf{A}$, $\mathbf{B}$, and $\mathbf{C}$ are of the same order then the following properties can be easily verified:

$$\mathbf{A} + \mathbf{B} = \mathbf{B} + \mathbf{A}, \tag{A2.2a}$$

$$(\mathbf{A} + \mathbf{B}) + \mathbf{C} = \mathbf{A} + (\mathbf{B} + \mathbf{C}), \tag{A2.2b}$$

$$\mathbf{A} + (-1)\mathbf{A} = \mathbf{A} - \mathbf{A} = \mathbf{0}, \tag{A2.2c}$$

$$(k_1 + k_2)\mathbf{A} = k_1\mathbf{A} + k_2\mathbf{A}, \tag{A2.2d}$$

$$k(\mathbf{A} + \mathbf{B}) = k\mathbf{A} + k\mathbf{B}, \tag{A2.2e}$$

$$k_1(k_2\mathbf{A}) = (k_1 k_2)\mathbf{A}. \tag{A2.2f}$$

A2.2.2 Transposition

If **A** is $(m \times n)$ then the matrix $\mathbf{A}^t$ (read "**A** transpose" or "the transpose of **A**") is a matrix of order $(n \times m)$ and the (i, j)th element of **A** is the (j, i)th element of $\mathbf{A}^t$. Thus the ith row of **A** becomes the ith column of $\mathbf{A}^t$; the jth column of **A** becomes the jth row of $\mathbf{A}^t$. The transpose of a row vector of m components is a column vector of m components; the transpose of a column vector of n components is a row vector of n components. For example, the column vector

$$\begin{bmatrix} 4 \\ -1 \\ 0 \\ 5 \end{bmatrix}$$

can also be written as $[4 \quad -1 \quad 0 \quad 5]^t$.

A2.2.3 Multiplication of a Row and a Column Vector

Let $\boldsymbol{r} = [r_1 \, r_2 \cdots r_p]$ be a row vector with p components and

$$\boldsymbol{c} = \begin{bmatrix} c_1 \\ c_2 \\ \vdots \\ c_p \end{bmatrix}$$

be a column vector of p components. The product of $\boldsymbol{r}$ and $\boldsymbol{c}$, written $\boldsymbol{rc}$, is the single number

$$\boldsymbol{rc} = \textstyle\sum_{i=1}^{p} r_i c_i. \tag{A2.3}$$

A2.2.4 Multiplication of Matrices

Let **A** be $(m \times p)$ and **B** be $(p \times n)$. Note that the number of components in a row of **A** is assumed to be the same as the number of components in a column of **B**. The product of **A** and **B**, written **AB**, is defined as a matrix **C** of order $(m \times n)$ where the (i, j)th element of **C** is defined as the ith row of **A** times the jth column of **B**. That is,

$$\mathbf{AB} = \mathbf{C} = [c_{ij}] \qquad \begin{cases} \mathbf{A} \text{ is } m \times p, \\ \mathbf{B} \text{ is } p \times n, \\ \mathbf{C} \text{ is } m \times n, \end{cases} \tag{A2.4a}$$

where

$$c_{ij} \equiv \textstyle\sum_{k=1}^{p} a_{ik} b_{kj}. \tag{A2.4b}$$

Notice, for example, that if **A** is (4×3) and **B** is (3×5), then **AB** is defined but **BA** is not defined. Notice also that if **A** is (3×5) and **B** is (5×3) then **AB** is (3×3) whereas **BA** is (5×5). Finally notice that if **A** is (2×2) and if **B** is (2×2), then **AB** and **BA** are both defined but it does not necessarily follow that **AB** = **BA**.

The following properties can be easily verified:

$$\mathbf{A}(\mathbf{B}+\mathbf{C}) = \mathbf{AB}+\mathbf{AC} \qquad \begin{cases}\mathbf{A} \text{ is } (m \times p), \\ \mathbf{B} \text{ and } \mathbf{C} \text{ are } (p \times n);\end{cases} \tag{A2.5a}$$

$$(\mathbf{A}+\mathbf{B})\mathbf{C} = \mathbf{AC}+\mathbf{BC} \qquad \begin{cases}\mathbf{A} \text{ and } \mathbf{B} \text{ are } (m \times p), \\ \mathbf{C} \text{ is } (p \times n);\end{cases} \tag{A2.5b}$$

$$(\mathbf{AB})\mathbf{C} = \mathbf{A}(\mathbf{BC}) \qquad \begin{cases}\mathbf{A} \text{ is } (m \times p), \\ \mathbf{B} \text{ is } (p \times q), \\ \mathbf{C} \text{ is } (q \times n);\end{cases} \tag{A2.5c}$$

$$\mathbf{A}^{tt} = \mathbf{A} \tag{A2.5d}$$

$$(\mathbf{A}+\mathbf{B})^t = \mathbf{A}^t + \mathbf{B}^t \qquad \mathbf{A} \text{ and } \mathbf{B} \text{ are } (m \times n), \tag{A2.5e}$$

$$(\mathbf{AB})^t = \mathbf{B}^t\mathbf{A}^t \qquad \begin{cases}\mathbf{A} \text{ is } (m \times p), \\ \mathbf{B} \text{ is } (p \times n);\end{cases} \tag{A2.5f}$$

$$\mathbf{A}(k\mathbf{B}) = k(\mathbf{AB}) = (k\mathbf{A})\mathbf{B} \qquad \begin{cases}\mathbf{A} \text{ is } (m \times p), \\ \mathbf{B} \text{ is } (p \times n).\end{cases} \tag{A2.5g}$$

The rules of operation given in (A2.2) and (A2.5) are valid only if the matrices are *conformable*; that is, the orders of the matrix are such that the operations involved are defined. It is useful to note that if the matrices are conformable on one side of any equality in (A2.2) or (A2.5) they will also be conformable on the other side.

A2.3 Inverse of a Matrix

A2.3.1 The Identity Matrix

The matrix **I** of order $(n \times n)$ which consists of 1s down the main diagonal and 0s elsewhere is called the *identity matrix*. Symbolically,

$$\mathbf{I} = [\delta_{ij}] \quad \text{where} \quad \delta_{ij} = \begin{cases}1 & \text{if} \quad i = j, \\ 0 & \text{if} \quad i \neq j,\end{cases}$$

where $i = 1, \ldots, n$ and $j = 1, \ldots, n$. The identity matrix satisfies

$$\mathbf{AI} = \mathbf{A} \quad \text{and} \quad \mathbf{IB} = \mathbf{B}, \tag{A2.6}$$

for all appropriate conformable **A** and **B**.

A2.3.2 The Inverse Matrix

Let **A** be a square matrix of order $(n \times n)$. If there exists a matrix **B** such that

$$\mathbf{BA} = \mathbf{AB} = \mathbf{I}$$

then **B** is said to be the *inverse* of **A**. The matrix **B** is usually written as $\mathbf{A}^{-1}$. If **A** has an inverse then **A** is said to be *nonsingular*.

The following properties of inverses are important:

1. The inverse of a nonsingular matrix **A** is unique.
2. If **A** and **B** are both nonsingular of the same order, then

$$(\mathbf{AB})^{-1} = \mathbf{B}^{-1}\mathbf{A}^{-1}. \tag{A2.7}$$

3. If $\mathbf{A}$ is nonsingular, then $\mathbf{A}^t$ is nonsingular and

$$(\mathbf{A}^t)^{-1} = (\mathbf{A}^{-1})^t. \tag{A2.8}$$

Proofs[1] 1. If $\mathbf{B}$ and $\mathbf{C}$ are both inverses of $\mathbf{A}$ then

$$\mathbf{B} = \mathbf{BI} = \mathbf{B}(\mathbf{AC}) = (\mathbf{BA})\mathbf{C} = \mathbf{IC} = \mathbf{C}.$$

2. Observe that

$$(\mathbf{B}^{-1}\mathbf{A}^{-1})(\mathbf{AB}) = \mathbf{B}^{-1}(\mathbf{A}^{-1}\mathbf{A})\mathbf{B} = \mathbf{B}^{-1}\mathbf{IB} = \mathbf{B}^{-1}\mathbf{B} = \mathbf{I},$$

and

$$(\mathbf{AB})(\mathbf{B}^{-1}\mathbf{A}^{-1}) = \mathbf{A}(\mathbf{BB}^{-1})\mathbf{A}^{-1} = \mathbf{AIA}^{-1} = \mathbf{AA}^{-1} = \mathbf{I}.$$

3. From (A2.5f),

$$\mathbf{I} = \mathbf{I}^t = (\mathbf{AA}^{-1})^t = (\mathbf{A}^{-1})^t\mathbf{A}^t,$$

and

$$\mathbf{I} = \mathbf{I}^t = (\mathbf{A}^{-1}\mathbf{A})^t = \mathbf{A}^t(\mathbf{A}^{-1})^t.$$

Later on we shall be in a position to show that if $\mathbf{A}$ is square, then

$$\mathbf{AB} = \mathbf{I} \quad \Leftrightarrow \quad \mathbf{BA} = \mathbf{I},$$

so that either one of these two conditions suffices to make $\mathbf{A}$ nonsingular and $\mathbf{B} = \mathbf{A}^{-1}$.

If

$$A = \begin{bmatrix} a_{11} & a_{12} \\ a_{21} & a_{22} \end{bmatrix},$$

then it is easy to verify that

$$\mathbf{A}^{-1} = \frac{1}{\Delta}\begin{bmatrix} a_{22} & -a_{12} \\ -a_{21} & a_{11} \end{bmatrix} \tag{A2.9a}$$

where

$$\Delta = a_{11}a_{22} - a_{12}a_{21}, \tag{A2.9b}$$

provided that $\Delta \neq 0$. If $\Delta = 0$ then it can be shown that $\mathbf{A}$ is not nonsingular (or simply is *singular*).

If $\mathbf{A}$ is $(n \times n)$ and nonsingular the running time to obtain $\mathbf{A}^{-1}$ on a digital computer is approximately $5n^3(\mu + \nu)$, where μ and ν are the multiply and add times respectively of the computer.

A2.4 Partitioned Matrices

Let $\mathbf{A}$ be a $(m \times p)$ matrix, partition the m rows of $\mathbf{A}$ into the first m_1 rows and the last m_2 rows where $m_1 + m_2 = m$; partition the p columns of $\mathbf{A}$ into the first p_1 columns and the last p_2 columns where $p_1 + p_2 = p$. Define the submatrices $\mathbf{A}_{11}$, $\mathbf{A}_{12}$, $\mathbf{A}_{21}$, and $\mathbf{A}_{22}$ where

$\mathbf{A}_{11}$ is $(m_1 \times p_1)$ consisting of the first m_1 rows and first p_1 columns of $\mathbf{A}$,

$\mathbf{A}_{12}$ is $(m_1 \times p_2)$ consisting of the first m_1 rows and last p_2 columns of $\mathbf{A}$,

1. All proofs are optional.

$\mathbf{A}_{21}$ is $(m_2 \times p_1)$ consisting of the last m_2 rows and first p_1 columns of $\mathbf{A}$,
$\mathbf{A}_{22}$ is $(m_2 \times p_2)$ consisting of the last m_2 rows and last p_2 columns of $\mathbf{A}$.

Symbolically

$$A = \begin{bmatrix} \mathbf{A}_{11} & \mathbf{A}_{12} \\ \mathbf{A}_{21} & \mathbf{A}_{22} \end{bmatrix} \quad \text{where} \quad \begin{cases} \mathbf{A} \text{ is } m \times p, \\ \mathbf{A}_{11} \text{ is } m_1 \times p_1. \end{cases}$$

Let $\mathbf{B}$ be $(p \times n)$, partitioned as

$$\mathbf{B} = \begin{bmatrix} \mathbf{B}_{11} & \mathbf{B}_{12} \\ \mathbf{B}_{21} & \mathbf{B}_{22} \end{bmatrix} \quad \text{where} \quad \begin{cases} \mathbf{B} \text{ is } p \times n, \\ \mathbf{B}_{11} \text{ is } p_1 \times n_1. \end{cases}$$

Notice that the number of columns of $\mathbf{A}_{ik}$ and the number of rows of $\mathbf{B}_{kj}$ agree. If $\mathbf{A}$ and $\mathbf{B}$ are partitioned in the above manner it is not difficult to show that

$$\mathbf{AB} = \begin{bmatrix} \mathbf{A}_{11} & \mathbf{A}_{12} \\ \mathbf{A}_{21} & \mathbf{A}_{22} \end{bmatrix}\begin{bmatrix} \mathbf{B}_{11} & \mathbf{B}_{12} \\ \mathbf{B}_{21} & \mathbf{B}_{22} \end{bmatrix} = \begin{bmatrix} \mathbf{A}_{11}\mathbf{B}_{11} + \mathbf{A}_{12}\mathbf{B}_{21} & \mathbf{A}_{11}\mathbf{B}_{12} + \mathbf{A}_{12}\mathbf{B}_{22} \\ \mathbf{A}_{21}\mathbf{B}_{11} + \mathbf{A}_{22}\mathbf{B}_{21} & \mathbf{A}_{21}\mathbf{B}_{12} + \mathbf{A}_{22}\mathbf{B}_{22} \end{bmatrix}, \tag{A2.10}$$

where the order of the submatrix in the upper left of the product is $(m_1 \times n_1)$. Notice the relation of this formula to the formula for the product of two (2×2) matrices.

The following two easily verified theorems about inverses of partitioned matrices are often useful in applications.

1. If $\mathbf{A}$ is a partitioned square matrix of the form

$$\mathbf{A} = \begin{bmatrix} \mathbf{A}_{11} & \mathbf{A}_{12} \\ \mathbf{0} & \mathbf{A}_{22} \end{bmatrix},$$

where $\mathbf{A}_{11}$ and $\mathbf{A}_{22}$ are square matrices with inverses, then $\mathbf{A}$ has an inverse and

$$\mathbf{A}^{-1} = \begin{bmatrix} \mathbf{A}_{11}^{-1} & -\mathbf{A}_{11}^{-1}\mathbf{A}_{12}\mathbf{A}_{22}^{-1} \\ \mathbf{0} & \mathbf{A}_{22}^{-1} \end{bmatrix}. \tag{A2.11}$$

2. If

$$\begin{bmatrix} \mathbf{A}_{11} & \mathbf{A}_{12} \\ \mathbf{A}_{21} & \mathbf{A}_{22} \end{bmatrix}\begin{bmatrix} \mathbf{B}_{11} & \mathbf{B}_{12} \\ \mathbf{B}_{21} & \mathbf{B}_{22} \end{bmatrix} = \begin{bmatrix} \mathbf{I} & \mathbf{0} \\ \mathbf{0} & \mathbf{I} \end{bmatrix}, \tag{A2.12a}$$

where $\mathbf{A}$ and $\mathbf{B}$ are square of the same order, $\mathbf{A}_{11}$ and $\mathbf{B}_{22}$ are also square of the same order, and $\mathbf{A}_{11}$ and $\mathbf{B}_{22}$ are nonsingular, then

$$\mathbf{A}_{11}^{-1} = \mathbf{B}_{11} - \mathbf{B}_{12}\mathbf{B}_{22}^{-1}\mathbf{B}_{21}, \tag{A2.12b}$$

and

$$\mathbf{A}_{11}^{-1}\mathbf{A}_{12} = \mathbf{B}_{12}\mathbf{B}_{22}^{-1}. \tag{A2.12c}$$

Proof To verify (A2.11), multiply $\mathbf{A}$ by the right-hand side of (A2.11) using (A2.10) and verify that it yields the identity matrix. To prove formulas (A2.12b) and (A2.12c) observe that (A2.12a) implies that

$$\mathbf{A}_{11}\mathbf{B}_{11} + \mathbf{A}_{12}\mathbf{B}_{21} = \mathbf{I}, \qquad \mathbf{A}_{11}\mathbf{B}_{12} + \mathbf{A}_{12}\mathbf{B}_{22} = \mathbf{0}.$$

Premultiplying the second equation of this pair by $\mathbf{A}_{11}^{-1}$ and postmultiplying by $\mathbf{B}_{22}^{-1}$ gives (A2.12c). Premultiplying the first equation by $\mathbf{A}_{11}^{-1}$ and making the substitution (A2.12c) then gives (A2.12b).

A2.5 Transformations and Inverses

A matrix of $\mathbf{A}$ of order $(m \times n)$ can be thought of as a special kind of transformation (or function, or mapping) that transforms a column n-tuple $\boldsymbol{x} = [x_1\, x_2 \cdots x_n]^t$, say, into a column

m-tuple $y = [y_1\, y_2 \cdots y_m]'$, say

$$\mathbf{A}x = y, \qquad \begin{cases} \mathbf{A} \text{ is } (m \times n) \\ x \text{ is } (n \times 1), \\ y \text{ is } (m \times 1). \end{cases} \tag{A2.13}$$

$$x = \begin{bmatrix} x_1 \\ x_2 \\ \vdots \\ x_n \end{bmatrix} \longrightarrow \quad \mathbf{A} \quad \longrightarrow y = \begin{bmatrix} y_1 \\ y_2 \\ \vdots \\ y_m \end{bmatrix},$$

(Input) (Transformation) (Output)

There are transformations sending a column n-tuple into a column m-tuple that are not representable as a matrix product. For example, let $\alpha(x) = y = [y_1 y_2]'$ where

$y_1 = \sum_{i=1}^{n} x_i^2$ and $y_2 = x_1 x_2 \cdots x_n$.

In this example there is *no* matrix of order $2 \times n$ such that

$\alpha(x) = \mathbf{A}x$ for all x.

However, the following theorem can be proved.

Theorem Let $\alpha(\cdot)$ be a transformation sending column n-tuples into column m-tuples. A $(m \times n)$ matrix $\mathbf{A}$ exists such that

$$\alpha(x) = \mathbf{A}x \quad \text{for all } x \tag{A2.14a}$$

if and only if $\alpha(\cdot)$ is a *linear* transformation, that is

$$\alpha(k_1 x_1 + k_2 x_2) = k_1 \alpha(x_1) + k_2 \alpha(x_2) \tag{A2.14b}$$

for all real numbers k_1, k_2 and all column n-tuples x_1, x_2. In this case, the jth column of $\mathbf{A}$ is $\alpha(\delta^{(j)})$, where $\delta^{(j)}$ is the column n-tuple with a 1 in the jth position and 0s elsewhere.

Proof If (A2.14a) holds, then (A2.14b) follows by (A2.5). Suppose conversely that (A2.14b) holds. Define $\mathbf{A}$ to have jth column $\alpha(\delta^{(j)})$, $j = 1, \ldots, n$. Then (A2.14a) holds for $x = \delta^{(j)}$, $j = 1, \ldots, n$. Now any $x = [x_1 \cdots x_n]'$ is representable as $\sum_{j=1}^{n} x_j \delta^{(j)}$ and by (A2.14b)

$$\alpha(x) = \alpha\left(\textstyle\sum_{j=1}^{n} x_j \delta^{(j)}\right) = \textstyle\sum_{j=1}^{n} x_j \alpha(\delta^{(j)})$$
$$= \textstyle\sum_{j=1}^{n} x_j \mathbf{A}\delta^{(j)} = \mathbf{A} \textstyle\sum_{j=1}^{n} x_j \delta^{(j)} = \mathbf{A}x.$$

A2.5.1 Iterated Transformations

Let A be $(m \times n)$, B be $(n \times r)$, and x be $(r \times 1)$ and consider the matrix identity

$$\mathbf{A}(\mathbf{B}x) = (\mathbf{AB})x. \tag{A2.15}$$

The left-hand side can be interpreted as follows: the r-tuple x is sent by $\mathbf{B}$ into the n-tuple $\mathbf{B}x$ which in turn is sent into the m-tuple $\mathbf{A}(\mathbf{B}x)$. Schematically,

$$\underset{(r\text{-tuple})}{x} \xrightarrow{\mathbf{B}} \underset{(n\text{-tuple})}{(\mathbf{B}x)} \xrightarrow{\mathbf{A}} \underset{(m\text{-tuple})}{\mathbf{A}(\mathbf{B}x)}.$$

The right-hand side of (A2.15) says that this iterated procedure can be combined into one step that sends the r-tuple directly, by an $(m \times r)$ matrix, into an m-tuple. This $(m \times r)$ matrix is $(\mathbf{AB})$. Schematically,

$$\underset{(r\text{-tuple})}{x} \xrightarrow{\mathbf{AB}} \underset{(m\text{-tuple})}{(\mathbf{AB})x}$$

A2.5.2 Inverse Transformations

A matrix $\mathbf{A}$ of order $(m \times n)$ can be regarded as a function that sends n-tuples $\boldsymbol{x}$ *into* m-tuples $\mathbf{A}\boldsymbol{x}$. The function is said to be *onto* if for every $\boldsymbol{y}$ there is at least one $\boldsymbol{x}$ such that $\mathbf{A}\boldsymbol{x} = \boldsymbol{y}$. The function $\mathbf{A}$ can only be onto if $m \leq n$. The function $\mathbf{A}$ is said to be *one-to-one* if $\mathbf{A}$ always sends distinct $\boldsymbol{x}$s into distinct $\boldsymbol{y}$s. The function $\mathbf{A}$ can only be one-to-one if $m \geq n$. When $m = n$ the function $\mathbf{A}$ which sends n-tuples into m-tuples can possibly be both one-to-one and onto. In this case it has an *inverse function* which we shall denote α^{-1} and which has the properties

$$\alpha^{-1}(\mathbf{A}\boldsymbol{x}) = \boldsymbol{x} \quad \text{for all } \boldsymbol{x}, \tag{A2.16}$$

$$\mathbf{A}\alpha^{-1}(\boldsymbol{y}) = \boldsymbol{y} \quad \text{for all } \boldsymbol{y}. \tag{A2.17}$$

Conversely, if there is a function α^{-1} with these properties, then $\mathbf{A}$ is one-to-one and onto, that is, having an inverse function is equivalent to being one-to-one and onto. If the matrix $\mathbf{A}$ is nonsingular, then its inverse matrix $\mathbf{A}^{-1}$ gives a function inverse to the function $\mathbf{A}$, that is, $\alpha^{-1}(\boldsymbol{y}) = \mathbf{A}^{-1}\boldsymbol{y}$ satisfies (A2.16) and (A2.17), as is easily verified. According to the following theorem, the function $\mathbf{A}$ is both one-to-one and onto only in this case.

Theorem The function $\mathbf{A}$ carrying $\boldsymbol{x}$ into $\mathbf{A}\boldsymbol{x}$ is both one-to-one and onto (has an inverse function) if and only if the matrix $\mathbf{A}$ is nonsingular. In this case, the matrix $\mathbf{A}^{-1}$ gives the inverse function.

Proof Suppose $\mathbf{A}$ has an inverse function α^{-1}. It can be shown that α^{-1} must be linear in the sense of (A2.14b). Therefore there is a matrix, which we label $\mathbf{A}^{-1}$, such that

$$\alpha^{-1}(\boldsymbol{y}) = \mathbf{A}^{-1}\boldsymbol{y} \quad \text{for all } \boldsymbol{y}. \tag{A2.18}$$

It remains to show that this matrix $\mathbf{A}^{-1}$ satisfies our earlier definition. From (A2.16), (A2.17), and (A2.18) we have that

$$(\mathbf{A}^{-1}\mathbf{A})\boldsymbol{x} = \mathbf{A}^{-1}(\mathbf{A}\boldsymbol{x}) = \alpha^{-1}(\mathbf{A}\boldsymbol{x}) = \boldsymbol{x} \quad \text{for all } \boldsymbol{x},$$

$$(\mathbf{A}\mathbf{A}^{-1})\boldsymbol{y} = \mathbf{A}(\mathbf{A}^{-1}\boldsymbol{y}) = \mathbf{A}\alpha^{-1}(\boldsymbol{y}) = \boldsymbol{y} \quad \text{for all } \boldsymbol{y}.$$

Now the only transformation that sends every n-tuple into itself is the identity transformation, represented by $\mathbf{I}$, so that we have

$$\mathbf{A}^{-1}\mathbf{A} = \mathbf{I}, \qquad \mathbf{A}\mathbf{A}^{-1} = \mathbf{I}.$$

Thus our previous definition of $\mathbf{A}^{-1}$ is satisfied.

A2.6 Linear Combinations of Vectors, Rank of a Matrix

A2.6.1 Linear Combinations

Let $\boldsymbol{w}_1, \boldsymbol{w}_2, \ldots, \boldsymbol{w}_n$ be n column vectors each having m components. If a column vector $\boldsymbol{w}$ is expressible as

$$\boldsymbol{w} = c_1\boldsymbol{w}_1 + c_2\boldsymbol{w}_2 + \cdots + c_n\boldsymbol{w}_n$$

for suitably chosen real numbers $c_1, c_2, \ldots, c_n$, then $\boldsymbol{w}$ is said to be a linear combination of vectors $[\boldsymbol{w}_1, \ldots, \boldsymbol{w}_n]$. This could be written: $\boldsymbol{w} = \mathbf{W}\boldsymbol{c}$ where $\mathbf{W}$ is the $(m \times n)$ matrix with columns $\boldsymbol{w}_1, \boldsymbol{w}_2, \ldots, \boldsymbol{w}_n$, and $\boldsymbol{c}$ is the $(n \times 1)$ column vector $[c_1, c_2, \ldots, c_n]^t$.

A2.6.2 Rank of a Set of Vectors

Let S be a set of column vectors each with m components. The number of vectors belonging to S may be finite or infinite. We are concerned with the extent to which the vectors in S may be expressed as linear combinations of one another. Of course any vector is a linear combination of itself: $\boldsymbol{w} = c_1\boldsymbol{w}$ for $c_1 = 1$.

If no vector in S can be written as a linear combination of other vectors in S, then the vectors in S are said to be *linearly independent*. It can be shown that in this case there are at most m vectors in S. It is not hard to see that the columns of a matrix $\mathbf{W}$ are linearly independent if and only if

$$\mathbf{W}c = \mathit{0} \quad \text{implies} \quad c = \mathit{0}.$$

(Technically, we require the convention that if $\mathit{0}$ is the only vector in S, then we shall not consider the vectors in S linearly independent.)

In general, we may ask the following question: What is the smallest number of vectors we can choose from S such that every vector in S can be expressed as a linear combination of the chosen vectors? This number is called the rank of S. It can be shown that if T is a subset of S, if every vector in S but not in T can be expressed as a linear combination of vectors in T, and if the vectors in T are linearly independent, then the number of vectors in T is exactly the rank of S. (It is at least the rank by the definition of rank.) The subset T is not unique, but the number of vectors in T will be unique. It can be shown that if the vectors in S have m components, then the rank of S is *at most m*.

Instead of column vectors we could have used row vectors throughout.

Example Let

$$w_1 = \begin{bmatrix} 0 \\ 1 \end{bmatrix}, \quad w_2 = \begin{bmatrix} 1 \\ 1 \end{bmatrix}, \quad w_3 = \begin{bmatrix} 2 \\ 1 \end{bmatrix}$$

and let set $S = \{w_1, w_2, w_3\}$. Since $w_3 = -w_1 + 2w_2$, the rank of S is at most 2. Since w_2 is not a multiplier of w_1 we can let $T = [w_1, w_2]$. Notice also that $w_1 = 2w_2 - w_3$, so that we could have taken $T = [w_2, w_3]$. The subset T is not unique but the number of vectors in T will always be 2. The rank of S is 2.

A2.6.3 Rank of a Matrix

Let $\mathbf{A}$ be a given $(m \times n)$ matrix. Consider the set of n columns of $\mathbf{A}$, each with m components. The rank of this set, that is, the maximum number of linearly independent columns of $\mathbf{A}$, is called the *column rank* of $\mathbf{A}$. Next, consider the set of m row vectors of $\mathbf{A}$, each with n components. The rank of this set, the maximum number of linearly independent rows of $\mathbf{A}$, is called the *row rank* of $\mathbf{A}$.

Theorem For any matrix $\mathbf{A}$, the row rank equals the column rank.

Because of this theorem we can refer simply to *the rank* of $\mathbf{A}$ without specifying "row" or "column."

Observe that if $\mathbf{A}$ is $(m \times n)$ the rank of $\mathbf{A}$ is at most the smaller of the two numbers m and n (Why?).

Theorem Let $\mathbf{A}$ be a square matrix of order $(n \times n)$. The inverse of $\mathbf{A}$ exists if and only if $\mathbf{A}$ has rank n.

A2.7 Positive-Definite and Positive-Semidefinite Matrices and Quadratic Forms

A $(n \times n)$ matrix $\mathbf{A}$ is said to be symmetric if $a_{ij} = a_{ji}$ for all i, j, or equivalently, if $\mathbf{A} = \mathbf{A}'$. For any symmetric matrix $\mathbf{A}$ of order $(n \times n)$, the *quadratic form* of $\mathbf{A}$ is defined as the real valued function $Q_A(\cdot)$ defined on column n-tuples by

$$Q_A(x) \equiv x'\mathbf{A}x = \sum_{i,j=1}^{n} x_i a_{ij} x_j = \sum_{i=1}^{n} a_{ii} x_i^2 + 2 \sum_{i=1}^{n} \sum_{j=1}^{i-1} a_{ij} x_i x_j, \tag{A2.19}$$

where the last equality follows from the symmetry of $\mathbf{A}$. The reason for taking $\mathbf{A}$ to be symmetric is that for $\mathbf{B}(n \times n)$ but nonsymmetric, $x'\mathbf{B}x$ can be rewritten in the form $x'\mathbf{A}x$ with $\mathbf{A}$ symmetric. Specifically, if $\mathbf{A} = \frac{1}{2}(\mathbf{B} + \mathbf{B}')$, then $\mathbf{A}$ is symmetric and $x'\mathbf{A}x = x'\mathbf{B}x$ for all x.

Let $\mathbf{A}$ be a $(n \times n)$ symmetric matrix and let x be a $(n \times 1)$ vector. The $\mathbf{A}$ is said to be positive-semidefinite if

$$x^t\mathbf{A}x \geq 0 \quad \text{for all } x; \tag{A2.20a}$$

$\mathbf{A}$ said to be positive-definite if

$$x^t\mathbf{A}x > 0 \quad \text{for all } x \neq 0. \tag{A.20b}$$

Only symmetric matrices will be called positive-definite or positive-semidefinite.

The following theorems on positive-definite and positive-semidefinite matrices will be required in the applications; proofs can be found in the literature. [Some hints are given in brackets.]

1. If $\mathbf{A}$ is any matrix, then $\mathbf{A}^t\mathbf{A}$ is positive-semidefinite.

$[x^t\mathbf{A}^t\mathbf{A}x = \sum y_i^2 \geq 0 \quad \text{where} \quad y = \mathbf{A}x.]$

2. A positive-semidefinite matrix $\mathbf{B}$ is positive-definite if and only if it is nonsingular.
3. If $\mathbf{A}$ is a $s \times r$ matrix of rank $r \leq s$, then $\mathbf{A}^t\mathbf{A}$ is positive-definite symmetric.

$[x^t\mathbf{A}^t\mathbf{A}x = \sum y_i^2 = 0 \Rightarrow y = \mathbf{A}x = 0 \Rightarrow x = 0.]$

4. If $\mathbf{C}$ is a $(r \times r)$ positive-semidefinite matrix and $\mathbf{B}$ is a $(p \times r)$ matrix, then $\mathbf{BCB}^t$ is positive-semidefinite. If, in addition, $\mathbf{C}$ is positive-definite and $\mathbf{B}$ is of rank p, then $\mathbf{BCB}^t$ is positive-definite.

$[x^t\mathbf{BCB}^tx = (\mathbf{B}^tx)^t\mathbf{C}(\mathbf{B}^tx) \geq 0$. Under the additional hypotheses,
$x^t\mathbf{BCB}^tx = 0 \Rightarrow \mathbf{B}^tx = 0 \Rightarrow x = 0.]$

5. If $\mathbf{C}$ is positive-definite, then $\mathbf{C}^{-1}$ is positive-definite.

$[x^t\mathbf{C}^{-1}x = (\mathbf{C}^{-1}x)^t\mathbf{C}(\mathbf{C}^{-1}x) \geq 0$ and if $= 0$ then $\mathbf{C}^{-1}x = 0$ and therefore $x = 0.]$

6. If $\mathbf{C}$ is positive-definite and $\mathbf{D}$ is formed by deleting any number of columns of $\mathbf{C}$ together with the corresponding rows, then $\mathbf{D}$ is positive-definite.
$[x^t\mathbf{D}x = w^t\mathbf{C}w$ where w is obtained from x by inserting zeros for deleted rows.]

7. If $\mathbf{C}$ is positive-definite, there exist nonsingular matrices $\mathbf{B}$ and $\mathbf{U} = (\mathbf{B}^t)^{-1}$ such that

$$\mathbf{BCB}^t = \mathrm{I}, \qquad \mathbf{U}^t\mathbf{I}\mathbf{U} = \mathbf{C}.$$

8. If the $r \times r$ matrix $\mathbf{D}$ is positive-definite and the $r \times r$ matrix $\mathbf{S}$ is positive-semidefinite, then there exists a nonsingular matrix $\mathbf{T}$ such that $\mathbf{TDT}^t$ is the identity matrix and $\mathbf{TST}^t$ is a diagonal matrix with all elements nonnegative and with strictly positive elements equal in number to the rank of $\mathbf{S}$.

Remark This remark is for motivation only. The reader may omit it if he or she does not understand it. In probabilistic applications, if $\tilde{w} = [\tilde{w}_1, \tilde{w}_2, \ldots, \tilde{w}_n]^t$ is a random vector its variance matrix will be a symmetric matrix, $\mathbf{A}$, say, where $a_{ij} \equiv V[\tilde{w}_1 \tilde{w}_j]$. Now if we let

$$\tilde{v} = \mathbf{B}\tilde{w} \quad \text{where} \quad \begin{array}{l} v \text{ is } (m \times 1), \\ \mathbf{B} \text{ is } (m \times n), \\ w \text{ is } (n \times 1), \end{array}$$

then the variance matrix of $\tilde{v}$ can be shown to be $\mathbf{BAB}^t$. In particular, if $\mathbf{B}$ is $1 \times n$, that is, if $\mathbf{B}$ is some row vector x^t, then

$$\tilde{v} = x^t\tilde{w} = \textstyle\sum_{i=1}^n x_i\tilde{w}_i$$

and $\tilde{v}$ is a scalar rv. The variance of $\tilde{v}$ is then the single *nonnegative* number $x^t\mathbf{A}x$. In this manner we see why a variance matrix is always positive-semidefinite and why it is natural to consider expressions of the form $\mathbf{BAB}^t$.

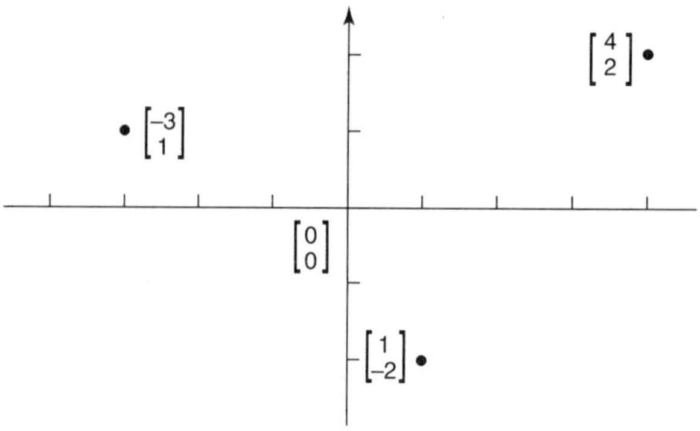

Figure A2.1
Vectors in two-space

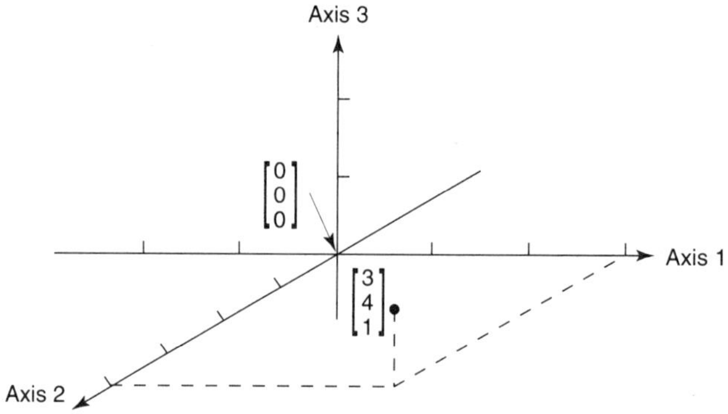

Figure A2.2
Three-space

A2.8 Geometrical Representation of Vectors and Quadratic Forms

A2.8.1 Geometrical Representation of Vectors

In two-space imagine an origin and two orthogonal axes along which units of measurement are marked off in positive and negative directions (see figure A2.1). Vectors of two components can be identified as points in this two-space as depicted. The vector with both coordinates 0 is identified as the origin. Similarly in three-space we can imagine an origin and three orthogonal axes along which units of measurement are marked off in positive and negative directions (see figure A2.2). Vectors of 3 components can be identified as points in this three-space. Although we cannot physically "see" a space of four or more dimensions, we can imagine a vector with n components as being represented as a point in n-space. Either row vectors or column vector may be represented in this way, though it is not natural to represent both in the same n-space.

A2.8.2 Geometrical Representation of Quadratic Forms

Let a quadratic form be given by a symmetric matrix $\mathbf{A}$ of order $(n \times n)$. We shall consider the set (or "locus") S of all $(n \times 1)$ vectors $\boldsymbol{x}$ such that

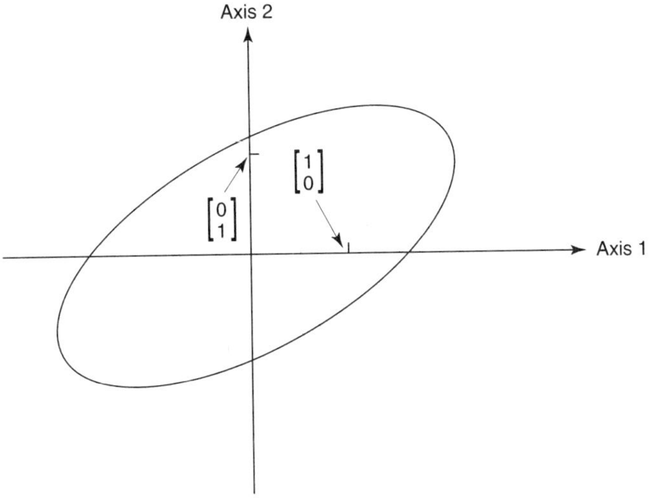

Figure A2.3
Elliptical contour of positive definite quadratic form

$$Q_A(\boldsymbol{x}) = \boldsymbol{x}^t\mathbf{A}\boldsymbol{x} = 1. \tag{A2.21}$$

The set S is symmetric with respect to the origin (i.e., $\boldsymbol{x} \in S \Rightarrow (-\boldsymbol{x}) \in S$), since $Q_A(-\boldsymbol{x}) = Q_A(\boldsymbol{x})$. Furthermore, if the constant on the right-hand side of (A2.21) were changed from 1 to any positive number k, the resulting locus would be "proportionately similar" to the original one, since

$$Q_A(\boldsymbol{x}) = 1 \quad \Leftrightarrow \quad Q_A(\sqrt{k}\boldsymbol{x}) = k.$$

If $\mathbf{A}$ is positive-definite then by (A2.20b), $Q_A(\boldsymbol{x}) > 0$ for all $\boldsymbol{x} \neq 0$, and therefore there exists a unique number ρ, depending on $\boldsymbol{x}$, such that $Q_A(\rho\boldsymbol{x}) = 1$. Geometrically this asserts that if $\mathbf{A}$ is positive-definite then any ray from the origin pierces S in one and only one point, and therefore S is a surface that completely encloses the origin. The converse also holds, so that the surface S given by (A2.21) encloses the origin if and only if $\mathbf{A}$ is positive-definite.

If $\mathbf{A}$ is (2×2), the set S of all $\boldsymbol{x} = [x_1\, x_2]$ such that

$$Q_A(\boldsymbol{x}) = \boldsymbol{x}^t\mathbf{A}\boldsymbol{x} = a_{11}x_1^2 + 2a_{12}x_1x_2 + a_{22}x_2^2 = 1$$

can be represented as a locus in a two-space. Consider, for example, a two-space comprising all points in the plane of a sheet of paper. Now suppose we arbitrarily choose:

1. A point to be designated as the *origin*.
2. Two orthogonal axes, labelled Axis 1 and Axis 2.
3. A unit of measurement.

In terms of this so-called "coordinate system" a one-to-one correspondence can be set up between a column vector $\boldsymbol{x}$ and a point p in this plane. In particular the set S can now be represented as a locus L of points whose $\boldsymbol{x}$ representations satisfy the algebraic requirement $Q_A(\boldsymbol{x}) = 1$. This locus of points L is recognized to be a two-dimensional conic. The locus is an ellipse if and only if $\mathbf{A}$ is positive-definite (see figure A2.3).

A (3×3) positive-definite matrix $\mathbf{A}$ gives rise similarly to an ellipsoid in three-space, and a $(n \times n)$ positive-definite matrix $\mathbf{A}$ to the generalization of this in n-space.

As already remarked, the set of $\boldsymbol{x}$ such that $Q_A(\boldsymbol{x}) = k$, $k \geq 0$, is "proportionately similar" to the set of $\boldsymbol{x}$ such that $Q_A(\boldsymbol{x}) = 1$. Thus, we see that if $\mathbf{A}$ is positive-definite of order $(n \times n)$, then the contours of the quadratic form of $\mathbf{A}$ are proportionately similar generalized ellipses in n-space.

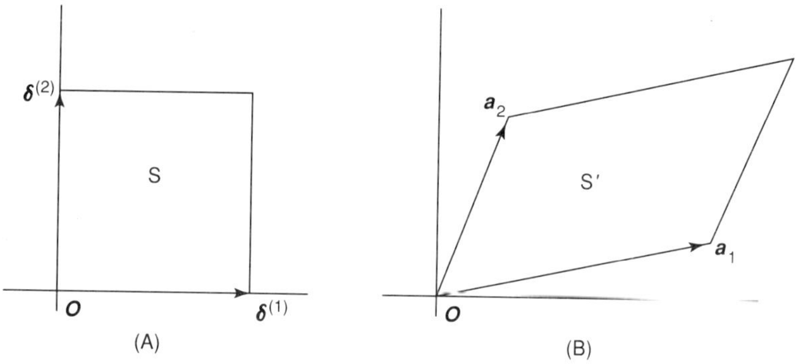

Figure A2.4
Linear transformation of a square

A2.9 Determinants

In most treatments of determinants found in algebra books, the determinant of a matrix is first defined in a mysterious way and then this notion is used for solving linear equations and for finding the inverse of a matrix. Determinants are not needed for these purposes since there are other more efficient ways of inverting a matrix; however, determinants are encountered in this text when changes of variables are made in multiple integrals. Hence the approach to determinants we shall take emphasizes at the outset the interpretation of a determinant as a (signed) volume in n space.

Suppose we make a transformation sending a column n-tuple $\boldsymbol{x}$ into a column n-tuple $\boldsymbol{y}$ by the transformation

$$\boldsymbol{y} = \mathbf{A}(\boldsymbol{x} - \boldsymbol{b}) \tag{A2.22}$$

for some fixed column n-tuple $\boldsymbol{b}$. Then the set of points constituting an n-dimensional set in n-space is sent into another n-dimensional set. The ratio of the volume of the transformed set to the volume of the original set is a number that depends only on the matrix $\mathbf{A}$ and it is the absolute value of the determinant of $\mathbf{A}$.

More precisely, in two-space consider the square (a two-dimensional "cube") two of whose sides are $\boldsymbol{0}$ to $\boldsymbol{\delta}^{(1)} = [1 \quad 0]^t$ and $\boldsymbol{0}$ to $\boldsymbol{\delta}^{(2)} = [0 \quad 1]^t$. Call this set S (see figure A2.4A). Assuming $\boldsymbol{b} = 0$ in (A2.22), the transformed set consisting of all points $\mathbf{A}\boldsymbol{x}$ where $\boldsymbol{x} \in S$ is denoted in figure A2.4B by S'. Segment $(\boldsymbol{0}, \boldsymbol{\delta}^{(1)})$ goes over to $(\boldsymbol{0}, \boldsymbol{a}_1)$ and segment $(\boldsymbol{0}, \boldsymbol{\delta}^{(2)})$ goes over to $(\boldsymbol{0}, \boldsymbol{a}_2)$, where $\boldsymbol{a}_1$ and $\boldsymbol{a}_2$ are the first and second columns of $\mathbf{A}$. The set S' is a parallelogram. The determinant of $\mathbf{A}$, written $\det(\mathbf{A})$ or $\det(\boldsymbol{a}_1, \boldsymbol{a}_2)$, is defined as the area of S' provided the angle $(\boldsymbol{a}_1, \boldsymbol{0}, \boldsymbol{a}_2)$ is less than 180° counterclockwise, as in figure A2.4B. If the points $\boldsymbol{a}_1$ and $\boldsymbol{a}_2$ must be interchanged to satisfy this condition on the angle, then we define

$$\det(\boldsymbol{a}_2, \boldsymbol{a}_1) \equiv -\det(\boldsymbol{a}_1, \boldsymbol{a}_2) = -[\text{area of } S']$$

to indicate the change in the orientation.

With the above motivation in mind, we now characterize the real valued function $\det(\cdot)$ on $n \times n$ matrices as follows:

1. $\det(\mathbf{I}) = 1$.
2. If $\mathbf{A}$ is modified to $\mathbf{A}^*$ by the interchange of two adjacent columns then $\det(\mathbf{A}) = -\det(\mathbf{A}^*)$.
3. $\det(k_1\boldsymbol{a}_1, k_2\boldsymbol{a}_2, \ldots, k_n\boldsymbol{a}_n) = k_1 k_2 \cdots k_n \det(\boldsymbol{a}_1, \boldsymbol{a}_2, \ldots, \boldsymbol{a}_n)$.
4. $\det(\boldsymbol{a}_1' + \boldsymbol{a}_1'', \boldsymbol{a}_2, \ldots, \boldsymbol{a}_n) = \det(\boldsymbol{a}_1', \boldsymbol{a}_2, \ldots, \boldsymbol{a}_n) + \det(\boldsymbol{a}_1'', \boldsymbol{a}_2, \ldots, \boldsymbol{a}_n)$.
5. If $\mathbf{A}$ has two identical columns then $\det(\mathbf{A}) = 0$.

We are using the notation $\det(\boldsymbol{a}_1, \boldsymbol{a}_2, \ldots, \boldsymbol{a}_n) = \det \mathbf{A}$ when $\mathbf{A}$ has columns $\boldsymbol{a}_1, \boldsymbol{a}_2, \ldots, \boldsymbol{a}_n$. From these properties it is not difficult to prove that

$$\det(\mathbf{A}) \equiv \sum \pm a_{1j_1} a_{2j_2} \cdots a_{nj_n} \tag{A2.23}$$

where the second subscripts $j_1, j_2, \ldots, j_n$ run through all the $n!$ possible permutations of the numbers $1, 2, \ldots, n$, and where the sign of each term is $+$ or $-$ depending on whether the corresponding permutation is even or odd. For example, the permutation $(3, 2, 1, 4)$ is odd because starting with $(1, 2, 3, 4)$ it arises from an odd number of adjacent interchanges, to wit: $1 \leftrightarrow 2$, $1 \leftrightarrow 3$, $2 \leftrightarrow 3$. In particular, $\mathbf{A}$ is (2×2)

$$\det(\mathbf{A}) = a_{11}a_{22} - a_{12}a_{21}. \tag{A2.24}$$

We shall indicate the proof of (A2.24) since the more general case follows in an analogous manner.

$$\begin{aligned}
&(1) \quad \det[\boldsymbol{a}_1, \boldsymbol{a}_2] = \det[a_{11}\boldsymbol{\delta}^{(1)} + a_{12}\boldsymbol{\delta}^{(2)}, a_{21}\boldsymbol{\delta}^{(1)} + a_{22}\boldsymbol{\delta}^{(2)}] \\
&\qquad = \det[a_{11}\boldsymbol{\delta}^{(1)}, a_{21}\boldsymbol{\delta}^{(1)}] + \det[a_{11}\boldsymbol{\delta}^{(1)}, a_{22}\boldsymbol{\delta}^{(2)}] \\
&(2) \qquad + \det[a_{12}\boldsymbol{\delta}^{(2)}, a_{21}\boldsymbol{\delta}^{(1)}] + \det[a_{12}\boldsymbol{\delta}^{(2)}, a_{22}\boldsymbol{\delta}^{(2)}] \\
&\qquad = a_{11}a_{21} \det[\boldsymbol{\delta}^{(1)}, \boldsymbol{\delta}^{(1)}] + a_{11}a_{21} \det[\boldsymbol{\delta}^{(1)}, \boldsymbol{\delta}^{(2)}] \\
&(3) \qquad + a_{12}a_{21} \det[\boldsymbol{\delta}^{(2)}, \boldsymbol{\delta}^{(1)}] + a_{12}a_{21} \det[\boldsymbol{\delta}^{(2)}, \boldsymbol{\delta}^{(2)}] \\
&\qquad = a_{11}a_{21}(0) + a_{11}a_{22}(1) + a_{12}a_{21}(-1) + a_{12}a_{22}(0) \\
&\qquad = a_{11}a_{22} - a_{12}a_{21},
\end{aligned}$$

where (1) uses properties 4 and 2; (2) uses property 3; (3) uses properties 1, 2, and 5.

From the motivation of a determinant as a ratio of two volumes one would expect the result

$$\det(\mathbf{AB}) = \det(\mathbf{A})\det(\mathbf{B}) \tag{A2.25}$$

which is indeed the case. Heuristically, a set S in n-space

$$\text{Set } S \xrightarrow{\mathbf{B}} \text{Set } S' \xrightarrow{\mathbf{A}} \text{Set } S''$$
$$\mathbf{AB}$$

is taken by $\mathbf{B}$ into set S', which in turn is taken by $\mathbf{A}$ into set S''. Also, set S is taken by $\mathbf{AB}$ directly into S''. Hence

$$\begin{aligned}
\det(AB) &= \frac{\operatorname{vol}(S'')}{\operatorname{vol}(S)} = \frac{\operatorname{vol}(S'')}{\operatorname{vol}(S')} \cdot \frac{\operatorname{vol}(S')}{\operatorname{vol}(S)} \\
&= \det(\mathbf{A})\det(\mathbf{B}).
\end{aligned}$$

A formal proof can be given using (A2.23).

The following can now be proved:

1. $\det(\mathbf{A}^{-1}) = [\det(\mathbf{A})]^{-1}$ if $\mathbf{A}^{-1}$ exists.
2. $\det(\mathbf{A}^t) = \det(\mathbf{A})$.
3. $\det(\mathbf{P}) = \pm 1$ if $\mathbf{PP}^t = \mathbf{I}$.
4. If $\mathbf{A}$ is $(n \times n)$ then $\det(\mathbf{A}) \neq 0 \Leftrightarrow \mathbf{A}$ is nonsingular.

Result 1 follows easily from (A2.25). Result 2 is derived from (A2.23). Result 3 follows from (A2.25) and result 2. Result 4 follows from properties 4 and 5 characterizing the $\det(\cdot)$ function.

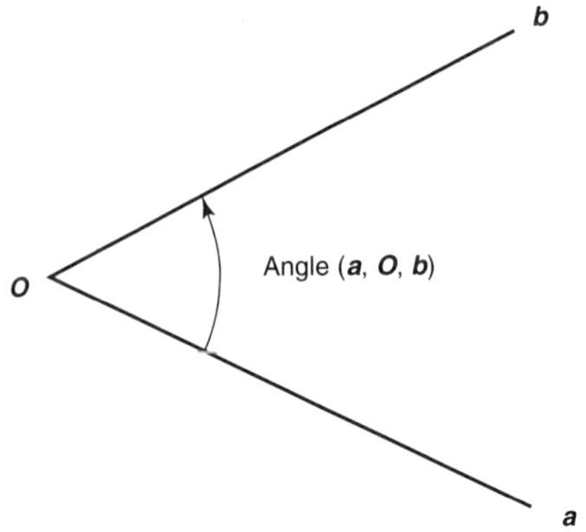

Figure A2.5
Angle between two vectors

A2.10 Inner Products, Distance, and Orthogonality

This section discusses further aspects of the geometrical representation of n-vectors as points in n-space. We use column vectors for definiteness.

A2.10.1 Distance and Norm

The *distance* from the origin $\boldsymbol{0} = [0 \quad 0 \cdots 0]'$ to the point $\boldsymbol{a} = [a_1\, a_2 \cdots a_n]'$ is defined as

$$\|\boldsymbol{a}\| = [\textstyle\sum_{i=1}^{n} a_i^2]^{1/2} = (\boldsymbol{a}'\boldsymbol{a})^{1/2}. \tag{A2.26}$$

The square of this distance is

$$\|\boldsymbol{a}\|^2 = \boldsymbol{a}'\boldsymbol{a}.$$

The symbol $\|\boldsymbol{a}\|$ is read "the *norm* of $\boldsymbol{a}$". The student should specialize and interpret this and other definitions to follow in two-space.

A2.10.2 Inner Product and Orthogonality

The *inner product* of two vectors $\boldsymbol{a} = [a_1 \cdots a_n]'$ and $\boldsymbol{b} = [b_1 \cdots b_n]'$ is defined to be the real number (scalar)

$$(\boldsymbol{a}, \boldsymbol{b}) \equiv \boldsymbol{a}'\boldsymbol{b} = \boldsymbol{b}'\boldsymbol{a} = \textstyle\sum_{i=1}^{n} a_i b_i. \tag{A2.27}$$

If $n = 2$ or 3 it can be shown by trigonometry that

$$(\boldsymbol{a}, \boldsymbol{b}) = \boldsymbol{a}'\boldsymbol{b} = \|\boldsymbol{a}\|\ \|\boldsymbol{b}\| \text{ cosine } [\text{angle } (\boldsymbol{a}, \boldsymbol{0}, \boldsymbol{b})]$$

(see figure A2.5).

For any n it can be shown that

$$-1 \leq \frac{(\boldsymbol{a}, \boldsymbol{b})}{\|\boldsymbol{a}\|\ \|\boldsymbol{b}\|} \leq 1 \tag{A2.28}$$

and equality holds on one side or the other if and only if $\boldsymbol{a}$ and $\boldsymbol{b}$ lie on the same line through the origin, that is, $\boldsymbol{b} = k\boldsymbol{a}$ for some k. If $(\boldsymbol{a}, \boldsymbol{b}) = 0$ then for $n = 2$ or 3, angle $(\boldsymbol{a}, \boldsymbol{0}, \boldsymbol{b})$ is 90°, or a right angle; equivalently, the line segment $\boldsymbol{0}$ to $\boldsymbol{a}$ is orthogonal to line segment $\boldsymbol{0}$ to $\boldsymbol{b}$. For any n, if $(\boldsymbol{a}, \boldsymbol{b}) = 0$ we say $\boldsymbol{a}$ and $\boldsymbol{b}$ are orthogonal.

The following two important properties of orthogonality are easily verified:

1. If $\boldsymbol{y}$ is orthogonal to $\boldsymbol{x}_1, \boldsymbol{x}_2, \ldots, \boldsymbol{x}_n$ then $\boldsymbol{y}$ is orthogonal to any linear combination of the $\boldsymbol{x}$'s.

2. If $\boldsymbol{x}_1, \boldsymbol{x}_2, \ldots, \boldsymbol{x}_n$ are nonzero vectors all orthogonal to each other then they are linearly independent.

Assertion 1 follows from $(\boldsymbol{y}, \sum_i c_i \boldsymbol{x}_i) = \boldsymbol{y}^t(\sum_i c_i \boldsymbol{x}_i) = \sum_i c_i \boldsymbol{y}^t \boldsymbol{x} = \sum_i c_i \cdot 0 = 0$. To prove assertion 2, suppose $\boldsymbol{x}_n$ were a linear combination of $\boldsymbol{x}_1, \ldots, \boldsymbol{x}_{n-1}$, say, $\boldsymbol{x}_n = c_1 \boldsymbol{x}_1 + \cdots + c_{n-1}\boldsymbol{x}_{n-1}$. Premultiplying both sides by $\boldsymbol{x}_n$ gives

$$\boldsymbol{x}_n^t \boldsymbol{x}_n = c_1 \boldsymbol{x}_n^t \boldsymbol{x}_1 + \cdots + c_{n-1} \boldsymbol{x}_n^t \boldsymbol{x}_{n-1} = 0.$$

But this implies $\boldsymbol{x}_n = 0$ contrary to our assumption.

A2.10.3 Orthogonal Matrices

A square matrix $\mathbf{P}$ is said to be orthogonal if

$$\mathbf{P}\mathbf{P}^t = \mathbf{I}. \tag{A2.29}$$

If $\mathbf{P}$ is orthogonal then it follows easily that:

1. $\mathbf{P}^t = \mathbf{P}^{-1}$.
2. $\mathbf{P}^t\mathbf{P} = \mathbf{P}\mathbf{P}^t = \mathbf{I}$.
3. Each row of $\mathbf{P}$ has unit norm and any two distinct rows are orthogonal.
4. Each column of $\mathbf{P}$ has unit norm and any two distinct columns are orthogonal.
5. If $\mathbf{P}$ is $(n \times n)$ then $\mathbf{P}$ orthogonal $\Leftrightarrow \boldsymbol{x}_1^t \boldsymbol{x}_2 = (\mathbf{P}\boldsymbol{x}_1)^t(\mathbf{P}\boldsymbol{x}_2)$ for all $\boldsymbol{x}_1, \boldsymbol{x}_2$ of order $(n \times 1)$.

The last assertion says that an orthogonal $\mathbf{P}$ is characterized by the property that the inner product of two vectors is the same as the inner product of their transforms under $\mathbf{P}$, so that the transformation $\mathbf{P}$ leaves angles and distances invariant. In other words, a transformation leaving the origin fixed is "rigid" if and only if it is given by an orthogonal matrix. Rotations about the origin and reflections about hyperplanes through the origin and combinations thereof have this property. No other transformations do.

A2.11 Canonical Representation of Quadratic Forms

Consider again the geometrical representation of a quadratic form (section A2.8.2). If instead of having chosen the orthogonal axes 1 and 2 in figure A2.3 we had chosen axes 1* and 2* in figure A2.6 the physical point p would have one representation

$$\begin{bmatrix} x_1 \\ x_2 \end{bmatrix} \text{say,}$$

in terms of axes 1 and 2 and another representation,

$$\begin{bmatrix} y_1 \\ y_2 \end{bmatrix}^* \text{say,}$$

in terms of axes 1* and 2*. The algebraic relation connecting y_1 and y_2 with x_1 and x_2 would take the form

$$y_1 = p_{11}x_1 + p_{12}x_2$$

$$y_2 = p_{11}x_1 + p_{22}x_2$$

or

$$\boldsymbol{y} = \mathbf{P}\boldsymbol{x},$$

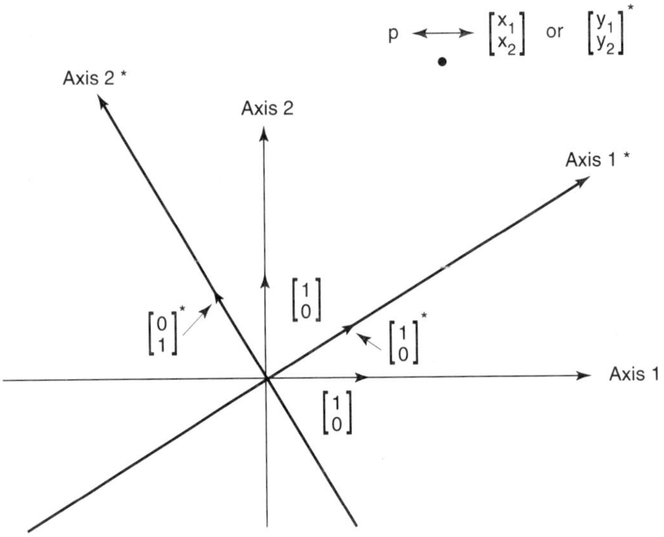

Figure A2.6
Orthogonal change of axes

where $\mathbf{P}$ is an orthogonal transformation. Since for an orthogonal matrix $\mathbf{P}^t = \mathbf{P}^{-1}$ it follows that

$$\boldsymbol{x} = \mathbf{P}^t\boldsymbol{y}.$$

The (physical) point p belongs to the locus L if and only if its representation $\boldsymbol{x}$, in terms of coordinate axes 1 and 2, is such that $\boldsymbol{x}^t\mathbf{A}\boldsymbol{x} = 1$. Hence in terms of coordinate axes 1* and 2* a point p belongs to L if and only if its $\boldsymbol{y}$ representation is such that

$$(\mathbf{P}^t\boldsymbol{y})^t\mathbf{A}(\mathbf{P}^t\boldsymbol{y}) = \boldsymbol{y}^t(\mathbf{P}\mathbf{A}\mathbf{P}^t)\boldsymbol{y} = 1.$$

If $\mathbf{A}$ is positive-definite, or equivalently if L is an ellipse, then $\mathbf{P}$ can be chosen (by choosing axes 1* and 2* to be the axes of the ellipse L) such that

$$\mathbf{P}\mathbf{A}\mathbf{P}^t = \begin{bmatrix} \lambda_1 & 0 \\ 0 & \lambda_2 \end{bmatrix}, \quad \lambda_1 \geq \lambda_2 > 0,$$

and therefore L consists of all points p whose $\boldsymbol{y}$ representations satisfy

$$\boldsymbol{y}^t\begin{bmatrix} \lambda_1 & 0 \\ 0 & \lambda_2 \end{bmatrix}\boldsymbol{y} = \lambda_1 y_1^2 + \lambda_2 y_2^2 = 1,$$

which is an ellipse in standardized or canonical form.

This discussion generalizes to n-space. Let $\mathbf{A}$ be positive-definite symmetric of order $(n \times n)$. Imagine in n-space that an orthogonal coordinate system has been chosen and define the natural one-to-one correspondence between a (physical) point p and a column n-tuple $\boldsymbol{x}$. The set of all n-tuples $\boldsymbol{x}$ such that

$$Q_A(\boldsymbol{x}) = \boldsymbol{x}^t\mathbf{A}\boldsymbol{x} = 1$$

is the representation of some locus of points in n-space and the locus is called an n-dimensional ellipse. There always exists an orthogonal matrix $\mathbf{P}$ such that

$$\mathbf{PAP}^t = \begin{bmatrix} \lambda_1 & & & 0 \\ & \lambda_2 & & \\ & & \ddots & \\ 0 & & & \lambda_n \end{bmatrix}, \quad \lambda_1 \geq \lambda_2 \geq \cdots \geq \lambda_n > 0, \tag{A2.30}$$

and if one chooses a new orthogonal coordinate system where the point p with original representation $\boldsymbol{x}$ is now represented by

$$\boldsymbol{y} = \mathbf{P}\boldsymbol{x} \quad \text{or} \quad \boldsymbol{x} = \mathbf{P}^t\boldsymbol{y}, \tag{A2.31}$$

then the locus L of points can be represented in the new coordinate system by

$$\boldsymbol{y}^t \begin{bmatrix} \lambda_1 & & & 0 \\ & \lambda_2 & & \\ & & \ddots & \\ 0 & & & \lambda_n \end{bmatrix} \boldsymbol{y} = \textstyle\sum_{i=1}^n \lambda_i y_i^2 = 1. \tag{A2.32}$$

The ellipse cuts axis 1* at the point p_1 whose representation is $\boldsymbol{y}_1 = [1/\sqrt{\lambda_1} \ \ 0 \ \ 0 \cdots 0]^t$ in the new coordinate system. This same point p_1 has representation

$$\boldsymbol{x}_1 = \mathbf{P}^t\boldsymbol{y}_1 = \mathbf{P}^t \begin{bmatrix} 1/\sqrt{\lambda_1} \\ 0 \\ 0 \\ \vdots \\ 0 \end{bmatrix}$$

in the old coordinate system. Thus the first column of $\mathbf{P}^t$, or equivalently the first row of $\mathbf{P}$, is merely $\sqrt{\lambda_1}\boldsymbol{x}_1$. It can be shown that

$$1/\lambda_1 = \boldsymbol{x}_1^t\boldsymbol{x}_1 = \max[\boldsymbol{x}^t\boldsymbol{x}]$$

where the maximum is taken over all $\boldsymbol{x}$ such that $\boldsymbol{x}^t\mathbf{A}\boldsymbol{x} = 1$.

More generally, the ellipse cuts axis i* at the point p_i whose representation in the new coordinate system is $\boldsymbol{y}_i$ consisting of 0s except for $1/\sqrt{\lambda_i}$ in the ith position. This same point p_i has representation

$$\boldsymbol{x}_i = \mathbf{P}^t\boldsymbol{y}_i$$

in the old coordinate system. Thus the ith column of $\mathbf{P}^t$, or equivalently the ith row of $\mathbf{P}$, is merely $\sqrt{\lambda_i}\boldsymbol{x}_i$. It can also be shown that

$$1/\lambda_i = \boldsymbol{x}_i^t\boldsymbol{x}_i = \max[\boldsymbol{x}^t\boldsymbol{x}]$$

where the maximum is taken over all $\boldsymbol{x}$ which are orthogonal to $\boldsymbol{x}_1, \boldsymbol{x}_2, \ldots, \boldsymbol{x}_{i-1}$ and which satisfy $\boldsymbol{x}^t\mathbf{A}\boldsymbol{x} = 1$.

A2.12 Characteristic Roots and Vectors

If $\mathbf{A}$ is positive-definite, then from (A2.30), remembering that $\mathbf{P}^t = \mathbf{P}^{-1}$ for an orthogonal matrix, we get

$$\mathbf{PA} = \mathbf{\Lambda P} \quad \text{or} \quad \mathbf{AP}^t = \mathbf{P}^t\mathbf{\Lambda} \tag{A2.33}$$

where $\mathbf{\Lambda}$ is the matrix with $\lambda_1, \ldots, \lambda_n$ down the main diagonal and zeros elsewhere. If we let $\boldsymbol{P}^{(j)}$ be the jth column vector of $\mathbf{P}^t$, then (A2.33) says that

$$\mathbf{A}\boldsymbol{P}^{(j)} = \lambda_j\boldsymbol{P}^{(j)}, \tag{A2.34}$$

or that $\mathbf{A}$ sends $\boldsymbol{P}^{(j)}$ into a scalar multiple of itself.

More generally, if $\mathbf{B}$ is a $(n \times n)$ matrix, if $\boldsymbol{v}$ is a non-$\boldsymbol{0}$ column n-tuple, if λ is a number, and if

$$\mathbf{B}\boldsymbol{v} = \lambda\boldsymbol{v} \tag{A2.35}$$

then λ is said to be an *eigenvalue*, $\boldsymbol{v}$ an *eigenvector*, and $(\lambda, \boldsymbol{v})$ an *eigenpair*. Observe that if $(\lambda, \boldsymbol{v})$ is an eigenpair of $\mathbf{B}$ so is $(\lambda, k\boldsymbol{v})$ for any number k.

If $(\lambda, \boldsymbol{v})$ is an eigenpair of $\mathbf{B}$ then from (A2.35)

$$(\mathbf{B} - \lambda\mathbf{I})\boldsymbol{v} = \boldsymbol{0}. \tag{A2.36}$$

If $(\mathbf{B} - \lambda\mathbf{I})$ were nonsingular, then the only $\boldsymbol{v}$ satisfying (A2.36) would be $\boldsymbol{v} = \boldsymbol{0}$. Hence, if λ is an eigenvalue then $(\mathbf{B} - \lambda\mathbf{I})$ is singular. The converse can also be shown to be true. Therefore, the problem of finding eigenvalues is equivalent to the problem of finding λ values that make $(\mathbf{B} - \lambda\mathbf{I})$ singular, which in turn is equivalent to finding λ values for which

$$\det(\mathbf{B} - \lambda\mathbf{I}) = 0. \tag{A2.37}$$

But now it is not hard to show that the left-hand side of the above equation is a polynomial of degree n in λ and therefore has at most n distinct roots. This proves that there are at most n distinct eigenvalues.

If $\mathbf{B}$ is symmetric it is not difficult to show that all the roots of equation (A2.37), that is, all eigenvalues, are real and not complex numbers.

The following assertion is easy to prove: if $\mathbf{A}$ is symmetric, if $(\lambda_1, \boldsymbol{v}_1)$ and $(\lambda_2, \boldsymbol{v}_2)$ are two eigenpairs, and if $\lambda_1 \neq \lambda_2$, then $\boldsymbol{v}_1$ is orthogonal to $\boldsymbol{v}_2$.

By hypothesis, $\mathbf{A}\boldsymbol{v}_1 = \lambda_1\boldsymbol{v}_1$ and $\mathbf{A}\boldsymbol{v}_2 = \lambda_2\boldsymbol{v}_2$. Premultiplying the first equation by $\boldsymbol{v}_2$, premultiplying the second equation by $\boldsymbol{v}_1^t$, and subtracting, gives the result that $\lambda_1\boldsymbol{v}_2^t\boldsymbol{v}_1 = \lambda_2\boldsymbol{v}_1^t\boldsymbol{v}_2$, or $(\lambda_1 - \lambda_2)\boldsymbol{v}_2^t\boldsymbol{v}_1 = 0$, from which the result follows.

An eigenvalue λ will be said to have multiplicity r (where $r \geq 1$) if the set of vectors $\boldsymbol{v}$ that satisfy

$$\mathbf{A}\boldsymbol{v} = \lambda\boldsymbol{v}$$

has rank r. In this case it is possible to find vectors $\boldsymbol{v}_1, \boldsymbol{v}_2, \ldots, \boldsymbol{v}_r$ orthogonal to each other such that

$$\mathbf{A}\boldsymbol{v}_k = \lambda\boldsymbol{v}_k, \qquad k = 1, 2, \ldots, r.$$

We wish now to show that if $\mathbf{A}$ is symmetric then by completely solving the eigenproblem we can very simply find an orthogonal matrix $\mathbf{P}$, say, such that $\mathbf{PAP}^t$ is a diagonal matrix (i.e., a matrix whose (i, j)th element is 0 whenever $i \neq j$). This is the way we can proceed. First, find all the eigenvalues, and for each eigenvalue of multiplicity r find r orthogonal associated eigenvectors. Happily, it turns out that the sum of multiplicities of the distinct eigenvalues equals n so that we can label the eigenpairs by $(\lambda_1, \boldsymbol{v}_1), (\lambda_2, \boldsymbol{v}_2), \ldots, (\lambda_n, \boldsymbol{v}_n)$ and we are assured that $\boldsymbol{v}_i$ is orthogonal to $\boldsymbol{v}_j$ if $i \neq j$. Since

$$\mathbf{A}\boldsymbol{v}_i = \lambda_i\boldsymbol{v}_i, \qquad i = 1, 2, \ldots, n$$

it is a simple exercise to show that

$$\mathbf{AP}^t = \mathbf{P}^t\mathbf{\Lambda} \tag{A2.38}$$

where $\mathbf{P}^t$ is defined by letting its ith column be $\boldsymbol{v}_i$ for $i = 1, 2, \ldots, n$ and where $\mathbf{\Lambda}$ is the diagonal matrix with $\lambda_1, \ldots, \lambda_n$ running down the main diagonal. Since the columns of $\mathbf{P}^t$ are orthogonal to each other, each having unit norm, the matrix $\mathbf{P}^t$ is orthogonal and its inverse is $(\mathbf{P}^t)^t = \mathbf{P}$. Premultiplying (A2.38) by $\mathbf{P}$ we get

$$\mathbf{PAP}^t = \mathbf{PP}^t\mathbf{\Lambda} = \mathbf{\Lambda}$$

as we announced.

From this result about the diagonalization of a symmetric matrix $\mathbf{A}$ it is easy now to prove the following simple results.

1. If $\mathbf{PAP}^t = \Lambda$ then $\det(\mathbf{A}) = \lambda_1 \lambda_2 \ldots \lambda_n$.
2. If $\mathbf{A}$ is positive-semidefinite, then $\lambda_i \geq 0$ for all i.
3. If $\mathbf{A}$ is positive-definite, then $\lambda_i > 0$ for all i.

Proofs

1. This follows from the fact that $\det(P) = \pm 1$, and $\det(\mathbf{AB}) = \det(\mathbf{A})\det(\mathbf{B})$.

2. For any column n-tuple $\boldsymbol{x}$,

$\boldsymbol{x}^t(\mathbf{PAP}^t)\boldsymbol{x} = \boldsymbol{x}^t \Lambda \boldsymbol{x} = \sum_{i=1}^n \lambda_i x_i^2.$

But since $\mathbf{A}$ is positive-semidefinite,

$\boldsymbol{x}^t(\mathbf{PAP}^t)\boldsymbol{x} = (\mathbf{P}^t\boldsymbol{x})^t \mathbf{A}(\mathbf{P}^t\boldsymbol{x}) \geq 0.$

Therefore

$\sum_{i=1}^n \lambda_i \boldsymbol{x}_i^2 \geq 0 \quad \text{for all } x_i,$

and the result follows.

3. Same as above except that the inequality holds strictly if $\boldsymbol{x} \neq \boldsymbol{0}$, since in that case $\mathbf{P}^t\boldsymbol{x}$ is also $\neq \boldsymbol{0}$.

Exercises

1. Let

$$\mathbf{A} = \begin{bmatrix} 1 & 3 & -3 & 1 \\ 4 & 0 & 2 & 0 \\ -4 & -1 & 0 & 0 \end{bmatrix}$$

a. What is a_{11}? a_{12}? a_{21}? a_{32}?

b. What is the order of $\mathbf{A}$?

c. Is $\mathbf{A}$ a row vector? column vector?

2. Let $\mathbf{A}$ be defined as above and let

$$\mathbf{B} = \begin{bmatrix} 2 & 6 & 6 & 2 \\ 8 & 4 & 0 & 0 \\ 8 & 2 & 0 & 0 \end{bmatrix}$$

a. Is $\mathbf{A} + \mathbf{B}$ defined? If so, what is it?

b. Does $2\mathbf{A} = \mathbf{B}$??

c. What is $-\mathbf{A}$?

d. What is the sum of the third column of $\mathbf{A}$ and the third column of $\mathbf{B}$? Does it equal the third column of $\mathbf{A} + \mathbf{B}$?

3. Prove A2.2.

4. Let $\mathbf{A}$ and $\mathbf{B}$ be defined as above.

a. In $\mathbf{A}^t$, what is the $(1, 1)$ element? the $(1, 2)$ element? the $(2, 1)$ element? the $(3, 2)$ element?

b. Is $\mathbf{A} + \mathbf{A}^t$ defined? If so, what is it?

d. What is the first column of $\mathbf{B}^t$?

e. Is the product of the first row of **A** and the first column of **B** defined? If so, what is it?

f. Same as (e) for first row of **A** and first column of $\mathbf{B}'$.

g. Same as (e) for first row of **A** and second column of $\mathbf{B}'$.

h. Same as (e) for third row of **A** and second column of $\mathbf{B}'$.

i. Is **AB** defined? If so, what is it?

j. Is $\mathbf{AB}'$ defined? If so, what is it?

k. Which of the following are defined, and what are their orders:

$\mathbf{AB}, \mathbf{AB}'\mathbf{A}'\mathbf{B}, \mathbf{A}'\mathbf{B}', \mathbf{BA}, \mathbf{BA}', \mathbf{B}'\mathbf{A}, \mathbf{B}'\mathbf{A}'$?

l. Are any two of the products in (k) equal? If so, which?

5. Prove (A2.5).

6. Let

$$\mathbf{C} = \begin{bmatrix} 2 & -3 \\ 1 & -2 \end{bmatrix}, \qquad \mathbf{D} = \begin{bmatrix} 0 & 1 \\ 1 & 0 \end{bmatrix}.$$

a. What is **CD**? **DC**? Are they equal?

b. What is **CC**? **DD**?

7. Prove (A2.6).

8. Prove that $(k\mathbf{A})^{-1} = k^{-1}\mathbf{A}^{-1}$ if either side is defined.

9. Prove (A2.9).

10. Let **C** and **D** be defined as above. Using (A2.10) and the answers to exercise 6, find

$$\begin{bmatrix} \mathbf{C} & \mathbf{C} \\ \mathbf{D} & \mathbf{C} \end{bmatrix}\begin{bmatrix} \mathbf{C} & \mathbf{D} \\ \mathbf{C} & -\mathbf{D} \end{bmatrix} \quad \text{and} \quad \begin{bmatrix} \mathbf{D} & \mathbf{C} \\ \mathbf{0} & \mathbf{I} \end{bmatrix}\begin{bmatrix} \mathbf{D} & \mathbf{D} \\ \mathbf{0} & \mathbf{C} \end{bmatrix}$$

11. Let **C** and **D** be defined as above. Using (A2.11) and the answers to exercise 6, find

$$\begin{bmatrix} \mathbf{C} & \mathbf{D} \\ \mathbf{0} & \mathbf{D} \end{bmatrix}^{-1} \quad \text{and} \quad \begin{bmatrix} \mathbf{D} & -\mathbf{D} \\ \mathbf{0} & -\mathbf{C} \end{bmatrix}^{-1}.$$

12. Show that if **B** is square and $A = \frac{1}{2}(\mathbf{B} + \mathbf{B}')$ then **A** is symmetric and $\boldsymbol{x}'\mathbf{A}\boldsymbol{x} = \boldsymbol{x}'\mathbf{B}\boldsymbol{x}$ for all $\boldsymbol{x}$.

13. Show that a singular matrix is not positive-definite.

14. If **A** is (1×1), say, $\mathbf{A} = [a]$, what is the locus S of points $\boldsymbol{x} = [x]$ such that $\boldsymbol{x}'\mathbf{A}\boldsymbol{x} = 1$? Consider separately the cases $a > 0$, $a = 0$, and $a < 0$.

15. What is the locus of points $\boldsymbol{x}$ such that $\boldsymbol{x}'\mathbf{A}\boldsymbol{x} = 1$ for

a. $\mathbf{A} = \begin{bmatrix} 1 & 0 \\ 0 & 1 \end{bmatrix}$, b. $\mathbf{A} = \begin{bmatrix} 1 & 0 \\ 0 & 4 \end{bmatrix}$, c. $\mathbf{A} = \begin{bmatrix} 1 & 0 & 0 \\ 0 & 1 & 0 \\ 0 & 0 & 1 \end{bmatrix}$?

16. What is the locus of points $\boldsymbol{x}$ such that $\boldsymbol{x}'\mathbf{A}\boldsymbol{x} = 1$ for

a. $\mathbf{A} = \begin{bmatrix} 1 & 0 \\ 0 & 0 \end{bmatrix}$, b. $\mathbf{A} = \begin{bmatrix} 1 & 2 \\ 2 & 4 \end{bmatrix}$, c. $\mathbf{A} = \begin{bmatrix} 1 & -2 \\ -2 & 4 \end{bmatrix}$?

17. Why was there no consideration of the set of $\boldsymbol{x}$ such that $\boldsymbol{x}'\mathbf{A}\boldsymbol{x} = k$ for $k < 0$ in the discussion of positive-definite quadratic forms (section A2.8.2)?

Appendix 3: Properties of Utility Functions for Monetary Consequences

A3.1 Introduction

In chapter 4 we introduced utility functions and some of their properties. In particular, in section 4.2.5 we defined risk aversion and noted that it is equivalent to concavity of the utility function, and in section 4.3.2 we described briefly some further possibly desirable properties. In this appendix we will define these and other properties and provide convenient analytical conditions for them and simple utility functions satisfying them. We will also answer various questions about rational risk attitudes and behavior. We will have to be concise, however. References may be found in Pratt (1992).

A3.2 Measuring Risk Aversion

For any random variable $\tilde{z}$, denote its expectation by $E\tilde{z}$. If $\tilde{x}$ is the payoff of a lottery, then $E\tilde{x}$ is the *expected monetary value* of the lottery.

If a decision maker has current wealth w and utility function u defined on total wealth, then he is indifferent between receiving the uncertain payoff $\tilde{x}$ and the certain amount c that satisfies $u(w + c) = Eu(w + \tilde{x})$. Thus the *cash equivalent* is $c = C(\tilde{x}, w) = u^{-1}(Eu(w + \tilde{x})) - w$, where the notation $C(\tilde{x}, w)$ indicates the dependence on both w and the probability distribution of $\tilde{x}$.

The *risk premium* of a risk $\tilde{x}$ is the difference between the expected monetary value and the cash equivalent of $\tilde{x}$, namely

$$\pi(\tilde{x}, w) = E\tilde{x} - C(\tilde{x}, w). \tag{A3.1}$$

It is a measure in monetary units of the effect of risk aversion on the value of $\tilde{x}$ to the decision maker. Like the cash equivalent, it depends on the decision maker's utility function and current wealth and on the probability distribution of $\tilde{x}$. For small risks $\tilde{x}$, however, we will see that this complicated dependence can be greatly simplified approximately. (The notation $\pi(\tilde{x}, w)$ for risk premium is standard. Accordingly we will not use $\pi(x)$ for utility below, although the two uses can be distinguished by the variables appearing as arguments.)

Let

$$r(w) = -u''(w)/u'(w) \qquad \text{for all } w. \tag{A3.2}$$

We call r the *local risk aversion function* for reasons that will emerge.

Assuming throughout that $u' > 0$, note first that $r \geq 0$ is equivalent to $u'' \leq 0$ and hence to concavity of u (risk aversion).

The local risk aversion $r(w)$ turns out to be an appropriate measure of concavity for a utility function u at w. (Neither u'' or $-u''$ nor the curvature $u''(1 + u'^2)^{-3/2}$ could be appropriate, because they change—even though preferences do not—when u is multiplied by a positive constant. Although $-u''(w) = r(w)$ if u is scaled so that $u'(w) = 1$, this scaling depends on w.) Much as the second derivative determines a function up to constant and linear terms, so r determines u up to change of utility scale: integrating $-r(w)$ gives $\log u'(w) + c$; exponentiating and integrating again then gives $e^c u(w) + d$. Since $e^c > 0$, the constants of integration, c and d, merely rescale u. Conversely, if $v(w) = a + bu(w)$ for all w, then $-v''/v' = -u''/u'$, that is, u and v have identical local risk aversion everywhere (exercise 1). Briefly we may write

$$u \sim \int e^{-\int r} \tag{A3.3}$$

where $\sim$ denotes equality except for change of utility scale. Thus r captures everything essential and eliminates everything arbitrary about u. We shall also see that it has not only local but also far-reaching implications.

For small risks, the risk premium is to first approximation simply a product of two terms, one being the variance $V(\tilde{x})$ of the risk and the other being one half of the decision maker's local risk aversion at the mean. Specifically, expanding the utility function u around $w + E\tilde{x}$

gives (exercise 2)

$$\pi(\tilde{x}, w) = \tfrac{1}{2}r(w + E\tilde{x})V(\tilde{x}) + \text{terms of smaller order}, \tag{A3.4}$$

where r is the local risk aversion function defined by (A3.2).

Thus the risk premium is approximately one-half the variance times the local risk aversion at the mean. When the risk premium equals the expected monetary value, the decision maker is indifferent between having and not having $\tilde{x}$. Hence the decision maker has a mean-variance tradeoff rate of $\frac{1}{2}r(w)$ at w, approximately. Note that the factor is the variance, not the standard deviation, because (A3.4) is really a second-order formula. To first order, any differentiable utility function is linear and a small gamble's cash equivalent is its expected monetary value.

The quadratic effect of variance is surprising and powerful here: a decision maker who would pay \$100 more than expected value to insure against a chance of losing \$10,000 should pay only \$1 more than expected value to insure against the same chance of losing \$1,000, approximately, and only \$.01 more to insure against losing \$100 (exercise 3). Similarly, if a gamble $\tilde{x}$ has positive expected monetary value, then $\varepsilon\tilde{x}$ has positive cash equivalent for some positive ε; that is, if transaction costs are proportional, any security offering a gain in mean is worth at least minimal investment (exercise 4, regularity conditions omitted).

A3.3 Examples

1. Constant Risk Aversion

If $r(w) = c > 0$ for all w, then by (A3.3), $u(w) \sim -e^{-cw}$. This utility function has the property that changes in wealth have no effect on preferences between risks, since for any constant h, $u(w + h) = -e^{-ch}e^{-cw} \sim -e^{-cw}$ as a function of w. Thus $\pi(\tilde{x}, w)$ does not depend on w, and $Eu(w + \tilde{x}) - Eu(w + \tilde{y})$ has the same sign for all w (exercise 5).

This example illustrates vividly the difficulty of inferring risk aversion from graphical appearances. As $w \to \infty$, the exponential curve $-e^{-cw}$ approaches a horizontal asymptote and appears more and more linear, yet as a utility function it has the same shape on any interval as on any other of the same length; horizontal translation merely rescales it vertically.

2. Constant Relative Risk Aversion

If $r(w) = b/w$ for all $w > 0$, then $u(w) \sim \log w$ if $b = 1$, and otherwise $u(w) \sim (1 - b)w^{1-b}$. In this case, changes in wealth have no effect on preferences between risks that are *proportional* to wealth, since for any constant h, $u(hw) \sim u(w)$, and $Eu(w\tilde{x}) - Eu(w\tilde{y})$ has the same sign for all w. In general, the *relative risk aversion* $r^*(w) = wr(w)$ plays a role for risks proportional to wealth like that played by the "absolute" risk aversion $r(w)$ for "absolute" risks. (Here "absolute" does not mean absolute value but merely contrasts with proportional or relative.)

3. Hyperbolic Absolute Risk Aversion (HARA)

Let $r(w) = 1/(a + bw)$ for all $w > -a/b$, with $b \geq 0$. Then $u(w) \sim -e^{-w/a}$ if $b = 0$, $u(w) \sim \log(w + a)$ if $b = 1$, and otherwise $u(w) \sim (1 - b)(w + a/b)^{1-1/b}$. The case $b = 0$ gives constant risk aversion, while $b > 0$ gives constant relative risk aversion with wealth measured from the origin $-a/b$. HARA preferences play a special role in problems of sharing risks among two or more parties.

4. Quadratic Utility

It would be convenient if quadratic utility functions could serve as an adequate approximation, but they have some properties that make this dubious. The only possibility with u increasing and concave is $u(w) \sim -(a - w)^2$ for $w \leq a$. Thus we must restrict w and $\tilde{x}$ to satisfy $w + \tilde{x} \leq a$. The risk premium is

$$\pi(\tilde{x}, w) = w + E\tilde{x} - a + [E\{(a - w - \tilde{x})^2\}]^{1/2} \tag{A3.5}$$

This is *increasing* in w, opposite to the usual assumption (exercise 6). Furthermore the risk premium cannot be as large as one might wish: it is always less than the standard deviation; for a nonnegative gamble, it is less than half the mean; and it is less than 42% of the mean for a 50-50 gamble between two positive values (exercise 7). Note that approximating by (A3.4) is not the same as using a quadratic utility function even though both depend only on the mean and variance of the gamble, because the quadratic approximation used in (A3.4) is not the same for all gambles.

A3.4 Decreasing Risk Aversion

A decision maker is called *decreasingly risk averse* if the risk premium of every gamble is decreasing in wealth: $\pi(\tilde{x}, w)$ is decreasing in w for every $\tilde{x}$. Equivalently, the cash equivalent $C(\tilde{x}, w)$ is increasing in w, and an acceptable gamble cannot be made unacceptable by an increase in w. (More precisely, "decreasing" should be replaced by "nonincreasing," etc., and the range of w may be restricted.)

The relation (A3.4) between the risk premium of a small gamble and the local risk aversion function r implies that r is decreasing if u is decreasingly risk averse, and the converse also holds (exercise 18). For the case of constant risk aversion we have already seen this in example 1 above. For hyperbolic absolute risk aversion, example 3, the local risk aversion $r(w) = 1/(a + bw)$ is decreasing on the entire range $w > -a/b$, so HARA utility functions are decreasingly risk averse. Quadratic utility, example 4, has increasing local risk aversion $r(w) = 1/(a - w)$, $w < a$.

If two utility functions u_i and u_2 are decreasingly risk averse, then so is their sum, say $u = u_1 + u_2$ (exercise 12). The same follows (by induction on n) for finite positive linear combinations, say $u = \sum_{i=1}^{n} b_i u_i$ where $b_i > 0$ and u_i is decreasingly risk averse for all i. Indeed, a further generalization adds substantial intuitive meaning and applicability to this result. Replace the index i by a variable s, which may be discrete or continuous in any number of dimensions, and let $\tilde{s}$ have any probability distribution whatever.

> If $u(w, s)$ is decreasingly risk averse as a function of w for each value of s, then $U(w) = Eu(w, \tilde{s})$ is decreasingly risk averse as a function of w.

In brief, mixing preserves decreasing risk aversion.

Multiplying $u(w, s)$ by $b(s) > 0$ is not a significant generalization because $b(s)u(w, s) \sim u(w, s)$ as a function of w, and it replaces the expectation by $Eb(\tilde{s})u(w, \tilde{s})$, which is harder to interpret.

As an example, a sum of exponentials $-e^{-ax} - be^{-cx}$ with a, b, $c > 0$ is decreasingly risk averse. So is any mixture of exponentials $U(w) = \int_0^\infty (g(s) - e^{-sw})\, dF(s)$. This class of functions is broader than it might appear, and includes among others all HARA utility functions (exercise 13).

The foregoing result has a natural interpretation in the context of multiattribute utility, that is, when consequences are multidimensional. One might think of a choice of uncertain wealth $\tilde{w}$ in the face of uncertain health $\tilde{s}$. Suppose that the choices available affect the distribution of $\tilde{w}$ but not the distribution of $\tilde{s}$. Then the expected utility of any decision is $EU(\tilde{w})$ where $\tilde{w}$ has the distribution chosen and U is defined as above. Thus U serves as a utility function for decisions about $\tilde{w}$. The result above states that if the multiattribute utility $u(w, s)$ is decreasingly risk averse in w for each s, then the "derived" utility $U(w)$ is decreasingly risk averse. In brief, a derived utility function inherits decreasing risk aversion from its components. A proof follows.

Decreasing relative risk aversion is also inherited, but increasing is not (exercise 21).

Proof Let $\tilde{u}'(w) = \partial u(w, \tilde{s})/\partial w$, and similarly for higher derivatives and $\tilde{r} = -\tilde{u}''/\tilde{u}'$. By hypothesis

$$\tilde{r}' = -\frac{\tilde{u}'''}{\tilde{u}'} + \left(\frac{\tilde{u}''}{\tilde{u}'}\right)^2 \leq 0. \tag{A3.6}$$

Let $R = -U''/U'$ be the local risk aversion function of U. Then,

$$R' = -\frac{U'''}{U'} + \left(\frac{U''}{U'}\right)^2 = -\frac{E\tilde{u}'''}{E\tilde{u}'} + \left(\frac{E\tilde{u}''}{E\tilde{u}'}\right)^2. \tag{A3.7}$$

The last term satisfies

$$\left(\frac{E\tilde{u}''}{E\tilde{u}'}\right)^2 = \left(E\left\{\frac{\tilde{u}''}{\tilde{u}'}\frac{\tilde{u}'}{E\tilde{u}'}\right\}\right)^2 \le E\left\{\left(\frac{\tilde{u}''}{\tilde{u}'}\right)^2 \frac{\tilde{u}'}{E\tilde{u}'}\right\} \tag{A3.8}$$

by the Schwarz inequality or by squared mean ≤ mean square applied to $\tilde{u}''/\tilde{u}'$, regarding $\tilde{u}'/E\tilde{u}'$ as a probability distribution. It follows that

$$R' \le -\frac{E\tilde{u}'''}{E\tilde{u}'} + E\left\{\left(\frac{\tilde{u}''}{\tilde{u}'}\right)^2 \frac{\tilde{u}'}{E\tilde{u}'}\right\}$$

$$= E\left\{\tilde{r}'\frac{\tilde{u}'}{E\tilde{u}'}\right\} \le 0 \tag{A3.9}$$

by (A3.6). Hence U is decreasingly risk averse. ■

A3.5 More Risk Averse

We turn briefly to a fundamental aspect of the theory of risk aversion, the comparison of two or more utility functions. They could for instance belong to different individuals, or to one individual in different circumstances—different levels of wealth or states of health, say. They could be under consideration by an individual assessing a utility function, or by a researcher analyzing observed behavior.

We call u_1 *more risk averse* than u_2 if u_1 assigns a larger risk premium (smaller cash equivalent) to every gamble than u_2 does. This implies by (A3.4) that $r_1 \ge r_2$ where $r_i = -u_i''/u_i'$, and again the converse holds. We list here and in exercise 17 a number of equivalent conditions, all of which are both useful and intuitive:

u_1 is more risk averse than u_2 ⇔

u_1 is a concave function of u_2 ⇔

u_1'/u_2' is decreasing ⇔ $r_1 \ge r_2$. (A3.10)

The condition on the ratio of the slopes, for example, says that u_1 bends over faster than u_2. The second condition says $u_1(w) = k(u_2(w))$ for all w where k is a concave function, or equivalently, $k(t) = u_1(u_2^{-1}(t))$ is a concave function of t. In the order given, the equivalences are not hard to prove (exercise 17). The equivalence of decreasing risk aversion to decreasing r follows by letting $u_2(w) = u_1(w + h)$, $h > 0$ (exercise 18).

Notice that if u_1 is more risk averse than u_2 and u_2 than u_3, then u_1 is more risk averse than u_3. Thus "more risk averse" is a transitive relation, or partial ordering, equivalent to inequality everywhere between local risk aversion functions. It can happen, though, that u_1 is neither more nor less risk averse than u_2 because their risk aversion functions cross, for example, exponential and logarithmic utility on $(0, \infty)$. However, if two utility functions have constant relative risk aversion (section A3.3), then the one with the larger value of b is more risk averse; the well-known inequalities between arithmetic, geometric, and harmonic means follow (exercise 19).

Greater risk aversion is not preserved by mixing as decreasing risk aversion is. It is easy to construct examples where u_1 is more risk averse than u_2 and u_3 is more risk averse than u_4, yet $u_1 + u_3$ is not more risk averse than $u_2 + u_4$ (exercise 20).

A3.6 Allocations to a Single Risk

The foregoing comparisons of individuals and wealth levels refer to choices between a risk and a certainty. Similar comparisons hold for choices of how much to invest in or insure against a single risk. We discuss investment, leaving insurance to exercise 21.

Suppose that an amount a is invested in a single risk while remaining wealth $w - a$ is held in cash without interest—or with interest if w is reinterpreted as in exercise 22. The risk could be a stock or mutual fund or an "efficient" or other portfolio. Let $\tilde{x}$ be the gain per unit invested in the risk. Thus final wealth will be $w + a\tilde{x}$. It can be shown that (exercise 23)

a. If $E\tilde{x} > 0$ then $a\tilde{x}$ is desirable for sufficiently small positive a.

b. If also u is concave, then $Eu(w + a\tilde{x})$ is a concave function of a. Thus investing more is better up to some amount $A(w)$ and worse beyond.

c. If u_1 is more risk averse than u_2, then the optimum amount to invest is smaller for u_1 than u_2.

d. If u has decreasing risk aversion, then the optimum $A(w)$ is increasing in w.

e. If u has monotonic relative risk aversion $r^*(w) = wr(w)$ then $A(w)/w$ is monotonic in the opposite direction.

Thus the effect of greater risk aversion on optimum investment in a single risk is as expected. Other comparative statics are unfortunately less simple. For example, an increase in the risk-free interest rate can lead a decreasingly risk-averse individual to invest more in the risk (exercise 25). And for multiple-risk and portfolio decisions, general results are even harder to obtain and require more complex conditions. The surprising results that are possible show weaknesses in our intuition about risk, and improve it, we hope. Some suggest further restrictions on utility functions (see below), but others should be allowed or the risks further restricted (exercises 26 and 27).

A3.7 Independent Risks

Next we discuss some properties of utility functions relating to *independent* risks. Note first that if $\tilde{w}$ and $\tilde{x}$ are independent, then $Eu(\tilde{w} + \tilde{x}) = EU(\tilde{x})$ where $U(x) = Eu(\tilde{w} + x)$ for each x. Thus the derived U governs decisions about risks independent of $\tilde{w}$. This is a special case of the derived utility in section A3.4, and as there, U is increasing, concave, and decreasingly risk averse if u is.

A stronger condition is motivated as follows (Pratt and Zeckhauser, 1987). An individual finds each of two independent risks undesirable. If required to take one, should he not continue to find the other undesirable? If in all such cases he would, his utility function is called *proper*. Specifically, proper is defined by the condition that, for all independent $\tilde{w}$, $\tilde{x}$, and $\tilde{y}$,

$$\text{if } \tilde{w} + \tilde{x} \precsim \tilde{w} \quad \text{and} \quad \tilde{w} + \tilde{y} \precsim \tilde{w} \quad \text{then} \quad \tilde{w} + \tilde{x} + \tilde{y} \precsim \tilde{w} + \tilde{y}. \tag{A3.11}$$

The reader should verify that decreasing risk aversion is the case of nonrandom y. Thus decreasing risk aversion says that a reduction in wealth cannot make an undesirable gamble $\tilde{x}$ desirable; proper says that an independent undesirable change $\tilde{y}$ cannot do so either. Apparently nonrandom w does not suffice for (A3.11), although it does in the case of nonrandom y (decreasing risk aversion).

Under the assumption of decreasing risk aversion, proper is equivalent to requiring all sums of independent undesirable gambles to be undesirable, and to the even weaker condition using indifference that, for all independent $\tilde{w}$, $\tilde{x}$, and $\tilde{y}$,

$$\text{if } \tilde{w} + \tilde{x} \sim \tilde{w} + \tilde{y} \sim \tilde{w} \quad \text{then} \quad \tilde{w} + \tilde{x} + \tilde{y} \precsim \tilde{w}. \tag{A3.12}$$

These conditions do not imply decreasing risk aversion, however, and hence are not sufficient without it, being satisfied for example by quadratic utility functions (exercise 29).

The cash equivalent $C(\tilde{x}, \tilde{w})$ for random $\tilde{w}$ is naturally defined as the certain amount c such that $Eu(\tilde{w} + c) = Eu(\tilde{w} + \tilde{x})$. Properness implies that, for all independent $\tilde{w}$, $\tilde{x}$, and $\tilde{y}$, if $C(\tilde{x}, \tilde{w}) \leq 0$ and $C(\tilde{y}, \tilde{w}) \leq 0$, then

$$\tilde{w} + \tilde{x} + \tilde{y} \precsim \tilde{w} + C(\tilde{x}, \tilde{w}) + \tilde{y} \precsim \tilde{w} + C(\tilde{x}, \tilde{w}) + C(\tilde{y}, \tilde{w}) \tag{A3.13}$$

and hence (exercise 30)

$$C(\tilde{x} + \tilde{y}, \tilde{w}) \leq C(\tilde{x}, \tilde{w}) + C(\tilde{y}, \tilde{w}), \tag{A3.14}$$

$$C(\tilde{x}, \tilde{y} + \tilde{w}) \leq C(\tilde{x}, \tilde{w}). \tag{A3.15}$$

(A3.14) is stronger than (A3.11) and weaker though more suggestive intuitively than (A3.15). We emphasize that these relations hold for *undesirable* $\tilde{x}$ and $\tilde{y}$, and may well reverse if $\tilde{x}$ or $\tilde{y}$ is desirable (exercise 31).

Proper utility implies regularities such as: the desirability of n independent repetitions of a gamble is increasing in n up to some number and decreasing thereafter (exercise 28), whereas every ordering is possible under decreasing risk aversion alone (exercise 26).

The local necessary condition for proper obtained from small gambles is $r'' \geq r'r$ everywhere, or equivalently $u'r'$ is increasing (exercise 32). Unfortunately this condition is not sufficient, and analytical necessary and sufficient are not convenient. A convenient sufficient condition is (exercise 39):

$$\text{If both } -u''/u' \text{ and } -u'''/u'' \text{ are decreasing, then } u \text{ is proper.} \tag{A3.16}$$

It is easy to verify that all HARA utility functions satisfy this condition (exercise 33). Furthermore the condition is preserved under mixing of the type appearing in section A3.4 (exercise 34). Hence all exponential mixtures are proper.

Mathematical Note. It is easy to see that exponential mixtures have positive odd derivatives and negative even derivatives everywhere (exercise 40). Surprisingly, the converse is also true. A positive function with positive even derivatives and negative odd derivatives is called *completely monotone*, and a classical theorem of S. Bernstein states that a function is completely monotone on some interval (w_0, ∞), possibly $(-\infty, \infty)$ if and only if it is the Laplace transform of a measure on $[0, \infty)$, a measure being like a probability distribution where probabilities are allowed to be more than 1 and even infinite. Thus u' is completely monotone if and only if u is an exponential mixture.

A3.8 Further Comments on the Choice of a Utility Function

We now add to the discussion of section 4.3 on constructing a utility function for money.

First we note the significance of taking the monetary outcome alone as an adequate description of the consequence. The desirability of \$1,000—or \$100,000—is treated as the same whatever any other decision or luck would have produced. No role is given to considerations such as anxiety, regret, disappointment, elation, envy, salience (is a loss in your mutual fund account the same as it would be out of your pocket?). Such emotions and other psychological factors are real and one might want to reflect them in a descriptive or prescriptive analysis by enriching the consequences or even by departing from our model of rational behavior. Empirical evidence and common sense confirm that even in making decisions about monetary matters, people do not consistently maximize expected utility for money alone. They are even so inconsistent as to react differently to exactly equivalent questions framed differently—a half empty piggy bank is different from a half full one. Expected utility of money is a starting point and stalking horse for other theories and models, however, and analyses based thereon are often useful in themselves, either because other considerations are or should be secondary or because we want to compare cold-blooded analysis with emotional or irrational behavior.

Next we emphasize that plausible risk premiums for large gambles imply tiny risk premiums for small gambles. This results from the quadratic nature of the risk premium, (A3.4). We have already seen examples, and the exercises give others (exercises, 3, 4, 42, 43). We mention just one more here (exercise 45): a decision maker who would pay \$200 more than actuarial value to insure against a chance of losing \$10,000 should pay only about \$2 more than actuarial value to insure against the same chance of losing \$1,000, and \$0.02 for \$100. We conclude that the choice of a utility function for money should be based on specific judgments about large (and simple) gambles and on general qualitative principles such as how and how rapidly absolute and relative risk premiums should vary as a function of

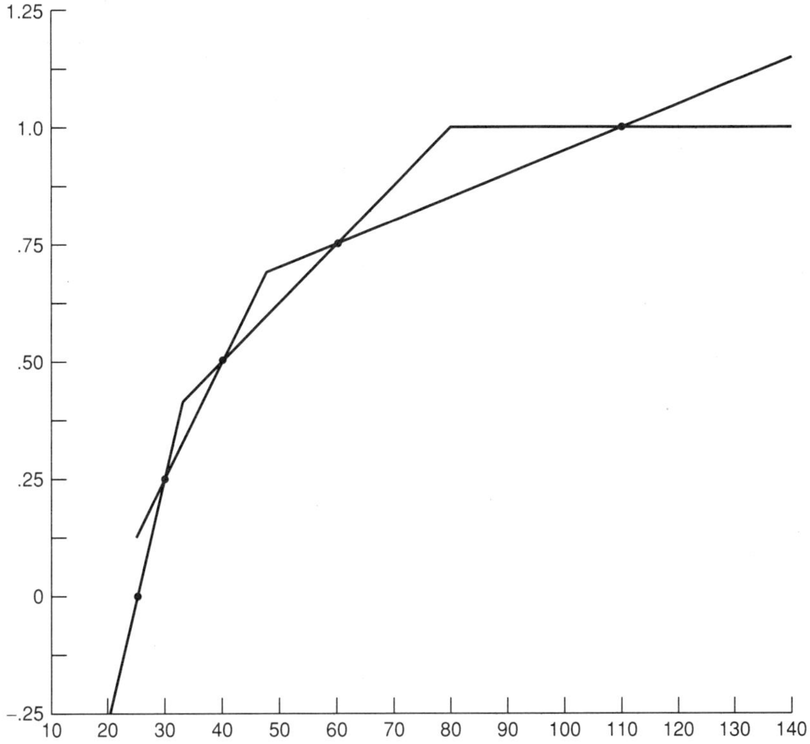

Figure A3.1

wealth. Evaluations of small gambles may differ from expected monetary value because of "noise," emotion, inconsistency (for example, in reactions to a \$100 change in all payoffs, in a bank account, or both), or other factors (it is unpleasant to explain a small uninsured auto accident to a spouse or employer). But these differences should not distort the choice of a utility function to guide decisions about major risks.

Finally, we illustrate how accurately a combination of specific judgments and general principles can determine a utility function for money. Suppose that, by the method suggested in section 4.3 or otherwise, we have obtained some points on a utility function; that is, some pairs $[x_i, u(x_i)]$ are given. Let us require that u be everywhere increasing and continuous except perhaps where it is $-\infty$. If u is also required to be risk averse, then it is not hard to see that it must lie between two piecewise linear, risk-averse utility functions that cross at the given points as shown in figure A3.1, and that all points between are possible in the absence of any further requirement (exercise 46). We would like to require some additional kind of smoothness—but what kind? Requiring differentiability—even infinitely often—has only the effect of eliminating the corners in figure A3.1. Requiring decreasing risk aversion does much more, however, replacing the boundaries by piecewise exponential functions. (For one piece see exercise 47.)

Figure A3.2 gives an example of the bounds obtained by requiring decreasing risk aversion when a utility function is given at five points whose utility values are equally spaced. (The points result from three judgments of 50-50 gambles in the Waterman case at the end of chapter 4.) This example is typical in that five (or more) reasonably spaced points together with the requirement of decreasing risk aversion usually determine a utility function up to a small margin of error within the given range except near the smallest point.

The algorithm that determines the piecewise exponential boundaries also determines feasibility, that is, whether a decreasingly risk-averse utility passing through the given points

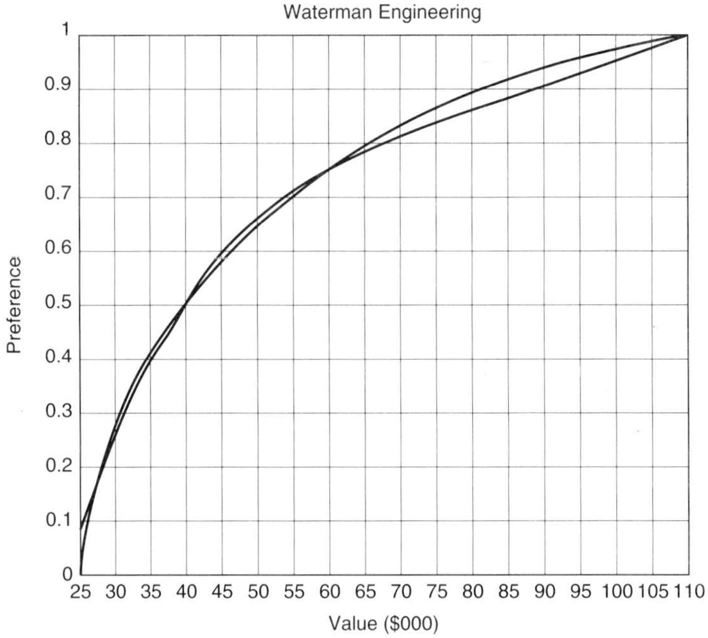

Figure A3.2

exists. A simple or weighted average of the two boundary functions is an analytically tractable, decreasingly risk-averse utility through the given points. A mixture of exponentials, when feasible, is even more convenient analytically and smoother—indeed proper. For five points, a sum of two exponentials has just enough parameters and often does the job. If the exponents are fixed and only the weights adjusted, more terms are needed but the problem becomes linear for any number of points (exercise 48).

Requiring properness would produce even tighter bounds than decreasing risk aversion, or perhaps infeasibility, since utility functions very close to piecewise exponential must violate the local necessary condition for properness (exercise 49). However, a method of determining the boundaries under properness is not known.

All this strengthens and amplifies the suggestions in section 4.3 for constructing a utility function for money by combining qualitative and quantitative judgments analytically.

Exercises

1. Fill out the justification given for (A3.3).

2. Verify the expression (A3.4).

3. If $\tilde{x}$ is the lottery $\{(p, -1), (1-p, 0)\}$ and $\pi(10{,}000\tilde{x}, w) = 100$, show that

   a. $\pi(1000\tilde{x}, w) = 1$ and $\pi(100\tilde{x}, w) = .01$, approximately.

   b. $\pi(1000\tilde{x}, w) \leq 1$ and $\pi(100\tilde{x}, w) \leq .01$ under decreasing risk aversion.

4. If $E\tilde{x} > 0$, show (under some regularity conditions) that $C(\varepsilon\tilde{x}, w) > 0$ for some $\varepsilon > 0$.

5. Verify the properties of constant risk aversion stated in section A3.3, example 1.

6. Show directly that the risk premium (A3.5) for quadratic utility is increasing in w.

7. For an increasing, concave, quadratic utility function, show that:

a. $\pi(\tilde{x}, w) \leq [V(\tilde{x})]^{1/2}$.

b. If $\tilde{x} = \{(q:0),(p:h)\}$ with $h > 0$ and $q = 1 - p$, then $\pi(\tilde{x}, w) \leq h\sqrt{q} - hq$; when $p = \frac{1}{2}$, this gives $\pi(\tilde{x}, w) \leq (\sqrt{2} - 1)E\tilde{x}$.

c. If $\tilde{x} \geq 0$, then $\pi(\tilde{x}, w) \leq \frac{1}{2}E\tilde{x}$.
Hint The "worst case" is (b) as $p \to 0$.

8. Suppose $\tilde{x}_1$, $\tilde{x}_2$, ... are independently, identically distributed gambles with positive mean. Suppose you have an increasing, concave utility function u and $E\{u(w + \tilde{x}_1)\} \leq u(w)$ for all w.

a. If you must decide in advance how many gambles to accept, what would you decide, or how?

b. If you could decide after each gamble whether to accept or reject the next one, might your answer change? Why or why not?

c. Suppose also that each $\tilde{x}_i$ has only two possible values. Show that u is bounded from above. (You can do the next part without doing this one.)

d. Show that a utility function is bounded from above if and only if the certainty equivalent of a 50-50 gamble between 0 and w is a bounded function of w.

9. If $u(w) \sim -(a - w)^2$ for $w \leq a$, then by (A3.5) the risk premium of a loss $\tilde{x}$ at $w = a$ is $\pi(\tilde{x}, a) = E\tilde{x} + [E(\tilde{x}^2)]^{1/2}$, which is linear, not quadratic in the scale of $\tilde{x}$ (e.g., in ε when $\tilde{x} = \varepsilon\tilde{z}$). Why does (A3.4) not apply here?

10. Due to an unfortunate miscalculation, I have caused my friend Z (Richard Zeckhauser of Harvard's Kennedy School of Government) damage for which I am legally liable. Z argues that, in order to make him "whole" (as well off as he would have been had I not damaged him), I will have to pay him more in the upcoming time period than the amount I caused him to lose in the previous time period, because he is risk averse. To be specific, he says that his utility is $u(x_1) + u(x_2)$ where x_1 is his income in period i, $i = 1, 2$. Absent the damage, his income would have been the same in both periods, say z. The damage reduced his income in period 1 by 10%.

a. Suppose $u(x) = \log(x)$. What payment in period 2 would make him whole?

b. Show that he is correct—as usual—that is, if u is risk averse, then his period 2 payment must be bigger than his period 1 loss to make him whole.

c. What qualitative difference would it make in (a) if $u(x) = 1 - e^{-x}$ instead of $\log(x)$?

d. *Mirabile dictu*, the court accepts Z's argument. (Z actually did suggest this argument, but the rest of the story is a fabrication. *Mirabile dictu* is a legal term meaning "miraculously.") Show that if Z persuades the cour that he is more risk averse than he really is, then I will have to pay more than I should, that is, replacing u by a more risk-averse utility function increases the period 2 payment required to make Z whole.

e. No probabilities are mentioned above. Why is risk aversion relevant?

11. Let $r = -u''/u'$ be the local risk aversion function of the utility function u. Show that the following conditions are equivalent: (a) r is decreasing; (b) $\log u'$ is convex; (c) u' is a convex function of u; (d) $u''^2 \leq u'u'''$.

12. Let $u = u_1 + u_2$ and let r_1, r_2, and r be the local risk aversions of u_1, u_2, and u respectively. Show that

a. $$r' = \frac{u_1' r_1' + u_2' r_2'}{u_1' + u_2'} - u_1' u_2' \left(\frac{r_1 - r_2}{u_1' + u_2'}\right)^2.$$

b. From (a) show that if r_1 and r_2 are decreasing then r is decreasing.

c. When can you conclude that r is strictly decreasing?

d. How this this relate to (A3.6)–(A3.9)?

13. Show constructively that all HARA utility functions are mixtures of exponentials.

14. Show that $C(\tilde{x}, w) = C(\tilde{x} - a, w + a) + a$ and $\pi(\tilde{x}, w) = \pi(\tilde{x} - a, w + a)$.

15. The lottery $\{(p : h), (q : -h)\}$ with $q = 1 - p$ has probability advantage $p - q$. Show that, as $h \to 0$, the probability advantage that makes the lottery indifferent to the status quo is $\frac{1}{2}hr(w)+$ terms of smaller order.

16. You must hold most of your wealth in cash, but can invest up to ε in risky securities. Security i will return $\tilde{x}_i$ per dollar invested. Thus, if you invest ε_i in security i, you will end up with $w + \sum_i \varepsilon_i \tilde{x}_i$. Under suitable conditions, show that, if ε is small enough, you should invest everything possible in the security or securities with maximum expected return. How can you reconcile "plunging" this way with risk aversion?

17. Show that u_1 more risk averse than u_2 is equivalent to the conditions given in section 4.5.5 and to the condition that $Q_1^a \leq Q_2^a$ for all w, x with $w \leq x$, where $Q_i^a = u_i'(x)/u_i'(w)$; and similarly for $Q_i^b = [u_i(y) - u_i(x)]/u_i'(w)$, $w \leq x < y$; $Q_i^c = u_i'(x)/[u_i(w) - u_i(v)]$, $v < w \leq x$; and $Q_i^d = [u_i(y) - u_i(x)]/[u_i(w) - u_i(v)]$, $v < w \leq y$, $v \leq x < y$. *Hint:* one step applies Jensen's inequality (exercise 13 of chapter 4) to $k(\tilde{t})$ where $\tilde{t} = u_2(\tilde{z})$. The others are mainly calculus, including the Mean Value theorem.

18. Use section A3.5 to show that decreasing risk aversion is equivalent to decreasing r.

19. a. Use section A3.5 to show that $[E(\tilde{x}^p)]^{1/p}$, the cash equivalent for $u_p(w) \sim \pm w^p$, is increasing in p. (Use appropriate limits for $p = 0$.)

b. Show that the arithmetic, geometric, and harmonic means correspond to $p = 1, 0$, and -1.

20. Let $u_i(w) = -c_i e^{-a_i w}$, $i = 1, 2, 3, 4$.

a. Show that there exist positive a_i and c_i such that u_i is more risk averse than u_{i+2}, $i = 1, 2$, but $u_1 + u_3$ is less risk averse than $u_2 + u_4$ on an arbitrary finite interval. Thus mixing does not always preserve greater risk aversion.

b. Mixing preserves decreasing risk aversion. Why so different?

21. a. Show that mixing preserves decreasing relative aversion $r^*(w) = wr(w)$.
Hint Use (A3.9).

b. Show that mixing need not preserve increasing relative risk aversion.

22. a. Show that allowing risk-free interest in section A3.6 merely replaces w by the final wealth that would be obtained by risk-free investment alone and $\tilde{x}$ by the difference between the risky and risk-free rates of return.

b. What if more than one risk-free security is available?

c. What if some assets are illiquid, that is, already committed and unavailable for new investments?

23. Prove the investment allocation results of section A3.6.
Hint Prove c by introducing $V_i(a) = Eu_i(w + a\tilde{x})$ and using the monotonicity of u_1'/u_2' to show that $V_1'(a)/u_1'(w) \leq V_2'(a)/u_2'(w)$. Then prove d by letting $u_2(w) = u_1(w + h)$ and e by letting $u_2(w) = u_1(kw)$.

24. Coinsurance means that if you incur a loss $\tilde{y}$, an insurance company reimburses you an amount $b\tilde{y}$. Suppose such insurance were available for any fraction b at a premium proportional to b.

a. How do the results of section A3.6 apply to this situation?

b. Why do you think such insurance is not more widely available?

25. In problem 22a, show that an increase in the risk-free interest rate can decrease the optimum risk-free investment by a decreasingly risk-averse individual enough even to decrease the interest earned.
Hint Let u' be very large below some minimum acceptable wealth.

26. Let $\tilde{S}_n$ be the sum of n independent repetitions of a gamble $\tilde{x}$ with positive mean and finite extrema a, b, $a < 0 < b$. Let $\tilde{S}_0 = 0$.

a. Show that, for some utility function u_0 with constant risk aversion, $Eu_0(\tilde{S}_n)$ is the same for all $n = 0, 1, 2, \ldots$.

b. Show that, for some decreasingly risk-averse utility functions v_m and V_m, $Ev_m(\tilde{S}_n)$ is the same for all $n < m$ and smaller for $n = m$ while $EV_m(\tilde{S}_n)$ is the same for all $n < m$ and larger for $n = m$.
Hint Modify u_0 below $(m-1)\,a$ or above $(m-1)\,b$.

c. Given any preference ordering of $S_0, S_1, \ldots, S_N$, show that there exists a decreasingly risk-averse utility that produces this ordering.
Hint Let $u = \sum_{n=1}^{N} d_n v_n + D_n V_n$ where d_n and D_n are chosen recursively to produce agreement with the ordering of $S_0, S_1, \ldots, S_n$.

27. Define the partial-insurance premium $\pi_i(\tilde{w}, \tilde{x})$ as the most an individual with utility u_i would be willing to pay to insure $\tilde{x}$ when facing $\tilde{w} + \tilde{x}$.

a. Show that $Eu_i(\tilde{w} - \pi_i(\tilde{w},\tilde{x})) = Eu_i(\tilde{w} + \tilde{x})$.

In parts b–d, fix w_1, assume $0 < x < y < w_1$, and let $(\tilde{w}, \tilde{x})$ have the possible values (y, x), $(y, -x)$, and $(0, 0)$ with probabilities $\frac{1}{2}p$, $\frac{1}{2}p$, and $1 - p$ respectively.

b. Show that $E(\tilde{x}|\tilde{w}) = 0$.

c. Given any x, y, u_2 with $\pi_2(\tilde{w}, \tilde{x}) > 0$, show that there exists a *more* risk-averse utility u_1 with *smaller* partial-insurance premium $\pi_1(\tilde{w}, \tilde{x})$.

d. Show that if $\pi_1(\tilde{w}, \tilde{x}) > \pi_2(\tilde{w},\tilde{x}) > 0$ for all x, y, then $u_1'(0)$ and $u_2'(0)$ are finite and $u_1''(y)/u_1'(0) \leq u_2''(y)/u_2'(0)$ for all y.
Hint Let $x \to 0$ and $p \to 0$.

e. Show the converse of (d) for all $\tilde{w}$, $\tilde{x}$ with $E(\tilde{x}|\tilde{w}) = 0$ provided $\tilde{w} + \tilde{x}$ and $\tilde{w} - \pi_2(\tilde{w}, \tilde{x})$ are in $[0, w_1]$ with probability 1.
Hint Let $G = u_1 - \lambda u_2$ for $\lambda = u_1'(0)/u_2'(0)$. Show G is concave and decreasing, hence $EG(w + \tilde{x}) \leq G(w) \leq G(w - \pi)$ if $E\tilde{x} = 0 < \pi$, hence

$$E\{u_1(\tilde{w} + \tilde{x}) - u_1(\tilde{w} - \pi)\} \leq \lambda E\{u_2(\tilde{w} + \tilde{x}) - u_2(\tilde{w} - \pi)\}.$$

f. Restrict $\tilde{w} + \tilde{x}$ and $\tilde{w} - \pi_2(\tilde{w}, \tilde{x})$ to an interval $[w_0, w]$ and assume $u_1'(w_0)$ and $u_2'(w_0)$ are finite. Show that $\pi_1(\tilde{w}, \tilde{x}) \geq \pi_2(\tilde{w}, \tilde{x})$ for all $\tilde{w}$, $\tilde{x}$ with $E(\tilde{x}|\tilde{w}) = 0$ if and only if $u_1''(y)/u_1'(w_0) \leq u_2''(y)/u_2'(w_0)$ for all $y \in [w_0, w_1]$.

g. One might say that u_1 is more partial-risk averse than u_2 on $[w_0, w_1]$. Show that if the condition in *f* holds then u_1 is more risk averse than u_2 on $[w_0, w_1]$.

h. Let each u_i have constant risk aversion a_i. Show that the condition in *f* is satisfied if and only if $a_1 = a_2$ or $a_1 > a_2$ and the interval has length

$$w_1 - w_0 \leq \frac{\log(a_1/a_2)}{a_1 - a_2}.$$

Therefore the condition can hold on overlapping intervals yet not on their union. Also the length of the interval on which it holds decreases as a_1 increases and approaches 0 as $a_1 \to \infty$ with a_2 fixed. This illustrates that the condition is not as natural as it might seem and that partial insurance is tricky.

28. Let $\tilde{S}_n$ be the sum of n independent repetitions of a gamble, independent of $\tilde{w}$. If u is proper, show that $Eu(\tilde{w} + \tilde{S}_n)$ is increasing in n up to some m (perhaps 0 or ∞) and decreasing thereafter, in contrast to exercise 26.

29. Show that quadratic utility satisfies (A3.11) if the final $\tilde{y}$ is omitted.

30. a. Prove (A3.14) and (A3.15) from (A3.13). (Proving (A3.13) itself is surprisingly hard.)

b. Show that (A3.11) corresponds to dropping one term on the right-hand side of (A3.14).

c. Show that (A3.15) is stronger than (A3.14) and (A3.14) than (A3.11).

31. Show that under decreasing risk aversion, if $\tilde{y}$ is a positive constant, then the inequalities in (A3.14) and (A3.15) are reversed for all x.

32. a. Show that if u is proper then $r'' \geq r'r$.

 b. Show that $r'' \geq r'r$ if and only if $u'r'$ is increasing.

33. Show directly that all HARA utility functions satisfy the condition (A3.16).

34. Show that the condition in (A3.16) is preserved under mixing.
Hint $-u'''/u''$ is the risk aversion function for the utility function $-u'$.

35. Show that u is decreasingly risk averse if and only if $-u'$ (viewed as a utility function in its own right) is more risk averse than u.

36. Show that u_1 is more risk averse than u_2 if and only if, for all w and y,

$$\frac{u_1(y) - u_1(w)}{u_1'(w)} \leq \frac{u_2(y) - u_2(w)}{u_2'(w)}.$$

37. Show that u is decreasingly risk averse if and only if, for every y, $(u(w + y) - u(w))/u'(w)$ is decreasing in w.
Hint Use exercise 36.

38. If $-u'''/u''$ is decreasing, show that

 a. $u'(w + z + y) - u'(w + z) - u''(w + z)[u'(w + y) - u'(w)]/u''(w)$ has the same sign as z for all w, y, z.
Hint Replace u by $-u'$ in exercise 37.

 b. $u(w + x + y) - u(w + x) - u(w + y) + u(w) \geq [u'(w + x) - u'(w)][u'(w + y) - u'(w)]/u''(w)$ for all w, x, y.
Hint Integrate over z in part a, or use the Mean Value theorem.

 c. If $\tilde{x}$ and $\tilde{y}$ are independent and $Eu'(w + \tilde{x})$ and $Eu'(w + \tilde{y})$ are both larger or both smaller than $u'(w)$, then

$$E\{u(w + \tilde{x} + \tilde{y}) - u(w + \tilde{x}) - u(w + \tilde{y}) + u(w)\} \leq 0.$$

39. If $-u''/u'$ and $-u'''/u''$ are both decreasing, show that u is proper using exercises 34, 35, and 38c.

40. Show that if u is an exponential mixture then

 a. u has positive odd derivatives and negative even derivatives.

 b. $0 \geq u''/u' \geq u'''/u'' \geq \ldots$.

 c. u_i is more risk averse than u_{i-1} for every i, where $(-1)^i u_i$ is the ith derivative of u.

41. Mr. Mensch is decreasingly risk averse but there is a gamble so small that he would be exactly indifferent between the gamble and its EMV. Show that if another gamble has minimum payoff at least as great, then he would be indifferent between that gamble and its EMV, no matter how risky it may be.

42. Show that a person with total assets $w = \$1{,}000$ and utility $-1/w^2$ would pay only \$229 for a 50% chance at a \$1,000 prize, but \$4.96 for a 50% chance at \$10 and \$0.4995 for a 50% chance at \$1.

43. For constant risk aversion c, show that for any Δ the cash equivalent of a 50% chance at Δ determines c and verify the following table of cash equivalents.

Δ	\$10,000	5,000	1,000	500	100	50	10
c							
0.00008222	4,000	2,244.83	489.73	247.43	49.90	24.97	4.999
0.00018011	3,000	1,955.22	477.52	244.37	49.78	24.94	4.998
0.00032813	2,000	1,572.43	459.17	239.76	49.59	24.90	4.996

Would it make more sense to determine c by assessing the cash equivalent of a 50% chance at \$10, \$100, or \$10,000?

44. For constant risk aversion c, show that if the risk premium of a 50% chance at Δ is less than $.1\Delta$, then it is within 3% of $c\Delta^2/8$.

45. Suppose a decreasingly risk averse individual would pay \$200 + 10,000p to insure against a chance p of losing \$10,000. Show that, if $p < \frac{1}{2}$, he would pay less than \$2.002 + 1,000p to insure against a chance p of losing \$1,000 and less than \$0.02002 + 100p to insure against a chance p of losing \$100.

46. Given n points on a concave function u, how can the range of possible values $u(x)$ at a given x be determined graphically? Analytically?

47. a. Show that if $r_1 - r_2$ changes sign n times then $u_1 - u_2$ changes sign at most $n + 2$ times, where r_i is the risk aversion function of the utility function u_i.
Hint On any interval, f changes sign at most one more time than f', and if φ is strictly monotonic, $\varphi(f_1(x)) - \varphi(f_2(x))$ changes sign the same number of times as $f_1 - f_2$.

b. Show that a decreasingly risk averse utility function can cross an exponential utility function at most three times.

c. Given three points on a decreasingly risk averse utility function u, say $[x_i, u(x_i)]$ for $i = 1, 2, 3$ with $x_1 < x_2 < x_3$, let u_0 be an exponential utility passing through these three points. Show that $u(x) \leq u_0(x)$ for $x \leq x_1$ and for $x \in [x_2, x_3]$ while $u(x) \geq u_0(x)$ elsewhere.

d. Obtain from (c) a necessary and sufficient condition for the existence of a decreasingly risk averse utility function u passing through four given points and a tight upper or lower bound for $u(x)$ at each x if u exists. (The other bounds and bounds for more points are harder to obtain. See Meyer and Pratt, 1968.)

48. Show that for $u(x) = a - \sum_{i=1}^{n} b_i e^{-c_i x}$ with the c_i given, it is a linear programming problem to find the maximum and minimum possible value of $u(x)$ subject to the conditions that all $b_i \geq 0$ and u passes through each of m given points (Richard F. Meyer, unpublished).

49. Show that a utility function cannot be proper if it is too close to piecewise exponential.

50. Drax Industries (DI) must decide what to do about next year's theft insurance policy on its Moonraker. It has just finished manufacturing this exotic piece of equipment, which is to be delivered a year hence, along with another on which production is just beginning. The loss to DI if the completed Moonraker is stolen will be \$1 million. The probability of theft is unrelated to any other DI business and is assessed at the same value p by both DI and the insurance company. Insurance is expensive, unfortunately, but DI can insure for less than the full amount. Specifically, the insurance company offers to pay DI any amount w up to \$1 million, in case of theft, in return for an insurance premium of $3pw$. DI is tax-exempt, of course.

a. Suppose that DI is solely owned by a Mr. John W. Drax whose utility function for a change of \$$x$ in DI's assets is $-e^{-ax}$ where a is a constant. Derive the optimum choice of w. (It is $1{,}000{,}000 - (1/a)\ln(3 - 3p)/(1 - 3p)$ when the solution is "interior.")

b. What is the relevance of the statement that theft is unrelated to other DI business?

c. What would the optimum w be if DI were owned in equal shares by five people each having the same utility function $-e^{-ax}$ for his or her share?

d. Would the optimum in (c) be Pareto optimal?

e. Give an equation satisfied by an interior optimum w when Mr. Drax has an arbitrary utility function.

f. How would the analysis change for five equal-shared owners with arbitrary concave utility functions, possibly all the same, possibly not?

51. Jack and Jill each have wealth 1 Utopian Crown. Jack's utility function is $\sqrt{v}$, Jill's is $-1/v$, where v is wealth in Crowns. A lottery ticket is available that costs 1 Crown and gives a chance p of winning 10 Crowns (gaining 9 Crowns).

Show that there is a probability p such that they would not agree to buy the ticket, yet the ticket's availability permits them to make a deal whereby both gain.

52. Kahneman and Tversky (1982) discuss S-shaped utility functions with some interesting properties. For instance, they are risk averse for gains and risk seeking for losses. The certainty equivalent of a 50% chance of a prize x is always the same multiple of x and similarly for losses. A "loss has a greater subjective effect than an equivalent gain." Kahneman and Tversky graph a case where utility is proportional to $x^{2/3}$ for $x > 0$ and proportional to $-(-x)^{3/4}$ for $x < 0$.

    Let $u(x) = 1/(1 + e^{-cx})$ for fixed $c > 0$. The function u is sometimes called S-shaped. (In fact it is shaped rather like the Normal cumulative distribution.) How does u compare to Kahneman and Tversky's S-shaped functions with respect to the foregoing properties and any others you think of? How do they behave for very small and very large gains and losses?

53. Mr. Daniel R. Amos (R stands for Rational) has the utility function suggested by Kahneman and Tversky, namely $ux = x^{2/3}$ for gains $x > 0$ and $u(-y) = -by^{3/4}$ for losses $y > 0$, where b is a positive constant to be determined below.

    a. Kahneman and Tversky say, "A 50 percent chance to win a given amount is just as acceptable as a sure gain of [P] percent of that amount." Derive a formula for P and show that it doesn't depend on the amount. (Kahneman and Tversky use the approximation $P = 35$.)

    b. Is Mr. Amos decreasingly risk averse for gains? (Justify your answer. His initials are strictly coincidental.)

    c. Define $f(x)$ for $x > 0$ so that Mr. Amos finds an even chance of winning x or losing $f(x)$ just acceptable. Suppose that $f(200) = 100$, as in Kahneman and Tversky's example. Derive formulas for the constant b (mentioned above) and for $f(x)$.

    d. Evaluate $\lim f(x)/x$ as $x \to 0$ and explain its behavioral meaning.

    e. Mr. Amos faces a 10% chance, in his judgment, that before June 1 his car will be stolen from his parking place in the slum where his limited financial resources force him to live. He would need to replace it with a similar heap (vehicle) at a cost of \$1,000. He is considering buying insurance. What would he be charged by an insurance company that is risk neutral, agrees with his 10% and adds no charge for commission, overhead, and profit, if he were so lucky as to find one?

    f. Show that Mr. Amos would be unwilling to pay that much.

    g. Find the maximum amount that Mr. Amos would be willing to pay.

Appendix 4: Tables

STANDARDIZED NORMAL LINEAR LOSS FUNCTION

	EXP	0	1	2	3	4	5	6	7	8
0.	0	3989	3940	3890	3841	3793	3744	3697	3649	3602
0.1	0	3509	3464	3418	3373	3328	3284	3240	3197	3154
0.2	0	3069	3027	2986	2944	2904	2863	2824	2784	2745
0.3	0	2668	2630	2592	2555	2518	2481	2445	2409	2374
0.4	0	2304	2270	2236	2203	2169	2137	2104	2072	2040
0.5	0	1978	1947	1917	1887	1857	1828	1799	1771	1742
0.6	0	1687	1659	1633	1606	1580	1554	1528	1503	1478
0.7	0	1429	1405	1381	1358	1334	1312	1289	1267	1245
0.8	0	1202	1181	1160	1140	1120	1100	1080	1061	1042
0.9	0	1004	986	968	950	933	916	899	882	865
1.0	-1	8332	8174	8019	7866	7716	7568	7422	7279	7138
1.1	-1	6862	6727	6595	6465	6336	6210	6086	5964	5844
1.2	-1	5610	5496	5384	5274	5165	5059	4954	4851	4750
1.3	-1	4553	4457	4363	4270	4179	4090	4002	3916	3831
1.4	-1	3667	3587	3508	3431	3356	3281	3208	3137	3067
1.5	-1	2931	2865	2800	2736	2674	2612	2552	2494	2436
1.6	-1	2324	2270	2217	2165	2114	2064	2015	1967	1920
1.7	-1	1829	1785	1742	1699	1658	1617	1578	1539	1501
1.8	-1	1428	1392	1357	1323	1290	1257	1226	1195	1164
1.9	-1	1105	1077	1049	1022	996	970	945	920	896
2.0	-2	8491	8266	8046	7832	7623	7418	7219	7024	6835
2.1	-2	6468	6292	6120	5952	5788	5628	5472	5320	5172
2.2	-2	4887	4750	4616	4486	4358	4235	4114	3996	3882
2.3	-2	3662	3556	3453	3352	3255	3159	3067	2977	2889
2.4	-2	2720	2640	2561	2484	2410	2337	2267	2199	2132
2.5	-2	2004	1943	1883	1826	1769	1715	1662	1610	1560
2.6	-2	1464	1418	1373	1330	1288	1247	1207	1169	1132
2.7	-2	1060	1026	993	961	929	899	870	841	814
2.8	-3	7611	7359	7115	6879	6650	6428	6213	6004	5802
2.9	-3	5417	5233	5055	4883	4716	4555	4398	4247	4101
3.0	-3	3822	3689	3560	3436	3316	3199	3087	2978	2873
3.1	-3	2672	2577	2485	2396	2311	2227	2147	2070	1995
3.2	-3	1852	1785	1720	1657	1596	1537	1480	1426	1373
3.3	-3	1273	1225	1179	1135	1093	1051	1012	973	937
3.4	-4	8666	8335	8016	7709	7412	7127	6852	6587	6331
3.5	-4	5848	5620	5400	5188	4984	4788	4599	4417	4242
3.6	-4	3911	3755	3605	3460	3321	3188	3059	2935	2816
3.7	-4	2592	2486	2385	2287	2193	2103	2016	1933	1853
3.8	-4	1702	1632	1563	1498	1435	1375	1317	1262	1208
3.9	-4	1108	1061	1016	972	931	891	853	816	781
4.0	-5	7145	6835	6538	6253	5980	5718	5468	5227	4997
4.1	-5	4566	4364	4170	3985	3807	3637	3475	3319	3170
4.2	-5	2891	2760	2635	2516	2402	2292	2188	2088	1992
4.3	-5	1814	1730	1650	1574	1501	1431	1365	1301	1241
4.4	-5	1127	1074	1024	976	930	886	844	804	765
4.5	-6	6942	6610	6294	5992	5704	5429	5167	4917	4679
4.6	-6	4236	4029	3833	3645	3467	3297	3135	2981	2834
4.7	-6	2560	2433	2312	2197	2088	1984	1884	1790	1700
4.8	-6	1533	1456	1382	1312	1246	1182	1122	1065	1011
4.9	-7	9096	8629	8185	7763	7362	6982	6620	6276	5950

MT-4R

9	10	Tenths of Mean Tabular Difference				
3556	3509	5	10	14	19	24
3111	3069	4	9	13	18	22
2706	2668	4	8	12	16	20
2339	2304	4	7	11	15	18
2009	1978	3	7	10	13	16
1714	1687	3	6	9	12	15
1453	1429	3	5	8	10	13
1223	1202	2	5	7	9	11
1023	1004	2	4	6	8	10
849	833	2	3	5	7	9
6999	6862	15	29	44	59	73
5726	5610	13	25	38	50	63
4650	4553	11	21	32	42	53
3748	3667	9	18	27	35	44
2998	2931	7	15	22	29	37
2380	2324	6	12	18	24	30
1874	1829	5	10	15	20	25
1464	1428	4	8	12	16	20
1134	1105	3	6	10	13	16
872	849	3	5	8	10	13
6649	6468	20	40	61	81	101
5028	4887	16	32	47	63	79
3770	3662	12	25	37	49	61
2804	2720	9	19	28	38	47
2067	2004	7	14	21	29	36
1511	1464	5	11	16	22	27
1095	1060	4	8	12	16	20
787	761	3	6	9	12	15
5606	5417	22	44	66	88	110
3959	3822	16	32	48	64	80
2771	2672	11	23	34	46	57
1922	1852	8	16	25	33	41
1322	1273	6	12	17	23	29
901	867	4	8	12	16	20
6085	5848	28	56	85	113	141
4073	3911	19	39	58	77	97
2702	2592	13	26	40	53	66
1776	1702	9	18	27	36	44
1157	1108	6	12	18	24	30
747	715	4	8	12	16	20
4777	4566	26	52	77	103	129
3027	2891	17	33	50	67	84
1901	1814	11	22	32	43	54
1183	1127	7	14	21	27	34
729	694	4	9	13	17	22
4452	4236	27	54	81	108	135
2694	2560	17	34	50	67	84
1615	1533	10	21	31	41	51
959	910	6	12	19	25	31
5640	5346	38	75	113	150	188

FRACTILES OF THE BETA DISTRIBUTION

n	r	k: .01	.05	.10	.15	.20	.25	.30	.35	.40	.45
2	1	0100	0500	1000	1500	2000	2500	3000	3500	4000	4500
3	1	0050	0253	0513	0780	1056	1340	1633	1938	2254	2584
4	1	0033	0170	0345	0527	0717	0914	1121	1338	1566	1807
4	2	0589	1354	1958	2444	2871	3264	3633	3986	4329	4666
5	1	0025	0127	0260	0398	0543	0694	0853	1021	1199	1388
5	2	0420	0976	1426	1794	2123	2430	2724	3010	3292	3573
6	1	0020	0102	0209	0320	0436	0559	0689	0825	0971	1127
6	2	0327	0764	1122	1419	1686	1938	2180	2418	2656	2895
6	3	1056	1893	2466	2899	3266	3594	3898	4186	4463	4733
7	1	0017	0085	0174	0267	0365	0468	0577	0693	0816	0948
7	2	0268	0628	0926	1174	1399	1612	1818	2022	2226	2433
7	3	0847	1532	2009	2374	2686	2969	3233	3486	3731	3973
8	1	0014	0073	0149	0229	0314	0403	0497	0597	0704	0819
8	2	0227	0534	0788	1001	1195	1380	1559	1737	1916	2098
8	3	0708	1288	1696	2011	2283	2531	2763	2987	3206	3423
8	4	1423	2253	2786	3176	3501	3788	4052	4301	4539	4771
9	1	0013	0064	0131	0201	0275	0353	0436	0524	0619	0720
9	2	0197	0464	0686	0873	1044	1206	1365	1523	1682	1844
9	3	0608	1111	1469	1746	1986	2206	2413	2614	2811	3007
9	4	1210	1929	2397	2742	3032	3291	3530	3756	3975	4189
10	1	0011	0057	0116	0179	0245	0315	0389	0467	0552	0643
10	2	0174	0410	0608	0774	0926	1072	1214	1355	1498	1645
10	3	0533	0977	1295	1542	1757	1955	2142	2324	2502	2681
10	4	1053	1688	2104	2414	2675	2910	3127	3335	3535	3733
10	5	1710	2514	3010	3367	3661	3920	4156	4378	4590	4796
11	1	0010	0051	0105	0161	0221	0284	0350	0422	0498	0580
11	2	0155	0368	0545	0695	0833	0964	1093	1221	1351	1485
11	3	0475	0873	1158	1381	1576	1756	1926	2092	2255	2419
11	4	0932	1500	1876	2156	2394	2609	2808	2999	3184	3367
11	5	1504	2224	2673	2998	3268	3507	3726	3932	4131	4325
12	1	0009	0047	0095	0147	0201	0258	0319	0384	0454	0529
12	2	0141	0333	0495	0631	0756	0876	0994	1111	1230	1353
12	3	0428	0788	1048	1251	1429	1593	1750	1902	2052	2204
12	4	0837	1351	1692	1949	2167	2364	2548	2724	2896	3067
12	5	1344	1996	2405	2704	2953	3173	3377	3570	3755	3938
12	6	1940	2712	3177	3508	3779	4016	4232	4434	4627	4815
13	1	0008	0043	0088	0135	0184	0237	0293	0353	0417	0486
13	2	0128	0305	0452	0577	0693	0803	0911	1020	1130	1242
13	3	0390	0719	0957	1143	1307	1459	1603	1744	1883	2024
13	4	0759	1229	1542	1778	1979	2162	2332	2496	2656	2815
13	5	1215	1810	2187	2463	2693	2898	3088	3268	3443	3614
13	6	1746	2453	2882	3189	3441	3663	3866	4057	4240	4418
14	1	0008	0039	0081	0124	0170	0219	0271	0326	0385	0449
14	2	0118	0281	0417	0532	0639	0741	0841	0942	1044	1149
14	3	0358	0660	0880	1053	1204	1345	1479	1610	1740	1871
14	4	0695	1127	1416	1635	1822	1991	2150	2303	2453	2602
14	5	1108	1657	2005	2261	2476	2668	2845	3014	3178	3340
14	6	1588	2240	2637	2923	3160	3368	3559	3740	3913	4082
14	7	2129	2870	3309	3618	3870	4090	4290	4477	4656	4829

MT-5a-R

.50	.55	.60	.65	.70	.75	.80	.85	.90	.95	.99
5000	5500	6000	6500	7000	7500	8000	8500	9000	9500	9900
2929	3292	3675	4084	4523	5000	5528	6127	6838	7764	9000
2063	2337	2632	2953	3306	3700	4152	4687	5358	6316	7846
5000	5334	5671	6014	6367	6736	7129	7556	8042	8646	9411
1591	1810	2047	2308	2599	2929	3313	3777	4377	5271	6838
3857	4147	4445	4756	5084	5437	5825	6265	6795	7514	8591
1294	1476	1674	1894	2140	2421	2752	3157	3690	4507	6019
3138	3389	3650	3925	4220	4542	4902	5321	5839	6574	7779
5000	5267	5537	5814	6102	6406	6734	7101	7534	8107	8944
1091	1246	1416	1605	1818	2063	2353	2711	3187	3930	5358
2644	2864	3094	3339	3604	3895	4224	4613	5103	5818	7057
4214	4458	4708	4967	5239	5532	5854	6222	6668	7287	8269
0943	1078	1227	1393	1580	1797	2054	2374	2803	3482	4821
2285	2480	2685	2905	3143	3407	3709	4067	4526	5207	6434
3641	3863	4092	4331	4586	4861	5168	5523	5962	6587	7637
5000	5229	5461	5699	5948	6212	6499	6824	7214	7747	8577
0830	0950	1082	1230	1397	1591	1822	2111	2501	3123	4377
2011	2186	2371	2570	2786	3027	3304	3635	4062	4707	5899
3205	3408	3618	3839	4075	4332	4621	4959	5382	5997	7068
4402	4616	4835	5061	5299	5555	5837	6159	6554	7108	8018
0741	0849	0968	1101	1252	1428	1637	1901	2257	2831	4005
1796	1955	2123	2304	2501	2723	2978	3285	3684	4291	5440
2862	3048	3242	3446	3665	3905	4177	4496	4901	5496	6563
3931	4131	4336	4550	4776	5020	5291	5605	5994	6551	7500
5000	5204	5410	5622	5844	6080	6339	6633	6990	7486	8290
0670	0767	0876	0997	1134	1294	1487	1728	2057	2589	3690
1623	1767	1921	2087	2269	2474	2710	2996	3368	3942	5044
2586	2757	2936	3126	3330	3554	3809	4111	4496	5069	6117
3551	3738	3930	4131	4345	4577	4837	5139	5517	6066	7029
4517	4710	4907	5111	5325	5555	5809	6100	6458	6965	7817
0611	0700	0799	0910	1037	1184	1361	1584	1889	2384	3421
1480	1613	1755	1908	2077	2266	2486	2753	3102	3644	4698
2358	2517	2683	2860	3050	3261	3501	3786	4152	4701	5723
3238	3413	3593	3782	3984	4205	4452	4742	5108	5644	6604
4119	4302	4489	4684	4889	5111	5357	5642	5995	6502	7378
5000	5185	5373	5566	5768	5984	6221	6492	6823	7288	8060
0561	0644	0735	0838	0955	1091	1255	1462	1746	2209	3187
1360	1483	1615	1757	1914	2091	2296	2546	2875	3387	4395
2167	2315	2470	2635	2814	3012	3238	3508	3855	4381	5373
2976	3140	3309	3488	3679	3888	4124	4401	4753	5273	6222
3785	3958	4136	4322	4518	4731	4968	5245	5590	6091	6976
4595	4772	4953	5140	5336	5547	5779	6047	6377	6848	7651
0519	0596	0681	0776	0885	1011	1164	1358	1623	2058	2983
1258	1373	1496	1629	1775	1941	2133	2368	2678	3163	4128
2004	2143	2288	2443	2611	2798	3011	3267	3598	4101	5062
2753	2907	3067	3235	3416	3615	3839	4105	4443	4946	5878
3502	3666	3835	4011	4199	4403	4631	4899	5234	5726	6609
4251	4420	4593	4773	4963	5167	5394	5657	5982	6452	7271
5000	5171	5344	5523	5710	5910	6130	6382	6691	7130	7871

FRACTILES OF THE BETA DISTRIBUTION

n	r	k: .01	.05	.10	.15	.20	.25	.30	.35	.40	.45
15	1	0007	0037	0075	0115	0158	0203	0252	0303	0358	0418
15	2	0110	0260	0387	0494	0593	0688	0781	0875	0970	1068
15	3	0331	0611	0815	0975	1117	1248	1373	1495	1617	1739
15	4	0640	1040	1309	1513	1688	1846	1995	2138	2279	2419
15	5	1019	1527	1851	2090	2291	2471	2638	2797	2952	3104
15	6	1457	2061	2432	2699	2921	3117	3298	3468	3633	3794
15	7	1947	2636	3046	3336	3574	3782	3972	4151	4321	4487
16	1	0007	0034	0070	0108	0148	0190	0235	0283	0335	0391
16	2	0102	0242	0360	0461	0553	0642	0729	0817	0906	0998
16	3	0307	0568	0759	0909	1041	1163	1281	1395	1510	1625
16	4	0594	0967	1218	1408	1572	1720	1860	1995	2128	2260
16	5	0944	1417	1720	1944	2132	2301	2459	2609	2755	2900
16	6	1346	1909	2256	2507	2716	2902	3072	3234	3390	3544
16	7	1795	2437	2822	3096	3321	3518	3699	3869	4032	4191
16	8	2287	3000	3415	3707	3944	4150	4337	4512	4679	4840
17	1	0006	0032	0066	0101	0138	0178	0220	0266	0314	0367
17	2	0095	0227	0337	0431	0518	0602	0684	0766	0850	0937
17	3	0287	0531	0710	0850	0975	1090	1200	1308	1416	1525
17	4	0554	0903	1138	1317	1471	1611	1743	1870	1995	2121
17	5	0878	1321	1606	1816	1994	2154	2303	2445	2583	2721
17	6	1251	1778	2104	2341	2539	2714	2876	3030	3178	3324
17	7	1665	2267	2629	2888	3101	3289	3461	3623	3779	3931
17	8	2117	2786	3178	3455	3680	3877	4056	4224	4384	4540
18	1	0006	0030	0062	0095	0130	0168	0208	0250	0296	0346
18	2	0090	0213	0317	0406	0488	0566	0644	0722	0801	0883
18	3	0269	0499	0667	0799	0916	1025	1129	1232	1333	1436
18	4	0519	0846	1068	1237	1382	1514	1639	1760	1879	1997
18	5	0822	1238	1506	1705	1873	2024	2165	2300	2432	2562
18	6	1168	1664	1972	2196	2383	2549	2703	2849	2991	3131
18	7	1552	2119	2461	2707	2909	3088	3252	3406	3555	3702
18	8	1971	2601	2973	3235	3450	3638	3809	3970	4124	4275
18	9	2422	3108	3504	3780	4004	4199	4376	4541	4698	4850
19	1	0006	0028	0058	0090	0123	0159	0196	0236	0280	0327
19	2	0085	0201	0299	0383	0460	0535	0608	0682	0757	0834
19	3	0254	0470	0629	0754	0865	0968	1066	1163	1260	1358
19	4	0488	0797	1006	1166	1304	1429	1547	1662	1775	1888
19	5	0772	1164	1418	1606	1765	1909	2043	2171	2297	2422
19	6	1096	1563	1855	2067	2245	2404	2550	2690	2825	2958
19	7	1454	1990	2314	2547	2740	2910	3067	3215	3357	3497
19	8	1844	2440	2792	3042	3247	3427	3591	3746	3894	4039
19	9	2263	2912	3288	3552	3767	3954	4124	4283	4434	4582
20	1	0005	0027	0055	0085	0117	0150	0186	0224	0265	0310
20	2	0080	0190	0283	0363	0436	0507	0576	0646	0717	0791
20	3	0240	0445	0595	0714	0819	0916	1010	1102	1194	1287
20	4	0461	0753	0951	1103	1233	1353	1465	1574	1682	1789
20	5	0728	1099	1339	1518	1670	1806	1934	2057	2176	2295
20	6	1032	1475	1751	1953	2123	2274	2414	2547	2676	2804
20	7	1368	1875	2183	2405	2589	2752	2902	3043	3180	3315
20	8	1733	2297	2633	2871	3067	3239	3397	3545	3688	3827
20	9	2124	2739	3098	3351	3556	3736	3900	4053	4199	4342
20	10	2540	3201	3579	3843	4056	4241	4408	4565	4713	4858

MT-5b

.50	.55	.60	.65	.70	.75	.80	.85	.90	.95	.99
0483	0554	0634	0722	0824	0943	1086	1267	1517	1926	2803
1170	1278	1393	1517	1655	1810	1992	2213	2507	2967	3891
1865	1995	2131	2277	2436	2612	2814	3057	3372	3854	4783
2561	2700	2857	3017	3189	3377	3592	3845	4170	4657	5567
3258	3413	3574	3742	3921	4117	4336	4594	4920	5400	6274
3954	4116	4282	4455	4637	4835	5055	5311	5631	6096	6920
4651	4816	4984	5157	5339	5535	5751	6001	6309	6750	7512
0452	0518	0593	0676	0771	0883	1017	1188	1423	1810	2644
1094	1195	1303	1420	1550	1697	1868	2077	2356	2794	3679
1743	1866	1995	2133	2283	2450	2641	2872	3173	3634	4532
2394	2531	2675	2826	2989	3169	3373	3616	3928	4398	5285
3045	3193	3346	3506	3678	3865	4076	4325	4640	5108	5969
3697	3852	4010	4176	4352	4543	4756	5005	5317	5774	6597
4348	4507	4669	4836	5013	5204	5415	5660	5965	6404	7177
5000	5160	5321	5488	5663	5850	6056	6293	6585	7000	7713
0424	0487	0557	0635	0725	0830	0957	1118	1340	1707	2501
1027	1122	1224	1335	1457	1596	1758	1957	2222	2640	3488
1637	1752	1874	2005	2147	2306	2488	2709	2996	3438	4305
2247	2378	2514	2658	2813	2985	3180	3413	3712	4166	5029
2859	3000	3145	3299	3463	3642	3845	4085	4389	4844	5690
3471	3619	3771	3930	4099	4283	4489	4731	5035	5483	6299
4082	4235	4391	4553	4724	4909	5116	5355	5654	6090	6866
4694	4849	5006	5168	5339	5522	5726	5960	6250	6666	7393
0400	0459	0525	0599	0684	0783	0903	1056	1267	1616	2373
0968	1058	1154	1259	1375	1507	1661	1850	2102	2501	3316
1542	1652	1768	1892	2027	2178	2352	2562	2837	3262	4099
2118	2242	2371	2509	2657	2821	3008	3231	3519	3956	4796
2694	2828	2968	3114	3271	3444	3639	3869	4164	4605	5434
3270	3412	3558	3711	3874	4051	4251	4485	4781	5219	6025
3847	3994	4144	4300	4466	4646	4846	5080	5374	5803	6577
4423	4573	4725	4883	5049	5229	5428	5658	5945	6360	7094
5000	5150	5302	5459	5624	5801	5996	6220	6496	6892	7578
0378	0434	0496	0567	0647	0741	0855	1000	1201	1533	2257
0915	1001	1092	1192	1302	1427	1574	1754	1995	2377	3160
1458	1563	1673	1791	1920	2064	2230	2431	2694	3103	3912
2002	2121	2244	2375	2517	2674	2853	3067	3344	3767	4583
2547	2676	2809	2949	3100	3265	3453	3676	3960	4389	5199
3092	3228	3368	3515	3672	3843	4036	4263	4550	4978	5772
3637	3778	3923	4074	4235	4409	4604	4832	5118	5540	6309
4182	4327	4474	4628	4789	4964	5159	5385	5667	6078	6814
4727	4873	5022	5175	5336	5510	5702	5923	6198	6594	7290
0358	0412	0471	0538	0614	0704	0812	0950	1141	1459	2152
0868	0949	1036	1131	1236	1355	1495	1668	1898	2264	3018
1383	1482	1587	1700	1823	1961	2120	2312	2565	2958	3741
1899	2012	2130	2255	2391	2541	2713	2919	3186	3594	4387
2415	2538	2666	2801	2945	3105	3285	3500	3775	4191	4983
2932	3063	3197	3339	3490	3655	3841	4061	4340	4758	5538
3449	3585	3725	3871	4026	4195	4384	4606	4886	5300	6060
3966	4106	4249	4397	4554	4725	4915	5136	5413	5819	6553
4483	4625	4769	4919	5076	5246	5435	5653	5925	6319	7020
5000	5142	5287	5435	5592	5759	5944	6157	6421	6799	7460

FRACTILES OF THE BETA DISTRIBUTION

n	r	k: .01	.05	.10	.15	.20	.25	.30	.35	.40	.45
21	1	0005	0026	0053	0081	0111	0143	0177	0213	0252	0294
21	2	0076	0181	0269	0344	0414	0481	0547	0614	0682	0752
21	3	0227	0422	0564	0677	0777	0870	0959	1047	1135	1224
21	4	0436	0714	0902	1046	1170	1284	1391	1495	1598	1701
21	5	0688	1041	1269	1440	1584	1714	1836	1953	2068	2182
21	6	0975	1396	1659	1851	2013	2157	2291	2418	2542	2665
21	7	1292	1773	2067	2278	2454	2610	2753	2889	3021	3150
21	8	1634	2171	2491	2719	2906	3071	3223	3365	3503	3637
21	9	2001	2587	2929	3171	3368	3541	3699	3846	3988	4126
21	10	2390	3020	3382	3635	3840	4018	4180	4331	4476	4616
22	1	0005	0024	0050	0077	0106	0136	0168	0203	0240	0281
22	2	0072	0172	0256	0328	0394	0458	0521	0585	0650	0717
22	3	0216	0401	0537	0644	0740	0828	0914	0997	1081	1166
22	4	0414	0678	0858	0995	1114	1222	1325	1424	1522	1621
22	5	0653	0988	1206	1369	1507	1631	1748	1860	1969	2079
22	6	0925	1324	1575	1759	1914	2052	2180	2302	2421	2539
22	7	1223	1682	1962	2164	2333	2482	2620	2750	2877	3001
22	8	1546	2057	2363	2582	2762	2920	3066	3203	3335	3465
22	9	1891	2450	2778	3010	3199	3366	3517	3660	3797	3930
22	10	2257	2858	3205	3448	3646	3818	3974	4121	4261	4397
22	11	2642	3281	3644	3896	4100	4277	4436	4585	4727	4865
23	1	0005	0023	0048	0074	0101	0130	0161	0194	0230	0268
23	2	0069	0164	0244	0313	0376	0437	0498	0558	0620	0684
23	3	0206	0382	0512	0615	0706	0790	0872	0952	1032	1113
23	4	0394	0646	0817	0949	1062	1166	1264	1359	1453	1548
23	5	0621	0941	1149	1304	1436	1556	1667	1775	1880	1985
23	6	0879	1260	1500	1676	1824	1956	2079	2197	2311	2425
23	7	1162	1599	1867	2061	2223	2366	2498	2624	2746	2866
23	8	1468	1956	2248	2458	2631	2783	2923	3056	3183	3309
23	9	1793	2327	2642	2864	3047	3207	3353	3491	3623	3753
23	10	2138	2713	3046	3280	3471	3637	3788	3930	4065	4198
23	11	2501	3113	3462	3705	3902	4073	4228	4372	4510	4644
24	1	0004	0022	0046	0070	0097	0124	0154	0186	0220	0257
24	2	0066	0157	0234	0299	0360	0418	0476	0534	0594	0655
24	3	0196	0365	0489	0587	0675	0756	0834	0911	0988	1066
24	4	0376	0617	0781	0906	1015	1114	1209	1300	1390	1481
24	5	0593	0898	1097	1246	1372	1487	1594	1697	1799	1899
24	6	0838	1202	1432	1601	1742	1870	1988	2101	2211	2320
24	7	1107	1525	1782	1968	2123	2260	2388	2509	2626	2742
24	8	1397	1863	2144	2345	2512	2658	2793	2921	3044	3165
24	9	1705	2216	2518	2732	2908	3062	3204	3337	3465	3590
24	10	2031	2582	2903	3128	3312	3472	3619	3756	3888	4016
24	11	2374	2961	3297	3532	3722	3887	4038	4178	4312	4443
24	12	2733	3351	3701	3943	4139	4308	4461	4603	4739	4870
25	1	0004	0021	0044	0067	0093	0119	0148	0178	0211	0246
25	2	0063	0150	0224	0287	0345	0401	0456	0512	0569	0628
25	3	0188	0350	0468	0563	0646	0724	0799	0873	0947	1022
25	4	0360	0590	0747	0868	0972	1068	1158	1246	1333	1420
25	5	0566	0859	1050	1192	1314	1424	1527	1626	1724	1821
25	6	0800	1149	1369	1532	1668	1790	1904	2013	2119	2224
25	7	1056	1457	1703	1882	2031	2164	2287	2403	2517	2628
25	8	1332	1780	2049	2243	2403	2544	2675	2798	2917	3034
25	9	1625	2116	2406	2612	2782	2931	3067	3196	3320	3441
25	10	1935	2464	2772	2989	3167	3322	3464	3597	3725	3849
25	11	2260	2824	3148	3374	3558	3718	3864	4001	4131	4258
25	12	2599	3194	3532	3766	3955	4120	4268	4407	4539	4668

MT-5c

.50	.55	.60	.65	.70	.75	.80	.85	.90	.95	.99
0341	0391	0448	0511	0584	0670	0773	0905	1087	1391	2057
0825	0903	0986	1076	1176	1290	1424	1589	1810	2161	2888
1315	1410	1510	1618	1736	1867	2020	2205	2448	2826	3583
1805	1913	2026	2147	2277	2421	2586	2785	3042	3437	4207
2297	2414	2537	2666	2805	2959	3133	3340	3607	4010	4783
2788	2913	3043	3179	3325	3484	3665	3878	4149	4556	5321
3280	3411	3545	3686	3836	4000	4184	4400	4673	5078	5829
3771	3906	4044	4189	4341	4507	4692	4908	5180	5580	6309
4263	4400	4541	4686	4840	5006	5191	5405	5673	6064	6766
4754	4893	5034	5180	5333	5498	5680	5891	6152	6531	7199
0325	0373	0427	0488	0557	0639	0738	0864	1038	1329	1969
0786	0860	0940	1026	1122	1232	1360	1518	1729	2067	2768
1253	1344	1440	1543	1656	1783	1929	2107	2340	2706	3439
1721	1824	1933	2048	2173	2312	2471	2662	2910	3292	4041
2189	2302	2420	2544	2678	2826	2994	3194	3452	3844	4598
2657	2778	2903	3034	3175	3329	3503	3710	3973	4370	5120
3126	3252	3382	3519	3664	3823	4001	4211	4477	4874	5613
3594	3725	3859	3999	4147	4308	4489	4700	4966	5359	6082
4063	4196	4333	4475	4624	4787	4967	5178	5442	5828	6528
4531	4667	4804	4946	5097	5258	5438	5646	5905	6281	6953
5000	5135	5273	5415	5564	5723	5900	6104	6356	6719	7358
0310	0356	0408	0466	0533	0611	0705	0826	0994	1273	1889
0751	0822	0898	0981	1073	1178	1301	1453	1656	1981	2658
1197	1284	1376	1475	1584	1705	1846	2017	2242	2595	3305
1644	1743	1847	1958	2078	2212	2365	2550	2789	3159	3887
2091	2200	2313	2433	2562	2705	2867	3061	3310	3691	4426
2538	2655	2775	2902	3038	3187	3355	3556	3812	4198	4933
2986	3108	3234	3366	3506	3660	3833	4037	4297	4685	5412
3433	3560	3690	3825	3969	4126	4302	4508	4768	5155	5868
3881	4011	4143	4281	4427	4585	4762	4968	5227	5609	6304
4329	4460	4594	4733	4880	5039	5215	5419	5675	6048	6720
4776	4909	5043	5182	5328	5486	5660	5862	6112	6475	7119
0297	0341	0391	0446	0510	0585	0676	0792	0953	1221	1815
0719	0787	0860	0939	1028	1128	1247	1393	1588	1902	2557
1146	1229	1318	1413	1517	1634	1770	1935	2152	2492	3181
1573	1669	1769	1876	1992	2120	2268	2446	2678	3036	3745
2001	2106	2215	2331	2455	2593	2750	2938	3180	3549	4267
2430	2542	2658	2780	2912	3056	3220	3414	3663	4039	4758
2858	2976	3098	3225	3362	3511	3679	3878	4131	4510	5224
3286	3409	3535	3666	3806	3959	4130	4331	4586	4964	5669
3715	3840	3969	4103	4246	4400	4573	4775	5029	5405	6094
4143	4271	4402	4538	4681	4836	5009	5210	5462	5832	6502
4572	4701	4832	4969	5112	5267	5438	5637	5885	6246	6892
5000	5130	5261	5397	5539	5692	5861	6057	6299	6649	7267
0285	0327	0375	0428	0489	0561	0649	0760	0915	1173	1746
0690	0755	0825	0901	0986	1083	1197	1337	1526	1829	2462
1099	1179	1264	1356	1456	1569	1700	1859	2069	2398	3066
1509	1601	1697	1800	1912	2036	2179	2351	2575	2923	3612
1919	2020	2125	2237	2357	2490	2642	2824	3059	3418	4118
2330	2438	2550	2669	2796	2936	3094	3283	3525	3891	4595
2741	2855	2972	3096	3228	3373	3536	3730	3976	4347	5048
3151	3270	3392	3520	3656	3804	3971	4167	4416	4787	5481
3562	3684	3809	3940	4079	4229	4398	4596	4845	5214	5896
3973	4098	4225	4357	4497	4649	4819	5016	5264	5629	6295
4384	4510	4639	4772	4912	5064	5233	5429	5674	6032	6678
4795	4921	5050	5184	5324	5475	5642	5835	6076	6424	7047

FRACTILES OF THE BETA DISTRIBUTION

n	r	k: .01	.05	.10	.15	.20	.25	.30	.35	.40	.45
26	1	0004	0020	0042	0065	0089	0114	0142	0171	0202	0236
26	2	0060	0144	0215	0275	0331	0385	0438	0492	0546	0603
26	3	0180	0335	0449	0540	0620	0695	0767	0838	0909	0981
26	4	0345	0566	0717	0832	0933	1024	1111	1196	1279	1364
26	5	0542	0823	1006	1143	1260	1366	1465	1561	1655	1749
26	6	0765	1101	1312	1468	1599	1717	1827	1932	2034	2136
26	7	1010	1395	1632	1804	1947	2075	2194	2306	2416	2524
26	8	1273	1703	1962	2149	2303	2440	2566	2685	2800	2914
26	9	1553	2024	2303	2502	2666	2810	2942	3066	3186	3304
26	10	1848	2356	2653	2863	3034	3184	3322	3451	3575	3696
26	11	2156	2699	3011	3230	3408	3564	3705	3838	3965	4088
26	12	2479	3051	3377	3604	3788	3947	4092	4227	4356	4482
26	13	2814	3414	3751	3985	4173	4335	4482	4619	4749	4876
27	1	0004	0020	0040	0062	0085	0110	0136	0164	0195	0227
27	2	0058	0138	0206	0264	0318	0370	0421	0473	0526	0580
27	3	0173	0322	0432	0519	0596	0668	0738	0806	0874	0944
27	4	0331	0543	0688	0800	0896	0985	1068	1150	1230	1312
27	5	0520	0790	0966	1098	1211	1313	1409	1501	1591	1682
27	6	0734	1056	1260	1410	1536	1650	1756	1857	1956	2054
27	7	0968	1338	1566	1732	1870	1994	2108	2217	2323	2427
27	8	1220	1633	1883	2062	2212	2344	2465	2581	2692	2802
27	9	1487	1940	2209	2401	2559	2698	2826	2947	3063	3178
27	10	1768	2257	2544	2746	2912	3058	3191	3316	3436	3554
27	11	2062	2584	2886	3098	3271	3421	3559	3688	3811	3931
27	12	2369	2921	3236	3456	3634	3789	3930	4061	4187	4310
27	13	2688	3266	3593	3820	4002	4161	4304	4437	4565	4688
28	1	0004	0019	0039	0060	0082	0106	0131	0158	0187	0219
28	2	0056	0133	0199	0255	0306	0356	0406	0455	0506	0559
28	3	0166	0310	0415	0499	0574	0643	0710	0776	0842	0909
28	4	0318	0522	0662	0770	0862	0948	1029	1107	1185	1263
28	5	0500	0759	0929	1057	1165	1264	1356	1445	1533	1620
28	6	0705	1015	1211	1356	1478	1588	1690	1788	1883	1978
28	7	0929	1285	1505	1665	1799	1918	2029	2134	2237	2338
28	8	1170	1568	1809	1983	2127	2255	2372	2484	2592	2699
28	9	1426	1862	2122	2308	2461	2596	2719	2837	2950	3061
28	10	1695	2166	2443	2639	2800	2941	3070	3192	3309	3423
28	11	1976	2479	2771	2976	3144	3290	3424	3549	3669	3786
28	12	2268	2801	3106	3319	3492	3643	3780	3908	4031	4150
28	13	2572	3131	3448	3668	3845	4000	4139	4270	4394	4515
28	14	2887	3470	3796	4021	4203	4360	4501	4633	4759	4880
29	1	0004	0018	0038	0058	0079	0102	0127	0153	0181	0211
29	2	0054	0128	0192	0245	0295	0344	0391	0439	0488	0539
29	3	0160	0298	0400	0481	0553	0620	0685	0748	0812	0877
29	4	0306	0503	0638	0742	0831	0914	0992	1068	1143	1219
29	5	0481	0731	0895	1018	1123	1218	1307	1393	1478	1563
29	6	0678	0977	1166	1306	1424	1530	1629	1724	1816	1908
29	7	0894	1237	1449	1604	1733	1848	1956	2058	2157	2255
29	8	1125	1509	1741	1909	2049	2172	2286	2395	2499	2603
29	9	1370	1791	2042	2221	2370	2500	2621	2734	2844	2952
29	10	1627	2082	2350	2540	2696	2833	2958	3076	3190	3301
29	11	1896	2383	2665	2864	3026	3169	3298	3420	3537	3651
29	12	2176	2691	2987	3193	3361	3508	3641	3766	3886	4002
29	13	2467	3007	3314	3528	3701	3851	3987	4114	4236	4354
29	14	2767	3331	3648	3867	4044	4197	4335	4464	4587	4706

MT-5d

.50	.55	.60	.65	.70	.75	.80	.85	.90	.95	.99
0273	0314	0360	0411	0470	0539	0623	0731	0880	1129	1682
0662	0725	0793	0866	0948	1041	1151	1287	1469	1761	2375
1055	1133	1215	1303	1400	1509	1635	1788	1991	2310	2959
1449	1538	1631	1730	1838	1958	2096	2263	2480	2817	3488
1843	1941	2043	2150	2267	2396	2543	2719	2947	3296	3979
2238	2343	2451	2566	2689	2824	2978	3161	3397	3754	4443
2632	2743	2857	2977	3105	3246	3405	3593	3833	4195	4884
3027	3142	3260	3384	3517	3661	3823	4015	4258	4622	5306
3422	3540	3662	3789	3924	4071	4236	4429	4673	5036	5711
3816	3937	4062	4191	4328	4476	4642	4836	5080	5439	6100
4211	4334	4460	4590	4728	4877	5042	5235	5477	5832	6476
4605	4730	4856	4987	5124	5273	5438	5629	5867	6214	6837
5000	5124	5251	5381	5518	5665	5827	6015	6249	6586	7186
0263	0302	0346	0396	0453	0519	0600	0704	0848	1088	1623
0637	0698	0763	0834	0913	1002	1108	1239	1415	1698	2293
1015	1090	1169	1254	1348	1453	1575	1723	1920	2229	2859
1394	1480	1570	1666	1770	1886	2020	2181	2392	2719	3372
1774	1868	1966	2070	2183	2308	2450	2621	2842	3182	3849
2153	2254	2359	2470	2590	2721	2870	3048	3277	3626	4300
2532	2639	2750	2866	2991	3128	3282	3465	3700	4054	4729
2912	3024	3139	3259	3388	3528	3687	3873	4111	4468	5140
3292	3407	3525	3649	3781	3924	4085	4274	4513	4870	5535
3671	3789	3910	4036	4170	4315	4478	4668	4907	5262	5916
4051	4171	4294	4421	4556	4702	4865	5055	5293	5643	6284
4431	4552	4676	4804	4939	5085	5247	5436	5671	6016	6639
4810	4932	5056	5184	5319	5464	5625	5811	6043	6379	6982
0253	0291	0334	0381	0436	0500	0579	0679	0817	1050	1568
0614	0672	0735	0803	0880	0966	1069	1195	1366	1640	2217
0978	1050	1127	1209	1299	1401	1519	1663	1853	2153	2766
1343	1426	1513	1606	1706	1819	1948	2105	2309	2627	3264
1709	1800	1895	1996	2105	2226	2364	2530	2745	3076	3727
2074	2172	2274	2382	2497	2625	2770	2943	3166	3506	4166
2440	2544	2651	2764	2885	3018	3168	3347	3575	3921	4584
2806	2914	3026	3143	3268	3405	3559	3741	3974	4323	4984
3171	3283	3399	3519	3647	3787	3944	4129	4364	4714	5370
3537	3652	3770	3893	4023	4165	4324	4510	4746	5095	5742
3903	4020	4140	4265	4397	4540	4699	4886	5120	5466	6102
4268	4387	4508	4634	4767	4910	5070	5255	5488	5829	6450
4634	4754	4876	5001	5134	5277	5436	5620	5849	6184	6787
5000	5120	5241	5367	5499	5640	5797	5979	6204	6530	7113
0245	0281	0322	0368	0421	0483	0559	0655	0789	1015	1517
0592	0649	0709	0775	0849	0933	1032	1155	1319	1585	2146
0944	1013	1087	1167	1254	1353	1467	1606	1791	2082	2679
1296	1376	1460	1550	1647	1756	1882	2034	2232	2542	3162
1648	1737	1829	1927	2033	2150	2284	2445	2655	2977	3613
2001	2096	2195	2299	2412	2536	2677	2845	3062	3394	4039
2354	2454	2559	2668	2786	2915	3062	3236	3459	3797	4447
2707	2812	2920	3034	3156	3290	3440	3618	3845	4187	4837
3059	3168	3281	3398	3523	3660	3813	3994	4224	4567	5214
3412	3524	3639	3759	3887	4025	4181	4364	4594	4938	5578
3765	3879	3997	4118	4248	4388	4544	4728	4958	5300	5930
4118	4234	4353	4476	4606	4746	4903	5086	5316	5654	6271
4471	4588	4707	4831	4961	5102	5258	5440	5667	6000	6602
4824	4941	5061	5184	5314	5454	5609	5789	6013	6338	6922

MT-6

NORMAL ORDINATE

	EXP	0	1	2	3	4	5	6	7	8	9	10					
0.	0	3989	3989	3989	3988	3986	3984						0	0	0	0	0
	0						3984	3982	3980	3977	3973	3970	0	1	1	1	1
0.1	0	3970	3965	3961	3956	3951	3945						0	1	1	2	2
	0						3945	3939	3932	3925	3918	3910	1	1	2	3	3
0.2	0	3910	3902	3894	3885	3876	3867						1	2	3	3	4
	0						3867	3857	3847	3836	3825	3814	1	2	3	4	5
0.3	0	3814	3802	3790	3778	3765	3752						1	2	4	5	6
	0						3752	3739	3725	3712	3697	3683	1	3	4	6	7
0.4	0	3683	3668	3653	3637	3621	3605						2	3	5	6	8
	0						3605	3589	3572	3555	3538	3521	2	3	5	7	8
0.5	0	3521	3503	3485	3467	3448	3429						2	4	5	7	9
	0						3429	3410	3391	3372	3352	3332	2	4	6	8	10
0.6	0	3332	3312	3292	3271	3251	3230						2	4	6	8	10
	0						3230	3209	3187	3166	3144	3123	2	4	6	9	11
0.7	0	3123	3101	3079	3056	3034	3011						2	4	7	9	11
	0						3011	2989	2966	2943	2920	2897	2	5	7	9	11
0.8	0	2897	2874	2850	2827	2803	2780						2	5	7	9	12
	0						2780	2756	2732	2709	2685	2661	2	5	7	10	12
0.9	0	2661	2637	2613	2589	2565	2541						2	5	7	10	12
	0						2541	2516	2492	2468	2444	2420	2	5	7	10	12
1.0	0	2420	2396	2371	2347	2323	2299						2	5	7	10	12
	0						2299	2275	2251	2227	2203	2179	2	5	7	10	12
1.1	0	2179	2155	2131	2107	2083	2059						2	5	7	10	12
	0						2059	2036	2012	1989	1965	1942	2	5	7	9	12
1.2	0	1942	1919	1895	1872	1849	1826						2	5	7	9	12
	0						1826	1804	1781	1758	1736	1714	2	5	7	9	11
1.3	0	1714	1691	1669	1647	1626	1604						2	4	7	9	11
	0						1604	1582	1561	1539	1518	1497	2	4	6	9	11
1.4	0	1497	1476	1456	1435	1415	1394						2	4	6	8	10
	0						1394	1374	1354	1334	1315	1295	2	4	6	8	10
1.5	0	1295	1276	1257	1238	1219	1200						2	4	6	8	10
	0						1200	1182	1163	1145	1127	1109	2	4	5	7	9
1.6	0	1109	1092	1074	1057	1040	1023						2	3	5	7	9
	0						1023	1006	0989	0973	0957	0940	2	3	5	7	8
1.7	-1	9405	9246	9089	8933	8780	8628						16	31	47	62	78
	-1						8628	8478	8329	8183	8038	7895	15	29	44	59	73
1.8	-1	7895	7754	7614	7477	7341	7206						14	28	41	55	69
	-1						7206	7074	6943	6814	6687	6562	13	26	39	52	64
1.9	-1	6562	6438	6316	6195	6077	5959						12	24	36	48	60
	-1						5959	5844	5730	5618	5508	5399	11	22	34	45	56

2.0	-1	5399	5292	5186	5082	4980	4879						10	21	31	42	52
	-1						4879	4780	4682	4586	4491	4398	10	19	29	38	48
2.1	-1	4398	4307	4217	4128	4041	3955						9	18	27	35	44
	-1						3955	3871	3788	3706	3626	3547	8	16	24	33	41
2.2	-1	3547	3470	3394	3319	3246	3174						7	15	22	30	37
	-1						3174	3103	3034	2965	2898	2833	7	14	20	27	34
2.3	-1	2833	2768	2705	2643	2582	2522						6	12	19	25	31
	-1						2522	2463	2406	2349	2294	2239	6	11	17	23	28
2.4	-1	2239	2186	2134	2083	2033	1984						5	10	15	20	26
	-1						1984	1936	1888	1842	1797	1753	5	9	14	18	23
2.5	-1	1753	1709	1667	1625	1585	1545						4	8	12	17	21
	-1						1545	1506	1468	1431	1394	1358	4	7	11	15	19
2.6	-1	1358	1323	1289	1256	1223	1191						3	7	10	13	17
	-1						1191	1160	1130	1100	1071	1042	3	6	9	12	15
2.7	-1	1042	1014	0987	0961	0935	0909						3	5	8	11	13
	-2						9094	8846	8605	8370	8140	7915	24	47	71	94	118
2.8	-2	7915	7697	7483	7274	7071	6873						21	42	63	83	104
	-2						6873	6679	6491	6307	6127	5953	18	37	55	74	92
2.9	-2	5953	5782	5616	5454	5296	5143						16	32	49	65	81
	-2						5143	4993	4847	4705	4567	4432	14	28	43	57	71
3.0	-2	4432	4301	4173	4049	3928	3810						12	25	37	50	62
	-2						3810	3695	3584	3475	3370	3267	11	22	33	43	54
3.1	-2	3267	3167	3070	2975	2884	2794						9	19	28	38	47
	-2						2794	2707	2623	2541	2461	2384	8	16	25	33	41
3.2	-2	2384	2309	2236	2165	2096	2029						7	14	21	28	36
	-2						2029	1964	1901	1840	1780	1723	6	12	18	25	31
3.3	-2	1723	1667	1612	1560	1508	1459						5	11	16	21	26
	-2						1459	1411	1364	1319	1275	1232	5	9	14	18	23
3.4	-2	1232	1191	1151	1112	1075	1038						4	8	12	16	19
	-2						1038	1003	0969	0936	0904	0873	3	7	10	13	17
3.5	-3	8727	8426	8135	7853	7581	7317						28	56	85	113	141
	-3						7317	7061	6814	6575	6343	6119	24	48	72	96	120
3.6	-3	6119	5902	5693	5490	5294	5105						20	41	61	81	101
	-3						5105	4921	4744	4573	4408	4248	17	34	51	69	86
3.7	-3	4248	4093	3944	3800	3661	3526						14	29	43	58	72
	-3						3526	3396	3271	3149	3032	2919	12	24	36	49	61
3.8	-3	2919	2810	2705	2604	2506	2411						10	20	30	41	51
	-3						2411	2320	2232	2147	2065	1987	8	17	25	34	42
3.9	-3	1987	1910	1837	1766	1698	1633						7	14	21	28	35
	-3						1633	1569	1508	1449	1393	1338	6	12	18	24	29

MT-7

NORMAL RIGHT TAIL

	EXP	0	1	2	3	4	5	6	7	8	9	10					
0.	0	5000	4960	4920	4880	4840	4801						4	8	12	16	20
	0						4801	4761	4721	4681	4641	4602	4	8	12	16	20
0.1	0	4602	4562	4522	4483	4443	4404						4	8	12	16	20
	0						4404	4364	4325	4286	4247	4207	4	8	12	16	20
0.2	0	4207	4168	4129	4090	4052	4013						4	8	12	16	19
	0						4013	3974	3936	3897	3859	3821	4	8	12	15	19
0.3	0	3821	3783	3745	3707	3669	3632						4	8	11	15	19
	0						3632	3594	3557	3520	3483	3446	4	7	11	15	19
0.4	0	3446	3409	3372	3336	3300	3264						4	7	11	15	18
	0						3264	3228	3192	3156	3121	3085	4	7	11	14	18
0.5	0	3085	3050	3015	2981	2946	2912						3	7	10	14	17
	0						2912	2877	2843	2810	2776	2743	3	7	10	14	17
0.6	0	2743	2709	2676	2643	2611	2578						3	7	10	13	16
	0						2578	2546	2514	2483	2451	2420	3	6	10	13	16
0.7	0	2420	2389	2358	2327	2296	2266						3	6	9	12	15
	0						2266	2236	2206	2177	2148	2119	3	6	9	12	15
0.8	0	2119	2090	2061	2033	2005	1977						3	6	9	11	14
	0						1977	1949	1922	1894	1867	1841	3	5	8	11	14
0.9	0	1841	1814	1788	1762	1736	1711						3	5	8	10	13
	0						1711	1685	1660	1635	1611	1587	2	5	7	10	12
1.0	0	1587	1562	1539	1515	1492	1469						2	5	7	9	12
	0						1469	1446	1423	1401	1379	1357	2	4	7	9	11
1.1	0	1357	1335	1314	1292	1271	1251						2	4	6	8	11
	0						1251	1230	1210	1190	1170	1151	2	4	6	8	10
1.2	0	1151	1131	1112	1093	1075	1056						2	4	6	8	9
	0						1056	1038	1020	1003	0985	0968	2	4	5	7	9
1.3	-1	9680	9510	9342	9176	9012	8851						17	33	50	66	83
	-1						8851	8691	8534	8379	8226	8076	16	31	47	62	78
1.4	-1	8076	7927	7780	7636	7493	7353						14	29	43	58	72
	-1						7353	7215	7078	6944	6811	6681	13	27	40	54	67
1.5	-1	6681	6552	6426	6301	6178	6057						12	25	37	50	62
	-1						6057	5938	5821	5705	5592	5480	12	23	35	46	58
1.6	-1	5480	5370	5262	5155	5050	4947						11	21	32	43	53
	-1						4947	4846	4746	4648	4551	4457	10	20	29	39	49
1.7	-1	4457	4363	4272	4182	4093	4006						9	18	27	36	45
	-1						4006	3920	3836	3754	3673	3593	8	17	25	33	41
1.8	-1	3593	3515	3438	3362	3288	3216						8	15	23	30	38
	-1						3216	3144	3074	3005	2938	2872	7	14	21	28	34
1.9	-1	2872	2807	2743	2680	2619	2559						6	13	19	25	31
	-1						2559	2500	2442	2385	2330	2275	6	11	17	23	28

2.0	-1	2275	2222	2169	2118	2068	2018						5	10	15	21	26
	-1						2018	1970	1923	1876	1831	1786	5	9	14	19	23
2.1	-1	1786	1743	1700	1659	1618	1578						4	8	13	17	21
	-1						1578	1539	1500	1463	1426	1390	4	7	11	15	19
2.2	-1	1390	1355	1321	1287	1255	1222						3	7	10	13	17
	-1						1222	1191	1160	1130	1101	1072	3	6	9	12	15
2.3	-1	1072	1044	1017	0990	0964	0939						3	5	8	11	13
	-2						9387	9137	8894	8656	8424	8198	24	48	71	95	119
2.4	-2	8198	7976	7760	7549	7344	7143						21	42	63	84	105
	-2						7143	6947	6756	6569	6387	6210	19	37	56	75	93
2.5	-2	6210	6037	5868	5703	5543	5386						16	33	49	66	82
	-2						5386	5234	5085	4940	4799	4661	14	29	43	58	72
2.6	-2	4661	4527	4396	4269	4145	4025						13	25	38	51	64
	-2						4025	3907	3793	3681	3573	3467	11	22	33	45	56
2.7	-2	3467	3364	3264	3167	3072	2980						10	19	29	39	49
	-2						2980	2890	2803	2718	2635	2555	8	17	25	34	42
2.8	-2	2555	2477	2401	2327	2256	2186						7	15	22	30	37
	-2						2186	2118	2052	1988	1926	1866	6	13	19	26	32
2.9	-2	1866	1807	1750	1695	1641	1589						6	11	17	22	28
	-2						1589	1538	1489	1441	1395	1350	5	10	14	19	24
3.0	-2	1350	1306	1264	1223	1183	1144						4	8	12	16	21
	-2						1144	1107	1070	1035	1001	0968	4	7	11	14	18
3.1	-3	9676	9354	9043	8740	8447	8164						30	61	91	121	151
	-3						8164	7888	7622	7364	7114	6871	26	52	78	103	129
3.2	-3	6871	6637	6410	6190	5976	5770						22	44	66	88	110
	-3						5770	5571	5377	5190	5009	4834	19	37	56	75	94
3.3	-3	4834	4665	4501	4342	4189	4041						16	32	48	63	79
	-3						4041	3897	3758	3624	3495	3369	13	27	40	54	67
3.4	-3	3369	3248	3131	3018	2909	2803						11	23	34	45	57
	-3						2803	2701	2602	2507	2415	2326	10	19	29	38	48
3.5	-3	2326	2241	2158	2078	2001	1926						8	16	24	32	40
	-3						1926	1854	1785	1718	1653	1591	7	13	20	27	34
3.6	-3	1591	1531	1473	1417	1363	1311						6	11	17	22	28
	-3						1311	1261	1213	1166	1121	1078	5	9	14	19	23
3.7	-3	1078	1036	0996	0957	0920	0884						4	8	12	16	19
	-4						8842	8496	8162	7841	7532	7235	32	64	96	129	161
3.8	-4	7235	6948	6673	6407	6152	5906						27	53	80	106	133
	-4						5906	5669	5442	5223	5012	4810	22	44	66	88	110
3.9	-4	4810	4615	4427	4247	4074	3908						18	36	54	72	90
	-4						3908	3747	3594	3446	3304	3167	15	30	44	59	74

−∞

A \ D	0.0	0.2	0.4	0.6	0.8	1.0	1.2	1.4	1.6	1.8	2.0
0.3	-0.8519										
0.4	-0.6733	-1.7895									
0.5	-0.5007	-1.2235									
0.6	-0.3344	-0.8789									
0.7	-0.1744	-0.6119									
0.8	-0.0207	-0.3864	-1.3363								
0.9	0.1273	-0.1875	-0.7858								
1.0	0.2699	-0.0072	-0.4601								
1.1	0.4077	0.1593	-0.2104	-1.1711							
1.2	0.5411	0.3151	-0.0004	-0.5827							
1.3	0.6706	0.4624	0.1849	-0.2551							
1.4	0.7968	0.6029	0.3534	-0.0080	-0.8312						
1.5	0.9199	0.7377	0.5095	0.1985	-0.3403						
1.6	1.0403	0.8678	0.6563	0.3803	-0.0392	-2.9730					
1.7	1.1583	0.9939	0.7958	0.5454	0.1940	-0.5094					
1.8	1.2743	1.1167	0.9294	0.6985	0.3914	-0.1084					
1.9	1.3885	1.2365	1.0582	0.8425	0.5666	0.1638	-0.9564				
2.0	1.5010	1.3540	1.1830	0.9796	0.7266	0.3818	-0.2451				
2.1	1.6121	1.4692	1.3045	1.1110	0.8757	0.5696	0.0961				
2.2	1.7220	1.5827	1.4232	1.2379	1.0165	0.7381	0.3449	-0.5474			
2.3	1.8307	1.6945	1.5396	1.3610	1.1507	0.8931	0.5501	-0.0330			
2.4	1.9385	1.8050	1.6538	1.4810	1.2798	1.0382	0.7297	0.2700			
2.5	2.0454	1.9142	1.7663	1.5984	1.4047	1.1758	0.8924	0.5019	-0.2944		
2.6	2.1515	2.0224	1.8774	1.7135	1.5261	1.3075	1.0430	0.6973	0.1351		
2.7	2.2569	2.1296	1.9871	1.8267	1.6446	1.4345	1.1847	0.8704	0.4142	-1.6362	
2.8	2.3618	2.2360	2.0956	1.9383	1.7607	1.5576	1.3197	1.0284	0.6345	-0.1230	
2.9	2.4661	2.3416	2.2031	2.0485	1.8747	1.6774	1.4492	1.1756	0.8229	0.2650	
3.0	2.5699	2.4467	2.3098	2.1574	1.9870	1.7947	1.5743	1.3146	0.9912	0.5300	-1.0672
3.1	2.6733	2.5511	2.4157	2.2653	2.0977	1.9096	1.6959	1.4474	1.1459	0.7431	-0.0113
3.2	2.7763	2.6551	2.5209	2.3723	2.2072	2.0227	1.8145	1.5751	1.2905	0.9270	0.3594
3.3	2.8790	2.7586	2.6256	2.4785	2.3155	2.1341	1.9306	1.6988	1.4276	1.0923	0.6182
3.4	2.9814	2.8617	2.7297	2.5839	2.4228	2.2441	2.0446	1.8192	1.5587	1.2447	0.8278
3.5	3.0835	2.9645	2.8333	2.6887	2.5292	2.3529	2.1568	1.9367	1.6852	1.3877	1.0095
3.6	3.1854	3.0670	2.9365	2.7930	2.6349	2.4606	2.2675	2.0520	1.8077	1.5234	1.1734
3.7	3.2871	3.1692	3.0394	2.8968	2.7400	2.5674	2.3769	2.1652	1.9271	1.6534	1.3247
3.8	3.3886	3.2711	3.1419	3.0001	2.8444	2.6734	2.4851	2.2768	2.0439	1.7789	1.4667
3.9	3.4900	3.3729	3.2442	3.1031	2.9484	2.7787	2.5924	2.3869	2.1585	1.9008	1.6017
4.0	3.5912	3.4744	3.3462	3.2057	3.0519	2.8834	2.6988	2.4958	2.2712	2.0196	1.7312
4.1	3.6922	3.5758	3.4480	3.3081	3.1550	2.9876	2.8045	2.6037	2.3823	2.1358	1.8562
4.2	3.7932	3.6770	3.5496	3.4102	3.2577	3.0913	2.9095	2.7105	2.4920	2.2500	1.9777
4.3	3.8940	3.7781	3.6510	3.5120	3.3602	3.1945	3.0139	2.8166	2.6005	2.3623	2.0961
4.4	3.9948	3.8791	3.7523	3.6137	3.4624	3.2974	3.1178	2.9220	2.7081	2.4730	2.2121
4.5	4.0954	3.9799	3.8534	3.7151	3.5643	3.4000	3.2213	3.0267	2.8147	2.5825	2.3260
4.6	4.1960	4.0807	3.9544	3.8164	3.6660	3.5023	3.3243	3.1309	2.9205	2.6907	2.4381
4.7	4.2966	4.1814	4.0553	3.9176	3.7675	3.6043	3.4271	3.2346	3.0256	2.7980	2.5487
4.8	4.3970	4.2820	4.1561	4.0186	3.8689	3.7061	3.5295	3.3379	3.1302	2.9044	2.6580
4.9	4.4975	4.3825	4.2568	4.1195	3.9701	3.8077	3.6316	3.4409	3.2342	3.0101	2.7661
5.0	4.5978	4.4830	4.3574	4.2204	4.0712	3.9092	3.7335	3.5434	3.3378	3.1151	2.8733
5.1	4.6982	4.5835	4.4580	4.3211	4.1721	4.0104	3.8352	3.6457	3.4410	3.2195	2.9796
5.2	4.7985	4.6838	4.5585	4.4217	4.2730	4.1116	3.9367	3.7478	3.5438	3.3234	3.0852
5.3	4.8987	4.7842	4.6589	4.5223	4.3737	4.2126	4.0381	3.8496	3.6462	3.4269	3.1901
5.4	4.9990	4.8845	4.7593	4.6228	4.4744	4.3135	4.1393	3.9512	3.7485	3.5300	3.2944
5.5	5.0992	4.9848	4.8597	4.7233	4.5750	4.4142	4.2403	4.0527	3.8504	3.6327	3.3983
5.6	5.1994	5.0850	4.9600	4.8237	4.6756	4.5150	4.3413	4.1539	3.9522	3.7351	3.5017
5.7	5.2995	5.1852	5.0603	4.9241	4.7760	4.6156	4.4421	4.2551	4.0537	3.8373	3.6047
5.8	5.3997	5.2854	5.1605	5.0244	4.8765	4.7161	4.5429	4.3561	4.1551	3.9392	3.7074
5.9	5.4998	5.3856	5.2607	5.1247	4.9768	4.8166	4.6435	4.4570	4.2563	4.0409	3.8098
6.0	5.5999	5.4857	5.3609	5.2249	5.0772	4.9171	4.7441	4.5578	4.3574	4.1424	3.9119
6.1	5.7000	5.5859	5.4611	5.3252	5.1775	5.0175	4.8447	4.6585	4.4584	4.2437	4.0138
6.2	5.8001	5.6860	5.5613	5.4254	5.2777	5.1178	4.9451	4.7591	4.5592	4.3449	4.1154
6.3	5.9002	5.7861	5.6614	5.5256	5.3780	5.2182	5.0456	4.8597	4.6600	4.4460	4.2169
6.4	6.0003	5.8862	5.7615	5.6257	5.4782	5.3184	5.1459	4.9602	4.7607	4.5469	4.3182
6.5	6.1004	5.9863	5.8616	5.7259	5.5784	5.4187	5.2463	5.0606	4.8613	4.6478	4.4194
6.6	6.2004	6.0864	5.9617	5.8260	5.6786	5.5189	5.3466	5.1610	4.9618	4.7485	4.5205
6.7	6.3005	6.1864	6.0618	5.9261	5.7787	5.6191	5.4468	5.2614	5.0623	4.8492	4.6214
6.8	6.4005	6.2865	6.1619	6.0262	5.8788	5.7193	5.5471	5.3617	5.1628	4.9498	4.7222
6.9	6.5006	6.3865	6.2620	6.1263	5.9790	5.8194	5.6473	5.4620	5.2631	5.0503	4.8229
7.0	6.6006	6.4866	6.3620	6.2264	6.0791	5.9196	5.7475	5.5622	5.3635	5.1508	4.9236
7.1	6.7006	6.5866	6.4621	6.3264	6.1792	6.0197	5.8476	5.6625	5.4638	5.2512	5.0242
7.2	6.8007	6.6867	6.5621	6.4265	6.2792	6.1198	5.9478	5.7627	5.5641	5.3515	5.1247
7.3	6.9007	6.7867	6.6622	6.5266	6.3793	6.2199	6.0479	5.8628	5.6643	5.4519	5.2252
7.4	7.0007	6.8867	6.7622	6.6266	6.4794	6.3200	6.1480	5.9630	5.7645	5.5522	5.3256
7.5	7.1007	6.9868	6.8623	6.7266	6.5794	6.4201	6.2481	6.0631	5.8647	5.6524	5.4259
7.6	7.2007	7.0868	6.9623	6.8267	6.6795	6.5201	6.3482	6.1633	5.9649	5.7527	5.5263
7.7	7.3007	7.1868	7.0623	6.9267	6.7795	6.6202	6.4482	6.2633	6.0650	5.8529	5.6266
7.8	7.4007	7.2868	7.1623	7.0267	6.8795	6.7202	6.5484	6.3634	6.1651	5.9531	5.7268
7.9	7.5007	7.3868	7.2623	7.1267	6.9795	6.8202	6.6484	6.4635	6.2652	6.0532	5.8270
8.0	7.6008	7.4868	7.3623	7.2267	7.0795	6.9202	6.7484	6.5636	6.3653	6.1533	5.9273
PSI	-0.3991	-0.5130	-0.6374	-0.7730	-0.9201	-1.0793	-1.2510	-1.4357	-1.6337	-1.8454	-2.0711

Λ \ D	2.0	2.2	2.4	2.6	2.8	3.0	3.2	3.4	3.6	3.8	4.0
3.0	-1.0672										
3.1	-0.0113										
3.2	0.3594										
3.3	0.6182	-1.0639									
3.4	0.8278	0.0460									
3.5	1.0095	0.4191									
3.6	1.1734	0.6785									
3.7	1.3247	0.8883	0.0441								
3.8	1.4667	1.0702	0.4417								
3.9	1.6017	1.2341	0.7096								
4.0	1.7312	1.3853	0.9238	-0.0414							
4.1	1.8562	1.5273	1.1083	0.4214							
4.2	1.9777	1.6623	1.2738	0.7087							
4.3	2.0961	1.7917	1.4262	0.9323	-0.2998						
4.4	2.2121	1.9167	1.5691	1.1223	0.3429						
4.5	2.3260	2.0381	1.7047	1.2915	0.6691						
4.6	2.4381	2.1566	1.8347	1.4465	0.9102						
4.7	2.5487	2.2725	1.9601	1.5913	1.1100	0.1636					
4.8	2.6580	2.3864	2.0818	1.7283	1.2855	0.5782					
4.9	2.7661	2.4985	2.2005	1.8594	1.4448	0.8510					
5.0	2.8733	2.6090	2.3167	1.9858	1.5928	1.0674	-0.3238				
5.1	2.9796	2.7183	2.4308	2.1083	1.7323	1.2531	0.4029				
5.2	3.0852	2.8264	2.5430	2.2276	1.8654	1.4193	0.7416				
5.3	3.1901	2.9335	2.6537	2.3443	1.9932	1.5723	0.9874				
5.4	3.2944	3.0398	2.7630	2.4588	2.1169	1.7155	1.1898	0.0129			
5.5	3.3983	3.1454	2.8713	2.5714	2.2373	1.8514	1.3668	0.5500			
5.6	3.5017	3.2503	2.9785	2.6824	2.3548	1.9815	1.5273	0.8557			
5.7	3.6047	3.3546	3.0849	2.7920	2.4700	2.1071	1.6761	1.0875			
5.8	3.7074	3.4585	3.1905	2.9005	2.5832	2.2290	1.8161	1.2821	0.1527		
5.9	3.8098	3.5619	3.2955	3.0079	2.6948	2.3478	1.9496	1.4542	0.6367		
6.0	3.9119	3.6649	3.3998	3.1145	2.8048	2.4640	2.0778	1.6112	0.9296		
6.1	4.0138	3.7676	3.5037	3.2202	2.9137	2.5781	2.2018	1.7575	1.1555		
6.2	4.1154	3.8699	3.6072	3.3253	3.0214	2.6904	2.3223	1.8956	1.3467	0.1811	
6.3	4.2169	3.9720	3.7102	3.4298	3.1283	2.8011	2.4401	2.0276	1.5166	0.6716	
6.4	4.3182	4.0739	3.8129	3.5338	3.2343	2.9105	2.5554	2.1546	1.6721	0.9661	
6.5	4.4194	4.1756	3.9153	3.6373	3.3396	3.0187	2.6687	2.2776	1.8172	1.1928	
6.6	4.5205	4.2771	4.0175	3.7405	3.4443	3.1260	2.7804	2.3974	1.9545	1.3844	0.0877
6.7	4.6214	4.3784	4.1194	3.8432	3.5485	3.2324	2.8905	2.5144	2.0858	1.5546	0.6528
6.8	4.7222	4.4795	4.2210	3.9457	3.6521	3.3380	2.9994	2.6292	2.2122	1.7102	0.9644
6.9	4.8229	4.5806	4.3225	4.0479	3.7554	3.4430	3.1073	2.7421	2.3348	1.8555	1.1987
7.0	4.9236	4.6815	4.4239	4.1498	3.8583	3.5474	3.2142	2.8533	2.4542	1.9929	1.3947
7.1	5.0242	4.7823	4.5250	4.2516	3.9608	3.6513	3.3202	2.9631	2.5709	2.1242	1.5677
7.2	5.1247	4.8831	4.6261	4.3531	4.0631	3.7547	3.4256	3.0717	2.6854	2.2507	1.7253
7.3	5.2252	4.9837	4.7270	4.4545	4.1651	3.8578	3.5303	3.1793	2.7981	2.3733	1.8720
7.4	5.3256	5.0843	4.8279	4.5557	4.2669	3.9605	3.6345	3.2859	2.9091	2.4928	2.0105
7.5	5.4259	5.1848	4.9286	4.6567	4.3685	4.0629	3.7382	3.3918	3.0187	2.6095	2.1426
7.6	5.5263	5.2853	5.0293	4.7577	4.4699	4.1650	3.8415	3.4970	3.1272	2.7241	2.2698
7.7	5.6266	5.3857	5.1298	4.8586	4.5712	4.2669	3.9444	3.6016	3.2347	2.8367	2.3930
7.8	5.7268	5.4861	5.2304	4.9593	4.6723	4.3686	4.0470	3.7056	3.3412	2.9478	2.5129
7.9	5.8270	5.5864	5.3308	5.0600	4.7733	4.4701	4.1493	3.8092	3.4470	3.0574	2.6300
8.0	5.9273	5.6867	5.4312	5.1606	4.8742	4.5714	4.2513	3.9124	3.5521	3.1659	2.7449
8.1	6.0274	5.7869	5.5316	5.2611	4.9750	4.6726	4.3531	4.0152	3.6566	3.2734	2.8578
8.2	6.1275	5.8872	5.6319	5.3616	5.0757	4.7737	4.4547	4.1177	3.7606	3.3799	2.9691
8.3	6.2277	5.9873	5.7322	5.4620	5.1763	4.8746	4.5562	4.2199	3.8641	3.4857	3.0790
8.4	6.3279	6.0874	5.8325	5.5624	5.2769	4.9754	4.6574	4.3219	3.9673	3.5908	3.1876
8.5	6.4279	6.1876	5.9327	5.6627	5.3774	5.0762	4.7586	4.4237	4.0700	3.6953	3.2952
8.6	6.5279	6.2878	6.0328	5.7630	5.4778	5.1768	4.8596	4.5252	4.1725	3.7993	3.4019
8.7	6.6279	6.3878	6.1330	5.8633	5.5782	5.2774	4.9605	4.6266	4.2747	3.9029	3.5078
8.8	6.7280	6.4878	6.2332	5.9634	5.6785	5.3780	5.0613	4.7278	4.3766	4.0060	3.6130
8.9	6.8282	6.5878	6.3333	6.0636	5.7789	5.4784	5.1620	4.8289	4.4783	4.1088	3.7176
9.0	6.9284	6.6880	6.4332	6.1639	5.8790	5.5788	5.2626	4.9299	4.5799	4.2112	3.8217
9.1	7.0285	6.7883	6.5333	6.2640	5.9792	5.6792	5.3632	5.0308	4.6812	4.3134	3.9253
9.2	7.1285	6.8884	6.6334	6.3639	6.0796	5.7795	5.4636	5.1315	4.7825	4.4154	4.0285
9.3	7.2286	6.9885	6.7337	6.4639	6.1797	5.8797	5.5641	5.2322	4.8835	4.5171	4.1313
9.4	7.3286	7.0886	6.8340	6.5641	6.2797	5.9799	5.6645	5.3328	4.9845	4.6186	4.2338
9.5	7.4286	7.1886	6.9340	6.6644	6.3797	6.0803	5.7647	5.4333	5.0853	4.7200	4.3361
9.6	7.5287	7.2887	7.0341	6.7647	6.4797	6.1803	5.8650	5.5338	5.1861	4.8212	4.4380
9.7	7.6287	7.3887	7.1342	6.8648	6.5801	6.2803	5.9654	5.6343	5.2868	4.9223	4.5398
9.8	7.7287	7.4887	7.2342	6.9649	6.6805	6.3803	6.0656	5.7345	5.3873	5.0233	4.6414
9.9	7.8288	7.5888	7.3343	7.0650	6.7806	6.4805	6.1656	5.8348	5.4879	5.1241	4.7428
10.0	7.9288	7.6888	7.4343	7.1650	6.8807	6.5810	6.2656	5.9353	5.5884	5.2249	4.8440
PSI	-2.0711	-2.3110	-2.5654	-2.8345	-3.1186	-3.4178	-3.7322	-4.0622	-4.4077	-4.7689	-5.1460

−∞

Λ \ D	0.0	0.2	0.4	0.6	0.8	1.0	1.2	1.4	1.6	1.8	2.0
0.3	-0.9414										
0.4	-0.7943	-0.9100									
0.5	-0.6587	-0.7327									
0.6	-0.5343	-0.5854									
0.7	-0.4200	-0.4573						−∞			
0.8	-0.3148	-0.3433	-0.4585								
0.9	-0.2175	-0.2400	-0.3227								
1.0	-0.1269	-0.1452	-0.2091								
1.1	-0.0419	-0.0573	-0.1089	-0.2269							
1.2	0.0382	0.0249	-0.0182	-0.1081							
1.3	0.1142	0.1026	0.0655	-0.0075							
1.4	0.1867	0.1764	0.1438	0.0820	-0.0328						
1.5	0.2563	0.2470	0.2178	0.1640	0.0714						
1.6	0.3234	0.3148	0.2884	0.2405	0.1619	0.0183					
1.7	0.3883	0.3804	0.3560	0.3126	0.2438	0.1304					
1.8	0.4513	0.4439	0.4213	0.3814	0.3197	0.2241					
1.9	0.5127	0.5058	0.4846	0.4475	0.3912	0.3074	0.1693				
2.0	0.5727	0.5662	0.5461	0.5113	0.4592	0.3839	0.2693				
2.1	0.6316	0.6253	0.6062	0.5733	0.5245	0.4555	0.3557				
2.2	0.6893	0.6833	0.6650	0.6337	0.5876	0.5235	0.4339	0.2963			
2.3	0.7462	0.7404	0.7228	0.6928	0.6489	0.5887	0.5066	0.3885			
2.4	0.8023	0.7966	0.7796	0.7507	0.7087	0.6516	0.5752	0.4700			
2.5	0.8576	0.8521	0.8356	0.8076	0.7672	0.7126	0.6408	0.5447	0.4041		
2.6	0.9123	0.9070	0.8909	0.8637	0.8246	0.7722	0.7039	0.6146	0.4912		
2.7	0.9665	0.9613	0.9456	0.9191	0.8811	0.8304	0.7651	0.6811	0.5693	0.3978	
2.8	1.0202	1.0151	0.9998	0.9738	0.9368	0.8876	0.8247	0.7450	0.6416	0.4954	
2.9	1.0735	1.0685	1.0534	1.0280	0.9918	0.9439	0.8831	0.8067	0.7097	0.5793	
3.0	1.1265	1.1215	1.1067	1.0817	1.0462	0.9994	0.9403	0.8667	0.7747	0.6553	0.4772
3.1	1.1791	1.1742	1.1596	1.1350	1.1000	1.0542	0.9966	0.9253	0.8373	0.7259	0.5720
3.2	1.2314	1.2266	1.2121	1.1878	1.1535	1.1085	1.0520	0.9828	0.8981	0.7928	0.6541
3.3	1.2834	1.2787	1.2644	1.2404	1.2065	1.1622	1.1068	1.0392	0.9572	0.8568	0.7288
3.4	1.3352	1.3305	1.3164	1.2927	1.2592	1.2155	1.1611	1.0948	1.0151	0.9186	0.7985
3.5	1.3868	1.3822	1.3682	1.3447	1.3115	1.2684	1.2148	1.1498	1.0719	0.9787	0.8646
3.6	1.4383	1.4337	1.4197	1.3965	1.3636	1.3210	1.2680	1.2041	1.1279	1.0373	0.9281
3.7	1.4896	1.4850	1.4712	1.4481	1.4155	1.3733	1.3209	1.2579	1.1831	1.0947	0.9894
3.8	1.5407	1.5361	1.5224	1.4995	1.4672	1.4253	1.3735	1.3112	1.2376	1.1511	1.0490
3.9	1.5917	1.5872	1.5735	1.5507	1.5186	1.4771	1.4257	1.3641	1.2916	1.2067	1.1072
4.0	1.6426	1.6381	1.6245	1.6018	1.5699	1.5286	1.4777	1.4167	1.3450	1.2615	1.1643
4.1	1.6934	1.6889	1.6754	1.6528	1.6211	1.5801	1.5295	1.4690	1.3981	1.3158	1.2205
4.2	1.7441	1.7396	1.7262	1.7037	1.6721	1.6313	1.5811	1.5211	1.4508	1.3695	1.2758
4.3	1.7948	1.7903	1.7769	1.7545	1.7230	1.6824	1.6324	1.5729	1.5032	1.4228	1.3305
4.4	1.8453	1.8409	1.8275	1.8052	1.7738	1.7334	1.6837	1.6244	1.5553	1.4757	1.3846
4.5	1.8958	1.8914	1.8781	1.8558	1.8246	1.7843	1.7348	1.6758	1.6072	1.5282	1.4381
4.6	1.9463	1.9418	1.9285	1.9064	1.8752	1.8351	1.7857	1.7271	1.6588	1.5805	1.4913
4.7	1.9967	1.9923	1.9790	1.9568	1.9258	1.8857	1.8366	1.7782	1.7103	1.6325	1.5441
4.8	2.0470	2.0426	2.0294	2.0073	1.9763	1.9364	1.8874	1.8292	1.7616	1.6842	1.5965
4.9	2.0973	2.0929	2.0797	2.0577	2.0268	1.9869	1.9381	1.8801	1.8127	1.7358	1.6487
5.0	2.1476	2.1432	2.1300	2.1080	2.0772	2.0374	1.9887	1.9308	1.8638	1.7871	1.7006
5.1	2.1979	2.1935	2.1803	2.1583	2.1275	2.0878	2.0392	1.9815	1.9147	1.8384	1.7523
5.2	2.2481	2.2437	2.2306	2.2086	2.1778	2.1382	2.0897	2.0321	1.9655	1.8894	1.8037
5.3	2.2983	2.2939	2.2808	2.2588	2.2281	2.1886	2.1401	2.0827	2.0162	1.9404	1.8551
5.4	2.3485	2.3441	2.3310	2.3091	2.2784	2.2389	2.1905	2.1332	2.0668	1.9913	1.9062
5.5	2.3986	2.3943	2.3811	2.3593	2.3286	2.2891	2.2408	2.1836	2.1174	2.0420	1.9573
5.6	2.4488	2.4444	2.4313	2.4094	2.3788	2.3394	2.2911	2.2340	2.1679	2.0927	2.0082
5.7	2.4989	2.4945	2.4814	2.4596	2.4290	2.3896	2.3414	2.2843	2.2183	2.1433	2.0590
5.8	2.5490	2.5447	2.5316	2.5097	2.4791	2.4398	2.3916	2.3346	2.2687	2.1938	2.1098
5.9	2.5991	2.5948	2.5817	2.5598	2.5293	2.4900	2.4419	2.3849	2.3191	2.2443	2.1604
6.0	2.6492	2.6449	2.6318	2.6100	2.5794	2.5401	2.4920	2.4352	2.3694	2.2947	2.2110
6.1	2.6993	2.6949	2.6819	2.6601	2.6295	2.5903	2.5422	2.4854	2.4197	2.3451	2.2615
6.2	2.7494	2.7450	2.7319	2.7101	2.6796	2.6404	2.5924	2.5356	2.4699	2.3954	2.3119
6.3	2.7994	2.7951	2.7820	2.7602	2.7297	2.6905	2.6425	2.5857	2.5202	2.4457	2.3623
6.4	2.8495	2.8451	2.8321	2.8103	2.7798	2.7406	2.6926	2.6359	2.5704	2.4960	2.4127
6.5	2.8995	2.8952	2.8821	2.8604	2.8299	2.7907	2.7427	2.6860	2.6205	2.5462	2.4630
6.6	2.9496	2.9452	2.9322	2.9104	2.8799	2.8407	2.7928	2.7361	2.6707	2.5964	2.5133
6.7	2.9996	2.9953	2.9822	2.9605	2.9300	2.8908	2.8429	2.7863	2.7208	2.6466	2.5636
6.8	3.0496	3.0453	3.0322	3.0105	2.9800	2.9409	2.8930	2.8364	2.7710	2.6968	2.6138
6.9	3.0997	3.0953	3.0823	3.0605	3.0301	2.9909	2.9430	2.8864	2.8211	2.7469	2.6640
7.0	3.1497	3.1454	3.1323	3.1106	3.0801	3.0410	2.9931	2.9365	2.8712	2.7971	2.7142
7.1	3.1997	3.1954	3.1823	3.1606	3.1302	3.0910	3.0432	2.9866	2.9213	2.8472	2.7643
7.2	3.2498	3.2454	3.2324	3.2106	3.1802	3.1411	3.0932	3.0366	2.9713	2.8973	2.8145
7.3	3.2998	3.2954	3.2824	3.2607	3.2302	3.1911	3.1432	3.0867	3.0214	2.9474	2.8646
7.4	3.3498	3.3454	3.3324	3.3107	3.2802	3.2411	3.1933	3.1367	3.0715	2.9975	2.9147
7.5	3.3998	3.3955	3.3824	3.3607	3.3303	3.2911	3.2433	3.1868	3.1215	3.0476	2.9648
7.6	3.4498	3.4455	3.4324	3.4107	3.3803	3.3412	3.2933	3.2368	3.1716	3.0976	3.0149
7.7	3.4998	3.4955	3.4825	3.4607	3.4303	3.3912	3.3434	3.2869	3.2216	3.1477	3.0650
7.8	3.5498	3.5455	3.5325	3.5107	3.4803	3.4412	3.3934	3.3369	3.2717	3.1977	3.1151
7.9	3.5999	3.5955	3.5825	3.5608	3.5303	3.4912	3.4434	3.3869	3.3217	3.2478	3.1651
8.0	3.6499	3.6455	3.6325	3.6108	3.5803	3.5412	3.4934	3.4369	3.3717	3.2978	3.2152
PHI	-0.3501	-0.3544	-0.3674	-0.3891	-0.4195	-0.4586	-0.5064	-0.5629	-0.6280	-0.7018	-0.7844

R ∞ *Optimal Sample Size, ∞ Degrees of Freedom* MT-9

D Λ	2.0	2.2	2.4	2.6	2.8	3.0	3.2	3.4	3.6	3.8	4.0
3.0	0.4772										
3.1	0.5720										
3.2	0.6541										
3.3	0.7288	0.5407									
3.4	0.7985	0.6346									
3.5	0.8646	0.7161									
3.6	0.9281	0.7904									
3.7	0.9694	0.8597	0.6837								
3.8	1.0490	0.9255	0.7658								
3.9	1.1072	0.9887	0.8403					−∞			
4.0	1.1643	1.0498	0.9098	0.7188							
4.1	1.2205	1.1092	0.9757	0.8028							
4.2	1.2758	1.1673	1.0389	0.8784							
4.3	1.3305	1.2242	1.1000	0.9486	0.7388						
4.4	1.3846	1.2802	1.1594	1.0151	0.8265						
4.5	1.4381	1.3355	1.2175	1.0786	0.9044						
4.6	1.4913	1.3900	1.2744	1.1400	0.9761						
4.7	1.5441	1.4440	1.3305	1.1997	1.0435	0.8358					
4.8	1.5965	1.4975	1.3857	1.2580	1.1079	0.9174					
4.9	1.6487	1.5506	1.4403	1.3151	1.1698	0.9915					
5.0	1.7006	1.6033	1.4942	1.3712	1.2300	1.0606	0.8276				
5.1	1.7523	1.6557	1.5477	1.4265	1.2886	1.1262	0.9159				
5.2	1.8037	1.7078	1.6008	1.4812	1.3460	1.1891	0.9939				
5.3	1.8551	1.7597	1.6535	1.5352	1.4024	1.2500	1.0657				
5.4	1.9062	1.8113	1.7059	1.5888	1.4579	1.3092	1.1332	0.8967			
5.5	1.9573	1.8628	1.7580	1.6419	1.5127	1.3671	1.1976	0.9815			
5.6	2.0082	1.9141	1.8099	1.6946	1.5669	1.4239	1.2595	1.0575			
5.7	2.0590	1.9652	1.8615	1.7471	1.6206	1.4798	1.3196	1.1279			
5.8	2.1098	2.0163	1.9130	1.7992	1.6739	1.5349	1.3783	1.1944	0.9505		
5.9	2.1604	2.0672	1.9642	1.8511	1.7267	1.5893	1.4356	1.2580	1.0338		
6.0	2.2110	2.1180	2.0154	1.9028	1.7792	1.6432	1.4920	1.3194	1.1089		
6.1	2.2615	2.1687	2.0664	1.9542	1.8314	1.6966	1.5475	1.3791	1.1787		
6.2	2.3119	2.2193	2.1173	2.0055	1.8834	1.7496	1.6023	1.4373	1.2447	0.9899	
6.3	2.3623	2.2699	2.1681	2.0567	1.9351	1.8023	1.6565	1.4943	1.3079	1.0733	
6.4	2.4127	2.3204	2.2188	2.1077	1.9866	1.8546	1.7102	1.5504	1.3690	1.1484	
6.5	2.4630	2.3708	2.2694	2.1586	2.0380	1.9066	1.7634	1.6057	1.4284	1.2181	
6.6	2.5133	2.4212	2.3200	2.2094	2.0891	1.9585	1.8162	1.6603	1.4865	1.2841	1.0148
6.7	2.5636	2.4716	2.3705	2.2602	2.1402	2.0101	1.8687	1.7144	1.5434	1.3474	1.0998
6.8	2.6138	2.5219	2.4210	2.3108	2.1912	2.0615	1.9209	1.7679	1.5993	1.4084	1.1759
6.9	2.6640	2.5722	2.4713	2.3614	2.2420	2.1127	1.9729	1.8210	1.6545	1.4678	1.2463
7.0	2.7142	2.6224	2.5217	2.4119	2.2927	2.1639	2.0246	1.8737	1.7090	1.5259	1.3127
7.1	2.7643	2.6726	2.5720	2.4623	2.3434	2.2148	2.0761	1.9261	1.7630	1.5828	1.3763
7.2	2.8145	2.7228	2.6223	2.5127	2.3940	2.2657	2.1274	1.9782	1.8164	1.6387	1.4377
7.3	2.8646	2.7730	2.6725	2.5631	2.4445	2.3165	2.1786	2.0301	1.8695	1.6939	1.4973
7.4	2.9147	2.8232	2.7228	2.6134	2.4950	2.3672	2.2297	2.0817	1.9221	1.7484	1.5555
7.5	2.9648	2.8733	2.7730	2.6637	2.5454	2.4178	2.2806	2.1332	1.9745	1.8023	1.6125
7.6	3.0149	2.9234	2.8231	2.7139	2.5957	2.4683	2.3314	2.1845	2.0265	1.8558	1.6686
7.7	3.0650	2.9735	2.8733	2.7642	2.6461	2.5188	2.3822	2.2356	2.0784	1.9088	1.7239
7.8	3.1151	3.0236	2.9234	2.8144	2.6964	2.5693	2.4328	2.2867	2.1300	1.9615	1.7784
7.9	3.1651	3.0737	2.9735	2.8645	2.7466	2.6197	2.4834	2.3376	2.1814	2.0138	1.8325
8.0	3.2152	3.1238	3.0237	2.9147	2.7968	2.6700	2.5339	2.3884	2.2327	2.0659	1.8860
8.1	3.2652	3.1739	3.0738	2.9648	2.8470	2.7203	2.5844	2.4391	2.2838	2.1177	1.9390
8.2	3.3153	3.2239	3.1238	3.0150	2.8972	2.7706	2.6348	2.4897	2.3348	2.1693	1.9918
8.3	3.3653	3.2740	3.1739	3.0651	2.9474	2.8208	2.6852	2.5403	2.3857	2.2208	2.0441
8.4	3.4154	3.3240	3.2240	3.1152	2.9975	2.8710	2.7355	2.5908	2.4365	2.2720	2.0962
8.5	3.4654	3.3741	3.2740	3.1653	3.0477	2.9212	2.7858	2.6412	2.4872	2.3231	2.1481
8.6	3.5154	3.4241	3.3241	3.2153	3.0978	2.9714	2.8360	2.6916	2.5378	2.3741	2.1997
8.7	3.5654	3.4742	3.3742	3.2654	3.1479	3.0215	2.8863	2.7420	2.5884	2.4250	2.2512
8.8	3.6155	3.5242	3.4242	3.3155	3.1980	3.0717	2.9365	2.7923	2.6388	2.4758	2.3025
8.9	3.6655	3.5742	3.4742	3.3655	3.2481	3.1218	2.9867	2.8426	2.6893	2.5265	2.3536
9.0	3.7155	3.6242	3.5243	3.4156	3.2981	3.1719	3.0368	2.8928	2.7397	2.5771	2.4046
9.1	3.7655	3.6743	3.5743	3.4656	3.3482	3.2220	3.0870	2.9430	2.7900	2.6277	2.4555
9.2	3.8155	3.7243	3.6243	3.5157	3.3983	3.2721	3.1371	2.9932	2.8403	2.6782	2.5063
9.3	3.8655	3.7743	3.6744	3.5657	3.4483	3.3222	3.1872	3.0434	2.8906	2.7286	2.5570
9.4	3.9156	3.8243	3.7244	3.6157	3.4983	3.3722	3.2373	3.0936	2.9408	2.7790	2.6077
9.5	3.9656	3.8743	3.7744	3.6658	3.5484	3.4223	3.2874	3.1437	2.9911	2.8293	2.6582
9.6	4.0156	3.9243	3.8244	3.7158	3.5984	3.4723	3.3375	3.1938	3.0413	2.8796	2.7087
9.7	4.0656	3.9744	3.8744	3.7658	3.6485	3.5224	3.3876	3.2439	3.0914	2.9299	2.7592
9.8	4.1156	4.0244	3.9244	3.8158	3.6985	3.5724	3.4376	3.2940	3.1416	2.9802	2.8096
9.9	4.1656	4.0744	3.9745	3.8658	3.7485	3.6225	3.4877	3.3441	3.1917	3.0304	2.8599
10.0	4.2156	4.1244	4.0245	3.9159	3.7985	3.6725	3.5377	3.3942	3.2418	3.0806	2.9102
PHI	-0.7844	-0.8756	-0.9754	-1.0840	-1.2013	-1.3272	-1.4619	-1.6052	-1.7572	-1.9179	-2.0872

TABLES OF THE BINOMIAL MASS FUNCTION MT-12R

The following tables give the binomial probability of exactly R successes in N trials given that the probability of a success is P on any trial regardless of the outcomes of previous trials. The values of R at the <u>left</u> of any section of the tables are to be used in conjunction with the values of P at the <u>top</u> of that section; the values of R at the <u>right</u> of any section are to be used in conjunction with the values of P at the <u>bottom</u> of that section.

Example: the probability of R = 3 successes in N = 8 trials when P = .25 is .2076 and is the same as the probability of R = 5 successes in N = 8 trials when P = .75.

N = 1

R	P	01	02	03	04	05	06	07	08	09	10		
0		9900	9800	9700	9600	9500	9400	9300	9200	9100	9000		1
1		0100	0200	0300	0400	0500	0600	0700	0800	0900	1000		0
		99	98	97	96	95	94	93	92	91	90	P	R

R	P	11	12	13	14	15	16	17	18	19	20		
0		8900	8800	8700	8600	8500	8400	8300	8200	8100	8000		1
1		1100	1200	1300	1400	1500	1600	1700	1800	1900	2000		0
		89	88	87	86	85	84	83	82	81	80	P	R

R	P	21	22	23	24	25	26	27	28	29	30		
0		7900	7800	7700	7600	7500	7400	7300	7200	7100	7000		1
1		2100	2200	2300	2400	2500	2600	2700	2800	2900	3000		0
		79	78	77	76	75	74	73	72	71	70	P	R

R	P	31	32	33	34	35	36	37	38	39	40		
0		6900	6800	6700	6600	6500	6400	6300	6200	6100	6000		1
1		3100	3200	3300	3400	3500	3600	3700	3800	3900	4000		0
		69	68	67	66	65	64	63	62	61	60	P	R

R	P	41	42	43	44	45	46	47	48	49	50		
0		5900	5800	5700	5600	5500	5400	5300	5200	5100	5000		1
1		4100	4200	4300	4400	4500	4600	4700	4800	4900	5000		0
		59	58	57	56	55	54	53	52	51	50	P	R

N = 2

R	P	01	02	03	04	05	06	07	08	09	10		
0		9801	9604	9409	9216	9025	8836	8649	8464	8281	8100		2
1		0198	0392	0582	0768	0950	1128	1302	1472	1638	1800		1
2		0001	0004	0009	0016	0025	0036	0049	0064	0081	0100		0
		99	98	97	96	95	94	93	92	91	90	P	R

R	P	11	12	13	14	15	16	17	18	19	20		
0		7921	7744	7569	7396	7225	7056	6889	6724	6561	6400		2
1		1958	2112	2262	2408	2550	2688	2822	2952	3078	3200		1
2		0121	0144	0169	0196	0225	0256	0289	0324	0361	0400		0
		89	88	87	86	85	84	83	82	81	80	P	R

R	P	21	22	23	24	25	26	27	28	29	30		
0		6241	6084	5929	5776	5625	5476	5329	5184	5041	4900		2
1		3318	3432	3542	3648	3750	3848	3942	4032	4118	4200		1
2		0441	0484	0529	0576	0625	0676	0729	0784	0841	0900		0
		79	78	77	76	75	74	73	72	71	70	P	R

R	P	31	32	33	34	35	36	37	38	39	40		
0		4761	4624	4489	4356	4225	4096	3969	3844	3721	3600		2
1		4278	4352	4422	4488	4550	4608	4662	4712	4758	4800		1
2		0961	1024	1089	1156	1225	1296	1369	1444	1521	1600		0
		69	68	67	66	65	64	63	62	61	60	P	R

R	P	41	42	43	44	45	46	47	48	49	50		
0		3481	3364	3249	3136	3025	2916	2809	2704	2601	2500		2
1		4838	4872	4902	4928	4950	4968	4982	4992	4998	5000		1
2		1681	1764	1849	1936	2025	2116	2209	2304	2401	2500		0
		59	58	57	56	55	54	53	52	51	50	P	R

N = 3

R	P	01	02	03	04	05	06	07	08	09	10		
0		9703	9412	9127	8847	8574	8306	8044	7787	7536	7290		3
1		0294	0576	0847	1106	1354	1590	1816	2031	2236	2430		2
2		0003	0012	0026	0046	0071	0102	0137	0177	0221	0270		1
3		0000	0000	0000	0001	0001	0002	0003	0005	0007	0010		0
		99	98	97	96	95	94	93	92	91	90	P	R

R	P	11	12	13	14	15	16	17	18	19	20		
0		7050	6815	6585	6361	6141	5927	5718	5514	5314	5120		3
1		2614	2788	2952	3106	3251	3387	3513	3631	3740	3840		2
2		0323	0380	0441	0506	0574	0645	0720	0797	0877	0960		1
3		0013	0017	0022	0027	0034	0041	0049	0058	0069	0080		0
		89	88	87	86	85	84	83	82	81	80	P	R

R	P	21	22	23	24	25	26	27	28	29	30		
0		4930	4746	4565	4390	4219	4052	3890	3732	3579	3430		3
1		3932	4015	4091	4159	4219	4271	4316	4355	4386	4410		2
2		1045	1133	1222	1313	1406	1501	1597	1693	1791	1890		1
3		0093	0106	0122	0138	0156	0176	0197	0220	0244	0270		0
		79	78	77	76	75	74	73	72	71	70	P	R

R	P	31	32	33	34	35	36	37	38	39	40		
0		3285	3144	3008	2875	2746	2621	2500	2383	2270	2160		3
1		4428	4439	4444	4443	4436	4424	4406	4382	4354	4320		2
2		1989	2089	2189	2289	2389	2488	2587	2686	2783	2880		1
3		0298	0328	0359	0393	0429	0467	0507	0549	0593	0640		0
		69	68	67	66	65	64	63	62	61	60	P	R

R	P	41	42	43	44	45	46	47	48	49	50		
0		2054	1951	1852	1756	1664	1575	1489	1406	1327	1250		3
1		4282	4239	4191	4140	4084	4024	3961	3894	3823	3750		2
2		2975	3069	3162	3252	3341	3428	3512	3594	3674	3750		1
3		0689	0741	0795	0852	0911	0973	1038	1106	1176	1250		0
		59	58	57	56	55	54	53	52	51	50	P	R

N = 4

R	P	01	02	03	04	05	06	07	08	09	10		
0		9606	9224	8853	8493	8145	7807	7481	7164	6857	6561		4
1		0388	0753	1095	1416	1715	1993	2252	2492	2713	2916		3
2		0006	0023	0051	0088	0135	0191	0254	0325	0402	0486		2
3		0000	0000	0001	0002	0005	0008	0013	0019	0027	0036		1
4		0000	0000	0000	0000	0000	0000	0000	0000	0001	0001		0
		99	98	97	96	95	94	93	92	91	90	P	R

R	P	11	12	13	14	15	16	17	18	19	20		
0		6274	5997	5729	5470	5220	4979	4746	4521	4305	4096		4
1		3102	3271	3424	3562	3685	3793	3888	3970	4039	4096		3
2		0575	0669	0767	0870	0975	1084	1195	1307	1421	1536		2
3		0047	0061	0076	0094	0115	0138	0163	0191	0222	0256		1
4		0001	0002	0003	0004	0005	0007	0008	0010	0013	0016		0
		89	88	87	86	85	84	83	82	81	80	P	R

R	P	21	22	23	24	25	26	27	28	29	30		
0		3895	3702	3515	3336	3164	2999	2840	2687	2541	2401		4
1		4142	4176	4200	4214	4219	4214	4201	4180	4152	4116		3
2		1651	1767	1882	1996	2109	2221	2331	2439	2544	2646		2
3		0293	0332	0375	0420	0469	0520	0575	0632	0693	0756		1
4		0019	0023	0028	0033	0039	0046	0053	0061	0071	0081		0
		79	78	77	76	75	74	73	72	71	70	P	R

R	P	31	32	33	34	35	36	37	38	39	40		
0		2267	2138	2015	1897	1785	1678	1575	1478	1385	1296		4
1		4074	4025	3970	3910	3845	3775	3701	3623	3541	3456		3
2		2745	2841	2933	3021	3105	3185	3260	3330	3396	3456		2
3		0822	0891	0963	1038	1115	1194	1276	1361	1447	1536		1
4		0092	0105	0119	0134	0150	0168	0187	0209	0231	0256		0
		69	68	67	66	65	64	63	62	61	60	P	R

R	P	41	42	43	44	45	46	47	48	49	50		
0		1212	1132	1056	0983	0915	0850	0789	0731	0677	0625		4
1		3368	3278	3185	3091	2995	2897	2799	2700	2600	2500		3
2		3511	3560	3604	3643	3675	3702	3723	3738	3747	3750		2
3		1627	1719	1813	1908	2005	2102	2201	2300	2400	2500		1
4		0283	0311	0342	0375	0410	0448	0488	0531	0576	0625		0
		59	58	57	56	55	54	53	52	51	50	P	R

N = 5

R	P	01	02	03	04	05	06	07	08	09	10		
0		9510	9039	8587	8154	7738	7339	6957	6591	6240	5905		5
1		0480	0922	1328	1699	2036	2342	2618	2866	3086	3280		4
2		0010	0038	0082	0142	0214	0299	0394	0498	0610	0729		3
3		0000	0001	0003	0006	0011	0019	0030	0043	0060	0081		2
4		0000	0000	0000	0000	0000	0001	0001	0002	0003	0004		1
		99	98	97	96	95	94	93	92	91	90	P	R

R	P	11	12	13	14	15	16	17	18	19	20		
0		5584	5277	4984	4704	4437	4182	3939	3707	3487	3277		5
1		3451	3598	3724	3829	3915	3983	4034	4069	4089	4096		4
2		0853	0981	1113	1247	1382	1517	1652	1786	1919	2048		3
3		0105	0134	0166	0203	0244	0289	0338	0392	0450	0512		2
4		0007	0009	0012	0017	0022	0028	0035	0043	0053	0064		1
5		0000	0000	0000	0001	0001	0001	0001	0002	0002	0003		0
		89	88	87	86	85	84	83	82	81	80	P	R

R	P	21	22	23	24	25	26	27	28	29	30		
0		3077	2887	2707	2536	2373	2219	2073	1935	1804	1681		5
1		4090	4072	4043	4003	3955	3898	3834	3762	3685	3601		4
2		2174	2297	2415	2529	2637	2739	2836	2926	3010	3087		3
3		0578	0648	0721	0798	0879	0962	1049	1138	1229	1323		2
4		0077	0091	0108	0126	0146	0169	0194	0221	0251	0283		1
5		0004	0005	0006	0008	0010	0012	0014	0017	0021	0024		0
		79	78	77	76	75	74	73	72	71	70	P	R

R	P	31	32	33	34	35	36	37	38	39	40		
0		1564	1454	1350	1252	1160	1074	0992	0916	0845	0778		5
1		3513	3421	3325	3226	3124	3020	2914	2808	2700	2592		4
2		3157	3220	3275	3323	3364	3397	3423	3441	3452	3456		3
3		1418	1515	1613	1712	1811	1911	2010	2109	2207	2304		2
4		0319	0357	0397	0441	0488	0537	0590	0646	0706	0768		1
5		0029	0034	0039	0045	0053	0060	0069	0079	0090	0102		0
		69	68	67	66	65	64	63	62	61	60	P	R

R	P	41	42	43	44	45	46	47	48	49	50		
0		0715	0656	0602	0551	0503	0459	0418	0380	0345	0313		5
1		2484	2376	2270	2164	2059	1956	1854	1755	1657	1562		4
2		3452	3442	3424	3400	3369	3332	3289	3240	3185	3125		3
3		2399	2492	2583	2671	2757	2838	2916	2990	3060	3125		2
4		0834	0902	0974	1049	1128	1209	1293	1380	1470	1562		1
5		0116	0131	0147	0165	0185	0206	0229	0255	0282	0312		0
		59	58	57	56	55	54	53	52	51	50	P	R

N = 6

R	P	01	02	03	04	05	06	07	08	09	10		
0		9415	8858	8330	7828	7351	6899	6470	6064	5679	5314		6
1		0571	1085	1546	1957	2321	2642	2922	3164	3370	3543		5
2		0014	0055	0120	0204	0305	0422	0550	0688	0833	0984		4
3		0000	0002	0005	0011	0021	0036	0055	0080	0110	0146		3
4		0000	0000	0000	0000	0001	0002	0003	0005	0008	0012		2
5		0000	0000	0000	0000	0000	0000	0000	0000	0000	0001		1
		99	98	97	96	95	94	93	92	91	90	P	R

R	P	11	12	13	14	15	16	17	18	19	20		
0		4970	4644	4336	4046	3771	3513	3269	3040	2824	2621		6
1		3685	3800	3888	3952	3993	4015	4018	4004	3975	3932		5
2		1139	1295	1452	1608	1762	1912	2057	2197	2331	2458		4
3		0188	0236	0289	0349	0415	0486	0562	0643	0729	0819		3
4		0017	0024	0032	0043	0055	0069	0086	0106	0128	0154		2
5		0001	0001	0002	0003	0004	0005	0007	0009	0012	0015		1
6		0000	0000	0000	0000	0000	0000	0000	0000	0000	0001		0
		89	88	87	86	85	84	83	82	81	80	P	R

R	P	21	22	23	24	25	26	27	28	29	30		
0		2431	2252	2084	1927	1780	1642	1513	1393	1281	1176		6
1		3877	3811	3735	3651	3560	3462	3358	3251	3139	3025		5
2		2577	2687	2789	2882	2966	3041	3105	3160	3206	3241		4
3		0913	1011	1111	1214	1318	1424	1531	1639	1746	1852		3
4		0182	0214	0249	0287	0330	0375	0425	0478	0535	0595		2
5		0019	0024	0030	0036	0044	0053	0063	0074	0087	0102		1
6		0001	0001	0001	0002	0002	0003	0004	0005	0006	0007		0
		79	78	77	76	75	74	73	72	71	70	P	R

R	P	31	32	33	34	35	36	37	38	39	40		
0		1079	0989	0905	0827	0754	0687	0625	0568	0515	0467		6
1		2909	2792	2673	2555	2437	2319	2203	2089	1976	1866		5
2		3267	3284	3292	3290	3280	3261	3235	3201	3159	3110		4
3		1957	2061	2162	2260	2355	2446	2533	2616	2693	2765		3
4		0660	0727	0799	0873	0951	1032	1116	1202	1291	1382		2
5		0119	0137	0157	0180	0205	0232	0262	0295	0330	0369		1
6		0009	0011	0013	0015	0018	0022	0026	0030	0035	0041		0
		69	68	67	66	65	64	63	62	61	60	P	R

R	P	41	42	43	44	45	46	47	48	49	50		
0		0422	0381	0343	0308	0277	0248	0222	0198	0176	0156		6
1		1759	1654	1552	1454	1359	1267	1179	1095	1014	0937		5
2		3055	2994	2928	2856	2780	2699	2615	2527	2436	2344		4
3		2831	[illegible]	2945	2992	3032	3065	3091	3110	3121	3125		3
4		1475	1570	1666	1762	1861	1958	2056	2153	2249	2344		2
5		0410	0455	0503	0554	0609	0667	0729	0795	0864	0937		1
6		0048	0055	0063	0073	0083	0095	0108	0122	0138	0156		0
		59	58	57	56	55	54	53	52	51	50	P	R

N = 7

R	P	01	02	03	04	05	06	07	08	09	10		
0		9321	8681	8080	7514	6983	6485	6017	5578	5168	4783		7
1		0659	1240	1749	2192	2573	2897	3170	3396	3578	3720		6
2		0020	0076	0162	0274	0406	0555	0716	0886	1061	1240		5
3		0000	0003	0008	0019	0036	0059	0090	0128	0175	0230		4
4		0000	0000	0000	0001	0002	0004	0007	0011	0017	0026		3
5		0000	0000	0000	0000	0000	0000	0000	0001	0001	0002		2
		99	98	97	96	95	94	93	92	91	90	P	R

R	P	11	12	13	14	15	16	17	18	19	20		
0		4423	4087	3773	3479	3206	2951	2714	2493	2288	2097		7
1		3827	3901	3946	3965	3960	3935	3891	3830	3756	3670		6
2		1419	1596	1769	1936	2097	2248	2391	2523	2643	2753		5
3		0292	0363	0441	0525	0617	0714	0816	0923	1033	1147		4
4		0036	0049	0066	0086	0109	0136	0167	0203	0242	0287		3
5		0003	0004	0006	0008	0012	0016	0021	0027	0034	0043		2
6		0000	0000	0000	0000	0001	0001	0001	0002	0003	0004		1
		89	88	87	86	85	84	83	82	81	80	P	R

R	P	21	22	23	24	25	26	27	28	29	30		
0		1920	1757	1605	1465	1335	1215	1105	1003	0910	0824		7
1		3573	3468	3356	3237	3115	2989	2860	2731	2600	2471		6
2		2850	2935	3007	3067	3115	3150	3174	3186	3186	3177		5
3		1263	1379	1497	1614	1730	1845	1956	2065	2169	2269		4
4		0336	0389	0447	0510	0577	0648	0724	0803	0886	0972		3
5		0054	0066	0080	0097	0115	0137	0161	0187	0217	0250		2
6		0005	0006	0008	0010	0013	0016	0020	0024	0030	0036		1
7		0000	0000	0000	0000	0001	0001	0001	0001	0002	0002		0
		79	78	77	76	75	74	73	72	71	70	P	R

R	P	31	32	33	34	35	36	37	38	39	40		
0		0745	0672	0606	0546	0490	0440	0394	0352	0314	0280		7
1		2342	2215	2090	1967	1848	1732	1619	1511	1407	1306		6
2		3156	3127	3088	3040	2985	2922	2853	2778	2698	2613		5
3		2363	2452	2535	2610	2679	2740	2793	2838	2875	2903		4
4		1062	1154	1248	1345	1442	1541	1640	1739	1838	1935		3
5		0286	0326	0369	0416	0466	0520	0578	0640	0705	0774		2
6		0043	0051	0061	0071	0084	0098	0113	0131	0150	0172		1
7		0003	0003	0004	0005	0006	0008	0009	0011	0014	0016		0
		69	68	67	66	65	64	63	62	61	60	P	R

R	P	41	42	43	44	45	46	47	48	49	50		
0		0249	0221	0195	0173	0152	0134	0117	0103	0090	0078		7
1		1211	1119	1032	0950	0872	0798	0729	0664	0604	0547		6
2		2524	2431	2336	2239	2140	2040	1940	1840	1740	1641		5
3		2923	2934	2937	2932	2918	2897	2867	2830	2786	2734		4
4		2031	2125	2216	2304	2388	2468	2543	2612	2676	2734		3
5		0847	0923	1003	1086	1172	1261	1353	1447	1543	1641		2
6		0196	0223	0252	0284	0320	0358	0400	0445	0494	0547		1
7		0019	0023	0027	0032	0037	0044	0051	0059	0068	0078		0
		59	58	57	56	55	54	53	52	51	50	P	R

N = 8

R	P	01	02	03	04	05	06	07	08	09	10		
0		9227	8508	7837	7214	6634	6096	5596	5132	4703	4305		8
1		0746	1389	1939	2405	2793	3113	3370	3570	3721	3826		7
2		0026	0099	0210	0351	0515	0695	0888	1087	1288	1488		6
3		0001	0004	0013	0029	0054	0089	0134	0189	0255	0331		5
4		0000	0000	0001	0002	0004	0007	0013	0021	0031	0046		4
5		0000	0000	0000	0000	0000	0000	0001	0001	0002	0004		3
		99	98	97	96	95	94	93	92	91	90	P	R

R	P	11	12	13	14	15	16	17	18	19	20		
0		3937	3596	3282	2992	2725	2479	2252	2044	1853	1678		8
1		3892	3923	3923	3897	3847	3777	3691	3590	3477	3355		7
2		1684	1872	2052	2220	2376	2518	2646	2758	2855	2936		6
3		0416	0511	0613	0723	0839	0959	1084	1211	1339	1468		5
4		0064	0087	0115	0147	0185	0228	0277	0332	0393	0459		4
5		0006	0009	0014	0019	0026	0035	0045	0058	0074	0092		3
6		0000	0001	0001	0002	0002	0003	0005	0006	0009	0011		2
7		0000	0000	0000	0000	0000	0000	0000	0000	0001	0001		1
		89	88	87	86	85	84	83	82	81	80	P	R

R	P	21	22	23	24	25	26	27	28	29	30		
0		1517	1370	1236	1113	1001	0899	0806	0722	0646	0576		8
1		3226	3092	2953	2812	2670	2527	2386	2247	2110	1977		7
2		3002	3052	3087	3108	3115	3108	3089	3058	3017	2965		6
3		1596	1722	1844	1963	2076	2184	2285	2379	2464	2541		5
4		0530	0607	0689	0775	0865	0959	1056	1156	1258	1361		4

5		0113	0137	0165	0196	0231	0270	0313	0360	0411	0467		3
6		0015	0019	0025	0031	0038	0047	0058	0070	0084	0100		2
7		0001	0002	0002	0003	0004	0005	0006	0008	0010	0012		1
8		0000	0000	0000	0000	0000	0000	0000	0000	0001	0001		0
		79	78	77	76	75	74	73	72	71	70	P	R
R	P	31	32	33	34	35	36	37	38	39	40		
0		0514	0457	0406	0360	0319	0281	0248	0218	0192	0168		8
1		1847	1721	1600	1484	1373	1267	1166	1071	0981	0896		7
2		2904	2835	2758	2675	2587	2494	2397	2297	2194	2090		6
3		2609	2668	2717	2756	2786	2805	2815	2815	2806	2787		5
4		1465	1569	1673	1775	1875	1973	2067	2157	2242	2322		4
5		0527	0591	0659	0732	0808	0888	0971	1058	1147	1239		3
6		0118	0139	0162	0188	0217	0250	0285	0324	0367	0413		2
7		0015	0019	0023	0028	0033	0040	0048	0057	0067	0079		1
8		C001	0001	0001	0002	0002	0003	0004	0004	0005	0007		0
		69	68	67	66	65	64	63	62	61	60	P	R
R	P	41	42	43	44	45	46	47	48	49	50		
0		0147	0128	0111	0097	0084	0072	0062	0053	0046	0039		8
1		0816	0742	0672	0608	0548	0493	0442	0395	0352	0312		7
2		1985	1880	1776	1672	1569	1469	1371	1275	1183	1094		6
3		2759	2723	2679	2627	2568	2503	2431	2355	2273	2187		5
4		2397	2465	2526	2580	2627	2665	2695	2717	2730	2734		4
5		1332	1428	1525	1622	1719	1816	1912	2006	2098	2187		3
6		0463	0517	0575	0637	0703	0774	0848	0926	1008	1094		2
7		0092	0107	0124	0143	0164	0188	0215	0244	0277	0312		1
8		0008	0010	0012	0014	0017	0020	0024	0028	0033	0039		0
		59	58	57	56	55	54	53	52	51	50	P	R

N = 9

R	P	01	02	03	04	05	06	07	08	09	10		
0		9135	8337	7602	6925	6302	5730	5204	4722	4279	3874		9
1		0830	1531	2116	2597	2985	3292	3525	3695	3809	3874		8
2		0034	0125	0262	0433	0629	0840	1061	1285	1507	1722		7
3		0001	C006	0019	0042	0077	0125	0186	0261	0348	0446		6
4		0000	0000	0001	0003	0006	0012	0021	0034	0052	0074		5
5		0000	0000	0000	0000	0000	0001	0002	0003	0005	0008		4
6		0000	0000	0000	0000	0000	0000	0000	0000	0000	0001		3
		99	98	97	96	95	94	93	92	91	90	P	R
R	P	11	12	13	14	15	16	17	18	19	20		
0		3504	3165	2855	2573	2316	2082	1869	1676	1501	1342		9
1		3897	3884	3840	3770	3679	3569	3446	3312	3169	3020		8
2		1927	2119	2295	2455	2597	2720	2823	2908	2973	3020		7
3		0556	0674	0800	0933	1069	1209	1349	1489	1627	1762		6
4		0103	0138	0179	0228	0283	0345	0415	0490	0573	0661		5
5		0013	0019	0027	0037	0050	0066	0085	0108	0134	0165		4
6		0001	0002	0003	0004	0006	0008	0012	0016	0021	0028		3
7		0000	0000	0000	0000	0000	0001	0001	0001	0002	0003		2
		89	88	87	86	85	84	83	82	81	80	P	R
R	P	21	22	23	24	25	26	27	28	29	30		
0		1199	1069	0952	0846	0751	0665	0589	0520	0458	0404		9
1		2867	2713	2558	2404	2253	2104	1960	1820	1685	1556		8
2		3049	3061	3056	3037	3003	2957	2899	2831	2754	2668		7
3		1891	2014	2130	2238	2336	2424	2502	2569	2624	2668		6
4		0754	0852	0954	1060	1168	1278	1388	1499	1608	1715		5
5		0200	0240	0285	0335	0389	0449	0513	0583	0657	0735		4
6		0036	0045	0057	0070	0087	0105	0127	0151	0179	0210		3
7		0004	0005	0007	0010	0012	0016	0020	0025	0031	0039		2
8		0000	0000	0001	0001	0001	0001	0002	0002	0003	0004		1
		79	78	77	76	75	74	73	72	71	70	P	R
R	P	31	32	33	34	35	36	37	38	39	40		
0		0355	0311	0272	0238	0207	0180	0156	0135	0117	0101		9
1		1433	1317	1206	1102	1004	0912	0826	0747	0673	0605		8
2		2576	2478	2376	2270	2162	2052	1941	1831	1721	1612		7
3		2701	2721	2731	2729	2716	2693	2660	2618	2567	2508		6
4		1820	1921	2017	2109	2194	2272	2344	2407	2462	2508		5
5		0818	0904	0994	1086	1181	1278	1376	1475	1574	1672		4
6		0245	0284	0326	0373	0424	0479	0539	0603	0671	0743		3
7		0047	0057	0069	0082	0098	0116	0136	0158	0184	0212		2
8		0005	0007	0008	0011	0013	0016	0020	0024	0029	0035		1
9		0000	0000	0000	0001	0001	0001	0001	0002	0002	0003		0
		69	68	67	66	65	64	63	62	61	60	P	R
R	P	41	42	43	44	45	46	47	48	49	50		
0		0087	0074	0064	0054	0046	0039	0033	0028	0023	0020		9
1		0542	0484	0431	0383	0339	0299	0263	0231	0202	0176		8
2		1506	1402	1301	1204	1110	1020	0934	0853	0776	0703		7
3		2442	2369	2291	2207	2119	2027	1933	1837	1739	1641		6
4		2545	2573	2592	2601	2600	2590	2571	2543	2506	2461		5

5		1769	1863	1955	2044	2128	2207	2280	2347	2408	2461		4
6		0819	0900	0983	1070	1160	1253	1348	1445	1542	1641		3
7		0244	0279	0318	0360	0407	0458	0512	0571	0635	0703		2
8		0042	0051	0060	0071	0083	0097	0114	0132	0153	0176		1
9		0003	0004	0005	0006	0008	0009	0011	0014	0016	0020		0
		59	58	57	56	55	54	53	52	51	50	P	R

N = 10

R	P	01	02	03	04	05	06	07	08	09	10		
0		9044	8171	7374	6648	5987	5386	4840	4344	3894	3487		10
1		0914	1667	2281	2770	3151	3438	3643	3777	3851	3874		9
2		0042	0153	0317	0519	0746	0988	1234	1478	1714	1937		8
3		0001	0008	0026	0058	0105	0168	0248	0343	0452	0574		7
4		0000	0000	0001	0004	0010	0019	0033	0052	0078	0112		6
5		0000	0000	0000	0000	0001	0001	0003	0005	0009	0015		5
6		0000	0000	0000	0000	0000	0000	0000	0000	0001	0001		4
		99	98	97	96	95	94	93	92	91	90	P	R

R	P	11	12	13	14	15	16	17	18	19	20		
0		3118	2785	2484	2213	1969	1749	1552	1374	1216	1074		10
1		3854	3798	3712	3603	3474	3331	3178	3017	2852	2684		9
2		2143	2330	2496	2639	2759	2856	2929	2980	3010	3020		8
3		0706	0847	0995	1146	1298	1450	1600	1745	1883	2013		7
4		0153	0202	0260	0326	0401	0483	0573	0670	0773	0881		6
5		0023	0033	0047	0064	0085	0111	0141	0177	0218	0264		5
6		0002	0004	0006	0009	0012	0018	0024	0032	0043	0055		4
7		0000	0000	0000	0001	0001	0002	0003	0004	0006	0008		3
8		0000	0000	0000	0000	0000	0000	0000	0000	0001	0001		2
		89	88	87	86	85	84	83	82	81	80	P	R

R	P	21	22	23	24	25	26	27	28	29	30		
0		0947	0834	0733	0643	0563	0492	0430	0374	0326	0282		10
1		2517	2351	2188	2030	1877	1730	1590	1456	1330	1211		9
2		3011	2984	2942	2885	2816	2735	2646	2548	2444	2335		8
3		2134	2244	2343	2429	2503	2563	2609	2642	2662	2668		7
4		0993	1108	1225	1343	1460	1576	1689	1798	1903	2001		6
5		0317	0375	0439	0509	0584	0664	0750	0839	0933	1029		5
6		0070	0088	0109	0134	0162	0195	0231	0272	0317	0368		4
7		0011	0014	0019	0024	0031	0039	0049	0060	0074	0090		3
8		0001	0002	0002	0003	0004	0005	0007	0009	0011	0014		2
9		0000	0000	0000	0000	0000	0000	0001	0001	0001	0001		1
		79	78	77	76	75	74	73	72	71	70	P	R

R	P	31	32	33	34	35	36	37	38	39	40		
0		0245	0211	0182	0157	0135	0115	0098	0084	0071	0060		10
1		1099	0995	0898	0808	0725	0649	0578	0514	0456	0403		9
2		2222	2107	1990	1873	1757	1642	1529	1419	1312	1209		8
3		2662	2644	2614	2573	2522	2462	2394	2319	2237	2150		7
4		2093	2177	2253	2320	2377	2424	2461	2487	2503	2508		6
5		1126	1229	1332	1434	1536	1636	1734	1829	1920	2007		5
6		0422	0482	0547	0616	0689	0767	0849	0934	1023	1115		4
7		0108	0130	0154	0181	0212	0247	0285	0327	0374	0425		3
8		0018	0023	0028	0035	0043	0052	0063	0075	0090	0106		2
9		0002	0002	0003	0004	0005	0006	0008	0010	0013	0016		1
10		0000	0000	0000	0000	0000	0000	0000	0001	0001	0001		0
		69	68	67	66	65	64	63	62	61	60	P	R

R	P	41	42	43	44	45	46	47	48	49	50		
0		0051	0043	0036	0030	0025	0021	0017	0014	0012	0010		10
1		0355	0312	0273	0238	0207	0180	0155	0133	0114	0098		9
2		1111	1017	0927	0843	0763	0688	0619	0554	0494	0439		8
3		2058	1963	1865	1765	1665	1564	1464	1364	1267	1172		7
4		2503	2488	2462	2427	2384	2331	2271	2204	2130	2051		6
5		2087	2162	2229	2289	2340	2383	2417	2441	2456	2461		5
6		1209	1304	1401	1499	1596	1692	1786	1878	1966	2051		4
7		0480	0540	0604	0673	0746	0824	0905	0991	1080	1172		3
8		0125	0147	0171	0198	0229	0263	0301	0343	0389	0439		2
9		0019	0024	0029	0035	0042	0050	0059	0070	0083	0098		1
10		0001	0002	0002	0003	0003	0004	0005	0006	0008	0010		0
		59	58	57	56	55	54	53	52	51	50	P	R

N = 11

R	P	01	02	03	04	05	06	07	08	09	10		
0		8953	8007	7153	6382	5688	5063	4501	3996	3544	3138		11
1		0995	1798	2433	2925	3293	3555	3727	3823	3855	3835		10
2		0050	0183	0376	0609	0867	1135	1403	1662	1906	2131		9
3		0002	0011	0035	0076	0137	0217	0317	0434	0566	0710		8
4		0000	0000	0002	0006	0014	0028	0048	0075	0112	0158		7

5		0000	0000	0000	0000	0001	0002	0005	0009	0015	0025		6
6		0000	0000	0000	0000	0000	0000	0000	0001	0002	0003		5
		99	98	97	96	95	94	93	92	91	90	P	R

R	P	11	12	13	14	15	16	17	18	19	20		
0		2775	2451	2161	1903	1673	1469	1288	1127	0985	0859		11
1		3773	3676	3552	3408	3248	3078	2901	2721	2541	2362		10
2		2332	2507	2654	2774	2866	2932	2971	2987	2980	2953		9
3		0865	1025	1190	1355	1517	1675	1826	1967	2097	2215		8
4		0214	0280	0356	0441	0536	0638	0748	0864	0984	1107		7
5		0037	0053	0074	0101	0132	0170	0214	0265	0323	0388		6
6		0005	0007	0011	0016	[illegible]	[illegible]	0044	0058	0076	0097		5
7		0000	0001	0001	0002	0003	[illegible]	[illegible]	[illegible]	0013	0017		4
8		0000	0000	0000	0000	0000	0000	0001	0001	0001	0002		3
		89	88	87	86	85	84	83	82	81	80	P	R

R	P	21	22	23	24	25	26	27	28	29	30		
0		0748	0650	0564	0489	0422	0364	0314	0270	0231	0198		11
1		2187	2017	1854	1697	1549	1408	1276	1153	1038	0932		10
2		2907	2845	2768	2680	2581	2474	2360	2242	2121	1998		9
3		2318	2407	2481	2539	2581	2608	2619	2616	2599	2568		8
4		1232	1358	1482	1603	1721	1832	1937	2035	2123	2201		7
5		0459	0536	0620	0709	0803	0901	1003	1108	1214	1321		6
6		0122	0151	0185	0224	0268	0317	0371	0431	0496	0566		5
7		0023	0030	0039	0050	0064	0079	0098	0120	0145	0173		4
8		0003	0004	0006	0008	0011	0014	0018	0023	0030	0037		3
9		0000	0000	0001	0001	0001	0002	0002	0003	0004	0005		2
		79	78	77	76	75	74	73	72	71	70	P	R

R	P	31	32	33	34	35	36	37	38	39	40		
0		0169	0144	0122	0104	0088	0074	0062	0052	0044	0036		11
1		0834	0744	0662	0587	0518	0457	0401	0351	0306	0266		10
2		1874	1751	1630	1511	1395	1284	1177	1075	0978	0887		9
3		2526	2472	2408	2335	2254	2167	2074	1977	1876	1774		8
4		2269	2326	2372	2406	2428	2438	2436	2423	2399	2365		7
5		1427	1533	1636	1735	1830	1920	2003	2079	2148	2207		6
6		0641	0721	0806	0894	0985	1080	1176	1274	1373	1471		5
7		0206	0242	0283	0329	0379	0434	0494	0558	0627	0701		4
8		0046	0057	0070	0085	0102	0122	0145	0171	0200	0234		3
9		0007	0009	0011	0015	0018	0023	0028	0035	0043	0052		2
10		0001	0001	0001	0001	0002	0003	0003	0004	0005	0007		1
		69	68	67	66	65	64	63	62	61	60	P	R

R	P	41	42	43	44	45	46	47	48	49	50		
0		0030	0025	0021	0017	0014	0011	0009	0008	0006	0005		11
1		0231	0199	0171	0147	0125	0107	0090	0076	0064	0054		10
2		0801	0721	0646	0577	0513	0454	0401	0352	0308	0269		9
3		1670	1566	1462	1359	1259	1161	1067	0976	0888	0806		8
4		2321	2267	2206	2136	2060	1978	1892	1801	1707	1611		7
5		2258	2299	2329	2350	2360	2359	2348	2327	2296	2256		6
6		1569	1664	1757	1846	1931	2010	2083	2148	2206	2256		5
7		0779	0861	0947	1036	1128	1223	1319	1416	1514	1611		4
8		0271	0312	0357	0407	0462	0521	0585	0654	0727	0806		3
9		0063	0075	0090	0107	0126	0148	0173	0201	0233	0269		2
10		0009	0011	0014	0017	0021	0025	0031	0037	0045	0054		1
11		0001	0001	0001	0001	0002	0002	0002	0003	0004	0005		0
		59	58	57	56	55	54	53	52	51	50	P	R

N = 12

R	P	01	02	03	04	05	06	07	08	09	10		
0		8864	7847	6938	6127	5404	4759	4186	3677	3225	2824		12
1		1074	1922	2575	3064	3413	3645	3781	3837	3827	3766		11
2		0060	0216	0438	0702	0988	1280	1565	1835	2082	2301		10
3		0002	0015	0045	0098	0173	0272	0393	0532	0686	0852		9
4		0000	0001	0003	0009	0021	0039	0067	0104	0153	0213		8
5		0000	0000	0000	0001	0002	0004	0008	0014	0024	0038		7
6		0000	0000	0000	0000	0000	0000	0001	0001	0003	0005		6
		99	98	97	96	95	94	93	92	91	90	P	R

R	P	11	12	13	14	15	16	17	18	19	20		
0		2470	2157	1880	1637	1422	1234	1069	0924	0798	0687		12
1		3663	3529	3372	3197	3012	2821	2627	2434	2245	2062		11
2		2490	2647	2771	2863	2924	2955	2960	2939	2897	2835		10
3		1026	1203	1380	1553	1720	1876	2021	2151	2265	2362		9
4		0285	0369	0464	0569	0683	0804	0931	1062	1195	1329		8
5		0056	0081	0111	0148	0193	0245	0305	0373	0449	0532		7
6		0008	0013	0019	0028	0040	0054	0073	0096	0123	0155		6
7		0001	0001	0002	0004	0006	0009	0013	0018	0025	0033		5
8		0000	0000	0000	0000	0001	0001	0002	0002	0004	0005		4
9		0000	0000	0000	0000	0000	0000	0000	0000	0000	0001		3
		89	88	87	86	85	84	83	82	81	80	P	R

R	P	21	22	23	24	25	26	27	28	29	30		
0		0591	0507	0434	0371	0317	0270	0229	0194	0164	0138		12
1		1885	1717	1557	1407	1267	1137	1016	0906	0804	0712		11
2		2756	2663	2558	2444	2323	2197	2068	1937	1807	1678		10
3		2442	2503	2547	2573	2581	2573	2549	2511	2460	2397		9
4		1460	1589	1712	1828	1936	2034	2122	2197	2261	2311		8
5		0621	0717	0818	0924	1032	1143	1255	1367	1477	1585		7
6		0193	0236	0285	0340	0401	0469	0542	0620	0704	0792		6
7		0044	0057	0073	0092	0115	0141	0172	0207	0246	0291		5
8		0007	0010	0014	0018	0024	0031	0040	0050	0063	0078		4
9		0001	0001	0002	0003	0004	0005	0007	0009	0011	0015		3
10		0000	0000	0000	0000	0000	0001	0001	0001	0001	0002		2
		79	78	77	76	75	74	73	72	71	70	P	R

R	P	31	32	33	34	35	36	37	38	39	40		
0		0116	0098	0082	0068	0057	0047	0039	0032	0027	0022		12
1		0628	0552	0484	0422	0368	0319	0276	0237	0204	0174		11
2		1552	1429	1310	1197	1088	0986	0890	0800	0716	0639		10
3		2324	2241	2151	2055	1954	1849	1742	1634	1526	1419		9
4		2349	2373	2384	2382	2367	2340	2302	2254	2195	2128		8
5		1688	1787	1879	1963	2039	2106	2163	2210	2246	2270		7
6		0885	0981	1079	1180	1281	1382	1482	1580	1675	1766		6
7		0341	0396	0456	0521	0591	0666	0746	0830	0918	1009		5
8		0096	0116	0140	0168	0199	0234	0274	0318	0367	0420		4
9		0019	0024	0031	0038	0048	0059	0071	0087	0104	0125		3
10		0003	0003	0005	0006	0008	0010	0013	0016	0020	0025		2
11		0000	0000	0000	0001	0001	0001	0001	0002	0002	0003		1
		69	68	67	66	65	64	63	62	61	60	P	R

R	P	4[illegible]	42	43		45	46	47	48	49	50		
0		0018	0[illegible]14	012	0010	0008	0006	0005	0004	0003	0002		12
1		0148	0126	0106	0090	0075	0063	0052	0043	0036	0029		11
2		567	0[illegible]2	0442	0388	0339	0294	0255	0220	0189	0161		10
3		1314	1211	1111	1015	0923	0836	0754	0676	0604	0537		9
4		2054	1973	1886	1794	1700	1602	1504	1405	1306	1208		8
5		2284	2285	2276	2256	2225	2184	2134	2075	2008	1934		7
6		1851	1931	2003	2068	2124	2171	2208	2234	2250	2256		6
7		1103	1198	1295	1393	1489	1585	1678	1768	1853	1934		5
8		0479	0542	0611	0684	0762	0844	0930	1020	1113	1208		4
9		0148	0175	0205	0239	0277	0319	0367	0418	0475	0537		3
10		0031	0038	0046	0056	0068	0082	0098	0116	0137	0161		2
11		0004	0005	0006	0008	0010	0013	0016	0019	0024	0029		1
12		0000	0000	0000	0001	0001	0001	0001	0001	0002	0002		0
		59	58	57	56	55	54	53	52	51	50	P	R

N = 13

R	P	01	02	03	04	05	06	07	08	09	10		
0		8775	7690	6730	5882	5133	4474	3893	3383	2935	2542		13
1		1152	2040	2706	3186	3512	3712	3809	3824	3773	3672		12
2		0070	0250	0502	0797	1109	1422	1720	1995	2239	2448		11
3		0003	0019	0057	0122	0214	0333	0475	0636	0812	0997		10
4		0000	0001	0004	0013	0028	0053	0089	0138	0201	0277		9
5		0000	0000	0000	0001	0003	0006	0012	0022	0036	0055		8
6		0000	0000	0000	0000	0000	0001	0001	0003	0005	0008		7
7		0000	0000	0000	0000	0000	0000	0000	0000	0000	0001		6
		99	98	97	96	95	94	93	92	91	90	P	R

R	P	11	12	13	14	15	16	17	18	19	20		
0		2198	1898	1636	1408	1209	1037	0887	0758	0646	0550		13
1		3532	3364	3178	2979	2774	2567	2362	2163	1970	1787		12
2		2619	2753	2849	2910	2937	2934	2903	2848	2773	2680		11
3		1187	1376	1561	1737	1900	2049	2180	2293	2385	2457		10
4		0367	0469	0583	0707	0838	0976	1116	1258	1399	1535		9
5		0082	0115	0157	0207	0266	0335	0412	0497	0591	0691		8
6		0013	0021	0031	0045	0063	0085	0112	0145	0185	0230		7
7		0002	0003	0005	0007	0011	0016	0023	0032	0043	0058		6
8		0000	0000	0001	0001	0001	0002	0004	0005	0008	0011		5
9		0000	0000	0000	0000	0000	0000	0000	0001	0001	0001		4
		89	88	87	86	85	84	83	82	81	80	P	R

R	P	21	22	23	24	25	26	27	28	29	30		
0		0467	0396	0334	0282	0238	0200	0167	0140	0117	0097		13
1		1613	1450	1299	1159	1029	0911	0804	0706	0619	0540		12
2		2573	2455	2328	2195	2059	1921	1784	1648	1516	1388		11
3		2508	2539	2550	2542	2517	2475	2419	2351	2271	2181		10
4		1667	1790	1904	2007	2097	2174	2237	2285	2319	2337		9
5		0797	0909	1024	1141	1258	1375	1489	1600	1705	1803		8
6		0283	0342	0408	0480	0559	0644	0734	0829	0928	1030		7
7		0075	0096	0122	0152	0186	0226	0272	0323	0379	0442		6
8		0015	0020	0027	0036	0047	0060	0075	0094	0116	0142		5
9		0002	0003	0005	0006	0009	0012	0015	0020	0026	0034		4
10		0000	0000	0001	0001	0001	0002	0002	0003	0004	0006		3
11		0000	0000	0000	0000	0000	0000	0000	0000	0000	0001		2
		79	78	77	76	75	74	73	72	71	70	P	R

R	P 31	32	33	34	35	36	37	38	39	40	
0	0080	0066	0055	0045	0037	0030	0025	0020	0016	0013	13
1	0469	0407	0351	0302	0259	0221	0188	0159	0135	0113	12
2	1265	1148	1037	0933	0836	0746	0663	0586	0516	0453	11
3	2084	1981	1874	1763	1651	1538	1427	1317	1210	1107	10
4	2341	2331	2307	2270	2222	2163	2095	2018	1934	1845	9
5	1893	1974	2045	2105	2154	2190	2215	2227	2226	2214	8
6	1134	1239	1343	1446	1546	1643	1734	1820	1898	1968	7
7	0509	0583	0662	0745	0833	0924	1019	1115	1213	1312	6
8	0172	0206	0244	0288	0336	0390	0449	0513	0582	0656	5
9	0043	0054	0067	0082	0101	0122	0146	0175	0207	0243	4
10	0008	0010	0013	0017	0022	0027	0034	0043	0053	0065	3
11	0001	0001	0002	0002	0003	0004	0006	0007	0009	0012	2
12	0000	0000	0000	0000	0000	0000	0001	0001	0001	0001	1
	69	68	67	66	65	64	63	62	61	60 P	R

R	P 41	42	43	44	45	46	47	48	49	50	
0	0010	0008	0007	0005	0004	0003	0003	0002	0002	0001	13
1	0095	0079	0066	0054	0045	0037	0030	0024	0020	0016	12
2	0395	0344	0298	0256	0220	0188	0160	0135	0114	0095	11
3	1007	0913	0823	0739	0660	0587	0519	0457	0401	0349	10
4	1750	1653	1553	1451	1350	1250	1151	1055	0962	0873	9
5	2189	2154	2108	2053	1989	1917	1838	1753	1664	1571	8
6	2029	2080	2121	2151	2169	2177	2173	2158	2131	2095	7
7	1410	1506	1600	1690	1775	1854	1927	1992	2048	2095	6
8	0735	0818	0905	0996	1089	1185	1282	1379	1476	1571	5
9	0284	0329	0379	0435	0495	0561	0631	0707	0788	0873	4
10	0079	0095	0114	0137	0162	0191	0224	0261	0303	0349	3
11	0015	0019	0024	0029	0036	0044	0054	0066	0079	0095	2
12	0002	0002	0003	0004	0005	0006	0008	0010	0013	0016	1
13	0000	0000	0000	0000	0000	0000	0001	0001	0001	0001	0
	59	58	57	56	55	54	53	52	51	50 P	R

N = 14

R	P 01	02	03	04	05	06	07	08	09	10	
0	8687	7536	6528	5647	4877	4205	3620	3112	2670	2288	14
1	1229	2153	2827	3294	3593	3758	3815	3788	3698	3559	13
2	0081	0286	0568	0892	1229	1559	1867	2141	2377	2570	12
3	0003	0023	0070	0149	0259	0398	0562	0745	0940	1142	11
4	0000	0001	0006	0017	0037	0070	0116	0178	0256	0349	10
5	0000	0000	0000	0001	0004	0009	0018	0031	0051	0078	9
6	0000	0000	0000	0000	0000	0001	0002	0004	0008	0013	8
7	0000	0000	0000	0000	0000	0000	0000	0000	0001	0002	7
	99	98	97	96	95	94	93	92	91	90 P	R

R	P 11	12	13	14	15	16	17	18	19	20	
0	1956	1670	1423	1211	1028	0871	0736	0621	0523	0440	14
1	3385	3188	2977	2759	2539	2322	2112	1910	1719	1539	13
2	2720	2826	2892	2919	2912	2875	2811	2725	2620	2501	12
3	1345	1542	1728	1901	2056	2190	2303	2393	2459	2501	11
4	0457	0578	0710	0851	0998	1147	1297	1444	1586	1720	10
5	0113	0158	0212	0277	0352	0437	0531	0634	0744	0860	9
6	0021	0032	0048	0068	0093	0125	0163	0209	0262	0322	8
7	0003	0005	0008	0013	0019	0027	0038	0052	0070	0092	7
8	0000	0001	0001	0002	0003	0005	0007	0010	0014	0020	6
9	0000	0000	0000	0000	0000	0001	0001	0001	0002	0003	5
	89	88	87	86	85	84	83	82	81	80 P	R

R	P 21	22	23	24	25	26	27	28	29	30	
0	0369	0309	0258	0214	0178	0148	0122	0101	0083	0068	14
1	1372	1218	1077	0948	0832	0726	0632	0548	0473	0407	13
2	2371	2234	2091	1946	1802	1659	1519	1385	1256	1134	12
3	2521	2520	2499	2459	2402	2331	2248	2154	2052	1943	11
4	1843	1955	2052	2135	2202	2252	2286	2304	2305	2290	10
5	0980	1103	1226	1348	1468	1583	1691	1792	1883	1963	9
6	0391	0466	0549	0639	0734	0834	0938	1045	1153	1262	8
7	0119	0150	0188	0231	0280	0335	0397	0464	0538	0618	7
8	0028	0037	0049	0064	0082	0103	0128	0158	0192	0232	6
9	0005	0007	0010	0013	0018	0024	0032	0041	0052	0066	5
10	0001	0001	0001	0002	0003	0004	0006	0008	0011	0014	4
11	0000	0000	0000	0000	0000	0001	0001	0001	0002	0002	3
	79	78	77	76	75	74	73	72	71	70 P	R

R	P 31	32	33	34	35	36	37	38	39	40	
0	0055	0045	0037	0030	0024	0019	0016	0012	0010	0008	14
1	0349	0298	0253	0215	0181	0152	0128	0106	0088	0073	13
2	1018	0911	0811	0719	0634	0557	0487	0424	0367	0317	12
3	1830	1715	1598	1481	1366	1253	1144	1039	0940	0845	11
4	2261	2219	2164	2098	2022	1938	1848	1752	1652	1549	10
5	2032	2088	2132	2161	2178	2181	2170	2147	2112	2066	9
6	1369	1474	1575	1670	1759	1840	1912	1974	2026	2066	8
7	0703	0793	0886	0983	1082	1183	1283	1383	1480	1574	7
8	0276	0326	0382	0443	0510	0582	0659	0742	0828	0918	6
9	0083	0102	0125	0152	0183	0218	0258	0303	0353	0408	5

10		0019	0024	0031	0039	0049	0061	0076	0093	0113	0136	4
11		0003	0004	0006	0007	0010	0013	0016	0021	0026	0033	3
12		0000	0000	0001	0001	0001	0002	0002	0003	0004	0005	2
13		0000	0000	0000	0000	0000	0000	0000	0000	0000	0001	1
		69	68	67	66	65	64	63	62	61	60 P	R

R	P	41	42	43	44	45	46	47	48	49	50	
0		0006	0005	0004	0003	0002	0002	0001	0001	0001	0001	14
1		0060	0049	0040	0033	0027	0021	0017	0014	0011	0009	13
2		0272	0233	0198	0168	0141	0118	0099	0082	0068	0056	12
3		0757	0674	0597	0527	0462	0403	0350	0303	0260	0222	11
4		1446	1342	1239	1138	1040	0945	0854	0768	0687	0611	10
5		2009	1943	1869	1788	1701	1610	1515	1418	1320	1222	9
6		2094	2111	2115	2108	2088	2057	2015	1963	1902	1833	8
7		1663	1747	1824	1892	1952	2003	2043	2071	2089	2095	7
8		1011	1107	1204	1301	1398	1493	1585	1673	1756	1833	6
9		0469	0534	0605	0682	0762	0848	0937	1030	1125	1222	5
10		0163	0193	0228	0268	0312	0361	0415	0475	0540	0611	4
11		0041	0051	0063	0076	0093	0112	0134	0160	0189	0222	3
12		C007	0009	0012	0015	0019	0024	0030	0037	0045	0056	2
13		C001	0001	0001	0002	0002	0003	0004	0005	0007	0009	1
14		0000	0000	0000	0000	0000	0000	0000	0000	0000	0001	0
		59	58	57	56	55	54	53	52	51	50 P	R

N = 15

R	P	01	02	03	04	05	06	07	08	09	10	
0		8601	7386	6333	5421	4633	3953	3367	2863	2430	2059	15
1		1303	2261	2938	3388	3658	3785	3801	3734	3605	3432	14
2		0092	0323	0636	0988	1348	1691	2003	2273	2496	2669	13
3		0004	0029	0085	0178	0307	0468	0653	0857	1070	1285	12
4		0000	0002	0008	0022	0049	0090	0148	0223	0317	0428	11
5		0000	0000	0001	0002	0006	0013	0024	0043	0069	0105	10
6		0000	0000	0000	0000	0000	0001	0003	0006	0011	0019	9
7		0000	0000	0000	0000	0000	0000	0000	0001	0001	0003	8
		99	98	97	96	95	94	93	92	91	90 P	R

R	P	11	12	13	14	15	16	17	18	19	20	
0		1741	1470	1238	1041	0874	0731	0611	0510	0424	0352	15
1		3228	3006	2775	2542	2312	2090	1878	1678	1492	1319	14
2		2793	2870	2903	2897	2856	2787	2692	2578	2449	2309	13
3		1496	1696	1880	2044	2184	2300	2389	2452	2489	2501	12
4		0555	0694	0843	0998	1156	1314	1468	1615	1752	1876	11
5		0151	0208	0277	0357	0449	0551	0662	0780	0904	1032	10
6		0031	0047	0069	0097	0132	0175	0226	0285	0353	0430	9
7		0005	0008	0013	0020	0030	0043	0059	0081	0107	0138	8
8		0001	0001	0002	0003	0005	0008	0012	0018	0025	0035	7
9		0000	0000	0000	0000	0001	0001	0002	0003	0005	0007	6
10		0000	0000	0000	0000	0000	0000	0000	0000	0001	0001	5
		89	88	87	86	85	84	83	82	81	80 P	R

R	P	21	22	23	24	25	26	27	28	29	30	
0		0291	0241	0198	0163	0134	0109	0089	0072	0059	0047	15
1		1162	1018	0889	0772	0668	0576	0494	0423	0360	0305	14
2		2162	2010	1858	1707	1559	1416	1280	1150	1029	0916	13
3		2490	2457	2405	2336	2252	2156	2051	1939	1821	1700	12
4		1986	2079	2155	2213	2252	2273	2276	2262	2231	2186	11
5		1161	1290	1416	1537	1651	1757	1852	1935	2005	2061	10
6		0514	0606	0705	0809	0917	1029	1142	1254	1365	1472	9
7		0176	0220	0271	0329	0393	0465	0543	0627	0717	0811	8
8		0047	0062	0081	0104	0131	0163	0201	0244	0293	0348	7
9		0010	0014	0019	0025	0034	0045	0058	0074	0093	0116	6
10		0002	0002	0003	0005	0007	0009	0013	0017	0023	0030	5
11		0000	0000	0000	0001	0001	0002	0002	0003	0004	0006	4
12		0000	0000	0000	0000	0000	0000	0000	0000	0001	0001	3
		79	78	77	76	75	74	73	72	71	70 P	R

R	P	31	32	33	34	35	36	37	38	39	40	
0		0038	0031	0025	0020	0016	0012	0010	0008	0006	0005	15
1		0258	0217	0182	0152	0126	0104	0086	0071	0058	0047	14
2		0811	0715	0627	0547	0476	0411	0354	0303	0259	0219	13
3		1579	1457	1338	1222	1110	1002	0901	0805	0716	0634	12
4		2128	2057	1977	1888	1792	1692	1587	1481	1374	1268	11
5		2103	2130	2142	2140	2123	2093	2051	1997	1933	1859	10
6		1575	1671	1759	1837	1906	1963	2008	2040	2059	2066	9
7		0910	1011	1114	1217	1319	1419	1516	1608	1693	1771	8
8		0409	0476	0549	0627	0710	0798	0890	0985	1082	1181	7
9		0143	0174	0210	0251	0298	0349	0407	0470	0538	0612	6
10		0038	0049	0062	0078	0096	0118	0143	0173	0206	0245	5
11		0008	0011	0014	0018	0024	0030	0038	0048	0060	0074	4
12		0001	0002	0002	0003	0004	0006	0007	0010	0013	0016	3
13		0000	0000	0000	0000	0001	0001	0001	0001	0002	0003	2
		69	68	67	66	65	64	63	62	61	60 P	R

R	P 41	42	43	44	45	46	47	48	49	50	
0	0004	0003	0002	0002	0001	0001	0001	0001	0000	0000	15
1	0038	0031	0025	0020	0016	0012	0010	0008	0006	0005	14
2	0185	0156	0130	0108	0090	0074	0060	0049	0040	0032	13
3	0558	0489	0426	0369	0318	0272	0232	0197	0166	0139	12
4	1163	1061	0963	0869	0780	0696	0617	0545	0478	0417	11
5	1778	1691	1598	1502	1404	1304	1204	1106	1010	0916	10
6	2060	2041	2010	1967	1914	1851	1780	1702	1617	1527	9
7	1840	1900	1949	1987	2013	2028	2030	2020	1997	1964	8
8	1279	1376	1470	1561	1647	1727	1800	1864	1919	1964	7
9	0691	0775	0863	0954	1048	1144	1241	1338	1434	1527	6
10	0288	0337	0390	0450	0515	0585	0661	0741	0827	0916	5
11	0091	0111	0134	0161	0191	0226	0266	0311	0361	0417	4
12	0021	0027	0034	0042	0052	0064	0079	0096	0116	0139	3
13	0003	0004	0006	0008	0010	0013	0016	0020	0026	0032	2
14	0000	0000	0001	0001	0001	0002	0002	0003	0004	0005	1
	59	58	57	56	55	54	53	52	51	50 P	R

N = 16

R	P 01	02	03	04	05	06	07	08	09	10	
0	8515	7238	6143	5204	4401	3716	3131	2634	2211	1853	16
1	1376	2363	3040	3469	3706	3795	3771	3665	3499	3294	15
2	0104	0362	0705	1084	1463	1817	2129	2390	2596	2745	14
3	0005	0034	0102	0211	0359	0541	0748	0970	1198	1423	13
4	0000	0002	0010	0029	0061	0112	0183	0274	0385	0514	12
5	0000	0000	0001	0003	0008	0017	0033	0057	0091	0137	11
6	0000	0000	0000	0000	0001	0002	0005	0009	0017	0028	10
7	0000	0000	0000	0000	0000	0000	0000	0001	0002	0004	9
8	0000	0000	0000	0000	0000	0000	0000	0000	0000	0001	8
	99	98	97	96	95	94	93	92	91	90 P	R

R	P 11	12	13	14	15	16	17	18	19	20	
0	1550	1293	1077	0895	0743	0614	0507	0418	0343	0281	16
1	3065	2822	2575	2332	2097	1873	1662	1468	1289	1126	15
2	2841	2886	2886	2847	2775	2675	2554	2416	2267	2111	14
3	1638	1837	2013	2163	2285	2378	2441	2475	2482	2463	13
4	0658	0814	0977	1144	1311	1472	1625	1766	1892	2001	12
5	0195	0266	0351	0447	0555	0673	0799	0930	1065	1201	11
6	0044	0067	0096	0133	0180	0235	0300	0374	0458	0550	10
7	0008	0013	0020	0031	0045	0064	0088	0117	0153	0197	9
8	0001	0002	0003	0006	0009	0014	0020	0029	0041	0055	8
9	0000	0000	0000	0001	0001	0002	0004	0006	0008	0012	7
10	0000	0000	0000	0000	0000	0000	0001	0001	0001	0002	6
	89	88	87	86	85	84	83	82	81	80 P	R

R	P 21	22	23	24	25	26	27	28	29	30	
0	0230	0188	0153	0124	0100	0081	0065	0052	0042	0033	16
1	0979	0847	0730	0626	0535	0455	0385	0325	0273	0228	15
2	1952	1792	1635	1482	1336	1198	1068	0947	0835	0732	14
3	2421	2359	2279	2185	2079	1964	1843	1718	1591	1465	13
4	2092	2162	2212	2242	2252	2243	2215	2171	2112	2040	12
5	1334	1464	1586	1699	1802	1891	1966	2026	2071	2099	11
6	0650	0757	0869	0984	1101	1218	1333	1445	1551	1649	10
7	0247	0305	0371	0444	0524	0611	0704	0803	0905	1010	9
8	0074	0097	0125	0158	0197	0242	0293	0351	0416	0487	8
9	0017	0024	0033	0044	0058	0075	0096	0121	0151	0185	7
10	0003	0005	0007	0010	0014	0019	0025	0033	0043	0056	6
11	0000	0001	0001	0002	0002	0004	0005	0007	0010	0013	5
12	0000	0000	0000	0000	0000	0001	0001	0001	0002	0002	4
	79	78	77	76	75	74	73	72	71	70 P	R

R	P 31	32	33	34	35	36	37	38	39	40	
0	0026	0021	0016	0013	0010	0008	0006	0005	0004	0003	16
1	0190	0157	0130	0107	0087	0071	0058	0047	0038	0030	15
2	0639	0555	0480	0413	0353	0301	0255	0215	0180	0150	14
3	1341	1220	1103	0992	0888	0790	0699	0615	0538	0468	13
4	1958	1865	1766	1662	1553	1444	1333	1224	1118	1014	12
5	2111	2107	2088	2054	2008	1949	1879	1801	1715	1623	11
6	1739	1818	1885	1940	1982	2010	2024	2024	2010	1983	10
7	1116	1222	1326	1428	1524	1615	1698	1772	1836	1889	9
8	0564	0647	0735	0827	0923	1022	1122	1222	1320	1417	8
9	0225	0271	0322	0379	0442	0511	0586	0666	0750	0840	7
10	0071	0089	0111	0137	0167	0201	0241	0286	0336	0392	6
11	0017	0023	0030	0038	0049	0062	0077	0095	0117	0142	5
12	0003	0004	0006	0008	0011	0014	0019	0024	0031	0040	4
13	0000	0001	0001	0001	0002	0003	0003	0005	0006	0008	3
14	0000	0000	0000	0000	0000	0000	0000	0001	0001	0001	2
	69	68	67	66	65	64	63	62	61	60 P	R

R	P 41	42	43	44	45	46	47	48	49	50	
0	0002	0002	0001	0001	0001	0001	0000	0000	0000	0000	16
1	0024	0019	0015	0012	0009	0007	0005	0004	0003	0002	15
2	0125	0103	0085	0069	0056	0046	0037	0029	0023	0018	14
3	0405	0349	0299	0254	0215	0181	0151	0126	0104	0085	13
4	0915	0821	0732	0649	0572	0501	0436	0378	0325	0278	12

5	1526	1426	1325	1224	1123	1024	0929	0837	0749	0667	11
6	1944	1894	1833	1762	1684	1600	1510	1416	1319	1222	10
7	1930	1959	1975	1978	1969	1947	1912	1867	1811	1746	9
8	1509	1596	1676	1749	1812	1865	1908	1939	1958	1964	8
9	0932	1027	1124	1221	1318	1413	1504	1591	1672	1746	7
10	0453	0521	0594	0672	0755	0842	0934	1028	1124	1222	6
11	0172	0206	0244	0288	0337	0391	0452	0518	0589	0667	5
12	0050	0062	0077	0094	0115	0139	0167	0199	0236	0278	4
13	0011	0014	0018	0023	0029	0036	0046	0057	0070	0085	3
14	0002	0002	0003	0004	0005	0007	0009	0011	0014	0018	2
15	0000	0000	0000	0000	0001	0001	0001	0001	0002	0002	1
	59	58	57	56	55	54	53	52	51	50 P	R

N = 17

R	P 01	02	03	04	05	06	07	08	09	10	
0	8429	7093	5958	4996	4181	3493	2912	2423	2012	1668	17
1	1447	2461	3133	3539	3741	3790	3726	3582	3383	3150	16
2	0117	0402	0775	1180	1575	1935	2244	2492	2677	2800	15
3	0006	0041	0120	0246	0415	0618	0844	1083	1324	1556	14
4	0000	0003	0013	0036	0076	0138	0222	0330	0458	0605	13
5	0000	0000	0001	0004	0010	0023	0044	0075	0118	0175	12
6	0000	0000	0000	0000	0001	0003	0007	0013	0023	0039	11
7	0000	0000	0000	0000	0000	0000	0001	0002	0004	0007	10
8	0000	0000	0000	0000	0000	0000	0000	0000	0000	0001	9
	99	98	97	96	95	94	93	92	91	90 P	R

R	P 11	12	13	14	15	16	17	18	19	20	
0	1379	1138	0937	0770	0631	0516	0421	0343	0278	0225	17
1	2898	2638	2381	2131	1893	1671	1466	1279	1109	0957	16
2	2865	2878	2846	2775	2673	2547	2402	2245	2081	1914	15
3	1771	1963	2126	2259	2359	2425	2460	2464	2441	2393	14
4	0766	0937	1112	1287	1457	1617	1764	1893	2004	2093	13
5	0246	0332	0432	0545	0668	0801	0939	1081	1222	1361	12
6	0061	0091	0129	0177	0236	0305	0385	0474	0573	0680	11
7	0012	0019	0030	0045	0065	0091	0124	0164	0211	0267	10
8	0002	0003	0006	0009	0014	0022	0032	0045	0062	0084	9
9	0000	0000	0001	0002	0003	0004	0006	0010	0015	0021	8
10	0000	0000	0000	0000	0000	0001	0001	0002	0003	0004	7
11	0000	0000	0000	0000	0000	0000	0000	0000	0000	0001	6
	89	88	87	86	85	84	83	82	81	80 P	R

R	P 21	22	23	24	25	26	27	28	29	30	
0	0182	0146	0118	0094	0075	0060	0047	0038	0030	0023	17
1	0822	0702	0597	0505	0426	0357	0299	0248	0206	0169	16
2	1747	1584	1427	1277	1136	1005	0883	0772	0672	0581	15
3	2322	2234	2131	2016	1893	1765	1634	1502	1372	1245	14
4	2161	2205	2228	2228	2209	2170	2115	2044	1961	1868	13
5	1493	1617	1730	1830	1914	1982	2033	2067	2083	2081	12
6	0794	0912	1034	1156	1276	1393	1504	1608	1701	1784	11
7	0332	0404	0485	0573	0668	0769	0874	0982	1092	1201	10
8	0110	0143	0181	0226	0279	0338	0404	0478	0558	0644	9
9	0029	0040	0054	0071	0093	0119	0150	0186	0228	0276	8
10	0006	0009	0013	0018	0025	0033	0044	0058	0074	0095	7
11	0001	0002	0002	0004	0005	0007	0010	0014	0019	0026	6
12	0000	0000	0000	0001	0001	0001	0002	0003	0004	0006	5
13	0000	0000	0000	0000	0000	0000	0000	0000	0001	0001	4
	79	78	77	76	75	74	73	72	71	70 P	R

R	P 31	32	33	34	35	36	37	38	39	40	
0	0018	0014	0011	0009	0007	0005	0004	0003	0002	0002	17
1	0139	0114	0093	0075	0060	0048	0039	0031	0024	0019	16
2	0500	0428	0364	0309	0260	0218	0182	0151	0125	0102	15
3	1123	1007	0898	0795	0701	0614	0534	0463	0398	0341	14
4	1766	1659	1547	1434	1320	1208	1099	0993	0892	0796	13
5	2063	2030	1982	1921	1849	1767	1677	1582	1482	1379	12
6	1854	1910	1952	1979	1991	1988	1970	1939	1895	1839	11
7	1309	1413	1511	1602	1685	1757	1818	1868	1904	1927	10
8	0735	0831	0930	1032	1134	1235	1335	1431	1521	1606	9
9	0330	0391	0458	0531	0611	0695	0784	0877	0973	1070	8
10	0119	0147	0181	0219	0263	0313	0368	0430	0498	0571	7
11	0034	0044	0057	0072	0090	0112	0138	0168	0202	0242	6
12	0008	0010	0014	0018	0024	0031	0040	0051	0065	0081	5
13	0001	0002	0003	0004	0005	0007	0009	0012	0016	0021	4
14	0000	0000	0000	0001	0001	0001	0002	0002	0003	0004	3
15	0000	0000	0000	0000	0000	0000	0000	0000	0000	0001	2
	69	68	67	66	65	64	63	62	61	60 P	R

R	P 41	42	43	44	45	46	47	48	49	50	
0	0001	0001	0001	0001	0000	0000	0000	0000	0000	0000	17
1	0015	0012	0009	0007	0005	0004	0003	0002	0002	0001	16
2	0084	0068	0055	0044	0035	0028	0022	0017	0013	0010	15
3	0290	0246	0207	0173	0144	0119	0097	0079	0064	0052	14
4	0706	0622	0546	0475	0411	0354	0302	0257	0217	0182	13

5		1276	1172	1070	0971	0875	0794	0697	0616	0541	0472		12
6		1773	1697	1614	1525	1432	1335	1237	1138	1040	0944		11
7		1936	1932	1914	1883	1841	1787	1723	1650	1570	1484		10
8		1682	1748	1805	1850	1883	1903	1910	1904	1886	1855		9
9		1169	1266	1361	1453	1540	1621	1694	1758	1812	1855		8
10		0650	0733	0822	0914	1008	1105	1202	1298	1393	1484		7
11		0287	0338	0394	0457	0525	0599	0678	0763	0851	0944		6
12		0100	0122	0149	0179	0215	0255	0301	0352	0409	0472		5
13		0027	0034	0043	0054	0068	0084	0103	0125	0151	0182		4
14		0005	0007	0009	0012	0016	0020	0026	0033	0041	0052		3
15		0001	0001	0001	0002	0003	0003	0005	0006	0008	0010		2
16		0000	0000	0000	0000	0000	0000	0001	0001	0001	0001		1
		59	58	57	56	55	54	53	52	51	50	P	R

N = 18

R	P	01	02	03	04	05	06	07	08	09	10		
0		8345	6951	5780	4796	3972	3283	2708	2229	1831	1501		18
1		1517	2554	3217	3597	3763	3772	3669	3489	3260	3002		17
2		0130	0443	0846	1274	1683	2047	2348	2579	2741	2835		16
3		0007	0048	0140	0283	0473	0697	0942	1196	1446	1680		15
4		0000	0004	0016	0044	0093	0167	0266	0390	0536	0700		14
5		0000	0000	0001	0005	0014	0030	0056	0095	0148	0218		13
6		0000	0000	0000	0000	0002	0004	0009	0018	0032	0052		12
7		0000	0000	0000	0000	0000	0000	0001	0003	0005	0010		11
8		0000	0000	0000	0000	0000	0000	0000	0000	0001	0002		10
		99	98	97	96	95	94	93	92	91	90	P	R

R	P	11	12	13	14	15	16	17	18	19	20		
0		1227	1002	0815	0662	0536	0434	0349	0281	0225	0180		18
1		2731	2458	2193	1940	1704	1486	1288	1110	0951	0811		17
2		2869	2850	2785	2685	2556	2407	2243	2071	1897	1723		16
3		1891	2072	2220	2331	2406	2445	2450	2425	2373	2297		15
4		0877	1060	1244	1423	1592	1746	1882	1996	2087	2153		14
5		0303	0405	0520	0649	0787	0931	1079	1227	1371	1507		13
6		0081	0120	0168	0229	0301	0384	0479	0584	0697	0816		12
7		0017	0028	0043	0064	0091	0126	0168	0220	0280	0350		11
8		0003	0005	0009	0014	0022	0033	0047	0066	0090	0120		10
9		0000	0001	0001	0003	0004	0007	0011	0016	0024	0033		9
10		0000	0000	0000	0000	0001	0001	0002	0003	0005	0008		8
11		0000	0000	0000	0000	0000	0000	0000	0001	0001	0001		7
		89	88	87	86	85	84	83	82	81	80	P	R

R	P	21	22	23	24	25	26	27	28	29	30		
0		0144	0114	0091	0072	0056	0044	0035	0027	0021	0016		18
1		0687	0580	0487	0407	0338	0280	0231	0189	0155	0126		17
2		1553	1390	1236	1092	0958	0836	0725	0626	0537	0458		16
3		2202	2091	1969	1839	1704	1567	1431	1298	1169	1046		15
4		2195	2212	2205	2177	2130	2065	1985	1892	1790	1681		14
5		1634	1747	1845	1925	1988	2031	2055	2061	2048	2017		13
6		0941	1067	1194	1317	1436	1546	1647	1736	1812	1873		12
7		0429	0516	0611	0713	0820	0931	1044	1157	1269	1376		11
8		0157	0200	0251	0310	0376	0450	0531	0619	0713	0811		10
9		0046	0063	0083	0109	0139	0176	0218	0267	0323	0386		9
10		0011	0016	0022	0031	0042	0056	0073	0094	0119	0149		8
11		0002	0003	0005	0007	0010	0014	0020	0026	0035	0046		7
12		0000	0001	0001	0001	0002	0003	0004	0006	0008	0012		6
13		0000	0000	0000	0000	0000	0000	0001	0001	0002	0002		5
		79	78	77	76	75	74	73	72	71	70	P	R

R	P	31	32	33	34	35	36	37	38	39	40		
0		0013	0010	0007	0006	0004	0003	0002	0002	0001	0001		18
1		0102	0082	0066	0052	0042	0033	0026	0020	0016	0012		17
2		0388	0327	0275	0229	0190	0157	0129	0105	0086	0069		16
3		0930	0822	0722	0630	0547	0471	0404	0344	0292	0246		15
4		1567	1450	1333	1217	1104	0994	0890	0791	0699	0614		14
5		1971	1911	1838	1755	1664	1566	1463	1358	1252	1146		13
6		1919	1948	1962	1959	1941	1908	1862	1803	1734	1655		12
7		1478	1572	1656	1730	1792	1840	1875	1895	1900	1892		11
8		0913	1017	1122	1226	1327	1423	1514	1597	1671	1734		10
9		0456	0532	0614	0701	0794	0890	0988	1087	1187	1284		9
10		0184	0225	0272	0325	0385	0450	0522	0600	0683	0771		8
11		0060	0077	0097	0122	0151	0184	0223	0267	0318	0374		7
12		0016	0021	0028	0037	0047	0060	0076	0096	0118	0145		6
13		0003	0005	0006	0009	0012	0016	0021	0027	0035	0045		5
14		0001	0001	0001	0002	0002	0003	0004	0006	0008	0011		4
15		0000	0000	0000	0000	0000	0000	0001	0001	0001	0002		3
		69	68	67	66	65	64	63	62	61	60	P	R

R	P	41	42	43	44	45	46	47	48	49	50		
0		0001	0001	0000	0000	0000	0000	0000	0000	0000	0000		18
1		0009	0007	0005	0004	0003	0002	0002	0001	0001	0001		17
2		0055	0044	0035	0028	0022	0017	0013	0010	0008	0006		16
3		0206	0171	0141	0116	0095	0077	0062	0050	0039	0031		15
4		0536	0464	0400	0342	0291	0246	0206	0172	0142	0117		14

5	1042	0941	0844	0753	0666	0586	0512	0444	0382	0327		13
6	1569	1477	1380	1281	1181	1081	0983	0887	0796	0708		12
7	1869	1833	1785	1726	1657	1579	1494	1404	1310	1214		11
8	1786	1825	1852	1864	1864	1850	1822	1782	1731	1669		10
9	1379	1469	1552	1628	1694	1751	1795	1828	1848	1855		9
10	0862	0957	1054	1151	1248	1342	1433	1519	1598	1669		8
11	0436	0504	0578	0658	0742	0831	0924	1020	1117	1214		7
12	0177	0213	0254	0301	0354	0413	0478	0549	0626	0708		6
13	0057	0071	0089	0109	0134	0162	0196	0234	0278	0327		5
14	0014	0018	0024	0031	0039	0049	0062	0077	0095	0117		4
15	0003	0004	0005	0006	0009	0011	0015	0019	0024	0031		3
16	0000	0000	0001	0001	0001	0002	0002	0003	0004	0006		2
17	0000	0000	0000	0000	0000	0000	0000	0000	0000	0001		1
	59	58	57	56	55	54	53	52	51	50	P	R

N = 19

R	P	01	02	03	04	05	06	07	08	09	10		
0		8262	6812	5606	4604	3774	3086	2519	2051	1666	1351		19
1		1586	2642	3294	3645	3774	3743	3602	3389	3131	2852		18
2		0144	0485	0917	1367	1787	2150	2440	2652	2787	2852		17
3		0008	0056	0161	0323	0533	0778	1041	1307	1562	1796		16
4		0000	0005	0020	0054	0112	0199	0313	0455	0618	0798		15
5		0000	0000	0002	0007	0018	0038	0071	0119	0183	0266		14
6		0000	0000	0000	0001	0002	0006	0012	0024	0042	0069		13
7		0000	0000	0000	0000	0000	0001	0002	0004	0008	0014		12
8		0000	0000	0000	0000	0000	0000	0000	0001	0001	0002		11
		99	98	97	96	95	94	93	92	91	90	P	R

R	P	11	12	13	14	15	16	17	18	19	20		
0		1092	0881	0709	0569	0456	0364	0290	0230	0182	0144		19
1		2565	2284	2014	1761	1529	1318	1129	0961	0813	0685		18
2		2854	2803	2708	2581	2428	2259	2081	1898	1717	1540		17
3		1999	2166	2293	2381	2428	2439	2415	2361	2282	2182		16
4		0988	1181	1371	1550	1714	1858	1979	2073	2141	2182		15
5		0366	0483	0614	0757	0907	1062	1216	1365	1507	1636		14
6		0106	0154	0214	0288	0374	0472	0581	0699	0825	0955		13
7		0024	0039	0059	0087	0122	0167	0221	0285	0359	0443		12
8		0004	0008	0013	0021	0032	0048	0068	0094	0126	0166		11
9		0001	0001	0002	0004	0007	0011	0017	0025	0036	0051		10
10		0000	0000	0000	0001	0001	0002	0003	0006	0009	0013		9
11		0000	0000	0000	0000	0000	0000	0001	0001	0002	0003		8
		89	88	87	86	85	84	83	82	81	80	P	R

R	P	21	22	23	24	25	26	27	28	29	30		
0		0113	0089	0070	0054	0042	0033	0025	0019	0015	0011		19
1		0573	0477	0396	0326	0268	0219	0178	0144	0116	0093		18
2		1371	1212	1064	0927	0803	0692	0592	0503	0426	0358		17
3		2065	1937	1800	1659	1517	1377	1240	1109	0985	0869		16
4		2196	2185	2151	2096	2023	1935	1835	1726	1610	1491		15
5		1751	1849	1928	1986	2023	2040	2036	2013	1973	1916		14
6		1086	1217	1343	1463	1574	1672	1757	1827	1880	1916		13
7		0536	0637	0745	0858	0974	1091	1207	1320	1426	1525		12
8		0214	0270	0334	0406	0487	0575	0670	0770	0874	0981		11
9		0069	0093	0122	0157	0198	0247	0303	0366	0436	0514		10
10		0018	0026	0036	0050	0066	0087	0112	0142	0178	0220		9
11		0004	0006	0009	0013	0018	0025	0034	0045	0060	0077		8
12		0001	0001	0002	0003	0004	0006	0008	0012	0016	0022		7
13		0000	0000	0000	0000	0001	0001	0002	0002	0004	0005		6
14		0000	0000	0000	0000	0000	0000	0000	0000	0001	0001		5
		79	78	77	76	75	74	73	72	71	70	P	R

R	P	31	32	33	34	35	36	37	38	39	40		
0		0009	0007	0005	0004	0003	0002	0002	0001	0001	0001		19
1		0074	0059	0046	0036	0029	0022	0017	0013	0010	0008		18
2		0299	0249	0206	0169	0138	0112	0091	0073	0058	0046		17
3		0762	0664	0574	0494	0422	0358	0302	0253	0211	0175		16
4		1370	1249	1131	1017	0909	0806	0710	0621	0540	0467		15
5		1846	1764	1672	1572	1468	1360	1251	1143	1036	0933		14
6		1935	1936	1921	1890	1844	1785	1714	1634	1546	1451		13
7		1615	1692	1757	1808	1844	1865	1870	1860	1835	1797		12
8		1088	1195	1298	1397	1489	1573	1647	1710	1760	1797		11
9		0597	0687	0782	0880	0980	1082	1182	1281	1375	1464		10
10		0268	0323	0385	0453	0528	0608	0694	0785	0879	0976		9
11		0099	0124	0155	0191	0233	0280	0334	0394	0460	0532		8
12		0030	0039	0051	0066	0083	0105	0131	0161	0196	0237		7
13		0007	0010	0014	0018	0024	0032	0041	0053	0067	0085		6
14		0001	0002	0003	0004	0006	0008	0010	0014	0018	0024		5
15		0000	0000	0000	0001	0001	0001	0002	0003	0004	0005		4
16		0000	0000	0000	0000	0000	0000	0000	0000	0001	0001		3
		69	68	67	66	65	64	63	62	61	60	P	R

R	P 41	42	43	44	45	46	47	48	49	50		
1	0006	0004	0003	0002	0002	0001	0001	0001	0001	0000		18
2	0037	0029	0022	0017	0013	0010	0008	0006	0004	0003		17
3	0144	0118	0096	0077	0062	0049	0039	0031	0024	0018		16
4	0400	0341	0289	0243	0203	0168	0138	0113	0092	0074		15
5	0834	0741	0653	0572	0497	0429	0368	0313	0265	0222		14
6	1353	1252	1150	1049	0949	0853	0761	0674	0593	0518		13
7	1746	1683	1611	1530	1443	1350	1254	1156	1058	0961		12
8	1820	1829	1823	1803	1771	1725	1668	1601	1525	1442		11
9	1546	1618	1681	1732	1771	1796	1808	1806	1791	1762		10
10	1074	1172	1268	1361	1449	1530	1603	1667	1721	1762		9
11	0611	0694	0783	0875	0970	1066	1163	1259	1352	1442		8
12	0283	0335	0394	0458	0529	0606	0688	0775	0866	0961		7
13	0106	0131	0160	0194	0233	0278	0328	0385	0448	0518		6
14	0032	0041	0052	0065	0082	0101	0125	0152	0185	0222		5
15	0007	0010	0013	0017	0022	0029	0037	0047	0059	0074		4
16	0001	0002	0002	0003	0005	0006	0008	0011	0014	0018		3
17	0000	0000	0000	0000	0001	0001	0001	0002	0002	0003		2
	59	58	57	56	55	54	53	52	51	50	P	R

N = 20

R	P 01	02	03	04	05	06	07	08	09	10		
0	8179	6676	5438	4420	3585	2901	2342	1887	1516	1216		20
1	1652	2725	3364	3683	3774	3703	3526	3282	3000	2702		19
2	0159	0528	0988	1458	1887	2246	2521	2711	2818	2852		18
3	0010	0065	0183	0364	0596	0860	1139	1414	1672	1901		17
4	0000	0006	0024	0065	0133	0233	0364	0523	0703	0898		16
5	0000	0000	0002	0009	0022	0048	0088	0145	0222	0319		15
6	0000	0000	0000	0001	0003	0008	0017	0032	0055	0089		14
7	0000	0000	0000	0000	0000	0001	0002	0005	0011	0020		13
8	0000	0000	0000	0000	0000	0000	0000	0001	0002	0004		12
9	0000	0000	0000	0000	0000	0000	0000	0000	0000	0001		11
	99	98	97	96	95	94	93	92	91	90	P	R

R	P 11	12	13	14	15	16	17	18	19	20		
0	0972	0776	0617	0490	0388	0306	0241	0189	0148	0115		20
1	2403	2115	1844	1595	1368	1165	0986	0829	0693	0576		19
2	2822	2740	2618	2466	2293	2109	1919	1730	1545	1369		18
3	2093	2242	2347	2409	2428	2410	2358	2278	2175	2054		17
4	1099	1299	1491	1666	1821	1951	2053	2125	2168	2182		16
5	0435	0567	0713	0868	1028	1189	1345	1493	1627	1746		15
6	0134	0193	0266	0353	0454	0566	0689	0819	0954	1091		14
7	0033	0053	0080	0115	0160	0216	0282	0360	0448	0545		13
8	0007	0012	0019	0030	0046	0067	0094	0128	0171	0222		12
9	0001	0002	0004	0007	0011	0017	0026	0038	0053	0074		11
10	0000	0000	0001	0001	0002	0004	0006	0009	0014	0020		10
11	0000	0000	0000	0000	0000	0001	0001	0002	0003	0005		9
12	0000	0000	0000	0000	0000	0000	0000	0000	0001	0001		8
	89	88	87	86	85	84	83	82	81	80	P	R

R	P 21	22	23	24	25	26	27	28	29	30		
0	0090	0069	0054	0041	0032	0024	0018	0014	0011	0008		20
1	0477	0392	0321	0261	0211	0170	0137	0109	0087	0068		19
2	1204	1050	0910	0783	0669	0569	0480	0403	0336	0278		18
3	1920	1777	1631	1484	1339	1199	1065	0940	0823	0716		17
4	2169	2131	2070	1991	1897	1790	1675	1553	1429	1304		16
5	1845	1923	1979	2012	2023	2013	1982	1933	1868	1789		15
6	1226	1356	1478	1589	1686	1768	1833	1879	1907	1916		14
7	0652	0765	0883	1003	1124	1242	1356	1462	1558	1643		13
8	0282	0351	0429	0515	0609	0709	0815	0924	1034	1144		12
9	0100	0132	0171	0217	0271	0332	0402	0479	0563	0654		11
10	0029	0041	0056	0075	0099	0128	0163	0205	0253	0308		10
11	0007	0010	0015	0022	0030	0041	0055	0072	0094	0120		9
12	0001	0002	0003	0005	0008	0011	0015	0021	0029	0039		8
13	0000	0000	0001	0001	0002	0002	0003	0005	0007	0010		7
14	0000	0000	0000	0000	0000	0000	0001	0001	0001	0002		6
	79	78	77	76	75	74	73	72	71	70	P	R

R	P 31	32	33	34	35	36	37	38	39	40		
0	0006	0004	0003	0002	0002	0001	0001	0001	0001	0000		20
1	0054	0042	0033	0025	0020	0015	0011	0009	0007	0005		19
2	0229	0188	0153	0124	0100	0080	0064	0050	0040	0031		18
3	0619	0531	0453	0383	0323	0270	0224	0185	0152	0123		17
4	1181	1062	0947	0839	0738	0645	0559	0482	0412	0350		16
5	1698	1599	1493	1384	1272	1161	1051	0945	0843	0746		15
6	1907	1881	1839	1782	1712	1632	1543	1447	1347	1244		14
7	1714	1770	1811	1836	1844	1836	1812	1774	1722	1659		13
8	1251	1354	1450	1537	1614	1678	1730	1767	1790	1797		12
9	0750	0849	0952	1056	1158	1259	1354	1444	1526	1597		11
10	0370	0440	0516	0598	0686	0779	0875	0974	1073	1171		10
11	0151	0188	0231	0280	0336	0398	0467	0542	0624	0710		9
12	0051	0066	0085	0108	0136	0168	0206	0249	0299	0355		8
13	0014	0019	0026	0034	0045	0058	0074	0094	0118	0146		7
14	0003	0005	0006	0009	0012	0016	0022	0029	0038	0049		6

R	P											
15		0001	0001	0001	0002	0003	0004	0005	0007	0010	0013		5
16		0000	0000	0000	0000	0000	0001	0001	0001	0002	0003		4
		69	68	67	66	65	64	63	62	61	60	P	R

R	P	41	42	43	44	45	46	47	48	49	50		
1		0004	0003	0002	0001	0001	0001	0001	0000	0000	0000		19
2		0024	0018	0014	0011	0008	0006	0005	0003	0002	0002		18
3		0100	0080	0064	0051	0040	0031	0024	0019	0014	0011		17
4		0295	0247	0206	0170	0139	0113	0092	0074	0059	0046		16
5		0656	0573	0496	0427	0365	0309	0260	0217	0180	0148		15
6		1140	1037	0936	0839	0746	0658	0577	0501	0432	0370		14
7		1585	1502	1413	1318	1221	1122	1023	0925	0830	0739		13
8		1790	1768	1732	1683	1623	1553	1474	1388	1296	1201		12
9		1658	1707	1742	1763	1771	1763	1742	1708	1661	1602		11
10		1268	1359	1446	1524	1593	1652	1700	1734	1755	1762		10
11		0801	0895	0991	1089	1185	1280	1370	1455	1533	1602		9
12		0417	0486	0561	0642	0727	0818	0911	1007	1105	1201		8
13		0178	0217	0260	0310	0366	0429	0497	0572	0653	0739		7
14		0062	0078	0098	0122	0150	0183	0221	0264	0314	0370		6
15		0017	0023	0030	0038	0049	0062	0078	0098	0121	0148		5
16		0004	0005	0007	0009	0013	0017	0022	0028	0036	0046		4
17		0001	0001	0001	0002	0002	0003	0005	0006	0008	0011		3
18		0000	0000	0000	0000	0000	0000	0001	0001	0001	0002		2
		59	58	57	56	55	54	53	52	51	50	P	R

N = 50

R	P	01	02	03	04	05	06	07	08	09	10		
0		6050	3642	2181	1299	0769	0453	0266	0155	0090	0052		50
1		3056	3716	3372	2706	2025	1447	0999	0672	0443	0286		49
2		0756	1858	2555	2762	2611	2262	1843	1433	1073	0779		48
3		0122	0607	1264	1842	2199	2311	2219	1993	1698	1386		47
4		0015	0145	0459	0902	1360	1733	1963	2037	1973	1809		46
5		0001	0027	0131	0346	0658	1018	1359	1629	1795	1849		45
6		0000	0004	0030	0108	0260	0487	0767	1063	1332	1541		44
7		0000	0001	0006	0028	0086	0195	0363	0581	0828	1076		43
8		0000	0000	0001	0006	0024	0067	0147	0271	0440	0643		42
9		0000	0000	0000	0001	0006	0020	0052	0110	0203	0333		41
10		0000	0000	0000	0000	0001	0005	0016	0039	0082	0152		40
11		0000	0000	0000	0000	0000	0001	0004	0012	0030	0061		39
12		0000	0000	0000	0000	0000	0000	0001	0004	0010	0022		38
13		0000	0000	0000	0000	0000	0000	0000	0001	0003	0007		37
14		0000	0000	0000	0000	0000	0000	0000	0000	0001	0002		36
15		0000	0000	0000	0000	0000	0000	0000	0000	0000	0001		35
		99	98	97	96	95	94	93	92	91	90	P	R

R	P	11	12	13	14	15	16	17	18	19	20		
0		0029	0017	0009	0005	0003	0002	0001	0000	0000	0000		50
1		0182	0114	0071	0043	0026	0016	0009	0005	0003	0002		49
2		0552	0382	0259	0172	0113	0073	0046	0029	0018	0011		48
3		1091	0833	0619	0449	0319	0222	0151	0102	0067	0044		47
4		1584	1334	1086	0858	0661	0496	0364	0262	0185	0128		46
5		1801	1674	1493	1286	1072	0869	0687	0530	0400	0295		45
6		1670	1712	1674	1570	1419	1242	1055	0872	0703	0554		44
7		1297	1467	1572	1606	1575	1487	1358	1203	1037	0870		43
8		0862	1075	1262	1406	1493	1523	1495	1420	1307	1169		42
9		0497	0684	0880	1068	1230	1353	1429	1454	1431	1364		41
10		0252	0383	0539	0713	0890	1057	1200	1309	1376	1398		40
11		0113	0190	0293	0422	0571	0732	0894	1045	1174	1271		39
12		0045	0084	0142	0223	0328	0453	0595	0745	0895	1033		38
13		0016	0034	0062	0106	0169	0252	0356	0478	0613	0755		37
14		0005	0012	0025	0046	0079	0127	0193	0277	0380	0499		36
15		0002	0004	0009	0018	0033	0058	0095	0146	0214	0299		35
16		0000	0001	0003	0006	0013	0024	0042	0070	0110	0164		34
17		0000	0000	0001	0002	0005	0009	0017	0031	0052	0082		33
18		0000	0000	0000	0001	0001	0003	0007	0012	0022	0037		32
19		0000	0000	0000	0000	0000	0001	0002	0005	0009	0016		31
20		0000	0000	0000	0000	0000	0000	0001	0002	0003	0006		30
21		0000	0000	0000	0000	0000	0000	0000	0000	0001	0002		29
22		0000	0000	0000	0000	0000	0000	0000	0000	0000	0001		28
		89	88	87	86	85	84	83	82	81	80	P	R

R	P	21	22	23	24	25	26	27	28	29	30		
1		0001	0001	0000	0000	0000	0000	0000	0000	0000	0000		49
2		0007	0004	0002	0001	0001	0000	0000	0000	0000	0000		48
3		0028	0018	0011	0007	0004	0002	0001	0001	0000	0000		47
4		0088	0059	0039	0025	0016	0010	0006	0004	0002	0001		46
5		0214	0152	0106	0073	0049	0033	0021	0014	0009	0006		45
6		0427	0322	0238	0173	0123	0087	0060	0040	0027	0018		44
7		0713	0571	0447	0344	0259	0191	0139	0099	0069	0048		43
8		1019	0865	0718	0583	0463	0361	0276	0207	0152	0110		42
9		1263	1139	1001	0859	0721	0592	0476	0375	0290	0220		41
10		1377	1317	1226	1113	0985	0852	0721	0598	0485	0386		40

11	1331	1351	1332	1278	1194	1089	0970	0845	0721	0602	39
12	1150	1238	1293	1311	1294	1244	1166	1068	0957	0838	38
13	0894	1021	1129	1210	1261	1277	1261	1215	1142	1050	37
14	0628	0761	0891	1010	1110	1186	1233	1248	1233	1189	36
15	0400	0515	0639	0766	0888	1000	1094	1165	1209	1223	35
16	0233	0318	0417	0529	0648	0769	0885	0991	1080	1147	34
17	0124	0179	0249	0334	0432	0540	0655	0771	0882	0983	33
18	0060	0093	0137	0193	0264	0348	0444	0550	0661	0772	32
19	0027	0044	0069	0103	0148	0206	0277	0360	0454	0558	31
20	0011	0019	0032	0050	0077	0112	0159	0217	0288	0370	30
21	0004	0008	0014	0023	0036	0056	0084	0121	0168	0227	29
22	0001	0003	0005	0009	0016	0026	0041	0062	0090	0128	28
23	0000	0001	0002	0004	0006	0011	0018	0029	0045	0067	27
24	0000	0000	0001	0001	0002	0004	0008	0013	0021	0032	26
25	0000	0000	0000	0000	0001	0002	0003	0005	0009	0014	25
26	0000	0000	0000	0000	0000	0001	0001	0002	0003	0006	24
27	0000	0000	0000	0000	0000	0000	0000	0001	0001	0002	23
28	0000	0000	0000	0000	0000	0000	0000	0000	0000	0001	22
	79	78	77	76	75	74	73	72	71	70 P	R

R P	31	32	33	34	35	36	37	38	39	40	
4	0001	0000	0000	0000	0000	0000	0000	0000	0000	0000	46
5	0003	0002	0001	0001	0000	0000	0000	0000	0000	0000	45
6	0011	0007	0005	0003	0002	0001	0001	0000	0000	0000	44
7	0032	0022	0014	0009	0006	0004	0002	0001	0001	0000	43
8	0078	0055	0037	0025	0017	0011	0007	0004	0003	0002	42
9	0164	0120	0086	0061	0042	0029	0019	0013	0008	0005	41
10	0301	0231	0174	0128	0093	0066	0046	0032	0022	0014	40
11	0493	0395	0311	0240	0182	0136	0099	0071	0050	0035	39
12	0719	0604	0498	0402	0319	0248	0189	0142	0105	0076	38
13	0944	0831	0717	0606	0502	0408	0325	0255	0195	0147	37
14	1121	1034	0933	0825	0714	0607	0505	0412	0330	0260	36
15	1209	1168	1103	1020	0923	0819	0712	0606	0507	0415	35
16	1188	1202	1189	1149	1088	1008	0914	0813	0709	0606	34
17	1068	1132	1171	1184	1171	1133	1074	0997	0906	0808	33
18	0880	0976	1057	1118	1156	1169	1156	1120	1062	0987	32
19	0666	0774	0877	0970	1048	1107	1144	1156	1144	1109	31
20	0463	0564	0670	0775	0875	0965	1041	1098	1134	1146	30
21	0297	0379	0471	0570	0673	0776	0874	0962	1035	1091	29
22	0176	0235	0306	0387	0478	0575	0676	0777	0873	0959	28
23	0096	0135	0183	0243	0313	0394	0484	0580	0679	0778	27
24	0049	0071	0102	0141	0190	0249	0319	0400	0489	0584	26
25	0023	0035	0052	0075	0106	0146	0195	0255	0325	0405	25
26	0010	0016	0025	0037	0055	0079	0110	0150	0200	0259	24
27	0004	0007	0011	0017	0026	0039	0058	0082	0113	0154	23
28	0001	0003	0004	0007	0012	0018	0028	0041	0060	0084	22
29	0000	0001	0002	0003	0005	0008	0012	0019	0029	0043	21
30	C000	0000	0001	0001	0002	0003	0005	0008	0013	0020	20
31	0000	0000	0000	0000	0001	0001	0002	0003	0005	0009	19
32	0000	0000	0000	0000	0000	0000	0001	0001	0002	0003	18
33	0000	0000	0000	0000	0000	0000	0000	0000	0001	0001	17
	69	68	67	66	65	64	63	62	61	60 P	R

R P	41	42	43	44	45	46	47	48	49	50	
8	0001	0001	0000	0000	0000	0000	0000	0000	0000	0000	42
9	0003	0002	0001	0001	0000	0000	0000	0000	0000	0000	41
10	0009	0006	0004	0002	0001	0001	0001	0000	0000	0000	40
11	0024	0016	0010	0007	0004	0003	0002	0001	0001	0000	39
12	0054	0037	0026	0017	0011	0007	0005	0003	0002	0001	38
13	0109	0079	0057	0040	0027	0018	0012	0008	0005	0003	37
14	0200	0152	0113	0082	0059	0041	0029	0019	0013	0008	36
15	0334	0264	0204	0155	0116	0085	0061	0043	0030	0020	35
16	0508	0418	0337	0267	0207	0158	0118	0086	0062	0044	34
17	0706	0605	0508	0419	0339	0269	0209	0159	0119	0087	33
18	0899	0803	0703	0604	0508	0420	0340	0270	0210	0160	32
19	1053	0979	0893	0799	0700	0602	0507	0419	0340	0270	31
20	1134	1099	1044	0973	0888	0795	0697	0600	0506	0419	30
21	1126	1137	1126	1092	1038	0967	0884	0791	0695	0598	29
22	1031	1086	1119	1131	1119	1086	1033	0963	0880	0788	28
23	0872	0957	1028	1082	1115	1126	1115	1082	1029	0960	27
24	0682	0780	0872	0956	1026	1079	1112	1124	1112	1080	26
25	0493	0587	0684	0781	0873	0956	1026	1079	1112	1123	25
26	0329	0409	0497	0590	0687	0783	0875	0957	1027	1080	24
27	0203	0263	0333	0412	0500	0593	0690	0786	0877	0960	23
28	0116	0157	0206	0266	0336	0415	0502	0596	0692	0788	22
29	0061	0086	0118	0159	0208	0268	0338	0417	0504	0598	21
30	0030	0044	0062	0087	0119	0160	0210	0270	0339	0419	20
31	0013	C020	0030	0044	0063	0088	0120	0161	0210	0270	19
32	0006	0009	0014	0021	0031	0044	0063	0088	0120	0160	18
33	0002	0003	0006	0009	0014	0021	0031	0044	0063	0087	17
34	0001	0001	0002	0003	0006	0009	0014	0020	0030	0044	16
35	0000	0000	0001	0001	0002	0003	0005	0009	0013	0020	15
36	0000	0000	0000	0000	0001	0001	0002	0003	0005	0008	14
37	0000	0000	0000	0000	0000	0000	0001	0001	0002	0003	13

38	0000	0000	0000	0000	0000	0000	0000	0000	0001	0001	12
	59	58	57	56	55	54	53	52	51	50 P	R

N = 100

R P	01	02	03	04	05	06	07	08	09	10	
0	3660	1326	0476	0169	0059	0021	0007	0002	0001	0000	100
1	3697	2707	1471	0703	0312	0131	0053	0021	0008	0003	99
2	1849	2734	2252	1450	0812	0414	0198	0090	0039	0016	98
3	0610	1823	2275	1973	1396	0864	0486	0254	0125	0059	97
4	0149	0902	1706	1994	1781	1338	0888	0536	0301	0159	96
5	0029	0353	1013	1595	1800	1639	1283	0895	0571	0339	95
6	0005	0114	0496	1052	1500	1657	1529	1233	0895	0596	94
7	0001	0031	0206	0589	1060	1420	1545	1440	1188	0889	93
8	0000	0007	0074	0285	0649	1054	1352	1455	1366	1148	92
9	0000	0002	0023	0121	0349	0687	1040	1293	1381	1304	91
10	0000	0000	0007	0046	0167	0399	0712	1024	1243	1319	90
11	0000	0000	0002	0016	0072	0209	0439	0728	1006	1199	89
12	0000	0000	0000	0005	0028	0099	0245	0470	0738	0988	88
13	0000	0000	0000	0001	0010	0043	0125	0276	0494	0743	87
14	0000	0000	0000	0000	0003	0017	0058	0149	0304	0513	86
15	0000	0000	0000	0000	0001	0006	0025	0074	0172	0327	85
16	0000	0000	0000	0000	0000	0002	0010	0034	0090	0193	84
17	0000	0000	0000	0000	0000	0001	0004	0015	0044	0106	83
18	0000	0000	0000	0000	0000	0000	0001	0006	0020	0054	82
19	0000	0000	0000	0000	0000	0000	0000	0002	0009	0026	81
20	0000	0000	0000	0000	0000	0000	0000	0001	0003	0012	80
21	0000	0000	0000	0000	0000	0000	0000	0000	0001	0005	79
22	0000	0000	0000	0000	0000	0000	0000	0000	0000	0002	78
23	0000	0000	0000	0000	0000	0000	0000	0000	0000	0001	77
	99	98	97	96	95	94	93	92	91	90 P	R

R P	11	12	13	14	15	16	17	18	19	20	
1	0001	0000	0000	0000	0000	0000	0000	0000	0000	0000	99
2	0007	0003	0001	0000	0000	0000	0000	0000	0000	0000	98
3	0027	0012	0005	0002	0001	0000	0000	0000	0000	0000	97
4	0080	0038	0018	0008	0003	0001	0001	0000	0000	0000	96
5	0189	0100	0050	0024	0011	0005	0002	0001	0000	0000	95
6	0369	0215	0119	0063	0031	0015	0007	0003	0001	0001	94
7	0613	0394	0238	0137	0075	0039	0020	0009	0004	0002	93
8	0881	0625	0414	0259	0153	0086	0047	0024	0012	0006	92
9	1112	0871	0632	0430	0276	0168	0098	0054	0029	0015	91
10	1251	1080	0860	0637	0444	0292	0182	0108	0062	0034	90
11	1265	1205	1051	0849	0640	0454	0305	0194	0118	0069	89
12	1160	1219	1165	1025	0838	0642	0463	0316	0206	0128	88
13	0970	1125	1179	1130	1001	0827	0642	0470	0327	0216	87
14	0745	0954	1094	1143	1098	0979	0817	0641	0476	0335	86
15	0528	0745	0938	1067	1111	1070	0960	0807	0640	0481	85
16	0347	0540	0744	0922	1041	1082	1044	0941	0798	0638	84
17	0212	0364	0549	0742	0908	1019	1057	1021	0924	0789	83
18	0121	0229	0379	0557	0739	0895	0998	1033	1000	0909	82
19	0064	0135	0244	0391	0563	0736	0882	0979	1012	0981	81
20	0032	0074	0148	0258	0402	0567	0732	0870	0962	0993	80
21	0015	0039	0084	0160	0270	0412	0571	0728	0859	0946	79
22	0007	0019	0045	0094	0171	0282	0420	0574	0724	0849	78
23	0003	0009	0023	0052	0103	0182	0292	0427	0576	0720	77
24	0001	0004	0011	0027	0058	0111	0192	0301	0433	0577	76
25	0000	0002	0005	0013	0031	0064	0119	0201	0309	0439	75
26	0000	0001	0002	0006	0016	0035	0071	0127	0209	0316	74
27	0000	0000	0001	0003	0008	0018	0040	0076	0134	0217	73
28	0000	0000	0000	0001	0004	0009	0021	0044	0082	0141	72
29	0000	0000	0000	0000	0002	0004	0011	0024	0048	0088	71
30	0000	0000	0000	0000	0001	0002	0005	0012	0027	0052	70
31	0000	0000	0000	0000	0000	0001	0002	0006	0014	0029	69
32	0000	0000	0000	0000	0000	0000	0001	0003	0007	0016	68
33	0000	0000	0000	0000	0000	0000	0000	0001	0003	0008	67
34	0000	0000	0000	0000	0000	0000	0000	0001	0002	0004	66
35	0000	0000	0000	0000	0000	0000	0000	0000	0001	0002	65
36	0000	0000	0000	0000	0000	0000	0000	0000	0000	0001	64
	89	88	87	86	85	84	83	82	81	80 P	R

R P	21	22	23	24	25	26	27	28	29	30	
7	0001	0000	0000	0000	0000	0000	0000	0000	0000	0000	93
8	0003	0001	0001	0000	0000	0000	0000	0000	0000	0000	92
9	0007	0003	0002	0001	0000	0000	0000	0000	0000	0000	91
10	0018	0009	0004	0002	0001	0000	0000	0000	0000	0000	90
11	0038	0021	0011	0005	0003	0001	0001	0000	0000	0000	89
12	0076	0043	0024	0012	0006	0003	0001	0001	0000	0000	88
13	0136	0082	0048	0027	0014	0007	0004	0002	0001	0000	87
14	0225	0144	0089	0052	0030	0016	0009	0004	0002	0001	86
15	0343	0233	0152	0095	0057	0033	0018	0010	0005	0002	85
16	0484	0350	0241	0159	0100	0061	0035	0020	0011	0006	84

R											
17	0636	0487	0356	0248	0165	0106	0065	0038	0022	0012	83
18	0780	0634	0490	0361	0254	0171	0111	0069	0041	0024	82
19	0895	0772	0631	0492	0365	0259	0177	0115	0072	0044	81
20	0963	0881	0764	0629	0493	0369	0264	0182	0120	0076	80
21	0975	0947	0869	0756	0626	0494	0373	0269	0186	0124	79
22	0931	0959	0932	0858	0749	0623	0495	0376	0273	0190	78
23	0839	0917	0944	0919	0847	0743	0621	0495	0378	0277	77
24	0716	0830	0905	0931	0906	0837	0736	0618	0496	0380	76
25	0578	0712	0822	0893	0918	0894	0828	0731	0615	0496	75
26	0444	0579	0708	0814	0883	0906	0883	0819	0725	0613	74
27	0323	0448	0580	0704	0806	0873	0896	0873	0812	0720	73
28	0224	0329	0451	0580	0701	0799	0864	0886	0864	0804	72
29	0148	0231	0335	0455	0580	0697	0793	0855	0876	0856	71
30	0093	0154	0237	0340	0458	0580	0694	0787	0847	0868	70
31	0056	0098	0160	0242	0344	0460	0580	0691	0781	0840	69
32	0032	0060	0103	0165	0248	0349	0462	0579	0688	0776	68
33	0018	0035	0063	0107	0170	0252	0352	0464	0579	0685	67
34	0009	0019	0037	0067	0112	0175	0257	0356	0466	0579	66
35	0005	0010	0021	0040	0070	0116	0179	0261	0359	0468	65
36	0002	0005	0011	0023	0042	0073	0120	0183	0265	0362	64
37	0001	0003	0006	0012	0024	0045	0077	0123	0187	0268	63
38	0000	0001	0003	0006	0013	0026	0047	0079	0127	0191	62
39	0000	0001	0001	0003	0007	0015	0028	0049	0082	0130	61
40	0000	0000	0001	0002	0004	0008	0016	0029	0051	0085	60
41	0000	0000	0000	0001	0002	0004	0008	0017	0031	0053	59
42	0000	0000	0000	0000	0001	0002	0004	0009	0018	0032	58
43	0000	0000	0000	0000	0000	0001	0002	0005	0010	0019	57
44	0000	0000	0000	0000	0000	0000	0001	0002	0005	0010	56
45	0000	0000	0000	0000	0000	0000	0000	0001	0003	0005	55
46	0000	0000	0000	0000	0000	0000	0000	0001	0001	0003	54
47	0000	0000	0000	0000	0000	0000	0000	0000	0001	0001	53
48	0000	0000	0000	0000	0000	0000	0000	0000	0000	0001	52
	79	78	77	76	75	74	73	72	71	70 P	R

R P	31	32	33	34	35	36	37	38	39	40	
15	0001	0001	0000	0000	0000	0000	0000	0000	0000	0000	85
16	0003	0001	0001	0000	0000	0000	0000	0000	0000	0000	84
17	0006	0003	0002	0001	0000	0000	0000	0000	0000	0000	83
18	0013	0007	0004	0002	0001	0000	0000	0000	0000	0000	82
19	0025	0014	0008	0004	0002	0001	0000	0000	0000	0000	81
20	0046	0027	0015	0008	0004	0002	0001	0001	0000	0000	80
21	0079	0049	0029	0016	0009	0005	0002	0001	0001	0000	79
22	0127	0082	0051	0030	0017	0010	0005	0003	0001	0001	78
23	0194	0131	0085	0053	0032	0018	0010	0006	0003	0001	77
24	0280	0198	0134	0088	0055	0033	0019	0011	0006	0003	76
25	0382	0283	0201	0137	0090	0057	0035	0020	0012	0006	75
26	0496	0384	0286	0204	0140	0092	0059	0036	0021	0012	74
27	0610	0495	0386	0288	0207	0143	0095	0060	0037	0022	73
28	0715	0608	0495	0387	0290	0209	0145	0097	0062	0038	72
29	0797	0710	0605	0495	0388	0292	0211	0147	0098	0063	71
30	0848	0791	0706	0603	0494	0389	0294	0213	0149	0100	70
31	0860	0840	0785	0702	0601	0494	0389	0295	0215	0151	69
32	0833	0853	0833	0779	0698	0599	0493	0390	0296	0217	68
33	0771	0827	0846	0827	0774	0694	0597	0493	0390	0297	67
34	0683	0767	0821	0840	0821	0769	0691	0595	0492	0391	66
35	0578	0680	0763	0816	0834	0816	0765	0688	0593	0491	65
36	0469	0578	0678	0759	0811	0829	0811	0761	0685	0591	64
37	0365	0471	0578	0676	0755	0806	0824	0807	0757	0682	63
38	0272	0367	0472	0577	0674	0752	0802	0820	0803	0754	62
39	0194	0275	0369	0473	0577	0672	0749	0799	0816	0799	61
40	0133	0197	0277	0372	0474	0577	0671	0746	0795	0812	60
41	0087	0136	0200	0280	0373	0475	0577	0670	0744	0792	59
42	0055	0090	0138	0203	0282	0375	0476	0576	0668	0742	58
43	0033	0057	0092	0141	0205	0285	0377	0477	0576	0667	57
44	0019	0035	0059	0094	0143	0207	0287	0378	0477	0576	56
45	0011	0020	0036	0060	0096	0145	0210	0289	0380	0478	55
46	0006	0011	0021	0037	0062	0098	0147	0211	0290	0381	54
47	0003	0006	0012	0022	0038	0063	0099	0149	0213	0292	53
48	0001	0003	0007	0012	0023	0039	0064	0101	0151	0215	52
49	0001	0002	0003	0007	0013	0023	0040	0066	0102	0152	51

50		0000	0001	0002	0004	0007	0013	0024	0041	0067	0103		50
51		0000	0000	0001	0002	0004	0007	0014	0025	0042	0068		49
52		0000	0000	0000	0001	0002	0004	0008	0014	0025	0042		48
53		0000	0000	0000	0000	0001	0002	0004	0008	0015	0026		47
54		0000	0000	0000	0000	0000	0001	0002	0004	0008	0015		46
55		0000	0000	0000	0000	0000	0000	0001	0002	0004	0008		45
56		0000	0000	0000	0000	0000	0000	0000	0001	0002	0004		44
57		0000	0000	0000	0000	0000	0000	0000	0001	0001	0002		43
58		0000	0000	0000	0000	0000	0000	0000	0000	0001	0001		42
59		0000	0000	0000	0000	0000	0000	0000	0000	0000	0001		41
		69	68	67	66	65	64	63	62	61	60	P	R

R	P	41	42	43	44	45	46	47	48	49	50		
23		0001	0000	0000	0000	0000	0000	0000	0000	0000	0000		77
24		0002	0001	0000	0000	0000	0000	0000	0000	0000	0000		76
25		0003	0002	0001	0000	0000	0000	0000	0000	0000	0000		75
26		0007	0003	0002	0001	0000	0000	0000	0000	0000	0000		74
27		0013	0007	0004	0002	0001	0000	0000	0000	0000	0000		73
28		0023	0013	0007	0004	0002	0001	0000	0000	0000	0000		72
29		0039	0024	0014	0008	0004	0002	0001	0000	0000	0000		71
30		0065	0040	0024	0014	0008	0004	0002	0001	0001	0000		70
31		0102	0066	0041	0025	0014	0008	0004	0002	0001	0001		69
32		0152	0103	0067	0042	0025	0015	0008	0004	0002	0001		68
33		0218	0154	0104	0068	0043	0026	0015	0008	0004	0002		67
34		0298	0219	0155	0105	0069	0043	0026	0015	0009	0005		66
35		0391	0299	0220	0156	0106	0069	0044	0026	0015	0009		65
36		0491	0391	0300	0221	0157	0107	0070	0044	0027	0016		64
37		0590	0490	0391	0300	0222	0157	0107	0070	0044	0027		63
38		0680	0588	0489	0391	0301	0222	0158	0108	0071	0045		62
39		0751	0677	0587	0489	0391	0301	0223	0158	0108	0071		61
40		0796	0748	0675	0586	0488	0391	0301	0223	0159	0108		60
41		0809	0793	0745	0673	0584	0487	0391	0301	0223	0159		59
42		0790	0806	0790	0743	0672	0583	0487	0390	0301	0223		58
43		0740	0787	0804	0788	0741	0670	0582	0486	0390	0301		57
44		0666	0739	0785	0802	0786	0739	0669	0581	0485	0390		56
45		0576	0666	0737	0784	0800	0784	0738	0668	0580	0485		55
46		0479	0576	0665	0736	0782	0798	0783	0737	0667	0580		54
47		0382	0480	0576	0665	0736	0781	0797	0781	0736	0666		53
48		0293	0383	0480	0577	0665	0735	0781	0797	0781	0735		52
49		0216	0295	0384	0481	0577	0664	0735	0780	0796	0780		51
50		0153	0218	0296	0385	0482	0577	0665	0735	0780	0796		50
51		0104	0155	0219	0297	0386	0482	0578	0665	0735	0780		49
52		0068	0105	0156	0220	0298	0387	0483	0578	0665	0735		48
53		0043	0069	0106	0156	0221	0299	0388	0483	0579	0666		47
54		0026	0044	0070	0107	0157	0221	0299	0388	0484	0580		46
55		0015	0026	0044	0070	0108	0158	0222	0300	0389	0485		45
56		0008	0015	0027	0044	0071	0108	0158	0222	0300	0390		44
57		0005	0009	0016	0027	0045	0071	0108	0158	0223	0301		43
58		0002	0005	0009	0016	0027	0045	0071	0108	0159	0223		42
59		0001	0002	0005	0009	0016	0027	0045	0071	0109	0159		41
60		0001	0001	0002	0005	0009	0016	0027	0045	0071	0108		40
61		0000	0001	0001	0002	0005	0009	0016	0027	0045	0071		39
62		0000	0000	0001	0001	0002	0005	0009	0016	0027	0045		38
63		0000	0000	0000	0001	0001	0002	0005	0009	0016	0027		37
64		0000	0000	0000	0000	0001	0001	0002	0005	0009	0016		36
65		0000	0000	0000	0000	0000	0001	0001	0002	0005	0009		35
66		0000	0000	0000	0000	0000	0000	0001	0001	0002	0005		34
67		0000	0000	0000	0000	0000	0000	0000	0001	0001	0002		33
68		0000	0000	0000	0000	0000	0000	0000	0000	0001	0001		32
69		0000	0000	0000	0000	0000	0000	0000	0000	0000	0001		31
		59	58	57	56	55	54	53	52	51	50	P	R

COMMON LOGARITHMS

	0	1	2	3	4	5	6	7	8	9	10					
1.0	0000	0043	0086	0128	0170	0212						4	8	13	17	21
						0212	0253	0294	0334	0374	0414	4	8	12	16	20
1.1	0414	0453	0492	0531	0569	0607						4	8	12	15	19
						0607	0645	0682	0719	0755	0792	4	7	11	15	18
1.2	0792	0828	0864	0899	0934	0969						4	7	11	14	18
						0969	1004	1038	1072	1106	1139	3	7	10	14	17
1.3	1139	1173	1206	1239	1271	1303						3	7	10	13	16
						1303	1335	1367	1399	1430	1461	3	6	9	13	16
1.4	1461	1492	1523	1553	1584	1614						3	6	9	12	15
						1614	1644	1673	1703	1732	1761	3	6	9	12	15
1.5	1761	1790	1818	1847	1875	1903	1931	1959	1987	2014	2041	3	6	8	11	14
1.6	2041	2068	2095	2122	2148	2175	2201	2227	2253	2279	2304	3	5	8	11	13
1.7	2304	2330	2355	2380	2405	2430	2455	2480	2504	2529	2553	2	5	7	10	12
1.8	2553	2577	2601	2625	2648	2672	2695	2718	2742	2765	2788	2	5	7	9	12
1.9	2788	2810	2833	2856	2878	2900	2923	2945	2967	2989	3010	2	4	7	9	11
2.0	3010	3032	3054	3075	3096	3118	3139	3160	3181	3201	3222	2	4	6	8	11
2.1	3222	3243	3263	3284	3304	3324	3345	3365	3385	3404	3424	2	4	6	8	10
2.2	3424	3444	3464	3483	3502	3522	3541	3560	3579	3598	3617	2	4	6	8	10
2.3	3617	3636	3655	3674	3692	3711	3729	3747	3766	3784	3802	2	4	6	7	9
2.4	3802	3820	3838	3856	3874	3892	3909	3927	3945	3962	3979	2	4	5	7	9
2.5	3979	3997	4014	4031	4048	4065	4082	4099	4116	4133	4150	2	3	5	7	9
2.6	4150	4166	4183	4200	4216	4232	4249	4265	4281	4298	4314	2	3	5	7	8
2.7	4314	4330	4346	4362	4378	4393	4409	4425	4440	4456	4472	2	3	5	6	8
2.8	4472	4487	4502	4518	4533	4548	4564	4579	4594	4609	4624	2	3	5	6	8
2.9	4624	4639	4654	4669	4683	4698	4713	4728	4742	4757	4771	1	3	4	6	7
3.0	4771	4786	4800	4814	4829	4843	4857	4871	4886	4900	4914	1	3	4	6	7
3.1	4914	4928	4942	4955	4969	4983	4997	5011	5024	5038	5051	1	3	4	6	7
3.2	5051	5065	5079	5092	5105	5119	5132	5145	5159	5172	5185	1	3	4	5	7
3.3	5185	5198	5211	5224	5237	5250	5263	5276	5289	5302	5315	1	3	4	5	6
3.4	5315	5328	5340	5353	5366	5378	5391	5403	5416	5428	5441	1	3	4	5	6
3.5	5441	5453	5465	5478	5490	5502	5514	5527	5539	5551	5563	1	2	4	5	6
3.6	5563	5575	5587	5599	5611	5623	5635	5647	5658	5670	5682	1	2	4	5	6
3.7	5682	5694	5705	5717	5729	5740	5752	5763	5775	5786	5798	1	2	3	5	6
3.8	5798	5809	5821	5832	5843	5855	5866	5877	5888	5899	5911	1	2	3	5	6
3.9	5911	5922	5933	5944	5955	5966	5977	5988	5999	6010	6021	1	2	3	4	5
4.0	6021	6031	6042	6053	6064	6075	6085	6096	6107	6117	6128	1	2	3	4	5
4.1	6128	6138	6149	6160	6170	6180	6191	6201	6212	6222	6232	1	2	3	4	5
4.2	6232	6243	6253	6263	6274	6284	6294	6304	6314	6325	6335	1	2	3	4	5
4.3	6335	6345	6355	6365	6375	6385	6395	6405	6415	6425	6435	1	2	3	4	5
4.4	6435	6444	6454	6464	6474	6484	6493	6503	6513	6522	6532	1	2	3	4	5
4.5	6532	6542	6551	6561	6571	6580	6590	6599	6609	6618	6628	1	2	3	4	5
4.6	6628	6637	6646	6656	6665	6675	6684	6693	6702	6712	6721	1	2	3	4	5
4.7	6721	6730	6739	6749	6758	6767	6776	6785	6794	6803	6812	1	2	3	4	5
4.8	6812	6821	6830	6839	6848	6857	6866	6875	6884	6893	6902	1	2	3	4	4
4.9	6902	6911	6920	6928	6937	6946	6955	6964	6972	6981	6990	1	2	3	4	4
5.0	6990	6998	7007	7016	7024	7033	7042	7050	7059	7067	7076	1	2	3	3	4
5.1	7076	7084	7093	7101	7110	7118	7126	7135	7143	7152	7160	1	2	3	3	4
5.2	7160	7168	7177	7185	7193	7202	7210	7218	7226	7235	7243	1	2	2	3	4
5.3	7243	7251	7259	7267	7275	7284	7292	7300	7308	7316	7324	1	2	2	3	4
5.4	7324	7332	7340	7348	7356	7364	7372	7380	7388	7396	7404	1	2	2	3	4
5.5	7404	7412	7419	7427	7435	7443	7451	7459	7466	7474	7482	1	2	2	3	4
5.6	7482	7490	7497	7505	7513	7520	7528	7536	7543	7551	7559	1	2	2	3	4
5.7	7559	7566	7574	7582	7589	7597	7604	7612	7619	7627	7634	1	2	2	3	4
5.8	7634	7642	7649	7657	7664	7672	7679	7686	7694	7701	7709	1	1	2	3	4
5.9	7709	7716	7723	7731	7738	7745	7752	7760	7767	7774	7782	1	1	2	3	4
6.0	7782	7789	7796	7803	7810	7818	7825	7832	7839	7846	7853	1	1	2	3	4
6.1	7853	7860	7868	7875	7882	7889	7896	7903	7910	7917	7924	1	1	2	3	4
6.2	7924	7931	7938	7945	7952	7959	7966	7973	7980	7987	7993	1	1	2	3	3
6.3	7993	8000	8007	8014	8021	8028	8035	8041	8048	8055	8062	1	1	2	3	3
6.4	8062	8069	8075	8082	8089	8096	8102	8109	8116	8122	8129	1	1	2	3	3
6.5	8129	8136	8142	8149	8156	8162	8169	8176	8182	8189	8195	1	1	2	3	3
6.6	8195	8202	8209	8215	8222	8228	8235	8241	8248	8254	8261	1	1	2	3	3
6.7	8261	8267	8274	8280	8287	8293	8299	8306	8312	8319	8325	1	1	2	3	3
6.8	8325	8331	8338	8344	8351	8357	8363	8370	8376	8382	8388	1	1	2	3	3
6.9	8388	8395	8401	8407	8414	8420	8426	8432	8439	8445	8451	1	1	2	2	3
7.0	8451	8457	8463	8470	8476	8482	8488	8494	8500	8506	8513	1	1	2	2	3
7.1	8513	8519	8525	8531	8537	8543	8549	8555	8561	8567	8573	1	1	2	2	3
7.2	8573	8579	8585	8591	8597	8603	8609	8615	8621	8627	8633	1	1	2	2	3
7.3	8633	8639	8645	8651	8657	8663	8669	8675	8681	8686	8692	1	1	2	2	3
7.4	8692	8698	8704	8710	8716	[illegible]	[illegible]	[illegible]	[illegible]	[illegible]	[illegible]	1	1	2	2	3

MT-13

7.5	8751	8756	8762	8768	8774	8779	8785	8791	8797	8802	8808	1	1	2	2	3
7.6	8808	8814	8820	8825	8831	8837	8842	8848	8854	8859	8865	1	1	2	2	3
7.7	8865	8871	8876	8882	8887	8893	8899	8904	8910	8915	8921	1	1	2	2	3
7.8	8921	8927	8932	8938	8943	8949	8954	8960	8965	8971	8976	1	1	2	2	3
7.9	8976	8982	8987	8993	8998	9004	9009	9015	9020	9025	9031	1	1	2	2	3
8.0	9031	9036	9042	9047	9053	9058	9063	9069	9074	9079	9085	1	1	2	2	3
8.1	9085	9090	9096	9101	9106	9112	9117	9122	9128	9133	9138	1	1	2	2	3
8.2	9138	9143	9149	9154	9159	9165	9170	9175	9180	9186	9191	1	1	2	2	3
8.3	9191	9196	9201	9206	9212	9217	9222	9227	9232	9238	9243	1	1	2	2	3
8.4	9243	9248	9253	9258	9263	9269	9274	9279	9284	9289	9294	1	1	2	2	3
8.5	9294	9299	9304	9309	9315	9320	9325	9330	9335	9340	9345	1	1	2	2	3
8.6	9345	9350	9355	9360	9365	9370	9375	9380	9385	9390	9395	1	1	2	2	3
8.7	9395	9400	9405	9410	9415	9420	9425	9430	9435	9440	9445	0	1	1	2	2
8.8	9445	9450	9455	9460	9465	9469	9474	9479	9484	9489	9494	0	1	1	2	2
8.9	9494	9499	9504	9509	9513	9518	9523	9528	9533	9538	9542	0	1	1	2	2
9.0	9542	9547	9552	9557	9562	9566	9571	9576	9581	9586	9590	0	1	1	2	2
9.1	9590	9595	9600	9605	9609	9614	9619	9624	9628	9633	9638	0	1	1	2	2
9.2	9638	9643	9647	9652	9657	9661	9666	9671	9675	9680	9685	0	1	1	2	2
9.3	9685	9689	9694	9699	9703	9708	9713	9717	9722	9727	9731	0	1	1	2	2
9.4	9731	9736	9741	9745	9750	9754	9759	9763	9768	9773	9777	0	1	1	2	2
9.5	9777	9782	9786	9791	9795	9800	9805	9809	9814	9818	9823	0	1	1	2	2
9.6	9823	9827	9832	9836	9841	9845	9850	9854	9859	9863	9868	0	1	1	2	2
9.7	9868	9872	9877	9881	9886	9890	9894	9899	9903	9908	9912	0	1	1	2	2
9.8	9912	9917	9921	9926	9930	9934	9939	9943	9948	9952	9956	0	1	1	2	2
9.9	9956	9961	9965	9969	9974	9978	9983	9987	9991	9996	10000	0	1	1	2	2

Bibliography

Almost all of the analytical results in this book were drawn from *ASDT* (Raiffa and Schlaifer 1961) and other works by the authors. These and a few other references cited in the text are listed below, with apologies for the inevitable overrepresentation of ourselves. We have added a number of books and papers related to our subject that we think the reader would find useful and interesting, including several of historical importance that are still very worth reading today. Our bibliography should not be taken as comprehensive or balanced, but further references may easily be found in the works we list. In particular, Berger (1985), an impressive book more advanced and broader in scope than ours, has an extensive bibliography on statistical decision theory. We used it as an aide-mémoire in developing a brief list emphasizing the subjective point of view and relating to our more focused coverage.

Abramowitz, M., and Stegun, I. A. (eds.), 1964. *Handbook of Mathematical Functions.* National Bureau of Standards. Republished by Dover, New York.

Allais, M., 1953. Le comportement de l'homme rationnel devant le risque: critique des postulats et axioms de l'école Américaine. *Econometrica* **21**, 503–546.

Anscombe, F. J., 1963. Sequential medical trials. *J. Amer. Statist. Assoc.* **58**, 365–383.

Antelman, G. R., 1965. Insensitivity to non-optimal design in Bayesian decision theory. *J. Amer. Statist. Assoc.* **60**, 584–601.

Bayes, T., 1763. An essay towards solving a problem in the doctrine of chances. *Phil. Trans. Roy. Soc.* **53**, 370–418. [Reprinted with a biographical note and some editing by G. A. Barnard in *Biometrika* **45**, 293–315 (1958) and in Pearson and Kendall (1970).]

Bell, D. E., 1991. *Risk, Return, and Utility.* Manuscript, Harvard Business School.

Berger, J. O., 1985 (2nd ed.). *Statistical Decision Theory and Bayesian Analysis.* Springer-Verlag, New York.

Berger, J. O., and Sellke, T., 1987. Testing of a point null hypothesis: the irreconcilability of significance levels and evidence (with discussion). *J. Amer. Statist. Assoc.* **82**, 112–139.

Berger, J. O., and Wolpert, R., 1984. *The Likelihood Principle.* Institute of Mathematical Statistics Monograph Series, Hayward, California.

Berkson, J., 1938. Some difficulties of interpretation encountered in the application of the chi-square test. *J. Amer. Statist. Assoc.* **33**, 526–542.

Bernardo, J. M., Berger, J. O., Dawid, A. P., and Smith, A. F. M. (eds.), 1992. *Bayesian Statistics IV.* Clarendon Press, Oxford.

Bernardo, J. M., DeGroot, M. H., Lindley, D. V., and Smith, A. F. M. (eds.), 1980. *Bayesian Statistics.* University Press, Valencia.

——— 1984. *Bayesian Statistics II.* North-Holland, Amsterdam.

——— 1988. *Bayesian Statistics III.* Clarendon Press, Oxford.

Birnbaum, A., 1962. On the foundations of statistical inference (with discussion). *J. Amer. Statist. Assoc.* **57**, 269–326.

Blackwell, D., and Girshick, M. A., 1954. *Theory of Games and Statistical Decisions.* Wiley, New York.

Blyth, C. R., 1986. Approximate binomial confidence limits. *J. Amer. Statist. Assoc.* **81**, 843–855.

Box, G. E. P., and Tiao, G. C., 1973. *Bayesian Inference in Statistical Analysis.* Addison-Wesley, Reading, Massachusetts.

Box, G. E. P., Leonard, T., and Wu, C.-F. (eds.), 1983. *Scientific Inference, Data Analysis, and Robustness.* Academic Press, New York.

Bracken, J., and Schleifer, A., Jr., 1964. *Tables for Normal Sampling with Unknown Variance: The Student Distribution and Economically Optimal Sampling Plans.* Harvard Business School, Boston.

Chernoff, H., and Moses, L. E., 1959. *Elementary Decision Theory.* Wiley, New York.

Clemen, R. T., 1991. *Making Hard Choices.* PWS-Kent Publishing, Boston.

Cochran, W. G., 1977 (3rd ed.). *Sampling Techniques.* Wiley, New York.

Cox, D. R., 1958. Some problems connected with statistical inference. *Ann. Math. Statist.* **29**, 357–372.

Dalal, S. R., and Hall, W. J., 1983. Approximating priors by mixtures of natural conjugate priors. *J. Roy. Statist. Soc. (B)* **45**, 278–286.

Dawid, A. P. Stone, M., and Zidek, J. V., 1973. Marginalization paradoxes in Bayesian and structural inference (with discussion). *J. Roy. Statist. Soc. (B)* **35**, 189–233.

de Finetti, B., 1937. La prévision: ses lois logiques, ses sources subjectives. *Ann. Inst. Henri Poincaré* **7**, 1–68. Reprinted in translation (Foresight: its logical laws, its subjective sources) in Kyburg and Smokler (1964).

——— 1962. Does it make sense to speak of "good probability appraisers"? In *The Scientist Speculates*, I. J. Good (ed.). Basic Books, New York.

——— 1972. *Probability, Induction, and Statistics.* Wiley, New York.

——— 1974, 1975. *Theory of Probability*, Vols. 1 and 2. Wiley, New York.

DeGroot, M. H., 1970. *Optimal Statistical Decisions.* McGraw-Hill, New York.

Diaconis, P., and Ylvisaker, D., 1979. Conjugate priors for exponential families. *Ann. Statist.* **7**, 269–281.

DuMouchel, W. M., and Harris, J. E., 1983. Bayes methods for combining the results of cancer studies in humans and other species (with discussion). *J. Amer. Statist. Assoc.* **78**, 293–315.

Edwards, W., Lindman, H., and Savage, L. J., 1963. Bayesian statistical inference for psychological research. *Psychol. Rev.* **70**, 193–242.

Ellsberg, D., 1961. Risk, ambiguity, and the Savage axioms. *Quart. J. Econ.* **75**, 644–661.

Ericson, W. A., 1963. *Optimum Stratified Sampling Using Prior Information.* Ph.D. dissertation, Harvard University.

Ferguson, T. S., 1967. *Mathematical Statistics: A Decision-Theoretic Approach.* Academic Press, New York.

Fienberg, S. E., and Zellner, A. (eds.), 1975. *Studies in Bayesian Econometrics and Statistics.* North-Holland, Amsterdam.

Fishburn, P. C., 1981. Subjective expected utility: a review of normative theories. *Theory and Decision* **13**, 139–199.

Fisher, R. A., 1935. The fiducial argument in statistical inference. *Ann. Eugenics* **6**, 391–398.

Goel, P. K., and A. Zellner (eds.), 1986. *Bayesian Inference and Decision Techniques with Applications: Essays in Honor of Bruno de Finetti.* North-Holland, Amsterdam.

Good, I. J., 1950. *Probability and the Weighing of Evidence.* Charles Griffin, London.

——— 1965. *The Estimation of Probabilities: An Essay on Modern Bayesian Methods.* MIT Press, Cambridge, Massachusetts.

——— 1983. *Good Thinking: The Foundations of Probability and Its Applications.* University of Minnesota Press, Minneapolis.

Grayson, C. J., 1960. *Decisions under Uncertainty: Drilling Decisions by Oil and Gas Operators.* Harvard Business School, Boston.

Greenwood, J. Arthur, and Hartley, H. O., 1962. *Guide to Tables in Mathematical Statistics.* Princeton University Press, Princeton.

Hansen, M. H., Hurwitz, W. N., and Madow, W. G., 1953. *Sample Survey Methods and Theory*, vol. 1. Wiley, New York.

Harvard University, 1955. *Tables of the Cumulative Binomial Probability Distribution.* Annals of the Computation Laboratory of Harvard University, vol. 35. Harvard University Press, Cambridge, Massachusetts.

Jeffreys, H., 1939 (3rd ed. 1961). *Theory of Probability.* Clarendon Press, Oxford.

Kadane, J. B., Dickey, J. M., Winkler, R. L., Smith, W. S., and Peters, S. C., 1980. Interactive elicitation of opinion for a normal linear model. *J. Amer. Statist. Assoc.* **75**, 845–854.

Kahneman, D., Slovic, P., and Tversky, A. (eds.), 1982. *Judgment under Uncertainty: Heuristics and Biases.* Cambridge University Press, New York.

Kahneman, D., and Tversky, A., 1982. The psychology of preferences. *Scientific American,* **246** no. 1 (Jan.), 160–173.

Keeney, R. L., and Raiffa, H., 1976. *Decisions with Multiple Objectives.* Wiley, New York.

Kendall, M. G., 1943 (vol. 1), 1946 (vol. 2). *The Advanced Theory of Statistics.* Later editions (3 vols.) with A. Stuart and J. K. Ord. Current edition *Kendall's Advanced Theory of Statistics* by Stuart and Ord. Griffin, London.

Kotz, S., and Johnson, N. L. (eds.), 1982–1988. *Encyclopedia of Statistical Sciences.* Wiley, New York.

Kyburg, H. E., Jr., and Smokler, H. E. (eds.), 1964. *Studies in Subjective Probability.* Wiley, New York.

LaValle, Irving, 1970. *An Introduction to Probability, Decision, and Inference.* Holt, Rinehart and Winston, New York.

Leamer, E. E., 1978. *Specification Searches.* Wiley, New York.

Lehmann, E. L, 1959 (2nd ed. 1986). *Testing Statistical Hypotheses.* Wiley, New York.

——— 1983. *Theory of Point Estimation.* Wiley, New York.

Lieberman, G. J., and Owen, D. B., 1961. *Tables of the Hypergeometric Probability Distribution.* Stanford University, Stanford, California.

Lindley, D. V., 1957. A Statistical Paradox. *Biometrika* **44**, 187–192.

——— 1965. *Introduction to Probability and Statistics from a Bayesian Viewpoint* (Parts 1 and 2). Cambridge University Press, Cambridge.

——— 1971. *Bayesian Statistics, A Review.* SIAM, Philadelphia.

Lindley, D. V., and Smith, A. F. M., 1972. Bayes estimates for the linear model (with discussion). *J. Roy. Statist. Soc. (B)* **34**, 1–41.

Ling, R. F., 1978. A study of the accuracy of some approximations for t, χ^2, and F tail probabilities. *J. Amer. Statist. Assoc.* **73**, 274–283.

Ling, R. F., and Pratt, J. W., 1984. The accuracy of Peizer approximations to the hypergeometric distribution, with comparisons to some other approximations. *J. Amer. Statist. Assoc.* **79**, 49–60.

Luce, R. D., and Raiffa, H., 1957. *Games and Decisions.* Wiley, New York.

Maindonald, J. H., 1984. *Statistical Computation.* Wiley, New York.

Maritz, J. S., and Lwin, T., 1989. *Empirical Bayes Methods.* Methuen, London.

Markowitz, H., 1959. *Portfolio Selection: Efficient Diversification of Investments.* Wiley, New York.

Meyer, R. F., and Pratt, J. W., 1968. The consistent assessment and fairing of preference functions. *IEEE Trans. Systems Science and Cybernetics* SSC-4, no. 3, 270–278.

Miller, R. W., 1962. How to plan and control with PERT. *Harvard Business Review* **40** no. 2, 93–104.

Molenaar, W., 1970. *Approximations to the Poisson, Binomial and Hypergeometric Distribution Functions.* Mathematisches Centrum, Amsterdam.

Molina, E. C., 1942. *Poisson's Exponential Binomial Limit.* Van Nostrand, New York.

Mosteller, F., and Wallace, D. L., 1984. *Applied Bayesian and Classical Inference: The Case of the Federalist Papers.* Springer-Verlag, New York. (2nd ed. of *Inference and Disputed Au horship: The Federalist.* Addison-Wesley, Reading, Massachusetts, 1964.)

Pearson, E. S., and Hartley, H. O. (eds.), 1966. *Biometrika Tables for Statisticians,* Vol. 1. Cambridge University Press, Cambridge.

Pearson, E. S., and Kendall, M. G. (eds.), 1970. *Studies in the History of Statistics and Probability.* Griffin, London.

Pearson, K. (ed.), 1922. *Tables of the Incomplete Γ-Function.* Biometrika, London.

——— 1934. *Tables of the Incomplete Beta Function.* Biometrika, London.

Peizer, D. B., and Pratt, J. W., 1968. A normal approximation for binomial, F, beta, and other common, related tail probabilities, I. *J. Amer. Statist. Assoc.* **63**, 1416–1456.

Pratt, J. W., 1964. Risk aversion in the small and in the large. *Econometrica* **32**, 122–36. Correction **44**, 420.

——— 1965. Bayesian interpretation of standard inference statements (with discussion). *J. Roy. Statist. Soc. (B)* **27**, 169–203.

——— 1966. The outer needle of some Bayes sequential continuation regions. *Biometrika* **53**, 455–467.

——— 1992. Risk aversion. *The New Palgrave Dictionary of Money and Finance* **3**, 365–371. Macmillan.

Pratt, J. W., Raiffa, H., and Schlaifer, R., 1964. The foundations of decision under uncertainty: a simplified exposition. *J. Amer. Stat. Assoc.* **59**, 353–375.

Pratt, J. W., and Schlaifer, R., 1988. On the interpretation and observation of laws. *J. Econometrics* **39**, 23–52.

Pratt, J. W., and Zeckhauser, R., 1987. Proper risk aversion. *Econometrica* **55**, 143–154.

——— 1989. The impact of risk sharing on efficient decision. *J. Risk and Uncertainty* **2**, 219–234.

Press, S. J., 1982 (2nd ed.). *Applied Multivariate Analysis: Using Bayesian and Frequentist Measures of Inference.* Kreiger, New York.

Raiffa, H., 1968. *Decision Analysis: Introductory Lectures on Choices under Uncertainty.* Addison-Wesley, Reading, Massachusetts.

Raiffa, H., and Schlaifer, R., 1961. *Applied Statistical Decision Theory.* Harvard Business School, Boston.

Ramsey, F. P., 1926. Truth and probability. In *The Foundations of Mathematics and Other Logical Essays*, 1931, Kegan Paul, London. Reprinted in Kyburg and Smokler (1964).

Savage, L. J., 1954. *The Foundations of Statistics.* Wiley, New York. (2nd ed. 1972, Dover, New York.)

Schlaifer, R., 1956. *Probability and Statistics for Business Decisions.* McGraw-Hill, New York.

——— 1969. *Analysis of Decisions under Uncertainty.* McGraw-Hill, New York. Reprinted by Robert E. Krieger Publishing Company, Melbourne, Florida.

——— 1971. *Computer Programs for Elementary Decision Analysis.* Harvard Business School, Boston.

Sittig, J., 1951. The economic choice of a sampling system in acceptance sampling. *Bull. Internat. Statist. Inst.* **33**, part 5, 51–84.

Tobin, J., 1958. Liquidity preference as behavior towards risk. *Rev. Econ. Studies* **25**, 68–85.

Trotter, H. F., 1959. An elementary proof of the central limit theorem. *Archiv der Mathematik* **10**, 226–234.

U.S. Army, Ordinance Corps, 1952. *Tables of the Cumulative Binomial Probabilities.* Pamphlet ORDP 20–1. Washington, D.C.

Von Neumann, J., and Morgenstern, O., 1944 (3rd ed. 1953). *Theory of Games and Economic Behavior.* Princeton University Press, Princeton.

Wald, A., 1950. *Statistical Decision Functions.* Wiley, New York.

Winkler, R. L., 1972. *Introduction to Bayesian Inference and Decision.* Holt, Rinehart and Winston, New York.

Zellner, A., 1971. *An Introduction to Bayesian Inference in Econometrics.* Wiley, New York.

Zellner, A. (ed.), 1980. *Bayesian Analysis in Econometrics and Statistics.* North-Holland, Amsterdam.

Index